BRITISH
WARSHIP LOSSES
in the Modern Era
1920–1982

BRITISH WARSHIP LOSSES in the Modern Era 1920–1982

DAVID HEPPER

First published in Great Britain in 2022 by
Seaforth Publishing
An imprint of Pen & Sword Books Ltd
47 Church Street, Barnsley
S Yorkshire S70 2AS

www.seaforthpublishing.com
Email info@seaforthpublishing.com

British Library Cataloguing in Publication Data
A CIP data record for this book is available from the British Library

978 1 3990 9766 6 (HARDBACK)
978 1 3990 9767 3 (EPUB)
978 1 3990 9768 0 (KINDLE)

Pen & Sword Books Limited incorporates the imprints of Atlas,
Archaeology, Aviation, Discovery, Family History, Fiction, History,
Maritime, Military, Military Classics, Politics, Select, Transport,
True Crime, Air World, Frontline Publishing, Leo Cooper,
Remember When, Seaforth Publishing, The Praetorian Press,
Wharncliffe Local History, Wharncliffe Transport, Wharncliffe
True Crime and White Owl.

Typeset by Mac Style
Printed and bound in Great Britain by
CPI Group (UK) Ltd, Croydon, CR0 4YY

Contents

List of Illustrations

Introduction: Losses in the Modern Era from 1920

THE PURPOSE OF THIS BOOK is to detail those ships and vessels of the Royal Navy which were lost by accident or enemy action during the twentieth century, from the end of the Great or First World War to the last years of the century. The six years of conflict between 1939 and 1945 predictably dominate these accounts.

It is inevitable that during a war that ships will be lost; it is their purpose to go in harm's way, and thereby run the risk of damage and danger. To this may be added the hazardous nature of the sea – storm force winds and heavy seas regularly take their toll on ships. It must also be understood that human error or plain foolishness may sometimes play a part.

The main bulk of the book is taken up by the losses experienced during the Second World War. The basis for identifying the losses has been the officially-produced *Ships of the Royal Navy: Statement of Losses during the Second World War*, which was published in 1947 to list the casualties of 1939–45, but despite being a Government production, had several omissions and errors. These were partly rectified by an Amendment produced two years later, but I have found that there were still gaps – the capture of *BYMS 2072* in 1943 for example was not listed. The Director of Naval Construction issued *H M Ships Sunk or Damaged by Enemy Action* as a Confidential Book (CB) in 1952 but this was not a public document, and rather than a simple listing of names, gives details of the damage suffered.

I hope that the list contained here is complete, but with the minor war craft there is still some uncertainty, and the smaller landing craft seem to have been frequently written off with little or no information recorded on what caused the loss.

The details come from research using primary source material wherever possible. For the Second World War, the collected loss and damage reports (National Archives ref: ADM.267) were most important, and these have been supported by the reports from a resulting court of enquiry or court martial into a loss. Where these did not take place or have not survived, then entries in War Diaries (ADM.199 – series) and casualty reports (ADM.358 – series) help to fill the gap. I have also used reliable secondary sources for some entries – in the case of submarine losses, then I acknowledge the work done by A S Evans and the excellent uboat.net website must also be recognised as a first-class source of information. For the smaller craft, such as motor torpedo and motor gun boats, then the series of volumes by Reynolds and

Cooper were invaluable. I have included the wartime losses of the Dominions, and Vic Cassells *For those in peril … and* McKee and Darlington's *Canadian Naval Chronicle* were the main sources of information

For the more recent period, then the casualties lessen: as much a reflection of the shrinking size of the Royal Navy as anything else. The short, sharp conflict of the Falklands in 1982 demonstrated a lesson that had been learned during earlier conflicts: that warships operating in confined inshore waters whilst supporting operations ashore are vulnerable to air attacks. The loss of *Ardent* and *Antelope* in that war could be compared the *Bittern* in 1940.

Lenton's *British and Empire Warships of the Second World War* and Conway's *All the World's Fighting Ships* provided the outline details of the vessels, whilst the courts of enquiry, published casualty lists or Navy Lists established the name of the commanding officer in most cases. I regret that I have not always been able to find the name of an officer, particularly with the so-called minor war vessels – landing craft in particular. The contemporary Navy Lists did not show these craft and reports often only list the number of the vessel, and not the names of any officers.

The terminology used is that of the contemporary sources, so Imperial measurements will predominate, rather than metric. The underwater detection system employed by the Royal Navy was referred to as Asdic for much of this period, although the term sonar became increasingly common, and indeed supplanted the earlier term after 1945 and I have followed this convention.

It should be noted that with some losses, particularly those of submarines, then dates are shown as a time period in brackets. This indicates that the precise date of the loss is uncertain but is likely to have been within the date range shown. Submarines were usually posted as missing on the date that the patrol was due to end and only after researching German and Italian records after the war could any firmer date be ascribed. Despite this, the cause for the loss of several submarines is still unclear.

The term constructive total loss will be seen for some entries. This is used to indicate a ship that is damaged so badly that repairs are not cost effective, and they are usually disposed of by being broken up. Some did manage a second life – the *Porcupine* being a particular example. This has made the inclusion of some CTLs as a loss problematic, but I have generally included them.

When defining the ships, the following format is used for each entry:

Date of Loss and name and type of ship. For some of the amphibious craft, a figure in brackets indicates the Mark of the design, so LCT(3) indicates a Mark 3 tank landing craft.

Location where built and the year of launch with any previous names noted in brackets; standard displacement in tons; perpendicular length and beam in feet and inches; outline details of weapons carried where known. The name of the commanding officer is shown, and the † marker indicates that he did not survive the loss.

The notation after each entry shows the principal source of information used.

For the photographs I must acknowledge the cooperation of the Imperial War Museum, British Pathé News, Mary Evans Picture Library and Portland Museum.

1 | Losses between 1 January 1920 and 2 September 1939

THE PERIOD THAT FOLLOWED the armistice of 1918 saw the Royal Navy adjusting to a new order; the heady days of accelerated building programmes and the 'dreadnought race' prior to 1914 was replaced with cutbacks and cancellations and a painful adjustment to a smaller fleet. Between 1921 and 1936 the major naval powers agreed a series of treaties which limited the size and armament of larger warships, which encouraged a climate of 'parsimony and parity' and the Royal Navy scrapped or discarded numbers of wartime-built ships.

Despite the limitations, for the Royal Navy the Empire still stretched around the globe and with it the Navy's responsibility for policing and protecting the trade routes and fleets were still maintained in the Far East and Mediterranean. This is reflected in the losses which occurred in the Far East, Mediterranean and North American waters apart from those closer to home.

The losses between the World Wars are dominated by submarine disasters – ten boats were lost between 1921 and 1939, which emphasised the hazardous nature of the service. Most of the surface ship losses can be attributed to adverse weather conditions, although human error also features. The loss of the cruiser *Raleigh* in 1922 was avoidable and the circumstances surrounding the wrecking of the sloop *Petersfield* in 1931 did not reflect well on the Royal Navy.

1920

16 January JAMES FENNELL trawler
Paisley 1918; 215 tons; 115ft × 22ft; 1 × 12pdr
Lieutenant – White RNR
Returning to Portsmouth from Gibraltar she ran ashore in thick fog near Blacknor Point, Portland. The firing of rockets alerted a local man, Albert Saunders, who assisted in the rescue of the crew, catching and securing a line thrown to him by which means all seventeen men on board were rescued. Saunders was subsequently awarded a Royal Humane Society Bronze Medal. The trawler remained aground until March when she was finally hauled off the rocks but capsized and sank.
[www.britishnewspaperarchive.co.uk: Portsmouth Evening News 17 January 1920 p10; Dundee Evening Telegraph 26 January 1920 p10]

16 January ST COLOMB tug
Chester 1918; 800 tons; 135ft × 29ft
Lieutenant Ernest Martin Jehan DSC
Laying at anchor at the small port of Marzameni, Sicily, when, with the winds increasing to gale force from the north-east, their position became untenable, it was decided to make for the open sea. As they were clearing the entrance, their boat, which was being towed astern, parted the tow, and in the efforts to retrieve it, with little sea-room, the tug ran aground and swung beam-on to the wind and sea. The destroyer *Tobago* was despatched to her aid from Malta, and found the vessel laying on her beam-ends on a rocky shore, badly holed fore and aft, her engine room full of water and with signs of having a broken back. She was abandoned as a wreck and was subsequently sold.
[TNA: BT.110/612/4; Dawson pp130–1]

19 February MICHAEL MALONEY trawler
Middlesbrough 1917; 275 tons; 125ft × 23.6ft
Manned by a civilian crew, undertaking commercial fishing, the Admiralty remained the managing owners of the trawler, which ran aground near Egersund, Norway. She was hauled off the rocks the following day but foundered.

Note: most printed sources, including contemporary newspapers, report the date of loss as 19 February, but curiously the Board of Trade register of shipping cites the date 13 July for the wreck – she was struck from the register 10 September.
[www.britishnewspaperarchive.co.uk: The Globe 23 February 1920 p12; TNA: BT 110/365/3]

24 March MOORVIEW mooring vessel
Paisley 1918; 720 tons; 138ft × 29ft
Master R E Robinson
Bound from Londonderry for Devonport, as the ship entered the western approaches to the English Channel the visibility was poor, with thick fog, and after sighting the Longships light at Land's End, a course was laid for the Lizard. The fog became thicker, obscuring all lights and landmarks, and at 03.00 she ran onto the Runnelstone, off Land's End. The impact was so severe that some of the crew were thrown from their bunks. She was badly holed and within minutes water had flooded several compartments, including the engine room. As she was clearly sinking, all nineteen members of the crew took to the boats, one of which was picked

up by the steamer *Fleswick*, the other successfully reached St Ives.

[www.britishnewspaperarchive.co.uk: Western Morning News 25 March 1920 p8]

10 June ST BOSWELLS tug
Leith 1919; 800 tons; 135ft × 29ft
Master John Corsie†

Manned by a civilian crew, she remained Admiralty property, and it was whilst towing a merchant vessel, the *Santa Theresa*, from Iquique in Chile to Hamburg, that she struck a mine near the island of Terschelling. She sank in 2 minutes with fourteen members of the crew, including the captain, being lost. Dutch tugs went to the scene and rescued six survivors.

[www.britishnewspaperarchive.co.uk: Portsmouth Evening News 12 June 1920 p10; The Scotsman 14 June 1920 p9]

9 September CMB 99 coastal motor boat
Gosport 1919; 11 tons; 60ft × 11ft; 1 × torpedo

Whilst leaving Portsmouth at 06.00 in company with other CMBs, a fire broke out in the engine compartment. The other boats closed and took off the crew and she then began to drift down towards the old cruiser *Arrogant* moored off Fort Blockhouse. She was eventually taken in tow by dockyard craft, and they moved her to Stokes Bay where she was allowed to burn out.

[www.britishnewspaperarchive.co.uk: Hampshire Telegraph 10 September 1920 p3]

9 September WILLIAM WILLMOT trawler
Middlesbrough 1917; 275 tons; 125ft × 23.6ft
Skipper William Kingston RNR

Manned by a civilian crew, undertaking commercial fishing, the Admiralty remained the managing owners of the trawler. The *William Willmot* sailed from Swansea for the Irish fishing grounds and was steering west-north-west at 9 knots when just before 01.00, then being about 14 miles to the south-west of the Smalls light, she saw the lights of a ship on her port bow, about 3 or 4 miles distant. The ship was the *Meissonier* (7,206 tons), bound for Liverpool, which was steering a north-easterly course at 12 knots. The bridge crew of the *Meissonier* observed the masthead light of the trawler on their starboard bow, but it was not until they saw a red, port side light, that they realised how close they were. They commenced a turn to starboard and sounded a blast on the siren. On board the trawler, the wheelhouse crew were confused, as they believed the stranger would pass ahead, but now seemed to be attempting to pass under their stern, so maintained their course and speed. The *Meissonier*, now closing fast, put her engines astern, but was still underway when she struck the trawler, cutting a hole in her side. The eleven members of the crew quickly took to their boat, just clearing away as the trawler's bows rose clear and she sank stern first.

[TNA: HCA 20/1625; BT.110/659; www.britishnewspaperarchive. co.uk: Western Mail 13 September 1920 p6]

1 November STONEHENGE destroyer
Hebburn 1919; 1,075 tons; 276ft × 27ft; 3 × 4in,
4 × torpedo tubes
Commander Richard Lloyd Hamer

The destroyer sailed from Constantinople on 31 October, and initially proceeded to the island of Mudros to collect mail and some ratings for passage. She weighed during the early afternoon of 1 November in poor weather, to make for Smyrna (Izmir). As she approached the coast the weather deteriorated, with Force 7 winds from the north-east, rain and a rising sea. At 21.00 she reduced speed, fearing that she was close to the shoreline, which could not be seen in the gloom. Just 15 minutes later breakers were seen ahead, and despite going full astern and putting the helm over, she ran hard aground, about 30 miles from Smyrna. Sounding around her, she found she had about 2 fathoms of water near her, but all efforts to free the ship, by using engines and having the crew mustered aft to jump, failed to move her. She fired rockets and flares to attract attention. The destroyer *Serapis* arrived and over the next few days efforts were made to free her, but she was abandoned as a total loss on 6 November. Her stores and guns were salvaged.

[TNA: ADM.53/61443; www.britishnewspaperarchive.co.uk: Hampshire Telegraph 12 November 1920 p7]

12 November TOBAGO destroyer
Woolston 1918; 1,087 tons; 276ft × 27.5ft; 3 × 4in,
4 × torpedo tubes
Lieutenant Humphrey Edward Archer

Stationed in the Black Sea, she was damaged by a mine explosion soon after sailing from Trebizond (Trabzon). The Italian steamer *Praga* stood by her, taking off most of the crew and towing her into Trebizond. The cruiser *Calypso* arrived the following day and assisted with the shoring of bulkheads, and removing ammunition, and then towed her to Istanbul. She was temporarily repaired at Istanbul and then towed back to Malta, but was written off as a constructive total loss, and sold for scrapping in February 1922.

[TNA: ADM.53/72333; various secondary]

1921

17 January MARJORAM sloop
Greenock 1917; 1,290 tons; 262.6ft × 35ft; 2 × 4in,
2 × 12pdr

Laid up at Queenstown (Cobh), Ireland she was selected for conversion to a Reserve drill ship to be stationed in the River Thames as *President*, the conversion work to be done at Pembroke Dock, west Wales. A small naval party of ten ratings under a Petty Officer embarked on the sloop and the large tug *Dainty* commenced the tow at 09.00 on 16 January and was able to maintain a speed of 5 knots, despite a large swell running. The barometer fell steadily during the day, and the wind increased, so that by the early hours of the following morning she was experiencing difficult conditions, with a high sea and strong westerly winds and regular rain squalls. At midday, with the sloop rolling 20 degrees in the swell, the tow parted. Efforts were made to re-connect, but it proved impossible, and Master Albert Rann of the *Dainty* decided that it was now too dangerous for the small towing party to stay on the sloop. With some difficulty the tug came up on her port quarter and the eleven men jumped over to the tug. An attempt was made in the late afternoon to board her, but again failed due to the pitching and rolling of the vessels. The sloop was now being carried by the wind and tide and disappeared into the night, last being seen drifting towards the shore near St Anne's Head. The destroyer *Velox* arrived on scene at 23.00 to assist with a search for the missing vessel, but she could not be found. During the night, the sloop went ashore just south of Linney Head, Milford Haven and broke up in the heavy seas. The court of enquiry agreed that the poor weather was the cause of the loss, but some blame was attributable to the towing crew; there was no organised communication between tug and tow, relying on shouted messages and no thought seems to have been given to anchoring. Master Rann had the opportunity to sail the previous evening but had delayed until the morning and the delay was a contributory factor.
[TNA: ADM.1/8598/16]

20 January K 5 submarine
Portsmouth 1916; 1,880/2,650 tons; 330ft × 26.6ft; 2 × 4in,
1 × 3in, 10 × torpedo tubes
Lieutenant Commander John Austin Gaimes†

Sailed from Torbay on 19 January in company with other 'K' class submarines and surface units to conduct exercises about 120 miles south-west of Scilly. The following day the submarines commenced diving at 11.30 as surface forces approached and *K 5* was seen to submerge at a normal angle, with no obvious signs of difficulty. A few moments later the submarines were brought to the surface, which included *K 5*, which was seen at 11.45. A few moments later she evidently dived again as ships of the Third Destroyer Flotilla were closing, although she was not seen to do so. Nothing was suspected until 14.09 when she failed to respond to radio calls. The senior ship, *Inconstant*, ordered the area to be searched and at 17.42 the submarine *K 9* found a large patch of oil in position 48.53N 08.52.05W, about 1½ miles from the diving position. The oil steadily spread and later debris and wreckage identified as belonging to *K 5* came to the surface. The cause of her loss could not be ascertained but some of the wreckage recovered showed clear evidence of being crushed under pressure, and she had clearly lost trim and dived beyond her safe depth. Captain Max Horton suggested that she may have failed to properly close the external vents, especially if she had dived slightly heavy by the head. Six officers and fifty-one ratings died.
[TNA: ADM.116/2125]

3 March GLOAMING drifter
Fraserburgh 1919; 94 tons; 86ft × 20ft; 1 × 6pdr
Sub-Lieutenant George Whitfield

The drifter sailed from Pembroke Dock, acting as part of an escort to the First Submarine Flotilla which was on passage to Torbay. Whitfield fixed the position of his vessel at midnight and then handed the watch to Commissioned Gunner Kennedy, with details of the course to be steered. The Lizard light was seen at 03.00 on the port bow, but at 03.30 she drove onto the Cledges Reef off Lizard Point with considerable violence. She was wedged firmly in between rocks, with a heel to starboard. Distress rockets were fired, and this brought the local Lizard lifeboat, which saved all fifteen members of the crew. The drifter broke up over the next few days. At a subsequent court martial it was judged that Lieutenant Whitfield had failed to lay out the correct course on the chart and had failed to give the Lizard a wide enough berth and failed to give orders that he was to be called when the Lizard was sighted; he was reprimanded. Commissioned Gunner Timothy Kennedy was also court-martialled and it was found that he had failed to keep a proper watch and later had failed to hand over charts and books in a timely manner, altering the chart before submitting them. He was severely reprimanded and dismissed his ship.
[Larn vol 1 sec 4; www.britishnewspaperarchive.co.uk:
Western Morning News 4 March 1920 p5, 29 June 1921 p3
& 1 July 1921 p3]

1922

23 March H 42 submarine
Walker on Tyne 1918; 423/510 tons; 171.9ft × 15.9ft;
1 × 3in, 4 × torpedo tubes
Lieutenant Douglas Carteret Sealy DSC[†]

With four other submarines of the Third Submarine Flotilla that had been deployed to Gibraltar for spring exercises, *H 42* was ordered to carry out a practice submerged attack on ships of the First Destroyer Flotilla. Led by *Wallace*, the destroyers would be in divisions, zigzagging at speed. At 09.30 the destroyers passed about half a mile south of the ordered start position at 20 knots and 10 minutes later an alteration of course was ordered. Just as they had completed this, a submarine broke surface about 40 yards ahead of the *Versatile*, giving the destroyer no chance to avoid a collision. Despite putting the helm to port and ordering engines full astern she rammed the submarine just abaft the conning tower after which the boat disappeared. Her position was then 35.59.30N 05.20.41W. It was believed that *H 42* had probably conducted an attack on the *Wallace* and believing herself to be to the northward, and clear of the line of destroyers she had surfaced to indicate a successful attack. Three officers and twenty-three ratings died.
[TNA:ADM.1/8623/60]

13 June BLUE SKY drifter
Lowestoft 1918; 94 tons; 86ft × 20ft
Lieutenant Francis Henry Cecil Jennings[†]

Acting as tender to the *Queen Elizabeth* she was ordered to sail from Portsmouth for Invergordon to support the battleship during fleet gunnery practice. She sailed on 12 June and after an overnight stop at Newhaven she set out again the next morning, being sighted off Beachy Head at 12.15 and was heard calling Dover by radio at 17.53 after which she disappeared. During the 15th· a lifebelt was found off Foreness Point and over the next few days wreckage came ashore between Herne Bay and Margate. The destroyer *Starfish* was ordered to search the area, but could only find two small ladders, similar to those used in drifters. The wreckage continued to come ashore on the north Kent coast over several days, including a boat, part of the deckhouse and two bodies, which were identified as a stoker and signalman from the drifter. The cause of her loss was uncertain; there was no indication in the wreckage of any explosion or fire, ruling out a mine. The weather in the area at the time was not ideal, with a strong wind from the north-east, but the drifter should have been capable of surviving this. The drift of the wreckage suggested that she had run aground on the Kentish Knock sand and subsequently broken

up. One officer, two midshipmen and twelve ratings were lost.
[TNA:ADM.1/8627/109]

1 July INSOLENT boom defence vessel
Pembroke 1881; 265 tons; 87.4ft × 26.1ft

Former gunboat converted for harbour use, she was laid up, listed for sale at Portsmouth when she foundered at her moorings in the harbour. Raised and sold in June 1925.
[Dittmar & Colledge p317]

8 August RALEIGH light cruiser
Dalmuir 1919; 9,750 tons; 605ft × 65ft; 7 × 7.5in, 6 × 12pdr, 4 × 3in, 6 × torpedo tubes
Captain Arthur Bromley

Acting as flagship of Admiral Sir William Pakenham, Commander-in-Chief, North American station, the Admiral was not embarked as the cruiser sailed from Hawke Bay, Nova Scotia, for Forteau Bay, Labrador. They experienced varying visibility, with the horizon often being obscured by patches of thick drifting fog, but a good fix on points of land was obtained at 12.47 and another an hour later. Thereafter the fog closed in preventing any further sightings of the coast, but they continued to steam at 12 knots, confident that they were clear of land. At 15.25, by dead reckoning, they were 2 miles from the shore and course was altered for Forteau Bay. After they had done so, the fog seemed to thicken and at 15.39 breakers were seen close ahead, only seconds before she ran hard aground on a rocky shore. She was held fast and started to bump badly in the surf and took a slight list to starboard. Captain Bromley, fearing that the ship might roll over, ordered the vessel to be abandoned and the boats were hoisted out. The cutter, whilst attempting to make the shore, overturned throwing the occupants into the water, drowning ten ratings, who were the only casualties. Lines were made safe to the shore and over the next 3 hours everybody was successfully landed, where they found that the ship had gone ashore about 5 cables (1,000 yards) from Point Armour lighthouse. Subsequent to the loss, courts martial were held on Captain Bromley and the navigating officer, Commander Leslie Charles Bott, being accused of losing the ship by negligence or default. Both officers claimed in their defence that the wreck occurred because of an error in the charts, it being found that Point Armour was shown 1 minute (0.65 miles) to the east of the true position. However, the courts were unsympathetic, ruling that any fault in the charts had no bearing on the subsequent stranding. It emerged that Bromley had not been on the bridge for much of the afternoon, arriving only at 15.30, after the course change and immediately before the ship struck. Only then was a reduction in speed ordered, which was far too late. If he had been

on the bridge, he would have realised that she was in as a perilous situation, steaming into thickening fog at 12 knots; as it was, valuable time had been lost acquainting him with the situation. Both Bromley and Bott had relied on a dead reckoning position for a course change when close to a dangerous shore having allowed the ship to run 25 miles in waters known to have a strong tidal current, where it might be expected that they would be slightly out of position. The Navigation Officer had failed to order a speed reduction when sight of the Labrador coast was lost. No sounding party had been closed up until after the fateful course change, again too late to be of any use. Both officers were dismissed their ship and severely reprimanded. Although the stores and valuable items from the ship, such as guns, anchors and cables, were recovered, the wreck lay on the shore for many years. In 1926, embarrassed by the sight, the Admiralty approved plans to demolish her 'sufficiently to obliterate resemblance to a man of war' by use of explosives. This was accomplished during the course of the following year.
[TNA: ADM.1/26770; ADM.156/57; www.britishnewspaperarchive.co.uk: Portsmouth Evening News 25 October 1922 p5]

29 August ML 196 motor launch
Bayonne, New Jersey 1917; 37 tons; 80ft × 12.3ft; 1 × 3pdr
Lieutenant John Ernest Padwick Brass
Part of a small squadron deployed to the river Danube, the launch was lying alongside the gunboat *Glowworm* at Porzony (modern Bratislava). At 00.40 the alarm was raised when smoke was seen rising from the engine compartment of the launch. The crew of the gunboat went to fire stations, and as it was clear that the fire had a good hold, at 01.05 she was veered astern of the gunboat. She eventually drifted clear, now completely ablaze, made worse by exploding ammunition. On the flames reaching the bows there was a final explosion and at 03.45 she rolled over and sank. No lives were lost.
[TNA: ADM.53/78042; www.britishnewspaperarchive.co.uk: The Scotsman 30 August 1922 p7; Kemp p88]

24 September SPEEDY destroyer
Woolston 1918; 1,087 tons; 276ft × 27.4ft; 3 × 4in, 4 × torpedo tubes
Commander Ralph Wilmot Wilkinson
Part of the Mediterranean Fleet deployed to the Aegean she was en-route to Constantinople, proceeding through the Sea of Marmara in clear weather at 16 knots. At 22.40 when about 24 miles east-north-east of Faranesi Light a small white light was seen ahead and estimated to be about 4 miles distant. Over the next 10 minutes the stranger caused some confusion as to her course; a green, or starboard light, could be glimpsed but no red or port light. The officer of the watch, Gunner Hector

Stanton, made a small alteration of course to port, but after doing so resumed his previous course. It was now realised that the stranger was approaching rapidly, and Stanton ordered the helm hard to port, but at 23.03 she was struck hard on the starboard side between the engine room and officers' quarters by the steamer *Kara Bigha*. She immediately started to flood and assumed a 10-degree list. Collision stations were piped, and doors and hatches closed. Attempts were made to shore up the after engine room bulkhead, but it was too severely damaged, and the engine room was soon flooded. Boats were hoisted out and Carley floats thrown overboard and as the ship settled, she was abandoned. The Captain was the last to leave, with the telegraphist who had stayed to transmit a distress message, the pair walking down the side of the ship as it slipped under, stern first, less than 10 minutes after the collision. In a subsequent court martial, Gunner Stanton was found guilty on two charges of negligently performing his duty. It was agreed that the *Kara Bigha* had poor navigation lights – on inspection the port light was 'miserable', being 'so dim as to be almost invisible at anything but very close distance'. This had contributed to Stanton's confusion, and his failure to appreciate that the oncoming steamer was on a collision course, the ships meeting head-on. The court felt that if he was uncertain, then he should have ensured his safety by making a bolder alteration of course; the brief and tentative alteration had done nothing to relieve the situation. The *Kara Bigha* had seen the bow and starboard lights of the destroyer and acted correctly under Rule 18 of the regulations to avoid collision and had ported her helm. Further, Stanton had failed to inform the Captain of the presence of a closing ship as standing orders required and had failed to make sound signals when altering course. He was dismissed his ship and reprimanded. One officer and nine ratings were drowned.
[TNA: ADM.156/58]

11 November WAYWARD despatch vessel
Wivenhoe 1914 (ex- *Wave*; ex-*BuyukAda*); 400 tons; 165ft × 26ft
Having been based at Mudros, she was under tow from the Aegean to Malta, when she foundered.
[Dittmar & Colledge p316]

1923

18 August L 9 submarine
Dumbarton 1918; 890/1,080 tons; 238.7ft × 23.5ft; 1 × 4in, 6 × torpedo tubes
Laid up in reserve at Hong Kong with several other 'L' class submarines, when the colony was threatened by a typhoon, it was decided that for their safety the boats

should be moved away from the piers and secured to buoys in the harbour. In addition, a small party of three men were put aboard *L.9* under Petty Officer Willie Gordon. By the morning of 18 August, the wind was increasing and by mid-morning it was blowing at storm force, with the centre of the typhoon passing over the southern side of the colony. At 10.15 the cable securing the submarine to the buoy parted under the strain and the boat was adrift. Petty Officer Gordon attempted to release the starboard anchor but could not keep a foothold on the deck which was being lashed by wind and waves and the party below were being thrown around as the boat rolled and were unable to close all the bulkhead doors. Red flares were fired as the submarine was carried across the harbour until she crashed against the north wall of the tidal basin. She was thrown violently against the wall, and with no sign of any assistance, Gordon ordered his small party to abandon ship, and with great difficulty they jumped onto the pier. She continued to bounce along the wall and at this stage Lieutenant Thomas Dickson, who had been checking on the safety of other vessels in the basin, saw her. Thinking someone may still be on board, at considerable risk to himself he jumped on board the drifting boat. After finding no one on board he managed to throw a lifebelt attached to a line to the shore, but this soon parted. The submarine continued to crash her way along the jetty until she collided with the Japanese merchant ship *Ginyo Maru*. Dickson managed to hold onto a wire from the merchant ship, being rescued by a rating who hauled him to safety. The submarine sank bows first. In the ensuing enquiry, no blame was attached to Petty Officer Gordon for the loss, but it was felt that he may have been too hasty in leaving her and could have closed watertight doors earlier. Lieutenant John Cresswell, the senior Submarine Officer and Lieutenant Thomas Williams, in charge of reserve ships, took some responsibility in failing to give definite orders regarding the securing of the boats, in particular ensuring the closure of doors and hatches. However, as this was the first typhoon to strike the colony since the submarines had arrived, they had no precedent to guide them, and no action was taken. *L 9* was successfully raised on 6 September and refitted for further service.
[TNA: ADM.1/8646/206; Evans p145]

1924

10 January L 24 submarine
Barrow 1919; 890/1,080 tons; 238.7ft × 23.5ft; 1 × 4in, 6 × torpedo tubes
Lieutenant Commander Paul Leathley Eddis[†]
Participating in a major Atlantic Fleet exercise *L 24* was deployed with other submarines to the south of

Portland Bill, to intercept a force of battleships which would pass through the area. Having sailed from Weymouth Bay, she was in position by 08.10 and then dived to await the columns of ships approaching from the east. By 11.00 the attacks were under way, and the submarines *H 23* and *H 48* came to the surface having completed dummy attacks. A few moments later staff on the bridge of the battleship *Revenge*, third ship in a column of four, clearly saw a periscope break surface about 300 yards on her port quarter. Before it disappeared, the periscope was seen to move to cross the stern, directly into the path of the last ship in the line, the battleship *Resolution*. On board that ship, the bridge staff saw a disturbance in the water off the port bow immediately ahead of them before they ran over the disturbed patch and felt a slight shudder. When the *L 24* failed to surface as expected, a search was started as it was feared that she had been rammed and sunk. With the weather worsening, locating the wreck proved difficult and she was not found until 28 January, in position 50.22.30N 02.37.49W. Divers examining the wreck found that both planes were set to dive, and damage was evident on the starboard side. An examination of the *Resolution* revealed that her port paravane chain had been severed, with the remains showing impact damage, and it became clear that she had indeed collided with the submarine. It was thought probable that Eddis had carried out an attack on the *Revenge*, thinking that she was the last ship in the line. Having done so, he was bringing the submarine to the surface when he suddenly realised that there was another ship bearing down on him. A rapid dive must have been ordered, and the disturbance seen by the *Resolution* may well have been the swirl caused by the submarine propellers. Forty-three officers and ratings were lost.
[TNA: ADM.116/2250; Evans p149; Larn vol 1 sec 6]

1925

23 January ML 307 motor launch
Bayonne New Jersey 1917; 37 tons; 80ft × 12.3ft; 1 × 3pdr
Lieutenant John Gibbons Henderson
One of two launches sent out to China in late 1924 for service on the river Yangtze. Whilst shifting berth at Hankow, a petrol vapour explosion occurred in the engine room which blew a hole in the side of the launch and started a fire. She was towed into shallow water where she sank. One leading stoker was injured.
[www.britishnewspaperarchive.co.uk: Portsmouth Evening News 29 January 1925 p4]

29 January ELPHINSTONE sloop
Walker 1917 (*Ceanothus*) transferred 1922; 1,290 tons;
250ft × 35ft; 2 × 4in, 2 × 12pdr
Commander Richard Hart Garstin RIM
Royal Indian Marine. When on a periodical visit to
the Andaman and Nicobar Islands, she ran onto an
uncharted rock off Castle Point, Tillanchong Island and
subsequently sank. All the crew took to boats and were
saved by the survey ship *Investigator*.
[various secondary]

12 November M 1 submarine
Barrow 1917; 1,594/1,946 tons; 295.9ft × 24.8ft; 1 × 12in,
4 × torpedo tubes
Lieutenant Commander Alec Murray Carrie†
One of the big 'submarine monitors' armed with a
large-calibre gun, she was in company with her sister
M 3, engaged in an exercise in the English Channel off
the south coast of Devon. This would involve a group of
ships acting as a convoy, accompanied by the submarine
monitors, who would act as escorts defending against
an attacking force. At 03.00 the pair sailed from
Plymouth to take up position and the 'enemy' ships
were identified at 07.00 and a few minutes later the
pair dived to approach. At 07.26 the pair surfaced to
conduct a gun action. At 07.37, *M 1* after exchanging
signals with the minesweeper *Newark*, was seen to dive,
her approximate position then was 49.58N 03.53W;
this was the last time she was seen. Nothing untoward
was suspected until she failed to surface as expected
and failed to respond to radio messages. A search was
instigated, but nothing could be found and no clue as
to what had happened to her emerged for several days.
Then a Swedish captain, having heard news reports
of the missing submarine, reported that his ship, the
Vidar, had been in the area at that time and at 07.45
had felt two distinct shudders, as if they had struck a
submerged object. An examination of the *Vidar*'s hull
revealed that her forefoot was bent and there was a
deep indentation on the port side about 1ft abaft the
stem running for 5ft. A scrape was visible further along
the hull and the keel showed a deep scar about 12ft
from the stern. Grey-green paint was recovered from
the indentation and analysis showed that it matched
that used on submarines. The first shudder felt by the
Vidar was probably the bow striking the submarine,
and as she pitched down with the sea, her stern had
delivered another blow. Despite searching for the lost
submarine for some time, she was not found, and the
search was abandoned on 1 December. Sixty-nine
officers and men died. In September 1967 it was
claimed that her remains had been found, but this was
never proved, and it was not until June 1999 that divers
finally found her, lying in 240ft of water. The wreck
is upright and with her gun mounting lying a short

distance from the wreck; it would suggest that this was
the point of impact of the *Vidar*.
*[TNA: ADM.116/2292; Evans p1.55; Larn vol 1 sec 5;
www.msac.org.uk/wrecks/affray.htm]*

1926

28 February ML 287 motor launch
Bayonne New Jersey 1917; 37 tons; 80ft × 12.3ft; 1 × 6pdr
One of several motor launches that had served since
1919 on the river Rhine, based at Cologne, the flotilla
was withdrawn in January 1926 and the vessels returned
to England. Having made their way through the canal
system, the launches gathered at Le Havre for the
transit across the Channel. The group set out on the
morning of Saturday 27 February under the escort of
the destroyer *Turquoise*, the weather at that time being
fine. Just 3 hours after leaving, *287* suffered an engine
breakdown and was taken in tow by the *Turquoise*, the
crew being taken off at the same time. The wind steadily
increased from the south-west and the craft started to
labour in the high seas and at 01.00 it was clear that she
had begun to fill with water, and a small party with hoses
and pumps were sent over to clear her. That complete,
the party was recovered, and the ships got under way
again, but at 04.10 when it again appeared that she was
settling, the destroyer manoeuvred close to the launch
during which she rammed her, and the launch sank.
Her position was then 50.31.25N 00.48.50W.
*[TNA: ADM.53/88257; www.britishnewspaperarchive.co.uk:
Portsmouth Evening News 1 March 1926 p8]*

9 August H 29 submarine
Barrow 1918; 423/510 tons; 171.9ft × 15.9ft; 1 × 3in,
4 × torpedo tubes
Lieutenant Frank Harold Elcho Skyrme
Having recently completed a refit at Devonport dockyard,
she was lying alongside the south wall of number 2 basin
for a series of basin trials with various power cables and
lines connected from the shore. Part of the trials involved
testing the torpedo tube firing mechanism which
required the boat to be trimmed down to submerge
the tubes. At 13.30 under the supervision of the First
Lieutenant of *H.29*, Lieutenant Malcolm Edgar Wevell,
the trial got underway. He announced that he intended
'putting a drop of water' in the main ballast tanks which
would bring the boat down to the required trim,
however this intention was misheard by Petty Officer
George Aske as an order to flood the tanks. With the
tanks filling the boat steadily settled, until the stern was
underwater, and as several hatches were open and could
not be closed because of the tubes and lines from the
shore, water flooded in. She now started to sink rapidly
by the stern, despite trying to blow the ballast tanks clear.

Lieutenant Skyrme, who had just returned on board made desperate efforts to close the hatches, including cutting the pipes, but it was too late and there was a scramble for the men on board to clear the boat before she sank. One rating and five dockyard workers were drowned. The sinking resulted in a civilian inquest on the dead workmen and a series of courts martial. Wevell was found guilty of hazarding his ship by negligence or by default. He had failed to give clear orders, which had resulted in confusion, had failed to realise or investigate why the tanks had been flooded and further, he had failed to ensure that all the hatches were shut. He was dismissed his ship and severely reprimanded. Lieutenant Skyrme was found guilty of failing to take charge of the submarine and had been unclear of his executive officer's intentions; he was reprimanded. Petty Officer Aske was cleared of negligence as it was found that he had believed he was acting as ordered. The submarine was later successfully raised, but not returned to service, being sold for scrap in October 1927.

[TNA: ADM.156/96; Evans p159; www.britishnewspaperarchive.co.uk: Exeter & Plymouth Gazette 10 August 1926 p8 & 21 August 1926 p4]

13 October LEVANTER drifter

Aberdeen 1918; 94 tons; 86ft × 18.6ft

Sub-Lieutenant Honourable Neville Archibald John Watson Ettrick Napier

Tender to the battleship *Iron Duke*, she sailed from Invergordon in company with several other drifters bound for Port Edgar, but the wind increased until by the evening it was blowing a strong south-easterly gale with driving rain. When off Rattray Head she was struck by a particularly big wave which dislodged her boat and jammed the steering gear. Another wave broke over her, water flooding into the engine room and putting all the lights out. Control was regained, but the little flotilla steered for the refuge at Peterhead. As the *Levanter* was entering the harbour, she suffered another steering gear failure and she was again swamped by a wave, stopping the engine. The anchor was let go but this would not hold, and she was driven broadside on to the rocks and holed. Another of the flotilla, the *Coldsnap*, tried to go to her aid, but had to haul off when she bumped onto rocks. One man was swept overboard but managed to hold onto a rock for some time until hauled back on board. A raft was made, and two men volunteered to swim ashore with it, and in spite of the dreadful conditions made it ashore. By now the shore authorities were fully alerted and the local lifeboat was launched which lifted off the remaining thirteen members of the crew. She was eventually salvaged, but did not re-enter service, being sold out in September 1927.

[www.britishnewspaperarchive.co.uk: The Scotsman 14 October 1926 p5; Dundee Courier 14 October 1926 p7]

22 October VALERIAN sloop

South Shields 1916; 1,250 tons; 268ft × 33.6ft; 2 × 4.7in, 2 × 3pdr

Commander William Arthur Usher

Part of the North America and West Indies squadron, the sloop was returning to Bermuda from the Bahamas, where she had been employed taking the Governor to outlying islands. She sailed from Nassau 18 October, and when about 200 miles from Bermuda they received warnings of an approaching hurricane, and speed was increased to try and make the island before the storm arrived. By 08.00 on 22 October, they were about 5 miles from Gibbs Hill, the southernmost extremity of Hamilton Island and experiencing strong winds and high seas. At about 09.00 the hurricane came ashore on the island, with winds of over 130mph causing widespread damage. With the conditions worsening rapidly, the possibility of entering harbour became remote and the ship put her head to the south-east to try and ride out the storm. It was soon found that they were unable to make any headway, and at about 13.00 she was hit by a series of very violent squalls, the ship heeling over 70 degrees, but righted herself. Lashed by a further series of squalls she heeled over again, and lost power and swung broadside on to the sea. This time she did not recover and slowly rolled over, until the funnels became submerged at which the boilers exploded, and she sank. Carley floats were released, and the survivors scrambled on board. When the storm abated the cruisers *Capetown* and *Curlew* commenced a search, the former finding two rafts, with twenty survivors. Eighty-seven officers and men died.

[www.britishnewspaperarchive.co.uk: Portsmouth Evening News 25 October 1926 p7 & 3 November 1926 p8]

1927

11 November FUMAROLE drifter

Lowestoft 1919; 94 tons; 86ft × 18.6ft

Tender to the *Revenge*, the drifter was acting as a 'liberty boat' whilst the battleship was anchored at Portland. At 18.00 that evening, the submarine *L 56* was entering harbour and steered to clear the stern of the battleship to proceed to her moorings when she suddenly encountered the drifter as she pulled away from the *Revenge* loaded with men heading for Weymouth. She struck the drifter hard, heeling her over to port, throwing two men into the water and the drifter quickly filled and sank in less than 5 minutes. Other drifters and steam pinnaces were quickly on scene and assisted by searchlights picked up all the men from the water. The drifter lay in about 7 fathoms and was successfully raised on 18 November and was refitted for further service.

[www.britishnewspaperarchive.co.uk: Western Morning News 12 November 1927 p7]

1929

9 July H 47 submarine
Dalmuir 1918; 423/510 tons; 171.9ft × 15.9ft; 1 × 3in,
4 × torpedo tubes
Lieutenant Robert James Gardner

Having completed exercises in the Irish Sea with other boats of the Sixth Submarine Flotilla, the submarines sailed from Lamlash bound for Milford Haven on 8 July, but *H 47* was delayed due to an engine defect, and so proceeded independently. The following morning saw her about 15 miles west of Strumble Head, south Wales, proceeding south at 8.75 knots in calm weather and light winds. At 07.30, two submarines, identified as 'L' class boats, were sighted on the port quarter, and it appeared that they were steering to pass close astern. The pair was *L 12* and *L 14*, bound for St Ives, and at 12 knots were steadily overhauling *H 47* on a slightly converging course. The leading submarine of the pair, *L 12*, was commanded by Lieutenant Commander H P K Oram, an experienced submariner. The officer of the watch was an officer under training, Sub-Lieutenant Wise, under the supervision of Lieutenant Claude Keen RNR. At a little after 08.00 with *L 12* fast approaching the other boat, Keen became concerned that they were getting uncomfortably close and ordered an alteration in course to pass astern. After doing so it became clear that *H 47* was actually going astern, which made the situation worse, and a collision was inevitable. On the bridge of *H 47*, Lieutenant Gardner at 08.03 observed that *L 12* after appearing to intend to pass ahead, had altered course. He had at first believed that the approaching submarine would pass clear, but now feared that she would not, and ordered full astern and altered course, but it was too late, and she was struck heavily on the port side abaft the control room's foremost bulkhead, the bows of *L 12* penetrating about 2ft into the hull. *H 47* remained upright for several seconds before slowly heeling over to starboard and then sank bows first. The bows of *L 12* remained wedged in the side of *H 47* and as she sank, she was pulled down, sweeping her bridge staff into the sea, before being released to regain her trim. Twenty-one men from *H 47* died, with just three survivors; three men from *L 12* died. In the courts martial that followed, it was agreed that *L 12* was largely to blame. As the overhauling ship, she had failed to take avoiding action soon enough. Lieutenant Keen was found guilty of hazarding his ship through negligence and failing to take proper action to avoid a collision and was dismissed his ship and severely reprimanded. It was thought that a better course of action would have been to reduce speed and inform Oram of the situation. This was perhaps a little harsh; Keen had only taken over the watch just before 08.00 and rapidly realised that the

boats were too close to each other and on a converging course and *H 47* going astern had not helped matters. He had passed a message down to the control room to inform the Captain, but this does not seem to have reached Oram before the collision. Oram was cleared of any blame. Lieutenant Gardner was cleared of negligence but found guilty of failing to handle *H 47* in manner that would have avoided collision and was reprimanded.
[TNA: ADM.156/99; Evans p163]

1930

12 January ST GENNY tug
Chester 1919; 800 tons; 135ft × 29ft
Lieutenant Charles Frederick Paul†

A unit of the Fleet Target Service, she was attached to the Atlantic Fleet. Sailing from Portland on 11 January for Gibraltar, in company with the sloop *Snapdragon* and sister tug *St Cyrus*, they were able to maintain a speed of 8 knots, despite worsening weather. At first light on 12 January, then being about 32 miles to the west of Ushant, the high wind and seas forced them to reduce speed and put their heads into the sea. By that evening the wind was gusting at over 80mph with frequent violent squalls. The ships were all maintaining a close group, but at 19.55 the *St Genny* was seen to haul out of formation, apparently to keep clear of her companions. At 20.20 survivors testified that she shuddered when hit by a particularly heavy sea and soon after took a distinct list to starboard. An attempt was made to signal to her companions, but she continued to heel over until the waist was submerged and water poured into the stokehold and she sank stern first. Five men were picked up, but twenty-three officers and men drowned. The cause of her loss was evidently due to water entering her starboard fuel bunker although how this happened was uncertain, but it was possible that the bunker had been holed when the rubbing strake had been damaged in the storm.
[TNA: ADM.1/8745/155; ADM.1/8743/111]

28 April C 64 / ROSA fuel lighter
Paisley 1903 (*C.21*); 615 tons
Master W J Freeman

A steam-powered collier operated by the Naval Stores Department, she was en-route from Rosyth to Chatham with a cargo of coke, when she ran ashore about 300 yards north of Flamborough Head at about 02.00 in dense fog and high seas. Unsuccessful attempts were made to launch the ship's boats, but they were swept away before they could be manned. A rocket was fired from the shore to put a line aboard, and the Flamborough lifeboat was called out and despite heavy seas sweeping the deck, successfully lifted off all sixteen crew members. The lifeboat was damaged in doing so, several oars being broken. The wreck lay beam-on to the shore, wedged between rocks and battered by a heavy north-east swell and was declared a total loss. *[www.britishnewspaperarchive.co.uk: Yorkshire Post 29 April 1930 p9; Larn vol 3 sec 5]*

1931

9 June POSEIDON submarine
Barrow 1929; 1,475/2,040 tons; 289.2ft × 29.11ft; 1 × 4in, 8 × torpedo tubes
Lieutenant Commander Bernard William Galpin

Deployed to the China station and based at Wei Hai Wei (modern Weihai) in Shandong province, she was conducting exercises with the sloop *Marazion* in the Yellow Sea to the north of that port. In the late morning she was stationary on the surface and preparing to take up a position to allow the First Lieutenant to conduct a submerged attack on the sloop. At 12.03 she got under way, the sloop then being 4 miles distant on the port bow; a Chinese merchant ship, the *Yuta*, was also in sight about 5 miles away on the port beam heading towards them. Before they dived however, Galpin advised the First Lieutenant to turn to port, to give him a better chance of an attack on the sloop. His intention was to pass to starboard of the oncoming *Yuta*. The submarine was now underway at about 5 knots and started to alter round to port, but as they did so they realised that the *Yuta* had also altered course, to starboard. Galpin hastily ordered full astern and stopped the turn, but it was too late and at 12.12 the submarine was struck at right angles on the starboard side a few feet forward of her gun mounting. She immediately started to flood and sank rapidly, taking most of the crew with her in position 37.49.5N 122.16E, those on the conning tower being thrown into the water. The watertight doors had all been closed as she sank, which meant that some of the men trapped inside survived. A group of eight men were trapped forward and made the first use of the Davis Submarine Escape Apparatus (DSEA), when after waiting in rising water for over 2 hours for the pressure to rise, made their escape to the surface 130ft above them. Two of these failed to reach the surface, probably after fouling something, and of the other six, one later died. Petty Officer Ellis, who had been the senior rating of the party, was later awarded the Albert Medal. None of the eighteen men from the after end survived. Twenty-one men died in total. Lieutenant Commander Galpin was court-martialled for the loss of his vessel and found guilty on the charge of hazarding the submarine by negligence or default. It was found that the Japanese captain of the *Yuta* had decided to alter course to starboard to pass astern of the submarine.

Galpin had apparently not realised how close the *Yuta* was before ordering his turn. He was dismissed his ship and severely reprimanded.
[TNA: ADM.156/101; ADM.1/9502; Evans p174]

11 November PETERSFIELD sloop
Renfrew 1919; 800 tons; 231ft × 28.6ft; 1 × 4in, 1 × 12pdr
Commander Douglas Cuthbert Lang

Stationed in the Far East, the sloop acted as despatch vessel for the Commander-in-Chief, China Station, which at this time was Vice Admiral Sir William A H Kelly. The flagship was in the course of changing from *Suffolk* to *Kent*, and Kelly, accompanied by his wife and daughter, had embarked on board *Petersfield* to convey him from Shanghai to Foochow (Fuzhou). Kelly took an active interest in the navigation and ship handling skills of his officers, and the commanding officer, Lang, did not immediately impress him. As they sailed from Woosung, Lang seemed uncertain of his actions when they entered a fog bank and later, when the mist cleared the ship collided with a fairway buoy. The following day they encountered a disabled junk and his ship handling skills in dealing with the vessel were judged less than perfect by Kelly. The following day they continued their journey south, with Kelly regularly joining the Navigating Officer, Lieutenant Geoffrey Pratt, and Lang in discussions over the planned course. The pair appear to have been dominated by the Admiral, who let them know that he had been a navigator since 1892. The course for the night of 10/11 November was to take them to Tung Yung Island, about 60 miles north-east of Foochow. Kelly discussed the proposed course with Lang and Pratt and stated his belief that they might hold this course until the light on the island was raised or 03.00 at the latest. During the early hours of the morning the visibility worsened, with a thick fog obscuring the horizon, but the sloop steamed on at 12 knots, relying on dead reckoning. They should have raised the light on the island soon after midnight, but when nothing had been seen by 02.00 Lieutenant Pratt called Lang and proposed an alteration of course. Lang refused, and when asked if he thought it was safe to go on, replied 'We have damn well got to, because the Commander-in-Chief says so'. At 02.43 breakers were reported ahead and to port, and despite the helm being put over she struck the ground heavily. She heeled over and it soon became evident that she had gone ashore on Tung Yung Island (26.23N 120.30E). She was held fast and at first light it was clear that nothing could be done, and the ship was abandoned. Most of the crew were taken off by the German liner *Derfflinger*, the cruiser *Suffolk* arriving on scene later. The circumstances of the loss revealed in the subsequent courts martial of Lang and Pratt made headlines in Britain. Lang attempted to shift the whole

blame onto the Commander-in-Chief, who was called as one of the main witnesses. Lang claimed that Kelly had constantly interfered with his decisions and had undermined his confidence. The conference about the course to be steered that night had been the last straw, and he believed that Kelly expected his suggestions to be treated as orders and had effectively taken command from him. This was dismissed by the court – if he had believed that Kelly was now in command, then why did Lang not ensure that the Admiral was informed when the fog arose? Or that the light had not been sighted as expected? Kelly freely admitted that his actions may well have been regarded as 'tiresome', but a better officer would have been able to deal with this. The Admiral strongly denied 'leaning' on Lang and Pratt, who he claimed were inexperienced and lacked confidence. He later wrote that he regretted ever going on board the 'disgusting little ship' and attacked Lang, claiming he had displayed 'poor judgement, poor ship handling and lack of confidence and experience'. Kelly seems to have failed to understand the effect he was having on the ship's officers, both of whom were in their first seagoing appointments as commanding officer and navigating officer respectively, and both clearly felt intimidated by the domineering personality of Kelly. Lang was found guilty of stranding his ship by negligence and also hazarding his ship by negligence. He was dismissed his ship and severely reprimanded. Pratt was also found guilty of hazarding the sloop and was severely reprimanded. In reviewing the case the Admiralty backed Kelly to the hilt. Vice Admiral Preston, the Fourth Sea Lord, opined that Lang had 'allowed resentment to affect his judgement', a view agreed by Captain Geoffrey Layton, Chief of Staff to Kelly, who wrote that Lang had acted 'in a fit of bad temper and sulkiness' by deliberately allowing the ship to continue in poor visibility towards a known hazard. Lang resigned from the Navy in March 1933.
[TNA: ADM.156/70; ADM.156/103; ADM.116/2840]

numerous contacts were investigated, but all proved to be old wrecks. Then the master of a coasting vessel, the *Tynesider*, came forward and reported that he had been approaching Portland from the west that morning and had seen a submarine. She had been about 2 miles from the shore and seemed to be half out of the water, with conning tower and fore part showing, stern submerged. As the master watched it remained like this for some minutes before submerging completely, stern first and a steep angle. The search continued until finally on 3 February the destroyer *Torrid* located a possible contact. Investigated by *Dunoon*, her sweep wires fouled a large object and later that night divers from the *Tedworth* and *Albury* successfully located the sunken submarine, in position 50.34N 02.33W. Investigation over the next few days by divers ascertained that the door to the hangar, which housed the small seaplane, was open and the upper conning tower hatch was also open. The submarine was in a bows-up attitude, with damage visible to the propellers. Efforts were made over the next few weeks to salvage her, but all failed, and on 8 December this was finally abandoned, and she was left on the seabed. Two bodies were recovered during these operations, a Leading Aircraftman and a Leading Seaman, apparently part of the aircraft launching party. The precise cause of her loss was uncertain; the open door and discovery of some of the aircraft team would suggest that she was surfacing to launch her aircraft when lost. The hangar door may have been opened too soon and flooded the boat, but if so then she would have been more likely to sink bows first, rather than stern first, which she obviously had. An alternative theory was that the vent valves of the aft ballast tanks had been left open when surfacing, causing the tanks to start refilling. As the stern slowly submerged, water would have flooded into the hangar before the fault could be rectified. Seven officers and fifty-three ratings died.
[TNA: ADM.116/2925; ADM.1/8673/287]

1932

26 January **M 2** submarine
Barrow 1918; 1,594/1,946 tons; 295.9ft × 24.8ft; 1 × 3in, 4 × torpedo tubes, 1 × seaplane
Lieutenant Commander Duncan de Mursenden Leathes†
Exercising in the vicinity of Portland, at 10.11, *M 2* signalled her depot ship *Titania* that she intended diving at 10.30; this was to be the last heard from her. When she failed to return to harbour at 16.15 and did not respond to radio calls, ships were immediately despatched to her exercise area, about 3 miles west of Portland Bill. Ships scoured the area with Asdic, and

1938

12 February **WALRUS** destroyer
Govan 1917; 1,300 tons; 312ft × 29.6ft; 4 × 4in, 1 × 3in, 6 × torpedo tubes
Laid up in reserve at Rosyth, she was ordered to be taken to Sheerness under tow by the tug *St Mellons* for refitting, with a small crew of four men on board. When off the North Yorkshire coast, at just after noon on 12 February in a strong northerly gale, with winds of 70mph and heavy falls of snow, the tow parted. The tug called for assistance by radio, and the towing crew on board dropped anchor, but this failed to hold them,

and the ship was swept away, the tug losing contact. The Coastguards were alerted and the Teesmouth lifeboat was launched and spent 16 hours in a vain search for the destroyer. The destroyer was taken by the wind and tide into North Bay, Scarborough and was driven ashore about 200 yards from the high water mark. A rocket brigade was called out and great efforts were made to haul the Scarborough lifeboat to the scene, but a raft was seen to be launched and all four men reached the shore. She remained aground, battered by the storms and on 16 February it was decided to abandon her, and she was put up for sale. Eventually refloated on 29 March, she was towed away, this time to the scrapyard.

[www.britishnewspaperarchive.co.uk: Yorkshire Post 14 February 1938 p9]

1939

1 June THETIS submarine
Birkenhead 1938; 1,090/1,222 tons; 275ft × 26.7ft; 1 × 4in, 10 × torpedo tubes
Lieutenant Commander Guy Howard Bolus†

Newly completed and escorted by the tug *Grebecock*, the submarine sailed from Liverpool for her first diving trials, with a large number of civilian personnel from Cammell Laird and Vickers, plus Admiralty officials in addition to her crew. At 13.40 she was about 15 miles north of Great Ormes Head and signalled that she would shortly be diving and 20 minutes later she commenced her dive. This proved to be difficult and despite flooding both main and auxiliary ballast tanks, only her deck was awash, and the conning tower remained above water. It was believed that the trim, or weight required to submerge her, had been miscalculated, and a check of the bow torpedo tubes was ordered, to confirm that the bottom tubes were full of water, a necessary condition for her trim. This was supervised by Lieutenant Frederick Woods, who started checking the state of all the tubes, using the test cock. This involved aligning a lever with an indicator, which allowed adjacent holes at the rear of each tube to be lined up and a resulting spurt of water would demonstrate a full tube. As they worked through the tubes in sequence each proved to be dry, a fact which was then verified by Woods who opened the rear door of each tube after failing to find any water using the indicator. As the team checked tube number 5, no water emerged on testing, indicating another empty tube, so Woods ordered the door opened. As Leading Seaman Hambrook tried to open the door he found it very stiff, but then it suddenly shot open, and a flood of water poured into the submarine at great pressure. Realising that something was wrong, Bolus ordered tanks to be blown and all watertight doors to be shut. This latter order proved difficult to implement in the

bow compartment, as it was filling with water giving the boat a bows-down attitude, so men in this space were trying to pull the door shut 'uphill'. Further, the securing arrangements were complicated, requiring a number of clips to be secured by butterfly nuts and in the confusion one of the nuts fell off and jammed the door. The attempt was eventually abandoned, and the men finally secured the door of the next compartment. This meant that the submarine had her forward compartments flooded. She had dived at a steep angle and her bows struck the bottom with force, burying her nose in the mud. She was far too heavy forward to successfully surface and it was decided to attempt to enter the flooded compartment using escape apparatus via the escape chamber, close the bow tube door, and then open valves to allow the water to be pumped clear of one of the compartments. This was attempted three times, but each time it failed as the pressure in the escape chamber as they waited for it to flood proved too great for the volunteers. Bolus now blew his tanks which successfully raised his stern nearer to the surface. The tug which had been waiting on the surface became worried when the submarine had failed to surface as expected and alerted the shore authorities, who were already concerned at the silence from the boat. A search was therefore implemented with several ships and aircraft ordered to the area, the first on scene being the destroyer *Brazen* which arrived at 21.00 by which time it was dark. Indicator buoys had been released by *Thetis*, but despite being seen, the position was misreported and only added to the delay. It was not until first light on 2 June that *Brazen* found the submarine, her stern just clear of the water. She dropped explosive charges to indicate her presence. A few minutes later Captain Oram (Captain Fifth Submarine Flotilla) and Lieutenant Woods successfully used the escape chamber to come to the surface where they were picked up. Later that morning another two men escaped, who reported that oxygen was perilously low. No further men escaped, the crew being disorientated and finally overcome by carbon dioxide. The number of ships on the surface grew, and included the salvage vessel *Vigilant*, and a line was secured around the submarine's stern. During the afternoon of the 2nd an attempt was made to open a hole in the exposed stern. A top cover plate was removed, but they could go no further before the boat started to move with the tide making it impossible to keep a foothold and finally at 15.10 the securing wire broke, and the submarine disappeared beneath the waves again. In all ninety-nine men died. She was finally raised on 23 October and towed to Birkenhead where she was rebuilt and renamed *Thunderbolt*. She had been lost because the rear door to number 5 torpedo tube was opened whilst the bow cap was open to the sea and the watertight doors could not be closed in time. It was discovered that the test cock for the tube, which should have indicated the presence of water, had been jammed by a coating of bitumen enamel, used to paint the inside of the tube. The arrangement of the indicators showing the state of the bow caps was unnecessarily complicated and confusing, and had been read incorrectly, Lieutenant Woods and the fore ends team wrongly believing that it was closed. Finally, the watertight doors were too difficult to shut in an emergency situation. As a direct result of this accident several changes were introduced in British submarine construction. A clip (subsequently known as the 'Thetis clip'), was fitted to the rear doors of torpedo tubes which prevented them opening more than a fraction of an inch after the operating lever had been moved to open. Further, all watertight doors were made quick-closing and easy securing, eliminating the complicated nut and screw arrangement.

[TNA: ADM.1/10230; ADM.116/3812 – 3823; Evans p184; Kemp p95]

30 August SUNDOWN drifter

Aberdeen 1918; 94 tons; 86ft x 18.6ft

Tender to the battlecruiser *Repulse*, she arrived at Scapa Flow on 11 August, but was stranded at Sullom Voe and written off.

[Dittmar & Colledge p229; https://canmore.org.uk/ site/290560]

2 | Losses between 3 September 1939 and 15 August 1945

THE NAZI PARTY HAD GAINED POWER in Germany in 1933 and immediately began to re-arm. This increase in military spending, coupled with an increasingly aggressive foreign policy, made the likelihood of Europe remaining at peace doubtful. At the end of 1936, at the insistence of Japan, the restrictive Naval Treaties which had limited the size and number of ships were abandoned, but the increased building programmes of the late 1930s were unable to provide sufficient numbers of ships before Europe was catapulted into war. On 1 September 1939 Germany invaded Poland, to gain 'living space' in the east. Two days later Great Britain and France declared war on Germany to protect Polish independence.

It was realised that the submarine would be a major threat, as it had been in 1914–18, but it was expected that Asdic (sonar) would be able to counter this threat. Merchant ships were organised into convoys immediately, but the new 'pack' tactics used by the enemy, whereby a number of U-boats were positioned across the likely line of advance of a convoy, and then converge after it had been located, proved to be difficult to overcome. Anti-submarine tactics devised before the war, such as aggressive sweeps, were not as successful as had been hoped, and with the loss of the *Courageous*, the use of aircraft carriers on such tasks was exposed as dangerous. The mass production of small escorts and increased use of aircraft, coupled with advances in technology, such as the fitting of radar on escorts and the use of radio direction finding (HF/DF), finally mastered the submarine threat. The introduction of an acoustic homing torpedo for use in German submarines from 1943, designed to home onto the sound of a ship's cavitating propeller, added a further level of threat, and despite the introduction of countermeasures, such as the noise-generating Foxer streamed astern of the ship, several escorts were lost to the weapon.

Aircraft proved to be more of a threat to ships than had been anticipated and pre-war anti-aircraft defences on board British ships were found to be woefully inadequate. Further, it did not always require a direct hit from a bomb to incapacitate a ship, as the blast and shock damage from near-misses also proved fatal to many smaller craft. This was forcibly demonstrated by the losses to aircraft off Dunkirk and Norway in 1940 and the anti-shipping raids of 1940–1 in the North Sea. The technique employed by the enemy, with numbers of aircraft dropping bombs from a steep dive,

was responsible for the loss of several ships. In addition to strengthening the armament, the increasing use of radar on smaller ships provided long-range warning and could also assist with giving accurate ranges for the guns. The introduction by the Luftwaffe of guided weapons, such as the Hs 293, dropped and controlled from aircraft, added to the threat and caused several casualties before radio countermeasures such as jamming could be deployed.

It was expected that enemy minelaying would be a problem, as in the First World War, and to deal with the threat, dozens of fishing vessels were taken up to assist with the task of minesweeping. Although they could deal with moored contact mines, the unexpected deployment of influence mines, with magnetic or acoustic triggers, easily laid in shallow water by aircraft or small craft such as torpedo boats, caused major difficulties in keeping estuaries and harbours clear, and many of the requisitioned vessels fell victim before countermeasures could be put in place. To deal with magnetic mines, at first towed 'skids' were used, whereby a large electromagnet was towed astern or alternatively housed in the hold of a suitable mercantile conversion, to generate a magnetic field, strong enough to trigger the mine, but was found not to answer, as the mines were triggered close to the ship and vessels were lost using these methods. Reducing a ships' magnetic signature by degaussing was introduced, and from 1940 the 'LL' sweep came into service. This required the installation of diesel generators to provide a pulsed signal and the fitting of lengthy electric cables to be streamed astern, which detonated the mines at a safe distance. The somewhat crude method of dangling an electric hammer in a metal box overboard, which became the 'SA' sweep, dealt with the acoustic mine.

The surface threat from the enemy proved to be less of a threat than submarines, aircraft and mines, but the presence of a small number of large enemy combatants led to much effort being diverted to deal with them. The occasional forays into the Atlantic by enemy surface raiders had varying success, but never matched the threat posed by the submarine. In home waters, there was a continuous threat from enemy fast torpedo boats, usually referred to at the time as E-boats, particularly along the eastern coast. The desire to take similar action against the enemy led to frequent encounters between coastal forces.

It was anticipated that amphibious landings on a hostile shore would result in the loss of numbers of landing craft, but these operations also cost some of the supporting larger units. The losses after the Normandy landings highlighted the difficulty and danger of ships operating in close proximity to the coast whilst supporting the army ashore – circumstances that were repeated 40 years later in the Falklands campaign.

The entry into the war by Japan opened a new theatre of war, and the British forces, insufficient in number and with little or no air cover, were completely outnumbered and this led to the heavy losses suffered by British naval forces in the Far East between January and April 1942.

In addition to the hazards of facing the enemy, accidents, poor weather and poor judgement also feature. Petrol vapour explosions were all too common, particularly in the smaller craft. There were also several losses in so-called 'friendly fire' incidents, and these were invariably due to poor communications.

The level of violence required to sink a ship varied; *Repulse* and *Prince of Wales* finally succumbed to numerous bomb and torpedo strikes, able to withstand a level of punishment due to armour. The *Hood* was lost to a single plunging 38cm shell hit, which detonated a magazine. Smaller vessels, without the protection of armour, could succumb very quickly and some of the corvettes and armed trawlers lost simply disappeared in seconds.

In describing the losses, I have, where necessary, given an outline of the background of the loss, but the circumstances were often shaped by other, external events, and the role of intelligence should not be underestimated. This may be seen with the example of *Narwhal* in 1940, lost due to successful deciphering of British signals traffic by the German intelligence service, but similar losses occurred, for example the interception and torpedoing of the *Eridge* in 1942 followed the breaking of British encoded signals by the Italian Navy.

1939

10 September OXLEY submarine
Barrow 1926; 1,354/1,872 tons; 275ft × 27.7ft; 1 × 4in, 8 × torpedo tubes
Lieutenant Commander Harold Godfrey Bowerman
One of the opening hostile acts carried out by the Royal Navy was to deploy a number of submarines in the North Sea, along the coast of Norway, with the intention of intercepting enemy shipping. The boats were stationed just 12 miles apart, and during the afternoon of 10 September, *Oxley* had been in communication with the *Triton* in the adjoining sector using sound telegraphy (SST). Through this, at about

15.00, Bowerman estimated that he was about 7 miles from the *Triton*. That evening, the *Triton* came to the surface at 20.04 to recharge batteries and fix her position. At 20.55 the *Triton* saw the silhouette of a surfaced submarine on the starboard side and course was altered to bring the stranger on the bow. Lieutenant Commander Steel of the *Triton* ordered tubes to be readied for firing and prepared the boat for diving. To be certain that the stranger was not a friendly submarine, the night challenge was made by light three times, but they received no reply. This was followed by the firing of a green grenade, a flare which burnt brightly for several seconds. With still no reply or response from the stranger, Steel decided that she must be hostile and fired two torpedoes. Just after firing a flashing light was seen from the stranger, but no sense could be made of it before one of the torpedoes struck and the submarine disappeared in a cloud of smoke. The *Triton* closed the scene and found three men swimming in a patch of oil and debris and with difficulty picked up two of them, finding them to be Lieutenant Commander Bowerman and an able seaman from the *Oxley*. The subsequent enquiry into the disaster found that the *Oxley* had been out of position. Bowerman had surfaced at 20.30 but the sighting of shore lights was confused by misty rain. He believed himself to be about 2 miles inside his own sector, when he was actually 4 miles inside the adjoining sector. The lookouts had failed to see the repeated challenges made by the *Triton* and had only realised that that there was another submarine in the area when they saw the green flares. An attempt was then made to fire a grenade, but the rifle had malfunctioned. Bowerman then arrived on the bridge and ordered the night challenge to be made, but this had hardly started when they were hit amidships by a torpedo. The *Oxley* had probably been taken out of position by a strong tidal set to the east. Four officers and forty-eight ratings were lost.
[TNA: ADM 178/194; Evans p195]

17 September COURAGEOUS aircraft carrier
Walker on Tyne 1916; 22,500 tons; 786.7ft × 90.6ft; 16 × 4.7in, 48 aircraft
Captain William Tofield Makeig-Jones†
Escorted by four destroyers, the carrier sailed from Devonport on 16 September and proceeded to the south-west of Ireland to carry out offensive operations against enemy submarines, using air patrols. Another group based around the carrier *Hermes* was operating further to the south. At 15.45 on the 17th a distress message was received from the merchant ship *Kafiristan* that she was being attacked by a U-boat about 150 miles to the west of their position and two of the escorting destroyers were detached to proceed to the scene, whilst *Courageous* launched several Swordfish

aircraft to carry out searches. That complete, the carrier with her remaining escorts headed towards the area of the *Kafiristan* at 26 knots. At 18.40 the first of the searching aircraft returned, and after reducing speed, the carrier was busy for the next hour manoeuvring to recover her aircraft. At 19.45 the last of the Swordfish was on deck and she again turned towards the west and prepared to increase speed. At 19.58 she was hit by two torpedoes, the explosions being close together and she immediately suffered a loss of power, all the lights went out and she started to list to port. The escorting destroyers busily searched the area, and *Ivanhoe* carried out depth-charge attacks on a submerged contact, but without result. Within 10 minutes of the explosions, she had assumed an alarming list of 40–45 degrees and the engine rooms were ordered to be cleared as cracking noises were heard, indicating that bulkheads were collapsing. The list continued to increase, and she slowly rolled over until at 20.17 she capsized and sank with the loss of 518 officers and men. Her position was approximately 50.10W 14.50W; her attacker had been the *U 29* (Schuhart). The subsequent court of enquiry was critical of the officers. The immediate damage was limited to the section between 40 and 80 stations, but she flooded very rapidly, making her unstable. This could only have happened if water had entered compartments outside the damaged area – through bulkheads where hatches and doors were not closed. It was found that the rapid sinking had been due to the majority of the doors and all the ventilation flaps being open. There was also evidence that damage control was not well organised – several watertight markings had not been painted up and the ship's company had not been exercised sufficiently to deal with major damage. It was appreciated that the ship had only been in commission for 6 weeks, but some responsibility must lay with her officers. The senior surviving officer, Commander Claude Woodhouse was informed that he had ' … incurred their Lordships' displeasure'.
[TNA: ADM.156/195; ADM.267/67]

14 October **ROYAL OAK** battleship

Devonport 1914; 29,150 tons; 624.3ft × 88.6ft; 8 × 15in, 12 × 6in, 8 × 4in, 8 × 2pdr
Captain William Gordon Benn

During the night of 13/14 October the *Royal Oak* was lying at a single anchor at Scapa Flow; the night was fine and clear, the sky lit by the Northern Lights. At 01.04 an explosion occurred forward on the starboard side. Its effect was to break the slips on the anchor cables, which allowed the port cable to run out completely and also let go the starboard anchor. The noise of the explosion and the cable running out woke most of the officers and ship's company. Despite witnesses reporting seeing a column of water which had drenched the fo'c'sle, it

was at first thought to be an internal explosion in the inflammable store. Investigation showed that water was entering the compartment and pumps were ordered to be prepared and the adjacent compartments ordered checked. There was no thought of an external threat, so no orders were given for closing watertight doors or deadlights. At 01.16 there were three shattering explosions, all on the starboard side and they had an immediate effect. The ship at once started to heel to starboard and with only a slight hang for a few moments, rolled over with increasing speed until she capsized at 01.29. The explosions had occurred forward, the first under the bridge, then abreast the forward boiler room and the last just forward of number 3 dynamo room. The bulkhead between the dynamo room and the engine room immediately bulged and distorted. Fires were started and compartments filled with thick choking smoke. Following the explosions, all power was lost and the lights went out, rendering it impossible to do anything effective to save the ship. Carley floats were hastily thrown overboard before she capsized. Those men that had managed to reach the upper deck soon found themselves in the water, and there were many terrifying experiences – some men tried to man the launch at the starboard boom, but saw the ship rolling over on top of them; the funnel came down into the water between the launch and the ship's side and one man was sucked into the funnel and then blown out again. Others saw 'A' and 'B' turrets swing round and fall off into the sea. She lay bottom up for some time before sinking. The drifter *Daisy-II* did sterling work picking up over 300 survivors up from the water, but 835 men lost their lives, with 424 survivors. She had been attacked by the *U 47* (Prien), which had successfully penetrated the anchorage. In the first attack, at midnight, Prien had fired three torpedoes, aiming at the ship beyond the *Royal Oak*, which he had misidentified as the *Repulse* (it was actually the aircraft repair ship *Pegasus*). These had missed, but one had detonated near the bows of the battleship. All of the torpedoes from the second salvo had hit.
[TNA: ADM.1/9840]

30 October **NORTHERN ROVER** trawler

Wesermünde 1936 requisitioned 1939; 655 tons; 188ft × 28ft; 1 × 4in
Skipper Martin Hugh MacPherson RNR†

A London-registered trawler converted for use as an armed boarding vessel, searching neutral shipping. Tasked to patrol between Fair Isle and Kirkwall, she was last seen in the morning of 30 October. When she failed to return to Kirkwall as expected on 5 November a search was initiated, but no trace was ever found of her. After the war it was found that she had been hit by a single torpedo fired by *U 59* (Jürst), at 23.35 on

30 October to the west of Papa Westray. Twenty-seven men were lost.
[TNA: ADM.1/11077]

13 November BLANCHE destroyer

Hebburn on Tyne 1930; 1,360 tons; 323ft × 32.3ft;
4 × 4.7in, 2 × 2pdr, 8 × torpedo tubes
Lieutenant Commander Robert Marriot Aubrey

The destroyer sailed from the Humber 12 November in company with her sister *Basilisk*, acting as escort to the minelayer *Adventure* on her passage to Portsmouth. By that evening the trio were in the Thames estuary, but the weather was poor, with thick patches of fog, and they anchored near the Barrow Deep. In the early hours, the mist started to clear and at 03.00 they weighed and proceeded. By 05.00 they were approaching the Tongue light vessel and they were about 3 miles from the light vessel when at 05.26 the *Adventure* detonated a mine. The destroyers stopped, and then whilst *Basilisk* went alongside the minelayer the *Blanche* carried out an anti-submarine sweep, as it was initially thought to have been a torpedo. By 07.45 the situation on the minelayer had stabilised and she was able to get underway, heading towards Sheerness at slow speed, led by *Basilisk*, with the *Blanche* stationed on the starboard bow of the pair. At 08.10 there was a large explosion on the port side under the stern of the *Blanche*. All steam was lost, the upper deck was split, the after engine room bulkhead buckled, and she flooded quickly aft, the water spreading to the cabin flat and the engine room, but she remained afloat. At 09.10 a tug arrived on scene and soon after she was under tow for Sheerness. However, she continued to settle by the stern and the list to port increased until by 09.30 the stern was awash, and all men were then ordered to the upper deck. At 09.50 she took a lurch to port and did not recover, slowly rolling over until she sank. Several local craft on hearing the explosion had closed the area, a trawler picking up over sixty men from the water including the captain, many of them covered in oil. Two ratings were lost. The minefield had been laid by four German destroyers, *Karl Galster*, *Wilhelm Heidkamp*, *Hermann Künne* and *Hans Lüdemann*, during the night of 12/13 November. The same minefield claimed thirteen merchant ships that were lost on the barrier. The wreck has been found and lies in position 51.27.34N 01.27.15E.
[TNA: ADM.1/10357; Larn vol 2 sec 7]

16 November MTB 6 torpedo boat

Hythe 1936; 22 tons; 60.4ft × 13.10ft; 2 × torpedoes, machine guns
Lieutenant Hardress Llewellyn Lloyd

Part of the First MTB Flotilla based in Malta, the boats were ordered to return to home waters in November. Half of the flotilla was shipped back as deck cargo, with the remainder making their way through the French canal system, *MTB 6* being one of these. As they made their way across the western Mediterranean to Marseilles, escorted by the destroyer *Dainty*, the weather was poor and worsened until it was blowing a gale from the north-west. The small boats suffered badly, pounding in the high waves and regularly swamped by seas which washed over them. At first light on 15 November *MTB 6* was in a poor state, with a flooded engine room. The *Dainty* closed and took off her crew and also embarked her torpedoes. That complete, a tow was rigged and the destroyer got underway for the shelter of Ajaccio, but during the night the tow parted. In the darkness and high seas reconnecting the tow was a difficult and dangerous task, and with the torpedo boat now low in the water, it was decided that she could not be saved. The *Dainty* therefore deliberately rammed the craft, cutting her in two; the stern half sank immediately but the bow portion was rammed again to ensure that she sank.
[Jefferson pp16–18; Reynolds & Cooper, *Mediterranean MTBs* p8]

20 November MASTIFF trawler

Leith 1938; 520 tons; 150t × 27.6ft; 1 × 4in, 1 × 20mm
Lieutenant Commander Aymé Arthur Carrington Ouvry

Fitted out as a minesweeper, she was working in conjunction with another converted trawler, the *Cape Spartel*, to recover a floating mine which had been discovered 1 mile to the east of the Tongue Light Vessel in the Thames estuary. At 10.23 as she was in the process of recovering the mine it detonated and this was followed by a second explosion, probably as her boiler exploded, and she sank very quickly. *Cape Spartel* picked up survivors, and the Margate lifeboat was launched to search the area, but five men were killed and a sixth died later of his injuries. She was probably a victim of the mines laid by a force of German destroyers some days earlier.
[TNA: ADM.1/10077; ADM.358/3595]

21 November GIPSY destroyer

Govan 1935; 1,350 tons; 323ft × 33ft; 4 × 4.7in, 10 × torpedo tubes
Lieutenant Commander Nigel John Crossley[†]

During the evening of 21 November, at about 19.30, German He 59 seaplanes were observed from Landguard fort at Felixstowe to fly low over the approaches to Harwich and drop objects in the harbour. It was suspected that these were mines, and the senior officer at Harwich closed the harbour to all traffic and ordered all destroyers in the haven to sea. From cross bearings taken from the shore, it was believed the mines were on the northern side of the channel, so the destroyers were ordered to keep to the southern side when leaving. Sailing at 21.00

the *Gipsy* was following 2 or 3 cables (400–600 yards) astern of her sister destroyer the *Griffin* and ahead of the *Keith* and *Boadicea*, when at 21.20 there was a terrific explosion under the hull as they passed the Cliff Foot buoy off Landguard Point. The explosion was so violent that the staff on the bridge were thrown onto the forward decks. The engine and boiler rooms had taken the full force of the blast and the ship broke in two amidships and settled to the bottom, the bow and stern sections being visible at low water. Thirty men died in the explosion or of their injuries. She remained a hazard, blocking the fairway, and efforts continued for some time to clear her remains, eventually both halves being raised and dragged a short distance into shallow water (51.56N 01.18E) where they remained until sold for scrap in 1969.
[TNA: ADM.1/22793; Shores, Fledgling Eagles p113; Warship Supplement 89 p9]

22 November **ARAGONITE** trawler
Beverley 1934 requisitioned 1939; 315 tons; 133.2ft × 24.5ft
Skipper George Kinnaird RNR
A former Hull trawler, converted for naval use as a minesweeper, she was returning to Deal from an uneventful patrol when at 15.45 as they passed the South Brake buoy there was a dull explosion on the port side which lifted the ship up and put all the lights out. She settled in the water until the decks were awash but remained afloat and was assisted by two tugs which closed and securing themselves on each side headed for the shore. However, she continued to fill with water and the tugs slipped the wires and allowed her to sink; she was then about three-quarters of a mile to the north-east of Deal Coastguard station. There were no casualties. Her wreck has been found and lies in sections, part in position 51.14.14N 01.25E, another in position 51.14.08N 01.24.59E, which suggests that the wreck was later dispersed. The mine that she had detonated was probably one of those laid by He 59 seaplanes during the night of 20/21 November.
[TNA: ADM.1/10335; Larn vol 2 sec 5]

23 November **RAWALPINDI** armed merchant cruiser
Greenock 1925 requisitioned 1939; 16,297 tons; 547.7ft × 71.3ft; 8 × 6in, 2 × 12pdr
Captain Edward Coverley Kennedy†
A former P & O line steamer armed and engaged in patrolling the north Atlantic to the south-east of Iceland as part of the blockade of Germany. At 15.30 when in position 63.35N 11.40W she sighted a ship closing which was identified as being a German cruiser. It was actually the battlecruiser *Scharnhorst* accompanied by her sister, the *Gneisenau*, the pair having had the *Rawalpindi* in sight for over 20 minutes. Kennedy altered course

to present his starboard quarter and dropped smoke floats in attempts to confuse the enemy. With a second hostile ship coming into view, at 15.48 the closing cruiser signalled *Rawalpindi* to stop, which was ignored, and then opened fire just after 16.00. The *Rawalpindi* returned fire with her starboard guns, but she was hit by the third salvo from the hostile cruiser which put the lights out and disabled the electric winches for the ammunition hoists. The next salvo hit the bridge. Both German ships were now firing and hitting repeatedly, with *Rawalpindi* continuing to return fire when she could, managing to hit the *Scharnhorst* with a 6in round, but not inflicting any serious damage. With fires now taking hold she was unable to continue to reply and at 16.15 her attacker ceased fire as she was clearly disabled. The crew managed to launch three boats and two of these, with twenty-six men on board, were picked up by the Germans. The third, with eleven men, made off, to be picked up later by the *Chitral*. The German pair continued to search the area for survivors, but sighted a large warship closing, believed to be a British cruiser (it was the *Newcastle*), and both German units took the opportunity to escape into a rain squall. The *Rawalpindi* continued to burn until 20.20 when she slowly rolled over to starboard and sank. In all 238 men died.
[TNA: ADM.1/19900; ADM.199/725; ADM.267/113]

29 November **BIRCHOL** oiler
Whiteinch 1917; 2,365 tons; 210ft × 34.7ft
Master William McEver RFA
Birchol sailed from Rothesay in company with the oiler *Montenol* and escorted by the patrol vessel *Sheldrake*, the trio steamed towards the Hebrides, intending to pass through the Sound of Eriskay. The weather was poor, and worsened, with a strong south-westerly wind, a high swell and constant rain. At about 17.30 that night the ships lost contact with each other in the darkness, but the *Birchol* continued on her course through the pitch-dark night and driving rain, relying on dead reckoning. At 18.05 land loomed out the darkness right ahead and she ran hard aground on South Uist, near Ru Melvich in position 57.05N 007.13.44W. Investigation showed that she had settled onto the rocks and could not be salved and was abandoned after all useable stores had been removed. The court of enquiry found that Mr McEver was to blame for the loss; he had been too reliant on his dead reckoning and was actually 5 miles to the eastward of his estimated position. Further, he had not made a sufficient alteration of course after he had sighted Barra Head, and had not ordered soundings to be taken, although entering coastal waters. There was some question over his future employment, but it was felt that his services could not be spared in wartime, and he was later given command of the *War Nawab*.
[TNA: ADM.178/195]

6 December **WASHINGTON** trawler

Selby 1909 requisitioned 1939; 209 tons; 117ft × 21.6ft
Skipper Joseph Anson Jennison RNR†

A former Grimsby-based trawler, she was newly requisitioned and was en-route to take up her duties as a 'look out vessel', on local patrol off Great Yarmouth when there was a large explosion, as she detonated a mine at 10.32 near the Cockle Light Vessel off Caister, in position 52.39N 01.45E. Seven men were killed with one survivor. The mine was probably one of those laid by the submarine *U 59* (Jürst).

[TNA: ADM.1/10077; www.britishnewspaperarchive.co.uk: Western Daily Press 8 December 1939 p8]

10 December **RAY OF HOPE** drifter

Lowestoft 1925 requisitioned 1939; 98 tons; 87.5ft × 19.6ft
Skipper Walter Hayes RNR

A former Lowestoft drifter, she was based at Ramsgate with the Mine Recovery Flotilla, which was employed in 'fishing' for air-dropped mines, using a small trawl sweep to drag along the bottom, aiming to find an intact mine. The *Ray of Hope* was working in company with another drifter, *Silver Dawn*, in the Thames Estuary to the east of the swept war channel where parachute mines had been seen to drop. The *Ray of Hope* found her sweep had become entangled with an underwater obstruction, but at 15.00 as they heaved in on the winch to recover the wire there was a large explosion as she detonated a mine which demolished the drifter. The skipper was blown off the bridge into the water but survived. Nine men were killed. The wreck lies in position 51.30.14N 01.25.39E.

[TNA: ADM.1/10077; Lund & Ludlam, Trawlers go to War p28; Larn vol 2 sec 7]

12 December **DUCHESS** destroyer

Hebburn 1932; 1,375 tons; 329ft × 33ft; 4 × 4.7in, 2 × 2pdr, 8 × torpedo tubes
Lieutenant Commander Robert Charles Meadows White†

The *Duchess* had been stationed in the Far East, but along with other 'D' class ships she was ordered to return to home waters in late 1939. From Gibraltar she formed part of the escort to the battleship *Barham* bound for the Clyde. By the early hours of 12 December, the group were in the North Channel, to the north-east of Rathlin Island, each ship zigzagging. At 04.25 as part of her zigzag the battleship made a 45-degree alteration in the course steered, but in the darkness the close proximity of her escorts was evidently not realised, as 2 minutes later she struck the *Duchess*, hitting her forward and rolling her over. Her upturned hull remained afloat for some time before she sank at 04.51, her depth charges exploding as she did so. Efforts were made by *Barham* to rescue men, but most were trapped in the upturned hull.

One hundred and thirty-five men were lost, with just twenty-three survivors. The *Barham* fixed her position as 293 degrees Kintyre Light 8.6 miles.
[TNA: ADM.53/107659]

13 December **WILLIAM HALLETT** trawler

Wivenhoe 1918 requisitioned 1939; 202 tons; 115.4ft × 22ft
Skipper Charles William Hannant RNR†

Former North Shields registered trawler, converted for use as a patrol vessel and stationed in the River Tyne. Following reports of moored mines being located off the Tyne, she investigated, streaming her trawl net. A mine was detonated in her trawl and then a few moments later she detonated a mine under the hull and rapidly sank. She was then about 3.5 miles east-south-east of St Mary's Light. Eight men died with one survivor being picked up by the *Ben Arthur*. The mine was one of those laid by German destroyers during the previous night. The wreck lies in position 55.03.45N 01.21.18W.

[TNA: ADM.1/1077; ADM.199/973; Larn vol 3 sec 7]

14 December **JAMES LUDFORD** trawler

Selby 1918; 438 tons; 138.4ft × 23.9ft; 2 × 12pdr
Lieutenant Commander Harry Richard John Lewis RNR†

In the early morning of 14 December there were two explosions as a northbound convoy passed the entrance to the River Tyne and coupled with the loss of the *William Hallett* (above), it was feared that either a submarine was in the area or mines had been laid. A further casualty occurred during the morning when the *James Ludford* was destroyed. Survivors stated that a floating mine was sighted, and as they manoeuvred to close and sink it with gunfire, there was a large explosion under the ship, evidently as she ran over another, unseen mine, and she rapidly sank. The mine was almost certainly one of those laid by German destroyers during the night of 12/13 December. The ship's boat was washed ashore at Cambois. Seventeen officers and men died with three survivors. The wreck lies in position 55.02.30N 01.16.15W

[TNA: CAB.66/4; Larn vol 3 sec 7]

14 December **EVELINA** trawler

Wivenhoe 1918 requisitioned 1939; 202 tons; 115.4ft × 22ft
Skipper John William Cowling RNR†

Former North Shields trawler converted for naval use as a patrol vessel. She failed to return from her night patrol off the River Tyne as expected during the morning of 15 December and was presumed lost on a mine, probably one of those laid by German destroyers. Nine men died.

[TNA: ADM.1/10077; ADM.358/3278]

14 December SEDGEFLY trawler
Middlesbrough 1939 requisitioned 1939; 520 tons;
175.8ft × 28.5ft
Chief Skipper Royce William Stocks RNR[†]
Converted for use as a patrol vessel, she was in company
with the *Evelina* (above), and also failed to return from a
night patrol off the Tyne and presumed lost by striking
a mine, probably in the extensive field laid by German
destroyers. All seventeen men on board died.
[TNA: ADM.1/10077; ADM.358/3278]

20 December NAPIA tug
South Shields 1914 requisitioned 1939; 155 tons;
90.3ft × 22.1ft
Master Charles Frederick Blake[†]
Engaged in the examination service, stopping and
checking on merchant vessels as they approached
ports, she was stationed off the Goodwin Sands when
she detonated a mine and sank rapidly. The wreck has
been found and lies in position 51.15.41N 01.25.11E.
The mine was probably one of those laid by German
destroyers. All ten crew members died.
[Larn vol 2 sec 5]

21 December BAYONET boom defence vessel
Blyth 1938; 530 tons; 159ft × 30.6ft; 1 × 3in
Boom Skipper Archibald Lamont RNR
Based at Leith, the *Bayonet* worked during the day to
install a new section of the boom barrier off the port,
completing the task by mid-afternoon. At 15.00 she got
underway and steered towards the harbour, but at 15.10
there was an explosion abaft the bridge. The detonation
did not seem to be large, but water flooded into the
machinery spaces and it soon became clear that she was
settling. Power was lost and she sank stern first in position
55.59N 03.09W. Three men were killed. An investigation
showed that the vessel had crossed the southern end
of a line of defensive mines laid by the *Plover* and
Skipper Lamont was deemed to be blameable, having
failed to properly fix his position, relying on eyesight
alone. However, the Director of Navigation supported
Lamont – the navigational restrictions imposed by the
position of the mines so close to the boom did not leave
a reasonable margin of safety to manoeuvre, indeed the
existing layout of mines and boom was dangerous. As a
direct result of this intervention the southern end of the
minefield was ordered to be swept.
[TNA: ADM.199/539]

22 December DROMIO trawler
Beverley 1929 requisitioned 1939; 380 tons;
140.9ft × 25.5ft; 1 × 6pdr
Lieutenant Commander George Dibley RNR
A former Hull trawler converted to a minesweeper, she
was leading a column of trawlers off the Northumbrian

coast, when during the night she crossed the bows of
the Italian steamer *Valdarno* (5,696 tons). The steamer
went astern and sounded her whistle but was unable
to prevent a collision, the larger ship striking the
trawler on the starboard side and she heeled over and
sank. After the collision, all seventeen members of the
crew were taken on board the Italian ship but were
later transferred to the trawler *Colonio* which put them
ashore at a north-east port. The *Dromio* was taken in
tow but sank approximately 3 miles north of Whitby.
There were no casualties.
[https://www.pastscape.org.uk; Yorkshire Post 23 December
1939 p1]

23 December GLENALBYN drifter
Findochty 1909 requisitioned 1939; 82 tons; 86.1ft × 18.3ft
The threat posed by magnetic mines became clear in the
opening days of the war, and to tackle the menace, the
generation of a powerful electrical field which would
prematurely detonate a mine offered a solution. At
Aultbea on Loch Ewe, designated as a convoy assembly
point, several elderly drifters were taken over and fitted
with a large coil. Unmanned, they would be connected
to another vessel, fitted with a high power generator,
which would tow the 'coil-drifters'. As mines had been
found at the entrance to the loch, they were set to work
in the convoy anchorage and then establishing a swept
channel to the sea. It was whilst engaged in this work
that two of the coil-drifters were blown up as they
detonated mines. *Glenalbyn* was one of them.
[Hardy p59]

23 December PROMOTIVE drifter
Great Yarmouth 1908 requisitioned 1939; 78 tons;
82.6ft × 18.8ft
As with *Glenalbyn* (see above), the *Promotive* was based
at Aultbea, Loch Ewe, and was fitted with a large coil,
energised by a generator in a towing drifter. During the
course of sweeping a mine detonated under her and she
was blown up. The mines had been laid by *U 31* on 27
October.
[Hardy p59]

25 December LOCH DOON trawler
Middlesbrough 1939 requisitioned 1939; 534 tons;
173.6ft × 28.6ft; 1 × 4in
Skipper George Henry Alexander Thompson RNR[†]
Failed to return from a patrol off Blyth, she was last
heard from during the morning of 25 December, when
she reported sighting a floating mine, which she was
proceeding to deal with. The mine was probably one
of those laid by *U 22* on 20 December. All fifteen men
on board died.
[TNA: CAB.66/4; ADM.358/3604]

28 December BARBARA ROBERTSON trawler
Selby 1918 requisitioned 1939; 325 tons; 135ft × 23.9ft;
1 × 12pdr
Skipper E – Hall

In November 1939, the *Barbara Robertson* had been armed by the Navy but retained the original crew on a T.124 agreement (subject to naval discipline whilst retaining Merchant Navy rates of pay). She was returning to Hull from the Icelandic fishing grounds when she was attacked in the early hours by the submarine *U 30* (Lemp), which surfaced on the port quarter of the trawler when she was about 35 miles north-west of the Butt of Lewis. The first the crew knew of the presence of the submarine was when two shells dropped nearby. Unable to see her attacker, only the flashes of the gun, all the men were ordered up, just as the third shell went through the wheelhouse, putting the steering gear out of operation. Unable to defend herself and with more shells hitting her, the boat was hoisted out and she was abandoned. As the boat cleared the trawler the submarine fired several more shells into her and she went down by the head. The survivors were in the open boat for 12 hours before being picked up by the destroyer *Isis*. One man was lost.
[TNA: ADM. 199/2131; www.britishnewspaperarchive.co.uk:
Fleetwood Chronicle 5 January 1940]

1940

January SEAHORSE submarine
Chatham 1932; 640/927 tons; 187ft × 24ft; 1 × 3in,
6 × torpedo tubes
Lieutenant Dennis Staunton Massey-Dawson[†]

The submarine sailed on 26 December 1939 from Blyth to conduct a patrol in the southern North Sea, between Heligoland and the Elbe but was not seen again and failed to return as expected on 9 January. The cause of her loss is uncertain; it was believed at the time that she had been mined, and this remains a distinct possibility. She would have been in the vicinity of a newly-laid minefield in position 55.26N 07.02E on 29 December and off Heligoland on the 30th. Various attacks on possible sonar contacts were made by German vessels during 6/7 January which offer an alternative fate. Minesweeper *M 5* carried out a series of depth-charge attacks to the north-west of Heligoland, during the afternoon of 6 January in approximate position 54.19N 07.30E, but with no obvious results. The following day at 13.18 in the same area *M 122* and *M 132* sighted a surfaced submarine which dived, and a sustained depth-charge attack was then carried out, although no results were evident. *M 5* returned to the area on 11 January to carry out a series of depth-charge attacks which produced some oil. Thirty-nine men were lost.
[Evans p205; TNA: ADM 358/8]

5 January KINGSTON CORNELIAN trawler
Beverley 1934, purchased 1939; 449 tons; 160.6ft × 26.6ft;
1 × 4in
Skipper William Green RNR[†]

Former Hull-based trawler, she was converted for use as an anti-submarine escort and stationed at Gibraltar. She sank very quickly after a collision at 23.00 with the French merchant ship *Chella* (8,920 tons) to the east of the port in position 36.02N 05.23W. Her depth charges exploded as she sank and there were no survivors, all nineteen men of the crew being lost.
[TNA: ADM. 199/2199; ADM. 358/3605]

7 January UNDINE submarine
Barrow 1937; 540/730 tons; 180ft × 16.1ft; 6 × torpedo
tubes
Lieutenant Commander Alan Spencer Jackson

The *Undine* sailed from Blyth on 31 December 1939 to conduct a patrol in the North Sea in the vicinity of Heligoland. During the morning of 7 January, about 20 miles west of the island, two armed trawlers were seen, and an attack carried out at 09.50, but without success, both torpedoes missing. The trawlers, which were *M 1201* and *M 1204*, immediately responded with the dropping of several depth charges, but these caused no damage. The Asdic and hydrophones of the *Undine* were not working properly, and Jackson was unable to determine where his opponents were, so after a period of silence came to periscope depth, only to find a trawler close on his starboard side. Despite ordering the boat to be taken down to 60ft, depth charges were dropped at close range, which started several leaks and shattered lights and glass. The hydroplanes were found to be jammed at rise and the fore-ends were reported to be flooding. The submarine broke surface and came under fire from the trawlers, although the firing was inaccurate. Unable to submerge and clearly in danger of being rammed or sunk by gunfire, without being able to respond, she was ordered to be abandoned. The evacuation was rapidly completed, the confidential books being burnt as they left, all of the crew being taken prisoner. The submarine settled, but the conning tower remained above water, and a small party of Germans managed to board, to search for papers and books, and attempt to rig a tow, but the boat sank before this could be accomplished.
[Evans p200]

9 January STARFISH submarine
Chatham 1933; 640/927 tons; 187ft × 24ft; 1 × 3in,
6 × torpedo tubes
Lieutenant Thomas Anthony Turner

The submarine sailed from Blyth on 5 January to conduct a patrol in the southern North Sea, near Heligoland. The first days of her patrol were uneventful, and she moved to the southern part of her patrol area in the early hours of 9 January, to re-position herself 5 miles to the south-west of the island. At 09.30 a German warship was sighted, originally thought to be a destroyer, but later ascertained to be a minesweeper. A torpedo attack was attempted, but not completed due to an internal communications error. The submarine was then brought to periscope depth to try and restart the attack, but the periscope was sighted by her target, which was the minesweeper *M.7*, and a depth-charge attack was the result. The boat was taken down to the bottom, at 90ft. After lying silent for some time, as she got underway a further depth-charge attack was carried out, with four charges exploding close to her, which shook the boat considerably, but she remained undamaged. They remained bottomed and as they listened to German sonar, it became clear that the hunt was continuing. At 14.40 the enemy evidently regained contact and a very heavy depth-charge attack took place, about twenty charges exploding all around the bottomed submarine. The explosions shattered glass and popped rivets, and several leaks were started, but the submarine remained lying on the bottom, hoping to evade further detection. No further charges were dropped, but engine noises were still audible above her. By 18.00 the situation on board was deteriorating; despite attempting to stem the leaks, several compartments were flooding with water and it was clear that unless she surfaced soon, the engines would become inoperable. At 18.20 she blew tanks and came to the surface, at a stern first angle. As she broke surface, two German warships were seen nearby, both of which illuminated her with searchlights, and the submarine came under fire from small arms. One ballast tank was then flooded, and as the submarine started to heel over, the crew were ordered to abandon her, and she sank rapidly bows first, the stern rising clear as she went under. All the crew was picked up by her attackers. [*Evans p206; TNA: ADM 267/114*]

11 January PRINCESS yacht
Haverton Hill 1924 requisitioned 1939; 730 tons; 186ft × 30ft
Captain William Gabbett Ashton Shuttleworth RNVR
Fitted out as an armed vessel, she was on station in the Bristol Channel, and ordered to patrol between Bull Point and Foreland. She was steering west when at 04.10 she sighted a white light right ahead. It was estimated to be about a quarter of a mile distant, and she altered course to starboard, blowing her siren as she did so. She then saw the bow lights of the oncoming ship right ahead, and evidently turning to port. The engines were stopped, but she was struck on the port side amidships by the steamer *Blairmore* (4,141 tons). The hole in the side was large, and as the *Blairmore* went

astern, the water entered at a fast rate. The *Princess* was turned in towards the shore and all boats were ordered to be turned out. After about 10 minutes, it was clear that she was sinking by the stern and the port anchor was ordered to be let go, and the hands were ordered into the boats and Carley floats, which was completed before she sank. She was then about 9.5 miles to the south-west of Bull Point, in approximate position 51.16N 03.55W. The *Blairmore* had stopped, and she picked up all the survivors, taking them to Breaksea anchorage. The subsequent inquiry was critical of the fact that a Chief Petty Officer was acting as the officer of the watch at the time but accepted that this had no bearing on the subsequent collision. The blame for that was placed firmly on the *Blairmore*, which had turned the wrong way. A sum of £37,500 was subsequently won in compensation from the owners of the *Blairmore*. [*TNA: ADM.1/12519*]

12 January VALDORA trawler
Selby 1916 (*Topaz*) requisitioned 1939; 251 tons; 121.8ft × 22.6ft
Skipper Albert Potterton RNR†
A former Grimsby trawler employed as a patrol vessel, she sailed from Dover on 11 January bound for Grimsby, but she failed to arrive and with no news of her she was presumed lost with all hands, one officer and nine ratings. During the day there was much enemy air activity in the area, with several vessels being attacked, mostly by He 111 aircraft. It is likely that she was the trawler seen by *Light Vessel 85* off Cromer to blow up at 17.00 on 12 January after an attack by a German aircraft. [*TNA: ADM.199/2199; ADM.358/10*]

19 January GRENVILLE destroyer
Scotstoun 1935; 1,465 tons; 319ft × 34.6ft; 5 × 4.7in, 8 × torpedo tubes
Captain George Elvey Creasey
In company with her sisters *Griffin* and *Grenade*, the trio were heading east in line abreast, 1 mile apart, and steaming at 20 knots conducting a patrol in the southern North Sea. At 12.45 there was the dull thud of an explosion and black smoke was seen to cover the *Grenville*. This was followed a second or so later by a large quantity of steam, as her boilers exploded. As the smoke and steam cleared her companions could see that her back had been broken, both her bows and stern sections coming out of the water and were almost vertical before sinking. They both closed to pick survivors up from the water, and as they did so there was another explosion close astern of *Grenade*, but she was not seriously damaged. Her position was 51.38N 02.17E. It was believed that either a magnetic or acoustic mine was responsible, and it was later

found that the group had entered an extensive field of magnetic mines laid by German destroyers. Seventy-five men lost their lives.

[TNA: ADM.116/4518]

21 January EXMOUTH destroyer
Portsmouth 1934; 1,460 tons; 332ft × 33.9ft; 5 × 4.7in, 8 × torpedo tubes
Captain Richard Stoddart Benson†

Ordered to escort the *Cyprian Prince* laden with military stores from Aberdeen to Kirkwall, the pair sailed at 20.30, the merchant vessel following in the wake of the destroyer. At 04.44 when in position 58.18N 02.25E an explosion was heard by the personnel on the bridge of the *Cyprian Prince*, which was thought to be the *Exmouth* dropping depth charges, but a few moments later, at 04.48 there was another, larger explosion and a column of flames and smoke was seen on the starboard bow. The observers were initially confused as to the identity of the ship involved, as they also saw a small white light on the starboard bow, which they thought might be the *Exmouth*. A short time later, they saw a number of small flashing lights in the water ahead – evidently lifejacket lights – and clearly heard the shouts and cries of men in the water. The master of the *Cyprian Prince*, Mr Wilson, was now on the bridge and stopped his engines, and ordered life rafts to be thrown overboard. He was now in a difficult position; clearly a ship had been torpedoed, but by stopping he feared that he would merely give the submarine another target to fire at. He therefore decided that he could not loiter and proceeded at full speed out of the area. A subsequent search of the area found wreckage, but failed to find any survivors, all 189 men on board were lost. The court of enquiry cleared Captain Wilson of any responsibility, informing him that 'his action … was entirely correct' and confirmed that Admiralty instructions to masters stressed the need to press on and not stop to pick up survivors. Her attacker had been the surfaced *U 22* (Jenisch) who had fired a single torpedo at a destroyer, which hit the starboard side. The second explosion was probably the forward magazine blowing up.

[TNA: ADM.1/10733]

27 January RIANT drifter
Oulton Broad 1919 requisitioned 1939; 95 tons; 86.2ft × 18.5ft
Skipper George Henry Kersey RNR

Ordered to proceed to Oban where she would be stationed, the drifter departed Lamlash during the morning of 26 January. As they steamed north the weather deteriorated, with the winds picking up and the sea rising. During the afternoon water was found to be entering, and they were having difficulty in keeping the bilges clear. They decided to lay to for the night, off Otter Rock, and by 08.00 the next morning the weather had improved and the water in the bilges had dropped, and they again got under way. Just an hour later it was found that water was again entering, and the engineer believed that a plate had split around the discharge pipe aft. It became evident that they could not clear the water, so Skipper Kersey decided to head for the island of Gigha, which was then in sight. When about a mile off, they found they would have to abandon her, as the port rail was then under water and the stern awash. The boat was hoisted out and the small crew pulled for 2 hours to reach safety. The wreck has been located on the west side of Gigha in position 55.40N 005.46W.

[TNA: ADM.1/10687]

3 February SPHINX minesweeper
Glasgow 1938; 815 tons; 245.6ft × 33.6ft; 2 × 4in
Commander John Robert Newton Taylor†

In company with her sisters, the *Speedwell* and *Skipjack*, the trio were carrying out a sweep off north-east Scotland, in the vicinity of 57.37N 01.59W. The ships were in line abreast formation, 4 cables (800 yards) apart, steaming at 6 knots. At 09.15 two aircraft were seen approaching from the south at about 1,000ft and they were identified as hostile – 'Dornier 17 type' – by the crew (they were in fact a pair of Ju 88s). At 09.18 the aircraft began a bombing attack in line astern concentrating on the *Sphinx*. A single bomb was dropped by each aircraft; the first dropped ahead but the second hit *Sphinx*, passing through the bridge and upper deck to explode in the forward mess deck and destroying much of the forward part of the ship. The aircraft then circled to carry out a second attack, this time a bomb exploded close on her starboard side whilst the second went astern of her. After carrying out some strafing runs on the ships, the aircraft then departed. *Sphinx* was taken in tow by the *Speedwell*, stern first, heading for Kinnaird Head. All went well until 12.50 when the tow parted, and *Skipjack* took over. When at 22.00 the tow again parted again, it proved impossible to re-connect. The weather had deteriorated considerably, with high seas and strong winds. Another minesweeper, the *Harrier* had now joined and made another attempt to rig a tow but could not do so and all the wounded and non-essential personnel were taken off. At 03.00 the *Sphinx* was reported to be filling with water and at 04.30 when struck by a particularly large wave she rolled over and capsized at 04.45. Fifty-four men lost their lives. It was believed that she had sunk, but the wreck was washed ashore 2 days later, at Occumster Beach, near Lybster, where it lay until sold for scrap.

[TNA: ADM.1/10785]

9 February FORT ROYAL trawler

Aberdeen 1931 requisitioned 1939; 351 tons;
140.3ft × 24ft

Chief Skipper William Craig RNR[†]

Converted to a minesweeper, this former Aberdeen-based trawler remained stationed at her homeport. She was working to maintain the swept channels in company with the sweepers *Robert Bowen*, *Thomas Altoft* and *Ohm*, about 20 miles east of Aberdeen when they came under air attack by a pair of Ju 88 aircraft. At 11.45 she was hit by two bombs and sank very quickly in position 57.20N 01.45W with the loss of seven men, including the Port Minesweeping Officer, Lieutenant Commander Edgar King.

[TNA: ADM.199/364; ADM.199/2200; ADM.358/3319]

9 February ROBERT BOWEN trawler

Beverley 1918 requisitioned 1939; 290 tons;
125.5ft × 23.5ft

Skipper-Lieutenant John Clark RNR[†]

Former Fleetwood trawler, converted for use as a minesweeper, and based at Aberdeen, she was in company with the *Fort Royal* and two other armed trawlers which came under attack by a pair of Ju 88 aircraft from 1/KG 30. On the first pass of the aircraft, she was hit amidships by a bomb and sank with the loss of all fifteen hands. One of the Ju 88 aircraft was hit by defending fire from the trawlers and subsequently crashed into the sea north of Sylt.

[TNA: ADM.199/364; ADM.199/2200; Shores, Fledgling Eagles p166]

18 February DARING destroyer

Woolston 1932; 1,375 tons; 317.9ft × 33ft; 4 × 4.7in,
8 × torpedo tubes

Commander Sydney Alan Cooper[†]

Part of the escort to Convoy HN12, bound for Methil from Bergen, Norway, she had joined the ships to provide extra cover from Orkney, taking station 2 cables (400 yards) on the port beam of the last ship of the port column. When the convoy was about 40 miles to the east of Duncansby Head, at 02.57 those on board felt the ship shudder and a dull red glow lit up the ship. The ship had been hit on the port side aft by a torpedo and was then blown apart by a large explosion which followed, probably as her after magazine ignited. The stern section heeled over to port and did not recover, continuing to roll over, capsizing in about 30 seconds before standing on end and sinking. Although the stern rapidly disappeared, the bow section continued to float for about 30 minutes before disappearing. The submarine *Thistle* was also in the convoy, stationed on the port wing astern of the *Daring*. She heard two distinct explosions and saw a huge column of black smoke that rose over the destroyer. She closed, to discover the bow

section pointing vertically from the sea. Survivors were seen in the water, and she tried her best to rescue as many as she could, but it proved impossible to haul men covered in thick oil over the casing. The submarine did raise the other escorting destroyer, *Ilex*, by light, and she closed to assist with the search, but they could only rescue one man clinging to wreckage. A further four men were found by the *Inglefield*, the only survivors, 156 men being lost. She had been torpedoed by the *U 23* (Kretschmer)

[TNA: ADM.1/10667]

20 February FIFESHIRE trawler

Middlesbrough 1938 requisitioned 1939; 540 tons;
175.8ft × 28.6ft

Sub-Lieutenant John Valentine Searles-Wood RNR[†]

In company with her sister trawler *Ayrshire*, they were patrolling to the east of Orkney, in approximate position 58.54N 00.58W; the weather was poor, with strong winds and overcast skies, when a pair of aircraft, believed to be He 111s, emerged from low cloud astern of them. One of them headed straight for *Fifeshire*, dropping three bombs, which straddled her, and she sank very quickly be the stern. The pair of aircraft then turned their attentions to the *Ayrshire*, but she survived. Twenty-one men lost their lives, with just one survivor.

[TNA: ADM.199/99]

23 February BENVOLIO trawler

Selby 1930 requisitioned 1939; 352 tons; 140.3ft × 24.6ft

Chief Skipper Samuel Melhuish Aldred RNR[†]

Whilst engaged in sweeping the channel at the entrance the river Humber she fouled her propeller with the sweeping gear. Whilst attempting to clear it, the trawler was carried northward by the strong tidal stream into a danger area, containing moored mines. A mine became entangled in the sweep gear and at 09.57 it exploded under the ship which sank very quickly in position 53.36N 00.21.3E. Ten men were killed, with five survivors.

[TNA: ADM.199/1171]

2 March FAIRPLAY TWO tug

Hamburg 1921 (*Fairplay XIV*) requisitioned 1939; 282 tons;
118.8ft × 24.3ft

Lieutenant William James Boyce RNR

Employed as a rescue tug and based at Harwich, at 11.19 in poor weather she went aground on Salt Scar near Redcar, all the men managing to reach safety. Salvage operations were attempted but had to be abandoned after 2 days due to the continuing poor weather, and she was written off as a total loss. The wreck lies in position 54.37.37N 01.03W.

[TNA: ADM.199/366; Larn vol 3 sec 5]

15 March PERIDOT trawler
Middlesbrough 1933 (*Barry Castle*), purchased 1939; 398 tons; 155ft × 26.4ft
Skipper Walter Hartcourt Burgess RNR

Former Grimsby trawler converted to an anti-submarine vessel and stationed at Dover. At 02.55 whilst on local patrol off the port, near number 8 buoy, she was struck on the starboard bow by a floating mine. The explosion holed the ship and fractured the foredeck, and the forward compartments started to flood. Another patrol trawler, the *Saon*, closed and took off most of the crew and a little later the destroyer *Brilliant* arrived on scene and although the trawler was down by the head, she seemed to be stable, and a tow was rigged. At first, light the destroyer commenced towing her, stern first towards Dover. At about 08.30 the Admiralty Salvage Officer arrived on the scene in the tug *Lady Duncannon* and took over the towing duties. The tow seemed to be going well, until at 09.30 the trawler gave a lurch, heeled over and then dipped her bows underwater, stood on her end and sank. Her position was then 51.06N 01.25E. It was believed that the fish hold bulkhead had probably collapsed, causing her to flood.
[TNA: ADM.178/2001; ADM.267/89]

16 March MAIDA drifter
Aberdeen 1914 (*Chestnut*) requisitioned 1939; 107 tons; 88.7ft × 18.7ft
Skipper Roland Morton Utting RNR†

Acting as a dan layer to a group of trawlers attempting to clear a minefield between the Kentish Knock and the Goodwin sands, laid by *Schiff II* on 9 March, she was about 10 miles to the east of North Foreland, when at 10.45 she struck a mine and rapidly sank. Six men were lost, but six survivors were picked up by the drifter *Mare*.
[TNA: ADM. 199/360; ADM.358/36; Foynes p32]

22 March LOCH ASSATER trawler
Aberdeen 1910, purchased 1940; 210 tons; 115.1ft × 22.6ft
Skipper George Douglas Greening RNR

Based at Aberdeen she was patrolling about 60 miles to the north-east of Kinnaird Head and took the opportunity to trawl for fish. At 14.30 as she hauled in her trawl, two mines detonated in the nets and then a third was seen caught in the net. In attempting to clear the menace it detonated close to the ship, which was badly shaken by the explosions, and filled and sank. All the crew was picked up, although three were injured, including the skipper, after spending several uncomfortable hours in an open boat. It was found that she had almost certainly trawled across a defensive British minefield. Skipper Greening was criticised for the loss; although patrolling trawlers might pretend to fish, they were prohibited for doing so.
[TNA: ADM.1/10441]

4 April GOLDEN DAWN drifter
Banff 1913 requisitioned 1940; 79 tons; 87ft × 19.2ft
Newly hired, she foundered at Ardrossan, Scotland whilst waiting to be fitted out.
[Statement of War Losses p9]

April 1940 – the Norway Campaign

Both Germany and the Allies had been concerned over the position of the Scandinavian countries since the outbreak of war. Sweden was a major supplier of iron ore to Germany, some of which was routed through northern Norway to the port of Narvik, from where ships could hug the Norwegian coast to reach Germany. Germany therefore wished to ensure the security of this supply, and the prospect of controlling Norwegian ports was attractive. For the Allies various intervention schemes for Norway were considered, with similar aims; to deny Swedish ore shipments to Germany and the securing of Norwegian ports to prevent German ships using them. On 5 April, the Royal Navy commenced Operation 'Wilfred', the laying of mines in Norwegian waters, to disrupt the coastal traffic. Two days later the Germans initiated the invasion of Denmark and Norway (Operation '*Weserübung*'), with several groups of ships departing ports to stage landings. The large-scale movement of German naval forces into the North Sea where British forces were already deployed led to the first clashes off the Norwegian coast.

8 April GLOWWORM destroyer
Woolston 1935; 1,350 tons; 312ft × 33ft; 4 × 4.7in, 10 × torpedo tubes
Lieutenant Commander Gerard Broadmead Roope†

With three other destroyers in company, she sailed from Scapa Flow on 5 April to join the battlecruiser *Renown* to provide cover for minelaying operations off the coast of Norway. The weather proved to be poor, and during 6 April she lost a man overboard and was allowed to detach from the force to carry out a search. After spending several hours fruitlessly searching in deteriorating weather, she gave up the hunt and turned back to try and re-locate the main force. In Force 7 winds and high seas she hove to during the night but reported by radio at 04.30 on the morning of 8 April that she was about to get under way. At about 07.30 as she was heading north-west, a strange destroyer was seen which turned away after an unsatisfactory reply to a visual challenge. Soon afterwards a second destroyer emerged from a rainsquall, which opened fire. *Glowworm* returned fire and saw her opponents turn away. The pair, which was the German destroyers *Bernd von Arnim* and *Hans Lüdeman*, broke off the action and headed north. Lieutenant Commander Roope realised that the pair were unlikely to be alone and may well be leading him towards a larger force, but decided to continue to chase, sending an enemy report at 07.59, stating that he was engaging enemy destroyers in position 65.04N 06.04E. The *Glowworm* chased her opponents into the gloom of rainsqualls, with occasional glimpses of the enemy, until at 08.50 when as the *Glowworm* emerged from a rain squall, she sighted the heavy cruiser *Admiral Hipper*. An enemy report was sent, but Roope realised that because of the heavy weather, attempting to shadow the enemy force would be impossible, so it was decided to attack. The *Hipper* engaged the destroyer, but the heavy seas did not make shooting easy, and it was not until the fourth salvo that a hit was claimed on the British destroyer. The *Glowworm* made smoke and turned back into the screen, the German cruiser continuing to fire into the smoke. At about 09.10 Roope emerged from the smokescreen and fired a salvo of torpedoes, which was avoided by the cruiser, the destroyer dodging back into the screen after being hit several times by both 203mm and 105mm shells. The *Hipper* now entered the smokescreen to emerge on the other side. The pair were now very close, and the destroyer collided with the cruiser, striking her opponent on the starboard side forward. She scraped down the cruiser's side, tearing away guardrails, wrecking a torpedo mounting and puncturing the hull, causing several compartments to be flooded. The bows of the destroyer were crushed, and she drew away, now being hit regularly by fire from the *Hipper*. Covered in smoke she heeled over to starboard, and orders were given to abandon her. Shortly after this she rolled over and sank at 09.24 in position 64.27N 06.28E. The *Hipper* stayed in the area for over an hour picking up the survivors from a sea covered in oil and debris but could only find thirty-one survivors, 111 men being lost. Roope subsequently received a posthumous award of the Victoria Cross; Lieutenant Robert Archibald Ramsay received the DSO and three ratings the CGM.

[TNA: ADM267/110; The London Gazette 6 July 1945; Haar, The German Invasion pp90–6]

9 April GURKHA destroyer
Govan 1937; 1,960 tons; 355.6ft × 36.6ft; 8 × 4.7in, 4 × 2pdr, 4 × torpedo tubes
Commander Anthony Wass Buzzard
During 7/8 April, the major units of the Home Fleet deployed to take station off the coast of southern Norway, hoping to intercept German units supporting the invasion. During the morning of 8 April, a force of cruisers and destroyers were detached to carry out an attack on the port of Bergen, where it was believed that enemy surface forces were assembling. Late in the afternoon this raid was cancelled, and the force reversed course to rejoin the fleet which were already heading north. During the following afternoon with the force

about 30 miles to the west of Korsfjord, and still some way astern of the fleet, the expected air attacks started. The destroyers were allowed to break formation and became separated whilst manoeuvring to engage. A large force of Ju 87 and Ju 88 aircraft carried out bombing attacks, and a large four-engined aircraft joined at 15.07 dropping bombs from high level. During these attacks, a stick of bombs exploded close along the starboard side. The ship was badly shaken by the explosions, and the starboard side was peppered with shrapnel. The gear room started to fill with water, followed shortly afterwards by the engine room and several of the after compartments. A fire was started in the after superstructure and the ship took a list to starboard bringing the upper deck to within 2ft of the waterline amidships. The forward part of the ship remained unaffected, and she continued to engage the circling aircraft. Another high-level bombing attack saw another stick of bombs exploding about 200 yards from her, causing more shock damage. Loss of fire main pressure made it impossible to fight the fire still burning aft, and as night fell work went on to jury rig wireless aerials, and she was able to get in touch with the rest of the force from which she had become detached. The cruiser *Aurora* was sent back to find her. In an attempt to stabilise the ship, and correct the heel, it was decided to pump out the forward starboard oil fuel tanks, and it did seem to ease the list. At 18.55 the *Aurora*, guided by shell bursts fired as a guide, found her and started to take off the men by boat. This proved a difficult task in high winds and sea and only half of the men had been taken off by 20.45 when the destroyer swung round so the wind was brought from port to starboard. This caused the ship to right herself, but then heel over alarmingly to port. With men now jumping into the sea, she continued to roll over until she lay on her beam-ends and then sank, stern first, her bows rising into the air. She was then to the west of Karmoy Island, Norway in position 59.13N, 04.00E. Five officers and eleven ratings were lost. The pumping out of the fuel was later criticised and deemed to have been ' … the worst thing that could have been done'. It had made the ship unstable and was a contributory factor to her loss.
[TNA: ADM.267/99]

10 April First Battle of Narvik
The furthest north that German forces had been landed was at the port of Narvik, where a force of destroyers landed 2,000 troops on 9 April. Already in the vicinity were the destroyers of the Second Destroyer Flotilla under Captain Warburton-Lee, who were screening the ships that would be laying mines off the Norwegian coast near Bodö. On 8 April on receipt of the enemy reports from the *Glowworm* (see above), the Second Flotilla joined the battlecruiser *Renown* to move to the vicinity of the Lofoten Islands and during 9 April

took part in a brief engagement between the *Renown* and the battlecruisers *Gneisenau* and *Scharnhorst*, firing torpedoes, but without effect. They were subsequently ordered to proceed to Narvik, but on arrival off Tranoy at about 16.00 that evening was warned that the enemy naval forces were substantial, and there was a possibility of mines having been laid. Despite this, Captain Warburton-Lee decided to attack at dawn, relying on surprise. *Hardy*, *Hunter* and *Havock* would attack ships in the harbour of Narvik, whilst the *Hotspur* and *Hostile* would engage shore batteries and any ships seen outside the anchorage. The five destroyers entered the long fjord leading to the harbour that night in a blinding snowstorm, and achieved complete surprise, arriving off the port at 04.15. In the subsequent action, two German destroyers, the *Wilhelm Heidkamp* and *Anton Schmitt*, were sunk and a further two damaged, and several merchant ships were sunk or damaged and the German supply ship *Rauenfels* sunk. As they withdrew, two of the attacking British destroyers were lost.
[The London Gazette 7 June 1940 and 1 July 1947]

HARDY destroyer
Birkenhead 1936; 1,340 tons; 312ft × 33ft; 4 × 4.7in, 8 × torpedo tubes
Captain Bernard Armitage Warburton-Lee[†]
Leading the line of destroyers into the fjord, she identified an enemy destroyer in the north-east corner of the harbour, closed and engaged her with gunfire and torpedo, having the satisfaction of seeing a large explosion as a torpedo hit the target amidships. As she moved away a second destroyer was identified and engaged with gunfire, with the other destroyers of the flotilla busily firing at the ships in the harbour and launching torpedoes, and a second enemy destroyer being seen to be hit. Warburton-Lee then led his ships out of the anchorage to assess the situation. There was concern that there were clearly some enemy destroyers unaccounted for, so at 05.20 the *Hardy* led the flotilla round to form up in line astern for another attack. After another flurry of gunfire and torpedoes the ships withdrew, heading down the fjord towards the open sea, working up to 30 knots. At 05.40 when about halfway along Ofot Fjord, three enemy destroyers were seen emerging from Herjangs Fjord and a few minutes later another hostile ship appeared ahead, crossing from port to starboard. A fierce gun battle ensued, with *Hardy*, as the leading destroyer, taking the brunt. At about 05.58 the *Hardy* was hit by a salvo of shells, being covered in water and smoke. The bridge suffered a direct hit, killing or wounding all the personnel and the after boiler room was also hit, flames being seen to spurt out of the after funnel. She rapidly lost way and with her helmsman killed she turned inshore, out of control. Despite being wounded, Paymaster Lieutenant Geoffrey

Stanning took over the wheel to regain control and she was steered into shallow water to ground about 300 yards from the shore, now on fire forward. She was then ordered to be abandoned, about 160 men making it safely to the shore, from where they took shelter in the village of Ballangen and were rescued by the *Ivanhoe* 3 days later. The torpedo officer, Lieutenant George Heppel, returned on board before leaving the scene to set off an explosive charge to destroy the safes containing confidential books. Nineteen men were lost. Captain Warburton-Lee was awarded a posthumous Victoria Cross.

HUNTER destroyer
Wallsend 1936; 1,340 tons; 312ft × 33ft; 4 × 4.7in, 8 × torpedo tubes
Lieutenant Commander Lindsay de Villers[†]
Following astern of the *Hardy*, she was repeatedly hit by several large-calibre shells, which blew her forward torpedo tubes overboard and, losing steam and covered in smoke, she slowed. The destroyer immediately astern, the *Hotspur*, was also hit, which put her steering gear out of action, and before control could be regained, she rammed the *Hunter*, and the pair became locked together. Eventually, by setting up a chain of verbal command from the upper deck to the tiller flat, the *Hotspur* was able to re-establish her steering and extricated herself. The *Hunter* however was so severely damaged that she was run inshore and run aground. She was last seen heeled over to her side and covered in smoke before she sank stern first with the loss of 106 men killed, with forty-six survivors who were taken prisoner.

★ ★ ★

10 April THISTLE submarine
Barrow 1938; 1,090/1,573 tons; 265.6ft × 26.7ft; 1 × 4in, 10 × torpedo tubes
Lieutenant Commander Wilfred Frederick Haselfoot[†]
Part of the Second Submarine Flotilla, she sailed from Scapa on 7 April to conduct a patrol off the Norwegian coast. During the afternoon of the 9th carried out an attack on a surfaced U-boat off Skudesnes, which failed. After she had reported this, she was ordered to remain in the area, in the hope that she might again find the enemy submarine. However, at 01.13 the situation was reversed, when her target, the *U 4* (Hinsch) caught the *Thistle* on the surface, recharging batteries off Utsira in position 59.06N 05.05E. Her attack was successful, and the *Thistle* was hit amidships by a torpedo and she broke up and sank rapidly with no survivors; five officers and forty-eight ratings were lost.
[Evans p211]

10 April TARPON submarine

Greenock 1939; 1,090/1,573 tons; 265.6ft × 26.7ft; 1 × 4in,
10 × torpedo tubes

Lieutenant Commander Herbert James Caldwell†

Sailed from Portsmouth on 5 April to take passage with
Convoy FN39 for Rosyth but was detached on 7 April
to conduct a patrol in the North Sea on the Norwegian
coast, following reports of the German invasion. She
reported her position at 18.10 the following day, but
this was the last heard from her. At 07.24 on 10 April in
position 56.43N 06.33E the German auxiliary *Schürbeck
/ Schiff-40* sighted two torpedo tracks which passed close
astern and a periscope was sighted soon after. Assisted
by the minesweeper *M 6*, an immediate depth-charge
attack was carried out, followed by a search with sonar,
which gained a contact. Prosecution was delayed when
she came under surveillance of RAF Hudson aircraft, and
it was not until 09.00 that attacks could resume. A pattern
of sixteen charges were dropped over the contact with
immediate results. A large quantity of air bubbles burst on
the surface followed by oil. Further attacks were carried
out during the morning until at 12.52 a large quantity
of debris came to the surface, identifiable as being from a
British submarine. Five officers and forty-eight men were
lost. The wreck of *Tarpon* was found in March 2016, with
severe damage behind the conning tower.

[Evans p212]

(18?) April STERLET submarine

Chatham 1937; 670/927 tons; 193.3ft × 24ft; 1 × 3in,
6 × torpedo tubes

Lieutenant Gerard Henry Stackpoole Haward†

Sailed from Harwich on 8 April for a patrol in the
Skagerrak, she was last heard from at 21.30 on 12 April
when she reported having carried out an unsuccessful
attack on a coastal convoy in position 57.47N 09.30E.
She then disappeared, and the circumstances of her loss
are unclear. The German gunnery training ship *Brummer*
was torpedoed by a submarine at 23.07 on 15 April,
inflicting damage which resulted in her sinking. Although
it was slightly out of her patrol area, it is accepted that the
Sterlet must have been responsible for this. Several depth
charges were dropped in the area by escort vessels after
the attack, but with no obvious results. At 21.42 on 18
April a German southbound convoy was attacked by a
submarine in position 58.57N 10.12E, a torpedo just
missing the leading ship. Immediately after, a submarine
broke surface about 60 yards from one of the escorts, the
minesweeper *M 75*, which attacked as she submerged
dropping five depth charges. The escorting trawlers
Uj 125, *Uj 126* and *Uj 128* joined the hunt. This must
have been the *Sterlet*, and this attack may have been
responsible for her end, but there was no debris or oil to
confirm her destruction. If she had survived the attack by
M 75, then a likely explanation would be the minefields

which had been laid since her sailing, between 58.02N
07.57E to 57.49N to 07.51E and were right across her
return route to Harwich. It is likely that these were the
cause of her loss. Six officers and thirty-five men were lost.

[Evans p215]

Operations in Norway – 'Maurice' and 'Sickle'

Although initial German advances had gone well in
the southern half of Norway following their invasion,
they had been unable to properly support the landings
that had been made at Trondheim and Narvik further
north. It was decided to exploit this weakness, and an
expeditionary force was hastily assembled, to be landed
at Namsos, to move south (Operation 'Maurice') and
at Åndalsnes, to move north (Operation 'Sickle'), both
with the aim of recovering the port of Trondheim.
Although the Allies had control of the sea, they lacked
air support, and the enemy with air bases firmly
established to the south took full advantage of this.

20 April RUTLANDSHIRE trawler

Middlesbrough 1936 requisitioned 1939; 458 tons;
164.6ft × 27.1ft; 1 × 4in

Chief Skipper John Wilson RNR

Former Grimsby-registered trawler, fitted as an anti-
submarine vessel, she was part of a force of armed
trawlers that was sent to cover the landing operations of
French troops at Namsos. At 09.00, having just screened
a troop convoy out of the fjord, she was returning to
Namsos when an air raid by He 111 aircraft developed.
The *Rutlandshire* increased speed and started to zigzag,
but a bomb exploded close on the starboard quarter,
which buckled plates and peppered her side with holes.
The main steam pipe was fractured, filling the engine
spaces with steam. The trawler was turned inshore until
she finally grounded at 10.15 when she was about
100 yards from the shore, and she was abandoned as
her stern settled under the water and sank. There were
no casualties.

Note: it is claimed in some sources that she was later
salvaged by the Germans and entered their service as
the *Ubier;* this is not correct. Part of the wreck was
salvaged but broken up.

*[TNA: ADM.199/476; http://www.royal-naval-reserve.co.uk/
trawlers/rutlandshire.htm]*

25 April BRADMAN trawler

Selby 1937 requisitioned 1939; 452 tons; 161.8ft × 27.1ft;
1 × 4in

Lieutenant Arthur Allison Fitzroy Talbot

One of the 'Cricketer' class of former Grimsby trawlers
that made up the Twenty-Second Anti-Submarine

Striking Force that was deployed to Norway, arriving in Molde Fjord on 22 April to support the landings at Åndalsnes. The 25th was a bright clear day, and the *Bradman* was commencing a local patrol when enemy aircraft were sighted at 08.00 and she immediately steered inshore, to take shelter in the lee of a steep cliff. Despite this precaution, she was attacked, about twenty bombs dropping close to her, but escaped injury. Getting underway as the aircraft cleared, she headed towards Molde but was again forced to take shelter inshore as more enemy aircraft came into view. At 09.15 as she was manoeuvring close inshore to avoid the bombs she ran aground in shallow water. All efforts to get her afloat failed and as more aircraft were seen closing, it was decided to abandon her; she was then about 200 yards offshore opposite Sattirvik point, near the village of Hjelkirkstrand. The ship's company went ashore in boats and a float, to take shelter among the trees. The ship was then continuously bombed through the day, by Ju 88 and He 111 aircraft. Although there were no direct hits, one salvo dropped close to the port bow, after which she was seen to heel over to port by 35 degrees. She subsequently slowly settled by the head and her foredeck submerged as far as the wheelhouse. The crew boarded her as night fell to destroy the confidential books and the Asdic set. She was later salvaged by the Germans and became patrol boat *V 6112/Friese*.
[TNA: ADM.199/477; ADM.199/478]

25 April HAMMOND trawler
Selby 1936 requisitioned 1939; 452 tons; 161.8ft × 27.1ft; 1 × 4in
Skipper Alexander McKay RNR

Sister to the *Bradman* (see above), she was attacked by aircraft on 22 April, their first day in Molde Fjord, when they were machine gunned, causing damage to the wheelhouse and bridge, wounding four men, including Skipper McKay. The ship steamed to Åndalsnes and transferred the casualties to the cruiser *Curacoa*, before returning to patrol duties in the fjord under the temporary command of Skipper John Crockett. On 25 April she got underway at 05.00 to proceed to Julsundet to relieve the *Larwood* on patrol, but at 08.15 aircraft were sighted and they commenced an attack. For the next 90 minutes she manoeuvred and zigzagged to avoid the bombs and was successful until at last a bomb detonated close under her stern. This fractured and split plates and put all the lights out. The engine room reported that they were making water and so she was run into shallow water, eventually grounding on a small island near Lervag. The crew went ashore after destroying the Asdic equipment. Over the next 2 days the ship was repeatedly attacked until she finally sank, leaving only her funnel and masts showing. The

crew used the boats to reach Molde. The wreck was eventually salvaged by the Germans to become the patrol vessel *V 6115/Salier*.
[TNA: ADM.ADM.199/477; ADM.199/478]

26 April LARWOOD trawler
Selby 1936 requisitioned 1939; 452 tons; 161.8ft × 27.1ft; 1 × 4in
Skipper Patrick Joseph Quinlan RNR

Another of the 'Cricketer' class former Grimsby trawlers that arrived in Norwegian waters with other ships of the Anti-Submarine Striking Force on 22 April. All attempts to carry out patrols in the fjords attracted very heavy air raids, and during the 25th the *Larwood* was damaged in the early morning when several bombs landed around her, shaking the ship considerably. The following morning the ship was taken as close to the shore as was possible, not far from the wreck of the *Hammond*, the crew landing to take shelter during daylight hours. During the day there were constant attacks by aircraft, and the trawler was near missed by several bombs, although no immediate damage could be seen from the shore. That evening the crew boarded her and found that she had suffered during the attacks, the hull and upperworks being peppered with shrapnel holes and the bunkers were seen to be smouldering. When the door of the bridge was opened there was an explosion and a sheet of flame burst out, causing the rapid evacuation of the ship. The fire rapidly spread, and she was soon well ablaze. By daylight, the fire had died down, but the crew remained ashore, fearing more air attacks, but were able to board her at dusk. She was a wreck, but as the hull seemed sound, there were hopes that she could be towed to Molde during the night. Most of the crew were ordered to leave by boat with a small party remaining with her. Hopes of a tow evaporated and on 28 April she was boarded for the last time to ensure that the Asdic equipment had been destroyed and the breech blocks of the guns thrown overboard; a local fishing boat took the last of the crew to Molde. The wreck was salvaged by the Germans and became the patrol boat *V 6111/Franke*.
[TNA: ADM.199/477; ADM.199/478]

28 April CAPE SIRETOKO trawler
Selby 1939 requisitioned 1939; 590 tons; 178.3ft × 30.1ft; 1 × 4in, 1 × 20mm
Lieutenant Arthur Norman Blundell RNR

A former Hull-based trawler, converted for naval use as an anti-submarine vessel, in company with other trawlers of the Eleventh Anti-Submarine Striking Force sailed from Aberdeen on 25 April to arrive in the Molde Fjord at 06.00 on 28 April to support the landings at Åndalsnes. Scarcely had they arrived when they came under air attack, with He 111

aircraft carrying out a bombing raid, although all the vessels escaped damage. Abandoning any plans for anti-submarine patrols, they took separated and took shelter close inshore, near cliffs, the *Siretoko* going into Mordalsvagen Bay. More raids developed during the morning, aircraft continuing to attack, evidently undeterred by the proximity of the cliffs. At 11.00 a bomb exploded close to her, shaking the vessel considerably; all the lights went out and she developed a list to port. At 11.15 another raid was under way, by several Ju 87 Stuka aircraft, during which she was straddled by a stick of bombs. Whipped by the blast, the list increased until the port gunwale was under water and it was decided to beach the ship. She was run into shallow water and at 11.45 ran aground in position 62.43.7N 06.59.6E and the crew went ashore after destroying all confidential books. The next morning a party went back on board to smash the Asdic set and remove the breech blocks of the guns. Before she was left for the final time a depth charge, set to explode on shallow setting, was placed in a boat which was then scuttled alongside the ship, but this was not seen to detonate. The wreck was later salvaged by the Germans and to become the patrol boat *V 6113/Gote*.
[TNA: ADM.199/477]

29 April CAPE CHELYUSKIN trawler
Selby 1936 requisitioned 1939; 494 tons; 166ft × 27.6ft; 1 × 4in
Skipper Harold Ernest Moran RNR
Armed trawlers of the Twelfth Anti-Submarine Striking Force, including *Chelyuskin*, arrived in Molde Fjord on 27 April, to give support to the allied forces at Åndalsnes. For the next 2 days the ships in the area were subjected to constant air raids from enemy aircraft and were ordered to separate and take shelter. During the early hours of 29 April, the *Chelyuskin* was taken to lay close to a cliff in Romdalsfjord near the village of Vaagestranden and the crew went ashore to take shelter. The ship avoided detection until late morning when at 11.30 several aircraft were seen approaching which then attacked the ship, the first stick of bombs breaking the lines securing the ship to the shore, causing her to drift out clear of the land. Bombing and machine-gunning of the ship continued through the day, although there were no direct hits, eighteen bombs were counted falling near to the ship, and she was seen to be settling slowly by the stern. At 19.00 at attempt was made to get back on board, and despite being machine-gunned by an aircraft, a small party succeeded. They found that shock damage had shattered the Asdic dome, damaged the engines and wrecked the steering gear and bridge. In addition, the hull and upperworks were peppered with shrapnel holes, a crack was found in the upper deck and side plates had been buckled. She remained

afloat until 05.00 on 30 April when she finally sank, an explosion occurring as she did, presumed to be the boiler blowing up.
[TNA: ADM. 199/477]

30 April BITTERN sloop
Cowes 1937; 1,190 tons; 282ft × 37ft; 4 × 4in
Lieutenant Commander Robert Henry Mills
During 30 April, the evacuation of Allied forces from Namsos commenced and the ships supporting this came under intense air attack. The *Bittern* was subjected to a series of attacks during the day by Ju 87 aircraft, the number varying from three to nine, but despite avoiding action being difficult due to restricted sea room, by using full rudder and varying speed she avoided any damage. In the final attack in the afternoon, however, she was closed by Ju 87 aircraft, with a pair closing from the port bow whilst the third passed down the starboard side to attack from the stern. All aircraft pressed home their attacks despite being engaged by everything that *Bittern* could fire; both aircraft that attacked from forward missed, but the third, from astern, hit her. A bomb struck the quarterdeck, close to the locker containing demolition charges which also exploded. The stern of the ship was blown off and the flash ran forward starting a fierce fire in the after lobby which spread to the small arms magazine, causing some of the stored ammunition to explode. The pumps were put out of action, meaning the fire could only be tackled by extinguishers and buckets. The engines had been stopped by the explosion, and to stop her drifting she anchored, with the smoke spreading through the ship. Unable to properly fight the fires and an obvious target for any future attacks, which were believed imminent, the destroyer *Janus* closed to put her bows alongside the sloops fo'c'sle and lifted off her crew. When that was complete, at 16.29 the destroyer fired a torpedo into the burning wreck to ensure that she sank. Twenty men were lost.
[TNA: ADM.267/100]

30 April BOARDALE oiler
Govan 1937; 17,388 tons; 466.3ft × 62ft
Master Leonard Elford
Sailed from Scapa in company with two cargo ships, all bound for Norway, escorted by the destroyers *Grafton* and *Burza*. The weather was poor, preventing sun or star sights and they approached the land cautiously. At 23.05 on 29 April *Grafton* ordered the convoy to heave to as land was visible ahead, to the north-west. At 02.00 *Grafton* signalled that they were in Vesteraels Fjord, but Mr Elford disagreed, and indicated (correctly) that he believed they were in Asanfjord. *Grafton* ordered the convoy to weigh soon after, and the *Boardale* weighed at 02.53 and got under way, steering to the west, to exit

from the fjord. At 02.55 she struck the ground, to the surprise of all on board, as they believed themselves to be in deep water. Sounding around them found 30 to 60 fathoms of water, and they appeared to have become stranded on a rocky pinnacle. She was rapidly filling with water and took on a pronounced list to starboard and the boats were hoisted out. At 16.15 that afternoon with the weather worsening she rolled over to port, broke in half and sank. Her stern was seen to rise, and an explosion occurred before she sank. Her position was approximately 68.42N 14.21E.

[TNA: ADM.1/10916]

30 April JARDINE trawler
Selby 1936 requisitioned 1939; 452 tons; 161.8ft × 27.1ft;
1 × 4in, 1 × 2pdr
Lieutenant Keith Burne Hopkins RNVR

Deployed to Norway with the Twenty-Second Anti-Submarine Striking Force, she had been subjected to constant air raids since arriving on 22 April, and her sisters *Bradman* and *Larwood* had been sunk earlier. At 14.30 on 27 April, she was heavily bombed, with near misses causing considerable damage and she was taken inshore to go alongside Molde pier. Here she remained for the night with base repair staff working to repair the damage, and then sailed to take shelter under cliffs nearby in Romsdalfjord. During 28 April, more attacks were made on her, causing more shock damage, and riddling the hull with shrapnel holes, and a bomb landed on shore near where the crew were sheltering, wounding six men. That night the crew returned on board, but found her in a poor state, and it was decided that she should be abandoned. During the night, the Asdic equipment was destroyed, and confidential books burned. During 29 April most of the crew made their way to Molde by boat, leaving a small party standing by the wreck, which were to ensure her destruction. After dark, the local ferry appeared, and with some persuasion, agreed to assist. A tow line was rigged and at 01.30 on 30 April, she hauled the *Jardine* off the ground and towed her to the middle of the fjord. The seacocks were then opened, valves removed, and the magazine flood valves opened and at 02.10 she was abandoned in a sinking condition. An hour later she was found, low in the water, but still afloat, by HMS *Northern Pride*. She speeded her end by using her 4in gun, hitting her four times after which she sank.

Note: it is claimed in some sources that the Germans salvaged her, to become the patrol vessel *Cherusker*; this is incorrect.

[TNA: ADM.199/477; ADM.199/478]

30 April WARWICKSHIRE trawler
Middlesbrough 1936 requisitioned 1939; 466 tons;
164ft × 27ft; 1 × 4in
Commander York McCleod Cleeves RNR

Leader of the Anti-Submarine Striking Force, like her sister trawlers she had been subjected to constant air raids ever since arriving in Molde Fjord on 22 April. In an attempt to avoid being attacked, she lay up during the day in Grundefjord, taking shelter close into the shore under cliffs. She was still attacked, however, and although not hit, suffered several near misses which caused considerable shock and whipping damage. When the ship was inspected during the evening of 29 April she was found to be in a poor state, with several leaks and the mast unstopped and it was decided to abandon her. The confidential books were burned, and the Asdic equipment smashed. A depth charge was then placed on the fore deck and another on the stern rail, both set to explode in shallow water. When all of this was complete, she was scuttled, the ship steadily settling until at 03.00 the depth charges exploded. The crew went ashore by boat to land at Mordal Point. Despite the confidence that she was effectively wrecked, the vessel was later salvaged by the Germans to become the patrol boat *V 6114/Alane*.

[TNA: ADM.199/477; ADM.199/478]

1 May ST GORAN trawler
Beverley 1936 requisitioned 1939; 564 tons;
172.2ft × 29.1ft; 1 × 4in, 1 × 20mm
Lieutenant William Clark McGuigan RNR†

In company with other units of the Fifteenth Anti-submarine Striking Force, she had arrived at Namsos, during 28 April, to conduct patrols at the entrance to the fjord. During 30 April there were intense air raids, the trawlers taking shelter close to the cliffs in an effort to avoid being hit. Despite this precaution the *St Goran* was badly damaged when a stick of three bombs exploded very close along the starboard side. The commanding officer and three ratings were killed, the hull was peppered with holes and a small fire was started in the messdeck. The fire was extinguished, and the wounded transferred to the *Arab*, and then the ship taken further inshore, the crew being landed. During the afternoon the air raids continued. The crew returned at nightfall to find the trawler in a poor state, holed and slowly filling with water. With reports of enemy forces closing it was decided to scuttle her and at 02.00 seacocks were opened and she settled, the *Cape Passaro* speeding her end with gunfire.

[TNA: ADM.199/478]

1 May ASTON VILLA trawler

Middlesbrough 1937 requisitioned 1939; 546 tons;
173.6ft × 28.6ft; 1 × 4in

Lieutenant Commander Sir Geoffrey Cecil Congreve

Tasked to patrol the Namsos fjord with other armed trawlers, with her companions the *Aston Villa* found themselves the target for an intense air raid during 29 April. To avoid being hit the ships moved further inshore and some rigged tree branches and canvas screens to camouflage themselves and the crew moved ashore. The camouflage had little effect as on 1 May the air raids resumed from 06.00 and continued during the day. At 17.00 the *Aston Villa* received a direct hit from a bomb dropped by a Ju 87 aircraft and was set on fire. She continued to burn until she exploded and sank at 20.00.

[TNA: ADM.199/476]

1 May GAUL trawler

Middlesbrough 1936 requisitioned 1939; 531 tons;
170.7ft × 28.6ft; 1 × 4in

Lieutenant Henry McLean Duff-Still RNVR

As with the other armed trawlers (see *St Goran* and *Aston Villa* above), the *Gaul* was based in Namsos fjord to carry out anti-submarine patrols but found herself the target for an intensive series of air raids. During the afternoon of 30 April, she suffered severe damage when a bomb exploded close under her bows, and she was sent into Krokan Bay as it was feared that she might founder. Air raids continued over the next 2 days, but the *Gaul* avoided further damage until at midday on 1 May when she was bracketed by a stick of bombs and started to settle. She finally sank at 13.00. There were no casualties.

[TNA: ADM.199/476]

3 May AFRIDI destroyer

Walker on Tyne 1937; 1,960 tons; 355.6 ft × 36.6ft;
8 × 4.7in, 4 × 2pdr, 4 × torpedo tubes

Captain Philip Louis Vian

Part of the force coving the evacuation of forces from Norway, the *Afridi* joined the cruiser *York* and several other destroyers, in screening transport ships entering Namsos fjord to take off allied troops. At 02.30 the main force sailed, with the *Afridi* remaining behind to bring off the rear guard and any stragglers. She sailed an hour later with thirty-six soldiers embarked to rejoin the main force, which now included the cruisers *Carlisle* and *Devonshire*. As the group were clearing the coast, they came under several intense air attacks, and at 10.10 the French destroyer *Bison* was struck by a bomb which exploded her forward magazine and blew off the forward part of the ship. The *Afridi* was one of the ships that went to her assistance, picking up sixty-nine survivors as she sank. The air raids continued, and

at 14.00 a large group of Ju 87 aircraft commenced a dive-bombing attack. The *Afridi* was at the rear of the force and was singled out for attention and was hit twice during an attack by one of the aircraft. She was steaming at 25 knots and under port rudder at the time. The first bomb passed through the galley and forward boiler room to exit through the starboard side. The second penetrated the port side abreast 'B' gun and the explosion killed several of the soldiers and survivors and started a fire in the forward mess decks and flooded forward compartments. Covered in dense smoke she lost power. The destroyers *Griffin* and *Imperial* closed to lift off the embarked troops and *Bison* survivors, and the *Imperial* passed a tow. It soon became clear that she would be not able to be towed, as the ship was quickly settling by the bows. She continued to settle by the head before rolling over to port to float bottom-up for a while before sinking bows first. Forty-nine of her own men were lost, along with thirty men from the *Bison* and seven soldiers.

[TNA: ADM.267/100}

★ ★ ★

29 April UNITY submarine

Barrow 1938; 540/730 tons; 180ft × 16.1ft; 1 × 12pdr,
6 × torpedo tubes

Lieutenant Francis John Brooks

Based at Blyth, she sailed at 17.30 for a patrol in the North Sea, the weather at the time being poor, with thick patches of fog. As they entered the main channel to clear the harbour, the fog closed in further, reducing visibility to less than 100 yards making it difficult to locate the channel marker buoys. At 19.07 the blast of a ship's siren was heard ahead in the mist and Lieutenant Brooks ordered a course alteration to starboard, but then another siren was heard, apparently close on the starboard bow. Now alarmed, Brooks ordered the engines astern and all watertight doors to be closed. As he did so a ship loomed out of the fog, no more than 50 yards away and before any avoiding action could be taken, at 19.10 the Norwegian steamer *Atle Jarl* (1,173 tons) rammed the *Unity* by the port forward hydroplane. With the submarine going astern, and the steamer only proceeding slowly, the impact was not great, but the hull was punctured, and she started to flood rapidly forward. The bows slowly dipped under and the crew were ordered to abandon the boat, which they did in good order, swimming to boats lowered by the *Atle Jarl* which had stopped after the collision. She sank about 5 minutes after the collision, the stern rising high out of the water as she went under. Two men were lost, Lieutenant John Low and Able Seaman Henry Miller, who had remained below to ensure that the main motors were shut down; both were awarded a posthumous George Cross. The subsequent court of enquiry established that the *Atle Jarl* had been part on a convoy from Methil to the Tyne, but Lieutenant Brooks had never been informed of the expected arrival of the inbound convoy. This was due to the mishandling of a signal, although who was responsible for this was uncertain. Further, Brooks should have exercised more caution in the foggy conditions, having failed to make any sound signals until he heard the siren of another vessel. However, this was mitigated by his cool and rapid decisions after the collision, which ensured that most of his crew escaped.

[TNA: ADM 1/12025; Evans p218]

30 April DUNOON minesweeper

Glasgow 1919; 710 tons; 231ft × 28.6ft; 1 × 4in, 1 × 12pdr
Lieutenant Commander Hugh Alan Barclay[†]

Following the mining of the merchant vessel *Cree*, the *Dunoon* was tasked to sweep for contact mines in the channel to the east of Great Yarmouth, working in company with her sister *Elgin*, in the vicinity of 52.45N 02.23E and employing a double Oropesa sweep. During the afternoon, several mines were brought to the surface and others exploded in the sweeps. At 15.40 the pair stopped sweeping and were engaged in recovering floats and sweeps and sinking floating mines with rifle fire. At 16.53 there was a large explosion under the forward part of the vessel as she ran over an unseen mine. This was followed by a further two distinct detonations, probably the fore magazine and then the boilers exploding, which demolished the forward part of the ship, the bridge and wheelhouse disappearing. The after section remained afloat, but steadily settled in the water. The *Elgin* launched her whaler and a skiff, and a Carley float was lowered for the survivors, but the ship sank about 40 minutes after the explosion. Three officers and twenty-four ratings lost their lives.

[TNA: ADM.1/10646; ADM.199/220]

5 May SEAL submarine

Chatham 1939; 1,520/2,157 tons; 271.6ft × 25.6ft; 1 × 4in, 6 × torpedo tubes, 50 mines
Lieutenant Commander Rupert Philip Lonsdale

Sailed from Immingham on 29 April to carry out a minelaying mission in the Kattegat, she was running on the surface during the early hours of the morning of 4 May, recharging her batteries as she was approaching her operating area, when at 02.30 she was surprised by a German aircraft which forced her to dive. Soon after this, she sighted a group of armed trawlers, who seemed to be searching, clearly having been alerted to her presence by the aircraft. Despite this, she commenced laying mines at 09.00, completing this at 09.45 after which she headed out of the area. The presence of the surface vessels did not make this easy and more vessels were detected joining the hunt. However, she remained undetected, and moved slowly but steadily clear of the area, until at 19.00 there was a loud explosion close astern. She had entered a hostile minefield, and had triggered a mine, probably after fouling the wire. The boat shuddered and with water entering the after ends went down stern first until she struck the bottom hard, burying her stern into the mud. Lonsdale decided that it was safer to remain where she was for a while, as he feared the explosion must have been noticed by the ships on the surface. At 22.30 they commenced blowing tanks to try and reach the surface, but found they were held firmly in the mud. It was with considerable difficulty that she finally managed to break free, resorting to moving all crew members as far forward as possible. At 01.30 she finally reached the surface; her air having been almost exhausted by this time, the crew suffering from the effects of carbon dioxide poisoning. It was then found that she was not answering the rudder, almost certainly because it was damaged, and it was decided to try and reach the neutral waters of Sweden, stern first but then one of the engines stopped working. This meant that they were crippled, unable to dive or manoeuvre. At first light an Arado 196 seaplane appeared overhead, which then commenced attacking her, dropping bombs which exploded nearby. A second seaplane joined later, and the pair attacked with cannon fire, causing further damage, puncturing the port ballast tank. It was clear that the boat would not escape, so Lonsdale ordered confidential books to be burnt and Asdic equipment smashed. To save casualties, a white tablecloth was hung over the conning tower to indicate surrender. One of the seaplanes then landed nearby and took Lonsdale prisoner. At 06.30 an armed trawler arrived on scene and took the crew off whilst they rigged a tow. It was believed by the *Seal*'s officers that the boat was in a sinking condition, listing to port and her stern being awash; however, she remained afloat and by late afternoon was in Frederikshavn. Eventually taken to Kiel, she was commissioned by the German Navy as a prize, *UB A*, but was only used as a training vessel.

[TNA: ADM 156/283; Evans p230]

6 May LOCH NAVER trawler

Troon 1919 (*Edward Cattelly*) requisitioned 1939; 278 tons; 125.5ft × 23.5ft; 1 × 12pdr
Skipper George Robert Burwood RNR

Sank off number 20 buoy, about 4.5 miles off Hartlepool, following a collision with the collier *Cordene* (2,345 tons) at 01.00. None of the crew were lost, all being all taken off by the armed yacht *Breda* before she foundered.

[TNA: ADM.199/366]

12 May **YPRES** trawler

Toronto 1917; 440 tons; 130ft × 23ft
Lieutenant Antoine Herbert Cassivi RCNVR

Royal Canadian Navy. Employed as a boom gate vessel at Halifax, she tended the nets to allow ships to pass through. A small convoy, with the battleship *Revenge*, prepared to sail during the afternoon and the gate was opened at the scheduled time. The ships, however, were delayed, so the boom gate was closed. *Revenge* finally got under way at 20.15, but this was not promptly communicated to the gate vessels, which were still working to open the barrier when the battleship arrived at the boom. Only realising at the last moment that the gate was not fully open, *Revenge* went astern, but momentum carried her forward and she rammed the *Ypres*, which, still connected to the net and cables, was dragged about 500 yards before the battleship stopped. Heeling over to starboard, she filled and sank. There were no casualties. Poor communication was blamed for the collision.

[McKee & Darlington p15]

15 May **VALENTINE** destroyer

Birkenhead 1917; 1,188 tons; 300ft × 29.6ft; 4 × 4in
Commander Herbert James Buchanan RAN

In company with the destroyer *Whitley* the pair were ordered to patrol in the Westerschelde estuary, the Netherlands, and provide cover for the movement of allied troops, in particular the ferrying of French troops from Terneuzen to the island of South Beveland. At 14.30 they were closed by a single aircraft, identified as a Ju 88, which carried out a steep dive-bombing attack from directly overhead. It dropped a number of bombs, which straddled her. One bomb went down the after funnel and exploded in number 2 boiler room, causing the boiler to blow up. Another detonated close to the starboard side, just forward of the bridge, blowing a hole in the side. She was clearly severely damaged, and the engine room was filling with water from a fractured fire main. Commander Buchanan decided to run into shallow water. The helm was put over and she was beached on the southern bank of the river, just under a mile to the east of the Nieuw Neuzenpolder light. She lay with a list of 20 degrees, with all her stern compartments flooded. Twenty-six men had been killed in the attack, and another eight died of their wounds later. Some of the crew were transferred to the *Whitley*, but the wounded were transferred to a local Dutch hospital and a party remained to stand by the wreck, building a bonfire on the upper deck of confidential books and papers. After sheltering for the evening in a nearby farmhouse, it was felt that little more could be done, and the wreck was abandoned, and the party left that night for Oostburg. The wreck remained in place for several years, until the stern section was broken up post-war.

[TNA: ADM.1/10805; ADM.199/100; ADM.199/667]

18 May **EFFINGHAM** cruiser

Portsmouth 1921; 9,550 tons; 605ft × 65ft; 9 × 6in, 8 × 4in, 8 × 2pdr, 4 × torpedo tubes
Captain John Montagu Howson

In Norway, the enemy had made a steady advance northwards and as Allied forces were withdrawn from central Norway, they reinforced various points further to the north. In an effort to send more forces to Bodø, the cruisers *Cairo*, *Coventry* and *Effingham* embarked troops and equipment and on 17 May sailed from Harstad, the *Effingham* having 1,000 soldiers on board in addition to extra stores. At 19.15 as they approached Bodø by the Bliksvaer Channel the group formed up in line ahead, the *Effingham* acting as guide led the other cruisers, with the destroyers *Matabele* and *Echo* stationed ahead and on the beam. It had been decided that a fast transit was necessary, to reduce the time exposed to possible air attack, with the navigating officer of *Effingham*, Lieutenant Michael Blake using a Norwegian chart for the passage. The ships threaded their way past small islands and rocky outcrops at 22 knots, making small alterations of course as they did so. At 19.44 another slight alteration in course was ordered by *Effingham*, and the *Matabele* altered to the new heading, but was then seen to suddenly shudder as she struck something, make a turn to starboard and reduce speed. On seeing this, the *Effingham*, close behind, reacted promptly and altered to starboard, but at 19.48 she grounded heavily. She seemed to have hit something under the port bow and then a series of heavy bumps occurred as she ran further onto the obstruction. She immediately started to settle on an even keel and both the engine and boiler rooms reported they were flooding, and soon after, all the power failed. Bulkheads were ordered to be shored, but it soon became clear that the hull had been pierced for much of the ship's length and water was entering in many places at a speed which could not be controlled. The *Echo* was ordered to lift off some of the troops and rigged a tow to haul her free, but little headway had been made in moving her before the destroyer was ordered to cast off at 20.45. The Rear Admiral commanding ordered her to be sunk in deep water if she could not be saved, but it became clear that with limited manoeuvring room and the rate at which she was settling made this difficult. Hauled free of the rocks, she drifted a little way until she grounded in shallow water. The destroyers then closed to lift off all the troops, transferring them to the cruisers. She remained lying on an even keel overnight, and the following morning work started to lift off the embarked stores. Several local steamers closed to assist but attempts to haul her free failed. The *Echo* returned to the scene and after removing as much ammunition and valuable stores as she could, fired a single torpedo into the starboard side of the wreck, which made her heel over and settle further. She was then abandoned in position 67.16.7N 14.03.5E.

It was later determined that she had struck rocks at the southern edge of the Faksen shoal and Captain Howson, and Lieutenant Blake were both found to have been partly to blame and informed that they had incurred their Lordships' displeasure. The reason for the grounding is somewhat obscure – it has been variously suggested that the rocks had been uncharted or that Lieutenant Blake had either failed to realise the significance of a cross marked on the Norwegian chart, which meant a rock, or even that he had used a thick pencil to chart his course and obscured the marks for the shoal. However, a more recent investigation shows that the presence and dangers of the Faksen shoal were well known to the navigating staff, and a more plausible explanation lays in mistaken identification of the numerous small islands in the channel which were being used as marks for plotting the line of advance and determining course changes – taking visual bearings on the wrong island would have incurred an error which would have led them over the edge of the shoal.
[TNA: ADM.1/99/485; Richard Wright in Warship 2011 pp165–74]

18 May PRINCESS VICTORIA minelayer
Dumbarton 1939 requisitioned 1939; 2,197 tons;
309.9ft × 48ft; 1 × 4in, 2 × 12pdr, 244 mines
Captain John Buller Edward Hall†
Returning to Grimsby from a minelaying operation escorted by two destroyers, she was passing about half a mile to the port of the Humber light vessel when at 23.15 there was a terrific explosion on the starboard side, just forward of the bridge, as she detonated a mine. The engines stopped, and all power was lost, the ship being plunged into darkness. She lost way and went down by the head and assumed a list to starboard. The explosion had wrecked the forward compartments which allowed rapid flooding and she started to sink bows first whilst continuing to roll to starboard until she was heeling over at an angle of 45 degrees. After hanging for some time, she slowly recovered, probably after her forefoot struck the ground. She steadily settled and eventually sank on an even keel with her masts, funnel and bridge exposed. Three officers and thirty-one ratings were killed.
[TNA: ADM.1/110807]

19 May WHITLEY destroyer
Sunderland 1918; 1,090 tons; 300ft × 29.6ft; 4 × 4in
Lieutenant Commander Guy Neville Rolfe
Operating off the Dutch coast, screening the movement of French troops retreating to Dunkirk, at 06.26 she came under attack by several Ju 87 dive bombers off Nieuport. Despite vigorous manoeuvring she was near missed several times and then struck by at least one bomb which penetrated the upper deck to detonate in the boiler room. The ship was turned inshore and then deliberately run into shallow water between Nieuport and Ostend, with both of her boiler rooms flooded. The salvage tug Lady Brassey was despatched from Dover, and the destroyer Vimiera and the flotilla leader Keith were also ordered to the scene. They found that her back was broken, and it would be impossible under the constant threat of further air attacks to salvage her, so she was abandoned. The Keith fired several rounds into the stranded ship to ensure her destruction. Four men, all stokers on watch in the boiler room, were killed.
[TNA: ADM.358/3656; Smith pp221–2]

20 May RIFSNES trawler
Beverley 1932 requisitioned 1939; 423 tons;
144.7ft × 25.1ft
Skipper Cecil Gordon Chudley Coombe RNR
Working in company with the trawler Lord Inchcape, the pair was attempting to sweep for magnetic mines between Dunkirk and Ostend. They came under sustained air attacks as they did so, being unable to manoeuvre due to the sweep gear. The Rifsnes suffered severe damage from several near misses and foundered off Ostend, near the Middle Peike Bank buoy. Two men were killed, one of whom was the Minesweeping Unit Officer, Lieutenant Lawrence Thornton RNR.
[TNA: ADM.1/99/795; Smith p23]

21 May CORBURN mine destructor
Burntisland 1936 requisitioned 1939; 3,060 tons;
257ft × 39.5ft; 2 × 12pdr
Lieutenant Commander Mark Edlin Welby
A former Cory line collier, she was one of several such vessels taken over and converted to house a large electromagnet in the fore hold. It was intended that this would create a magnetic field to deal with the magnetic mine. Following reports of mines being dropped by aircraft in French harbours, the Corburn was ordered to Le Havre arriving during the afternoon of 21 May. A French naval officer boarded her and after briefing on the mining situation, asked if they could sweep the inner harbour and approaches. At 19.00 that night they commenced the work and at 19.40 a magnetic mine exploded about 150 yards on the starboard bow. This shook the ship considerably, causing loss of electrical power. This was restored and as she recommenced her work a second mine was detonated about 20 yards to starboard, abreast the bridge. The shock damage was extensive, leaks being started, and the boilers flooded with a noisy escape of steam. Boats were ordered to be hoisted out and at 20.10 she was abandoned, the evacuation being assisted by a French drifter. About an hour later she sank, stern first. One man was killed in the second blast.
[TNA: ADM.1/99/220]

21 May CAPE PASSARO trawler

Selby 1939 requisitioned 1939; 590 tons; 178.2ft × 30.1ft;
1 × 4in
Lieutenant Commander Martyn Butt Sherwood

One of the Anti-Submarine Striking Force trawlers that had been deployed to Norway in late April, the ships found life exceedingly difficult, being under constant air attack. The *Cape Passaro* was in Bogen Bay near Narvik when she was attacked and sunk by an He 111 bomber. Four men were killed, the survivors being picked up by the cruiser *Cairo*.
[TNA: ADM.358/3133]

22 May MELBOURNE trawler

Middlesbrough 1936 requisitioned 1939; 466 tons;
164.1ft × 27.1ft; 1 × 4in
Lieutenant Commander Arthur John Cinammond
Pomeroy RNVR

Melbourne had arrived in Norway in mid-April, to act as senior officer of one of the Anti-Submarine Striking Groups, with Lieutenant Commander Alan Holt Davies RNVR embarked. The ships were immediately subjected to constant attacks by the Luftwaffe. *Melbourne* was in the fjords north of Narvik, off Gratangsbotn, when attacked by a group of He 111 aircraft and severely damaged by several near misses. The trawler was run into shallow water where she grounded, capsizing onto her port side; no men were lost.
[Statement of Losses p7]

24 May WESSEX destroyer

Hebburn 1918; 1,090 tons; 300ft × 29.6ft; 4 × 4in, 1 × 2pdr,
6 × torpedo tubes
Lieutenant Commander William Archibald Rosebery
Cartwright

Ordered to carry out a bombardment of shore positions around Calais, she was joined by the destroyers, *Wolfhound*, *Vimiera* and the Polish *Burza*, but was frustrated by a lack of targets until 13.30 when they were able to engage positions about 3 miles to the south of the town. At 16.45 a large group of aircraft was sighted, closing from the north-east, identified as Ju 87 aircraft. These commenced a dive-bombing attack on the destroyers, and the *Burza* was damaged and forced to leave the formation. *Wessex* meanwhile had worked up to full speed and engaged with all available guns whilst manoeuvring. She was the target of two dive-bombing attacks, both of which missed, but a third succeeded, hitting three times, all of the bombs hitting her amidships. They penetrated the upper deck and exploded in the boiler room, killing all the personnel, and both compartments were wrecked. The foremost engine room bulkhead was damaged, causing the

engine to start flooding. The bottom and sides of the compartment had also been damaged, and this added to the flooding. All her boats and deck fittings were wrecked, the after funnel fell over and the foremast was broken, falling over the bridge. It was clear that she was sinking, and the *Vimiera* closed to place her starboard bow alongside her port quarter to remove all the personnel. When this was complete, she rolled over and sank. Five men were lost.
[TNA: ADM.199/103]

25 May MASHOBRA base ship

Glasgow 1920 requisitioned 1939; 8,324 tons;
450ft × 58.3ft
Lieutenant Commander Percy Taylor RNR

A former British India steamship, she was taken over for use as a depot and mobile base ship. Arriving in Norwegian waters on 10 May, she was sent to Harstad, where she arrived on 17 May to commence disembarking the guns and equipment of the Royal Marine Fortress Unit. German air attacks were a constant menace and on 23 May at 17.15 she was damaged by a near miss from a bomb, being shaken badly and was subsequently run into shallow water where she grounded. Examination showed a hole on the waterline abreast number 3 hold which caused numbers 2 and 3 holds to flood. All boats on the port side were wrecked and there was considerable blast and shock damage to the bridge and cabin area. All personnel were evacuated except essential crew. Over the next 2 days work continued to offload stores using LCMs although she was again subject to high-level air bombing which caused further damage and she settled by the stern. During the evening of 25 May orders were received to evacuate the area and return to the UK and as it was clear that she would be unable to sail, the forepart was blown up. There were no casualties.
[TNA: ADM.199/483]

25 May CHARLES BOYES trawler

Beverley 1918 requisitioned 1939; 275 tons; 125ft × 23.5ft;
1 × 12pdr
Skipper George Reynolds RNR‡

Fitted out as a minesweeper, when returning to Great Yarmouth, she detonated a mine at 14.10 in position 52.40.5N 01.46.5E. The Caister lifeboat was launched and went to her assistance and saved three men they found surrounded by wreckage, clinging to lifebelts, but fifteen of her crew were lost. It was found that she had taken a course that took her through an area that had not been swept.
[TNA: ADM.199/1171]

26 May LOCH SHIN boom defence vessel
Aberdeen 1930 requisitioned 1939; 255 tons;
121ft × 22.6ft
Boom Skipper Harry Sizer RNR
One of the numerous support vessels deployed to
Norway, she was attacked by five He 111 aircraft off
Harstad and severely damaged by a near miss. She
subsequently capsized as attempts were being made to
beach her. There were no casualties.
[TNA: ADM.199/2225]

26 May CURLEW cruiser
Walker on Tyne 1917; 4,190 tons; 425ft × 43.5ft; 10 × 4in,
8 × 2pdr
Captain Basil Charles Barrington Brooke
Supporting the Allied forces ashore in Norway, she was
in Lavang Fjord, giving protection to an airfield under
construction ashore. During the afternoon, her radar
detected four aircraft approaching at a range of 19 miles.
The aircraft were approaching from the starboard beam,
and she increased speed and headed for the entrance to
the Fjord, engaging the hostile aircraft as soon as she
could. The aircraft initially dropped bombs from high
level, very ineffectively, one stick dropping half a mile
off the port bow, another exploded along the shoreline.
The third aircraft dropped five bombs which landed
about 100 yards away. Still undamaged, the ship was
now close to the entrance of the Fjord when the fourth
aircraft, estimated to be at 20,000ft closed from the stern
and dropped four bombs, none of which hit her, but all
exploded close along the starboard side. The 'whipping'
effect of the blast was terrific. The whole ship shuddered
and vibrated, which lifted the floor plates in the engine
room and with water and oil flooding in, both engine and
boiler rooms had to be evacuated. The ship's side opened,
parting from the upper deck plates. All power was lost,
and the ship lost way, taking a sheer to port to head for
the shore, but Captain Brooke let go the anchors when
about 2 cables (400 yards) from the shore to bring her up.
She was settling by the stern and soon the quarterdeck
was awash, and with the forward engine room reported
to be filling, she was ordered to be abandoned. Floats and
boats were hoisted out and lowered and all men were
safely put ashore. She continued to settle until she finally
rolled over at 17.00. Nine men were lost. The attacking
aircraft were He 111s from KG 100.
[TNA: ADM.267/84]

28 May OCEAN REWARD drifter
Aberdeen 1912 requisitioned 1939; 95 tons; 86.1ft × 18.6ft
Lieutenant Hugh Clunas Slater RNR[†]
Stationed at Dover, she was assigned to the examination
service, checking neutral shipping entering harbour.
During the evening of 28 May, the steamer *Isle of
Thanet*, which was acting as a hospital ship, was ordered

to proceed from Dover to Newhaven. She got under
way and saw the *Ocean Reward* stationary on her port
bow. As the *Thanet* increased speed, the drifter was seen
to get underway and then alter course to pass across the
bows of the oncoming steamer. Despite the helm being
put over and the engines put to full astern the drifter
was struck hard on the starboard side. She rolled over
and sank immediately with the loss of all eight men
on board. The *Ocean Reward* had been tasked to carry
orders to various ships off Dover, one of them being the
Isle of Thanet; she may have been attempting to close the
steamer but miscalculated her course and speed.
[TNA: ADM.1/12602]

30 May CAMBRIAN trawler
Selby 1924 requisitioned 1939; 338 tons; 138.8ft × 23.8ft
Boom Skipper Alexander Livingstone Wood RNR
Employed as a boom defence vessel, she sank after
striking a mine at 15.30 when 8.5 cables (1,700 yards)
to the east of the Horse Sand Fort, Spithead. There were
two survivors, with twenty-one men lost.
[TNA: ADM.199/370; ADM.358/3121]

26 May–4 June: Operation 'Dynamo' – Withdrawal of troops from north-eastern France

On 10 May the German army invaded the Netherlands,
Belgium and France. They advanced rapidly through
the Low Countries to push into northern France and
within 10 days it was clear that it might be necessary
to carry out an evacuation of the troops of the British
Expeditionary Force to prevent them being cut off.
With the fall of Boulogne and Calais, the evacuation
became concentrated on the port of Dunkirk and
during the afternoon of 26 May, Operation 'Dynamo',
the evacuation of British troops from that port, was
initiated. Numerous merchant ships, ranging from
passenger ships to cargo vessels and drifters were taken
up for the role, and as the evacuation got under way
many small craft were employed. Admiral Ramsay at
Dover was given operational control, and ships of the
Royal Navy were to lead the evacuation, which was
subject to constant air attack with the added menace of
surface and sub-surface attacks.

27 May PAXTON drifter
Lowestoft 1911 requisitioned 1939; 92 tons; 86ft × 19.5ft
Skipper Alfred Manning Lovis RNR
Based at Dover as a flare-burning drifter, she was ordered
to proceed to Dunkirk, where she became the first of
the naval casualties of the evacuation. *Paxton* arrived off
Dunkirk during the afternoon of 27 May. At 16.30 as she

steered to enter the harbour, she came under air attack, with a bomb exploding nearby peppering her with shrapnel. Filling with water, she was able to proceed to a position out of the fairway where she settled into shallow water and was abandoned. There were no casualties.
[TNA: ADM.267/126; Winser, BEF Ships p15]

27 May BOY ROY drifter
Lowestoft 1911 requisitioned 1939; 95 tons; 86.3ft × 19.5ft
Skipper Edward Frederick Dettman RNR

Another Dover–based drifter like the *Paxton*, she arrived in Dunkirk roads during the late afternoon and was also promptly subjected to an air attack. Badly shaken by a near miss, she was run clear of the channels and beached in shallow water. There were no casualties.
[TNA: ADM.267/126; Winser, BEF Ships p15]

28 May THOMAS BARTLETT trawler
Beverley 1918 requisitioned 1939; 290 tons;
125.5ft × 23.5ft
Skipper John Jeffrey Tomlinson RNR

One of a group of minesweeping trawlers ordered to carry out a sweep along the channel off the northern French coast between Calais and Dunkirk that would be used by ships from Dover. The group came under fire from the shore and at 10.17 whilst manoeuvring to get out of range of the shellfire she ran into a British minefield, detonated a mine and sank. Eight men were killed.
[TNA: ADM.267/126; Winser, BEF Ships p15]

28 May BRIGHTON BELLE paddle minesweeper
Kinghorn 1900 requisitioned 1939; 320 tons; 200ft × 24ft;
1 × 12pdr
Lieutenant Leonard Kaye Perrin RNVR

Having successfully embarked 350 troops from the beach at Zuydcoote, she sailed to return to Dover, but manoeuvring during an air attack, she collided with a submerged object, believed to be a wreck, near the Gull Light Buoy in the Downs. The paddle steamers *Sandown* and *Medway Queen* and the Belgian launch *Yser* all closed to assist, taking off her troops and rigged a tow. However, at 13.00 she settled and subsequently broke up and sank. The main part of the wreck lies in position 51.17.53N 01.30.10E. One man was killed and two wounded during the air attack.
[TNA: ADM.267/126; Winser, BEF Ships p16; Larn vol 2 sec 6]

28 May THURINGIA trawler
Selby 1936 (*Rockflower*), purchased 1939; 396 tons;
150.5ft × 25.6ft
Chief Skipper David William Leonard Simpson RNR†

Ordered to proceed to Dunkirk to carry out patrols and cover the evacuation, she was passing to the north of the

Sandettie Bank when she detonated a mine and sank. Fourteen men were killed, with four survivors. Her wreck has been found and lies in position 51.20.5N 02.02.4E.
[TNA: ADM.267/126; Winser, BEF Ships p15]

28 May GIRL PAMELA drifter
Great Yarmouth 1912 (*Oburn*) requisitioned 1939; 93 tons;
88.2ft × 19.7ft
Skipper Charles Sansom RNR

Arrived at Dunkirk mid-morning, she went into the harbour to assist transferring troops to the larger ships. That night the visibility was restricted by thick smoke from burning oil fuel tanks and in the crowded harbour, at 23.18, as the minesweeper *Lydd* entered, she encountered the *Girl Pamela* which loomed out of the murk close on the port bow. Despite going full astern the *Lydd* struck the starboard side of the drifter and she subsequently sank. There were no casualties.
Note: Statement of Losses records this loss on 29 May
[TNA: ADM.199/790]

28 May ALICE coaster
1939 Westerbroek requisitioned 1940; 291 tons;
94.2ft × 23.2ft
Lieutenant Hubert Duncan McLauchlan Slater

One of a number of Dutch coasters, or schuyts, which were taken up for service for the evacuation. *Alice* arrived off the beaches of La Panne, to the east of the harbour in the early hours and was run into shallow water to allow unloading of food and water for the troops. Lieutenant Slater went ashore to try and gain more information, and in his absence the beach came under air attack, and although she did not receive any direct hits, the ship was peppered with shrapnel. Late in the day, when she attempted to weigh, her engines seized because of the damage, and with no sign of Lieutenant Slater returning, she was abandoned, the crew transferring to another requisitioned coaster, the *Kaap Falga*, reporting that they believed their commanding officer was probably dead. This latter fact was confounded some days later when Lieutenant Slater reappeared; he had returned to find his ship abandoned. He eventually managed to get aboard another vessel and return to Dover.
[Gardner p30; TNA: ADM.358/117]

29 May WAKEFUL destroyer
Dalmuir 1917; 1,090 tons; 300ft × 29.6ft; 4 × 4in,
6 × torpedo tubes
Commander Ralph Lindsay Fisher

Having embarked over 600 troops from the beaches at Bray, to the north of Dunkirk, she sailed at 23.00 to return to Dover. As she approached the Kwinte Whistle buoy she was able to increase to 20 knots. At 00.45 just after she had started to zigzag, two torpedo tracks were seen and the helm was put over; the first torpedo missed ahead, but the second hit the destroyer amidships, with a brilliant flash. The explosion was violent, and she broke in half, and both halves sank in less than a minute, with each section remaining vertical, standing clear of the water with the amidships end resting on the bottom. The drifters *Nautilus* and *Comfort* arrived on the scene about 30 minutes after the explosion to start a search for survivors, and they were joined by the minesweepers *Gossamer* and *Lydd*. Despite their efforts, all but two of the soldiers had been lost, and only a handful of men were picked up, 104 members of her crew having been killed. Her attacker had been the torpedo boat *S 30*. The wreck has been located, in position 51.22.72N 02.43.35E.

[TNA: ADM.199/789; ADM.267/126]

29 May **COMFORT** drifter
Fraserburgh 1901 requisitioned 1939; 60 tons; 70ft × 20ft
Skipper John Dougal Mair RNR†
One of the first on scene at the sinking of the *Wakeful* (see above), she picked up sixteen survivors, including Commander Fisher. When they saw the *Grafton* approaching, Commander Fisher was concerned that they must be warned of the danger of torpedo boats in the area, and the drifter steered toward the destroyer. They had just reached her when *Grafton* was hit by a torpedo, and the shock wave from the explosion 'whipped' the drifter, throwing several men overboard. Still under full power she cleared the destroyer and circled round but as she emerged from the spray and smoke, she was seen by the *Grafton* and presumed to be an enemy torpedo boat. The destroyer promptly opened an accurate fire on the drifter, and was joined by the minesweeper *Lydd*, and they soon reduced her to a sinking wreck. The *Lydd* then closed and rammed the *Comfort* to ensure that she sank. Just one survivor from the *Comfort* was picked up and four from the *Wakeful*. Commander Fisher of the *Wakeful* was left swimming for a second time and was eventually picked up at 05.15 by a merchant vessel. Six men died.

[TNA: ADM.267/126; Winser, BEF Ships pp16–17]

29 May **GRAFTON** destroyer
Woolston 1935; 1,350 tons; 312ft × 33ft; 4 × 4.7in,
8 × torpedo tubes
Commander Cecil Edmund Charles Robinson†
Busily engaged in evacuating troops from the beaches near Dunkirk, she had taken on board about 800 soldiers, had cleared the shore and at 02.45 was approaching the scene of the search for survivors from the *Wakeful* (see above). As she slowed as they neared the incident, they were hit by a torpedo on the port side aft, scattering debris, and there was a second, smaller explosion on the bridge which killed Commander Robinson. Her back

was broken, and the bridge wrecked, but she remained afloat, which allowed the passenger ship *Malines* to be brought alongside to lift off the troops. The destroyer *Ivanhoe* closed, and found her listing and with her stern awash, and sank her, firing several shells into the wreck. The wreck lies in position 51.24.42N 02.49.08E. Her attacker was unclear at the time, and it was widely assumed to be from an enemy torpedo boat, but it is now clear that she was torpedoed by the submarine *U 62* (Michalowski) which reported attacking a destroyer, one torpedo hitting the target aft. Sixteen crew members died, along with thirty-five soldiers.

[TNA: ADM 267/126; Winser, BEF Ships pp16–17]

29 May **GRENADE** destroyer
Linthouse 1935; 1,350 tons; 312ft × 33ft; 4 × 4.7in,
8 × torpedo tubes
Commander Richard Courtney Boyle
During the late morning of 29 May, the *Grenade*, having successfully completed one evacuation trip, arrived off Dunkirk, and almost immediately found herself under a determined air attack by a large number of Ju 87 dive bombers. They survived this, although her sister *Gallant* had to return to Dover with damage. *Grenade* then moved into the harbour to berth at the outer end of the east pier, to take her place with numerous other vessels which were embarking troops. By 15.30 the first of the fully-laden vessels started to leave, and the pier again came under air attack, during which she was damaged by splinters. A further air raid developed at about 17.50, and it was during this attack that a bomb exploded close to her, blowing a hole in her starboard side. Soon after this she received two direct hits. This immobilised her engines and started a fire. At 18.15 she was towed clear of the pier by the trawler *John Cattling* and beached in shallow water where she burned for 7 hours before she blew up. Nine men were lost.

[Gardner pp43–4; Winser p18]

29 May **CRESTED EAGLE** anti-aircraft ship
Cowes 1925 requisitioned 1939; 1,110 tons;
299.7ft × 34.6ft; 3 × 2pdr
Lieutenant Commander Bernard Ralph Booth RNR
Arrived at Dunkirk during the morning and berthed outboard of the east pier. During the air raids of the afternoon, she escaped damage, and took on board about 600 troops from the bomb-damaged passenger ship *Fenella*. Still with the air raids underway, she swung clear of the pier and got under way but was almost immediately hit by a stick of four bombs. She caught fire and, burning fiercely, was run inshore and beached at about 18.30. The wreck lies in position 51.04.56N 02.29.46E. Four members of the crew were lost and perhaps 300 of the embarked soldiers,

[TNA: ADM.267/126; Winser, BEF Ships p18]

29 May NAUTILUS drifter
Findochty 1930 requisitioned 1939; 64 tons
Skipper Robert MacLean RNR

Arrived at Dunkirk during the morning, she was employed in ferrying troops to the destroyers *Harvester* and *Greyhound*. During the afternoon, in the intense air raids, at 16.30, she was damaged by a near miss from a bomb, which knocked her steering gear and engines out of action and started a fire. She managed to get alongside the *Greyhound* and transfer the 150 troops she was carrying and was then run into shallow water and abandoned, petrol being thrown around below decks and then set on fire. There were no casualties.
[TNA: ADM.199/789; Winser, BEF Ships p19]

29 May WAVERLEY paddle minesweeper
Glasgow 1899 requisitioned 1939; 537 tons; 235ft × 26.1ft
Lieutenant Sydney Frederick Harmer-Elliott RNVR

Fully laden with about 600 troops lifted from the beach at La Panne, *Waverley* sailed for Dover, but as she cleared the harbour at 14.00 came under air attack from several dive bombers. A bomb exploded as a near miss and caused some shock damage, with lights and fittings being broken. She then suffered two direct hits which struck her aft, with the bomb which struck the port quarter passing through several compartments, killing four soldiers in its passage, before going through the bottom. The steering gear was put out of action and the after bulkhead of the saloon compartment held out for about 20 minutes until it gave way. She then rapidly filled with water and heeled over to port and started to sink by the stern and she finally sank at 14.46, with the troops left swimming in the debris. The French destroyer *Cyclone* and paddle minesweeper *Golden Eagle* picked up more than 400 men from the water. The wreck is in position 51.17.02N 02.41.23E. Two ratings were killed.
[TNA: ADM.267/101; Gardner p42; Winser, BEF Ships p19]

29 May CALVI trawler
Beverley 1930 (*Galleon*) requisitioned 1939; 553 tons; 145.9ft × 24.2ft
Skipper Bertie David Spindler RNR

Arrived in Dunkirk harbour during the day, and berthed at the east pier, outboard of another two trawlers. At about 18.00 there was another intense air raid, and she suffered a direct hit from a bomb which apparently went through the counter stern and exploded beneath her. She sank very quickly, her masts and funnel remaining above water. Her crew all survived, scrambling on board the trawler *John Cattling*, which was alongside, but one man subsequently died of his wounds.
[Winser, BEF Ships p18; Gardner p43]

29 May POLLY JOHNSON trawler
Beverley 1918 (*John Aikenhead*) requisitioned 1939; 408 tons; 125.5ft × 23.6ft
Chief Skipper Leonard Lake RNR

Crossed to Dunkirk during the day, she was directed to berth at the east pier, outboard of two other trawlers, and ahead of two destroyers. From 15.30 a series of air raids commenced, with more than twenty bombs being dropped in the harbour, none scored a direct hit, but a near miss peppered the *Polly Johnson* with shrapnel. Despite the damage, she was able to get under way at about 18.00 with a load of troops, but it was discovered that she was making water. Unable to proceed, the troops were taken off by the trawler *Arley*, which, when complete, fired several rounds into the *Polly Johnson* which sank her.
[TNA: ADM.199/792]

30 May GRACIE FIELDS paddle minesweeper
Woolston 1936 requisitioned 1939; 393 tons; 195.9ft × 24.9ft
Lieutenant Alfred Clifford Weeks RNVR

Having made a successful trip from Dunkirk on 28 May, when she had taken over 200 troops to England, she arrived back off the French port during the afternoon the following day. She embarked about 700 troops from the beach at La Panne, and got under way at 20.00, but 30 minutes later she was attacked by several Ju 87 bombers and received a direct hit amidships, the bomb bursting in the engine room, wrecking the compartment and putting the engines out of action and jammed her steering with 15 degrees of starboard wheel on. Several ships came to her aid, and the coasters *Jutland* and *Twente* managed to get alongside and lifted off the troops, and the minesweeper *Pangbourne* rigged a tow. She was towed until 02.00 when, with the paddle sponsons awash and the engine and stokeholds flooded to a depth of 10ft, it was decided to abandon her. She continued to settle until she heeled over and sank at 02.30. Her wreck lies in position 51.12.55N 02.39.39E. Eight men were lost.
[TNA: ADM.267/101; Gardner p41; Winser, BEF Ships p19]

30 May KING ORRY armed boarding steamer
Birkenhead 1913 requisitioned 1939; 1,877 tons; 300ft × 43.1ft; 1× 4in, 1 × 12pdr
Commander Jeffrey Elliott DSO RNR

Arrived in Dunkirk roads during the heavy air raids of the late afternoon of 29 May, and although she had escaped a direct hit, she was badly shaken by several near misses. These had damaged her steering gear, and as she attempted to come alongside the east pier, she struck the wharf heavily. A little later she was further damaged by bombs exploding right next to her; these peppered her hull with shrapnel, burst steam pipes

on the starboard side, and started fires. The fires were tackled and extinguished, but fearing that she would prevent other ships berthing, she was ordered to leave the harbour. At 00.30 she attempted to put to sea, but as she got underway, stern first, she developed a heavy list to starboard, and attempts to put her head to seaward proved difficult. Water was reported entering the engine room, and she was eventually run aground on a sandbank and at 02.00 rolled over onto her starboard side and sank. The yacht *Bystander* stood by her during this time, to lift off the crew, and the trawlers *Lord Grey* and *Clythness* assisted in taking off the survivors. Five men were lost.
[TNA: ADM.267/101; Gardner p45; Winser, BEF Ships p20]

31 May DEVONIA paddle minesweeper
Clydebank 1905 requisitioned 1939; 642 tons; 245ft × 29ft; 1 × 12pdr
Lieutenant George Clifford Spong RNR
Arrived off the beaches at La Panne, to the east of Dunkirk during the morning only to become the target for an air attack in which she was damaged by several near misses and was then further damaged by hits from shells from shore artillery. With the need to improve conditions for boat work on the beach, and effectively form a pier, at 16.00 she was ordered to be run ashore onto the beach and abandoned, which was done at full speed at 19.30. The wreck now lies in position 51.04.77E 02.30.16E. One man was killed.
[Winser, BEF Ships p107; Gardner p83]

31 May HORST coaster
Foxhol 1939 requisitioned 1940; 400 tons; 149.8ft × 27ft
Lieutenant Thomas Edward Sargent RNR
Employed off the beaches to the east of Dunkirk transferring troops to larger ships offshore, during the evening she embarked a large number of troops, intending to return to Dover. When she attempted to weigh, she found that her anchor cable was fouled, and could not be freed. It was decided to abandon her, and troops were transferred to other ships.
[Winser, BEF Ships p26]

31 May SURSUM CORDA coaster
Waterhuizen 1933 requisitioned 1940; 199 tons; 108.5ft × 21.8ft
Lieutenant Christopher Louis George Philpotts
Arrived off the beaches of La Panne to the east of the port during the early hours of 30 May, and successfully went close inshore to embark troops over the bows and then ferry them to large ships offshore. When attempting to take on board more troops, she was found to be aground. The coaster *Hebe-II* attempted to tow her free, but she would not move. Work to shift her continued during 31 May, but her engines were

damaged in the efforts and it was decided to abandon her as a wreck.
[Winser, BEF Ships p20]

1 June ST ACHILLEUS trawler
Beverley 1934 requisitioned 1939; 484 tons; 164.4ft × 27.3ft
Lieutenant Harry Alfred Gellett RNR[†]
On patrol off Dunkirk, she disappeared during the night of 31 May/1 June; an explosion heard in the early hours of the morning was believed to have marked her loss. Some wreckage from *St Achilleus* was seen the next morning by a patrolling aircraft, which directed the sloop *Sheldrake* to the scene, and she rescued eleven men found clinging to wreckage, but four died before they could be got to harbour. Sixteen men were lost in all. Her wreck has been found, about 7 miles to the west of Nieuport, with a large hole on the port side, consistent with striking a mine.
[Gardner p93; http://www.wrecksite.eu/wreck.aspx?132178]

1 June ST FAGAN tug
Lytham 1918; 860 tons; 135.5ft × 29ft; 1 × 12pdr
Lieutenant Commander George Henry Warren MBE
With two lighters in tow, the tug approached Dunkirk at night, and at 03.00, when about 3 miles to the east of the harbour, slipped the lighters, to allow them to be taken into shallow water by her boats. Although an aircraft was heard overhead, there was little warning when at 03.55 she was struck by a single bomb which hit her amidships, and she 'practically disintegrated' and sank immediately, settling on an even keel. The tug *Tanga* picked up seven survivors, but seventeen men were lost. The wreck lies in position 51.04.31N 02.18.55E.
[TNA: ADM.199/793; Gardner p88]

1 June HAVANT destroyer
Cowes 1939; 1,350 tons; 312ft × 33ft; 3 × 4.7in, 8 × torpedo tubes
Lieutenant Commander Anthony Frank Burnell-Nugent
After completing three round trips to Dunkirk, lifting off 2,100 men, she returned for a fourth time in the early hours of 1 June. They arrived off Dunkirk at 08.00 and initially went alongside the jetty just as the first air raids of the day were developing. The destroyer *Ivanhoe* was hit and damaged and the *Havant* immediately slipped and proceeded to her assistance, taking off a number of soldiers. At 09.00 she got under way, intending to proceed to Dover, but as they steamed along the western end of the channel parallel to the beach, she came under attack herself from a large group of Ju 87 dive bombers. At 09.06 she was hit by two bombs which passed through her starboard side to explode in the engine room, with another exploding close under her bows. Her steering gear was put out of

action and she circled out of control to starboard. Her starboard anchor was then let go while Chief Stoker Martin Gallon gallantly entered the steam-filled boiler room to let steam out of the boiler, and these actions brought her up. The minesweeper *Saltash* and yacht *Grive* came alongside, to take off all the troops on board and tried to rig a tow, despite the air attacks continuing. Whilst this was underway a bomb exploded between *Saltash* and *Havant*, and another bomb then exploded under the stern of the destroyer, wrecking the tiller flat. She was now heeling over to port and as there was no hope of getting her back to England, it was decided to abandon her, the coaster *Aegir* taking off the last of the men, before she rolled over and sank at 10.15. The wreck lies in position 51.08.07N 02.15.77E. Eight men were killed, and twenty-five of the embarked soldiers were lost. Chief Stoker Gallon was awarded the DSM for his actions.

[TNA: ADM.199/101; Gardner p91; Winser, BEF Ships p28]

1 June KEITH destroyer

Barrow 1930; 1,400 tons; 312ft × 32.3ft; 4 × 4.7in, 2 × 2pdr, 8 × torpedo tubes
Captain Edward Lyon Berthon DSC

Having embarked Admiral Wake-Walker and several army staff officers at Dunkirk, she came under sustained attack from a large group of Ju 87 aircraft at the same time as the *Basilisk* and *Havant* (see above). She witnessed those destroyers hit and only by violent manoeuvres avoided being hit. The attacks continued, with one bomb exploding close astern, and the shock caused a steering gear failure. Emergency steering was rigged, but with all of her 2pdr ammunition expended, the only defence she had was to turn in tight circles, and during a hard turn to starboard, two bombs exploded close on the port side, causing shock damage and distorting some of the side plates. As she straightened up, still under attack, a bomb went down the aft funnel to explode in the engine room, Power was immediately lost, she heeled over to port and the after part of the ship was covered in a huge cloud of smoke and escaping steam. It soon became clear that she could not survive, the list increased, and the stern went down until the quarterdeck was awash. *MTB 102* was called alongside and successfully took of the Admiral and the staff officers; the coaster *Hilda* and minesweeper *Salamander* took off the troops who had been embarked. The tug *St Abbs* closed and positioned herself alongside the fo'c'sle to try and rig a tow. Air attacks were still underway, and as the men were being taken off by the tug, an attacking Me 109 was shot down into the water close alongside. She continued to list to port which increased and Carley floats were released before she capsized and sank at about 09.40 with more men being picked up by the tug *Vincia*.

Thirty-four men were lost. The wreck has been found in position 51.04.75N 02.26.70E.

[TNA: ADM.199/101; Gardner pp89–90; Winser, BEF Ships p26]

1 June SKIPJACK minesweeper

Clydebank 1934; 815 tons; 230ft × 33.6ft; 2 × 4in
Lieutenant Commander Francis Babington Proudfoot

Arriving off Dunkirk in the early hours of the morning, *Skipjack* commenced embarking troops using several small boats to ferry the men from the beaches. Air raids began with the daylight, but by constant manoeuvring she avoided any damage. At 08.45, now heavily laden with troops, she was only half a mile from the destroyers (above), when she became the target for Ju 87 dive bombers. She was hit twice in quick succession, the first bomb penetrated the oil fuel tank on the port side, and the second struck the starboard side by the boat davits. The ship stopped and took a pronounced list to port. Whilst in this position a second aircraft scored a direct hit with a stick of three bombs which exploded down the centreline, from forward to aft. The first struck the fo'c'sle, the next passed through the bridge, whilst the third pierced the upper deck to explode in the boiler room. She immediately heeled further to port, and less than a minute later she rolled over and capsized at 08.49. The survivors were picked up by *St Abbs* and *Hilda*, but twenty crew and about 275 troops were lost. The wreck has been located in position 51.05.28N 02.28.42E.

[TNA: ADM.267/101; Winser, BEF Ships p26]

1 June ST ABBS tug

Port Glasgow 1918; 860 tons; 135.5ft × 29ft; 1 × 12pdr
Lieutenant Thomas Ernest Brooker[†]

Having loaded a number of troops from the beaches, she was still off the beaches when the destroyers came under sustained air attack. She closed the stricken *Keith*, running alongside the fo'c'sle taking off many survivors. The attacks continued as the tug continued to pick up survivors from the water from the destroyers and the *Skipjack*. At about 09.00 the tug received a direct hit, the blast of the explosion scattering those men on the upper deck into the water, and she sank in less than a minute. Twenty men of the crew were killed and perhaps eighty other men were lost, troops and survivors. The wreck has been found in position 51.04.95N 02.27/57E.

[TNA: ADM.116/4121; Winser, BEF Ships p26]

1 June BASILISK destroyer

Clydebank 1930; 1,360 tons; 312ft × 32.3ft; 4 × 4.7in, 2 × 2pdr, 8 × torpedo tubes
Commander Maxwell Richmond

The *Basilisk* performed several trips to Dunkirk, during which she had evacuated several hundred soldiers, embarking them from the mole. On 1 June they were

ordered further to the east of Dunkirk to carry out a shore bombardment around the area of La Panne. At 08.00 as they were steaming along the coast several Ju 87 dive bombers were seen approaching from the east which commenced a concentrated bombing attack. The destroyer manoeuvred violently, and there were several near misses until a single bomb hit her amidships, exploding between the engine room and number 3 boiler room. Her engine and boiler rooms flooded, as did her after magazine. The ship drifted, having lost all power, ditching depth charges and torpedoes overboard to lighten her. Attempts to take her in tow were made, but the air attacks continued, being strafed by fighters and a further bombing attack during which the ship was shaken by several near misses. She was settling all the time, and when the ship heeled over to starboard, she was abandoned at 12.13, the survivors being taken off by the trawler *Jolie Mascotte* and destroyer *Whitehall*, the latter of which fired several rounds into her to speed her sinking. Nine men were killed. Her wreck lies in position 51.08.22N 02.35.02E
[Gardner pp90–1; Winser, BEF Ships pp27–8]

1 June **BRIGHTON QUEEN** paddle minesweeper
Clydebank 1905 requisitioned 1939; 807 tons; 245ft × 29ft; 1 × 12pdr
Lieutenant Archie Stubbs RNR
Brighton Queen had performed one trip evacuating troops to Dover and arrived back at the harbour during the morning, as the air raids were at their height. She managed to avoid being hit, went alongside and embarked a large number of French troops and left at approximately 12.30pm to return, in company with another steamer, the *Scotia*. They had not cleared the coast before they came under air attack, and a bomb exploded close under the starboard quarter. She took on a heavy list as she rapidly settled, and the tug *C9* and the minesweeper *Saltash* came alongside to lift off some of the soldiers before she sank on an even keel in about 5 fathoms of water. Two men were lost and perhaps 300 troops. The wreck lies in position 51.06.45N 02.11.41E.
[Winser, BEF Ships p28]

1 June **FAIRBREEZE** drifter
Selby 1925 requisitioned 1939; 92 tons; 85.2ft × 18.6ft
Skipper J – Kemp
Having been employed as an examination vessel at Ramsgate, she was sent to assist at Dunkirk. Having completed one successful trip to Dover loaded with troops, she returned to Dunkirk during the day to embark a further load despite constant air attacks and shelling. On her way home at 02.45 she struck a sunken wreck and had to be abandoned, the Dutch schuyt *Atlante* lifting off the troops.
[TNA: ADM.199/787; ADM.358/3284; Winser, BEF Ships p30]

1 June **MOSQUITO** river gunboat
Scotstoun 1939; 585 tons; 197ft × 33ft; 2 × 4in
Lieutenant Denis Harold Palmer Gardiner
The gunboat had made two round trips to Dover, carrying over 1,000 troops, and as she approached the beaches during the late morning of 1 June for the third time, she was the target for an attack by a Ju 87 dive bomber. By putting the wheel hard over the bombs were avoided, but they exploded close alongside, peppering her hull with shrapnel. She steamed on and after embarking some thirty French troops from the motor boat *Rapid-I*, headed towards the passenger steamer *Scotia* which was sinking after a heavy air attack. She had barely got under way when at 13.30 she herself became the target for attack by a large group of about twenty Ju 87 aircraft. Avoiding action was taken, and the first three attacks missed, but the fourth aircraft was more successful. A bomb exploded right ahead of the ship, throwing up a large quantity of mud and water over the forecastle and bridge, then another bomb scored a direct hit amidships, blowing a hole in the boiler and engine rooms and putting the steering gear out of action. Listing heavily to port, she was ordered to be abandoned, just as another attack took place, with the ship being enveloped in water and smoke as bombs burst around her. The Carley floats were released and the drifters *Lord Cavan* and *Jackeve* and the motor boat *Rapid-I* closed to run alongside, which allowed the survivors to escape as the ship sank in shallow water, with her upper works still exposed. The wreck was later bombed again by enemy aircraft and eventually the gunboat *Locust* closed her and placed depth charges on board to blow her up. Eight men were lost.
[TNA: ADM.199/1792; ADM.199/793]

1 June **STELLA DORADO** trawler
Hull 1935 requisitioned 1939; 416 tons; 152.8ft × 25.6ft; 1 × 12pdr
Skipper William Henry Burgess RCNR†
A unit of an Anti-Submarine Group, the *Stella Dorado*, along with the other ships of the group commenced patrolling the approaches to Dunkirk. The presence of enemy fast torpedo boats became evident in the early hours of 1 June when Asdic operators on board the *Kingston Galena* detected the hydrophone effect of a fast diesel engine, and bridge staff caught a glimpse of a small fast craft in the mist. At 02.30 ships in the patrol group heard a large explosion, followed immediately after by the sound of a ship's whistle sounding for several seconds before it cut out. The *Kingston Galena* steered towards the sound and found wreckage and then four survivors from the *Stella Dorado* on a Carley float and another clinging to the wreckage of the Asdic hut. She had fallen victim to a torpedo fired by *S 34*. Fifteen men lost their lives.
[TNA: ADM.199/792]

1 June ARGYLLSHIRE trawler
Middlesbrough 1938 requisitioned 1939; 540 tons;
175.8ft × 28.6ft; 1 × 12pdr
Sub-Lieutenant John Sturdee Weddle RNVR
As with the *Stella Dorado* (above), the *Argyllshire* was
one of several armed trawlers ordered to patrol the
approaches to Dunkirk. She was in company with the
Stella Rigel and *Lord Melchett*, when at 02.45 they sighted
what they believed to be a surfaced submarine but was a
fast torpedo boat. The *Argyllshire* altered course towards
the threat, which was then about 1,800 yards on the
starboard beam. They had barely commenced the turn
when there was a large explosion as she was hit on the
starboard quarter by a torpedo. The bows reared up clear
of the water, all the fittings on the upper deck broke
loose and she went down stern first very quickly, the
bows standing vertically before disappearing; she was
another victim of the *S 34*. Twenty men were lost, with
five survivors being picked up by the trawler *Malabar*.
[TNA: ADM.199/793]

1 June LORD CAVAN drifter
Lowestoft 1920 requisitioned 1939; 96 tons; 86.5ft × 19.5ft
Skipper James Henry Mugridge RNR
Arriving at Dunkirk during 28 May, she was employed
as a local depot ship for the Senior Naval Officer.
During the evening of 1 June, she embarked a senior
army officer and his staff at Dunkirk pier, with the
intention of transferring them to a waiting destroyer.
As they left the pier at 22.00, she was hit by a shell on
the port side on the waterline, the shell passing through
the mess deck to exit on the starboard side, exploding
on the pier. She flooded and sank in 3 minutes. There
were no casualties.
[TNA: ADM.199/793]

1 June AMULREE yacht
Delfzijl 1938 requisitioned 1939; 88 tons; 84.3ft × 16.5ft
Sub-Lieutenant Graham Phineas Probert RNVR
Arrived off the beaches at La Panne during 31 May, she
was busily employed during the day towing pontoons
full of troops out to destroyers, despite running aground
at one point and being under constant fire. At 20.00
she was ordered back to Dover, but at 01.56 as she
approached the Downs, she encountered the destroyer
Vimy, which was heading in the opposite direction.
The destroyer sighted a single white light close ahead,
and despite going full astern and putting the helm to
starboard, she struck the starboard bow of the *Amulree*,
which sank as the destroyer pulled clear. They were then
200 yards to the west of the north-west Goodwin buoy.
All the crew were picked up.
[TNA: ADM.199/787; ADM.199/790; ADM.199/791]

1 June GRIVE yacht
Govan 1905 (*Narcissus*) requisitioned 1939; 688 tons;
222.7ft × 27.7ft; 2 × 12pdr
Captain Lionel John Olive Lambart DSO†
The armed yacht first arrived off the beaches during
the afternoon of 30 May, and worked both as a ferry,
taking troops to waiting destroyers, and then taking
troops back to England. She made three round trips and
having landed her third load of troops at Dover during
the afternoon of 1 June she again headed back to
Dunkirk, arriving in the evening. At 22.30 she slowed
as she entered the channel to the harbour when there
was a terrific explosion under the hull, and she rapidly
broke up and sank immediately. The trawler *Gula* was
immediately astern and closed to pick up survivors,
but twenty-three men lost their lives. An aircraft had
been heard overhead some minutes before, and it was
believed that it may have sown magnetic mines, with
the *Grive* being an immediate victim. The wreck has
been found in position 51.03.31N 02.24.48E.
[TNA: ADM.199/792]

1 June PELLAG II yacht
Tarbert 1937 requisitioned 1940; 44 tons; 60.7ft × 13.5ft;
1 × 3pdr
Lieutenant Frederick William Richard Martino RNVR
Arrived at Dunkirk during the morning of 31 May,
and after avoiding a determined air attack, closed the
beaches, and picked up over thirty men from small
rowing boats. She then went to the aid of the trawler
Fyldea, which was aground, rigging a tow. However, she
burnt out her clutch and damaged her rudder as she
attempted to haul the trawler clear. Steering by engines
alone she managed to reach the destroyer *Worcester*, who
took off her troops. Requests for a tow could not be
met, and she was ordered to be abandoned and was run
ashore in shallow water. She was later found by troops
who succeeded in getting her under way, and managed
to beg a tow, but she foundered in mid-Channel.
[TNA: ADM.199/791; Winser, BEF Ships p117]

2 June BLACKBURN ROVERS trawler
Middlesbrough 1934 requisitioned 1939; 422 tons;
157ft × 26.7ft
Skipper William Martin RNR
In company with the trawlers *Westella* and *Saon*, the
group were conducting a patrol off the approaches to
Dunkirk. At 16.18 whilst investigating a possible Asdic
contact, there was a large explosion as she detonated
a mine and sank immediately. As she went under her
depth charges exploded, causing more casualties. Six
men were killed. The wreck has been found in position
51.19.09N 02.06.21E.
[TNA: ADM.199/793]

2 June WESTELLA trawler

Selby 1934 requisitioned 1939; 413 tons; 152.8ft × 25.6ft

Chief Skipper Andrew Gove RNR

In company with the armed trawler *Blackburn Rovers*, engaged in patrolling the approaches to Dunkirk. When that ship exploded a mine (see above), the *Westella* promptly closed, and was damaged when the depth charges on the sinking ship exploded, the ship being lifted out of the water by the shock, putting her Asdic and pumps out of action. Some 30 minutes after this, as she was engaged in rescuing survivors, there was another explosion under the port bow as she herself hit a mine. The bows were damaged and 10 minutes after the explosion she was ordered to be abandoned. The survivors were picked by the trawlers *Saon* and *Grimsby Town*, the latter sinking the wreck by gunfire. One man subsequently died of his wounds. Her wreck lies in position 51.24.97N 02.13.32E.

[TNA: ADM.199/793]

4 June LENA coaster

Martenshoek 1938 requisitioned 1940; 383 tons; 136.9ft × 24.8ft

Lieutenant Commander Richard Pennell Caesar Hawkins

Sailed from Dover during the afternoon of 3 June, in company with other requisitioned Dutch schuyts, she arrived off Dunkirk at 23.00. She went into the inner harbour in an attempt to go alongside one of the inner piers but ran aground. A tug was called for, but none was available and attempts by another requisitioned coaster, the *Bornrif* and a drifter to haul her free failed. At 10.45 the next morning, 2 hours after high water, with orders that no further embarkation should take place in daylight, she was abandoned, the crew being taken off by a drifter.

[Gardner p116]

Note: There was, in addition to the vessels detailed above, a number of small craft, including lifeboats, motorboats, launches, barges, wherries and punts that were lost, some of which were manned by the Royal Navy. I have not detailed them here, but the names may be found in Winser, *BEF Ships* and Gardner, *The Evacuation from Dunkirk* (Naval Staff History).

★ ★ ★

2 June ASTRONOMER boom carrier

Glasgow 1917 requisitioned 1940; 8,401 tons; 482.7ft × 58.2ft

Master John James Egerton

Former Harrison line cargo ship, taken up to be employed by the Navy as a base ship for boom defences, she was en-route from Rosyth to Scapa Flow when at 23.50 on 1 June, then being to the south-east of Wick, in position 58.01N 02.12W, there was a large explosion under the stern of the ship. The blast blew a large hole, several feet across, in the main deck and the stern was laid open. She settled by the stern, but remained afloat, but there were a further two explosions, at 03.18 and 04.43 after which she started to sink by the stern. The armed trawlers *Stoke City* and *Leicester City* picked up the survivors, but four men lost their lives. She had been torpedoed by *U 58* (Kuppisch).

[TNA: ADM.1/10237]

4 June OCEAN LASSIE drifter

Aberdeen 1919 requisitioned 1939; 96 tons; 86.2ft × 18.5ft

Lieutenant Cyril Hector Burns RNR

Employed in the examination service, boarding incoming steamers, she was based at Harwich. During the afternoon she detonated a mine near the Outer Ridge Buoy and sank rapidly. It was believed that she had strayed out of the designated swept channel. Six men were killed. The wreck has been found in position 51.55.01N 01.21.02E.

[TNA: ADM.199/1171; ADM.358/4479; Larn vol 3 sec 1]

7 June CARINTHIA armed merchant cruiser

Barrow 1925 requisitioned 1939; 20,227 tons; 600.7ft × 73.8ft; 8 × 6in

Captain John Francis Benjamin Barrett

To enforce a blockade of Germany, several ocean liners had been fitted out as armed merchant cruisers, and one of their tasks was to form the Northern Patrol, stopping and searching vessels in the North Atlantic that might be heading for continental Europe. At 14.07 on 6 June, when in position 55.13N 10.38W as she was heading out to take up her station on the Northern Patrol, she was struck on the port side by a torpedo. The torpedo exploded at frame 69 (number 8 bulkhead) and this caused the engine room to flood rapidly, the water then spreading to number 4 hold and the after 6in magazine and all power was lost. A sharp watch was ordered to be kept for periscopes, and occasional glimpses of a periscope were made over the next 20 minutes, which were engaged by gunfire. At 14.35 the submarine attempted another attack; the track of a torpedo being seen to pass ahead of the ship. Meanwhile emergency power had restored, and some facilities and pumping had commenced, but despite all efforts the flow of water could not be checked, and water started to enter number 5 hold. She remained stable, and after the failed attack at 14.35 the submarine had left them alone, and the crew continued to pump and shore up bulkheads. Her distress calls brought assistance to the scene, the destroyer *Volunteer* being the first to arrive the following morning at 03.25 and by 07.00 she was being screened by three destroyers and the sloop *Gleaner* had rigged a tow. The ship's company was transferred to the other ships over the next 3 hours, leaving only essential personnel on board. At 10.00 the salvage tug *Marauder* arrived, to take over the towing duties, but the situation was worsening, with water still rising in the engine room. By 19.30 number 5 hold was filling and water was now entering number 6 hold and was lapping over onto 'C' deck. She was clearly settling, and the last members of the crew were removed before she sank at 21.40, her position then being 55.12N 09.30W. Her attacker had been the *U 46* (Endrass). Four men were killed.

[TNA: ADM.1/10806]

8 June 1940 Loss of the *Glorious* and escorts

GLORIOUS aircraft carrier
Belfast 1916; 22,500 tons; 735ft × 90.6ft; 16 × 4.7in, 24 × 2pdr, 48 aircraft
Captain Guy D'Oyley-Hughes DSO DSC†

During the first week of June the *Glorious*, in company with the *Ark Royal* with supporting light forces, was despatched to the coast of Norway to cover the evacuation of Allied troops. During 7 June, seven Royal Air Force Hurricane and ten Gladiator aircraft had successfully landed on board the *Glorious*. That complete, the group headed south-west, with the *Glorious* being detached at 02.50 on the following morning to proceed independently to Scapa Flow, accompanied by two destroyers. Speed was reduced to 17 knots, and aircraft were placed on 10 minutes notice for flying, but not ranged on deck. At 16.00 ships were sighted on the horizon to the north-west and the escorting destroyer *Ardent* was detached to investigate, whilst orders were given to range five Swordfish aircraft on deck. At 16.20 the *Ardent* was seen to be under fire and the *Glorious* went to action stations. The ships could now be seen to be two large enemy battlecruisers (they were the *Scharnhorst* and *Gneisenau*). The pair concentrated on the carrier, and taking up positions on her quarters, opened fire at 16.30. The third salvo straddled her, with a shell striking the flight deck and penetrating the upper hanger where it exploded. This caused widespread damage and started a fire, the smoke spreading through the ship and affecting the boiler rooms. She was hit again soon after, the bridge being struck, killing the commanding officer. More hits followed, with one shell entering the engine room, which 'shook the whole ship'. After this she lost speed, developed a list to starboard, and with the steering gear out of action circled to port. At 17.20 the fire was out of control and with the heel increasing she was ordered to be abandoned. She sank at about 17.40, her position being 68.45N 04.30E. Several hundred men entered the water, clinging to rafts, floats and pieces of wood. Before she had sunk, an enemy report had been transmitted, but it was made on the wrong frequency, using the wavelength in use for the Narvik operations

off Norway, when other British ships had shifted to the Home frequencies. It was received by both the cruiser *Devonshire* and the battleship *Valiant*, but neither ship could act on it; the former was too far distant, and the latter had the King of Norway embarked, and it was decided that his safety took precedence. No one was aware of her sinking for some time, and many of the men left in the freezing waters of the northern North Sea died before they could be picked up. On 11 June, the Norwegian fishing vessels *Borgund* and *Svalbard II* picked up forty-three men from the carrier – they were the only survivors: 1,203 men from *Glorious* died. The subsequent enquiry was critical of the actions of Captain D'Oyley-Hughes. He had evidently not believed that an attack from surface forces likely, so was insufficiently prepared for a possible surface action. Not only had no aerial reconnaissance had been carried out for 12 hours prior to the action but the aircraft had been placed on a long notice for flying. There was a lack of a proper lookout on board and the only shells provided for the guns were for anti-aircraft attack. The First Sea Lord, Admiral Sir Dudley Pound, noted on the enquiry findings that he found the state of readiness '… deplorable … they … seem to have forgotten they were a man o' war'. Since then, the sinking has been a matter of debate and controversy, largely focussing on why *Glorious* was allowed to proceed independently. It has been suggested that Captain D'Oyley-Hughes had wished to proceed directly to Scapa Flow for the court martial of one of his officers or because of a shortage of fuel. Neither theory is particularly strong. An alternative hypothesis is that *Glorious* had been detached to take part in a secret operation to lay mines off the Swedish port of Luleå.

[TNA: ADM178/201; ADM.1/19984; Roskill vol 1 p195; Mariner's Mirror vol 86 p302; www.hmsglorious.com]

ARDENT destroyer
Greenock 1929; 1,350 tons; 312ft × 32.3ft; 4 × 4.7in, 2 × 2pdr, 8 × torpedo tubes
Lieutenant Commander John Frederick Barker DSC†

One of the escorts to the *Glorious*, she was despatched at 16.00 to investigate and challenge the strange warships seen on the horizon. As she closed it became clear that they were enemy battlecruisers, which was confirmed when they opened fire. *Ardent* worked up to full speed and started laying a smokescreen, in an effort to screen the carrier. She returned fire and fired a salvo of torpedoes before she was hit and brought to a halt. After being hit repeatedly she rolled over and sank at 17.28. Only two men survived, being picked up 3 days later by a German seaplane. One hundred and fifty-two officers and men died.

[TNA: ADM178/201; ADM.1/19984; Roskill vol 1 p195; Mariner's Mirror vol 86 p302; Kemp p119]

ACASTA destroyer

Clydebank 1929; 1,350 tons; 312ft × 32.3ft; 4 × 4.7in,
2 × 2pdr, 8 × torpedo tubes
Commander Charles Eric Glasfurd†

The second of the escorts to the *Glorious*, she initially
stayed near the carrier, but as the *Ardent* steered
towards the enemy she was seen to come under fire
and then start laying smoke. The *Acasta* also laid a thick
smokescreen, in a vain attempt to screen the carrier,
although it did mask the *Acasta*. With the *Ardent*
stopped and surrounded by a cloud of smoke, and
the *Glorious* clearly badly hit, Commander Glasfurd
decided to attack the enemy, and went through the
smokescreen. As they emerged, they achieved surprise
and were able to launch a torpedo attack, firing a salvo
of four torpedoes, and were rewarded by the sight of
an explosion on one of the enemy ships (it was the
Scharnhorst), before retiring into the smoke. Glasfurd
then had the opportunity to escape, still masked by the
screen, but decided to make a further attack. This time
as they emerged from the smoke she came under heavy
fire and was hit amidships. She came to a halt and took
a list to port, but the guns continued to engage, and
the last torpedoes were fired. She was then hit again,
and there was a large explosion aft, which lifted her out
of the water. She heeled over and sank at about 18.10.
There was only one survivor from her complement of
160.
[TNA: ADM178/201; ADM.119984; Roskill vol 1 p195;
Mariner's Mirror vol 86 p302; Kemp p119]

★ ★ ★

8 June OLEANDER oiler

Pembroke 1922; 7,045 tons; 430.2ft × 57.1ft
Master Frederick Murison Harvey

Deployed to support the forces in Norway, she was
damaged during an air attack off Harstad on 26 May by
He 111 bomber aircraft, which scored a near miss, the
bomb exploding under her stern. Badly shaken, the ship
was run into shallow water and grounded. When Allied
forces were ordered to evacuate the area she was taken
into deep water and scuttled in Harstad Bay.
[TNA: ADM.199/484]

8 June JUNIPER trawler

Renfrew 1939; 530 tons; 150ft × 27.6ft; 1 × 12pdr
Lieutenant Commander Geoffrey Seymour Grenfell†

Sailed from Malanger Fjord, Norway, during the
afternoon of 6 June to escort the oil tanker *Oil Pioneer*
to Scapa Flow, but not seen again. It later emerged that
they had been located at 06.00 by a large enemy force
led by the battlecruisers *Scharnhorst* and *Gneisenau* in
position 67.26.5N 04.23E. *Juniper* initially closed,
believing that the ships in sight were Allied, but soon

realised her mistake. The cruiser *Admiral Hipper* tackled
the trawler, using her secondary armament of 105mm
guns to great effect, hitting her immediately. The *Juniper*
was set on fire and was seen to heel over until at 07.14
there was an explosion, apparently when her depth
charges exploded, and she capsized and sank. Four
survivors were picked up by the *Hipper*, but twenty-
three men died.
[TNA: ADM.116/4121; ADM.358/3701; Haar, The Battle for
Norway p326]

8 June BOOMERANG VI yacht

Gourock 1938 requisitioned 1940; 19 tons; 34ft × 9ft

Based at Glasgow for local patrols in the river Clyde,
she was destroyed by accidental fire (when fitting out?)
[Statement of Losses p8]

9 June DEWY EVE drifter

Findochty 1916 requisitioned 1940; 109 tons;
93.2ft × 19.3ft

Based at Scapa Flow, she foundered at 10.14 after a
collision with the trawler *Gold Crown*, 200 yards from
number 6 buoy, Gutter Sound, sinking in 7 fathoms.
There were no casualties.
[TNA: ADM.199/377]

10 June VANDYCK armed boarding steamer

Belfast 1921 requisitioned 1939; 13,241 tons;
510.6ft × 64.3ft; 2 × 6in, 1 × 12pdr
Captain Graham Francis Winstanley Wilson

Sailed 6 June from Harstad, Norway at the evacuation
of that place, and ordered to cruise independently
approximately 130 miles to seaward, and then proceed
to a rendezvous to join other troopships but failed
to arrive as expected. Destroyers were sent along the
track to investigate but failed to find any trace of her,
although a troop transport reported seeing her during
the morning of 9 June in the vicinity of 70.44N 10E. It
was later found that she had been attacked by German
aircraft during the morning of 10 June and sunk. Seven
men were killed, the rest taking to lifeboats, 161 men
being picked up by the Germans to be taken into
captivity.
[TNA: ADM.199/485]

11 June HEBE II coaster

Delfzijl 1932 requisitioned 1940; 176 tons; 102.2ft × 20.9ft
Lieutenant Dennis Robert Bennett-Jones RNVR

Used during the operations to evacuate troops from
Dunkirk, she was subsequently ordered to assist with
Operation 'Cycle', the evacuation of troops from the
ports of St Valery and Le Havre. *Hebe-II* successfully
lifted off troops during 10 June, ferrying them to larger
ships offshore, but during the early morning, as she
went inshore between St Valery and Veules-les-Roses to

repeat the exercise the tide was already on the ebb, and after loading a number of troops, at 06.00 it was found that she had grounded. It was hoped that she be refloated later in the day, but during the morning German troops were seen, and the ship became a target for heavy fire, being shelled and machine-gunned. As it was clear that she could not escape, Lieutenant Bennett-Jones ordered the crew to abandon the ship and surrender. Despite being gravely wounded, he was the last to leave. He was subsequently awarded the Distinguished Service Cross.
[TNA:ADM 358/171]

12 June **CALYPSO** cruiser

Hebburn 1917; 4,180 tons; 425ft × 42.9ft; 5 × 6in, 2 × 2pdr, 8 × torpedo tubes
Captain Henry Audley Rowley

Stationed in the Mediterranean, she was part of a force under the command of Admiral Cunningham, which was ordered to carry out an offensive sweep in the eastern Mediterranean against Italian shipping. In company with the destroyer *Dainty*, she was stationed on the port wing of the main force, when at 02.02 (local time) in position 33.45N 24.32E there was an explosion below the waterline near station 70, the main watertight bulkhead immediately before 'A' boiler room. The shock of the explosion was such that rangefinders and signal projectors jumped out of their mountings. All the lights went out and she lost power. The ship took an immediate list to starboard, and her head swung to port as she lost way. By 02.30 she was stopped, with a 15-degree list. She settled slowly and it was hoped to tow her, but by 03.10 it was clear that she was sinking. At 03.27 with the fo'c'sle awash the order was given to abandon ship. She continued to heel over until at 03.35 she was laying on her beam ends with her bows submerged until she went under, her stern rising vertically as she disappeared. One officer and thirty-eight ratings were lost. The court of enquiry was not convinced that everything possible had been done to save the ship. Far more effort could have been made to maintain steam pressure and conduct damage control efforts. Evidence was heard that much of the flooding of mess decks had been due to poor watertight discipline, with doors open or poorly secured. Further, the officers and senior petty officers, responsible for damage control and those in charge of the engine room and 'B' boiler room had reacted slowly or ineffectively. The court commented that they seemed to have been 'elderly, or considerably above the age at which maximum efficiency and energetic action … were likely to be forthcoming'. The senior engineer officer was a reserve officer of little experience and had had only been in the ship for a few weeks. Her attacker had been the Italian submarine *Bagnolini* (Tosoni-Pittoni).
[TNA:ADM.1/10507]

12 June **SISAPON** trawler

Beverley 1928 requisitioned 1939; 326 tons; 137.2ft × 23.6ft; 1 × 12pdr
Skipper Frederick Alfred Henson RNR†

Employed as a minesweeper and based at Harwich, she had spent the morning in company with the armed trawler *Lord Irwin* sweeping the war channel at the entrance to that port. On completion of the task the pair proceeded to the Cork Light Vessel for boat exercises, this being a regular practice of the pair, the competitive evolutions being aimed at smartening up the crews. This was complete by 11.00 and the pair got underway, to head back to Harwich, *Lord Irwin* in the lead. As they passed about 200 yards to the east-north-east of the light vessel the *Sisapon* disappeared in a cloud of smoke and spray as she detonated a mine – the *Lord Irwin* had passed over the spot minutes earlier. Her stern was lifted out of the water by the explosion, and she settled rapidly, rolled over to starboard and sank. Her companion turned back and picked up two survivors, another seven being saved by a boat launched from the light vessel and attendant craft *MAC.5*. Lieutenant J P Kelly RNVR of the *Lord Irwin* was informed that he had 'incurred their Lordships' displeasure' by taking the trawlers into waters close to the Cork light vessel that were known to have been mined. Twelve men were killed. Wireman Joseph Warne was mentioned in despatches for his bravery in saving the life of a shipmate, keeping him afloat in the water for some time before being picked up.
[TNA:ADM.1/10898]

12 June **TWENTE** coaster

Groningen 1937 requisitioned 1940; 239 tons; 119.3ft × 21.5ft
Lieutenant Commander Humphrey Gilbert Boys-Smith RNR

A former Dutch coaster, she had been busily employed in evacuating troops from Dunkirk and was then ordered to support the evacuation of Allied troops from other French ports. Loaded with petrol and ammunition for the port of St Valery, in the early hours, as she approached the port, she came under fire from a shore battery. She was hit twice on the starboard side amidships and once in the stern. She filled rapidly, rolled over to starboard and sank at 06.32. There were no casualties.
[Winser, BEF Ships p39]

13 June **SCOTSTOUN** armed merchant cruiser

Glasgow 1925 requisitioned 1939; 17,046 tons; 553ft × 70.4ft; 8 × 6in, 2 × 12pdr
Captain Sydney Keith Smyth

As part of the Northern Patrol, stopping and searching neutral merchant ships, she sailed from Greenock on 12 June to take up station in the North Atlantic. At

06.20 the following morning when in the vicinity of 57N 10W there was a loud explosion aft on the port side when she was hit by a torpedo. The port engine immediately 'raced' and then stopped, apparently caused by the port shaft having been blown away, and the port tunnel filled with water. Flooding was also reported in number 7 hold. Over the next 20 minutes there were reported sightings of torpedo tracks and the cruiser fired occasionally at claimed sightings of periscopes. At 06.47 the ship was hit for a second time, a torpedo hitting the starboard side aft, just before the after magazine, which seems to have triggered a secondary explosion. All the lights went out and steam pipes fractured in the engine room, flooding it with steam. The ship now took a pronounced list to starboard, before righting herself slightly and then starting to sink quickly by the stern. All boats were turned out and at 07.10 she was ordered to be abandoned, the last survivors having to jump into the water and swim for the Carley floats that had been released. She sank at 07.27, the bows rising clear of the water as she disappeared. Assistance appeared in the shape of the destroyer *Highlander*, which arrived on scene at 13.40, spending the next hour picking up all the survivors. Six men were lost. Her attacker had been the *U 25* (Beduhn).
[TNA: ADM.1/10808]

13 June KHARTOUM destroyer
Wallsend 1939; 1,690 tons; 339.6ft × 35.8ft; 6 × 4.7in, 4 × 2pdr, 10 × torpedo tubes
Commander Donald Thorn Dowler
Patrolling at the southern end of the Red Sea, she was about 7 miles to the north of Perim Island, when at 11.50 there was a large explosion in the starboard wing tube of the after set of torpedo tubes. The tube burst open, with the metal folding back, and the torpedo broke up, the warhead being blown out with considerable force. The warhead smashed through the officer's galley, starting a fire, which was fuelled by an oil pipe which was broken by the impact. It then passed through a gun support and power unit before finishing up on the quarterdeck. It did not explode. The fire in the galley spread rapidly, and thick choking smoke filled the after part of the ship. Fire fighting started, but it was found that the after rising main had been shattered and hoses severed. Hoses were eventually rigged from forward, although pressure was low. There was a real fear that the after magazines would explode, particularly when efforts to flood the magazines were frustrated by the thick smoke and damaged controls. About 12–13 minutes after the initial explosion, it was reported that the fire was out of control, and course was altered to take her inshore, to Perim Island. To minimise the danger, all torpedoes were jettisoned (except for the after ones, which were inaccessible), and depth charges

and ready-use ammunition was dropped overboard. As they passed Princes Shoal, steam failed, and they lost all electrical power soon after. With way still on her, she continued until she was in 7 fathoms of water, when the anchors were let go to bring her up. With the fire now burning fiercely, the boats and floats were lowered, and the ship's company was ordered to leave her. As they were doing so, at 12.45 there was a large explosion as one of the magazines blew up, showering the area with shrapnel, killing one Boy Seaman and severely injuring several men. The ship now settled quickly by the stern and she was felt to touch the ground. At 12.59 there was a second, much heavier explosion, which was probably some or all the twenty-nine depth charges stowed in the warhead magazine detonating. This blew the stern off. She heeled over 25 degrees to port and settled, righted herself, and then sank with her bridge and funnel still showing. Her position was noted as 12.38.52N 43.24.55E. The subsequent investigation found that the initial detonation had been caused by the pressurised air vessel inside a torpedo exploding, which split the torpedo tube and blew the warhead off. Why this had happened was uncertain; the most likely cause was a manufacturing fault which had left an unsuspected flaw in the vessel. Some pitting had been noted on the torpedo previously, and such pitting had been seen on other torpedoes, but it was not thought likely to have been deep enough to have caused the vessel to split.
[TNA: ADM.1/11210]

13 June ABEL TASMAN coaster
Groningen 1937 requisitioned 1940; 314 tons; 126.6ft × 24ft
Lieutenant Edward Terence Mudie†
A former Dutch coaster, she had been taken over during May to assist with the evacuation of troops from northern France. She took part in Operation 'Dynamo', taking men from Dunkirk, and was then assigned to Operation 'Cycle', the lifting of troops from other French ports. She sailed from Poole on 11 June to proceed to St Valery in company with several other naval manned coasters, but failed to make the port, as she became detached from the main force in fog. Returning to Poole, she was in the Swash Channel, following another Dutch coaster/store ship, the *Wega*, when she detonated a mine and sank. There were no survivors, with all eleven men on board being killed.
[TNA: ADM.116/4121; Winser, BEF Ships p40]

13 June OCEAN SUNLIGHT drifter
Aberdeen 1929 requisitioned 1939; 131 tons; 94.3ft × 20.1ft
Skipper Reginald James Crane RNR
Sank at 19.45, when she was 4 cables (800 yards) to the south-east of the West Breakwater Light, Newhaven

following an explosion whilst minesweeping. It was believed likely that she had triggered a magnetic mine. Ten men were lost.

[TNA: ADM.116/4121; ADM.199/2206]

(13–16?) June ODIN submarine

Chatham 1928; 1,475/2,038 tons; 265ft × 26.11ft; 1 × 4in, 8 × torpedo tubes

Lieutenant Commander Kenneth MacIver Woods[†]

Stationed in the Far East at the outbreak of the war, she was moved to the Mediterranean in April 1940. In June *Odin* conducted her first war patrol, in the Gulf of Taranto, but failed to return, the last contact with her being by radio in the early hours of 11 June. The exact circumstances of her loss are uncertain. During 13–14 June, Italian warships reported several contacts with submarines, which resulted in depth-charge attacks, but it is uncertain whether any were effective, and indeed some must have been on non-submarine contacts. Of all of these incidents, the attacks by *Strale* and *Baleno* may possibly be responsible for the loss of *Odin*. During the evening of 13 June, at 23.21, a large submarine was sighted by the torpedo boat *Strale*. She immediately closed at high speed, firing a torpedo and hearing a detonation, they believed they had scored a hit. They also opened fire and managed to fire four shots at the submarine before it dived. As it disappeared the *Strale* ran over the position and dropped seven depth charges, then turned to drop a further two charges. It was hoped that she had disposed of the enemy, but they could see no obvious signs of destruction, and the squadron remained in the area. At 01.57 about 9 miles from the original attack position, the torpedo boat *Baleno* claimed she had sighted a submarine on the surface, about half a mile distant. She again reacted immediately, heading towards the enemy at high speed. The submarine started to dive but had hardly submerged before the *Baleno* ran over the position, dropping two depth charges. She conducted a sharp turn and dropped a further three charges into the disturbed water, but again, no visible signs of success were seen. An air search of the area was conducted at first light, and found patches of oil, which was taken as being from a sunken submarine, but no other wreckage was seen. To counter this, reports of submarine activity continued, with claims of torpedo tracks being seen and more prosecutions of sonar contacts during 16–17 June by the escorts *Folgore* and *Saetta*, which included the claimed sighting of a surfaced submarine. Again, none of these attacks resulted in any visible signs of success. It is possible that *Odin* was lost in one of these attacks, or she may have strayed into a defensive minefield off Taranto. Five officers and forty-eight men were lost.

[Evans pp251–2; https://www.uboat.net/allies/warships/ ship/3394.html]

14 June MYRTLE trawler

Beverley 1928 purchased 1939 (*St. Irene*); 357 tons; 140.4ft × 24ft; 1 × 12pdr

Chief Skipper William Garwood Cleveland RNR[†]

Detonated a mine at 15.53 and quickly sank when 2 miles to the south of the East Shingle buoy in the Thames estuary; there were no survivors, all twenty-two men on board were killed.

[TNA: ADM.199/2206]

16 June ANDANIA armed merchant cruiser

Hebburn 1922 requisitioned 1939; 13,950 tons; 520.2ft × 65.3ft; 8 × 6in, 2 × 12pdr

Captain Donald Keppel Bain

Part of the Northern Patrol, she was on station to the south of Iceland, in position 62.36N 15.09W, when at 23.30 on 15 June there was a heavy explosion as a torpedo hit the starboard side aft, between numbers 5 and 6 holds. She quickly settled by the stern, took a list to starboard and lost headway. The rudder was found to be out of action and the lights went out. Emergency generators restored some power, and work started to pump out the water and shore up bulkheads. She became the target for more torpedo attacks, but all of them missed, with tracks being seen to pass astern at 23.45, 00.20 and 00.50. In choppy sea conditions, there were regular sightings of a periscope, which was engaged by gun crews. Number 5 and 6 holds had filled rapidly, and it was reported that number 7 hold and the after magazines were also flooding. At 01.15 the boats were ordered to be hoisted out and an hour later all non-essential personnel were ordered to leave the ship. At 02.30 water was reported to be entering the engine room, and was soon at chest height, at which point everyone was ordered to the upper deck and 10 minutes later she was abandoned. The ship was then deep in the water, down by the stern and with a list to port. She finally went under at 06.55, by which time the Icelandic trawler *Skallagrimur* had arrived to assist the survivors, and the destroyer *Forester* was on scene that afternoon. There were no casualties. Her attacker had been the *UA* (Cohausz).

[TNA: ADM.1/10897]

16 June GRAMPUS submarine

Chatham 1936; 1,520/2,157 tons; 271.6ft × 25.6ft; 1 × 4in, 6 × torpedo tubes, 50 mines

Lieutenant Commander Charles Alexander Rowe[†]

Stationed in the Far East at the outbreak of the war, she was re-deployed to the Mediterranean in May 1940. On 10 June, she sailed from Malta to lay mines off the coast of Sicily, between Augusta and Syracuse. On 13 June she reported by radio that she had successfully completed the lay but failed to return as expected. The circumstances of her loss are uncertain. It is possible that

an attack by the patrol vessel *Polluce* was responsible. At 18.30 on the 16th, the *Polluce* off Syracuse reported what she believed were torpedo tracks, and this led to an extensive search of the area by several patrol vessels, and at 19.02 *Circe* sighted a periscope and altered course to attack, seeing the tracks of torpedoes as they did so. The *Circe* ran over the position of the submarine and dropped several depth charges, and this was followed by another of the squadron, the *Clio*, repeating the action. The *Polluce* having apparently avoided the torpedoes which had been fired at her then joined her companions to drop more depth charges. This brought a mass of air bubbles to the surface, and the *Polluce* returned to the attack dropping a series of charges into the disturbed water. This brought up a large column of water to the surface, followed by oil which left a large slick on the surface. A total of sixty-one charges had been dropped in 15 minutes in a small area. Five officers and fifty-four men were lost.
[Evans p254]

19 June MURMANSK trawler
Beverley 1929 (*Night Watch*) requisitioned 1940; 348 tons; 140.2ft × 24.6ft; 1 × 12pdr
Newly fitted out, she sailed from Plymouth on 16 June and proceeded to Brest to assist with the evacuation of Allied troops but ran aground on the falling tide the following day, when attempting to leave the French port. Unable to be freed she was abandoned in the early hours of 19 June as a wreck. She was later salvaged and entered German service as patrol vessel *KFK 76*.
[TNA:ADM.116/4121;ADM.199/371]

(20–22?) June ORPHEUS submarine
Dalmuir 1929; 1,475/2,038 tons; 265ft × 26.11ft; 1 × 4in, 8 × torpedo tubes
Lieutenant Commander James Anthony Surtees Wise[†]
Based at Malta, she sailed on 10 June to conduct a patrol initially intended to be in the area of Corfu but amended to the coast of Sicily on 11th. On 18 June, another change was ordered, when she was directed to shift her area to the North African coast. She failed to return from patrol, with the last positive contact being at 21.15 on 19 June, when she acknowledged a signal from Alexandria, ordering her to patrol the approaches to Benghazi. At that time, she would have been about 100 miles north-west of the port. The cause of her loss is uncertain. One popular theory is that she was sunk by the Italian destroyer *Turbine*, which dropped depth charges during the afternoon of 19 June around position 32.30N 24E, following reports of a submarine in the area, but this seems highly doubtful, as this puts her at an impossible distance from her last known position, and was before the last radio message. She was expected to arrive in the new patrol area during the morning of

the 21st and leave the following night. The most likely cause for her loss is by striking a mine off the North African coast, near Benghazi. Five officers and forty-nine men were lost.
[Evans p256; https://www.uboat.net/allies/warships/ship/3396.html]

21 June CHARDE drifter
Lowestoft 1919 (*Hurricane*) requisitioned 1939; 99 tons; 86ft × 19.11ft
Skipper Alfred James Henry Taylor RNR
Foundered after colliding with the hopper barge *Foremost-101* (833 tons) in Portsmouth harbour.
[TNA:ADM.116/4121]

21 June CAPE HOWE (Prunella) special service vessel
Glasgow 1930 requisitioned 1939; 4,443 tons; 375ft × 53 ft; 7 × 4in, 4 × torpedo tubes
Commander Eric Langton Woodhall[†]
Former merchant ship taken over to be fitted out as a decoy vessel, in the hope of luring a submarine to the surface, she operated under the false identity of *Prunella*. She sailed from Scapa on 14 June to cruise initially off the west coast of Ireland until during 20 June she was ordered to shift to the western approaches. She heard a distress call from the British merchant ship *Otterpool* that same day and steered towards the area. Her disguise was ineffective however, as she was torpedoed by a submerged *U 28* (Kuhnke) at 06.46 when in position 49.44N 08.52W. The torpedo hit in the fore end of number 1 hold on the starboard side; the explosion caused some shock damage, hatches were blown open, the forward messdeck was wrecked and the steering was put out of action, but the ship remained stable and there was no fire. Most of the crew were sent away by boats, playing the 'panic party', to try and fool the submarine in coming to the surface, the gun crews remaining closed up. However, about 30 minutes after the explosion and not long after the last boat had cleared away a second torpedo hit her, this time on the port side, just forward of the cross-bunker bulkhead. The ship, however, was carrying a 'buoyant cargo', to slow her sinking and this worked perfectly, the vessel remaining upright and settling very slowly. By noon there was no sign of the submarine surfacing and the boats were recalled to the ship. An inspection showed that she was slowly filling with water forward and was visibly going down by the head. It was decided to leave her, and all the men were evacuated in good order. As the last boat cleared away, she sank, bows first, standing on end before disappearing. Only one man had been killed in the initial explosion, and with an orderly evacuation using two lifeboats and two Carley floats, with the jolly boat and a raft, it was hoped that all would soon be rescued. However, the

weather worsened, and the boats became scattered. The corvette *Calendula* was directed to proceed to the area, but when she arrived during the afternoon, she reported she could find no trace of her. Destroyers were tasked to sweep towards the area, searching both for the U-boat and any survivors. This was rewarded on 27 June when the *Versatile* reported that she had picked up thirteen survivors from a small raft, and the French merchant ship *Casamance* rescued twenty-seven men from a lifeboat on 23 June, but the other boats were not found. Fifty-seven men died.
[TNA: ADM.199/150; ADM.199/371]

22 June **CAMPEADOR** yacht
Dartmouth 1938 requisitioned 1939; 213 tons; 120ft × 20ft
Commander Charles Henry Davey OBE[†]
Whilst proceeding out on local patrol from Portsmouth, at 09.00, when 3 miles to the west of the Nab Tower, she detonated a mine and foundered; there were just two survivors from a crew of twenty-two. The wreck of the vessel was towed into the shallows near Bembridge and abandoned in 5m of water.
[TNA: ADM.116/4121; ADM.199/370; Larn vol 2. sec 2]

23 June **CORINGA** tug
Dumbarton 1914 requisitioned 1940; 294 tons; 135.4ft × 25.1ft
Lieutenant Thomas Adrian Dexter RNR
During 21–22 June, as Atlantic Convoy HX49 entered the western approaches to the English Channel, it came under attack from several U-boats and three ships were torpedoed as the convoy dispersed, one of them being the Norwegian tanker, *Eli Knudsen*. The *Coringa* sailed at 14.00 from Milford Haven to proceed to her assistance, escorted by the armed trawler *Agate*. The pair found the stricken vessel in the early hours, but before they could assist, the *Knudsen* sank at 04.25. As the *Coringa* cleared the area, water was reported to be entering engine spaces, and then there was a rush of water into the stokehold, and she heeled over to port and sank 20 minutes later. Fourteen men were lost.
[TNA: ADM.199/371]

24 June **PATHAN** patrol sloop
Belfast 1918 (*PC 69*) transferred 1921; 660 tons; 233ft × 26.5ft; 1 × 4in, 2 × 12pdr
Lieutenant Commander Karl Durston[†]
Royal Indian Navy. Stationed at Bombay, she was conducting an anti-submarine patrol in the approaches to Bombay, when at 06.30 on 23 June, a violent explosion occurred in the after part of the ship, followed after a few seconds by two more explosions. The after part of the ship was blown away and the deck was forced up over the after gun and on to the boat deck. Assistance was

sent, and attempts made to tow the ship into harbour, but the engine room reported slow flooding and by the early hours of the following morning there was 6ft of water present. With the weather worsening, she was abandoned and foundered in position 18.56N 72.45E. Five men died in the explosion and another died later of his injuries. The survivors were rescued by the patrol vessel *Dipvati*. The cause of the blast was uncertain. It was initially believed to be a mine, and Bombay harbour was closed for some time whilst sweeping operations were conducted, but no mines were found. It was later ascribed to the Italian submarine *Galvani*, but this is impossible, as she was then operating in the Gulf of Oman. An accident is therefore more likely, perhaps due to an explosion of a depth charge.
[TNA: ADM.199/368; CB.4273 p347]

25 June **FRASER** destroyer
Barrow (*Crescent*) 1931; 1,375 tons; 317.7ft × 33ft; 4 × 4.7in, 1 × 12pdr, 2 × 2pdr, 4 × torpedo tubes
Commander Wallace Bourchier Creery RCN
Royal Canadian Navy. Having deployed to St Jean de Luz in south-west France to support the evacuation of troops, she sailed with forty-four soldiers on board, in company with the cruiser *Calcutta* and destroyer *Restigouche* to return to Plymouth. At 22.00 with the *Fraser* on the starboard bow of the cruiser and the *Restigouche* on the port quarter, the cruiser ordered ships to form single line ahead. *Fraser* initiated a turn, intending to pass down the starboard side of *Calcutta* to take station. However, as the manoeuvre started, it became clear that there was insufficient room for this, and instead, attempted to cross the bows of the cruiser. On board *Calcutta*, they saw that the destroyer was attempting to cross the bows and doubting that there was sufficient room, altered to starboard. The ships closed rapidly and despite both putting engines astern, the cruiser struck *Fraser* on the port side abreast 'B' gun and cut her two. Several men managed to scramble onto the forecastle of the *Calcutta*, and *Restigouche* ran alongside the remains of the stern of the wrecked ship to take off survivors. Sixty-three men were lost.
[McKee & Darlington p18]

29 June **WILLAMETTE VALLEY** (**Edgehill**) special service vessel
Glasgow 1930 requisitioned 1939; 4,702 tons; 401.1ft × 54.2ft; 9 × 4in, 4 × torpedo tubes
Commander Robert Edward Dudley Ryder
Fitted out as a decoy vessel or 'Q' ship, she operated under the false identity of *Edgehill*, with the aim of deceiving a submarine into believing that they were an easy target and would surface to carry out or complete an attack. To help this, the ship was loaded with a buoyant cargo, to keep her afloat for as long as possible

if she should be torpedoed. Having sailed from Gibraltar on 11 June she had orders to steam as far as the 15th meridian, and then proceed to Halifax. She was painted to resemble a Greek steamer and carried a false identity of '*Ambea*'. She succeeded in attracting attention late on 28 June when at just after 21.00 (local) without warning she was hit by a torpedo which exploded on the port side forward of the bridge, abreast number 2 hatch. It did little harm, but the organised 'panic party' was sent away. This was a group of seamen who made off in a boat, to give the impression to a watching submarine that the ship had been abandoned. The remainder of the crew remained closed-up at the concealed weapons. At about 22.10 there was a second torpedo attack, and she was hit on the starboard side of the engine room. This caused a tremendous flash, which extended through most of the 'tween deck spaces; all the lights went out and the fire main was severed. A fire was started amidships, the flames reaching as high as the funnel. Until this time everyone had remained at action stations, but after this half of them were ordered to fall out and tackle the blaze. A bucket chain was organised and some control over the flames was gained. However, 20 minutes later a third torpedo hit, on the port side abreast the main mast. In less than a minute the ship had rolled over although the ship remained afloat for some considerable time, settling by the stern until her bows came clear of the water. The bows then pointed upwards, and she sank by the stern. Because of the explosions and fire, the abandonment was somewhat chaotic, with Commander Ryder clinging to a piece of wreckage before being picked up 3 days later. A single lifeboat was found by the French trawler *Donibane* on 4 July with twenty-three survivors; sixty-seven men were lost. The attacker had been *U 51* (Knorr)
[TNA: ADM.1/11660; ADM.199/149]

4 July FOYLEBANK anti-aircraft ship
Belfast 1930 requisitioned 1940; 5,582 tons;
426.8ft × 57.3ft; 8 × 4in, 8 × 2pdr, 4 × 20mm
Captain Henry Percival Wilson

The harbour and anchorage at Portland became the target for a heavy air raid by a large number of Ju 87 dive bombers, which commenced their attack at 08.45, concentrating on the *Foylebank* which was laying at anchor at Admirals' buoy. She suffered at least three direct hits abaft the funnel which started extensive fires, which were only subdued by flooding compartments. The ship eventually settled on an even keel, the machinery spaces and fuel tanks still on fire, and the wreck burnt for 36 hours until she finally disappeared. Seventy men lost their lives. A posthumous Victoria Cross was awarded to Able Seaman Jack Mantle who had continued to engage the enemy aircraft, refusing to leave his gun although mortally wounded.
[TNA: ADM.267/113; London Gazette 3 September 1940]

5 July WHIRLWIND destroyer
Wallsend 1917; 1,100 tons; 300ft × 29.6ft; 4 × 4in,
6 × torpedo tubes
Lieutenant Commander John Malcolm Rodgers

Part of the escort to the outward-bound Atlantic Convoy OB178 which had sailed from Liverpool on 3 July, they were to the south-west of Ireland when at noon on 5 July a report was received of a suspected submarine sighting, some 20 miles distant. *Whirlwind* detached from the convoy and made her best speed to the reported position and at 13.00 an object was sighted fine on the starboard bow. This appeared to be the conning tower of a submarine, which was trimmed down, deck awash. As they closed, the submarine disappeared, the range was then estimated at 7 miles. She commenced an Asdic search, zigzagging either side of the mean course every 10 minutes. She continued her hunt throughout the afternoon, but without success until at 17.00 when in approximate position 50.17N 08.48W, she was hit by a torpedo forward. The torpedo exploded just forward of the bridge, and this blew the bows off, and with the engine and boiler rooms reporting flooding, she appeared to have broken her back. Both the whaler and motorboat had been wrecked by the explosion, but Carley floats were ordered to be cut free and kept close by the ship. She settled but remained afloat and soon after this a Sunderland flying boat appeared, which directed another destroyer to the scene. This was the *Westcott*, who arrived at 20.00. The commanding officers conferred, and it was decided to abandon the *Whirlwind*, as she was clearly doomed, with her bows gone and her back broken. The *Westcott* then came alongside and removed all the survivors, stood off and opened fire on the wreck. She was hit several times, the shells puncturing the hull and appearing to go straight through rather than exploding. At 22.44 she fired a torpedo which hit her amidships and she sank in a few minutes. The subsequent court of enquiry believed the regular zigzag carried out whilst hunting may have assisted the submarine in deducing her future movements. They were also concerned that insufficient effort had been made to tow her, taking the example of the destroyer *Kelly*, which had survived serious torpedo damage and been towed over 250 miles to safety. Fifty-seven ratings were lost. Her attacker had been the *U 34* (Rollmann).
[TNA: ADM.1/11217]

6 July SHARK submarine
Chatham 1934; 640/927 tons; 193ft × 24ft; 1 × 3in,
6 × torpedo tubes
Lieutenant Commander Peter Noel Buckley

Ordered to conduct a patrol off the coast of Norway, near Skudesnes, she sailed 3 July from Rosyth. At 22.00 on 5 July as they approached the patrol area, the submarine was brought to the surface to recharge batteries, although this was a hazardous undertaking, as at this time of year it was never completely dark in those latitudes. They had only been on the surface for 15 minutes when they were attacked by a seaplane which dropped two bombs as they were diving. This was followed a few minutes later by another two bombs, whilst the submarine was only barely submerged. The explosions caused widespread damage – glass was shattered, the lights went out, the hydroplanes were reported as being out of action, the starboard motor stopped, and an electrical fire started in the engine room. As they were tackling these problems, it was found that the after hydroplanes were jammed hard to rise, and despite all their efforts the submarine rose to the surface. She wallowed on the surface for several minutes, immediately becoming the target for a machine–gun attack before some control was regained and the boat dived. She was found to be difficult to control, with water reported entering aft and the engines not responding, and she dived to 256ft before she could be steadied. High pressure air was now low, and it decided that they must go to the surface before it was expended completely in attempts to stabilise her. She rose at a very steep angle and finally surfaced at 22.45, finding that the aircraft had left the scene. She managed to put her head to the west, but an examination revealed that she was in a sorry state – the stern was severely damaged, being twisted to starboard for about 20ft, and the hull had opened from the after escape chamber, which was causing a flood in the after ends, which could barely be controlled. The port shaft had been knocked out of alignment; the rudder was jammed; most electrical circuits were out of action and the batteries smoking. Buckley realised that it was only a matter of time before they were spotted and at midnight as they threw overboard the confidential books an aircraft flew overhead. From then on, they were subjected to constant air attacks. Bombs were dropped, which exploded close by her, and there were regular strafing runs by an He 111 bomber aircraft, the submarine responding with the deck gun and a Lewis machine gun. By 03.00 the submarine was full of smoke and fumes from the overheating engines, and several men had been wounded. Me 109 fighter aircraft then appeared which carried out a series of devastating runs, peppering the submarine with cannon fire, which left the bridge ' … a shambles of wounded men, blood and empty cartridge cases'. After this Buckley signalled that he surrendered, and after a 30-minute lull a seaplane landed astern – only to sink. Both of the crewmen swam to the submarine, and a nervous truce was observed, with the wounded men being treated for their injuries. At 05.00 a larger seaplane landed to take off Lieutenant

Buckley and another wounded officer. At 06.30 the first of several armed trawlers arrived on scene to take off the survivors and attempted to rig a tow. However, at 09.00 the *Shark* heeled over and sank, stern first. She was then about 30 miles south-west of Stavanger. Four men were killed in the air attacks; thirty-two men survived to be taken prisoner.
[Evans pp232–40]

8 July CAYTON WYKE trawler
Selby 1932 purchased 1939; 373 tons; 150.5ft × 25.5ft; 1 × 12pdr
Skipper David Forbes Noble RNR[†]
During the evening of 7 July, radio intercepts indicated that a number of enemy surface craft, probably torpedo boats, were at sea in the area of the Dover straits. No firm positions could be ascertained, but it was clear that a small vessel, probably a trawler was being shadowed. At midnight warning messages were issued to ships in the area, which included the information that enemy surface ships bore 140 degrees from North Foreland. At 01.10 the *Cayton Wyke* was torpedoed and sank very quickly, about half a mile to the west of the South Goodwin lightship. Eighteen men were lost, with just one survivor being picked up by an MTB. She had been torpedoed by *schnellboot S 36*. The wreck lies in position 51.19.05N 01.30.20E.
[TNA: ADM.199/360; Larn vol 2 sec 6]

(9?) July SALMON submarine
Birkenhead 1934; 640/927 tons; 193ft × 24ft; 1 × 3in, 6 × torpedo tubes
Commander Edward Oscar Bickford[†]
Sailed from Rosyth on 4 July for a patrol off the Norwegian coast and never seen or heard from again. It is almost certain that she was lost by striking a mine. Her route to the operational area took her through a freshly-laid enemy minefield which was unknown to the British at the time. She would have passed through the minefield in position 57.22N 05.00E during 9 July. Five officers and thirty-six men were lost.
[Evans p240]

9 July FOXGLOVE sloop
Glasgow 1915; 1,165 tons; 255.3ft × 33.5ft; 2 × 4in
Lieutenant Commander Thomas Ian Scott Bell
On completion of providing an escort to a group of minesweepers, during the afternoon the sloop was returning to Portsmouth, and was about 8 miles to the south of the Nab Tower, when she became the target for a group of Ju 87 aircraft, which commenced a series of dive-bombing attacks. The ship suffered three direct hits, with two bombs hitting the boat deck near the after funnel. The first burst on impact, whilst the second demolished most of the boat deck across

the width of the ship and caused widespread splinter damage. A third bomb went through the upper deck to explode on contact with the boiler room bulkhead. The ship remained stable and was towed into Portsmouth but was considered a constructive total loss and not repaired. She was later taken to Londonderry to act as an accommodation ship. Twenty-two men were killed or died subsequently of their injuries.
[TNA: ADM.267/101; CB.4273 p334]

11 July ESCORT destroyer
Greenock 1934; 1,405 tons; 318.3ft × 33.3ft; 4 × 4.7in,
8 × torpedo tubes
Lieutenant Commander John Bostock
Part of a force screening the major units of Force 'H' in the western Mediterranean, at 02.15 the officer of the watch sighted an object on the surface which was identified as the conning tower of a submarine. The submarine was on the starboard bow and seemed to be turning to port, across the destroyer's track. No Asdic contact had been reported, but as the destroyer headed towards the submarine it was seen to be diving and as it did so, HE (hydrophone effect) was reported, indicating a torpedo had been fired, presumably from a stern tube. Before any avoiding action could be taken, the Escort was hit by the bulkhead between number 1 and 2 boiler rooms. Both boiler rooms were wrecked and flooded very quickly, and number 3 boiler room started to slowly flood, due to the sheering of several rivets in the dividing bulkhead. By 06.30 she had developed a list of 25 degrees to port and was abandoned at 08.00. The list steadily increased until by 10.45 she was heeling by 35 degrees at which point she rolled over onto her beam ends revealing the hole made by the torpedo, about 20ft in length. She then broke in half, the stern sinking immediately the fore end remaining afloat, bottom up for about 15 minutes before sinking. The position was noted as 36.07N 03.40W. Two men were killed. The submarine had been the Italian Marconi (Chialamberto).
[TNA: ADM.267/90]

11 July WARRIOR-II yacht
Troon 1904 requisitioned 1939; 1,124 tons;
298.7ft × 32.7ft; 1 × 4in
Captain Archibald Edward Johnston
During the morning of 11 July Portland harbour came under intense air attack, some fifty aircraft being reported in the area. The Warrior foundered at 08.55 during an attack by several Ju 87 dive bombers, being struck aft by a single bomb after a series of near misses. The wreck lies in position 50.21.34N 02.12.14W. One man was killed in the attack.
[TNA: ADM.199/2208; Larn vol 1 sec 6]

16 July IMOGEN destroyer
Hebburn 1936; 1,370 tons; 312ft × 33ft; 4 × 4.7in,
10 × torpedo tubes
Commander Charles Leslie Firth
On 15 July, a force of German minelayers was detected deploying into the North Sea, and in the early hours of the following day, Force 'C' was sailed from Scapa Flow to intercept them. This consisted of four cruisers and eight destroyers, one of which was Imogen. During the afternoon it became clear that the German force had returned into the Baltic, so Force 'C' reversed course to return to Scapa. The cruisers were deployed in single line ahead, the destroyers in two lines, each of four ships, a mile astern of the cruisers. The officer commanding the force, Rear Admiral Marshall Clarke, embarked on board Southampton, decided to carry out manoeuvring exercises on the way back. From 22.30 a series of turns together were executed, although the fading light of the late day was complicated by banks of thick fog. At 23.22 the group assumed a new course of 330°, steaming at 15 knots but 20 minutes later, at 23.42, the Admiral ordered another course change, ships to turn in succession, to 130°, indicating a radical change of course of 160 degrees. At this time, the cruisers were still in line ahead, and the destroyers were in divisions, on either quarter of the last cruiser in line. This order placed the ships on the starboard quarter in a difficult position. If they altered round to starboard as ordered, they would foul the cruisers as they turned; if the course were held then they would interfere with the line of destroyers on their port beam as they turned. The situation was further complicated by the ships running into a thick bank of fog at this time. Just one minute after the order was given, it was executed. Now blanketed in thick fog, the Imogen, following her leader Inglefield, heard siren blasts and realised that the cruisers were turning, but could do nothing until the bows of a large ship loomed out of the mist on the port bow, only 200 yards away. Unable to avoid the collision, she was rammed by the Glasgow, the last ship in the line of cruisers. She was struck on the port side of the fo'c'sle abreast 'A' gun. The cruiser cut deep into the smaller ship and they were locked together. There was then an explosion, and a sheet of flame shot along the port side of the destroyers' bridge. This was probably caused by the 5-gallon drums of petrol stowed by the break in the fo'c'sle being smashed in the collision. The burning fuel spread to the forward fuel tanks and shortly after the whole of the fore part of the ship was burning fiercely. All the lights went out and steam power failed. Water gushed into the split in the hull, and she started to go down by the head. The starboard whaler was lowered, and the Carley floats were prepared for release. Fire-fighting efforts were going on, but it could not be got under control, and 30 minutes after the collision she

was ordered to be abandoned, all the men going on board the *Glasgow*. She was last seen at 00.45, low in the water, surrounded by burning oil. An air search the following morning failed to find her. The position was in the vicinity of 58.34N 02.54W. Seventeen men on the destroyer died, and another died later of his injuries. Two men were lost from the *Glasgow*, having been thrown overboard. The subsequent enquiry placed the blame on Vice Admiral Clarke. He had shown a '… lamentable lack of appreciation of his responsibility … and failed to exercise control during a dangerous manoeuvre'. He had evidently believed that the destroyers were also in single line ahead, not in divisions; he had failed to confirm the position of all his ships before ordering a radical change of course; and to carry out such a manoeuvre in half-light with patches of thick fog was dangerous. He was informed that he had incurred their Lordships' displeasure and was ordered to haul down his flag and go ashore. The senior officer of the destroyers, Captain Philip Vian of the *Cossack*, was also blameable. He had shown a lack of judgement in failing to order the destroyers to form a single line when ordered to take station astern as the manoeuvres began. He was informed that he had incurred their Lordships' displeasure.

[TNA: ADM.1/10869]

(16?) July PHOENIX submarine

Birkenhead 1929; 1,475/2,040 tons; 270ft × 29.11ft; 1 × 4in, 8 × torpedo tubes

Lieutenant Commander Gilbert Hugh Nowell[†]

In the Far East at the outbreak of war, she was moved to the Mediterranean in May 1940 and based at Alexandria she sailed from that port on 3 July to conduct a patrol off the south-east corner of Sicily but failed to return as expected. The cause of her loss is uncertain. One possible cause was an attack by the Italian torpedo boat *Albatros* acting as escort to an oil tanker. At 06.30 on 16 July, off the lighthouse of San Croce, Augusta, the *Albatros* saw the tracks of torpedoes, which passed ahead and astern of the tanker, and she promptly turned and steamed down the tracks, dropping ten depth charges as she did. Although there were no obvious signs of success, it is possible that the *Phoenix* was the target of the attack, and that she was fatally damaged. However, *Phoenix* had been ordered to return to Malta on 14 July, so should have departed from her patrol area by the 16th. An alternative fate was by striking a mine, a field having been laid to the south-east of Augusta. Five officers and fifty men were lost.

[Evans p25; https://www.uboat.net/allies/warships/ship/3402. html]

17 July STEADY mooring vessel

Renfrew 1916; 758 tons; 135ft × 27ft; 1 × 12pdr

Master G Castle

Normally based at Portsmouth, she had been deployed to Newhaven to lay and control booms and nets across the harbour entrance. At 07.00 she proceeded out of harbour to lay a new set of nets and was then used to drag nets to the east to allow ships to enter. Whilst doing so her recovery gear broke, requiring her to return to harbour. It was whilst manoeuvring to enter at 12.40, then about 250 yards to the south of the east pier, that there was a large explosion on the starboard side between the boiler room and mess deck. She started to sink immediately, and a raft was hastily launched from the starboard side and the dinghy from the fo'c'sle before she went under. Ten men were killed and two were injured including the skipper. Her wreck was noted in position 50.46.45N 00.03.40E.

[TNA: ADM.199/220]

19 July WAR SEPOY oiler

West Hartlepool 1919; 5,557 tons; 400ft × 52.3ft

Master Thomas George Bennett RFA

During 19 July there were several large air raids on targets in southern England, including the port of Dover. At 15.50 several bomber aircraft, identified as Do 17s with fighter escort, were seen approaching, which then carried out an attack on Dover harbour, with twenty-two high explosive bombs being dropped. The *War Sepoy*, secured at the detached mole, was hit amidships in the engine room. A survey assessed the damage as so severe, that the ship was beyond economical repair. She was further damaged during an air raid on 25 July, being set on fire and she subsequently broke in half. After several weeks were spent in removing the oil from the wreck, the remains were filled with concrete and scuttled at western entrance of the harbour, to act as a blockship.

[TNA: ADM.199/360; Lloyd's War Losses vol 1 p103; www. historicalrfa.org/rfa-war-sepoy-ships-details]

19 July CRESTFLOWER trawler

Selby 1930 requisitioned 1939; 367 tons; 150.3ft × 24.5ft; 1 × 12pdr

Skipper George Henry Goodinson RNR

Whilst sweeping off Portsmouth harbour, at 12.50 she became the target for an attack by enemy aircraft. No direct hits were obtained but she subsequently foundered after her hull was holed by splinters from several near misses. Two ratings were killed. The wreck lies in position 50.29.02N 01.18.53W.

[TNA: ADM.199/370; Larn vol 2 sec 2]

20 July BRAZEN destroyer

Jarrow 1930; 1,360 tons; 312ft × 32.3ft; 4 × 4.7in,
1 × 12pdr, 2 × 2pdr, 4 × torpedo tubes
Lieutenant Commander Sir Michael Culmer-Seymour

On patrol between the South Goodwin and Lydd light vessels, *Brazen* was ordered to remain in the vicinity to give extra cover for a coastal convoy, CW7, due to pass through the area. This duly arrived in the late afternoon, and by 18.20 *Brazen* had taken station on the flank of the convoy, with the destroyers *Boreas* and *Windsor* being positioned ahead and astern of the convoy. When they were about 1.5 miles south of the Folkestone light, a large number of aircraft were seen approaching from the east, at a height of about 8,000ft, with twenty-two Ju 87 aircraft being counted, and these were followed by a number of twin-engined aircraft. Fire was opened at long range from the 4.7in and the 12pdr, and the aircraft broke up into groups. Speed had been increased to 24 knots and several of the groups appeared to single out the *Brazen* for attack. The attacks came from the port side and about ten Ju 87s and six twin-engined aircraft made a series of dive bombing and shallow dive attacks. The wheel was put hard over and then reversed as the attacks commenced, and this continued. Several sticks of bombs were dropped which fell around her, but all missed until an attack by a large twin-engined aircraft. A stick of two heavy and four smaller bombs were dropped which could not be avoided. These did not actually hit the ship but burst all around and underneath her. This caused a most violent concussion to the ship. The steering gear failed, and all the lights went out, but the engines continued working. Further bombing runs were made, but without success. One of the attacking aircraft was shot down, crashing into the sea near the ship. Both engine and boiler rooms reported they had water entering and it was found that the upper deck had been distorted by the blast, being raised about 8in above the engine room bulkhead, and the deck had ripples either side of it. The side plating bulged outboard at the same station. As the water steadily gained, so power was lost, and she came to a stop. The *Boreas* closed and took her in tow, but this parted soon after. As a tug was now closing, all non-essential personnel were taken off, a small towing party of twenty-one officers and men remaining. With a new tow rigged by the tug, she started to make her way towards Dover, but after 45 minutes she broke apart amidships. The stern section floated free and then sank. The bow continued to float, slowly rising vertically. The fore part was eventually sunk by gunfire from *Boreas*. No one was killed in the incident, although six ratings were wounded, and one man subsequently died of his injuries. The wreck lies in position 51.01.05N 01.17.15E.

[TNA: ADM.1/31009; Larn vol 2 sec 4]

22 July CAMPINA trawler

Selby 1913 requisitioned 1939; 289 tons; 133.5ft × 23ft
Skipper Frederick Welburn RNR†

Based at Holyhead, North Wales, that port became the target of an air raid on the night of 21/22 July, when an aircraft was seen to fly low over the harbour and drop an object by parachute. This was believed to be a magnetic mine, and from observations from the shore the position was fixed as being 4 cables (800 yards) from the outer breakwater light. The port was therefore ordered to be closed until the menace could be cleared. There were no magnetic minesweepers at the port, and some were ordered to the scene from Liverpool, but would take some time to arrive, so Commander Critchlow, the local Group minesweeping officer, used a 'lash-up' magnetic sweep of 200 yards length. Using this from the trawler *Sheldon*, he swept the area suspected, but without result. On completion of this, at 13.00 the harbour was re-opened, the first movement being the sailing of the mail steamer which passed the spot without incident. The five ships which had been waiting outside the harbour were then ordered to enter, which they did in line ahead formation, the *Campina* being the fourth ship in line. When they were about 100 yards off the breakwater light, she was blown up, the time then being 13.45. She sank immediately, her bows showing for a short time. Twelve men were killed. It was believed that the magnetic mine had probably employed a time delay fuse.

[TNA: ADM.1/10903]

23 July NARWHAL submarine

Barrow 1935; 1,520/2,157 tons; 271.6ft × 25.6ft; 1 × 4in,
6 × torpedo tubes, 50 mines
Lieutenant Commander Ronald James Burch DSO†

Sailed from Blyth at 15.00 on 22 July to lay a minefield in the approaches to Kristiansund, Norway, in the vicinity of 63.16N 07.13E and not heard from again. She failed to confirm by radio that the operation had been completed and failed to respond to radio calls. It was later found that the German B-Dienst intelligence service had broken British naval codes, and through the deciphering of several messages addressed to *Narwhal*, they became aware of her mission and likely course. Aircraft were then deployed to hunt for her, and this brought success at 14.55 the day after she sailed, when a patrolling Do 17 bomber sighted and attacked a submarine on the surface in the vicinity of 55.30N 01.10E, which they had identified as a British *Porpoise* class vessel. This must have been the *Narwhal*, as she would have been in this position at this time. Fifty-nine men lost their lives. In May 2017, the wreck of *Narwhal* was found by a Polish expedition, close to the position reported by the attacking German aircraft.

[Evans p24; https://www.uboat.net/allies/warships/ship/3414.html]

24 July KINGSTON GALENA trawler

Beverley 1934, purchased 1939; 415 tons; 151.7ft × 25.9ft;
1 × 4in
Skipper Sidney Jackson RNR†

During the morning, a coastal convoy attracted the attention of enemy aircraft as it passed through the Dover straits. At 08.30 and again at 09.00 the convoy was attacked, but with no losses. The *Kingston Galena* had escorted the convoy past Dover, and at 11.20, having completed her escort duties, was returning to Dover when she was attacked by sixteen bombers. She took a direct hit amidships and sank very quickly. Eighteen men died. The wreck has been found and lies in position 51.07.18N 01.24.52E.
[TNA: ADM.199/160; Larn vol 2 sec 4]

24 July RODINO trawler

Beverley 1913 requisitioned 1939; 230 tons; 117.5ft × 22ft;
1 × 12pdr
Skipper Joseph Charles Winning RNR

A Dover-based minesweeping trawler, she was newly equipped to sweep for magnetic mines, and was busy sweeping a known mined area, when a large air raid developed. Having successfully attacked the *Kingston Galena* (see above), the aircraft then shifted their attention to the *Rodino*, which was hit by a bomb forward and sank immediately. Three men died. The wreck lies in position 51.07N 01.23.55E.
[TNA: ADM.199/360; Larn vol 2 sec 4]

24 July FLEMING trawler

Beverley 1929 requisitioned 1939; 356 tons; 140.2ft × 24ft;
1 × 12pdr
Skipper Ernest George Gurney RNR

In company with two other armed trawlers, she was in the Thames estuary, in the vicinity of the Longsand, having completed recovering her gear on completion of minesweeping duties for the day, and was preparing to return to harbour. Earlier that afternoon a twin-engined Dornier aircraft had flown overhead, which appeared to be on a reconnaissance mission. This seemed to be borne out when at 17.20 aircraft engines were heard, and then four aircraft, thought to be Ju 88s, emerged from the low cloud to fly straight towards the group, splitting into pairs as they did so. The first pair concentrated on the *Fleming*, dropping three bombs, with one exploding as a near miss, the others hitting her. The first bomb struck her between the bridge and the funnel, the second on her stern and she broke up and sank immediately. The second pair of aircraft attacked the *Berberis* nearby, but all the bombs missed. Nineteen men were killed in the attack, with three survivors being picked up by the *Corena*.
[TNA: ADM.1/10890]

27 July CODRINGTON destroyer

Wallsend 1929; 1,540 tons; 332ft × 33.9ft; 5 × 4.7in,
2 × 2pdr, 8 × torpedo tubes
Captain George Frederick Stevens-Guille DSO

Undergoing a period of maintenance which included a boiler clean, she was secured alongside the depot ship *Sandhurst* which was berthed on the north wall of submarine basin at Dover when the harbour came under air attack. At about 18.00 the 'all clear' was sounded, but very soon afterwards three enemy aircraft approached from the west and a further two from the north and they commenced a dive-bombing attack on the harbour. Two bombs fell in the submarine basin close to the ships and then one struck *Codrington* amidships. The engine and boiler rooms rapidly flooded and it was clear that her back was broken. The bow and stern rose clear of the water and the stern half rolled over and sank, although the forward half remained buoyant for some time before settling into the shallow water. There were no casualties.
[TNA: ADM.267/101]

27 July WREN destroyer

Scotstoun 1919; 1,120 tons; 300ft × 29.6ft; 4 × 4.7in,
2 × 2pdr, 6 × torpedo tubes
Lieutenant Commander Frederick William George Harker

In company with the destroyer *Montrose*, the pair was acting as escort to a group of minesweeping trawlers off the coast of Suffolk, providing anti-aircraft cover. At 13.30, just as the trawlers had altered course round to the west, a solitary He 111 aircraft appeared ahead. It swept overhead without attacking, but the group were now on the alert as they had obviously been seen. At 16.55 the *Wren* was stationed on the port side of the sweepers, the *Montrose* on the starboard, when a group of fifteen aircraft were seen closing from the starboard quarter. Both destroyers worked up to full speed, as the aircraft attacked, breaking up into sections of three and attacking in steep dives. Two bombs struck her on the starboard side aft, bursting below the waterline abreast the wardroom and cabin flat, causing severe damage to the bulkheads and the structure abaft the engine room. She listed heavily to port, and the stern settled until the upper deck was awash as far as the after torpedo tubes. The boats and floats were ordered to be turned out as she started to fill rapidly with water from aft. She then broke in half, splitting across the deck. She was still under attack, and another bomb either hit her amidships or close to her. All bulkheads abaft the engine rooms collapsed and she sank stern first, the bows remaining above water for about 20 minutes before sinking. Thirty-six men died.
[TNA: ADM.199/101]

27 July STAUNTON trawler
Beverley 1907 requisitioned 1940; 283 tons; 130ft × 22.2ft;
1 × 6pdr
Skipper Sidney Wilfred Campbell RNR†
Ordered to carry out a night patrol in the local area,
she sailed from Brightlingsea, Essex, at 18.00 on 26 July.
She was seen by the yacht *Sarawara* at 22.00 that night,
but no further contact with her was ever made. When
she failed to return to harbour the following morning
a search was instigated, and at 11.30 on the 28th the
armed yacht *Giroflée* found the wreck of a trawler, with
just the masts showing, 8 cables (1,600 yards) to the
south-east of the Knoll buoy, which was believed to be
the *Staunton*. It was presumed that she had fallen victim
to an air-laid magnetic mine. There were no survivors:
thirteen men died.
[TNA: ADM.199/220]

29 July DELIGHT destroyer
Govan 1933; 1,375 tons; 317ft × 33ft; 4 × 4.7in, 2 × 2pdr,
8 × torpedo tubes
Commander Mark Fogg-Elliott
Having completed a maintenance period in Portsmouth
dockyard, she was ordered to proceed to Greenock
without delay, for convoy escort duties. As she was
steering south-west in the English Channel at 23 knots,
at 18.35 a large formation of aircraft was sighted on
the port beam, her position then being about 20 miles
south-west of Portland Bill. The aircraft turned to
attack, there being about fifteen aircraft, which appeared
to be Me 109s, each armed with a single bomb, which
divided themselves into groups of three. The ship
increased speed to 27 knots and turned to starboard. The
aircraft dived from a steep angle, dropping their bombs
from about 500ft, machine-gunning the destroyer as
they did. Most of the bombs missed, but the second
wave of attackers was the most effective, with one bomb
striking a glancing blow on the fo'c'sle to detonate at
the break of the fo'c'sle on the port side. All the lights
went out, the main steam pipe was fractured, and the
ship was swathed in a cloud of steam and black oily
smoke as an oil fire broke out. She steadily lost way, and
as a precaution the boats were lowered and as they had
evidently lost wireless communications, the motorboat
was sent away to Portland to request assistance. The
fires were tackled, but the flames could not be brought
under, slowly spreading through the amidships section.
At 20.45 a pair of MA/SBs arrived on the scene to
assist and lifted off the wounded. The flames were now
leaping above the superstructure and burning oil could
be seen pouring out of her. She was abandoned, the
boats and MA/SBs picking up the survivors. At 21.30
there was a large explosion forward and she sank. Her
position was 50.15N 02.43W. Seventeen men were
killed. It was believed that the explosion had split an

oil fuel tank, and the fire had been started by severed
electrical cables. The fire could not be controlled
because the flames were constantly fed by the oil.
[TNA: ADM.178/199]

29 July GULZAR yacht
Southampton 1934 requisitioned 1939; 201 tons;
108.3ft × 21.1ft
Lieutenant Cedric Victor Brammall RNR
Based at Dover, she was alongside in the harbour when
the port came under an intense air attack, from about
forty Ju 87 Stuka aircraft from 07.30. One large bomb
exploded close to the *Gulzar*, accompanied by some
incendiary bombs which set her on fire. Her diesel and
petrol fuel seeped out from damaged fuel tanks and this
caused a fierce fire which spread across the water, helped
by fuel oil leaking from the bomb-damaged depot ship
Sandhurst, moored nearby. She eventually sank alongside
the jetty. None of the crew was lost, as all had taken
shelter ashore when the air raid started.
[TNA: ADM.199/360]

30 July LADY SLATER examination vessel
Georgetown 1934 requisitioned 1939; 273 tons;
109.1ft × 23.6ft
(Civilian master)
Employed at Jamaica as an examination vessel –
checking incoming merchant ships – she was lying at
a buoy at the Palisadoes, Kingston, when a ship was
observed approaching. As preparations were made to
get underway, a fire was reported in the engine room.
The fire spread rapidly through the ship and she was
abandoned, a launch moored at the stern being used
to take off most of the crew, although others, including
the master, had to clamber down the mooring hawser
to the buoy, from where they were picked up. The ship
continued to burn until she sank. An enquiry found
that the cause was due to the practice of using a petrol
pressure lamp to pre-heat the engine, the compression
of which was poor. It appeared that the lamp had been
left unattended, standing next to a wooden partition.
[TNA: CO 137/846/16]

1 August OSWALD submarine
Barrow 1928; 1,475/2,038 tons; 265ft × 29.11ft; 1 × 4in,
8 × torpedo tubes
Lieutenant Commander David Alexander Fraser
Based at Alexandria, she was conducting a patrol to the
east of Sicily. During the afternoon of 30 July, she carried
out an attack on a small convoy about 20 miles to the
south of Cape delli'Armi. The attack failed but did alert
the enemy to the presence of a submarine, and an anti-
submarine sweep of the area was carried out by Italian
destroyer squadrons. At 23.50 on 1 August the destroyer
Ugolino Vivaldi, one of a group of five ships, sighted a

submarine on the surface on the port beam at a range of 2,500m. The *Vivaldi* reacted promptly, increasing speed and turning towards the submarine. On board the *Oswald* an alert lookout had spotted the destroyer on their starboard quarter, but Lieutenant Commander Fraser, who was below at the time, on hearing the shout 'Enemy ship in sight', instead of ordering the submarine to dive, decided to go to the bridge, but it took some time for him to climb the ladder and for eyes to become accustomed to the dark. Meanwhile all torpedo tubes were ordered to be readied for firing, and the boat made an alteration of course, to turn away from the oncoming threat. It was hoped that she had not been seen, but it soon became clear that the destroyer was rapidly closing on a collision course, at which Fraser gave the order to abandon ship. At 23.58 the *Vivaldi* struck the *Oswald* on the starboard side aft, puncturing the ballast tanks. The destroyer then passed along the submarine's starboard side, dropping depth charges as she did so. When clear the *Vivaldi* came around at high speed to open fire with her 120mm gun. On board the *Oswald*, the crew, led by the Executive Officer, were already abandoning her, with water flooding into the after compartments and it was found that the after hatch was distorted by the collision, so that it could not be closed. The crew took to the water, the order to open main vents being given as they did so, to ensure that the submarine would sink. The boat, still under way and under helm continued her way, circling around with an increasing list to port until she slowly filled and sank. The *Vivaldi*, after firing several rounds at the boat, closed preparing to ram again, but found the water was full of men calling for help. Heaving to, a boat was lowered and over the next 30 minutes they picked up fifty-two survivors. Three men did not survive. In April 1946 Lieutenant Commander Fraser was court-martialled for the loss of his vessel through negligence and failing to have his vessel in a proper state to engage the enemy. The Executive Officer, Lieutenant Commander Grahame Roy Marsh, was court-martialled for negligence and unbecoming conduct. During these procedures, it became clear that neither officer was popular, and the ship's company clearly believed that the *Oswald* could have been handled better. Fraser had failed to wear red goggles when in the control room, as recommended, which meant that he was night-blind when he went onto the bridge. He had then wasted considerable time in trying to locate the enemy himself, instead of immediately ordering the boat to dive. Finally, it was found that he had ordered 'Abandon ship' before she was rammed. He was cleared of charges of not having his vessel in a proper state of readiness, but he was found guilty of three counts of negligence – failing to dive when the destroyer was first seen, failing to engage the enemy and failing to issue orders to the officer of the

watch on actions to be taken when sighting a ship. He was sentenced to forfeit all seniority, to be dismissed his ship and to be severely reprimanded. Marsh was found guilty on two counts; firstly, of negligence, by failing to ensure that the order to abandon ship was carried out in an orderly fashion, and secondly of conduct unbecoming an officer, by leaving his position in the control room and going to the bridge, without first ensuring that those inside the submarine had succeeded in clearing the boat. He was dismissed from the service.
[TNA: ADM.156/280; Evans pp258–62; Kemp p128; www. britishnewspaperarchive.co.uk: Hampshire Telegraph 18 April 1946 pp1, 3 & 8]

1 August SPEARFISH submarine
Birkenhead 1936; 670/960 tons; 193ft × 24ft; 1 × 3in, 6 × torpedo tubes
Lieutenant Commander John Hay Forbes DSO[†]
Sailed from Rosyth on 31 July to conduct a patrol in the North Sea and not heard from again. A few days later the German press announced that she had been torpedoed and sunk by a German U-boat, and a solitary survivor had been picked up. Her attacker had been *U 34* (Rollmann), who had sighted a surfaced submarine at 18.17 in position 58.28N 01.06E and carried out an attack at 19.04, a single torpedo hitting the target amidships, with a large explosion. On surfacing, they found just a few pieces of debris and Able Seaman William Pester, who had been on the bridge, and was carried to the surface in a large air bubble. Forty-one men died.
[Morgan & Taylor pp53–5]

2 August EMBRACE drifter
Govan 1907 requisitioned 1940; 94 tons; 86.2ft × 18.5ft
Skipper Arnott Herbert Smith Besford RNR
Based at Loch Alsh, western Scotland as a local patrol craft, she ran aground and sank in shallow water and was condemned as a total loss. The wreck has been found off Ornsay in the Sound of Sleat, Skye.
[TNA: ADM.199/2210; https://canmore.org.uk/site/102014]

2 August CAPE FINISTERRE trawler
Selby 1939 requisitioned 1940; 594 tons; 178.2ft × 30.1ft; 1 × 12pdr
Skipper John Pagley Grantham RNR
Based at Harwich, she was employed in conducting local anti-invasion patrols. She was engaged on such a patrol when at 19.05 aircraft were seen approaching from the port beam. The aircraft, believed to be Me 110s, crossed her bows to come down the starboard side in line ahead and then attack from the starboard quarter. Each plane dropped a single bomb, none of them hit her, but two were near misses, falling close on the port side. These shook the ship considerably, with the gun's crew being blown overboard by the blast. The

main steam pipe was fractured, filling the engine room with scalding steam. The ship heeled over to port and started to sink, and she foundered about 10 minutes after the attack, sinking stern first. One man was killed. The gun layer, Able Seaman Joseph Dunn, had shot down one of the attacking aircraft and was subsequently awarded the Conspicuous Gallantry Medal. Not only had he displayed ' … coolness and skill in withholding his fire until the one round able to be fired ensured the destruction of the enemy', but on discovering that a trimmer was missing, he had gone down into the steam-drenched engine room to try and find him.

[TNA: ADM.178/199; London Gazette 6 September 1940]

(2/3) August THAMES submarine
Barrow 1932; 1,830/2,680 tons; 325ft × 28.3ft; 1 × 4in, 6 × torpedo tubes
Lieutenant Commander William Donald Dunkerley[†]

Based at Dundee, she sailed 22 July to conduct a war patrol in the North Sea, off the south-western coast of Norway. She was not heard from again. The last time she may perhaps be identified, is with a submarine attack on the battlecruiser *Gneisenau* and her escorts in position 58.26N 04.10E during the afternoon of 26 July. During this attack, the 900-ton torpedo boat *Luchs* was sunk by a torpedo. It is considered likely that the *Thames* was responsible for this attack. During the afternoon of 2 August all submarines in the North Sea were ordered to return to harbour. If the attack on the *Gneisenau* group was indeed conducted by the *Thames*, as is believed probable, then her course to obey this order would have taken her through a German minefield, which was not known to the British, during the night of 2/3 August, in position 56.45N 03.26E. This is the most likely cause of her loss. Six officers and fifty-six men lost their lives.

[Evans pp241–4]

4 August DRUMMER trawler
Middlesbrough 1915 requisitioned 1940; 297 tons; 138.7ft × 23.5ft; 1 × 12pdr
Skipper Harry Cecil Hall RNR

Engaged in minesweeping off the Essex coast near Brightlingsea, she was wrecked at 18.30 by a large detonation, believed to have been a magnetic mine exploding close to her, and she sank with the loss of two men. The wreck has been located lying in position 51.43.57N 01.07.11E.

[TNA: ADM.199/1171; Larn vol 3 sec 1]

4 August MARSONA trawler
South Shields 1918 (*James Christopher*) requisitioned 1939; 276 tons; 125.3ft × 23.4ft; 1 × 12pdr
Skipper-Lieutenant Alfred Daniel Ellis RNR

A former Fleetwood trawler, *Marsona* was converted for use as a minesweeper, being fitted for LL or magnetic minesweeping. In company with two other trawlers, the *George Cousins* and *Industry*, she had been deployed to the Cromarty Firth off Nigg Bay, mines having been reported in the area. At 07.20, when about 3 miles off Sutor the trio commenced veering out their sweeps and magnets, but before this was complete there was a large explosion which covered the *Marsona* in smoke and water. When it cleared the only thing visible was the bow section, from the wheelhouse forward, her stern having been demolished. The wreck disappeared in 3 minutes. Six survivors were picked up by the other trawlers, twelve men being killed. The remains of the wreck lie in position 57.40N, 003.55W

[TNA: ADM1/10767]

4 August OSWALDIAN trawler
Beverley 1917 requisitioned 1940; 261 tons; 120ft × 22.5ft
Skipper James Darkins RNR

Sank after she detonated a mine about 1 mile to the south-east of Breaksea lighthouse in the Bristol Channel. Seven survivors were landed at Barry, but twelve men died.

[TNA: ADM.199/372; Lloyd's War Losses vol 1 p110]

5 August RIVER CLYDE trawler
Ayr 1919 requisitioned 1939; 276 tons; 125.3ft × 23.5ft; 1 × 12pdr
Skipper James Leslie Grant RNR

In company with the trawler *Berberis*, the pair were conducting an Oropesa sweep for contact mines off the Essex/Suffolk coast. At 17.00 they had completed the work for the day, and were lying with engines stopped, hauling in sweeps. The *Clyde*'s Oropesa sweep float was about 4 yards off the starboard quarter when there was an explosion under the stern and the ship 'caved in' abaft the funnel. She had disappeared in 20 seconds. The trawler *Joseph Button* nearby, closed and rescued nine survivors, but eleven men were killed and one of those picked up later died of his injuries. Her position was noted as 52.07.9N 01.54.4E. It was believed that a moored mine had been caught in the sweep but had not been cut free. It was ascertained that when conducting Oropesa sweeps, cutters were not always employed.

[TNA: ADM.1/10902]

8 August BOREALIS barrage balloon vessel
Emden 1935 requisitioned 1940 (*Pilote no.15*); 451 tons; 154.3ft × 25.9ft
Lieutenant Arthur Hague RNR

Assigned as an escort to coastal convoy CW9, she was leading the starboard column, flying her barrage balloon at 3,200ft. At 12.19 as they were passing St Catherine's light, Isle of Wight, several aircraft approached from the south-east. An enemy fighter aircraft carried out several attacks on her balloon, finally setting it on fire. This was

scarcely over when a Ju 87 attacked her from the port quarter. The crew replied with machine guns, the only weapons they had, but this did not deter the attacker, which dropped a single bomb, which scored a direct hit. The bomb struck the foremast bringing it down over the starboard side, then pierced the upper deck and exploded below, blowing a hole in the starboard side on the water line. The forward part of the ship was wrecked, but the collision bulkhead held, and she still had power. The tug *Elan-II* took her in tow, stern first, but as it proved difficult to control her, secured alongside. They headed towards Spithead, but were subject to another air attack, during which, as they could offer no resistance, all the crew took to their boat. She was either hit again, or suffered a near miss, and when the aircraft departed, they returned on board to find her filling with water. She was then abandoned, and she sank by the head at 17.20, being about 4.5 miles from St. Catherine's Light. There were no casualties.
[TNA:ADM.199/163]

10 August TRANSYLVANIA armed merchant cruiser
Govan 1925 requisitioned 1939; 16,293 tons; 552.4ft × 70.3ft; 8 × 6in, 2 × 12pdr
Captain Francis Nigel Miles
Part of the Northern Patrol, she sailed from Greenock 9 August to take up her duties. At midnight, a course alteration was ordered, and the ship was still swinging under starboard helm when there was an explosion on the port side, just before the funnel. The ship took a list to port, and the engine room reported flooding, and several of the after compartments also reported that water was entering. She slowly stabilised, but the water could not be controlled and by 02.30 the water was lapping onto 'B' deck and the list was increasing. The lights had failed, including emergency lighting, and it was decided to abandon her. Boats were ordered to be hoisted out and most of the ship's company were ordered to leave, a small party remaining on board, to continue pumping and shoring bulkheads. By 04.15 she was clearly sinking, the last men left the ship, and she sank at 04.30. Her position was approximately 55.50N 08.30W. Several destroyers arrived on scene shortly before she sank to pick up the crew, but in choppy waters, two of the boats capsized, with the loss of thirty-six men. The court of enquiry was not impressed with the actions of her engineering officers; the Engineer Commander had failed to take charge of the situation and had not conducted a personal examination of the damage. Further, there was evidence of '… insufficient attention being paid to the shutting of bulkhead valves, with the result that the water was penetrating to other compartments'. It was found that the officers in charge of the watch in the engine and boiler rooms had ordered the evacuation of those spaces without ordering the closing of various outlets or attempting any damage control measures. The enquiry feared that they had '… abandoned their places of duty without any reason other than the consideration of their own safety.'. As a result, three officers were disciplined, Engineer Commander Donald Nicholson RNR, Engineer Lieutenant Thomas Phillips RNR and Engineer Lieutenant Ian Haldane RNR were all informed that they would not be employed again by the Navy. Her attacker had been the *U 56* (Harms).
[TNA:ADM.1/10889]

10 August YOUNG SID drifter
Aberdeen 1912 requisitioned 1940; 100 tons; 86.1ft × 18.7ft
Whilst on passage from Invergordon to Oban, the drifter was in collision at 10.00 off Tarbet Ness with the collier *The Duke* (820 tons) and subsequently foundered. All the crew were rescued by the *Duke* which landed them at Invergordon. A wreck, which may be her, has been located lying in position 57.45W 03.40W.
[TNA:ADM.199/365; https://canmore.org.uk/sit/101704]

12 August PYROPE trawler
Beverley 1932 requisitioned 1939; 295 tons; 129ft × 24ft; 1 × 12pdr
Skipper Arthur James Folkard RNR
During August 1940, the Luftwaffe made coastal convoys and shipping a primary target. During 12 August as a group of minesweeping trawlers from Sheerness were employed sweeping, they became the target for an attack by a large group of Ju 87 aircraft. At 11.20, when near the north-east Spit Buoy in the Thames Estuary the *Pyrope* suffered a direct hit and sank with the loss of six men. The wreck has been found and lies in position 51.28.02N 01.25.20E.
[TNA:ADM.199/2210; Larn vol 2 sec 7]

12 August TAMARISK trawler
Beverley 1925 (*St Gatien*), purchased 1939; 352 tons; 140.3ft × 24ft; 1 × 4in
Skipper Samuel Charles William Bavidge RNR
Another of the Sheerness-based minesweepers attacked during the late morning (see *Pyrope* above); she was also hit and sank with the loss of seven men. The Margate lifeboat rescued the survivors. The wreck has been found and lies in position 51.27.52N 01.26.06E.
[TNA:ADM.199/2210; Larn vol 2 sec 6]

13 August ELIZABETH ANGELA trawler
Glasgow 1928 (*Hannah Reynolds*) requisitioned 1939; 253 tons; 120.7ft × 23.1ft; 1 × 12pdr
Skipper Frederick Arthur Meggitt RNR
In company with the trawler *Taipo* off the coast of Kent, when four aircraft, identified as Ju 87s, were seen

approaching from the east, which circled around and then, dividing into pairs, headed towards the ships. The aircraft commenced dive bombing attacks, each dropping two bombs. The *Taipo* escaped injury, but a bomb landed close alongside the *Elizabeth Angela*, and she sank in 3 minutes from the damage received, the mast and funnel remaining visible. The wreck lies in position 51.19.51N 01.33.05E. One man was killed.
[TNA: ADM.237/126; Larn vol 2 sec 6]

16 August MANX LAD drifter
Sandhaven 1937 requisitioned 1939; 24 tons; 44.3ft × 14.3ft
Employed as an examination vessel at Holyhead, she went alongside the Irish registered steamer *Lady Meath* about 6 cables (1,200 yards) to the north-east of Breamer Rock lighthouse to check the vessels paperwork, when at 07.40 there was a large explosion as she detonated a mine. Both the *Lady Meath* and the *Manx Lad* foundered. All the crew were saved.
[TNA: ADM.199/372; Lloyd's War Losses vol 1 p114]

20 August RESPARKO trawler
Beverley 1916 requisitioned 1939; 248 tons; 120.5ft × 22ft
Skipper James Fountain RNR
She was lying at the southern end of the western arm of Falmouth Docks, outboard of the trawler *Royalo*, when the port came under air attack. At 21.08 she was straddled by a stick of bombs which exploded around her. She was badly shaken and holed by a near miss forward, and a second bomb then scored a direct hit aft. She sank in 2 minutes. The wreck now lies in position 50.09.10N 05.03.04W. There were no casualties as the crew had taken shelter ashore.
[TNA: ADM.199/163; Larn vol 1 sec 4]

21 August KYLEMORE paddle net layer
Port Glasgow 1897 (*Vulcan*) requisitioned 1939; 319 tons; 200.5ft × 24.1ft; 1 × 12pdr
Lieutenant Commander William McEver
Having sailed from Boston at 20.00 on 20 August for Great Yarmouth, she was off the coast of Norfolk at just after noon the following day when two aircraft approached from seaward, emerging from low cloud. They promptly attacked despite defensive fire from the ship, and a number of bombs exploded across her stern. The deck was pierced by at least one bomb, which entered the deck abaft the engine room and exploded in the after messdeck. She started settling quickly by the stern. A second attack was pressed home, and she was again hit aft, which speeded her sinking. The boats were cleared away with difficulty, the skiff being swamped, and as she sank the crew were forced to jump into the water, clinging to debris, such as gangways and ladders. The survivors were picked up by the trawlers *Loch*

Eriboll and *Loch Leven*. Eight men were lost. The wreck lies in position 53.08.3N 01.14.8E.
[TNA: ADM.199/101]

23 August HOSTILE destroyer
Greenock 1936; 1,340 tons; 312ft × 33ft; 4 × 4.7in, 8 × torpedo tubes
Lieutenant Commander Anthony Frank Burnell-Nugent
On passage from Malta to Gibraltar in company with two other destroyers, the *Mohawk* and *Hero*, the trio were in line ahead formation, the *Hostile* bringing up the rear. At 02.17 as they were steaming westwards along the coast of Tunisia, then being 17.6 miles off the coast, Cape Bon Light bearing 125 degrees, there was an explosion just abaft the engine room as she detonated a mine. The ship started to flood rapidly, from the fore end of the engine room to the after magazine and it became clear that her back had been broken near the after torpedo tubes, which had been blown overboard. She lost all power and took a pronounced list to starboard and as she was clearly sinking she was ordered to be abandoned. The *Hero* then torpedoed the wreck the to ensure her despatch. By this time, her stern was under water, and the explosion broke her in half, the stern section quickly disappearing, the depth charges exploding as it went under. The bow section remained stubbornly afloat, rising vertically into the air and a second torpedo had to be fired, which produced a huge explosion and she disappeared. Five men lost their lives. The mines had been laid between 8–10 August by Italian destroyers.
[TNA: ADM.1/10784]

24 August PENZANCE sloop
Devonport 1930; 1,025 tons; 250ft × 34ft; 2 × 4in
Commander Allan John Wavish
Sailed from Sydney, Cape Breton, Canada on 15 August as escort to slow Convoy SC1, composed of forty-two ships, bound for Liverpool. Speed should have been 7.5 knots, but poor weather reduced this to just 6.5 knots, but even so ships straggled and were dropped from the convoy. On 24 August at 17.35 the convoy was in position 56.20N 28.20W, the sloop being stationed ahead, zigzagging at 8 knots when a torpedo track was seen on the port side, about 500 yards from the ship. Engines were put to full ahead and the helm put hard over, but before the orders could take effect, she was hit on the port side amidships, below the foremast. The explosion blew the ship in two and she capsized over to starboard and turned turtle, broke up and sank rapidly. The bows and stern section rose clear of the water before sinking, disappearing in less than 5 minutes. Explosions continued immediately after she sank, as her depth charges detonated, killing some of the men in the water. Ninety men died and just thirteen survivors

were picked up by two of the convoy, the *Blairmore* and *Fylingdale* which lowered boats. Her attacker had been the *U 37* (Oehrn).
[*TNA: ADM.199/157*]

27 August WHITE FOX II   yacht

Looe 1933 requisitioned 1940; 23 tons; 43.3ft × 11ft
Second Hand J B Buck RNR

A private yacht taken over by the Admiralty in July, she was taken to Aldous Ltd Shipyard at Brightlingsea to be fitted out for naval service. Work was being carried out on the engines, and it was just after the starboard engine had been started up following repairs that a fire broke out in the bilges. The flames spread rapidly and in a short time she was burnt out. It was believed that petrol had built up in the bilges, and the vapour had probably ignited when the starter motor had been used.
[*TNA: ADM.199/675*]

28 August DUNVEGAN CASTLE   armed merchant cruiser

Belfast 1936 requisitioned 1939; 15,007 tons; 540ft × 72ft;
7 × 6in, 2 × 12pdr
Captain Hubert Ardill

Employed as an Ocean Escort, she had escorted homeward-bound Convoy SL43 from Freetown, and when approaching home waters, was detached to proceed independently to Belfast. She was in approximate position 55.05N 11W, steaming at 14 knots and had just stopped zigzagging, prior to commencing an alteration to a new course, when at 22.50 there was an explosion on the starboard side abreast the generating room. All the generators were immediately stopped, and she lost all power. The emergency generators were successfully started to restore some lighting and power, and pumps were started to try and clear the water which was entering. At 23.20 there was a second attack, a torpedo hitting on the port side, exploding in the engine room and 30 minutes later a third torpedo hit her further aft. This last ignited ready-use ammunition and started a fire aft. As a precaution the other magazines were ordered to be flooded, and at the same time all men were ordered to the upper deck and to hoist out all the boats. When number 3 hold was reported to be flooding, and the fires prevented all magazine spaces being flooded, she was ordered to be abandoned. This was done in good order, apart from the last boat, which had slipped in the davits until, with the commanding officer on board, it cleared at 01.30, the falls having to be cut to make it drop away. They remained by her as she steadily settled lower in the water, the corvette *Primrose* arriving at 04.00 to start picking them out of the water, the destroyer *Harvester* joining soon after. She finally disappeared at 06.00. Her attacker had been the *U 46* (Endrass). Twenty-seven men were lost.
[*TNA: ADM.1/10812*]

31 August EMELLE   yacht

Jersey City 1916 requisitioned 1940; 43 tons; 79.9ft × 12ft

Employed as a tender at Scapa Flow, she was driven from her moorings during a strong south-westerly gale and was driven ashore in Ore Bay, where she later caught fire and burnt out.
[*TNA: ADM.199/377*]

1 September IVANHOE   destroyer

Scotstoun 1937; 1,370 tons; 312ft × 33ft; 4 × 4.7in,
10 × torpedo tubes
Commander Philip Henry Hadow

Sailed from Immingham in company with other destroyers to lay a minefield in the southern North Sea. The first indication that they had entered waters already mined by the enemy was at 23.05 when her port paravane was carried away, followed by an explosion astern. It was soon after this that the *Express* was mined, losing her bows. *Ivanhoe* closed the damaged destroyer and lifted off twenty men, before proceeding with care to retrace her course. Despite this at 23.24 there was a large explosion forward as she detonated a mine. She remained afloat and after shoring up bulkheads found that she was able to proceed, stern first, at about 7 knots. The strain proved too great, however, and at 04.00 she shuddered and lost way, and it was believed that she had lost her propellers. At first light the destroyer *Garth* joined, with four motor torpedo boats and after taking off most of *Ivanhoe*'s men, a tow was rigged, despite coming under air attack during the morning from a German floatplane. Pumps were kept working, but it was found to be impossible to clear the engine rooms of water and at 13.45 all steam pressure was lost, and it was clear that she was settling, with a list that was slowly increasing. The survivors were removed by ships in company, including the *Kelvin* which had now joined. She remained stubbornly afloat and finally at 16.55 the *Kelvin* despatched her with a single torpedo. Her position was then 53.23N 03.50E. One officer and fifty-two men were lost. The subsequent enquiry was critical of the actions of Commander Hadow; the *Express* had survived and made it back to harbour after having her bows blown off, but *Ivanhoe* had been abandoned whilst still afloat. It was judged that adequate steps to localise the flooding had not been taken. When the steam failed for the last time, the decision to abandon her was made after a perfunctory examination. It was found that Hadow had prematurely abandoned his ship and Engineering Lieutenant Andrew Mahoney did not have a good knowledge of methods of damage control and had recommended the abandonment without sufficient reason.
[*TNA: ADM.1/12012; ADM.199/220*]

1 September ESK destroyer

Wallsend 1934; 1,405 tons; 318.3ft × 33.3ft; 4 × 4.7in, 8 × torpedo tubes, 60 mines

Lieutenant Commander Richard John Hollis Couch†

One of the consorts to the *Ivanhoe* during a mining operation in the southern North Sea that ran into an enemy-laid minefield. After the *Express* had been damaged by a mine, the *Esk* initially stopped, but was then seen to proceed, and in company with the *Icarus* and *Intrepid* passed to starboard of the stricken vessel. They were scarcely clear, when at 23.10 there was a large explosion forward when she detonated a mine which brought her to a halt. About 15 minutes later there was a second explosion amidships which broke her in two and she rapidly sank. There was just one survivor: 127 men died.

[TNA: ADM.1/12012]

1 September ROYALO trawler

Beverley 1916 requisitioned 1939; 248 tons; 120.5ft × 22ft; 1 × 12pdr

Skipper William Durrant Warford RNR†

After aircraft were seen to drop objects into the water, which were believed to be mines, the *Royalo* was one of a group of minesweeping trawlers ordered to sweep Mounts Bay. At 12.12 in position 50.06.47N 05.30.56W as she was under helm, a mine exploded under the after part of the ship and she rapidly sank. Twelve men were lost, with eight survivors. It was believed that she had continued to sweep in shallow water at low tide; orders clearly stated that mines in such waters should only be tackled at high water.

[TNA: ADM.1/10975; Larn vol 1 sec 4]

4 September SAUCY tug

Hessle 1918 requisitioned 1939; 579 tons; 155ft × 31ft

Lieutenant Archibald McFarlane Paton RNR

Employed as a salvage and rescue tug and based at Rosyth, she had completed the task of towing in a damaged Dutch merchant ship, when at 19.55, then being 1 mile to the west of Inchkeith light, she detonated an air-laid magnetic mine, which blew her stern off. Twenty-seven men were lost, with three survivors. The wreck has been found in position 56 02 11.5N, 003 10 45W.

[TNA: ADM.199/363; ADM.358/252]

6 September GODETIA corvette

Middlesbrough 1940; 940 tons; 190ft × 33ft; 1 × 4in

Lieutenant Commander George Victor Legassick RNR

Sailed from Methil on 31 August, in company with the Canadian destroyer *St Laurent* to escort a fourteen-ship convoy, OA207, to the south-west approaches. The convoy was routed around northern Scotland and the Hebrides, before entering the Irish Sea through the North Channel. On 6 September, the convoy was covered by a thick fog, reducing visibility to less than half a mile. At 23.00 when about 3 miles off Altacarry Head, in position 55.18N 05.57W, the corvette was rammed by the merchant ship *Marsa* (4,405 tons), which was a straggler from another convoy, OA209, the corvette being hit on the starboard side amidships. The tugs *Superman* and *Salvonia* were ordered to the scene and the destroyer *Duncan* was diverted to the area. Before any assistance could arrive at 02.15 the *Marsa* reported that the corvette had sunk in position 55.17N 06W and the *Lairdsgrove* had assisted in picking up the survivors, but thirty-three men died.

[TNA: ADM.199/372; ADM.199/837]

7 September RHODORA yacht

Southampton 1929 requisitioned 1939; 688 tons; 187ft × 29.2ft

Captain Charles Thomas Alexander Bunbury OBE

On patrol in the Bristol Channel, she was in collision with the steamship *Ngatira* (525 tons) at 05.00 when 12.5 miles to the west of Bull Point. The trawlers *Lord Wakefield* and *Kirkella* went to her assistance, but she steadily filled and sank. *Lord Wakefield* took her crew to Swansea.

[TNA: ADM.199/372]

7 September SHASHI III yacht

Rosneath 1934 requisitioned 1940; 16 tons; 41ft × 9.6ft

Based on the river Clyde for local patrols, she was lost at Port Glasgow as the result of an accidental fire after which she subsequently sank.

[TNA: BT.110/1282; Statement of Losses p8]

9 September DERVISH trawler

Beverley 1911 (*Norman*) requisitioned 1940; 346 tons; 140ft × 24ft; 1 × 6pdr

Skipper Ambrose Arthur Ashcroft RNR

Detonated a mine at 13.00 whilst in the approaches to the river Humber when about 2.6 miles to the south-east of the Humber Light vessel and subsequently sank. The wreck was reported to be awash with mast still visible. Four men were lost. The wreck was dispersed by explosives in 1948–9. The remains lie in position 53.31.17N 00.23.47E.

[TNA: ADM.199/2212; Larn vol 3 sec 4]

12 September SALVAGE KING tug

Paisley 1925 requisitioned 1940; 1,164 tons; 186.3ft × 36.2ft

Lieutenant Robert Hill RNR

Based at Kirkwall as a salvage tug, she carried Lieutenant Hill (who held a temporary commission as a Reserve officer) as the naval officer in charge, but the other officers were drawn from the merchant navy. Late on 11 September she received orders to

sail immediately to proceed to the assistance of a ship reported in difficulty off Noss Head, north-east of Wick. Although the night was very dark, the tug headed out of Scapa Flow at just after midnight, in a fresh breeze and a slight sea. Lieutenant Hill's actions soon disturbed Second Officer Corke, who had to point out that the course then being steered would take them uncomfortably close to the island of Swona. With some reluctance Hill altered course slightly, but then had to alter sharply when Swona appeared right ahead. The Second Officer then left the bridge, and was surprised when he and the First Officer, Ernest Fudge, returned a little later to find that Hill had also left the bridge, leaving the ship with no officer of the watch. First Officer Fudge then reduced the ship's speed, initiated a series of course alterations to take them clear of the island of Stroma, and then worked out a course to take the ship to the landfall of Duncansby Head. At 01.30 Hill re-appeared and ordered speed to be increased and an alteration in course. Fudge protested at this, warning that the new course would take them dangerously close to land, but this was ignored. A little later the faint outline of land could be discerned ahead. Although this was reported, Hill failed to react, and when, at 01.50 breakers were seen ahead, it was the First Officer who stepped in to order the wheel to put hard over. Despite that she took the ground and drove ashore, about 1.5 miles west of Duncansby Head. Efforts over the next few days by the tug *Buccaneer* and escort destroyer *Eglinton* to free her failed and she was abandoned as a total loss. The loss resulted in the court martial of Hill, who, by steering improper courses and absenting himself from the bridge, was found guilty of negligence. He was severely reprimanded and dismissed his ship. The Admiralty was thoroughly annoyed by the unnecessary loss; a valuable ship had been lost, '... thrown away by negligence.' It was ruled that Hill was 'unfitted for command' and his temporary commission was ordered to be cancelled, and he was not to be employed by the Navy again.
[TNA:ADM.156/201]

15 September DUNDEE sloop
Chatham 1932; 1,105 tons; 265ft × 35ft; 2 × 4in
Captain Oliver Maurice Fitzgerald Stokes DSO
Part of the escort to the eastbound Atlantic Convoy SC3 which had sailed on 4 September from Sydney, Cape Breton. At 22.34, when in position 56.50N 15.04W, the *Dundee*, stationed ahead of the right-hand column of the convoy was rocked by a large explosion aft when she was hit by a torpedo fired by the submerged *U 48* (Bleichrodt). This was followed at short intervals by two small, dull explosions, which were believed to be depth charges which had been blown off

the stern exploding. Investigation revealed that the after part of the ship had been wrecked. The engines were stopped, the lights went out and she was reported to be flooding rapidly from aft, so it was decided to abandon her. Boats were cleared away and floats launched, men transferring the escorts *Wanderer* and *St Laurent*. The latter destroyer stood by her and at 03.25 as she was still afloat, put a boarding party on board to rig a tow. The tow went well until a check later that morning showed that she was settling by the stern. At 10.00 the tow was slipped; the damaged sloop having then developed a list to port. At 12.45 her bows rose clear of the water and she disappeared 15 minutes later. Her position was then 56.45N 14.40W. Fourteen men were lost in the initial explosion. The subsequent Board of Enquiry was not impressed with the actions of the commanding officer in abandoning her so soon. When the party from the *St Laurent* had arrived onboard, over 4 hours after being abandoned, although the ship had been largely destroyed aft of 102 bulkhead the damage was concentrated on the port side aft. There was some water in the engine room, but the boiler room was found to be dry and the after bulkheads holding. With some effort steam could have been maintained and power restored. There was slow leakage through shaft glands and through strained plates, but this could have been kept under control by pumping and the *St Laurent* came in for some criticism by failing to bring more pumps into operation. Captain Stokes was informed that he had incurred their Lordships' displeasure at abandoning his ship too soon. It was noted that he was not to be employed at sea in command on one of His Majesty's Ships again.
[TNA:ADM.178/250]

23 September LOCH INVER trawler
Beverley 1930 requisitioned 1940; 356 tons;
140.3ft × 22.5ft; 1 × 12pdr
Skipper Thomas Hardcastle RNR†
Fitted as a patrol vessel and based at Harwich, she was part of a group of armed trawlers conducting a night patrol off the Suffolk coast, her station being about 3.5 miles off the Aldeburgh light float. In the early hours of the morning the trawler *Edwina*, in the adjacent sector, observed tracer fire and heard an explosion, and a short time later, was attacked by two enemy torpedo boats, engaging them with her 12pdr and machine guns as they disappeared into the night. When the *Loch Inver* failed to return to harbour as expected, a search of the area was conducted, and the *Lady Shirley* found a patch of wreckage, including a hammock and Carley float belonging to her. It would seem likely that she was the ship claimed to have been hit by torpedo by one of the torpedo boats, *S 13*. Fifteen men were killed.
[TNA:ADM.1/10786]

24 September MTB 15 motor torpedo boat
Hythe 1939; 22 tons; 60.4ft × 13.10ft; 2 × torpedoes
Lieutenant John Assheton Eardley-Willmott
In company with *MTBs 14, 16* and *17* sailed from
Felixstowe at 19.30 on 23 September to patrol in the
vicinity of the Sunk light vessel. At 20.53 as they were
about to alter course to make for the West Hinder buoy
there was a dull explosion, with a flash either side of
the boat and a cloud of black smoke rose to a height of
about 50ft. Water started entering immediately and she
started settling, stern first, but remained afloat, her bows
rising clear of the water. The other boats closed and
picked up the crew, most of whom were in the water.
She remained afloat until 01.30 when she finally slipped
under. She had probably run over a magnetic mine.
[TNA: ADM.199/220]

25 September WHITE DAISY drifter
Banff 1910 requisitioned 1940; 79 tons; 89ft × 19ft
Attached to the base at Lerwick in the Shetland Isles,
she went aground at 20.00 on 23 September on Baa
of Hascosay whilst attempting to enter Mid Yell Voe.
The crew abandoned the vessel. The Skipper and crew
managed to return with some assistance at 01.30 but
found that she had already refloated on the rising tide
and was taken by a strong wind towards Whalsey. She
eventually filled and sank at 07.00 between Whalsey
and Lunna Ness.
[TNA: ADM.199/377]

25 September STELLA SIRIUS trawler
Middlesbrough 1934 requisitioned 1939; 404 tons;
158.7ft × 26.7ft; 1 × 4in
Lieutenant Commander Alan Newhouse Benson RNVR
Based at Gibraltar, she was secured alongside the South
Mole, when the colony became the target for an air
raid mounted by Vichy French aircraft as retaliation for
the British attack on Dakar. A bomb struck the trawler
forward, causing major damage and starting an intense
fire. Lieutenant Commander Benson ordered the
magazines to be flooded, and fire-fighting commenced,
being aided both by dockyard workers and the crew of
the *Arctic Ranger*, berthed astern. Despite all their efforts
the fire gained, and it was feared that her depth charges
would 'cook' in the intense heat, so she was abandoned,
Kingston valves being opened and the intake pipe for
the condenser being broken to ensure that she sank.
[TNA: ADM.1/10776]

28 September RECOIL trawler
Emden 1938 (*Blankenburg*) requisitioned 1939; 344 tons;
135.8ft × 25.3ft
Lieutenant Ian Martin Wilson RNVR[†]
Ordered to carry out an anti-invasion patrol, she sailed
from Portsmouth during the evening of 27 September,

her station being to the south-west of Portland Bill.
She was last heard from soon after 21.00 when she
acknowledged a radio signal but failed to respond
when called at 04.00 and failed to return to harbour
the following morning as expected. A search of the area
by an RAF Lysander aircraft failed to find any trace of
her. Another trawler, the *Angle*, which had been in the
adjoining station, later reported hearing an explosion
the previous evening at approximately 21.16 and later at
03.15 when at the end of her patrol line, noted a strong
smell of oil. It was presumed that she had been mined
and lost with all twenty-five hands.
[TNA: ADM.199/239]

29 September SAPPHO yacht
Bowling 1935 requisitioned 1939; 386 tons; 135ft × 24.1ft
Commander Wilfred Ireland[†]
Fitted out as a patrol vessel, she disappeared whilst
conducting a night patrol in Falmouth Bay. Watchers
from the shore at Cadgwith saw a flash and heard the
rumble of an explosion at 20.33 which probably marked
her end. Attempts to raise her by radio in the early hours
failed. A search of the area the next morning failed to
find anything, although the drifter *United Boys* reported
seeing a patch of oil and debris 2 miles south-east of
Black Head, which included a lifebuoy from the *Sappho*.
She was probably a victim of the minefield laid by
German destroyers in Falmouth Bay during the night of
28/29 September. All thirty-two men on board were lost.
[TNA: ADM.1/10780; ADM.199/239]

30 September COMET trawler
Middlesbrough 1924 (*Tamura*) requisitioned 1939; 301
tons; 130.2ft × 24ft
Second Hand George Herbert Smith RNR
Part of an escort to a coastal convoy heading for
Falmouth, after they had arrived safely in the early
morning, she was ordered to put about to search for
the yacht *Sappho* that was missing (see above). As she
headed seaward across Falmouth Bay at 07.05, she
disappeared in a large cloud of black smoke and spray
as she detonated a mine. Two survivors were picked up,
but fifteen men were lost. Her position was noted as
50.06.5N 04.58.33W. Subsequent sweeping of the area
brought up three moored mines. The mines were part
of a field laid during the night of 28/29 September by
German destroyers.
[TNA: ADM.1/10780; ADM.199/239]

4 October RAINBOW submarine
Chatham 1930; 1,475/2,040 tons; 270ft × 29.11ft; 1 × 4in,
8 × torpedo tubes
Lieutenant Commander Lewis Peter Moore[†]
The fate of the *Rainbow* is somewhat uncertain. She
sailed from Alexandria 23 September to conduct a

patrol in the Gulf of Taranto but failed to return as expected on 19 October and was posted missing on that date. It was initially believed that she had been sunk whilst on the surface by the Italian submarine *Enrico Toti* on 15 October, but a re-assessment of that engagement has identified the victim as the *Triad*. On 3 October, the *Rainbow* had been ordered to shift her patrol area to the Straits of Otranto, to intercept Italian traffic to Albania. At 03.30 on 4 October the Italian merchant ship *Antonietta Costa* (5,900 tons), one of a small four-ship convoy under the escort of an armed merchant cruiser, struck an underwater object, when in approximate position 41.28N 18.05E. This was followed by what appeared to be an underwater explosion. The *Costa* was able to continue to Bari, and on examination in dry dock was found to have suffered damage from striking a large submerged object. This would have been in the new patrol area ordered for the *Rainbow* and the collision is believed to be the likely cause of her loss. Fifty-six officers and men were lost.
[*Hezlet vol 1 p60; http://uboat.net/allies/warships/ship/3405. html*]

5 October KINGSTON SAPPHIRE trawler
Beverley 1929 requisitioned 1939; 352 tons; 140.3ft × 24ft; 1 × 4in
Lieutenant Louis Alan Sayers RNR
En-route for Gibraltar, the trawler was about 30 miles to the west of Cape Trafalgar, on a dark, moonless night, when at 03.00 the bridge staff heard a strange hissing noise and were astonished when, a few moments later, a submarine broke the surface about 200ft away on the starboard beam. Action stations were immediately sounded, full speed called for and the course altered to steer for the enemy. The submarine was seen to turn to starboard and manoeuvred adeptly to avoid a collision. At 03.10 the 4in gun was able to open fire but had not had any success before the trawler was hit by a torpedo at 03.13. Seconds later there was another explosion as a depth charge that had been dislodged from the stern by the torpedo hit, exploded close under her stern. The *Kingston Sapphire* took a lurch to port, trimmed by the bow, the stern rose clear of the water and she sank very quickly. Her assailant had been the Italian submarine *Nani* (Polizzi). Two men were lost.
[*TNA: ADM.267/91*]

6 October SCOTCH THISTLE drifter
Portgordon 1913 requisitioned 1939; 84 tons; 88ft × 18.8ft
Skipper Walter Sheales RNR
Sailed from Lowestoft at 13.00 on 5 October bound for Burnham-on-Crouch but ran aground during the night off Frinton near the Whitaker beacon and was abandoned in the early hours of 6 October, the entire crew of eleven being taken off by the *Ipswich Trader*. She

was later reported to have sunk about 1 mile north-east by north from the Whitaker beacon.
[*TNA: ADM.199/2214*]

9 October SEA KING trawler
Selby 1916 requisitioned 1939; 321 tons; 138.6ft × 23.5ft; 1 × 12pdr
Skipper Leslie Rushby RNR[†]
Based in the Humber, she was one of several trawler-sweepers ordered to clear the convoy anchorage near the Chequer Shoal buoy, following reports of mines being dropped by aircraft. With the Group senior officer embarked they commenced sweeping along the swept channel with three other trawlers in company. At 18.43 there was a large explosion close astern, on the starboard quarter, as she detonated a mine. This covered her in spray and smoke, and she rapidly sank. Two officers and eleven men were killed. There was some criticism levelled at the other sweepers for failing to render prompt assistance, the survivors being rescued by a pilot cutter.
[*TNA: ADM.1/10782*]

11 October AISHA yacht
Selby 1934 requisitioned 1940; 117 tons; 102.5ft × 18ft
Lieutenant Leslie Ernest Humphries Brunton RNVR
Patrolling in the Thames Estuary, she was near the East Knob buoy as the destroyer *Jersey* approached from astern when there was a large explosion about 40 yards off the port side of the destroyer. This was presumed to be an influence mine detonating, and both ships reversed course, but as they did so there was an explosion close astern of *Aisha* and she immediately started settling by the stern. The *Jersey* closed, and a tow was rigged, but she foundered 7 cables (1,400 yards) to the east of the East Oaze buoy.
[*TNA: ADM.116/4353*]

12 October RESOLVO trawler
Beverley 1913 requisitioned 1939; 231 tons; 117.4ft × 22ft; 1 × 12pdr
Skipper Alexander Affleck RNR
Heading east at 7 knots in the Thames Estuary, at 20.30 as she was about 6 cables (1,200 yards) from the Knob Bell Buoy, she was rocked by a large underwater explosion as she triggered an influence mine close nearby. Making water she was run into shallow water to the south of the Outer Bar buoy at Sheerness and sank. The wreck lies in position 51.27.26N 00.50.54E.
[*TNA: ADM.267/127; Lloyd's War Losses vol 1 p136; Larn vol 2 sec 7*]

12 October WARWICK DEEPING trawler

Selby 1934 requisitioned 1939; 445 tons; 154ft × 26ft;
1 × 4in
Skipper John Robert Bruce RNR

Ordered to carry out a night patrol to the south of the Isle of Wight, she sailed from Spithead in company with the patrol vessel *Listrac*. At 22.35 a lookout sighted darkened ships on the port quarter, which appeared to be warships. Their identity remained uncertain until the leading ship came around to port and opened fire, the others following. The *Warwick Deeping* immediately increased power and altered round to starboard and commenced a zigzag. However, she was coming under a concentration of fire and was hit by two shells. The first struck the gun mounting, slewing the gun round so that the muzzle was resting on the deck. The next struck her on the port side just above the waterline, blowing a hole in the fish hold. Unable to return fire she tried to withdraw to the north, making a distress signal in the clear as she did so. The enemy had by now shifted their target to her consort, the *Listrac*, so the *Warwick Deeping* was able to make off into the dark, steadily settling, hoping to beach the ship. At 23.46 she was labouring so much it was clear that she could not make it to the shore and was abandoned, sinking rapidly. Her attackers had been ships of the Fifth Torpedo Boat Flotilla (*Falke, Greif, Kondor, Seeadler* and *Wolf*). Her wreck has been found and lies in position 50.34.21N 01.27.69W. There were no casualties.
[TNA: ADM.1/11212]

12 October LISTRAC auxiliary patrol vessel

Le Havre 1907 seized 1940; 778 tons; 196ft × 27.8ft;
1 × 100mm, 1 × 37mm
Lieutenant Kenneth Powell Kirkup RNR[†]

In company with the *Warwick Deeping* (above), for a night patrol off the Isle of Wight, she was ahead of her consort and was taken completely by surprise at the start of the action. The first they know that something was wrong was when gun flashes were seen, and shells splashed around the *Warwick Deeping*. The ship's company were sent to Action Stations, but fire was held, as they were not certain of the targets identity and range was difficult to ascertain in the darkness and confusion. At 23.40 she became the object of the enemy's fire and was immediately hit by a shell which burst in the boiler room. She started filling with water and settled quickly and sank. The only boat had been smashed, so rafts and floats were thrown overboard. Eleven men were killed in the action.
[TNA: ADM.1/11212]

12 October CH 06 submarine chaser

Dunkerque 1939 seized 1940; 107 tons; 116.6ft × 18.7ft;
1 × 75mm
Lieutenant William Brodie Galloway Galbraith[†]

In company with her sister *CH 07* (see below), conducting a night patrol to the south of the Isle of Wight when they encountered the aggressive Fifth Torpedo Boat Flotilla, who had already despatched 2 patrol ships (see above) and she was quickly overwhelmed. Firing was heard onshore at 01.00 and again at 01.14, which was supposed to mark the end of the submarine chasers. German radio transmissions were monitored throughout the night and the actions heard as they unfolded, and they confirmed the sinking of *CH 6* and that some survivors had been picked up. Nine men were lost.
[TNA: ADM.1/11212]

12 October CH 07 submarine chaser

Dunkerque 1939 seized 1940; 107 tons; 116.6ft × 18.7ft;
1 × 75mm
Sub-Lieutenant George Arthur Gabbett-Mulhallen DSC[†]

Consort to the *CH 06* (see above), and also taken by surprise and sunk in the same action. Twelve men were killed, with nine survivors being picked up by the German patrol craft *Greif*.
[TNA: ADM.1/11212]

13 October SUMMER ROSE drifter

Northwich 1919 requisitioned 1939; 96 tons;
86.5ft × 18.5ft
Skipper Walter George Robert Howes RNR

Ordered to sweep the area off Seaham harbour for magnetic mines using a towed 'skid' fitted with electric coils, she picked up her equipment at Sunderland and headed north. At 09.30 the skid was veered out and switched on, but as she altered course to take her clear of two other minesweepers, there was a large explosion close abaft the beam as she triggered a magnetic mine. She was thrown about violently, and the explosion covered the ship in water and smoke. As it cleared, she started to fill with water and sank, then being 4.9 cables to the north-east of Roker Light Pier. Two men were killed.
[TNA: ADM.267/91]

13 October DANUBE III tug

Selby 1924 requisitioned 1939; 234 tons; 110.2ft × 27.6ft;
1 × 12pdr
Lieutenant Richard Sullivan

Employed on examination service and based at Sheerness, they were ordered to investigate the wreck of the *Resolvo* (see 12 October) and fix the position, the Senior Examining Officer being embarked. At 08.30 they were approaching the site at slow speed,

when a few moments later there was a heavy explosion under the port quarter. The vessel heeled over to port, the stern lifting clear of the water before settling back with the decks awash aft. After 5 minutes she started to slowly heel over to port and was clearly sinking by the stern, the bow rising out of the water. She continued to roll over and sank stern first. She was then 2 cables (400 yards) from the Outer Bar buoy. It was presumed that she had triggered a magnetic mine. Eleven men were lost.
[TNA: ADM.1/11209]

14 October LORD STAMP trawler
Selby 1935 requisitioned 1939; 448 tons; 157.3ft × 26.1ft
Chief Skipper James Donald McKay RNR[†]
One of the escorts for a convoy on passage from Dartmouth to Spithead, she blew up and sank at 01.30 off Portland Bill in position 50.19N 02.47W, presumably after hitting a mine. An initial search was made by the *Hertfordshire* for survivors, and at first light *MA/SB1* continued the search being joined by Lysander and Roc aircraft, and although wreckage was found, there were no survivors. Twenty-five men were lost.
[TNA: ADM.199/369]

15 October APPLETREE drifter
1907 requisitioned 1939; 84 tons; 85ft × 16ft
Boom Skipper William Percy Waters RNR
Employed as a local patrol vessel based at Oban, she was patrolling the approaches to that harbour, the night being dark and the weather poor, with heavy rain. At 20.00 a masthead and starboard light of a vessel was seen, apparently heading for Lismore Island. It was difficult to make out the craft in the weather conditions and the night visual challenge was ordered to be made, which was done, but received no response. The masthead lights were switched on and visual signals continued for several minutes, but the stranger still showed no reply, and Skipper Waters ordered the Lewis gun to be manned as a precaution. At 20.17 in position 56.27.10N 005.34.20W the stranger drove straight into the drifter, hitting her on the port side, just abaft the beam. Water poured in and the crew hastily scrambled on board their assailant, which had her bows still firmly embedded into their side. The Skipper and Chief Engineer remained on board in the hope that they could keep her afloat long enough to beach her, but she filled and sank about 4 minutes after the impact. The stranger was revealed as *RAF Pinnace-50*, on a high-speed transit from Colonsay to Oban, and had not seen the drifter until the last minute and despite putting the engines astern could not avoid a collision.
[TNA: ADM.1/10773]

15 October TRIAD submarine
Barrow 1939; 1,090/1,575 tons; 265.6ft × 26.7ft; 1 × 4in, 10 × torpedo tubes
Lieutenant Commander George Stevenson Salt[†]
Sailed from Malta 9 October to conduct a patrol in the Gulf of Squillace, southern Italy, in the vicinity of Punta Stilo, and then proceed to Alexandria on completion. When she failed to return on 20 October she was posted as missing. Her fate was at first uncertain, and it was believed she may have fallen victim to either an air attack or a minefield. However, it is now reasonably certain that she was the victim of a surface gun action with the Italian submarine *Enrico Toti* – an action originally believed to have involved the *Rainbow* (see 4 October). At a little after midnight on 14 October, the *Toti*, proceeding on the surface in bright moonlight sighted a surfaced submarine ahead. The *Toti* altered course to close and as she did so the stranger opened fire with a deck gun, but the shells passed overhead. The Italian submarine opened fire with machine guns and rifles as well as the deck gun, and evidently caused casualties amongst the stranger's deck crew. The pair passed on opposite courses about 20ft apart, still firing at each other, the Italian submarine being hit and several sailors wounded. The *Toti* executed a turn to port and fired a torpedo at her opponent, which was then attempting to submerge, but missed. As the stranger was submerging the *Toti* continued to fire with her deck gun and scored a direct hit, setting off a multi-coloured explosion, and she sank. The position given for the engagement, 38.16N 17.37E, is at the eastern edge of the patrol area of the *Triad*, and it is now accepted that she was probably the victim. Fifty-two men were lost.
[Evans pp263–5]

15 October MISTLETOE drifter
Plymouth 1890 requisitioned 1939; 46 tons; 59ft × 18.2ft
Skipper Donald Charles Hockney RNR[†]
Employed as a tender in the river Humber, she was despatched to warn local fishing vessels that aircraft had been seen dropping what were believed to be mines during the early hours of the morning. At 07.45 she was seen approaching the North Middle buoy when there was a large explosion and she disappeared in a cloud of smoke and spray. The *Better Hope* and *Chameleon* closed the position and picked up two survivors. Four men lost their lives.
[TNA: ADM.199/220]

16 October MTB 106 motor torpedo boat
Hampton 1940 (ex-*DCTB 2*); 9 tons; 44.3ft × 9.6ft; 1 × torpedo tube
Lieutenant Ian Andrew Bryant Quarrie RNVR
The difficulty of dealing with influence mines, both magnetic and acoustic, led to some hazardous practices,

including the use of high-speed craft. It was hoped they could detonate the mines as they ran over them, their speed carrying them clear of the main explosion. This was the task undertaken by *106;* to clear the way in the Thames Estuary for the passage of an important convoy, she dutifully sped at 35 knots in a series of laps in a designated area near the Nore Light Vessel. As she slowed to turn, ready to commence her next lap, she detonated a mine underneath her, which demolished the boat, throwing the crew into the sea. Luckily, all survived, but *106* disappeared.

[Reynolds & Cooper, Mediterranean MTBs p18]

17 October **DUNDALK** minesweeper

Port Glasgow 1919; 710 tons; 220ft × 28.6ft; 1 × 4in, 1 × 12pdr

Lieutenant Commander Frederick Arthur Kirkpatrick

During 16 October, *Dundalk* was working in company with three other minesweepers, the *Sutton, Speedwell* and *Fitzroy*, around number 54A buoy, off Orfordness, sweeping for moored contact mines. At 17.27 sweeps were ordered to be taken in and when this was complete, they formed up in line ahead, 3 cables (600 yards) apart, to return to Harwich, the *Dundalk* being second in line. At 18.31 then being about 4 miles from 54A buoy, a very heavy explosion took place on the *Dundalk's* starboard side. This blew a 30ft hole in the side, which extended from the waterline to the upper deck and the ship was swathed in steam from a fractured steam pipe. Water flooded number 1 boiler room, and number 2 boiler room started to slowly flood, forcing the fires to be quenched. Her sister, the *Sutton*, took her in tow, all except the towing crew being taken off. At 02.00 the tug *Muria* arrived on scene but she had scarcely taken over when the minesweeper rolled over and sank at 02.43 in position 51.56.54N 01.26.42E. Four men were killed.

[TNA: ADM.267/91; ADM.116/4353]

18 October **H 49** submarine

Dalmuir 1919; 410/510 tons; 164.6ft × 15.9ft; 4 × torpedo tubes

Lieutenant Commander Richard Evelyn Coltart DSC†

Ordered to conduct a patrol in the southern North Sea off the Dutch coast, she sailed from Harwich on 17 October. The following day at 15.10 when off the Texel, with a heavy mist cloaking the area, the opportunity was taken to bring the submarine to the surface. Very soon after she had done so several surface ships loomed out of the mist and she was ordered to submerge. The ships were a group of armed trawlers who sighted the conning tower of the submarine as it disappeared underwater and promptly commenced a sonar search of the area, which resulted at 16.20 in two of the trawlers, *Uj 116* and *Uj 118* obtaining a contact

at 1,800m range. This was immediately prosecuted, with six depth charges being dropped in two groups. As a result of this attack, power was lost in the submarine and she sank to lie on the bottom. The crew worked to restore some power, but it was found that water was entering at several points. At 17.00 the attacks recommenced with another six charges, which resulted in oil and large bubbles of air coming to the surface and more depth charge runs brought up a large quantity of oil and debris. As they investigated the site, the attackers found one survivor swimming in the oil, which proved to be Leading Stoker George Oliver, who seems to have been blown out of the boat as it was crushed by the explosions. Twenty-six men were lost.

[Evans pp246–8]

18 October **KINGSTON CAIRNGORM** trawler

Beverley 1935 requisitioned 1939; 448 tons; 160.6ft × 26.6ft; 1 × 4in

Former Hull-based trawler, used as a patrol vessel, the *Kingston Cairngorm* was damaged when she grounded off Chichester during a winter storm in January 1940, and was subsequently paid off. In October she was taken in tow by the *Caroline Moller* to be refitted for further service but detonated a mine to the south of Portland. The patrol trawler *Cape Comorin* proceeding from Yarmouth to meet an east coast convoy heard a large explosion at 03.18 and on investigation discovered the *Kingston Cairngorm* still afloat, but in a sinking condition. Believing a submarine may have been responsible the trawler *Ruby* closed to investigate the area with Asdic and did gain a possible contact which resulted in a depth charge being dropped, but without result. A tow was rigged, but she steadily settled and eventually sank. She had probably run over a mine. The wreck lies in position 50.23N 02.42W. There were no casualties.

[TNA: ADM.199/220]

19 October **VENETIA** destroyer

Govan 1917; 1,090 tons; 300ft × 29.6ft; 4 × 4in

Lieutenant Commander Desmond Lisburn Curtis Craig†

Returning to Dover, in company with the destroyers *Walpole* and *Garth*, following a night patrol in the southern North Sea the ships were in line ahead, the *Venetia* leading. At 08.50 as they were approaching the East Knob buoy there was a large explosion under the hull as she detonated a mine. The explosion took place under the searchlight platform and seemed to be followed immediately after by a second detonation, further aft. Her back was broken by the explosion, the amidships section becoming awash, with the bow and stern rising clear of the water. She eventually broke up, the stern remaining afloat for about 20 minutes, the bow rolling over to starboard and floated for an hour

before sinking. Forty men were killed. Her position was noted as 51.31.2N 01.08E.
[TNA: ADM.1/10792]

19 October **VELIA** trawler

Selby 1914 (*Sitvel*) requisitioned 1940; 290 tons; 130.2ft × 23.5ft
Second Hand Cyril Kaiser RNR

Ordered to conduct a patrol between the Sunk light vessel and the Longsand Head buoy, it was decided to anchor for the night due to thick fog. At 07.40 the anchor was weighed with the intention of resuming her patrol when it was seen that there was a mine and mooring hooked over the flukes of the anchor. The brake was hastily released, and the anchor promptly dropped back into the water. The cable ran out and a moment later there was a large explosion, when the mine, carried by the anchor, hit the bottom. The forward part of the trawler was demolished, the bows disappearing back to the fish room bulkhead although she remained afloat. Other trawlers, hearing the explosion had closed the area, and the *Stella Carina* lifted off the crew, whilst the *Hekla* rigged a tow. Despite their efforts, she steadily settled and finally went under at 15.30. There were no casualties. Mr Kaiser was praised for his efforts after the explosion, although the Admiralty was not impressed with the actions on sighting the mine – one officer commented that to drop the anchor with a mine attached was 'lunatic'.

Note – announcing the loss, the Admiralty named Sub-Lieutenant Lionel John George Shoobridge RNVR as the commanding officer, but the court of enquiry established that the senior man on board at the time of the loss was Mr Kaiser.
[TNA: ADM.199/239]

19 October **BRAS D'OR** trawler

Sorel 1919 (*Lightship 25*) requisitioned 1939; 265 tons; 124.6ft × 23.6ft; 1 × 4in
Lieutenant Charles Avery Hornsby RCNR†

Royal Canadian Navy. Ordered to sail from Clarke City, Quebec, to follow the Romanian steamer *Inginer Vlassopol* to Sydney, Nova Scotia, and on arrival, detain her. The pair sailed on 18 October, to transit the St Lawrence, but the merchant vessel arrived at Sydney alone. On being questioned, the ship's officers indicated that they had seen the trawler's lights disappear at 03.50 on the 19th but otherwise had seen nothing untoward. No trace of her was found, and it was presumed that she was lost due to stress of weather. She had grounded shortly before sailing, and this may have strained her hull. Thirty men were lost.
[McKee & Darlington p21]

21 October **MTB 17** motor torpedo boat

Hythe 1939; 22 tons; 60.4ft × 13.10ft; 2 × torpedoes
Lieutenant Robert Ian Tardrew Falkner

Part of a group ordered to carry out a night patrol off the Dutch coast, she sailed from Felixstowe in company with her sisters *MTB 14* and *MTB 16*, at 20.00 on 20 October. The trio investigated Nieuwpoort roads, but found no suitable targets, so continued to the north-east. At 23.59 as they approached the Stroombank they made out the darkened shape of a ship, which seemed to be about 400 tons and they turned out to seawards, intending to attack her from the north. *MTB 17* led as they closed the target at speed, but when she tried to release her torpedo from the stern trough, it failed to leave the rails. The target, now aware of their presence, fired flares and opened an inaccurate fire with small arms. *14* and *16* then made attack runs, but both of their torpedoes missed the target. *MTB 17* had circled round and made a second attempt. By now the area was fully alert and was lit by searchlights and star shell. Several shore batteries were now firing, and several shells were landing uncomfortably close. At 00.11 she fired her torpedo, but seconds later, as she started a turn to starboard there was an explosion under the boat, which blew overboard several of the crew, and she started to sink. With some difficulty the small skiff carried on board was launched, the stern sinking as they did so. Her companions closed and picked up the crew, all of whom survived, and before they left the scene fired repeatedly into the bow section which was then floating vertically. It was believed that the explosion was caused by her own torpedo. The firing arrangements on the early torpedo boats meant launching the torpedo from a trough that extended out of the stern, and it seems reasonably certain that after firing, the torpedo had run under the boat and struck the seabed where it exploded directly underneath her. The engineer testified that the bottom of the boat had been blown out, with the centre engine falling out. Despite the damage done, the wreck of the boat drifted into shallow water and was found the next morning by German naval forces which towed her into Ostend. However, she was so severely damaged that she was scrapped.
[TNA: ADM.1/10731: Warship 1992 p138]

21 October **WAVEFLOWER** trawler

Selby 1929 requisitioned 1939; 368 tons; 150.3ft × 24.5ft; 1 × 12pdr
Skipper Robert McKay MacDonald RNR†

One of a force of three armed trawlers engaged in a night patrol along the swept channels off the Essex/Suffolk coastline, the group were under the charge of Lieutenant William James Curtayne RNVR, who was embarked in the *Waveflower*. They proceeded in line ahead, the *Waveflower* leading, until at 20.30 the

William Wesney next in line, realised that they could no longer see the leader, who had evidently stretched ahead. The result was that *Waveflower* found herself on her own, and at 22.00 decided to turn back to try and regain contact with her consorts. On failing to do this, she resumed her course to the north-east, but as she did so, she detonated a mine. This was at 23.55, about 3 miles to the west of the Aldeburgh light float. The explosion was just abaft the wheelhouse on the starboard side and broke the trawler's back. She broke up and sank in less than a minute after taking a rapid list to starboard. The other vessels, meanwhile, having realised that they had lost their leader, made no effort to rejoin, but decided to anchor. They heard the explosion but did not think it 'anything out of the ordinary' and did not bother to investigate. They could make out the shape of another trawler at anchor some distance away and presumed that this was the *Waveflower*. Only at first light, about 04.00, did they realise their mistake, and got under way to try and regain contact. At 07.50 they found wreckage, and then a Carley float with the survivors onboard. The court of enquiry was disturbed by the lack of action that night. Lieutenant Curtayne in the *Waveflower*, as the Group Commander, had not been concerned about stretching ahead and had only turned back on the advice of the skipper. As senior officer of the detached ships, Lieutenant Martin Gardner RNVR in the *Joseph Button* apparently failed to understand which of the trawlers should be in which station. Skipper Farrow in the *William Wesney* had lost contact with the leader by steaming at the wrong speed and had failed to make any attempt to keep station. No one had taken charge of the detached ships and no one had thought to investigate the explosion. All were informed that they had 'incurred their Lordships' displeasure' and Lieutenants Curtayne and Gardner were additionally informed that were to serve as watchkeeping officers only, not being placed in a position of responsibility until they had gained further experience and training. Fourteen men died.
[TNA: ADM.1/10891]

21 October JOSEPH BUTTON trawler
Beverley 1917 requisitioned 1939; 290 tons;
125.5ft × 23.5ft; 1 × 12pdr
Skipper James Drennan RNR

Part of the group, along with the *Waveflower* and *William Wesney*, that had been sent to carry out a night patrol off the Essex/Suffolk coast, she had Lieutenant Martin Gardner RNVR embarked as senior officer. With the loss of the *Waveflower* (see above), they spent much of the early part of the morning searching for survivors, and this caused a delay in their next task, which was to 'sweep through' the passage of a southbound

coastal convoy. Because of their late arrival at the start position, they found that fleet minesweepers with the convoy had passed and that they were consequently forced to sweep on the starboard side of the channel, abreast of the convoy. This meant that the water they were sweeping did not overlap that covered by the fleet sweepers. At 09.05 in position 52.06N 01.48E a mine exploded under *Joseph Button*'s stern. A high black plume of smoke and spray was thrown up and the trawler sank rapidly by the stern in less than a minute. Five men were lost.
Note: often (and wrongly) listed as *Joseph Burton*
[TNA: ADM.1/10891]

22 October MARGAREE destroyer
Hebburn 1932 (*Diana*) transferred 1940; 1,375 tons;
317.7ft × 33ft; 4 × 4.7in, 2 × 2pdr, 8 × torpedo tubes
Commander Joseph Wilton Rouer RCN

Royal Canadian Navy. Sailed 20 October from Liverpool as escort to Convoy OL8 into the Atlantic, where the ships would be dispersed. The destroyer took station ahead of the convoy which was steaming in two columns. At 01.00 the *Port Fairy* (8,072 tons), leading ship of the port column, saw the *Margaree* fine on the starboard bow and moving across the line of advance. Engines were put astern, and the helm put over to port, but moments later she struck the destroyer under the bridge and cut her in half. The forward section rolled over and sank immediately. The after section remained afloat and thirty-four survivors managed to get aboard the *Port Fairy*. The merchant ship then used her 4in gun to fire several rounds into the wreck, with little obvious effect, but she was abandoned, listing heavily to starboard and sinking by the stern. A total of 142 men died. With the loss of all the bridge personnel it was impossible to determine why the destroyer had steered across the bows of the advancing convoy but it was presumed to have been either an error of judgement or mechanical failure.
[McKee & Darlington p23]

22 October HICKORY trawler
Leith 1940; 530 tons; 150ft × 27.6ft; 1 × 12pdr
Lieutenant Ralph Eric Hardinge RNZVR

Engaged in sweeping in the area of Portland with two of her sisters, the *Birch* and *Pine*, they were 12.5 miles to the east of the Bill when at 12.50 she detonated a mine under her bows. A large column of water, smoke and debris was thrown up and the whole of the bridge structure collapsed. She at once heeled over to port and sank rapidly by the bows. The stern rose clear with her propellers still turning as she sank her position being noted as 50.26.24N 02.45.48W. Twenty-three men were lost.
[TNA: ADM.267/91]

25 October DUTHIES drifter

Sandhaven 1914 requisitioned 1939; 89 tons;
88.7ft × 19.4ft

Employed as a range safety vessel at Arbroath, she was entering the port of Montrose when an air raid took place, with He 111 aircraft dropping fifteen bombs in the harbour. The *Duthies* was sunk following a near miss as she was securing to the jetty. All the crew were saved.
[TNA: ADM.199/364]

25 October LORD INCHCAPE trawler

Selby 1924 requisitioned 1939; 338 tons; 138.8ft × 23.8ft;
1 × 12pdr

Skipper Oliver Bert Bell RNR

In company with two other trawlers, *Lord Grey* and *St Melante*, she was employed in sweeping Cawsand Bay for contact mines. A mine was brought to the surface at 09.00 and disposed of, and at 09.25 as they formed up to carry out another sweep, there was an explosion close to the stern of the *Inchcape*. As the smoke and water thrown up cleared, she started to settle by the stern as water entered, hull plates evidently having been sprung. The engine room reported a steam pipe had fractured forcing the engines to stop. They dropped anchor and the boat was ordered to be hoisted out, but as this was being done a man fell overboard and disappeared. This caused some confusion and any work on clearing water from the trawler was delayed in the search for him. Not until 10.55 was the drifter *Salpa* called alongside to rig a tow, and more time elapsed whilst this was achieved. The tow finally got under way for Plymouth with the trawler steadily getting lower in the water, and at 11.55 when 7 cables from Mount Batten breakwater she sank. The subsequent enquiry criticised the lack of urgency in the officers of all the trawlers; if one of her companions had promptly taken her in tow, she would have been saved. One man was lost.
Note: the ship was salvaged during 1942 and again taken into service.
[TNA: ADM.267/92]

27 October PERSEVERE drifter

1937 requisitioned 1939; 20 tons

Employed as a dockyard tender at Rosyth, she sank following a large explosion, presumed to have been a mine, when the drifter was about 100 yards from the East Gunnet Ledge Buoy, Firth of Forth. Both men on board at the time were saved.
[Lloyd's War Losses vol 1 p146; TNA: ADM.199/363]

28 October HARVEST GLEANER drifter

Oulton Broad 1918 requisitioned 1939; 96 tons;
86.2ft × 18.5ft

Skipper Victor James Thompson RNR

The drifter sailed from Lowestoft at 11.00, with Lieutenant G C Herbert RNVR embarked, to carry out an inspection of the boom defences off Sizewell. The weather was fine, with low cloud. At 12.51 when she was off Southwold, an aircraft emerged from the cloud almost overhead, and dived straight down on them, dropping a number of bombs. One bomb struck the ship on the starboard side of the engine room, where it exploded, and a second went through the upper deck and entered the mess deck to exit through the side, just below the waterline. She immediately lost power and she started to flood fore and aft. She was ordered to be abandoned, the men jumping into the water, to be picked up about 30 minutes later by the drifter *Quicksilver*. Four men were lost. Her wreck lies in position 52.20.15N 01.42.19E.
[TNA: ADM.199/102; Larn vol 3 sec 2]

30 October STURDY destroyer

Greenock 1919; 905 tons; 265ft × 26.8ft; 2 × 4in, 1 × 2pdr,
40 mines

Lieutenant Commander George Tyndale Cooper

In company with her sister *Shikari*, sailed from Londonderry on 26 October to rendezvous with inbound Convoy SC8 at first light of 28 October. The wind was freshening, until by the morning of the 28th it was blowing a Force 7 to 8 gale with a high sea. There was no sign of the expected convoy, but with visibility little more than 4 to 5 miles, and poor weather, it was presumed that the convoy had been delayed. That evening the pair received a new position of the convoy and a new course was set. The night was dark and at approximately 20.20 she lost sight of the *Shikari* but maintained her course and speed. At daylight on 29 October her companion was nowhere in sight. The weather continued to be poor, with a full gale from the south-east and with fuel running low it was decided to return to Londonderry. Course was set for Inistrahull Light at reduced speed. At 04.30 white water was seen on the port bow and it was realised that it was breakers. Engines were stopped, but she hit the ground hard, immediately heeling over to starboard. Attempts to free her by putting the engines astern failed, and it was clear that she was held fast, and the wind and waves were driving her further onto the rocks. It was decided to launch a raft through the surf with two volunteers to take a line to the shore, but although they made it ashore, the line was lost, and the pair indicated that they would try and find help. The ship was pounding heavily, and it was feared that she was breaking up, and another attempt to get a line ashore was made. For this the whaler was launched but this capsized, throwing the men into the water, drowning five of them. At 05.10 the ship broke in half. The stern portion was swept round to port until it was at right angles to the bows. Soon after this, people could be seen on the shore, who signalled by light 'help is coming'. Despite this another attempt to take a line

ashore was made by two ratings swimming through the surf, which succeeded, and the line was safely secured. However, the party ashore signalled for the ship to wait until the tide turned. Later that morning with the tide having largely left her and the weather having moderated somewhat, all the men made the shore along the line. The subsequent enquiry into the loss convened by Flag Officer in Charge, Greenock, ruled that Lieutenant Commander Cooper was not to blame for the loss and there was no evidence of neglect. This decision created ripples of disapproval in the Admiralty. Their Lordships, on reviewing the case, thought there certainly was evidence of neglect and the proper procedure was for Cooper to have been court-martialled. A valuable destroyer had been lost, largely because the commanding officer, uncertain of his position due to a lack of sun-sights, had steered towards the land on a dark and stormy night. The enquiry had established that bearings of a radio beacon could have been taken to assist in fixing his position but had not been. The Admiralty Board opined that soundings could also have been taken, using the Kelvin sounding machine, but Cooper did not seem to have been prepared for this. Vice Admiral Watson at Greenock was informed that he had incurred their Lordships' displeasure for failing to order a court bmartial, and '… stating an illogical opinion on the merits of the case'. Watson defended himself by pointing out the officer's inexperience and suggested that the Kelvin machine was practically unworkable in the weather conditions of the time. Lieutenant Commander Cooper was informed that he had incurred their Lordships' displeasure and was reduced to half-pay for 6 weeks. It was also noted that he should not be given another destroyer command.
[TNA: ADM.1/11542]

30 October ML 109 motor launch
Littlehampton 1940; 57 tons; 110ft × 17.5ft; 1 × 3pdr
Lieutenant Anthony Kirk RNR[†]
Based at Grimsby, she was ordered to sail in company with ML 106 to rendezvous with a southbound convoy. Soon after sailing however, 109 suffered engine problems, and was forced to shut down two of her three engines as they were overheating but decided to press on. At 17.55 when 1.85 miles south of Spurn Point Light there was a large explosion under her hull as she detonated a mine, followed almost immediately afterwards by a second explosion, about 20 yards astern as another mine was set off. Her back was broken, and she settled rapidly. 106 closed and picked the survivors up from the water and she was left in a waterlogged condition and believed to have sunk soon after. Three men were lost.
[TNA: ADM.1/11211]

(30) October SEAGEM tug
Hardinxveld 1939 requisitioned 1939; 92 tons; 75ft × 20.1ft
Master Albert James Corps[†]
Sailed from Dundee en-route for Middlesbrough and was seen at 05.15 on 30 October as she passed the South Gare signal station, at the entrance to the river Tees, but was not seen or heard from after. It was presumed that she had been lost, probably through striking a mine sometime after this. All seven men on board were killed.
[Lloyd's War Losses vol 2 p1286]

30 October ATTENDANT salvage tender
Govan 1913 requisitioned 1940; 357 tons; 124.7ft × 27.2ft
Vaguely listed in the official Statement of Losses as being 'Lost, cause and place unknown' in 1943, she actually ran aground on the northern side of the Isle of Canna in poor weather at this time, whilst on passage from Stornaway to Oban. The crew of eight men abandoned her and spend 5 hours in the lifeboat before getting ashore at Tarbert Bay. Written off as a loss, the vessel was subsequently salvaged but was sold out of service in 1942.
[TNA: BT.358/125; http://clydesite.co.uk/clydebuilt/viewshipasp?id=6177;www.nts.org.uk/stories/john-lorne-campbells-canna-diaries]

31 October MTB 16 motor torpedo boat
Hythe 1939; 18 tons; 60.4ft × 13.10ft; 2 × torpedo tubes
Lieutenant Philip Francis Gould
In company with her sister MTB 15, the pair sailed at 08.15 from Felixstowe heading for Sheerness. An hour later, at 09.15 when 2 miles from the Barrow Deep light vessel, a mine detonated about 30 yards off the port beam of MTB 16. The boat was shaken considerably, and was stopped to check for damage, but all appeared well, and the pair got under way again. They had barely done so, when at 09.35 another mine exploded, this time directly underneath her. She was lifted out of the water and as she crashed back down the engine room started to flood. The other torpedo boats nearby, MTB 34 and MTB 81, closed, took off the crew and attempted to take her in tow, but the tow parted. It was reconnected, but at 13.32 again parted as she settled deeper into the water and the boat sank by the stern.
[TNA: ADM.267/91]

1 November TORBAY- II drifter
Selby 1910 requisitioned 1940; 83 tons; 83.3ft × 18.2ft
Skipper William Benjamin Jenner RNR
In company with the drifters Ut Prosim and Young Mun, she sailed from Dover at 16.00 to carry out a local patrol, the ships forming up into a line ahead formation, the Torbay being the sternmost ship. When the group was about 3 miles off Dover, a large group of aircraft

identified as Ju 87 dive bombers were seen approaching from the south-east. The aircraft carried out a sustained attack on the drifters, which replied with machine guns – the only armament they had. None of the ships were hit, but the *Torbay-II* suffered several near misses, which shook her considerably and caused sufficient damage to start leaks. She was turned inshore, intending to run into shallow water, but before this could be achieved, she filled and sank. One man was killed.
[TNA: ADM.116/4353; ADM.199/102]

1 November TILBURY NESS trawler
Beverley 1917 (*Joseph Barrett*) requisitioned 1939; 279 tons; 125.5ft × 23.5ft; 1 × 12pdr
Skipper Sherad James Catchpole RNR
Based at Sheerness, the trawler was working in company with the LL (magnetic sweep) equipped tugs *Salvo* and *Solitaire*, the group operating near to the East Oaze Lightship in the Thames Estuary. At 14.30 a large group of aircraft was observed to be closing from the east, over twenty being counted, with several fighter escorts. They commenced a dive-bombing attack on the ships, the *Salvo* having bombs bursting all around her. The *Tilbury Ness* then became the target, with up to six aircraft dive-bombing her. Most bombs exploded around her, but she was hit twice. One bomb struck the starboard quarter, the second went through the upper deck to explode in the engine room. She rapidly filled with water, broke in half and sank. Ten of her crew were killed. The aircraft went on the attack and sink the light vessel and a merchant ship, the *Letchworth*. Skipper Catchpole was rebuked by an enquiry for not having his ship in an efficient state of readiness.
[TNA: ADM.199/1175; ADM.116/4353; Hardy p146]

1 November PLACIDAS FAROULT lighter
Martenshoek (*Apollinaris*) 1927 seized 1940; 136 tons; 85ft × 20.4ft
A former French merchant vessel forcibly taken over by the Royal Navy whilst laying at Salcombe in June 1940, she was pressed into service locally as a gate vessel for the boom. During the night of 31 October, the port was affected by a strong south-west gale and despite being secured by five anchors, she dragged, and one of her anchor cables parted, allowing her to swing with the tide. Heavy seas prevented any attempt to board her. At 10.30 the next morning another anchor cable parted, and she was carried onto the Blackstone rock, and was wrecked.
[TNA: ADM.199/372]

2 November GOODWILL drifter
Requisitioned 1940; 28 tons
Sub-Lieutenant Charles Alexander Whitney-Smith RNVR
Fitted out as a local patrol vessel and based at Rosyth, she foundered after she detonated a mine at 11.15 when

3.1 miles to the north-east of Inchkeith. There were no casualties.
[TNA: ADM.199/363]

2 November RINOVIA trawler
Beverley 1931 (*Blakkur*) requisitioned 1939; 403 tons; 142.7ft × 25.1ft; 1 × 12pdr
Chief Skipper Thomas Fraser DSC
Whilst off Falmouth, she detonated a mine which exploded under her stern, when about 2.9 miles off St Anthony Light, and quickly sank with the loss of fourteen men. The wreck lies in position 50.05.50N 04.58.57W
[TNA: ADM.199/372; Larn vol 1 sec 4]

3 November LAURENTIC armed merchant cruiser
Belfast 1927 requisitioned 1939; 18,724 tons; 578.2ft × 75.4ft; 8 × 5.5in, 3 × 4in
Captain Eric Paul Vivian
Returning to Liverpool following an Atlantic patrol to the east of the Azores, they were to the west of Ireland, when at 21.00 they received a message from the merchant ship *Casanare* indicating that they had been torpedoed. The position was only a few miles ahead of them, and Captain Vivian was discussing the course to take to avoid the danger area, when at 21.50 she was hit by a torpedo on the starboard side of the engine room. The ship took an immediate list to port as the engine room flooded. Boats were ordered to be hoisted out, floats readied for release and the crew were sent to Abandon Ship stations except for some gun crews and essential personnel. As this was being completed a submarine broke surface on the starboard bow. There was some confusion, as only the aft gun crews had remained closed-up, the forward guns had been abandoned, but after some moments she was able to open fire, with both high explosive and star shell. The submarine promptly submerged. Shortly after this she was hit by another torpedo, this exploding on the starboard side in number 4 hold. The boats were now cleared away and floats released, the ship settling and heeling quickly, and she sank slowly by the stern. Her approximate position was 54.09N 13.44W. The survivors were picked up the following morning by the destroyer *Achates*. Fifty-one men died. The court of enquiry found that Captain Vivian could have acted more promptly in steering clear of the danger area around the *Casanare*. Vivian was severely affected by the loss and was later diagnosed as suffered from 'profound melancholia' and it was noted that he would be invalided from the service. Her attacker had been *U 99* (Kretschmer).
[TNA: ADM.1/11215]

4 November PATROCLUS armed merchant cruiser
Greenock 1923 requisitioned 1939; 11,314 tons;
498.8ft × 62.3ft; 6 × 6in, 2 × 12pdr
Captain Gerald Charles Wynter†

Like the *Laurentic* (above), she was returning to Liverpool from an Atlantic patrol, being routed to the west of Ireland. She also received the distress message at 21.00 from the *Casanare*, and the position given was only 30 miles away. Captain Wynter decided that rather than steer a course to avoid the danger, she should proceed to her assistance, despite the objections of other officers. She arrived on the scene and sighted several lifeboats, and slowed to recover the occupants, when at 22.55 she was hit on the starboard side, forward, by a torpedo. Some minutes later a second torpedo hit, exploding in number 4 hold. The ship heeled to starboard and started settling. The boats were ordered to be cleared away, and the crew ordered to leave her, apart from a gun crew and essential personnel. This was underway when she was hit by a further two torpedoes, one exploding in the cross bunker, the other in number 6 hold, the latter blowing one of the starboard guns overboard. However, the engine room reported they were dry, and the bulkheads were holding. She remained stable, and there were hopes that she might be saved, but was though unlikely as she was very slowly settling in the water. The boats remained close by, and the party on board settled down for a long night. At 01.00 they were startled by an explosion, and they realised that the submarine had come to the surface and was shelling the ship. The starboard 3in gun was hastily manned, and they returned fire. They were pleasingly accurate, one shell exploding close the submarine, which submerged. Ten minutes later the ship was hit by another torpedo, which exploded in number 3 hold, but the ship remained upright and stubbornly afloat, so the party onboard gathered around the gun and tried to get some sleep. This was disturbed at 04.00 by another torpedo, this one exploding under the bridge. This collapsed the bridge completely and broke her back just forward of the bridge structure. Unbelievably, 5 minutes later yet another torpedo hit her, this time in the engine room. This was the final blow; the ship could take no more and she heeled over and started to sink. The last of the crew then abandoned her as she rolled over to starboard and went down stern first, her bow remaining above the water for some time before sinking. The survivors were picked up by the destroyer *Achates* at 08.30. Fifty-six men were lost. The later enquiry into the loss blamed Captain Wynter, who had not survived, for the loss. He should not have risked his ship by taking her into a known danger area. Her attacker had been *U 99* (Kretschmer).

[TNA: ADM.1/11215]

5 November JERVIS BAY armed merchant cruiser
Barrow 1922 requisitioned 1939; 14,164 tons;
530.6ft × 68.3ft; 7 × 6in, 2 × 12pdr
Captain Edward Stephen Fogarty Fegen†

Acting as the ocean escort to eastbound Convoy HX84, consisting of thirty-eight ships, which sailed from Halifax, Canada on 28 October. At 16.50 (local time), then in position 52.45N 32.13W, a strange warship was seen approaching the convoy from the north-west. The *Jervis Bay* altered course towards the stranger and challenged her by flashing light but received no reply. Shortly after this, the stranger altered course to the west and could be seen to be a 'pocket-battleship'. The *Jervis Bay* increased speed, made an enemy report by radio and then ordered the convoy to scatter. The enemy warship, which was the *panzerschiff Admiral Scheer*, opened fire, with her first salvo falling short of the *Jervis Bay*. At 16.55, at a range of 29,000 yards (14.5 miles), with her third salvo, the *Scheer* hit the *Jervis Bay*, a shell exploding amidships putting the forward fire-control position and the steering gear out of action. From 17.00 onwards, as the range decreased, the *Jervis Bay* was hit repeatedly, with two of her starboard guns being put out of action within 10 minutes. Fire was being returned, but all her shots were falling short. By 17.05 she was out of control and fell off to port, a hit in the engine room stopping her engines. By 17.20 she was on fire aft, and the smoke spread throughout the ship and she was clearly out of action, without being able to return fire, and the *Scheer* ceased firing soon after. Some boats were able to be launched, along with Carley floats and the crew were ordered to abandon her soon after this. She continued to burn until 20.00 when she finally sank. Sixty-five survivors were picked up by the Swedish steamer *Stureholm* of Goteborg, but thirty-three officers and 147 ratings were lost. The *Admiral Scheer* went on to sink five ships of the convoy, but the losses would undoubtedly have been higher but for the defence of the *Jervis Bay*. Captain Fegen was posthumously awarded the Victoria Cross for the action, ' … challenging hopeless odds and giving his life to save the many ships it was his duty to protect'.

[TNA: ADM.1/10506; London Gazette 22 November 1940]

6 November GIRL HELEN drifter
Buckie 1934 requisitioned 1939; 63 tons; 73.7ft × 18.3ft
Skipper William Whittaker Scarborough RNR

Fitted out as a dan layer, she was based in the River Tyne. At 10.26 when about 1,600 yards off the North Tyne Pier she detonated a mine and sank. One man was killed.

[TNA: ADM.116/4353]

6 November SEVRA whaler

Middlesbrough 1929 requisitioned 1940; 253 tons;
116ft × 24.2ft
Sub-Lieutenant Francis Brooks Richards RNVR

During October 1940, the *Sevra* was one of the first
minesweepers to be fitted with an acoustic hammer,
which generated sound waves to trigger the newly
deployed acoustic mine. However, it was found not to
be working properly and was removed. It was therefore
unfortunate that she was destroyed when she detonated
an acoustic mine when she was 5.5 cables (1,100 yards)
to the south-south-east of St Anthony Point off
Falmouth. The ship had just completed sweeping and
was in the process of laying dan-buoys to mark the
limits, when at 11.00 she was lifted into the air with an
enormous column of water under her stern as the mine
exploded, and quickly sank. There were no casualties.
[TNA: ADM.116/4353; ADM.199/372; Hewitt pp122–3]

7 November REED drifter

Govan 1911 requisitioned 1939; 99 tons; 86.5ft × 18.5ft
Skipper George Ernest Utting RNR†

Based at Brightlingsea, she was sunk when she
detonated a mine at 16.30 when off Holland on Sea,
in approximate position 51.46N 01.14E. Sixteen men
were killed, with only one survivor being picked up, the
Group Officer Lieutenant Kenneth Empson RNVR,
but he died later of his wounds.
[TNA: ADM.116/4353]

7 November SWORDFISH submarine

Chatham 1931; 640/927 tons; 187ft × 24ft; 1 × 3in,
6 × torpedo tubes
Lieutenant Michael Armitage Langley DSC†

Ordered to conduct a patrol off the port of Brest, she
sailed from Gosport on 7 November, but was never seen
or heard from again. When she had failed to respond to
radio calls by 16 November, she was presumed lost and
was posted as missing. It was assumed that she must have
been lost somewhere in her patrol area, either because of
hitting a mine or surface attack by destroyers. However,
in July 1983 her remains were found to the south of the
Isle of Wight lying in 150ft of water, broken in half just
forward of her gun mounting. It would seem that she
had been lost on the day that she sailed, almost certainly
by striking a mine soon after diving. Five officers and
thirty-six men were lost.
[Evans pp249–50]

7 November WILLIAM WESNEY trawler

Beverley 1930 requisitioned 1939; 364 tons;
145.9ft × 24.2ft; 1 × 12pdr
Skipper Frederick James Farrow RNR

Based at Harwich, she sailed in company with other
trawler-minesweepers to conduct sweeping operations
around the Shipwash buoy, being astern of the *Stella
Rigel*, in a line ahead formation. At 08.58 when in
position 51.33.48N 01.33.36E she detonated a mine
which exploded close under the starboard quarter,
throwing up a large column of water, and blowing the
stern of the trawler to pieces. She foundered rapidly,
stern first, the survivors clinging to a Carley float which
had been thrown clear by the explosion. Six men
were killed.
[TNA: ADM.1/10793; ADM.116/4353]

8 November MURIA tug

Bowling 1914 requisitioned 1940; 192 tons;
106.3ft × 23.1ft
Master James Walker

Employed as a rescue tug at Sheerness, she was sunk
when she detonated a mine at 14.25 when off North
Foreland in position 51.26.30N 01.27E. Ten men lost
their lives. The wreck was later dispersed.
[TNA: ADM.199/2216]

8 November AN 2 whaler

Tonsberg 1926 requisitioned 1940; 223 tons;
109.4ft × 22.4ft; 1 × 12pdr
Skipper Alfred William Pearson RNR

Employed as a dan layer, she sailed from Falmouth at
10.40 to join minesweeping trawlers to mark the area
swept and deal with any stray floating mines they may
bring to the surface. At 13.10 she developed engine
trouble and was ordered to return to harbour. When she
was abeam Pendennis Point and steering for the boom
entrance there was a large explosion immediately astern
of her, on the starboard quarter. The shock severed steam
pipes and the ship was covered in a cloud of steam. She
started to sink, stern first, the boat and a Carley float
being launched before she submerged. It was believed
that she had succumbed to an acoustic mine probably
laid by aircraft. The wreck lies in position 50.07.42N
05.01.10W.
[TNA: ADM.1/10768; Larn vol 1 sec 4]

10 November MARCELLE drifter

1925, requisitioned 1940; 64 tons

A former Belgian fishing vessel, she was fitted to carry
a barrage balloon controlled by an RAF team. She sank
after exploding a mine in position 51.21.48N 00.38W,
to the north-east of the Mackenzie Shoal in the Bristol
Channel. Of the crew of five, one man died, as did three
airmen; the rest were all picked up by the steamship
Downleaze and landed at Barry.
[TNA: ADM.199/367; AIR 81/4171]

10 November KINGSTON ALALITE trawler
Beverley 1933 requisitioned 1939; 412 tons;
151.7ft × 25.9ft; 1 × 12pdr
Skipper Samuel Herbert Cullings RNR

Former Hull trawler converted to an anti-submarine patrol vessel and based at Devonport. At 17.30 she was proceeding out of harbour to conduct a night patrol and was 5.6 cables off the Breakwater lighthouse when there was a large explosion on the starboard side, forward of the bridge. She lost all power, then broke up and sank in less than 3 minutes, the boiler exploding as she went under. Six men were killed. She had probably detonated an air-dropped influence mine.
[TNA:ADM.1/10769]

11 November STELLA ORION trawler
Selby 1935 requisitioned 1939; 417 tons; 152.8ft × 25.6ft
Skipper Walter Johnson Barlow RNR

Detonated a mine at 19.40 when she was about 2 cables (400 yards) to the north-west from the Shingles buoy, in the Thames estuary and subsequently foundered; all the crew were saved.
[TNA:ADM.116/4353]

14 November RISTANGO trawler
Beverley 1913 requisitioned 1940; 178 tons; 106.7ft × 21ft
Boom Skipper Harry Edward Myhill RNR

Employed as the gate vessel at the Medway boom, Sheerness, she foundered during heavy weather, the wreck fouling the boom, preventing its use until the following day.
[TNA:ADM.199/375]

14 November SHIPMATES drifter
Great Yarmouth 1911 requisitioned 1939; 82 tons;
84.5ft × 18.3ft; 1 × 3pdr
Skipper Alexander Pirie RNR

Based at Dover she was berthed at the inner end of West Pier in the Submarine Basin when the port came under air attack. At 14.25 a group of about twenty-five Ju 87 aircraft escorted by fighters carried out a sustained attack, with bombs landing in the harbour, the castle grounds and around a coastal battery. One bomb scored a direct hit on the foredeck of the *Shipmates*, just abaft the gun platform, and blew the forward part of the ship to pieces. One man was killed, being the only man on board, all the rest of the crew having taken refuge in a nearby air raid shelter.
[TNA:ADM.199/102]

14 November THE BOYS drifter
Lowestoft 1914 requisitioned 1939; 92 tons; 86.4ft × 19.4ft
Skipper Andrew Buchan DSC RNR

Carrying out a night patrol off Dungeness in poor weather, she started making water at about midnight and attempted to return to harbour. A tug was despatched to assist and successfully took her in tow, but she continued to settle and eventually foundered at 08.00 when near the south-west Goodwin buoy. All the crew were rescued. The wreck lies in position 51.08.30N 01.32.12E
[TNA:ADM.116/4353; Larn vol 2 sec 6]

15 November DUNGENESS trawler
Selby 1914 requisitioned 1940; 263 tons; 125.2ft × 22.5ft;
1 × 12pdr
Skipper Charles William Neesham RNR

Bombed by an enemy aircraft off Hammonds Knoll, off the north Norfolk coast, she avoided any direct hits but was severely shaken by near misses. Making water, she steered inshore to run herself onto the beach off Happisburgh at 03.25. Tugs and the local lifeboat were sent to her assistance, but she was found to be irreparably damaged and was written off as a constructive total loss.
[TNA:ADM.116/4353]

15 November GUARDSMAN tug
Ayr 1905 requisitioned 1939; 102 tons; 90ft × 18.1ft

Employed in the examination service, she was en-route to Ramsgate and the Downs anchorage from Gravesend when she detonated a mine near the North East Spit buoy off North Foreland. Seven men were rescued by the Margate lifeboat, but two men were lost. The wreck lies in position 51.27.29N 01.26.1E.
[Lloyd's War Losses p156; Larn vol 2 sec 4]

16 November ARSENAL trawler
Middlesbrough 1933 purchased 1939; 398 tons;
155ft × 26.4ft
Skipper Charles Robert Radford RNR

The trawler was about 4 miles south of Toward light in the river Clyde, when at 07.45, in thick fog, she collided with the Polish destroyer *Burza* and was severely damaged. The destroyer *Arrow* closed to stand by her, and the tug *Superman* was despatched to the scene to assist. As they arrived there was an explosion, which also damaged the tug, and she subsequently sank about 2.5 miles south of Runnaneum Point (Rubh' an Eun). There were no casualties.
[TNA:ADM.116/4353; https://canmore.org.uk/site/102738]

18 November GO AHEAD drifter
Oulton Broad 1919 requisitioned 1939; 100 tons;
89.9ft × 20ft
Skipper William Norman Hurn RNR

Based at Sheerness, she was in collision with the destroyer *Watchman* during a gale and subsequently foundered about 3 cables (600 yards) off Garrison Point.
[TNA:ADM.116/4353]

19 November FONTENOY trawler
Paisley 1918 (*Siam Duffy*) requisitioned 1940; 276 tons; 125.5ft × 23.4ft; 1 × 12pdr
Skipper John Couch Coaker RNR

In company with other minesweeping trawlers, sailed from Great Yarmouth at 09.30 to commence sweeping the channels in the area. At 10.05 the group came under air attack by a single aircraft, which despite dropping about ten bombs, all missed. At 12.05 another aircraft, identified as an He 111, closed, attacking from out of the sun and making the *Fontenoy* its target, dropping two bombs which exploded close on the port side. The effect was to lift her out the water and 'whip' the whole vessel. Within minutes the Chief Engineer reported that she was making water in both the engine and boiler rooms. On inspection it was found that the circulator pump inlet valve was fractured. In the magazine the flood valve had been cracked and consequently that compartment was slowly flooding. At 12.30 the *Tamora* took the *Fontenoy* in tow and headed back for Great Yarmouth, but within 5 minutes *Fontenoy* was down by the head and would no longer steer. At 14.00 the tow parted. By now the tug *Krooman* was on scene, and a new tow was rigged, and she was again heading for safety. However, at 14.15 the boiler room reported that the pumps could no longer stem the flow of water, and it was evident that she could not last much longer. She was therefore ordered to be abandoned. At 14.20 she capsized over to starboard and sank. There were no casualties. The wreck has been found and lies in position 52.29.52N 01.56.26E
[*TNA: ADM.1/11548; Larn vol 3 sec 2*]

20 November GOORANGAI armed trawler
Newcastle NSW 1919 requisitioned 1939; 223 tons; 117.1ft × 22.1ft; 1 × 12pdr
Commissioned Warrant Officer David MacGregor RANVR[†]

Royal Australian Navy. Fitted as a minesweeper, she was in Port Philip Bay, Victoria, making for an anchorage, where it was intended to stay for the night. At 20.37 she was in collision with the outward-bound passenger liner *Duntroon* (10,364 tons), which struck the trawler on the port side amidships. The trawler was cut in half and sank in less than a minute, taking all twenty-four members of the crew with her. The subsequent inquiry found that the *Duntroon* was overtaking the smaller vessel and believed that they were on a parallel course. When they realised that they were converging, it was too late to avoid the collision. Initially, blame was placed on the captain of the *Duntroon*, but this was modified as it was believed that the navigation lights of *Goorangai* were poorly positioned.
[*http://www.navy.gov.au/hmas-goorangai*]

21 November XMAS ROSE drifter
Aberdeen 1918 (*Jean Patterson*) requisitioned 1939; 96 tons; 86.2ft × 18.5ft
Skipper John Merson RNR[†]

Sank after she detonated a mine at 15.45 in the Thames Estuary, near the North East Gunfleet buoy, in position 51.47.45N 01.25.30E. Three men were killed, and Skipper Merson died later of his wounds.
[*TNA: ADM.116/4353*]

22 November ML 127 motor launch
Oulton Broad 1940; 75 tons; 112ft × 18.4ft; 1 × 3pdr
Lieutenant Francis Beaumont Morice RNVR

Destroyed when she detonated an influence mine in the Thames Estuary, off Clacton, in position 51.49N 01.25.30E. Lieutenant Eric Kneen and ten ratings were killed.
[*TNA: ADM.116/4353; ADM.358/337*]

22 November ETHEL TAYLOR trawler
Middlesbrough 1916 (*Cremlyn*) requisitioned 1940; 276 tons; 125.5ft × 23.4ft; 1 × 12pdr
Skipper Robert Cowling RNR

When she was 7.5 cables (1,500 yards) to the east of the North Pier Light in the River Tyne she detonated a mine, causing serious damage. The Cullercoats lifeboat and a drifter went to her assistance and attempted to rig a tow, but she filled and sank in position 55.00.34N 01.22.08W. Two men were killed.
[*TNA: ADM.116/4353*]

22 November GLEN stores lighter
1909; 130 tons
Mr Robert Alexander Johnstone[†]

Based at Rosyth, she sailed from Grangemouth for Crombie whilst loaded with 5.25in ammunition and armament stores. At approximately 12.50 she detonated a mine, probably an air-laid magnetic mine, which exploded when she was off Bo'ness and she sank immediately with the loss of all five men on board. Her wreck lies in position 56.01.99N, 03.34.14W
[*TNA: ADM.1/19244*]

24 November AMETHYST trawler
Middlesbrough 1934 (*Phyllis Rosalie*) purchased 1935; 627 tons; 157.3ft × 26.4ft; 1 × 4in
Lieutenant Honourable William Keith Rous RNVR

Sank at 16.45 after detonating a mine in the Barrow Deep in the Thames Estuary. Although several men were injured, none were killed in the blast, all being picked by the armed trawler *le Tiger*. The loss position was noted as 51.41.3N 01.20.3E.
[*TNA: ADM.1/11171*]

24 November GAEL yacht

Renfrew 1904 requisitioned 1940; 101 tons; 90.6ft × 17ft
Lieutenant Frederick James Brister Hart RNVR

Stationed at Immingham in the river Humber as a local patrol craft, at 08.24 she had just shoved off from the drifter *Gemara*, and was getting under way, when there was a large explosion under the port quarter as she detonated a mine. She subsequently foundered about 2 miles off Spurn Point, in position 53.31.5N 00.07.30E. There were no casualties.

[TNA: ADM.116/4353]

25 November ML 111 motor launch

Rosneath 1940; 66 tons; 110ft × 17.5ft; 1 × 3pdr
Lieutenant Austin Victor Coates Hoadley RNVR

In company with *ML 108* proceeding up the river Humber in line ahead, having escorted Convoy FD42, with *111* leading her sister. At 09.00 when she was off Spurn Point, about half a mile to the east of the Chequer Shoal buoy, there were two large explosions under her hull as she set off mines. When the smoke and spray had cleared *111* was seen to have been blown in half just forward of the funnel. The after half of the wreck lay at an angle of 30 degrees, with the stern out of the water. A dinghy was launched from *108* which took men off the forward half and picked up three men from the water. Attempts were made to tow the wreck, but this proved impossible, and she was abandoned, last seen drifting, low in the water towards Binks Shoal, where it was believed that she sank. Three men died.

[TNA: ADM.1/11208]

25 November KENNYMORE trawler

Beverley 1914 requisitioned 1939; 225 tons; 117ft × 22ft
Skipper Joseph William Greene RNR

With the Senior Officer of the minesweeping group embarked, she was engaged in sweeping for magnetic mines using LL gear in the Thames Estuary. At 19.30, when she was 2 miles to the east of the East Oaze buoy a mine detonated close under her stern, and she sank with the loss of three men.

[TNA: ADM.116/4353; ADM.199/1171]

25 November CONQUISTADOR trawler

Aberdeen 1915 (*Glenbervie*) requisitioned 1939; 224 tons; 120.7ft × 22.7ft
Skipper John Paterson RNR

In company with the *Kennymore* (see above), she was engaged in minesweeping in the Thames Estuary, when her consort exploded a mine and sank. The *Conquistador* recovered her gear as quickly as she could and then went to the aid of the survivors and picked up several men. As she was returning to Sheerness she was rammed by another trawler, the *Capricornus*, which was proceeding to the area as relief. The latter was only slightly damaged, but *Conquistador* steadily filled with water and sank. There were no casualties.

[TNA: ADM.199/1171; Hardy p148]

27 November PORT NAPIER auxiliary minelayer

Wallsend 1940 requisitioned 1940; 9,847 tons; 503.6ft × 68.3ft; 2 × 4in, 2 × 2pdr, 550 mines
Captain John Norman Tait DSC

Lying at Loch Alsh off the Isle of Skye, the motor vessel *Rudderman* came alongside to supply her with 140 tons of diesel oil. Fuelling commenced at 12.30 and was complete by 13.25 and the *Rudderman* prepared to cast off. As she did so black smoke could be seen rising from the engine room and there were reports of a fire below. The thick smoke spread throughout the ship and it proved to be difficult for men to enter the engine room to fight the fire; furthermore it was found that there were no arrangements to flood the engine room from outside. Flames were soon coming out of hatches and ventilators, and the heat was intense. With a full load of mines on board, the situation was clearly becoming dangerous, and mines were ordered to be jettisoned. Many of the mines were thrown overboard, but when the mining room bulkheads were reported to be dangerously hot, it was decided to abandon her. The *Rudderman* was still alongside, and about 150 men managed to scramble on board her before she cast off. The tug *Pleto* had now come alongside and found herself picking up men from the water as they jumped overboard. Thick smoke was now blanketing everything, pouring out of doors and hatches and by 15.00 flames could be seen around the funnel and boat deck. At 15.40 there was a large explosion, apparently in the engine room, and after this the ship listed over to starboard and started to settle by the stern. A further two smaller explosions occurred and then at 16.30 another, very heavy explosion, which scattered debris over a large distance, and she rolled over onto her port side. She lay on her beam ends, still burning furiously, throughout the night before she disappeared the following morning. The Board of Enquiry found that the blaze was caused by an oil pipe from the double bottom oil tank breaking, the oil being sprayed onto one of the boilers. This had happened because the Assistant Engineer Officer, Mr Ronald Haagensen, had failed to close off the double bottom oil tank and it had been overfilled. It was also found that there had been no fire-fighting drill and no fire exercises had been carried out. Mr Haagensen was informed that he had incurred their Lordships' displeasure and directed to obey orders promptly in future. Commander (E) Hector Weir RNR also incurred displeasure, over his lack of organisation and failure to train his department in fire-fighting. Captain Tait was also held to be blameworthy, as he had failed to ensure that ship had an efficient fire-fighting

organisation. It was ordered that he not be given command of a fighting ship again.
[TNA: ADM.178/249]

27 November ELK trawler

Beverley 1902 requisitioned 1939; 181 tons; 108.7ft × 21ft
Chief Skipper James Samuel Bush RNR

Fitted with experimental gear designed to tackle acoustic mines developed by the RN Engineering College at Keyham, she was sweeping the approaches to Plymouth harbour, when at 15.25 a mine exploded directly under the ship. She was covered in a large quantity of smoke and spray, and the explosion fractured the hull under the engine room. She steadily filled with water and sank about 45 minutes after the explosion, then being 11.4 cables south of Penlee Point. There were no casualties.
[TNA: ADM.199/239]

28 November MANX PRINCE trawler

Selby 1910 requisitioned 1939; 221 tons; 117.5ft × 21.5ft
Skipper Alfred Arthur Grounds RNR

Based at Immingham, she was getting under way at 05.05 from her overnight anchorage off Spurn Point Light, when there was a large explosion under her port quarter as she detonated a mine. She filled and sank, about 3.5 miles to the south-east of Spurn Point. There were no casualties, all the crew being rescued by the *Cortina*.
[TNA: ADM.116/4353]

29 November PILOT VESSEL NUMBER 4

examination vessel
Amsterdam 1905 (*Stoomloodsvaartuig No 4/Hellevoetsluis*)
requisitioned 1940; 461 tons; 137ft × 24ft
Lieutenant Reginald Henry Whiteley RNR[†]

A sortie was made into the western approaches of the English Channel by a group of German destroyers from Brest, the *Galster*, *Lody* and *Beitzen*, which attacked a small convoy off Start Point, sinking a tug and barge. As they cleared the area, they encountered *Pilot Vessel 4* which had sailed from Plymouth bound for Milford Haven, with a small number of Royal Navy personnel onboard, and a number of merchant seamen making up the crew. She was hit several times by gunfire from the *Beitzen*, which left her bunkers on fire and flooding fore and aft. Several armed trawlers were sent to search the area, and destroyers from Plymouth had a brief, unsatisfactory encounter with the German force. The destroyer *Jackal* found the burning wreck in position 49.49N 04.49W and picked up six survivors, but seven men were lost.
Note: incorrectly shown in the *Statement of Losses* as being lost in February 1941 – place and circumstances unknown
[TNA: ADM.199/372; ADM 358/3797; Statement of Losses p16; Young p67]

29 November YOUNG FISHERMAN drifter

Lowestoft 1914 requisitioned 1940; 83 tons; 86ft × 19.5ft

Ran aground when attempting to berth alongside the Railway Pier at Oban. Subsequent efforts to refloat her were unsuccessful and she was eventually written off as a constructive loss.
[TNA: ADM.199/2217]

29 November CALVERTON trawler

Beverley 1913 (*Loroone*) requisitioned 1939; 214 tons; 117.2ft × 21.5ft; 1 × 6pdr
Skipper James Fountain RNR

Based at Immingham, she was engaged in sweeping the area to the south-east of Spurn Point Light, using LL (magnetic) sweeps. At 02.30 there was a large explosion under her starboard quarter, with a 60ft column of water being thrown up. She slowly filled with water and sank after listing to port. She was then about 4 miles from Spurn Point. Two men were lost.
[TNA: ADM.116/4353]

30 November CHESTNUT trawler

Goole 1940; 530 tons; 150ft × 27.6ft; 1 × 12pdr
Lieutenant John Everard Finch RNZVR

In company with her sister *Ash*, engaged in sweeping the approaches to Portsmouth. When she was close to the North East Spit buoy at 12.34, a mine exploded close on the port side, just abaft the bridge. A few minutes later a second mine exploded about 100 yards away. The *Ash* closed, and she was taken in tow, but at 14.00 she foundered, then being 2 cables to the west of the East Shingles buoy. There were no casualties.
[TNA: ADM.116/4353]

2 December FORFAR armed merchant cruiser

Govan 1922 requisitioned 1939; 16,402 tons;
548.7ft × 70.2ft; 8 × 6in, 2 × 12pdr
Captain Norman Arthur Cyril Hardy[†]

Sailed from the Clyde on 30 November, being escorted clear of coastal waters by HMCS *St Laurent*, to steer into the Atlantic to rendezvous with an inbound Atlantic Convoy HX90. At 02.50 (local), in approximate position 54.35N 18.18W, she was hit on the starboard side of the engine room by a torpedo. All the lights went out, but the emergency diesel generator was able to restore some lighting some minutes later. Star shell was ordered to be fired to illuminate the area, hopefully to deter any surfaced submarine. The boats were hoisted out, but not put into the water and bulkheads were ordered to be shored. The engine room flooded and after a while she lost power, but she remained stable. About 40 minutes after the first attack, she was hit by a second torpedo, this one hitting the port side, again in the engine room. As she was clearly settling, she was ordered to be abandoned, with a further attack taking place as this was happening. The third torpedo hit the port side, almost in the same position as the second; this caused the boat deck to collapse. The fourth hit the port side, just abaft the engine room and detonated one of the magazines. This seemed to 'crumple the ship up'. With her back broken, she sagged and the bow and stern both rose clear of the water. As the last of the men were jumping into the sea a fifth and final torpedo hit her, again on the port side. The bow and stern continued to rise to meet each other, and she sank the stern going under first, followed soon after by the bows. The destroyer *Viscount* picked up some survivors several hours later, as did the merchant ship *Dunsley*, but 176 men were lost. The submarine responsible was the *U 99* (Kretschmer). [TNA:ADM.1/11216]

November / December REGULUS submarine
Barrow 1930; 1,475/2,040 tons; 270ft × 29.11ft; 1 × 4in, 8 × torpedo tubes
Lieutenant Commander Frederick Basil Currie†
Sailed from Alexandria 18 November for a patrol in the Adriatic and Straits of Otranto and when she failed to return as expected on 6 December, she was posted missing. The date and circumstances of her loss are not known, but she was presumed to have been lost before that date, perhaps in a minefield near the straits of Otranto in late November/early December. Fifty-five men were lost.
[Evans p266]

5 December CAMERON destroyer
Quincy (USA) 1919 (*Welles*) leased 1940; 1,215 tons; 311ft × 30.7ft; 3 × 4in, 1 × 3in, 6 × torpedo tubes
One of the fifty ex-US Navy destroyers transferred under the Lend/Lease agreement in September 1940. Newly transferred and not yet in commission, *Cameron* was in number 8 dry dock at Portsmouth when an air raid targeted the dockyard. During the raid, a bomb fell into the dock on the port side of the ship, exploding abreast 77 station. The side of the ship was blown in and she was lifted off the blocks to turn onto her port side, and a fire was started onboard. The dock was flooded to help extinguish the fire. The bomb, fire and flood caused extensive damage, and she was written off as a constructive total loss. The hull was later used for experimental purposes before being scrapped in 1944.
[TNA:ADM.267/103; CB.4273 p153]

December TRITON submarine
Barrow 1937; 1,095/1,579 tons; 265.6ft × 26.7ft; 1 × 4in, 10 × torpedo tubes
Lieutenant Guy Claude Ian St Barbe Watkins†
Based in the Mediterranean, she sailed from Malta on 28 November to carry out a patrol in the Adriatic, between 40N and 42N. When she failed to return on 18

December, she was posted as missing. She was probably responsible for an attack on the Italian merchant ship *Olimpia* at 05.30 on 6 December, in position 41.06N 18.39E, but this is the last known of her. The possibility remains that she suffered a diving accident, but the most likely cause would seem to be that she struck a mine, probably soon after 7 December, in the lower Adriatic or the Otranto Straits. Five officers and forty-nine ratings were lost.
[Evans pp266–7]

7 December LORMONT guardship
Greenock 1927 (*Woodcock*) requisitioned 1939; 1,561 tons; 241.4ft × 40.2ft; 2 × 12pdr
Lieutenant Kenneth Maurice Cutler RNR
Stationed in the river Humber, she was near the Humber Light Vessel when she was rammed by the inbound merchant ship *Olaf Bergh* (5,811 tons), part of Convoy FS354, and subsequently foundered. There were no casualties.
[TNA:ADM.116/4353]

7 December CORTINA trawler
Beverley 1913 requisitioned 1939; 213 tons; 117.1ft × 21.5ft; 1 × 12pdr
Skipper Thomas Arthur Phillipson RNR
Based in the river Humber, she was alerted to the difficulties of the *Lormont* (see above) and closed to render assistance. Whilst manoeuvring to close her, she was in collision with the trawler *War Duke* (246 tons), the damage being such that she settled and sank.
[TNA:ADM.116/4353]

7 December CAPRICORNUS trawler
Goole 1917 requisitioned 1939; 219 tons; 117.2ft × 22ft; 1 × 12pdr
Skipper Edward Tom Bridge RNR
Sailed from Sheerness with three other minesweeping trawlers, heading through the Thames Gate, to conduct a magnetic mine or LL sweep, with Skipper-Lieutenant James White RNR embarked as the senior officer of the group. At 19.25 when about 2 miles to the east of the Nore light vessel there was a large explosion about 60ft abeam of the *Capricornus* as they detonated a magnetic mine. The ship was shaken violently and several men, without any orders, evidently thinking that the ship was doomed, launched the Carley float and abandoned her. Other members of the crew, coming onto the upper deck, thought that they must have missed the order to abandon ship, so hastily launched the sea boat and followed their mates. The ship was now abandoned except for Skipper-Lieutenant White, who was bewildered to find himself alone on the trawler. He decided that they must know something he did not and jumped into the sea to swim

to the boat. All were picked up by the other trawlers. White now questioned them and ascertained that after the shock of the explosion, water had been entering the engine space, causing the flight. As the *Capricornus* was still afloat, White then returned on board with a small number of volunteers and found that the vessel was dry except for the engine room which was about half full of water. The vessel was turned into shallow water and run aground where she heeled over, her position being noted as 51.28.36N 00.56.36E. The court of enquiry was not impressed with the actions of the crew and believed that a determined effort could have saved the trawler if it had been made promptly. The inexperience of the crew and the unfamiliarity with naval discipline was believed to be a major factor in her loss. One man was lost, having been blown overboard from the gun platform.
[TNA:ADM.1/10774]

14 December BRANLEBAS torpedo boat
Le Havre 1937 seized 1940; 610 tons; 249.4ft × 26.1ft; 2 × 3.9in, 4 × 13.7mm, 2 × torpedo tubes
Lieutenant Commander Hugh Charles James McRae[†]
A former French warship, taken earlier in the year, she sailed from Dartmouth 13 December to act as an escort to a westbound coastal convoy. The weather encountered in the Channel was poor and steadily worsened, until blowing a full gale. She was last seen at 18.40 on 13 December, but then disappeared. The French warship *Mistral* subsequently found and picked up three survivors, who testified that the ship had broken in half at the break of the fo'c'sle and rapidly sank at about 09.10 on 14 December, between Land's End and the Lizard. The Director of Naval Construction opined that the design was fundamentally weak, and the hull had probably fractured due to sagging and bending, conditions likely to be encountered in heavy seas. It was also noted that a considerable amount of topweight had been added since the completion of the ship. Ninety-six men died.
[TNA:ADM.267/127;ADM.199/372]

15 December ANTOINE WILLY boom defence tender
1919 requisitioned 1940; 19 tons
Former Belgian fishing boat, she was employed at Dartmouth as a boom defence tender and was lost by 'marine causes' with no further detail.
[Statement of Losses Amendment p2;ADM.199/24129]

17 December ACHERON destroyer
Woolston 1930; 1,350 tons; 312ft × 32.3ft; 4 × 4.7in, 8 × torpedo tubes
Lieutenant John Rees Wilson[†]
Having sailed from Portsmouth to conduct post-refit trials, she was about 9.5 miles to the south of the

Needles, Isle of Wight, and steaming at 27 knots, when at 06.40 there was a large explosion on the port side forward as she hit a mine. All the lights went out, and the ship immediately took a list to port of 10 degrees, and a fierce fire started in the forward section, which had been wrecked. The ship continued to heel to port and was abandoned as she sank bows first. Her stern rose high out of the water to the vertical before disappearing in less than 5 minutes. One hundred and sixty-seven men were lost from her complement plus twenty-five dockyard workers who were on board.
[TNA:ADM.267/91]

17 December THOMAS CONNOLLY trawler
Beverley 1918 requisitioned 1939; 290 tons; 125.5ft × 23.5ft
Lieutenant Richard Lionel Langridge RNR[†]
Employed as a boom defence vessel, she sailed from Sheerness in company with other boom working vessels to carry out maintenance on local defences. At 09.40 she closed the senior officer of the group, in the tug *Kestrel*, and asked permission to proceed to the Medway Gate. As the pair was manoeuvring close to each other, about 100 yards apart, the *Thomas Connolly* suddenly blew up and sank immediately. The *Kestrel* threw overboard floats and lowered her boat, and picked up eight survivors, but seventeen men were killed. It was presumed that she had detonated a mine.
[TNA:ADM.199/239]

17 December CARRY ON drifter
Lowestoft 1919 requisitioned 1939; 93 tons; 87.4ft × 19.4ft
Skipper Ernest Harper Smith RNR[†]
Fitted out to act as a barrage balloon vessel, she was sunk by a large explosion when to the east of the Nore Sand Lightvessel, off Sheerness; it was believed that a mine, either acoustic or magnetic was responsible. The loss position was noted as 51.28.5N 00.45.5E. Six men were lost.
[TNA:ADM.199/1171]

18 December REFUNDO trawler
Beverley 1917 requisitioned 1939; 258 tons; 120.5ft × 22ft
Skipper Alexander Smith Dorward RNR
Based at Harwich, she was engaged in conducting trials of new sweeping gear, which involved the use of a noise source suspended over the bows, which would trigger acoustic mines. At 13.55 a mine was detonated about 20 yards immediately ahead of her. This stove in her bow plates and she went down by the head but did not immediately sink. A tow was rigged, but about 45 minutes later she sank. Two men were lost. Her wreck lies in position 51.56.06N 01.21.02E.
[TNA:ADM.116/4353; Larn vol 3 sec 1]

19 December **PROFICIENT** drifter

Brixham 1910 requisitioned 1940; 58 tons; 71ft × 19.3ft

Ran aground and stranded on Whitby sands about 400 yards north of West Pier, the crew of four all landed safely. She was subsequently written off as a constructive total loss.

[TNA: ADM.199/2219]

21 December **SUN IX** tug

Selby 1919 requisitioned 1939; 196 tons; 100.3ft × 25.6ft

Lieutenant Thomas Michael Rumbold RNVR†

Detonated a mine at 12.43 when in the Yantlet Channel, Thames Estuary, between numbers 1 and 2 buoys, and rapidly sank. Four men were lost, the survivors being landed at Southend. The wreck was later raised and broken up.

[TNA: ADM.199/2219]

22 December **HYPERION** destroyer

Wallsend 1936; 1,340 tons; 312ft × 33ft; 4 × 4.7in, 8 × torpedo tubes

Commander Hugh St Lawrence Nicolson

Based in the Mediterranean, she was acting as escort to the battleship *Malaya* which was covering the passage of Convoy MG1 from Malta to Gibraltar. At 01.27 when 24 miles to the east of Cape Bon, *Hyperion* obtained a good Asdic contact and altered course to carry out a depth-charge attack and then came around to carry out a second run. That complete, she steamed 1,000 yards clear of the datum point then started a turn with the intention of making a third attack. At 01.56 as she was still under helm there was a heavy explosion under 'Y' gun. This resulted in the after compartments up to the bulkhead of the office flat flooding. The stern of the ship dropped by about 10 degrees, indicating that her back was broken, and the stern could be seen to be working in the sea. Bulkheads were shored, and she was stabilised although the engines stopped. The *Ilex* closed, and a tow was rigged, and they were underway at 03.45. An hour later Captain (Destroyers) in the *Jervis* arrived on scene and assessed the situation. They were a long way from a friendly port, and they would certainly be a target for further attacks at first light. It was therefore reluctantly decided to abandon her. By 05.10 all the crew had been removed and the *Janus* fired a torpedo into her to ensure that she sank. It was believed probable that her propellers had struck a moored contact mine, and it was later found that the Italians had recently laid a minefield (4AN) in the area. The Italians confused the picture by claiming that she had been torpedoed by the submarine *Serpente*, a claim which has been repeated by other authorities, but has no substance. Two men were lost.

[TNA: ADM.267/92]

24 December **LORD HOWARD** drifter

Stromness 1917 (*Thule Rock*) requisitioned 1939; 98 tons; 90.1ft × 18.8ft

Skipper Leonard Inwood Batchelor RNR

Foundered in the Submarine Basin, Dover at 03.00 following a collision with the armed yacht *Radiant* (503 tons); there were no casualties.

[TNA: ADM.116/4353]

24 December **PELTON** trawler

Beverley 1925 requisitioned 1939; 358 tons; 140.4ft × 24ft

Skipper James Alexander Sutherland RNR†

During the evening of 24 December several flotillas of enemy torpedo boats staged an attack on a northbound east coast convoy, FN366, off the coast of Norfolk. Whilst the convoy escorts attempted to find and engage the torpedo boats, at 23.44 one of them, *S 28*, found the *Pelton* laying near number 5 buoy off Aldeburgh and hit her with a single torpedo. She blew up with the loss of twenty men, with just one survivor. The wreck lies in position 52.31.33N 02.04.12E.

[TNA: ADM.358/3808; Foynes p103; Larn vol 3 sec 2]

25 December **MERCURY** paddle minesweeper

Glasgow 1934 requisitioned 1939; 621 tons; 223.8ft × 30.1ft; 1 × 12pdr

Lieutenant Commander Bertram Aubrey Palmer RNVR

A former Caledonian Steam Packet Company steamer, she was converted into a minesweeper, and joined the 11th Minesweeping Flotilla, which was based at Milford Haven from late 1940. On Christmas Day she was in company with her sister paddle sweepers, engaged in clearing a defensive British minefield near the Coningbeg Light vessel, near the Saltee Islands, Eire. They had completed several laps when *Mercury*'s Oropesa float, which marked the outer end of the sweep wire, dipped, and then disappeared, which was supposed to indicate that they had snagged a mine. One mine did indeed come to the surface, but the float remained submerged, evidently still fouled. They obtained permission to drop out of line and clear the snag. After attempting to solve the problem by manoeuvring and varying speeds without success, it was decided to recover the wire. At 15.50 speed was reduced to slow ahead and the wire was hauled in. As they did so the otter board, a metal board designed to act as a kite, to keep the sweep at a distance from the ship, came into view, and a mine could clearly be seen snagged to it. Hauling-in was ceased, and it was decided to grapple the Oropesa float, which could now be seen, and haul this into the ship so that it could be recovered, then the wire could be cut. The float was successfully grappled and then unshackled. During this time the otter board, complete with mine, was suspended under the ship. As they prepared to veer out the wire, to distance themselves from the menace there was a

large explosion close astern as the mine exploded. The stern was lifted, and the rudder put out of action, and on checking for internal damage it was discovered that she was making water. The armed trawler *Mangrove* was sent to her aid in response to her call for assistance, and a tow was rigged by 18.00. However, progress was slow and by 20.20 water was covering the wardroom floor. At 20.30 the tow parted as she settled by the stern. The trawler *Almond* came alongside to lift off the crew. At 21.15 she sank in position 51.58.3N 06.24.2W. Lieutenant Commander Palmer was subsequently court-martialled for the loss. He was found guilty of hazarding his ship through negligence. He had contravened both local standing orders and the instructions in the Manual of Minesweeping, in not veering out and then cutting the wire when the mine was first seen. By concentrating on the recovery of the float rather than dealing with the mine, he had allowed the otter and mine to drift under her stern. He was reprimanded.
[TNA: ADM.156/216]

26 December TRUE ACCORD drifter
Grimsby 1921 (*Catherine Charlton*) requisitioned 1939; 92 tons; 87.3ft × 18.4ft
Skipper Richard Henry Alexander RNR
Engaged in a night patrol, she foundered after colliding with the armed trawler *Saronta* (316 tons) off Smith's Knoll, Norfolk. There were no casualties.
[TNA: ADM.199/375]

26 December MAC 5 motor attendant craft
Hythe 1936 (*MTB 5*); 18 tons; 60.4ft × 13.10ft
Sub. Lieutenant Walter Alexander Edmenson RNVR†
Based at Harwich, she sailed from Harwich at 09.00 with the Admiralty Salvage Officer embarked, to examine the wreck of the Dutch steamer *Stad Maastricht*, at the northern end of the Barrow Deep in the Thames estuary. At 10.00 the patrolling trawlers *Strive* and *Lord St Vincent* heard a large explosion, and when called by radio at 10.04, *MAC.5* did not respond. A search of the area failed to find any trace of the craft, but it was believed that she had probably detonated a mine to the south of the North East Gunfleet buoy, near the wreck of the *Xmas Rose*. Eight men died.
[TNA: ADM.199/239]

30 December BANDOLERO trawler
Middlesbrough 1935 purchased 1939; 440 tons; 162.1ft × 26.7ft
Lieutenant Commander Francis Mervyn Wynter Harris RNR
Whilst patrolling in the Gulf of Sollum, Egypt, she was in collision at 21.05 with the Australian destroyer *Waterhen*. Severely damaged, she steadily filled with water and foundered at 21.50. There were no casualties.
[TNA: ADM.116/4353]

1941

3 January NEW SPRAY drifter
Lowestoft 1912 requisitioned 1939; 70 tons; 80.6ft × 18ft
Fitted out as a boom defence vessel, she was not manned when she foundered at her moorings at Sheerness in poor weather.
[TNA: ADM.199/407]

9 January DUSKY QUEEN inshore trawler
Oulton Broad 1920 requisitioned 1939; 40 tons; 59ft × 17.3ft
Based at Ramsgate, she was conducting a night patrol, but managed to wander off station and ran aground in Pegwell Bay, being badly holed in the process. With her radio not working, the only way she could attract attention was to fire rockets, which caused some confusion ashore, as she used the pyrotechnics which were only to be used in case of invasion. She was eventually found, and the crew taken off by motorboat. She lay on the rocks until, with the aid of salvage pumps, she was cleared of water and refloated and towed into Ramsgate but was subsequently written off as a constructive total loss.
[TNA: ADM.199/405]

10 January GALLANT destroyer
Linthouse 1935; 1,350 tons; 312ft × 33ft; 4 × 4.7in, 8 × torpedo tubes
Lieutenant Commander Cecil Powis Frobisher Brown
The *Gallant* sailed from Alexandria with other destroyers to screen the battleships *Barham* and *Valiant*, as part of the force escorting the passage of a convoy to Malta as Operation 'Excess'. At 08.30 in position 36.24.5N 12.10N with no warning there was a large explosion under the ship near 'A' gun as she detonated a contact mine. The explosion wrecked the forward part of the ship, and with the ship still being driven forward at 17 knots, the bows broke off to float away down the starboard side. In the boiler rooms safety valves were lifted and she came to a stop in clouds of smoke and steam. Her sister, *Griffin*, came alongside and the *Mohawk* closed to prepare a tow. Despite the damage the destroyer remained upright and stable, and hard work by damage control parties shored up bulkheads and controlled the flooding. This complete, the *Mohawk* commenced towing her, stern first, towards Malta. At noon, the following day a tug arrived to take over towing duties and she arrived at Malta without further damage later that afternoon. Sixty-five men were killed. Docking revealed the extent of the damage; not only had the forward section of the ship been blown away, the keel, side plating and upper deck were buckled and distorted, with shock damage to equipment and fittings. There were some optimistic

plans (Job 7044) for steel to be shipped to Malta to allow a new bow section to be erected and built on to the ship, but with Malta under siege this proved impossible. On 5 April she suffered extensive splinter damage during an air raid and was written off as a constructive total loss to be cannibalised and in September 1943 was towed to St Paul's Bay and scuttled.
[TNA: ADM.267/94]

11 January SOUTHAMPTON light cruiser
Clydebank 1936; 558ft × 61.8ft; 12 × 6in, 8 × 4in, 8 × 2pdr, 6 × torpedo tubes
Captain Basil Charles Barrington Brooke

In company with the cruiser *Gloucester*, departed from Malta on 11 January to provide distant cover for Operation 'Excess', the passage of a convoy to the eastern Mediterranean. At 15.20 that afternoon a group of Ju 87 bombers were observed closing rapidly, having approached undetected. Diving out of the sun they were seen only moments before commencing the attack, achieving complete surprise, with only the after quadruple 2pdr being able to open fire. She was hit by two bombs; the first penetrated into 'A' boiler room, putting it out of action whilst another hit aft, passing through the wardroom flat to burst on the deck above the wireless office, piercing the oil tank adjacent to the 4in magazine. This killed or injured a number of men. A third bomb was a near miss, with splinters piercing the side and causing more casualties. Small fires had been started aft and 'A' boiler room was evacuated. Many of those killed were in the after fire and repair party and this hindered the initial tackling of the fires. New parties attacked the fires, but they were hampered by lack of fire main pressure and the fire gained a good hold. It was found that the main portable pump for the after section had been lost in the fire. The ship remained under power from 'B' boiler room, until water was found to have contaminated the oil fuel, probably because of the bomb damage, water from a leaking fire main having entered the punctured tank. A second air raid then took place, apparently by Ju 88 bombers at high level, but no damage was inflicted. The fire steadily gained until it had spread through four compartments and the engine and boiler rooms were now being affected by the heat and smoke and all had to be evacuated. At 18.00 a fire was observed in the foremost funnel, probably from an oil fire in 'A' boiler room, and 5 minutes later all power was lost. Captain Brooke was now concerned for the safety of the ship as it had proved impossible to flood the after magazines, and he decided to abandon ship. The destroyer *Diamond* was called alongside and at 19.00 men started leaving her and evacuation was complete an hour later. The *Gloucester* then fired a torpedo into her, but this seemed to have little effect. By 21.30 the cruiser *Orion* had arrived on scene and

she fired four torpedoes into the burning wreck, and she rolled over and sank. The approximate position was 34.54N 18.24E. Eighty men were killed.
[TNA: ADM.116/4354]

11 January UBEROUS drifter
Sandhaven 1918 requisitioned 1939; 92 tons; 86.5ft × 19.6ft
Skipper Monypenny Macpherson Anderson RNR

Ran aground in the early hours of the morning in the channel in Lough Foyle approaching Londonderry, and eventually heeled over and sank.
[TNA: ADM.199/658]

11 January MTB 108 motor torpedo boat
Portsmouth; 10 tons; 46ft × 10.5ft

Under construction at the Vosper yard at Portsmouth, she was destroyed on the building slip when the port came under air attack on the night of 10/11 January.
[Secondary]

16 January DESIRÉE trawler
Beverley 1912 requisitioned 1939; 117.2ft × 21.5ft
Skipper Ernest Lubbock Fiske RNR

Employed in sweeping along the Knob Channel in the Thames Estuary, she sank after she exploded a mine when 5 cables (1,000 yards) from the north-west Shingles buoy in position 51.31.52N 01.11.08E. All the crew were saved.
[TNA: ADM.199/407; Lloyd's War Losses vol 1 p179]

20 January RELONZO trawler
Beverley 1914 requisitioned 1939; 245 tons; 120.5ft × 22ft; 1 × 12pdr
Skipper Albert Edward Slater RNR[†]

A Grimsby-registered fishing vessel converted to an armed patrol trawler after being taken over by the Navy and attached to the Minesweeping Group based at Birkenhead. She detonated a mine at 10.15 when near C10 Red buoy in Crosby Channel and broke up with the loss of nineteen men with two survivors.
[TNA: ADM.199/220]

21 January ENGLISHMAN rescue tug
Selby 1937 requisitioned 1939; 487 tons; 135ft × 30.3ft
Master George Henry Spence[†]

Admiralty controlled, civilian manned, she was based at Campbeltown, and sailed from that port during the evening of 20 January, in company with the tug *Restive*, to render assistance to a merchant ship. The weather was poor, and the pair became separated, and *Englishman* was not seen again. The following day at 12 noon an Fw 200 Condor aircraft from 1/KG 40 attacked a tug, sinking her with a single 250kg bomb which struck her amidships. This was evidently the *Englishman*. The

estimated position of the attack was translated as being '40 miles west of Tory Island', but in the prevailing weather, this is doubtful. During 2003 divers discovered her wreck, lying on the seabed 6 miles to the west of the Kintyre village of Bellochantuy. If correct, it is likely that she had taken shelter overnight during the poor weather. The reported position to the 'west' of Tory Island was evidently a mistake for 'east'.
[https://canmore.org.uk/event/940029]

22 January LUDA LADY trawler
Selby 1914 (*Mona; St Elmo*) requisitioned 1939; 234 tons; 122.2ft × 22.2ft
Skipper William Francis Somers RNR
Carrying out an LL sweep for magnetic mines in the approaches to Immingham in company with the trawler *War Duke*, the first lap had been completed and they were returning on the opposite course when at 10.15, about 7 cables (1,400 yards) north of the Middle light vessel, there was a large explosion close on the starboard beam. She started filling with water and the *War Duke* closed to take off the crew. The tug *Negro* arrived on scene and attempted to rig a tow, but before this could be achieved, she filled and sank in position 53.56.33N 00.01.09W. There were no casualties.
[TNA: ADM.199/239; ADM.199/777]

22 January ST CYRUS tug
Chester 1919; 860 tons; 135.4ft × 29ft; 1 × 12pdr
Lieutenant Peter Alan Allan RNR[†]
Searching along the Gateway Channel at the entrance to the river Humber, near the Middle light vessel, for the *Luda Lady* (see above), when at 12.00 there was a large explosion under the vessel as she detonated a mine, and she quickly sank. Eight men lost their lives. The loss position was noted as 53.35.2N 00.03.2E.
[TNA: ADM.119/1172]

27 January DAROGAH trawler
Middlesbrough 1914 requisitioned 1939; 221 tons; 117.5ft × 20ft
Skipper Joseph Harrison RNR
Whilst engaged in sweeping in the Thames Estuary using Sound Acoustic or SA gear, to clear acoustic mines, she was 1,600 yards to the south-west of the Sea Reach buoy when a mine was detonated at 09.13 which exploded close to her. The trawler was badly shaken, and she slowly filled and sank at 10.56.
[TNA: ADM.199/777]

31 January HUNTLEY minesweeper
South Shields 1919; 710 tons; 220ft × 28.6ft; 1 × 4in, 1 × 12pdr
Lieutenant Commander Ernest Sprent Cotsell RNR[†]
Engaged in supplying the garrison at Tobruk, she had sailed from Mersa Matruh. As she steamed along the North African coast, at 17.40 when about 4 miles off Ras Abu Lahu, a pair of He 111 aircraft approached her at low level and conducted a number of attacks. During the first attack she was strafed with machine-gun fire, which caused several casualties on the bridge, including the commanding officer who was mortally wounded. Several bombs were also dropped, one of which hit her, perforating the upper deck to explode in the boiler room. This caused the collapse of both boilers and the consequent loss of power; several rivets were also blown out, leading to water entering. The subsequent attacks saw more strafing and bombs, during which she was near missed by a bomb which exploded close to the stern. This dislodged two depth charges, and as they had not been set to 'safe', they exploded at 150ft underneath her. This blew the stern off the ship as far as the minesweeping winch. She heeled over and started to sink by the stern, and at 18.10 she sank, in position 31.30.5N 26.58E. Eighteen men were killed.
[TNA: ADM.267/103]

2 February ALMOND trawler
Ardrossan 1940; 530 tons; 150ft × 27.6ft; 1 × 12pdr
Skipper Albert Edward Johnson RNR[†]
Returning to Falmouth on completion of sweeping duties, she struck a moored mine at about 14.00 in position 50.30N 04.55W and sank rapidly with the loss of nineteen men with three survivors.
[TNA: ADM.199/220; ADM.358/3006]

3 February MIDAS drifter
Lowestoft 1910 requisitioned 1939; 89 tons; 84.6ft × 19.6ft; 1 × 3pdr
Skipper Herbert Holden RNR
Whilst conducting a night patrol off Dungeness she was in collision at 05.30 with another armed patrol drifter, the *Girl Gladys*. All the crew were taken off as she steadily settled, and she was left at daylight, decks awash but still afloat. A subsequent search was unsuccessful, and she was presumed to have sunk shortly after being abandoned.
[TNA: ADM.199/889]

3 February MGB 12 motor gun boat
Hythe 1940 (*MA/SB 12*); 31 tons; 70ft × 20ft; 1 × 2pdr
Severely damaged by the near explosion of a mine when near the boom at Milford Haven, she lost power and subsequently drifted until she fouled the boom. The following day she was hauled clear of the boom but then subsequently sank when under tow for the harbour. The wreck lies in position 51.43N 06.45W.
[TNA: ADM.196/220; ADM.199/658]

James Fennell ashore at Blacknor Point, Portland. (*Portland Museum*)

Raleigh on the rocks at Point Amour, Labrador. (*Mary Evans – Pharcide*)

Salvage attempts underway over the site of the sunken *M 2*. (*John Barrett Collection – Mary Evans*)

The *Walrus* in the surf off Scarborough having lost her tow. (*British Pathé*)

Walrus high and dry on the beach at Scarborough. (*Mary Evans – Imagno*)

Salvage vessels struggle to keep the stern of *Thetis* above water. (*British Pathé*)

Courageous heels over after being torpedoed by U 29. (*Mary Evans – SZPhoto-Scherl*)

Requisitioned trawler *Aragonite* sunk in shallow water after being mined. (*British Pathé*)

The remains of the *Glowworm* sinking, as seen through *Admiral Hipper*'s rangefinder. (*Imperial War Museum*)

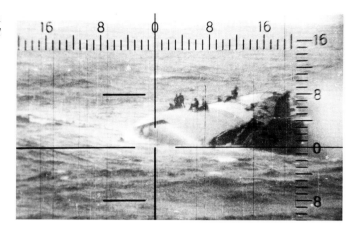

Bittern ablaze in Namsos Fjord after air attacks. (*Imperial War Museum*)

The damaged *Mashobra* in shallow water near Harstad. (*Imperial War Museum*)

Shark on the surface and about to be boarded. (*Imperial War Museum*)

Destroyer *Ivanhoe* is despatched by torpedo from HMS *Kelvin*. (*Imperial War Museum*)

Right: Bombs fall around *Chakla* during an air attack at Tobruk. (*British Pathé*)

Left: *Ladybird* resting on the bottom of Tobruk harbour. (*British Pathé*)

Attackers' view of the *Gloucester* under air attack off Crete. (*Imperial War Museum*)

Defender, her back broken after air attack, just before sinking, seen from HMAS *Voyager*. (*Imperial War Museum*)

Ark Royal torpedoed and listing to starboard; the view from HMS *Hermione*. (*Imperial War Museum*)

Barham rolls over before exploding after being torpedoed. (*British Pathé*)

Prince of Wales sinking; HMS *Express* is alongside as the crew abandons ship. (*Imperial War Museum*)

Destroyer *Gallant* with bows blown off, reduced to a hulk at Malta. (*Imperial War Museum*)

3 February CRISPIN ocean boarding vessel
Birkenhead 1935 requisitioned 1940; 5,051 tons;
412.2ft × 55.8ft; 2 × 6in, 1 × 12pdr
Lieutenant Commander Bernard Moloney RNR[†]
Part of the escort assigned to Convoy OB280, she
loitered astern of the convoy as it was dispersed on 3
February to the south of Iceland. At 23.35 when in
position 56.36N 21.35W, she was struck by a torpedo
which exploded on the port side beneath the bridge.
This probably destroyed the bulkhead of number 2 hold,
which rapidly flooded, and then through the bilges into
the engine and boiler rooms. She settled steadily and
an hour after being hit the boats were ordered to be
cleared away before she capsized over to port and sank,
her boilers exploding as she disappeared. Eight officers
and twelve ratings were killed; the survivors were found
by the destroyer *Harvester*. Criticism was subsequently
made of the lack of cooperation between the convoy
escorts, which had led to a delay in the rescue of the
survivors. Her attacker had been the *U 107* (Hessler).
[*TNA: ADM.267/92*]

3 February ARCTIC TRAPPER trawler
Selby 1928 (*Sprayflower*) requisitioned 1940; 352 tons;
140.3ft × 24ft; 1 × 12pdr
Skipper Louis Martin Harvey RNR[†]
Bombed by a group of Ju 87 Stuka aircraft when 3 miles
to the east of Ramsgate pier, in position 51.19.45N
01.31.45E, she suffered a direct hit amidships, and she
sank very quickly. Three men were picked up from a
Carley float, but none survived, all seventeen men on
board losing their lives.
[*TNA: ADM.199/777; ADM.358/3017*]

4 February IMBAT drifter
Buckie 1918 requisitioned 1940; 92 tons; 87.1ft × 19.7ft
Based at Scapa Flow, she was damaged in a collision
off Lyness pier and subsequently foundered. The cost of
salvage and repair was considered to be excessive, and
the hull was dispersed by explosives.
[*TNA: ADM.199/2224*]

5 February TOURMALINE trawler
Middlesbrough 1936 (*Berkshire*); 446 tons; 164.1ft × 27.1ft;
1 × 4in
Lieutenant Henry Patterson Carse RNVR
Part of the escort to northbound coastal Convoy
CE24 which passed through the Dover area during
the early hours of 5 February, at 09.00 the ships were
approaching the North East Spit buoy when an enemy
reconnaissance aircraft was seen, clearly shadowing the
convoy. An hour later, when off North Foreland, a large
group of Ju 87 Stuka aircraft appeared and commenced
an attack on the ships. A flight of RAF fighter aircraft

intercepted and shot down one of the enemy aircraft,
and another attacker was shot down by anti-aircraft fire
from the convoy. Despite this, the enemy pressed home
their attack and the *Tourmaline* was straddled by three
bombs and sank rapidly in position 51.23.44N 01.31.
11E. Twenty-four men were picked up, but two men
were killed.
[*TNA: ADM.199/405; ADM.199/777*]

6 February HOPPER NUMBER 39 auxiliary
minesweeper
Requisitioned 1941; 1,500 tons
During January and February 1941 there was extensive
minelaying in the Suez Canal by German aircraft.
Several craft were hastily requisitioned and converted
to minesweeping, which included four canal hopper-
dredgers. Fitted with LL gear to trigger magnetic mines,
Hopper 39 was working between kilometre markers 136
and 137 when she detonated a magnetic mine which
exploded with a double concussion close ahead of her.
She rapidly sank with the loss of four lives.
[*TNA: ADM. 199/250; ADM.199/413*]

10 February BOY ALAN drifter
Lowestoft 1914 requisitioned 1939; 109 tons;
89.5ft × 20.3ft; 1 × 6pdr
Skipper Ernest Henry Crowe DSC
On passage for conversion to a minesweeper, she was
damaged in collision with the trawler *Ben Glas* (234 tons)
off Sheerness in the Thames Estuary and subsequently
foundered in position 51.29.33N 00.45.21E.
[*TNA: ADM.199/777*]

(11?) February SNAPPER submarine
Chatham 1934; 670/960 tons; 193ft × 24ft; 1 × 3in,
6 × torpedo tubes
Lieutenant Geoffrey Vernon Prowse[†]
Sailed from the Clyde 29 January for a patrol off
the southern coast of Brittany, she failed to return as
expected on 12 February. The reason for her loss remains
uncertain; hitting a mine is likely, although it is possible
that an attack by German minesweepers *M 2*, *M 13*
and *M 25* in position 47.52.5N 05.47W in the early
hours of 11 February may be responsible. This followed
a torpedo attack on the group by a submarine at 02.39
which failed and resulted in the attacker broaching.
The minesweepers gained a sonar contact and dropped
fifty-six depth charges in a small area. Although no oil
or debris came to the surface, the submerged contact
was subsequently lost. This was in the patrol area of the
Snapper, although she should have finished her patrol on
the 10th to return home. Five officers and thirty-seven
ratings were lost.
[*Evans pp268–9*]

11 February **SOUTHERN FLOE** whaler

Vegesack 1936 requisitioned 1940; 344 tons;
139.3ft × 26.1ft; 1 × 3pdr, 1 × 20mm
Lieutenant John Edward Joseph Lewis SANF†

South African Navy. Deployed to Tobruk, she was detailed to carry out a night patrol off the port, but when her relief, *Southern Sea*, arrived during the morning, she found no sign of her. Later that day a patch of wreckage was found by HMAS *Voyager* and a single survivor, who testified that at approximately 04.00 there had been a heavy explosion, and the ship had broken in half and sunk very quickly. It was presumed that she had struck a floating mine. Twenty-seven men were lost.
[TNA: ADM 358/3826; https://samilhistory.com]

13 February **RUBENS** trawler

Ostend 1937 requisitioned 1940; 320 tons; 138.3ft × 26ft
Lieutenant Henry Gardiner Pyle RNR†

Sailed with Convoy OG52 for Gibraltar but failed to arrive as expected. It emerged that she had parted company with the convoy during the night of 10/11 February, probably when she mistook a signal with the intended future course of the convoy as an instruction to herself. It was later discovered that *Rubens* had been sunk when attacked by an Fw 200 aircraft at 14.28 in position 48.50N 14.20W with the loss of all twenty-one men onboard.
[TNA: ADM.199/1173; ADM.358/3346]

14 February **MTB 41** motor torpedo boat

Cowes 1940; 37 tons; 72.1ft × 18.2ft; 2 × torpedo tubes
Lieutenant Commander John Colin Cole†

Acting as Senior Officer of the Fifth MTB Flotilla, the boat was blown to pieces when she detonated a mine in the southern North Sea in position 51.57.30W 02.27.30E. The boat sank very quickly, and only three ratings were picked up, eight men being lost.
[TNA: ADM.199/777]

16 February **SOUTHSEA** paddle minesweeper

Govan 1930 requisitioned 1940; 825 tons; 244ft × 30.1ft;
1 × 12pdr
Lieutenant Commander Charles Clifford Matthews Pawley
RNR

Former ferry converted for use as a minesweeper, she joined the minesweeping flotilla based at North Shields. At 13.55 she was entering the River Tyne and was about 4 cables (800 yards) to the west of North Tyne Pier when there was a large underwater explosion under her stern, and a column of water rose on either side of the after part of the ship. The shock blew a machine gun mounted aft onto the fo'c'sle and killed several men, some of whom were thrown some distance forward. The after end of the ship was shattered, being enveloped in a cloud of smoke and steam. The explosion had been

seen by the pilot vessel *Vigilant*, which immediately closed, to find her settling by the stern. A rope was quickly passed, and the pilot vessel towed her out of the main channel until she ran aground in shallow water on the Herd Sand. By now a fire had broken out on board, started by hot coals having been scattered by the blast. With the help of the harbour fire float this was tackled, and the flames extinguished. Examination of the ship found that about a third of the hull was missing, and 65 per cent of the superstructure had been destroyed. She was therefore declared a constructive total loss and subsequently sold to the British Iron and Steel Corporation (Salvage) Ltd., for scrapping. She proved difficult to remove completely, and remains of the wreck were causing problems as late as 1949. Eight men were killed.
[TNA: ADM.1/21232]

16 February **ORMONDE** trawler

Selby 1906 requisitioned 1939; 250 tons; 125ft × 22ft
Skipper William Thompson Coull RNR†

In company with two other minesweeping trawlers, the *Chrysolite* and *Ligny*, engaged in sweeping about 7 miles to the east of Cruden Scaur, Peterhead. During the morning, a mine was brought to the surface, and the *Ligny* was detached to dispose of it. Whilst the other pair formed up to resume sweeping an aircraft, identified as an He 111, was seen closing from the east at low level. The aircraft headed straight for the *Ormonde* and as it passed overhead dropped two bombs, one or both of which hit her. She was seen to be covered in a cloud of smoke, steam and spray and sank in less than 2 minutes. The aircraft then attacked the *Chrysolite* but failed to secure any hits and made off. A search of the area failed to find any survivors, and a search by the Peterhead lifeboat also found nothing. Some days later a solitary lifebuoy from the ship was washed ashore at Cruden Bay. All eighteen men on board were lost.
[TNA: ADM.267/102]

20 February **LINCOLN CITY** trawler

Middlesbrough 1933 (*Pembroke Castle*) requisitioned 1939;
398 tons; 155ft × 26.4ft
Lieutenant Francis Albert Seward RNR

Whilst laying at anchor at Tórshavn in the Faeroe Islands, the port was attacked by a pair of He 111 aircraft, taking the ships in the anchorage by surprise when they appeared over the hills behind the town. One aircraft dropped bombs on the oil storage depot but missed; this aircraft came under intense anti-aircraft fire, and after dropping more bombs which landed in open water, force-landed in the sea. The second aircraft attacked *Lincoln City*, dropping a single bomb, which hit the water about 10 yards from her port side to enter the hull below the waterline and after about 5 seconds detonated. She rolled over and sank quickly, with the loss of eight men.

[TNA: ADM.199/1173]

20 February OUSE trawler

Selby 1917 (Andrew King); 462 tons; 138.6ft × 23.9ft

Lieutenant John Edmund Grice

The ship arrived at Tobruk from Alexandria during 18 February, to commence sweeping the port with acoustic minesweeping equipment or SA gear. The following morning, she commenced work and at 10.39 a double explosion was seen, as mines detonated under her, and she sank immediately, then being about 120 yards from number 133 buoy. Twelve men lost their lives.

[TNA: ADM.199/220]

24 February TERROR monitor

Belfast 1916; 7,720 tons; 380ft × 88.2ft; 2 × 15in, 8 × 4in, 2 × 2pdr

Commander Henry John Haynes DSC

Based in the eastern Mediterranean, she arrived at Benghazi on 16 February, to provide coastal defence for that port, berthing at the end of the breakwater. For the next week, the harbour was subjected to constant air raids, although she remained undamaged until 22 February. During the afternoon, another raid developed, and this time several dive bombers concentrated on the *Terror*. Most of the bombs missed, but one landed close to the port bulge, lifting the whole ship and causing extensive shock damage. The bulges flooded, bulkheads were buckled, and leaks were reported in shell rooms and magazines. Later that afternoon she was ordered to proceed to Tobruk without delay, but at 19.10 as they were preparing to leave there was another air raid, which saw several near misses around the monitor. By 21.00 she was under way, but as she proceeded down the swept channel two mines, presumed to be acoustic, detonated about 200 yards away off the port beam. They shook the ship considerably. The following morning (23 February) saw her proceeding slowly along the coastline, with the minesweeper *Fareham* going ahead, with sweeps streamed. An assessment of her damage revealed that the double bottom was reported to be flooding; she was estimated to have nearly 400 tons of water in her bulges, oil fuel tanks and bottom, and the pumps were working constantly. At 18.20 she again came under attack, when five Ju 88 bombers accompanied by fighter aircraft were seen approaching from the starboard quarter. They commenced a dive-bombing attack, being engaged by both ships with AA fire. The bombers concentrated on the *Terror*, each of them dropping three bombs; the first aircraft put all the bombs wide and the second dropped across the port bow. The third aircraft, however, was more accurate, with all the bombs dropping close to her starboard side, at least one exploding underneath her. She was lifted out of the water and the shock of the bombs 'gave her a most severe shaking'. This wrecked all small fittings on board and caused considerable structural damage. The ship's back seemed to be broken between the turret and the bridge, the fo'c'sle was buckled and distorted, the deck being separated from the side plating. Below decks, the engine room and boiler rooms reported that they were flooding with oil and water. As the oil spilled into the boiler room it caught fire and a thick cloud of smoke enveloped the ship. The engine and boiler rooms were abandoned and shored up as she took a list to starboard. The *Fareham* closed and prepared to take her in tow. Towing got under way, but the monitor was settling lower into the water all the time and it was clear that she could not last long. At 23.30 it was decided to abandon her, and all the men were taken off by *Fareham* and the corvette *Salvia* which had now joined. When this was complete, during the early hours of the 24th depth charges were dropped along her starboard side and at 04.00 she slowly rolled over to starboard, capsized and sank at 04.15. There were no casualties.

[TNA: ADM.1/11292]

24 February DAINTY destroyer

Govan 1932; 1,375 tons; 317.9ft × 33ft; 4 × 4.7in, 2 × 2pdr, 8 × torpedo tubes

Commander Mervyn Somerset Thomas

In company with the destroyer *Hasty*, the pair sailed from Tobruk at 18.30 to carry out a night patrol between Bomba and Ras Azzaza. They had scarcely cleared the harbour when the sound of an aircraft was heard, but in the gloom of twilight it could not be seen. At 18.57 the sound of a falling bomb was heard and there was a large explosion aft as she was struck by a bomb which penetrated the upper deck to explode in the officers' cabins. The stern was wrecked with the ships side being opened for over 15ft on the port side and the upper deck was blown upwards. Oil fuel in the after tank ignited and burning oil poured out into the sea. The ship continued steaming at 20 knots and managed to clear the patch of burning oil until the engines came to a stop at 19.00. The fire took hold and spread through the after compartments. The heat caused the depth charges and torpedoes to burst open in the heat and their contents burned fiercely. At 19.05 there was a large explosion, probably caused by the depth charges stored in the warhead magazine exploding. This broke her back, and she sank very quickly, the *Hasty* and other small vessels from the harbour picking up survivors. Fourteen men were lost. Her unseen attacker had been a low-flying He 111 bomber.

[TNA: ADM.267/104]

24 February MANISTEE ocean boarding vessel
Birkenhead 1920 requisitioned 1940; 5,360 tons;
400.2ft × 51.1ft; 2 × 6in, 1 × 12pdr
Lieutenant Commander Eric Haydn Smith RNR†
Part of the Western Patrol, to intercept and search
suspect shipping, she joined Convoy OB288 that had
sailed from Liverpool on 18 February, to proceed to her
station to the west of Ireland. The convoy was only to
be escorted to 15 degrees East, about 750 miles to the
west of Land's End, where it would be dispersed, and
the escorts withdrew. The convoy was located during
the morning of 22 March by an Fw 200 aircraft, which
also carried out a bombing attack. To avoid the enemy
submarines that were concentrating on the course of
the convoy, CinC Western Approaches ordered the
convoy to alter course, but this was not carried out.
On 23 February, the escorts left the convoy, and it was
expected that ships would disperse. Several submarines
were now in position to attack the ships, but it was
U 107 (Hessler) that found *Manistee* and was able to
make an attack at 21.45 in position 58.13N 21.33W.
Hit by a torpedo on the port side, she reported that she
was making water in her main bunker but was stable
and was steering north at 6 knots. The corvette *Heather*
was ordered to proceed to her aid and the destroyer
Churchill was also later directed to the area. At 06.18
the following morning a brief message was received
from her indicating that she had been torpedoed
again, but nothing more was heard from her and the
searching ships could find no trace of her. It was later
found that she had been attacked for a second time at
07.58 on 24 February by *U 107* in position 59.30N
21W, securing a hit in the aft cargo hold, at which she
started to sink by the stern. There were no survivors:
141 men died.
[TNA: ADM.199/658; ADM.199/1051]

25 February EXMOOR escort destroyer
Walker 1940; 1,000 tons; 264.2ft × 29ft; 4 × 4in, 4 × 2pdr
Lieutenant Commander Robert Tindle Lampard†
Part of the escort to North Sea Convoy FN17 they
were to the east of Lowestoft when *Exmoor* was
detached to speak to a broken-down merchant ship.
That complete she was underway at 10 knots when at
21.00 and then being about 5 cables (1,000 yards) to
the south of number 5 buoy, with no warning there
was a large explosion under the ship. The centre of
the explosion was 66-67 station, midway between the
forward fuel tank and the aft oil fuel group. The ship,
from the pom-pom deck to the stern, was enveloped
in a sheet of flame which rose about 40ft into the air.
The ship heeled over to port as the fire spread forward
and burning oil from the punctured tanks poured out
to cover the sea around her. With a list of 20 degrees to
port, the ship 'hung' for a while and then capsized to

lay on her beam ends surrounded by burning fuel. The
stern then began to sink, and her bows rose clear until
she stood on end and sank in approximate position
52.29N 02.40E. The time from the explosion to her
disappearance was less than 10 minutes, leaving a large
patch of burning oil. The patrol vessel *Shearwater* saw
the blaze and closed to pick up thirty-two survivors,
but 106 men were killed. There was some uncertainty
at the time over the cause of the explosion, only later
did it emerge that she had been attacked by a torpedo
boat, the *S 30*.
[TNA: ADM.199/670; ADM.267/92; Foynes pp110–12]

25 February SARNA whaler
Middlesbrough 1930 requisitioned 1940; 268 tons;
121.4ft × 24.6ft
Skipper Walter Thomas Allen RNR
Stationed in Egypt she was ordered to sweep the Suez
Canal, after several mines had been discovered. At 13.10
when adjacent to the 138.5km marker there was an
explosion under the engine room. She was covered in
steam which came out in vast quantities, and the engine
room was abandoned. The Skipper put his helm hard to
starboard and made for the west bank of the canal and
ran close alongside the tug *Atlas* and dropped anchor.
The tug responded quickly by rigging lines to her, but
she was sinking fast and 7 minutes after the explosion
went under. One man was killed.
[TNA: ADM.199/239]

27 February REMILLO trawler
Beverley 1917 (*Robert Betson*) requisitioned 1940; 281
tons; 125.2ft × 22ft; 1 × 3pdr
Skipper Herbert Henry Jarvis RNR†
Fitted as a dan-layer, *Remillo* foundered after she
detonated a mine in the river Humber, when she was
1.76 miles to the east of Spurn Point lighthouse. She
sank in shallow water with her masts and funnel awash
at low water. Seventeen men were lost.
[Lloyd's War Losses vol 1 p196]

28 February MA/SB 3 motor anti-submarine boat
Hythe 1939; 19 tons; 60ft × 13.11ft; small arms and depth
charges
Lieutenant John Duff Ritchie
Stationed in Egypt, she was pressed into service to help
clear mines in the Suez Canal (see 25 February *Sarna*).
It was hoped that by running a high-speed craft over
the area, mines would be detonated, but the speed of
the vessel would take her clear. *MA/SB 3* made several
high-speed runs along the canal, but with no result.
Having completed her work, she slowed and headed
inshore to berth, but as she approached the bank there
was a large explosion as she set off a mine. The craft
rapidly filled with water and settled in shallow water

next to the bank. Although all the crew suffered injuries, none were killed. The boat was later salvaged from the canal but found to be so severely damaged that it was written off as a total loss.
[Reynolds & Cooper, Mediterranean MTBs at War p15]

1 March ST DONATS trawler
Beverley 1924 requisitioned 1939; 349 tons; 140.3ft × 24ft
Skipper Frederick Lawrence Atkinson RNR
Foundered at 00.15 in approaches to the river Humber in position 53.29N 01.01E following a collision with the escort destroyer *Cotswold* some 45 minutes earlier.
[TNA: ADM.199/777]

3 March COBBERS trawler
Aberdeen 1919 (*William Knight*) requisitioned 1940; 276 tons; 125ft × 23.4ft; 1 × 12pdr
Skipper Lawrence Turner RNR†
Sunk by enemy air attack at about noon near 'A' buoy off Lowestoft; four survivors were picked up but eleven men, including the skipper, were lost.
[TNA: ADM.199/407; ADM.199/2225]

3 March KNIGHT OF MALTA transport vessel
Newcastle 1929 requisitioned 1940; 1,553 tons; 260.5ft × 37.3ft
Lieutenant Commander Frederick Walter Johnson RNR
Employed as a stores and transport ship, she departed Alexandria on 1 March with several troops on board bound for Tobruk, but in the early hours of the morning in poor weather ran aground 2 miles from Ras Azzass, near Bardia. Salvage of the ship was abandoned on 10 March, following bombing attacks on the corvette *Peony* and tug *St Issey*, which had been sent to the scene.
[Statement of Losses, Amendment p3; www.naval-history.net.]

6 March KERYADO trawler
Hamburg 1920, seized 1940; 252 tons; 121.8ft × 23ft; 1 × 12pdr
Skipper Henry Charles Gue DSC RNR
Ex-French trawler, taken over by the French Navy as minesweeper *AD112* she was forcibly taken into British service in 1940. In company with the trawlers *Lois* and *Gulfoss*, the latter of which was towing the lighter *X218*, sailed from Dover 6 March, all being bound for Swansea. At 10.48 when to the south of Beachy Head, in position 50.36.5N 00.09E, there was a large explosion close under her starboard bow when she detonated a mine. The ship heeled over to starboard and sank bows first, in about 3 minutes. A secondary explosion occurred before she sank, probably the magazine exploding. *Lois* picked up twelve survivors, but nine men were killed. Wreck lies in position 50.37.7N 00.04.9W.
[TNA: ADM.199/239]

6 March SUN VII tug
Wivenhoe 1918 requisitioned 1939; 202 tons; 105.2ft × 25.5ft
Master George Cawsey
Detonated a mine and foundered, position reported to be 1–2 miles 60 degrees North Knob Buoy, Barrow Deep, Thames Estuary. Five crew members were lost.
[TNA: ADM.358/3835; Lloyd's War Losses p198]

7 March MTB 28 motor torpedo boat
Hampton 1940; 37 tons; 70ft × 16.7ft; 2 × torpedo tubes
Sub-Lieutenant William King Croxton RNVR
Whilst berthed alongside at HMS *Hornet*, the coastal forces base at Gosport, she suffered an internal explosion and fire and was burnt out. Two people were killed in the explosion.
[TNA: ADM.199/777]

9 March GULLFOSS trawler
Selby 1929 requisitioned 1939; 358 tons; 140.4ft × 25ft; 1 × 12pdr
Skipper Alfred Hill RNR
Conducting sweeping operations off Dover, a mine exploded at 08.00 whilst she was heaving in her sweeps, probably because of a mine lodging in her gear, and she rapidly sank with the loss of ten men. Wreck lies at 50.51.30N 00.56.42E.
[TNA: ADM.199/239; Larn vol 2 sec 4]

March MGB 98 motor gun boat
Nantes 1940 (*VTB11*) seized 1940; 26 tons; 65.7ft × 13ft; 1 × 20mm
Lost in an air raid on *Hornet* at Gosport; the date is uncertain but probably during the night of 10/11 March which was a particularly heavy raid on Portsmouth and Gosport.
[Statement of Losses p13 and Amendment p2]

16 March LADY LILIAN trawler
Beverley 1939 requisitioned 1940; 581 tons; 178.1ft × 30ft; 1 × 4in
Lieutenant the Honourable William Keith Rous RNVR
In company with four other armed trawlers of the Third Escort Group, she sailed from Greenock to rendezvous with the incoming Convoy HG55. At 09.55 on 16 March, with one trawler detached with engine trouble, the remaining ships were about 150 miles to the west of Ireland, in position 54.18N 12.10W, steaming in line abreast, when an aircraft was seen approaching from ahead. The aircraft, now identified as an Fw 200, then turned to close them from their starboard side, and ran over the group, dropping a number of bombs, two of which dropped off the starboard quarter of the *Lady Lilian* but caused no damage. The aircraft then turned to carry out a second attack, with all the bombs bursting

around the *Lilian*. This gave her a violent shaking, lifting her out of the water. Water was found to be entering the engine room, and the ship's side was seen to be split from gunwale to the waterline by the amidships bunker. She was abandoned, rapidly filled with water, and sank 10 minutes later. There were no casualties.
[TNA: ADM.199/1173]

16 March **CHABOOL** tug
Requisitioned 1940; 48 tons
Lieutenant John Mumford RNR[†]
Sailed from Aden at 17.30 on 15 March for Berbera with one officer and seven ratings, ex-HMS *Glasgow*, as crew, with fuel and provisions for 4 days, and never seen again. An air search of the area failed to find any trace of her, and she was presumed lost, probably by hitting a mine. She was formally paid off on 22 March.
Note: the *Statement of Losses* wrongly lists her name as *Chabook*.
[TNA: ADM.199/777; ADM.358/3148]

17 March **MOLLUSC** yacht
Southampton 1906 (*Medusa*) requisitioned 1939; 598 tons; 199.1ft × 26.1ft; 1 × 12pdr
Lieutenant Nicholas Percy Doyle RNR
Employed as an examination vessel, she was laying off St Mary's lighthouse, Blyth, having anchored due to poor visibility. When the weather showed signs of clearing, she prepared to weigh, but as she was doing so a single aircraft, believed to be a Ju 88, appeared from astern and headed straight towards her. The yacht managed to engage the oncoming aircraft with machine guns, but it had no effect, and two bombs were dropped which exploded close on the port side, starting leaks which led her to sink 15 minutes later. There were no casualties. The wreck lies in position 55.06.15N 01.26.06W.
[TNA: ADM.199/1173; ADM.267/28; Larn vol 3 sec 7]

18 March **ROSAURA** armed boarding vessel
Govan 1905 (*Dieppe*) requisitioned 1939; 1,552 tons; 273.5ft × 34.8ft
Captain Ronald Keith Spencer RNVR
In company with three merchant ships, and escorted by the whaler *Southern Maid*, the *Rosaura* sailed from Tobruk for Alexandria, carrying 400 Italian prisoners of war and their guards, in addition to three passengers. The group proceeded slowly toward the gate in the boom at the entrance to the harbour, and the *Southern Maid* and one of the merchant ships had passed through when the corvette *Gloxinia* was seen approaching from seawards. The *Rosaura*, next in line, waited for the *Gloxinia* to enter, and on being signalled that it was clear to proceed, went through the gate. When clear the engines were put to half ahead and she steered to join the escort, but moments later, at 12.22 there was a large explosion under the hull. The rudder would not answer the helm and attempts to put the engines to full astern also failed, as the telegraphs were broken. The engine room reported that they were flooding, and she took heavy list to port. Within 2 minutes the stern was awash, and she continued to rapidly sink by the stern until it rested on the bottom, the bows rising clear of the water. At that point, the forward bulkhead of number 1 oil bunker then apparently gave way and the ship rapidly flooded. She righted herself and then sank, with her foremast showing above water. Her position was noted as being 146 degrees Tobruk Point Light 9 cables (1,800 yards). An acoustic mine, probably air-dropped during a raid on 13 March, was believed to have been responsible. Thirteen members of her crew, with five military guards and fifty-nine prisoners of war, were lost.
[TNA: ADM.1/11291]

20 March **HELVELLYN** auxiliary anti-aircraft vessel
Govan 1937 (*Juno*) requisitioned 1939; 642 tons; 223ft × 30ft
Lieutenant Percy Baker RNVR
Fitting out in Surrey Commercial Docks, London, she was hit by a bomb at 23.00 during a very heavy air raid and so damaged that she was written off as a constructive total loss. One man died of his wounds.
[TNA: ADM.199/1173]

20 March **GLOAMING** drifter
1928 requisitioned 1939; 28 tons
Skipper Daniel Main RNR
Employed as a local patrol vessel, the drifter was returning to Grimsby after a night patrol, when at 10.15 off Grimsby hydraulic tower she detonated a mine, capsized, and sank. Three men were killed, with two survivors.
[TNA: ADM.196/220]

20 March **SOIZIC** drifter
(France) 1937; seized 1940; 72 tons
Former Breton fishing vessel, requisitioned by the French Navy to serve as the minesweeper *AD414* before being taken over by the Royal Navy, she was based at Plymouth. The craft is listed as 'Lost' in the *Statement of Losses*, with no further detail, but it was probably during the heavy enemy air raid on the city that took place on the night of 20/21 March.
[Statement of Losses p15]

20 March **DOX** fishing vessel
(Belgium) 1931 requisitioned 1940; 35 tons
The vessel, employed as a local patrol vessel, is listed as being lost on this date, but with no further detail; she was probably lost because of the enemy air raid on the city of Plymouth during the night of 20/21 March.
[Statement of Losses p14; TNA: ADM.199/2429]

21 March ASAMA trawler
Middlesbrough 1929 requisitioned 1939; 303 tons;
131ft × 24ft; 1 × 12pdr
Lieutenant Noel Page RNR[†]

Lying at anchor 4 cables (800 yards) from the breakwater at Plymouth during an intensive air raid, in which numerous fires had been started in the town which lit up the horizon. At 23.35 a number of bombs were dropped which exploded around her, with one hitting her on the starboard side, near the funnel, and detonating on the bottom plates. She sank immediately with the loss of six men.
[TNA:ADM.199/1173]

24 March WILNA yacht
Gosport 1939 requisitioned 1940; 461 tons; 165ft × 26ft;
1 × 4in
Lieutenant Llewellyn Winston Cleverley RNR

Heading out of Portsmouth harbour, she was about 1.5 miles to the west of the Nab Tower when at 08.00 she saw an aircraft closing from seaward, which was seen to bank and turn towards them. The twin rudders identified it as being a probable enemy aircraft and the yacht went to action stations. The aircraft ran straight over them, firing with machine guns with some effect, wrecking the Asdic hut on the fo'c'sle before circling round for a second attack. This time two bombs were released which exploded close on the starboard side. She lost steering and the after compartments were reported to be flooding so the boats were hoisted out and she was abandoned, the water being up to the main deck as the last men left her. The trawlers *Cypress* and *Dalmatia* closed to pick them up as the yacht sank at 08.35 one mile to the west of Nab Tower. The wreck lies in position 50.40.42N 00.55.34W.
[TNA:ADM.267/128; Larn vol 2 sec 3]

26 March YORK heavy cruiser
Jarrow 1928; 8,250 tons; 540ft × 57ft; 6 × 8in, 4 × 4in,
6 × torpedo tubes
Captain Reginald Henry Portal

In early March Operation 'Lustre', the British reinforcement of Greece, got under way and as part of the force screening the passage of ships the *York*, in company with the cruiser *Gloucester*, arrived at Suda Bay, north-western Crete at 14.00 on 25 March, with the intention of refuelling and then sailing the next morning. Both ships had competed the fuelling by 18.00 and *York* then moved out to anchor for the night in the bay, which was full of ships. The crew remained closed-up, as air attacks were thought possible. At 05.11 lookouts reported the sound of high-speed engines, and it was thought to be aircraft approaching, although nothing could be seen. A minute later there was an explosion on the starboard side amidships. The explosion ruptured the bulkhead between 'B' boiler room and the forward engine room, and both immediately flooded. She took a list to starboard and started to settle by the stern. All power and lights failed, plunging the ship into darkness. Damage control parties worked hard to tackle the damage, but by 06.30 the flood had spread into 'A' boiler room and she had settled 6ft by the stern. It was thought likely that she might sink where she was, so a tug, the *Irini Veronicos*, was brought alongside and with the assistance of the destroyer *Hasty*, the *York* was moved inshore into shallow water where she ran aground. Salvage operations were then started to clear the water, with portable pumps being embarked, and this was aided by the arrival of the salvage tug *Protector* on 14 April which had some success in pumping out some flooded compartments. At this time hopes were high that she could be salvaged, but from 22 April she became the target for a sustained aerial bombing campaign. On that day, a number of bombs exploded alongside, causing extensive shock damage and causing the engine room to flood again. In a further raid 2 days later, a bomb exploded close to the port side causing heavy concussion and opening more leaks in the hull, causing 'B' magazine to flood. Work continued, but on 28 April all salvage work was stopped, and she was ordered to be stripped and abandoned. Over the next few days stores and ammunition was landed, and her crew started to be sent away. The air raids continued unabated, and she was hit several more times; on 18 May one bomb exploded on 'B' turret and 'Y' turret suffered a direct hit on 20 May. On 19 May orders were issued that what could not be removed should be destroyed, and the last man left her on the night of 20 May. She had been hit not by aircraft but by two Italian explosive motorboats which had successfully penetrated the anchorage. In addition to the *York*, the tanker *Pericles* was also hit. Two men were killed in the attack.
[TNA:ADM.199/777]

26 March OTTER armed yacht
New York 1921 (*Conseco*) requisitioned 1940; 419 tons;
160ft × 25ft; 1 × 12pdr
Lieutenant Dennis Sinclair Mossman RCNR

Royal Canadian Navy. Sailed from Halifax to rendezvous with the incoming submarine *Talisman*, she took station off Sambro Light Vessel. The weather was poor, with bitterly cold, strong winds and heavy seas. At 08.45 flames burst up through the upper deck from the engine room, and the fire rapidly spread. Fire-fighting efforts made little impression and she was ordered to be abandoned. The crew left her in two dinghies and a Carley float, but were exposed to the freezing conditions and were in poor condition when the *Talisman* arrived on scene. In addition, an inbound merchant ship, the *Wisla* came to their aid. Between them, in difficult conditions, they managed to save twenty-two men, but nineteen men died. The cause of the fire was uncertain, but probably due to the starboard generator being overloaded.

[McKee & Darlington p30]

31 March BONAVENTURE cruiser

Greenock 1939; 5,600 tons; 485ft × 50.6ft; 8 × 5.25in, 1 × 4in, 6 × torpedo tubes

Captain Henry Jack Egerton

During March British forces in Greece were reinforced from Alexandria, the convoys being covered by the Royal Navy. During the evening of 29 March, the *Bonaventure* joined the escort to Convoy GA8, which consisted of the troopships *Breconshire* and *Cameronia*, returning to Egypt after offloading their troops, with three destroyers. The cruiser took station astern of the convoy, which was in line abreast. At 02.55 in position 33.09N 26.57E, she was hit by two torpedoes fired by the Italian submarine *Ambra* (Arillo). The first hit abreast the foremost engine room, the second further aft, in the after engine room. The bulkheads between them were probably blown in as she flooded very quickly and immediately heeled over to starboard. The order was given to lower boats, but none were able to get away, although some floats and rafts were released before she sank. The ship continued to steadily roll over until she was almost on her beam ends, recovered slightly, then still with a list of about 60 degrees, sank stern first, only 5 minutes after the first explosion. The destroyers *Hereward* and *Stuart* picked up 300 survivors, but twenty-three officers and 115 ratings were lost.

[TNA:ADM.267/76]

31 March LORD SELBOURNE trawler

Beverley 1917 requisitioned 1940; 247 tons; 117.2ft × 22ft; 1 × 12pdr

Skipper Frank Watkinson RNR†

Sank at 11.10 after she detonated a mine at the entrance to the river Humber; she was then to the east of Spurn Head signal station and to the north of the swept channel. Seventeen men were lost. The position of the sinking was noted as 53.34.2N 00.12.4E.

[TNA:ADM.1/11172; Lloyd's War Losses vol 1 p212]

2 April CRAMOND ISLAND trawler

Govan 1910 requisitioned 1939; 180 tons; 112.3ft × 21.9ft; 1 × 6pdr

Skipper Eric Cyril Garnett RNR

Ordered to patrol near St Abb's Head, she was lying-to about 5 miles off the coast. The weather was overcast, with low cloud. At 14.04 a twin-engined aircraft was seen approaching from seaward and was believed to be a British coastal patrol plane, until it opened fire with machine guns as it closed. The engines were ordered to full ahead, but far too late to take effect as the aircraft dropped three bombs as it passed overhead. One hit the water close to the ship and exploded, blowing a hole in the side below the waterline. The second struck the side, penetrated the engine room and there it lodged, unexploded. The third fell about 60 yards clear. The main steam pipe was fractured, water was pouring out of the boiler and water was also entering through the hole in the side. The boat was hoisted out, and with the decks awash, she was abandoned. As they pulled clear there was a large explosion aft, believed to be the bomb in the engine room detonating. This blew the stern off and she rapidly sank. The Eyemouth lifeboat was launched and picked up the survivors from the boat and the local fishing vessel *Milky Way* picked up a further two men from a float. Five men lost their lives.

[TNA:ADM.199/1174; ADM.267/128]

2 April FORTUNA trawler

Beverley 1906 requisitioned 1940; 259 tons; 128.4ft × 22ft; 1 × 6pdr

Skipper William Todd Matthews Charlton RNR†

Patrolling between Berwick and the Farne Islands, she was last heard from at 18.05 on 2 April, when she signalled that she was going to assist the *Cramond Island* (see above) which was under attack off St Abb's Head. The next morning lifebuoys and wreckage was washed ashore, which was identifed as coming from the *Fortuna* and two bodies came ashore later at Berwick. It was presumed that she had also been sunk by air attack with the loss of fifteen men.

[TNA:ADM.199/777]

3 April BAHRAM drifter

Hamburg 1924 (*Standard*) requisitioned 1940; 72 tons; 69.7ft × 20.8ft

Second Hand John Neve Crawford RNR

Based at Grimsby, she had completed a night patrol and was to the west of Spurn Point with her engines stopped when at 07.20 she got underway to return to harbour. Immediately after she started her engines there was a large explosion underneath her and the ship disintegrated. The fishing vessel *Prospecto*, nearby, closed the scene but could find only one survivor, who had been blown out of the wheelhouse. Eight men were killed. It was presumed she had triggered an influence mine.

[TNA:ADM.199/239]

4 April VOLTAIRE armed merchant cruiser

Belfast 1923 requisitioned 1939; 13,248 tons; 510.5ft × 64.3ft; 8 × 6in, 2 × 12pdr

Captain James Alexander Pollard Blackburn DSC

Having sailed from Trinidad bound for Freetown, with orders to pass through areas to the west of the Cape

Verde Islands, when she failed to arrive as expected on 9 April it was presumed that she had been lost. An enemy surface raider – 'Raider-E' – was known to be active and was feared to have been responsible for her loss, and this was confirmed by a German announcement. The Canadian armed merchant cruiser *Prince David* was ordered to carry out a search and found a patch of oil and wreckage in position 14.31N 40.32W, and this was believed to mark the remains of the *Voltaire*. The details of her loss were not discovered until after the war. During the early morning of 4 April, the *Voltaire* had encountered the raider *Thor*, which was disguised as a Greek merchant vessel. On closing and challenging by light, the raider had opened fire. The first salvo hit the *Voltaire*, putting her radio out of action. She returned the fire, but was hit repeatedly and was soon on fire, with her steering gear out of action, which caused her to steam in circles. The engagement lasted less than an hour and ceased when no fire was being returned and white flags were seen to be waved. The *Thor* closed and lowered boats to rescue 197 survivors, but seventy-two men were killed.

[TNA: ADM.234/324; http://www.bismarck-class.dk/ hilfskreuzer/thor.html]

5 April **BUFFALO** mooring vessel
Paisley 1916; 750 tons; 135ft × 27ft; 1 × 12pdr
Master T W Airs†

Based at Singapore, she was called on to assist with the recovery of an RAF Blenheim aircraft that had crashed into the sea close to a defensive minefield. The officer in charge of the local survey unit, Lieutenant Commander Michael Beach-Thomas was instructed to fix the position of the wreck and then guide the mooring vessel past the minefield to the site. After embarking an RAF salvage team, she anchored near HMS *Dauntless* to take on board Commander Richard Airey who would oversee the operation. At 05.45 she got underway, and moved slowly towards the crash site, directed by Beach-Thomas in a motorboat. At 06.45 there was a large explosion under the ship, and as the smoke and spray cleared it could be seen that she had broken in half. The after part sank rapidly, but the fore part remained afloat. Several small craft closed the wreck, including Beach-Thomas's motorboat, to assist rescuing survivors, Airey Thomas scrambling on board. As they did so she 'gave an ominous lurch' and then capsized and sank. Neither Airey nor Beach-Thomas survived. In addition, six British dockyard staff, fourteen locally employed personnel and eight members of the RAF salvage team were killed. The court of enquiry placed the blame firmly on the shoulders of the late Beach-Thomas. It was found that he had been negligent by failing to properly acquaint himself with the orders for the operation, had failed to appreciate the danger

of the operation, had used out of date charts and had failed to constantly fix his position when nearing the minefield. In addition, Captain Loveband, Captain of the Dockyard, and Captain Bell, Chief of Staff, failed to ensure that the orders for the operation were fully understood by all, and were informed that they had incurred the severe displeasure of their Lordships.
[TNA: ADM.178/275; https://eresources.nlb.gov.sg/ newspapers/Straits Times 8 April]

6 April **COMORIN** armed merchant cruiser
Glasgow 1925 requisitioned 1939; 15,241 tons;
523.5ft × 70.2ft; 8 × 6in, 2 × 12pdr
Captain John Ignatius Hallett

Sailed from the Clyde 4 April in company with the steamship *Glenarty* and the destroyer *Lincoln* bound for Freetown carrying 135 passengers, most of them service personnel for the ships and shore base established in Sierra Leone. At 14.30 on 6 April, then being in position 54.44N 20.50W, steering to the west at 15 knots, with a strong south-easterly wind and a heavy swell, there was a report of a fire in the boiler room. The engineer of the watch reported that there were flames between number 4 and 5 boilers. The oil supply was immediately shut off and the blaze was initially tackled by hand extinguishers, but the fire spread rapidly and soon the boiler room was filled with thick black oily smoke. Fire-fighting teams were now in action, and did have some success, extinguishing the flames in the bilges, but the fire had taken a firm hold on top of the boilers, and smoke was spreading, affecting much of the ship. The engines had been stopped when the fire had been reported and this caused her to swing round lay beam on to the sea, causing her to roll heavily, which did not help with the fire-fighting efforts. The fire took a firm hold, and woodwork in surrounding compartments caught fire. Non-essential personnel were ordered to be evacuated, boats and floats being lowered and cleared away, taking people to the *Lincoln* and *Glenarty*, and the destroyer *Broke*, which fortuitously happened to be in the vicinity, also closed. Captain Hallett then decided that as it was impossible to bring the blaze under control, to flood the magazines, and then abandon her. *Broke* came alongside and men jumped across to her, and others jumped into the sea to cling to Carley floats that had been released. When all the men were clear the *Broke* torpedoed her. She settled, but stubbornly remained afloat, and she was not sunk until noon the following day (7 April), assisted by gunfire from the *Lincoln*. The enquiry found that the fire had been started by red-hot sparks dropping into the bilges when stokers were cleaning the fires of number 4 boiler. This had ignited oil leaking from a fractured pipe. It was found that the officers and engine and boiler room crews were not well trained in fire-fighting, never having drilled

or exercised. Captain Hallett was informed that he had incurred their Lordships' displeasure for failing to ensure the efficiency of the engine room department's fire-fighting organisation.
[TNA: ADM.178/219]

6 April SURF yacht
Leith 1902 requisitioned 1939; 496 tons; 185.7ft × 25.6ft; 1 × 12pdr
Lieutenant Dudley Cyril Wilson RNVR
On 6 April, a large force of German aircraft carried out an air raid on the harbour of Piraeus, and successfully hit the British freighter *Clan Fraser* (7,529 tons), which was laden with a variety of military stores which caught fire. Several explosions subsequently took place and another freighter, the *City of Roubaix*, was set on fire. She was also laden with military stores, including 50 tons of explosives. She subsequently exploded and set fire to several surrounding ships, including the *Surf*, which was completely burnt out.
[Lloyd's War Losses vol 1 p216; TNA: ADM.199/414]

6 April VIKING salvage tug
Copenhagen 1904; 386 tons; 155.5ft × 27.2ft
Listed in the *Statement of Losses* as being sunk during the heavy air attack on Piraeus, her inclusion in that document as a British naval vessel is questionable. In *Lloyd's War Losses*, the *Viking* is stated to have been taken over by the Greek Government on 28 October 1940 and in TNA:CAB.66/17 she is also listed as being Greek. She is included here for completeness.
[Statement of Losses p15; Lloyd's War Losses p218; TNA: CAB.66/17 p19]

6 April TORRENT yacht
Southampton 1930 (*Anna-Marie*) requisitioned 1939; 337 tons; 137.5ft × 23.9ft
Commander Montague Wriothesley Noel
Whilst on patrol off Falmouth, she detonated a mine at 19.00, in position 50.05.10N 04.57.25W. Four officers and fifteen ratings were killed, with just five survivors being picked up by the yacht *Hiniesta*.
[TNA: ADM.196/220; ADM.199/655]

7 April ROCHE BONNE trawler
Middlesbrough 1913 requisitioned 1940; 258 tons; 125ft × 23.5ft
Chief Skipper William Richard Setterfield RNR†
Bombed and sunk when attacked by a single He 111 aircraft at 10.50 when about 3 miles to the south-south-east of the Lizard, Cornwall. Eight survivors were picked up, but eleven men lost their lives.
[TNA: ADM.199/655; ADM.199/1174]

8 April MOOR mooring vessel
Paisley 1919; 670 tons; 137.5ft × 29ft; 1 × 12pdr
Based at Malta, she detonated a mine at 17.15 when about 270 yards from Ricasoli breakwater as she was returning to the dockyard after completing maintenance on the boom defence nets at the entrance to Grand Harbour and sank in 12 fathoms. It appeared that she had steered an unauthorised shortcut across a known danger area. Twenty-eight locally employed Maltese personnel were killed, with one survivor.
Note: this loss is incorrectly recorded as being in 1942 in the official *Statement of Losses*, a mistake copied by others.
[TNA: ADM.199/413; Lloyd's War Losses p219; Warships Supplement number 132 p8]

9 April D'ARCY COOPER drifter
Selby 1928 requisitioned 1940; 127 tons; 94.3ft × 19.6ft
Skipper Richard Brown RNR
Employed on the Examination Service at Harwich, she was berthed outboard of the paddle vessel *Marmion*, at the Trinity pier, when the port came under a night-time air raid. At 01.00 she took a direct hit from a large bomb which blew her apart. She broke in half with the fore part lying 60ft from the after. The remains were eventually dragged further inshore to clear the jetty. Most of the ship's company were on shore, so casualties were limited – four men were killed with three survivors.
[TNA: ADM.199/777; ADM.358/3210]

9 April MARMION paddle minesweeper
Glasgow 1906 requisitioned 1939; 490 tons; 210ft × 24ft; 1 × 12pdr
Lieutenant Douglas McNeil MacFarlane RNR
Laying at Trinity Pier Harwich when the port came under air attack, the drifter *D'Arcy Cooper* berthed alongside her took a direct hit and sank immediately (see above). The *Marmion* was damaged by the blast, her upperworks being carried away and the side and mess decks peppered with holes and a fire was started. The fire was extinguished but she was making water, and salvage pumps were used to try and clear the water but failed to make any impression. Attempts were made to move her into shallow water, but she became jammed between the wreck of the *D'Arcy Cooper* and the pier, and she sank alongside the jetty. One man was killed. The wreck was eventually refloated on 10 May but was then towed to Tilbury to be broken up.
[TNA: ADM.199/1174; Foynes pp306–07]

11 April OTHELLO trawler
Selby 1907 requisitioned 1939; 201 tons; 115ft × 21.6ft
Boom Skipper Walter Trench RNR†
Employed as a boom defence vessel, she was working in company with the yacht *Yorkshire Belle* on the boom

defences close to the Haile Sand Fort in the River Humber, when she detonated a mine at 14.30 and sank with the loss of twelve men. The wreck lies in position 53.32.40N 00.02.31E

[TNA: ADM.199/1172; Larn vol 3 sec 4]

11 April **YORKSHIRE BELLE** yacht

Beverley 1938 requisitioned 1939; 56 tons; 76ft × 17ft

Acting as tender to the *Othello* (see above), she was also at the boom at the entrance to the river Humber when the trawler exploded. She went to her assistance but as she did so, she also detonated a mine and quickly sank with the loss of all nine ratings onboard. Position given as 3.5 cables (700 yards) to the north of the Haile Sand Fort.

[TNA: ADM.199/1172; ADM.358/3853]

13 April **RAJPUTANA** armed merchant cruiser

Govan 1925 requisitioned 1938; 16,644 tons; 547.7ft × 71.3ft; 8 × 6in, 2 × 12pdr

Captain Frederick Henry Taylor DSC

Originally part of the escort to Convoy HX117 which had sailed from Halifax on 27 March bound for Liverpool, after handing over to the main escorts, she detached from the convoy at 22.00 on 9 April in position 62N 25W, to patrol the Denmark Strait before returning to Halifax. Four days later, at 06.00, when she was to the south-west of Iceland, in position 64.50N 27.25W she was hit by a torpedo on the port side, abreast the engine room, fired by the submerged *U 108* (Scholtz). The engines stopped and both engine rooms started to flood, as did the after stokehold, but she remained stable and upright. Fire was opened on a periscope which could now be seen, but this did not stop another attack. At 07.40 she was hit by a second torpedo, on the starboard side, between numbers 4 and 5 holds, which immediately flooded. As it was clear that she was now sinking she was abandoned 10 minutes later. She foundered shortly after; forty-two men were lost. The survivors were picked up about 12 hours later by the destroyer *Legion*.

[TNA: ADM.267/112]

16 April **MOHAWK** destroyer

Woolston 1937; 1,960 tons; 355.6ft × 36.6ft; 8 × 4.7in, 4 × 2pdr, 2 × torpedo tubes

Commander John William Musgrave Eaton

In company with the destroyers *Jervis*, *Janus* and *Nubian*, sailed from Malta to patrol in the vicinity of the Kerkenah Bank to intercept an enemy convoy which was believed to be en-route to North Africa. At 01.30 objects were seen on the port bow and course was altered to close them, and speed increased to 25 knots. By 01.45 they could be made out to be five large merchant ships, screened by three destroyers.

The *Jervis* led the group around to close from their starboard quarter. At 02.05 the destroyers opened fire on the convoy, the *Mohawk* concentrating her fire on the rearmost merchant ship. She hit her target with the second salvo and after eight salvoes checked fire, as the target was burning fiercely. At 02.23 an enemy destroyer was seen on a parallel course closing at high speed. *Mohawk* engaged, and immediately hit her object, which caught fire amidships. The British destroyers were now led round to cross the bows of the convoy and one leading merchantman, still unengaged, was seen to turn to starboard, apparently to ram a British destroyer. *Mohawk* put the helm over to starboard to avoid a collision, and it was with the ship turning to starboard that she was rocked by an explosion on the starboard side abreast 'Y' gun. The stern of the ship was blown off and she came to a stop, although the forward guns were still firing at the convoy, hitting another merchant ship. Although the stern had gone, the shafts and propellers were apparently still in place, and she was able to get under way. As she did so, she was hit by a second torpedo, this time on the port side, exploding on the bulkhead between numbers 2 and 3 boiler rooms. Now rapidly filling with water, she started to sink on an even keel. About one minute after the explosion, she took a heavy list to port and then rolled over onto her beam ends, with the after part submerged as far as the after torpedo tubes. The Carley floats were released, and the ship was ordered to be abandoned. *Nubian* and *Jervis* closed her to pick up survivors. At 03.30 the *Janus* fired four rounds into her hull, and she slowly sank. Her position was 34.56N 11.42E, lying in 7 fathoms of water. It was difficult to ascertain where the torpedoes had come from. The first was almost certainly fired from the destroyer *Luca Tarigo*, which was the vessel engaged and set on fire earlier. She was lying about a mile away, burning, and had been dismissed as not posing any further threat. The second must have come from either *Baleno* or *Lampo* that was being engaged at that time by *Nubian*. The enemy lost all five merchant ships of the convoy, with two of the destroyers.

[TNA: ADM.1/11299]

18 April **FIONA** ocean boarding vessel

Dundee 1933 requisitioned 1939; 2,198 tons; 286.3ft × 44.1ft; 2 × 4in, 1 × 12pdr, 2 × 2pdr

Commander Arthur Harold Hildreth Griffiths RNR[†]

Sailed from Alexandria to proceed to Tobruk, she was off Sidi Barrani when a group of aircraft were sighted closing her from ahead. Speed was increased, and the ship went to action stations as the aircraft, now identified as Ju 88s, commenced a dive-bombing attack. One bomb exploded close to the starboard bow, and another penetrated the deck alongside the starboard pom-pom gun to explode in the port boiler room. The explosion

blew a hole in the side and the ship was covered in debris, smoke and steam. A third bomb then hit abaft the bridge and exploded in the galley. The bridge collapsed, and the ship heeled over to take a heavy list to port as she started to fill with water. The attack continued, with another bomb striking forward, detonating in the hold. She was now blanketed in smoke and steam and continued to slowly roll over until she lay on her beam ends. The order was given to abandon her as she started to capsize, but men were forced to jump into the water, there being no time to release boats, but some Carley floats were released. She sank within minutes of the commencement of the attack, with violent explosions as she went under, probably as the boilers exploded. Sixty-seven men died.
[TNA: ADM.199/1177]

18 April YOUNG ERNIE drifter
Lowestoft 1924 requisitioned 1939; 88 tons; 85.7ft × 19.6ft
Skipper Robert Milligan RNR
Damaged in a collision with the examination steamer *Ben Idris* (232 tons) off Tynemouth, she subsequently foundered about 3,800 yards to the east of Tynemouth war signal station. There were no casualties.
[TNA: ADM.199/777; ADM.199/2226]

19 April KOPANES trawler
Beverley 1914 (*Sir John Jellicoe*) requisitioned 1940; 351 tons; 140.2ft × 24.1ft; 1 × 12pdr
Skipper Edward Matthews Charlton RNR
Laying at 'G' buoy off Coquet Island in the River Tyne, she was in company with the trawler *Morgan Jones*, when a single He 111 aircraft came out of a hazy sky, approached from astern and dropped two bombs. The first exploded close under the stern, the second by the port bow. The aircraft then circled and returned for a second run, releasing three bombs. These exploded close along the port side, shaking her considerably, popping rivets and splitting plates. She started to fill with water and the engines stopped. The boat was launched, and she was abandoned, sinking 25 minutes after the attack.
[TNA: ADM.199/1174]

20 April HDML 1003 / HDML 1037 motor launches
East Molesey (*1003*); Lymington (*1037*) 1940; 46 tons; 70ft × 15ft
Ordered to the Mediterranean, they were embarked as deck cargo on board the *Empire Endurance* which sailed independently from Swansea for Alexandria, via the Cape of Good Hope. At 03.32, to the west of Ireland, in position 53.05N 23.14W she was hit amidships by a single torpedo, fired by the *U 73*, broke in two and sank taking both launches with her.
[https://www.uboat.net/allies/merchants/ships/881.html]

20 April TOPAZE trawler
Middlesbrough 1936 (*Melbourne*) purchased on stocks; 421 tons; 157ft × 26.7ft; 1 × 4in
Chief Skipper George Richard Gale RNR†
Foundered after being rammed by the battleship *Rodney* at 00.57, when 2.9 miles to the south of Cumbrae Light. There were only two survivors: eighteen men were lost. The wreck lies in position 55.40N 004.59W.
[TNA: ADM.199/837; https://canmore.org.uk/site/102487]

23 April SATURNUS barrage balloon vessel
Delfzijl 1935 requisitioned 1940; 200 tons; 111.2ft × 21.2ft
A former Dutch coaster fitted out as a balloon vessel and stationed in the river Mersey, on 31 January she broke from her moorings in poor weather and drifted out to sea. She was eventually towed into the harbour at Douglas, Isle of Man. On 23 April, she was under tow to return to her station, when, in poor weather, she broke adrift and went ashore at Onchan Head, Isle of Man. She was subsequently written off on 1 May as a total loss.
[TNA: ADM.199/658]

24 April LCT (1) 1 landing craft, tank
Barrow 1940; 226 tons; 135ft × 28ft; 2 × 2pdr
Sub-Lieutenant Louis Dennis Peters RNVR
Deployed from North Africa to Greece, to assist with the evacuation of Allied troops, she arrived at Megara near Piraeus on 23 April. The following day she was the target for an attack by Ju 87 dive bombers and severely damaged by near misses, sank in shallow water off the port of Pachi in the Gulf of Megara. Some stores and equipment were able to be salvaged, after which she was broken up with demolition charges. Despite this, the Germans later salvaged and refitted the craft for further service as a *Lokfähre* in German service.
[TNA: ADM.199/806]

25 April CALANTHE yacht
Govan 1898 requisitioned 1941; 370 tons; 164ft × 24ft
In early 1941 the yacht was hired to carry civilian evacuees from Greece to Alexandria. On her return to Piraeus in April she was taken over by British forces to assist with the evacuation of British Legation staff and other civilians, with the Assistant Naval Attaché, Commander John Brass, taking charge. Retaining her Greek master and crew, several soldiers, detached from their units, along with two Royal Navy seamen and one Royal Marine were recruited to assist, and four Lewis guns were installed as the sole armament. The yacht sailed from Piraeus at dusk on 24 April arriving in the shelter of Polyaigos Island, near Milos, at dawn the following day. They hoped to avoid detection, but during the late afternoon a single Ju 88 aircraft spotted them and circled round to attack. Commander Brass

advised the master to weigh anchor and try to give themselves room to manoeuvre. During the first attack, several bombs were dropped, but all exploded well clear of the yacht. She was still trying to get underway as the aircraft carried out a second attack. This was more successful, three bombs being dropped, which straddled the ship, two being near misses the third hitting between the funnel and wheelhouse to penetrate the boiler room. A fire was started on the upper deck, and there was another explosion, probably as the boiler exploded. Everyone on board was evacuated to shore as she settled and sank, still burning. Five men were killed in the attack.

[TNA:ADM.199/806]

25 April ULSTER PRINCE victualling store ship

Belfast 1929 requisitioned 1940; 3,757 tons; 346ft × 46.2ft
Commander Frank Albert Bond RNR

Based in the Mediterranean, she was sent to Piraeus to assist with the embarkation of troops from Greece. On 24 April as she attempted to go alongside the quay at Nauplia (Nafplio) she grounded. Despite all efforts to free her, including towing, she would not move, and this left her very exposed the following morning from enemy air attacks. She was heavily bombed and set on fire, becoming a total loss. There were no casualties.

[Statement of Losses p16; Supplement to the London Gazette of 18 May 1948]

26 April LCT (1) 19 landing craft, tank

Linthouse 1940; 226 tons; 135ft × 28ft; 2 × 2pdr
Skipper Reginald Stanley Cooper RNR

Sent to Greece from North Africa, to assist with the Allied evacuation, she arrived at Megara on 23 April. She was busily employed over the next few days, ferrying troops and equipment from the shore to transports. At 02.00 on 26 April, she fouled her starboard screw, a wire wrapping itself around the shaft, putting it out of action. With the port engine defective, she was effectively immobile, and so all useful equipment was removed during the day, the engine room 'wrecked' and she was then taken into shallow water and scuttled by opening the sea outlets. She was later salvaged by the Germans and refitted for further service under their flag as a Lokfähre.

[TNA:ADM.199/806]

27 April DIAMOND destroyer

Barrow 1932; 1,375 tons; 317.9ft × 33ft; 4 × 4.7in, 1 × 3in, 2 × 2pdr, 8 × torpedo tubes
Lieutenant Commander Philip Alexander Cartwright[†]

In company with the destroyer Wryneck, the pair was part of the force tasked to evacuate Allied troops from Greece and were despatched to the aid of the transport Slamat, which had been attacked by enemy aircraft. By mid-afternoon they had taken off the 500 troops that had been embarked on the transport, and then, when all were clear, the Diamond sank the Slamat with a torpedo. The pair then got underway, heading for Crete at 28 knots. An hour later, when they were about 20 miles to the east of Cape Maleas, 'unseen and unheard' an aircraft appeared from low cloud, having approached with engines cut off. This carried out a strafing and bombing run, initially concentrating on the Diamond. A number of bombs was released, one of which was a near miss, but caused much splinter and shock damage, and this was followed by a direct hit amidships. The bomb penetrated the upper deck to explode in the engine room and brought down the mast and forward funnel. Steam blew off in all directions, covering the ship in a cloud of steam and smoke until an emergency valve was released. The ship sank rapidly, stern first, her bows rising clear as floats were released. One hundred and forty-eight men died.

[TNA:ADM.267/110]

27 April WRYNECK destroyer

Jarrow 1918; 1,090 tons; 300ft × 29.6ft; 4 × 4in, 1 × 2pdr, 6 × torpedo tubes
Commander Robert Henry Douglas Lane[†]

Consort to the Diamond (see above), she became the object of an intense air attack by several Ju 87 dive bombers after that ship was hit. A bomb struck 'A' gun, killing or wounding everyone forward, and this was followed by a second bomb which entered the engine room, bursting all the steam pipes. A third bomb hit aft, starting a fire in the ready-use ammunition locker. The ship rolled over to port and she did not recover, heeling over until she capsized and sank about 4 minutes after being hit. One hundred and eight men died.

[TNA:ADM.267/110]

27 April PATIA fighter catapult ship

Birkenhead 1922 requisitioned 1940; 5,355 tons; 400ft × 51.1ft; 2 × 6in, 1 × 12pdr, 2 × 2pdr
Commander David Marion Burson Baker RNR[†]

After completing a refit at Rosyth, she sailed at 18.30 on 27 April for trials before proceeding to Belfast. At 21.20 she was off the Farne Islands, when an aircraft was seen on the starboard beam. It closed rapidly from the east at low level to run over the ship, releasing one bomb, which fell wide. The aircraft, identified as an He 111, turned to carry out a second attack, this time the bomb near missing on the port side. The aircraft then cleared the area to the north, only to reappear, again closing at low level, about 5 minutes later. Having initially been taken by surprise, the crew were now at action stations, and engaged the aircraft as it closed, but the starboard pom-pom jammed. Two bombs were dropped which fell clear of the ship on the port quarter. The aircraft banked and

turned, to rake the ship with machine-gun fire, before again clearing the area to the east. There followed a lapse of several minutes, before the aircraft was seen again, this time closing from the port quarter at low altitude. This time three bombs were dropped; the first exploded close astern, the second hit the starboard side, entering the engine room. The third narrowly missed the upper works to land close to the starboard side, resulting in some shock damage. It was the second bomb that had done the fatal damage, having exploded at the bulkhead between the engine room and number 3 hold and probably blew a hole in the bottom. This allowed two large compartments to rapidly flood. The aircraft had been engaged all the time it had performed its attacking run, and was seen to be hit and fly off trailing smoke. The ship heeled over to port and started sinking immediately. The boats and floats were cleared away with difficulty, the ship listing by 30 degrees, before she sank. The survivors in boats, rafts and floats were rather surprised to find themselves joined by three German airmen in a small rubber dinghy; the crew of the bomber, which had been shot down. They were informed by Chief Petty Officer Edward Prior that they were now prisoners of war. All were picked up by the trawler *Chassiron*, but thirty-nine men were lost. The wreck lies in position 55.31.4N 01.25.09E.
[TNA: ADM.1/11240]

27 April MUNDON boom defence vessel
Sittingbourne 1868; 44 tons
A spritsail barge employed locally at Harwich as a boom tender, she foundered in a storm off that port.
[Statement of Losses – Amendment p2]

28 April LCT (1) 5 landing craft, tank
Birkenhead 1940; 226 tons; 135ft × 28ft; 2 × 2pdr
Boatswain Harold Robert Paxton
Deployed to Greece to assist with the evacuation of personnel, she arrived on 24 April at Nauplia (Nafplio), and was busily employed, working as a ferry taking men from the shore to transports. Late on 27 April she moved to Monemvasia, but due to the increasing air threat, she was run inshore and laid up during the day near rocks. Despite this precaution, the following morning she was spotted and attacked by several Ju 87 dive bombers. The ship was set on fire and the upperworks and hull wrecked, and she sank in shallow water. There were no casualties.
[TNA: ADM.199/806: Burn p7]

28 April LCT (1) 15 landing craft, tank
Greenock 1940; 226 tons; 135ft × 28ft; 2 × 2pdr
Boatswain Charles William Dennis†
Sent from North Africa to Crete to help with troop movements, she was initially stationed at Suda Bay,

but during the evening of 27 April she sailed for the Greek mainland with Lieutenant Commander Peter Hutton, Senior Officer Western Desert Lighter Flotilla embarked, to assist with the evacuation of allied troops. At 10.00 the next day as she entered Monemvasia Bay she came under attack from several dive bombers and was sunk with the loss of sixteen men.
[TNA: ADM.199/806; ADM.358/3432]

29 April CHAKLA ocean boarding vessel
Glasgow 1914 requisitioned 1939; 3,081 tons; 330.5ft × 46.2ft; 2 × 4in, 1 × 12pdr
Commander Leslie Charles Bach RNR
Having sailed from Mersa Matruh during the afternoon of 28 April loaded with stores and troops, she arrived at Tobruk the following day. After disembarking her load, she anchored in the harbour in 6 fathoms. During the day there had been several air raids, but none of them had affected the harbour, but at 17.00 another raid developed, with about fifteen aircraft attacking shipping. Several bombs fell around the *Chakla*, and finally she was hit twice, one of the bombs penetrating number 1 hold. She started to flood and took a bows-down attitude. At 17.10 the ship took a lurch to port and as it was feared that she was about to roll over, she was ordered to be abandoned, the foredeck being under water by this time. The ship however steadied itself but continued to settle and sank on an even keel with her upper works still above water. Over the next few days considerable efforts were made to salvage her guns, ammunition and stores. She was finally abandoned on 4 May.
[TNA: ADM.199/1177]

30 April PARVATI auxiliary patrol vessel
Grangemouth 1927, requisitioned 1939; 1,542 tons; 250ft × 38ft
Lieutenant Hajee Mohammed Siddiq Choudri RIN
Royal Indian Navy. Operations against the Italian forces in Eritrea advanced in early 1941, but the harbour at Assab remained in enemy hands. The *Parvati* was directed to the vicinity of the port where she met the light cruiser *Ceres*, who advised Lieutenant Choudri that the intention was to enter the port if possible, where they would destroy or capture any remaining craft. It was feared that defensive minefields had been laid, but the cruiser would stream paravanes, the patrol vessel was to follow, with a Eureka motor launch. At 15.52 *Ceres'* starboard paravane cut a mine free. The *Parvati* slowed until she sighted the drifting mine, then manoeuvred around it. *Ceres* now signalled that the operation was cancelled as the mission was not worth the risk, and commenced a turn to starboard, to reverse course. The *Parvati* was now at some distance from the cruiser but increased to full speed and started to follow in her track when there was a large explosion abreast the forward

well deck as she detonated a mine. The forward section was severely damaged, and she started to sink by the bows immediately. The ship then slowly rolled over to starboard and sank bows first within 2 minutes of the explosion. Some rafts had been released, and the motor launch assisted to pick up survivors, the *Ceres* sending her motor cutter to help. Fifty-six survivors were picked up, but sixteen men died.
[*TNA: ADM.156/221*]

30 April PEUPLIER tug

Lorient 1918, seized 1940; 371 tons; 121.5ft × 24.6ft
A former French Navy tug, she had been taken over for service at Devonport dockyard. She was sunk during a heavy air raid on the town of Plymouth and the dockyard.
[*TNA: ADM.199/655*]

April USK submarine

Barrow 1940; 540/730 tons; 180ft × 16ft; 1 × 12pdr,
4 × torpedo tubes
Lieutenant Godfrey Paul Darling†
Sailed from Malta 19 April to conduct a patrol off the north-west coast of Sicily but failed to return as expected on 5 May. The reason for her loss is uncertain. She was last heard from at 23.25 on 25 April when she was in contact with Malta by radio when she indicated that she was shifting to the area of Cape Bon, Tunisia. The most likely cause is by hitting a mine. A new minefield had been laid by the enemy between Cape Bon and Marettimo after her sailing and would have been on the route taken by the *Usk*. Four officers and twenty-eight ratings were lost.
[*Evans pp269–70*]

2 May JERSEY destroyer

Cowes 1938; 1,690 tons; 339.6ft × 35.8ft; 6 × 4.7in,
4 × 2pdr, 10 × torpedo tubes
Lieutenant Commander Anthony Frank Burnell-Nugent DSC
Sailed from Malta in company with other ships of the Fifth Destroyer Flotilla to intercept an Axis convoy bound for North Africa but returned to harbour when they failed to find their target. At 07.00, with the ships in a line ahead formation, the destroyers started to enter the harbour, but as the fourth ship in line, *Jersey*, passed the breakwater at the entrance to Grand Harbour, she detonated a mine. She sank at once, completely blocking the channel. Thirty-five men were lost. The cruiser *Gloucester* and destroyers *Kashmir* and *Kipling* could not enter and were diverted to Gibraltar. Her wreck caused much inconvenience, and the stern section was later blown up to clear the entrance.
[*TNA: ADM.199/414*]

2 May NYULA yacht

Sandbank 1936 requisitioned 1940; 48 tons; 65ft × 14.4ft
Lieutenant William Harry Findlay Kelly RNVR
Foundered at 04.40 about 500 yards south of T1 buoy in the River Tyne, following a collision with the yacht *Yarta* (357 tons); there were no casualties.
[*TNA: ADM199/837*]

3 May ALBERIC trawler

Selby 1910 requisitioned 1940; 286 tons; 130.2ft × 23.5ft
Lieutenant Robert Murray Johnston RNR
At 23.55 on 2 May she was in collision with the destroyer *St Albans* off Scapa Flow, Orkney, and subsequently foundered with the loss of fourteen men and just nine survivors.
[*TNA: ADM.199/397; ADM.358/3000*]

4 May FERMOY minesweeping sloop

Dundee 1919; 710 tons; 220ft × 28.6ft; 1 × 4in, 1 × 12pdr
Lieutenant Commander John Guy Douglas Wetherfield
Taken into dry dock in Malta for routine boiler cleaning and maintenance, the sloop suffered damage during the incessant air raids mounted on the island. During a raid on the night of 29/30 April she suffered significant damage, receiving a direct hit on the bridge, the bomb penetrating down to pierce the hull. In another raid on the night of 4/5 May she was again damaged when struck by a bomb on the port side amidships, and she flooded and was displaced off the chocks. A survey on the ship on 17 May found that she was a constructive total loss and she was written off, to be stripped of all useable equipment and then scrapped in the dock in situ. She was officially paid off on 1 June.
[*TNA: ADM.199/1777; ADM.267/130*]

4 May BEN GAIRN trawler

Aberdeen 1916; 204 tons; 122.5ft × 22.1ft
Lieutenant Robert Hugh le Masurier RNVR
Based at Lowestoft, she was secured alongside in the Waveney Basin, with several other trawlers. During the night of 3 May a single aircraft was heard overhead which dropped two parachute mines. One of them exploded on landing in the dock area but the other was seen to land in the basin near the trawlers. The ships nearest to the point of impact were evacuated and all engine movements ordered to be stopped, and it was planned to tackle the mine at first light. However, at 05.30 the mine exploded, with the nearest trawlers, *Ben Gairn* and *Niblick*, taking the full force. The latter was damaged but remained afloat. The *Ben Gairn* however filled and sank. There were no casualties.
[*TNA: ADM.199/239*]

4 May VAN ORLEY trawler

Beverley 1927 (*Kingston Garnet*) requisitioned 1940; 352 tons; 140.3ft × 24ft

Liverpool suffered a series of very heavy air raids during the first week of May 1941; the *Van Orley* in Huskisson Dock was damaged during the night of 3/4 May and was subsequently written off as a constructive total loss. [*TNA: ADM.199/2227*]

4/5 May Air Raid on Belfast

During the night of 4/5 May Belfast suffered a very heavy air raid, which particularly affected the Harland and Wolff shipyard, with several ships under construction being damaged. Several motor launches under construction were destroyed.

HDML 1092 / HDML 1093 / HDML 1094 / HDML 1095

Belfast (incomplete); 46 tons; 70ft × 15ft

★ ★ ★

5 May FIDELIA trawler

Hull 1891, purchased 1941; 147 tons; 100ft × 20.5ft

Employed as a boom defence vessel, she was stationed at the entrance to the harbour at Lowestoft when the town came under attack from an aircraft during the night of 4/5 May. Several bombs were scattered across the town and during the early hours, the trawler was struck by a single bomb which broke her in half, and she rapidly sank, her upperworks still above water. All eight men on board survived,

[*TNA: ADM.199/407; Foynes p163; http://www.oldlowestoft. co.uk/ajt/?The_letters-1941*]

6 May CAMITO ocean boarding vessel

Glasgow 1915 requisitioned 1940; 6,828 tons; 426.3ft × 54.2ft; 2 × 6in, 1 × 12pdr

Commander Avon Alexander Barnet RNR

On 1 May, the ocean boarding vessel *Cavina* had successfully intercepted a blockade runner, the Italian tanker *Sangro*, attempting to reach France from Brazil and the *Camito* was ordered to escort the prize back to England. Having put a prize crew on board, the pair then steered a course to make a rendezvous with a corvette in position 50N 22W. At 00.50 on 6 May, the *Camito* was hit by a torpedo on the starboard side amidships. This caused a hold to flood, and water penetrated the engine room through buckled watertight doors. By 01.30, with bulkheads shored up, the situation had stabilised and with one engine functioning she was able to proceed at 3 knots. The prize *Sangro* was now ahead of her, when at approximately 01.30 she was seen to be engulfed by a tremendous explosion. A great sheet of flame illuminated the sea for miles around for several

minutes until it died down into a fierce glow which burned for about 30 minutes and then suddenly went out. *Camito* meanwhile was now zigzagging, and when a second engine was brought back on-line, she was able to increase speed, despite having a list of about 10 degrees to starboard. At 04.45 the starboard engine stopped and, with water entering the compartment until it was waist deep, 30 minutes later the port engine stopped. The shored bulkheads, however, were still holding and it was hoped that she might yet be saved, but with the weather worsening, it was decided to launch the lifeboats with most of the crew, a small party remaining on board. This was achieved smoothly and without incident, the boats remaining close by. By 10.00 it was blowing a Force 7 from the north-east with a heavy sea. The list was increasing, and she was showing signs of settling by the stern. Seas were washing over her after decks and water was pouring down fans and hatches into the holds. At 11.00 after sending a final signal with their position, the last men left her; the ship was then lying almost on her beam ends. She went down a few minutes later, her bows rearing up into the air until they were vertical before sinking. Her position was 51.14N 21.45N. Twenty-eight men died in the incident. The corvette *Orchis* picked up the survivors later that day, and the *Heather* found four men from the *Sangro*. Both ships had been torpedoed by *U 97* (Heilmann). [*TNA: ADM.1/11546*]

7 May GOWANHILL drifter

Oilton Broad 1920 (*Puff*) requisitioned 1939; 96 tons; 86.2ft × 18.5ft

During the night of 6/7 May Glasgow came under intense air attack; the *Gowan Hill* was under refit at Greenock and was blown off the blocks by a bomb and was written off as a total loss. [*TNA: ADM.199/2227*]

7 May STOKE minesweeper

South Shields 1918; 710 tons; 220ft × 28.6ft; 1 × 4in, 1 × 12pdr

Commander Cyril John Percy Hill

One of the few operational minesweepers based at Tobruk, she and her sisters gallantly worked to keep the approaches to the harbour free of mines, despite the regular attacks from aircraft. During 7 May, the *Stoke* arrived in the harbour having escorted several ships from Alexandria, and anchored. At 16.05 numerous aircraft, identified as Ju 87s, were sighted approaching and they commenced a dive-bombing attack on the shipping. Almost immediately the *Stoke* was hit, being struck by a bomb amidships, between the boats, shattering both and a second went through the upper deck to explode in the flat below. Several other bombs burst around her, covering her with water and smoke

and shaking the ship. She started to settle by the stern and within a minute had rolled over to port and sank. Nine men were lost.
[TNA: ADM.199/1177]

7 May SUSARION trawler
Beverley 1916 requisitioned 1940; 261 tons; 120ft × 22.5ft; 1 × 12pdr
Skipper Peter Coull RNR
The trawler was lying at anchor about 3 miles to the south-east of the Humber Light vessel, when a single aircraft approached from the direction of the land at 00.30 and attacked her. Two bombs were dropped which fell within 10ft of her, on the port quarter and beam. She was lifted out of the water by the blast and shaken considerably, starting numerous leaks. The engine room steadily flooded, and she was abandoned at 04.00 in a sinking condition. Three men were killed. The wreck lies in position 53.31.13N 00.22.42E
[TNA: ADM.199/1175; Larn vol 3 sec 4]

8 May SILICIA trawler
Beverley 1912 requisitioned 1940; 250 tons; 120ft × 22.6ft
Lieutenant Frederick Arthur Matson RNR
Based at Grimsby and tasked to sweep the area of the docks following reports of aircraft dropping objects into the water. She commenced her work at 12.00 and completed one lap along all the dock entrances, then anchored half a mile to the west of the docks, awaiting high tide. At 15.30 she weighed and proceeded to sweep off Albert Dock with acoustic or SA gear when at 15.44 a mine detonated close astern. The ship was lifted out of the water by the explosion and started to break up and sank rapidly. Seven men were killed.
[TNA: ADM.199/239]

8 May THISTLE drifter
North Shields 1904 requisitioned 1940; 79 tons; 80ft × 18.1ft
Skipper Charles Sansom RNR[†]
Employed in the examination service, the drifter was sunk at 08.30 when off Lowestoft, near the Newcombe buoy, in position 52.28N 01.47.3E after detonating a mine. There was just one survivor, with eleven men being killed.
[TNA: ADM.199/777]

8 May UBERTY drifter
Aberdeen 1912 requisitioned 1939; 93 tons; 86ft × 18.6ft
Skipper Richard Henry Alexander RNR[†]
In company with the drifters John & Norah, Cula and Craig Miller, the group were proceeding to the area of 54F buoy off Lowestoft, when at 22.30 they saw a pair of twin-engined aircraft approaching from the north. The aircraft were very low, and headed straight for the group, opening fire with machine guns as they closed. They both ran right over the Uberty dropping a number of bombs, which exploded around her, with at least one being a direct hit. The drifter blew up in a huge sheet of flame, a large spread of oil and debris marking her end. Thirteen men were killed.
[TNA: ADM.199/1175]

8 May VIVA II yacht
Gosport 1929 requisitioned 1939; 522 tons; 166.2ft × 26ft
Captain Myles Aldington Blomfield OBE[†]
Escorting a coastal convoy from Falmouth to Milford Haven, the ships were off Trevose Head when they came under a night air attack. From 01.15 several bombs were dropped around the convoy, and at 01.37 she suffered a direct hit and sank. Twenty-one men were lost.
[TNA: ADM.199/1175]

9 May QUEENWORTH mine destructor
Sunderland 1924 requisitioned 1940; 2,047 tons; 275ft × 39.9ft; 2 × 12pdr
Lieutenant Commander Robert William Wainewright
Laying at anchor near the Outer Dowsing Light Vessel, to east of the river Humber, at 01.20 a single aircraft approached her from seaward, flying at high level. As it passed overhead, three bombs were dropped. The first detonated on the starboard side amidships whilst the second penetrated the deck between the bridge and the engine room before it exploded. The third was a near miss, detonating on the waterline on the port side. She flooded rapidly and sank. There were no casualties.
[TNA: ADM.199/1175]

11 May GYPSY accommodation ship
London 1893 (Carlotta) requisitioned 1941; 261 tons; 124.7ft × 32.5ft
A former Tilbury ferry, latterly used as a yacht club HQ vessel, she was moored at Tower Pier, London for use by the auxiliary patrol. She sank after being damaged during a night-time air attack.
[Lloyd's War Losses p247]

(3–12) May UNDAUNTED submarine
Barrow 1940; 540/630 tons; 180ft × 16.1ft; 1 × 12pdr, 4 × torpedo tubes
Lieutenant James Lees Livesay[†]
This is yet another Mediterranean submarine with no firm explanation as to her loss. She sailed from Malta on 29 April for a patrol in the area off Tripoli, Libya and failed to return as expected by 13 May. She was last heard from on 1 May and the Italian merchant vessel Lusiana reported being attacked by torpedo on 3 May off Tripoli, which, if correct, may well have been by Undaunted. Loss by accident or by striking a mine are the most likely options – Italian destroyers

laid mines to the north of Tripoli on 1 May, and the *Upright* reported hearing an explosion on 7 May from the direction of the area allocated to *Undaunted* which could have been a mine detonating. Claims have been made for an attack by an Italian escort ship *Pegaso* on 12 May, which dropped depth charges following a report of a submarine by an aircraft, about 80 miles north of Tripoli. However, it is unlikely to have been responsible, as the *Undaunted* should have been out of the area, having completed her patrol. Four officers and twenty-eight men were lost.
[*Evans p271; http://uboat.net/allies/warships/ship/4222.html*]

12 May **LADYBIRD** river gunboat
Renfrew 1916; 625 tons; 230ft × 36ft; 2 × 6in, 1 × 3in, 1 × 20mm, 2 × 2pdr
Commander John Fulford Blackburn
Although built for service in the rivers of China, she was one of three gunboats transferred to the Mediterranean for service with the Inshore Squadron, being worked hard as shore bombardment vessels. During the afternoon of 12 May she was at Tobruk when the port came under air attack. At 14.55 several enemy aircraft carried out bombing attacks on the western defence lines, but three Ju 87s turned their attention to the harbour and *Ladybird* became the main target. One bomb struck the stern of the ship which killed or wounded the crew of the after pom-pom. A further hit followed which penetrated the upper deck to explode in the boiler room, which blew the sides out of the ship. She started to sink immediately, taking a heavy list to starboard. The wounded were evacuated by boat as she was covered in thick black smoke as a fierce oil fire broke out. She was abandoned at 15.20, the ship sinking into the harbour, although her upper works remained above water, and the wreck was later used by the army as a flak platform. Three men were lost.
[*TNA: ADM.199/1177*]

13 May **SALOPIAN** armed merchant cruiser
Govan 1926 (*Shropshire*) requisitioned 1939; 10,519 tons; 483.6ft × 60.3ft; 6 × 6in, 2 × 12pdr
Captain Sir John Meynell Alleyne
Assigned to the Halifax Escort Force, she escorted Convoy SC30 from Canada during 12 May and handed the ships over to a destroyer to take them to UK waters. That complete, at 16.00 she reversed course to head back to Halifax. At 03.30 the alarms were sounded, and the helm put over when she sighted a submarine on the surface, which submerged. A few minutes later a torpedo hit the starboard side, just abaft the bridge between numbers 3 and 4 holds. She took a heel to starboard and settled by the bows, the engines stopped, and the engine room reported that they were flooding. A moment later a second torpedo hit her forward, under the fo'c'sle.

The ship was now lying stopped, but appeared to be stable, and pumps were ordered rigged to try and clear the engine spaces of water. Despite the damage, and a list to starboard, the ship remained stable, and the ship's armament engaged the periscope whenever possible. At 04.00 a third torpedo was fired which hit the port side, by number 5 hold. The ship righted herself, then took a slight heel to port and settled a little by the stern, which effectively brought her onto an even keel. The holds had been packed with empty oil drums, and these were effective in acting to keep her afloat. The pumps in the engine rooms were not having any effect, and despite the buoyant cargo, she was slowly settling. Her attacker, which was the *U 98* (Gysae), was evidently curious, and briefly came to the surface, only to be engaged by the ships' guns. A fourth torpedo was then fired, hitting the starboard side by number 5 hold. The fore peak was now flooded, numbers 1, 3, 4 and 5 holds and the engine room were filling. It was decided to abandon her, and the boats were hoisted, and the crew left her. At 06.45 she was still afloat, although very low in the water, the boats clustered nearby. Another torpedo was fired after which there was a large explosion, and she broke in two with the bow and stern rising clear of the surface before she sank. Two hundred and seventy-eight survivors were picked up the following day by the destroyer *Impulsive*, but three men died.
[*TNA: ADM.267/92*]

14 May **PURIRI** auxiliary minesweeper
Leith 1938 requisitioned 1940; 927 tons; 180ft × 35ft; 1 × 4in
Lieutenant Douglas William Blacklaws RNZNR[†]
Royal New Zealand Navy. On 13 May a floating mine was caught in the nets of a fishing vessel about 9 miles north-east of Bream Head, in Hauraki Gulf, North Island. The minesweepers *Gale* and *Puriri* were ordered to search for the mine which had been marked by a buoy. The pair searched the area but could not find the buoy. At 11.00 The *Puriri* checked her position by taking a four-point bearing, which placed her about a mile and half from the reported position of the buoy. She was preparing to alter course to follow in the wake of the *Gale*, when there was a large explosion. The commanding officer was killed by the blast, and she rolled over and sank very quickly, not allowing any boats to be launched, the survivors being forced to jump into the water. The *Gale* picked up twenty-six men, but five men lost their lives. The Board of Inquiry found that she had been lost on the mine they had been searching for. Some blame was attributable to the *Gale* by failing to carry out an organised search. The mine was one of those laid in June 1940 by the German raider *Orion*.
[*http://nzetc.victoria.ac.nz/tm/scholarly/tei-WH2Navy-c12.html*]

14 May M A WEST drifter
Lowestoft 1919 (*Broil*) requisitioned 1939; 96 tons;
86.2ft × 18.5ft
Underway at slow speed, she was about a mile off the harbour mouth of Great Yarmouth when at 14.12 a single He 111 aircraft approached her from the north-west. Running in at low level the aircraft dropped four bombs as it passed overhead which exploded all around her causing considerable shock damage, the seams of the hull opening. The engine room and accommodation started to fill with water, and she heeled over to port and sank, stern first at 14.27; all the crew were picked up.
[TNA: ADM.199/777; ADM.199/1175]

14 May MINICOY launch
Old Kilpatrick 1918 requisitioned 1940; 5 tons;
26.1ft × 7.1ft
Lieutenant Ernest Francis Pegg RNVR[†]
Stationed at Milford Haven, she went to the assistance of RAF launch *316* after she was engulfed by a large explosion. As they approached the scene at 13.00, she herself was sunk by a large explosion. Her position then was 1 mile to the west of St Annes Light; three men were killed, with two survivors. It was believed that both vessels had been sunk by acoustic mines.
[TNA: ADM.199/239]

18 May JEWEL drifter
Buckie 1908 (*Lily Oak*) requisitioned 1940; 84 tons;
85.2ft × 19ft
Sub-Lieutenant George Hubert Joseph Cresswell RNVR[†]
Whilst on passage, she detonated a mine and rapidly sank just outside the swept channel about 1 mile to the west of the Pile Light, in Belfast Lough. There were no survivors, all fourteen men on board were lost.
[TNA: ADM.199/658]

18 May OLNA oiler
Devonport 1921; 7,023 tons; 430ft × 57ft
Lieutenant Commander Douglas Noel James Williams RNR
Part of the Mediterranean Fleet, she used Suda Bay in Crete as a base from November 1940. From late April the port came under regular air attack, and during one of these on 21 April she was damaged when a bomb exploded nearby. During another air raid on 18 May by a large group of Ju 87 dive bombers, she received a direct hit and was set on fire forward, leading to her being abandoned in a sinking condition. One rating subsequently died of his injuries.
[TNA: ADM.199/810]

19 May CITY OF ROCHESTER paddle minesweeper
Kinghorn 1904 requisitioned 1939; 235 tons;
160.2ft × 22.2ft; 1 × 12pdr
Laid up and not in commission, she was lying at Acorn's Yard, Gas House Point, Rochester, where she foundered after the explosion of an air-dropped mine.
[TNA: ADM.199/407]

19 May SEA ANGLER yacht
(*Steam Pinnace 339*) requisitioned 1940; 23 tons;
50.5ft × 9.7ft
Employed as a harbour tender, she is reported to have been destroyed by accidental fire at Plymouth.
[Statement of Losses p15; TNA: BT.110/1503]

21 May HANYARDS yacht
Littlehampton 1931 requisitioned 1940; 17 tons;
40.4ft × 10.3ft
Lieutenant Somerset Stafford Brooke RNVR
Employed as a boom patrol vessel at Cardiff and Swansea, she is listed as being lost on this date – cause unknown.
[Statement of Losses p15; TNA: ADM.1/24129]

Invasion and Evacuation from Crete 20–29 May

On 20 May the Germans launched Operation '*Merkur*', the invasion of Crete. The extensive use of airborne troops frustrated the defenders and in heavy fighting the Allies retreated. The Royal Navy gave what support it could by intercepting or disrupting enemy seaborne reinforcements, but with no air cover, ships found themselves very exposed and suffered badly from air attacks. On 27 May it was decided to evacuate the troops from the island, and this had to be performed under constant air attack. In the operations two cruisers, six destroyers, one sloop, three armed whalers and five torpedo boats plus two motor launches and three landing craft were lost; a further fifteen ships were damaged.

20 May WIDNES minesweeping sloop
Glasgow 1918; 710 tons; 220ft × 28.6ft; 1 × 4in, 1 × 12pdr
Lieutenant Commander Robert Bruce Chandler
Whilst anchored in Suda Bay, Crete, she had been subjected to an air attack on 18 May, when Ju 87 Stuka aircraft had carried out a determined attack on her. This assault had resulted in several near misses by bombs, all landing within 30ft, and she was badly shaken and peppered with shrapnel. She was underway off Cape Drepano 2 days later when at 14.55 she was again attacked by Ju 87s. The results were like the

earlier attack: she escaped any direct hits, but three bombs landed around her, with one under her stern and another close to her starboard side. This latter bomb threw her over to port, and she assumed a 10-degree list from which she did not recover. The starboard engine was reported out of action due to fractured pipes and all electrical power was lost. Water was reported entering the engine and boiler rooms, and with the pumps out of action the rush of water could not be stemmed. She was steered inshore and ran onto a sandy beach at 15.55 in position 35.26.42N 24.12.42E. With the steady advance of German troops, salvage was not considered possible, and after removing valuable stores, she was abandoned on 24 May. There were no casualties. The Germans subsequently salvaged her, and she was repaired to become *Uj 2109*, to be sunk by Allied forces in October 1943.
[TNA: ADM.199/621]

20 May KOS XXIII whaler

Middlesbrough 1937 requisitioned 1941; 353 tons; 134.8ft × 26.5ft; 1 × 4in

Berthed at the north end of Suda Bay in Crete, she came under repeated air attack. At 14.35 she became the target for a sustained attack by Ju 87 Stuka dive bombers. Although there were no direct hits, several bombs landed close around her, with one exploding under the bows, another two on the starboard side and another under her stern. The ship was covered with smoke and water, and she was severely shaken, which ruptured an oil tank. Oil spilled out, surrounding the ship, and water was reported entering several compartments. To prevent her sinking she was run on to the shore at 14.47. Subsequently she was declared a constructive total loss and all useful equipment was removed or smashed, and she was abandoned some days later as a wreck. Later, the occupying forces raised her and after repair she entered German service as the patrol vessel *Uj 2104*. She was eventually sunk in September 1943 in Stampalia Bay by the destroyers *Eclipse*, *Faulknor* and *Vasilissa Olga*.

Note: the name of the commanding officer of *Kos XXIII* is somewhat obscure. Secondary sources indicate 'Lieutenant Commander J J Reid RNVR' as being in command, but there is no officer of that name and rank carried in the contemporary Navy List. Possibly Lieutenant Commander Lawrence Alexander St John Reid RNVR (SA)?
[TNA: ADM.199/810]

21 May JUNO destroyer

Govan 1938; 1,690 tons; 339.6ft × 35.8ft; 6 × 4.7in, 4 × 2pdr, 10 × torpedo tubes
Commander St. John Reginald Joseph Tyrwhitt

Stationed in the eastern Mediterranean, she sailed from Alexandria joining three other destroyers escorting the cruisers *Naiad* and *Perth* to proceed to Crete as Force 'C'. They established a patrol line to the north of the island and successfully intercepted a force of Italian torpedo boats during the night of 20/21 May, forcing them to retire. The following morning at daybreak the force withdrew through the Kaso Strait heading southward. As they did so they came under a series of heavy air attacks being bombed continuously from 09.50. At 11.49 during a high-level attack by five Italian Cant Z1007 aircraft the *Juno* was hit by three bombs, with another two exploding close nearby. The ship broke up abaft the bridge and sank very quickly, disappearing in 2 minutes. The casualties were very heavy, with five officers and 111 ratings being lost.
[TNA: CAB.106/640]

22 May GLOUCESTER light cruiser

Devonport 1937; 9,400 tons; 558ft × 62.4ft; 12 × 6in, 8 × 4in, 16 × 2pdr
Captain Henry Aubrey Rowley[†]

Deployed to the area west of Crete with the cruiser *Fiji*, during the night of 21 May as Force 'A1', they were ordered to enter the Aegean to intercept German surface craft. The following morning, they came under attack by aircraft from first light onwards, formations of Ju 87 and Ju 88 aircraft constantly dive bombing the group. By 07.00 they were in the Anti-Kithera channel and *Gloucester* suffered a near miss on her port quarter, which shook the ship. The attacks went on throughout the day until at 14.15 the cruisers were ordered to cover the rescue of survivors from the *Greyhound* (see below), and they circled the survivors, trying to keep the aircraft from attacking and rescue the men in the water. From 15.00, as they cleared the area, they again came under attack, and at 15.27 she was hit by two bombs in quick succession; the first entered through 'X' barbette and exploded in the gunroom flat. *Gloucester* disappeared in a cloud of smoke and spray as she was hit, the ship shaking violently, but as she reappeared, was almost immediately hit again, on the port side amidships blowing the after-director tower overboard. Both masts were seen to be leaning sideways and she took a heel to port. She was hit again by another bomb which exploded on the upper deck between 'P.1' and 'P.2' guns and then another which went through the port pom-pom platform, to explode in the canteen flat. She lost steam and slowed to a halt. As the *Fiji* closed her, fires could be seen burning in the port hanger and the port side was a 'mass of destruction'. With the air attacks still under way, the *Fiji* would endanger herself by stopping, so dropped Carley floats and then left the scene. The cruiser steadily settled and then rolled over and sank. Seven hundred and twenty-two men were lost with just eighty-five survivors.
[TNA: ADM.1/18695; ADM.199/1177]

22 May FIJI light cruiser
Clydebank 1939; 8,525 tons; 538ft × 62ft; 12 × 6in, 8 × 4in, 8 × 2pdr
Captain Peveril Barton Raby Wallop William-Powlett

On 21 May, in company with the cruiser *Gloucester*, the pair moved into the Aegean (see *Gloucester* above). They found no targets but attracted a great deal of attention from enemy aircraft, being attacked frequently. The airborne assault continued during the 22nd, and although she had suffered considerable damage, much of it was superficial. Far more worrying was the steady diminution of ammunition; and by the afternoon the *Fiji* had only forty rounds per 4in gun remaining. At 14.15 *Fiji* and *Gloucester* were ordered to go the assistance of the destroyers *Kandahar* and *Kingston* which were attempting to rescue survivors of the *Greyhound* (see above). At 15.15 they came under another intense air attack during which a bomb landed close to the port side of *Fiji*, exploding abreast the forward engine room. This caused considerable structural damage, wrecking the port crane, and dislodging the port torpedo tubes. A hole approximately 6ft by 4ft was blown in the side and about twenty-five rivets were blown out, the side plating being buckled around the area. The air attacks continued, usually by Ju 87 dive bombers approaching from the stern or bow, and ammunition was now dangerously low. When the *Gloucester* was immobilised, it was reluctantly agreed to leave her and head south for safety. There followed a lull but at 18.50 three aircraft emerged out of clouds with little warning to attack her. The wheel was put hard to starboard and she managed to avoid a direct hit, but a bomb exploded close to the port side abreast 'A' boiler room. The ship was heeling because of the turn and never recovered. She assumed a list which slowly increased as the boiler room flooded, and her speed fell away. The forward engine room then reported that they were flooding, and the water spread rapidly. By now all 4in ammunition had been expended and both 'A' and 'B' turrets were reported to be jammed due to lack of power. By 19.15 the ship had stopped and had a list of 25 degrees to port. At this point a single Ju 88 aircraft appeared, circled her, and then carried out a dive-bombing attack from forward, dropping three bombs, all of which struck her; one hit the port side of the hanger deck, and penetrated through to 'A' boiler room where it exploded. This sealed her fate as she heeled further over to port and the order was given to abandon her. At 20.15 she rolled over and remained afloat, bottom up for some time before sinking. Two hundred and forty-eight men died.
[TNA:ADM.267/82]

22 May GREYHOUND destroyer
Barrow 1935; 1,350 tons; 312ft × 33ft; 4 × 4.7in, 1 × 3in, 4 × torpedo tubes
Commander Walter Roger Marshall-A'Deane[†]

Part of Force 'B', she was sent into the Aegean in company with the cruisers *Gloucester* and *Fiji* to intercept enemy surface craft that may attempt to cross to Crete. During the late morning she was detached to investigate a small vessel that was seen close to the island of Pori, and as they closed it could be seen to be a caique, flying a Nazi ensign. The boat was engaged and sunk with gunfire, and this complete, she increased speed to rejoin the force when at 13.51 several Ju 87s were sighted approaching her. She manoeuvred and worked up to full speed, and avoided the first attacks, but then suffered three direct hits from bombs. One struck amidships, near the 3in gun mounting, the others hit aft, exploding in the officers' cabins and on 'Y' gun deck. She started sinking very quickly by the stern, and the port whaler was ordered to be lowered, but only one Carley float was released before she was ordered to be abandoned. About 5 minutes after the attack, she had sunk, leaving many men in the water. After about an hour the destroyers *Kingston* and *Kandahar* appeared and lowered boats to pick up survivors but were forced to retire to another air attack. They returned, screened by the cruisers *Gloucester* and *Fiji*, and successfully picked up many of the men, but seventy-nine men died. Commander A'Deane was rescued by the *Kandahar*, and later that day when that destroyer went to the aid of the sinking *Fiji* (see above), he dived into the water to help men struggling in the water, but in the gathering darkness he was not seen again. He was granted a posthumous award of the Albert Medal.
[TNA:ADM.199/1177]

23 May KASHMIR destroyer
Woolston 1939; 1,690 tons; 339.6ft × 35.8ft; 6 × 4.7in, 4 × 2pdr, 10 × torpedo tubes
Commander Henry Alexander King

In company with four other ships of the Fifth Destroyer Flotilla, she sailed from Malta at 21.30 on 21 May, to proceed to Crete, with orders to join the cruisers of Force 'A1' to the west of the island. They successfully rendezvoused with the cruisers during the afternoon of 22 May and were initially tasked to search for survivors from the *Gloucester* (see above). That complete, they closed the coast to bombard enemy shore positions and sank two small surface craft. At dawn they retired at full speed to the south but were located by enemy aircraft and suffered air attacks until at 07.55 there was a determined attack by a large number of Ju 87 Stuka aircraft during which *Kashmir* was hit by at least one large bomb and sank in 2 minutes. The survivors were picked up by her sister *Kipling*. Eighty-one men died.
[TNA: CAB.106/640]

23 May KELLY destroyer
Hebburn 1938; 1,690 tons; 339.6ft × 35.8ft; 6 × 4.7in,
4 × 2pdr, 10 × torpedo tubes
Captain Lord Louis Mountbatten

Leader of the Fifth Destroyer Flotilla, she had been with *Kashmir* (see above), sailing from Malta to join the forces off Crete. During the intense air attacks at 07.55 as the force retired from the coast of the island, after the *Kashmir* had been sunk, the aircraft concentrated on the *Kelly*. She was doing 30 knots and under full starboard rudder when she was hit by a large bomb. The ship took a heavy list to port and then rolled over, still with way on the ship which sheered away, out of control, to starboard, before she capsized. She floated for about 30 minutes, bottom up, before sinking. Seven officers and 122 men were lost. The survivors were picked up by the *Kipling*, despite the heavy air raids continuing.
[TNA: ADM.199/810; CAB.106/640]

23 May Air attack on Suda Bay, Crete
To support the hard-pressed British forces in the Aegean, part of the 10th MTB Flotilla was deployed to northern Crete, being based at Suda Bay. Following the invasion of Crete on 20 May, they conducted several night patrols off the coast, leaving the harbour at dusk, and returning at dawn. At 11.50 on the 23rd the port became the target for an attack by the German air force, when four Me 109s flew low over the harbour strafing the boats with cannon fire. At 12.10 there was a second, stronger attack, by nine Me 109s, some carrying bombs, and by the end of this attack all the boats were either on fire or so severely damaged that they sank. The attackers were from 111/JG 77. In all, five boats were lost.
[TNA: ADM.199/1177; Reynolds & Cooper, Mediterranean MTBs at War pp24–5]

MTB 67 motor torpedo boat
Hampton 1940; 17 tons; 55ft × 11ft; 2 × torpedo tubes
Lieutenant Charles Courtney Anderson

With hull and bows badly damaged by cannon fire and splinters, she was the last of the boats to sink, finally going under during mid-afternoon.

MTB 213 motor torpedo boat
Hampton 1940; 17 tons; 55ft × 11ft; 2 × torpedo tubes
Lieutenant Theodore Patrick Kenneth Kemble RNVR

Catching fire when hit by cannon fire, she was abandoned as the fire spread and was burned out.

MTB 214 motor torpedo boat
Hampton 1940; 17 tons; 55ft × 11ft; 2 × torpedo tubes
Lieutenant Commander Edward Copson Peake

Set on fire during the second attack, she caught fire and eventually blew up at 12.45.

MTB 216 motor torpedo boat
Hampton 1940; 17 tons; 55ft × 11ft; 2 × torpedo tubes
Lieutenant Charles Leslie Coles RNVR

Secured to a tug alongside a wooden jetty when the attacks commenced and hit by cannon fire she was set on fire during the initial attack. This was extinguished, and she was hauled clear of the tug which was also on fire and moved to be alongside the other boats. Hit again during the second attack she was burned out.

MTB 217 motor torpedo boat
Hampton 1940; 17 tons; 55ft × 11ft; 2 × torpedo tubes
Lieutenant Richard Millet Rickards RNVR

Caught fire during the second attack and burnt steadily until she eventually blew up.

24 May HDML 1011 motor launch
Hamworthy 1940; 46 tons; 70ft × 15ft; 1 × 3pdr
Lieutenant Alan Holland Blake RNR

Based at Suda Bay in Crete, she was tasked to carry portable radios and naval ciphers to Sphakia where the HQ of the General Officer Commanding troops in Crete had been established. She sailed from Suda Bay after dark on 23 May but was forced to take shelter at Selinos Kastelli because of poor weather anchoring close inshore, with most of the crew ordered ashore to take shelter. At 06.30 several aircraft were seen approaching, a mixture of Me 110 fighter and Ju 88 bomber aircraft, some of which circled around and commenced an attack. During the first attack the launch was riddled with bullets and a bomb burst close on the starboard side, which blew the forward section in, the gun going overboard, and killing one man. She heeled over to starboard and then sank bows first, still being strafed by the aircraft.
[TNA: ADM.199/810]

27 May LCT (1) 16 landing craft, tank
Greenock 1940; 226 tons; 135ft × 28ft; 2 × 2pdr
Boatswain Edward John Boissel

Originally part of the North African lighter flotilla, she had been deployed to Crete to support the Allied efforts, arriving at Suda Bay on 21 April. The next day *LCT 16* was badly shaken by a bomb which landed 50ft away. When the situation deteriorated on the island, small craft were ordered to leave on 26 May; as it was doubted that she could make it to Alexandria, she was scuttled in shallow water, the crew being taken off by the *Abdiel*.
[TNA: ADM.199/810]

27 May KOS XXII whaler
Middlesbrough 1937 requisitioned 1941; 353 tons;
134.8ft × 26.5ft; 1 × 12pdr
Lieutenant Herbert Duncan Foxon SANF

Part of the forces assembled at Suda Bay in Crete, she had just secured alongside the wharf to embark stores and replenish her ammunition, when at 22.30 she received the order to sail forthwith to Alexandria, travelling only by night. She cleared the harbour at midnight, but was unable to unship the Asdic dome, necessary for maximum speed, so was restricted to 11 knots. At first light she went inshore, to anchor under cliffs to the south-east of Suda Bay, most of the crew being landed. Lieutenant Foxon also prepared for any march overland, should it be necessary. At 08.00 the *Syvern* arrived and anchored nearby (see below), and the pair escaped detection by the enemy until 16.30 when a single aircraft carried out a strafing run. Two hours later there was a determined attack by a number of aircraft. At 19.00 the *Kos* was hit by two bombs, both exploding forward. The ready-use ammunition was set on fire and the blaze soon spread aft, covering the ship in smoke. With the ship on fire from forward to aft, and settling, she was abandoned. There were no casualties.
[TNA: ADM.199/810]

27 May SYVERN whaler
Sandefjord 1937 requisitioned 1940; 307 tons;
125.5ft × 28.6ft; 1 × 75mm
Lieutenant Commander Reginald Edkins Clarke RNR

Deployed to Suda Bay in Crete, she was damaged on 21 May when a Ju 88 aircraft attacked her with cannon and machine-gun fire. During the attack, most of the men on the upper deck were wounded and one man killed, and a tracer shell struck the starboard ready-use ammunition locker, which exploded and started a fire. There was some consolation as the attacker flew low over the whaler, it struck the foremast, carrying it away, but causing the aircraft to lose control and crash into the sea. The fire was brought under control and she was taken back into harbour for repairs. Ordered to sail during the evening of 26 May, she was able to sail at 06.00 the following morning, steering east along the coast for 2 hours when she headed inshore to anchor near the armed whaler *Kos-22* (see above). With the crew landed ashore for their safety, they escaped attention from passing aircraft until 16.30. During an attack at 18.45 the *Kos* was set on fire. At 20.00 a further air attack commenced, and during this raid, a stick of three bombs fell across the stern, all of which either hit or exploded close around the ship. A fire was started which was seen to spread quickly and she sank with a series of explosions at 21.00.
[TNA: ADM.199/810]

28 May HDML 1030 motor launch
Clynder 1940; 46 tons; 70ft × 15ft; 1 × 3pdr
Lieutenant William Octavius Cooksey RNVR

Stationed at Suda Bay, Crete, after the German invasion she was ordered to proceed west around the island and head for Alexandria. She sailed during the evening of 27 May but at 05.30 the next morning when about 15 miles west of Gavdo Pulo, she was attacked by two German aircraft. The first attack was avoided, but the second resulted in a bomb exploding under her bows, blowing away the fore part as far back as the engine room bulkhead. She came to a stop, and as it was clear that she was sinking she was abandoned. All the crew survived, taking to one boat and a raft to make it to the shore.
[TNA: ADM.199/810; http://www.naval-history.net/WW2MemoirAndSo06.htm]

(28) May LCT (1) 6 landing craft, tank
Birkenhead 1940; 226 tons; 135ft × 28ft; 2 × 2pdr
Sub-Lieutenant John Digby Sutton RNVR

Having earlier supported the evacuation of Allied forces from Greece to Crete, she was then employed at Suda Bay, where she arrived on 29 April. With the deterioration of the situation on 26 May she was ordered to make her way direct to Alexandria, via Sphakia, with Lieutenant Benjamin Weston Waters RNVR (Flotilla Senior Officer) embarked, and sailed the next morning but was lost en-route by air attack off the west coast of Crete. The precise date of loss is uncertain but seems likely to have been on 28 May.
[TNA: ADM.199/415; ADM.358/3432]

(28) May LCT (1) 20 landing craft, tank
Linthouse 1940; 226 tons; 135ft × 28ft; 2 × 2pdr
Sub–Lieutenant Allen Howarth RNVR

Having supported Allied troops in Crete, when the island was evacuated she was ordered on 26 May to proceed from Suda Bay to Sphakia and having collected troops, to make her way independently to Alexandria and sailed the next morning in company with *LCT 6*. She was sunk by air attack off south-west Crete whilst on passage to Alexandria, the precise date is uncertain, but 28 May is most likely.
Note: the wreck of an LCT has been found at Falasarna, evidently having been bombed – this may well be either *LCT 6* or *LCT 20*.
[TNA: ADM.199/415; ADM.199/810]

29 May IMPERIAL destroyer
Hebburn 1936; 1,370 tons; 312ft × 33ft; 4 × 4.7in,
10 × torpedo tubes
Lieutenant Commander Charles Arthur de Winton Kitcat

Part of a force of six destroyers and three cruisers under the command of Rear Admiral Rawlings that were sent to Crete to assist with the evacuation of Allied troops from Crete, they were subjected to air attacks during 28 May. During one attack by a formation of Ju 87 aircraft, the *Imperial* avoided any direct hits, but about five bombs exploded around the stern of the ship. She was badly shaken, and suffered superficial splinter damage, but otherwise appeared to have survived well. During that night they entered Heraklion and embarked a large number of troops. At 03.25 the force sailed, but as they cleared the harbour the *Imperial* suffered a steering gear breakdown, and only narrowly avoided a collision with the cruiser *Dido*. The destroyer showed little inclination to obey the wheel and slewed erratically from port to starboard. Steering from the tiller flat was attempted, to no effect, and steering by engines had little success. Investigation revealed an extensive oil leak in the hydraulic system, and it was believed that ram cylinders had been fractured, probably during the air raid. The problem meant that the rudder was swinging freely side to side. This would normally be a repairable problem and she could have been towed, but the situation was dangerous. The senior officer, Rear Admiral Rawlings was acutely aware that at daybreak they would be very vulnerable to air attack. The embarked troops were therefore transferred to other ships and the *Hotspur* fired a torpedo into her to sink her, in position 35.23N 25.38.6E.

[TNA: ADM.199/675]

29 May HEREWARD destroyer

Walker 1936; 1,340 tons; 312ft × 33ft; 4 × 4.7in, 8 × torpedo tubes
Lieutenant William James Munn

Another of the units of Force 'B', six destroyers and three cruisers, deployed to Crete (see above). As they cleared the coast, they came under intense air attack and at 06.25 during a dive-bombing attack by Ju 87 Stuka aircraft, the *Hereward* was hit by a bomb. She lost power and fell out of formation. Admiral Rawlings was in a difficult position; the force was in the middle of the Kaso strait and for other ships of his already-depleted force to go to her aid would only endanger them. *Hereward* was therefore left, last being seen heading slowly inshore, still engaging the enemy. She continued to come under attack by both German and Italian aircraft and was hit again before she rolled over and sank. All the ship's boats had been smashed, and the survivors were forced to cling to wreckage or the few Carley floats that had survived for several hours before being picked up by Italian patrol boats. Seventy-six members of the crew and an indeterminate number of soldiers lost their lives.

[TNA: ADM.199/810; WO.361/142]

★ ★ ★

24 May HOOD battlecruiser

Clydebank 1918; 42,100 tons; 810ft × 95ft; 8 × 15in, 14 × 4in, 24 × 2pdr, 5 × rocket projectors
Captain Ralph Kerr†

In the spring of 1941, the Admiralty was much exercised with the threat of major German surface units breaking out into the Atlantic to attack convoys. The *Scharnhorst*, *Gneisenau* and *Admiral Hipper* were all located in French ports and the new battleship *Bismarck* was in the Baltic and reportedly ready for sea. Various capital units had been disposed to counter the threat; the battlecruiser *Hood*, with the flag of Vice Admiral Lancelot Ernest Holland onboard, with four destroyers in company was deployed to Hvalfjord in Iceland. Three battleships were stationed at Scapa Flow whilst cruisers patrolled the Iceland-Faeröes gap and the Denmark Strait. On 18 May the *Bismarck* sailed from Gydnia, accompanied by the heavy cruiser *Prinz Eugen* to re-position in the waters of northern Norway. The movement was detected and in anticipation of an Atlantic raid by the pair, the *Hood* and her destroyers were ordered to sea, and the battleship *Prince of Wales* was deployed from Scapa to join her to the south of Iceland. On the afternoon of 22 May aerial reconnaissance confirmed that both German units had left their anchorage in Korsfjord and at 22.45 that night the main fleet of two battleships, the aircraft carrier *Victorious*, three cruisers and seven destroyers sailed from Scapa, to steam to take up a position to the south of Iceland and cover whichever passage the enemy might take. At 19.22 on 23 May the heavy cruiser *Suffolk*, patrolling to the north-west of Iceland, sighted the *Bismarck* and her consort steaming to the south-west. The cruiser promptly took advantage of the fog patches to take cover but maintained contact by use of her radar. She continued to shadow throughout the night, passing accurate positions. She was joined by her sister, the *Norfolk*, but she was seen, and had to hastily retreat under a smokescreen as she came under fire. The pair then stationed themselves astern of the German group, and using radar, kept themselves at a range outside of their guns whilst sending a stream of position reports. Admiral Holland with his two ships was the nearest force, and whilst Admiral Tovey, with the force from Scapa, was closing, it was clear that Holland would intercept first. *Hood* and *Prince of Wales* along with four destroyers steered towards the *Bismarck*, clearly with the intention of intercepting in the early hours of 24 May. However, the shadowing cruisers were having difficulty in maintaining contact by radar alone, and they lost touch. The sudden loss of reports led to Holland altering course and slowing. At 02.00 *Hood* and *Prince of Wales* turned to the south, to wait for contact to be regained and the destroyers were detached to the north to assist with the search. At 02.47 the *Suffolk* reported that she had regained contact and Holland was able to alter course to intercept. This manoeuvring had the unfortunate result that when the *Bismarck* and *Prinz Eugen* were sighted, at 05.35, they were fine on the starboard bow of the British ships. To the Germans, the British were seen closing from the port beam. This meant that Holland's force could only employ the forward armament for the opening part of the engagement, whilst facing the full broadsides of the enemy. *Hood*, leading the *Prince of Wales*, opened fire at 05.53, the enemy then being at a range of 26,500 yards. Initially the *Hood* targeted the wrong ship, believing that the leading vessel was the *Bismarck*. This was ordered to be corrected, but it meant that the *Bismarck* was only being engaged by the forward armament of the *Prince of Wales*, whilst both German units were able to concentrate their entire broadsides against *Hood*. At 05.55 Holland ordered a turn together of 20 degrees to port, which would allow her after turrets to engage. The firing of both sides was of markedly different accuracy. It was not until her sixth salvo that the *Prince of Wales* managed to straddle her target, and the *Hood*, wrongly firing at the cruiser *Prinz Eugen*, failed to achieve any hits. The *Bismarck*, on the other hand, straddled the *Hood* with her third salvo. One shell from this salvo exploded on the boat deck of the *Hood* and another fell just short. Shortly after this a fire was observed on the port after end of the deck. It burned with a clear flame and appeared to spread, and then died down. The shell had exploded next to one of the Unrotated Projectile (UP) mountings, which had resulted in the ready-use ammunition catching fire and exploding. As the ammunition was destroyed, so the fire died down. At 06.00 Holland ordered a further turn of 20 degrees to port, but it was never executed. *Hood* was straddled twice, by the fifth and sixth salvoes from the *Bismarck* and after the last, she blew up. The explosion occurred amidships; it was not a sudden flash, but '… a great sheet of flame with several bright balls of fire visible'. To another observer, it was 'like a vast blow torch'. The boat deck appeared to rise in the middle before the mainmast and huge chunks of debris were seen to be scattered, and the whole ship then disappeared in a vast cloud of smoke. As the *Prince of Wales* drew abreast the scene, the *Hood* was seen to have broken in half, with the fore part sticking out of the water, turning over before sinking. The after part was just a mass of twisted framework which turned over to port and sank. She had gone in 3 minutes. The battle continued for only a few minutes longer. The *Prince of Wales* was now faced with both of the German ships concentrating their fire on her, and at 06.13 she turned away and withdrew under the cover of smoke, although before doing so she had obtained two hits on the *Bismarck*, one of which caused a leak of fuel oil, and this forced the *Bismarck* to abandon her sortie and shape course for France. Ninety-four

officers and 1,321 ratings died. There were just three survivors, who were picked up by the destroyer *Electra*. Midshipman Dundas had been stationed on the upper bridge. He could recall a tremendous explosion which knocked everyone off their feet and the ship heeling rapidly to port. He scrambled out of a window to find himself in the water and he swam clear, seeing the bows rising clear of the water before sliding under. Able Seaman Tilburn was stationed on the boat deck. He had witnessed the explosion of the ready-use ammunition, and then the main explosion, which seemed to him to be between the control tower and 'B' turret, which had blown him into the water. Signalman Briggs, on the compass platform, also found himself in the water after the explosion. The subsequent enquiry found that the fire on the boat deck in the ready-use ammunition for the rocket projectiles was not thought to have been relevant and was not a contributory factor. The most likely cause of her loss was by the penetration of one of her magazines by a 38cm shell. One of the 4in magazines probably exploded first, and this triggered another explosion in the forward 15in magazine. The *Bismarck* was successfully intercepted for a second time by Admiral Tovey, with the *Rodney* and *King George V*, which sank her.

[TNA: ADM. 1/11726; Roskill vol 1 pp394–406]

24 May **AURORA II** drifter

Banff 1906 requisitioned 1941; 74 tons; 84.7ft × 18.6ft
Run ashore at Tobruk during 23 May during a sandstorm, she was then attacked by aircraft the following day and destroyed.
[TNA: ADM.199/413]

25 May **GRIMSBY** sloop

Devonport 1933; 990 tons; 250ft × 34ft; 2 × 4.7in,
1 × 12pdr
Commander Kenneth Judge D'Arcy
In company with the armed whaler *Southern Maid*, ordered to escort a valuable tanker, the *Helka*, from Alexandria to Tobruk. At 12.35, when in approximate position 32N 24.42E, the group were attacked by a number of Ju 88 aircraft, which dived out of the sun, but none of the bombs scored hits. One bomb, however, did explode about 20ft from the starboard side of the sloop. The shock put the pusher hoist for the forward gun out of action. At 15.40 Tobruk reported that another large group of aircraft was approaching, and these duly appeared overhead at 15.57 and commenced a dive-bombing attack. Some of these concentrated on the tanker, and the second aircraft hit the *Helka* amidships, and she almost immediately broke in half. Further attacks were made on her, which confirmed her destruction. Meanwhile the *Grimsby* had been subjected to a succession of steep dive-bombing attacks from a

large number of Italian aircraft. By manoeuvring hard, the ship managed to avoid all except one. An aircraft dived steeply out of the sun from the port quarter and scored two direct hits on the port side aft. One bomb passed through the after end of the engine room, the other went through the wardroom flat. It is likely that the bottom was blown out of the ship aft as she immediately took a list to port and settled by the stern as she flooded. The boiler and engine rooms reported that they were rapidly filling with water and were evacuated. The *Southern Maid* closed, and the wounded were transferred to her by boat although the heel continued to increase. As it was clear that she was sinking, she was ordered to be abandoned, the men taking to the boats. By 16.50 all survivors except the gun crews had been evacuated, and 5 minutes later she gave a lurch, and the last men left her. At 17.09 the *Southern Maid*, with two whalers, a skiff and a boat from the *Helka* in tow, got under way, heading for Mersa Matruh, but the boats were difficult to tow, and one by one they broke free, and the men were picked up by the whaler. When they last saw her, the *Grimsby* was listing 30 degrees to port and her stern was awash. Her position then was approximately 32.33N 25.40E. Eleven men were lost. [TNA: ADM.1/11841]

27 May EVESHAM trawler

Selby 1915 requisitioned 1939; 239 tons; 116ft × 22.5ft; 1 × 6pdr
Skipper George Russell Bull RNR

Bound for a night patrol off the Essex/Suffolk coast, she proceeded in company with three other patrol trawlers, steaming in line ahead northwards along the swept channel off the coast. At 22.10, when they were approaching 54W buoy off Southwold, an aircraft was seen approaching from the east at low level. It crossed the bows of the group and then turned towards them. All the group responded by opening fire with deck guns and machine guns, but the aircraft pressed home an attack, dropping a stick of six bombs. All exploded around the *Evesham*. Although none of them was a direct hit, the shock of the explosions brought down the mast and the engine room reported that it was flooding. The 6pdr gun was reported to be out of action due to shock damage. The aircraft circled around to press home another attack, again concentrating on the *Evesham*. Another six bombs were dropped, which again straddled the trawler and lifted her out of the water. She was now making water rapidly and clearly settling. The floats were cut free and the *Aurilla* closed to come alongside to lift off the crew before she sank, but several of the men had to jump into the water as the ship went under. There were no casualties. [TNA: ADM.1/11296]

28 May MASHONA destroyer

Walker 1937; 1.960 tons; 355.6ft × 36.6ft; 8 × 4.7in, 4 × 2pdr, 4 × torpedo tubes
Commander William Halford Selby

Part of the force gathered in the Atlantic to the west of Ireland, to hunt for the battleship *Bismarck*, she had acted as part of the escort the battleships *King George V* and *Rodney*. At 07.20 on 27 May the *Mashona*, in company with her sister *Tartar*, were ordered to detach and return to harbour and refuel. The initial intention was to proceed to Devonport, but this was changed, and the pair headed for Londonderry. At 08.30 an Fw 200 aircraft was sighted, which stayed out of range of the guns, and was evidently shadowing the pair. About 10 minutes later several more aircraft appeared, which they identified as He 111s, but were actually Ju 88s, closed and commenced an attack. The attacks were pressed home continuously, the destroyers being restricted in their speed due to low fuel. At 09.12 the *Mashona* was straddled by a stick of bombs, with 3 falling close along the port side, but a fourth striking the port side abreast the bridge, to penetrate number 1 boiler room where it exploded, blowing a large hole in the side. A further two bombs passed over her to explode on the starboard side. Extensive damage was done to the port side compartments, and the starboard side was peppered by shrapnel holes. All the lights went out and she heeled over to port. A fire broke out in 'B' magazine, probably caused by splinters, but partially flooding the compartment extinguished the blaze. The rudder was found to be jammed to starboard resulting in her constantly turning a circle, but emergency hand steering was eventually rigged to restore control. The air attacks continued, and she was near missed again, splinters hitting her, causing further damage and casualties. Despite efforts to lighten her, by jettisoning torpedoes and depth charges, the list increased, until at 10.30 with the list nearing 60 degrees, she was ordered to be abandoned. Survivors were picked up by the *Tartar* and two 'Town' class destroyers that had arrived on scene, the *St Clair* and *Sherwood*. The *St Clair* was ordered to sink the wreck and she attempted to do so by torpedo; the first fired dived and went off course; the second ran straight but went under her. The third torpedo fired struck her amidships and the destroyer then fired several rounds of 4in into the wreck to ensure that she sank. Forty-six men died, and a further ten expired later of their wounds or hypothermia. [TNA: ADM.199/1175; ADM.267/104]

29 May SINDONIS trawler

Middlesbrough 1934 (*Sudanese*) requisitioned 1939; 440 tons; 162.1ft × 26.7ft; 1 × 4in
Skipper Reginald Walter Denny RNR

Based in the Mediterranean, she was in Tobruk harbour and became the target during an air raid. A group of three Ju 87s dive-bombed her, with all the bombs

exploding close along the port side. She settled and sank. There were no casualties.
[TNA: ADM.156/236]

30 May CAIRNDALE oiler
Belfast 1939 (*Erato*); 8,129 tons; 465.6ft × 59.5ft
Master Stanley Guy Kent

Proceeding independently to Gibraltar, she was ordered to rendezvous with two corvettes to the south-west of Cape Trafalgar. At 07.20 on 30 May the corvettes *Fleur de Lys* and *Coreopsis* duly appeared, with the former taking up station astern of the tanker, on her port quarter, and the *Coreopsis* on her starboard bow. Initially all the units were zigzagging, but at 08.29 Lieutenant Commander Leslie Carter RNR, the commanding officer of the *Fleur de Lys*, and senior officer, ordered to tanker to stop zigzagging, as he believed that as she was only making 9.5 knots, the zigzag served no purpose. At 09.15 bridge staff on the *Cairndale* saw a torpedo track approaching from the port side. They reacted immediately by ringing full speed and putting the wheel hard to starboard. The track passed ahead of them, but about 15 seconds later, there was a large explosion near number 3 tank, and about 5 seconds later there was a second explosion in the main engine room. She heeled over to port and settled by the stern. The Master ordered the boats to be swung out and three boats were manned and launched before she foundered, and he was the last to leave, having to jump into the sea and swim for a boat as she sank. Her bows rose up and she disappeared at 09.45. Her position was 35.20N 08.30W. Four men lost their lives. The two corvettes carried out a vigorous anti-submarine sweep, dropping seventy-six depth charges over the next hour, but without any obvious result. Her attacker had been the Italian submarine *Marconi* (Pollina). The subsequent enquiry into the loss considered that Lieutenant Commander Carter had been guilty of a serious error of judgement in ordering the cessation of the zigzag. A submarine was known to be operating in the area, a merchant ship having reported being attacked the previous day. He had then compounded this error by poor positioning of the escorts. The *Fleur de Lys* should have been ahead, not astern of her charge. Vice Admiral Edward-Collins, Vice Admiral, North Atlantic, considered that Carter had displayed '… a combination of stupidity and lack of experience'. Carter was informed that he was considered unsuitable for command and relieved as commanding officer of the corvette.
[TNA: ADM.178/260]

1 June CALCUTTA anti-aircraft cruiser
Walker 1918; 4,290 tons; 425ft × 43.6ft; 8 × 4in, 4 × 2pdr
Captain Dennis Marescaux Lees DSO

In company with the *Coventry*, the pair sailed from Alexandria at 04.00 to rendezvous with the cruiser *Phoebe* and destroyers that were carrying evacuated troops from Crete. The pair was in line astern, *Coventry* leading, zigzagging at 20 knots, and were about 100 miles to the north-west of Alexandria when at 09.00 the *Coventry* detected approaching aircraft on radar. Despite this warning, no aircraft were seen until the last minute, when two Ju 88s dived out of the sun. The wheel was put hard to starboard and the first cluster of bombs missed on the port side, but the second aircraft placed their bombs accurately, straddling the cruiser, with two bombs hitting her. One struck the upper deck near the after funnel, the other just before the bridge, both penetrating the deck to detonate below. One exploded between the boiler rooms, wrecking both and filling the ship with smoke. She started to rapidly fill with water and settled on an even keel, but it was believed that her back was broken and 4 minutes after the attack had begun, she took a list to starboard and the bows went down, the stern rose into the air and she sank with the loss of 109 men.
[TNA: ADM.199/1177]

1 June STORA whaler
Middlesbrough 1929 requisitioned 1940; 341 tons;
135.6ft × 26.2ft; 1 × 12pdr
Skipper John Baxter RNR

Having arrived at Aberdeen on 25 April for leave and a refit, she undocked on 23 May and after re-embarking her stores and ammunition during 30–31 May was preparing for sea. At 19.00 the following day, she was blown apart by a large explosion and she sank rapidly, bows first. The detonation scattered debris and shrapnel over a wide distance and caused damage to dockside buildings. An investigation by divers established that the ship had been split across the forward part of the hull, with the deck lifted and folded back across the bridge, and plates buckled outwards, all indicative of an internal explosion in the bows of the ship. It was believed that the most likely cause of the explosion was the detonation of the demolition charge, fitted in the Asdic well. This consisted of a depth charge with special primers. As the primers were not normally fitted in harbour and had to be removed from their stowage and inserted into the depth charge before they could be lit, the court of enquiry was concerned that sabotage may have been the cause. To follow this, Mr William Skardon of MI5 was called to investigate, but nothing definite was found. There was some criticism of Skipper Baxter, who had taken little interest in the ammunitioning of the ship and displayed little knowledge of the fire-watching organisation on board. He was admonished and warned to be more assiduous in his duties in the future. One man was killed in the explosion. The ship was later raised, rebuilt and returned to service.
[TNA: ADM.1/11836]

2 June IRINI VERNICOS tug

Odessa 1911 (*Tchenomor; Atrato*) requisitioned 1941; 663 tons; 179.8ft × 30.6ft

Master Emmanuel Vernicos

The tug was attacked 27 May by a Ju 88 bomber and damaged in Suda Bay, Crete, and subsequently abandoned in a sinking condition when Allied forces evacuated the island. She was later taken into German service.

[Statement of Losses p15; various secondary]

4 June VAN MEERLANT convoy escort/minelayer

Schiedam 1919 transferred 1941; 687 tons; 180.4ft × 28.5ft; 3 × 75mm

Commander Arnold Stewart Piggott

Part of the Thames local defence flotilla, she was patrolling in the Thames estuary to the north of the Isle of Sheppey, when at 08.07 she detonated an air-dropped mine near the Nore light vessel and quickly sank. Three officers and thirty-eight men died. Commander Piggott survived, but lost a leg. Her position was noted as 51.28.29 N 00.052.06 E.

[TNA: ADM.199/407; ADM.358/3359]

4 June MAMARI ('Fleet Tender C') fleet tender

Belfast 1911 (*Zealandic*) requisitioned 1939; 7,924 tons; 477.5ft × 63.1ft

Taken over by the Navy in 1939 for use as a dummy warship, she was converted to resemble the aircraft carrier *Hermes*, with a superstructure of wood and canvas to resemble the real ship as closely as possible. On 2 June she was en-route to Chatham in an east coast convoy when she came under air attack. An aircraft, identified as an He 111, was seen closing, and it was feared that she had dropped a torpedo; the helm was put over to avoid the threat, but the aircraft continued to close, dropping a stick of four bombs which all exploded around her stern, shaking the ship violently. A further attack followed by a second aircraft that released five bombs, which exploded all around her. The engine room and boiler room lighting went out and she lost power. Unable to manoeuvre, later that day she struck the wreck of the merchant vessel *Alamo* in 53.22N 00.59E and remained stuck fast. In the early hours of 4 June, she was the target for an attack by torpedo-boats, with one torpedo striking her forward at 04.32. She settled further until the foredeck was awash and she was abandoned, the crew being taken off by the tug *Sabine* and patrol sloop *Kittiwake*.

[TNA: ADM.267/129: Lloyd's War Losses p262]

5 June ASH trawler

Selby 1939; 530 tons; 150ft × 27.6ft; 1 × 12pdr

Lieutenant Arthur George Newell RNZVR

In company with her sister *Birch*, ordered to sweep ahead of Convoy CW37 as it proceeded clear of the Thames estuary. The pair had sailed from Sheerness and were heading toward the Knock John buoy and were about half a mile to the south-west of the buoy when at 18.25 there was a large explosion just abaft the amidships section on the starboard side as she detonated a mine. The engine room and after flat commenced filling immediately and the engines stopped. The *Birch* closed and came alongside, to take off stores and injured personnel, and a tow was rigged. At 19.30 the tug *Mammouth* came alongside and rigged pumps, but her equipment was in poor condition. It barely kept the water in check and when the pumps failed the water rose rapidly. At 20.30 the tow was cast off and the trawler sank in position 51.29.24N 00.59.36W.

[TNA: ADM.1/11295]

7 June PILOT VESSEL NUMBER TEN examination vessel

Amsterdam 1911 (*Stoomloodsboot no.10*) requisitioned 1940; 281 tons

Former Dutch vessel employed at Milford Haven in the examination service, she was lost when she detonated a mine off St Ann's Head, sinking 3 cables (600 yards) from the Dale Point Flagstaff. There was no loss of life.

[Statement of Losses p16; Lloyd's War Losses p 264]

8 June COR JESU drifter

(Belgian) 1931 requisitioned 1940; 97 tons

Sailed from Swansea in company with another requisitioned drifter, the *Alex Gabrielle*, for passage to the Humber, where they were to be fitted out for naval service, still manned by a small crew of Belgian seamen. The pair had been routed north around Scotland, and were off Alnmouth, heading south at 23.00 when two aircraft closed them from the east. The aircraft were identified as He 111s, which passed across their bows, and then circled around to run in towards them from astern. The wheel was put over and speed increased, but a number of bombs was dropped which exploded all around *Cor Jesu*. She was lifted and shaken considerably, starting numerous leaks, from which she subsequently foundered in position 55.29.30N 01.27W.

[TNA: ADM.199/1176; ADM.267/129]

10 June PINTAIL patrol sloop

Dumbarton 1939; 580 tons; 234ft × 25.6ft; 1 × 4in

Lieutenant John Leopold Elphinstone McClintock†

Engaged in escorting convoys along the east coast of England, she was protecting Convoy FN77 as it approached the Humber estuary. Fog during the previous evening had caused several convoys to anchor for the night, and consequently there was a large concentration of ships in the area. As they approached the Humber, they overtook another, smaller and slower convoy, escorted by the destroyer *Quantock*.

The destroyer was concerned about the yacht *Caterina*, which was labouring in the swell, and requested that the *Pintail* escort the small vessel into shelter, as they were faster than his convoy. The *Pintail* was closing her new charge when at 11.50 the *Royal Scot*, part of FN77, and about 2.5 miles away, detonated a mine. Both *Quantock* and *Pintail* immediately altered course towards her, the destroyer leading, but as the pair approached, the *Pintail* blew up. She immediately took a 45-degree list to starboard and sank rapidly by the head, disappearing in 3 minutes. The *Quantock* was joined by other escort vessels, but there was little to be done except pick up the survivors. Seven officers and forty-eight men died. It was believed that due to the congestion of shipping, the *Royal Scot* had probably strayed slightly outside the swept channel. The wreck was noted as lying in position 53.30.20N 00.52.00E.
[TNA: ADM.1/11294]

12 June LCT (1) 12 landing craft, tank
Belfast 1940; 226 tons; 135ft × 28ft; 2 × 2pdr
Caught fire whilst discharging a cargo of cased petrol at number 3 Pier, Tobruk, and burnt out. No overt reason was found for the fire, but the cases used had a poor reputation for leaks, and a petrol vapour explosion was the most likely cause.
Note: Statement of Losses vaguely gives the loss as 'August' with no details.
[TNA: ADM.199/799]

13 June KING HENRY trawler
Grimsby 1900 requisitioned 1940; 162 tons; 105.7ft × 21.1ft
Stationed at Lowestoft and employed as a boom gate vessel, she was not manned when the port came under attack during the night of 13 June by a single enemy aircraft. Several bombs were dropped which caused damage to dockside offices and a near miss caused the *King Henry* to sink.
[TNA: ADM.199/407]

20 June RESMILO trawler
Beverley 1917 requisitioned 1940; 258 tons; 120.5ft × 22ft; 1 × 12pdr
Skipper Robert Duthie Stephen RNR
In company with two other armed trawlers, the *Lord Ashfield* and *Craig Coilleach*, lying at anchor off Peterhead. At 01.26 a single aircraft was heard approaching from the south and about 10 minutes later two bombs were dropped on the group, one of which hit the *Resmilo* on the starboard side amidships. She started filling with water, and was closed by an examination vessel, the *Silver Sky*, which rigged a tow. However, before this could take effect she settled and sank on an even keel 30 minutes later, then being about 150 yards from the

end of the southern breakwater. The Peterhead lifeboat rescued all the crew.
[TNA: ADM.199/1176]

22 June BEECH trawler
Selby 1929 (*Lord Dawson*) purchased 1939; 346 tons; 140.3ft × 24ft; 1 × 12pdr
Lieutenant Arthur Patrick Cocks RNVR†
At anchor in the harbour at Scrabster, at 01.30 several enemy aircraft were detected closing northern Scotland. They headed out to Cape Wrath before turning back to approach Orkney from the west, evidently intending to attack Scapa Flow. At 02.28 an air raid warning was sounded as one aircraft closed Scrabster from over the land and dropped a number of bombs one of which scored a direct hit on the *Beech*, which sank immediately. Eleven men were killed.
[TNA: ADM.199/1176]

24 June NOGI trawler
Middlesbrough 1923 requisitioned 1939; 299 tons; 130.3ft × 24ft; 1 × 12pdr
Lieutenant Commander John Noel Caris RNR
Tasked to sweep the channels off the north Norfolk coast, she was working with the trawler *Irvana* when just before midnight on 23 June the noise of an aircraft could be heard approaching. A few moments later the aircraft materialised on the starboard bow, banked to port, and then ran over the pair, dropping three bombs, all of which fell wide. At 00.20 the aircraft returned, running in from ahead of the trawlers, at low altitude. Both vessels opened fire, and hit the aircraft, but it pressed on to drop two bombs, both of which exploded close to the *Nogi*, blowing the gun's crew into the sea, and damaging the hull. As the aircraft passed overhead it was seen to be hit by tracer bullets fired by the machine guns and it crashed into the sea a short distance away. Meanwhile it was found that water was entering the storeroom and magazine. The trawlers *Solon* and *Contender* closed and, placing themselves on either side of the *Nogi*, steered towards Great Yarmouth. But the water gained on the pumps, and hand bailing had to be resorted to, but she continued to fill. By 01.25 she was ordered to be abandoned, and she sank by the head 10 minutes later in position 52.59.30N 01.25E. There were no casualties.
[TNA: ADM.1/11548; ADM.199/1176]

24 June AUCKLAND sloop
Dumbarton 1938; 1,250 tons; 276ft × 37.6ft; 8 × 4in
Commander Mervyn Somerset Thomas
In company with the Australian destroyer *Parramatta*, she sailed from Alexandria to escort the petrol tanker *Pass of Balmaha* to Tobruk. At 08.40 the following morning the group came under air surveillance from an Italian

S 79 aircraft, and during the morning they came under attack several times from more S 79s, dropping bombs and torpedoes, but all were evaded. At 17.36 a large formation of aircraft was sighted closing from the south-east, which were identified as a force of sixteen Ju 87s. The aircraft divided themselves into smaller formations and commenced a series of attacks on the group, much of it concentrated on the sloop. She avoided the initial attacks by violent manoeuvring, but at 17.50 she suffered a direct hit on 'Y' gun, which jammed the steering gear. She veered wildly out of control and lost speed. She was then hit by three bombs in rapid succession. The first detonated in the sick bay, the second went through the bridge and then out through the ship's side. The third struck her amidships. The ship heeled over to port and the gunwale was soon under water and she was ordered to be abandoned. As the men jumped overboard there was a large explosion, probably as a magazine exploded, although a delayed-action bomb was possible. This broke her back and she as she rolled over onto her beam ends, she folded up, bows and stern rising, before she capsized to port and sank at 18.29 in position 32.13N 24.30E. Thirty-eight men were killed.
[TNA:ADM.199/1177]

27 June TRANIO trawler
South Shields 1917 (*George Clarke*) requisitioned 1939; 276 tons; 125.3ft × 23.4ft; 1 × 12pdr
Lieutenant Alexander Leonard Gustav Gillies RNR
Part of the escort to the northbound east coast Convoy EC38, she was stationed on the port side of the convoy when at 23.12 on 26 June, then being near Number 57 buoy, off Happisbugh, a 'Dornier type' aircraft attacked her from dead astern. Fire was opened on the aircraft with machine guns, but the aircraft dropped three bombs which exploded close along her port side, covering her in smoke and spray. The shock damage was extensive with machinery and fittings thrown around and several leaks had been started. At 23.25 the aircraft returned to carry out a second attack, but the bombs fell wide. She was taken in tow by the armed trawler *Tango*, but steadily settled, and at 01.30 the tow was slipped as the main deck was nearly awash, and she was abandoned. She rolled over and sank at 03.25 when near 56B buoy, off Cromer. There were no casualties.
[TNA:ADM.1/1176; ADM.199/621]

27 June FORCE trawler
Selby 1917 (*James Buchanan*) requisitioned 1940; 324 tons; 138.5ft × 23.7ft; 1 × 12pdr
Skipper-Lieutenant Walter Jonsen RNR
Acting as an escort to the southbound east coast Convoy FS26, they were off the Norfolk coast in position 52.50N 01.48E, when at 23.35 they were attacked by a group of aircraft. One attacker dropped several

bombs around the Dutch merchant ship *Montferland*, which was brought to a stop by three near misses. The *Force* closed to confirm whether she needed assistance when another attack developed. This time, two aircraft passed overhead, but did not drop anything, but served as a distraction to a third aircraft which flew in at low level, straight at the *Force* and released two bombs. One exploded close on the starboard side, the second hit her abaft the funnel, entering the engine room. There was a 'terrible explosion' and the bridge collapsed, and she rolled over and sank almost immediately, with men being thrown into the sea. The escort destroyer *Meynell* picked up ten survivors, but eleven men were killed. Skipper Jonsen was subsequently awarded the Distinguished Service Cross for placing himself alongside a stationary merchant ship to give assistance during an air raid.
[TNA:ADM.1/11551; London Gazette 5 September 1941]

30 June WATERHEN destroyer
Jarrow 1918; 1,100 tons; 300ft × 29.7ft; 4 × 4in, 1 × 2pdr, 6 × torpedo tubes
Lieutenant Commander James Hamilton Swain
Royal Australian Navy. Engaged in supplying the garrison at Tobruk, she was on her thirteenth run, in company with the *Defender*, loaded with 50 tons of stores and a number of troops. At 19.45 they were about 50 miles north-west of Sidi Barani, when they were attacked by several Ju 87 dive bombers. *Defender* was the target at first, but then they shifted to *Waterhen*. Several bombs exploded off the port bow which shook the ship. Then another three bombs exploded close along the port side, which whipped the hull, jamming the helm, splitting plates and fracturing bulkheads between the engine room and fuel tank. This caused slow flooding to engine and boiler rooms and she showed a list to port. The deck cargo was jettisoned, and torpedoes released to reduce top weight. *Defender* closed and took her in tow, aiming to return to Mersa Matruh, but the flooding steadily increased, and the list became greater. All the crew were successfully transferred to *Defender* before she slowly rolled over at 01.50 and sank in position 32.15N 25.20E. There were no casualties.
[TNA:ADM.267/103; https://www.awm.gov.au/articles/blog/reports-of-proceedings-the-tobruk-ferry-and-hmas-waterhen

30 June CRICKET river gunboat
Whiteinch 1915; 625 tons; 230ft × 36ft; 2 × 6in, 1 × 12pdr
Lieutenant Commander Edwin Beadnell Carnduff
Sailed from Mersa Matruh during the afternoon of 29 June as part of the escort to a small coastal convoy of two merchant ships, bound for Tobruk, the other escorts being the sloop *Flamingo* and armed whaler *Southern Isle*. The following day the ships came under repeated air attacks, but damage was avoided until a simultaneous attack by two aircraft, a Ju 87 and a Ju 88. The former

closed from the beam whilst the latter attacked from ahead. Whilst the first attack missed, the Ju 88 attack was successful, a bomb exploding under her hull amidships. The blast lifted the ship and shook her violently causing extensive shock damage. Power was lost, and the engine room reported that it was flooding. The *Flamingo* rigged a tow, and the gunboat was taken back to Mersa Matruh, where portable pumps were embarked to tackle the flooding. When she was stabilised, she was towed by the *St Issey* to Port Said. Examination found that there was severe structural damage over the whole length of the ship, and she was written off 9 September as a constructive total loss.
[The Review pp44–54; CB.4273 p402]

1 July DEVON COUNTY drifter
Great Yarmouth 1910 (*Scadaun*) requisitioned 1939; 86 tons; 83.9ft × 18.9ft; 1 × 6pdr
Skipper George Herbert Barnard RNR
On patrol in the Thames estuary, she was near the South Oaze buoy when she exploded a mine and sank in position 51.28.51N 00.59.14E. Three men were killed.
[TNA: ADM.199/407; Lloyd's War Losses vol 1 p275]

3 July RECEPTIVE drifter
Lowestoft 1913 requisitioned 1940; 86 tons; 85.1ft × 18.9ft
Lieutenant Raymond Harmon Arthur Remington RNVR†
Equipped to attend boom defences, the drifter sailed from Sheerness in company with another drifter, the *Phyllis Rose*, to proceed to Whitstable. At about 18.30 as they moved up the river Swale and were about 150 yards to the west of Swale Boom, there was a large explosion under the stern of *Receptive* and she was covered in water and dirty-coloured smoke. As it cleared, she was seen to roll over onto her side, her stern having been blown away. Her bows remained afloat for a few minutes before disappearing. Nine men lost their lives, and there were four survivors.
[TNA: ADM.1/11549]

4 July AKRANES trawler
Selby 1929 requisitioned 1939; 358 tons; 140.4ft × 25ft
Lieutenant Walter Arthur Charles Harvey RNR
Lying at anchor in Bridlington Bay, it was a bright moonlit night when the sound of an approaching aircraft was heard. The aircraft then appeared to shut down the engines, and closed silently, as it was not seen until the engines restarted as it was nearly overhead. As it passed over it opened fire with a machine gun and two bombs were dropped, which exploded on each side of the trawler. The vessel was badly shaken, with rivets driven out and plates split. She rapidly filled with water and sank. The crew escaped in their own boat. The wreck has been found and lies in position 54.05.45N 00.07.33W
[TNA: ADM.199/1175; Larn vol 3 sec 5]

5 July SNAEFELL paddle minesweeper
Clydebank 1907 (*Waverley*) requisitioned 1939; 471 tons; 225.6ft × 26.6ft; 1 × 12pdr
Lieutenant Commander Frank Brett RNR†
The senior officer's ship of the Eighth Minesweeping Flotilla, she was based at North Shields. She was in the war channel near Number 20A buoy, approaching the River Tyne when attacked by an aircraft and was struck by a bomb which blew the bows off, and she sank at 23.55 (local time). Three men were killed, including the commanding officer.
[TNA: ADM.199/1172]

7 July LORD ST VINCENT drifter
Lowestoft 1929 requisitioned 1939; 115 tons; 92ft × 20.1ft
Skipper James Samuel Alexander RNR
Ordered to patrol in the area of the Sunk Head buoy in the Thames Estuary, at 14.45, then being 3 cables (600 yards) to the north-east of the North-East Gunfleet buoy, there was a large explosion just abaft the beam as she detonated a mine. She soon began to sink, and the boats were ordered to be hoisted out and the Carley float put into the water. She steadily settled by the stern before she sank. The boats joined the float and tried to row to the Cork light vessel but were carried south by the tide. After spending an uncomfortable night at sea, they were found the following morning by a vessel from Harwich and rescued. One man was killed.
[TNA: ADM.196/220]

11 July DEFENDER destroyer
Barrow 1932; 1,375 tons; 317.9ft × 33ft; 4 × 4.7in, 2 × 2pdr, 8 × torpedo tubes
Lieutenant Commander Gilbert Lescombe Farnfield
In company with the Australian destroyer *Vendetta*, she sailed at 01.00 from Tobruk with military personnel embarked bound for Alexandria, and when well clear of the harbour the *Vendetta* took station on the starboard beam of *Defender*. At 05.18 when in position 31.49N 25.50E with no warning, the sound of a falling bomb was heard and there was a large explosion under the starboard side amidships, which lifted the ship upwards, and she was covered in a column of water and smoke. It was believed a 1,000kg bomb had detonated under the ship. The engine and boiler rooms started to slowly flood, all power failed, and the ship listed to starboard, and the upper deck was distorted and buckled. A little before 06.00 the *Vendetta* was called alongside to lift off 275 soldiers, and a tow was rigged. At 07.52 the ship was seen to be sagging amidships, and it was believed that her back was broken. The crew was removed except for a small towing crew, and the tow then resumed. She was slowly settling, and by 10.30 the torpedo tubes were awash and metallic rending noises could be heard. At 11.15 the last men were removed, and she sank, then

being 7 miles north of Sidi Barrani. There were no casualties.
[TNA: ADM.199/1178; ADM.267/104]

13 July TUNA stores carrier
Leith 1907 requisitioned 1940; 662 tons; 190ft × 30.1ft
A local coasting vessel used to carry stores and personnel between Aden and Berbera, she was loaded with petrol in drums and cases when she caught fire in Aden harbour. Fire-fighting failed to control the blaze, necessitating the vessel being scuttled at her berth to avoid further damage.
[TNA: ADM.199/410]

15 July LADY SOMERS ocean boarding vessel
Birkenhead 1929; 8,194 tons; 420.3ft × 60.2ft; 2 × 6in, 1 × 12pdr
Commander George Learmouth Dunbar RNR
Part of the escort to Gibraltar-bound Convoy OG67, at 03.10 on 15 July, she was in position 37.12N 20.32W, zigzagging at 12 knots, when the lookouts saw a torpedo track on the port beam. The helm was put hard over to starboard and full speed was run up, and the torpedo was seen to pass ahead, whilst a second track passed close under the stern. The ship was now swinging round to starboard when a third track was seen on the port quarter, and this could not be avoided, and struck the stern. The explosion blew the rudder off and fractured both propeller shafts, which brought the ship to a halt. A submarine was then seen on the surface on the port beam, and it was engaged, several rounds being fired before it disappeared, with star shell being fired to illuminate the area. The boats were lowered as a precaution, but efforts were made to deal with the damage. She remained afloat and upright, but the flooding could not be stemmed, and by 05.00 the engine room reported that water was entering. Fifteen minutes later the ship took a 'lurch' and settled quickly by the stern. It was decided to abandon her, and most of the crew left her, a small party remaining on board. By 06.15 the poop was awash, but a Spanish ship, the *Campeche*, came into sight, and closed her to render assistance, and there were hopes that a tow might be rigged. However, at 07.55 there was another large explosion on the starboard side as she was hit by another torpedo. The ship heeled over to port and the stern reared up into the air. Those remaining on board hastily left her, jumping into the water as the bows rose vertically clear of the water before sinking. By 08.40 *Campeche* had picked up all the survivors – there were no casualties. Her attacker had been the Italian submarine *Morosini* (Fraternale).
[TNA: ADM.267/129]

15 July PRINCE PHILIPPE landing ship, infantry
Hoboken 1940 requisitioned 1940; 2,938 tons; 360ft × 46ft; 2 × 12pdr, 2 × 2pdr, 6 × 20mm
Commander Robert Edward Dudley Ryder
In collision at 02.45 in thick fog with the steamship *Empire Wave* (7,463 tons) in the North Channel off western Scotland, to the north-west of Corsewall Point, in position 55.04N 05.21W and subsequently foundered. The *Empire Wave* picked up twenty-nine survivors and the rescue tug *Salvonia* picked up a further forty-two, but two men died.
[TNA: ADM.199/659; ADM.199/2229]

16 July MGB 92 motor gun boat
New London 1941; 32 tons; 70ft × 20ft; 1 × 20mm
Lieutenant Ronald John Chesney RNVR
Part of the Seventh MGB Flotilla, based at Portland, several boats were alongside undergoing maintenance; *MGB 92* was berthed outboard of *MGB 90*, with *MGB 89* and *MGB 96* ahead of them. Lieutenant Chesney was on shore, leaving Sub-Lieutenant John Waller RNVR, the First Lieutenant as the senior officer onboard. Able Seaman Chadwick was busy stripping and servicing a Lewis gun, the gun resting on the platform of the port machine gun turret. Finding that the trigger group was stiff, he used a mallet to loosen it. Unfortunately, a round had been left in the breech, and as he struck the weapon, it fired. The round pierced the canopy of the turret and entered a box of 20mm ammunition that had been stowed there. The resulting explosion scattered debris and ammunition over a wide area, blew a hole in the deck and punctured the inner starboard petrol tank. The petrol vapour ignited, starting a very fierce fire. All available fire extinguishers on board were used but to no effect. With the fire getting out of control, Sub-Lieutenant Waller ordered the boat to be slipped and allow her to drift clear of the other boats, but this proved impossible, as the wind was blowing the burning *92* back into the jetty. A fire boat arrived on scene, and with a dockyard trailer pump, water was played onto *MGB 92*, and the force of the water drove her clear. She was eventually taken in tow by a launch and towed inshore to be run onto the beach and allowed to burn out. There were no casualties.
[TNA: ADM.178/259]

16 July MGB 90 motor gun boat
New London 1941; 32 tons; 70ft × 20ft; 1 × 20mm
Sub-Lieutenant Cornelius Burke RCNVR
A boat of the Seventh MGB Flotilla, she was berthed inboard of *MGB 92* at Portland, when that boat caught fire, following an ammunition explosion (see above). Initially they attempted to assist with fighting the fire on board *92*, and then, after the burning boat had been slipped, to haul their own boat clear. The

wind, however, prevented this, and the fire spread to *90*. The flames rapidly gained hold forcing the crew to abandon her. She was towed clear by a launch, to be run onshore nearby and allowed to burn out. There were no casualties.

[TNA:ADM.178/259]

17 July FERTILE VALE drifter
Sandhaven 1917 requisitioned 1939; 91 tons;
87.8ft × 19.3ft
Skipper Frederick Leonard Stather RNR

Whilst patrolling off the port of Aberdeen, she was run down and sunk at night by the 402-ton *Empire Isle*, about 2 cables (400 yards) south of Number 1 buoy in the approaches the harbour. Her remains caused problems for ships entering the harbour and considerable effort had to be made to clear the wreck. Initially four depth charges were used to break her up, and then the trawler *Dane* dragged her boiler out of the main channel.

[TNA:ADM.1/11039]

17 July LCT (1) 10 landing craft, tank
Govan 1940; 226 tons; 135ft × 28ft; 2 × 2pdr
Sub-Lieutenant John Dermont Thom RNVR

When attempting to take supplies to the garrison at Tobruk, as she tried to enter harbour at dusk, she was attacked by several dive bombers. Damaged by several near misses, she started to sink. Her sister landing craft, *LCT 11*, secured a tow, but she steadily settled and eventually sank in shallow water. The wreck was later attacked again by dive bombers.

[TNA:ADM.199/799]

19 July MALVERNIAN ocean boarding vessel
West Hartlepool 1937 requisitioned 1940; 3,133 tons;
345.9ft × 50ft; 2 × 6in, 1 × 12pdr
Commander John William Baillie Robertson RNR

Bound for Gibraltar, the ship was to the south-west of Ireland, near 47N 19W, when at 08.28 on 1 July, an aircraft was sighted closing them from the east. It was identified as an Fw 200, and although the alarms were sounded, and fire ordered to be opened on the aircraft, it dropped two bombs, both of which struck her. The first hit the ship's superstructure amidships and went through the radio room into the engine room to explode. The second exploded just abaft the bridge. The engines stopped, power was lost, and fires were started in the engine room and the main superstructure. The aircraft had circled round and ran in for a second attack. The 12pdr gun and machine guns were able to engage this time but had no effect before the aircraft passed overhead dropping a further three bombs, all of which exploded in the water around her. An assessment of the situation showed that although the engines were out of action, all the boats on the starboard side were wrecked,

the superstructure was damaged with the bridge being wrecked and a fire had taken hold amidships. The port-side boats were hoisted out as a precaution and ammunition ordered to be ditched overboard as the fire was tackled. This proved difficult, but with bucket chains organised the blaze was contained, although it had hold of the centre of the ship. The cutter was stored and manned and sent away that evening with a small party of men, hoping to make Ireland or England. Over the next few days, the crew continued to work at containing the fire, the ship drifting slowly south-eastwards. On 7 July, with no sight of any other ship, it was decided to send away more of the men, and that day another boat was cleared away to try and make land. The remaining men on board continued to work and containing the fire and clearing the ship of water, but she seemed to be settling deeper into the water. On 11 July, with food and fresh water running low, and the men exhausted, it was decided to send away the last boat, and that day, manned with 'married men and the oldest of the single men', it was cleared away. The small party of men left on board now employed themselves in lashing together empty oil drums and pieces of wood to make rafts. The weather was deteriorating, with a rising sea, and it was feared that the ship would not stay above water for much longer; however, she remained afloat, still drifting. It was not until 19 July that a ship hove into sight. This proved to be the small French fishing vessel *Chloé*, from Camaret. The survivors had little choice but to abandon her, and Captain Robertson with thirty-one men, the last onboard, scrambled on board the fishing vessel, leaving the *Malvernian* low in the water, a gutted wreck, her bunkers still burning, and all the holds flooded. The *Chloé* made for the nearest port which proved to be Corunna, in northern Spain, where they arrived on 21 July. Of the boats sent away, one was found by Spanish fishing vessels and taken to Vigo, the others by patrolling German minesweepers. Twenty-six men were lost in the bombing.

[TNA:ADM.199/1175]

19 July UMPIRE submarine
Chatham 1940; 540/730 tons; 180ft × 16ft; 1 × 12pdr,
4 × torpedo tubes
Lieutenant Commander Mervyn Robert George Wingfield

Newly completed, she was en route the Clyde to commence training, and joined an east coast convoy heading north. During the day, the port engine developed problems and had to be shut down, which meant that she lagged behind the convoy, and although a Motor Launch (ML) was detailed to stay with her, it lost contact in the night. Just before midnight, then being about 12 miles off Cromer, the shapes of ships ahead could be made out, and it was realised that this must be a south bound convoy. Usually, vessels meeting

in a swept channel would keep to starboard and pass, port to port. However, it was found that because the oncoming ships were so close, that any move to take her to the starboard side of the channel would mean crossing their bows, a potentially dangerous situation. The submarine was therefore taken to the port side of the channel, and it was hoped that the convoy would pass her on the starboard side. This seemed to work, and the column of ships started to pass her, but an escort trawler, evidently stationed on the starboard wing of the convoy, was spotted right ahead and steering straight for the submarine. The correct procedure should have been to turn to starboard, but Wingfield felt unable to do this, as it would have taken him directly into the path of the column of ships in the convoy. He therefore ordered a turn to port. However, as he did so, the trawler spotted him right ahead and turned to starboard. The inevitable happened, and the trawler, which was the *Peter Hendriks* (266 tons), rammed the *Umpire* about 25ft from the bow. The submarine immediately took a bow-down attitude and sank within minutes, washing the bridge staff, who included Wingfield, into the water. A quick reaction from the control room crew closed the conning tower hatch, and all watertight doors were rapidly closed. The submarine sank in 80ft of water, with her bows buried in the mud. Attempts to blow tanks and surface failed, and it was decided to escape, using the engine room and conning tower hatches. The small group of men in the control room were the first to exit, allowing the conning tower to flood before opening the hatch and swimming to the surface. About 30 minutes later, the men from the engine room started coming to the surface. Although all successfully exited the submarine, several did not survive the ascent and others reached the surface but expired before they could be picked up. Sixteen men survived, twenty-two died. Chief ERA George Killan was awarded the British Empire Medal for organising the engine room survivors, with great coolness and courage, and was the last man to leave the boat.
[*Evans pp271–4*]

20 July UNION submarine
Barrow 1940; 540/730 tons; 180ft × 16ft; 1 × 12pdr, 4 × torpedo tubes
Lieutenant Robert Malcolm Galloway†

Ordered to carry out a patrol in the vicinity of Pantelleria, she sailed from Malta 14 July, intelligence having indicated the passage of a large convoy from Tripoli. She seems to have missed the convoy as it passed the island on 15 July, and the only attack reported was by another British submarine, *P33*. The *Union* evidently continued to patrol her area, and on 20 July about 25 miles south-west of Pantelleria, located a German merchant ship being towed by

two Italian tugs, and escorted by the Italian patrol vessel *Circe*. At 11.18 the *Circe* saw the track of an approaching torpedo, and immediately altered course towards the point of firing, the small convoy being ordered to alter to starboard at the same time. *Circe* sighted a periscope, and in the clear waters could see the masts of a submarine below the water. The patrol vessel ran right over the submarine and dropped a pattern of six depth charges, after which a large bubble of air came to the surface. *Circe* came about and made a second run, releasing another three depth charges into the disturbed water, after which she broke off to return to her convoy. An escorting seaplane then took over the attack; immediately after the second depth-charge attack by the escort, the crew of the aircraft saw another large bubble of air come to the surface about 150m from where the attack had taken place. The seaplane closed and dropped a bomb into the patch of water, and soon after a large quantity of oil came to the surface. At 12.00 the *Circe* returned to the scene and confirmed that there was a large spreading patch of oil, which almost certainly marked the end of the *Union*. Thirty-two men were lost.
[*Evans pp274–6*]

23 July FEARLESS destroyer
Birkenhead 1934; 1,405 tons; 318.3ft × 33.3ft; 4 × 4.7in, 1 × 12pdr, 4 × torpedo tubes
Commander Anthony Follett Pugsley

On 21 July Operation 'Substance' commenced, which was the passage of seven transport ships from Gibraltar for Malta, *Fearless* being one of the escorts. On 23 July when the convoy was to the south of Sardinia, they came under sustained attack from Italian bombers. They were detected at 09.10, and a synchronised attack by torpedo bombers and high-level bombers commenced 20 minutes later. Two of the torpedo bombers concentrated on the *Fearless*, releasing their weapons from a height of 70ft and at ranges of about 1500 and 800 yards, respectively. Avoiding action was taken, and the first torpedo passed about 90 yards ahead. The second torpedo ran shallow and could be seen to be running to pass close astern. When about 30 yards from the ship the torpedo broke surface and seemed to alter to port to hit the ship abreast the 12pdr gun. Both engines were put out of action, the rudder jammed hard a-port, all electric power failed due to the switchboard being destroyed, and a fuel fire was started aft. The fire was spreading, and any attempt to tow her was not considered justified in the hazardous conditions, and the survivors were ordered to be taken off and her sister the *Forester* sank her with a torpedo. One officer and thirty-four ratings were killed.
[*TNA: ADM.199/830; Simpson: Somerville Papers pp286–7*]

29 July LCT (1) 8 landing craft, tank
Govan 1940; 226 tons; 135ft × 28ft; 2 × 2pdr
Sub-Lieutenant Roy Maurice Wright RNVR[†]
In company with another landing craft, *LCT 14*, the pair was attempting to take supplies to Tobruk from Alexandria, when they were attacked at 19.00 off Bardia by a number of Ju 87 dive bombers. Damaged by near misses, she then took a direct hit aft, after which she sank, with the loss of eight men.
[TNA: ADM.199/799]

30 July CACHALOT submarine
Greenock 1937; 1,520/2,117 tons; 271.6ft × 25.6ft; 1 × 4in, 6 × torpedo tubes
Lieutenant Commander Hugo Rowland Barnwell Newton
Laden with stores and personnel for Alexandria, she sailed from Malta 26 July, having been warned of the expected transit of an enemy tanker, bound for Benghazi, which they might encounter en-route. During the early hours of 30 July then being to the north of Benghazi in position 32.49N 20.11E, she surfaced, to charge batteries and keep a watch for the tanker. At 01.55 a vessel, identified as a destroyer, was sighted closing them, and they crash dived. This proved full of incident, as due to a series of drill errors, it took several moments to gain control and stabilise the boat. The submarine was then brought to the surface, to again attempt to recharge batteries. The visibility was poor, being a dark night with patches of mist. At 03.35 a ship was sighted on the starboard beam. It appeared to be the expected tanker, and a gun action was ordered. After eleven rounds had been fired, the target made considerable quantities of smoke, and this, combined with the mist, obscured her. One minute later a destroyer emerged from the mist and smoke, heading straight for them at high speed. The upper deck was ordered to be cleared, and they prepared to dive, but the crew took longer than expected to clear the gun platform. By the time they commenced the dive, the approaching destroyer was only 300 yards away, firing with all the guns that could bear. Lieutenant Newton was the last man on the bridge, and it was clear that they were doomed; the destroyer was closing so fast that it was inevitable that they would be rammed, and if they had succeeded in submerging, would have been blown apart by depth charges. He therefore took the decision to stop the dive and ordered the boat to be abandoned. Moments later the destroyer *Achille Papa* struck the *Cachalot* just astern of the conning tower. Realising that the submarine was not diving, her commanding officer had ordered full astern, to slow the impact. The crew then abandoned ship, the *Papa* having ceased firing, and took to the water. As they left, the main vents were opened, and she slowly sank, bows first. All the crew except one were picked up out of the water by the *Papa*. It was later

realised that the ship they had seen at 03.35 was the *Achille Papa*, not the anticipated tanker.
[Evans pp276–80]

4 August ESCAUT store carrier
Hoboken 1938 requisitioned 1940; 1,087 tons; 280ft × 36.3ft
Master Oscar Adam[†]
Loaded with 1,000 tons of government stores, including ammunition, she was laying in Attika Bay, Suez, Egypt, when attacked by enemy aircraft at 23.30 and sank in position 1.73 miles from the South Beacon, with the loss of the master and two of the crew.
[Lloyd's War Losses p281]

6 August AGATE trawler
Middlesbrough 1934 (*Mavis Rose*), purchased 1935; 627 tons; 157.3ft × 26.4ft; 1 × 4in
Lieutenant Commander Leonard Harry Cline RNR[†]
Part of the escort to the ill-fated east coast Convoy FS59, which sailed from Methil Roads in Scotland, and after picking up more ships off the Tyne and from Sunderland, headed south for the Thames estuary, forty-two ships in all, with an escort of nine warships. The weather was poor, with a strong north-westerly Force 8 gale, with torrential rain and frequent thunder and lightning. Despite the weather, the convoy made good their passage down the swept channel until they reached Number 8B buoy, off Cromer. The leading ships of the convoy passed this at 01.50, at which point they were to alter to a new course, to take them to the next buoy in the channel, number 8A. The required course was 140 degrees, but the convoy commodore, embarked in the Dutch steamer *Kentar*, ordered a course change to 120 degrees. This effectively 'cut the corner' and took them directly onto the south-west edge of the dangerous Haisborough Sands. The port column of the convoy followed the commodore, as did the escorting destroyer *Wolsey*. At 03.25 (approximately) the lookouts in both the *Kentar* and *Wolsey* reported sighting breakers ahead on the port bow. Both altered course but apart from the commodore sounding one long blast on the siren, neither ship took any steps to warn the ships astern of the danger. The sudden alteration of course was not seen by the next ship astern, and the siren went unheard in the storm. In consequence the ships in the column steamed on and between 04.00 and 04.20, seven ships ran hard aground on the sands and were wrecked. The *Agate*, also on the port wing of the convoy, seems to have realised the danger at the last minute, and may have tried to shepherd them away from the sands, but it was too late, and she also ran aground and was wrecked. The armed trawler *Bassett* sighted the *Agate* at first light, lying on her beam ends on the sand with the sea breaking over her, and she located a Carley float from

her, with four survivors. Another four were picked up by other searching ships, but nineteen men died. Apart from the *Agate*, the merchant ships lost were *Oxshott* (1,241 tons), *Gallois* (2,684 tons), *Aberhill* (1,516 tons), *Taara* (1,402 tons), *Deerwood* (1,914 tons), *Betty Hindley* (1,737 tons) and *Afon Towy* (682 tons). All were laden with coal. Thirty-seven seamen were lost from them, but the toll would have been far higher if it had not been for the great efforts by several ships that took part in the rescue of men from the wrecks; the destroyers *Wolsey* and *Vimiera*, trawler *Bassett* and patrol vessel *Puffin* all took part. The commanding officer of the *Puffin* wrote '... the scene of those ships stranded on the sands was the most grim sight I have ever seen; five of them awash to the level of the boat deck and terrific seas breaking over them every few moments'. The local lifeboats were also launched, from Cromer and Gorleston. Coxswain Blogg of the Cromer lifeboat was instrumental in saving many lives that night, being 'outstanding in his skill and fearlessness', repeatedly taking his boat into very hazardous conditions to rescue men clinging to the wrecks. The subsequent enquiry was scathing in their findings. The convoy commodore, Lieutenant Commander Robert John Stephens RNR, was held principally to blame for the disaster by steering a wrong course and then making no effort to warn the convoy when he realised the danger. The enquiry was also unhappy with the evidence given to them by Stephens, who seemed to vacillate and 'disclosed an ignorance of his duties'. His claims to have steered the correct course were flatly contradicted by others – there was 'abundant evidence that an incorrect course had been ordered, steered and followed'. Lieutenant Commander Campbell DSC of the escorting destroyer *Wolsey* also shared some of the blame, for failing to warn the commodore that he was steering a dangerous course. The Masters of the merchant ships immediately astern of the *Kentar* were blameable for blindly following the ship ahead, failing to appreciate the danger. Lieutenant Commander Stephens was informed that he had incurred their Lordships' severe displeasure and he was not to be employed as a convoy commodore again.
[TNA:ADM.178/271]

7 August   MMS 39   motor minesweeper
Lowestoft 1941; 225 tons; 105ft × 23ft; machine guns
Lieutenant George Stanley Peyton RNVR
In company with her sister minesweeper *MMS 40*, she sailed at 10.00 from Queenborough to sweep the war channels. During the afternoon several mines, believed to be acoustic, were detonated in Princes Channel, and the pair continued sweeping, heading towards the north-west Long Sand buoy. At 17.30 when 200 yards to the west of the buoy, there was a large explosion under the bows of *MMS 39* as she detonated a mine,

which blew away the fore part of the ship to the forward bulkhead. She immediately started sinking, and *MMS 40* closed to pick up the survivors, but three men were lost. She finally disappeared at 19.00.
[TNA:ADM.199/239]

9 August   MGB 62   motor gun boat
Hythe 1940; 28 tons; 70ft × 20ft; 1 × 20mm
Lieutenant Peter Arthur Whitehead
One of a unit of three gunboats tasked to conduct a patrol in the southern North Sea, to the east of the Brown Bank, as they were nearing the Dutch coast the dark shape of a vessel was seen. *MGB 60*, the nearest boat, altered course towards the stranger and opened fire until it was realised that it was a small fishing vessel. The leader, *MGB 62*, called off the chase and altered course to starboard, but in the confusion, she was in collision with *MGB 67* which was close astern. *62*'s bows were pushed back several feet and she quickly filled, and all the crew were taken off and she was sunk by gunfire.
[TNA:ADM/199/407; Hichens p172]

12 August   LCT (1) 14   landing craft, tank
Clydebank 1940; 226 tons; 135ft × 28ft; 2 × 2pdr
Lieutenant Amos Stuart Mullins RNR
Having arrived at Tobruk from Mersa Matruh during the evening of 12 August she was ordered to secure at Mengar Halgh el Teah. When she was about 150 yards from the inlet there was a very heavy explosion, and the vessel sank in less than 10 minutes. All those on board were saved. It was believed that she had triggered a magnetic mine, which had probably been dropped during the previous evening by enemy aircraft.
[TNA:ADM.196/220]

12 August   PICOTEE   corvette
Belfast 1940; 940 tons; 190ft × 33ft; 1 × 4in
Lieutenant Ronald Arthur Harrison RNR†
In company with the armed trawler *Ayrshire*, the pair were acting as escort to the Iceland-bound Convoy ON(S)4, which consisted of eight ships. During the morning of 11 August, the escorts were warned by a patrolling aircraft of the presence of a submarine, which had been detected about 30 miles to the east of the convoy late the previous evening. *Ayrshire* was stationed on the port bow of the convoy and during the day the *Picotee* swept ahead. The corvette was last seen by her consort at 01.50 on the 12th, when she crossed ahead of the trawler to proceed down the starboard side of the ships; the position of the convoy was then approximately 62.15N 16W. Sometime later the trawler heard six dull thuds of explosions, which they believed were depth charges, but did not believe anything was amiss even though there was no sign of

the corvette. Later investigation revealed that some of the merchant ships had witnessed her demise, but not appreciated what they had seen. Several ships had heard the explosions, and some had seen smoke. Staff on board the *Delaware* saw a large cloud of dark smoke in the direction of the *Picotee* and when it cleared, she seemed to be in a bow-up attitude. The other convoy escort, the *Ayrshire*, made no attempt to find what had happened to her consort and it was not for another 4 days that searches commenced, which failed to find any trace of her. There were no survivors, five officers and sixty ratings were lost. After the war it was confirmed that she had been torpedoed at a little after 02.00 by the *U 568* (Preuss), which saw the torpedo hit abreast the bridge, and she broke up and sank immediately, her depth charges exploding immediately afterwards.

[TNA: ADM.199/621; Morgan & Taylor pp109–11]

13 August **KEPHALLINIA** stores ship

Birkenhead 1893 (*City of Belfast*) requisitioned 1941; 1,267 tons; 280.6ft × 32.1ft

Lieutenant Commander Benjamin Andrew Rogers RNR

Taken over by the Royal Navy at Alexandria, Egypt, the ship was to be used to carry stores and personnel between Tobruk and Egypt. She had successfully completed a round trip, and on 12 August sailed for her second journey, laden with 300 tons of military stores, the armed whaler *Thorbryn* acting as escort. The weather was poor, with a heavy swell and strong wind. The ship was rolling deeply and regularly shipping water into the shelter deck. At 19.30 that day it was reported that the mess decks were flooding and on inspection other compartments were also affected, with the reserve bunker space being full of water. She hove to in position 31.19N 29E and contacted Alexandria by radio to request assistance. Coal was jettisoned to lighten her, and by midnight the weather had eased somewhat, and she was able to start pumping out the stokehold bilges, but it proved difficult to clear the water, with the reserve bunker and fore hold still full. The destroyer *Hero* arrived at first light, and with the pumps working constantly she took the *Kephallinia* in tow. At noon two tugs arrived, the *St Issy* and *Roysterer*, and the latter came alongside to pass over another pump whilst a new tow was prepared. However, it was too late; the water in the stokehold completely overwhelmed the pumps and she steadily settled until the foredeck was awash, at which point she was abandoned. She sank later that afternoon, her position then being 31.07N 29.24E. It was believed that damaged scuttle ports in the reserve bunker space, coupled with the low freeboard (just 2ft 6in) had caused the flooding, made worse by being overloaded, but it was agreed that she was generally in a poor material condition.

[TNA: ADM.1/12603]

August **P 33** submarine

Barrow 1941; 540/730 tons; 180ft × 16ft; 1 × 12pdr, 4 × torpedo tubes

Lieutenant Reginald Dennis Whiteway-Wilkinson†

Sailed from Malta 6 August, for a patrol to the west of Tripoli, being part of a group of three submarines deployed to intercept an Italian convoy that intelligence had indicated was bound for North Africa. When she failed to return to harbour on 20 August, she was posted missing. The circumstances are unknown. It was probably before 15 August, when her sister *P 32* attempted to call her by sound telegraphy (SST) but received no reply. A claim by the Italian Navy patrol vessel *Partenope* to have sunk a submarine off Pantellaria on 23 August may be dismissed, as being out of area and after her patrol was due to finish. *P 32* had heard prolonged depth charging during the afternoon of 18 August, which may perhaps be responsible, but the Italians made no claim for a sinking, and the charges seem to have been a precautionary measure ahead of the convoy. Several new minefields had been laid around Tripoli, which were unknown to the British at this time, and the most likely explanation for her loss is due to striking a mine (see *P 32* below). Four officers and twenty-eight men were lost.

[Evans pp282–3]

18 August **P 32** submarine

Barrow 1940; 540/730 tons; 180ft × 16ft; 1 × 12pdr, 4 × torpedo tubes

Lieutenant David Anthony Baily Abdy

Sailed from Malta 12 August for a patrol off Tripoli, joining *P 33* (see above), as part of a group which was deployed to intercept an Italian convoy bound for North Africa. At 15.30 on 18 August Lieutenant Abdy sighted the convoy heading into the port, but it was too distant to carry out an attack, and Abdy went deep and headed underneath a known minefield to gain the safety of the swept channel entrance to the harbour, to get closer and carry out an attack. As the submarine was brought to periscope depth there was a large explosion on the port side forward as she struck a mine. All the lights went out, the boat took a pronounced list to port and as the bow compartments flooded, the head went down, and she started to dive. Despite the confusion, and darkness, the foreplanes were set to rise and tanks were blown, but it could not stop the dive and she struck the bottom with some force. Checks found that the forward compartments were full of water, and it had to be presumed that the eight men stationed forward were all dead. Efforts were made to free the submarine, but it was clear that she could not be saved, and it was decided that the surviving crew should make an ascent to the surface from the engine room, with Abdy and two ratings volunteering to try and escape through the conning tower. A successful escape was made by these three, although one of them failed to make it to the surface alive. The two survivors were spotted by an Italian aircraft investigating the explosion, and they directed a patrol boat to the area which picked them up. Despite waiting for some time for the expected engine room party, none ever appeared. Three officers and twenty-seven men died.

[Evans pp283–5]

19 August **THORBRYN** whaler

Sandefjord 1936 requisitioned 1940; 305 tons; 125.5ft × 25.6ft

Lieutenant Francis Albert Seward RNR

Whilst engaged in towing two lighters to Tobruk, she was attacked off the port at 08.30 by a group of Ju 88s, receiving two direct hits and she quickly sank. Nine men were killed. Her two lighters drifted away into enemy waters, and a rescue schooner despatched from Tobruk was also attacked and sunk.

[TNA: ADM.199/794]

20 August **LORINDA** trawler

Beverley 1928 requisitioned 1939; 348 tons; 140.2ft × 24.6ft

Lieutenant John Henry Seelye RNZVR

In company with the armed trawler *Balta*, bound for Freetown, west Africa, when in the early hours of 19 August, she suffered an engine breakdown, in position 06.30N 11.37W. The *Balta* took her in tow, and the corvette *Lavender* was ordered to the scene to assist. Twenty-four hours later the *Balta* reported that the *Lorinda* was leaking, putting the boiler fires out, but there was no immediate danger. However, at 06.10 it was clear that she was settling quickly, and she sank at 08.45.

[TNA: ADM.199/794]

22 August **TONBRIDGE** net layer

Glasgow 1924 requisitioned 1940; 682 tons; 220.4ft × 33.6ft; 2 × 2pdr

Lieutenant Duncan Edward Brown RNR

A former cross-Channel ferry, she was employed at Great Yarmouth as a net layer. During 21 and 22 August she was engaged in laying five half-mile lengths of net obstructions, and by late morning of the second day she was completing the final lay. At 12.15 all was complete, and she got underway to return to harbour. At 16.25 she was approaching Yarmouth roads, and then being about 2 cables (400 yards) from the Scroby Elbow buoy, when a twin-engined aircraft was seen approaching from seaward. It flew directly towards the *Tonbridge* and dropping down to masthead height strafed her with machine-gun fire and then dropped two bombs. Both hit her, one exploding on the port side forward of the

funnel, the second struck amidships, penetrating the boiler room before exploding. This opened the ships side along the waterline and caused the collapse of the after bulkhead of the fore hold, which allowed her to fill with water very rapidly. She sank quickly on an even keel, bows first, a single Carley float being released before she went down. Thirty-three men were killed. Lieutenant Brown was subsequently court-martialled for the loss, being charged with negligence, in failing to ensure that his ship was in readiness for action. It was found that neither of the 2pdr guns was manned, and only one machine-gunner was closed-up at a Hotchkiss gun. In defence, Brown explained that he did not have enough crew to both man the guns and lay nets, and that during the net-laying operations gun crews had been fallen out. He admitted that on completion of laying, he had failed to order them to resume action stations. He was reprimanded. The wreck has been found and lies in position 52.37.12N 01.46.06E

[TNA: ADM.156/219; Larn vol 3 sec 3]

23 August **ZINNIA** corvette

Middlesbrough 1940; 940 tons; 190ft × 33ft; 1 × 4in

Lieutenant Commander Charles George Cuthbertson DSO RNR

Part of the escort of Convoy OG71 from Liverpool to Gibraltar, she was stationed on the port beam and carrying out an irregular zigzag. At 04.21 in position 40.11N 11.30W as the ship had started swinging to port for the next leg of the zigzag there was a blinding flash and an explosion on the port side, abreast the funnel. The ship heeled over to starboard to lie on her beam ends. She did not recover and after hanging for several seconds slowly rolled over and broke in half. Her bows rose vertically out of the water before sinking, whilst the stern section disappeared rapidly, with a series of detonations, probably the boilers and depth charges exploding. Several men that had been thrown clear or jumped found themselves trying to cling to scattered wreckage in a sea covered in thick fuel oil. The corvettes *Campion* and *Campanula* closed, to pick up sixteen men, one of whom subsequently died of his injuries. Fifty men were lost. She had been torpedoed by *U 564* (Suhren).

[TNA: ADM.199/621]

24 August **KOS XVI** whaler

Middlesbrough 1932 requisitioned 1940; 258 tons; 119.7ft × 24.1ft; 1 × 12pdr

Lieutenant M Fredericksen RNoN

Taken over for use as a minesweeper, she was manned by a largely Norwegian crew. At 11.45 in clear weather, she was rammed by the destroyer *Wolsey*, when to the north of number 62B buoy off Hull, the destroyer striking her on the starboard side, aft. The ship was ordered to make her way to the nearest port, but despite the pumps

working, the engine rooms slowly flooded, and at about midnight, the after engine room bulkhead gave way. She quickly filled, rolled over and sank. There was no loss of life. The wreck was reported to be in position 53.50.15N 00.35.12E.
[TNA: ADM.199/794; http://www.warsailors.com/singleships/kos.html]

27 August SKUDD 3 whaler
Oslo 1929 requisitioned 1940; 245 tons; 115.1ft × 23.1ft
Lieutenant Robert Cunningham MacMillan RCNVR
Based in the Mediterranean, she had just completed storing and watering and was secured alongside the jetty at Tobruk next to the trawler *Urania* when the port came under a low level and dive-bombing attack which commenced at 17.45. *Skudd 3* took a direct hit on the signal deck, the bomb penetrating below into the fuel tanks which started a fierce fire. There were also several near misses, which caused rivets to sheer and sprung plates in the sides. The fire steadily spread aft and despite the best efforts of fire parties from the ship and shore it proved impossible to get under control. She was hauled free of the jetty by the tugs *Jeddah* and *C307* and towed to the wreck of the *Chakla* where she sank, her upperworks still showing. Five men were killed.
[TNA: ADM.199/1178]

6 September BRORA trawler
Beverley 1940; 545 tons; 150ft × 27.6ft; 1 × 12pdr;
3 × 20mm
Lieutenant Leonard Anthony Enevoldson RNVR
During the early hours of the morning, she ran aground onto rocks near the leading beacon to the entrance to Obbe, on the island of South Harris, in the Outer Hebrides. The tug *Marauder* was sent to the scene but found that she had capsized and was laying on her beam ends. She was abandoned as a constructive total loss. The position was determined as 57.46.14N 07.02.06W.
[TNA: ADM.199/837]

6 September STRATHBORVE trawler
Aberdeen 1930 requisitioned 1940; 216 tons;
117.6ft × 22.1ft; 1 × 12pdr
Lieutenant Albert William Johnstone RNR†
In company with other trawlers, she was engaged in sweeping the approaches to the river Humber in line abreast, or 'Q' formation. At 12.35 a magnetic mine was detonated nearby and 3 minutes later another exploded, this time close astern. This probably damaged her sweeping gear as at 13.05 there was another explosion, this time right under her, immediately below the funnel. By the time the smoke and spray had cleared only her bows were visible and she sank very quickly. Fifteen men were killed. Her position then was 53.33.04N 00.18.11E.
[TNA: ADM.1229/239]

8 September CORFIELD mine destructor
Burntisland 1937 requisitioned 1939; 3,060 tons;
257ft × 39.5ft; 2 × 12pdr
Lieutenant William John Tucker RNVR
Sailed in company with another mine destructor ship, the *Borde*, and escorted by HNoMS *Draug* from Immingham to carry out a combined acoustic and magnetic mine sweep in the vicinity of the Humber Light vessel. The *Borde* developed an engine defect which forced her to anchor, but the *Corfield* and *Draug* continued. The *Corfield* had completed two laps of the designated area on her own by 15.50, and then proceeded to recover her magnetic sweep. This was a tedious operation, requiring the recovery of a long tail of cable and this normally occupied about 45 minutes. During this time, she had her engines stopped. At the same time the tide was flooding at about 2 knots. Some difficulty was experienced in recovering the sweep and the commanding officer went aft to personally investigate. At about 17.00 when 2 miles south of the Humber Light vessel, a mine detonated under the ship on the starboard side abreast the foremast. The ship took a slight list to starboard, and this increased over the next 2 hours until she sank. Lieutenant Tucker ordered her to be abandoned very soon after the explosion, and boats were hoisted out and all were taken off by the *Draug* and the armed trawler *Sangarius*. However, about 45 minutes after she had been abandoned, when it was clear that she was still afloat and not in any immediate danger of sinking, a party returned on board. The *Sangarius* came alongside, and a wire was shackled to the anchor of *Corfield* to allow her to commence towing. The party on board tried to counter-flood the port side to counteract the list, but failed, and she continued to slowly heel further over. At 19.00 it was becoming dangerous, and she was abandoned for a second time. She continued to heel further over until she capsized and sank at 19.15. The circumstances surrounding her loss led to Lieutenant Tucker being court-martialled for hazarding his ship by negligence and prematurely abandoning his ship. He was found guilty on both counts. He had failed to appreciate the strength of the tide and in consequence the ship had drifted out of swept water and into a dangerous unswept area; further he had ordered her to be abandoned before properly ascertaining her state. He was dismissed his ship and reprimanded. The wreck has been found and lies in position 53.26.59N 00.19.20E.
[TNA: ADM.156/218; Larn vol 3 sec 4]

10 September CHRISTINE ROSE drifter
France? (*Christine Rose*), seized 1940; 91 tons
Skipper Richard William Griffiths RNR†
A French-registered fishing vessel, originally taken over by the French Navy and commissioned as a patrol vessel, *VP5*, she had been seized by the Royal Navy at

Southampton in July 1940. In 1941 she was engaged in government-sponsored trials collecting plankton to investigate the possibility of using it as food, under the guidance of Professor A C Hardy from the University of Hull. In poor weather she ran aground and was wrecked at Knap Point, Loch Coalisport. Ten survivors, including the Professor and his assistant, took to the boats and made it to the shore safely, but five men, including the skipper, were lost.
[TNA: ADM.199/659; ADM.358/3159]

12 September TAIKOO tug
Hong Kong 1937 requisitioned 1941; 688 tons;
156ft × 35ft
Master James Thomas Thirlwell†
Based at Aden, she was ordered to proceed to the islands in the Dahlak Archipelago in the Red Sea and assist with the salvage of a grounded lighter and investigate reports of a wrecked submarine. The voyage was uneventful until 19.00 on 12 September when there was a large explosion on the port side. The vessel shuddered, rolled over to starboard, recovered, then slowly heeled over to port. The boats were ordered out and rafts ordered to be cut away as it was clear that she was sinking, and this had barely been started before she sank bows first, leaving the survivors clinging to wreckage. Her position was then approximately 16.45N 40.05E. The men in the water endured a night in the water, until daylight revealed an island nearby, and they found they were drifting towards it. By the time they reached the island, later identified as Harmil, only a handful of them were still alive and only six survived to be picked up by an Arab dhow. It was presumed that she had struck an Italian-laid mine, the Master having ignored his routing instructions and taken the tug through a hazardous area. Twenty-six men died.
[TNA: ADM.1/12022]

19 September LÉVIS corvette
Lauzon 1941; 940 tons; 190ft × 33ft; 1 × 4in
Lieutenant Charles Walter Gilding RCNR
Royal Canadian Navy. Part of the escort to Convoy SC44 from Canada to Liverpool, the corvette was zigzagging on the port side of the convoy, when at 02.05 she was hit on the port side forward by a torpedo. The bow was almost severed by the blast and as her head dipped it was feared that she was about to sink. She was ordered to be abandoned, the corvette *Mayflower* closing to stand by her. To everyone's surprise, she remained afloat, and a party returned onboard 2 hours later to assess the damage and a tow was rigged to *Mayflower*. The tow initially went well, but it soon became clear that she was settling, and the boarding party was removed. At 17.10 she slowly rolled over and sank. Eighteen men were lost in the initial blast. The subsequent Board of Inquiry found that the order to

abandon her was precipitate and criticism was made of the lack of damage control equipment provided and poor organisation onboard. Her attacker had been *U 74* (Kentrat) which fired a salvo of five torpedoes into the convoy at this time, only one of which found a target.
[Morgan & Taylor p119]

20 September MARCONI trawler
Selby 1916 requisitioned 1940; 322 tons; 136.2ft × 24ft;
1 × 12pdr
Skipper George Noble RNR
Having completed her sweeping duties in local waters, she was returning to Harwich when she was in collision with another armed trawler, the *Lord Beaconsfield* when near the Rough buoy, and subsequently foundered in position 51.54 N 001.30E.
[TNA: ADM.199/407]

22 September ML 144 motor launch
Hamworthy 1940; 85 tons; 112ft × 18.4ft; 1 × 3pdr
Lieutenant John Edward Gibbons RNVR
Sailed from Dungeness at 20.00 in company with *ML 143* for a night patrol off the coast, but only 20 minutes later there was a large explosion as *144* detonated a mine when 3 miles to the east of the port. The explosion blew the launch apart, the after part disappeared and was believed to have sunk, but the fore part remained afloat and *143* closed to pick up the survivors. Lieutenant Gibbons, who had been blown overboard, swam through burning fuel to rescue a crew member. The following morning patrolling trawlers found the forepart floating bottom-up and attempted to tow it into Dungeness, but the tow parted, and it sank. The remains of the stern were found by an ML and towed into shallow water, with the intention of taking it to Dover, but it sank 1 mile to the west of Dungeness. Four men were lost in the explosion, and one man died of his injuries the next day. Lieutenant Gibbons was awarded the Albert Medal for his gallant action.
[TNA: ADM.199/406; London Gazette 11 August 1942]

26 September KANTARA schooner
The schooner *Kantara* is listed in *Statement of Losses* as being lost on this date, 'place and cause unknown', but I have been unable to find any details of this vessel or the loss.
[Statement of Losses p15]

27 September SPRINGBANK auxiliary anti-aircraft ship
Govan 1926 requisitioned 1939; 5,155 tons;
420.3ft × 53.9ft; 8 × 4in, 8 × 2pdr, 6 × 20mm
Captain Claude Herbert Godwin DSO
Part of the escort to Convoy HG73, bound for Liverpool, they sailed from Gibraltar on 17 September.

Several contacts with enemy U-boats were made over the next few days, and on 24 September the *Springbank* launched her Fulmar aircraft to drive off an Fw 200 reconnaissance aircraft. In the early hours of the following morning, the first attack on the convoy by a submarine took place, and these attacks, by several U-boats continued. *Springbank* was stationed between the fourth and sixth columns when at 23.00 on 26 September a merchant ship was hit by a torpedo in the port column. She went to action stations and commenced a zigzag. At 01.10 Asdic reported HE (Hydrophone Effect) on the port beam indicating a submarine on the surface, which then seemed to draw ahead of them. At 01.13 there was an explosion on the port bow, believed to be a merchant ship being hit, and star shell was ordered to be fired to illuminate the area. Before this could be completed, she was hit on the port side aft by a torpedo, immediately followed by another one, on the port side forward. The effect was devastating; the rudder did not answer the helm, the bridge was wrecked, and numbers 2 and 3 holds were filling rapidly with water, which was also penetrating the forward magazine and Asdic compartment. Aft, water was reported to be in numbers 6, 7 and 8 holds, although the engine room reported that it was dry, but it seemed the propellers had gone. Pumps were used to keep the water in the holds at bay, but with the heavy sea running it proved difficult to keep her under control. At 03.30 it was clear that it was a losing battle, and floats and rafts were launched, to allow men to start leaving her in a controlled way, a party of essential personnel remaining onboard. At 05.00 she heeled to port and became 'heavy in the water'. The corvette *Jasmine* was ordered to come alongside and managed to take off sixty men. With water now entering the engine room the last men jumped off onto the upper deck of the *Fowey*, which despite the difficult conditions, had put herself alongside. The ship continued to settle, but despite her upper decks being awash, she did not sink. The *Jasmine* fired several rounds of 4in into her and dropped depth charges alongside, but she did not finally disappear until 19.15. The position was approximately 49.10N 20.05W. Thirty-two men were lost. The attacking submarine had been *U 201* (Schnee).
[TNA: ADM.1/11300]

30 September EILEEN DUNCAN trawler

Selby 1910 requisitioned 1940; 223 tons; 120.1ft × 22ft
Lieutenant George Neville Ward RNVR
On the night of 30 September/1 October there was a very heavy air raid on Tyneside, with a large number of He 111 aircraft dropping bombs over North and South Shields, causing widespread damage. *Eileen Duncan* was laying alongside the T I C quay, South Shields, and she suffered a direct hit, broke up and sank. Eight men were

killed. The wreck was later dragged clear of the wharf onto the Herd Sand and later dispersed.
[TNA: ADM.1/21232; ADM.199/407]

30 September STAR OF DEVERON trawler

Aberdeen 1916 (*Star of Peace*) requisitioned 1939; 220 tons; 120.5ft × 22.5ft
Skipper George Frederick Durrant RNR[†]
Moored alongside the *Eileen Duncan* (see above) at the T I C quay, South Shields, when the harbour came under air attack, she sank alongside the wharf when the pair was hit by a stick of four bombs. Five men were killed. The wreck was later hauled away to clear the wharf, being placed on the Herd Sand, where she was broken up for scrap in 1945.
[TNA: ADM.1/21232; ADM.199/407; ADM.199/794]

4 October WHIPPET whaler

Middlesbrough 1937 (*Kos XXI*) requisitioned 1940; 353 tons; 134.8ft × 26.5ft; 1 × 4in
Lieutenant Arthur Robert James Tilston SANF
Escorted by the armed whaler *Svana* she sailed at 07.10 from Mersa Matruh for Tobruk, towing the lighter *SD 28*. At 19.30 aircraft were heard in the area, and at 20.00 a Ju 88 appeared and carried out a dive-bombing attack, a bomb exploding on the port beam. The aircraft continued their attentions, with several flares being dropped to illuminate the ships, and more dive-bombing attacks took place, but again without result. At 21.00 yet another attack took place, this time the aircraft scored a direct hit, a bomb striking the whaler astern of the funnel. It went through into the boiler room where it burst, blowing a hole in the bottom. The engine room quickly filled, and the ship heeled over to port and sank. The survivors were picked up by the *Svana*. One man was killed.
[TNA: ADM.199/1178]

10 October LCT (2) 102 landing craft, tank

Belfast 1941; 296 tons; 143ft × 30ft
Embarked in sections as deck cargo on the merchant ship *Nailsea Manor*, part of Convoy OS7 from Liverpool en-route for Egypt, via Freetown and South Africa, which was forced to drop astern in poor weather. The ship was torpedoed at 05.43 by the submerged *U 126* (Bauer), when in position 18.45N 21.18W and sank complete with cargo.
[TNA: ADM.199/2233; http://www.uboat.net/allies/merchants/shiphtml?shipID=1148]

10 October LCT (2) 103 landing craft, tank

Belfast 1941; 296 tons; 143ft × 30ft
Being carried as deck cargo on board the merchant ship *Ger-y-Bryn*, which sailed in Convoy OS7 from Liverpool on 23 September, en-route to Freetown and South Africa, the craft was lost overboard in poor weather.
[TNA: ADM.199/2233]

11 October ML 288 motor launch
Marylandsea 1941; 85 tons; 112ft × 18.4ft; 1 × 3pdr
On passage to Methil from the Thames Estuary, she was in Convoy EC83. The weather was poor, and the launch was labouring badly, and lost touch with the convoy at about 23.15 on 10 October. The sloop *Lowestoft* closed to stand by her, but during the morning she was abandoned, the crew transferring to the sloop. At this time, her decks were reportedly 'stove in' and she was flooding. The sloop fired several rounds into her, which set her on fire, and she burned for some time before finally sinking, about 4 miles to the east of Hartlepool.
[TNA: ADM.199/675]

12 October LCT (1) 2 landing craft, tank
Barrow 1941; 226 tons; 135ft × 28ft; 2 × 2pdr
Sub-Lieutenant Edmund Leonard Clark RNVR†
In company with *LCT 7* (see below), sailed from Tobruk at 19.00 on 11 October after unloading, bound for Alexandria, but not seen again. It was believed at the time that the most likely cause of her loss was by air attack, but she had been sunk by the submarine *U 75* (Ringelmann) at 01.24 the following morning in position 32.08N 24.56E. After being shelled, she was hit by a single torpedo at which she disappeared. There were no survivors, sixteen members of the ship's company being lost, with several soldiers.
[TNA: ADM.199/794; ADM.358/3504]

12 October LCT (1) 7 landing craft, tank
Govan 1941; 226 tons; 135ft × 28ft; 2 × 2pdr
Sub-Lieutenant Arthur Charles Bromley RNVR†
In company with *LCT 2* (see above), she was carrying some Italian prisoners of war from Tobruk with soldiers embarked as guards. The pair was taken by surprise by *U 75*, which commenced her attack with gunfire. *LCT 7* was hit almost immediately, killing several soldiers. *LCT 2* initially attempted to close and render assistance but disappeared in an explosion. Men were seen struggling in the water, and despite still being under attack, *LCT 7* attempted to pick them up, but was then rocked by a large explosion and she quickly sank. Eight soldiers and prisoners of war and thirteen members of her crew died, with one survivor, Petty Officer William Henley, being picked up by the submarine.
[TNA: ADM.199/794: ADM.358/3504; WO.361/170]

14 October FLEUR DE LYS corvette
Middlesbrough 1940 (*la Dieppoise*); 940 tons; 190ft × 33ft; 1 × 4in
Lieutenant Alexander Collins RNR†
Based at Gibraltar, she sailed to patrol the western approaches to the Straits, to screen the approach of inward-bound Convoy OG75. At 02.40 when about 55 nautical miles to the west of Gibraltar, in position 36.00N 05.40W, she was hit on the port side under the bridge by a torpedo fired from the submerged *U 206* (Opitz). The initial explosion was immediately followed by a large detonation as the magazine blew up. She immediately broke in half and both parts sank rapidly. Seventy men were lost with only three survivors, who were picked up by the Spanish freighter *Castillo Villafranca*.
[TNA: ADM.199/794]

14 October FORERUNNER drifter
Lowestoft 1911 requisitioned 1939; 92 tons; 88.8ft × 19.3ft
Skipper William Harmon RNR
Foundered in position 51.30N 04.40E following a collision at 19.00 with the Dutch tanker *Ocana* (6,256 tons) near the Nore light vessel.
[TNA: ADM.199/407; ADM.199/794]

16 October GLADIOLUS corvette
Middlesbrough 1940; 940 tons; 190ft × 33ft; 1 × 4in, 1 × 2pdr
Lieutenant Commander Harris Marcus Crews Sanders DSO DSC RNR†
Gladiolus sailed from St Johns, Newfoundland, to join the escort to Convoy SC48, meeting the convoy on 15 October. The previous night the convoy had came under constant attacks from U-boats and three ships had been lost and the assault continued the next night. All that can be said with certainty on the loss of *Gladiolus* is that she was lost at some stage during the night of 16/17 October, probably torpedoed, in the vicinity of 57N 25W. The Canadian corvette *Wetaskiwin* was in communication with the *Gladiolus*, which was stationed on the port side, astern of the convoy, at 19.30 on the 16th, after which she disappeared. The *Wetaskiwin* received a call from a station 'purporting to be *Gladiolus*' at 22.00, but the authenticity was doubted, and when challenged, there was no reply. This may suggest that she was lost soon after this. The identity of her attacker is uncertain, as the convoy suffered a series of torpedo attacks from three submarines that night – *U 432*, *U 553* and *U 558* – and it is not clear which was responsible. Careful modern research would suggest that if she was lost soon after the *Wetaskiwin* call, then an attack by *U 553* (Thurmann) at 22.00 was most likely. At that time, the submarine, after three unsuccesful attacks, fired a single torpedo, having adjusted the depth setting, and this resulted in a vessel on the port side of the convoy, thought by the submarine to have been a tanker, to explode in a fireball, having been hit amidships. This is now believed to have been *Gladiolus*, and the large column of fire may well have been her magazines exploding. Sixty-four men were lost.
[TNA: ADM.237/187; Morgan & Taylor pp128–36; uboat.net – Articles/73.html]

18 October BROADWATER destroyer
Newport News 1919 (*Mason*) transferred RN 1940; 1190 tons; 309ft × 31.9ft; 4 × 4in, 2 × 20mm
Lieutenant Commander William Maurice Lloyd Astwood
Part of the escort to Atlantic Convoy SC48 that sailed from Canada 5 October for Liverpool. From 15 October it came under sustained attack by a group of U-boats (see *Gladiolus* above). She was at the rear of the convoy when at 01.35 in position 51N 19W she was hit by a torpedo which struck the bows. A second torpedo was seen to pass close astern. The forward part of the ship from the bow to the after hatch of the forward mess deck was blown away and the upper bridge disappeared. The mast collapsed and the upper deck was buckled. The engines had stopped immediately, and she lost all power and light. Two armed trawlers, the *Cape Warwick* and *Angle*, closed and started to lift off the survivors, who were transferred by her boat, which had successfully been launched. By 09.45 this was complete. Water was now washing over the well deck and daylight showed that her back was broken, and she was visibly lower in the water and settling. It was therefore decided to sink her, and the *Cape Warwick* and *St Apollo* fired several rounds into her after which she sank at about midday. Her attacker had been *U 101* (Mengersen). Forty-five men were lost.
[TNA: ADM.1/12013; ADM.237/187]

18 October ASSURANCE rescue tug
Selby 1940; 700 tons; 142.5ft × 33.2ft; 1× 12pdr, 1 × 20mm
Went ashore on Bluick rocks off Greencastle in Lough Foyle, Northern Ireland. Badly holed, she rolled over onto her side. Attempts to salvage the tug failed and she was written off as a total loss.
[TNA: ADM.199/837]

21 October GNAT river gunboat
Renfrew 1915; 625 tons; 230ft × 36ft; 2 × 6in, 1 × 12pdr
Lieutenant Commander Samuel Reginald Halls Davonport
Having successfully escorted two lighters from Alexandria to Tobruk, arriving on 19 October, the gunboat carried out a bombardment of an enemy gun position the following day in support of ground troops, before getting under way at nightfall to return. At 04.45 in position 32.06N 25.30E, there was an explosion forward as she was hit by a torpedo fired by *U 79* (Kaufmann). Her bows were blown off, and a small fire started, but she remained upright, and with bulkheads shored remained stable. It was found that with her damaged head so low in the water, little or no progress could be made, and she could not steer. The destroyers *Jaguar* and *Griffin* were ordered to her assistance, and they arrived later that morning, being joined by the escort destroyers *Eridge* and *Avon Vale*. The *Griffin* took her in tow, stern first, and she maintained the tow until the tug *St Monance* arrived to

take over. They finally arrived at Alexandria after dark on 23 October. It was hoped that she could be kept in service by rebuilding her bows, using the forward section of the *Cricket* (see above), but this could not be achieved, and she was written off as a constructive total loss on 7 December, to be cannibalised.
[TNA: ADM.199/415]

21 October HELEN BARBARA tug
Possibly 1937 USA transferred 1941; 56 tons; 61ft × 16ft? (details uncertain)
In the *Statement of Losses* listed as being 'abandoned in sinking condition, due to heavy weather' but further details of the loss have not been found.
[Statement of Losses p15; TNA: ADM.1/24129]

22 October ALDER trawler
Selby 1929 (*Lord Davidson*) purchased 1939; 346 tons; 140.3ft × 24ft; 1 × 4in
Skipper George Edward Yates RNR
In poor weather, she went ashore on rocks, about 100 yards to the west of Cairnbulg beacon, near Fraserburgh. Held fast, she assumed a 15-degree list and in heavy surf she was abandoned and subsequently written off as a wreck.
[TNA: ADM.199/837]

22 October DARKDALE oiler
Blythswood 1940; 8,145 tons; 483ft × 59.5ft; 1 × 4.7in
Master Thomas H Card
Hit at 01.42 by a salvo of four torpedoes fired by the *U 68* (Merten), while she was lying at anchor in James Bay, in the island of St Helena. A large explosion followed, lighting up the harbour and throwing debris over a considerable distance. The ship caught fire and continued to burn fiercely, the ship eventually rolling over onto her side, until at 05.30 there was a large explosion, and she sank in 5 minutes. Forty-one men were killed, but the master and seven crew members who were ashore survived. The wreck was the source of a slow but increasing leak of oil into the waters of St Helena and in 2012 a survey found her wreck to be in two parts. Work to clear the wreck of oil was finally completed in 2015.
[TNA: ADM.199/395; ADM.199/2232]

24 October EMILION trawler
Middlesbrough 1914 requisitioned 1939; 201 tons; 112.3ft × 21.6ft
Sub-Lieutenant Joseph William Sloan Allison RNVR
Tasked to sweep the Barrow Deep in the Thames estuary, where it was believed that mines had been laid by aircraft, she was near B6 buoy when there was a large explosion as she detonated a mine and sank; all the crew was saved.
[TNA: ADM.199/407]

24 October LUCIENNE JEANNE trawler

Middlesbrough 1917 (*Daniel Harrington*) seized from
French Navy 1940; 286 tons; 125.5ft × 23.4ft
Skipper Stanley Edward George RNR

Another of the minesweeping trawlers ordered to
sweep the Barrow Deep in the Thames estuary, she was
badly shaken when she detonated mine off B6 buoy
and she was run into shallow water near B4 buoy, off
Sheerness to prevent her from sinking. She rolled over
the following day and was abandoned as a wreck.
[TNA: ADM. I 99/407; Lloyd's War Losses vol 1 p305]

25 October LATONA minelayer

Woolston 1940; 2,650 tons; 400.6ft × 40ft; 6 × 4in,
4 × 2pdr, 2 × 20mm, 100+ mines
Captain Stuart Latham Bateson

Sailed from Alexandria at 06.00 in company with the
destroyers *Hero*, *Encounter* and *Hotspur* loaded with many
soldiers and their equipment, bound for Tobruk. The
ships took station in line abreast, a mile apart, steaming at
18 knots and despite coming under surveillance from an
Italian aircraft, remained unmolested until mid-afternoon.
The group then came under air attack, from Italian and
German aircraft, but escaped any damage, as they did
during a second attack, mounted at around 19.00. An
hour later a third air raid developed, with about ten Ju 87
dive bombers making a determined attack, concentrating
on the *Latona*. During this attack she was hit by a bomb
which passed through the side of the ship just below the
upper deck to burst in the engine room. The explosion
was particularly violent, cutting the starboard steam pipe
and the fire main, unseating 'Y' gun, the pom-pom and
20mm guns and starting a fire in the starboard side of
the engine room. The engine room spaces were filled
with steam and smoke, and with no pressure from the
shattered fire main, a human chain had to be formed
with buckets to fight the blaze. The *Encounter* was ordered
to close and lift off the soldiers, but as she did so there
was another explosion aft, apparently from the embarked
stores. The fire was now spreading, and the *Hotspur* came
close alongside to play fire hoses on the hull aft. *Hero*
joined, to place herself alongside the fo'c'sle to lift off
the remaining soldiers, and finally the crew. When all
were off, at 20.50, the destroyers stood off to search for
any survivors in the water. That complete, a torpedo was
fired into the burning wreck to ensure that it sank. The
position was 32.15N 25.14E. Twenty men were lost.
[TNA: ADM. I 99/1178]

27 October COSSACK destroyer

Walker 1937; 1,960 tons; 355.6ft × 36.6ft; 8 × 4.7in,
4 × 2pdr, 4 × torpedo tubes
Captain Edward Lyon Berthon DSC[†]

Acting as Senior Officer of the escort to Convoy
HG75, she sailed from Gibraltar on 22 October bound
for Liverpool. At 22.55 on 23 October, then being in

position 35.56N 10.04W, she was hit by a torpedo on
the port side abreast 'B' gun. The explosion destroyed the
forward part of the ship and wrecked the bridge, killing
the commanding officer. It also started a fire at the after
end of the fo'c'sle, which burned fiercely and ignited the
ready-use ammunition for the 2pdr pom-pom. Number
1 boiler room reported that it was flooding, and number
2 had to be abandoned when it started to fill. The senior
executive officer still alive was Lieutenant Brian Moth,
and as he feared that the forward magazine would
explode, ordered the ship to be abandoned. Various other
ships closed to take off the survivors, although this was
dangerous, as she was still burning fiercely forward, with
regular explosions of ready-use ammunition. When all
the men had been evacuated, consideration was given
on what to do with her. Commander (E) Robert Brian
Halliwell, the engineering officer of *Cossack*, believed
that the fire could be tackled successfully, and it might be
possible to tow her to safety. The destroyer *Legion* and the
corvette *Carnation* closed the burning ship and stationing
themselves on either side commenced spraying her with
fire hoses. This seemed to work, as the flames subsided.
When sufficiently subdued, at 01.45 on the 26th the
Carnation laid herself alongside and put men on board,
led by Halliwell. To their surprise they found three
injured ratings still on board, evidently overlooked. After
these had been transferred, the party started to tackle
the fire. By 05.45 Halliwell was able to report the fires
were out, but the forward boiler room was flooded, and
they were unable to get the pumps working. Hands were
employed in shoring up the bulkheads and removing top
weight. During the late morning, the corvette *Jonquil* and
the tug *Thames* arrived on scene and at 14.20 the *Cossack*
was taken in tow by the latter. At first light the next day,
the *Cossack* could be seen to be noticeably lower in the
water. It was found that the portable pumps could not be
used, as the sea was now washing over the decks, and at
18.30 it was decided to take the men off her for the night.
At 08.30 on 27th, the *Jonquil* again closed, to find that
she was trimmed down by the head, with her stern now
out of the water, with seas sweeping over her, making it
impossible to board her. At 10.37 the tug master reported
that he was releasing the tow, as the destroyer was sinking,
and 5 minutes later, in position 35.12N 08.17W her bows
went under, her stern rose until vertical, then slowly sank.
One hundred and fifty-nine men were lost. The attacker
was *U 563* (Bargsten).
[TNA: ADM. I/I 1846]

(27/28) October TETRACH submarine

Barrow 1939; 1,090/1,575 tons; 265.6ft × 26.7ft; 1 × 4in,
10 × torpedo tubes
Lieutenant Commander George Henry Greenway[†]

Sailed from Alexandria 17 October, bound for Gibraltar
via Malta, and having delivered a cargo of stores to
the island, sailed 26 October to continue her journey.

She was last heard from at 14.40 on 27 October, when she communicated with another submarine, *P 34*, by sound telegraphy (SST). At that time, her position was 37.28.5N 12.35.5E. She failed to report her position by radio when to the west of 7 degrees east as she had been ordered and failed to arrive at Gibraltar as expected on 2 November and did not respond to subsequent calls by radio. It was presumed that she had been lost on or about 27/28 October by striking a mine, probably off south-eastern Sardinia in the Sicilian Channel. Five officers, fifty-four ratings and three passengers were lost. [*Evans pp286–7*]

3 November OUZEL yacht

Dundee 1927 (*Wang, Urda*) requisitioned 1941; 76 tons; 76.2ft × 16ft

Lieutenant George William Wilkinson RNVR†

Fitted out as a local patrol vessel, she detonated a mine at 12.12 when half a mile to the east of Mablethorpe, killing all eight crew members and two army officers. [*TNA:ADM.199/794*]

4 November LCT (2) 105 – LCT (2) 109 – LCT (2) 110 landing craft, tank

Wallsend 1941; 296 tons; 143ft × 30ft; 2 × 2pdr

Listed as being 'lost in home waters', it would seem probable that they were lost overboard from merchant vessels whilst being taken, in sections, to the Mediterranean. The War Diary entry for 30 November noted that '… sections of 5 TLC's have recently been lost overboard in OS convoys' – two of these were *LCT 102* and *LCT 103* (see above) and these three craft are likely candidates for the others. [*TNA:ADM.199/2233; Statement of Losses p50*]

6 November FLOTTA trawler

Selby 1941; 545 tons; 150ft × 27.8ft; 1 × 12pdr, 3 × 20mm

Sub-Lieutenant Arthur Smith RNVR

Escorting the merchant ship *St Magnus*, in poor weather the trawler went aground at 05.00 on 29 October off Rattray Head, Aberdeenshire, the crew having to be taken off by the Coastguard using a breeches buoy. Salvage work was successful, and she was refloated on 6 November. The tug *Abeille IV* took her in tow for Aberdeen but at 21.09 she foundered 3 miles off Buchan Ness, with the loss of five men. The wreck has been found in position 57.27N 01.41W. [*TNA:ADM.199/397;ADM.199/794*]

8 November MONARDA drifter

Findochty 1916 requisitioned 1939; 108 tons; 91.1ft × 19.4ft

Lieutenant Vernon Esmond Kennard RNR

When leaving Queenborough, Kent, she damaged her bow whilst manoeuvring, but continued out of the harbour. As she steamed clear she started filling with water, and it became clear that the damage was more severe than realised and her sideplates were opening. She was deliberately turned inshore and run into shallow water and beached, to be written off as a total loss. [*TNA:ADM.199/802*]

9 November BOY ANDREW drifter

Aberdeen 1918 (*Sunburst*) requisitioned 1940; 97 tons; 85.8ft × 18.6ft

Skipper George Frederick Ball RNR†

Lost following a collision with the steamship *St Rognvald* (920 tons), which was overhauling the drifter in a swept channel in the Firth of Forth, the drifter turning across the bows of the steamer. All twelve men on board died in the sinking. The collision resulted in the owners of the *St Rognvald* being sued by the Admiralty. After several appeals, it was finally ruled in July 1947 that the blame should be shared, two-thirds to the *Boy Andrew*, by the action of the crew in turning across the bows of the steamer, and one-third to the *St Rognvald*, which had not shown good seamanship in passing so close to the drifter and should have allowed greater clearance. The wreck lies in position 56.03.31N 03.01.55W. [*TNA ADM.358/3092; Larn vol 4 sec 1; www.britishnewspaperarchive.co.uk: Aberdeen Journal 29 July 1947*]

9 November LETTIE tug

Rotterdam 1914 requisitioned 1940; 89 tons; 76.5ft × 19.6ft

Master Leonard Frank Simmons†

Sailed from Blyth bound for Inverness during the morning of 9 November, she was last seen during the late afternoon off St Abb's Head. Two bodies later washed ashore at Tentsmuir Point were identified as being crew members. The cause of her loss was uncertain; seven men were lost. [*TNA:ADM.199/2233*]

12 November FRANCOLIN trawler

Selby 1916 (*Faraday*) requisitioned 1939; 322 tons; 136.2ft × 24ft; 1 × 12pdr

Skipper-Lieutenant John Dinwoodie RNR

In company with the armed trawler *Commander Holbrook*, the pair was patrolling off the coast of Norfolk, steaming 3 cables (600 yards) apart at 7 knots. They were about 2 miles to the north-east of Happisburgh lighthouse when at 22.47 an aircraft was sighted approaching from seaward, which was identified as a Dornier bomber. The aircraft went into a shallow dive as it closed the *Francolin*. Four bombs were released, three of which exploded alongside, the fourth struck her on the foredeck, going through to the mess deck where it exploded, blowing holes in the port and starboard sides. The aircraft failed to recover from her dive and

struck the topmast of the trawler as it flew overhead and crashed into the sea nearby. The ship steadily filled with water and sank with the loss of one man.
[TNA: ADM.199/1176]

14 November ARK ROYAL aircraft carrier
Birkenhead 1937; 22,000 tons; 685ft × 94.9ft; 16 × 4.5in, 48 × 2pdr, 60 aircraft
Captain Loben Edward Harold Maund

Having successfully flown off Hurricane aircraft to Malta (Operation 'Perpetual'), the *Ark Royal* was returning to Gibraltar in company with the carrier *Argus*, the battleship *Malaya*, cruiser *Hermione* and seven destroyers. At 15.29 she altered course into the wind to commence flying operations. This took her outside the line of heavy ships, but still within the destroyer screen and she was still conducting a zigzag. Six Swordfish and two Fulmar aircraft were launched, and five Swordfish were recovered over the next few minutes. Flying operations complete, she altered course to resume her station at 24 knots. At 15.38 when nearly in station between *Argus* and *Malaya*, she again altered course to recover more aircraft. She had just recovered one aircraft when at 15.41 there was a large explosion on the starboard side abreast the Admiral's bridge. No torpedo track had been reported, and at first some on board thought it may have been an internal explosion but reports of a column of water disproved that. The explosion had been severe. The bomb lift doors had been blown open and smoke emerged; the ship had been 'whipped' so violently that aircraft parked on the forward end of the flight deck jumped into the air. She immediately listed 10 degrees to starboard and within 3 minutes this had increased to 12 degrees. She continued to slowly heel over, until half an hour after the explosion the list had grown to 18 degrees. The engines were put astern and the helm to amidships, but all telegraphs were found to have jammed. The telephone system was also put out of action, making internal communications difficult. This was due to the main switchboard and telephone exchange being damaged and flooded with oil because of the explosion. Communications were therefore carried out by bugle call and messengers, with a chain of ratings being formed to pass orders from the bridge to the engine rooms. It soon became evident that the starboard boiler room and surrounding passageways were flooding, but watertight doors had been closed to contain this. At 16.00 it was decided to evacuate all non-essential personnel and the destroyer *Legion* was called alongside, and in a short time had lifted off 1,487 officers and men, she left at 16.48. At the same time boats were lowered and Carley floats readied for slipping. The men left on board were organised into parties; one in the port engine room trying to raise steam; another on the fo'c'sle under the Gunnery

Officer to prepare a tow and a repair party, based in the lower hanger. All bulkheads were reported holding, and portable pumps were installed in after mess decks and flats to pump them clear of water. However, the situation in the starboard engine room was worsening. The starboard boiler room was now full of water, and this was overflowing into the centre boiler room via the uptake casing and the machinery control room was also being affected. By 17.00 steam could no longer be kept up in the port engine room due to the list. The destroyer *Laforey* was therefore called alongside, and she passed forty tons of fresh water for the boiler and electric cables to help power the pumps. At 19.45 the *Legion* was contacted, and volunteers called for to return on board to assist; eighty engine room and electrical ratings returned. By 21.30 steam had again been raised on one boiler, and later a second. Power was restored to the steering gear and the port shaft was operational. A tug, the *St Day*, had arrived earlier, but her performance in trying to rig a tow was condemned as 'pitiable' by Captain Maund. By the time, the tow was finally connected, the tug found herself 'facing aft, alongside the starboard side' and was forced to slip the tow. By now a second tug, the *Thames*, had arrived and quickly and efficiently had the carrier in tow by 20.30. The tow commenced at 2 knots. The *Laforey* slipped at 22.15, no longer needed as the ships' dynamos were now back on-line, powering ten portable pumps and a 150-ton pump, all working to keep the water at bay. Hopes at this time were high. The list had been stabilised, some power had been restored and pumping was underway to reduce the water. The *St Day* was then called alongside, and she was secured alongside the port side, and this increased the speed of advance. However, at 02.15 it was noticed that the list was again beginning to increase. Then smoke and fumes started to affect the port engine room and it was found that the funnel uptakes were flooded, and furnace gases could not escape. All salvage work came to a halt as they again lost power. The *Laforey* again came to their aid, coming alongside to pass cables to restore power, but it was too late. The list was now 20 degrees, and it was becoming difficult to work on sloping decks. The corvette *Penstemon* arrived at this stage, with a large pump, but it could not be passed as the list was too great. At 04.00 it was decided that little more could be done; the water was gaining and the list increasing. When it reached 28 degrees the *St Day* and *Laforey* took off the working parties, which was complete by 04.30. The carrier continued to slowly roll over until she reached 45 degrees, when she 'hung' for some time, before dipping again until the island reached the sea. She slipped under at 06.13. Only one man had been killed, in the initial explosion. Her attacker had been the *U 81* (Guggenberger), which had targeted the battleship *Malaya*, with a spread of four torpedoes,

but due to wrongly estimating the target speed, they all missed, only for one of them to find the *Ark Royal* by chance.
[*TNA:ADM.1/11816; ADM.156/203 – 206; ADM.199/2066; ADM.267/72*]

15 November **HARMONY** drifter
Middlesbrough 1910 (*Unison*) requisitioned 1940; 79 tons; 80ft × 18ft
Following a collision with buoy number 23, at the entrance to the harbour at Invergordon, she foundered at 07.50 about half a mile from the dockyard pier.
[*TNA:ADM.199/794*]

19 November **SYDNEY** light cruiser
Clydebank 1927; 7198 tons; 590ft × 61ft; 8 × 8in, 4 × 4in, 8 × 2pdr
Captain Joseph Burnett RAN†
Royal Australian Navy. Having completed escorting a convoy to the Sunda Strait, *Sydney* was returning to Fremantle, Western Australia, and signalled the shore authorities that she should arrive at that port on the afternoon of 20 November. When she failed to arrive, an air and sea search was instigated, but it was not until 24 November, when the merchant ship *Trocas* reported picking up twenty-five German sailors, that the first indication of her fate was known. Over the next several days more German sailors were recovered, who confirmed that they were survivors from a German auxiliary cruiser, or commerce raider, the *Kormoran*, which had been in action with the light cruiser on 19 November in position 26.31S 111.39E, and both ships had sunk. They testified that at about 16.00 they had sighted the cruiser, and had turned away, but the cruiser had followed them, and closed, until by 17.40 was at a range of approximately 1,000 yards. The commerce raider was a merchant ship, fitted with a heavy concealed armament, and when challenged by flashing light by the cruiser, had identified herself by flag hoist as the Dutch merchant ship *Straat Malakka*, and indicated by light that she was bound for Batavia. These actions were done slowly, to lure the cruiser to close. *Sydney* then signalled the raider to show her secret signal – a four-letter code which a stranger would not know. Realising that she could not do this, Captain Detmers of the *Kormoran* ordered the disguise to be dropped and to engage the cruiser, which was now steaming on a parallel course. All her guns that would bear then opened fire, with devastating effect. The initial salvo destroyed the bridge and director control tower of the *Sydney* and started a fire. At the same time two torpedoes were fired, one of which exploded under 'A' turret. *Sydney* returned fire only after some time, and her first salvos went over, but the third and fourth salvos hit *Kormoran*, starting a fire in the engine room. By now *Sydney* had been devastated

by the constant fire and performed a hard turn to port and passed under the stern of her attacker. As she passed, she was hit by another torpedo fired from *Kormoran*. She was then seen to proceed on a southerly course and over the horizon, burning fiercely. The engines of the *Kormoran* had been put out of action and a fire started which was out of control, so she was abandoned in an orderly fashion. Despite the extensive air and sea search, no survivors were found from *Sydney*, all 645 men onboard being lost, just one body being found, when on 6 February 1942 a Carley float containing the remains of a sailor was recovered off Christmas Island. The loss caused considerable distress in Australia, and the circumstances of the battle became the source of much speculation and rumour. The wrecks of both *Kormoran* and *Sydney* were located in March 2008. Examination of the wrecks showed that the damage suffered by the cruiser was significant, with at least eighty-seven hits from 15cm shells, plus multiple hits from 37mm and 20mm guns, and torpedo damage. Why Captain Burnett allowed his ship to get so close to the raider remains uncertain, but it is likely, that as there was no definite intelligence to indicate the presence of a commerce raider, he was using the approach procedure for a presumed innocent vessel, not a suspicious one.
[*http://www.naa.gov.au/collection/fact-sheets/fs111.aspx; http://www.defence.gov.au/sydneyii/FinalReport/*]

20 November **WAR MEHTA** oiler
Walker 1919; 5,503 tons; 400.2ft × 52.4ft; 1 × 12pdr
Chief Officer Stanley M Woodward RFA
Bound for Harwich laden with 7,000 tons of fuel oil, she sailed from Methil to join southbound coastal Convoy FS50. The convoy was a large one, with several escorts, and formed up into two long columns, *War Mehta* being the third ship in the starboard column. During the night of 19 November, the weather was fine with good visibility, and the opportunity was taken by a force of enemy torpedo boats to attack the convoy as it approached number 55A buoy, between Smith's Knoll and Hearty Knoll off Great Yarmouth. The first indication that Captain Woodward had that something was amiss was at 23.00 when the sound of an aircraft was heard, and flares were dropped over the convoy. Soon after this, ships' whistles were heard sounding and although no signals had been received from the convoy commodore, it was decided to take evasive action, and a turn to port was ordered. At the same time, the noise of powerful engines could be heard to seaward, but nothing seen. Then several torpedo tracks were clearly seen running towards the convoy; most passed the tanker, but one struck her on the port side abaft the engine room bulkhead. Two other explosions were heard, believed to be torpedoes finding their mark in the convoy. The engine and boiler rooms reported oil entering their

compartments, and engines were stopped. Inspection of the ship revealed a large hole in the ship's side, with the metal plating turned back about 30ft either side of the hole; the port after lifeboat had been demolished and hatch covers blown open. She was now beginning to heel over to port, and following a report of a fire breaking out, the ship was ordered to be abandoned. The remaining boats were hoisted out and the crew left her, being picked up very quickly by another ship in the convoy, the *Greenwood*. A short time later the tug *Superman* appeared, and embarking a small party from the survivors, managed to get alongside and a tow was rigged. The fire was tackled, and towing commenced. A second tug arrived at daybreak, but during the morning she was seen to be sagging amidships, and it was clear that her back was broken. When the engine room bulkheads gave way, she foundered, in position 52.35.45N 02.09.20E. Several enemy torpedo boats had taken part in the attack, but *S 104* claimed the hit on *War Mehta*.
[*TNA: ADM.199/2139; Lloyd's War Losses vol 1 p313*]

21 November ROWAN TREE drifter
Sandhaven 1917 requisitioned 1940; 91 tons;
87.5ft × 19.2ft
Skipper Stanley James Cutts RNR
As she was returning to port, the drifter ran aground on a newly-formed sandbank at the entrance to Lowestoft harbour, and subsequently capsized and sank.
[*TNA: ADM.199/407*]

21 November ML 219 motor launch
Littlehampton 1941; 85 tons; 112ft × 18.4ft; 1 × 3pdr
Irreparably damaged when she ran aground on Goat Island, Stornoway, a hole being ripped in the hull under the engine room. She was refloated but was written off as a constructive total loss.
[*TNA: ADM.199/2233*]

22 November MARIA DE GIOVANNA schooner
Martenshoek 1918 Italian prize 1941; 255 tons;
112.8ft × 27.8ft; 1 × 20mm
Lieutenant Alfred Brian Palmer DSC RNR
Attempting to carry supplies to the garrison at Tobruk, she was laden with ammunition and stores, when she ran aground to the west of the port during the night of 22/23 November and was captured by the enemy.
[*TNA: ADM.199/415*]

22 November ST APOLLO trawler
Beverley 1939 requisitioned 1940; 608 tons; 178.1ft × 30ft;
1 × 4in
Lieutenant Rupert Henry Marchington RNR
In poor weather, with winds gusting to Force 8, a dark overcast sky and a heavy sea, she was in collision with

the destroyer *Sardonyx*, to the north-west of the Isle of Lewis, in position 59.13N 07.41W, the destroyer only catching a brief glimpse of the trawler before she hit. The rescue tug *Marauder* was nearby and soon on the scene, finding the trawler in a sinking condition, with several men still on board and other men in the sea, clinging to a life raft. The men in the sea were picked up and the tug then tried to run alongside the trawler, urging those on board to jump. This was hazardous, with both ships moving wildly in the bad weather, and although several made it, others held back. After only a few minutes the trawler dipped and sank, slipping underneath the tug as she went, and several explosions followed, presumed to be the boilers and depth charges. Thirty-five men were saved, but three were lost.
[*TNA: ADM.199/837; ADM.199/802*]

24 November DUNEDIN light cruiser
Walker 1918; 4,850 tons; 445ft × 45.6ft; 6 × 6in, 3 × 4in,
2 × 2pdr, 12 × torpedo tubes
Captain Richard Stratford Lovatt[†]
Stationed in the South Atlantic from June 1941, the *Dunedin* was ordered to assist in the search for enemy supply ships that were refuelling submarines in mid-Atlantic. Having good intelligence that a supply ship was operating in the area between 0.N to 5.N, 25W to 30W, the cruiser was in approximate position 3N 26W, at 12.50 on 24 November, when a lookout reported a mast on the horizon. The cruiser altered towards the suspect, and speed increased. Sight was lost of the 'mast', and it was thought possible that it may have been a submarine, when at 13.26 she was struck by a torpedo on the starboard side, which exploded near the Seaman Petty Officer's mess. Seconds later there was a second explosion further aft, abreast the wardroom flat. The ship took a list to starboard of about 15 degrees and this steadily increased, to 35 degrees in 15 minutes. The second explosion had wrecked the after part of the ship, dislodging the after 6in gun and blowing off the port propeller. Attempts were made to close watertight doors and hatches, but several were found to have distorted due to the blast. With the list increasing it was feared that she was about to capsize, and boats were ordered to be hoisted out, but with the steep angle of the ship, this proved difficult. The cutter was swamped when it entered the water at an angle, and one whaler was waterlogged, but six Carley floats and a 'floatanet' were released before she slowly rolled over and capsized about 20 minutes after the first hit. Conditions on the rafts were poor, the men being cramped and with little supplies, the survivors being forced to rely on rainwater and a small quantity of biscuit for survival. They drifted for 4 days, in increasingly difficult conditions, with men being attacked by fish, particularly barracuda, and several became delirious and threw themselves into the

sea. On the evening of the fourth day, they were found by the American merchant ship *Nishmaya*, which picked up seventy-two survivors, but five of these subsequently died. Four hundred and twenty men lost their lives in all. Their attacker had been the *U 124* (Mohr).
[TNA: ADM.199/2067h; ADM.267/71]

25 November BARHAM battleship
Clydebank 1914; 31,350 tons; 600ft × 90.6ft; 8 × 15in, 12 × 6in, 8 × 4in, 32 × 2pdr
Captain Geoffrey Clement Cooke[†]
In late November intelligence indicated that two enemy convoys were making for Benghazi, and Admiral Cunningham determined to intercept them. Accordingly, a powerful force of cruisers and destroyers sailed from Alexandria and were provided with distant support by the Mediterranean Fleet Battle Squadron, consisting of three battleships, *Queen Elizabeth* (flagship of the CinC), *Barham* (flagship of Vice Admiral Pridham-Whipple, First Battle Squadron) and *Valiant*. They were escorted by eight destroyers who provided an anti-submarine screen. At 16.29 they were in position 32.39N 26.25E, steering to the west at 17 knots whilst zigzagging. The *Barham* was on the port 'leg' of her zigzag when she was attacked by a submarine which had penetrated the destroyer screen. As the submarine fired, she briefly broached, being seen about 400 yards on the port side of the battleship. This had barely been registered when she was hit by three torpedoes in rapid succession on the port side, concentrated in the area between the funnel and after turrets. The effects were immediate. She heeled over 10 degrees to port, then steadied herself somewhat, but after a few seconds again heeled to port and continued to roll over, assuming a very heavy list of more than 20 degrees. She appeared to 'hang' in this position for about a minute and then rolled over until she was lying on her side and water could be seen to enter the funnel. A moment or so after this there was a terrific explosion in the after part of the ship, abaft the mainmast as one of her magazines exploded. The explosion vented itself in different directions; upwards through the upper deck and sideways blowing out a portion of the starboard side. The ship was shrouded by a thick cloud of yellowish-black smoke and when it cleared, she had disappeared. Her attacker had been *U 331* (von Tiesenhausen). It later emerged that the submarine had probably penetrated the screen between the destroyers *Jervis* and *Griffin*. *Jervis* gained a contact on Asdic, at a range of 1,100 yards, but did not act, as it was classified as a 'non-sub', believing it to be the echo from the wake of a ship ahead. Fifty-six officers and 806 ratings died, including the commanding officer, with 450 survivors, which included Pridham-Whipple; 337 were picked up by the destroyer *Hotspur*.
[TNA: ADM.1/11948]

25 November FISHER GIRL drifter
Lowestoft 1914 requisitioned 1940; 85 tons; 83.7ft × 19.4ft
Skipper Frederick Melhuish RNR
Serving as a degaussing vessel, she was stationed at Falmouth. During the night of 25 November, the harbour and town came under attack from a single enemy aircraft, which dropped four bombs in the town at 19.45 and then 30 minutes later dropped another stick of bombs in the harbour which exploded all around the *Fisher Girl* causing her to sink.
[TNA: ADM.199/655]

27 November PARRAMATTA sloop
Sydney 1939 1,070 tons; 250ft × 36ft; 3 × 4in
Commander Jefferson Hirst Walker RAN[†]
Royal Australian Navy. Actively involved in the supply missions to Tobruk, *Parramatta* sailed from Alexandria 25 November in company with the escort destroyer *Avon Vale* and two South African armed whalers, to escort the supply ship *Hanne* to the garrison. At 00.46 she was hit by a torpedo, the initial explosion being followed by a second, larger detonation, probably as the magazine exploded. The ship rolled over to starboard, broke in half, and sank, although the stern section came to the surface and drifted away. The two whalers continued to Tobruk with the convoy whilst *Avon Vale* loitered to pick up twenty-one survivors from the water. Another three men managed to climb aboard the ship's boat and made it to the shore. One hundred and thirty crew members died, with two RN passengers. Her attacker had been *U 559* (Heidtmann), which had already carried out an unsuccessful attack on the convoy an hour before the sinking of the *Parramatta*.
[Morgan & Taylor p167]

29 November EGLAND whaler
Oslo 1912 requisitioned 1941; 153 tons; 104.5ft × 20.1ft
(Norwegian)
Fitted out as a minesweeper, and based at Alexandria with a Norwegian crew, she ran aground off Gaza. The corvette *Salvia* was despatched to her assistance, but found the whaler listing by 30 degrees and firmly aground. She was written off as a constructive total loss.
[TNA: ADM.199/413]

November LCT (2) 137 – LCT (2) 143 landing craft, tank
Stockton 1941; 296 tons; 143ft × 30ft; 2 × 2pdr
Both listed as being lost in home waters but with no details; possibly written off as constructive total losses after accidents but may have been lost overboard from a merchant vessel (see entry for *LCT 105/LCT 109/ LCT 110* above). Some sections of *LCT 137* and *LCT 143* were evidently recovered as they were re-used to build *LCT 421* in 1942.
[Statement of Losses p50]

5 December CHAKDINA armed boarding vessel
Leith 1914 requisitioned 1940; 3,033 tons; 330.7ft × 46.1ft;
2 × 4in, 1 × 12pdr, 2 × 2pdr
Lieutenant Commander Walter Raleigh Hickey RNR
Sailed from Tobruk for Alexandria in company with the merchant ship *Kirkland* with about 400 wounded men and 100 prisoners of war embarked, the pair made up Convoy TA1, with escorts *Eridge*, *Ferndale* and *Thorgrim*. At 21.30 they came under air attack, when an aircraft, believed to be an Italian S 79, closed from the port bow, and dropped a torpedo. The *Chakdina* put her helm over to starboard to avoid the torpedo which passed astern, but another aircraft was then seen closing from the starboard side. Despite the heavy fire which was opened, another torpedo was dropped, and it could not be avoided, striking her on the starboard quarter, about 50ft from the stern. The engines raced and then stopped, probably because the shafts were broken. The ship started flooding from the stern and the boats were ordered to be lowered into the water, to evacuate the wounded. Some boats were cleared away, but there was some panic by the prisoners as the ship started to sink. The bows rose quickly and reared up into the vertical position as she sank. The position was noted as 33.12N 24.30E. Seventy-one members of the crew and about 200 of the wounded and prisoners died.
[TNA: ADM.199/1178]

6 December PERSEUS submarine
Barrow 1929; 1,475/2,040 tons; 270ft × 29.11ft; 1 × 4in,
8 × torpedo tubes
Lieutenant Commander Edward Charles Frederick Nicolay[†]
Ordered to conduct a patrol in the Aegean, she sailed from Malta 26 November. At 22.00 on 6 December when off the island of Kefalonia there was a terrific explosion forward as she struck a mine, all the lights went out and the submarine heeled over to starboard and rapidly sank bows first. She struck the bottom and after remaining at a steep angle for some time settled down on the seabed, still with a list to starboard. In the after ends, one man, Stoker John Capes was alive and alert, and using a hand-held torch searched the compartments near him found five other stokers, all injured, still alive. All the forward compartments had flooded. The survivors managed to switch on some secondary lighting and decided to try and reach the surface using the after-escape hatch, using the DSEA breathing apparatus. With considerable difficulty, the boat being at an acute angle, the equipment was found and donned, and canvas trunking pulled down to form an escape compartment. Capes had to use the vent for the underwater gun, used for firing flares, to flood the compartment to equalise the pressure. The air was foul and as the water rose in the compartment it was covered in oil and paint from burst tins. By the time equalisation was achieved only Capes and one other survivor were still conscious and ready to make the ascent. Forcing open the outside hatch they left, and after a 90-second ascent, during which he passed close to a moored mine, Capes reached the surface. No one else came to the surface. Despite being exhausted, Capes started to swim to the island which was visible some distance away. He eventually reached the shore and hauled himself out of the water to take shelter in a cave, where he was found later that morning by local fishermen. For the next 6 months Capes evaded capture, being sheltered by local Greek families, regularly being moved, until in June 1943 he was rescued. He was subsequently awarded the British Empire Medal. The wreck of the *Perseus* has been found, lying in 170ft of water. Her hull shows a split on the port side near the bow, evidently the damage from the mine. The after escape hatch is open, just as Capes had left it. Five officers and fifty-four men were lost.
[Evans pp287–91; http://www.navy.gr/hms/ENGLISH/kathodos_en.htm]

7 December CHANTALA armed boarding vessel
Whiteinch 1920 requisitioned 1940; 3,129 tons;
330.2ft × 46ft; 2 × 4in, 1 × 2pdr
Lieutenant Commander Christopher Ernest Inman Gibbs
Loaded with personnel and stores for Tobruk, she sailed from Alexandria, arriving at her destination at first light on 6 December. Having disembarked the men and unloaded the stores, she took on 700 Italian and German prisoners of war and at 17.30 sailed for Alexandria. She got under way stern first, then turned her head to seaward assisted by the tug *C307*, when a mine exploded on the starboard side, throwing up a huge column of water. It was clear that her back was broken, and it was decided to beach her, and she was run aground about 100ft from the pier head. She heeled over and settled quietly, allowing the ship to be evacuated. Pumping commenced, and it was hoped to salvage her, but during the day she became the target for enemy aircraft and three or four bombs landed close to her, causing further damage. All stores were therefore removed, and she was abandoned, although it was hoped that the hulk could be used as an anti-aircraft platform. Two members of the crew and several prisoners of war were killed by the explosion.
[TNA: ADM.199/239]

7 December WINDFLOWER corvette
Lauzon 1940; 940 tons; 190ft × 33ft; 1 × 4in, 1 × 2pdr
Lieutenant John Price RCNR[†]
Royal Canadian Navy. Sailed from Sydney, Nova Scotia on 4 December as part of the escort to Convoy SC58. During the night of 6/7 December the convoy was

shrouded in thick fog, but it appeared that she took station ahead of the starboard column of the convoy, although her allotted position was on the beam of the leading ship. At just after 09.00 the fourth ship in the starboard column, the Dutch merchant ship *Zypenberg* (4,973 tons), suddenly saw the corvette loom out of the fog about 400 yards ahead and crossing her bows. Despite putting engines astern, the *Zypenberg* struck the *Windflower* on the port quarter, slicing off her stern. A few minutes after the impact there was a large explosion as a boiler exploded, and it was clear that the corvette was sinking. *Zypenberg* managed to pick up forty-seven survivors, but twenty-three men died. None of the bridge staff survived, so the reason for her movements were unclear, but it was presumed that she was attempting to gain her correct station but misjudged her position in the thick fog.

[McKee & Darlington p40]

8 December PETEREL river gunboat
Scotstoun 1927; 310 tons; 177ft × 29ft; 2 × 12pdr
Lieutenant Stephen Polkinghorn RNR
Based at Shanghai, she was lying at that port with a reduced crew, when in the early hours of 8 December; Lieutenant Polkinghorn was woken to be advised that war had been declared on Japan, and that troops were reported moving on Hong Kong. At 04.15 a motor launch came alongside carrying a party of Japanese officers and on meeting Polkinghorn, they demanded the surrender of the gunboat. This was refused, and it was stressed that they were in a neutral port. The Japanese party then left, but when about 100 yards clear a red flare was fired from the boat, clearly a signal. Moments later the gunboat was illuminated by a searchlight from the cruiser *Izumo*, and a fierce, well directed fire was opened from 3 Japanese warships anchored nearby. One shell from a ship anchored at the Customs Wharf hit the stern, starting a fire. Polkinghorn ordered demolition charges already prepared for this situation to be fired, and when this was done ordered his men to leave her. All were forced to jump into the water to escape the ship, swimming to the French Bund despite being fired on by machine guns from the Japanese ships. Five men were killed. Polkinghorn was later awarded the Distinguished Service Cross for his 'courage, determination and tenacity'.

[TNA: ADM.267/122; London Gazette 19 October 1945]

8 December PHINEAS BEARD trawler
Beverley 1917 requisitioned 1939; 278 tons;
125.5ft × 23.5ft; 1 × 12pdr
Skipper William Wood McRuvie RNR
Several ships of the Forty-First Minesweeping Group were under way in Lunan Bay, east Scotland, when they came under attack from several aircraft. *Phineas*

Beard received a direct hit amidships which demolished the wheelhouse and sank immediately with the loss of twelve men. The wreck has been found and lies in position 56.38.45N 02.26.06W.

[TNA: ADM.199/1172; https://canmore.org.uk/site/102797]

8 December MILFORD EARL trawler
Beverley 1919 (*Andrew Apsley*) requisitioned 1939; 290 tons; 125.5ft × 23.5ft; 1 × 12pdr
Lieutenant John Stuart Neate RNVR[†]
In company with the *Phineas Beard* (see above), when the group came under air attack in Lunan Bay, off the east coast of Scotland. The ship was badly shaken by several near misses and was further damaged and set on fire by strafing. She sank one hour after the attack; five men were killed. The wreck lies in position 56.38.42N 02.23.48W.

[TNA: ADM.199/1172; https://canmore.org.uk/site/102801]

8 December 1941 PRABHAVATI auxiliary patrol vessel
Glasgow 1933 requisitioned 1939; 556 tons;
199.7ft × 34.1ft
Lieutenant Douglas Murray Stafford RINR
Royal Indian Navy. Following reports of a Japanese submarine and possible parent ship being in the area, the light cruiser *Glasgow* sailed from Colombo on 6 December to search around the Laccadive Islands and then sweep north towards Goa. The concern that enemy forces were in the area was strengthened during 8 December, when the Indian patrol vessel *Dipavati* reported sighting a submarine off Goa. That evening, in position 15.14N 72.28E, *Glasgow* was heading towards that port, when a light was sighted on the port bow. She altered course to investigate and signalled 'What ship?' by light but received no response. *Glasgow* manoeuvred to place the stranger up-moon, and the silhouette seemed to resemble a submarine. They continued to close, and then illuminated the target with a searchlight, and the shape revealed appeared to confirm their suspicions, and at midnight, fire was opened on the target. Eight rounds of 6in were fired, and the target hit. When *Glasgow* closed the scene, they discovered the target was a small ship and two barges, the ship and one of the barges soon sinking. The survivors picked up from the water confirmed that they had sunk the patrol vessel *Prabhavati*, which was towing two lighters, the *Hetampur* and *Hingoli*, to Karachi. They testified that during the evening, a link had parted in the tow, and both lighters had been brought alongside, for a new hawser to be brought up and shackled on. The officers and crew were busily occupied with this, and had not seen any signal lamps, and only became aware of the presence of the *Glasgow* when illuminated by searchlight but could do little before attacked. Hit repeatedly by large shells, they were clearly sinking,

and she heeled over to port and sank, along with the lighter *Hingoli*. Twenty-four men were killed or died of wounds subsequently. The subsequent Board of Inquiry found that neither ship had been advised of the presence of the other. The primary cause was the misleading appearance of the target – *Glasgow* had been warned of the presence of a submarine and the small steamer with two lighters alongside did resemble the hull of a surfaced submarine. Furthermore the lamp used to signal when first sighted was probably too weak to be seen. However, the *Prabhavarti* was guilty of a poor lookout – it was a moonlit night and an object the size of *Glasgow* should have been seen.
[TNA: ADM.1/11949]

(7/8) December BANKA auxiliary minesweeper
Dordrecht 1914 (*Singkara*) requisitioned 1939; 623 tons;
185.6ft × 31.1ft; 1 × 12pdr
Lieutenant Arthur Ernest Stephenson RNR†
Based at Singapore, she was posted missing when she failed to return to the base as expected on completion of a patrol. Six survivors later landed at Pulau Tinggi, Johore, after being adrift for several hours, who confirmed that she had quickly sunk after suffering a night-time explosion when to the north of the island of Tioman. At the time it was believed that a British mine that had broken free from a defensive field was responsible, and the likely time of loss of 9/10 December. It was later discovered that a large minefield had been laid in the area by the Japanese *Tatsumiya Maru* on 6 December and was almost certainly responsible. Her wreck was found 12 miles north-east of Tioman. Four British officers and thirty-eight Malay ratings were lost.
[TNA: ADM.199/1172; ADM.199/1287]

10 December REPULSE battlecruiser
Clydebank 1916; 32,000 tons; 750ft × 90ft; 6 × 15in,
6 × 4in, 24 × 2pdr, 15 × 20mm
Captain William George Tennant†
During 1941, with Japan perceived as a growing threat, consideration was given to strengthening the fleet in the Far East, which mainly consisted of elderly ships of various classes. The *Repulse* was ordered to deploy to Ceylon in late August 1941 and after much discussion it was decided in October to send the new battleship *Prince of Wales* with four modern destroyers under the command of Admiral Sir Tom Phillips. The force had scarcely assembled in Singapore when the Japanese attacked Pearl Harbour on 7 December, with other attacks on Hong Kong and the Philippines and this was followed by landings in Thailand and in northern Malaya. During the night of 7/8 December Japanese troops were reported landing at Singora (modern Songkhla) in south-eastern Thailand and at Kota Baru

(Kota Baharu) in north-east Malaya. Admiral Phillips decided to attack the Japanese transports and warships at those places, and his force of two capital ships and four destroyers sailed from Singapore at 17.35 on 8 December. His intention was to arrive off Singora at dawn on 10 December to achieve the maximum surprise. He requested air support in the form of reconnaissance ahead of him and direct air support from fighters on his arrival off Singora. However, at the last minute the RAF indicated that although reconnaissance could be provided, they would not be able to comply with the request for fighter cover. Despite this, Admiral Phillips decided to press on, as they had a good chance of surprising the enemy. During the afternoon of 9 December however, this hope was also dashed as the Japanese submarine *I-65* sighted them as they steamed to the north-west and reported their course and speed. Although this was unknown to the British ships, the sighting led to increased air activity by the Japanese to locate them. This proved to be successful at 17.00 when a floatplane from the cruiser *Kinu* spotted them, and then by other search aircraft, which were seen by the British force. With no air cover and their presence in the area now known, their only advantage, surprise, had clearly been lost and the attempt was abandoned, and after nightfall Admiral Philips reversed course to head back to Singapore. Shortly before midnight a signal from shore indicated that more landings had been reported at Kuantan, which was just to the west of their present position. This was too good an opportunity to be missed and at 00.50 course was altered to the west, to steer for Kuantan. The Japanese, meanwhile, were now fully alerted to the presence of the British force and diverted all available resources to dealing with them. A large air search was initiated, and long-range bombers prepared for the attack. In fact, the British eluded the air search, which had assumed they were continuing to proceed north. Their bad luck continued, however, as they were sighted at just after midnight by the surfaced Japanese submarine *I-58* (Kitamura) which hastily dived and then carried out an attack, firing a full salvo of torpedoes, all of which missed. The sighting reports from *I-58* alerted the Japanese to the change of course, and the air search was shifted to the new area. At dawn, the British force arrived off Kuantan to find the reports had been false, and all was peaceful. They duly altered course to head south, to return to Singapore, but at about 10.15 they were again located by a Mitsubishi G3M2 'Nell' reconnaissance aircraft. A large force of Japanese bombers was already in the air searching for the enemy and they were immediately diverted to the newly reported position. The British force increased speed to 25 knots and prepared for action. The attacks began at 11.18 with a high-level attack by nine Mitsubishi 'Nell' bombers, which attacked the

Repulse from ahead. She received one direct hit from this, a bomb hitting the port hangar, penetrating the upper deck to burst on the armoured deck below. All the rest of the bombs missed. At 11.44 the next attack developed, with nine torpedo bombers which concentrated on the *Prince of Wales* (see below). *Repulse* became a target at 11.50 when she came under another high-level bomber attack from six 'Nells', which she again avoided and again at 11.56 when seven 'Nell' torpedo bombers closed from the port side, the ship turning to meet the threat, and avoided all the torpedoes by 'combing' the tracks. A brief lull in the action was broken at 12.20 when there was a sustained attack by eleven Mitsubishi G4M1 'Betty' torpedo bombers on both ships, and it was it was during this raid that *Repulse* was hit by a single torpedo amidships, which caused only local damage. A few moments later the air attack continued from different directions, and this time she could not avoid them. In a few minutes she was hit by four torpedoes, three of them on the port side. The first exploded abreast the gunroom, which jammed the rudder, causing her to steam in circles. The second hit the port side aft; the third exploded abreast the engine room and the fourth hit the starboard side, exploding abreast 'E' boiler room. The ship then listed to port and started to slowly roll over. Realising that she was not going to recover, Captain Tennant ordered the ship to be abandoned. The ship hung for some minutes at an acute angle of about 60 degrees, with men jumping into the sea and then capsized and sank at 12.33. The position was 03.45N 104.24E. The destroyers *Electra* and *Vampire* closed to pick up 796 survivors. Twenty-seven Officers and 486 men died.

[TNA: ADM.1/2006; ADM.234/330; Roskill vol 1 pp563–7]

10 December **PRINCE OF WALES** battleship
Birkenhead 1939; 36,730 tons; 700ft × 103ft; 10 × 14in, 16 × 5.25in, 32 × 2pdr
Captain John Catherall Leach[†]

In company with the *Repulse* (see above), she was the Flagship of Admiral Sir Tom Spencer Vaughan Philips in the doomed expedition to the Far East. When the air raids developed during the morning of 10 December, they initially concentrated on *Repulse*, but at 11.38 a formation of nine Mitsubishi G3M2 'Nell' torpedo bombers were seen closing from the starboard bow. They crossed the bow in line astern and then turned to attack from the port side at 11.44. She altered course to face the threat and 'comb the tracks' of the torpedoes, but one torpedo hit her in the vicinity of the mainmast, abreast 'P3' and 'P4' turrets, throwing up a large column of water. It is probable that a second torpedo hit the stern. This latter explosion caused widespread flooding aft with the water entering the shaft alley to penetrate 'B' engine room forcing it to be evacuated; the steering

gear failed and both port shafts were out of action; mechanical breakdowns occurred and both port side forward 5.25in turrets were put out of action. She took an 11-degree list to port and with only two shafts she slowed to about 16 knots. When at 12.22 there was a determined attack by six 'Betty' torpedo bombers the battleship was incapable of manoeuvring. She was hit at least three times on the starboard side, two torpedoes hitting her aft, the third abreast 'B' turret. These hits caused widespread damage, putting the starboard outer shaft out of action, reducing her speed further, and with more flooding aft she steadily settled, and heeled slowly to port. At 12.33 a further raid developed, when nine 'Nells' aircraft dropped bombs from high level, but all fell wide. The final air attack took place at 12.46 when eight 'Nells' aircraft carried out a bombing attack. She was hit by one bomb, which hit the upper deck by the catapult, penetrating to burst on the main deck. The flash from this penetrated 'X' boiler room, putting it out of action. With smoke spreading through the ship some of the after magazines were flooded, which caused her stern to trim even lower. She was clearly sinking and at 12.50 the destroyer *Express* was called alongside to take off the crew. She continued to slowly heel over until at 13.20 she capsized over to port, her starboard bilge keel hitting the *Express*, making her heel violently. She sank in position 03.36N 104.28E. The destroyers picked up 1,285 survivors; 327 men died.

[TNA: ADM.1/2006; ADM.116/4521; ADM.234/330; Roskill vol 1 pp563–7]

10 December **NYKEN** harbour tender
Kulstadjoen 1918 requisitioned 1940; 111 tons; 81.1ft × 19.9ft
Former Norwegian fishing vessel that escaped from Norway in May 1940 and later employed as a harbour tender in Scottish waters. She is listed as being written off as a constructive total loss; circumstances uncertain, 'off West Scotland'.

[Statement of Losses p24; TNA: ADM.1/24129]

11 December **LADY SHIRLEY** trawler
Beverley 1937 requisitioned 1940; 472 tons; 163.5ft × 27.2ft; 1 × 12pdr
Lieutenant Commander Arthur Henry Callaway RANVR[†]
Based at Gibraltar, she was last seen at 03.45 by another trawler, the *St Nectan*, as both vessels conducted an anti-submarine patrol in the Straits after which she disappeared without trace. Despite searching the area, nothing was ever found. After the war it emerged that she had been torpedoed at approximately 04.21 by the *U 374* (Fischel). There were no survivors. Four officers and twenty-nine men died.

[TNA: ADM.199/661; Lund & Ludlam, Trawlers go to War p132]

11 December ROSABELLE yacht
Leith 1902 requisitioned 1939; 526 tons; 192ft × 26.4ft;
1 × 12pdr
Lieutenant Hercules Scott Findlay RNR[†]
Employed as an armed boarding vessel and based at
Gibraltar, she was conducting a night patrol in the
Straits when she blew up at 04.42 and sank in less than a
minute. Twelve survivors were picked up by the armed
yacht *Sayonara*, but thirty officers and men with two
embarked soldiers were lost. It was later confirmed that
she had been attacked by the *U 374* (Fischel).
[*TNA: ADM.199/661; WO.361/144; Lund & Ludlam, Trawlers
go to War p133*]

12 December MOTH river gunboat
Sunderland 1915; 625 tons; 230ft × 36ft; 2 × 6in, 1 × 12pdr
Commander Charles Reginald Creer RAN
Based at Hong Kong, she was in dry dock at Kowloon
when hostilities began with some plates removed
and suffered shrapnel damage during an air raid on
8 December. On the night of 10/11 December the
Japanese forces were reported to have broken through
the lines to the north and the evacuation of Kowloon
was ordered, with the destruction of anything that
could not be moved. Air raids which had been regular
for the past few days intensified, and as the *Moth* could
not be moved from her dock in time, the dock was
flooded, and she was allowed to sink. During 1942 the
Japanese managed to salvage the gunboat and she was
pressed into service as the *Suma*, to be sunk again in
1945 in the river Yangtse.
[*TNA: ADM.199/357*]

12 December TAMAR base ship
London 1863; 4,650 tons; 320ft × 45ft
The elderly former troopship had served as a depot at
Hong Kong since 1897 and was ordered to be sunk
as the Japanese advanced through the colony. She was
scuttled at her buoy off the Wan Chai waterfront.
[*TNA: ADM.191/286*]

13 December KAMPAR auxiliary patrol vessel
Hong Kong 1915 requisitioned 1940; 971 tons;
223.2ft × 36ft; 1 × 4in
Lieutenant Robert Hamer RNR
Based at Penang, she was attacked by several Japanese
dive bombers whilst on patrol off Muka Head during
the late morning of 12 December. The attacks
continued during the afternoon, but all failed to cause
any damage, the bombs falling well clear until at 15.00
a bomb exploded close alongside the port beam, abreast
the boiler room. The ship was shaken badly, and several
leaks became evident. The ship broke off her patrol and
returned to port, to land one injured rating and inspect
for damage. It was found that water was entering the

ship which could not be controlled, so at 20.30 she was
run aground on the middle bank on an even keel and
all the crew left her. The following day she was again the
target for further air attacks, being bombed and strafed.
She was seen to be hit forward which started a fire,
which spread aft, with several explosions as ammunition
started to explode. The ship was boarded on 14
December but found to be a wreck and was abandoned.
She was subsequently salvaged by the Japanese and
entered their service as the transport *Kasumi Maru*.
[*TNA: ADM.199/357: http://www.bbc.co.uk/ww2peopleswar/
stories/41/a5897541.shtml*]

13 December TUNG WO auxiliary patrol vessel
Shanghai 1914 requisitioned 1940; 1,337 tons;
235ft × 40.1ft
Master William Rochester
Based at George Town, Penang, and employed as an
examination vessel, she was damaged during a series of
bombing raids on 12 December, in which one crew
member was killed. During further raids on the next
day, she was hit again and suffered further damage,
forcing the crew to abandon her. She was subsequently
salvaged by the Japanese after their occupation of the
port and served as the *Dowa Maru*.
[*Statement of Losses p16; http://www.combinedfleet.com/
dowa_t.htm*]

14 December GALATEA light cruiser
Greenock 1934; 5,220 tons; 480ft × 51ft; 6 × 6in, 8 × 4in,
6 × torpedo tubes
Captain Edward William Boyd Sim[†]
On 13 December Operation 'ME9' was ordered, an
attack on enemy units reported to be operating in
the Ionian Sea covering the passage of a convoy to
Libya. *Galatea*, in company with her sisters *Euryalus*
and *Naiad* sailed from Alexandria with nine destroyers.
The operation was abandoned the following day
when it was clear that the convoys had been recalled
and the ships returned to harbour. At 23.59 as she
was approaching the entrance to the swept channel
leading into Alexandria harbour, she was hit on the port
side amidships by two torpedoes in quick succession.
Internal compartments evidently rapidly flooded, and
the ship rolled over to port and sank in 3 minutes. The
destroyers *Griffin* and *Hotspur* picked up 13 officers and
141 men but 469 were lost. The attacking submarine
was *U 557* (Paulshen).
[*TNA: ADM.199/415*]

14 December MA/SB 30 motor anti-submarine boat
Hythe 1941; 20 tons; 63ft × 15ft
Employed on air-sea rescue duties, she was proceeding
out of harbour for rescue work during the night of
13/14 December, when she fouled the boom across the

river Humber. The following day she was successfully removed from the obstruction, but during the late afternoon the tow parted as she was being taken back to port and she disappeared into the dark and foundered.
[TNA: ADM.199/2234]

14 December MTB 68 motor torpedo boat
Hampton 1940; 17 tons; 55ft × 11ft; 2 × torpedo tubes
Lieutenant Richard Routledge Smith RNVR
Stationed in the eastern Mediterranean, with the 10th MTB Flotilla, she was based at Tobruk with her sister, *MTB 215*. Whilst returning to base after a night patrol along the Libyan coast she collided with *215*. The damage was such that *68* filled and sank rapidly, her crew scrambling onto *215*, which had damaged bows, but made it back to Tobruk.
[Reynolds & Cooper, Mediterranean MTBs at War pp29–30]

15 December INDIRA auxiliary patrol vessel
Middlesbrough 1918 (*Kildysart*) requisitioned 1940; 895 tons; 170ft × 30ft; 1 × 4in
Lieutenant Desmond Ernest Hindmarsh HKRNVR
Based at Hong Kong, she was laying alongside in Aberdeen harbour, when it came under a Japanese air raid and she foundered after two bombs exploded next to her. One man was lost.
[TNA: ADM.267/130; ADM.199/287]

16 December MTB 8 motor torpedo boat
Hythe 1937; 18 tons; 60.4ft × 13.10ft; 2 × torpedo tubes
Lieutenant Laurence Dudley Kilbee RNVR
Based at Aberdeen harbour, Hong Kong, she was out of the water and being maintained on a slipway when that the colony came under Japanese air attack. Although not directly hit, she was peppered by splinters and then caught fire, rapidly burning out.
[TNA: ADM.267/131; ADM.199/1286]

16 December GATLING armament tug
Hong Kong 1937; 151 tons; 85ft × 22ft
Based at Hong Kong, manned by a civilian crew provided by Jardine–Mathieson, she was lying alongside when the harbour came under intensive air attack. Damaged by splinters, several of her crew were injured and she caught fire. Towed clear of the wharf, she was allowed to settle in shallow water. Later salvaged by the Japanese, she was recovered at the end of the war and re-entered service as *Boomerang*.
[TNA: ADM.267/131]

16 December LCT (1) 11 landing craft, tank
Belfast 1940; 226 tons; 135ft × 28ft; 2 × 2pdr
Sub-Lieutenant Ronald George Sturdy RNVR
During September 1941 *LCT 11* had been damaged off Sidi Barrani by dive-bomber attack and subsequently

retired to Port Said for repair. That complete she resumed her hazardous task of supplying the garrison at Tobruk. Fully laden with stores, ammunition and two launches, she sailed from Mersa Matruh, but soon found that she was leaking. As she settled, the heavy seas washed over the sides and the flooding became serious. An attempt was made to return to Matruh, but this had to be abandoned as she became uncontrollable and eventually drifted ashore about a mile to the west of Buq-Buq. No salvage was possible, and she settled into the sand.
[TNA: ADM.199/799]

17 December THRACIAN destroyer
Hebburn 1918; 905 tons; 265ft × 26.9ft; 2 × 4in, 1 × 2pdr, 40 mines
Lieutenant Commander Arthur Beard Pears
Based at Hong Kong, the destroyer grounded on her way into the port in the early hours of 14 December and was taken into dry dock in Aberdeen harbour for an inspection the following day. During 16 December, the harbour was subjected to repeated air raids, and during one of these she was hit, suffering considerable damage, with oil fuel tanks flooded. On the night of 16 December, she was towed out and then deliberately run aground on Round Island, Repulse Bay. She was refloated by the Japanese in July 1942 and repaired to become patrol boat *PB 101*. She was recovered at Yokosuka in September 1945.
[TNA: ADM.267/130; ADM.267/131]

19 December NEPTUNE light cruiser
Portsmouth 1933; 7,175 tons; 522ft × 55.8ft; 8 × 6in, 8 × 4in, 8 × 2pdr
Captain Rory Chambers O'Conor[†]
In company with the cruisers *Penelope* and *Aurora*, and four destroyers, sailed from Malta at 18.30 on 18 December, to close the Libyan coast and intercept an Axis convoy believed to be en-route for Tripoli. Steaming south in line ahead, the *Neptune* was leading, when at 01.06 in position 33.09N 13.20.5E there was a large explosion under her bows as she ran over a mine. Two minutes later the *Aurora* was also mined, and another mine exploded close the *Penelope*. It was clear that they had run into an unsuspected minefield. The group came to a halt, and the cruisers went astern, to try and retrace their course, and clear the field. Although the other ships managed to extricate themselves, at 01.12 and again at 01.15 the *Neptune* detonated a further two mines under her stern. These blew her stern off, and she lost her rudder and propellers. She signalled her consorts that she was damaged and had lost all power. The *Aurora*, now free of the field, was ordered to proceed to Malta, escorted by two of the destroyers. The *Penelope*, with the other two destroyers, *Lively* and

Kandahar, remained near the stricken *Neptune*. Without any power, the *Neptune* drifted with the wind and tide, and Captain O'Conor hoped that this would take her free of the minefield, and at 02.18 signalled to the *Penelope* that he was preparing for a tow, when he was clear. An hour passed, and at 03.09 *Neptune* signalled that she was ready for a tow and the *Penelope* and the two destroyers closed to 2.5 miles. The *Kandahar* slowly went forward to close the cruiser, but when she was 7 cables (1,400 yards) from her a mine exploded under her stern. After this Captain O'Conor signalled 'keep away' to the others. The cruiser continued to slowly drift until at 04.00 she detonated a fourth mine, which exploded amidships. She was then seen to heel over to port and slowly sink. The position for the *Penelope* and *Lively* was now very difficult; before them they had a cruiser that had sunk and a destroyer that was sinking, and clearly they were still in the middle of a minefield. To go to their assistance, it seemed highly likely that they would meet the same fate. It would soon be daylight, and they were only 20 miles from the hostile Libyan coast which meant the added threat of enemy air activity. The decision was therefore taken to leave and return to Malta. The *Penelope* did break radio silence to inform Malta of the situation and suggested that a flying boat or submarine could be sent to the area to find survivors. The survivors of the cruiser found themselves swimming in a sea covered with oil and debris, and it was with difficulty that they hauled themselves onto floats and rafts. Several tried to swim to the *Kandahar*, but none made it. Over the next few hours and days, they died, one by one of hypothermia and exhaustion. Five days after the loss, an Italian patrol boat found a raft with one man alive. Able Seaman Norman Walton was picked up, the only survivor. Seven hundred and sixty-four men had died.
[TNA: ADM.1/11947]

19 December **STANLEY** destroyer

Quincy 1919 (*McCalla*), loaned 1940; 1,190 tons; 309ft × 30.10ft; 4 × 4in, 1 × 3in, 2 × 20mm
Lieutenant Commander David Byam Shaw[†]

Ordered to join the 36th Escort Group as additional escort to the thirty-two ships of Convoy HG76, which had a close escort of seven 'Flower' class corvettes and the escort carrier *Audacity*, she sailed from Gibraltar on 14 December. During the 16th the convoy came under the surveillance of a patrolling Fw 200 aircraft, and that evening and all through the following day, numerous contacts with submarines were made. Despite having both her Asdic Type 141 and radar Type 271 out of action, making her 'deaf and blind', she more than adequately played her part. At 09.06 on the 18th *Stanley* had sighted a submarine, trimmed down, on her port quarter, and altered course towards, being joined by

the escort destroyer *Blankney*. The pair had mounted a prompt depth-charge attack which had forced the *U 434* to the surface, to be abandoned before it sank. That evening both *Pentstemon* and *Convolvulus* carried out attacks on submarines forcing them to break off attacks. At 03.45 the next morning a torpedo track was seen by *Stanley*, and evasive action was immediately taken, altering course to starboard and increasing speed. After several moments she again altered, to resume her previous course. She was still under port helm when another torpedo track was seen on the port beam and before any avoiding action could be taken it struck her amidships; the time was then 04.08. The torpedo detonated abreast the forward mess deck and the explosion was violent, starting a fire in the immediate vicinity. Very soon after this she took a heavy list to starboard then broke in half. The stern sank after 5 minutes, the bows upending and remaining vertical for about 45 minutes before sinking. The *Stork* and *Samphire* picked up the survivors, 136 men died. Her assailant had been the *U 574*, which was attacked by the *Stork* and rammed a short while after her attack.
[TNA: ADM.1/12019]

19 December **MTB 12** motor torpedo boat

Hythe 1938; 18 tons; 60.4ft × 13.10ft; 2 × torpedo tubes
Lieutenant John Baxter Colls HKRNVR[†]

One of a small force of torpedo boats based at Aberdeen harbour, Hong Kong that undertook the hazardous task of tackling the Japanese invasion forces. During the night of 18/19 December the invasion of Hong Kong began and at first light the torpedo boats were sailed to intercept any enemy shipping they could find crossing to the island from Kowloon. There was a short, fierce fight, in which one landing craft was destroyed and another damaged by gunfire. Two of the attacking torpedo boats were damaged but managed to withdraw. *MTB 12* was hit on the bridge and covered in white smoke she was seen to career out of control and eventually ran aground after ramming the harbour wall at Kowloon. The commanding officer and six others were killed, with two survivors.
[TNA: ADM.267/131; Reynolds & Cooper, *Mediterranean MTBs at War* p174]

19 December **MTB 26** motor torpedo boat

Hampton 1938; 13 tons; 55ft × 11ft; 2 × torpedo tubes
Lieutenant Donald William Wagstaff HKRNVR[†]

Another of the torpedo boats based at Hong Kong that attacked the invading Japanese. She was last seen heavily engaged with the enemy but had been brought to a halt. She was sunk soon after with the loss of all nine men onboard.
[TNA: ADM.267/131; Reynolds & Cooper, *Mediterranean MTBs at War* p174]

19 December Scuttling of naval vessels, Hong Kong
With the Japanese gaining ground in the colony, on 19 December all auxiliary and support vessels were ordered to be taken to Deepwater Bay and scuttled:

REDSTART minelayer
Leith 1938; 498 tons; 149ft × 27.4ft; 1 × 20mm, 12 mines
Lieutenant Commander Henry Charles Selby

TERN river gunboat
Scotstoun 1927; 262 tons; 160ft × 27ft; 2 × 12pdr
Lieutenant John Douglas RNR

CORNFLOWER sloop
Glasgow 1916; 1,250 tons; 255ft × 33.6ft
Lieutenant Commander Richard John Vernall HKRNVR

EBONOL oiler
Glasgow 1917; 2,365 tons; 210ft × 34.7ft
Master Leslie Sonley
Ebonol proved to be reluctant to sink, so the *Cicala* fired several 6in rounds into her, to speed the process. She was salvaged by the Japanese and renamed *Enoshima Maru*. She was recovered in October 1945 and re-entered RFA service.
[TNA ADM.199/1286]

SHUN WO auxiliary minesweeper
Shanghai 1917 requisitioned 1941; 220 tons; 125ft × 22.1ft
Sub-Lieutenant William Ernest Baker HKRNVR

BARLIGHT boom defence vessel
Renfrew 1938; 730 tons; 150ft × 32+ft; 1 × 12pdr
Chief Skipper Andrew Flett RNR
Subsequently salvaged by the Japanese in 1942 and repaired to serve as an auxiliary vessel and designated *M-101*.

ALDGATE boom gate vessel
Hong Kong 1934; 290 tons; 98ft × 26ft; 1 × 12pdr

WATERGATE boom gate vessel
Hong Kong 1934; 290 tons; 98ft × 26ft; 1 × 12pdr

ALLIANCE tug
Chatham 1910; 615 tons; 145ft × 29ft

MATCHLOCK tug
Hong Kong 1940; 70 tons
Note: the official *Statement of Losses* strangely gives the loss of *Matchlock* as being in 1942 by mine at Canton – which had been in Japanese hands since 1938. TNA: ADM.267/131 gives the more likely cause as being scuttled at her base in Hong Kong, presumably during the mass scuttling on 19 December.

POET CHAUCER tug
Hong Kong 1919; 239 tons; 105ft × 25ft

MAN YEUNG auxiliary minelayer
Hong Kong 1933 requisitioned 1939; 225 tons; 128.1ft × 41.6ft

MINNIE auxiliary patrol vessel
Shanghai 1905 requisitioned 1941; 17 tons; 47.5ft × 9.5ft

HAN WO auxiliary patrol vessel
Shanghai 1919 requisitioned 1941; 248 tons; 140ft × 26.1ft
Sub-Lieutenant Thomas Hanson Hood HKRNVR
[TNA: ADM.199/357; ADM.199/1286; ADM.267/131: Lloyd's War Losses]

★ ★ ★

20 December KANDAHAR destroyer
Dumbarton 1939; 1,690 tons; 339.6ft × 35.8ft; 6 × 4.7in, 4 × 2pdr, 10 × torpedo tubes
Commander William Geoffrey Arthur Robson DSO DSC
Part of the group led by the *Neptune* that sailed from Malta to attack an enemy convoy and subsequently ran into a newly-laid Italian minefield in the early hours of 19 December (see above). With the *Neptune* helpless and the *Aurora* damaged, the group stopped and tried to extract themselves. The *Aurora* was successful and with the escort of two destroyers returned to Malta. The *Neptune* slowly drifted to the north-east, and just after 03.00 an attempt was made to take the cruiser in tow. *Kandahar* approached slowly, but at 03.18 a mine exploded under her stern. All power was immediately lost, the lights went out, and the engine room reported that they believed the propellers had been lost. Although she settled down by the stern, she did not seem to be in imminent danger of sinking. The *Penelope* and *Lively* were still waiting at a distance, and Commander Robson realised their dilemma, and signalled 'Suggest you go' and the pair reluctantly turned away from the minefield and headed back for Malta. The *Neptune* was seen to roll over and sink, but nothing could be done. The *Kandahar* was now alone and drifting slowly away to the north-east. The engine room bulkheads were ordered to be shored up, and top weight was shed, with ammunition being ditched overboard and torpedoes dumped. She fully expected to attract the attention of hostile aircraft, but none appeared. Later that night a searching RAF Wellington aircraft flew overhead. The destroyer *Jaguar* had been despatched from Malta to find her, and after searching for some time, finally found the wreck at 04.20 on 20 December. When she arrived, the *Kandahar* was awash astern of her funnel, being flooded abaft the engine room and she had a 15-degree list to port. It was agreed that she could not be saved, and

so *Jaguar* managed to put her bows alongside, which allowed about fifty men to jump on board before she was forced to back off as she was in danger of being damaged by the ships' constant scraping together. She then took station close by her and the remainder of the ship's company of *Kandahar* jumped into the water to be picked up. This was complete by 05.30 when *Jaguar* fired a torpedo into the wreck and the *Kandahar* sank at 05.45. Her position was then 32.53N 14.20E. Seventy-three men died.

[TNA: ADM.1/11947]

20 December ADVERSUS auxiliary patrol vessel

Orillia 1931 requisitioned 1939; 155 tons; 112.3ft × 19ft
Skipper William Ralph Chandler RCNR

Royal Canadian Navy. Employed at Halifax as a local patrol and examination vessel, she met the tug *Ocean Eagle* which was proceeding to Shelburne. The weather was poor, with gale force winds and regular snow squalls. The pair headed toward the harbour entrance, but *Adversus* ran hard aground on McNutt Island. The winds and sea drove her further inshore onto the beach where the crew were able to get ashore. She was subsequently written off as a total loss.

[McKee & Darlington p42]

21 December AUDACITY escort aircraft carrier

Bremen 1939 (*Hanover*), prize 1940; 8,600 tons;
434.4ft × 56.3ft; 1 × 4in, 4 × 2pdr, 4 × 20mm, 6 aircraft
Commander Douglas William MacKendrick†

Part of the escort to Convoy HG76 en-route to Liverpool from Gibraltar, the convoy had come under sustained attack since it had sailed. Aircraft from *Audacity* had successfully shot down two Fw 200 reconnaissance aircraft and had been invaluable in providing aerial surveillance around the convoy. Rather than stay with the convoy, she normally operated about 10 miles distant, to allow her room to manoeuvre. During the evening of 21 December, she took up station on the starboard side of the convoy, zigzagging at 14 knots. At 20.35 she was hit by a torpedo aft, which exploded under the squadron office abreast number 5 hold. It apparently holed the shaft tunnel and in about 10 minutes, due to a small bulkhead at the forward end of the tunnel giving way, the engine room flooded, putting the electric supply out of action. The ship remained on an even keel, although down by the stern. She stayed in this state until 21.45 when she was struck by another two torpedoes. One detonated under the bridge, the second exploded between that and the hole caused by the first torpedo which effectively broke her back. Her head dipped, and she steadily sank by the bow, the stern rising clear of the water as she sank. The corvettes *Marigold*, *Pentstemon* and *Convolvulus* picked up the survivors, but seventy-three men were lost. Her

position was 43.54N 19.15W. Her attacker was the *U 751* (Bigalk).

[TNA: ADM.1/11895]

21 December CICALA river gunboat

Whiteinch 1915; 625 tons; 230ft × 36ft; 2 × 6in, 1 × 12pdr
Lieutenant Commander John Christian Boldero DSC

Based at Hong Kong, during the Japanese attack on the colony she stationed herself in the West Lamma Channel, to bombard troops seen on the Middle Spur and Shousan Hills. She did this successfully for some time, until from 10.30 she was repeatedly attacked by several dive bombers. She was hit four times, and in the last attack a bomb passed through the ship to explode beneath the hull, others set her on fire, with one man being killed. Boats closed the crippled gunboat to remove the crew, and then hastened her end by use of depth charges dropped alongside her.

[TNA: ADM.267/119].

23 December TOKEN drifter

Banff 1914 requisitioned 1939; 89 tons; 89.7ft × 19.1ft

Employed as a tender at Scapa Flow, in poor weather, with a strong westerly gale she went aground in Skerry Sound and could not be salvaged, being written off as a constructive total loss.

[TNA: ADM.199/397]

23 December TIBERIO auxiliary schooner

Prize, ex-Italian captured 1941; 231 tons; 144.3ft × 22.4ft
Lieutenant Ian Horace Laing RNR

Employed as a store carrier, ferrying stores and munitions to garrisons in North Africa, she sailed from Mersa Matruh loaded with 212 tons of oil, contained in drums. Soon after this an aircraft reported seeing the vessel 'steering wildly in all directions', so the corvette *Protea* and tug *St Issey* were sent to her aid. They found that her cargo had shifted, and the oil drums had taken charge. The non-essential members of the crew were taken off and an attempt was made to return to Mersa Matruh, but in heavy seas she capsized and sank near the harbour entrance. One man lost his life.

[TNA: ADM.199/799]

24 December SALVIA corvette

Renfrew 1940; 940 tons; 190ft × 33ft; 1 × 4in
Lieutenant Commander John Isdale Miller DSO DSC RNR†

During the evening of 23 December, the British steamer *Shuntien*, carrying about 1,000 prisoners of war from Tobruk to Alexandria, was torpedoed and sunk by U-boat off the north coast of Egypt. The *Salvia* was ordered to her assistance and picked up a large number of survivors. She subsequently disappeared, and air and sea searches found nothing, until the *Peony* found a patch of wreckage and oil in position 31.46N 28E, about

90 miles to the east of the *Shuntien* sinking, which was presumed to be connected to her loss. it was assumed that she had been torpedoed, and probably capsized, overloaded with the survivors. This was later found to be correct, although not in the position suggested by the wreckage. She had been torpedoed at 01.35 by *U 559* (Heidtmann) in approximate position 32.09N 25.20E. The U-boat fired a salvo of four torpedoes at a warship, resulting in a single hit which was followed be secondary explosions. The target was seen to break in half, the stern sinking quickly, the fo'c'sle floated for several minutes before disappearing. There were no survivors from her ship's company of fifty-nine men or those she had rescued from the *Shuntien*.
[TNA: ADM.199/415; Morgan & Taylor pp175–8]

(20-24) December H 31 submarine
Barrow 1918; 410/510 tons; 164.6ft × 15.9ft; 4 × torpedo tubes
Lieutenant Frank Bridges Gibbs†
Since early 1941, the elderly *H 31* had been used for training, but in December of that year it was believed that the *Scharnhorst* and *Gneisenau* may be about to sail from Brest, and she was ordered to conduct an operational patrol. She sailed from Falmouth 19 December and was last seen that evening off Wolf Rock, heading for her patrol area but failed to return as expected on 24 December, so must have been lost between those dates, either from a diving accident or from striking a mine. Four officers and twenty-nine men died.
[Evans p291]

25 December ROBIN river gunboat
Scotstoun 1934; 226 tons; 150ft × 26.8ft; 1 × 3.7in, 1 × 6pdr
Lieutenant Commander Hugh Monthermer Montague
Based at Hong Kong, she had been positioned in Aberdeen harbour, assisting ground forces by carrying out supporting bombardments. On 22 December she was damaged by splinters from an air-dropped bomb which landed nearby, but she continued to provide fire support. On 25 December it was clear that the colony would have to surrender, and at 15.20 she was taken to the south-east channel off Aberdeen and scuttled.
[TNA: ADM.199/357]

26 December Coastal Forces, Hong Kong, scuttling
With the Japanese now in control of Hong Kong, and two of the boats damaged following the action of 18/19 December, it was decided during 25 December that they should be scuttled. The following day all four surviving boats were taken to Mirs Bay (22.33N 114.26E) and scuttled, the bottom in each boat being attacked with hatchets, and the sea water intakes opened.

MTB 7 motor torpedo boat
Hythe 1937; 18 tons; 60.4ft × 13.10ft; 2 × torpedo tubes
Lieutenant Ronald Robert Wilson Ashby RNVR

MTB 9 motor torpedo boat
Hythe 1937; 18 tons; 60.4ft × 13.10ft; 2 × torpedo tubes
Lieutenant Alexander Kennedy RNVR

MTB 10 motor torpedo boat
Hythe 1937; 18 tons; 60.4ft × 13.10ft; 2 × torpedo tubes
Lieutenant Commander Gerard Horace Gandy

MTB 11 motor torpedo boat
Hythe 1937; 18 tons; 60.4ft × 13.10ft; 2 × torpedo tubes
Lieutenant Cuthbert John Collingwood

MTB 27 motor torpedo boat
Hampton 1938; 13 tons; 55ft × 11ft; 2 × torpedo tubes
Lieutenant Thomas Maurice Parsons RNVR
[TNA: ADM.267/131; Reynolds & Cooper, Mediterranean MTBs at War p175]

★ ★ ★

26 December Hong Kong – other vessels abandoned at the surrender:

WAVE tug
Hong Kong 1939; 300 tons; 120ft × 24.7ft
Recovered after the war and taken back into service as *Wavelet*.

MINNIE MOLLER tug
Trondheim 1909 (*Nidaros*) requisitioned 1941; 377 tons; 154.8ft × 25.3ft

Ships on the stocks, captured. Several ships were under construction and fell into Japanese hands.

LANTAU minesweeper
Kowloon incomplete; 673 tons; 171.5ft × 28.5ft
Completed by the Japanese in 1943 as the *Gyosei Maru*.

LYEMUN minesweeper
Kowloon incomplete; 673 tons; 171.5ft × 28.5ft
Her end is unclear. Most secondary sources indicate that she was completed in 1943 by the Japanese as the gunboat *Nanyo*, but this is uncertain.
[www.combinedfleet.com/nanyo_t.htm]

TAITAM minesweeper
Hong Kong incomplete; 673 tons; 171.5ft × 28.5ft
About 60 per cent complete, she was launched by the Japanese in February 1943 as minesweeper *W 101*. She was sunk by US Navy aircraft 12 January 1945.

WAGLAN minesweeper
Hong Kong incomplete; 673 tons; 171.5ft × 28.5ft
About 30 per cent complete, she was launched by
the Japanese in March 1943 as minesweeper *W 102*.
Returned to RN control in 1947.

GRINDER tug
Hong Kong; 300 tons; 120ft × 24.7ft
Found by the Japanese on the building stocks, she was
completed for their service as *Nagashima*.

Ships on the stocks: Vessels at an early stage of
construction, all were destroyed on the stocks.

MMS 95 / MMS 96 / MMS 123 / MMS 124 motor
minesweepers
Hong Kong (incomplete); 225 tons; 105ft × 23ft

ML 434 / ML 435 motor launches
Hong Kong (incomplete); 85 tons; 112ft × 18.4ft

MOORBERRY boom defence vessel
Hong Kong (incomplete); 1,000 tons; 149ft × 34ft

SKILFUL tug
Hong Kong (incomplete); 300 tons; 120ft × 24.5ft

★ ★ ★

26 December HENRIETTE trawler
Rotterdam 1906, seized 1940; 261 tons; 123.9ft × 22.5ft
Lieutenant Arthur Vibert Pearce RNR
Tasked to sweep the approaches to the Humber in
company with the trawlers *John Fitzgerald* and *Rolls-Royce*,
employing both acoustic and magnetic sweep gear. At
11.24 when 1.4 miles from Spurn light a mine detonated
about 40 yards on the starboard beam. The ship was shaken
badly, the steering gear was put out of action, the galley
stove fell apart and water started entering. The *Rolls-Royce*
came alongside and took off most of the crew and rigged
a tow. This went well until 12.20 when she started to
settle by the stern, and she foundered at 12.34, then being
2.4 miles from Spurn Light bearing 153 degrees.
[TNA: ADM.199/239]

30 December KUDAT auxiliary patrol vessel
Dundee 1914 (*Barima*) requisitioned 1941; 1,725 tons;
250.5ft × 37.1ft
Lieutenant Frederick William Jannings RNR
Acting as the base depot ship for landing craft and
other light craft at Port Swettenham, Malaya (now Port
Klang), she was ordered to lie up by day, but was caught
at sea in the South Klang Straits by Japanese aircraft and
bombed. She caught fire and eventually sank with two
men killed.
[The London Gazette 20 February 1948]

1942

(1–8) January TRIUMPH submarine
Barrow 1938; 1,090/1,575 tons; 265.6ft × 26.7ft; 1 × 4in,
10 × torpedo tubes
Lieutenant Commander John Symonds Huddart[†]
Sailed from Alexandria for a patrol in the Aegean on 26
December and last heard from on 30 December, when
she reported by radio that she had landed a raiding party
ashore on the island of Antiparos. She was then due to
patrol between 36–39N to 25E and then return on 9/10
January to pick them up, but she failed to appear. It is
presumed that she was lost by striking a mine, perhaps
in the vicinity of 37.36N 23.59E, where a minefield
was laid by the enemy on 6 January. Seven officers and
fifty-five men lost their lives.
[Evans p292; TNA: HS5 1524]

2 January DAISY tug
Requisitioned 1941
A locally-employed vessel in North Africa, she is
reported to have foundered on passage from Alexandria
to Tobruk because of heavy weather; there were no
casualties.
[TNA: ADM.199/2235]

9 January VIMIERA destroyer
Wallsend 1917; 1,090 tons; 300ft × 29.6ft; 4 × 4in,
2 × 20mm
Lieutenant Commander Angus Alexander MacKenzie RNR
Part of the escort to a North Sea convoy, FS39, she was
stationed on the port side of a line of ships as they headed
west in the Thames Estuary. Another convoy, CE63, had
also arrived, and some bunching was occurring as the
ships were funnelled into the swept channel between
the East Spile buoy and J buoy off Garrison Point,
Sheerness and the *Vimiera* was endeavouring to keep
some order amongst the stragglers. At 13.52 there was
a large explosion under the ship as a mine detonated
under the forward boiler room. Amidst a cloud of
smoke and water the ship rapidly broke in half under
the bridge. The bow section remained afloat and drifted
for some time before sinking in position 51.28.30N
00.55.09E but the stern half sank rapidly. The position
of the stern section was noted as being exposed at low
water at 51.28.16N 00.54.56E. Survivors were picked
up by other escort vessels, but ninety-three men were
killed. It was believed that she had probably strayed just
outside the swept channel.
[TNA: ADM.1/12017; ADM.199/221]

16 January KELANA auxiliary patrol vessel
Kuantan 1936 requisitioned 1939; 83 tons; 80ft × 18ft;
1 × 6pdr
Lieutenant Cyril Joseph Windsor RNVR

Formerly a private craft owned by Mr Windsor, who offered it to the Royal Navy at Singapore in December 1939. He was granted a commission in the Reserves at the same time, to remain in command. Apart from Windsor and one other British officer, all the crew were locally-employed Malays. It was stationed at Kuantan, on the north-eastern coast of Malaya, although in January 1942 she was moored in the Endau River where Windsor used his local knowledge to employ local people to gather intelligence on the advancing Japanese forces. Windsor was evidently rather eccentric and was regarded with some suspicion by local colonial police and planters. His activities resulted in a visit in January 1942 by a Superintendent O'Connell from Singapore, who arrived with several constables. O'Connell informed Windsor that he was urgently required in Singapore. With Windsor out of the way, the police started a search of the ship claiming that they had information that the ship was working for the Japanese. Having found no evidence, they then left. Windsor, on arrival in Singapore, finding that he had been tricked, attempted to return to Endau, but he failed to arrive before her demise. Japanese aircraft were making regular attacks on positions in the area, and the *Kelana* was an obvious target. Lieutenant Owen Henman RNVR had been left in charge and fought the ship. Although not directly hit, she was raked with machine-gun fire and suffered damage from near misses and bomb splinters and two ratings were killed by shrapnel. On 16 January, with the enemy approaching, and the damage preventing her being moved, Henman scuttled her at Anak Endau. She was later salvaged by the Japanese, to become *Sukei No8*.
[TNA:ADM.178/373]

16 January IRVANA trawler
Middlesbrough 1917 (*Arthur Lessimore*) requisitioned 1940; 276 tons; 125.5ft × 23.4ft; 1 × 12pdr
Skipper John Leador Borrett RNR

In company with two other minesweepers, the *Contender* and *Solon*, the *Irvana* was laying at anchor in Yarmouth road, near the North Corton buoy on the coast of Norfolk. The weather was hazy, with low cloud, when at 08.30 the ships prepared to weigh and proceed. Before this could be completed a single aircraft emerged from the low cloud on the starboard quarter and flew towards the ships. The aircraft, now identified as a Ju 88, singled out the *Irvana*, machine-gunning her as she closed and then released four bombs, one of which struck her, the others exploded all around her. The bomb that hit went through the starboard side and

exploded as it exited through the port side. The aircraft was engaged with a Lewis gun, but to no effect. The trawler heeled over and started to make water, with the fore peak and mess deck rapidly flooding. The *Solon* attempted to take her in tow, but efforts were hampered by the *Irvana*'s windlass being damaged, preventing her anchor being lifted, and she filled and sank at 09.00. There were no casualties.
[TNA:ADM.267/119]

17 January GURKHA destroyer
Govan 1937; 1,960 tons; 355.6ft × 36.6ft; 8 × 4.7in,
4 × 2pdr, 4 × torpedo tubes
Commander Charles Nugent Lentaigne DSO

As part of a major effort to re-supply Malta, several ships sailed from Alexandria on 16 January as Convoy MW8B which was to rendezvous with another group, MW8A, 2 days later. *Gurkha* was one of escorts to MW8B. At 07.39 in position 31.50N 26.14E, to the north of Bardia, there was a large explosion on the starboard side aft as she was hit by a torpedo. The damage was extensive: compartments abaft the engine room flooded, the upper deck was ruptured and distorted, the after superstructure collapsed and a fierce fire broke out, the seat of which was the cabin flat and, with the fire main ruptured, flames and thick choking smoke filled the ship which prevented access to the portable pump. The ship came to a stop, with a slight list to port. The after oil tanks caught fire and as oil poured out into the sea, to burn on the surface, the ready-use ammuntion started to 'cook' and explode in the heat. Efforts were made to jettison ammunition and close watertight doors, but it became clear that she would not survive. Very gallantly the Dutch destroyer *Isaac Sweers* closed to come alongside her fo'c'sle and rigged a tow to haul the ship out of the pool of burning oil and took off all her crew. The list steadily increased until she finally rolled over to port to lie on her beam ends before sinking stern first at 09.02. Nine men were lost. Her attacker had been *U 133* (Hesse).
[TNA:ADM.267/93]

17 January MATABELE destroyer
Greenock 1937; 1,960 tons; 355.6ft × 36.6ft; 6 × 4.7in,
2 × 4in, 4 × 2pdr, 4 × torpedo tubes
Commander Arthur Caerlyon Stanford DSC†

Acting as part of the escort to the Murmansk-bound Convoy PQ8, they had sailed from Hvalfjordur, Iceland, on 8 January. During 17 January they encountered the first of a three-strong U-boat pack, when at 20.00 the *U 454* (Hackländer) torpedoed a merchant ship in the convoy. Escaping detection, Hackländer conducted a second attack at 23.25. This time he found the *Matabele*, which was hit amidships by a single torpedo. She heeled over, but then righted herself to an even keel but was

shrouded in steam and smoke. About 2 minutes later there was a large explosion under the bridge. She broke in two, the forward end disappearing in a sheet of flame and as the smoke from the explosion cleared her stern could be seen standing vertically into the air before it sank into a large area of burning oil. The position was 68.21N 35.24E. The violence of the explosion and the freezing waters meant a high death toll; 236 men died, the minesweeper *Harrier* picking up just three survivors, one of whom later died. The most likely cause of the second explosion was thought to be the forward magazine exploding, possibly triggered by an oil vapour explosion from ruptured tanks.
[*TNA:ADM.1/11951*]

17 January   MTB 47   motor torpedo boat
Cowes 1941; 33 tons; 72ft × 18ft; 2 × torpedo tubes
Lieutenant William Ivan Cecil Ewart RNVR
Sailed from Dover in company with *MTB 35* and *MTB 44* to conduct a night patrol off Boulogne and intercept coastal shipping. The night was dark, with no moon and as they closed the French coast, firing could be heard to the north-east, and it was presumed that an enemy convoy was probably making passage along the coast in a south-west direction. They slowly made their way towards the disturbance in line ahead, *47* being the stern most ship. At 21.30 the dark shapes of ships could be made out closing from ahead, which opened fire on the leading torpedo boat. *47* left the line and manoeuvred to make a torpedo attack but as they closed, the target saw them and made a radical alteration of course, and the boat found herself uncomfortably close to the towed flak ship *SF110*, manned by the Luftwaffe. The latter was able to pour a large amount of 20mm fire into the torpedo boat at short range. She was almost immediately hit on the port side on the waterline; her steering gear broke down and a fire started in the engine room. Slowing to a halt, the crew successfully tackled the fire and rigged hand steering. The port and centre engines were found to be out of action, but the starboard engine was still working, and she got under way and turned to the north. As she did so she encountered another vessel, the trawler *Vp 1806*, which loomed out of the dark to open fire on the torpedo boat hitting her several times. She staggered clear but was filling with water and was clearly sinking and the crew took to the Carley float which was launched. Before leaving the bilges were flooded with petrol and despite being wounded Ewart was the last to leave, firing a flare into the engine room to start a fire. The following morning, they were picked up by the German coaster *Dorothea Weber* and made prisoners.
[*TNA:ADM.199/176; Reynolds & Cooper, Home Waters MTBs pp35–6*]

18 January   ERIN   trawler
Middlesbrough 1933 (*Sheffield Wednesday*) requisitioned 1940; 399 tons; 155ft × 26.4ft; 1 × 12pdr
Lieutenant William Graham Swanston RNVR
Moored alongside the main wharf at Gibraltar, with the trawler *Imperialist* inboard and the *Honjo* outboard of her, the trio were immediately astern of the aircraft carrier *Argus*. At 18.28 there was a tremendous explosion in the stern of the *Erin*, which disappeared in a huge cloud of flame and smoke. Both of the nearby trawlers were set on fire and debris was scattered across the dockyard and nearby ships, killing the officer of the watch on board the *Argus*. Fire crews from the dockyard and town attended the scene as did fire parties from other ships, but the *Erin* could not be saved and sank. The cause of the explosion was a time bomb placed among the depth charges by a saboteur, a Spanish agent working for the Germans. Three of *Erin*'s men lost their lives.
[*TNA:ADM.199/649*]

18 January   HONJO   trawler
Middlesbrough 1928 requisitioned 1940; 308 tons; 129.4ft × 24ft; 1 × 12pdr
Chief Skipper Joseph Bowie RNR
Moored outside the *Erin* at the main wharf, Gibraltar, when the latter exploded (see above), she was set on fire, burning fiercely from stem to stern. The efforts of the fire-fighting teams extinguished the blaze, but she was severely damaged, and written off as a constructive total loss. Two men were killed.
[*TNA:ADM.199/649*]

19 January   ROSEMONDE   trawler
Middlesbrough 1910 seized 1940; 364 tons; 147.6ft × 23ft
Lieutenant Kristian Galteland RNR†
Formerly the French *AD 70*, she had been taken over at Southampton in July 1940 and refitted as a minesweeper and initially served at Harwich. In January 1942 she was ordered to proceed to the Far East. She sailed from Milford Haven on 13 January in company with the *Lord Gray* and *Rosalind* but became separated from her companions in poor weather and failed to arrive at Gibraltar as expected. All twenty-five men on board were lost. The most likely cause of her loss was a torpedo attack by *U 581* (Pfeifer), which reported that at 23.00 on 19 January she had attacked what she believed was a corvette, 400 miles west of the Azores. One torpedo exploded amidships, and the target broke up and sank rapidly.
[*TNA:ADM.199/802; http://uboat.net/allies/merchants/ships/1277.html*]

22 January LARUT armed trader
Aberdeen 1927 requisitioned 1941; 839 tons;
214.4ft × 35.7ft; 1 × 4in
Lieutenant Commander Charles Edward Cleaver RNR
Larut was bombed by Japanese aircraft and burnt
out at Sabang, northern Sumatra. Captain Cleaver,
his officers and crew then set off to on foot, heading
south through Sumatra, before taking over a train, his
engineers managing to run it from Belawan to the
south, eventually crossing to Java.
[TNA: ADM.199/2235; London Gazette 31 January 1947]

22 January RAUB armed trader
Hong Kong 1926 requisitioned 1939; 1,161 tons;
232ft × 42.7ft; 1 × 4in
Lieutenant Francis George Ryland Lawes RNVR
Bombed by Japanese aircraft on 20 January near
Belawan, north-east Sumatra, and damaged. Repairs
were attempted alongside, but she was bombed again 2
days later and subsequently capsized.
[TNA: ADM.199/2235]

25 January ISLEFORD naval armaments carrier
Ardrossan 1918; 414 tons; 149.8ft × 25.6ft; 1 × 12pdr
Master David Andrew Kevern Foalle†
En-route from Scapa to Inverness carrying fired
cartridge cases and empty packages, she sailed at 09.00
on 24 January, in weather that was poor, and forecast to
worsen. By late evening it was blowing a gale from the
south-east, with heavy rain, and at 22.05 the coastguard
at Wick received reports that distress flares had been
seen to the south-west of the town. Over the next 40
minutes flares were regularly seen. The lifeboat could
not be launched due to the bad weather, but the lifesaving apparatus team were called out. At 23.57 a vessel
was sighted, rolling helplessly, evidently having lost
power and out of control. She was being driven towards
the north shore, frequently engulfed by large waves. At
00.34 she went onto rocks on the north shore of Wick
Bay; a searchlight from an army anti-aircraft battery was
employed to light the scene, which showed several men
huddled together in the wheelhouse. Soon after the
vessel struck, she started to break up, the forepart of the
ship forward of the mast being swept away. At 00.40 a line
carrying rocket was fired which went over a boat davit,
and although a man was seen attempting to secure it, the
ship was being constantly swept by heavy waves, and he
failed. More attempts were made, and the fourth rocket
placed a line over the mast, but despite more efforts by
the crew, they could not secure the line. The vessel was
rolling and pounding heavily and at 01.25 was swept by
a particularly heavy sea which washed several men away,
and at 01.40 the last survivor was seen to be carried away
by a large wave. All fifteen men on board died.
[TNA: ADM.1/19244]

26 January SHUN ON auxiliary patrol vessel
Shanghai 1916 requisitioned 1941; 116 tons; 86ft × 15ft
Lieutenant Owen Robert Templer Henman SSRNVR
Damaged by bombing at Endau, eastern Malaya, she
was abandoned as a constructive total loss.
Note: misspelled in *Statement of Losses* as 'Shun An'.
[Lloyd's War Losses p978; Statement of Losses p24]

26 January SIROCCO channel patrol boat
Sydney 1939 requisitioned 1941; 13 tons; 42ft × 12ft
Warrant Officer Robert Elmo Faliere Dale RANR
Royal Australian Navy. Serving as a tender to the shore
establishment at Hobart, Tasmania, she was destroyed by
an accidental fire.
[Cassells p68]

27 January THANET destroyer
Hebburn 1918; 905 tons; 265ft × 26.8ft; 3 × 4in, 1 × 2pdr,
4 × torpedo tubes
Commander Bernard Sydney Davies
The Japanese had commenced their landings in north-
east Malaya in early December, and by late January
were well advanced in their progress towards Singapore.
During the evening of 26 January, the destroyers *Thanet*
and HMAS *Vampire* were ordered to sail from Singapore
and sweep up the east coast to the vicinity of the port
of Endau, to locate and destroy enemy transport ships
reported in the area. At 02.37 as the pair neared the
location, in good weather with a bright moon, a ship,
identified as a Japanese destroyer was sighted, but fire
was withheld as they evidently had not been seen and
they hoped to find transport ships. A few minutes later
another destroyer was sighted, and they decided to
attack, and the *Vampire* fired two torpedoes, but both
missed. Still evidently undetected, they pressed on, but
finding no sign of transports they reversed course to
carry out a second torpedo attack on the destroyers. At
03.18 they sighted the two enemy vessels, but as they
closed and launched a full salvo of four torpedoes they
were seen and challenged by light. When these were
ignored, searchlights illuminated the *Thanet*, followed
by gunfire. *Thanet*, astern of *Vampire*, returned fire as the
pair increased speed and steered to the east to escape,
but after firing three salvos, she was hit by a shell which
penetrated the port side to burst in the engine room.
Both main and auxiliary steam pipes were severed, and
the ship gave a violent lurch, swung to starboard and
stopped. All lighting failed, and she was enveloped in
steam and smoke. Still under fire, she was unable to offer
any resistance and was ordered to be abandoned. The
Japanese noted that at 04.18 she rolled over and sank,
her position then being approximately 02.41N 103.47E.
Commander Davies and about sixty-five of her crew
made it to the shore by boat and float, and eventually
reached Singapore. A significant number, believed to be

thirty ratings, were picked by the destroyer *Shirayuki* and later handed over to the control of the Japanese army, who apparently killed them all some days later. A total of forty-two men died either in the sinking or at the hands of their captors.
[TNA: ADM.267/107]

29 January SOTRA whaler
Middlesbrough 1925 requisitioned 1939; 313 tons; 130.4ft × 26ft; 1 × 12pdr
Lieutenant Frederick Roy Linfield DSC†
In company with the corvette *Gloxinia* and the French ship *Viking*, she sailed from Tobruk bound for Alexandria, escorting empty store ships. At 21.46 when the group were off Bardia, in position 32.06N 25.31E there was a large explosion, and she sank within minutes with the loss of twenty-two men. The source of the explosion was uncertain at the time, both air-dropped and submarine-fired torpedoes were believed as the most likely cause. After the war it was revealed that she had been attacked by *U 431* (Dommes).
[TNA: ADM.199/650; ADM.199/802]

30 January LOCH ALSH trawler
Beverley 1926 (*Lady Madeleine*) requisitioned 1939; 358 tons; 140.4ft × 24ft; 1 × 12pdr
Skipper William Fairclough Wright RNR
When close to number 59 buoy, about 30 miles to the north-east of Skegness, she was attacked by a single Ju 88 aircraft, which closed from the port quarter to drop two bombs which exploded under her stern. Lifted out of the water by the blast, she was badly shaken; her propellers shattered and suffered considerable internal damage. Several rivets and plates were sprung, and she started making water. She was taken in tow but foundered before she could make the shelter of the Humber.
[TNA: ADM.267/119; Lloyd's War Losses vol 1 p344]

31 January CULVER cutter
Quincy 1928 (*Mendota*) transferred 1941; 1,975 tons; 236ft × 42ft; 1 × 5in, 2 × 3in, 2 × 6pdr
Lieutenant Commander Randall Thomas Gordon-Duff†
Part of the escort to Convoy SL98 that had sailed from Freetown on 15 January bound for Liverpool. When the ships were about 500 miles to the south-west of Ireland, in position 47.18N 20.51W, at 20.30 the Asdic operator reported HE (hydrophone-effect) on the port beam, and at the same time the officer of the watch saw the outline of a surfaced submarine. Despite an order to increase speed and put the helm over, the *Culver* was hit by two torpedoes, the first striking forward and the next aft. These were followed by a third explosion, either a magazine exploding or the boiler blowing up. There were further explosions as depth charges thrown

clear by the first hits detonated. The ship rolled over to starboard, broke up and sank very quickly, with only thirteen survivors, 136 men losing their lives. She had been torpedoed by *U 105* (Schuch).
[TNA: ADM.267/115]

31 January BELMONT destroyer
Newport News 1918 (*Satterlee*) transferred 1940; 1,190 tons; 311ft × 30.10ft; 3 × 4in, 1 × 3in, 6 × torpedo tubes
Lieutenant Commander Geoffrey Bransby O'Brien Harding†
In company with the destroyer *Firedrake*, sailed from Halifax, Nova Scotia on 30 January to escort two large troopships, the *Volendam* and *Largs Bay*, to the Clyde. The troopships steamed in line abreast with the destroyers on each flank, zigzagging independently. At 22.12 in approximate position 42.08N 57.26N, the officer of the watch on board the *Firedrake* heard two explosions from the other side of the line of ships but could see nothing in the gloom but a cloud of smoke. The convoy was immediately turned away to starboard as it was presumed that the *Belmont* was in contact with a submarine. That belief was bolstered 5 minutes later when more reports were heard, believed to be depth charges, and later flashes were seen. At 22.50 the convoy resumed their course, but the *Firedrake* was now anxious, as nothing had been heard from her consort. On enquiry, the ship that had been nearest to her, the *Largs Bay*, reported that she had also heard an explosion, and had seen the *Belmont* wreathed in smoke. It was then realised that she must have been torpedoed. The captain of *Firedrake* took the difficult decision to remain guarding the convoy rather than turn back to search for survivors, which would have left his charges exposed. This decision was backed by the Commander-in-Chief, Western Approaches. There were no survivors, all 138 men being lost. Her attacker had been *U 82* (Rollmann).
[TNA: ADM.237/12]

31 January UNICITY drifter
Lowestoft 1919 (*Bubble*) requisitioned 1939; 96 tons; 86.2ft × 18.5ft
Skipper James Murray RNR
Capsized and sank just after noon in position 55.00.50N 01.29.10W whilst returning to Blyth after completing minesweeping duties in the area. Nine men died, including the group officer, Lieutenant B M T Wallace RNVR, who was on board.
[TNA: ADM199/802; ADM.358/3586]

2 February CAPE SPARTEL trawler
Selby 1929 requisitioned 1939; 346 tons; 140.4ft × 24ft; 1 × 12pdr
Lieutenant John Richard Grundy RNR
In company with three other armed trawlers, *Arctic Hunter*, *Nab Wyke* and *Remexo*, the group were engaged

Campbeltown lodged against the caisson at St Nazaire. (*Imperial War Museum*)

Right: The scene onboard *Breconshire*, set on
fire after bombing off Grand Harbour, Malta.
(*Imperial War Museum*)

Left: Submarine *P 36*, sunk by air attack in Grand Harbour,
Malta, is brought to the surface during salvage operations.
(*Imperial War Museum*)

Cornwall under air attack listing to starboard and sinking. (*Imperial War Museum*)

Eridge showing the hole in the starboard side caused by a torpedo hit. (*Imperial War Museum*)

Coventry on fire after being attacked by dive bombers in the Mediterranean. (*Imperial War Museum*)

Hartland on fire and sinking in Oran harbour. (*Imperial War Museum*)

D–Day: an unidentified landing craft burning after being hit by shore fire off Sword Beach, Normandy. (*Imperial War Museum*)

Fury on the beach after being driven ashore at Arromanches. (*Imperial War Museum*)

Nabob down by the stern after being torpedoed. (*Imperial War Museum*)

Bickerton dead in the water after she had been hit by a homing torpedo. (*Imperial War Museum*)

LCG(M) 101 being abandoned before sinking during the landings at Walcheren. (*Imperial War Museum*)

Minesweeper *Squirrel* at the moment of striking a mine. (*Imperial War Museum*)

Truculent breaks surface during salvage operations. (*British Pathé*)

Saumarez low in the water after being mined in the Corfu Channel. (*Illustrated London News – Mary Evans*)

Berkeley Castle on her side at Sheerness after tidal surge. (*Keystone Pictures USA – Zumapress – Mary Evans*)

Sidon on the surface in Portland harbour after being raised. (*British Pathé*)

A victim of Argentine air attack, the *Coventry* rolls over to port before sinking. (*Imperial War Museum*)

Antelope burning following a fatal bomb explosion; her magazines later detonated. (*Imperial War Museum*)

in sweeping to the east of the Humber. At 14.10, then being one mile off 62 buoy an aircraft was seen closing from the starboard quarter. Alarms were sounded as the aircraft, identified as an Me 110, circled the group before delivering a shallow dive attack on the *Cape Spartel*. Four bombs were dropped which straddled the ship, which engaged the attacker with her guns and fired PAC rockets. The aircraft then circled around to carry out a second attack from the starboard beam. Four bombs were dropped which exploded all around her, one particularly close to the starboard quarter. This caused considerable shock damage, and soon after water was reported to be entering the engine room. At 14.35 the boat was hoisted out and the *Arctic Hunter* closed as she sank, her position being noted as 53.28.42N 00.49.12E; all the crew were saved.

[TNA:ADM.267/119]

2 February CLOUGHTON WYKE trawler

Selby 1918 (*John Johnson*) requisitioned 1939; 324 tons; 138.5ft × 23.7ft; 1 × 12pdr
Skipper Charles Seymour Larter RNR
In company with other trawlers, she sailed from Gorleston to commence a sweep off Cromer. The weather was poor, with a choppy sea, low clouds and occasional rain showers. During the morning she became separated from her companions when she developed a mechanical defect, and whilst lying stationary in position 52.59N 01.28.30E an aircraft, identified as an Fw 200, emerged from the cloud to run straight at them dropping four bombs. All missed, but the aircraft circled around to conduct a second run, again releasing several bombs. Although there were no direct hits, one bomb exploded close under the stern and she sank quickly, the bows rising out of the water. Four men were killed.

[Personal recollection from a survivor: http://www.bbc.co.uk/ww2peopleswar/stories/76/a4183076.shtml]

2 February VAILLANT tug

Renfrew 1887 requisitioned 1941; 111 tons; 100ft × 18ft
Sub-Lieutenant John Easton Niels Carter RNR
Based at Tobruk, she was damaged by enemy action, and written off as a total loss.
[TNA:ADM.199/802; FO.371/41407]

5 February ARBUTUS corvette

Blyth 1940; 940 tons; 190ft × 33ft; 1 × 4in
Lieutenant Arthur Lionel Waldegrave Warren DSC RNR†
Part of the escort to Atlantic Convoy ON63 that had sailed from Liverpool on 2 February. At 19.20 the destroyer *Chelsea* in company with *Arbutus*, was detached to investigate a radio transmission from a submarine, detected by HF/DF (high frequency direction finding) on the starboard quarter of the convoy. At 19.50 the

Arbutus gained a radar contact at 3,000 yards and 5 minutes later sighted a submarine on the surface. The escorts increased speed and headed towards the submarine which was seen to dive as they approached. Asdic contact was gained and the *Arbutus* ran over the datum point to drop a pattern of depth charges, although some detonated immediately on entering the water, causing shock damage to the corvette, putting her out of action for several minutes before order was restored. The *Chelsea* and *Arbutus* commenced an Asdic search of the area, but although some brief contacts were gained, none of them could be held. At 21.30 the pair decided to return to the convoy, but at 21.38 the corvette was hit by a torpedo on the starboard side, exploding abreast the foremost bulkhead of number 1 boiler room. The submarine broached immediately after firing, and the *Chelsea* engaged her with gunfire and then carried out an immediate attack dropping depth charges. This was followed by a further two attacks, but no result was obvious. The corvette had been virtually broken in half, with the forward section of the ship being wrecked and she was wreathed in clouds of steam from broken pipes. She steadily settled, rolled over to starboard and had disappeared in 30 minutes, her position being 55.51N 19.15W. Forty-three men died. The submarine had been the *U 136* (Zimmerman), which escaped the counter-attacks.

[TNA:ADM.199/802]

5 February BOY PETER auxiliary

14 tons requisitioned
Listed in the *Statement of Losses* as being lost by fire but with no further details of the incident or the vessel have been found – possibly the motor boat listed as being stationed at Pembroke Dock in 1942
[Statement of Losses p24]

9 February HERALD survey ship

Blyth 1918 (*Merry Hampton*); 1,320 tons; 255ft × 35ft
Paid off in July 1939, she was laid up in reserve at Seletar, Singapore. As the Japanese army advanced and the harbour came under air attack, she was scuttled in the harbour. She was later salvaged and entered Japanese service as the *Heiyo*.
Note: the loss was omitted from *British Vessels Lost at Sea*.
[Various secondary]

10 February SPIKENARD corvette

Lauzon 1940; 940 tons; 190ft × 33ft; 1 × 4in, 1 × 2pdr
Lieutenant Commander Hubert George Shadforth, RCNR†
Royal Canadian Navy. Sailed from Sydney, Nova Scotia, 2 February as part of the escort to Convoy SC67 bound for Liverpool. During the night of 10/11 February the convoy came under submarine attack. *Spikenard* was

ahead of the starboard column of ships when the first attack materialised, when at 21.20 another escort, on the opposite side of the convoy, the corvette *Chilliwack*, sighted a submarine submerging and carried out a depth-charge attack on an Asdic contact. At 21.33 the merchant ship *Heina* was hit by a torpedo, and 2 minutes later the *Spikenard* was hit on the port side amidships. Her attacker was *U 136* (Zimmerman), who reported hitting a freighter first and then targeting a corvette immediately afterwards, the warship being covered in an enormous fiery glow and then sinking bows first. There was much confusion in the convoy after the attacks, and other escorts were uncertain how many ships had been hit. It was not until the morning that it was established that *Spikenard* was missing. The corvette *Gentian* was then despatched to search for survivors, and they found a raft with eight men, the only survivors; fifty-seven men died.
[Morgan & Taylor p205]

11 February **MAORI** destroyer
Govan 1937; 1,960 tons; 355.6ft × 36.6ft; 6 × 4.7in, 2 × 4in, 6 × 2pdr, 4 × torpedo tubes
Commander Ronald McLelland Powning Jonas
Stationed in the Mediterranean, she was moored at number 3 buoy in Grand Harbour, Malta, when the island came under air attack. At 01.15 she was hit by a single bomb which penetrated the upper deck to explode in the after end of the engine room, on the port side. The force of the explosion opened up the bulkhead between the engine room and the gearing room. The lubricating oil in the gearing room, about 2,000 gallons, caught fire and this spread to the midships fuel tanks. This effectively cut off the after part of the ship from the fore part. As the accommodation for the officers was aft, it meant that they were unable to direct any fire-fighting efforts. They, with a handful of ratings, gathered on the quarterdeck from where they were taken off by boats from the cruiser *Penelope* and destroyer *Decoy*, Commander Jonas going to the latter. However, two of the officers, Lieutenant Kenneth Innes-Hamilton, the First Lieutenant, and Lieutenant Commander Eric Michell, the engineer officer, decided to jump into the sea and then swim forward to climb inboard over the boom. They were then able to lead fire-fighting efforts. The fires however spread, and it was found that the fire main was out of action and hand pumps were inadequate. By the time a pump had been rigged it was too late, and she was ordered to be abandoned. Shortly after this order, about an hour after the bomb hit, there was a large explosion, probably the 4in magazine blowing up. The ship then sank, still moored to the buoy, her bows clear of the water. As she sank blazing fuel oil spread across the harbour, and this was not finally extinguished until 04.00. As many of the crew were sleeping ashore, the casualties were light, with two men being killed. The subsequent enquiry praised

the efforts to fight the fire, but were critical of the actions of Commander Jonas, who had remained on board the *Decoy* trying to organise assistance, whilst the First Lieutenant had stayed on board the burning destroyer. The Commander-in-Chief of the Mediterranean Fleet, Admiral Cunningham, thought he had been 'gravely at fault' for failing to make every endeavour to return and take charge. Lieutenant Commanders Innes-Hamilton and Michell were subsequently awarded the Distinguished Service Cross.
[TNA:ADM.178/280]

11 February **BOY ROY** drifter
Requisitioned 1941; 20 tons
Listed as being lost, 'cause and place unknown'; no further details of the vessel or cause have been found, but she is known to have been based at Loch Alsh.
[Statement of Losses p23]

11 February **LIPIS** armed trader
Greenock 1927 requisitioned 1939; 845 tons; 214.3ft × 35.6ft; 1 × 4in
Lieutenant William Edward Steel RNR[†]
Attacked by three Japanese aircraft when off Sultan Shoal, Singapore, the *Lipis* was damaged, and when the steering gear failed and with fires out of control the order to abandon ship was given, her commanding officer having been killed. She was later salvaged by the Japanese and towed into Singapore in a burnt-out condition, and eventually entered Japanese service as the *Risui Maru*.
[TNA:ADM.1/18479; Lloyd's War Losses vol 1 p1003]

11 February **PENGHAMBAT** motor launch
Singapore 1942; 60 tons; 76.5ft × 13.5ft; 1 × 3pdr
Lieutenant Frank Otto Stoe Man SSRNVR
After conducting several local patrols, she had returned from escorting a tug and lighter to Pulau Tekong and secured alongside Telok Ayer Basin, Singapore, when the dockyard became the target for an air raid. At 13.00 during one of these raids, she was damaged by a near miss, being peppered above and below the waterline with shrapnel, reducing her to a sinking condition. As it was clear that due to the rapid Japanese advance that she would not be able to be salvaged, she was stripped of all useful stores and at 16.00 she was scuttled.
[TNA:ADM.267/131; http://manfamily.org/PDFs/EVACUATION%20OF%20SINGAPORE.pdf]

13 February **TEMPEST** submarine
Birkenhead 1941; 1,090/1,575 tons; 263ft × 26.7ft; 1 × 4in, 11 × torpedo tubes
Lieutenant Commander William Alexander Keith Napier Cavaye[†]
Ordered to conduct a patrol in the Gulf of Taranto, she sailed from Malta 10 February. The following day, in

approximate position 39.20N 17.25E she sighted an Italian tanker, but recognised her as being the *Lucania*, which had been granted safe conduct through the area. However, the submarine *Una*, in the adjacent patrol area, not recognising her, carried out a successful torpedo attack. This brought a flurry of activity, with several Italian surface ships searching for the culprit. The night of 12/13 January saw the *Tempest* on the surface, recharging batteries, and the burning remains of the tanker could still be seen on the horizon. At 03.00, then being about 12 miles to the south-east of the wreck, they sighted an Italian torpedo boat closing and dived. The torpedo boat was the *Circe*, and although they had not seen the submarine, her hydrophone operator heard the noise of her diving, and she gained a sonar contact at 1,700 yards. At 03.32 she ran over the position and dropped several depth charges. These put out several lights, broke glass fittings and damaged a propeller shaft. Poor weather prevented the *Circe* from conducting a second attack but spent the next 4 hours regularly running over the position of the dived submarine, confirming her position by sonar. At 07.16 a second depth-charge attack was carried out, and a third followed at 07.55. These brought oil and air bubbles to the surface. The *Tempest* had indeed been damaged, with fittings smashed, oil tanks split, and she became increasingly difficult to control. At 09.17 the *Circe* carried out another depth-charge attack, which proved fatal. The battery boards burst open releasing chlorine gas, and as they could not survive this, the submarine was brought, with some difficulty, to the surface, which was achieved at 09.49. As they did so, the *Circe* opened fire with small arms, but when it was realised that she was being abandoned, firing was stopped. The crew from the *Tempest* abandoned her, with her motors still going ahead, but the planes set to dive, although these were seen to be damaged. The *Circe* spent some time picking up the survivors, and although all the men exited the boat, several drifted away in the heavy seas. Despite efforts to scuttle the submarine, she remained stubbornly afloat, and by 12.15, with no more survivors left to pick up, a small party from the *Circe* tried to get on board, but the high seas prevented this, and despite firing a dozen shells into her, she remained on the surface, although her stern was under water. At 14.30, with the weather moderating, another attempt was made to put a boarding party on the *Tempest*, and this time it was successful, and a tow was rigged. At 16.05, just as the *Circe* took up the strain of the tow, the stern of the submarine went under, and her bows reared up out of the water, and she sank stern first, the Italian seamen on board having to jump into the sea. Three officers and twenty men were saved, with two officers and thirty-seven men being lost.
[*Evans pp293–300*]

13 February MMS 180 minesweeper
Grimsby 1941; 225 tons; 105ft × 23ft
Newly built, she was on passage in a convoy from the builder's yard at Grimsby to Methil, when she was rammed by one of the other ships at 22.05 near number 20A buoy at the entrance to the Tyne. She eventually foundered at 04.45. There were no casualties.
[*TNA:ADM.199/802*]

13–18 February: The Evacuation of Singapore

The Japanese armed forces had staged a successful landing in northern Malaya on 8 December 1941 and made a rapid advance south towards Singapore. By the first week in February the city was being subjected to regular air raids and artillery fire. On 8 February, the invaders successfully crossed the Johore Straits to land on Singapore Island. With defeat inevitable the evacuation of the European civilian population started, and later military and naval personnel were ordered to leave. A wide range of merchant and naval shipping was employed, but with the Japanese having complete air and naval supremacy, many of the vessels were lost.
Note: the evacuation became increasingly disorganised, and the details of some losses are both unclear and disputed, with accounts from survivors sometimes contradicting each other. The dates and details below are hoped to be correct.

13 February SIANG WO auxiliary patrol vessel
Hong Kong 1926 requisitioned 1940; 2,595 tons; 275ft × 46.1ft; 1 × 4in
Lieutenant Commander Archie Woodley RNR
Loaded with personnel escaping from Singapore, she left the harbour during the evening of 12 February but the following morning she was subjected to repeated air attacks. At 16.30 with steering gear out of action, she was run aground on the north-west corner of Banka Island, not far from Muntok lighthouse and became a total loss. Three men were killed; the remainder were taken into captivity.
[*TNA:ADM.1/18479; Lloyd's War Losses vol 1 p823; Shores & Cull p86*]

13 February GIANG BEE auxiliary patrol vessel
Rotterdam 1908 (*Reijnierz*) requisitioned 1939; 1,646 tons; 270.5ft × 40.3ft; 1 × 4in
Lieutenant Samuel Kenneth Rayner SSRNVR†
Having landed all the locally-employed crewmen, and embarking over 300 men, women and children escaping from the colony, with several soldiers, some of them volunteering to assist as stokers and deck hands, she sailed from Singapore at 22.00 on 12 February. The

hope was to reach Java, but the following morning she came under air attack. With the old vessel manoeuvring as fast as she could, no hits were obtained, passengers manning machine guns to reply. Later that day the aircraft returned, and this time she was not so lucky, being hit by two bombs which penetrated the upper deck and exploded in the lower decks, killing two passengers and wounding many more. The ship remained structurally sound, however, and although she came under further air attacks, she escaped further damage. As dusk was falling, ships were seen on the horizon, and they could be seen to be a cruiser with destroyers. They closed, and two shots were fired across the bows which brought them to a halt, it being decided to anchor as they did so. The cruiser and one destroyer then moved off to the north, but the destroyers *Asagiri* and *Fubuki*, stayed close by. Attempts were made to communicate by light, but they could not understand the replies. By 19.30 it was understood that the passengers should leave the ship, and this was started, the scene now being lit by searchlights from the destroyers. The boats, when loaded, headed for the nearby shore. After 3 hours of this, and although all the boats had gone, and with many people assembled on the upper deck, the destroyers opened fire. Only six rounds seem to have been fired, but all hit her, and immediately started a fire. The remaining people were forced to jump into the sea as the ship continued to burn until she sank. One boatload of survivors successfully made it to Bangka and a second landed in Sumatra. Seventeen members of the crew were killed and approximately 200 passengers lost their lives.
[TNA: CO.980/233]

13 February **HUA TONG** auxiliary minesweeper
Hong Kong 1927 requisitioned 1939; 280 tons;
139.7ft × 26.2ft; 1 × 12pdr
Lieutenant Charles Lloyd Brown RNR
In company with the auxiliaries *Klias* and *Jerantut*, she successfully escaped from Singapore on 7 February, reaching Palembang, Sumatra. The Dutch authorities then ordered that they should proceed to Tandjong Priok, but as they were leaving the harbour, they had barely cleared the mouth of the river, when they were attacked by six Japanese aircraft. A near miss caused the windlass to malfunction, and both anchors ran out. Another near miss wrecked the steering gear and put the lights out. Now helpless, unable to manoeuvre, she was a sitting target, and took a direct hit, a bomb exploding by number 1 hatch. The forward bulkhead gave way and the ship rapidly flooded. She heeled over to port and sank. Lieutenant James Tongue RNVR was subsequently awarded the DSO for remaining at his post by the gun, although wounded, maintaining fire until the gun was dismantled. Casualties are uncertain.
[TNA: ADM.1/12244; London Gazette 25 August 1942]

13 February **HDML 1096** motor launch
Singapore 1941; 46 tons; 70ft × 15ft; 1 × 3pdr
Lieutenant Jack Gifford RNZVR
Fitting out at Singapore, the launch was incomplete when the arrival of the Japanese army was imminent. At 14.00 on 12 February, she was taken in tow by the tug *Trebova*, along with the *Panglima*, hoping to reach Batavia (Djakarta). Little headway was made however, and during the afternoon of 13 February she was scuttled.
[TNA: ADM.267/131]

13 February **PANGLIMA** motor launch
Singapore 1939; 60 tons; 76.5ft × 13.5ft; 1 × 3pdr
Lieutenant Harry Gordon Greatorex Riches SSRNVR
Along with *HDML 1096* (see above), taken in tow by the tug *Trebova*, leaving Singapore on 12 February she was also abandoned and scuttled as little progress had been made.
[TNA: ADM.267/131]

13 February **SCORPION** river gunboat
Cowes 1937; 670 tons; 200ft × 34.8ft; 2 × 4in, 1 × 3.7in, 2 × 3pdr
Lieutenant Commander George Christian Ashworth SSRNVR†
Built for service on the river Yangtze, following the Japanese incursions into China, she had moved to Singapore. During the first week of February, she had been employed in evacuating troops from the west coast of Malaya, but during 9 February as she was heading back to Singapore, she came under air attack and received a hit from a small bomb forward. This had penetrated the fore deck and partly exploded in the cabin flat below, starting a fire which destroyed forty rounds of 4in ammunition in the ready-use locker before being extinguished. She reached Keppel Harbour the following day, and still with her damage unrepaired was ordered to sail for Batavia after refuelling. After some delay, she finally departed at 18.00 on 11 February, with thirty-eight extra personnel embarked in addition to her normal crew. She proceeded to the island of Singkep Laut where she lay up during the following day, remaining undetected, raising anchor at 18.30 that evening. At 19.30 the sound of gunfire could be heard, and at 20.15 a large ship, identified as a cruiser along with two destroyers, was seen close ahead. Soon after this she was illuminated by a searchlight and then came under fire. The *Scorpion*, although clearly outclassed, returned fire, but was soon hit amidships. The main steam pipe in the engine room was fractured and all the engine room staff were killed or injured. Soon after this she was hit again forward, which started a fire. She slowly came to a halt, and the crew were ordered to abandon her. An attempt was made to lower the whaler, but this

immediately sank, evidently having been holed. Carley floats carried on board were successfully launched and with the gunboat now burning fiercely, the men jumped into the water. The enemy continued to fire into her, until she rolled over and sank by the bows. Her position was approximately 01S 104.40E. Seventy men were lost with forty-four survivors. Her assailants had been the cruiser *Yuru* and destroyers *Fubuki* and *Asagiri*.
[TNA:ADM.1/19288]

14 February ST BREOCK tug
Hong Kong 1919; 860 tons; 135.5ft × 29.1ft; 1 × 12pdr
Skipper Joseph Jappy RNR

Escaped from Singapore during the night of 12 February, towing four lighters loaded with ammunition, but two of these broke free during the night and were abandoned. Having laid up close inshore during the day, they again got underway in the evening of 13 February, losing another lighter as they did so. At first light on 14 February, when they were close to Singkep Island, Sumatra, the last lighter broke her tow, with the tow rope fouling the screw of the tug. It took 2 hours to clear the obstruction, and during this time two Japanese aircraft flew close overhead. As the tug was manoeuvring to pick up the drifting lighter the aircraft returned and attacked, each dropping a single bomb. All attempts to recover the tow were abandoned and she made for the shoreline at full speed but came under repeated strafing and bombing attack from the aircraft. A bomb exploded close under the starboard bow and she started to sink, bows first, and boats and rafts were released as she was abandoned. All the crew survived the attack and made it to the shore and eventually reached a Dutch settlement. One man, Chief Petty Officer Vernon, was found clinging to the wreckage by the gunboats *Dragonfly* and *Grasshopper* later that day and was picked up by the latter, only to be sunk again later.
[TNA:ADM.199/622A; http://users.tpg.com.au/borclaud/ranad/singapore_story.html]

14 February DRAGONFLY river gunboat
Woolston 1938; 625 tons; 190ft × 33.8ft; 2 × 4in, 1 × 3.7in
Commander Alfred William Sprott†

Stationed in the Far East, she and her sister *Grasshopper* were at Singapore as the Japanese advanced towards that port. Having embarked a party of about fifty soldiers from the Manchester Regiment and a reconnaissance unit, the pair sailed from Keppel Harbour at 01.00 on 14 February. They steamed through the night, but at 08.00 a Japanese floatplane flew overhead, which then carried out two bombing attacks, which caused no damage. The pair pressed on and deciding that it would be better if they lay up out of sight, they headed towards Sinkep Island. At 11.30 when about 2 miles off the island they found a patch of wreckage which

proved to be the site of the sinking of the tug *St Breock* (q.v.). Just before noon when off Rusuk Buaja Island a large number of Japanese aircraft appeared which commenced an attack. *Dragonfly* was hit at least three times, caught fire, rolled over and sank. One boat and a Carley float were launched before she sank, the survivors being taken prisoner by the Japanese. Three officers and twenty-nine ratings were lost, with several of the passengers.
[TNA:ADM.267/122]

14 February GRASSHOPPER river gunboat
Woolston 1939; 625 tons; 190ft × 33.8ft; 2 × 4in, 1 × 3.7in
Commander Jack Sanler Hoffman

Based at Singapore, the gunboat sailed at 01.00 on 14 February in company with her sister *Dragonfly* (see above). She embarked about fifty passengers, including a party of Japanese prisoners of war, with the intention of making Batavia (Djakarta). At about 12.00 they came under attack from a large group of Japanese aircraft which sank the *Dragonfly*, but the *Grasshopper* escaped the initial attacks. The *Grasshopper* was constantly manoeuvring, waiting until an aircraft committed itself to a dive, and then making a drastic alteration of course. After numerous attacks, all of which were foiled, she was finally hit by a single bomb which exploded in the after mess deck and started a fire. Attempts were made to flood the after magazine, but they failed as the control valve had been damaged. Fearing that the magazine might explode she was run inshore and beached in shallow water off Rusuk Buaja Island. When all the surviving crew were safely ashore, a camp was set up and Lieutenant Ian Forbes in company with Chief Petty Officer Vernon, the survivor from *St Breock*, were sent to try and contact the Dutch. After an epic journey, swimming, walking and using local boats they eventually made it to safety and allowed a rescue attempt to be made. Twenty men were lost. Commander Hoffman survived, only to be killed when he was taking passage in the destroyer *Stronghold* (q.v.)
[TNA:ADM.1/19493; ADM.267/122]

14 February KUALA auxiliary patrol vessel
Dundee 1911 requisitioned 1939; 954 tons;
225.2ft × 35.6ft; 1 × 4in
Lieutenant Franklin Caithness RNR

Having survived earlier bombing attacks, the *Kuala* arrived at Singapore on 13 February, embarked about 500 men, women and children and that night, in company with the *Hung Jao*, sailed for Sumatra. The following morning *Kuala* took shelter close to Pompong Island in company with other escaping ships, the *Tien Kwang* and *Kung Wo*. At about 10.00 a large number of Japanese aircraft appeared and commenced an attack on the ships. After initially attacking the *Kung Wo* they turned their

attentions to the *Kuala*. She was hit by three bombs, the first struck the bridge and others penetrated to the stokehold and engine room. She caught fire, rolled over and sank. Hundreds of survivors were left struggling in the water as the air attacks continued, with only about 150 making it to the shore. Many of these were later taken on board steamer *Tandjong Pinang*, which was sunk on the 17th. Only three survivors from *Kuala* survived this second sinking. About seventy others were rescued by a local fishing craft commandeered for use by other escaping refugees. Just how many people lost their lives in *Kuala* is uncertain, but would seem to be about 350, the majority civilian refugees.
[http://www.navyhistory.org.au/the-loss-of-hms-kuala-1942; Shores & Cull p82; http://www.bbc.co.uk/ww2peopleswar/ stories/55/a7697055.shtml]

14 February SHU KWANG auxiliary patrol vessel
Glasgow 1924 requisitioned 1941; 732 tons;
198.7ft × 32.9ft; 1 × 4in
Commander Alexander Duff Thomson DSO RNR
With 270 evacuees embarked, she sailed from Singapore at 01.20 on 14 February, aiming to escape to Sumatra. The following afternoon at 13.40, when in position 00.25N 104E, she was attacked by several Japanese aircraft. Hit several times, eleven men were killed, and several were injured, and the engine and boiler rooms were damaged which resulted in a loss of steam pressure. An hour later the aircraft returned, and this time the raid resulted in the engine room being wrecked and the vessel being holed on the starboard side. At 15.45 she was abandoned as she sank, the *Tengaroh* and *Hung Jao* taking off the survivors.
[TNA: ADM.267/131]

14 February CHANGTEH auxiliary minesweeper
Shanghai 1914 requisitioned 1939; 244 tons; 140ft × 26ft
Lieutenant James Craig SSRNVR
With a large number of evacuees embarked, many of them RAF personnel, she escaped from Singapore late in the evening on 13 February and headed for Sumatra. At 12.00 the following day she was attacked by five aircraft in the Rhio Straits. Although she received no direct hits, she was shaken when a large bomb near-missed her. The shock of the explosion cut the steam pipes near the boiler and she came to a stop. Unable to move, and still under air attack, boats and floats were launched and she was abandoned, sinking a few minutes later with heavy loss of life.
[TNA: ADM.267/131]

14 February VYNER BROOKE armed trader
Leith 1928 requisitioned 1941; 1,670 tons; 240.7ft × 41.3ft;
1 × 4in
Lieutenant Richard Edward Borton RNR
On the evening of 12 February *Vyner Brooke* was one of the last ships carrying evacuees to leave Singapore, having 181 passengers embarked, most of them women and children. Among the passengers were sixty-five Australian nurses. Throughout the daylight hours of 13 February *Vyner Brooke* laid up in the lee of a small jungle-covered island, but she sailed that evening, heading for the Banka Strait, hoping to reach Palembang in Sumatra. The following day she had little choice but to press on, although very conscious of being dangerously exposed. In the early afternoon, at about 14.00 she was approached by six twin-engined Japanese aircraft, which attacked in pairs. Her zigzagging successfully allowed her to avoid the initial attacks, but the final aircraft dropped a bomb which entered number 2 hatch and exploded in the hold. Another attack then developed, with several other bombs exploding nearby and a further two bombs hit her. About 30 minutes after the initial attack, she rolled over and sank. Approximately 150 survivors eventually made it ashore at Bangka Island, after periods of between 8 and 60 hours in the water. The island had already been occupied by the Japanese and most of the survivors were taken captive. For those that had landed on Radji beach, they joined other civilians and about sixty Commonwealth servicemen and merchant sailors, who had made it ashore after their own vessels were sunk. A short time later a party of Japanese troops arrived at Radji Beach, who shot and bayoneted the males and then forced twenty-two Australian nurses and one British civilian woman to wade into the sea, then shot them. There were only two survivors from the atrocity – Sister Vivian Bullwinkel, and Private Cecil Kinsley, a British soldier. After hiding in the jungle for several days the pair eventually gave themselves up to the Japanese. Kinsley died a few days later from his wounds, and Bullwinkel spent the rest of the war as an internee.
[TNA: CO.980/233; ADM.267/131; www.awm.gov.au/units/ events_301.asp]

14 February ML 310 motor launch
Singapore 1941; 75 tons; 112ft × 18.4ft; 1 × 3pdr
Lieutenant Herbert John Bull SSRNVR
During the afternoon of 13 February, the launch sailed from Singapore having embarked several officers and personnel, including Admiral Ernest Spooner (Rear Admiral, Malaya) and Air Vice Marshal Conway Pulford (AOC Far East). It was intended to make for Batavia (Djakarta), via Bangka Island, lying up during the day to avoid air attack. That evening they ran aground after suffering a steering gear breakdown, but a passenger, Lieutenant Pool volunteered to go in to the water to assist in clearing her, but badly cut his hand in doing so. They got under way in the early hours and continued until 10.00 where it was decided to lay up for the day in the shelter of an island. They again moved on during the night, to make it to Seven Brothers' island, about

30 miles to the north-east of Bangka to again lie up for the day. However, Lieutenant Pool was now seriously ill, with his hand turning septic, so it was decided to press on in daylight to try and reach safety and gain medical attention. However, at 14.30 they sighted a group of cruisers and destroyers and turned inshore. They were pursued by the destroyers, and the cruisers launched aircraft which bombed them. They ran into shallow waters until she grounded on Tjebia Island. One of the destroyers, the *Fubuki*, continued to close, and then sent a party on board the launch where they destroyed the lubricating system of the engines, before making off. The following morning a Japanese seaplane appeared which machine-gunned and bombed the grounded launch. The party set up a camp ashore with stores salvaged from the wreck of the launch. On 20 February, a small party led by Lieutenant Bull left on a local boat to try and bring assistance; they were picked up a week later by an Australian corvette and a rescue attempt was mounted by the US submarine *S-39*, but it failed to locate any survivors. Those left on the island became ill and during March and April several died, including Admiral Spooner and Air Vice Marshall Pulford. On 15 May the survivors used a local boat and made it to a former Dutch island where they surrendered to the Japanese.
[TNA: ADM.1/24307; ADM.1/18261; Shores & Cull p81]

14 February KUNG WO auxiliary minelayer
Hong Kong 1921 requisitioned 1940; 4,636 tons; 350ft × 48.5ft; 2 × 4in, 240 mines
Lieutenant Edward James Thomson RNR
Escaped from Singapore but attacked and damaged by Japanese air attack when about 6 miles north-west of Pompong Island, near the Lingga Archipelago, 80 miles to the south of Singapore. She was run inshore into shallow water and abandoned. One man was killed.
[TNA: ADM.1/18479; http://www.navyhistory.org.au/the-loss-of-hms-kuala-1942/]

14 February LI WO auxiliary minesweeper
Hong Kong 1938 requisitioned 1940; 707 tons; 163.8ft × 30.1ft; 1 × 4in, 1 × 3pdr
Lieutenant Thomas Wilkinson RNR†
At 03.00 she sailed from Singapore, with a mix of survivors from various ships, locally-employed Malay and Chinese ratings plus army and Air Force personnel, with orders to escape to Batavia via the Banka Straits. That afternoon she was subjected to a high-level bombing attack, but was not hit, although her hull was peppered with splinter holes. That evening, in company with the *Fuh Wo*, she anchored off a small island, shifting her anchorage in the early hours of the following morning. It was decided to lie up during the day, to avoid detection, but at 10.00 they were spotted by a Japanese aircraft which attacked them, although no damage was caused. It was decided that as they had been seen, there was little point in staying at the anchorage as they were bound to be attacked again, and the commanding officer wanted room to manoeuvre. At 10.30 the pair sailed, to act independently. During the afternoon they were subjected to an attack by a seaplane, but no hits were obtained. At 15.30 a convoy of about ten ships were seen to the north-east, and at 16.10 a second group of fifteen ships were sighted off the starboard bow, which were escorted by a cruiser and a destroyer. After conferring with his officers, Lieutenant Wilkinson decided to engage rather than surrender, believing they could 'inflict considerable damage on the enemy, before she could be sunk herself, and if we had to go, to take at least one with us'. They steamed straight at the nearest ship, a large transport. The 4in gun was manned with a scratch crew and despite having only thirteen shells, fired and with the third round hit the transport, starting a fire. As they closed, they came under fire from the escorts, but despite being hit, she continued to close until she was close enough to fire machine guns into the transport. She rammed the transport heavily amidships, making a sizeable hole. The *Li Wo* was now on fire following several hits and in a sinking condition, the steering gear broken, and main steam pipe burst. As she drifted clear of the transport, Wilkinson ordered the ship to be abandoned. There were only ten survivors from her crew, twenty-three men died. In 1946 when the events became known, Lieutenant Wilkinson was posthumously awarded the Victoria Cross, Sub-Lieutenant Ronald Stanton, the senior survivor, the DSO. Other awards were made to the survivors of the CGM and DSM and mentions in despatches.
[TNA: ADM.1/24321; London Gazette 17 December 1946]

14 February FUH WO auxiliary minesweeper
Glasgow 1922 requisitioned 1940; 953 tons; 204ft × 33ft; 1 × 4in
Lieutenant Norman Cook RNR
Sailed from Singapore 13 February and was initially in company with the *Li Wo* and after lying up at anchor off a small island during the morning of 14th, the pair decided to act independently. When it became clear from the level of enemy air and surface activity that she could not escape, she was run inshore and beached on Bangka Island and set on fire before being abandoned.
[TNA: ADM.1/18479: Lloyd's War Losses vol 1 p352]

14 February PENGAWAL motor launch
Singapore 1941; 60 tons; 76.5ft × 13.5ft; 1 × 3pdr
Lieutenant Leslie Gordon Jago SSRNVR
Left Singapore during the night of 13 February, she was bombed and sunk in the Durian Straits.
[TNA: ADM.1/18479; Lloyd's War Losses vol 2 p1735].

14 February HUNGJAO auxiliary patrol
Purchased 1941; 65 tons; 1 × 3pdr
Lieutenant Thomas Ewart Mellor RNZVR
A former yacht, she sailed from Singapore, loaded with refugees, in the same little convoy as *Kuala* (see above). She successfully made it Rengat, where she landed her passengers, but then returned in company with the steamer *Sungei Pinang* to try and rescue survivors from sunken ships. Her exact fate in uncertain; variously stated to have been either sunk by Japanese aircraft or scuttled at Rengat.
[*TNA: ADM.1/18479; http://www.naval-history.net/xDKWW2-4202-42FEB01.htm*]

15 February MATA HARI auxiliary patrol vessel
South Shields 1915 requisitioned 1939; 1,020 tons;
220ft × 35.2ft; 1 × 4in
Lieutenant Albert Charles Carston RNR
Sailed from Singapore during the evening of 12 February heavily loaded with evacuees – in addition to over 100 service personnel, she embarked 370 civilians, many of them women and children. She anchored later than same evening, to get underway at 04.00 to find shelter by False Durian Island, where she anchored close to the land. During the morning she was attacked by Japanese aircraft, but was not damaged, and late that afternoon she was able to get underway. At 01.00 on the following day (14 February), she was off Berhala Lighthouse, and hearing shouts was able to pick up six survivors from the sunken gunboat *Scorpion*. She made good progress and was undetected, being able at first light to anchor in a bay about 20 miles to the north of the Musi river in Sumatra. She lay up during the day, until at 20.30 she again got under way, and hugging the coast made her way south. Searchlights were seen to seaward, and she was illuminated at 00.15 (15 February), but after flashing her signal lamp at the stranger, the searchlight was turned off and the stranger made off. However, at 03.00, she was again illuminated from seaward, and this time she was closed by a ship that flashed 'stop' in international code. She did so, as it was evident that she was surrounded by several Japanese warships, including two cruisers. Unable to offer any effective resistance, and to save the lives of the passengers, it was decided to surrender. All confidential books were destroyed, the gun disabled, and the Asdic set destroyed. At first light she was boarded by a party of Japanese sailors, and was ordered to proceed to Muntok, where the passengers and crew were taken prisoner. The ship was commissioned by the Japanese as the *Nichirin Maru*.
[*TNA: ADM.1/17338*]

15 February TIEN KWANG auxiliary patrol vessel
Scotstoun 1925 requisitioned 1939; 731 tons;
198.5ft × 32.9ft; 1 × 4in
Lieutenant Wilfred Glandfield Briggs RNR
Laden with approximately 300 refugees she sailed from Singapore in company with the *Kuala* during the evening of 13 February. At 05.45 she took shelter during the day close to the island of Pompong at the southern end of the Rhio Strait, coming to anchor near the *Kuala* and attempts were made to hide the vessels by camouflaging them with branches and foliage gathered from the shore. At about 11.00 aircraft were seen overhead, but they escaped detection initially until two Japanese aircraft saw them and commenced a bombing attack and the *Tien Kwang* was damaged by near miss explosions. Unable to proceed she was abandoned and scuttled at 01.00 the next morning.
[*TNA: ADM.1/18479; www.navyhistory.org.au/the-loss-of-hms-kuala-1942/ www.bbc.co.uk/ww2peopleswar/stories/55/a7697055.shtml*]

15 February KLIAS auxiliary minesweeper
Penang 1927 requisitioned 1941; 207 tons; 126.2ft × 23ft;
1 × 12pdr
Lieutenant Harold Norman Smyth SSRNVR
Loaded with refugees, she successfully escaped from Singapore on 7 February, and reached safety at Palembang, Sumatra. With the rapidly deteriorating situation making any further progress impossible, she was abandoned and scuttled.
[*TNA: ADM.1/18479; Lloyd's War Losses vol 1 p352*]

15 February JERANTUT auxiliary minesweeper
Hong Kong 1927 requisitioned 1940; 217 tons;
110ft × 22.1ft; 1 × 12pdr
Lieutenant Leonard Lawton Cooper SSRNVR
Escaped from Singapore during 11 February, she managed to evade detection and reached Palembang. However, with the situation deteriorating and with Dutch demolition squads in action ashore, it was decided to scuttle her.
Note: the *Statement of Losses* gives the date of scuttling as 8 March, which is incorrect.
[*TNA: ADM.1/18479*]

15 February ST JUST tug
Old Kilpatrick 1919; 860 tons; 135.5ft × 29.1ft; 1 × 12pdr
Master Reginald Walter Henry Millen
Based at Singapore, on 2 February, as the Japanese invaders advanced, she successfully towed the Royal Australian Navy destroyer *Vendetta*, which had been under refit, clear of the harbour to Palembang. Along with the *Jerantut* and *Klias* (see above) she was taken into 12 fathoms of water and scuttled.

Note: the official *British Vessels Lost at Sea* indicates that she was bombed and sunk in the Durian Strait off Singapore, but this is incorrect.
[TNA: ADM.199/622A]

15 February ML 311 motor launch
Singapore 1941; 73 tons; 112ft × 18.4ft; 1 × 3pdr
Lieutenant Ernest Joseph Huson Christmas RANVR†
Laden with sixty army personnel she sailed from Singapore during the evening of 13 February, hoping to make Sumatra. During the next day she avoided detection, laying up in the shelter of an island, and then getting under way at night. In the early hours of 15 February, she was approaching the island of Bangka, but at first light a Japanese destroyer was seen on the port bow. The launch increased speed and commenced a zigzag, but the destroyer, which was the *Shiryuki*, opened fire, hitting the wheelhouse and killing the cox'n. A second hit put the steering gear out of action. Now out of control, and with a fire on board setting off the ready-use ammunition, she came to a stop and was abandoned before she sank. The survivors clung to anything that would float and made it ashore to the island. Six men were killed.
[TNA: ADM.267/131]

15 February ML 433 motor launch
Singapore 1942; 85 tons; 112ft × 18.2ft; 1 × 3pdr
Lieutenant Commander Harry Campey RANVR
Sailed from Singapore on the night of 13 February and in a similar manner to the other MLs laid up during the day to avoid detection. During the early morning of 15 February as she approached Bangka Island, she was intercepted by a Japanese destroyer which opened fire and sank her. Nine men were killed.
[TNA: ADM.1/18479]

15 February PAHLAWAN motor launch
Singapore 1937; 60 tons; 76.5ft × 13.5ft; 1 × 3pdr
Lieutenant Philip Dorian Cork SSRNVR
Escaped from Singapore during the night of 13 February, carrying twelve passengers from the RAF and army and successfully made the passage to Bangka Island undetected. During the afternoon of 15 February as she was approaching Muntok, two ships were sighted which were identified as a cruiser and a destroyer. The cruiser was seen to launch an aircraft which circled around before closing to drop two bombs, both of which dropped wide. At about 16.00 both ships opened fire on the launch and after six salvoes, with the shells dropping around her, Lieutenant Cork stopped the ship and struck his flag as a token of surrender. The destroyer came alongside to take possession.
Note: not listed in the *Statement of Losses*.
[TNA: ADM.1/18479]

15 February YIN PING tug
Shanghai 1914 requisitioned 1941; 191 tons; 105ft × 22.1ft; 1 × 4in
Lieutenant Patrick Ormond Howard Wilkinson SSRNVR
Based at Singapore, she sailed shortly before midnight 13 February, carrying several officers and officials from the naval base, including Captain Atkinson, the Captain Superintendent of the dockyard, hoping to make Batavia (Djakarta). The 14th was spent in the Cooper Channel, embarking more personnel from the stranded *Trang* to transfer to the *Malacca*, and dodge the regular air raids. During the 15th, still with many people on board, she headed for Bangka, but at 19.20, two warships were sighted, which appeared to be a cruiser and a destroyer. The warships closed to about 2 miles and then opened fire. Six rounds were fired, and three shells hit the tug; the first hit the bridge killing or wounding several people and starting a fire. The second exploded on the fo'c'sle whilst the third burst in the engine room. She was now on fire and sinking and she was ordered to be abandoned. Two boats and some floats were launched, but some of the passengers panicked and two men jumped into one of the boats, capsizing it. At 19.40 the tug rolled over to starboard and sank bows first, everyone having to jump clear, to cling to the remaining boat. Using boards as paddles they tried to make for the shore, which was about 6 miles off, the Japanese warships took no interest in them and made off. Sometime later *RAF Launch 56* appeared and took all the survivors on board. It was decided to make for Muntok light, where they were later made prisoner. Six men were lost.
[TNA: ADM.1/18261]

15 February TRANG auxiliary minesweeper
Butterworth 1912 requisitioned 1939; 205 tons; 111ft × 21.7ft
Lieutenant Henry Thomas Rigden SSRNVR
With over seventy RAF and army people on board, she sailed from Singapore at 21.00 on 13 February, aiming to reach Sumatra. The following day at 09.20 she ran aground in the Cooper Channel, and despite strenuous efforts to free her, she remained immobile. The situation was worsened when a rope from a launch manoeuvring to bring an escaping family and their baggage onboard fouled the screw. The work was given over in the early hours of the 15th, and she was abandoned at 02.00, being set on fire.
[TNA: ADM.267/131]

16 February HDML 1062 motor launch
Singapore 1941; 46 tons; 70ft × 15.10ft; 1 × 3pdr
Lieutenant Colin Edward McMillan RNZVR†
Heavily loaded with over fifty people evacuated from Singapore, she initially joined the gunboats *Dragonfly*

and *Grasshopper* (see above), when they took shelter at Singkep Island but escaped damage. She was intercepted in the eastern Bangka strait by Japanese surface forces and sunk by the destroyer *Hatsuyuki*.
[TNA: ADM.1/18479; ADM.358/615]

16 February FANLING launch
Requisitioned 1941; 65 tons; 1 × 3pdr
Lieutenant John Pierce Upton RNZNVR†
A former Shanghai customs launch, she sailed from Singapore during 13 February with over forty passengers, including several army officers and NCOs as passengers. They evaded detection until 06.30 on 16 February when she was in the Bangka Strait when two Japanese warships were sighted and identified as a cruiser and destroyer. Hoping that they had not been seen they continued their course, but the hostile ships turned in pursuit and at 07.00 opened fire. With the range rapidly closing she gallantly returned fire and continued to do so until the destroyer was just 800 yards away. Hit at least three times she filled with water and sank with heavy loss of life.
[TNA: ADM.1/18479; http://www.nzetc.org/tm/scholarly/tei-WH2Navy-c29.html]

17 February JARAK auxiliary minesweeper
Sungei Nyok 1927 requisitioned 1941; 208 tons; 127.2ft × 23ft; 1 × 6pdr
Lieutenant Edmund Albert Hooper RNVR
With several troops embarked, she sailed from Singapore during the early hours of 13 February, lying up at anchor close to a small island during the day to avoid being seen by patrolling Japanese aircraft. Getting underway the next night, it was decided to steam on through the day rather than again lay up. At 14.30 (14 February), then being about 6 miles to the north–east of Pulo Saya, strange warships were sighted on the horizon and they soon resolved themselves as being a Japanese cruiser with accompanying destroyers. After attempting to flash a recognition signal, the *Jarak* zigzagged vigorously, avoiding the shellfire, until she was attacked by an aircraft launched from the cruiser, and then by a destroyer which closed to within 2,000 yards. She was hit repeatedly, and the engines stopped, and a fire broke out. Boats were lowered and pulled away, the ship then listing and covered with smoke. Evidently satisfied that they had disposed of her, the Japanese moved off. When it was clear that they had gone the boats returned to board the steamer, the fire was put out and having successfully restarted the engines she was run inshore into shallow water off Saya. During the night work went on repairing the engines, and the following evening (16 February), despite oil leaks and 'steam blowing all over the place' she was able to get under way and made the island of Singkep, where she anchored just before

midnight. The stores and food were removed and in the early hours of 17 February she was scuttled off Tanjong Buku in 17 fathoms.
[https://www.navyrecords.org.uk/magazine_posts/the-loss-of-h-m-s-jarak-1942/; http://www.bbc.co.uk/ww2peopleswar/stories/13/a2162413.shtml]

17 February TANDJONG PINANG auxiliary patrol
Hong Kong 1936 requisitioned 1941; 133 tons; 97ft × 22.2ft; 1 × 12pdr
Lieutenant Basil Shaw RNZNVR
With over 100 civilian evacuees embarked, and about fifty army personnel, she sailed from Singapore on 13 February and made it to Tembilan, having picked up survivors of other vessels. She then returned to the vicinity of Lingga Island, to rescue more survivors from the ships and vessels that had been lost in the waters around Singapore. Having picked up over 100 survivors, on 17 February they sailed for Batavia, but that night, at about 21.30, when about 30 miles north of Tanjong Ular light, Bangka Island, she was illuminated by searchlights and then came under accurate fire. She suffered two direct hits which caused considerable damage and she started to sink, with another shell destroying a lifeboat as it was about to be launched. She disappeared under water in about 5 minutes, leaving people struggling in the sea, and clinging to rafts. Two members of the crew were killed with an uncertain number of passengers. Several survivors did make it to the shore, and others were picked up by Japanese warships; the exact number is uncertain but would appear to about twenty. Lieutenant Shaw was one of the survivors but was captured and executed by the Japanese.
[TNA: ADM.1/1879; WO.361/462]

17 February TAPAH auxiliary minesweeper
Penang 1926 requisitioned 1939; 208 tons; 125.7ft × 23ft; 1 × 12pdr
Lieutenant John Neil Coulter Hancock SSRNVR
Successfully escaped from Singapore on the night of 12 February, she evaded detection and made her way to Bangka Island. During the morning of 17 February when she was about 10 miles from Muntok, she was intercepted by a Japanese warship and captured, being taken back to Singapore.
[TNA: ADM/1/18479; Lloyd's War Losses p986]

17 February ML 432 motor launch
Singapore 1942; 85 tons; 112ft × 18.2ft; 1 × 3pdr
Lieutenant William Bourke RNZVR
Sailed from Singapore, with several soldiers embarked, during the night of 13 February, she evaded detection as they headed towards Bangka Island. They picked up some survivors of a sunken ship at Singkep Island but went aground when attempting to take shelter

from Japanese aircraft. Refloated the next day she encountered a cruiser and destroyer off Muntok, and they beached the craft, all the crew and evacuees being taken prisoner.
[TNA: ADM.1/18479; http://www.nzetc.org/tm/scholarly/tei-WH2Navy-c29.html]

18 February MALACCA auxiliary minesweeper
Hong Kong 1927 requisitioned 1939; 210 tons; 110ft × 22.1ft; 1 × 12pdr
Lieutenant William Benjamin Bevis RNVR
Heavily loaded with over sixty troops and several civilian evacuees, she escaped from Singapore during the evening of 13 February, hiding out during the following day by concealing themselves by the shoreline at False Durian Island. They were damaged by near misses from an air attack on 14 February and briefly ran aground but were able to get underway and made it to safely to Kuala Lajau in Sumatra during the morning of the 15 February. Moving on to Rengat, she could go no further as the fuel (coal) had run out and no stocks were available. It was decided to scuttle her and after sailing at 06.00 she was taken 1½ miles up the Tjimako River and scuttled, being left with her upper deck awash.
[TNA: ADM.267/131]

18 February PENGAIL motor launch
Singapore 1942; 60 tons; 76.5ft × 13.5ft; 1 × 3pdr
Lieutenant Norman George Bell SSRNVR
The launch escaped from Singapore, sailing at 23.30 on 13 February, and by lying up during the day under the shelter of the land, successfully escaped to Batavia (Djakarta). She was then moored in the river at Pakan Paroe and turned over to the Dutch authorities.
[TNA: ADM.267/131]

Vessels abandoned and lost at the surrender of Singapore 14–15 February:

SUI WO accommodation ship
Govan 1896 requisitioned 1941; 2,672 tons; 290ft × 43.1ft
Lieutenant Andrew Robertson RNVR

PENINGAT motor launch
Singapore 1941; 60 tons; 76.5ft × 13.5ft; 1 × 3pdr

HDML 1097 motor launch
Singapore 1941; 46 tons; 70ft × 15ft; 1 × 3pdr

RHU auxiliary minelayer
Penang 1940 requisitioned 1941; 254 tons; 126.9ft × 27.1ft

DOWGATE boom gate vessel
Hong Kong 1935; 290 tons; 98.5ft × 26ft; 1 × 12pdr
'Immobilised' and scuttled.

LUDGATE boom gate vessel
Hong Kong 1935; 290 tons; 98.5ft × 26ft; 1 × 12pdr
'Immobilised' and scuttled.

LANTAKA tug
Singapore; 300 tons; 120ft × 24.5ft
Captured incomplete on the stocks.

SILVIA yacht or auxiliary patrol launch
'Constructive total loss'.

MMS 93 / MMS 94 / MMS 125 / MMS 126 / MMS 127 / MMS 128 motor minesweepers
Singapore (incomplete) 225 tons; 105ft × 23ft
All listed as being under construction, and all destroyed on the stocks.

MOORWIND boom defence vessel
Singapore (incomplete); 1,000 tons; 149ft × 34ft
Shown as being destroyed on the stocks.

HDML 1167 / HDML 1168 / HDML 1169 / HDML 1170 / HDML 1213 / HDML 1214 / HDML 1215 / HDML 1216 / HDML 1217 / HDML 1218 / HDML 1219 / HDML 1220 motor launches
Singapore (incomplete); 46 tons; 70ft × 15ft
All listed as being under construction, and all destroyed on the stocks.

★ ★ ★

15 February ML 169 motor launch
Burnham 1940; 75 tons; 112ft × 18.4ft; 1 × 3pdr
Lieutenant John Eric Harrison RNVR
Based at Gibraltar, she caught fire and was burnt out after an explosion of petrol vapour in the engine room, triggered when the engines were started up to proceed on patrol. Four men were killed.
[TNA: ADM.199/802; ADM.358/4032]

18 February BOTANIC trawler
Selby 1928 requisitioned 1939; 348 tons; 140.3ft × 24ft; 1 × 12pdr
Lieutenant John Glendinning Paterson RNVR
In company with another armed trawler, the *Fyldea*, the pair was engaged in sweeping about 16 miles to the north-east of Spurn Head. At 12.30 aircraft, identified as Dorniers, were seen closing from the starboard quarter. Fire was opened by the trawlers, including by a party of soldiers from the Gloucestershire Regiment, who employed a Bren gun, but with no obvious effect. The first aircraft dropped a stick of four bombs as it passed over the *Botanic* all of which dropped clear, but the second aircraft was more successful. It released six bombs which exploded all around her; with one bomb hitting the starboard side

to pass through the ship, exploding as it exited the port side. A fire was started in the engine room and this spread as she settled. The *Fyldea* closed to run alongside to take off the crew and then stood off as *Botanic* exploded and sank soon after but without result. One man was killed.
[TNA: ADM. 267/119]

18 February WARLAND trawler
Beverley 1912 requisitioned 1940; 214 tons;
117.2ft × 21.5ft; 1 × 12pdr
Skipper Herbert Hopwood Firth RNR
At 13.50 the *Warland* was leading a group of armed trawlers out of the river Humber to meet an inward bound convoy. As they neared number 62D buoy, to the north-east of Spurn Head, they received an air raid warning from one of the escorting destroyers and they went to action stations. An aircraft, believed to be a Dornier, emerged from low cloud right ahead of the trawler and made straight for her. Four bombs were dropped which exploded all around her stern. She was badly shaken, and water started to enter very quickly, and steam flooded the engine room. The Carley float was released, and the merchant ship *High Wear* closed to drop her boat to render assistance. Fifteen minutes after the attack she foundered. One man was killed in the attack.
[TNA: ADM.267/120]

19 February Japanese attack on Darwin
On 19 February, a large force of aircraft was launched from four Japanese aircraft carriers to carry out a raid on the harbour of Darwin, Northern Territory, Australia. The aircraft began their attacks at 10.00 and the initial assault lasted about 30 minutes. One US destroyer (*Perry*) was sunk, along with two US Army transports, four merchant ships and two Australian Navy vessels. A second wave of land-based bomber aircraft continued the assault at midday, concentrating on shore facilities. The Australian craft destroyed:

MAVIE channel patrol boat
Fremantle WA 1903 requisitioned 1941; 19 tons;
38.6ft × 11.11ft
Royal Australian Navy. A sailing lugger, she had only just been taken over, and was laying alongside the depot ship *Platypus* at Darwin, when the harbour came under Japanese air attack. She was hit by a bomb from a dive bomber and broke up and sank immediately. There was no loss of life.
[Cassells p40]

KELAT coal hulk
Stockton on Tees 1881 requisitioned 1941; 1,894 tons;
261ft × 41ft
Royal Australian Navy. The *Kelat* was originally a fully-rigged ship that was used at Darwin as a coal store.

Kelat was fully laden with coal when she was strafed by fighter aircraft and subsequently sank at her buoy. There were no casualties.
[Cassells p34]

★ ★ ★

23 February P 38 submarine
Barrow 1941; 540/732 tons; 180ft × 16.1ft; 1 × 12pdr,
4 × torpedo tubes
Lieutenant Rowland John Hemingway[†]
P 38 sailed from Malta 8 February for a patrol in the Gulf of Hammamet, but this was shifted to the vicinity of Tripoli, Libya, to intercept a convoy that intelligence had indicated was about to arrive from Taranto, joining another two submarines. The convoy arrived in the British patrol area during the morning of 23 February. At 10.14, in position 32.48N 14.58E, one of the screening escorts, the torpedo boat *Circe* gained a sonar contact at 1,600 yards and altered course towards the target, sighting a periscope as she did so. At 10.22 the *Circe* ran over the contact and dropped a pattern of depth charges. Moments later a submarine was seen to come to the surface, her bows high out of the water. Others of the convoy escorts opened fire, and an escorting aircraft closed and dropped a bomb, just as the submarine submerged. As the *Circe* began to conduct a sonar search, to attempt to regain contact, the submarine burst to the surface for a second time, yet again with the bows rearing out of the water at a high angle before crashing back into the sea. She then dived at a very steep angle, her propellers rising out of the water before she disappeared. The destroyer *Emanuele Passagno* promptly ran over the position and dropped another pattern of depth-charges. The *Circe* then slowly closed the area, searching on her sonar, and found a large, spreading patch of oil with some debris. The target of these attacks can only have been *P 38*. Four officers and twenty-eight men died.
[Evans pp301–03]

27 February ELECTRA destroyer
Hebburn 1934; 1,405 tons; 318.3ft × 33.3ft; 4 × 4.7in,
8 × torpedo tubes
Commander Cecil Wakefield May
Having accompanied the doomed *Repulse* and *Prince of Wales* and rescued many survivors, she moved to Batavia (Djakarta) following the collapse of Singapore. Now part of the newly formed Anglo-Dutch-US-Australian force under the command of Admiral Doorman, they sailed during the evening of 26 February to locate and attack ships of the Japanese invasion fleet. At 08.30 the following morning as they steamed towards Bawean Island following reports of an enemy force, they came under enemy air reconnaissance, and the surveillance

continued through the day. At 16.14 several ships came into sight, which resolved themselves into a force of two heavy and two light cruisers, with two groups of destroyers. Fire was opened at 30,000 yards and the forces were led round to run on parallel courses. The action continued with patches of drifting smoke frequently obscuring the targets and attempts by the Japanese to stage destroyer torpedo attacks. At 17.14 the *Exeter* was hit by a large shell and was forced out of the line. This threw the Allied line into some confusion, and as the line reformed, the British destroyers were ordered to carry out a torpedo attack. At 17.30 the *Electra*, with *Encounter* and *Jupiter* steered towards the enemy through patches of thick drifting smoke. As they cleared the smoke, three enemy destroyers were seen on an opposite course at a range of about 6,000 yards. They were immediately engaged with main armament and hits were obtained on the leading ship. The *Electra* was hit once, a shell exploding in number 2 boiler room, shattering the boiler and carrying away the steering gear. She lost way and slowly came to a stop. One of the enemy destroyers closed out of the smoke and it was engaged, but as she could not manoeuvre, she was a 'sitting duck'. Hit repeatedly, a fire broke out forward and she developed a list to port. When only 'Y' gun was still in action she was ordered to be abandoned. The whaler got away with two Carley floats whilst the ship was listing heavily to port and then dipped by the bows. She turned slowly over and sank until only her screws and quarterdeck showed. She remained like this for some time before sinking at 18.00. One hundred and eight men were killed, with the survivors being picked up by the American submarine *S 38*.

[TNA: ADM.267/84; London Gazette 7 July 1948]

27 February JUPITER destroyer

Scotstoun 1938; 1,690 tons; 339.6ft × 35.8ft; 6 × 4.7in, 4 × 2pdr, 10 × torpedo tubes
Lieutenant Commander Norman Vivian Joseph Thompson Thew

Based in the Far East, she had been part of the Allied group that had fought a Japanese force in the Java Sea (see *Electra* above). After the *Exeter* had been forced to withdraw, and the failed destroyer attack, Admiral Doorman disengaged and steered away for Surabaya. At 21.00 in position 06.45.2N 112.05.5E there was an explosion on the starboard side, abreast the forward bulkhead of the engine room. The explosion left the starboard side with a hole 20ft long and the upper deck distorted. The engine room and after boiler room flooded immediately and the forward boiler room flooded slowly, and the ship was immobilised. She steadily filled and sank 4 hours later. It was believed at the time that she must have been the victim of torpedo attack by a Japanese submarine, but it later emerged that

the force had strayed through a minefield that had been laid by the Dutch minelayer *Gouden Leeuw*. Ninety-nine men died.

[TNA: ADM.267/84; CB.4273 p190; London Gazette 7 July 1948]

28 February SURPRISE yacht

Troon 1896 (*Razvet*) requisitioned 1939; 1,144 tons; 252.6ft × 33.7ft
Commander Lionel Carroll Ansdell

Employed as an armed patrol vessel, she was based at Lagos, Nigeria and was berthed at number 1 wharf alongside the boom defence vessel *Barbrook*. At 02.50 smoke was seen coming out of the sick bay, and when checked it was found to be full of smoke, but no fire was visible. The adjacent compartments were checked, and a fire was discovered in the wardroom, which lay directly below the sick bay. The wardroom had extensive wood panelling, and this was well alight, apparently around the refrigerator which was sited at one end of the compartment. All hands were called, and the fire was tackled with buckets of water and fire extinguishers, but there was an explosion, and what appeared to be burning paraffin sprayed all over the wardroom. The fire was now fierce, with flames and sparks bursting up through the skylight to the deck above. The one and only fire pump was then rigged with two hoses connected but were found to have little effect. Within 10 minutes the forward part of the ship was ablaze. Hoses were rigged from the shore and from *Barbrook* to pump water onto her, and the crew were ordered to evacuate the ship. At 03.25 the Lagos fire brigade arrived and shortly after a Nigerian Marine tug, the *Atlas*, was on scene. Both joined the fire-fighting efforts, spraying her with water. All this work had some effect and the flames visibly died down, and she was re-boarded by some of the crew, and Commander Ansdell ordered the bilges to be flooded to allow her to settle. However, before this could be achieved the fire broke out again, forcing all ashore again. She now had a pronounced list to starboard, and as the hoses continued to play on her, she steadily lost stability and rolled over onto her starboard side at 05.10. The enquiry found that the seat of the fire was probably a kerosene-powered Electrolux refrigerator. She had capsized due to the amount of water pumped into her; it was estimated that 500 tons were sprayed onboard.

[TNA: ADM.1/11896]

1–3 March Destruction of vessels escaping from Java

On 27 February, the various ships that had escaped from Singapore and had made it to the settlements in the Dutch East Indies were ordered to make their way south to Australia. The continued Japanese advance had now made this a dangerous journey, as the enemy had complete control of the air and superiority at sea.

1 March EXETER cruiser

Devonport 1929; 8,390 tons; 540ft × 58ft; 6 × 8in, 4 × 4in, 16 × 2pdr, 2 × 20mm, 6 × torpedo tubes
Captain Oliver Loudon Gordon

The *Exeter* had been part of the Allied force that had clashed with Japanese surface forces in the action on 27 February, known as the Battle of the Java Sea. During this the *Exeter* had been damaged by an 8in shell which had passed through 'S.2' 4in gun shield, entered 'B' boiler room and hit a boiler which exploded. She had retired to Surabaya and four of her boilers were restored to working order, allowing her to steam at about 24 knots. She sailed at 19.00 on 28 February in company with the destroyers *Encounter* and USS *Pope*, initially to head for Tjilatjap (Cilacap), and ultimately Colombo. The following morning, at just before 04.00 ships were seen to the west, and the group turned away to avoid contact. At 07.50 the exercise was repeated when smoke from ships was seen on the horizon. They hoped they had escaped detection, but at 09.35 the topmasts of two large cruisers were seen to the south and yet again the *Exeter* and her consorts altered away, but this time it was clear that they had been seen, as the strangers were following. Restricted by her limited speed, the strangers gradually overhauled *Exeter*, the nearest being seen to be a large destroyer. This was engaged at 20,000 yards, forcing the destroyer to turn away. As it did so, another two large cruisers were seen to the north-west. *Exeter* was now faced with four heavy cruisers – they were the *Nachi*, *Haguro*, *Ashigari* and *Myoko* – and four destroyers. She and her two destroyers altered away to the east and by strenuous efforts by her engineers managed to increase her speed to about 25 knots. The two cruisers to the north-west opened fire, the fire being returned by *Exeter*. The pursuers gradually overhauled her, and she was under constant fire, but with her escorting destroyers making smoke, she escaped any injury until 11.20 when she was hit in 'A' boiler room. This started a fire and losing steam pressure, power failed. After this the enemy was able to close and the fire became concentrated, and she was hit several times, with another fire breaking out aft. By 11.35 it was clear that she could resist no longer, and she was heeling over to port and was ordered to be abandoned. As this was underway one of the destroyers, the *Inazuma*, closed and fired a torpedo into her. This hit her on the starboard side amidships, throwing up a large column of water. She righted herself, and then slowly rolled over to starboard and sank at 11.50 in position 04.38S 112.28E. Fifty-four men died.

[London Gazette 7 July 1948; TNA: ADM.267/84]

1 March PERTH light cruiser

Portsmouth 1934 (*Amphion*); 6980 tons; 522ft × 56.7ft; 8 × 6in, 8 × 4in
Captain Hector McDonald Laws Waller DSO RAN

Royal Australian Navy. One of the ABDA force ships in the Dutch East Indies, she had taken part in the action of 26/27 February (see above) and with the other ships had gone to Tanjong Priok to refuel. At 19.00 on 28 February, she sailed in company with the USS *Houston*, intending to pass through the Sunda Strait to reach Tjilatjap (Cilacap). Soon after sailing, intelligence was received of the sighting of a force of Japanese transports, with escorts, to the north-east of Batavia (Djakarta). It was believed that these would be an invasion force heading for that place, and that they were unlikely to encounter them. The true force and location of the invasion force was unknown, and the Western Invasion convoy of transports, with a powerful escort, was ahead of them, in Bantam (or Banten) Bay, at the head of the Sunda Strait. At 23.06 a ship was seen by *Perth*, but when challenged by light, gave an unrecognised reply. Correctly assessing that this was a Japanese warship, she engaged the stranger, which was the destroyer *Harukaze*, which turned away, making smoke. Shortly afterwards, several other destroyers were sighted to the north, *Perth* and *Houston* firing at several targets, and the cruisers found themselves having to engage seven destroyers, which made several torpedo attacks. Ammunition was now running low in both ships, and *Perth* was reduced to practice shells and star shells. Unable to continue the fight, she increased speed and headed for the Sunda Strait. This allowed the Japanese destroyers to make a further torpedo attack, and she was hit by a torpedo on the starboard side at 00.05 followed by a second hit a few minutes later. She lost power, and when she received a third hit on the starboard side and a fourth torpedo on the port, it was clear that she was lost, and she was ordered to be abandoned. She rolled over and sank at approximately 00.25 about 3 miles off St Nicholas Point with the loss of 353 men.

[http://www.navy.gov.au/hmas-perth-i ; Cassells p52]

1 March ENCOUNTER destroyer

Hebburn 1934; 1,405 tons; 318.3ft × 33.3ft; 4 × 4.7in, 8 × torpedo tubes
Lieutenant Commander Eric Vernon St John Morgan

She accompanied the *Exeter* and the USS *Pope* when they sailed from Surabaya to head for Colombo. When the enemy forces were sighted (see *Exeter* above) she initially matched the movements of the cruiser and attempted to screen the force by laying smoke and engaged the enemy forces whenever they came within range. By 11.30 her ammunition was running low, and the engine room then reported that the main engines were out of action, the forced lubrication pumps having fractured. Losing power, she slowed, and enemy fire became intense, and she was hit several times. Clearly doomed, men were ordered up from below and floats were prepared for release. With the boiler room on fire and the engine room flooding, she was abandoned, the ship taking a list to starboard as the men entered the water. At 12.10pm she rolled over to starboard and sank. Seven men died.

[*London Gazette 7 July 1948*]

1 March WAR SIRDAR oiler

Sunderland 1919; 5,542 tons; 400ft × 52.4ft
Commander Murray William Westlake RNR

Having escaped from Singapore to reach Batavia (Djakarta), as the Japanese continued to advance through Java it soon became clear that this was also becoming untenable, and attacks on shipping by aircraft increased. During 25 February, at 11.30 the *War Sirdar* received a direct hit on number 2 port tank by a small calibre bomb and was also shaken by several near misses. The bulkheads from number 1 tank were carried away, allowing oil to discharge into the sea. Temporary repairs were made, but on 28 February all remaining British auxiliary craft were ordered to move. At midnight, the Australian sloop *Yarra* and the Indian Navy sloop *Jumna* sailed escorting a convoy for Tjilatjap (Cilacap) which included the *War Sirdar*, although she was barely seaworthy. At 04.04 she ran aground on the Jong reef, north-west of Batavia. Engines were put astern, but she refused to move and an attempt to tow her free also failed. It was therefore decided to abandon her, the ship's company setting her on fire before leaving her. The Japanese subsequently salvaged her, and she was later sunk by the US submarine *Bluegill* in March 1945 under the name *Honan Maru*.

[*TNA: ADM.1/19497; ADM.267/130*]

1 March RAHMAN auxiliary minesweeper

Sungei Nyok 1926 requisitioned 1940; 209 tons;
124.8ft × 23ft; 1 × 12pdr
Lieutenant Herbert Cooper Upton SSRNVR

Having successfully escaped from Singapore to Batavia (Djakarta), when that place was abandoned, she was condemned as unseaworthy, and unlikely to make the journey to Australia. Despite that, she sailed from Tandjong Priok during the afternoon of 1 March, but was intercepted by Japanese destroyers and sunk about 8 miles south-west of Pulo Babi in the Sunda Straits.

[*TNA: ADM.1/18479; https://www.navyhistory.org.au/the-rescue-yacht/*]

1 March SCOTT HARLEY auxiliary minesweeper

Rotterdam 1913 (*Singaradja*) requisitioned 1940; 620 tons;
185.2ft × 31.1ft

Under the command of Lieutenant John Rennie RNR, she escaped from Singapore on 12 February at daybreak, carrying 170 female and 30 male evacuees, they evaded detection and successfully arrived at Batavia on 15 February, where Rennie, passengers and crew disembarked. Ordered to make for Australia, she sailed on 27 February with a small crew, reportedly survivors from *Prince of Wales* and *Repulse*. She was in company with the Dutch motorship *Toradja* when they were intercepted south of Tjiatjap by a Japanese force of three cruisers (*Atago*, *Maya* and *Takao*) with two destroyers and sunk.

[*TNA: CO.980/217; http://www.combinedfleet.com/atago_t. htm; https://www.cofepow.org.uk/armed-forces-stories-list/ scott-harley-passenger-list*]

1 March SIN AIK LEE auxiliary minesweeper

Singapore 1928 requisitioned 1940; 198 tons;
110ft × 22.5ft; 1 × 12pdr
Lieutenant Joseph McPherson Brander SSRNVR

Another escapee from Singapore, she reached safety at Batavia (Djakarta), only to be moved on again as the Japanese advanced. She sailed from that port on 1 March in company with the *Rahman* and *HDML 1063* but was intercepted that evening in the Sunda Straits when about 8 miles south-west of Pulo Babi by two Japanese warships which opened fire. Her engines out of action she was ordered to be abandoned. The following day a Japanese warship found her still afloat but drifting and took her in tow, taking her to Singapore. One man died of his injuries. The survivors spent several days in boats before making the shore, to be taken prisoner.

[*TNA: ADM.1/18479; Lloyd's War Losses p992*]

1 March HDML 1063 motor launch

Singapore 1942; 46 tons; 72ft × 15.10ft; 1 × 3pdr
Lieutenant Geoffrey Daniel Inns RNZVR

Left Singapore on 13 February and successfully evaded detection to reach Batavia on 16 February. On 1 March she sailed from Tandjong Priok in company with the *Rahman* and *Sin Aik Lee* but were intercepted that evening, by Japanese destroyers as the group attempted to transit through the Sunda Straits and sunk after being hit repeatedly.

[*TNA: ADM.1/18479; https://www.navyhistory.org.au/the-rescue-yacht/*]

2 March STRONGHOLD destroyer

Greenock 1919; 905 tons; 265ft × 26.8ft; 2 × 4in, 1 × 2pdr,
40 × mines
Lieutenant Commander Giles Robert Pretor-Pinney[†]

Based in the Far East, following the collapse of Singapore, the destroyer was part of the Allied force that gathered in Java. As the Japanese advanced through that island, she sailed at 18.00 from Tjilatjap (Cilacap) on 1 March to provide cover for those vessels that were making their way to Australia. At 09.00 the following

morning a Japanese floatplane was sighted, and it was clear that her position was now compromised. At 17.50 a large warship was sighted on the starboard quarter. The *Stronghold* increased speed and made smoke, but the larger ship was overhauling her. At 17.52 the Japanese heavy cruiser *Maya* opened fire, but despite accurate firing with several salvoes dropping near, the destroyer avoided being hit by vigorous manoeuvring. After about 15 minutes of this, she was finally hit by an 8in shell amidships. Two destroyers, the *Arashi* and *Nowaki*, could now be seen, and they were also closing and opened fire. *Stronghold* was now hit several times. The forward torpedo tubes were hit, the galley flat was on fire and the bridge was hit, severely wounding the captain; the engine room was damaged, and she lost steam and power. An attempt was made to close and carry out a torpedo attack, and they successfully closed to within 4,000 yards and fired two torpedoes but were now being hit constantly and the engine room was on fire and had to be evacuated. She lay stopped in the water when at 19.30 she was ordered to be abandoned. As this was underway one of the Japanese destroyers closed and about 30 minutes later fired a torpedo into her and she sank rapidly in position 12.10S 112.00E. About fifty survivors were picked up by the Dutch steamer *Binthoehan*; eighty–three men died.
[TNA:ADM.1/19493]

2 March **JERAM** auxiliary minesweeper
Hong Kong 1927 requisitioned 1939; 210 tons; 110ft × 22.1ft; 1 × 12pdr
Lieutenant Joseph Horace Evans SSRNVR
The *Jeram* successfully escaped from Singapore, reaching Tandjong Priok in Sumatra on 22 February, where she refuelled to continue to Tjilatjap. It was here that she was attacked by Japanese aircraft and so severely damaged that she was abandoned and allowed to sink in shallow water. The Japanese subsequently salvaged her to become the *Suikei-21*.
[TNA:ADM.1/18479; Lloyd's War Losses vol 1 p364]

3 March **GEMAS** auxiliary minesweeper
Sungei Nyok 1925 requisitioned 1939; 207 tons; 125.1ft × 23ft; 1 × 12pdr
Lieutenant Frank Stanley Cable SSRNVR
Fitted out as a minesweeper, she was based in Singapore and had successfully escaped from the colony to reach Tjilatjap (Cilacap), Java. She was ordered to be scuttled, and after all sensitive equipment, including magnetic sweeping gear had been destroyed, she sailed during the evening of 2 March. At 01.20 she was scuttled, then being 7 miles off Tjilatjap Light.
[TNA:ADM.267/131]

★ ★ ★

1 March **SOPHIE MARIE** auxiliary patrol vessel
Wesermunde 1923 requisitioned 1939; 677 tons; 216.7ft × 34.5ft
Lieutenant Douglas George Cowan Courtney RINR
Royal Indian Navy. Stationed at Port Blair in the Andaman Islands, in March 1942 the small British garrison was being withdrawn and with increasing Japanese air activity it was decided to leave the harbour and take shelter further along the coast and only return during the evening. She sailed from Port Blair during the morning and headed south for the MacPherson Straits, where she anchored until 13.45, when she weighed to make her way back to the harbour. Soon after this there was a large explosion as she triggered a mine. She listed to port and continued to roll over until she sank. One boat managed to get clear, and several rafts were freed which allowed survivors to make the shore, about 1½ miles away. One man was lost. A Board of Inquiry was held at Madras, which found that the ship had no knowledge that the Strait had been mined.
[http://www.ibiblio.org/hyperwar/UN/India/RIN/RIN-6.html]

2 March **LCT (2) 155** landing craft, tank
Paisley 1941; 296 tons; 143ft × 30ft
Being carried out to the Mediterranean in sections, the largest, stern section, was lost overboard from the merchant ship *Empire Cameron* in poor weather, in position 43.30N 020.57W.
[TNA:ADM.199/2237]

4 March **Destruction of the *Yarra* convoy**
The Battle of the Sunda Strait on 1 March saw the last major naval units of the Allied forces in the Singapore area destroyed. The remnants of the force, a mixture of auxiliaries and small ships were ordered to make their way to Australia. A small convoy of the *Anking, Francol* and *MMS 51* sailed from Tjilatjap (Cilacap), Java, on 2 March under the escort of the Australian sloop *Yarra* to proceed to Western Australia. At 05.30 on 4 March a powerful Japanese squadron came into sight; consisting of the cruisers *Atago, Takao* and *Maya*, with two destroyers, which closed the small convoy at speed. The *Yarra*, despite being completely outmatched did what she could, by laying a smokescreen and engaging the enemy, but neither she nor any of her convoy survived.
[TNA:ADM.1/19497; Shores & Cull 319]

YARRA Sloop
Sydney 1935; 1,060 tons; 250ft × 36ft; 3 × 4in
Lieutenant Commander Robert William Rankin RAN†
Royal Australian Navy. The *Yarra* acted as escort to the three ships that sailed from Tjilatjap, and when, at dawn on 4 March, the Japanese squadron was sighted, ordered the ships to scatter and then put herself between the convoy and the oncoming threat. Smoke was laid to

obscure the fleeing ships and she engaged the enemy. She was hit several times, and at 08.00 she was hit by a heavy shell and it was clear that she could not survive. She was ordered to be abandoned, with two Japanese destroyers closing to fire at close range before leaving the area. The survivors were left in two rafts, and drifted for several days, and only thirteen men were still alive when picked up by the Dutch submarine *K XI*; 138 men died.

[*https://www.awm.gov.au/articles/encyclopedia/yarra/loss*]

ANKING base ship

Greenock 1925 requisitioned 1941; 3,472 tons; 338.4ft × 49.2ft

Lieutenant Stanley Leonard Garrett RNR[†]

Whilst some of the Japanese forces were engaged with the only armed escort, the *Yarra*, others turned their attentions to the convoy. At 06.15 the *Anking* was hit by a large-calibre shell which brought her to a stop. She heeled over with her decks awash and after being hit repeatedly she sank at about 07.00. The Japanese picked up sixteen survivors, but 261 men died.

[*TNA ADM.1/14284*]

4 March FRANCOL oiler

Hull 1917; 2,607 tons; 320ft × 41.5ft

Master John Harris Burman[†]

Hit several times, she was reduced to a hulk and was last seen at 07.30 covered in a swathe of white smoke and steam. One boatload of survivors was picked up by the Japanese before they made off. Seven men were killed.

[*TNA: ADM.267/122*]

4 March MMS 51 minesweeper

Singapore 1941; 225 tons; 105ft × 23ft

Lieutenant Francis Nixon RNR

The minesweeper attempted to escape by increasing to maximum speed and zigzagging. She was chased by a cruiser, which closed to 1,800 yards before opening fire. Hit almost immediately by a large-calibre shell, the vessel came to a stop. The boats and floats were ordered to be launched, despite still being under fire from the cruiser. The engine room was ordered to open the main inlets and flood the ship and she was then abandoned. The cruiser closed to about 400 yards, firing all the time, until the minesweeper caught fire, and she sank at 07.20 stern first. No attempt was made by the Japanese to pick up any of the men swimming in the water. Fourteen men gathered together on two floats, and they spent an uncomfortable 3 days before being picked up during the afternoon of 7 March by the Dutch ship *Tjimanoek*. Two men were killed in the attack.

[*TNA: ADM.267/131*]

★ ★ ★

5 March WO KWANG tug

Shanghai 1927 requisitioned 1940; 350 tons; 153.7ft × 28ft; 1 × 12pdr

Lieutenant John Robinson RNR[†]

Having escaped from Singapore on 11 February, she successfully reached Batavia (Djakarta) and subsequently moved on to Tjilatjap (Cilacap) in company with the *Jeram* and *Gemas* (see above). When those two ships were scuttled, she took on all the survivors and sailed on 3 March for Western Australia. During 5 March, when about 300 miles south of Java, smoke was seen on the horizon and during the afternoon it became clear that it was a force of a cruiser and two destroyers. Initially it was hoped that these were Allied ships, and *Wo Kwang* closed to signal the strangers, but as they neared it was realised that they were Japanese warships. The destroyers opened fire and almost immediately the bridge was hit, killing or wounding several men. After another hit, she was ordered to be abandoned, and the boat was lowered, only to capsize on hitting the water. One of the enemy destroyers closed and continued to fire at point blank range into the tug until she sank, when they made off leaving several men in the water. The survivors, eighteen in total, managed to right the boat and clamber aboard, but with no fresh water, little food and no means of propulsion. The boat drifted for 15 days before land was sighted and a further 9 days before they were washed ashore on the southern coast of Java near Wonosari. By that time there were only two men left alive who were taken prisoner. Approximately forty men were lost.

[*TNA: ADM.358/4047*]

5 March KARALEE lighter

Fremantle 1919 requisitioned 1941; 117 tons; 103.6ft × 23ft

Royal Australian Navy. Employed at Darwin as lighter, assisting with the unloading of ships, she was damaged during the Japanese raid on the harbour in February. Although repairs were carried out, on 2 March a temporary patch gave way, and she sank at her moorings. She was moved into shallow water, but the following day, during recovery, her bollards and upper works were so rusted and fragile, that they were ripped out. Two days later she drifted away and sank off the Boom Jetty.

[*Cassells p34*]

7/8 March NORTHERN PRINCESS trawler

Wesermunde 1936 requisitioned 1939; 655 tons; 188.1ft × 28.1ft; 1 × 4in

Lieutenant Dryden Byrne Phillipson RNR[†]

In company with several other trawlers, she was sent across the Atlantic to assist the Americans with anti-submarine duties. Having arrived in Canada, on 6 March a group of four trawlers sailed from St Johns,

Newfoundland to proceed to New York. The weather was poor and worsened, with a heavy sea and Force 8 gale, the ships pitching and pounding badly. The *Northern Princess* became separated during the night of 7 March, last being seen at 20.45 in position 45.22N 55.29W. When she failed to arrive, she was presumed lost with all thirty-eight hands, probably through force of weather, perhaps through a leaking Asdic dome or insecure hatch. After the war it emerged that she had probably been torpedoed during the early hours of 8 March by *U 587* (Borcherdt) who reported attacking a target in this vicinity.
[*TNA: ADM.199/802; Rohwer, Axis Submarine Successes p83*]

7 March ST SAMPSON tug
Hong Kong 1919; 451 tons; 135.2ft × 29.1ft
In July 1941 the liner *Georgic*, being used as a troop transport, was bombed and set on fire whilst lying at Port Tewfik, Egypt. The burnt-out hulk was later towed to Port Sudan and on 5 March she left under the tow of two tugs, the *Recorder* and *St Sampson*, bound for Karachi. The following day, as the tugs struggled in a strong north-westerly gale to bring the hulk head to wind, the *St Sampson* was damaged and was forced to cast off the towline. She steadily filled with water, and eventually foundered, her crew being picked up by the hospital ship *Dorsetshire*.
[*http://www.liverpoolships.org/britannic_and_georgic_cunard_white_star.html*]

8 March NOTTS COUNTY trawler
Middlesbrough 1938 requisitioned 1939; 197 tons; 175.8ft × 28.6ft; 1 × 4in
Skipper Ronald Hartley Hampton RNR†
Patrolling to the south-east of Iceland in company with armed trawler *Angle*, when at 23.30, in position 63.10N 13.16W, she was hit on the port side amidships by a torpedo. She was seen to break in half and roll over to port and disappeared very quickly, her depth charges exploding as she sank. The *Angle* searched the area, picking up one survivor, but forty-one men died. Her attacker had been the *U 701* (Degen).
[*TNA: ADM.199/423*]

9 March SHERA whaler
Middlesbrough 1929 requisitioned 1940; 253 tons; 116ft × 24.2ft; 1 × 20mm
Lieutenant William Edward Bulmer RNR†
En-route to Murmansk to be transferred to the Russian Navy, she sailed in company with three other whalers from Greenock 14 February to join Convoy PQ12. At 06.30 on 9 March, when in approximate position 70.50N 38.10E she capsized over to port and sank. The weather at the time was not abnormal, and although some icing of the upper deck had occurred, it was not severe. It was thought that the stability of the vessel was certainly affected by the ice, and this was aggravated by the low level of oil fuel on board and the excessive top hamper. Only three of her crew survived, with twenty men losing their lives.
[*TNA: ADM.1/12142*]

11 March NAIAD cruiser
Hebburn 1939; 5,600 tons; 485ft × 50.6ft; 10 × 5.25in, 8 × 2pdr, 5 × 20mm, 6 × torpedo tubes
Captain Guy Grantham DSO
Acting as the flagship of Rear Admiral Vian, commanding the Fifteenth Cruiser Squadron, she was based in the eastern Mediterranean as flagship of Force 'B'. Following reports of a damaged enemy warship to the south-east of Malta, she sailed from Alexandria in the early hours of 10 March in company with *Euryalus* and *Dido* to search the area. The reports proved false, and now joined by *Cleopatra* with another destroyer, the force turned back for Alexandria. During 11 March they were subjected to constant air attacks, but avoided any damage, but late in the day it was a submarine attack which had success. The force was in position 32.01N 26.20E, to the north of Mersa Matruh, heading east at 18 knots, when the escorting destroyer *Zulu* sighted a submarine as it was submerging, but before any avoiding action could be taken, at 20.05 *Naiad* was struck on the starboard side by a torpedo. The explosion took place at 99 station, the junction between the forward engine room and the after boiler room. All power was lost, and the ship was plunged into darkness as the ship took an immediate list to starboard of 10 degrees. The list steadily increased to 20 degrees as the engine and boiler rooms flooded. The ship then hung in this position for about 5 minutes before the heel again increased until she rolled over, capsizing and sinking by the stern at 20.40. Eighty-one men died. The attacking submarine was the *U 565* (Jebsen).
[*TNA: ADM.267/13*]

11 March STELLA CAPELLA trawler
Beverley 1937 (*Admiral Hawke*) purchased 1939; 507 tons; 166.2ft × 28.1ft; 1 × 4in
Lieutenant Walter Langdon Sadgrove RANVR†
Sailed from Seidisfjord, Iceland, at 19.00 on 10 March bound for Stornoway, but disappeared, and was posted missing on 19 March with the loss of all thirty-three hands. After the war it emerged that she had been torpedoed at 02.11 the morning after her departure by *U 701* (Degen) in position 64.48N 13.20W, about 12 miles south-east of Vattarnes Lighthouse, disappearing in less than 3 minutes.
[*TNA ADM.199/239; https://www.uboat.net/allies/merchants/1420.html*]

12 March ST BRIAC target vessel
Dumbarton 1924 requisitioned 1941; 2, 292 tons;
316ft × 41.1ft
Captain Rupert Egerton Lubbock
Based at Dundee, she was employed in acting as a target
and range safety vessel for Fleet Air Arm aircraft from
RNAS Arbroath. During the morning of 12 March, she
had operated to the east of Aberdeen, until at 12.00 she
altered course to proceed to a new area about 50 miles
off the port for the next period of exercise. At 14.05
there was a large explosion under the after part of the
engine room on the port side as she detonated a mine.
The engine room rapidly flooded, and the after hold
slowly started to fill, but the stokehold bulkhead held.
Boats were ordered to be hoisted out as she slowly settled
by the stern. At 14.20 there was a second explosion aft;
it was uncertain whether this was a second mine or
the sound of the plates separating as the vessel broke
her back. After this she went down rapidly by the stern,
the bows rising vertically, remaining visible for about
5 minutes before sinking. Two lifeboats with survivors
spent an uncomfortable night before being seen by a
searching Swordfish aircraft. One boat was found by the
tug *Empire Larch*, but the second went ashore at Old
Slains, Collieston, capsizing in the surf, only four of the
occupants being saved. It was found that she had strayed
into a defensive British minefield, the full extent of
which was unknown to them. Considerable confusion
was revealed to have existed over the distribution of the
relevant 'Q' signal, outlining the danger area. The Naval
Officer in Charge at Dundee was found to have failed
to ensure that the ship had been properly informed of
the extent of the minefield; the commanding officer
of RNAS Arbroath had failed to advise the NOIC
Dundee of the extent of his planned exercise area and
Captain Lubbock of the *St Briac* should have ensured
that the ship was in full possession of all information
necessary for safe navigation. Forty-seven men died.
[TNA: ADM.1/15063]

13 March SPARSHOLT mooring lighter
South Shields 1915 requisitioned 1940; 127 tons;
105.9ft × 21.1ft
Boatswain Edward William Dalby[†]
Based at Sheerness, she sailed to fix moorings for
spotting vessels on a target range, being accompanied by
the trawler *Sarba*. They intended placing a wire pendant
on the buoy marking the spotting position, but as they
heaved the buoy up on deck, they also weighed the
securing anchor and consequently drifted. They asked
the *Sarba* to assist in re-positioning the buoy and anchor.
As the *Sarba* heaved in on the wire, she also moved the
securing anchor, dragging it under the *Sparsholt*, and it
struck the hull, holing her. Mr Dalby decided to run
her into shallow water, heading for Marine Parade,

Sheerness to the west of Garrison Point Light. When he
was 3 cables (600 yards) off the shore a mine exploded
under her starboard quarter, the bridge taking the full
force of the blast, and she rapidly sank. Seven men were
killed, with four survivors.
[TNA: ADM.199/221]

15 March VORTIGERN destroyer
Cowes 1917; 1,090 tons; 300ft × 29.6ft; 3 × 4in, 1 × 12pdr,
2 × 2pdr, 3 × torpedo tubes
Lieutenant Commander Ronald Stanley Howlett[†]
Part of the escort to the southbound North Sea Convoy
FS49, they departed from Methil on 13 March, bound
for Southend, with more ships joining off the Tyne.
During the night of 14/15 March she was stationed
on the seaward flank of the convoy when it came
under attack by a force of enemy fast torpedo boats.
At 01.55 when they were about 17 miles to the north
of Cromer, she was hit by a torpedo fired by *S 104*.
With her forward section damaged she went down by
the head very quickly, her stern remaining clear of the
water, evidently as her bows struck the bottom. Her loss
was not immediately noticed, except by the patrol vessel
Guillemot, which continued to screen the ships against
the torpedo boats until it was daylight, when she turned
back. She picked up fourteen men, some still clinging
to the wreck, others in a Carley float, all covered in
oil and surrounded by wreckage and floating bodies.
A subsequent search by the Cromer and Sheringham
lifeboats failed to find any more survivors. One hundred
and ten men died.
[TNA: ADM.199/692; Foynes pp222–3]

17 March ADEPT tug
Selby 1941; 700 tons; 142.5ft × 33.3ft; 1 × 12pdr,
1 × 20mm
Lieutenant Arthur Godfrey Norton Hawkins RNR
In poor weather, she ran aground on Patterson's
Rock, Isle of Sanda. The Campbeltown lifeboat was
despatched to the scene to stand by her, and the tugs
Zwarte Zee and *Caroline Moller* were ordered to try and
haul her off. They found that she was immoveable, and
her oil tank bulkhead had fractured. She was abandoned
the following day and declared a constructive total loss.
[TNA: ADM.199/802]

20 March HEYTHROP escort destroyer
Wallsend 1940; 1,050 tons; 264.2ft × 31.6ft; 6 × 4in,
4 × 2pdr
Lieutenant Commander Robert Sydney Stafford
In company with other ships of the Fifth Destroyer
Flotilla, sailed from Alexandria during 19 March to
carry out an aggressive anti-submarine patrol between
25.40E and 27.30E, ahead of the passage of Convoy
MW10 from Alexandria for Malta. At 11.00 the

officer of the watch saw torpedo tracks approaching and ordered the helm over, but before this could take effect, she was struck on the port side. about 60ft from the stern, by a torpedo which had been fired by the *U 652* (Fraatz). The damage was extensive to the after part of the ship, losing a gun mounting, and the after compartments started to flood. She was taken in tow by the *Eridge*, but the port propeller gland plate fractured and the loss of steam from number 2 boiler made it impossible to operate pumps for removal of water. She had a heavy list to starboard and after 2 hours the tow was slipped and she was abandoned, then having a 50-degree list, until at about 16.00 she rolled over onto her starboard side and sank, stern first, in position 32.13N 25.33E. Sixteen ratings were lost.
[TNA: ADM.199/650; CB.4273 p192]

22 March **ML 129** motor launch
Cremyll 1940; 75 tons; 112ft × 18.4ft; 1 × 3pdr
Lieutenant Walter Symington Strang RNVR
In March 1942, the Third Motor Launch Flotilla was deployed to the Mediterranean, to be stationed in Malta. The passage from Gibraltar was recognised as being hazardous, and the flotilla was sent in pairs, hugging the North African shoreline and flying Italian flags as a disguise. One pair had successfully made the transit, but the next pair – *ML 129* and *ML 132* – failed to make the passage. The pair sailed from Gibraltar on the night of 17/18 March and made it as far as Cape Bon when they were recognised as being hostile by an enemy aircraft. At about 10.30 a group of aircraft carried out attacks, but without causing any damage. The attack resumed mid-afternoon, and *129* suffered a direct hit. She caught fire, and the crew were forced to jump into the water. The survivors were picked up after an hour in the water. Seven men were lost.
[TNA: ADM.199/802; ADM.223/546; ADM.358/4054; Pope pp43–4]

22 March **ML 132** motor launch
Itchenor 1940; 75 tons; 112ft × 18.4ft; 1 × 3pdr
Lieutenant Alfred Thomas Read RANVR
Consort to *ML 129* (see above), she was damaged during the air attack off Cape Bon, but after picking up the survivors from *129*, decided that it was unlikely that she would be able to make Malta. She therefore steered for the port of Bône (Annaba) and requested the Vichy French authorities leave to stay for 24 hours to effect repairs, but this was refused, and the launch with her crew was interned.
[TNA: ADM.199/802; ADM.223/546; ADM.358/4054; Pope pp43–4]

24 March **SOUTHWOLD** escort destroyer
Cowes 1941; 1,050 tons; 264.2ft × 31.6ft; 6 × 4in, 2 × 2pdr
Commander Christopher Theodore Jellicoe DSC
Another unit of the Fifth Destroyer Flotilla (see *Heythrop* above), covering the outward passage of Convoy MW10 from Alexandria. The convoy attracted much enemy attention and there was a distant engagement between Italian and British surface forces. As they approached Malta, they came under air attack, and during this assault one of the convoy, the *Breconshire* was hit by a bomb and damaged and anchored off St Elmo's. The *Southwold* was directed to go to her aid and as she closed to pass a tow line a mine exploded under the engine room. She was enveloped in clouds of steam and smoke but remained afloat, although listing to starboard. The engine and gearing rooms were wrecked, and the upper deck was split over the engine room. The engine and boiler rooms slowly flooded. Her sister *Dulverton* closed, and it was hoped to rig a tow, but it became clear that her back was broken, the amidships section sagging and settling. As the list was slowly increasing, it was decided to leave her, the *Dulverton* remained close by to take off the crew. She then became the target of another air attack, and a Ju 88 straddled her with a number of bombs. One of these exploded close to the port side, which speeded up her demise; she steadily heeled over to starboard and eventually capsized and sank. Five men lost their lives.
[TNA: ADM.199/221]

25 March **VICTORIA I** drifter
Requisitioned 1940; No details known
Apparently, a local vessel fitted out as a minesweeper, she is listed as being sunk by enemy action but 'cause and place unknown'; she was based in the Mediterranean, at Alexandria – so presumably lost locally.
[Statement of Losses p23; Lloyd's War Losses p379]

25 March **SULLA** whaler
Middlesbrough 1928 requisitioned 1940; 251 tons; 116ft × 24.2ft; 1 × 20mm
Skipper Thomas Meadows RNR†
One of a group of armed whalers to be transferred to Russia that joined Convoy PQ13 for Kola that sailed from Seidisfjord on 22 March. The *Sulla* was last seen by her companions at 20.00 on the night of 25 March and subsequently by the escort *Walney* at about midnight astern of convoy, in position 70.57N 006E. A subsequent search of the area failed to find any trace of her. The cause of her disappearance was uncertain, but it was thought probable that she had capsized in the night due to the weight of ice on the upper works, the crew being unable to compete with the hostile weather conditions. The other whalers testified that they were 'practically unmanageable', being top heavy with ice, the temperatures constantly below freezing.
[TNA: ADM.1/11214; ADM.358/4058]

26 March LEGION destroyer

Hebburn 1939; 1,920 tons; 345.6ft × 36.9ft; 8 × 4in,
4 × 2pdr, 2 × 20mm, 8 × torpedo tubes

Commander Richard Frederick Jessel DSC

Sailed from Malta 20 March in company with the cruiser *Penelope* to meet Convoy MW10, a group of supply ships bound for Malta from Alexandria. Having made the rendezvous 2 days later, a powerful Italian surface force attempted to intercept the convoy. This resulted in the Second Battle of Sirte, with both sides suffering some damage, including *Legion*, but the Italian force withdrew. The following day the convoy was subjected to air attacks as they neared Malta. The *Legion* was the target for an attack by a Ju 88 aircraft which dropped four bombs, which exploded close along the starboard side. The shock damage was considerable, with radar and Asdic being put out of action, bulkheads cracked and much of the auxiliary machinery damaged. Despite the damage, she maintained power and successfully made harbour to be run into shallow water at Marsa Sciroco. She was subsequently hauled clear and on 26 March was lying alongside Boiler House Wharf in the dockyard when the island was subjected to an intense air raid by Ju 87 and Ju 88 aircraft. She was hit by two bombs. Both struck forward on 'B' gun deck; one of them exploded on the port side, the second pierced the deck to explode in the mess deck below. The effect of the blasts was devastating, the side being split open, and she rolled over onto her port side and sank by the bow in 5 minutes. Eleven men were killed.

[TNA: ADM.267/107]

26 March BRECONSHIRE stores carrier

Hong Kong 1939, requisitioned 1939; 9,776 tons;
483ft × 66.4ft

Captain Colin Alexander Gordon Hutchinson

Part of Convoy MW10 from Alexandria to Malta, which was comprised of four supply ships with a powerful escort of several cruisers and destroyers, the ships sailing from the Egyptian port on 20 March. During 22 March, an attempted interception of the convoy by an Italian force led to a rather confused and distant action, but no serious damage to ships in the convoy. The following day as the ships approached Malta, they came under intense and regular air attacks. At 10.30 when she was about 5 miles from Grand Harbour the *Breconshire* suffered a direct hit in the engine room. She lost power and an attempt by the cruiser *Penelope* to rig a tow failed in the heavy swell. With the weather deteriorating, in the strong winds and swell she drifted inshore and during the afternoon managed to anchor off Zonkor Point. The weather abated during the night of the 24/25 March, sufficient for the tugs *Ancient* and *Robust* to connect a tow, getting underway at 02.00. Strong winds prevented her being taken into Grand Harbour, but they took her into Marsaxlokk Bay where she anchored at 10.45. Air attacks resumed, but by the morning of 26th it was hoped to take her into harbour later that day, but at 18.30 a Ju 88 aircraft hit her with a number of bombs which set her on fire, and she was abandoned in a sinking condition. She finally sank at 11.03 the next day with part of her side above water. Over the next few weeks intensive efforts saw some fuel and stores being salvaged. Two men were killed.

[TNA: ADM.199/650; ADM.267/113]

26 March JAGUAR destroyer

Dumbarton 1938; 1,690 tons; 339.6ft × 35.8ft; 6 × 4.7in,
4 × 2pdr, 10 × torpedo tubes

Lieutenant Commander Lionel Rupert Knyvet Tyrwhitt
DSO DSC†

In company with the Greek destroyer *Vasilissa Olga* and the armed whaler *Klo*, sailed from Alexandria bound for Tobruk at 06.30 on 25 March as escorts to the oil tanker *Slavol*. At 02.38 in position 31.53N 26.18E the *Jaguar* had just commenced a turn to port as part of her zigzag pattern when there was a large explosion on the starboard side amidships as she was hit by a torpedo. This was followed immediately after by a second explosion under the funnel. She took a heavy list to starboard and within minutes had broken in half. The fore part was engulfed in flames as a fierce fire broke out near the galley, which spread to the forward messdecks and bridge superstructure, before it broke away, rolled over and sank. The stern section remained afloat for several minutes before disappearing. The *Klo* and *Olga* closed to assist and pick up survivors, but 153 men lost their lives. The *U 652* (Fraatz) was her attacker.

[TNA: ADM.267/93]

26 March SLAVOL oiler

Greenock 1917; 2,623 tons; 320.1ft × 41.6ft; 1 × 12pdr,
1 × 20mm

Master George Sydney Perry

Sailed from Alexandria bound for Tobruk escorted by two destroyers and an armed whaler (see *Jaguar* above), after the *Jaguar* was hit, she continued on her own way, unescorted, as the *Olga* and *Klo* both stood by the torpedoed ship. At 04.40 in position 32N 25.57E she was hit on the starboard side forward by a torpedo. She was stuck 10 minutes later by a second torpedo, which exploded by the boiler room. She quickly settled by the head, and when the foredeck was awash, she was ordered to be abandoned, and she subsequently sank. Her sinking was originally credited to *U 205*, but modern research has established that her attacker was *U 652* (Fraatz). Thirty-six men were lost.

[TNA: ADM.199/117; Morgan & Taylor, pp222–3]

26 March P 39 submarine
Barrow 1941; 540/732 tons; 180ft × 16.1ft; 1 × 12pdr;
4 × torpedo tubes
Lieutenant Norman Marriott
Deployed to the Mediterranean, she was stationed at Malta. As she entered harbour on 27 February she was attacked by an enemy aircraft, which strafed her with machine-gun fire. The resulting damage had scarcely been repaired when she was damaged during an air raid on 6 March. This left her with distorted casing, motors lifted off mountings and damaged batteries. She was towed to the Stone Wharf, Grand Harbour, for repair. During the afternoon of 26 March, she received a direct hit from a bomb during another air raid, which almost broke her in two. It was clear that she was a total loss, and she was paid off, towed to Kalkara and run ashore in shallow water.
[Evans pp306–08]

27 March STAGHOUND distilling vessel
Troon 1894, requisitioned 1940; 468 tons; 170ft × 25.6ft
Stationed at Torquay, she was sunk during an air raid. She was subsequently raised and berthed alongside Haldon Pier to be used for 'experimental purposes' and was eventually moved to the air gunnery range and weapons test site on St Thomas's Head for use as a target.
[Statement of Losses p23; Lloyd's War Losses p381]

28 March Operation 'Chariot' – the raid on St-Nazaire
In January 1942, the battleship *Tirpitz* sailed from the Baltic, to take shelter in a fjord in northern Norway. The movement was watched anxiously by the Admiralty, fearing that she may attempt to break out into the Atlantic as her sister *Bismarck* had done the previous year. Although little could be done at this time to prevent her sailing, it was thought that her return to port from a sortie would mean her running the gauntlet of British forces, particularly if the choice of port were limited. The only dry dock capable of handling a ship of her size in German hands on the Atlantic was the Forme-Écluse at the French port of St-Nazaire. A plan was therefore formed to take a force of commandos to the port which could be landed from motor launches to place demolition charges, whilst a destroyer, packed with explosives on time-delay fuses, would ram the dock gates. A motor torpedo boat would also be used to fire delayed-action torpedoes into the gates. The elderly Lend-Lease destroyer *Campbeltown* was selected for the role, having her main armament removed with extra 20mm Oerlikon guns installed, and a large quantity of explosives embarked on top of the fuel tanks with two sets of fuses. Her appearance was modified to resemble a German torpedo boat. Sailing from Devonport during the evening of 26 March, the force arrived at the

entrance to the river Loire undetected, despite a brush with a U-boat the following morning. At 22.00 on 27 March the force rendezvoused with the submarine *Sturgeon*, acting as a marker, 40 miles from the port, and they formed up to start the assault. At 23.30 the planned air raid on the port by RAF aircraft got under way, but this was hampered by poor visibility, which prevented any meaningful bombardment. The force managed to penetrate the river and despite being briefly illuminated by searchlight, and challenged by light from the shore, successfully reached the harbour entrance. At 01.28 the Germans, now realising the danger, opened fire. The wooden-hulled motor launches suffered badly as they were subjected to a fierce crossfire but pressed on; the destroyer increased speed to head to the lock gates.
[TNA: ADM.1/11888; ADM.1/14753; ADM.1/20019; DEFE.2/125 – 133; Dorrian passim]

CAMPBELTOWN destroyer
Bath 1919 (*Buchanan*), transferred 1940; 1,090 tons; 309ft × 30.10ft; 1 × 12pdr, 8 × 20mm
Lieutenant Commander Stephen Halden Beattie
The destroyer became the main target for enemy fire, being hit repeatedly by small and large calibre shells, but returned fire as she headed towards the dry dock. She rammed the dock gates at 01.34, her bows riding up onto the top of the caisson, and there she remained, firmly wedged. Although the landing parties had suffered several casualties, the embarked troops landed over the bows onto the caisson to successfully knock out gun positions and lay demolition charges in various dockyard buildings. When all the troops had gone, Commander Beattie ordered steam to be shut off and condenser inlets opened to ensure her stern settled. To his relief *ML 177* then appeared, to lay herself alongside the destroyer to lift off the wounded men and when this was complete, she embarked Beattie and several of the surviving crew of the destroyer. The main fuses had been set to explode after 2.5 hours, but they evidently failed, as she was still in place at first light when she was boarded by the Germans. During the morning, many German officers swarmed over her, and there was also a crowd of interested spectators, when at 11.30 she exploded violently as her cargo of twenty-seven depth charges and 100lbs of TNT blew up. The explosion buckled the caisson, forcing one end from its seating and water flooded into the dock, which contained two merchant vessels. The remains of the *Campbeltown* were carried forward into the dock on a surge of water. The dock remained out of action for the rest of the war. It was presumed that the main fuses had failed, but the secondary, long-delay fuses had worked. They had been set to explode after 8.5 hours, but trials found that they regularly fired at least 2 hours late. Lieutenant Commander Beattie had been taken prisoner by the

Germans after *ML 177* was sunk was subsequently awarded the Victoria Cross. Thirty-two men were lost.

ML 192 motor launch
Southampton 1941; 75 tons; 112ft × 18.4ft; 2 × 20mm
Lieutenant Commander William Lawson Stephens RNVR
ML 192 was the leader of the column designated as Group Two, to land troops to attack the 'old entrance' to the basin. As they neared their target, they were hit repeatedly by small-calibre fire, which was returned by their own armament, but she was then hit by a large-calibre shell which struck the waterline under the bridge. This was followed by another two hits, one of which exploded in the engine room. On fire, with many of the embarked troops killed or wounded, her engines stopped, and steering gear disabled, momentum carried her forward and she crashed alongside the Old Mole. Now burning fiercely, she drifted clear of the jetty, and was abandoned, the men jumping into the water, Carley floats being released for them to cling to. The floats drifted inshore as the battle raged around them, the survivors scrambling ashore to be taken prisoner. Four of her crew were killed.

ML 262 motor launch
Lowestoft 1941; 75 tons; 112ft × 18.4ft; 2 × 20mm
Lieutenant Edward Alfred Burt RNVR
Part of Group Two, she was immediately astern of her leader as the column steered towards the harbour, and when *ML 192* was put out of action, she assumed the lead to head towards the old entrance. Lieutenant Burt made several violent alterations of course to try and shake the attentions of the searchlights that were illuminating her. In doing so he overshot his target and was forced to reverse course, the boat immediately astern of him (*ML 267*) dutifully following. At 01.40 she finally found a suitable berth and ran alongside to land her troops. After engaging shore targets for some time, they took on board several troops, who had returned in the belief that the recall signal had been made. As they cleared the jetty and headed out for the main stream, she was hit several times, the hull being punctured, and a small fire started but pushed on, despite taking several casualties. She stopped to try and give aid to the burning *ML 457*, but then worked up to full speed to clear the harbour. As they did so they suffered a series of hits from heavy shells, the bridge, engine room and mess deck all being struck. A fire started in the engine room and steering was lost and with the boat attracting a large amount of tracer fire she was ordered to be abandoned. Carley floats were lowered, and wounded men put in them, the others jumping into the water to cling to wreckage and made their way ashore to be captured. The launch blew up shortly afterwards. Seven of her crew were lost.

ML 267 motor launch
Sarisbury Green 1941; 75 tons; 112ft × 18.4ft; 2 × 20mm
Lieutenant Eric Harry Beart RNVR†
Assigned to Group Two, she followed *ML 262* as they overshot their target and were forced to reverse course and try and find the old entrance to the dock. After some time, they ran into shallow water near a landing stage to start disembarking their troops. This had scarcely begun when they came under heavy and accurate fire, being hit by large and small-calibre shells which started a fire. Lieutenant Beart attempted to go astern to pull her clear, but the engines stopped, and she started to sink, and her surviving crew and remaining troops jumped into the water to try and make the shore through the hail of machine-gun fire. Eight of the embarked Commandos were killed along with Beart with nine others of the crew.

ML 268 motor launch
Hamworthy 1941; 75 tons; 112ft × 18.4ft; 2 × 20mm
Lieutenant Arnold Bertram Kingsley Tillie RNVR
Part of the Group Two team, in the confusion of lights and gunfire, she lost sight of her leaders, and steered independently towards the jetty. As she neared, she was hit by a shell which brought her to a halt and set her on fire. The fire spread rapidly to her petrol tanks which had ruptured and burnt fiercely until she blew up with a violent explosion. Eight of her crew were killed.

ML 177 motor launch
Wallasea 1940; 75 tons; 112ft × 18.4ft; 1 × 3pdr;
2 × torpedo tubes
Sub-Lieutenant Mark Fleming Rodier RNVR†
Last in the doomed column that made up Group Two, she bore a charmed life initially, with the fire being concentrated on the boats ahead of her. Avoiding the burning wreckage in the water she was put alongside the jetty and the troops were landed. That complete, she ran alongside the *Campbeltown* to lift off Commander Beattie and many of her crew, plus several of the wounded men. When full of men, she got underway and working up to 20 knots, headed for open water, taking the opportunity to fire both her torpedoes at some vessels seen at anchor, although they appear to have struck the jetty. The launch then pulled clear of the harbour and the small arms fire, but they still attracted the attention of a shore battery which opened an accurate fire, and they were struck by a large-calibre shell in the engine room. All power was lost, the engines stopped, and she came to a halt. Now illuminated by a powerful searchlight, other gun batteries joined in, and she was hit again by another large shell which struck amidships. The launch now caught fire and she was abandoned as she broke in half, her bow and stern rising clear of the water before she sank. The survivors clung

to wreckage and several did make it ashore, including Beattie. Five of her men died, along with several of the *Campbeltown* men.

ML 447 motor launch
Horning 1941; 75 tons; 112ft × 18.4ft; 2 × 20mm
Lieutenant Thomas Douglas Laverick Platt RNR

ML 447 headed the column of launches known as Group One that were heading for the Old Mole; being the leader, she seemed to attract the attention of much of the shore fire and was hit repeatedly, and many of her embarked troops were killed or wounded. As Lieutenant Platt neared the jetty, he altered course to run alongside, but the launch ran aground as he did so. Her engines were put astern to pull her free but just as she got under way, she was hit by a large-calibre shell in the engine room, which stopped the engines and started a fierce fire. She drifted clear, still going astern. *ML 160* then gallantly ran alongside the burning launch to take off firstly the wounded and then the survivors, Lieutenant Platt being the last to leave. The launch continued to drift across the river burning fiercely, until she blew up some time later with a loud explosion. Five members of the crew and eight commandos were killed.

ML 457 motor launch
Leigh on Sea 1941; 75 tons; 112ft × 18.4ft; 2 × 20mm
Lieutenant Thomas Alexander Mackay Collier RNVR†

Immediately astern of *ML 447* as they headed towards the Old Mole, they escaped much of the incoming fire, and were able to pass their leader, not realising that she had been damaged, and the boat was successfully put alongside the jetty to land her troops. Having done so, she stood off, now becoming the target for small arms fire and grenades lobbed from the jetty, one of which exploded inside the bridge killing or wounding several men. As she attempted to make for the open sea, she was still under heavy fire from the shore, and after being hit repeatedly was brought to a halt, and a fire started. *ML 262* saw her difficulties and ran alongside to start taking off her men, but was then ordered away by Lieutenant Collier, as both vessels were still being hit. Those that did not make it then abandoned her, jumping into the water, to leave the launch burning and settling in the mainstream. Nine members of her crew died.

ML 298 motor launch
Hamworthy 1941; 75 tons; 112ft × 18.4ft; 2 × 20mm
Sub-Lieutenant Neville Rupert Nock RNVR

One of the launches that were to be used to pick up returning troops and provide fire support, the launch stayed clear of the other craft and engaged shore positions with her own armament. After some time, and with explosions being seen ashore, *298* was taken inshore, with the intention of picking up any returning

troops that they could find. They successfully made it to the jetty, near the old entrance, but finding no friendly troops to embark, they decided to clear the harbour. They steered around the burning wrecks of other launches and patches of burning fuel, but despite her manoeuvring she was illuminated by a searchlight and came under very heavy fire. A hit astern started a fire, and she was then hit several times by a variety of shells, peppering her hull and stopping her engines. Now drifting helplessly, she was ordered to be abandoned, survivors taking to a Carley float or clinging to wreckage. Ten of her crew were killed.

MTB 74 motor torpedo boat
Portsmouth 1941; 39 tons; 72.7ft × 19.2ft; 2 × torpedo tubes
Sub-Lieutenant Robert Charles Michael Vaughan Wynn RNVR

Having been towed across the Channel by the escort destroyer *Atherstone*, she was the last of the small craft to enter the estuary, her role being to assist in the destruction of the lock gates. She steered clear of the launches and escaped any injury to follow the destroyer. Having seen the *Campbeltown* had rammed the lock gates and confirming that she was firmly in place, Wynn fired his delayed-action torpedoes at the gates of the old entrance and then made her way down river, picking up men from the shore plus some survivors from the water from sunken launches. Putting the head to the sea, Wynn worked up to full speed to clear the harbour, but as they did so saw a Carley float full of men. Slowing down to close the float, she was hit twice by heavy shells. The boat promptly caught fire and was abandoned. Six men were killed with just four survivors, one of them being Wynn, who had lost an eye. Her torpedoes exploded during the afternoon, wrecking the outer caisson of the old lock.

ML 306 motor launch
Sarisbury Green 1941; 75 tons; 112ft × 18.4ft; 2 × 20mm
Lieutenant Ian Bernard Henry Henderson RNVR†

One of the launches assigned to Group One, tasked to land troops on the Old Mole, she was the fifth ship in line and found their way blocked by burning wreckage from the boats ahead of her, and ran along the jetty under constant fire, unable to find a safe landing place. Lieutenant Henderson therefore decided to turn back to the harbour entrance and was able to extract the launch relatively unscathed from the fierce fighting. At 05.30 she was well clear of the coast and heading for the rendezvous with the escort destroyers when dark shapes were seen ahead, which were resolved as five German destroyers. One of the enemy ships, the *Jaguar*, hauled out of line, increased speed, switched on her searchlight and attempted to ram the launch. Quick manoeuvring by Lieutenant Henderson meant that only a glancing blow was struck, but this threw several men into the water. The pair then parted, firing furiously at each other. The smaller vessel suffered, being riddled with shell holes and most of the men killed or wounded. When a shell exploded on the bridge of the launch, killing or incapacitating the occupants, she was leaderless. Several of the embarked soldiers continued to fire small arms for several minutes more but at about 06.00 when the destroyer ran alongside, resistance had ceased, and she was boarded. After removing the survivors and treating the wounded, she was taken in tow for St-Nazaire as a prize. Four of her crew and several of the embarked soldiers were killed. She was subsequently refitted and entered Kreigsmarine service as a motor minesweeper, *RA 9*. She was sunk by British air attack off Le Havre in June 1944.

ML 156 motor launch
Wallasea 1940; 75 tons; 112ft x 18.4ft; 1 x 3pdr,
2 x torpedo tubes
Lieutenant Leslie Fenton RNVR
Following astern of *ML 268* as part of Group Two, with troops embarked to attack installations around the main basin, her bridge was hit by a burst of small arms fire, seriously wounding Lieutenant Fenton. With the launch ahead of her (*ML 268*) exploding, and unable to find their landing place, Sub-Lieutenant Noel Gordon Machin RNVR assumed command, made smoke and tried to reverse course to take them out of the crossfire. However, she was hit repeatedly, one engine being knocked out and steering gear disabled. Swathed in smoke she staggered out of line and somehow pointed her bows to the open sea. At first light she successfully rendezvoused with the destroyers *Atherstone* and *Tynedale* and was able to transfer her wounded men. As it was believed that she would never make England in her damaged state, she was abandoned, slowly settling, the *Atherstone* firing several rounds into her as she drifted away. A Heinkel floatplane later appeared and dropped a bomb on her as she sank.

MGB 314 motor gun boat
Bangor 1941; 72 tons; 108ft x 17.5ft; 2 x 2pdr
Lieutenant Dunstan Michael Car Curtis RNVR
Designated as the command vessel for the actual assault, she was towed to the enemy coast by the escort destroyer *Atherstone*, when Commander R E D Ryder embarked. Initially she went ahead of the destroyer, engaging shore positions and a guardship as she did. As the destroyer went in to ram the gates, she circled round and ran alongside the jetty to land her party of troops. That complete, she took on board several wounded men, and some of the crew of the now abandoned *Campbeltown*. At about 02.30 with the headquarters staff re-embarked

she got underway, and unaware of the failure of the group designated to attack the old entrance, went along the jetty to investigate, and was surprised to come under very heavy fire from the shore. Fire was returned, that from the forward 2pdr, manned by Able Seaman Savage being particularly effective in silencing enemy gun positions. After some time attempting give some support to the troops remaining ashore, it eventually became clear that they could do little more, as the situation was very confused with the designated landing places clearly in enemy hands and fire from the shore coming uncomfortably close. Therefore, at about 03.00 she turned seaward and increased speed to clear the harbour. As they moved out of range of the harbour guns, she came into sight of the coastal batteries of heavy guns and the gunboat worked up to full speed, manoeuvring all the time to avoid the shells, which threw up large columns of smoke and water. They eventually cleared out of range of the guns only to see the shape of a large ship looming ahead in the darkness. This was a German patrol boat and the pair passed by each other on opposing courses at close range exchanging gunfire. The gunboat escaped any serious damage, but two men were killed, including Able Seaman William Savage who died at his gun. She met the *Atherstone* and *Tynedale*, and it was hoped that she would make it back to England, but she was struggling to keep the pace and was filling with water, a chain of buckets being used to try and clear the boat. She was therefore abandoned, and she was despatched by several rounds fired by the destroyers. Savage was subsequently awarded a posthumous Victoria Cross.

ML 446 motor launch
Falmouth 1941; 75 tons; 112ft x 18.4ft; 2 x 20mm
Lieutenant Henry George Richard Falconar RNVR
Sternmost of the vessels that made up the column of launches of Group One, she suffered a direct hit from a large calibre shell amidships as she approached the Mole, which killed or wounded many of the men on board. In the confusion of searchlights and heavy fire she overshot her designated landing place and was forced to reverse course. It was then found that the jetty was still clearly occupied by the enemy and burning wreckage from other launches baulked their approach. As they searched along the jetty they came under heavy fire from large and small-calibre guns, and took more casualties, and all her guns were put out of action. Lieutenant Falconar therefore decided to abandon the attempt and headed seawards, making smoke as he did. She successfully cleared the harbour and during the morning met the escort destroyers to transfer her wounded. It was decided that it was unlikely that she would make England in her damaged state, so she was abandoned and sunk by fire from the escorts.

ML 270 motor launch
Oulton Broad 1941; 75 tons; 112ft × 18.4ft; 1 × 3pdr;
2 × torpedo tubes
Sub-Lieutenant Charles Stuart Bonshaw Irwin RNR

Not assigned as a troop carrier, she was one of those launches to be employed initially as a fire-support vessel then to pick up troops from the shore. She kept clear of the columns approaching the jetty, staying midstream, but still attracted incoming fire, and a hit aft put the steering out of action. With emergency steering rigged, she headed out of the harbour, still under fire. Another hit had started a fire in the engine room, but this was extinguished. As they cleared the approaches, they passed close by an incoming enemy torpedo boat and exchanged fire, but escaped any serious damage, and finally rendezvoused with *MGB 314* and together they made the meeting with the escort destroyers. During the morning it became clear that she would not be able to make it back to England, so she was abandoned, the *Brocklesby* firing several rounds into her to ensure that she sank.

★ ★ ★

29 March MTB 215 motor torpedo boat
Hampton 1940; 17 tons; 55ft × 11ft; 2 × torpedo tubes
Lieutenant Alec Primrose Grahame Joy RCNVR

Based in the eastern Mediterranean, she was the last survivor of the 10th MTB Flotilla. She had been damaged in a collision with her sister *MTB 68* (see 14 December 1941), and although temporarily repaired at Tobruk, she remained out of action. It was decided to send her to Alexandria, but during the passage she started making water, and foundered in shallow water. The hull was later salvaged but written off as a total loss.
[*Reynolds & Cooper, Mediterranean MTBs at War pp29–30*]

March MMS 147 / MMS 153 / MMS 156 / MMS 161 / MMS 162 / MMS 163 / MMS 164
Rangoon; 225 tons; 105ft × 23ft

All motor minesweepers, under construction at Rangoon, they are shown as being destroyed on the stocks before the occupation of that city by the Japanese, which happened on 7 March, so presumably before that date.
[*Lenton; TNA: CAB.66/22*]

1 April P 36 submarine
Barrow 1941; 540/732 tons; 180ft × 16.1ft; 1 × 12pdr;
4 × torpedo tubes
Lieutenant Harry Noel Edmonds

Stationed in the Mediterranean, she arrived at Malta 29 March on completion of a patrol. She was alongside at Marsamxett when the island came under another heavy air attack. During the afternoon, a bomb exploded

between the submarine and the harbour wall which blew a large hole in the port side. To prevent her sinking a wire hawser was rigged, running around the conning tower and secured to buildings ashore. However, she steadily filled with water, until it was clear that the strain on the wire was close to breaking point. The wire was therefore severed, and *P 36* rolled over and sank in 50ft of water. She remained on the bottom until July 1958 when she was finally raised, and after lying in shallow water for 2 weeks, was towed out to sea and scuttled.
[*Evans pp309–10*]

1 April PANDORA submarine
Barrow 1929; 1,475/2,040 tons; 270ft × 29.11ft; 1 × 4in,
8 × torpedo tubes
Lieutenant Robert Love Alexander

Having completed a refit in the United States, the *Pandora* was ordered to return to the Mediterranean. After a stop at Gibraltar, she arrived at Malta on 31 March, laden with stores for the island. She was alongside Hamilton Wharf, discharging her cargo, when the island came under an intense air raid. Between 14.30 and 15.00 she received two direct hits and after the second hit, she sank in less than 4 minutes, with the loss of two officers and twenty-five men. The wreck was subsequently raised and towed to Kalkara Creek where she was beached. The remains lay there until 1957 when she was sold for scrap.
[*Evans p310*]

1 April SOLOMON trawler
Beverley 1928 (*Lady Rachael*) requisitioned 1939;
357 tons; 140.4ft × 24ft
Skipper-Lieutenant Charles Dale RNR

In company with the trawler *Kurd*, she was conducting a night patrol off the north Norfolk coast and the approaches to the River Humber. At 00.46 a mine detonated under her port quarter. The violence of the explosion lifted the ship bodily, extinguished all lights and flooded the upper deck. She was badly shaken, with water entering in several places, but she remained afloat. The *Kurd* closed and took her in tow, but she steadily settled and eventually sank, her position then being 53.11.25N 01.11.05E.
[*TNA: ADM.199/221*]

1 April SUNSET drifter
Goole 1918; 148 tons; 86ft × 18.6ft; 1 × 6pdr
Lieutenant John Reginald Lidgey RNR

Based at Malta, she had been fitted out as a minesweeper and was busily employed keeping Grand Harbour clear. The harbour was under constant air attack and during the afternoon she was damaged during an attack and subsequently foundered in shallow water in French Creek.
[*TNA: ADM.199/648; Warships Supplement no 133 p5*]

4 April PLUMLEAF oiler
Wallsend 1916; 5,916 tons; 405.5ft × 54.5ft
Master Leonard Elford
Damaged following several near misses during air raids, whilst moored at Parlatario wharf, Malta, she suffered a direct hit on 26 March, with her after end sinking in shallow water, although the ship remained upright. She was hit again during air raids on 4 April and sank to deck level in 46ft of water and written off as a total loss. The wreck was raised and sold for scrap in 1947.
[Lloyd's War Losses p380]

5 April Air raid on Ceylon
In late March 1942, the Japanese deployed a large and powerful force under Admiral Nagumo, comprising five large aircraft carriers and four battleships with escorting cruisers and destroyers, into the Indian Ocean with the intention of attacking British warships in the harbours of Trincomalee and Colombo. Warned of their approach by an RAF reconnaissance flight, Admiral Somerville ordered all ships that could sail to leave the harbours, but about twenty-one merchant ships and thirteen naval vessels were unable to leave. At first light on 5 April Admiral Nagumo launched fifty-three B5N 'Kate' torpedo bombers, with thirty-eight D3A 'Val' bombers escorted by thirty-six A6M 'Zero' fighters to carry out the attack. Because of the orders to leave the harbour, the targets were few, and the raid not as successful as Nagumo would have liked; two warships were sunk with another, the depot ship *Lucia* and the merchant ship *Benledi* damaged. The warships lost were:

5 April HECTOR armed merchant cruiser
Greenock 1924; 11,198 tons; 498.8ft × 62.3ft; 8 × 6in, 2 × 12pdr
Commander Arthur Kennett Baxendell RAN
Having just undocked after a period of repair, she was alongside number 4 berth at Colombo when the air raid developed. At 07.50 the first aircraft appeared, and a group of dive bombers attacked the *Hector*, and she was hit by four bombs, two of which entered through the engine room skylight, and another detonated in the boiler room having penetrated after hitting the base of the funnel. The fourth bomb hit the waterline on the port side abreast number 2 hold, blowing a large hole in the side. Fires immediately broke out in both engine and boiler rooms, power failed, and all the lights went out. Attempts to fight the fire were hindered by much of the fire-fighting equipment having been wrecked. A merchant ship, the *Tjibadak*, was moored nearby, and untouched by the air raid provided hoses to help fight the fire, but at 09.00 this had to be abandoned, as did assistance from the tug *Sinjabahu* which had come alongside, as they could do little. A more determined effort to tackle the blaze was organised with the boom

defence vessel *Barlane* coming alongside along with a dredger, and pumps were passed onboard. The fire, however, had a firm hold and at 10.00 Commander Baxendell ordered the men to start leaving her, and the last of the fire parties left her at 14.00 and she was allowed to burn herself out. A total of fourteen men were killed in the attack.
[TNA:ADM.199/623]

5 April TENEDOS destroyer
Hebburn 1918; 905 tons; 265ft × 26.9ft; 3 × 4in, 1 × 2pdr, 2 × 20mm, 4 × torpedo tubes
Lieutenant Commander Richard Dyer
Under repair at the time of the raid on Colombo, she became the target of high-level bombers. The destroyer was hit on the starboard side aft by two bombs and there were also near misses, with bombs exploding abreast the foremost funnel and near the stern. This resulted in the destroyer settling with her masts and upper works exposed. Three officers and twelve ratings were killed.
[TNA:ADM.199/623]

★ ★ ★

5 April DORSETSHIRE cruiser
Portsmouth 1929; 10,300 tons; 595ft × 66ft; 8 × 8in, 4× 4in, 16 × 2pdr, 6 × 20mm, 8 × torpedo tubes
Captain Augustus Wilmington Shelton Agar VC
In company with the *Cornwall*, she had sailed from Trincomalee on news of the approaching Japanese force under Nagumo (see above) intending to join the main fleet under Somerville. Enemy reports from friendly reconnaissance aircraft indicated the presence of a strong force continuing to close from the east and at 08.00 speed was increased to 27 knots. At 11.30 a spotter plane from the Japanese cruiser *Tone* discovered the cruisers as they headed south-east. On receiving this intelligence, Nagumo ordered a substantial force to attack the pair and launched fifty-three D3A 'Val' bomber aircraft which arrived at 13.40, consisting of several waves, in formations of three aircraft. The first wave concentrated on the *Cornwall*, but the second headed for the *Dorsetshire*. Avoiding action was taken, but as more aircraft arrived to attack her, she could not avoid being hit. A few moments after the attack had commenced, she was hit three times in quick succession. One bomb went through the quarterdeck which disabled the steering gear, and another went through the catapult to destroy the wireless offices. The third exploded on the port side amidships, putting out of action all the armament on the port side. The unremitting attack continued, and in the next few minutes several more hits were received, one bomb going through the base of the forward funnel, another exploding aft, putting the after turrets out of action whilst the after funnel was demolished by another hit.

She had now assumed a list to port; fires had broken out on the upper deck and in the stokers' mess deck. All the powered anti-aircraft guns were inoperative; she had lost communications and steering and was slowing as she lost power. Captain Agar ordered all the rafts, floats and boats to be lowered, but as this was under way another wave of attacks commenced. In the next few minutes, she was hit another four times, besides several near misses. She heeled further over to port and all hands were ordered to come on deck and abandon her over the starboard side. About 10 minutes after the attack had commenced, she rolled over onto her port side and sank, stern first. The survivors huddled in the boats and rafts and were picked up by the *Enterprise* and two destroyers later that evening. Two hundred and thirty-four men died.

[TNA: ADM.199/623; Shores & Cull p406]

5 April CORNWALL cruiser

Devonport 1926; 10,900 tons; 590ft × 68.4ft; 8 × 8in, 4 × 4in, 4 × 2pdr, 6 × 20mm, 8 × torpedo tubes
Captain Percival Clive Wickham Manwaring

Consort to the *Dorsetshire* (see above), it was realised at 11.30 that they were in danger from air attack after the sighting of a Japanese floatplane. At 13.40 many aircraft were seen closing from the east and the initial attack headed for the *Cornwall*. Diving out of the sun, the enemy aircraft pressed home the attack despite the heavy anti-aircraft fire put up by the cruisers. The numbers attacking were such that she was soon overwhelmed. Within 5 minutes she was hit at least eight times, the first bomb hitting her between the funnels, penetrating the boiler room flat; others exploded between 'X' and 'Y' turrets; amidships, which knocked out the dynamo room; the quarterdeck, the sick bay flat, the recreation spaces. She was also near missed about seven or eight times. The helm was jammed hard to starboard, all power failed, both engine and boiler rooms reported they were flooding, and numerous fires were started. The ship heeled over to port until the gunwale was awash, the starboard propellers breaking the surface, the ship wreathed in thick black smoke. It was clear that she was sinking and Captain Manwaring, wounded in the shoulder, ordered her to be abandoned, and about 5 minutes later she rolled over and sank by the bows, finally plunging bows first at an angle of 30 degrees. One hundred and ninety men died, with the survivors being picked up later that evening by the cruiser *Enterprise*.

[TNA: ADM.199/623]

5 April ABINGDON minesweeper

Troon 1918; 710 tons; 220ft × 28ft; 1 × 4in, 1 × 12pdr
Lieutenant Graham Allen Simmers RNR

Based at Malta, the *Abingdon* was hard worked keeping the approaches to Grand Harbour clear of mines, being attacked several times by enemy aircraft. The air attacks on the island intensified and on 1 April several bombs fell near her causing considerable damage. On 4 April she was lying in Kalkara creek when she was near missed by two bombs, and this caused more damage, and she started to flood. To save her she was towed into shallow water and run ashore near Bighi hospital but was written off as a constructive total loss.

[TNA: ADM.199/650; Williams p36]

6 April HAVOCK destroyer

Dumbarton 1936; 1,340 tons; 312ft × 33ft; 4 × 4.7in, 8 × torpedo tubes
Lieutenant Commander Geoffrey Robert Gordon Watkins DSC

The destroyers in the Mediterranean were a hard-pressed group, constantly in use and with little time given for repairs or recuperation. On 22 March, the *Havock* was involved in an action with Italian units whilst screening Convoy MW10 bound for Malta, during which she was damaged by a near miss from a heavy shell. She made Valetta for repair, where she was under constant air attack. Scarcely was she out of dockyard hands than she was employed screening a 500-ton lighter to the wreck of the *Breconshire*, so that much needed fuel oil could be extracted. During this, she again came under the constant attention of enemy aircraft before she regained Valetta harbour. She was then ordered to sail to Gibraltar for further repairs and to evacuate several wounded officers and troops. During all this time her officers and crew had been under great strain, Lieutenant Commander Watkins later complained that he had had little or no sleep for several days before sailing, and it was with some trepidation that he undertook the passage, having to trust the navigation to an inexperienced Reserve Sub-Lieutenant, Royston Lack. They sailed at 19.30 on 5 April, and after passing Pantelleria, to avoid minefields, altered course for the light at Kelibia, Tunisia, steaming at 30 knots. At 03.50 white water was seen ahead, and Watkins, who had been on the bridge for much of the time ordered an alteration of course, but soon realised that there was still broken water ahead. The engines were then put to full astern, but despite this she ran hard aground on a spit of sand about 100 yards from the shore. The ship was ordered to be lightened, and some ammunition was heaved overboard, but it was clear that this was futile. The passengers were ordered ashore, and preparations were made to destroy her. Cordite charges were laid everywhere, and a depth charge was placed into a forward compartment. As the last of the men left her, this was exploded, which blew out the sides of the fo'c'sle, and the resulting cordite explosions started fires through the ship. A messenger was sent to the nearby Fort Kelibia and later that morning a force of French soldiers arrived on scene to escort them to the

barracks. At 14.00 a large explosion was seen, which was probably the remaining depth charges blowing up, which destroyed much of the wreck. In the early hours of the next morning the Italian submarine *Aradam* fired a torpedo into her remains and claimed to have given her the *coup-de grâce*, but as she had already been destroyed by the explosion of her own ammunition, this was hardly necessary. One man, a stoker, was killed when a steam valve ruptured in the engine room and a second stoker, severely injured in the same incident, died later of his injuries. The loss resulted in a court martial which resulted in Watkins being found guilty of losing his ship through negligence. It was found that when he took his ship towards Kelibia at high speed, by steering between a minefield and a rocky shore, he had (i) failed to clarify the position of the ship before doing so; (ii) failed to ensure that the bearing and distance of Kelibia light showed that it was safe to make any alteration of course and finally (iii) failed to check Sub-Lieutenant Lack's calculations. In light of a distinguished war career, and testimonies from several officers including Admiral Somerville, Commander Watkins was not given a harsh punishment, being reprimanded.
[TNA ADM.1/12040; ADM.156/252]

6 April   INDUS   minesweeper
Hebburn 1934; 1,190 tons; 250ft × 34ft; 2 × 4.7in
Commander Jesser Evelyn Napier Coope, RIN
Royal Indian Navy. Deployed to Burma to provide support to the retreating British forces, she was at anchor in the harbour of Akyab when that harbour came under a series of air attacks. During the morning she suffered from several near-misses, until hit by at least two bombs, one of them exploding in the engine room. Another near miss under the stern caused her to start settling, and she capsized and sank in position 020.07N 092.54E. Although several men were wounded, there were no deaths.
[TNA: ADM. 358/4070; www.ibiblio.org/hyperwar/UN/India/RIN/RIN-6.html]

7 April   EMILY   tug
Greenock 1933 (*Emilia*) purchased 1934; 71 tons;
78ft × 18.1ft
Based at Malta, she was sunk in the harbour during a very heavy air raid.
[TNA: ADM.199/650]

7 April   HELLESPONT   tug
Hull 1910; 690 tons; 144ft × 27.4ft
Based at Malta, she was damaged by an air raid in September 1940 and was subsequently laid up at Sheer Bastion. She received a direct hit from a bomb during a very heavy air raid and sank alongside Somerset wharf,

apparently having her bows blown off. The wreck was later raised and subsequently dumped off Grand Harbour.
[TNA: ADM.199/413: http://www.marinefoundation.org/wreckshmshellespoint.htm]

8 April   THORGRIM   whaler
Sandefjord 1936 requisitioned 1940; 305 tons;
125.5ft × 25.6ft; 1 × 4in
Lieutenant Joseph Benjamin Sparkes RNR
Based at Alexandria, she had just completed a boiler clean, and to assist in raising steam the armed whaler *Svana* was brought alongside, and a steam hose rigged to the *Thorgrim*. During the early hours of 8 April an air raid took place on the harbour, and at 05.15 a large bomb exploded close under the sterns of the trawlers, with a second bomb landing on the quay, showering them with splinters. The blast lifted them out of the water, breaking the moorings and severing the steam pipe. Clouds of steam blanketed the pair, and *Thorgrim*, with plates split and rivets blown, settled by the stern and sank. There were no casualties.
[TNA: ADM.267/120]

8 April   SVANA   whaler
Middlesbrough 1930 requisitioned 1940; 268 tons;
121.4ft × 24.6ft; 1 × 4in
Lieutenant John McDonald Ruttan DSC RCNVR
Based at Alexandria, she was brought alongside the *Thorgrim* to expedite the raising of steam (see above). When the bombs landed close by, she was lifted out of the water by the blast, and then heeled over to port. With water flooding into the stokehold, she rapidly settled until she sank. Several men were injured, but there were no deaths.
[TNA: ADM.267/120]

9 April   HERMES   aircraft carrier
Walker 1919; 10,850 tons; 548ft × 65ft; 6 × 5.5in, 3 × 4in,
4 × 2pdr
Captain Richard Francis John Onslow MVO DSO†
Following the attacks on Ceylon, detailed above, Admiral Nagumo's force had remained to the east of Ceylon whilst his aircraft searched for the missing heavy units, but was sighted and reported by British reconnaissance aircraft. The harbour of Trincomalee was again cleared of shipping. The *Hermes*, her aircraft disembarked ashore, sailed at 01.00 on the 9th accompanied by the Australian destroyer *Vampire* and hugging the coast headed south until they were some 60 miles to the south of the harbour. Course was then reversed, intending to arrive back at dusk. However, at 08.55, when about 10 miles off Batticaloa light, she was seen by a floatplane from the battleship *Haruna* which reported locating an aircraft carrier escorted by three

destroyers. A powerful striking force was consequently launched from the Japanese carriers, with eighty-five D3A 'Val' bombers, escorted by several A6M 'Zero' fighter aircraft. At 10.35 aircraft were sighted closing from the east, and for the next 10 minutes *Hermes* was the target of a sustained attack by the bomber aircraft. The 4in guns opened fire as the Japanese aircraft closed, but the carrier was completely overwhelmed. Almost immediately there were two violent explosions as bombs hit the starboard side and the whole ship shuddered. More hits followed, with bombs hitting 'S1' gun, the port side aft and starboard side forward and the lights went out. When the forward lift was hit it caused a large explosion, scattering debris and starting a fire, with smoke pouring out of the hanger. She was hit or near missed by repeatedly by bombs and within 10 minutes was burning from a large fire in the hanger and had a 40-degree list to port. She continued to slowly roll over, sinking bows first, her stern rising clear of the water until it was almost vertical before it disappeared. Eighteen officers and 288 ratings were lost. The position was 07.45N 81.48E.

[TNA: ADM.199/623]

9 April VAMPIRE destroyer

Cowes 1917; 1,090 tons; 300ft × 30.7ft; 4 × 4in, 1 × 12pdr, 2 × 2pdr, 2 × 20mm, 6 × torpedo tubes

Commander William Thomas Alldis Moran RAN†

Royal Australian Navy. Escorting the aircraft carrier *Hermes*, as outlined above, the pair came under sustained air attack during the morning. After the carrier was set on fire, the attack shifted to the destroyer. About fifteen aircraft took part in the attack, and she suffered three near misses, with a bomb exploding under the stern, and another two in the water alongside 'B' gun, which put both forward guns out of action. A further near miss demolished the whaler. She then took a direct hit, which went through an upper deck locker to penetrate and explode in number 2 boiler room. Losing power, she slowed and further near misses followed until a second bomb struck an oil fuel tank. She developed a heavy list to port, and she was ordered to be abandoned. Attacks continued as this was underway, with another hit which struck the torpedo tubes, and although the warheads did not explode, the blast was sufficient to break her back. She broke up and the forward half sank very quickly, the stern section remained afloat for several minutes until the after magazine exploded and she sank at 11.05. Eight men were killed in the attack, but the remainder were picked up during the afternoon by the hospital ship *Vita*.

[TNA: ADM.267/106]

9 April HOLLYHOCK corvette

Sunderland 1940; 940 tons; 190ft × 33ft; 1 × 4in, 1 × 2pdr

Lieutenant Commander Thomas Edward Davies OBE RNR†

Acting as an escort to the oil tanker *Athelstane*, the pair sailed from Trincomalee for Colombo early on 9 April. At 10.05 they saw the attacks being made on the distant *Hermes* (see above) and altered to the south to close the shore. However, at about 12.00 when they were about 30 miles to the south of Batticaloa light, they were sighted by a group of 'Val' aircraft from the carrier *Akagi*. They immediately attacked the tanker, and she was hit by several bombs, setting her on fire, at which the crew abandoned her. More 'Val' aircraft, from the carrier *Hiryu*, had now arrived on scene and the focus of the attack shifted to the corvette and she was subjected to a sustained and intense air attack. The first damage came at 12.08 when two bombs exploded close on the starboard side, abreast the bridge. These shook the ship considerably, putting her boilers out of action and splitting the side fuel tanks. About 5 minutes later a second wave of attacks commenced and she was hit twice. One bomb exploded amidships on the engine room casing putting the engines and steering gear out of action, the second burst amidships causing a large explosion, either the 2pdr magazine or the boilers. The after part of the ship disintegrated and the ship sank in less than a minute. The position was approximately 07.21N 81.57E. Fifty-three officers and ratings were killed.

[TNA: ADM.199/623; ADM.199/2140]

9 April LANCE destroyer

Scotstoun 1940; 1,920 tons; 345.6ft × 36.9ft; 6 × 4.7in, 4 × 2pdr, 8 × torpedo tubes

Lieutenant Commander Ralph William Frank Northcott DSO

During January and February 1942, the *Lance* had been busily engaged in escorting convoys to Malta and had suffered damage which led to her being taken into number 2 dock at Malta for urgent repairs. Malta became the focus for a determined air campaign by the enemy, and the island was subject to a series of heavy bombing raids. During 4 April *Lance* was struck by two bombs, which fortunately failed to explode. The following day, during a heavy air raid, she was blown off the blocks with her starboard side blown in amidships by a bomb which exploded in the dock. She suffered further damage in more air raids, and on 9 April another bomb landed nearby, and she was partially submerged. The dockyard, under constant air attack and limited resources could not repair her, and she was written off as a constructive total loss. When the raids subsided, work on her recovery did continue and during 1943 she was eventually righted and cleared from the dock,

to be towed back to Chatham, but was sold for scrap during 1944.
[TNA: ADM.199/650; CB.4273 pp196–7]

9 April WEST COCKER tug
Dartmouth 1919; 131 tons; 88.5ft × 21ft
Based at Malta, she was damaged during an air raid on 26 March, and after further damage from subsequent raids, she foundered in Grand Harbour.
[Statement of Losses p22 and Amendment p4]

11 April KINGSTON destroyer
Cowes 1939; 1,690 tons; 339.6ft × 35.8ft; 6 × 4.7in, 4 × 2pdr, 10 × torpedo tubes
Commander Philip Somerville DSO DSC
In March 1942 during an action to screen the Malta convoy MW10, the *Kingston* was damaged when hit by a 38cm shell. She was taken into number 4 dock at Valetta, but, like the *Lance* (see above), was then subject to a series of heavy air raids. On 8 April she was struck by a bomb, which penetrated the upper deck, but failed to explode, but in a further air raid on 11 April, at about 17.30 she suffered a direct hit on the port side amidships. The bomb penetrated the engine room before exploding, the ship capsized over onto her port side in the dock. She was written off as a total loss. The wreck was cut in half during January 1943, the halves refloated and undocked in April of that year and towed away to be scuttled as a blockship near St Paul's Island.
[TNA: ADM.199/650; Warship Supplement no 146 p44]

11 April ST CATHAN trawler
Beverley 1936 requisitioned 1939; 564 tons; 172.2ft × 29.1ft; 1 × 4in
Lieutenant John MacKay RNR
Whilst on local patrol off the coast of South Carolina, she was involved in a collision with the Dutch merchant ship *Hebe* (1,140 tons) at 02.15 in position 33.10N 78.17W, the ships only sighting each other immediately before the collision. The trawler switched on her lights and ported her helm, but she was struck heavily on the starboard side aft. The trawler was cut in half and sank in 5 minutes with the loss of thirty men. The patrol yachts *Beryl* and *Azurlite* picked up the survivors. The merchant ship, which also sank, was held to blame, in having failed to have posted sufficient lookouts.
[TNA: ADM.199/802]

13 April LORD SNOWDEN trawler
Selby 1934 requisitioned 1939; 444 tons; 155.8ft × 26.1ft; 1 × 4in
Skipper-Lieutenant George McKay Sutherland RNR
Foundered at 15.03 after a collision with the merchant ship *Felspar* (799 tons) off Falmouth. The probable wreck site has been identified in position 50.04N 04.58W.
[TNA: ADM.199/802]

14 April (?) UPHOLDER submarine
Barrow 1940; 540/732 tons; 180ft × 16.1ft; 1 × 12pdr, 4 × torpedo tubes
Lieutenant Commander Malcolm David Wanklyn VC, DSO†
Sailed from Malta 6 April bound for the North African coast to conduct a war patrol. She landed a small party near Sousse on 9 April, and then made a rendezvous with the submarine *Unbeaten* the following night. She was last seen during the early hours of 11 April, after which she was ordered to patrol to the east of Djerba Island and then to join a patrol line with other submarines to the east of Tripoli, but no further contact was made. The cause of her loss is uncertain. It is probable that she was lost in a minefield near Tripoli, but another theory is that she was sunk on the afternoon of 14 April, in position 34.57N 16.55E when attempting to attack a convoy. At 15.47 that day, an aircraft covering an Italian supply convoy bound for Tripoli reported sighting a submarine. The aircraft attacked the submerged boat after which some oil was seen rising to the surface. This was outside the operating area of the *Upholder*, but no other British submarine was in the area, and Wanklyn had the reputation of being an aggressive commander and may well have taken his submarine searching for targets.
[Evans pp310–12]

18 April ANDROMEDA tug
Bremen 1910 requisitioned 1941; 658 tons; 180ft × 28.1ft
Lieutenant Leonard Charles Watson RNR
The tug suffered damage during a series of near misses by bombs during the constant air raids on Malta, until she foundered in Grand Harbour.
[TNA: ADM.199/650]

20 April FASTNET boom defence vessel
Goole 1920 (*Benjamin Hawkins*) purchased 1933; 444 tons 138.6ft × 23.9ft
Former trawler converted to a boom defence vessel she was deployed to the Far East, stationed in Singapore. Having escaped to Batavia, she was abandoned there, being officially turned over to Dutch control on 20 April, but evidently scuttled soon after to prevent capture.
[TNA: ADM.199/622A]

21 April JADE trawler
Beverley 1933 (*Lady Lillian*) purchased 1939; 615 tons; 151.9ft × 25.6ft; 1 × 4in
Lieutenant Arthur Roger James Tilston DSC RNR
Based at Malta, she was damaged on 10 April during an air raid, and when she suffered another bomb hit on 21 April she foundered in Grand Harbour.
[TNA: ADM.199/650]

25 April **CHORLEY** trawler
Middlesbrough 1914 (*Ceresia*) requisitioned 1940;
284 tons; 128.8ft × 23.5ft
Boom Skipper Albert James Beckett RNR†

Employed as a boom gate vessel, she was based at Dartmouth. After completing a boiler clean at Devonport Dockyard, she sailed to resume her station at 06.15, being ordered to follow astern of the minesweeping trawlers *Bilsdean* and *Lorraine*, as they swept the channel from Plymouth to Dartmouth. The *Chorley* tucked herself behind the sweepers, but slowly fell behind, and by mid-afternoon appeared to be in some difficulty, having virtually stopped. The *Bilsdean* tried to raise her by light but could get no answer. At 15.55 she was seen to have developed a list to port, and the sweepers turned back to investigate, but she sank, bows first. Her position was 50.10.4N 03.37.7W. By 16.26 the sweepers were on scene and lowered boats to pick up survivors, but three men were found to be missing, including Skipper Beckett. The enquiry into her loss found that she had been in poor material condition and was barely seaworthy. She had been involved in a collision with the steam tender *Sir Francis Drake* in February 1941 and although some repairs were made, some damage was never made good. She was constantly leaking through the seams and rivets of the deck over the forward mess and had unrepaired damaged bulwarks on the starboard side. The amount of water entering was such that the pumps could not cope. The poor weather had not helped, with seas regularly being shipped through hawse pipes which were not covered, and then coming through the skylight to enter the forward mess deck. It was ruled that Skipper Beckett could have done more to prevent the loss, either turning back when it became clear that she was shipping water, or signalled his difficulties to the minesweepers, but he had done neither. Some blame was also placed on the Boom Defence Officer, Plymouth, for allowing the ship to put to sea in an unfit condition.
[TNA: ADM.1/12031]

25 April **DAISY** drifter
1902 requisitioned 1940; 50 tons

Employed as a degaussing vessel, she was lost through stress of weather off Greenock.
[Statement of Losses p20]

(27) April **URGE** submarine
Barrow 1940; 540/730 tons; 180ft × 16ft; 1 × 12pdr,
4 × torpedo tubes
Lieutenant Commander Edward Philip Tomkinson†

In early April 1942 it was decided to transfer the submarines based at Malta to Alexandria, and the *Urge* sailed on 27 April to make the transit but failed to arrive as expected on 6 May and was posted as missing. The cause of her loss was uncertain, but she was judged that she was likely to have fallen victim to a mine soon after sailing – according to her route she would have passed through a field laid by German torpedo boats a few days earlier and was not known at the time. During 2019 a team from the University of Malta located the wreck off Grand Harbour in the north–east searched channel that she would have used, showing extensive damage to the bows, which confirmed that she had indeed fallen victim to a mine shortly after leaving the island.
[https://www.royalnavy.mod.uk/news-and-latest-activity/news/2019/october/31/191031-ww2-submarine-urge-found-off-malta; Evans pp314–15]

30 April **CORAL** trawler
Selby 1935 (*Cape Duner*) purchased 1939; 705 tons;
161ft × 26.5ft; 1 × 4in
Lieutenant Malcolm Christopher English RNR

After being seriously damaged during the air raids on Malta, she was taken into number 3 dock for repairs. However, during a very heavy air raid a large bomb fell on the dock caisson, causing it to flood. The *Coral*, with several openings in the hull for pipes and cables was overwhelmed and sank in the dock. She was subsequently cut up to be refloated to clear the dock.
[TNA: ADM.199/413; Warships Supplement no 133 p5 and no 146 p44]

April **ML 1100** motor launch
Rangoon 1941; 60 tons; 76.5ft × 13.5ft; 1 × 3pdr
Lieutenant Alistair Campbell BRNVR

Manned by the Burmese Royal Naval Reserve *1100*, in company with *1101*, gave active support to the army in the fight against the advancing Japanese forces in the Arakan region. Proceeding up the Mayu river, they continued to give support if they could, but with ammunition and fuel running out, and the Japanese now encircling them, they were both scuttled in the Naaf river at Taung Bazaar.
[Goulden p42]

April **ML 1101** motor launch
Rangoon 1941; 60 tons; 76.5ft × 13.5ft; 1 × 3pdr
Lieutenant Thomas Reginald Milsom Cole BRNVR

Acting in company with her sister *ML 1100* in supporting the army in the river Mayu, Burma, she was also abandoned and scuttled in the Naaf river at Taung Bazaar.
[Goulden p42]

1 May **PUNJABI** destroyer
Greenock 1937; 1,960 tons; 355.6ft × 36.6ft; 6 × 4.7in,
2 × 4in, 4 × torpedo tubes
Commander the Honourable John Montagu Granville Waldegrave

For the protection of Russian Convoy PQ15 a powerful force was assembled, consisting of the battleships *King George V* and USS *Washington*, the aircraft carrier *Victorious* and US Navy cruisers *Wichita* and *Tuscaloosa*. They were escorted by ten British and American destroyers, the *Punjabi* being stationed on the starboard side of the main body, being the second ship in the column, astern of *Inglefield*. The force was to the north-east of Iceland, steaming at 18 knots in poor visibility, with thick patches of fog. Because of the mist, Commander Waldegrave ordered the bridge staff not to lose touch with the *Inglefield*. To achieve this, they frequently resorted to using Asdic to confirm her position. When they entered a particularly thick patch of fog, Lieutenant Leonard Hollis, the officer of the watch, asked for a bearing of *Inglefield* from Asdic. This indicated that her leader was on the port bow, so 10 degrees of port helm was applied. This had scarcely been implemented, when the lookout shouted that he could see a floating mine on the starboard bow. Hollis promptly increased the turn to 15 degrees. Asdic then reported echoes on the port bow, range 1,400 yards. Hollis presumed that this must be *Inglefield*, which he thought must have reduced speed. He therefore stopped the turn to port and steadied his helm to parallel his still unseen leader. To everyone's horror, the bows of a large ship suddenly loomed out of the mist close on the port bow. The wheel was ordered full over, and engines put full ahead, but it was too late, and at 15.45 she was rammed by the *King George V*, which struck her between 'X' and 'Y' turrets cutting her in two. The stern section was seen to float away and then the depth charges exploded, and it sank, almost under the bows of the USS *Washington*. The wreck of the forepart took a list to starboard of about 35 degrees and it was clear that she could not last much longer. The whaler was successfully lowered and cleared away and a single Carley float released before Waldegrave was forced to order her to be abandoned. More Carley floats were released before she rolled over and sank at 16.21. The next destroyers astern, the *Martin* and *Marne*, then loomed out of the mist and almost collided with her but stopped to lower boats and over 200 men were picked up from the freezing water. Fifty-three men lost their lives. The loss resulted in both Commander Waldegrave and Lieutenant Hollis being court-martialled. It was found that Hollis had shown a lack of appreciation of the proximity of the main force and had been over-reliant on the reported Asdic bearings and had presumed that they must be *Inglefield* and consequently had altered round to port far too much. Ratings manning the Asdic later admitted that the picture was not as clear as Hollis had believed, being confused with numerous wakes, and contact was frequently lost. Hollis was severely reprimanded and ordered to lose 6 months seniority. Commander Waldegrave was criticised for not being on the bridge

whilst the ship was in such conditions. He was severely reprimanded and ordered to forfeit all seniority. [TNA:ADM.156/227]

2 May **EDINBURGH** cruiser

Wallsend 1938; 10,565 tons; 579ft × 63.4ft; 12 × 6in, 12 × 4in, 6 × 20mm, 6 × torpedo tubes
Captain Hugh Webb Faulkner

With the flag of Rear Admiral Bonham-Carter DSO embarked, she sailed from Vaenga in the Kola Inlet, Russia, during the evening of 28 April, to join Convoy QP11 the following day. Although a reconnaissance aircraft was observed at long range, no contact was made with the enemy. During the night *Edinburgh* stretched ahead of the convoy, stationing herself some 15 to 20 miles distant. She maintained this position, zigzagging at 19 knots, when at 16.07 on 30 April, when in position 73.08N 33E, as she was altering course for the next leg of the zigzag, she was hit by two torpedoes fired by *U 456* (Teichert). The first hit the starboard side forward, exploding between 70 and 87 stations; the second hit aft and caused considerable damage, distorting the deck so that it folded back. The ship continued to steam, slowly circling to starboard, and it was found that the rudder and starboard shafts had been damaged, but the port shafts appeared to be intact. She remained stable, although with a slight list, and attempts were made to steer her using engines, with limited success. The destroyer escorts to the convoy, the *Foresight*, *Forester* and the Russian *Kuibyshev* and *Sokrushitelnyi* closed, and preparations were made for a tow. At 18.30 the damaged portion of the stern broke off, just abaft 'Y' turret. At 19.05 the *Forester* took her in tow, but it proved difficult to control her movements, probably due to wreckage from two damaged shafts hanging down. Eventually the tow parted, and rather that re-connect, the *Foresight* was secured aft. This proved a better arrangement, and the cruiser was able to get underway and head back towards Kola at about 3 knots. At 06.00 on 1 May the two Russian destroyers were forced to leave, being low on fuel, and it was decided to release *Foresight* from her duties alongside, to join her sister *Forester* acting as a screen. By means of the useable shafts she was able to maintain headway, at a speed of 2 knots, although progress was slow as her head was still swinging wildly, and once went in a complete circle, and she frequently had to go astern to control the yawing. At 18.00 that evening the Russian patrol vessel *Rubin* joined, and at 23.45 the minesweepers *Harrier*, *Hussar*, *Gossamer* and *Niger* arrived with the welcome sight of a Russian tug. The tug was secured forward and with the *Gossamer* secured aft, she regained some control over her movements, and good progress was made during the night. At 06.27, however, German destroyers were reported closing from the starboard quarter. These were

the *Hermann Schoemann*, *Z 24* and *Z 25*. The tug and minesweeper were ordered to be slipped, and the cruiser managed to work herself up to 8 knots, but being unable to control her steering, she slowly circled around to port. The *Foresight* and *Forester* closed the incoming threat, and a sharp action commenced, with the cruiser joining in, with 'B' turret firing in local control. Despite her difficulties the firing was accurate, and the *Schoemann* was hit twice and put out of action. The *Forester* and *Foresight* were busily engaged, and the former was damaged by shell hits, which killed her commanding officer. Both groups of destroyers fired torpedoes at each other, which were avoided. However, those fired by *Z 24*, although they missed the intended target were seen by *Edinburgh* as they approached from the starboard beam. In normal circumstances they could have been avoided, but the ship was still swinging wildly, and she swung round to present her port side as they approached. One track was seen to pass ahead but a second hit on the port side amidships. She immediately took a list to port of about 12 degrees, and steam was reported to have failed. An inspection showed that the explosion had been almost opposite the earlier impact point. With no power, the list steadily increasing, and a high risk of her breaking in two, it was decided to abandon her. All men were ordered up from below and the *Gossamer* and *Harrier* were ordered to come alongside. When all the men had been transferred, the *Harrier* fired several 4in rounds into her, and dropped a depth charge close by her, but they seemed to have little obvious effect. The *Foresight* now closed and fired a single torpedo after which the cruiser rolled over and sank in 3 minutes. Fifty-eight men died.
[TNA:ADM.199/165]

3 May FERMOY minesweeping sloop
Dundee 1919; 710 tons; 220ft × 28.5ft; 1 × 4in, 1 × 12pdr
Lieutenant Commander John Guy Douglas Wetherfield
Based at Malta, she had been worked hard clearing the mines laid in the approaches to Grand Harbour. During April she was taken into number 5 dock for essential repairs, but never emerged. In an air raid on 30 April she received a direct hit which struck the bridge and went through the hull. She was damaged again during later raids, but at 20.55 on 3 May she suffered another direct hit on the port side amidships and fell off the supporting chocks. On inspection the following day she was written off as a constructive total loss.
[TNA:ADM.199/413]

6 May AURICULA corvette
Greenock 1940; 940 tons; 190ft × 33ft; 1 × 4in
Lieutenant Commander Sidney Lord Bannister Maybury
Part of the force gathered in the Indian Ocean to carry out an invasion of the island of Madagascar, held by the Vichy French she escorted an assault convoy from

Durban, arriving off the beachhead at Diego Suarez on 5 May. Many mines were encountered, and the minesweepers were fully engaged in trying to clear channels. By 10.30 the sweepers were busy widening the channel, and eighteen mines were cut within a few minutes. Several ships reported floating mines, and small arms fire was employed to sink or explode them. At 11.38 there was a large explosion under the *Auricula* as she struck a mine. She was holed and badly shaken, but remained stable and upright, slowly settling by the bows, but power was lost, and she slowly drifted. Several vessels went to her assistance and flooding was contained. During the afternoon, a damage control party from the *Devonshire* arrived, with more wood to help shoring, but by 18.30 it was clear that despite all their efforts she was still settling by the head. By nightfall she had drifted closer inshore, and the crew were removed into other ships. The following morning the *Freesia* closed, finding her low in the water, but a small party managed to get aboard, and a stern tow was rigged, hoping to take her into shallow water. However, at 08.23 she broke in half and sank. There were no casualties.
[Supplement to the London Gazette 4 March 1948]

5 May SAMBHUR whaler
Tonsberg 1926 (*AN1*) requisitioned 1940; 223 tons; 109.4ft × 22.4ft; 1 × 3pdr
Lieutenant Robert Blakeway Parry RNR
Based at Trincomalee, Ceylon, she was manned by personnel from the Ceylon Naval Volunteer Force. At 13.10 she ran aground on Kalappu Gala off Colombo, 1.8 miles north of the breakwater. Despite efforts to free her, she would not move and was written off as a total loss.
[TNA:ADM.199/2239]

6 May ML 160 motor launch
Sandbank 1940; 75 tons; 112ft × 18.4ft; 1 × 3pdr
Lieutenant Thomas Wilson Boyd DSO RNVR
At 11.48, a pair of Me 109 aircraft were seen approaching Brixham harbour from the south-east, flying low over the sea. One of them then broke off to attack *MMS 173* which was off Berry Head, inflicting damage to her upper works with machine-gun fire. The second aircraft attacked *ML 160* in the outer harbour at Brixham, dropping a bomb which exploded close to the launch. She was run into shallow water in a sinking condition and beached.
[TNA:ADM.199/2239]

6 May SENATEUR DUHAMEL trawler
Aberdeen 1927 seized 1941; 913 tons; 192.3ft × 31.2ft; 1 × 4in
Lieutenant Alexander Michael Sullivan RNVR
One of several British armed trawlers sent to the east coast of the United States to give anti-submarine

support, she was conducting a night patrol near Cape Lookout, North Carolina, when at 03.40 a light was sighted fine on the port bow. The stranger was the USS *Semmes*, also patrolling in the area, and she had detected the trawler on radar a little before at a range of 2 miles. The *Duhamel* challenged the stranger by light, but could not understand the reply, so signalled in plain language 'What ship?' The *Semmes* bridge staff later claimed that the use of an unshaded light blinded them and prevented them following the movements of the trawler; they believed that she would pass close to starboard, so made a radical alteration of course to port and went astern. After the *Semmes*' head had swung about 30 degrees, she struck the oncoming trawler hard amidships. The pair remained locked together until *Semmes* went astern and freed them. The USS *Roper* was called to the scene and assisted by lowering boats to take off the crew of the *Duhamel* which was quickly settling. Lieutenant Sullivan did return on board later but found the engine room to have flooded and she was again abandoned, to sink just after 05.00. There were no casualties. The enquiry found that the collision had been brought about by the ships approaching each other on a head-on course, but neither could work out whether they would pass clear. *Semmes* eventually took avoiding action but turned the wrong way. Blame should be shared between the ships. The *Duhamel* should have altered course on sighting the approaching lights instead of standing on. The *Semmes* made an error of judgement by turning to port. The British were critical of the management of the patrols, believing that poor organisation and lack of coordination had been the underlying cause. It seemed that neither of the ships was aware of the presence of the other and the orders given to them were vague.
[TNA: ADM.1/12037]

7 May ML 130 motor launch
Looe 1940; 75 tons; 112ft × 18.4ft; 1 × 3pdr
Lieutenant David Robert Hamilton Jolly RNVR
Having sailed at 20.52 from Grand Harbour, Malta, to conduct a night patrol off the approaches to the harbour, she failed to return as expected. She was last seen at 00.41, and a little over an hour later heavy tracer was seen and intermittent gunfire heard, which lasted until 02.00. A large explosion was head at 03.01. A search of the area at first light by RAF launch *HSL 128* found a patch of burning wreckage and debris, and it was presumed that she had been sunk. It later emerged that she had encountered a group of enemy torpedo boats as they were employed laying mines (see *Olympus* below). Three men were lost, the survivors being picked up by their attackers to become prisoners.
[TNA: ADM.199/177; ADM.199/802]

8 May OLYMPUS submarine
Dalmuir 1928; 1,475/2,038 tons; 265ft × 29.11ft; 1 × 4in, 8 × torpedo tubes
Lieutenant Commander Herbert George Dymott[†]
Bound for Gibraltar loaded with stores and several passengers, she sailed from Malta at 04.00 on 8 May. Just an hour later, when she was about 6 miles from St Elmo light, and running on the surface, there was a large explosion forward, when she ran onto a mine. She flooded forward and started to settle by the bow. Abandon ship was ordered, and it is believed that most, if not all, the men on board made it to the upper deck and into the water, before she sank, bows first, about 9 minutes later. Malta could be seen on the horizon, and the survivors, trying to keep together in groups, started to swim towards the island. Most did not make it, being overcome by exhaustion and the cold, and it was not until 10.00 that the first survivors reached a beach. A picket boat was then dispatched to the area, but only 12 men survived; eighty-six officers and men died. The mine was one of a large number laid by German torpedo boats.
[Evans pp316–19]

11 May LIVELY destroyer
Birkenhead 1941; 1,920 tons; 345.6ft × 36.9ft; 6 × 4.7in, 4 × 2pdr, 8 × torpedo tubes
Lieutenant Commander William Frederick Eyre Hussey DSO DSC
On 10 May the destroyers, *Jervis*, *Jackal*, *Kipling* and *Lively* were sailed from Alexandra on Operation 'MG2', the interception of an enemy convoy believed bound for Benghazi, which turned into a disaster. The operation became known to the enemy through signals intercept, and during the afternoon of 11 May, then being to the south-west of Crete, they were detected by enemy aerial reconnaissance. As the chance of surprise had been lost, the force reversed course to return to Alexandria. It was hoped that friendly air cover would be available, and at 16.30 contact was made with Beaufighter aircraft which were closing, but before they could reach the destroyers, radar indicated many hostile aircraft were closing. At 16.40 several Ju 88 and Fiat BR 20 aircraft came into view and they commenced a diving attack on the *Lively* from the starboard bow. Speed was increased, and the helm put over, but the first aircraft dropped four bombs which straddled her fo'c'sle, either hitting her or near missing. One bomb went through 'B' gundeck to explode in the mess deck below, whilst the others, exploding close by shook her considerably. She immediately heeled over to starboard and took a bow-down attitude. Another aircraft dropped several bombs which exploded close along her starboard side, peppering her hull with shrapnel and again shaking her considerably. The heel continued to increase and within a minute she was on her beam ends.

One Carley float was released as the men were ordered to abandon her, the men scrambling over the side as she capsized to float bottom up, her screws still turning. She lay like this for about 3 or 4 minutes and then sank. Two officers and sixty-five ratings were lost.
[TNA: ADM.267/101]

11 May KIPLING destroyer
Scotstoun 1939; 1,690 tons; 339.6ft × 35.8ft; 6 × 4.7in,
1 × 4in, 4 × 2pdr, 5 × torpedo tubes
Commander Aubrey St Clair Ford DSO

Consort to the *Lively* (above), when that ship was sunk the *Kipling* and *Jervis* closed and picked up the survivors, the *Kipling* rescuing over 100 men. The air attacks continued as she did so, but she escaped any damage. At 20.00 when in position 32.39N 26.19E, another air raid developed, about ten Ju 88 aircraft carrying out dive-bombing attacks in twilight from astern. Despite a heavy volume of fire and manoeuvring at high speed, the *Kipling* was straddled by a number of bombs. One exploded amidships, close to the waterline. This blew the torpedo tubes over the side and ripped a hole in the side. A second bomb exploded close to the port side aft, peppering the hull with shrapnel. The engine and boiler rooms were affected by the shock of the explosion, and water flooded in. The ship heeled over to port and it was clear that she was sinking, and she was ordered to be abandoned. Just 10 minutes after the attack had started, she sank stern first, the bows rising clear as she went under. Two officers, twenty ratings and one NAAFI assistant were killed.
[TNA: ADM.267/107]

11 May JACKAL destroyer
Clydebank 1938; 1,690 tons; 339.6ft × 35.8ft; 6 × 4.7in,
1 × 4in, 4 × 2pdr, 5 × torpedo tubes
Commander Christopher Theodore Jellicoe DSC

The third of the four destroyers engaged in the disastrous attempt to intercept an Italian convoy, after the loss of the *Lively* (above), the ships had continued to steam to the south-east, still a target for air attacks. At 19.50 the *Jackal* had detected another group of aircraft closing, and 10 minutes later Ju 88 aircraft had started another dive bombing attack. The *Kipling* had been their first victim (see above), and attention then focused on the *Jackal*. One aircraft dropped four bombs very accurately, with one of the missiles hitting the starboard cutter, passing through it to pierce the upper deck to enter number 2 boiler room where it exploded. The other bombs exploded close around her. The blast lifted the ship bodily and broke her back. The boiler and engine rooms reported they were rapidly flooding, all power was lost, and an oil fire broke out in number one boiler room. The fire was tackled, and was contained, but could not be extinguished, and hard work by damage

control parties prevented the flooding from spreading, and the ship remained stable and upright. With the area now in darkness air attacks ceased, enabling the *Jervis* to close, take off half the crew and rig a tow. The tow went on into the early hours, making slow progress to the south-west and safety, but the *Jackal* was settling all the time. The fire in the boiler room was still burning, flames occasionally bursting up through the funnel and the decks and bulkheads were hot to the touch. By 02.30 she was low in the water; the starboard side of the quarterdeck was awash. As they were still a long way from home and dawn would probably bring a resumption of air attacks, it was doubted that she would survive. At 03.06 the tow was slipped and the last of the crew taken off. When that was complete, at 04.45, the *Jervis* fired a torpedo into her and she sank immediately, in position 32.31N 26.28E. Ten men were killed.
[TNA: ADM.267/107]

11 May BEDFORDSHIRE trawler
Middlesbrough 1935 purchased 1939; 443 tons;
162.3ft × 26.7ft; 1 × 4in
Lieutenant Russell Bransby Davis RNR†

One of over twenty anti-submarine trawlers loaned to the United States Navy, to escort local convoys and shipping off the American east coast. On the night of 11 May the *Bedfordshire* was conducting an anti-submarine patrol off the North Carolina coast near Cape Lookout, steaming at 6 knots and operating Asdic, in company with another armed trawler, the *St Loman*. At just after 23.00 the pair came under attack from the submerged *U 558* (Krech), which fired two torpedoes, both of which missed. Krech then carried out a second attack at 23.40, and this time both struck *Bedfordshire* which blew up and sank immediately in position 34.10N 76.41W. There were no survivors, thirty-seven men being lost.
[The Review 18.2: Summer 2005)

11 May C 308 tug
Portsmouth 1932; 154 tons; 108ft × 24ft
Boatswain Cedric Martin Radcliffe†

Based at Malta, she was fitted out locally as a minesweeper and sailed at 20.30 on 10 May to sweep the approaches to Grand Harbour in company with the trawler *Beryl* and drifter *Eddy*. In the early hours of the morning as she was recovering her Oropesa sweep it was found that the kite was missing and was ordered to return to harbour. At 03.00, then being 1.5 miles south of Fort Rocco, a mine detonated under the port quarter and she immediately listed to port. An attempt was made to launch the boat, but this failed due to the rapidly increasing list, but a Carley float was released before she sank, only a minute after the explosion. Nine men were killed, with six survivors.
[TNA: ADM.199/239]

13 May BEN ARDNA trawler

Aberdeen 1917 (*John Bradford*) requisitioned 1939; 226 tons; 122.8ft × 22.2ft; 1 × 4in

Skipper William Christopher Cornick RNR

Employed as an examination vessel, inspecting neutral merchant vessels, she was stationed at a buoy at the entrance to the River Tyne, when she was in collision with the merchant ship *Bruce-M* in the east coast northbound Convoy FN41 and subsequently foundered to the east of Souter Point. There were no casualties.
[TNA: ADM.199/645; ADM.199/777]

13 May MTB 220 motor torpedo boat

Portsmouth 1941; 47 tons; 71ft × 19.3ft; 1 × 20mm, 2 × torpedo tubes

Lieutenant Eric Alfred Edward Cornish RNVR†

One of a group of motor torpedo boats that were conducting a night patrol in the English Channel, in the region of Ambleteuse, north-eastern France. At 01.45 a signal was received that a large enemy convoy was moving down channel, and the group split up and lay to, waiting for the approach of the enemy vessels. Their patience was rewarded when at 04.00 several vessels loomed out of the dark, and as the boats got under way and closed their target, they came under fire. Then a large 'destroyer type' (actually an ocean-going torpedo boat) appeared directly ahead of them and Cornish took the opportunity to fire a torpedo, which was seen to hit amidships with a large explosion. As they tried to clear the area, the hostile fire seemed to concentrate on them, and they were now being hit. A fire broke out in the mess deck, fuelled by petrol leaking from ruptured tanks, and the steering gear was found to be out of action. The fires were tackled, but the constant fire caused most of her small crew to be killed and Cornish with Telegraphist Albert Davis seemed to be the only ones standing. Cornish ordered the boat to be abandoned but was shot in the head immediately after this. Davis jumped into the sea and swam to the Carley float floating nearby, and to his surprise two other survivors popped up on the other side, a stoker and a seaman; they were the only survivors. The boat, still with some way on, it slowly moved off, burning fiercely. The three were picked up a short time later by a German 'R' boat, the water around them being covered with oil and wreckage. It was later found that two large enemy torpedo boats had been sunk, the *Iltis* and *Seeadler*, one of which must have been *220*'s target. Eight men died.
[TNA ADM.1/19573]

15 May TRINIDAD cruiser

Devonport 1940; 8,525 tons; 538ft × 62ft; 12 × 6in, 8 × 4in, 8 × 2pdr, 5 × 20mm, 6 × torpedo tubes

Captain Leslie Swain Saunders

In March 1942, the *Trinidad* had formed part of the escort to Russian Convoy PQ3 during which she had been damaged by one of her own torpedoes, fired to dispatch a German destroyer. Following emergency repairs at Murmansk, she sailed from the Kola Inlet at 23.00 on 13 May to return to England, with four destroyers forming a screen. The force was detected the following morning at 07.30 when a Ju 88 aircraft was sighted, clearly shadowing. The weather was poor, with low cloud and regular snow showers. During the day, more shadowers were detected, often by radar, and homing signals were being transmitted constantly. The anticipated air raid materialised at 21.00 when radar detected groups of aircraft approaching and at 21.50 several Ju 88s appeared to commence a dive-bombing attack on the force. Several near misses were scored, but there were no direct hits. At 22.37 a group of eight low-flying aircraft were seen, which circled the force and then split up into groups before forming into line abreast to commence a torpedo attack. The cruiser manoeuvred to 'comb the tracks', steaming towards the attackers. As this was underway a single Ju 88 appeared out of the clouds and carried out a dive-bombing attack from the starboard quarter. Four bombs were dropped, one of which hit the ship on the starboard side, narrowly missing the bridge structure to pass behind 'B' turret and penetrate below to detonate in the lower mess deck, where it exploded, killing or wounding all the forward damage control party and starting a fire. A second bomb either hit the starboard side or exploded close alongside. This blew a hole in the side and damaged the temporary patch on the previous area affected by the earlier torpedo hit; 'B' magazine and the adjacent compartments started to flood. The others were near misses, exploding close around her stern. The ship took a 14-degree list to starboard, but further torpedo attacks by aircraft and another dive-bombing attack were all avoided. The fire that had been started under the bridge structure gained a firm hold and by 23.59 was out of control and course was altered to allow the smoke to blow clear of the ship. It was decided to start evacuating the crew. The destroyer *Forester* was called alongside to remove the wounded, and when they were clear it was decided to abandon her. They needed dockyard support and the chances of safely making a friendly port was low, with further air raids expected, and attack by U-boat highly likely. Other destroyers were called alongside to remove the crew and after taking the last men off, the *Matchless* fired three torpedoes into the burning wreck and she sank at 01.20 in position 73.55N 22.53E. Sixty-two men were killed, in addition several men taking passage, some of them survivors from sunken merchant ships, were lost.
[TNA: ADM.267/84]

16 May MTB 338 motor torpedo boat
Montreal 1942; 22 tons; 60ft × 13.3ft; machine guns
Lieutenant Anthony Calvert Lewis RANVR
Caught fire following an explosion, when she was hauled up on the Archer Coal Company's slip at Trinidad for maintenance and subsequently written off as a constructive total loss.
[TNA: ADM.199/777]

21 May MONTENOL oiler
West Hartlepool 1917; 2,646 tons; 320ft × 41.5ft
Master Edward Emile August le Sage RFA
Bound from Greenock for Freetown, West Africa, in Convoy AS28, she was the third ship in the port column, when at 00.27, in position 36.41N 22.45W, she was hit by a torpedo on the port side. The torpedo exploded in the engine room near the stokehold bulkhead, and the ship came to a stop with a great rush of steam from the boilers. All power was lost, and she heeled over to port. All boats on the port side were found to be smashed, but boats on the starboard side were lowered, and she was abandoned, the sloop *Wellington* closing to pick them up. As it was evident that she was still afloat, the Master and a small team returned to stand by her, remaining in a boat alongside until first light, when they boarded her. She was low in the water, with the stokehold and the amidships section full of water. She was visibly settling and hopes that she could be towed were clearly impractical and were abandoned. The corvette *Woodruff* closed to take off the team and she was sunk by gunfire from the *Wellington*. She had been torpedoed by *U 159* (Witte); two men were lost.
[TNA: ADM.267/115]

25 May TANJORE armed trawler
Calcutta 1919 (*Madras*): 360 tons; 125ft × 23.5ft; 1 × 12pdr
Lieutenant Neville Charles Eric Little RIN
Royal Indian Navy. Sailed from Bombay 20 May for Karachi but suffered a complete engine-room failure 4 days later when 50 miles from Manora. Another ship, the patrol vessel *Bhadravati* was sent to her aid and anchored close by her, but poor weather prevented action. The *Tanjore* drifted inshore until she ran aground. Efforts were made over the next few weeks to haul her free, but it was not until late December that she was finally refloated and towed to Bombay but was written off as a constructive total loss.
[TNA: ADM.199/425]

26 May EDDY drifter
Aberdeen 1918; 199 tons; 86ft × 18.5ft; 1 × 6pdr
Lieutenant James Findlay RNR
Based at Malta and fitted out as a minesweeper. Following extensive minelaying operations by enemy torpedo boats, *Eddy* had been employed acting as a dan layer during sweeping operations off Valetta harbour, marking with buoys the boundary of the swept area. Operations having completed for the day she was returning to harbour by the swept channel when a mine was sighted in the channel. The vessel was stopped, and they prepared to lay a marker buoy, when other mines became visible, and it became clear that they had entered a minefield. All hands were brought up on deck and mustered amidships, and the engine shut down. It was hoped that they would drift clear of the menace, but at 16.30 a mine detonated on the starboard side forward, and then a second later another exploded aft. The drifter sank immediately. They were then 7 cables (1,400 yards) to the west of St Elmo breakwater. Four Maltese seamen were killed.
[TNA: ADM.199/239; Rohwer, Chronology p164]

27 May FITZROY minesweeper
Renfrew 1919; 710 tons; 220ft × 28.5ft; 1 × 4in, 1 × 12pdr
Commander Auberon Charles Alan Campbell Duckworth
In company with other ships of the Fourth Minesweeping Flotilla, she sailed from Great Yarmouth to clear a British defensive minefield. Arriving on scene she was detailed to act as a dan-layer, laying buoys marking the limits of the swept areas. She had just laid a buoy, with engines stopped but way still on the ship, when a mine exploded close to the port side, between numbers 1 and 2 boiler rooms, which immediately flooded. She lost power and the ship took a list to starboard and continued to slowly roll over until she lay on her beam ends and sank about 10 minutes after the explosion. Her position was then 52.38.45N 02.45.15E. The dan-laying trawler *Fisher Boy* picked up the survivors, but fifteen men died.
[TNA: ADM.199/221]

27 May ARCTIC PIONEER trawler
Beverley 1937 requisitioned 1939; 501 tons; 166.7ft × 27.6ft; 1 × 4in, 1 × 12pdr
Lieutenant George Walter Surtees Robinson RNVR
Laying at anchor near St Helens Fort in the Solent, when three aircraft were sighted at 15.00 closing from the south-east. They made straight for the trawler at low level, raked her with gunfire and dropped two bombs as they swept overhead. Both exploded on the waterline, close on the starboard quarter next to the engine room. The ship was lifted out of the water and was covered in smoke and spray and began to sink rapidly by the stern. She had disappeared in less than 5 minutes. The aircraft, identified as Me 109s, had not been engaged as they closed, and Lieutenant Robinson was subsequently informed by the Admiralty that he had incurred their Lordships' displeasure over the loss, being criticised for having a 'slipshod' organisation.
[TNA: ADM.199/173; ADM.199/174]

30 May ST ANGELO tug
Greenock 1935 purchased 1935, 71 tons; 78ft × 18.1ft
Sub-Lieutenant Gordon John Martyn RNVR
Based at Malta, she was fitted out locally as a minesweeper.
In company with the trawler *Beryl*, she was tasked to sweep
the approaches to Valetta harbour, to clear the field that
had claimed the *Eddy* (see 26 May). Several mines had
successfully been dealt with during the day, but as she
turned to conduct another 'lap' a mine was sighted directly
ahead. Immediate avoiding action was taken, but the mine
exploded under her port side and she sank quickly, with
the loss of four men, 1,600 yards off St Elmo.
[TNA: ADM.199/239]

31 May DINSDALE oiler
Govan 1941; 8,254 tons; 466ft × 62ft
Master Thomas H Card
Bound from Trinidad for Port Elizabeth, South Africa
with a full load of aviation spirit, she was sailing
independently without escort, when she was torpedoed
by the Italian submarine *Cappelini* (Revedin) at 02.30 in
position about 120 miles to the south-south-west of St
Paul Rocks, Brazil, in position 00.45S 29.50W. Thirteen
men were lost, with the forty-four survivors being
picked up by the Spanish merchant ship *Monte Orduna*.
[Lloyd's War Losses vol 1 p444; Tennant p2]

1 June KUTTABUL accommodation ship
Newcastle NSW 1922 requisitioned 1940; 448 tons;
418.2ft × 54.3ft
Lieutenant Commander Alan Gilbert Lewis RAN
Royal Australian Navy. Used to accommodate ratings
standing by ships in refit, the former ferry was secured
at Garden Island, Sydney, when the harbour came
under attack during the night of 31 May/1 June by
three Japanese midget submarines. One was caught in
an anti-torpedo net, and the crew destroyed the vessel
with demolition charges, and another was sunk by
depth-charge attack. The one vessel that made it into the
harbour was observed just before 22.00 and was fired on
by the US cruiser *Chicago*. The submarine then fired two
torpedoes at the cruiser, but both missed. One torpedo
beached itself on the shore, the second hit the seabed by
the jetty and exploded under the stern of *Kuttabul*. Her
back broken by the shock, the ship sank by the stern, the
forward section settled later, leaving the deckhouse and
funnel above water. Twenty-one men died.
[http://www.navy.gov.au/hmas-kuttabul; Cassells p35]

3 June COCKER whaler
Sandefjord 1936 (*Kos XIX*) requisitioned 1940; 305 tons;
125.5ft × 25.6ft; 1 × 12pdr
Lieutenant John Scott RNVR
In company with the corvette *Gloxinia*, the whaler sailed
from Tobruk during the evening of 2 June to escort the
merchant ship *Katie Moller* to Alexandria. At 01.01, then
on the port beam of the convoy, in position 32.06N
24.12E, she was hit on the port side amidships by a
torpedo. A second explosion occurred, either as a boiler
or ammunition exploded, and a fire broke out. She rolled
over to port and quickly sank by the head. Her attacker
was uncertain at the time and was thought at the time
to have been a submarine, the *Gloxinia* dropping depth
charges after the attack. The attacker was actually the
German fast torpedo boat *S 57* which had approached the
group undetected. Sixteen men were picked up by motor
launch later that morning, but fifteen men were killed.
[TNA: ADM.199/650]

4 June SONA yacht
Southampton 1922 purchased 1939; 520 tons;
169.8ft × 27ft
Employed as an accommodation ship at Poole, she
was alongside the jetty in the harbour, when the port
became the target for an air raid. The yacht took a direct
hit at 00.52 which broke her back and she sank. The
wreck was later lifted and repositioned and now lies in
position 50.38.37N 01.55.38W.
[TNA: ADM.199/777; Larn vol 1 sec 6]

8 June CATHERINE drifter
1914 requisitioned 1939; 78 tons
Based at Scapa she filled with water and foundered
during a strong northerly gale; all the crew were taken
off and there were no casualties.
[TNA: ADM.199/2242]

10 June TRUSTY STAR drifter
Goole 1920 (*Elie Ness*) requisitioned 1939; 96 tons;
86.2ft × 18.5ft
Boatswain William Henry McCarthy
Based at Malta, during 10 June she accompanied the
whaler *Swona* and trawler *Beryl*, to work to clear the
minefields laid by German torpedo boats off the island.
She acted as a dan layer, laying buoys marking the
boundary of the swept area until the *Beryl* brought up a
mine nearby. She closed to sink it, and after this had been
completed, at 16.40 whilst proceeding back to the line
of dan buoys a moored mine was sighted right ahead.
Before any avoiding action could be taken, she ran over
the mine which exploded. She was then about 2 miles
to the south-east of St Elmo light. One Maltese rating
was injured, but all were picked up by the other vessels.
[TNA: ADM.199/239]

12 June GROVE escort destroyer
Wallsend 1941; 1,050 tons; 264.2ft × 31.6ft; 6 × 4in,
4 × 2pdr, 2 × 20mm
Commander John Wolferstan Rylands
A group of five store ships, including the RFA *Brambleleaf*,
sailed from Alexandria on 9 June as Convoy AT49 bound

for Tobruk, escorted by the destroyers *Grove* and *Tetcott*, corvettes *Hyacinth* and *Peony* and whaler *Klo*. The *Grove* was operating on only a single shaft, but no other escorts were available. During the night of 9/10 June the convoy was attacked by the *U 559* and again the following night by two submarines, the *U 431* and *U 453*. Their attacks sank the cased petrol carrier *Havre* and set the petrol carrier *Athene* on fire leading her to be abandoned. The *Brambleleaf* was hit but taken in tow and the convoy arrived at Tobruk during night of 11 June. The *Grove* and *Tetcott* then turned back to return to Alexandria, but the *Grove* ran hard aground off Ras Azzaz. She was eventually refloated but was restricted to just 8 knots and was now faced with the passage in daylight. At 06.45 in position 32.05N 25.30W torpedo tracks were seen, but the order to put the helm over was too late, and she was hit by two torpedoes. The first struck the starboard side abreast the forward gun mounting, the second blew the stern off. She immediately took a heavy list and sank about 15 minutes after being hit. Her attacker was the *U 77* (Schonder). The *Tetcott* picked up the survivors but 111 men died.
[TNA: ADM.199/650]

13 June KINGSTON CEYLONITE trawler
Beverley 1935; 448 tons; 160.6ft × 26.6ft; 1 × 4in
Skipper-Lieutenant William Mackenzie Smith RNR†
One of a group of trawlers sent across the Atlantic to assist the United States with mine clearance, she was under the control of the US Navy, although remaining manned by the Royal Navy. Ordered to act as an escort to a convoy including a ship under tow off Virginia Beach, she proceeded from Moorehead City on a northerly course. At 20.18, as she was approaching a buoy in Chesapeake Bay an explosion occurred under the bows, and she sank in 3 minutes, breaking in half as she did. Subsequent sweeping of the area found five mines nearby. Twenty men were killed, with fifteen survivors. It emerged that she had not been operating her degaussing equipment at the time of the loss, as the generator could not carry the load of the radio and sonar as well as the degaussing equipment; further, there was no known threat from magnetic mines in the area. The mines had been laid the previous night by *U 701*. The wreck has been found and lies in position 36.44.47N 75.51.33W.
[TNA: ADM.199/239]

13 June FAROUK decoy schooner
Requisitioned 1942; 96 tons; 2 × 12pdr
Lieutenant Arthur Esmé Lockington RNR
A local sailing vessel, she was converted under the direction of Lieutenant Lockington into a submarine decoy, with guns concealed in a false deckhouse. It was intended to repeat the 'Q' ship exploits of the First World War, by patrolling in an area where submarines were known to be active. It was hoped that the submarine commander would be unwilling to use an expensive torpedo on such a humble vessel and would be more likely to approach on the surface, at which point the concealed armament of the decoy ship could be used. She sailed from Beirut on 12 June and made her way slowly north along the coast towards Iskenderun. At 11.10 a surfaced submarine was sighted, which closed her, but opened fire from a considerable distance, meaning the schooner could not get into range to use her own armament, and was hit by the fourth salvo. For the next 20 minutes the submarine shelled the schooner, setting it on fire. She finally sank at 11.50 in position 34.19N 35.33E. Throughout the bombardment Lockington and a small party remained on board trying to return fire, until they were forced to jump into the water. Her attacker was *U 83* (Kraus); eight men lost their lives. Lockington was subsequently awarded the DSC and two seamen the DSM.
[TNA: ADM.1/12282; ADM.199/650]

14 June MTB 259 motor torpedo boat
Bayonne NJ 1940 (*PT 10*) transferred 1941; 32 tons; 70ft × 20ft; 4 × torpedo tubes
Lieutenant Robert Alexander Allan RNVR
Part of the 10th MTB Flotilla in the Mediterranean, four boats of the flotilla were ordered to form part of the escort to the large supply convoy MW11, bound for Malta from Alexandria, given the codename Operation 'Vigorous'. The boats would be towed astern of a merchant vessel, with the intention that if the convoy came under attack from enemy surface craft, the MTBs could be slipped and counter the attack. However, it soon became clear that the plan was flawed; the towing arrangements were crude, with warps fitted round the hull, the boats were overloaded with supplies and the weather was poor, all of which combined to make the tow difficult. The boats were being battered by the seas and constantly surging forward to run over the tow, which then slackened, and the boats slowed until jerked forward again. It was decided to slip the boats to allow them to return to Alexandria independently. This proved difficult in the weather conditions; in some cases, tow wires having to be sawn through to be freed; *259*, being towed by the *Lincoln City*, lost one man overboard in the efforts to free her. She was already damaged, the towing warp and constant surging having strained the hull, and the engine room started to flood. Very soon the engine stopped and being constantly washed over by the sea she steadily settled until she foundered at 23.47. *MTB 268* had stood by her, and as it was clear that she had to be abandoned, with great difficulty her sister boat picked up her crew.
[TNA: ADM.199/1244; Pope pp47–8; Reynolds & Cooper, *Mediterranean MTBs at War* pp39–40]

15 June HASTY destroyer
Dumbarton 1936; 1,340 tons; 312ft × 33ft; 4 × 4.7in, 1 × 12pdr, 2 × 20mm, 4 × torpedo tubes
Lieutenant Commander Nigel Hubert George Austen DSO

Part of the escort to the Malta-bound Convoy MW11 from Alexandria, she was screening the cruiser *Newcastle*, with another two destroyers, and were zigzagging at 20 knots, about 15 miles on the starboard quarter of the convoy. At 05.27 in position 34.02N 22.08E, to the south-east of Crete, lookouts on the cruiser saw two torpedo tracks on the port side. The tracks passed along the port side of *Newcastle*, and one headed straight for the *Hasty*, which was taking up station ahead of the cruiser. The approaching track was seen at the last minute by lookouts on the destroyer and the wheel ordered hard over to starboard, but it was too late, and she was hit on the port side under 'A' gun. There was a large explosion, probably the result of the forward magazine exploding, and the bows were blown off forward of 'A' gun. The engines stopped, the boiler room filled with smoke and the ship was reported to be flooding. The *Hotspur* came alongside to take off survivors, and as it was clear that she would not survive was ordered to sink her by torpedo. Fourteen men lost their lives. They had been attacked by torpedo boats which had successfully approached unseen; *S 55* was credited with the sinking of *Hasty*. The attack continued, with the cruiser *Newcastle* being damaged.
[TNA:ADM.199/1244]

15 June AIREDALE escort destroyer
Clydebank 1941; 1,050 tons; 264.2ft × 31.6ft; 4 × 4in, 4 × 2pdr, 3 × 20mm, 2 × torpedo tubes
Lieutenant Commander Archibald George Forman DSC

One of the escorts to the Operation 'Vigorous' convoy to Malta, they were to the south of Crete, in position 33.55N 23.45E, when they came under a series of intense air attacks during the afternoon. At 15.25 several Ju 87 aircraft were seen on the starboard quarter of the *Airedale*, which increased speed to 22 knots and altered course to allow all guns to engage. A number of aircraft separated from the main group and concentrated their attack on her. Two bombs exploded close to the port side, and another near the starboard side before a fourth bomb hit the after gun mounting. This triggered a heavy explosion aft, probably the 4in and/or the depth-charge magazine blowing up. This blew the stern off abaft the searchlight platform, and the ship's sides were buckled, and distorted, jagged edges being folded back towards the bow. The ship settled by the stern and took a slight list to starboard. Number 2 boiler room was on fire and she was blanketed by a large amount of smoke and steam. At 15.45 she was clearly sinking by the stern and abandon ship was ordered; the whaler was

lowered, and Carley floats were released, the survivors being picked up by *Hurworth* and *Aldenham*, the latter of which despatched the wreck by torpedo. One hundred and twenty-three men died.
[TNA:ADM.199/1244]

15 June BEDOUIN destroyer
Dumbarton 1937; 1,960 tons; 355.6ft × 36.6ft; 6 × 4.7in, 2 × 4in, 4 × 2pdr, 4 × 20mm, 4 × torpedo tubes
Commander Bryan Gouthwaite Scurfield OBE

At the same time as Convoy MW11 was attempting to reach Malta from Alexandria, another convoy set out from Gibraltar, as Operation 'Harpoon'. The *Bedouin* was among the ships detached from the Home Fleet to act as escorts to this convoy which set out on 12 March. They soon became the target for air and submarine attacks, but no serious losses had occurred. At 06.00 on 15 June, the convoy had cleared the coast of North Africa and was approaching the island of Pantellaria. Fifteen minutes later enemy ships were sighted to the north-east; this was a powerful Italian surface force, consisting of the cruisers, *Raimondo Montecuccoli* and *Eugenio di Savoia* with five destroyers. *Bedouin*, along with other destroyers, increased speed to 20 knots and turned towards the threat, whilst the cruiser *Cairo* and escort destroyers with the convoy made smoke whilst it altered to the south. At 06.27 fire was opened, the British line continuing to close, despite the disparity in force. Several large shells near missed her, and at 06.50 she was hit, the director being put out of action, and she was then hit or near missed a further ten times, although the damage was largely superficial. When *Bedouin* was 4.500 yards from the nearest of the enemy cruisers, she executed a turn away, firing her torpedoes as she did. This forced the enemy to carry out a drastic alteration of course, turning away from the convoy, to avoid the threat. As the *Bedouin* completed her turn she was hit again, by a heavy shell in the engine room. All power was lost, the lights went out and she slowed down. She remained stable and upright, the guns continuing to work in local control. The destroyer *Partridge*, herself having suffered damage, closed and rigged a tow, the pair steering towards Malta, the convoy having steamed ahead. The pair were very conscious of being exposed to air attack, and at 13.00 a gaggle of Ju 87 aircraft were sighted, causing the tow to be cast off, but no attack materialised, and the tow was re-connected. The tow was again cast off a little later when the Italian surface ships were sighted, the *Partridge* gallantly making smoke and closing the threat, but the Italians turned away. At 14.15 a single Italian SM 79 aircraft closed and attacked the now solitary *Bedouin* with a torpedo, which struck the ship between the engine and gearing room on the starboard side. She immediately heeled over to port and she was clearly sinking. Boats and rafts were lowered or released, and she was abandoned. After several hours in the water the survivors were rescued by Italian ships, to be taken into captivity. Twenty-eight men were killed. [TNA: ADM.267/106]

15 June MTB 201 motor torpedo boat
Cowes 1941; 38 tons; 72ft × 18.2ft; 1 × 20mm,
2 × torpedo tubes
Lieutenant George Lennox Cotton RNVR

Based at Dover, she sailed in company with another two torpedo boats to loiter to the south of Calais, to intercept enemy shipping that was expected to sail from Boulogne; a group of motor gunboats was tasked to operate to the north of their position. At just before midnight the vague shapes of ships could be seen approaching, and as the torpedo boats started up to manoeuvre into an attacking position, they were illuminated by star shell. Despite this they attacked, meeting strong opposition, with fire from both the escorts and from the shore. *201* was withdrawing after firing her torpedoes, when she was hit by a burst of fire, including at least one large-calibre shell. The bridge was wrecked, wounding several men, one engine was put out of action and a fire had been started. The crew were forced to abandon her, but after 30 minutes, seeing the flames die down, went back alongside and re-embarked. The fire was put out and managed to restart an engine to proceed slowly towards Dover. She was spotted at daybreak, about 10 miles to the east of the port, low in the water and clearly seriously damaged. Efforts were made to tow her by two RAF air-sea rescue launches, but at 08.48 she rolled over and sank. Three men were killed in the action. Cotton was subsequently awarded the DSC and two crew members were awarded the DSM and CGM for their actions. [TNA: ADM.199/777; Reynolds, Home Waters MTBs pp52–5]

16 June HERMIONE cruiser
Linthouse 1939; 5,600 tons; 485ft × 50.6ft; 10 × 5.25in,
8 × 2pdr, 5 × 20mm, 6 × torpedo tubes
Captain Geoffrey Nigel Oliver DSO

Sailed from Alexandria on 11 June as part of the escort to the large supply Convoy MW11, bound for Malta from Alexandria, under the codename Operation 'Vigorous'. During 14 June, the convoy came under intense air attacks, and during the evening an attempted attack by submarine was driven off. The convoy then came under threat from a powerful Italian surface force and with the prospect of continuing air attacks over the next few days, and insufficient AA ammunition remaining to provide cover, they turned back during the evening of 15 June. At 01.00 the *Hermione* was stationed on the starboard side of the convoy as it headed south-east, just abaft the beam of the last ship in the column of merchant ships; two escort destroyers were stationed

on her starboard beam and ahead of her as she zigzagged at 13 knots. At 01.27 a 'swish' was heard which was followed immediately by a large explosion as she was hit by a torpedo which exploded at 117 station, between the after engine room and 'B' boiler room. The blast lifted the starboard torpedo tubes off their mounting, and there was widespread shock damage as the ship whipped in the explosion. The after engine room and 'B' boiler room rapidly flooded and the forward engine room was affected, with a mixture of oil and water starting to enter, which steadily increased to eventually force its evacuation. The ship settled by the stern as she heeled over to starboard, listing 22 degrees within one minute of the blast. The ship hung in this position for some moments, but then started to heel over further, at which the order to abandon ship was given. The ship slowly rolled further to starboard until she was almost on her beam ends, and then steadied herself, to remain in this precarious position for several more minutes before capsizing, her bows then rose vertically into the air and she sank at 01.48. Eighty-eight officers and men lost their lives. Her position was 33.17N 26.10E. Whether she was hit by a single torpedo is doubtful: her attacker, *U 205* (Reschke), claimed hearing three detonations in quick succession, and the escorting *Dido* saw two flashes. [TNA: ADM.199/2068; WSS Warship Supplement 134 pp28–30]

16 June NESTOR destroyer
Govan 1940; 1,773 tons; 339.6ft × 35.7ft; 6 × 4.7in, 1 × 4in,
4 × 2pdr, 4 × 20mm
Commander Alvord Sydney Rosenthal RAN

Royal Australian Navy. Part of the escort to Convoy MW11 for Malta, as part of Operation 'Vigorous'. The convoy came under heavy and repeated attacks, which led to the ships being turned back to Alexandria. At shortly after 18.00 on 15 June during another air attack, *Nestor* was straddled by bombs which caused the ship to 'whip' violently. Personnel were thrown off their feet and there was widespread damage to fixtures and fittings. The hull was distorted and punctured on the port side and the forward boiler room quickly flooded, and with the after boiler room slowly flooding, she lost all power. The ship listed to port and started to settle by the head, but quick action by damage control teams stabilised the ship and this allowed the ship to be taken in tow by *Javelin* although this parted at 23.00 and had to be re-rigged. During the early morning, the tow parted for the second time and it was decided that, with the slow progress of the tow and with over 200 miles to Alexandria, the threat of further attacks and being low on ammunition, she should be abandoned. *Javelin* lifted off all the crew and then dropped shallow-set depth charges to ensure her sinking. Four men lost their lives. [Cassells p44; TNA: ADM.267/106]

16 June JUSTIFIED drifter

Selby 1925 (*Marinus*) requisitioned 1940; 93 tons;
86.3ft × 18.6ft
Sub-Lieutenant Robert Lawrie RNVR

Employed as a minesweeper, she was based in Malta. Ordered to act as a marker for the arrival of the 'Harpoon' convoy, she took up station 3 miles to the west of St Elmo's light. She found it difficult to maintain her station, being unable to anchor, and laid a buoy as a marker. During the night she lost sight of the buoy and at first light hailed the minesweeper *Hythe* to lead her to safe water to allow her to fix her position and then return to her buoy. At 06.25, when astern of the *Hythe*, there was a large explosion amidships abaft the bridge as she detonated a mine. The boiler then exploded, and the vessel rapidly sank with the loss of three men.
[TNA: ADM.199/221; ADM.199/239]

16 June TRANQUIL trawler

Beverley 1912 (*Good Luck*) requisitioned 1940; 294 tons;
130ft × 23.5ft
Lieutenant William Postlethwaite RNR†

Employed in towing two barges from the river Thames, at 02.35 she was in collision when off North Foreland with the steamer *Deal* (829 tons), a ship in Convoy CE91 and subsequently sank. The survivors were picked up by convoy escorts, but five men lost their lives. The wreck lies in position 51.13.08N 01.27.51E.
[TNA: ADM.199/777; ADM.358/4095; Larn vol 2 sec 5]

17 June WILD SWAN destroyer

Wallsend 1919; 1,120 tons; 300ft × 29.6ft; 3 × 4in,
1 × 12pdr, 2 × 2pdr, 2 × 20mm, 3 × torpedo tubes
Lieutenant Commander Claude Edward Lutley Sclater

Having completed distant support duty for inward-bound Convoy HG84, the *Wild Swan* was heading for Devonport at 15 knots, when at 19.52, when about 100 miles west of Ushant, an Fw 200 reconnaissance aircraft was sighted. It evidently reported sighting the destroyer as at 21.16, as she was passing a group of Spanish fishing trawlers, a gaggle of twelve aircraft, identified as Ju 88s, was sighted closing, which commenced a bombing attack. Defensive fire was opened with all armament by the destroyer, and two aircraft were shot down, one of which was seen to crash onto one of the trawlers. Despite working up to full speed and manoeuvring, she was straddled by a stick of four bombs. The force of the explosions was such that she was lifted out of the water, and her back was broken. The steering gear jammed, the engine and boiler rooms reported flooding and she swung round, out of control, to ram one of the trawlers, which slowly sank, her crew clambering on board the destroyer. The attacking aircraft remained circling, and were then seen to start attacking the trawlers,

evidently mistaking them for part of the convoy. Two of the trawlers were sunk, although the *Wild Swan* continued to put up a fierce anti-aircraft barrage and claimed to have shot down a further two aircraft. At 21.56 she was stopped in the water and listing when she again came under attack. This time three bombs burst close to the starboard quarter, although she did dispose of another aircraft, which was seen to crash into the sea. She was clearly sinking and was ordered to be abandoned. The whaler and motor boat were successfully launched, and floats were released, the crew leaving her in an orderly manner, taking with them eleven Spanish fishermen from a sunken trawler. She finally sank at 23.15 in position 49.52N 10.44W. The *Vansittart* found them the next day, but thirty-one men had died, many of them during the night from exposure. Lieutenant Commander Sclater was subsequently awarded the DSC for the stubborn defence of his ship.
[TNA: ADM.267/110]

17 June VIXEN tug

Sydney 1938, purchased 1940; 12 tons; 39ft × 10.5ft
Based at Tobruk, she was abandoned when the port was evacuated, apparently having been damaged and sunk before the occupation by the enemy.
[TNA: ADM.199/799; Statement of Losses – Amendment p4]

18 June VISION tug

Sydney 1938 purchased 1941; 12 tons; 39ft × 10.5ft
Reported sunk at Mersa Matruh, Egypt; the circumstances uncertain but it was presumably either by enemy surface or air action.
[Statement of Losses p23]

19 June SGB 7 steam gun boat

Dumbarton 1941; 165 tons; 137.9ft × 23.4ft; 2 × 2pdr,
2 × torpedo tubes
Lieutenant Ronald Lewis Barnet (n.b. this was a 'cover' name for René Barnett a French officer)

During the night of 18/19 June, the escort destroyer *Albrighton* in company with the steam gunboats, *SGB 7* and *SGB 8*, attacked an enemy convoy between Le Havre and Cherbourg, which consisted of two ships with an escort of what appeared to be six to ten patrol and torpedo boats. The *Albrighton* hit one ship twice with 4in shells, and *SGB 7* claimed a torpedo hit on one of the merchant ships – this was the 800-ton *Turquoise*, which later sank. In the fierce exchange of fire that followed, *SGB 7* was hit in the boiler room, probably by the escort *M.3800* and came to a halt, covered in steam and smoke. She subsequently sank, the crew being picked up by the patrol ship *RA 2*. Four men were killed.
[TNA: ADM.267/124; Scott p69]

20 June The fall of Tobruk

In North Africa, the Afrika Korps was making rapid advances to the east, and as the British army fell back, the besieged garrison at the port of Tobruk came under increased pressure. On 17 June, all merchant ships were ordered to leave, and 3 days later a strong force of German tanks supported by infantry broke through the perimeter defences during the morning and by that afternon enemy tanks were shelling the harbour. The last craft under naval control still in the harbour were ordered to leave for Alexandria and did so under constant shelling and regular air attacks. The following were lost:

HDML 1039 motor launch
Teignmouth 1940; 46 tons; 70ft × 15ft; 1 × 3pdr
Lieutenant Robert Morton RNVR[†]
Suffered a direct hit as she left the wharf loaded with troops. There was another large explosion, probably as ammunition or depth charges exploded and she sank rapidly. Fourteen men of her complement were lost.
[TNA: ADM.199/799; Burns p48]

HDML 1069 motor launch
East Molesey 1941; 46 tons; 70ft × 15ft; 1 × 3pdr
Lieutenant Lionel Pierce Douglas RCNVR[†]
Having been ordered to wait to embark the NOIC Tobruk, she waited until German tanks were visible, but on sailing she was hit bit by an artillery shell as she left the jetty and a short while later by a shell fired by a tank. On fire, the vessel signalled for medical assistance and returned to the jetty. Five survivors were taken aboard *ML 355* and the vessel was abandoned to be captured by Axis forces. Three ratings were killed.
[TNA: ADM.199/802; ADM.358/4100; Burns pp45–50]

LCT (2) 117 landing craft, tank
Middlesbrough 1941; 296 tons; 143ft × 30ft; 2 × 2pdr
Sub-Lieutenant Eric Davies RNVR
Loaded with personnel, as she got underway to leave the harbour, she was still under helm to point to the entrance when they were hit by a heavy shell, wounding everyone on the upper deck. Another shell then hit in the engine room, severing the fuel lines and starting a fire. She was abandoned and allowed to drift ashore, still burning.
Note: this loss is not noted in the official *Statement of Losses*.
[Lund & Ludlam p42; http://www.bbc.co.uk/history/ww2peopleswar/stories/05/a4486205.shtml]

LCT (2) 119 landing craft, tank
Middlesbrough 1941; 296 tons; 143ft × 30ft; 2 × 2pdr
Hit repeatedly by shore fire as she attempted to leave the harbour, loaded with troops and stores, she was set on fire, drifted inshore and was abandoned.
[TNA: ADM.199/799; Lund & Ludlum pp43–5]

HIGHLAND QUEEN drifter
Requisitioned 1941; 23 tons
Reported to have been lost, apparently one of the small units intercepted by enemy *Schnellboot* patrol craft as she left the harbour and sunk by gunfire.

KHEIR-EL-DINE schooner
Requisitioned 1941; 150 tons
Lieutenant Ronald John Chesney RNVR
By 20.00 it was clear that the enemy were about to overrun the harbour, and the last craft attempted to leave. Loaded with troops the vessel was hit almost as soon as she got underway, and when another shell struck her bows, she slowed, and water was reported to be entering. An MTB closed and took off several of the troops, but she drifted across the harbour until she ran aground and was abandoned. Despite this, as the enemy's attention shifted away from her, she was later re-manned and sailed out, only to encounter several torpedo boats and the schooner was scuttled as they approached.
[TNA: ADM.199/799; IWM Doc 9664]

LARS RIISDAHL schooner
Rosendal 1904 requisitioned 1940; 143 tons; 103ft × 24.6ft
Skipper John Muttit RNR
Hit by two shells, she caught fire and was abandoned. As the men left her, to board *MTB 262* berthed astern of her, she was hit by another shell and became a mass of flames.
[TNA: ADM.199/802]

ESKIMO NELL schooner
Requisitioned 1941; 20 (?) tons
A former local fishing boat, she was taken into British service and classed as a 'schooner'. She was intercepted by enemy torpedo boats during the evening after she left the harbour and was sunk. All of her crew were taken prisoner.
[TNA: ADM.358/3272]

ALAISIA tug
1929 requisitioned 1941; 72 tons
Lieutenant Arthur Ramsey Gilmore RNVR
Having embarked about thirty soldiers, she got underway at about 19.30, but was hit in the after end of the wheelhouse, wounding the commanding officer. She kept going but then received another direct hit on a fuel tank which spread burning fuel, setting her on fire. The blaze was tackled, but the fire spread and some of the men jumped into the water. Still under fire she was turned inshore and beached near number 6 jetty and abandoned.
[TNA: ADM.199/799; ADM.358/2998; Burns p48]

Note: In addition, five LCMs, one LCP and an LCA were lost

★ ★ ★

21 June PARKTOWN whaler

Middlesbrough (*Southern Sky*) 1929 requisitioned 1940;
250 tons; 116ft × 24.2ft; 1 × 20mm
Lieutenant Leslie James Jagger SANF[†]

South African Navy. Successfully managed to leave Tobruk under heavy fire, with a small tug in tow full of soldiers, but was only able to proceed at about 5 knots. At 06.45 the following morning several torpedo boats were sighted, and these closed to attack. A direct hit on the bridge killed Lieutenant Jagger and the coxswain. Outnumbered, and damaged with the ship on fire, the crew started to leave, launching Carley floats, and the enemy craft left the scene. The tug, which had been ignored by the torpedo boats, was able to close and pick up survivors and an MTB approached later during the morning and sank the burning wreck. Five men were killed.

[*https://samilhistory.com/tag/hmsas-parktown/*]

21 June LCT (2) 150 landing craft, tank

Meadowside 1941; 296 tons; 143ft × 30ft; 2 × 2pdr
Skipper Ronald Nathaniel Buck RNR

The last vessel to leave Tobruk, she had taken on board dozens of wounded soldiers. As she got underway to clear the harbour she came under heavy fire from the shore, which caused several casualties amongst the crew and troops. With her steering gear out of action, she used engines to manoeuvre, and despite collisions with *LCT 119* and the *Kheir-el-Dine* (see above), she managed to clear the harbour. The following morning several small craft were seen approaching, and it became clear that they were enemy patrol boats. Unable to offer any resistance, and to save further casualties, they hoisted a white flag. The *S 55* came alongside and took possession of her, and she was taken back to Tobruk.

[*TNA: ADM.199/799; Lund & Ludlum, War of the Landing Craft p43; Rohwer, Chronology of the War at Sea p174*]

21 June P 514 submarine

San Francisco 1918 (*R 19*) transferred 1942; 530/684 tons;
179ft × 18ft; 1 × 3in, 4 × torpedo tubes
Lieutenant Walter Augustus Philimore[†]

One of several American submarines transferred to the Royal Navy, it was intended that she join the others as a training vessel. Commissioned at New London on 9 March, she arrived at the small port of Argentia, Canada, on 27 May where she remained until 20 June when she sailed in company with the corvette *Primrose*, to make the journey to St John's, Newfoundland. At the same time, two coastal convoys were transiting through the area. SC88 was heading east for St Johns, whilst CL43 was westbound for Sydney, Nova Scotia. Visibility was poor, with patches of thick drifting fog, when in the early hours of 21 June, the groups encountered each other in position 46.33N 53.40W. Part of the escort to CL43, the

Canadian minesweeper *Georgian*, was keeping a watch on hydrophones for the sound of the approaching convoy. At 03.00 she duly picked up the noise of the oncoming ships, but soon after picked up another hydrophone effect. *Georgian* stopped engines and carefully monitored the noise, which was clearly not from the convoy. When the dark low shape of a submarine was seen, she got underway, flashing the visual recognition signal as she did. When no reply was received it was assumed that she must be hostile and working up to full speed the *Georgian* rammed the submarine, the time then being 03.10, striking her on the port side amidships. The submarine rapidly disappeared, and despite a search of the area, no survivors were found; forty-two men died. It later emerged that *Georgian* had never been informed of the presence of a British submarine but had been warned that two German U-boats were operating off Cape Race. No blame was therefore placed on the officers of the *Georgian*.

[*Evans pp320–1*]

24 June GOSSAMER minesweeper

Port Glasgow 1938; 875 tons; 230ft × 33.6ft; 2 × 4in,
2 × 20mm
Lieutenant Commander Thomas Crosbie Crease

Based in northern Russia, the *Gossamer* was lying at anchor off Mishukov light in the Kola Inlet when at 09.00 an air raid warning was received. The weather was clear with no cloud and a very bright sun. Moments later several Ju 88 aircraft were seen approaching from the south, which started diving attacks on merchant ships anchored nearby. The minesweeper engaged the aircraft with 4in and 20mm. One aircraft which had broken away from the main group then carried out a diving attack out of the sun on the *Gossamer*. Blinded by the glare, the aircraft was not seen until the last minute as it released two bombs. At least one of the bombs struck the ship on the starboard side aft. The stern of the ship was wrecked, and her back was broken. Settling quickly by the stern, the port whaler was lowered, and floats and rafts ordered to be released as the minesweeper *Hussar* was signalled to standby her. The ship started to slowly roll over to starboard and the order was given for her to be abandoned. At 09.21, about 8 minutes after being hit, she rolled over and sank. Three officers and twenty ratings were lost.

[*TNA: ADM.1/12285*]

30 June MEDWAY depot ship

Barrow 1928; 14,650 tons; 545ft × 85ft; 6 × 4in
Captain Philip Ruck Keene CBE

With the steady advance of the Afrika Korps through North Africa to threaten Egypt and the Suez Canal, it was decided to shift the base of submarine operations from Alexandria to Beirut. The *Medway* sailed on 29

June in company with the cruiser *Dido* and escorted by seven destroyers. The following day, at 09.25 in position 32.03N 30.55E she was hit by three torpedoes on the starboard side. The swirl of the discharge or possibly the conning tower of the attacking submarine briefly breaking surface was seen from the lower bridge, but too late to take avoiding action. The first torpedo hit abreast the generator room about 12ft below the waterline. This blew down nearby bulkheads and caused immediate flooding. The second hit the after end of the engine room and immediately flooded the space. There was a third, lighter, explosion about 3 or 4 seconds after the second, which was believed to be a hit on the starboard propeller as the starboard engine stopped abruptly at this time. The port engine continued to run until stopped by telegraph order. The ship assumed a slight heel to starboard, but this steadily increased and in 3 minutes had reached 17 degrees, where she stabilised and hung for several minutes. She then started to slowly roll over to starboard and orders were given to abandon ship. By 09.40 she was lying on her beam ends and the stern sank, the bows rearing up vertically and she had disappeared by 09.42. The survivors were picked up by the destroyers *Hero* and *Zulu*. Her attacker had been *U 372* (Neumann), and Captain Ruck Keene commented that ' … if she had to be sunk, (it was) fitting that it was done by a submarine, who undoubtedly carried out a very fine unseen attack, passing through a strong Asdic screen'. Thirty men were lost.
[TNA: ADM.267/112]

2 July NEREUS channel patrol boat
Sydney 1939 requisitioned 1941; 36 tons; 66ft × 16ft
Lieutenant James Benison Griffin DSC RANVR
Royal Australian Navy. A motor launch employed by the Naval Auxiliary Patrol for local patrol duties, she was commissioned for service at Darwin, Northern Territories, but caught fire and burnt out in Sydney Harbour before she could take up her station.
[Cassells p42]

5 July SWORD DANCE trawler
Leith 1940; 530 tons; 150ft × 27.8ft; 1 × 4in, 3 × 20mm
Lieutenant James Joseph Allon RNR
In dense fog, during the early hours, whilst acting as escort to the east coast convoy WN5 off the Scottish coast she was rammed by one of the convoy, the *Thyra-II* (1,088 tons). Holed in the starboard coal bunker, the engine room rapidly flooded and she sank in less than an hour.
[TNA: ADM.199/777; Lund, Trawlers go to War p170]

5 July NIGER minesweeper
Cowes 1936; 815 tons; 230ft × 33.6ft; 2 × 4in, 2 × 20mm
Commander Arthur Jelfs Cubison DSC†
Acting as part of the escort to a westbound convoy, QP13, they sailed from Murmansk 27 June. On 4

July, the convoy divided, with the ships for Loch Ewe detaching, the remaining sixteen continued towards Iceland with an escort of two minesweepers, a corvette and two armed trawlers. The weather was poor, with strong north-easterly gales, and regular patches of fog. This meant that no sun or star sights could be obtained, and the position of the convoy was uncertain. By 5 July they were in the Denmark Strait to the north-west of Iceland, and the ships of the convoy were divided into two columns, with the minesweeper *Hussar* leading. The *Niger* was the senior officer and steamed ahead to make a landfall. On sighting what they believed was land, they signalled an alteration of course to the west. At 20.40 she was returning to rejoin the convoy, but as she crossed the bows of the *Lady Madeleine*, she altered course to port to take up her station ahead of the trawler, there was a large explosion on the port side amidships. She was seen to heel to port, then rolled to starboard, rolled back to port again, this time not recovering, capsizing over, to float bottom up, the stern clear of the water. She hung in this position for 5 minutes before rising perpendicularly and remained visible for nearly an hour before sinking. Eighty men died. It was found that the convoy had mistaken an iceberg for land, and the course alteration had taken them into the British minefield SN72. In addition to the *Niger*, six ships of the convoy also detonated mines, with four sinking immediately, another two being constructive losses.
[TNA: ADM.199/239; Woodman p196]

7 July ALDERSDALE oiler
Birkenhead 1937; 17,231 tons; 466.3ft × 62ft
Master Archibald Hobson
En-route for northern Russia, she joined Convoy PQ17 which sailed from Reykjavik on 27 June. On 4 July the Admiralty, fearing that the convoy was under immediate threat from a powerful surface force, including the battleship *Tirpitz*, ordered the convoy to scatter. This misguided decision, based on incomplete intelligence led to a disaster, with twenty-four ships being sunk by aircraft and submarine. When the dispersal was ordered, the *Aldersdale* initially steamed north, heading for Novaya Zemlya, and found herself in company with the minesweeper *Salamander*, the rescue ship *Zaafaran* and the cargo ship *Ocean Freedom*. The group kept together for mutual protection, but the following day they were found by four Ju 88 bombers which were searching the area. The aircraft attacked, and although she suffered no direct hits, several bombs exploded around the stern of the *Aldersdale*. The shock stopped her engines and she started rapidly making water. The *Salamander* ran alongside and lifted off the crew, but after some time it was clear that she was not immediately about to sink, and Captain Hobson and a few of the crew returned

onboard, with the hope of restarting her engines or perhaps rigging a tow. However, it became clear that the engines were quite useless, and with air attacks resuming on the *Zaafaran*, rigging a tow was out of the question. Hobson and his team were again evacuated, and the *Salamander* attempted to speed up her sinking by firing into her and dropping a depth charge under her stern. All failed to despatch her, and she was abandoned, slowly settling. She remained afloat, derelict and drifting for another 2 days, until she was sighted during the late morning of the 7th by the *U 457* (Brandenburg); after firing several high explosive shells into the wreck, at 14.56 she was despatched with a torpedo, the ship breaking up as she sank.

[*Woodman p230; Rohwer, Axis Submarine Successes p199*]

9 July TUNISIAN trawler
Beverley 1930 requisitioned 1939; 238 tons; 122.6ft × 22.1ft
Boom Skipper Thomas How Pattison RNR[†]

Former Grimsby trawler employed as a boom defence vessel and based at Harwich. She sailed from the anchorage off Felixstowe with the mooring barge *Porthos* in tow, to carry out maintenance work on a line of HABs (horizontal anti-boat defences) between Thorpeness and Minsmere off the Suffolk coast. At 07.43 as she passed the Wadgate Ledge buoy there was a large explosion as she detonated a mine, and she rapidly sank with the loss of twenty-nine men. Her position was noted as 51.56.32N 01.23.13E.

[*TNA: ADM.199/221*]

9 July MANOR trawler
Aberdeen 1913 requisitioned 1939; 314 tons; 130ft × 23.6ft; 1 × 4in
Skipper Benjamin Pile RNR[†]

Part of the escort to the westbound coastal Convoy WP183 passing through the English Channel, which consisted of fifteen ships being escorted by a destroyer and two armed trawlers. The convoy safely arrived off the Eddystone light during the morning of 8 July, where five ships were detached, the remainder reforming into two columns. At 17.00 an unidentified aircraft was seen at high level and was identified as a Ju 88 on reconnaissance. The aircraft stayed with them through the evening. At 00.45 flares were dropped ahead of the convoy and this was recognised as being a signal to waiting torpedo boats. The attack commenced at 01.00, with the *Brocklesby* firing star shell, but very soon after, one of the convoy was hit by a torpedo, followed by a second soon after. The escort destroyer *Brocklesby* engaged the enemy craft but could not stop the attacks continuing and a force of eight enemy torpedo boats carried out a devastating attack. The *Manor* was hit by a torpedo and sank very rapidly, with the loss of twenty-

nine men. In all, five ships of the convoy were sunk as well as the *Manor*.

[*TNA: ADM.199/420; ADM.199/421; ADM.199/287*]

11 July HDML 1090 motor launch
Wootton 1942; 46 tons; 70ft × 15ft

Being carried as deck cargo for transfer to the Royal New Zealand Navy, the launch was lost when the merchant ship *Port Hunter* was torpedoed at 11.00 by *U 582* (Schulte) about 370 miles south-west of Madeira.

[*https://uboat.net/allies/merchants/1925.html*]

21 July MGB 328 motor gun boat
Southwick 1941; 72 tons; 108ft × 17.5ft; 2 × 2pdr
Lieutenant Henry Patrick Cobb RNVR[†]

In company with *MGB 322* and *MGB 601*, ordered to conduct a night patrol in the Channel, with the aim of intercepting coastal traffic south of Boulogne. Soon after midnight the group were informed by Dover that a group of ships had been detected by shore radar off Cap Gris Nez which appeared to be a coastal convoy. The enemy ships were sighted 45 minutes later and found to be a single merchant ship escorted by several armed trawlers and patrol craft. This was not a favourable gun boat target, but an attack was decided on. Led by Cobb, the group ran at high speed towards the enemy, and initially it went well. Taking the enemy by surprise, they ran past several escort vessels, leaving them to port, then closed the merchant ship and engaged her at close range to starboard. It may well have been the intention to run under her bows and drop a depth charge, but by now they were coming under intense fire from the escorts, and *328* was hit several times and then disappeared in an enormous flash and flames. The other two boats managed to extricate themselves, although both were hit repeatedly and continued to engage the enemy which eventually turned back into Boulogne. Six men were lost.

[*Scott pp81–2; Reynolds, Dog Boats p17; TNA: ADM.199/782*]

23 July VASSILIKI harbour tender
Glasgow 1879 (*Jessie*), requisitioned 1941; 190 tons; 136.3ft × 17ft

Carrying a load of oil in drums and cases, she was on passage from Beirut to Famagusta when she was attacked by a surfaced submarine, *U 77* (Schonder). The submarine fired ten rounds into the ship in the early hours, setting her on fire and forcing the crew to abandon ship in position 34.45N 34.35E; there were no casualties.

[*Statement of Losses p24; Rohwer, Axis Submarine Sucesses p235*]

24 July MGB 601 motor gun boat

Teddington 1942; 90 tons; 115ft × 21.3ft; 1 × 2pdr,
2 × 20mm

Lieutenant Allan Arthur Gotelee RNVR

Part of the forces stationed at Dover, she had taken part in the action in the Channel on the night of 20/21 July, which had seen the destruction of *MGB 328* (see above) and during which she had suffered one man killed and three wounded, including Gotelee. During the fight she had been peppered with enemy shellfire – an examination later found twenty-six holes in the hull, mainly from 20mm shells. Her engines were unaffected, and she made it back to Dover. Whilst lying alongside at Dover under repair there was a large internal explosion and fire, and she was wrecked. It was found that the most likely cause was an ignition of petrol vapour. One of the fuel tanks seems to have been hit, and the petrol had subsequently leaked out but had been trapped between the tank and the self-sealing compound. One man was killed.

[TNA: ADM.267/121; Reynolds, Dog Boats pp17–18]

25 July LAERTES trawler

Beverley 1940; 545 tons; 150ft × 27.8ft; 1 × 12pdr,
3 × 20mm

Skipper-Lieutenant Patrick Joseph Quinland DSC RNR

Stationed at Freetown, Liberia, she was on night patrol in approximate position 6N 14.17W, when she gained an Asdic contact which she attacked, with no obvious result. She continued the search and contact was regained at 21.10 at 1,000 yards and she turned to carry out a second attack. As she did, she sighted a U-boat broaching. Seconds later she was hit by a torpedo and sank in less than 2 minutes after a violent explosion. Eleven survivors were picked up, but nineteen men died. Her attacker had been *U 201* (Schnee).

[TNA: ADM.199/777]

27 July MGB 501 motor gun boat

Gosport 1942; 95 tons; 110ft × 19.6ft; 1 × 2pdr, 1 × 20mm

Lieutenant Dunstan Michael Calvert Curtis RNVR

Engaged in exercises off the Scilly Isles in company with *MGB 318* and *MASB 6*, she was in position 49.56N 05.56W, heading west at 19.5 knots when without warning there was a large explosion forward on the port side. The boat came to a stop, covered in a thick cloud of smoke. The explosion was evidently internal, with the forward magazine being demolished, the galley being wrecked with the bulkhead between the galley and the magazine blown away. Both sides of the boat were blown out and the forward deck blown up and distorted. *MGB 318* closed to pass a tow aft, but she was already sinking by the bows and at 12.20 she broke in half. The fore part rolled over to float upside down with the after section rising to stand vertically out of the sea.

The wreck was sunk by gunfire from *318*. The court of enquiry believed the probable cause of the blast was a petrol vapour explosion, caused by fumes creeping along the bilges from the petrol compartment to be ignited by the flames of the burner on the galley stove. However, it was recognised that the bilges had been checked earlier and found dry and further, although the galley stove had been dislodged by the explosion, it would surely have been destroyed if it had been the seat of the blast. Therefore, an alternative theory, an explosion of overheated torpedo impulse charges, which had been improperly stowed in the forward magazine next to the galley bulkhead, was considered possible.

[TNA: ADM.267/13]

7 August THORN submarine

Birkenhead 1941; 1,090/1,575 tons; 263ft × 26.7ft; 1 × 4in,
11 × torpedo tubes

Lieutenant Commander Robert Galliano Norfolk[†]

Sailed from Beirut 21 July to conduct a patrol, initially off Tobruk, then move to the area of Cape Matapan on 6 August. At 12.55 on 7 August, 30 miles south-east of Gavdos Island, southern Crete, a Ju 88 aircraft supporting the passage of an Italian steamer and her escort sighted a submarine periscope. They immediately attacked with gunfire, and the escort, the torpedo boat *Pegaso*, closed the scene. Despite the action of the aircraft, the periscope was still clearly visible as they approached, until it finally disappeared. As it went under, at 12.58 the *Pegaso* gained a good sonar contact at 1,500 yards, and over the next hour carried out seven depth-charge attacks, after which the contact disappeared, and large air bubbles and oil came to the surface. There can be little doubt that this was the *Thorn*. Six officers and fifty-four men were lost.

[Evans pp323–4]

7 August MTB 44 motor torpedo boat

Cowes 1941; 33 tons; 71ft × 19.2ft; 1 × 20mm,
2 × torpedo tubes

Sub-Lieutenant Victor Frank William Clarkson RNVR

Sailed from Dover aiming to intercept the passage of an enemy coastal convoy, she had Lieutenant Christopher Dreyer DSC embarked as senior officer of a mixed force of coastal forces ships, three torpedo boats and three gun boats. The hostile group was sighted just after midnight, having been illuminated by star shell from another force of over anxious Germans. They approached from ahead of the convoy, and as the gun boats engaged the outer screen of enemy escorts, the torpedo boats increased speed and headed for the large merchant ship that was being protected. They came under fierce fire from other escorts, with *MTB 45* being hit on the bridge, killing her commanding officer and a second boat had her steering gear shot away. *MTB 44* then received a 40mm shell in the engine room which wounded all the engine room crew and put the engines out of action. She drifted away out of the action, being taken towards the French coast and as she was settling, it was decided to abandon her. The Carley float was hoisted out and mess deck cushions lashed together to act as a raft. The motor mechanic broke the fuel leads to flood the engine room with petrol. The crew then left her, the last being Lieutenant Dreyer who, after everyone was clear, fired a flare into the engine room. The resulting explosion started a large fire which attracted the attention of one of the gunboats which closed and picked up the crew.

[Scott pp83–6; Reynolds, Home Waters MTBs pp62–3]

7 August MTB 237 motor torpedo boat
Gosport 1942; 38 tons; 71ft × 19.2ft; 1 × 20mm,
2 × torpedo tubes
Lieutenant Richard Guy Fison RNVR

One of a group of three torpedo boats, that sailed from Gosport to carry out an offensive patrol off the northern French coast near Cap Barfleur. MTB 237 had the senior officer of the flotilla, Lieutenant Peter Dickens embarked. In the early hours of the morning, as the group loitered under auxiliary engines, the shapes of several ships were seen in the gloom on the starboard beam. The boats started main engines and altered around to attack, the ships sighted being a small coastal convoy with a heavy escort of five minesweepers and an armed trawler. MTB 237, uncertain of the distance and speed of the enemy steered between the escorts and she managed to discharge both torpedoes but then found herself uncomfortably close to the ocean tug Oceanie, the main body of the convoy. She was being fired on throughout this time and was hit several times. One hit severed a fuel pipe which brought the centre engine to a stop and this was followed by several more hits, one of which exploded in the wheelhouse. With hand steering rapidly rigged the torpedo boat steered out of the fire to head south. A fire had broken out in the radio cabin and galley, and despite valiant fire-fighting efforts the flames spread, to endanger the petrol tanks. They tried staring main engines to rejoin her consorts, but this only fanned the flames and when one of the fuel tanks exploded, it was clear that the boat was doomed. MTB 241 had seen the flames and closed, to run close alongside and evacuate the crew. Attempts to sink the burning craft by dropping a depth charge close alongside failed to achieve the aim, as did firing into the hull. As she was now burning from stem to stern 241 finally left her. Apart from three men slightly wounded, there were no casualties.

[Dickens p1 – 18]

9 August The Battle of Savo Island
On 7 August American forces commenced landing on Guadalcanal and Tulagi in the Solomon Islands. This was covered and supported by a powerful Australian-American naval force and they withstood the initial Japanese reaction which was by airstrikes. During the night of 8/9 August a Japanese task force of six cruisers and a destroyer successfully approached the Allied anchorage, undetected, to achieve tactical surprise. The Allied ships had been divided into three groups, designated Eastern, Northern and Southern Forces. The subsequent assault on the Allied ships resulted in the loss of four ships, one of them Australian.

CANBERRA heavy cruiser
Clydebank 1927; 9,850 tons; 590ft × 68.3ft; 8 × 8in, 4 × 4in,
4 × 2pdr
Captain Frank Edmond Getting RAN

Royal Australian Navy. Part of the Southern Force in company with the US cruiser Chicago, when at 01.43 the destroyer Patterson signalled that strange ships were entering the anchorage and the Canberra went to action stations as flares fired by the Japanese lit up the harbour. The ship was still preparing for action when the compass platform was hit by a shell. In the next few minutes, she was hit by at least twenty-four heavy shells. Power failed and listing to starboard, with a fire burning amidships, she limped out of action. Damage control work went on to stabilise the ship and fight the fires, but with no water pressure they were fighting a losing battle. Ships in the anchorage were ordered to be withdrawn, and orders were given that any ships unable to comply with the order should be abandoned. The destroyers Patterson and Blue came alongside to take off the crew after which the Selfridge fired repeatedly into her, with little effect, so the USS Ellet torpedoed her, at which she rolled over and sank. Eighty-four men died.

[Cassells p25]

★ ★ ★

9 August ML 301 motor launch
Brightlingsea 1941; 73 tons; 112ft × 18.4ft; 1 × 3pdr
Stationed at Freetown, West Africa, she suffered a petrol vapour explosion in the engine room and a subsequent fire whilst on escort duty. She sank at 14.40 in position 08.54N 14.37W. Three men were lost.

[TNA: ADM.199/777]

10–15 August Operation 'Pedestal': Supply Convoy to Malta
On 10 August, under the code name Operation 'Pedestal', a supply convoy for Malta consisting of thirteen merchant ships and one tanker sailed from Gibraltar with a powerful escort, and an additional

distant covering force. The convoy was subject to constant attack by enemy air, surface and sub-surface forces, and suffered serious losses, but four freighters and a tanker finally made it through to Malta.

11 August **EAGLE** aircraft carrier
Walker 1918; 22,600 tons; 627ft × 92.4ft; 9 × 6in, 4 × 4in, 8 × 2pdr, 12 × 20mm, 21 aircraft
Captain Lachlan Donald Mackintosh DSC
By 11 August, the convoy was to the south of Majorca, and refuelling was underway; the *Eagle* was stationed 1,600 yards astern of the starboard wing of the convoy which was formed into five columns. At 13.17, then being in position 38.05N 03.03E, an explosion took place on the port quarter of the ship, abreast 'P3' gun, throwing up a large column of smoke and water. This was followed over the next few seconds by a further three explosions, all of which hit between 'P2' and 'P3' guns, meaning that the port engine room took the full force of the blasts. The engine room rapidly flooded and the adjacent boiler rooms also quickly started to fill with water as bulkheads collapsed. The ship immediately took a 5-degree list to port, and then slowly started to heel further over, settling all the time. It was realised that she could not be saved, and floats and rafts were ordered to released, and men started leaving her almost immediately. She reached a list of about 30 degrees before she sank, just 6 minutes after the first explosion. Many of the survivors were picked up by the tug *Jaunty*. One hundred and sixty-three men were lost. Her attacker had been the *U 73* (Rosenbaum).
[TNA: ADM.267/13]

12 August **CAIRO** cruiser
Birkenhead 1918; 4,290 tons; 425ft × 43.6ft; 8 × 4in, 6 × 2pdr
Captain Cecil Campbell Hardy DSO
During the evening of 12 August, the convoy was approaching the Skerki Channel between Sardinia and the North African coast. At 19.45 the convoy was ordered to reform into two columns, and the escorting cruisers took up new stations, *Cairo* to lead the second column into their new position astern of the column led by the cruiser *Nigeria*. As they were doing so, they presented an ideal target for the Italian submarine *Axum* (Ferrini), which had manoeuvred undetected to position herself close to the port side of the convoy. At 19.55 *Axum* fired a salvo of four torpedoes, all of which hit; one hitting the tanker *Ohio* amidships, another struck the cruiser *Nigeria* on the port side below the bridge and two hit the *Cairo* on the port side aft. She immediately lost way, took a slight list to starboard and started to settle by the stern. It was clear that much of the stern had been blown off, and the propellers had been lost. The boats were ordered to be turned out and the floats released. Although she

was going down by the stern and the upper deck was awash up to the after superstructure, it was found that the watertight bulkheads were holding. An assessment of the situation showed that a tow was possible but unlikely to succeed, as she would clearly be a target for more attacks. The escort destroyer *Wilton* was called alongside to lift off the crew, and when this was complete the destroyer *Pathfinder* instructed to sink her with a torpedo. Embarrassingly three torpedoes were fired and hit but all failed to explode. A fourth finally did explode, but she stubbornly refused to sink. The destroyer then ran close alongside to drop depth charges, but these also failed to make any impression. Finally, the escort destroyer *Derwent* was ordered to close, and she fired 4in shells into the wreck until she finally disappeared at 21.30 in position 37.35E 10.25E. Twenty-four men were lost.
[TNA: ADM.267/71; Woodman, Malta Convoys pp410–11]

13 August **FORESIGHT** destroyer
Birkenhead 1934; 1,405 tons; 318.3ft × 33.3ft; 4 × 4.7in, 6 × 20mm, 4 × torpedo tubes
Lieutenant Commander Robert Augustus Fell
During 12 August, the convoy came under repeated air attacks, and it was during one of these, which developed in the late afternoon that the *Foresight* became a target. At 18.45 during a sustained attack by numerous Italian SM 79 torpedo bomber aircraft, a torpedo hit her aft, exploding abreast the tiller flat and she came to a halt swathed in black smoke. The after part of the ship flooded and she settled by the stern; the steering gear was put out of action and she developed a list to starboard. Strenuous efforts by the damage control parties stabilised her, and she slowly regained an even keel. The destroyer *Tartar* was ordered to stand by her, and at 19.30 she came alongside to pass a towing hawser, but towing was delayed, by fouling the hawser, air attacks and a scare over strange ships approaching, all of which involved slipping the tow and re-connecting, but the pair finally got under way at 22.30. *Tartar* towed her all through the night, but at first light an assessment of the situation led to concerns for their safety. They had travelled about 60 miles and were still a long way short of Malta. The day would certainly bring more air attacks and they offered a good target for an enemy submarine. At 08.39 Fell signalled the *Tartar*, voicing his concerns, suggesting that as they were 'in enemy territory' they might consider abandoning her. This was not immediately agreed, but soon after the tow parted, and the *Foresight*'s list was again slowly increasing, and her stern was awash. Shortly after this a shadowing enemy aircraft made an appearance followed by the sighting of a periscope, which caused the *Tartar* to again cast off the tow to carry out a depth-charge attack. Commander St John Tyrwhitt of the *Tartar* and Fell agreed that they would stand little chance of survival

if they came under another attack, which was thought highly likely. At 09.45 she was ordered to be abandoned, the crew moving by boat and float to the *Tartar*. She was then 13 miles south-west of Galite Island. When all were clear the *Tartar* fired a torpedo into the ship to sink her. Five men were killed in the original attack. Commander St John Tyrwhitt was subsequently court-martialled, for ordering the *Foresight* to be sunk whilst there was a reasonable change of bringing her into harbour. He was cleared of the charge and acquitted. *[TNA: ADM.156/225]*

13 August **MANCHESTER** cruiser
Hebburn 1937; 9,400 tons; 558ft × 62.4ft; 12 × 6in, 8 × 4in, 8 × 2pdr, 8 × 20mm, 6 × torpedo tubes
Captain Harold Drew DSC

At midnight on 12 August the convoy rounded Cape Bon when they came under attack from enemy fast torpedo boats. The first indication of this was at 00.15 when a fast-moving craft was reported on the port beam. This was engaged with main and secondary armament from *Manchester* for about 10 minutes, and it was believed at the time they may have sunk it. At 01.20 they were off Point Kilibia, and a suspicious object was sighted off the starboard bow. Course was altered to starboard to close the object, which resolved itself as a fast torpedo boat, which started up its engines and went off at high speed towards the shore. As it did so the tracks of two torpedoes were seen. One passed clear ahead, but the second hit the ship to explode abreast the after engine room. She had come under attack from two Italian vessels, *Ms 16* and *Ms 22*, both of which claimed to have hit her. When the torpedo hit, she was still under helm and remained under hard rudder for a while until the engines were stopped. The ship immediately assumed a 12-degree list to starboard. The after engine room quickly flooded, as did the 4in magazine and some adjacent compartments, including the main wireless office, although hard work by the damage control parties stopped further flooding. Power to the turrets was lost and three of the main engines and shafts were unusable. The main body of the convoy steamed on, but the destroyer *Pathfinder* was detailed to stand by her, which she did until released by Captain Drew to rejoin the convoy at 02.30. The cruiser was then on her own, just off the enemy coast. By 03.00 they were still without steam and it was estimated that it would be another 3 hours before power could be restored. Captain Drew's assessment of the situation was that a return to Gibraltar was impossibly far; he could probably make Malta, but this would put a strain on an already overstretched dockyard; further the cruiser would certainly become a target. It would be light soon which would certainly mean a resumption of air attacks. Without power to the armament, only

hand-trained weapons would be available, meaning that he could not properly fight the ship. The decision was therefore made to abandon her. At 05.00 charges over the condenser doors were fired and inlets opened. The ship was abandoned in an orderly fashion, taking to the boats and floats. As they were doing so two Italian aircraft flew in from the land and carried out a torpedo attack, although both torpedoes missed ahead. The ship listed heavily to starboard, rolling further over until she capsized at 05.20 and sank. The rafts and boats drifted inshore until they landed on the North African coast between 08.30 and 09.00, to be interned by the Vichy French. When the survivors were released, the loss generated a series of courts martial. Captain Drew was found guilty of prematurely abandoning his ship and was severely reprimanded. Lieutenant Commander Daniel Duff, the gunnery officer, was found to have failed to ensure the fighting efficiency of the armament and to have prematurely ordered the abandonment of weapons. He was reprimanded and ordered to forfeit 6 months seniority. Two control position officers were reprimanded for leaving their posts without orders; a warrant officer was severely reprimanded for failing to ascertain or properly report the state of the armament, or to affect the necessary repairs; a petty officer was reduced in rank when he abandoned his position prematurely, leaving it unmanned. Ten men were lost. *[TNA: ADM.156/209; ADM.156/210; ADM.156/211]*

★ ★ ★

13 August **PIERRE DESCELLIERS** trawler
Ostend 1933 seized 1940; 153 tons; 95.5ft × 20.7ft
Skipper William Mercer RNR

Former French trawler, taken over by French Navy in 1939 as minesweeper *AD 19*, she was seized by the Royal Navy the following year. After being taken over she was employed at Salcombe as a boom gate vessel. Whilst lying at that port she was attacked at 12.17 by an enemy aircraft which initially strafed her with machine-gun fire, and then dropped a single bomb which scored a direct hit. Three men were killed. A small boat, that was delivering fresh water to the trawler, was also sunk, killing one local woman. *[TNA: ADM.199/777; ADM.358/4124]*

13 August **INTREPIDE** drifter
Seized 1940; no details found

Former French fishing vessel, she was based at Newlyn as part of the local auxiliary patrol but was at Salcombe when it came under air attack (see *Pierre Descelliers* above), being alongside the larger vessel. When the *Descelliers* sank after receiving a direct hit, the *Intrepide* was dragged down with her. *[TNA: ADM.199/2248]*

18 August MTB 43 motor torpedo boat
Cowes 1941; 33 tons; 72.1ft × 18.2ft; 2 × torpedo tubes
Lieutenant Henry Eric Butler RNR
One of a group of six torpedo boats that were stationed independently along the length of the course of an enemy coastal convoy that was proceeding from Boulogne to Dunkirk; the convoy consisted of three ships, with five escorts. Each boat staged an attack as the enemy group passed. The plan had limited success, with the enemy being under constant threat, uncertain of when the next attack would take place, but all escaped being hit. The first casualty of the night's action was *MTB 43*. When she mounted her attack, she came under heavy fire and was hit several times and caught fire, forcing her to be abandoned, to the north of Gravelines. All the crew were picked up.
[Scott p90]

18 August MTB 218 motor torpedo boat
Portsmouth 1941; 35 tons; 72.7ft × 17.1ft; 2 × torpedo tubes
Lieutenant Henry Paddison Granlund, RNVR
Another of the group of torpedo boats from Dover that were positioned to allow a sustained attack on an enemy convoy as it passed along the northern French coast. As she closed to attack, she was hit repeatedly by heavy fire from the escorts, a shell exploding in her engine room. Despite this, an attempt was made to continue the attack, but losing power and making water fast this had to be abandoned. She began a slow journey home, but eventually the engines were flooded, and she stopped. She now drifted helplessly, and as she did, so she struck a mine and blew up. Five men were killed, including Sub-Lieutenant Ball RNR.
[Scott p90]

19 August GOLDEN SUNBEAM drifter
Oulton Broad 1920; 84 tons; 81ft × 19.4ft; 1 × 3pdr
Skipper Alfred Manning Lovis DSC RNR
During the night of 18/19 August, the coastal convoy CW116 passed Dover westbound, and the *Golden Sunbeam* was ordered to escort three ships from the convoy into Dover, and then resume her local patrol. The tug *Lynch*, with a lighter in tow, had sailed from Dover to join the convoy, but failed to catch them up. When she was off Dungeness, at 04.20, the tug met the *Golden Sunbeam*, which closed to give instructions, but as the pair manoeuvred close together, they collided, and the drifter rolled over and sank in less than 4 minutes. Seven men lost their lives.
[TNA: ADM.199/417; ADM.199/777]

19 August Operation 'Jubilee' – Raid on Dieppe
During the spring of 1942 consideration was given to the idea of a large-scale raid against German occupied France. Small raids had already been carried out in Norway and northern France, and the attack on St. Nazaire, although costly, was judged to be a success. It was thought necessary to maintain the momentum and a larger raid could further dent the enemies' confidence and raise Allied morale. It would gain experience of attacking an enemy-held coastline and offered the opportunity to try new weapons and equipment that were untested in war. An assault on the port of Dieppe was decided upon, the intention being to land approximately 6,000 men, the majority of which would be by frontal assault on the town, accompanied by smaller landings on the flanks. However, this was planned to be done with no aerial bombing and no sustained bombardment by large units such as battleships or cruisers. Indeed, only lightly-armed escort destroyers would accompany the force which would rely on surprise. Once ashore, the forces would destroy or capture any shipping found, along with the guns and radar emplacements, before withdrawing. The raid was a very costly failure. The reliance on obtaining complete surprise was always a tenuous belief. As it transpired, the attacking force encountered an enemy coastal convoy as they approached the French coast, and the subsequent battle alerted the forces ashore. With only destroyers or specially equipped landing craft to bombard shore targets, and no aerial bombing, the attackers lacked the punch necessary to knock out enemy guns; further, the size and likely reaction of the German forces in the area had been woefully underestimated. Therefore, when the assault began, they met an alerted enemy, who brought down heavy fire on the landing force from gun positions that had not been touched, with terrible results. Several landing craft were hit before they reached the beaches, and those troops that did make the shore were cut down. Unaware of the true scale of the disaster, more troops kept on being sent in to the beaches, to be slaughtered. Over 4,300 men were killed, captured or wounded; 106 aircraft were lost, and the Navy lost a destroyer and 33 landing craft of various sizes.
[TNA: ADM.1/11986; ADM.199/1079; London Gazette Supplement 14 August 1947; Roskill vol II pp240–52]

BERKELEY escort destroyer
Birkenhead 1940; 1,000 tons; 264.2ft × 29ft; 4 × 4in, 4 × 2pdr
Lieutenant James John Simon Yorke
Supporting the landings, she was in company with the other escort destroyers laying close off the port. There had been regular air attacks during the morning, but none had seriously threatened the ships until at 13.08 when a group of three enemy aircraft, identified as Dornier types, closed at low level. They pressed home their attack on the destroyers, with several bombs falling around the *Berkeley*. One bomb exploded directly

under her, the blast lifting the ship up and breaking her back. She heeled over to starboard, covered in steam and smoke and circled at high speed before she came to a stop, with her boiler and engine rooms rapidly flooding. *SGB 8* skilfully went alongside her port side to take off the crew as she was clearly sinking and *SGB 9* with LCAs *185* and *188* started to pick up men who had jumped overboard. As this was underway there was a further attack by several Fw 190 aircraft but all escaped damage. *Berkeley* was now stopped, down by the bows, with a heavy list to starboard. The *Albrighton* closed, to take off one man who had been left behind, then when clear fired a torpedo into the wreck. It hit under the bridge and blew the bows off, but the rest of the ship remained defiantly afloat. A second torpedo hit her aft and the after magazine evidently blew up as there was a large burst of flame and smoke and a huge column of smoke marked her end. Sixteen men were killed. Her wreck lies in position 49.59.43W 01.02.25E.
[TNA: ADM.267/108; Scott pp102–03]

LCF 2 landing craft, flak
Middlesbrough 1941; 369 tons; 143ft × 31ft; 8 × 2pdr, 4 × 20mm
Lieutenant Eric Leslie Graham RNVR†
Called in to provide close support, as she closed the landing beach, she was hit at 06.30 by a heavy shell which killed the commanding officer and wounded several other men. She continued to engage positions ashore, but the starboard engine was put out of action as she was hit again, the steering gear failed, and she drifted across the landing area. When the engine room reported a fire, she was ordered to be abandoned and 20 minutes later she sank. Two men were killed.
[TNA: ADM.199/1079]

LCT (2) 121 landing craft, tank
Middlesbrough 1942; 296 tons; 143ft × 20ft; 2 × 2pdr
She successfully made the shore to land her tanks directly in front of the Casino, but was hit repeatedly whilst laying on the beach, set on fire and disabled. With three men killed, she was abandoned.
[http://www.historyofwar.org/articles/battles_dieppe2.html]

LCT (2) 124 landing craft, tank
Middlesbrough 1942; 296 tons; 143ft × 20ft; 2 × 2pdr
Lieutenant Lennox Gwinner RNVR†
Hit several times by shellfire as she closed the beach, a small fire was started in one of the tanks, but she pressed on and all three tanks were put ashore. She made her withdrawal after the landing but was as she did so, the craft was hit aft by a heavy shell and set on fire and subsequently sank.
[TNA: ADM.199/1079]

LCT (2) 126 landing craft, tank
Middlesbrough 1942; 296 tons; 143ft × 20ft; 2 × 2pdr
Lieutenant Arthur Cheney RNVR
Despite being hit when about 300 yards from the shore which started a fire, she pressed on and ran up onto the beach, to discharge her three tanks. Whilst her cargo was unloading, they came under very heavy fire, one shell hitting the bow door and they were repeatedly hit on the waterline and fuel tanks, killing or wounding most of her crew. They managed to back off the beach but in a sinking condition with engine room flooded and quarterdeck awash. When far enough off the beach for safety, a motor launch came alongside to take off the crew and troops still on board. Lieutenant Cheney did return on board later to retrieve the confidential books, with *126* heeling over on her side before she sank.
[Lund & Ludlam, War of the Landing Craft p55; ADM.199/1079]

LCT (2) 145 landing craft, tank
Thornaby 1942; 296 tons; 143ft × 20ft; 2 × 2pdr
Lieutenant George Edward Hammond Reynolds RNVR
Despite coming under constant and heavy fire, she was hit several times, starting fires, but reached the beach and discharged her load of three Churchill tanks and a scout car. Still under fire, she succeeded in withdrawing from the beach, but was then hit by at least one shell in the engine room which flooded. Strenuous efforts were made to plug the holes and stem the flow of water, but she filled and sank just off the mole.
[TNA: ADM.1/30551]

LCT (2) 159 landing craft, tank
Old Kilpatrick 1942; 296 tons; 143ft × 20ft; 2 × 2pdr
Lieutenant Wilfred Hume Cooke RNVR†
She successfully ran onto the beach to start discharging her tanks, but was almost immediately hit by several shells, causing casualties amongst the embarked troops and killing the coxswain. Out of control she was washed broadside onto the beach in a wrecked condition. Lieutenant Cooke was one of those killed.
[TNA: ADM.199/176]

★ ★ ★

24 August ML 103 motor launch
Oulton Broad 1940; 57 tons; 110ft × 17.5ft; 1 × 3pdr
Sub-Lieutenant Ronald John Grahamslaw RNVR
During the night of 23/24 August enemy small craft activity, believed to be torpedo or patrol boats, was detected by shore-based radar at Dover, and coastal forces were deployed to intercept them. They failed to find the intruders, but *ML 103* and *ML 210* crossed the plotted track taken by the enemy craft about 3 miles to the east of the North-East Varne buoy. As they did so

there was a large explosion as *103* detonated a freshly laid mine. She caught fire, and at 05.25 exploded. The explosion put out the flames, and the trawler *Fyldea*, which had closed, tried to tow her into Dover, but she settled and sank at 07.30. Two men were killed.
[TNA: ADM.199/103]

29 August ERIDGE escort destroyer

Wallsend 1940; 1,050 tons; 246.3ft × 31.6ft; 6 × 4in, 4 × 2pdr, 2 × 20mm
Lieutenant Commander William Frank Nieman Gregory-Smith

In company with three other escort destroyers, *Aldenham*, *Croome* and *Hursley*, tasked to carry out a shore bombardment of positions around Ras-el-Daba on the Libyan coast. Having sailed from Alexandria the ships arrived in position at 04.20 and carried out fire support for 30 minutes. At 04.54 course was altered to the east and speed increased to 20 knots to clear the area. As they picked up speed an indistinct small dark object was seen ahead, then a small boat was seen in a patch of moonlight close on the starboard bow. This had not been detected by radar. *Eridge* altered to starboard and opened fire with a 20mm gun, but the craft was seen to alter course and pass close down the starboard side before disappearing into the night. A moment later there was a large explosion on the starboard side abreast the engine room. The ship was still under helm and took a list of 10 degrees to port. The engine room, gearing room and senior rates mess were reported to be flooding, and damage control parties worked to shore up bulkheads and keep the water down. The *Aldenham* closed to pass a tow, and at 05.50 the towing commenced, although it was found to be difficult to steer, and the pair twice went in complete circles before they could gain control. At first light they came under air attack, and these continued through the morning, but despite only managing 5 knots, they were not damaged further. By 16.00 they were off Alexandria and by 19.00 she was alongside. Examination of the ship showed such extensive damage that she was beyond repair and she was written off as a constructive total loss. She remained at Alexandria, being cannibalised for spares and was used as a local base shop until disposed of at the end of the war. It was later revealed that her attacker had been a small fast motor boat *MTSM 228* of the Italian Navy. Five men were lost.
[TNA: ADM.199/681]

7 September RACCOON armed yacht

Bath 1931 (*Halonia*) requisitioned 1940; 377 tons; 148ft × 25ft; 1 × 12pdr
Lieutenant Commander John Norman Smith RCNR†

Royal Canadian Navy. Employed as a local patrol vessel in the Gulf of St Lawrence, on 6 September, she joined the escort to Convoy QS33, bound from Quebec to Sydney, Nova Scotia, taking station astern of the ships. That night they came under attack from *U 165* (Hoffman), the merchant ship *Aeas* being torpedoed at 21.10. At 00.12, ships in the convoy heard two explosions in rapid succession, but the source was uncertain. In the morning it became clear that the *Raccoon* was missing but a search was delayed because of continued U-boat attacks on shipping in the St Lawrence. A body and wreckage were later found washed ashore. Thirty-seven men died.
[McKee & Darlington p65]

11 September CHARLOTTETOWN corvette

Kingston 1941; 940 tons; 190ft × 33ft; 1 × 4in, 1× 2pdr
Lieutenant John Willard Bonner, RCNR†

Royal Canadian Navy. Assigned to the Gulf of St Lawrence Escort Force, she had successfully escorted a convoy to Quebec, and in company with the minesweeper *Clayoquot* was returning to Gaspé. At 11.03, with no warning, she was hit twice by torpedoes. The first struck her starboard quarter, the second further forward, probably in the boiler room. The ship swung round to port and immediately took a heavy list to starboard before sinking, her depth charges exploding as she went under. The *Clayoquot* spent some time vainly hunting for the attacker and dropped several depth charges before rescuing the survivors. Ten men died. She had fallen victim to *U 517* (Hartwig) which had taken advantage of the difficult Asdic conditions of the St Lawrence, with its mix of salt and fresh water, to carry out the attack.
[Morgan & Taylor p265]

11 September MGB 335 motor gun boat

Bangor 1941; 67 tons; 108ft × 17.6ft ; 2 × 2pdr
Lieutenant Robert Alan Forbes RNVR

One of a group of four gunboats loitering off the Dutch coast, they were aware from radio traffic of a sharp action taking place further to the north of their position as another group of gunboats had tangled with a group of enemy fast patrol boats. They moved towards the action, to see if they could catch the German craft as they disengaged. Just as day was breaking and they were about to leave the scene the enemy came into sight. They proved to be a considerable force of nine torpedo boats and a fierce exchange of fire soon began between the opposing groups. *335* received a hit in the engine room which brought her to a halt, and a fire broke out below. She fell out of line and became the target for most of the fire from the enemy, which took up station about 500 yards away. Despite this, the senior officer, Lieutenant Thorpe, returned to put his gunboat alongside the burning *335* to lift off the survivors. As he drew away, he fired several rounds into her hull to speed sinking, but she remained afloat. The burning wreck was boarded by the Germans who found two wounded crew members still on board and towed her into harbour as a prize. Thorpe was subsequently awarded the DSO for his action. Three men were lost.

[Scott pp111–12]

13 September OTTAWA destroyer

Portsmouth 1931 (*Crusader*); 1375 tons, 317.7ft × 33ft; 4 × 4.7in, 4 × 20mm, 1 × 12pdr, 2 × 2pdr, 4 × torpedo tubes

Lieutenant Commander Clark Anderson Rutherford RCN†

Royal Canadian Navy. Sailed 5 September from Londonderry to join Convoy ON127 bound for New York. The convoy was attacked repeatedly in mid-Atlantic by U-boats, seven ships being lost, the *Ottawa* picking up survivors from the *Empire Oil*. At 23.00, then being ahead of the main body of the convoy, *Ottawa* picked up a radar contact and suspecting that it was a submarine, she altered towards the contact. At 23.06 as she was under helm to port, she was hit by a torpedo in the bows, the explosion removing most of the forepart of the ship, as far back as 'A' gun. The ship remained stable and there were hopes that she would survive, but at 23.15 she was hit again, on the starboard side, the torpedo exploding in the boiler room. She slowly rolled over onto her starboard side, breaking apart as she sank, the stern rising clear of the water. The other escorts searched for the attacker but returned 4 hours later to pick up the survivors, the *Celandine* and *Arvida* picking up sixty-nine men, but 119 men died, along with twenty-two survivors from the *Empire Oil*. Her assailant had been *U 91* (Walkering), who had carried out both attacks on *Ottawa*, believing that they were separate destroyers.

[Morgan & Taylor p268]

Operation 'Agreement' – Commando raid on Tobruk

During the summer of 1942, the British army in North Africa was under great strain; the German army under Rommel had pushed forward into Egypt, and urgent requests were made to relieve the pressure. Because of this, a plan was formed to carry out an attack on the port of Tobruk, which by then was a long way behind enemy lines. The plan was approved on 21 August and preparations were completed by early September. There would be an attack by Special Forces from inland followed by a seaborne assault, with troops being landed from coastal forces craft and destroyers. The whole operation would be covered by heavy air raids by the RAF. It was an extremely ambitious plan, requiring a force to travel overland, penetrate the enemy defences and then capture and hold the Mersa Sciausc inlet. They would then signal to the naval forces to land further troops to carry out demolition tasks. All would be evacuated by launch and torpedo boat. It proved to be an expensive failure with over 700 men being lost and the Navy losing several valuable ships and small craft.

[TNA: ADM.1 99/680; Rohwer, *Chronology of the War at Sea* p196; Roskill vol II pp309–10]

14 September COVENTRY cruiser

Wallsend 1917; 4,190 tons; 425ft × 43.5ft; 8 × 4in, 8 × 2pdr, 2 × 20mm

Captain Richard John Robert Dendy

Sailed from Port Said during the evening of 12 September in company with four 'Hunt' class destroyers, to join a force of two 'Tribal' and four 'Hunt' class destroyers the next morning. During the day they steadily moved westwards until the 'Tribals' were detached during the evening to make their way inshore to Tobruk. The cruiser, in company with the 'Hunt' class ships, remained off the coast to provide distant support, with the *Coventry* maintaining radar watch for enemy aircraft, using her Type 279 radar. The initial radio reports from *Zulu*, indicating that she had been hit, were not encouraging. Later that morning, the *Zulu* indicated that she was clearing the shore at 30 knots, and the group was turned towards the shore to provide close support for her. At the same time Captain Dendy detached two of the 'Hunt' class destroyers to return to Alexandria, as they were low on fuel. By 11.15 the *Coventry* and six escort destroyers were about 100 miles off the coast, steering to the west to rendezvous with the *Zulu*. Several aircraft movements had been detected by radar, but none of them closed, and friendly Beaufighter aircraft were in the area to provide support, being directed by the *Coventry*. Just 10 minutes later, radar reported aircraft closing from astern, and almost immediately after this a group of fifteen Ju 87 Stuka aircraft emerged from low clouds to carry out an attack. It was so sudden that only the 20mm Oerlikons were able to open fire before bombs were dropping around them. The cruiser was hit four times. The first bomb struck the bows, forward of 'A' gun, starting a fire; further bombs exploded immediately under the bridge. These demolished the bridge structure and penetrating below caused more damage and started another fire. The final hit was next to the after funnel, with the bomb penetrating the deck to explode in 'A' boiler room. The forward part of the ship was wrecked, and the fires were serious, and the forward magazines were ordered to be flooded. Captain Dendy was concerned that although the cruiser was upright and stable, and could be towed stern first, they were a long way from home, close to an enemy shore, and would present a sitting target for the next air raid, which was only a matter

of time. This would probably mean the loss of some of the escort destroyers as well as the cruiser. He therefore decided to abandon ship. The *Dulverton* and *Beaufort* closed and lifted off the men and were then detached to Alexandria. Dendy had hoped that the burning wreck could be despatched by torpedo, but then discovered that the 'Hunt' class ships were not fitted with torpedo tubes. He then ordered *Zulu* to continue to close, so that she could give the *coup de grace*. The *Zulu* arrived on scene at 14.45, just as another air attack by Ju 87 aircraft developed, but despite this, the destroyer closed and fired two torpedoes into the *Coventry*, and she rolled over and sank at 15.05. Sixty-four men lost their lives. The court of enquiry was critical of Captain Dendy. It was judged that he had failed to maintain his force at constant readiness for attack; the enemy could be expected to react violently after the raid had started, but despite that, only half of the action armament was closed up at the time of the attack and the long-range radar had not been properly employed. It was found that the Type 279 had been employed in directing the Beaufighter aircraft to the detriment of use as a warning set, and 'all round' sweeps were not being carried out. The incoming air raid had been detected at 11.10, but the radar team had been distracted in trying to vector the friendly fighters towards them, who in turn were frustrated by the heavy cloud cover. A warning had only been issued 2 minutes before the aircraft emerged from the cloud. Their Lordships informed both Captain Dendy and the radar officer, Sub-Lieutenant Edwin Flint Shales RCNVR that they had incurred their Lordships' displeasure. The attacking aircraft were from 8/StG 3.
[TNA: ADM.1/12134]

14 September SIKH destroyer

Linthouse 1937; 1,960 tons; 355.6ft × 36.6ft; 6 × 4.7in, 2 × 4in, 2 × 20mm, 4 × torpedo tubes
Captain St John Aldrich Micklethwait DSO

In company with her sister *Zulu* and four 'Hunt' class escort destroyers, the group sailed from Alexandria, to take part in the raid on Tobruk, having a party of Royal Marines embarked. It was intended that the Marines would be landed to the north of the port, the destroyers returning later to destroy any shipping and re-embark the troops. Having detached from the main group at 21.30 the destroyers closed the coast until at 03.10 they were 2 miles from the beach and lowered boats to disembark the troops. This took longer than expected and it was not complete until just before 04.00. That complete the pair stood out to sea for 30 minutes and then reversed course to close the shore and pick up the raiders. Signs of fighting on shore were evident, with explosions and tracer visible. Quite suddenly at 05.05 when about 2 miles off shore *Sikh* was lit up by

a searchlight from the shore. This was followed by well-directed fire. At 05.20 she was hit by an 88mm shell that struck aft. This knocked the steering gear out of action and wrecked the forced lubrication system. Both ships were now making smoke and returning the fire, and the *Zulu* closed her sister to pass a tow. At the same time small boats approached from the shore, with some of the returning landing party. In this difficult position, under fire from the shore and trying to recover men from the boats and with *Sikh* slowly circling, the *Zulu* managed to pass a tow at 06.30. It was now daybreak, and with the pair just a mile off shore, they were under intense fire. The *Sikh* was hit another three or four times, with one shell destroying 'A' turret's ready-use ammunition. Other shells destroyed the rangefinder and started fires aft. At 06.36 the tow line was severed. Now drifting, the *Sikh* was being hit regularly, and rather than continue to stand by her any longer, Captain Micklethwait ordered the *Zulu* to leave. The confidential books were thrown overboard, and scuttling charges fired which flooded the boiler and engine rooms. The ship heeled over to starboard and settled until she sank, still under shellfire. Two officers and twenty-one ratings were killed; 223 made prisoners of war.
[TNA: ADM.1/12134; English p42]

14 September ZULU destroyer

Linthouse 1937; 1,960 tons; 355.6ft × 36.6ft; 6 × 4.7in, 2 × 4in, 2 × 20mm, 4 × torpedo tubes
Commander Richard Taylor White DSO

Accompanied the *Sikh* (see above) to land a raiding party in the early hours and came under intense fire when the pair returned at 05.05. During her attempts to tow the *Sikh* clear of danger, she was herself hit several times, the worst being a shell explosion on the quarterdeck, which killed two men and parted the tow. It was after this that the *Sikh* ordered the *Zulu* to leave and save herself. Shortly after 07.00 she therefore turned to seaward and increased to 30 knots and cleared the area, heading towards the *Coventry* group. At 08.50 a single Ju 88 aircraft flew overhead, and then attacked, dropping a single bomb, which missed. This was followed by a series of intensive air raids, at 11.16, 12.34 and 14.30 by Ju 88 and Ju 87 aircraft, but she avoided further damage and continued to close the *Coventry*, having been requested to torpedo her (see above). At 14.45 she manoeuvred close to the burning cruiser, and despite another air raid developing, fired torpedoes into the wreck. Now in company with the 'Hunt' class escort destroyers, the group formed up in line abreast, with the *Zulu* in the centre, and headed east at 25 knots. At 16.00 there came another, final air attack, by twelve Ju 87 and six Ju 88 aircraft. They seemed to concentrate on the largest ship, and she found herself in 'a hail of falling bombs'. One hit the ship's side, entering the engine

room and bursting, which wrecked that compartment and number 3 boiler room. She promptly lost power, and the *Hursley* closed to take her in tow, however the tow parted after 15 minutes. All the crew, except for a small party, were then transferred to the other ships in company. Any further attempts to tow were abandoned as she was clearly settling, and at 20.00 she slowly rolled over to starboard and sank. Twelve men were killed and twelve reported missing.
[TNA: ADM.1/12134]

Operation 'Agreement' – the coastal forces

A force of sixteen motor torpedo boats with three motor launches were employed, each MTB embarking 10 army personnel with the MLs having demolition parties. It was intended that these would enter the small inlet of Mersa Sciausc and land their troops when signalled to do so by forces that had travelled overland. They sailed from Alexandria during the evening of 12 October. However, they suffered from a lack of co-ordination, with the changes of course and speed during the transit causing the formation to become dispersed, and instead of arriving as a coherent force, approached the target in several small groups. On arrival the boats found it extremely difficult in the darkness to find the entrance to Mersa Sciausc, and the expected signal from shore could not be seen. The noise of fighting and gun flashes ashore made it obvious that a fierce fight was going on, but as more boats arrived, they were unable to help. Finally two boats, *MTB 261* and *MTB 314*, found the inlet and landed their troops. Now under fire from the shore, it was clear that the raid was not going to plan, and the MTBs withdrew, but suffered badly from air attacks as they did so. The MLs meanwhile fared little better. They arrived off the port and with no signal from shore, closed to investigate, but also found it impossible to locate the landing place. As the first light of dawn was now appearing, they also withdrew and suffered as the MTBs had done.
[TNA: ADM.1/12771; ADM.223/565; Reynolds & Cooper, Mediterranean MTBs at War pp44–6; Pope pp56–61]

14 September   MTB 308   motor torpedo boat
Bayonne NJ 1942 (*PT 50*); 34 tons; 77ft × 20ft; 1 × 20mm, 2 × torpedo tubes
Lieutenant Ralph William Yates RNVR†
Unable to find the landing place, and under fire from the shore, she cleared the harbour and steered out to sea. As they cleared the coast, the first air attacks took place, with German and Italian bomber and fighter aircraft repeatedly attacking. *308* was damaged in one of the first attacks and slowed. In a subsequent attack a

Ju 88 was hit by fire from the MTBs but crashed into *308*, destroying it. There were no survivors, eleven men being lost.

14 September   MTB 310   motor torpedo boat
Bayonne NJ 1942 (*PT 52*); 38 tons; 77ft × 20ft; 1 × 20mm, 2 × torpedo tubes
Lieutenant Stuart Clarke Lane RCNVR†
Came under constant air attack as she cleared the shore, until a bomb exploded close under the bows during a dive bombing attack by a Ju 87. She started to go down by the head, and she was abandoned, the survivors taking to a small boat which landed on the desert coast. The survivors were not found for several days, during which several died from exposure and thirst. Ten men were lost.

14 September   MTB 312   motor torpedo boat
Bayonne NJ 1942 (*PT 54*); 38 tons; 77ft × 20ft; 1 × 20mm, 2 × torpedo tubes
Lieutenant Ian Andrew Bryant Quarrie RNVR
At 07.00 she was caught by an Italian Macchi fighter aircraft which attacked her, carrying out several strafing runs. Despite manoeuvring she was raked with machine-gun fire and a fire was started amongst some cased petrol being carried on the upper deck. The fire rapidly got out of control and with ammunition beginning to explode she was abandoned before she blew up. There were no casualties.
[TNA: ADM.267/110]

14 September   MTB 314   motor torpedo boat
Bayonne NJ 1942 (*PT 56*); 34 tons; 77ft × 20ft; 1 × 20mm, 2 × torpedo tubes
Lieutenant Harwin Woodthorpe Sheldrick RNVR
One of the only two MTBs that found the landing place, having disembarked her troops she attempted to make her way out of the harbour but ran hard aground on rocks. All efforts to free her failed and she was abandoned, scuttling charges having been set. Unfortunately, these failed to go off, and she was found by the enemy the next morning and successfully refloated. Refitted, she entered German service as the patrol boat *RA 10*. She was sunk during an attack by RAF aircraft off La Goulette in April 1943.

14 September   ML 352   motor launch
Cairo 1942; 73 tons; 112ft × 18.4ft; 1 × 2pdr
Lieutenant George Raymond Worledge RANVR
As the launches neared Tobruk, *ML 349* was sent closer inshore to try and locate the landing place, but could not, and when *352* and *353* followed, but they could make out nothing. They eventually decided to abandon the attempt and withdrew as a group, coming under fire from the shore as they did so. After taking the men off

the stricken *353* (see below), she steered to seaward in company with *349* at maximum speed but from 07.30 they came under constant air attack. The pair suffered five attacks during the next hour, being strafed and bombed. They escaped damage until *352* was hit by a cannon shell which pierced a petrol tank, which led to petrol escaping and pouring into the bilges. In the final attack at 08.20 she was again hit by a cannon shell and the petrol vapour exploded, starting a fierce fire. The survivors left her at 08.32, taking to a small boat, the ML then being rocked by explosions. They were picked up later that morning by the Italian destroyer *Castore*. Two men were killed.

14 September ML 353 motor launch
Cairo 1942; 73 tons; 112ft × 18.4ft; 1 × 2pdr
Lieutenant Edwin James Mitchelson RNZVR
With the failure of the assault, she was in company with *ML 349* and *ML 352* as they cleared the harbour under fire from the shore. At 07.00 *ML 353* was seen to lose way and then stop. *ML 352* then closed, took all her men off and continue the flight to seaward. *353* was last seen to be covered in smoke and blew up a short time later.

★ ★ ★

(16/17) September TALISMAN submarine
Birkenhead 1940; 1,090/1,575 tons; 265.6ft × 26.7ft; 1 × 4in, 10 × torpedo tubes
Lieutenant Commander Michael Willmott†
Bound for Malta with stores, she sailed from Gibraltar on 10 September, but failed to arrive as expected on 17 September. She was last heard from at 08.45 on 14 September, when they reported the sighting of a surfaced U-boat off Cape Bougaroni, Algeria. It is presumed that she was lost in the Sicilian Channel, probably by striking a mine. Six officers and fifty-four men were lost.
[Evans p325]

17 September WATERFLY trawler
Beverley 1931 (*Walpole*) requisitioned 1939; 387 tons; 142.2ft × 24.9ft; 1 × 4in
Lieutenant Commander Ritchie William Hawes RNVR†
Based at Dover; she was attacked at 14.15 when 4 miles to the west of Dungeness by a pair of Fw 190 aircraft, when she was returning from minesweeping operations. The aircraft emerged from low cloud to the east and there was little warning before both dropped bombs. The first exploded as a near miss, but the second scored a direct hit on the well deck. She sank quickly, with just three survivors, sixteen men being lost.
[TNA: ADM.199/621]

19 September ALOUETTE trawler
Middlesbrough 1939 requisitioned 1939; 520 tons; 175.9ft × 28.5ft; 1 × 4in
Lieutenant Richard Adams RNR
En-route for Gibraltar, she was about 7 miles west of Sesimbra, Portugal, when at 03.00 she was hit on the port side forward by a torpedo fired by *U 552* (Popp). The ship broke in half, the bow section sinking immediately, but the stern remained afloat. The U-boat carried out a second attack on the remains 30 minutes later, which resulted in a large explosion, and she disappeared. A large search was initiated by the Portuguese, employing boats and aircraft, and twenty-seven men were rescued, but fourteen men were killed.
[TNA: ADM.199/621; ADM.358/3007; https://uboat.net/ allies/merchants/ships/2184.html]

19 September PENTLAND FIRTH trawler
Beverley 1934, purchased 1939; 485 tons; 164.4ft × 27.3ft; 1 × 4in
Skipper Edward John Lockwood Davis RNR
One of group of British trawlers sent to the United States to boost the numbers of anti-submarine vessels available for use along the American eastern seaboard. Whilst patrolling between the Ambrose Lightship and Sandy Hook, she was rammed by the minesweeper USS *Chaffinch* (AM.81) at 02.00, which apparently mistook the darkened trawler for a U-boat. She sank very quickly, in position 40.25N 73.55W. There were no casualties.
[TNA: ADM.199/2249; www.bbc.co.uk/ww2peopleswar/ stories/83/a8848083.shtml]

20 September LEDA minesweeper
Devonport 1937; 815 tons; 230ft × 33.6ft; 2 × 4in, 2 × 20mm
Commander Arthur Hugh Wynne-Edwards
Part of the close escort to Convoy QP14 which sailed from Archangel on 13 September bound for Loch Ewe, by 20 September the ships were in the Greenland Sea, in position 76.26N 04.50E, the weather was overcast with heavy cloud and regular squalls. The *Leda* was stationed on the starboard quarter of the convoy when at 05.20, without warning, a torpedo struck the starboard side under the funnel, exploding between the forward and after boiler rooms. The initial explosion was followed by further small detonations, probably the boilers exploding. All power was lost, and a fierce fire broke out on the upper deck at the site of the impact and 'B' boiler room was filled with smoke and steam. The ship listed 20 degrees to port, and she gradually rolled over until she lay on her beam ends. She hung in this position for some time, until at 05.40 she capsized, to float bottom up, showing that her back was broken. The bow and stern remained projecting out of the water

until 06.30 when the remains were sunk by fire from the *Ayrshire*. Forty-four men died. Her attacker had been *U 435* (Strelow).

[TNA:ADM.267/115]

21 September ST OLAVES tug
Govan 1918 requisitioned 1939; 468 tons; 135.6ft × 29ft; 1 × 12pdr
Lieutenant Alexander Thomas Lewis RNR

Whilst towing the water boat *Golden Crown* south from Scapa, in poor weather, the tow line parted, and whilst manoeuvring to re-secure the tow, she ran onto rocks on the Ness of Duncansby. The Wick lifeboat was launched in strong winds and high seas and although four members of the water boat's crew managed to get ashore, the lifeboat successfully rescued thirty-one men from the vessels. The tug was subsequently written off as a total loss.

[http://www.hellsmouth.com/st-olaves.html]

22 September GRAY RANGER oiler
Dundee 1941; 3,313 tons; 339.7ft × 48ft; 1 × 4in, 1 × 12pdr
Master Howard Douglas Gausden DSO

Returning to the United Kingdom in Convoy QP14 from Russia, bound for Loch Ewe, the tanker was in ballast. The passage was uneventful until 20 September when submarine attacks began. On 22 September at 06.13 local time in position 71.23N 11.03W *Gray Ranger* was hit on the starboard side by a torpedo fired by the submarine *U 435* (Strelow). Two merchant ships were also hit during the attack. As the tanker lost power and steadily settled, she was abandoned, and at 07.30 several shells were fired into her by escorts to speed her sinking. Six men were lost, the thirty-two survivors being picked up by the rescue ship *Rathlin*.

[TNA:ADM.199/721]

23 September   SIESTA channel patrol boat
1931 requisitioned 1942; 11 tons; 40.6ft × 11.8ft
Sub-Lieutenant Ivan Egerton Tickle RANVR

Royal Australian Navy. Employed as a local patrol boat at Fremantle, at about 18.30, as she was leaving harbour, there was an explosion in the engine room, which started a fire, and she was burnt out before sinking. The patrol launch *Dolphin* picked up the crew, all of whom survived, although they suffered burns.

[Cassells p66]

24 September SOMALI destroyer
Wallsend 1937; 1,960 tons; 355.6ft × 36.6ft; 6 × 4.7in, 2 × 4in, 2 × 20mm, 4 × torpedo tubes
Lieutenant Commander Colin Douglas Maud DSC

Part of the escort to Convoy QP14 which sailed from Archangel on 13 September bound for Loch Ewe. During 20 September, the convoy came under submarine attack (see *Leda* above) and it was at 18.00, in position 75.12N 02.00E, that a patrolling aircraft was seen to drop a marker flare about 5 miles ahead of the convoy, evidently warning of the presence of another submarine. At 18.55 just as the *Somali* was altering to starboard as part of a zigzag, the Asdic operator reported the noise of a 'torpedo approaching port side'. Engines were ordered full ahead and the helm reversed to port to comb the tracks. Despite this, one minute later she was hit by a torpedo on the port side amidships, exploding abreast the engine room. The midships portion of the ship was wrecked, with a large hole extending from the upper deck to below the water line. The torpedo tubes were blown overboard, and the ship heeled over to assume a list of 15 degrees to starboard. The amidships section flooded, but it was found that the engine room bulkheads held, although buckled, and they were shored up to secure them. Topweight was jettisoned as the *Ashanti* closed to rig a tow. At 20.26 the tow commenced, and in good weather 7 knots was achieved for an hour until the tow parted. A second hawser was passed, and the tow resumed, and continued at a slightly slower pace. During the 21st the list slowly increased, to 20 degrees, and the ship was yawing badly. More weight equipment was thrown overboard to lighten her, and power was restored for a while and this helped the pumps to clear the water and by the evening the list had been reduced to 10 degrees. The trawler *Lord Middleton* tried to help with the tow, but this was abandoned. On the 22nd an electrical cable was passed from the *Ashanti* and after much effort and hard work in freezing temperatures some power was restored to *Somali* enabling her to run steering motors and submersible pumps. The oiler *Blue Ranger* appeared, to refuel the *Ashanti*. The following day the weather was showing signs of deteriorating, and *Blue Ranger* pumped some oil into the sea ahead of the tow to try and calm the sea. The wind steadily increased and despite the oil slick, the sea was now breaking over the *Somali*. By 02.30 on 24th it was blowing a full gale with regular snow showers and the ship broke her back near the engine room bulkhead. She became awash amidships with the fore and aft parts rising clear of the water. Within minutes the portions had separated, and each assumed a steep angle before sinking. The position was then 69.11N 15.32W. Seven officers and seventy-five ratings were lost. Her attacker had been the *U 703* (Bielfeld).

[TNA:ADM.267/93]

24 September KALGAH water carrier
Greenock 1917 (S 52) requisitioned 1942; 293 tons; 150ft × 33ft

Listed in the *Statement of Losses* as being lost, 'cause and place unknown', the vessel was a river steamer belonging to the Anglo–Persian Oil Company and was evidently being used by British army forces occupying Persia (Iran). She was burnt out 40 miles below Ahwaz, Karun River.

[Statement of Losses p23; http://www.clydesite.co.uk/ clydebuilt/viewshipasp?id=15818]

25 September VOYAGER destroyer

Linthouse 1917; 1,090 tons; 300ft × 29.5ft; 4 × 4in, 2 × 2pdr, 6 × torpedo tubes
Lieutenant Commander Rupert Cowper Robison RAN

Royal Australian Navy. In February 1942 Timor was occupied by the Japanese, but a small force of Australian soldiers remained on the island as a harassing force, and this required regular supply runs. In September it was decided to replace the men of the original force with new troops, and *Voyager* was given this task. The destroyer arrived in Betano Bay, southern Timor, at sunset on 23 September, and despite having no navigational aids, and only a rough sketch plan of the rendezvous, anchored as close to the shore as possible, to start the disembarkation. Soon after this had started, it became clear that there was a strong current, which was pushing the ship further inshore. Commander Robison waited until the troops were clear, and then attempted to get under way and gain sea room, but the ship immediately ran aground. Efforts went on through the night to free her, but she was held fast. The work went on the next morning, but they attracted the attention of the enemy and were attacked by two aircraft, although no damage was caused. It was now clear that she was settling into the soft sand, and it was decided to remove all her stores and destroy the ship, as further air attacks were inevitable. Explosive charges were laid in the engine room, and at 20.00 on 24 September they detonated, blowing holes in the sides of the hull. The following morning, after the last of the stores had been removed, the ship was set on fire, and burnt out.

[https://www.awm.gov.au/articles/blog/hmas-voyager-wrecked-and-burning-betano-bay]

26 September VETERAN destroyer

Clydebank 1919; 1,090 tons; 300ft × 29.6ft; 3 × 4in, 1 × 12pdr, 4 × 20mm, 3 × torpedo tubes
Lieutenant Commander Trevor Henry Garwood†

Converted to a short-range escort, she was in company with her sister *Vanoc*, the pair acting as escorts to a transatlantic convoy, RB1, consisting of eight coastal and river steamers from North America to the United Kingdom. The convoy sailed from St John's, Newfoundland on 21 September. During 24 September, the group encountered several enemy submarines, and unsuccessful prosecutions of contacts were made by the escorts. The following day two of the convoy were torpedoed and sunk, the *Veteran* dropping astern

to investigate Asdic contacts and search for survivors. Further attacks by submarines continued during the night. At 23.25 and 00.38 was in radio contact with *Vanoc*, when the *Veteran* reported that she had picked up twenty-eight survivors from one of the sunken ships and was rejoining the convoy. This was the last heard from her. One of the attacking submarines, *U 404* (Bulow), subsequently reported that at 07.36 local time he had carried out an attack in position 54.34N 25.44W on a destroyer just astern of the convoy, firing a spread of three torpedoes, which resulted in two detonations being heard, followed by 'hissing and breaking noises'. This must have been the *Veteran*. The convoy was evidently unaware of her loss, and it was not for another 2 days before a search was carried out for survivors, but no trace of anyone was found. One hundred and sixty officers and ratings were lost, in addition to the men she had rescued.

[TNA: ADM.199/719; Morgan & Taylor pp280–4]

30 September MGB 18 motor gun boat

Hythe 1940; 30 tons; 70ft × 20ft; 1 × 20mm
Lieutenant Edmund Fitzgerald Smyth RNVR

On the night of 30 September, a force of six coastal forces craft, a mix of torpedo boats and gunboats, sailed from Felixstowe for a night patrol off the coast of Holland, hoping to intercept a coastal convoy that had been sighted by reconnaissance aircraft. At 23.28 the dark shapes of several ships became clear on the port bow of the group and at the same time they were illuminated by star shell fired by the enemy escorts. The group accelerated towards the enemy, but were confused as to their course and direction, and crossed ahead of the convoy, now under constant fire. *MGB 18* found herself engaged with an armed trawler *Vp 2003*, and the pair exchanged gunfire at close range and the gunboat was hit several times, the coxswain being wounded in the face. Lieutenant Smyth then realised that the other gunboats had altered round to the south, so *18* then altered round to starboard, reversing course, to rejoin her companions. Travelling at high speed *18* crossed the stern of her leader, *MGB 21*, to find *MGB 82* immediately ahead of her. Unable to avoid a collision, she struck *82* heavily, shattering her bows. Despite that, she had to clear the action and steered to seawards. Once clear it was obvious that she could not survive; the centre engine had failed due to broken fuel lines and water was pouring in through the broken bows. At this point *MTB 234* emerged out of the darkness and smoke to put herself alongside. It was hoped to rig a tow, but as they were preparing this, several armed trawlers came into sight, which fired star shell, and were clearly heading towards them. *MGB 18* was then ordered to be abandoned, the crew leaping over to *234*. Before they left, the motor mechanic had smashed a

fuel pipe to flood the engine room. Lieutenant Smyth then fired a Verey pistol into the space, which started a fire. As Smyth jumped across to *234*, the closest enemy trawler being only 100 yards away, the torpedo boat was able to make smoke and then speed clear.
[*TNA: ADM.199/621; Dickens pp81–102; Reynolds pp71–2*]

September (?) HDML 1153 motor launch
Bideford 1942; 40 tons; 72ft × 15.10ft; 1 × 2pdr
In 1942 several warships were transferred to Turkey, which included nine harbour defence motor launches, one of which was *HDML 1153*. She was reported in September to have been shipped as deck cargo on a merchant but was later 'lost due to enemy action' before the transfer was made. The ship and date of loss have not been identified, but a possible candidate is the *City of Athens*, which sailed from the Clyde on 30 August, and her cargo included stores for Turkey. She was torpedoed by *U 179* on 8 October off the coast of South Africa. Another possibility is the *Ocean Honour*, loaded with military stores for the Middle East, sunk by the Japanese submarine *I-29* on 16 September in the Gulf of Aden.
[*TNA: ADM.116/4876; Statement of Losses p21*]

September HARLEQUIN accommodation ship
Greenock 1897 (*Strathmore*) purchased 1908; 528 tons; 200.5ft × 24.1ft
Ran aground, apparently in the Medway, when on passage from Chatham to the Clyde and subsequently written off as a constructive loss. The wreck was sold in March 1943 and broken up during 1945.
[*http://www.clydesite.co.uk/clydebuilt/viewship.asp?id=17751*]

2 October CURACOA cruiser
Pembroke 1917; 4,190 tons; 425ft × 43.5ft; 8 × 4in, 4 × 2pdr, 4 × 20mm
Captain John Wilfred Boutwood
The 81,235-ton Cunard liner *Queen Mary* was employed as a troopship, and could act independently of the convoy system, relying on her ability to travel at high speeds to avoid submarine attack, but escort would be provided as she entered coastal waters. The *Curacoa*, accompanied by six destroyers, was detailed to meet the liner to the north of Tory Island as she headed towards the Clyde, carrying 10,000 American troops. As the escort headed seaward, they met a heavy swell, and the destroyers found it difficult to do more than 20 knots. The larger cruiser pushed on towards the rendezvous and duly sighted the inbound liner during the morning as her masts and funnels appeared over the horizon. The cruiser came around to match the course of the *Queen Mary*, which seemed to be steering 108 degrees. This course was confirmed by the liner, who then indicated that she was maintaining a speed of 26.5 knots. *Curacoa*, being unable to keep at that speed

in the present weather conditions, signalled the liner to indicate that she would allow the liner to slowly overhaul her, and then drop astern. By 13.00 the *Queen* was about 5 miles on the port quarter of the cruiser, and Captain Boutwood decided that he would close the liner 'to provide adequate A/A cover'. He therefore altered round to port to bring him closer to the track of the liner as she passed. The *Queen* steadily overhauled her consort until she was about 5 cables (1,000 yards) on her port quarter when the liner was seen to be altering course to starboard. At first this was thought to be her yawing in the seaway, but after a moment or two, the Navigating Officer said, 'It looks as if she's turning'. The staff on the bridge of the cruiser watched as the liner continued to turn towards them and they realised that it was not a yaw, but a definite course alteration. Captain Boutwood exclaimed 'Is she mad?' and ordered his helm 15 degrees to starboard. It was far too late however, and at 14.10 the cruiser was struck by the *Queen Mary*, which hit the after superstructure in the vicinity of 'X' gun, the great liner slicing through the cruiser – 'she went into us and over us' – those on the upper deck having the amazing sight of the liner cutting right through the smaller ship and steaming on. The cruiser was thrown over onto her beam ends, and only slowly righted herself, to regain an even keel. The stern section sank quickly, but the forward half remained afloat, slowly settling by the stern with the bows lifting clear of the water. As she began to sink, she was ordered to be abandoned. The liner, under strict orders not to stop under any circumstances, carried on, and the destroyers, now visible in the distance, closed as fast as they could, but there was a heavy loss of life, with 337 men being killed. The enquiry found that the *Queen Mary* had expected the escort to keep clear of her as she was unable to manoeuvre rapidly. Further, the fatal alteration of course had been part of her planned zigzag; they had expected the cruiser to know she would make irregular alterations of course; indeed, this had been discussed between the respective captains prior to their rendezvous. By taking the cruiser into 1,000 yards, Captain Boutwood had shown a lack of appreciation of the situation, as it was well inside the larger ship's zigzag pattern. The *Queen Mary* was not entirely free of blame; her officers had presumed that their escort knew of her zigzag pattern and had consequently failed to inform the *Curacoa* of her planned alterations, again presuming that she would keep clear. The collision led to a protracted civil case for compensation, which ended in February 1949 with a final appeal to the House of Lords. This decided that *Curacoa* was two-thirds to blame, the *Queen Mary* one-third. It was the duty of the escort, being smaller and more manoeuvrable, to keep clear of the escorted ship. The cruiser should have realised that the *Queen* would be zigzagging and liable to alter to a

new course and that they were converging; she took no action until it was too late. The liner could have acted earlier as well. Making the course alteration clearly took them onto a collision course, but the size and speed of the *Queen Mary* made it difficult for them to make any rapid alteration after committing to the turn.
[*TNA: ADM.116/6158 to ADM.116/6164*]

2 October LORD STONEHAVEN trawler
Selby 1934 requisitioned 1939; 444 tons; 155.8ft × 26.1ft; 1 × 4in
Skipper-Lieutenant John Main RNR

Part of the escort to westbound coastal convoy PW226, which consisted of eight merchant ships, screened by a destroyer, a minesweeper and three armed trawlers, the group sailed from the Solent during the morning of 1 October. At 20.20 an aircraft was heard overhead, and soon after, flares were dropped ahead, evidently marking their course. Alert to the possibility of an attack, at 20.45 the destroyer *Krakowiak* detected on radar small surface contacts heading toward them. These were three motor launches (MLs), to be an addition to the escort, intending to join the convoy off Dartmouth. However, neither the convoy nor the launches were properly advised of the movements of the other. As a direct consequence of this, as the MLs continued to close, they were mistaken for enemy torpedo boats and engaged, causing casualties on both sides. During this skirmish, the convoy was turned to take them away from the supposed threat, but the shadowing aircraft kept with them, dropping flares to indicate their position. At 00.20 the real attack materialised when the group were near the Eddystone Light, five fast torpedo boats from the Fifth S-boot Flotilla carrying out attacks. Torpedo tracks were seen and avoided but at 00.50 there was a large explosion as *Lord Stonehaven* was hit by a torpedo fired by *S 112* and rapidly sank. Eighteen men were killed. Her wreck has been found and lies in position 50.11.15N 04.08.35W.
[*TNA: ADM.199/287; Warship 1996 p44*]

3 October   MGB 78 motor gun boat
Hythe 1942; 33 tons; 71.9ft × 20.7ft; 1 × 2pdr, 2 × 20mm
Lieutenant George Findlay Duncan DSC RCNVR†

One of a group of motor gun boats ordered to cover a force of motor launches that were tasked to lay mines in the Schelde estuary. On completion of the task the gunboats moved off to join with motor torpedo boats off the Hook of Holland. At 23.59 as they were making their way to the north, a group of enemy armed trawlers were seen. It was decided that *78* would attempt a depth-charge attack on the last of the line of trawlers under cover of the others, who would distract their attention. This was a very hazardous manoeuvre, as it meant running close under the bows of the target vessel, dropping a depth charge as they did so. Set to

explode at shallow depth, the resulting explosion might well disable the vessel. *78* was therefore detached and at 01.00 the action commenced. Working up to 36 knots, Duncan steered for the last ship in the line, which was probably *Vp 1340*, whilst the other gunboats, on the other side of the line opened an accurate fire at the enemy. They were seen when about 200 yards from the target which promptly opened a heavy and accurate fire. When she was only yards from the enemy, she received a direct hit on the bridge, which killed the commanding officer. The boat lost way and sheered off to starboard, passing close along the side of the trawler, which raked them with a very heavy fire. Most of the crew were either killed or wounded during this encounter. Acting Lieutenant Eggleston took command and disengaged from the enemy whilst directing fire into the enemy, and they repeatedly scored hits before they were out of range. The situation was now critical, with the upper deck a wreck and the engine room on fire. The boat was stopped, and after a determined effort the fire was extinguished, and the boat put into some sort of order. They got under way, but with no compass to steer by, it having been destroyed in the action, it was with difficulty that they could steer a safe course. Soon after this she ran hard aground onto a sandbank. Efforts to free her failed and it was clear that she could go no further. It was therefore decided that she should be abandoned, so the Carley float was hoisted out. Before leaving, petrol was released into the engine room and a fire started to ensure her destruction. The survivors drifted for 10 hours before being picked up by the Germans and made prisoner. After their release Acting Lieutenant Roy Major Eggleston was awarded the DSC and Chief Motor Mechanic Buchanan Heron the DSM for their actions that night. Lieutenant Duncan was the only casualty.
[*TNA: ADM.199/176*]

6 October   MGB 76 motor gun boat
Hythe 1942; 33 tons; 71.9ft × 20.7ft; 1 × 2pdr, 2 × 20mm
Lieutenant Leveson Granville Robert Campbell DSC RNVR

Deployed from Dover to intercept an expected enemy convoy off the coast of Belgium, she was one of a group of six torpedo boats and gunboats, *MGB 76* having Lieutenant Commander Robert Hichens, senior officer of the group, embarked. At just before midnight hydrophone effect (HE) on engine noises was detected to the south-west, indicating the approach of the ships, and the craft increased speed to attack from the north. As they ran in, they were seen, and were illuminated by star shell. They broke off the attack to re-group and then recommenced the attack from the south-west. A hectic and confused action resulted, with star shell and tracer fire lighting up the sky and during

this *76* received a hit in the petrol tank. The fire that resulted was quickly tackled and brought under control, although the engine room was filled with fumes, and she slowly made her way clear. At 06.40 the fire broke out again, and this time could not be brought under control, and an explosion forced the abandonment of the boat. The explosion was seen by other boats of the group who closed and picked up the crew. One man was killed in the action.
[TNA:ADM.199/621]

6 October MTB 29 motor torpedo boat
Gosport 1940; 34 tons; 71.9ft × 16.4ft; 2 × torpedo tubes
Lieutenant Felix Maxwell Tattersfield RNZVR[†]
One of the coastal forces craft on an offensive night patrol that *MGB 76* took part in (see above), she launched her torpedoes during the second attack, but as she was manoeuvring, she collided with another of the boats, *MTB 30*. The damage was such that she was ordered to return to harbour. As she made her way back independently, she encountered an enemy patrol which heard the noise of her engines and illuminated the area with star shell. This lit up the MTB and one of the enemy patrol, the large minesweeper *M 21*, being the nearest, altered course to ram. Having raked the torpedo boat with gunfire she struck her abreast the bridge. *29* drifted astern, still under heavy fire, until she sank, bows first. Ten men died.
[TNA:ADM.199/621; Warship 1996 p139]

7 October ML 339 motor launch
Wallasea 1941; 73 tons; 112ft × 18.4ft; 1 × 3pdr
Lieutenant Geoffrey Malvern Hobday RNVR
Part of the escort to coastal convoy FN32, which was subjected to a concerted attack by a force of 17 enemy torpedo boats during the night of 6/7 October between buoys 57F and 57B off the Norfolk coast. At 03.38 a ship in the convoy was torpedoed, and two torpedo tracks were seen heading for *339*. One passed close ahead of the launch the second hit under the stern with a large explosion and the after section of the launch was blown off. Despite the damage the forward section remained afloat for another hour until she caught fire and was abandoned, the launch exploding before it sank. Three men were lost.
[TNA:ADM.199/621; ADM.199/645; ADM.267/115]

7 October CAROLINE MOLLER tug
Hessle (*St Mabyn*) requisitioned 1940; 444 tons; 135.5ft × 29ft; 1 × 12pdr
Lieutenant John Henry Kennedy RNR
Based at Harwich as a rescue tug, she sailed to provide cover for the passage of the northward-bound Convoy FN32. When the convoy was attacked in the early hours of the morning (see *ML 339* above), she became

a target and was hit by a torpedo at 04.00 and quickly sank with the loss of sixteen men in position 53.05.42N 01.28.48E.
[TNA:ADM.199/645]

9 October RUBY fishing vessel
1902 requisitioned 1941; 46 tons
Lieutenant Nicholas Leadley Brown RNR
Employed as a ferry at Scapa Flow, she was driven ashore on Lamb Holm in a gale and completely wrecked.
[TNA:ADM.199/2250]

11 October THALIA pilot tender
Greenock 1904 (*Protector*) requisitioned 1940; 161 tons; 108.8ft × 21.1ft
Employed as a pilot vessel at Oban, she foundered after a collision with a merchant vessel off Lynn of Lorne, 15 miles south-west of 'Greig Island' (Creag Island?), West Scotland.
[TNA:ADM.199/2250]

(13?) October UNIQUE submarine
Barrow 1940; 540/732 tons; 180ft × 16.1ft; 1 × 12pdr; 4 × torpedo tubes
Lieutenant Robert Evelyn Boddington[†]
Ordered to deploy to the Mediterranean, she sailed from Holy Loch, Scotland 8 October. She was last sighted in the western approaches to the English Channel on 9 October but failed to arrive as expected at Gibraltar on 22 October. The cause of her loss is unknown, and an accident is a possibility. Her loss may be linked to an incident on 13 October, when the German blockade runner *Spichern* in the Bay of Biscay reported being attacked by a submerged submarine, in position 46.54N 06.03W. During the attack, a large explosion was seen on the port side, about 2,000 metres away, and a torpedo was seen to pass close to the port side. A few moments later there was another, duller explosion and more tracks were seen. The *Ursula*, also on passage to Gibraltar, also heard two underwater explosions at the same time on the same day. The only submarine in this area was the *Unique* and the explosions are likely to relate to her loss, probably by premature detonation of her torpedoes. Four officers and thirty men were lost.
[Evans p326; http://uboat.net/allies/warships/ship/3534.html]

14 October LCT (5) 2006 landing craft, tank
Manitowoc 1942; 143 tons; 105ft × 32.8ft; 2 × 20mm
In transit from the USA, she was being carried as deck cargo, along with several smaller landing craft, on board the former whale factory ship *Southern Empress* (12,398 tons), in Convoy SC104 which had sailed from New York on 3 October. At just after midnight on 13/14 October the convoy came under attack from *U 221* (Trojer). At 00.32 an attack was made when the

Southern Empress was hit and stopped. *U 221* fired a further torpedo at 03.21 in position 53.40N 40.40W which sent her to the bottom, complete with cargo.
[http://www.uboat.net/allies/merchants/ships/2276.html]

16 October INVERCLYDE trawler
Goole 1914 (*Perihelion*) requisitioned 1939; 215 tons; 120.4ft × 22ft
Foundered at 18.20 when 11.6 miles west of Beachy Head whilst under tow of the tug *Harold Brown* from Shoreham to Portsmouth. The small towing crew onboard were taken off by the trawler *Transvaal*.
[TNA: ADM.199/2250]

16 October LADY CRADDOCK fishing vessel
Requisitioned 1939; 80 tons
Lieutenant Cecil Arthur Tatam RINR
Royal Indian Navy. Fitted as a minesweeper, she was stationed at Calcutta, engaged in sweeping the approaches to the River Hooghly. In mid-October, the area was affected by a severe tropical cyclone. *Lady Craddock* was at anchor at Diamond Harbour and was caught by a 30ft wave and capsized and sank off Haldia River Buoy. The survivors managed to swim ashore, but six men died.
[http://www.ibiblio.org/hyperwar/UN/India/RIN/RIN-6.html]

27 October LCT (5) 2281 landing craft, tank
Kansas City 1942; 143 tons; 105ft × 32.8ft
Being carried as deck cargo on board the whale factory ship *Sourabaya* for transportation to England, sailing in Convoy HX212 which departed from New York on 18 October. At 23.00 on 27 October the *U 436* (Seibicke) commenced submerged attacks on the convoy which was then south-east of Cape Farewell in position 54.32N 31.02W. In the second attack a torpedo struck the *Sourabaya* and she sank, taking *2281* with her.
[http://www.uboat.net/allies/merchants/2302.html]

29 October LCT (5) 2190 / 2192 / 2284 landing craft, tank
North Tonawanda (*2190*); Buffalo (*2192*); Kansas City (*2284*); 143 tons; 105ft × 32.8ft
Loaded on board the whale factory ship *Kosmos-II* for transit to England, which sailed in Convoy HX212. She was hit by a torpedo fired by *U 606* at 05.37 on 28 October, and, severely damaged, fell behind from the convoy, some of the passengers embarked leaving on lifeboats, but most of the crew remained onboard. After extinguishing a fire and stabilising the flood, they set about rejoining the convoy, but at 03.05 she was torpedoed again, by *U 624* (Soden-Frauhofen) and caught fire, settled and sank, with the landing craft.
[http://www.uboat.net/allies/merchants/ships/2320.html]

30 October PANORAMA trawler
Savannah 1919 (*Rocroi*), purchased 1940; 408 tons; 140.1ft × 28.5ft
Boom Skipper Donald George RNR
Employed as a boom defence vessel, based at Freetown, Sierra Leone, she was en-route to Bathurst (Banjul) but stranded in shallow water at the mouth of the Saloum River, Senegal, and was detained by the French colonial authorities. She was released on 23 November when the French West African territories came under the control of the Free French forces.
[TNA: BT.373/242; ADM.199/2251]

31 October MTB 87 motor torpedo boat
Belfast 1942; 38 tons; 72.7ft × 19.2ft; 2 × torpedo tubes
Lieutenant Dennis John Long
In company with several other torpedo boats, she sailed at 17.00 on 30 October for a night patrol in the North Sea. The patrol proved to be uneventful and as the weather was deteriorating at 04.45 it was decided to terminate the patrol, and *87* in company with *MTB 232* withdrew to the west. The weather worsened, the wind rising to Force 6 with a strong swell. At 08.10 when descending into the trough of a wave a heavy shudder was felt and the bows of the boat disintegrated in an explosion. The force of the blast also demolished the wheelhouse and she started to break up, the stern section remaining afloat, sitting in a litter of debris and a dark patch of oil. *MTB 232* closed and picked up the crew, all of whom had survived the blast. *232* then fired into the shattered remains to set them alight, ensuring destruction before leaving the scene. It was thought that they might have strayed into a defensive British minefield, although this was not certain. The explosion had been small and was more likely to have been the type laid by German torpedo boats.
[TNA ADM.199/239]

3 November BAIA tug
Ancona 1912, captured 1941; 181 tons; 132.7ft × 19.1ft
Foundered whilst under tow between Mombasa and Mogadishu.
[Statement of Losses p23; TNA: ADM.1/24129]

6 November MGB 19 motor gun boat
Hythe 1941; 31 tons; 70ft × 20ft; 1 × 2pdr
Hauled onto the slipway of Robinson's Yard at Oulton Broad for repairs and maintenance she was destroyed when the yard was the target of an air raid. The boat was blown off the slip and landed upside down, breaking into two.
[TNA: ADM.267/120]

8 November Operation 'Torch' – landing and occupation of French North Africa

'Torch' was the operation to occupy Morocco and Algeria, with the aim of securing the Vichy-controlled North African coast and effectively creating a threat to the Axis forces in Italy. The main landings would be on beaches around Algiers, Oran and Arzeu by a large force of allied troops, many of them American. It was decided that the main harbours should be secured as soon as possible, and this led to Operations 'Reservist' and 'Terminal'.

Operation 'Reservist' – landing of troops in Oran harbour

This called for a force to be landed inside the harbour, to prevent ships being scuttled and to secure certain key points. For this, ex-United States Coastguard vessels would be used, which would fly both the US and British flags, in the hope that the French defenders may be more reluctant to fire on American vessels than British. The *Hartland* and *Walney* were to enter Oran harbour and launch canoes which would carry troops to various points around the harbour, before securing alongside. The operation would be under the control of Captain Frederick Thornton Peters DSO, who would be embarked in the *Walney*. It was uncertain whether the Vichy French occupants would resist or not, but it had to be presumed that they would. The pair were detached from the main invasion force at 23.00 and at 03.00 of the morning of 8 November, accompanied by two motor launches, *ML 480* and *ML 483*, they approached the entrance to the harbour which was barred by a timber boom. Each ship was carrying 240 troops, the majority of whom were American.

WALNEY cutter
Oakland 1930 (*Sebago*), transferred 1941; 1,983 tons; 236ft × 42ft; 1 × 5in, 3 × 12pdr
Lieutenant Commander Peter Capel Mayrick[†]
With Captain Peters embarked, she led the way to the harbour entrance, the motor launches laying a smokescreen as she approached. She struck the boom across the harbour at 15 knots and steamed into the basin. As she did so searchlights lit up the night, and a heavy fire was opened on the ships by a shore battery at Fort Lamoune, overlooking the harbour, followed by the ships in the harbour. The *Walney*, so far untouched, launched her canoes with some troops embarked and then proceeded further into the harbour at 4 knots, heading for the Mole Jules Giraud, the troops below ready for landing. She was now being hit regularly by shore fire, but the damage was not serious. As she steamed on, she encountered a French destroyer

outbound, and attempted to turn and ram, but did not have sufficient way to achieve this. The French vessel opened a fierce fire on the cutter at point blank range. She passed her opponent on the starboard side, and shortly afterwards received further hits in the boiler room and engine room, effectively stopping her engines. She was now being raked by intense fire from all sides and with her steering gear out of action, she drifted under momentum further into the harbour until she ran alongside the destroyer *Epervier*. By now she was a wreck, riddled with holes and burning fiercely, and the survivors abandoned her to be taken on board the French ship. The wreck continued to burn and eventually drifted to the northern side of the harbour where she grounded and burnt out. Eighty-one members of the crew were killed, with many the embarked troops.

HARTLAND cutter
Quincy 1928 (*Pontchartrain*) transferred 1941; 1,975 tons; 236ft × 42ft; 1 × 4in, 3 × 12pdr
Lieutenant Commander Godfrey Philip Billot RNR
Astern of the *Walney* when she broke through the boom, the *Hartland* followed, heading for the entrance. However, as the leader pushed forward into the harbour, several searchlights came on and these focused on the *Hartland* and the resulting fire was concentrated on her. Almost immediately the bridge was hit, killing or wounding all the staff and a hit in the boiler room severed a steam pipe. Out of control she swung out of control and rammed the jetty a few feet from the entrance. However, despite the hail of fire, control was regained and at the second attempt entered the port and she headed for objective, the Quai de Dunkerque. As she closed, she came under fire at point-blank range from a destroyer, and she was soon on fire with very many casualties. She somehow reached her objective and dropped the port anchor to hold them in position, but most of the troops were now dead or wounded, and the commanding officer was blinded in one eye and wounded in the leg and shoulder. With the ship now ablaze from stem to stern she was ordered to be abandoned and the survivors scrambled ashore, the French ceasing fire as they did so. She continued to lay off the Quai, burning, until she eventually blew up at 10.15. Thirty two men were killed.
[TNA ADM.1/11915]

Operation 'Terminal' – landing of troops at Algiers
As another key part of Operation 'Torch', it was planned that a force of Allied troops should be landed from two destroyers, *Malcolm* and *Broke*, to secure key points in the port of Algiers and prevent acts of sabotage. During the late afternoon of 7 November each destroyer embarked 350 US troops from the cruiser *Sheffield* and at 22.30

detached from the main force to make their way to the port.

9 November BROKE destroyer
Woolston 1920 (*Rooke*); 1,480 tons; 318.3ft × 31.6ft;
2 × 4.7in, 4 × 20mm, 6 × torpedo tubes
Lieutenant Commander Arthur Frank Capel Layard DSC

In the early hours of the morning of 8 November the destroyers approached the entrance to Algiers, but had difficulty in finding the correct channel, and searchlights illuminated them, blinding the bridge staff. Both turned away and attempted further runs at the harbour entrance and each time were forced to turn away, unable to find their way. As they turned in again for a fourth attempt, they came under fire from the shore, and the *Malcolm* was hit in the boiler room, forcing her to turn away and retire. The *Broke* continued, and at 04.30, with it now getting light she found the entrance and sighted the protective boom, which she rammed at 25 knots, going straight through it. She ran alongside a jetty to discharge her cargo of troops, all being off by 05.15. Only light small arms fire was experienced in the harbour until at 07.30 a shore battery at Musoir de Nord suddenly opened up, several shells dropping nearby and one hitting the bows. The destroyer quickly got under way, parting securing wires to get clear of the jetty, and deftly manoeuvring between moored merchant ships reached sheltered waters. Things again became quiet until 09.30 when she again came under fire, apparently from a field gun or howitzer, the fire becoming heavy, and she was again hit. A motor launch entered to lay a smokescreen as she got under way to clear the harbour, suffering several near misses from shells. It was found that several forward compartments were flooded; the after magazine and shell room were flooded by a shell hole on the waterline and the hull had numerous holes, the most serious being in the engine room. The damage control parties were kept fully employed plugging and shoring up, but with an increasing wind and a rising sea they struggled to keep the water at bay, and she slowly developed a list to starboard. At 22.00 the lubricating oil pumps failed, and the engines stopped. The ship fell away with the wind and sea and developed a considerable heel to port. The escort destroyer *Zetland* had closed to render assistance and a tow was rigged. The tow went on through the night, slowly heading west, but the following morning showed that she was down by the head and the list was increasing. At 14.00 the port side upper deck was awash and *Zetland* was ordered to slip the tow and take off the crew. This was initially done by boat but was too slow and the *Zetland* then put her bows alongside the bows of the *Broke*, allowing the men to leap across. The *Broke* finally sank at 17.00. Nine men lost their lives from the shellfire.
[TNA:ADM.199/904]

★　★　★

9 November GARDENIA corvette
Renfrew 1940; 940 tons; 190ft × 33ft; 1 × 4in, 2 × 20mm
Lieutenant Christopher James Jackson RNVR

Part of the assault convoy for Operation 'Torch' that arrived off Oran on 8 November. With the landings successfully made, she patrolled the area off 'X' beachhead, but at 01.35 was in collision with the armed trawler *Fluellen*. She steadily flooded and was finally abandoned and sank 7 miles to the north-east of Habibes light. The corvette *Vetch* lifted off all the survivors, but three men lost their lives.
[TNA:ADM.199/652]

9 November CROMER minesweeper
Renfrew 1940; 673 tons; 180ft × 28.6ft; 1 × 12pdr, 1 × 2pdr, 2 × 20mm
Commander Robert Hearfield Stephenson DSO[†]

Based in the eastern Mediterranean, she was in company with the *Cromarty* and *Boston*, and engaged in sweeping the approaches to Mersa Matruh. During the day, several moored mines had been brought to the surface and disposed of and at 17.00 the ships were ordered to approach a clutch of newly-exposed mines and sink them. They slowly closed the area and had started firing at a floating mine with rifles, when at 17.15 there was a large explosion on the port side just abaft the bridge when she ran over an unseen mine. The ship broke in half, with the after section capsizing to starboard and sinking. The forward part slowly rolled over, but remained afloat, upside down, for about 20 minutes before sinking. They were then 4 miles north of the harbour. Three officers and forty-one ratings were killed.
[TNA ADM.199/239]

10 November MARTIN destroyer
Walker 1940; 1,920 tons; 345.6ft × 36.9ft; 6 × 4.7in, 1 × 4in, 4 × 2pdr, 4 × 20mm, 4 × torpedo tubes
Commander Charles Richard Powys Thomson DSO

Part of the force assembled off Algeria to support Operation 'Torch', the Allied landings in north Africa, she was about 85 miles north-east of Algiers, in position 37.48N 03.50E, when at 02.59, an explosion took place aft, followed almost immediately by a further two. The first detonation had hit the cabin flat and started a fierce fire. The others had struck further forward, one impacting in the gearing room, which caused immediate flooding of the engine room and put all the lights out. The other detonated just forward of the bridge. This blew 'A' turret overboard and caused considerable structural damage and started another fire, and flames were seen bursting up through 'B' turret from below. The ship heeled over to starboard and started to sink by the bow, and within minutes of the first explosion the bridge was underwater. She then steadied somewhat, hanging at an angle of 60 degrees with the stern clear of the water for several minutes before sinking. As she disappeared there was another large explosion, probably her depth charges exploding. She had been torpedoed by the *U 431* (Dommes). One hundred and fifty-nine men died.

[TNA: ADM.267/94]

10 November IBIS sloop

Haverton 1940; 1,300 tons; 283ft × 37.6ft; 6 × 4in, 4 × 2pdr, 2 × 20mm
Commander Henry Maxwell Darell-Brown DSC[†]

Part of the force covering the landings in North Africa, she supported the landings at Algiers 'C' beachhead then joined the escort to the aircraft carrier *Argus*. At 16.40 the group was 12 miles off Cape Caxine, when a formation of twelve Ju 88 aircraft was sighted on the port beam which commenced a bombing attack, concentrating on the *Argus*. At 17.15 a second raid was sighted closing, and as before the *Ibis* engaged with main armament. This time two of the attackers turned to concentrate on the sloop, dropping low evidently to release torpedoes. The attack was pressed home and the first aircraft passed close over the bows after dropping a torpedo, only to crash into the sea, after being engaged by all the close-range weapons. The torpedo passed clear, but another aircraft was seen approaching from the port quarter, which dropped a torpedo. The wheel was put over to 'comb the track' but at 17.21 it hit the port side, aft of number 1 boiler room. Clouds of steam escaped to blanket the after part of the ship and she heeled over to take a list of 15 degrees to starboard. The ship did not recover and continued to slowly roll over and floats and nets were released as she was ordered to be abandoned. By 17.23 she was hanging at an angle of 45 degrees, and 5 minutes later she rolled over to starboard to float bottom up, a huge rent in her port side showing, from the upper deck to the keel, before sinking. One hundred and six men were killed.

[TNA: ADM.267/115]

11 November UNBEATEN submarine

Barrow 1940; 540/732 tons; 180ft × 16.1ft; 1 × 12pdr, 4 × torpedo tubes
Lieutenant Donald Eric Ogilvy Watson[†]

In order to carry out a patrol in the Bay of Biscay, she sailed from her base in Holy Loch on 23 October. She successfully landed agents on the northern Spanish coast on 2 November and on 6 November reported the sighting of a blockade runner. This was the last heard from her, and she failed to make her expected rendezvous off Bishop's Rock on 12 November. It is highly likely that she was the target attacked by a RAF aircraft of 172 Squadron. At 02.16 on 11 November a patrolling Wellington picked up a radar contact at 8

miles and turned to intercept. At 02.22 she illuminated the contact with her Leigh Light (a powerful searchlight) and confirmed that it was a submarine on the surface; she was then in position 46.50N 06.51W. The Wellington, which had not been warned of the presence of any British submarine, assumed the boat must be German and dived to attack, running over the target at 75ft and releasing depth charges and two large explosions were seen to envelop the submarine, which was apparently under helm to port. The aircraft then made a further three runs, with the gunners firing approximately 200 rounds at the target, before departing. No German submarine was lost at this time, and none reported an attack. The expected position of the *Unbeaten* would have been close to the position given. Four officers and thirty-two men were lost.

[Evans pp327–8]

12 November TYNWALD anti-aircraft ship

Barrow 1937 purchased 1940; 2,376 tons; 314.6ft × 46ft; 6 × 4in, 8 × 2pdr, 4 × 20mm
Captain Philip George Wodehouse DSO

Part of the force that covered the landings in North Africa, she had acted as a radar guard ship and provided anti-aircraft support whilst stationed off Algiers and Bougie (Béjaïa). The ships off the ports came under regular air attack and during an attack near Bougie on 11 November, the monitor *Roberts* had been hit and damaged. The *Tynwald* closed the *Roberts* and anchored in 7 fathoms for the night. At 04.45 she weighed anchor and drifted very slowly to the east, bows to the north. At 05.05 there were two violent explosions in quick succession on the starboard side as she was hit by torpedoes fired by the Italian submarine *Argo* (Gigli). The first exploded abreast the funnel, the second further aft, level with the pom-pom platform. The ship immediately heeled over to port and started to go down by the head. The forward mess decks, stokehold and engine room were all reported to be flooding rapidly. She sank by the head in shallow water, her upper works still showing. Three officers and twenty-one men were lost.

[TNA: ADM.199/904]

12 November KARANJA landing ship

Linthouse 1931 requisitioned 1941; 9,891 tons; 471.3ft × 64.2ft; 1 × 6in, 1 × 12pdr, 12 × 20mm
Commander Dyson Standish Hore-Lacey

Fully laden with troops with vehicles and petrol, the landing ship had supported the initial 'Torch' landings in North Africa, and then moved on to the east, sailing from Algiers 10 November to arrive at Bougie (Béjaïa) the following day. Having discharged her cargo of troops, she embarked about 100 soldiers and some crew from the *Cathay*, which had been damaged in an air attack. The following morning, she 'stood to' at 04.45 as more

air attacks were expected, and at 05.00 got underway. She made her way towards the *Roberts* and *Tynwald* (see above). At 05.15 the air attacks started, and a single Ju 88 was seen to dive out of a cloud astern of the *Karanja*, and despite defensive fire being opened, the aircraft carried out an attack, dropping four bombs. Two of them exploded as near misses either side of the bow, the other two hit her. The first penetrated the upper deck to enter the engine room where it exploded, starting a fierce fire. Another bomb entered a mess deck and burst outwards through the port side and setting fire to the petrol store. The amidships section of the ship was swathed in thick smoke as the starboard anchor was let go to stop her drifting. With the fire gaining, the boats were ordered to be hoisted out and several landing craft closed to assist. By 08.30 the fires were now very fierce and spreading, and it was decided to abandon her; there was some confusion and panic from the *Cathay* survivors, who rushed the boats, and several were lowered without orders. The fires continued to burn, the amidships section covered in smoke, steam and flames, until she sank. Thirty-eight men died, many of them from the spare crew of the RFA *Dewdale*, who had been in the mess deck where the bomb had exploded.
[TNA: ADM.199/904]

12 November HECLA depot ship
Barrow 1928; 14,650 tons; 545ft × 85ft; 6 × 4in
Captain Stephen Henry Tolson Arliss DSO
Having been repaired at Simonstown, South Africa, after suffering mine damage, she was en-route to Gibraltar, escorted by the destroyer *Venomous*, when at 23.15 on 11 November, then being in position 35.42N 09.54W, she was hit by a torpedo on the starboard side. There was flooding of the boiler rooms, and power was lost, but the damage was controlled, and she reported that she was in no danger of sinking but required a tow. The tug *Salvonia* was dispatched from Gibraltar, and the destroyer *Marne* was ordered to stand by her. At 00.50 she was hit by another torpedo, which hit the port side forward with a large explosion which resulted in flooding of a number of compartments. The ship now assumed a marked list to port, which steadily increased. Ten minutes later another torpedo struck her, on the port side aft, and she was clearly settling. At 01.05 the *Marne* reported that she was remaining by the *Hecla*, but as she manoeuvred to close the depot ship, she was herself torpedoed, her stern being blown off. Another tug, the *Jaunty*, was sent to the scene and the *Venomous* prosecuted a sonar contact but failed to prevent yet another torpedo attack. At 06.50 the *Hecla* was hit twice more, and quickly rolled over and sank. The *Venomous* picked up 493 survivors and reached Casablanca with only 4 tons of fuel left, but 281 men died. The attacking submarine had been the *U 515* (Henke).
[TNA: ADM.199/652; ADM.199/2013]

15 November AVENGER escort carrier
Chester 1940; 12,150 tons; 465ft × 69.6ft; 3 × 4in, 19 × 20mm, 15 aircraft
Commander Antony Paul Colthurst†
Having provided support for the landings in North Africa (Operation 'Torch'), she left Gibraltar to return to the river Clyde in Convoy MKF1. The convoy was drawn up in four columns, the distance between columns being 5 cables (1,000 yards), with *Avenger* being the second ship in the second column. At 02.55 in approximate position 36.15N 07.45W the escorting destroyers commenced an attack on a suspected submarine contact, and at 03.10 an emergency turn to starboard was ordered. At 03.15, as they were under helm, the *Avenger* was hit by a torpedo which detonated at number 75 frame, abreast the bomb room. She took an immediate list to port, then a vivid red glow appeared which lit up the side of the carrier, stretching the length of the ship for about 2 or 3 seconds. All the lights went out and she was covered in a great cloud of black smoke and she broke up and disappeared in less than 3 minutes. There were just twelve survivors with 516 fatalities. The cause of the rapid disintegration was uncertain, although it would seem likely that there was an explosion in the bomb room, triggered by the initial torpedo detonation. This led to a recommendation that the escort carriers have a new longitudinal bulkhead built into the existing bomb room and in future the bombs should be stored away from the ship's side. The attack had been conducted by the *U 155* (Piening), which had fired a fan of five torpedoes, which was remarkably successful, resulting in not only the loss of the *Avenger*, but also the merchant ship *Ettrick*, which had been immediately ahead of the carrier, and the damaging of the USS *Almaack* (AK 27).
[TNA: ADM.1/12605]

15 November ALGERINE minesweeper
Belfast 1941; 850 tons; 212.6ft × 35.6ft; 1 × 4in, 8 × 20mm
Lieutenant Commander Wilfred Allan Cooke†
Part of the force assembled for Operation 'Torch', she stood by the landing sites at Algiers from 8 November, then remained patrolling off the beachhead. During the night of 14/15 November she was conducting a patrol in company with the minesweeper *Alarm* and trawlers *Hoy* and *Mull*. At 03.55 when she was about 5 miles due north of Cape Carbon, she was hit by two torpedoes a few seconds apart and she sank in less than 5 minutes. There was another explosion as she submerged, probably a depth charge exploding. Due to rain squalls, the sinking was not observed by her consorts, and it was not until daylight that it was realised that she was missing, and a search started. Thirty-two survivors were picked up, but eighty-three men died. Her attacker had been the Italian submarine *Ascianghi* (Erler)
[TNA: ADM.199/652]

15 November SAGUENAY destroyer

Southampton 1930; 1,350 tons; 312ft × 32.9ft; 5 × 4.7in,
2 × 2pdr, 8 × torpedo tubes

Lieutenant Commander Dickson Carlisle Wallace RCNR

Royal Canadian Navy. Convoy WB13 was a local convoy from St Johns, Newfoundland to Sydney, Nova Scotia which departed 14 November, escorted by the *Saguenay*. At 08.45 the following morning in thick fog, then being about 12 miles south of Cape Race, one of the convoy, the Panamanian registered freighter *Azar* (1,700 tons) loomed out of the mist and rammed the destroyer's stern. This dislodged several depth charges, at least one of which exploded under the bows of *Azar* and another exploded under the stern of *Saguenay*. This blew away the destroyer's stern, along with the rudder and caused shock damage throughout the ship. Internal bulkheads held, and the ship remained stable and upright. The *Azar* was not so fortunate, as the ship foundered, with the loss of one of her crew. The damaged destroyer was towed to St Johns, Newfoundland and was declared a constructive total loss. Despite this, temporary repairs were made, and she was later employed as a static training ship.
[*www.forposterityssake.ca/Navy/HMCS_SAGUENAY_D79.htm*]

18 November WINSOME drifter

Burra 1902 requisitioned 1940; 46 tons; 65ft × 19.5ft

Used as a harbour tender, she foundered off Fairlie in the River Clyde.
[*Statement of Losses p23*]

19 November ULLSWATER whaler

Middlesbrough 1939 (*Kos XXIX*) purchased 1939; 560 tons; 138.5ft × 26.6ft; 1 × 4in, 1 × 20mm

Lieutenant Neil Black Cameron Ross RNR[†]

Coastal convoy PW250, one of the regular convoys that shuttled along the south-west coast of England, sailed from the Solent on 18 November with twelve ships and escort of a destroyer and five armed trawlers, including the *Ullswater*. At 01.00 as they headed west, an aircraft was heard overhead and over the next 2 hours regularly reappeared to drop flares ahead of the convoy, clearly marking its progress and course. This alerted the convoy to the probability of an attack, but this did not materialise until 03.00 when a group of six enemy torpedo boats, which had been loitering off Eddystone, commenced an attack. Star shell was fired to illuminate the area, but at 03.05 there was a flash and the *Ullswater* disappeared in a cloud of smoke as it was hit by a torpedo. The cargo ship *Yewforest* was just 2 cables (400 yards) astern of her at the time and reduced speed and lines were ordered to be thrown overboard for any survivors, but she was also hit. The torpedo boats completed an effective attack by sinking another two merchant ships without loss before retiring. Thirty-five men were lost from the *Ullswater*.
[*TNA: ADM.237/171; Warship 1996 p44*]

20 November LCT (2) 120 landing craft, tank

Middlesbrough 1941; 296 tons; 143ft × 31ft

Foundered at 07.47 in heavy weather off the coast of Libya, 35 miles to the north-east of Bardia
[*TNA: ADM.199/621*]

(24/25) November UTMOST submarine

Barrow 1940; 540/732 tons; 180ft × 16ft; 1 × 12pdr, 4 × torpedo tubes

Lieutenant John Walter David Coombe[†]

Ordered to carry out a patrol off the coast of Tunisia, she sailed from Malta on 17 November. She reported by radio on the night of 23 November that she had carried out a torpedo attack on an Italian ship earlier that day, off Cape Blanc. She was then due to return to Malta but failed to arrive as expected on 25 November. The cause of her loss is uncertain; if the boat had moved to the north to clear the area of Cape Blanc after her attack, to avoid the anti-submarine activity and head back to Malta, then her course would have taken her through a minefield, which is the most likely reason for her loss. Claims have been made that an attack by the Italian destroyer *Groppo* may have been responsible. Escorting a convoy between Palermo and Bizerta, during the afternoon of 25 November, the destroyer twice carried out depth-charge attacks on sonar contacts which subsequently disappeared, but no other evidence was seen. By the time of these attacks however, *Utmost* was due at Malta, and the position of the attacks was not on the route she would have taken. Four officers and twenty-nine men were lost.
[*https://uboat.net/allies/warships/ship/3540.html*]

25 November LEYLAND trawler

Selby 1936 requisitioned 1939; 452 tons; 161.8ft × 27.1ft; 1 × 4in

Lieutenant Arthur Kennedy Nears RNR[†]

Based at Gibraltar, she was on a night patrol when she was rammed and sunk by the American cargo ship *John Sergeant* (7,191 tons) 1.5 miles to the west of the port. Eight men were lost.
[*TNA: ADM.199/652; ADM.199/662*]

29 November ML 242 motor launch

Looe 1941; 73 tons; 112ft × 18.4ft; 1 × 3pdr

Lieutenant John Robert Walsh RNVR

Normally based at Freetown, Sierra Leone, she was at Lagos, Nigeria, undergoing repairs with some base staff on board, when at 09.20 a fire broke out in the galley. Despite tackling the blaze with all available equipment, it soon took hold. The local fire brigade was called and were soon on scene, but the launch was abandoned at 09.30. *ML1016* towed the burning vessel into shallow water where she was beached and allowed to burn out.
[*TNA: ADM.53/116296; ADM.199/621*]

November LCT (5) 2187 landing craft, tank
North Tonawanda (LCT 187); 143 tons; 112.3ft × 32.9ft
In the *Statement of Losses* listed as being lost in transit from the USA during November. This was presumably in sections, as part of the deck cargo on a merchant ship, but the vessel has not been identified. One possibility is the Panamanian merchant vessel *Buchanan* (5,614 tons), carrying crated aircraft and 'landing barges' as deck cargo, which was torpedoed and sunk by *U 224* (Kosbadt) at 21.35 on 12 November, whilst sailing independently.
[Statement of Losses p51]

1 December ARMIDALE minesweeper
Sydney 1942; 790 tons; 180ft × 31ft; 1 × 4in, 3 × 20mm
Lieutenant Commander David Herbert Richards RANR
Royal Australian Navy. Ordered to assist with carrying troops to Timor to reinforce the small force resisting the occupying Japanese, she sailed from Darwin 29 November, bound for Betano. Despite coming under air attack, they escaped damage and reached Timor the following day but failed to locate the expected launch that was to assist landing the troops, so put to sea. The following day, having met with the launch *Kuru*, the pair headed back for Betano. They came under regular air attack as they steamed north, but again avoided damage until the final attack at 15.00 by a force of thirteen aircraft which broke up into small groups to carry out simultaneous attacks. At 15:10, the ship was hit on the port side by two torpedoes, one of which exploded in the engine room. She immediately heeled over to port and started to sink by the bows. Floats were released as she sank, and two damaged boats remained, to which the survivors managed to swim, but they became separated over the next few days. HMAS *Kalgoorlie* found the dinghy on 7 December and the whaler on 9 December, but although a raft was seen by aircraft, no trace of it could be found by searching ships. Forty men lost their lives, along with sixty Dutch and native troops of the Dutch East Indies Army.
[http://www.navy.gov.au/hmas-armidale-i]

1 December JASPER trawler
Beverley 1931 (*Balthasar*) purchased 1935; 381 tons; 145.8ft × 25.1ft; 1 × 4in
Lieutenant William Thomason Hodson RNVR
Part of the escort to westbound convoy PW256 through the English Channel, with three other armed trawlers and the escort destroyer *Glaisdale*. At 02.50, as they crossed Lyme Bay, they were warned from the shore of unidentified radar contacts, believed to be enemy torpedo craft. At 03.30 the *Glaisdale* gained radar contact on a surface ship to the south, at a range of 6 miles. Correctly suspecting that this was one the anticipated enemy torpedo boats, she altered course to close, gaining more radar contacts as she did so. Just before 04.00 she

opened fire, and a running battle continued for the next 45 minutes before contact was lost. The convoy meanwhile had been turned away to steer to the north-west, but as they approached Bolt Head a second group of torpedo boats was seen to be lying in wait. The trawler *Cornelian* illuminated them at 04.10 and she was joined by the escort destroyer *Tynedale*, closing from the west, to engage the enemy craft which got under way at high speed. *Jasper* had seen the star shell being fired by the *Cornelian* and realised that another group of boats was close by but had not sighted any before a torpedo track was sighted on the port side. The wheel was put hard to starboard, but she was hit about 6ft from the stem. The ship was lifted out of the water and was covered with spray and smoke. When this cleared it was found that she had taken a 20-degree list to starboard and the 4in gun and its crew had disappeared, and a fire was reported in a forward compartment, next to the 4in ready-use locker. Rafts and floats were ordered to be cleared away, but Lieutenant Hodson did not immediately order her to be abandoned. The engine room reported that they had no water, and the engines were working and although much of her bow had been blown away, the forward bulkhead was holding. The fire was tackled and brought under control. It was hoped that by first light a tug could assist, and the ship could be saved. At 05.10 small fast-moving craft were seen approaching, and it was feared that it was the enemy returning, and the machine guns were manned, but they were found to be friendly motor launches, and at 05.25 *ML 179* was alongside. The engine room now reported that they had water entering the compartment, and it soon became clear that the pumps could not keep pace with the flooding. At 05.48 she slowly rolled over to starboard, and the crew were ordered to leave, which was done quickly and quietly. At 05.50 she partly righted herself and then sank bows first. Her position then was approximately 50.10N 03.49W. Eleven men lost their lives. Two gallantry awards were subsequently made: Lieutenant Hodson was awarded the DSC for his tenacity in refusing to leave the ship, and his efforts to try and save her, plus his willingness to engage the enemy which gave inspiring leadership. Engineman Toovey was awarded the DSM, for remaining at his place in the engine room, ensuring that the engines remained available until the very last and remaining cool and calm throughout, providing an excellent example to those around him.
[TNA:ADM.1/14211]

2 December QUENTIN destroyer
Cowes 1941; 1,692 tons; 339.6ft × 35.8ft; 4 × 4.7in, 4 × 2pdr, 6 × 20mm, 8 × torpedo tubes
Lieutenant Commander Allan Herbert Percy Noble DSC
On the evening of 1 December Force 'Q', consisting of three light cruisers and two destroyers, one of

which was the *Quentin*, sailed from Bône (Annaba) to intercept enemy shipping sailing from Italy to Tunisia. That night they successfully attacked a convoy of four merchant ships, sinking all of them, along with one of the destroyer escorts. They were heading back to Bône when they came under air attack when 50 miles north-east of Cap de Guarde from Ju 88 bombers. At 06.36 the *Quentin* suffered a large explosion on the starboard side, about 8ft from the after bulkhead of the engine room. The forward torpedo tubes were blown overboard, the starboard Oerlikon platform collapsed and both engine and boiler rooms started to flood. She heeled over to starboard, and it was clear that she was sinking. The *Quiberon* came alongside and took off most of the crew despite still being under attack, apart from a small number of men that managed to release a Carley float. A further attack by Ju 88s, which the British wrongly identified as being Italian aircraft, scored another hit amidships on the sinking vessel. There was a considerable explosion which threw debris over a wide area; this evidently broke her back, and she sank at about 06.40 in position 37.32N 08.32E. Twenty men were killed.
[TNA: ADM.267/94]

3 December PENYLAN escort destroyer
Barrow 1942; 1,050 tons; 264.2ft × 31.6ft; 4 × 4in, 4 × 2pdr, 3 × 20mm, 2 × torpedo tubes
Lieutenant Commander John Henry Wallace DSC
Escort to coastal convoy PW257, the ships sailed from the Solent on 2 December, being in two columns. At 03.25 the following morning shore-based radar detected the movement of small units in the channel which were approaching the convoy, but Plymouth HQ failed to pass on the warning, as they were uncertain whether the contacts were hostile. The subsequent attack by four enemy torpedo boats, about 5 miles south of Start Point took the convoy by surprise. One merchant ship of the convoy and the *Penylan* were both hit by torpedoes and quickly sank. Although five officers and 112 ratings were rescued, thirty-eight men died.
[TNA: ADM.237/172; Warship 1996 p45]

(2–4) December TRAVELLER submarine
Greenock 1941; 1,090/1,575 tons; 263ft × 26.7ft; 1 × 4in, 11 × torpedo tubes
Lieutenant Commander Drummond St Clair Ford†
As part of a planned attack by divers on the harbour of Taranto, the *Traveller* sailed from Malta 28 November to carry out a reconnaissance of the approaches to the harbour. No radio calls were ever received from her and she did not return as expected on 12 December. The date and cause of her loss is unknown but was presumed to be in one of the many minefields that

protected Taranto, probably between 2 and 4 December. Six officers and fifty-nine men were lost.
[Evans p330]

5 December Explosion and fire at Lagos, Nigeria
On the morning of 5 December, several armed trawlers were laying port side to, at number 3 jetty, Apapa Dockyard, Lagos, Nigeria. The *Bengali* was berthed inboard, with the *Spaniard* next to her and the *Canna* the outboard ship, all being secured to each other. A fourth trawler, the *Kelt*, was astern of them. All were under refit and in various stages of repair, with several locally-employed workmen onboard. Between 09.00 and 09.30 all trawlers noticed a strong smell of petrol and no smoking was ordered and galley fires were doused. At 10.25 a fire started, triggered by a large explosion of petrol vapour, at the Divisional Officer's Pier, immediately ahead of the trawlers. The fire spread very rapidly across the harbour, with flames reaching 100ft into the air and all of the trawlers were engulfed in the flames and a great grey-black mushroom cloud of smoke rose up into the sky. The outboard ship, the *Canna*, was seen to break free and settle slightly by the stern before there was a terrific explosion, about 5 minutes after the initial outbreak of the fire, when the heat 'cooked' the depth charges on some, or all, of the trawlers. The blast caused tremendous damage to the surrounding buildings, and three of the trawlers disappeared. The *Kelt* had her bows wrecked and her foredeck collapsed, but the blast effectively put out the worst of the flames, which enabled a small party led by Sub-Lieutenant Fowler to return on board to remove the primers of the depth charges. A tug now closed the scene and successfully extinguished the last of the flames on board *Kelt* and she survived. In addition to the three trawlers, seven dockyard craft were damaged and there was extensive damage to warehouses and offices. The remains of the trawlers were found to have shattered sterns, consistent with the explosion of the depth charges. It is unsure exactly how many people died, but the official count placed it at 101, with sixty-eight of those being dockyard workers and the rest on board the trawlers. An investigation ascertained that the cause of the disaster was a spillage from the oil tanker *Athelvictor*. She had been berthed about 400 yards from the trawlers at the oil storage berth and had been discharging her cargo. Her load of aviation spirit and gas oil had been discharged, and at 09.00 she prepared to commence pumping benzene ashore. However, it was soon realised that something was amiss, as the fuel could be seen to be escaping from the tanker into the sea. It was found that valves used to admit water ballast and to flush pipelines for cleaning had not been closed after her last discharge. Consequently about 60 tons of benzene had spilled into the harbour. After the war, the Admiralty

successfully brought a claim for compensation for the loss of the trawlers, winning £173,583 plus costs from Elder Dempster Lines.
[TNA: ADM.1/21671]

BENGALI trawler
Middlesbrough 1937 purchased 1939; 455 tons;
164ft × 27.1ft; 1 × 4in
Lieutenant Reginald Frederick Pembury RNR
Three ratings were killed, two of them local Kroomen.

CANNA trawler
Selby 1940; 545 tons; 150ft × 27.8ft; 1 × 12pdr, 3 × 20mm
Lieutenant Wilfred Noel Bishop-Laggett RNR
Fourteen men on board were killed, two of them local Kroomen.

SPANIARD trawler
Middlesbrough 1937, purchased 1939; 455 tons;
164ft × 27.1ft; 1 × 4in
Lieutenant Joseph Davison Love RNR
Three men died on board, one of them a local Krooman.

★ ★ ★

9 December PORCUPINE destroyer
Newcastle 1941; 1,540 tons; 338.5ft × 35ft; 4 × 4.7in,
8 × 20mm, 8 × torpedo tubes
Commander George Scott Stewart RAN
On passage from Gibraltar to Oran, acting as part of the escort screen to the depot ship *Maidstone* and two troopships. At 23.30, in position 36.40N 00.04E, there was an explosion on the port side by the after bulkhead to the engine room. This blew a large hole in the side, distorted plating and caused considerable internal damage. The forward torpedo tubes were blown overboard, and all power failed as the engine room, gearing rooms and after fuel tanks flooded and the ship heeled over to port. Non-essential personnel were transferred to the destroyer *Vanoc*, and a tow was rigged with the frigate *Exe*. The next day, after transferring the tow to a tug, she was taken into Arzeu, Algeria. After some temporary repairs, she was moved to Oran, and written off as a constructive total loss. The ship was then cut into two, and later both halves were towed back to Portsmouth where, in 1944, they were stationed in Stokes Bay, to act as accommodation hulks for landing craft crews. The remains were finally scrapped in 1946. Seven men were lost. Her attacker had been *U 602* (Schüler), who had targeted the *Maidstone*.
[TNA: ADM.267/43; CB.4273 p220]

9 December MARIGOLD corvette
Aberdeen 1940; 940 tons; 190ft × 33ft; 1 × 4in, 1 × 2pdr
Lieutenant James Alexander Smith Halcrow RNR[†]
Part of the escort to Convoy MKS3Y that had sailed on 6 December from Philippeville for the UK, she took station on the starboard bow of the convoy. During 9 December they were 5 miles to the north of Cap Caxine, the weather being cloudy with rain threatening. At 15.15 a group of Italian SM 79 bombers appeared from the low cloud in line abreast. One of them broke away to fly directly towards *Marigold*, to release a torpedo from close range. When the aircraft were first seen full speed had been ordered and alarms sounded, but she was unable to avoid the torpedo which struck her forward. The explosion blew the 4in gun overboard, wrecked the fore part of the ship and the mast collapsed over the bridge. The ship remained stable and upright for several minutes after the blast, but it was clear that she was sinking, and she was ordered to be abandoned. Carley floats were released but the ship then lurched to port, hung at an angle of 45 degrees for about 5 minutes then sank bows first. As she disappeared there was another explosion, presumed to be a depth charge exploding. Forty men lost their lives.
[TNA: ADM.199/172]

11 December BLEAN escort destroyer
Hebburn 1942; 1,050 tons; 264.2ft × 31.6ft; 4 × 4in,
4 × 2pdr, 3 × 20mm, 2 × torpedo tubes
Lieutenant Norman John Parker
Part of the escort to Convoy MK4, bound for the Clyde, she sailed from Algiers on 10 December, to accompany them to Gibraltar. At 16.30 the following day, then being about 11 miles to the west of Oran, in position 35.55N, 01.50W the convoy was attacked by the submarine *U 443* (Puttkamer). The *Blean* was hit twice on the starboard side by torpedoes, about 2 minutes apart. The first hit near the stern whilst the second struck amidships. She was covered in smoke before rolling over to port and sinking by the stern, the bows rising clear of the water. Eighty-seven officers and ratings were picked up by the destroyer *Wishart*, as were four RAF sergeant pilots who were taking passage, but eighty-nine men died.
[TNA: ADM.199/163; ADM.199/662]

12 December P 222 submarine
Barrow 1941; 715/990 tons; 201ft × 23.9ft; 1 × 3in,
6 × torpedo tubes
Lieutenant Commander Alexander James Mackenzie[†]
The submarine sailed from Gibraltar 30 November to conduct a patrol near Naples. She was in radio contact on 7 December but was not heard from again, being posted as missing when she failed to arrive at Algiers as expected on 21 December. The most likely cause of her loss was

from an attack on 12 December. On 17.34 on that day the destroyer *Fortunale*, part of the escort to a small convoy bound for Tunis from Naples, then being about 3 miles to the west of Capri, sighted a submarine surfacing about 3,500 yards away on the port bow, silhouetted against the dusk. The destroyer immediately ordered the convoy to turn away, whilst it closed the submarine, which dived as they approached. The *Fortunale* rapidly gained a sonar contact and carried out four attacks, dropping thirty-one depth charges. After the third attack, several large bubbles of air burst on the surface, and after the last run the sonar contact was lost. It is reasonably certain that this must have been *P 222*. Forty-seven men were lost.

[Evans pp331–2]

16 December **FIREDRAKE** destroyer
Walker 1934; 1,405 tons; 318.3ft × 33.3ft; 3 × 4.7in, 1 × 12pdr, 2 × 20mm, 4 × torpedo tubes
Commander Eric Henry Tilden DSC[†]
The destroyer sailed from Moville on 12 December, in company with the *Chesterfield*, *Pink* and *Snowflake* to join Convoy ON153 on its passage across the Atlantic. The presence of enemy submarines was clear from the intercept of radio transmissions (HF/DF) made during the night of 14/15 December and during 16 December the convoy twice came under attack. That evening the *Firedrake* took station of the starboard side of the convoy, about 4 miles from the outside column of merchant ships. At 22.10 she was hit by a torpedo fired by *U 211* (Hause), which exploded amidships, near number 1 boiler room. The ship rolled over to starboard, slowly righted herself and then broke in half, the whole process taking less than a minute. The bows floated vertically, about 20ft showing above the water, the larger stern section remained afloat on an even keel. The bows sank after about 30 minutes. The sea was rough, with a heavy swell, regularly breaking over the wreck, but the survivors busied themselves preparing the floats for release, and ditching torpedoes and depth charges overboard. It became clear that the attack had gone unnoticed by the rest of the convoy, so at 22.35 a star shell was fired from 'Q' gun to attract attention, but it was not until 00.15 that the corvette *Sunflower* was seen ahead. By now the wreck was settling and 30 minutes later the forward bulkhead collapsed, and she started to sink. The *Sunflower* picked up twenty-six survivors. One hundred and seventy-one men died.

[TNA:ADM.199/165]

18 December **PARTRIDGE** destroyer
Govan 1941; 1,640 tons; 328.9ft × 35ft; 5 × 4in, 4 × 2pdr, 4 × 20mm, 4 × torpedo tubes
Lieutenant Commander William Alan Frank Hawkins DSO
In company with three other destroyers, the *Partridge* was carrying out an anti-submarine sweep to the west of Oran, the ships forming up into line abreast, with the *Partridge* being the starboard wing ship. No contact had been made when at 08.06 in position 35.50N 01.35E there was a large explosion on the port side abreast the engine room as she was hit by a torpedo. She was swathed in a cloud of thick smoke and there was immediate flooding of the engine and gearing rooms. The stern of the ship listed to port and then broke away as the ship broke in two. The after part remained upright but quickly started to sink; the forward part listed to starboard then rose up until the bows were vertical and finally fell over backwards, almost touching the stern as it rose clear before sinking. Thirty-seven men were killed or died later of their wounds. Her attacker had been *U 565* (Franken).

[TNA:ADM.267/94]

18 December **MTB 30** motor torpedo boat
Gosport 1940; 34 tons; 70ft × 16.4ft; 2 × torpedo tubes
Lieutenant Anthony George Halstead RNVR
In company with two other torpedo boats, she sailed from Felixstowe to carry out a night patrol off the Dutch coast. They were still well clear of their objective when there was a flash under the bows of *MTB 30* as she detonated a mine. The fore part of the boat was blown off as far back as the wheelhouse, throwing the men on the bridge into the water. The other boats promptly altered course to close the wreck, finding the stern portion still afloat. After removing all the survivors an attempt was made to take the remains in tow, but this failed as the wreck steadily settled and finally sank. Four men were killed instantly and a fifth died of his injuries later.

[Dickens pp148–9]

19 December **SNAPDRAGON** corvette
Renfrew 1940; 940 tons; 190ft × 33ft; 1 × 4in, 1 × 2pdr
Commander Hugh Crofton Simms DSO[†]
Sailed from Benghazi with a small coastal convoy at 18.30 and took station ahead of the body of ships. They were about 6 miles off the port when at 20.00 anti-aircraft fire was observed over Benghazi indicating enemy air activity and soon after the noise of aircraft overhead could be heard, but nothing was seen. At 20.05 a stick of four bombs exploded around her. One burst about 30 yards off the port quarter, another two close to the port side, holing the fuel tanks whilst the fourth detonated close to the bridge causing considerable damage to the amidships section. She immediately took a 15-degree list to port and started to go down by the head, still moving forward at 7 knots. Efforts were made to locate and deal with the damage, but water was entering rapidly, and she was ordered to be abandoned, sinking 5 minutes after the attack. Twenty-three men lost their lives.

[TNA:ADM.267/121]

19 December **SOUTH SEA** trawler

Goole 1912 (*Ferriby*) requisitioned 1941; 322 tons;
140ft × 23.8ft

Lieutenant Peter Evelyn Bradley RNZR

Royal New Zealand Navy. Stationed at Wellington, she was patrolling the entrances to the harbour in company with the *Rata*, and was steering south by west, towards Point Halswell, when the steamer *Wahine* (4,436 tons) which was en-route to Lyttleton approached from her starboard beam. The pair continued to close, until the *Wahine* rammed the *South Sea* on the starboard side. The *Rata* closed and took her in tow, and a tug went alongside and attempted to stem the inrush of water with a portable pump. The efforts to save her were in vain as she steadily settled and sank about 1 mile from Point Halswell. It emerged at the Board of Inquiry, that the *South Sea* should have given way to the oncoming *Wahine*, but had failed to do so, as Lieutenant Bradley believed that he could pass clear. On realising that *South Sea* was not giving way as expected, the *Wahine* had put engines astern and the helm over, but this had not prevented the collision.

[*http://nzetc.victoria.ac.nz/tm/scholarly/tei-WH2Navy-c18.html*]

25 December **P 48** submarine

Barrow 1942; 540/730 tons; 180ft × 16ft; 1 × 12pdr;
4 × torpedo tubes

Lieutenant Michael Elliot Faber[†]

P 48 sailed for a patrol off the coast of Tunisia from Malta on 21 December. At 11.20 on Christmas Day, 16 miles north-west of Zembra Island the Italian destroyer *Ardente*, part of an escort to a small convoy, gained a sonar contact at a range of 2,600 yards. The destroyer ran over the contact and dropped twelve depth charges, turned, regained contact and carried out a second attack, again launching twelve depth charges. The *Ardente* then closed the position, but then stopped to allow the water to calm. During this time sonar contact was held, and oil could be seen coming to the surface in position 37.17N 10.32E. After 15 minutes a third attack was made after which several large air bubbles and a quantity of oil came to the surface. A fourth and final attack was carried out after which the *Ardente* rejoined her convoy. It is believed that the target must have been *P 48*. Four officers and thirty ratings died.

[*Evans pp332–3*]

26 December **BRØDRENE** harbour tender

1922 requisitioned 1942; 42ft

A small Norwegian fishing vessel that had escaped from Lofotodden in April 1942 to Iceland, where she was subsequently employed locally as a harbour tender. She foundered after being in collision at Hvalfjord.

[*Statement of Losses p24; http://www.warsailors.com/ shetlandbus/boatsb.html*]

28 December **ST ISSEY** tug

Old Kilpatrick 1918; 860 tons; 135.3ft × 29ft; 1 × 12pdr

Lieutenant John Henry West Howe[†]

Towing two lighters from Alexandria to Benghazi, at 06.10 in position 32.37N 20.22E she suddenly blew up with no warning. No torpedo tracks were seen, and no Asdic contact had been made by her escort, the trawler *Kingston Crystal*. A subsequent search of the area by the *Seaham* and *ML 348* failed to find any survivors; all thirty-six men onboard being lost. Her attacker had been the submarine *U.617* (Brandi).

[*TNA: ADM.199/649*]

30 December **FIDELITY** special service

Garston 1920 (*Rhin*) requisitioned 1940; 2,456 tons;
264.9ft × 41.3ft; 3 × 4in, 4 × torpedo tubes

Commander 'Jacques Langlais' (*real name* Claude André Michel Peri)

The *Fidelity* was an oddment in the Royal Navy; originally a French merchant ship, she had been sailed from Marseilles by Claude Peri – also known as Claude Costa – and taken to Gibraltar to be handed over to the British. Peri and several others who had accompanied him were given new identities and commissions in the Royal Navy, being allowed to continue to serve onboard. The ship was armed, equipped with a seaplane, two landing craft and a torpedo boat and employed during 1941 by the Special Operations Executive (SOE) in various covert operations, landing agents and picking up evaders. During 1942 she was further refitted, and ordered to the Far East, with a detachment of fifty-one Royal Marine Commando embarked. For the first leg of the voyage, she joined Convoy ON(S)154, which departed from Liverpool on 18 December. During 28 December, her main engine suffered a breakdown and she fell behind the convoy, and eventually stopped at 18.00 in position 42.45N 28.50W. She managed to get underway again the next morning, but again suffered a breakdown, and was ordered to proceed to Gibraltar for repairs when she could get underway. Whilst stopped, the aircraft was launched, and the torpedo boat put into the water, to conduct local patrols. The aircraft spotted crowded life rafts, and the landing craft were put into the water and successfully rescued forty-four men from the torpedoed *Empire Shackleton*. At 15.30 the *Fidelity*, having again repaired her engines, hoisted in the seaplane and landing craft, and got underway at 5 knots, the torpedo boat following behind. That night she was twice attacked by submarines, the *U 615* (Kapitzky) and *U 225* (Leimkühler) both fired torpedoes, but both missed. The *Fidelity* had responded to one of the attacks by dropping depth charges. She continued to slowly steam to the north-east, leaving her torpedo boat far astern of her and

was last heard from at 11.30 on the morning of 30 December, after which she disappeared. After the war it was found that she had been attacked for a third time by a submarine, this time successfully, when *U 435* (Strelow) torpedoed her at 16.38 that afternoon in position 43.23N 27.07W, one torpedo hitting under the bridge the second forward, and heard a third, large detonation a few minutes later. Although Strelow saw several survivors in life rafts both immediately after the sinking, and again the following morning, no one survived the sinking, although the torpedo boat crew survived (see entry for *MTB 105* later) and two of her aircrew had earlier been recovered by a Canadian destroyer following an accident. The two landing craft, *LCV 752* and *LCV 754*, both went down with her. In all 364 men died – 284 of the crew, 50 Royal Marines and the 44 survivors of the *Empire Shackleton*.
[TNA: ADM.199/837]

31 December **BRAMBLE** minesweeper
Devonport 1938; 815 tons; 230ft × 33.6ft; 2 × 4in, 2 × 20mm
Commander Henry Thew Rust DSO†
As part of the escort to the Russia-bound Convoy JW51B she sailed from Loch Ewe on 22 December. The weather was poor and worsened, with a Force 10 storm affecting the convoy on 26/27 December, with five merchant ships and two of the escorts losing touch. During the 29th some of the missing ships rejoined, and the *Bramble* was detached to search for the stragglers. The convoy had been shadowed since Christmas Day by the submarine *U 354*, and the long Arctic nights offered a good opportunity for an attack by surface units. On 30 December, the 'pocket battleship' *Lützow* and heavy cruiser *Admiral Hipper* accompanied by six destroyers sailed from their bases in northern Norway to head north-west for the convoy. As they approached, they divided into two groups, each of a major ship and three destroyers and they gained distant sight of the convoy at 07.15 on 31 December. *Bramble* by this time was about 30 miles astern and closing. At 10.43 she broke radio silence to report sighting a cruiser, but this message was only picked up by the corvette *Hyderabad*. This was the *Admiral Hipper*, which was manoeuvring to avoid what they had thought may have been a torpedo attack by British destroyers screening the convoy. The *Hipper* opened fire on the minesweeper and immediately gained hits, bringing her to a halt, the minesweeper responding with return fire. The cruiser then left her, to swing south to close the convoy, the destroyer *Friedrich Eckholdt* closing to finish her off. There were no survivors, eight officers and 113 ratings being killed.
[TNA: ADM.199/73]

31 December **ACHATES** destroyer
Clydebank 1929; 1,350 tons; 312ft × 32.3ft; 4 × 4.7in, 1 × 12pdr, 4 × 20mm, 4 × torpedo tubes
Lieutenant Commander Arthur Henry Tyndall Johns†
Another of the escorts to Convoy JW51B (see *Bramble* above), being stationed astern of the main body. As the attack from the German surface units developed, the senior officer, Commander Sherbrooke in the destroyer *Onslow*, took another three 'O' class destroyers to close the threat, placing himself between the convoy and the enemy. The *Achates* was tasked to start laying a smokescreen across the convoy, which altered away to the south-east. The *Admiral Hipper* initially believed that Sherbrooke was conducting a torpedo attack and altered away, but then swung back and engaged the destroyers, hitting and severely damaging the *Onslow*. As the *Achates* continued to close, the cruiser shifted target to her, just as she was clearing her own smokescreen to join *Onslow*. She was straddled after a few minutes with one near miss on the port side forward riddling the hull with innumerable small holes. The forward messdecks started to flood, but this was contained by pumping and securing and shoring bulkheads. At 11.15 she received a direct hit on the bridge, killing or wounding all the personnel, including Lieutenant Commander Johns, and starting a fire. 'B' gun's crew had been killed, and a cordite fire started, but this was put out by seas washing over the bows. The ship was straddled twice more, resulting in one hit on the port side, and a near miss abreast number 2 boiler room. These caused more flooding, and she developed a 15-degree list to port, and was difficult to steer, but the ship continued to lay smoke and return fire whilst damage control parties worked to stem the inrush of water from the numerous holes in the hull. They were still under fire from the *Hipper* and being peppered with shrapnel from shells exploding around her. She steadily lost steam and settled by the head, with the list slowly increasing. She finally requested assistance, and the trawler *Northern Gem* closed, and initially it was hoped that the destroyer could be towed, but it soon became clear that this could not be done. At 13.00 with her upper deck awash, the bows under water and with the list increasing, the trawler ran alongside to lift off the men, just as she rolled over onto her beam ends, and then capsized to float bottom up. She floated in this position for some minutes before her stern rose until it was vertical and then sank, her depth charges exploding as she did. The *Northern Gem* worked hard to pick up as many of the men from the freezing water and rescued eighty-one men, but 113 men were lost. The actions of the destroyers were not in vain. No ships of the convoy were lost, and the resistance had allowed the cruisers *Sheffield* and *Jamaica* to close, to sink one German destroyer and drive off the German

cruisers with damage. The First Lieutenant, Loftus Peyton-Jones, who had assumed command on the death of his commanding officer, was subsequently awarded the DSC for his gallantry in continuing the action.

[TNA: ADM. 267/107; Woodman pp321–4]

December LCT (5) 2054 / 2312 landing craft, tank
2054 – Kansas City (LCT 54) / 2312 – Omaha (LCT 312): 143 tons; 112.3ft × 32.9ft

In the *Statement of Losses* listed as being lost in transit from the USA during December, but with no further detail, presumably as part of a merchant vessels deck cargo.

[Statement of Losses p51]

1943

1 January MTB 105 motor torpedo boat
Hampton 1940; 9 tons; 46ft × 10.6ft
Lieutenant John Henry O'Neill

Carried as part of the armament of the special service vessel *Fidelity* (see 30 December 1942 above) she was put into the water on the evening of 28 December to carry out a local patrol whilst the ship was stopped with engine defects, but the main engine, a Rolls Royce Merlin, would not start due to defective carburettors. However, the auxiliary V8 engine was working and after embarking six depth charges and some provisions, started to patrol around the ship. At 15.30 on 29 December the *Fidelity* was able to get underway, and steered to the north-east at 5 knots, instructing the torpedo boat to follow. That night the ship came under submarine attack; the torpedo boat observing one of the attackers come to the surface about 600 yards away but could do little before it submerged. At 23.00 she lost sight of her parent ship in the dark and did not see her again. The following morning, she heard a faint radio message from her at 09.00, and they rigged a sea anchor, to hold them in position, hoping that the *Fidelity* would return, but as she failed to materialise during the day, it was clear that they were on their own. Lieutenant O'Neill therefore decided that they would have to make their own way to land, and with a makeshift sail rigged steered to the north-east, intending to try and make England(!) On 1 January at 11.15 they were sighted by the Canadian corvette *Woodstock* who took off the eight members of the crew. An attempt was made to tow the boat, but this proved impossible, the tow parting and the boat being swamped, so at 15.30 the corvette sank her with gunfire, in position 43.46N 28.26W.

[TNA: ADM. 199/837]

1/2 January P 311 submarine
Barrow 1942; 1,090/1,575 tons; 263ft × 26.7ft; 1 × 4in, 11 × torpedo tubes
Commander Richard Douglas Cayley DSO†

Tasked to carry two 'Chariot' manned torpedoes to attack shipping in Maddalena harbour as part of Operation 'Principal,' she sailed from Malta 28 December 1942. She was last heard from at 01.30 on 31 December, when she transmitted her position, which was 38.10N 11.30E. She failed to return to harbour as expected on 8 January, and it was presumed that she was lost in the approaches to Maddalena, very probably by mine. In 2015 her remains were found off the island of Tavolera, Sardinia, with extensive bow damage, indicative of striking a mine, probably one laid in the previous September. She would have passed through this area during 1/2 January.

[TNA: ADM.358/4191; Evans p330; https://www.uboat.net/allies/warships/ship/3506.html]

2 January ALARM minesweeper
Belfast 1942; 850 tons; 212.5ft × 35.5ft; 1 × 4in, 8 × 20mm
Lieutenant Commander Russell Patterson SANF(V)

Part of the 12th Minesweeping Flotilla that deployed to the Mediterranean to support the landings in North Africa. Whilst in the harbour at Bône (Annaba) the port came under air attack, and a bomb exploded under her stern, causing extensive shock damage and she was run into shallow water to prevent her sinking. A few days later, she suffered a direct hit, the bomb penetrating the upper deck to explode in the engine room. The ship's structure abaft the forward bulkhead of the engine was seriously damaged by the blast, and the ship was declared a constructive total loss. There were no fatalities.

[TNA: ADM 267/121; CB.4273 p308]

6 January LCT (2) 106 landing craft, tank
Wallsend 1941; 296 tons; 143ft × 30ft; 2 × 20mm
Having taken supplies of fuel, ammunition and water to troops at Benghazi, she was driven ashore in poor weather and lost.

[TNA: ADM.199/2254; http://www.bbc.co.uk/ww2peopleswar/stories/68/a1156268.shtml]

6 January LCT (2) 107 landing craft, tank
Wallsend 1941; 296 tons; 143ft × 30ft; 2 × 20mm
With her sister *106*, she was also driven ashore in poor weather after unloading supplies at Benghazi.

[TNA: ADM.199/2254]

7 January HORATIO trawler
Beverley 1940; 545 tons; 150ft × 27.9ft; 1 × 12pdr;
3 × 20mm
Lieutenant Charles Alfred Lemkey RNR†
Based at Bône, Algeria (modern Annaba), in North
Africa, she was ordered to carry out a patrol off Cape
de Garde and was last seen on 6 January at 17.45 to
the north of the Cape. That night radio traffic was
intercepted from German torpedo boats which had
detected a surface contact at 01.00 and then carried out
an attack, reporting a direct hit at 01.12. The Germans
managed to pick up two survivors from the *Horatio*,
but thirty-one men died. It later emerged that there
had been confusion over which patrol line she was
on. Although initially ordered to carry out a patrol to
seaward, because of the suspected presence of enemy
surface craft, she should have been warned and ordered
to shift her patrol line to the south, but this was never
done. The enemy surface craft were from the S-Boot
flotilla from Bizerte, and her attacker had been *S 58*.
[TNA:ADM.199/541]

7 January JURA trawler
Ardrossan 1941; 545 tons; 150ft × 27.6ft; 1 × 12pdr;
3 × 20mm
Lieutenant Eric Havercroft RNR†
The trawler was on passage from Algiers to Philippeville
(Skikda) in company with the trawlers *Ruskholm* and
Stronsay, when in position 36.58N 03.58E the *Ruskholm*
had an Asdic contact and moments later saw a torpedo
track, but had no time to alert her consort, and at 12.04
the *Jura* was hit on the port side forward by a torpedo.
She sank by the bows very quickly. The *Stronsay* picked
up twenty survivors and returned to Algiers, whilst the
Ruskholm remained in the area vainly hunting for the
submarine. Three officers and fourteen ratings were
killed. The attacker had been *U 371* (Mehl)
[TNA:ADM.199/648]

12 January KINGSTON JACINTH trawler
Beverley 1929 requisitioned 1939; 352 tons; 140.3ft × 24ft;
1 × 4in
Skipper Reginald Walter Denny RNR
In company with another armed trawler, the *Asie*, the
pair was conducting a night patrol off Portsmouth; the
unit commanding officer Lieutenant Neville Mangnall
RNVR was also on board. The weather was poor, with
strong winds and a heavy swell. At 06.58 there was an
explosion on the port side aft as she detonated a mine.
The engines stopped, all the lights went out, the bridge
windows were shattered, and she started to settle by the
stern. Skipper Denny went aft to investigate but found
the after compartments full of water. He then went
forward to check on the forward mess deck, hailing
down the hatch but had no response. When he shone

a torch down, he could see no one and presumed that
the men were either all out or were dead. She was
clearly going down by the stern the engine room was
reported to be making water and starting to flood. With
seas washing over her the skipper ordered her to be
abandoned. The boat was cleared away and seven ratings
got in and pulled away. Skipper Denny and Lieutenant
Mangnall and one other rating then jumped into the sea
to swim to the boat. The trawler continued to slowly
sink by the stern until she disappeared, her position then
was 50.33.50N 00.37.18W. The armed trawler *Asie* had
seen the flash of the explosion and closed to investigate
but because of faulty steering gear it was nearly an hour
after the explosion that she came alongside the boat.
When Skipper Mutton of the *Asie* asked if there were
other survivors, as he thought he had also seen a Carley
float, Skipper Denny informed his rescuers that they
were the only survivors. No further search was therefore
conducted. At 11.00 on 17 January off Newhaven,
Royal Air Force launch *HSL2548* spotted a Carley
float and on investigation found the bodies of six men.
They were identified as some of the missing men from
the *Kingston Jacinth*, who had died of exposure. As the
Carley float had not been launched before the survivors
left the sinking ship, it was presumed that the men must
have been below, and on coming on deck discovered
that the others had already abandoned her, and so used
the float to escape. This led to both Skipper Denny
and Lieutenant Mangnall being court-martialled for
negligence; Denny was charged with failing to use every
effort to ascertain the fate of those men who had been
below decks and Mangnall in failing to order a search
after being picked up. Both were found guilty. Skipper
Denny was dismissed his ship and severely reprimanded;
Lieutenant Mangnall was severely reprimanded. A total
of twenty men lost their lives.
[TNA:ADM.178/307;ADM.156/236;ADM.156/256]

16 January FABIOUS boom defence vessel
? Requisitioned 1941; 230 tons
A former dumb barge, in the *Statement of Losses* listed as
'sunk', with no further details.
[Statement of Losses p28;TNA:ADM.1/24129]

17 January LCT (5) 2239 / 2267 / 2344 landing
craft, tank
Decatur (2239, 2344); Evansville (2267); 134 tons;
105ft × 32.8ft
All loaded as deck cargo onto the Norwegian cargo
ship *Vestfold*, which sailed from Halifax, Nova Scotia,
on 8 January to join Convoy HX222. At 16.00 in
approximate position 61.25N 26.2W, the ship was
torpedoed by *U 268* (Heydemann) and rapidly sank,
taking all three craft with her.
[http://www.warsailors.com/singleships/vestfold1.html]

22 January   PATRICIA CAM   store carrier

Brisbane NSW 1940 requisitioned 1942; 301 tons;
120.9ft × 30.3ft

Lieutenant Alexander Cecil Meldrum RANR

Royal Australian Navy. Originally fitted as a minesweeper, she was latterly employed as a general-purpose vessel, based at Darwin, and used to supply outlying settlements. En-route to Marchinbar Island, she had stores and six passengers embarked, when at 13.30 off the coast of Arnhem Land, in position 11.19S 136.23E, she was attacked by a Japanese Aichi E13A 'Jake' floatplane. Passing over the ship a single bomb landed amidships, penetrating the upper deck and exploding below. The ship sank very quickly, disappearing in less than a minute. One man was killed in the explosion. The survivors found themselves in the water surrounded by wreckage, and one raft. As they struggled in the water, the floatplane returned, strafing them with machine-gun fire and dropping another bomb, which killed three men. The aircraft then landed nearby and ordered a survivor to swim across, one of the passengers, the Reverend Leonard Kentish swimming to the plane which took him aboard and then took off. During the night, the survivors became separated, but the raft made it a small, deserted islet where they were found by local people who took Lieutenant Meldrum to Marchinbar, from where a rescue was organised. Investigations after the war found that the Reverend Kentish was killed by his Japanese captors. In total nine men died – five ratings and four passengers.

[www.navy.gov.au/hmas-patricia-cam; Cassells p50]

25 January   CORNCRAKE   trawler

Selby 1942 (Mackerel); 670 tons; 146ft × 25.3ft; 3 × 20mm,
12 mines

Lieutenant Commander Lewis Russell Renfrew RNVR†

Sailed from the Clyde on 21 January to join Convoy KMS8 for the Mediterranean, the ships encountered strong winds and high seas. Labouring in the bad weather, she fell astern of the convoy and was last heard from at 09.13 on 25 January, reporting that she was in need of urgent assistance as she was in danger of sinking, in position 55.10N 13.30W. The minesweeper *Londonderry* was detached from the convoy to go to her assistance and the Canadian corvette *Regina* was despatched from Londonderry to go to the area and an air search was conducted during daylight hours. No trace of her was found and she was assumed to have foundered with the loss of all hands due to stress of weather. Twenty-three men died.

[TNA: ADM.199/631; ADM.358/1599]

30 January   SAMPHIRE   corvette

Middlesbrough 1941; 940 tons; 190ft × 33ft; 1 × 4in,
2 × 20mm

Lieutenant Commander Frederick Thomas Renny DSC RNR†

Part of the escort to Convoy TE14 along the North African coast, the ship was zigzagging at 10 knots, stationed 5,000 yards on the starboard side of the convoy, when at 00.15 a torpedo track was seen just abaft the starboard beam. The wheel was put over, but it was too late, and the torpedo struck her amidships, exploding by the engine room. There was a second explosion under stern a minute later, believed to be another torpedo. She began to sink by the stern very quickly, and by 00.23 she had gone. Her position was 37.02N 05.30E. After carrying out an unsuccessful Asdic search of the area, the *Zetland* closed to lower her whaler to pick up four survivors. Forty-three men died. She had been attacked by the Italian submarine *Platino* (Patrell-Campagnano).

[TNA: ADM.267/115]

31 January   BLOODHOUND   trials/tender

Woolston 1937; 35 tons; 68ft × 19ft

Lieutenant Archibald Joseph Knight RNVR

Used for trials and testing of torpedoes, she was based at Bincleaves, near Weymouth. During the night of 30/31 January bad weather affected the English Channel, with a force of destroyers having to take shelter from the storm. At the height of the gale the *Bloodhound* was driven ashore at Portland and wrecked.

[TNA: ADM.199/2254]

1 February   WELSHMAN   minelayer

Hebburn 1940; 2,650 tons; 400.6ft × 40ft; 6 × 4in, 4 × 2pdr,
156 mines

Captain William Howard Denis Friedberger DSO

Bound for Alexandria, she sailed from Malta on 31 January. At 18.42 the following day, when in position 32.12N 24.52E, zigzagging at 25 knots, there were two explosions under her stern. Both of her engines immediately stopped, the ship lost headway, with her bows swinging round to the north and she took a slight list to port. The engine room reported that they believed the port propeller had been lost, and the starboard shaft would not turn. The cause of the explosion was something of a mystery at the time; Asdic had detected hydrophone effect after the explosion, consistent with a submarine moving away, but the explosions did not seem to be violent enough for torpedoes. The ship started to slowly flood from aft, and bulkheads were shored, and when a fire broke out in a storeroom, this also had to be tackled. The boats were turned out, and although the list had slightly increased, the ship remained stable, and lighting and power had not been affected. A tow was requested, and they were informed that the escort destroyer *Tetcott*

would join her to assist. Quite suddenly, at 20.40 she lurched, heeling 30 degrees to starboard, hung for some moments, then continued to slowly roll over until she lay on her beam ends. A depth charge then went off aft, and the ship started to sink. She gave a shudder and her bows rose until they were vertical before disappearing. One hundred and sixty-five men died. The enquiry found that the stern had been damaged sufficiently to allow water to run from the storerooms aft onto the mining deck. As there was no watertight subdivision in this lengthy space, the water had been allowed a free run, resulting in a sudden loss of stability. The ship's officers had failed to appreciate the danger and should have treated the mining deck as the upper deck for the purposes of stability. Although it was uncertain at the time whether she had been mined or torpedoed, it subsequently transpired that she had been attacked by *U 617* (Brandi).
[*TNA: ADM.1/13090*]

1/2 February **LCT (3) 326** landing craft, tank
Middlesbrough 1942; 350 tons; 175ft × 31ft; 2 × 2pdr
Sub-Lieutenant William Norman Griffiths RNVR†
One of a number of landing craft that sailed from Troon on 31 January for Plymouth, being formed up into columns under the escort of the trawler *Cotillion*. As they headed south through the Irish Sea, the weather worsened, the wind picking up to Force 8. The landing craft laboured in the sea and had difficulty in maintaining their heading and several fell behind. *LCT 326* was last seen during the evening of 1 February, being missed at first light the next day, and was presumed to have foundered during the night. Fourteen men were lost. In May 2019, a team from Bangor University located the wreck to the south-west of Bardsey Island. The remains suggest that the vessel had broken in half just forward of the bridge and had probably foundered soon after she was last seen.
[*TNA: ADM.217/13; https://www.bangor.ac.uk/news/latest/discovery-of-a-ww2-landing-craft-off-wales-ends-77-year-old-mystery-43610*]

3 February **PREMIER** drifter
1914 requisitioned 1940; 14 tons
In collision at 08.35 with number 10 Holme Hook buoy off Killingholme oil jetty in the river Humber, she subsequently foundered. The collision was caused by jammed steering gear in a strong ebb tide.
[*TNA: ADM.199/778*]

5 February **STRONSAY** trawler
Glasgow 1942; 545 tons; 150ft × 27.6ft; 1 × 12pdr, 3 × 20mm
Lieutenant Stephen Crichton Dickinson RNVR
Patrolling off the port of Philippeville (modern Skikda) on the coast of Algeria, the trawler was about 2.5 miles

to the west of Île Srigina light when at 17.45 there was a large explosion under her stern. The engine room was reported to be flooding, and officer of the watch, Sub-Lieutenant Allen immediately ordered the boats to be hoisted out and prepare the Carley floats for launching. She quickly settled by the stern and it was decided to abandon her, and as motor launches *HDML 1221* and *1225* were closing, the crew took to the boats to transfer to them. Lieutenant Dickinson and a small crew remained on board and prepared for a tow. The tug *Jaunty* arrived on scene and it was with some difficulty that a tow was rigged, the stern now being awash, and all the men now left her, transferring to the tug as it started the tow. After only 5 minutes the towline parted; it was re-rigged, only to immediately part again. She then slowly drifted towards the shore, sinking steadily by the stern, until she ran aground in shallow water, decks awash, about 3.75 miles from Île Srigina. A subsequent enquiry was critical of the ship's officers; neither Dickinson nor the First Lieutenant, George Ireland Russell, had properly ascertained the condition of the ship before deciding to abandon her, and more could have been done to stem the flow of water rather than concentrate on hoisting out boats. The cause of the explosion was uncertain; it was believed that a mine was the most likely cause, and it was later ascertained that enemy torpedo boats had laid a field in the area.
[*TNA: ADM.199/243*]

6 February **LOUISBURG** corvette
Quebec 1941; 940 tons; 190ft × 33ft; 1 × 4in, 1 × 2pdr, 2 × 20mm
Lieutenant Commander William Franklin Campbell RCNVR
Royal Canadian Navy. Sailed from the River Clyde on 22 January to join the escort to Convoy KMS8 bound for North Africa. The convoy paused at Gibraltar 5/6 February, before continuing towards Bône (Annaba). They came under attack late that same afternoon, when about 60 miles north-east of Oran, by formations of German aircraft, with Ju 88s carrying out bombing attacks followed by torpedo-armed He 111s. At 19.00 an aircraft passed across the head of the columns of ships, to turn towards the corvette, dropping down to sea level as it did so, releasing a torpedo when about 700 yards from the ship. With little time to manoeuvre, the torpedo struck her on the starboard side amidships, exploding in the engine room. She immediately heeled over to port and sank stern first, within 3 minutes, her depth charges exploding as she went under. Forty-two men died.
[*McKee & Darlington p85*]

7 February TERVANI trawler

Beverley 1925 requisitioned 1939; 394 tons;
147.5ft × 25.1ft; 1 × 12pdr

Skipper Frederick George Blockwell RNR†

Tasked to tow the 762-ton water carrier *Mory-Mazout* from Algiers to Philipville (Skikda), she was escorted by three other trawlers, the *Achroite*, *Arnold Bennet* and the Free French *Petit Pierre*. At 22.20 in position 37.02N 05.55.30E she was hit on the port side aft by a submarine-fired torpedo. She heeled over to starboard and started sinking by the stern. Her escorts carried out a perfunctory search of the area for survivors before leaving the area. Twenty-two men died. The escorts also abandoned the *Mory-Mazout*, which, complete with a small crew, was left to drift away, to be found later by a convoy and towed in. All the commanding officers of the escorts were criticised for their inaction. Although not equipped with Asdic, all had passive hydrophone equipment, but it was not manned. The excuse that it would not work whilst underway was dismissed, as the group was moving at only 4 to 5 knots, a speed which did not inhibit use. The abandonment of the tow was evidently due to the failure of the senior officer of the group in *Achroite* to order anyone to stand by the *Mory-Mazout*. He believed that one of the group would have assisted her without prompting. Skipper-Lieutenant James Stewart RNR was informed that he had 'incurred their Lordships' displeasure'. Her attacker was the Italian *Platino* (Patrelli-Campagnano)
[TNA: ADM.1/15065]

7 February MGB 109 motor gun boat

Hythe 1942; 37 tons; 71.9ft × 20.7ft; 1 × 2pdr, 2 × 20mm

Lieutenant Arthur William Outen RNVR

The gunboat was about 16 miles to the east of South Foreland, when she detonated a mine, which blew away much of the bow, the 2pdr gun being blown overboard. She was soon flooded forward, but remained afloat, and she was taken in tow by *MGB 108* and *MGB 110*, later assisted by *MGB 324*. They successfully made it back to Dover, but subsequent examination judged that she was irreparable, and was formally paid off on 25 February. One rating was lost.
[TNA: ADM.199/778]

7 February LCI (L) 162 landing craft, infantry, large

Newark 1942; 234 tons; 150ft × 23.4ft; 4 × 20mm

Lieutenant Robert Henry Hanley RNVR†

In company with *LCI 7* and *LCI 210*, the three craft were en-route to Algiers from Oran. At 17.08 when in position 35.45N 00.45W, there was a large explosion amidships of *162* and when the smoke and water cleared it could be seen that she had broken in half, with the stern part on fire. The remains finally sank at about 17.45. Eighteen men were lost. At the time, the cause

of the explosion was uncertain; the water was believed to be too deep for a mine; no torpedo tracks had been observed and being unloaded her draught was thought to be too shallow for a torpedo to hit her. An internal cause was thought possible. Despite these reservations, it is probable that she was actually hit by a torpedo, as the submarine *U 596* (Jahn) reported attacking a landing craft at this time.
[TNA: ADM.199/837; http://www.uboat.net/allies/merchants/ships/2628.html]

8 February LCT (5) 2335 landing craft, tank

Decatur 1942 (*LCT 335*); 134 tons; 105ft × 32.8ft; 2 × 20mm

In transit to England, she was loaded as deck cargo onto the Norwegian steamship *Daghild* which sailed from St John's, Newfoundland, on 30 January to join convoy SC118. At 04.38 on 7 February the *Daghild* was hit by a single torpedo fired by the *U 402* (Forstner), which although abandoned by the crew, did not sink and at 02.37 on 8 February the wreck was torpedoed again, this time *U 608* (Struckmeier) after which she sank, taking *2335* with her.
[http://www.warsailors.com/singleships/daghild.html; http://www.uboat.net/allies/merchants/ships/2644.html]

8 February BREDON trawler

Beverley 1941; 750 tons; 166.3ft × 28ft; 1 × 12pdr, 3 × 20mm

Lieutenant John Reginald Fradgley RNVR†

Part of the escort to Convoy GIBR2 from West Africa to Gibraltar, she was hit by a torpedo fired by the submerged *U 521* (Bargsten) at 07.03 in position 29.55N 13.57W. She sank in a few minutes and although her sister trawler *Dunkery*, assisted by an RAF Hudson aircraft searched for survivors, only three were picked up, forty-three men being killed.
[TNA: ADM.199/637]

9 February ERICA corvette

Belfast 1940; 940 tons; 190ft × 33ft; 1 × 4in, 2 × 20mm

Lieutenant Adrian Charles Cuthbert Seligman RNR

Acting as escort to a convoy from Benghazi to Alexandria, when at 15.30, as they passed between a British laid defensive minefield and the shore, the escort *Southern Maid* reported an Asdic contact. *Erica* altered course to carry out an attack, dropping five depth charges over the reported position. When this was complete, she resumed her search of the area, and also obtained a contact, which appeared to be at the edge of the minefield. Putting her head towards the contact, she stopped her engines whilst the *Southern Maid* carried out an attack. When the noise of the explosions had died down, she recommenced her Asdic search, and gained a new contact which she closed. As she ran over the

position, ready to drop depth charges, there was a large explosion under her hull. Both boiler rooms and some forward compartments were flooded, and a fire broke out in number one boiler room and the wardroom flat. Flooding spread rapidly and she settled quickly, sinking 15 minutes after the explosion, *ML 351* picking up men from the water. One man was killed. An enquiry confirmed that she had been lost after detonating a mine in the British-laid defensive field, but it was felt that her actions were justified, as she was prosecuting a good Asdic contact.
[TNA:ADM.199/243]

13 February POZARICA auxiliary anti-aircraft ship
Sunderland 1938, purchased 1940; 1,893 tons;
295.6ft × 45ft; 6 × 4in, 8 × 2pdr, 4 × 20mm
Captain Laurence Bernard Hill DSO
On 29 January, whilst escorting Convoy TF14, she was subjected to an intensive air attack off Bougie (Béjaïa), North Africa, from He 111 and Italian SM 79 aircraft, during which she was hit by a torpedo. Fifteen men were killed. The corvette *Nasturtium* took her in tow and successfully took her into Bougie where she was run aground in shallow water. It was found that the stern was damaged, the boat deck was wrecked, and the guns blown out of the after mountings and several compartments aft were flooded. She was partly pumped clear, and it was intended that she be towed to Algiers for repairs, but on 13 February the engine room bulkhead collapsed, and she capsized and settled and was subsequently written off a constructive total loss.
[TNA:ADM.267/131]

22 February WEYBURN corvette
Port Arthur 1941; 940 tons; 190ft × 33ft; 1 × 4in, 1 × 2pdr, 2 × 20mm
Lieutenant Commander Thomas Maitland Wade Golby RCNR[†]
Royal Canadian Navy. The corvette sailed from Gibraltar 22 February to join westbound Convoys MKS8/GUS4 as part of the escort. At 10.00, then being about 5.5 miles to the north-west of Cape Spartel, the convoys started to separate. As *Weyburn* was moving up the port side of the column of ships, at 10.17 there was a large explosion under the port side amidships as she detonated a mine. The engine room was flooded, decks and plates were distorted, and she came to a halt. The destroyer *Wivern* came alongside, to take off some of the injured and preparations were made for a tow. But 20 minutes after the explosion, an after bulkhead collapsed and she rapidly flooded. The bows rose clear of the water and she quickly sank by the stern, with two of her depth charges exploding as she went under, despite having been set to safe. These explosions badly 'whipped' the *Wivern*, throwing machinery off their mounts and

causing several casualties. The *Black Swan* closed to take the *Wivern* in tow and rescue the survivors still in the water. Nine men died. The mine was part of a field laid by *U 118* on 1/2 February.
[McKee & Darlington p91]

24 February VANDAL submarine
Barrow 1942; 540/730 tons; 180ft × 16ft; 1 × 3in, 4 × torpedo tubes
Lieutenant John Stirling Bridger[†]
Newly completed, she had just completed acceptance trials and had arrived in Holy Loch on 20 February, to join the Third Submarine Flotilla. She sailed on the 23rd to conduct exercises in the local area of Kilbrannan Sound and Upper Inchmarnock, being due to return to the depot ship *Forth* by 19.00 on 24 February. She was observed lying at anchor off the village of Lochranza, on the isle of Arran, during the night of 23 February and was seen leaving the anchorage at 08.30 the next morning. After this, she disappeared. Due to an administrative oversight, it was not until the next morning that it was realised that she was missing, and a search was undertaken. The submarine *Templar*, also exercising in the area, reported that she had seen a white smoke candle about 2.5 miles north of Inchmarnock, which was believed may have been from the *Vandal*; the *Usurper* thought she had heard hull tapping in the area of More Light and a searching aircraft reported seeing a small patch of oil about 2 miles north-west of Lochranza. The submarine *Severn* checked the area, but no trace of her was found. It was presumed that she must have been lost, probably due to a diving accident. In 1995 the minehunter *Hurworth*, investigating reports of trawlers regularly snagging nets off Lochranza carried out a sonar search of the area, and revealed the image of a submarine lying on the seabed in 330ft of water. During 2003 a diving expedition to the site confirmed that it was the missing *Vandal*. Her position, not far from her overnight anchorage, would suggest that she sank soon after sailing. The divers found that the hydroplanes were in the stowed position, and this, coupled with the fact that mooring ropes were coiled up on the casing, rather than being stowed below, indicated that she must have been on the surface when disaster overtook her. The forward hatch was open, but the access ladder was not rigged, all other hatches were closed. This could suggest that some of the men in the forward compartment may have attempted to exit the submarine in a desperate attempt to escape as it foundered. If so, then it would have meant that the forward compartments were open to the sea, worsening her situation. The bows were damaged, indicating that she went down bows first. There is no obvious visual cause of her sinking, but it has been suggested that she may have been lost in the same way that her near sister *Untamed* was, some

weeks later (see 30 May), in the mishandling of the Ottway transducer, which was lowered and recovered through the bottom of the hull. This was retracted into a watertight tank, but procedural errors were not unknown, and if the tank was opened before the log was fully retracted, it would result in rapid flooding.
[TNA: ADM.1/14943; Evans pp333–4; http://www. deepimage.co.uk/wrecks/vandal/vandal_pages/vandal-mainpage.html]

24 February MTB 262 motor torpedo boat
Bayonne NJ 1940 (PT 13); 32 tons; 70ft × 20ft; 4 × torpedo tubes
Lieutenant Charles Leslie Coles RNVR
Based at Bône, Algeria (modern Annaba), in company with *MTB 95* she was sent on a mission to lay mines in the vicinity of Galite Island. However, *95* suffered an engine breakdown, so *262* continued on her own. She failed to return as expected, and an air search failed to find her. The first information as to her fate came some days later, when the Germans announced that they had captured eleven men from a motor boat adrift in the Sicilian Channel. It emerged that *262* had also suffered mechanical problems, having had a battery failure. Strenuous efforts were made to restore power, but all failed, and she drifted towards the island of Galite. It was decided that she would have to be destroyed to prevent her falling into enemy hands, and small charges were detonated to blow holes in the hull, allowing her to steadily settle. At the same time the depth charges were set to explode at 20ft, and the crew took to two small boats. Almost immediately after leaving her, it became clear that this had been a mistake, as the boats were tossed and thrown around in the high seas, and one sank. The decision was made to re-board her, and it was with difficulty that some did achieve this. There were others who were still struggling in the water, and failed to regain the boat, three men being swept away and drowned. The survivors managed to disarm the depth charges and the holes in the hull were blocked, and work started on bailing and pumping, but she was still low in the water. During the morning, a German aircraft flew low over the boat, and as it was feared that this would result in an air attack, and she was being taken further into the island, and was barely afloat, she was again abandoned, the survivors roping themselves together as they entered the water. They spent some time in the water before a fishing boat from the island spotted them and picked them up, although another two of the men had died in the water.
[TNA: ADM.199/541; Reynold & Cooper, Mediterranean MTBs at War pp59–60]

24 February LCT (3) 403 landing craft, tank
Meadowside 1942; 350 tons; 175ft × 31ft; 2 × 2pdr
Foundered due to stress of weather off Barra Head, whilst under tow of the tug *Freebooter*, the holds being flooded.
[TNA: ADM.1/15024]

27 February TIGRIS submarine
Chatham 1939; 1,090/1,575 tons; 265.6ft × 26.7ft; 1 × 4in, 10 × torpedo tubes
Lieutenant Commander George Robson Colvin DSO DSC†
Based in the Mediterranean, she sailed from Malta 18 February, to conduct a patrol in the Gulf of Naples. At 10.50 on 27 February a group of German anti-submarine trawlers en-route to Naples was 6 miles south-east of the island of Capri, when one of them, escort vessel *Uj 2201* gained a sonar contact. The contact was investigated by *Uj 2210*, which also gained a good contact, and closed to run over the datum at 11.14 to drop five depth charges. After waiting for the water to settle, at 11.35 she again prosecuted the contact, dropping a further batch of charges, after which several large air bubbles came to the surface and some oil. *Uj 2210* again waited for the water to settle, re-gained contact and ran in for a third attack, which brought up more air and oil to the surface. The fourth and final attack was carried out at 12.35, after which a huge quantity of air burst to the surface, along with some more oil and debris. Satisfied that she had disposed of the threat, *Uj 2210* rejoined her companions. It is believed that this attack was on the *Tigris*. Five officers and fifty-seven ratings died.
[Evans pp334–5; https://www.uboat.net/allies/warships/ ship/3492.html]

27 February LORD HAILSHAM trawler
Selby 1934, purchased 1940; 445 tons; 155.8ft × 26.1ft; 1 × 4in, 2 × 20mm
Lieutenant Peter Horace Gordon Clark RNVR
Part of an escort to Convoy WP300 through the English Channel, being stationed on the starboard quarter of the ships, abeam the steamship *Modavia*. At 20.00 as they approached Lyme Bay, the ship went to action stations, being aware of the threat of surface attack by enemy fast torpedo boats. At 01.10 a signal was received from shore that there were indications of torpedo-boat activity in the Channel, and just 5 minutes later the *Modavia* was hit by a torpedo. The helm was put over, and the trawler steered seawards, and almost immediately the Asdic operator reported HE (hydrophone effect) indicating a high speed craft on the starboard bow. Course was altered to put this right on the bow and star shell was ordered to be fired. As this burst, it revealed the shapes of two torpedo boats, which were crossing her bows.

Both of the craft immediately reacted by turning towards her and firing torpedoes. Two tracks were seen, the first of which passed astern, but the second hit the starboard bow abreast the foremast. The blast blew the 4in gun crew overboard, the ship heeled over and the mast collapsed over an Oerlikon gun. She continued to heel over and with the engine room reporting that it was filling fast, she was clearly sinking. Carley floats were released, and she was abandoned, sinking in less than 4 minutes. She was then about 23 miles to the east of Berry Head. The survivors were picked up by two motor launches 3 hours later, but eighteen men were lost. The attackers had been from the Fifth S-boot Flotilla.
[TNA: ADM.1/14345]

27 February   LCT (3) 381   landing craft, tank
Middlesbrough 1941; 350 tons; 175ft × 31ft; 2 × 2pdr
Lieutenant John Walter Casson RNVR
Part of the convoy that was attacked by enemy torpedo boats as they crossed Lyme Bay (see above), she was stationed in the column astern of the *Modavia*. The first indication they had of enemy activity was when that ship was hit by a torpedo. Very soon after this *381* was also hit and immediately began to sink. With her engines stopped she drifted clear of the convoy and an enemy torpedo boat ran alongside to lift off the crew, taking them prisoner. This complete, their captors fired a second torpedo into the landing craft to ensure that she sank. One man was killed when the first torpedo hit.
[TNA: ADM.199/2422]

28 February   MGB 79   motor gun boat
Hythe 1942; 37 tons; 71.9ft × 20.7ft; 1 × 2pdr, 2 × 20mm
Lieutenant David Pelham James RNVR
In company with four torpedo boats, *MGB 79* was one of a group of four gunboats ordered to conduct a joint night patrol in the southern North Sea, intending to intercept an enemy convoy of southbound merchantmen off the Dutch coast. At 03.00 they were in position and stopped. About 20 minutes later the shapes of approaching ships could be made out ahead and orders were given to start engines. All the torpedo boats closed up and steered to the north-west, but *79*, that should have fallen in astern, swung round to port to head south-east. Lieutenant James had actually spotted a small merchant ship and acting on his own initiative decided to engage. As he swung round to close, he came under heavy fire from the escort to the ship and the boat was hit on the port side. He continued to close, his guns registering hits on the merchant ship before the 2pdr jammed. The earlier hit had punctured the fuel tanks, and as the boat closed to within point-blank range, the tanks exploded, and the engines stopped. The engine room was filled with smoke, the stern was on fire and

several of the crew, including James were wounded at this time when they were raked by enemy fire. Despite this, James manned the 20mm Oerlikon and continued to fire at the enemy as they drifted clear. Meanwhile the main units had attempted to engage the other enemy ships, but never got into position to fire torpedoes, and were forced to withdraw. Seeing the tracer fire astern they steered towards, seeing the explosion and flames as they neared, realised that it must be *79*. Closing the burning wreck, they stopped to pick up the survivors who were now jumping into the water, with enemy patrol boats holding fire, apparently uncertain of the identity of the boats in the confusion and darkness. When it was realised that they were British, a fierce fire was opened, at which the torpedo boats were forced to withdraw. Lieutenant James was seen in the water just as this happened, and a heaving line thrown to him, but as the speed increased, he was forced to let go. He survived and was picked up by the Germans. Three men were lost.
[TNA: ADM.199/541; ADM.199/778; Scott p129; Hichens pp315–21]

2 March   UT PROSIM   drifter
Lowestoft 1925 requisitioned 1939; 91 tons;
82.6ft × 19.5ft; 1 × 3pdr
Skipper Arthur William Peak RNR
Based at Dover, she was lying at the Prince of Wales pier, at 2 hours' notice for steam. Several of the crew were ashore on liberty, the rest were all below on the mess deck. At 21.30 the port came under long-range shellfire from the French coast, and after 30 minutes there was a shock as a large-calibre shell exploded next to her. The ship lurched to starboard, then heeled over to port, water flooding into the forward compartments as the lights went out. The skipper ordered her to be abandoned, and by the time they had arrived on the upper deck the port gunwale was already awash. She foundered soon after. One man lost his life. It was believed that the shell exploded at the waterline, between the ship and the pier.
[TNA: ADM.199/778]

(3–18) March   TURBULENT   submarine
Barrow 1941; 1,090/1,575 tons; 263ft × 26.7ft; 1 × 4in,
11 × torpedo tubes
Commander John Wallace Linton DSO DSC†
Sailed from Algiers on 24 February for a patrol off the western coast of Italy, she was posted missing when she failed to return on 23 March. The cause and date of her loss is uncertain. She attacked a convoy on 1 March, sinking a steamer, and was probably responsible for an attack during 3 March off Milazzo, Sicily, which is the last positive contact known – some sources cite an attack and sightings on 11/12 March, but these seem to relate

to the submarine *Casabianca*. She failed to respond to radio calls on the 19th or 20th, which suggests that she was lost before then and after 3 March. She was expected to move to the coast of Sardinia during this time, and it is possible that she was lost by striking a mine. A distinct possibility is an attack by the escort *Ardito* on 6 March, 34 miles to the west of Punta Licosa. Investigating the report from an aircraft of a submarine, a sonar contact was gained, and two patterns of depth charges was dropped, but with no obvious result, and no further contact was gained. Six officers and sixty-one men were lost. Commander Linton was one of the most experienced of British submarine commanders, having conducted twenty-one war patrols, and had been responsible for sinking thirty enemy vessels. He was posthumously awarded the Victoria Cross in May 1943.

[Evans pp337–40]

6 March ML 251 motor launch

Looe 1941; 85 tons; 112ft × 18.4ft; 1 × 3pdr
Lieutenant Ernest Edward Lever RNVR

Stationed at Freetown, Sierra Leone, during 5 March the launch was ordered to patrol the approaches to the harbour during the day, and by late evening she was heading back to the port. As she did so, the corvettes *Burdock* and *Thyme* got underway from the harbour to escort a merchant ship clear of the coast. By 23.00 they were fast approaching each other. At 23.10 the *Burdock* obtained an Asdic contact and spent some time searching the area, leaving the *Thyme* and the merchant ship to continue. Having lost her contact, *Burdock* resumed her course to rejoin. At just before midnight the motor launch sighted a darkened ship on her port bow, and using a small signal lamp, flashed the night challenge, but received no response. Meanwhile on the *Burdock* a small radar contact was obtained ahead, and Asdic reported hydrophone effect (HE) from a small engine. The commanding officer of the *Burdock*, fresh from a frustrated hunt for a submarine, assessed that this contact must be his quarry and increased his ships speed and altered course towards the contact. *ML 251* managed to pass ahead of the oncoming corvette and passed down her port side, at about 700 yards, now flashing 'What ship?' to the stranger, before altering around to parallel the course of the corvette which had turned on navigation lights, a pre-arranged signal to *Thyme*, that they were making an attack. Meanwhile, the signals staff on the *Burdock* had replied to the flashing signals from the launch, and identified themselves, but they had scarcely done so when the corvette, with accurate timing, went to port and deliberately rammed the launch, which broke up and sank quickly. The commanding officer of *Burdock* took most of the blame; he had convinced himself that he was dealing

with a U-boat and failed to appreciate the implications of his 'target' signalling. The shore authorities were also blameable, as they had failed to inform the corvettes of the presence of the patrolling launch. There were no casualties.

[TNA: ADM.199/837]

8 March LCT (5) 2480 landing craft, tank

Camden 1942 (*LCT 480*); 134 tons; 105ft × 32.8ft; 2 × 20mm

The landing craft was loaded as deck cargo onto the cargo ship *Fort Lamy* for transfer to the UK, which sailed from New York 23 February to join Convoy SC121. She straggled from the convoy and at 18.23 was torpedoed and sunk by *U 527* (Uhlig) in approximate position 58.30N 31W.

[http://www.uboat.net/allies/merchants/shiphtml?shipID=2731]

10 March MTB 622 motor torpedo boat

Lowestoft 1942; 95 tons; 115ft × 21.3ft; 1 × 2pdr, 3 × 20mm, 2 × torpedo tubes
Lieutenant Francis William Carr RNVR

In company with other boats of the 31st MTB Flotilla, *622* sailed from Great Yarmouth for a patrol off the coast of Holland, a reconnaissance aircraft having reported a convoy assembling to the north of Wangeroog. At 23.00 a group of armed vessels was sighted and presumed to be the escort for the convoy. It was actually an independent group of patrolling armed trawlers, and a brief but sharp action ensued until they disengaged, and as a result the torpedo boats became separated, only *622* and *624* being able to join up subsequently. The pair continued the search for the convoy and with the aid of a co-operative aircraft, made contact at 01.16. The convoy consisted of eight ships with a strong escort of minesweepers and armed trawlers. The torpedo boats attacked from the port side of the convoy, firing torpedoes and then, making smoke, breaking off. The pair were now under heavy fire and at 01.50 *MTB 622* was hit by a large-calibre shell which disabled her. She now became the target of concentrated fire from the escorts, and was abandoned, the boat then being ablaze. Fifteen men were lost, the survivors being picked up by *Vp 1300*.

[TNA ADM.199/537; Reynolds, Dog Boats pp23–4; Warship 1996 p139]

10 March LCT (5) 2341 landing craft, tank

Decatur 1942; 134 tons; 105ft × 32.8ft; 2 × 20mm
The newly-completed landing craft was loaded onto the Norwegian cargo ship *Bonneville* for transfer to the UK, which sailed from New York 23 February in Convoy SC121. The ship was torpedoed at 22.35 in position 58.48W 22.00W and sank, taking *2341* with her. The attacker is not entirely certain; *U 405* (Hopman) is

generally credited, however new research appears to indicate that it is possible that *U 229* (Schetelig) may have been responsible.

[http://www.warsailors.com/singleships/bonneville.html]

11 March HARVESTER destroyer

Barrow 1939 (*Handy*); 1,350 tons; 312ft × 33ft; 3 × 4.7in, 2 × 20mm, 8 × torpedo tubes

Commander Arthur André Tait DSO†

Part of the escort to Convoy HX228 from New York to Liverpool that came under attack from several U-boats from 10 March. At 01.00 on 11 March the *Harvester* had carried out a depth-charge attack on an Asdic contact without result and was returning to rejoin the convoy when a radar contact was reported, 1,000 yards broad on the starboard beam. The destroyer altered course towards the contact, which was revealed as a submarine on the surface, which hastily dived as *Harvester* approached. The destroyer ran over the disturbed patch of water left by the submarine as it disappeared and dropped a pattern of depth charges. She steamed clear to turn and was preparing to carry out a second attack when the submarine came to the surface about 1,000 yards away. *Harvester* worked up to 26 knots, and turned to on a course to ram, firing at the submarine as she did so. Despite an attempt to turn away, the submarine was unable to avoid her, and the destroyer struck her target and rode up over the casing, until her shafts became entangled, and she came to a halt, the submarine wallowing under her stern. After 10 minutes in this confused situation, the submarine broke free and disappeared into the night, the *Harvester* being unable to pursue as she was disabled. By now the French corvette *Aconit* was on scene and at 01.37 she found the crippled *U 444* (Langfeld) still on the surface, about 400 yards off the port beam of the *Harvester*. She promptly engaged the submarine with gunfire and then rammed after which it sank. The state of the shafts and propellers of the *Harvester* were uncertain, but after engine repairs at 04.00 she was able to get under way on her starboard shafts only and slowly followed the convoy. She had suffered damage forward during the collision, losing her Asdic dome and several compartments forward had been flooded, but she was stable. At 08.30 the engines raced, and it was believed that her remaining propeller had been shed. She came to a halt in position 51.23N 28.42W and signalled for assistance. At 11.00 she gained an HF/DF radio intercept, evidently close, which alerted her to the presence of an enemy submarine, but she was unable to react. Five minutes later there was a large explosion on her starboard side as she was hit by a torpedo. She was covered in a cloud of smoke and steam and she heeled over, and it was clear that she was sinking. A few moments later there was a second explosion as a second torpedo hit her. This probably detonated a magazine as there was a large explosion and she broke up. The fore part rose up vertically before sinking; the after part rolled over and sank. Eight officers and 136 ratings were lost. The corvette *Aconit* was already in sight and carried out an Asdic search, gained a contact which was prosecuted by depth charges. This forced the *U 432* (Eckhardt) to the surface where she was despatched by gunfire and ramming by the corvette.

[TNA:ADM.267/94]

11 March LCT (5) 2398 landing craft, tank

Ironton 1942 (*LCT 398*); 134 tons; 105ft × 32.8ft; 2 × 20mm

Having been completed in the United States, *2398* was loaded on board the American cargo ship *William C Gorgas* for the transfer to the UK which sailed from New York 28 February to join Convoy HX228. At 02.42 in position 51.35N 28.30W the *Gorgas* was hit by a torpedo and abandoned in a sinking condition; a further torpedo hit at 04.38 sank her. The attacking submarine was *U 757* (Deetz).

[http://www.uboat.net/allies/merchants/ships/2768.html]

12 March LIGHTNING destroyer

Hebburn 1940; 1,920 tons; 345.6ft × 36.9ft; 6 × 4.7in, 1 × 4in, 4 × 2pdr, 2 × 20mm, 4 × torpedo tubes

Commander Hugh Greaves Walters DSC

During the night of 11 March Force 'Q', consisting of the light cruisers *Aurora* and *Sirius* accompanied by the destroyers *Lightning* and *Loyal*, carried out a sweep along the North African coast to the east of Bône (Annaba), to search for enemy shipping. The cruisers were in line astern, the destroyers stationed ahead to port and starboard. During the day they came under air attack but avoided any damage. At 22.45 as they neared Galite Island, German radio traffic was picked up by 'Headache' (radio intercept), which indicated the presence of surface craft, probably torpedo boats. Speed was increased to 28 knots, as a vessel was sighted on the port bow of the *Lightning*. She immediately opened fire on the stranger and altered course towards the contact, but they had scarcely done so when they were hit by a torpedo right forward. The engines stopped and she lost steerage in a cloud of smoke. A moment later there was a second hit, this time the torpedo struck amidships, abreast the engine room. This broke her back, and as she was clearly doomed was ordered to be abandoned, the stern and bows started to rise clear of the water as the men jumped into the water. Both ends stood vertically on end for some moments before sinking in position 37.53N 09.50E. Forty-six men lost their lives. A number of torpedo boats had been involved in the incident and it appears that torpedoes from both *S 158* and *S 55* found their mark.

[TNA:ADM.267/94]

13 March **MORAY** trawler

Wivenhoe 1918 (*Henry Jennings*) requisitioned 1940; 206 tons; 115.4ft × 22.1ft

Employed as a water boat, she left Milford Haven during the afternoon of 12 March under tow of the *Empire Minnow*, bound for Gibraltar. She developed a leak during the night and foundered at 03.05, then being about 20 miles to the west of Fastnet lighthouse. [TNA: ADM.199/631]

14 March **THUNDERBOLT** submarine

Birkenhead 1938 (*Thetis*); 1,090/1,575 tons; 265.6ft × 26.7ft; 1 × 4in, 10 × torpedo tubes
Lieutenant Commander Cecil Bernard Crouch DSO†

Built as the *Thetis*, which had foundered in tragic circumstances in 1939 (q.v.) she had been salvaged, rebuilt and renamed *Thunderbolt* in 1940. She had served with distinction in the Mediterranean since 1941 and sailed for her fifteenth war patrol from Malta on 9 March but failed to return. The exact circumstances of her loss are somewhat uncertain. Perhaps the strongest claim is by the Italian corvettes *Cicogna* and *Libra*. During the evening of 12 March an Italian convoy was subjected to a torpedo attack by Allied aircraft when 2 miles north of Capo San Vito, Sicily during which one tanker, the *Esterel*, was hit and forced to run inshore and beach herself. The escorts believed a submarine may also have been involved and a search of the area was conducted by the escort *Libra*, and less than an hour after the attack she gained a sonar contact in position 38.17N 12.57E. The *Libra* held the contact for 2 hours, and carried out seven attacking runs over the contact, dropping depth charges. During the next day, the *Libra* was joined by escorts the *Cicogna* and *Persefone*, and they recommenced an anti-submarine hunt which continued into the 14th. Their persistence was rewarded at 05.16 when the *Cicogna* gained a contact, which for the next 3 hours was pursued, contact often being lost and then regained. At 08.45 the echo became strong, and at the same time the staff on the bridge clearly saw a periscope show itself close ahead. The corvette ran right over the point, releasing several depth charges as she did. As the corvette turned to commence another run, the stern of a submarine briefly came to the surface at an acute angle before disappearing in a bubbling quantity of air and oil and leaving a haze of smoke hanging in the air. The *Cicogna* ran over the site again, dropping a further two depth charges, after which more oil came to the surface, with great bubbles of air. Despite searching, no further contact could be made. This would seem to be fairly conclusive, but at the time of the attack, the *Thunderbolt* should have been on patrol further to the east. An alternative is the attack which took place during the afternoon of the same day, about 130 miles away, by the escort to another small convoy which

gained a sonar contact at 13.10. This led to three attacks being made on the contact over the next 40 minutes by *Uj 2210*, with bubbles and oil coming to the surface after the last one. Several minutes later hydrophone operators heard two distinct deep explosions and a large amount of air and water bubbles came to the surface, which was presumed to be a submarine breaking up. It would seem likely that one of these attacks saw the destruction of *Thunderbolt*, but which one is uncertain. Six officers and fifty-six ratings died.
[Evans pp336–7; http://www.worldnavalships.com/forums/ HMS Thunderbolt 1940-1943]

14 March **MORAVIA** trawler

Beverley 1917 requisitioned 1940; 306 tons; 130.2ft × 23ft; 1 × 6pdr
Skipper-Lieutenant Hector Rawle Pook RNR

One of a group of five minesweeping trawlers based at Great Yarmouth that were ordered to sweep along the Suffolk coast between Southwold and Harwich. Several mines had been brought to the surface during the morning and at 12.45 the *Moravia* was detached to sink any drifting mines by gunfire. As they searched, a mine was seen immediately ahead of her. The engines were put to full astern, but she ran over the mine and there was an explosion on the starboard side amidships. She immediately heeled over and sank in 4 minutes. One man was killed in the blast. Her position was noted as 52.03.15N 01.48.18E.
[TNA ADM.199/243]

16 March **CAMPOBELLO** trawler

Ontario 1942; 545 tons; 150ft × 27.6ft; 1 × 12pdr, 3 × 20mm
Lieutenant Kenneth Alexander Grant RNVR

The *Campobello* had a short and rather unlucky career. Having been completed in October 1942, she was damaged when lying at Quebec by 'surging' alongside the wharf during high winds. This had caused structural damage, including buckling several plates. This had been repaired, but she was again placed under strain in December 1942 when she ran out of fuel when on passage to Halifax and had to be towed to safety. After further repairs at Shelburne she moved to St Johns, Newfoundland and deemed seaworthy, although this was disputed by her commanding officer. She sailed for England on 9 March. On 15 March, the weather was poor, with gale force winds gusting to Force 10 and high seas. At 02.00 it was reported that the stokehold was leaking, and on trying to clear the water it was found that the pump was defective, so a bucket chain was organised. The water steadily rose and at 02.45 the engines stopped. By 06.20 both the stokehold and the bunkers were flooded. At first light a sail was rigged from a canvas awning and a sea anchor streamed.

Her position then was 50.57N 35.22W. At 09.30 the corvette *Godetia* closed and attempted a tow, but the line parted after 20 minutes. As she continued to fill with water and was visibly settling, it was decided that afternoon to abandon her, and all the crew were transferred to the *Godetia*. This was complete by 18.00 when the corvette closed to one cable (200 yards) and dropped a depth charge to speed her end. She had gone by 18.30. It was assessed that she had been weakened by structural damage, and the repairs had not been effectively carried out.

[TNA:ADM.1/16875]

16 March HORSA tug

Selby 1942 (*Rescue*); 700 tons; 142.6ft × 33.3ft; 1 × 12pdr, 1 × 20mm

Lieutenant Ian Taylor RNR

Based in Iceland she was sent to the assistance of the torpedoed merchant ship *Richard Bland*, and in difficult conditions had successfully towed her into Seydisfjord on the eastern coast of Iceland. The weather conditions were appalling, with winds Force 7, high seas and regular snow storms. Finding it difficult to control the tow, Lieutenant Taylor decided to cut her free in Hjeradsfloi, where she would drift ashore onto a beach where salvage would be possible. She had been escorted by the armed trawler *Bute* and with the tow now complete, the pair steered back out to sea. Taking their departure from Bjarnaroy light, they steered 120 degrees, a course agreed by both ships. The weather now closed in again, with the thick black clouds covering the skies and the visibility down to a few yards with thick driving snow. At 16.53 broken water was seen close ahead. The engines were stopped, and the helm put over, but the tug struck the ground. As the snow eased it could be seen that they had grounded on Osfles rocks; the *Bute* had narrowly avoided a similar fate. She pounded on the rocks in the heavy seas, and water was reported entering. At 17.45 efforts to free her from the rock succeeded but she was still making water despite pumping. The *Bute* closed and took off the crew and she later settled into shallow water, being a total loss. The court of enquiry commended Taylor for his 'tenacious manner' in towing the *Richard Bland* but found that he had been overconfident in assessing his position in the fjord. A sounding had shown that his estimated position was wrong, but this was ignored as the sounding machine was thought unreliable – if he mistrusted it, then he should have checked the sounding by another means. He was informed that he had incurred their Lordships' displeasure.

[TNA:ADM.1/15032]

22 March HDML 1157/ HDML 1212 motor launch

Port Bannatyne (*1157*), Hampton (*1212*); 46 tons; 70ft × 15ft

The launches, with a third, *HDML 1229*, were embarked as deck cargo on board the merchant ship *City of Christchurch*, which sailed from Milford Haven to join Convoy KMS11G, bound for Gibraltar. On 21 March, in position 39.35N 12.46W, the convoy was attacked by a long-range Fw 200 aircraft and the *Christchurch* was damaged by near misses. She was detached from the convoy and ordered to make Lisbon, escorted by the Canadian corvette HMCS *Morden*. However, she steadily settled and the following day her stern was awash, and she was abandoned. The lashings of the launches were cut, and two of them did successfully float free when the ship went under, but it was found that one of them had been damaged and was scuttled. The survivor, *1229*, was manned by a scratch crew from the *Morden* and successfully made it to Gibraltar.

[Pope p95]

27 March DASHER escort aircraft carrier

Chester (USA) 1941; 12,150 tons; 465ft × 69.6ft; 3 × 4in, 8 × 20mm, 15 aircraft

Captain Lennox Albert Knox Boswell DSO

Having spent the day in the approaches to the river Clyde, she had completed flying exercises for the day and all except one aircraft were struck down below, she was to the south of Cumbrae Island, proceeding towards Greenock at 15 knots, when at 16.48 there was a large explosion aft. The force of the explosion vented itself forward through the engine room, upwards into the hangar and outwards through the starboard side, and very probably downwards through the bottom. The aircraft lift was blown upwards and overboard, as was a 4in gun. The stern was swathed in thick black smoke, and several fierce fires were started, which rapidly spread through the hangar and along the tops of the fuel tanks. All power was lost, and the ship took a list to starboard and went down by the stern. It rapidly became clear that she was sinking, and she was ordered to be abandoned. She slowly regained her upright position, but continued to settle by the stern, her bows rising up out of the water under a rising cloud of thick black smoke. The bows continued to rise until they became vertical, and 8 minutes after the explosion, she sank. Several nearby ships, including *ML 582*, the training ship *Isle of Sark* and the corvette *la Capricieuse* all came to the assistance of the dozens of men struggling in the water surrounded by fuel oil, as did the merchant ships, *Lithium* and *Cragside*. As they did so, there was another explosion as fuel vapour ignited, sending flames 60ft into the air. In all 379 men were lost, with 149 survivors. The cause of the disaster was uncertain but was believed 'almost certainly' to be ignition of petrol vapour in the

main petrol compartment. Testimony was heard that there was a persistent, albeit slow, leak from the petrol stowage. Further, the initial explosion was reported to be a muffled, rumbling report, rather than that of a sudden detonation of explosives. Several aircraft were in the hanger, being refuelled, and this would have aided the spread of the fires and smoke. The later explosion of fuel in the sea was probably due to a calcium flare going off. The wreck lies in position 55.49.32N 05.15.40W.
[TNA: ADM.267/132]

31 March CAULONIA trawler

Selby 1912 requisitioned 1939; 296 tons; 136.8ft × 23ft
Skipper Arthur Christy RNR

Acting as escort to a group of landing craft in 'Haulabout Group-67' heading for Portsmouth, the weather was poor and in high seas and strong winds, the *Caulonia* ran aground at 01.00 at Jury's Gap, in Rye Bay, about 600 yards from the coastguard station. Some men attempted to swim to the shore but were lost. The Hastings lifeboat was called out and lifted off seven men, and others successfully reached the shore during the morning. Three men lost their lives.
[TNA: ADM.199/778; ADM.358/3145]

2 April MTB 267 motor torpedo boat

Bayonne NJ 1941 (*PT 18*); 32 tons; 70ft × 20ft; 4 × torpedo tubes
Lieutenant Alec Primrose Grahame Joy RCNVR

In company with *MTB 313*, she sailed from Benghazi at 16.00 on 1 April en-route to Malta. The weather was poor, and she suffered badly in the worsening weather conditions. She was found to be making water and in the early hours of 2 April, it became clear that she had broken her back in the constant pounding in the high seas. The side had split and come away from the chine; the bottom was also apparently coming apart, the engine room flooding. *313* initially tried to take her in tow, but she could not be kept afloat, she was abandoned in position 34.26N 16.14W, *313* firing several rounds into her to ensure that she sank.
[TNA: ADM.199/778; Reynolds & Cooper, Mediterranean MTBs at War p60]

2 April MTB 63 motor torpedo boat

Portchester 1942; 35 tons; 70ft × 14.9ft; 1 × 20mm, 2 × torpedo tubes
Lieutenant Roger George Bowlby Keyes

In company with *MTB 64*, the pair sailed from Benghazi during the afternoon of 1 April, to make their way to Malta (see *MTB 267* above). The weather deteriorated during the passage, and at 05.00 in position 33.35N 17.11E, the pair collided heavily, causing both considerable damage. They gave up any attempt to reach Malta, turning back to Benghazi. However, an engine

breakdown in *63* left her alone and drifting. A search was instituted from Malta, and she was found and taken in tow, but this had to be abandoned due to the weather and the crew was taken off and she was sunk by gunfire.
[TNA: ADM.199/638]

2 April MTB 64 motor torpedo boat

Portchester 1942; 35 tons; 70ft × 14.9ft; 1 × 20mm, 2 × torpedo tubes
Sub-Lieutenant Paul William Rickards RNVR (?)

Consort to *MTB 63*, as the pair attempted to reach Malta from Benghazi (see above) but were frustrated by poor weather. After the pair collided during the early morning of 2 April, they turned back, and following *63*'s breakdown, *64* pressed on alone, intending to reach Benghazi. However, the weather continued to worsen, and she eventually foundered before she reached her destination.
[TNA: ADM.199/638]

2 April HAIDERI auxiliary patrol vessel

Vegesack 1920 (*Doros*) requisitioned 1939; 1,510 tons; 239.7ft × 34.2ft
Lieutenant Geoffrey Henry Gordon Scott RINR

Royal Indian Navy. Towing six lighters from Vizagapatnam to Madras, in poor weather she ran aground on the Sacramento Shoal at the entrance to the Godaveri River. The armed trawler *Lahore* was despatched to the scene but found the ship hard aground and in the early hours of the following morning she was abandoned. There were hopes that she may be salvaged, but on inspection it was found that the forward hold was full of water and she was written off as a constructive total loss.
[TNA: ADM.199/769]

6 April GOLDEN GIFT drifter

Lowestoft 1910 requisitioned 1939; 90 tons; 84.6ft × 19.4ft

Based at Oban, western Scotland, she was damaged in a collision at 13.58 with the MacBrayne steamer *Lochinvar* (178 tons) and subsequently sank in 9 fathoms in the harbour.
[TNA: ADM.199/631; ADM.199/778]

7 April MOA minesweeper

Leith 1941; 600 tons; 150ft × 30ft; 1 × 4in, 1 × 20mm
Lieutenant Commander Peter Phipps DSC RNZVR

Royal New Zealand Navy. After arriving in Tulagi Harbour, British Solomon Islands, she went alongside the US Navy oil storage barge *Erskine M Phelps* to refuel. At about 15.00 a large number of Japanese aircraft approached the harbour and commenced attacking shipping. *Moa* received a direct hit by a bomb which passed through the bridge before detonating. There were also at least two near misses. The ship listed heavily before sinking, bows first, in just 4 minutes, the crew jumping into the sea. Five men were killed.

[TNA: ADM.1/14363; https://nzhistory.govt.nz/war/bird-class-minesweepers/sinking-of-the-moa]

11 April **BEVERLEY** destroyer

Newport News 1919 (*Branch*) transferred 1940; 1,190 tons; 309ft × 30.10ft; 1 × 4in, 1 × 3in, 4 × 20mm, 3 × torpedo tubes
Lieutenant Commander Rodney Athelstan Price[†]

Detailed to act as one of the escorts to westbound North Atlantic Convoy ON176 with two other destroyers and five corvettes, the convoy sailed from Liverpool on 31 March bound for New York City. During 9 April she closed the corvette *Clover* for a personnel transfer which was successfully completed despite a blanket of dense fog, but as she cleared to take up her screening position, she was in collision with the merchant ship *Cairnvalona*, suffering severe damage to her starboard side, and putting her Asdic equipment out of action. It was decided that although damaged, she should not be detached but remain with the convoy, stationed at the rear. During the next day HF/DF radio intercepts showed that the convoy had been found by a patrolling U-boat, and attacks were therefore anticipated. There was, however, no warning, when at 03.52 the *Clover* saw the flash of an explosion and heard several detonations in the direction of *Beverley*. Believing that the destroyer may be engaging a submarine, she turned to investigate and gained an Asdic contact at a range of 2,500 yards. A depth-charge attack was carried out after which a strong smell of oil was detected and shouting from men in the water could be heard. Any hopes that these may have been from a submarine were dispelled when it was realised that they were in the patch of wreckage left by the *Beverley*. They managed to pick up seven men from the water, but only four survived. They testified that there had been an explosion on the port side between the forward and after boiler rooms. All the lights went out and she rolled over to sink quickly by the stern, there being further explosions as she went under, probably from her boilers and depth charges exploding. She had been torpedoed by the *U 188* (Ludden). One hundred and fifty-one men died.

[TNA: ADM.237/98]

11 April **YAMPI LASS** stores lighter

Fremantle 1912 requisitioned 1942; 28 tons; 63ft × 16ft
Royal Australian Navy. Employed as a tender to HMAS *Melville* at Darwin, Northern Territories, she was blown ashore in a storm and written off as a total loss. There were no casualties.

[Cassells p109]

15 April **ADONIS** trawler

Hull 1914 (*Ocean, Nordhav 1*) requisitioned 1940; 644 tons; 175.9ft × 29.1ft; 1 × 12pdr
Skipper Henry Draper RNR[†]

Ordered to conduct a night patrol along the east coast between Harwich and Aldeburgh, she was abreast number 54B buoy at the northern end of the patrol line, when at 00.53 a radar contact was obtained at 3,500 yards range. A star shell was fired which illuminated three torpedo boats in line ahead, heading north. More star shells were fired, it being intended to engage, but immediately after the last shell had been fired an explosion occurred on the port side amidships. The detonation was abreast the cross bunker, and the machinery compartments rapidly filled, and she rolled over and quickly sank. It was thought that she had been torpedoed by a second group of torpedo boats that she had not detected. The eleven survivors spent an uncomfortable night in a Carley float until picked up the following morning by an RAF rescue launch. Twenty-one men died. The commanding officer of the armed trawler *Milford Prince*, senior officer that night, was criticised. It emerged that he had failed to report a hydrophone effect (HE) contact indicating a fast-moving surface contact some time before the action. He had also displayed a lack of seamanship in not making allowances for the tide when searching for survivors.

[TNA: ADM.199/541; Lund & Ludlam, Trawlers go to War pp198–202]

16 April **PAKENHAM** destroyer

Hebburn 1941; 1,640 tons; 328.9ft × 35ft; 5 × 4in, 4 × 2pdr, 4 × 20mm, 4 × torpedo tubes
Commander Basil Jones DSC

Based at Malta, in company with her sister *Paladin*, she was ordered to investigate and intercept enemy traffic believed passing between Pantellaria and Sicily. The first indication that enemy units were nearby was at 22.52 when 'Headache' (radio intercept) reported the presence nearby of an Italian patrol boat. The pair continued to run northwards with *Pakenham* leading, until 02.42 when a ship was seen on the starboard bow. Course was altered to put the stranger right ahead, which appeared to be steering to the west. The radar reported the range as 7,200 yards and visually it could be made out to be two small destroyers in line ahead. The British pair continued to close until they were at 2,700 yards and then opened fire. It was then 02.48. At the same time the searchlight was switched on to illuminate the target. Hits were immediately observed on the leading enemy ship, and the *Pakenham* also fired two torpedoes, and observed an explosion amidships. Attention was then shifted to the second ship, and again hits were observed. Fire was now being returned,

which was vigorous and included some bright tracer and a torpedo track passed near the *Pakenham*. All of the enemy fire was concentrated on *Pakenham*, and she was hit at least five times by 100mm shells, which including hits on the stern, which started a fire in the engine room and the searchlight was knocked out. The British pair continued to engage and at 03.12 the second enemy destroyer was seen to blow up. With the leading enemy ship on fire, it was decided to break off the action and they turned away. The engine room reported that high pressure steam was escaping and it became clear that the ship had been hit twice in the machinery spaces, damaging main steam pipes. At 03.50 the *Pakenham* was forced to a stop. Her sister *Paladin* closed, and a tow was rigged, but with her steering gear out of action, she was an awkward tow. At daylight, a pair of Ju 88 aircraft were seen approaching from the west which divided to attack from each side but were driven off. Then the tow parted, and more aircraft were seen approaching. These turned out to be Italian Macchi fighters, with Ju 88s and Me 109s. Although British fighters from Malta arrived overhead to drive away the attackers soon after, they were at the limit of their range and clearly could not stay long. As the *Pakenham* was steadily settling it was decided to abandon her, which was complete by 07.18 when the *Paladin* fired a torpedo into her. The position was approximately 37.26N 12.30E. Nine men were killed in the encounter. Their opponents had been the *Cigno*, which was sunk and the *Cassiopeia*, which survived, although damaged.
[TNA: ADM.1/14402]

18 April REGENT submarine
Barrow 1930; 1,475/2,040 tons; 270ft × 29.11ft; 1 × 4in, 8 × torpedo tubes
Lieutenant Walter Neville Ronald Knox DSC†
Sailed for a patrol on 11 April from Malta for a patrol in the southern Adriatic but failed to arrive at Alexandria on 2 May as expected. The last time she can be identified is at 15.45 on 18 April, when a submarine carried out a torpedo attack on an Italian merchant ship off Monopoli, which must have been *Regent*. That evening an explosion was heard on the shore, evidently to seaward. On 1 May the body of a British seaman wearing an escape apparatus (DSEA) hood was washed ashore at Brindisi, and it was estimated that he had been dead for 6 to 8 days. On the 15th and 16th, a further three bodies came ashore, between Castro Marina and Torre Santo Stefano, one of whom was also wearing a DSEA; the advanced state of deterioration of the bodies suggested that they may have dead for up to 4 weeks. Although there were no minefields off Monopoli, it is presumed that the *Regent* must have struck a mine that had come adrift from the nearest field about 15 miles away on the night of 18 April. Some of the crew had

evidently survived the explosion and made an escape but did not make it to shore alive.
[Evans pp340–1]

18 April P 615 submarine
Barrow 1940 (*Uluc Ali Reis*); 624/861 tons; 193ft × 22.3ft; 1 × 3in, 5 × torpedo tubes
Lieutenant Charles Walderne St Clair Lambert†
Employed as a training submarine, exercising surface forces, she was based at Freetown, Sierra Leone. She sailed on 17 April bound for Takoradi, being escorted by the minesweeper *MMS 107*. The pair lost sight of each other in poor visibility during the night, but regained contact at 07.00. When they did so, *MMS 107* reported that at 04.00 the track of what appeared to be a torpedo was sighted, which had passed underneath her. Lieutenant Lambert was apparently doubtful, as they had no intelligence of any enemy submarines in the area but suggested that if they were certain that it had been an attack, then an enemy report should be made. No report had been made by 09.05 when a merchant ship, which proved to be the *Empire Bruce*, came into view. A few moments later, as *MMS 107* was attempting to call the ship by light, *P 615* was blown up by a large explosion, evidently having been hit on the starboard side by a torpedo and she had disappeared within 10 seconds. There was no sign of any survivors, all forty-four men onboard being lost. The position was 06.49N 13.09W. *MMS 107* warned the *Empire Bruce* of the presence of a U-boat and then turned towards the coast, to establish radio contact and make an enemy report. As she was doing so, at 10.50 the *Empire Bruce* was hit on the port side, and rapidly sank. *MMS 107* closed to pick up the survivors and then returned to Freetown. The attacker had been *U 123* (Schroeter).
[Evans pp341–3]

21 April SPLENDID submarine
Chatham 1942; 715/990 tons; 201ft × 23.9ft; 1 × 3in, 7 × torpedo tubes
Lieutenant Ian Lauchan McGeoch
Based at Malta, the submarine sailed on 18 April to carry out a patrol in the Gulf of Naples. At 08.38, about 3 miles south-south-east of Capri, the German destroyer *Hermes* sighted a periscope, about 3,000 yards off the port bow. She immediately altered course towards and soon after picked up a sonar contact. The destroyer then ran over the contact and carried out a depth-charge attack. Sonar contact was regained, and between 08.38 and 09.24 a further six attacks were made. The last caused serious damage to the submarine; one shaft was distorted and jammed; a fire broke out in the engine room; she took a sharp stern down attitude and plunged to 500ft. McGeoch ordered main ballast tanks to be blown and slowly the submarine stopped her descent

and came to the surface, where it came under fire from the *Hermes*, the boat being hit several times killing and wounding several men, including McGeoch, who lost an eye. When it was clear that the submarine was sinking, the destroyer ceased fire, and started picking up the survivors from the water, the Italian patrol boat *VAS 226* joining the rescue efforts. Eighteen men were lost.
[*Evans pp346–9*]

21 April LCI (L) 7 landing craft, infantry, large

Camden 1942; 234 tons; 150ft × 23.3ft; 4 × 20mm
Lieutenant George Donald King McCormick RNVR
The craft was one of a number of vessels that were sent to Djedjelli from Algiers, to form a new operating base for landing craft. At 05.00 the base was attacked by at least four Ju 88 aircraft, one of which scored a direct hit on *LCI 7*. Set on fire, with several casualties, she was run onto a beach and allowed to burn out. Four men were killed.
[*TNA: ADM.199/638; ADM.358/1540*]

22 April HERRING trawler

Selby 1942; 670 tons; 146ft × 25.3ft; 1 × 4in, 3 × 20mm
Herring was escorting Convoy FN108 when she was in collision with the French merchant ship *Cassard* (1,596 tons), at 03.00, when about 2 nautical miles to the north of number 20E Buoy, north-east of Blyth. All the crew was picked up by the *Cassard*. The wreck has been found and lies in 51.19N 001.21W.
[*TNA: ADM.199/837*]

24 April SAHIB submarine

Birkenhead 1942; 715/990 tons; 201ft × 23.6ft; 1 × 3in, 6 × torpedo tubes
Lieutenant Commander John Henry Bromage DSO DSC
Ordered to conduct a patrol in the Messina straits, she carried out a submerged attack against a strongly protected merchant ship off Capo Milazzo, Sicily, and successfully torpedoed the Italian transport *Galiola* at 04.58. After firing the torpedoes, the submarine broached, her periscope standards being exposed for some moments before control was regained and she dived. The attack brought about a rapid counter-attack from a patrolling aircraft, which saw the swirl of water as she disappeared and dropped a bomb. This did not cause any damage but did serve as a marker for the convoy escorts *Climene*, *Euterpe* and *Gabbiano*, who turned to close. The submarine was taken to 250ft. At 05.26 the *Gabbiano* gained sonar contact at 1,000 yards and carried out a depth-charge attack. At 05.45 the *Euterpe* carried out a very precise depth-charge attack which ruptured pipes, shattered glass and most seriously of all, blew the compressor outlet valve out, leaving a hole in the hull, through which water poured in at an alarming rate. The boat took a stern down angle and

started to dive. Tanks were blown and she was held at 270ft, and then when it was clear that she could not be saved, all tanks were blown to take her to the surface. As they burst to the surface in a bows up attitude the Italian ships all opened fire, and they were joined by the patrolling Ju 88, which carried out a machine-gun attack. All of the crew escaped and took to the water as she sank, the bows rearing up as she did so, being almost perpendicular as she disappeared.
[*Evans pp352–8*]

25 April LCG (L) 15 landing craft, gun, large

Old Kilpatrick 1942 (*LCT 369*); 491 tons; 175ft × 31ft; 2 × 4.7in, 3 × 20mm
Lieutenant Donald Herbert Goldsmith RNVR†
Newly refitted at Belfast in her new role as a gunfire support ship, she sailed in company with her sister *LCG 16* for Falmouth. The pair called at Holyhead to refuel and then continued their journey to the south. The weather had deteriorated steadily during the passage, and the pair suffered, pitching and rolling deeply. Particularly troublesome was the water being shipped over the blunt landing craft bows, which led to forward compartments being flooded, with the space between the forward gun mounting and the bows being particularly difficult to clear of water, which led to a bows down attitude. In the worsening weather, she altered course to head for the shelter of Milford Haven. She reported that she would be unable to enter harbour unaided, and three harbour tugs were despatched, but in the high seas found themselves unable to close her. The sloop *Rosemary* and the trawler *Bern* were both directed to the scene but could do little to assist in the poor weather. At 18.15 she reported that she was waterlogged and was unable to maintain her course in the strong winds and currents and was being carried inshore. The local lifeboats at Angle and St David's were called out to go to her assistance, and the Life Saving Association were directed to Sheep Island, where it was believed she was going to be wrecked. Local troops and men from a local RAF base also went to the coastline to help. Despite all of their efforts at 18.50 she was driven onto rocks and broke up in the heavy seas. Several men from the craft tried to make it to the shore, but none survived. The wreck broke up in the storm, and bodies were washed ashore along the coast. There were no survivors, thirty-seven men losing their lives.
[*TNA: ADM.199/837; Lund & Ludlam, The War of the Landing Craft pp92–104*]

26 April LCG (L) 16 landing craft, gun, large

Meadowside 1942 (*LCT 393*); 491 tons; 175ft × 31ft; 2 × 4.7in, 3 × 20mm
Lieutenant Douglas Arthur Burgass RNVR†
Consort to *LCG 15* (see above), she fell astern of her companion, with a loss of engine power and the

compass developed a fault. Also suffering from the forward compartments flooding, as it was impossible to clear water from the space immediately abaft the bows, it was found that the increasing bows-down attitude and the deep rolling of the craft made her difficult to handle. She followed *LCG 15* to head inshore towards the shelter of Milford Haven, with the water now flooding into other compartments, and the pumps were having difficulty in keeping the water clear. As they closed Milford, the sloop *Rosemary* arrived on scene and made several attempts to pass a line to rig a tow, but all failed in the poor weather conditions. The sloop then lowered her whaler, with six volunteers, to pull to the landing craft, but soon after being launched the small boat was rolled over, throwing the men into the sea, and despite all wearing lifejackets, all were drowned. With the flooding now gaining on the pumps and the light now failing, it was decided to run her inshore and try to run her onto a beach, but it was found that she did not have the power to carry her, and she was carried along by powerful currents. The St David's lifeboat was launched to go to her assistance at 22.45 but had not reached the scene before the landing craft foundered. She had become increasingly unstable until she took a pronounced list to port and then rolled over and sank. The lifeboat arrived at 01.20 and a search of the area found one survivor in the water, surrounded by oil and debris. Another two survivors were washed ashore onboard a raft. These three were the only survivors from both landing craft; including the six men from the *Rosemary*, seventy-eight men had died.
[TNA: ADM.199/837; Lund & Ludlam, The War of the Landing Craft pp92–104]

26 April **THORA** drifter
1930 requisitioned 1940; 37 tons
Mr George Allen Beet†
Former Dutch fishing vessel employed as a barrage balloon vessel in the river Humber, manned locally employed civilians with a detachment from the Royal Air Force. In poor weather, at 02.50 she was driven down onto the boom at Grimsby and subsequently foundered. Six men were picked up, but two men, including Mr Beet the skipper, were lost.
[TNA: ADM.199/778; ADM.358/1535]

28 April   **MTB 639** motor torpedo boat
Lowestoft 1943; 95 tons; 115ft × 21.3ft; 1 × 2pdr, 2 × 20mm
Lieutenant George Lambert Russell†
639 sailed from Sousse, Tunisia, in company with *MTB 633* and *MTB 637* to carry out a reconnaissance of the coast as far north as Cape Bon. The trio successfully passed along the coast as far as the Cape, noting important gun emplacements and military positions, the

enemy evidently believing that they were friendly. After they had passed Cape Bon, and considering that their work was complete, they decided to attack an enemy 'R' or patrol boat which was seen in a creek by Ras el Amar, along with two Italian minesweepers. This was carried out with some success, the enemy craft being set on fire, and they then shifted their attention to aircraft parked near the shore and destroyed a Ju 52 transport and a Fieseler Storch reconnaissance aircraft. As they moved clear of the land, they sighted a large merchant ship which being escorted by two warships, believed to be destroyers. They promptly attacked, and at the time, believed they had hit the merchant ship, which was the *Teranio*, but had actually missed. The boats turned away, but as they attempted to clear the area, they came under attack from enemy aircraft. These concentrated on *639* which was badly hit by cannon fire and set on fire. *MTB 637* closed to take off the men, and *633* picked up several men that had jumped into the water. Before they left the scene *633* and *637* fired several rounds in the burning hull of *639* to ensure that she sank. Six men were killed.
[TNA: ADM.199/778; Pope pp84–7; Reynolds, Dog Boats pp51–5]

2 May **MTB 311** motor torpedo boat
Bayonne NJ 1942 (*PT 53*); 34 tons; 77ft × 20ft; 1 × 20mm, 2 × torpedo tubes
Lieutenant James Donald Lancaster RNVR
Patrolling from Bône (modern Annaba) in company with *MTB 316*, they were to the north of Bizerte when at 21.05 there was a 'shattering explosion' under the hull. After the water and smoke had subsided it was discovered that the stern had disappeared, leaving the engine room exposed and flooding. All hands were brought to the upper deck and moved forward, and *MTB 316* closed to lift off the crew. This was complete by 21.35 after which *316* fired her 20mm gun repeatedly at the wreck, to ensure that it sank. Amazingly no one was killed, although three were injured. Her position was noted at 37.26N 09.52E. It was assessed that she had run over a mine, although the waters were expected to be hazardous, they had passed along the route several times in the recent past without incident.
[TNA: ADM.199/243]

3 May **LCT (4) 613** landing craft, tank
Stockton 1943; 200 tons; 171ft × 38.8ft
One of a convoy of landing craft on passage along the North African coast towards Oran, the weather was heavy, and the pounding opened up the plates and *613* started to make water. At 09.10 she broke her back. The escorting minesweeper, *Rhyl*, took her in tow, heading inshore intending to anchor at Beni Saf, but at 15.28 the craft broke in half. The forepart was holed by gunfire

and sank; the stern remained afloat and was towed into Oran by the *Rhyl*.
[TNA:ADM.199/639]

7 May ADELE examination vessel
Leith 1906 requisitioned 1939; 288 tons; 145ft × 22.4ft
Lieutenant John Kennedy RANR
Royal Australian Navy. At Port Kembla, New South Wales, she was thrown against a breakwater by high winds and written off as a constructive total loss.
[Cassells p14]

8 May DANEMAN trawler
Selby 1937 requisitioned 1939; 516 tons; 173.2ft × 28.6ft; 1 × 4in
Lieutenant Stanley William Lock RNVR
As part of the escort covering the westward passage of Atlantic Convoy ON181, she sailed from Londonderry to join, taking up station astern of the ships. During 6 May the engine room reported flooding and despite constant pumping, it proved difficult to clear the water. A bucket chain was organised, but she lost speed and fell astern of the convoy and the following day a rescue tug, the *Growler*, was despatched to her aid and a corvette, the Free French *la Renoncule*, was ordered to stand by her. By the time the tug arrived the trawler was listing to starboard with 200 tons of water in the engine and boiler rooms. There was a high sea running and it was with difficulty that a tow was rigged, and the pair was able to get under way. During the late morning, the weather had moderated sufficiently to allow the tug to slip the tow and go alongside to attempt to use her salvage pumps to clear the water, but the constant rolling crushed the pipe, forcing this to be abandoned. However, she passed across a portable pump for the trawler to use. The deep rolling made this difficult, but it was finally achieved, and the tug was able to resume the tow. The weather continued poor and despite all the pumping and bailing the water did not seem to be clearing, and the trawler continued to list, heeling over to about 40 degrees, making towing increasingly difficult. In the early hours of 8 May the tow parted. Seas were now washing over the trawler; the list was not easing, and the water was gaining in the hold. At 02.20 the trawler signalled that they were sinking, and both the tug and corvette closed her to take the men off. A Carley float was put into the water, and men jumped on board, but three men failed to reach the raft and were swept away. The float then drifted down towards the *Renoncule*, which picked all the men up, although one subsequently died of cold and exhaustion. The *Growler* fell back and tried to come alongside, but the heel of the trawler, and the high seas made this a dangerous manoeuvre, with the pair crashing together in the swell and then falling apart. Men jumped across when they thought the moment was right, but two men fell into the

sea and were lost. All the rest made it across. The corvette then fired several rounds of 4in into the wreck to ensure that she sank. A subsequent enquiry found that the most likely cause was damage caused by the trawler striking a piece of floating ice, the area being thick with drifting patches of ice and icebergs.
[TNA:ADM.217/194; ADM.199/837; Lund & Ludlam, Trawlers go to War pp207–11]

9 May MTB 61 motor torpedo boat
Portchester 1942; 35 tons; 70ft × 19.2ft; 1 × 20mm, 2 × torpedo tubes
Lieutenant Timothy James Bligh RNVR
Stationed in North Africa, she was conducting a night patrol off the coast of Tunisia, in the vicinity of Bizerte, in company with *MTB 77* and the American *PT 203*. At just after midnight the trio approached the harbour at Kelibia, and Lieutenant Bligh was ordered to move inshore and attack any targets found inside. *61* did so, closing to within a mile from the shore, where she saw four or five vessels, lying across the north of the anchorage. It was decided to close and destroy them with gunfire, but as they did so, at 01.04 she ran hard aground about 100 yards off the shore. Despite putting the engines to full astern, she would not move, even when depth charges, ammunition and stores were heaved overboard. Bligh stripped off and went over the side to investigate and found that the water was shallow for some distance around her. A Carley float was lowered and used to take out an anchor but attempts to kedge her free also failed. It was clear that she could not be moved, and as there were indications of activity ashore, preparations were made to abandon her. At 02.30 *PT 203* closed to about 50 yards and all the crew jumped into the water and swam to the patrol boat. By now sporadic fire was coming from the shore, from machine guns and rifles. The last man to leave was Lieutenant Bligh who fired a signal flare into the mess deck, the lower decks having been flooded with fuel oil. The resulting explosion blew Bligh clear and set the boat on fire. One man was lost, apparently having been swept away between the boats.
[TNA:ADM.199/541; Pope pp90–3; Reynolds & Cooper, Mediterranean MTBs at War pp61–2]

10 May MTB 264 motor torpedo boat
Bayonne NJ 1940 (*PT.15*); 32 tons; 70ft × 20ft; 4 × torpedo tubes
Lieutenant Harwin Woodthorpe Sheldrick RNVR
Whilst on patrol off Sousse, she detonated a mine at 18.20 in position 35.52N 10.40E, which blew most of her stern off, but she remained afloat. Taken in tow, she was brought into Sousse harbour and beached but was written off as a constructive total loss.
[TNA:ADM.199/639; Reynolds & Cooper, Mediterranean MTBs at War p62]

10 May MAROUBRA stores support vessel
Townsville 1930 requisitioned 1942; 21 tons; 61.3ft × 18.3ft
Royal Australian Navy. Employed supplying stores and fuel for local vessels in the Northern Territories, she had completed a voyage to Thursday Island, and was lying off Milingimbi, Arnhem Land, when that place came under attack by Japanese aircraft. Hit by cannon fire she caught fire and sank soon afterwards. There were no casualties.
[Cassells p38]

11 May ML 133 motor launch
Isleworth 1940; 73 tons; 112ft × 18.3ft; 1 × 3pdr
Lieutenant Commander John Magnus Hurrie Garrioch RNVR
Based at the training establishment at Fort William, Scotland, she was laying at Camusnagell when she suffered a large internal explosion which blew out the side of the boat and started a fierce fire. The crew of the local Loch Linnhe ferry saw the fire and ran alongside the burning launch to lift off the crew. A series of further explosions wrecked the launch as her depth charges and magazines exploded before she sank. One man lost his life. The explosion was probably caused by petrol vapour igniting when the engines were started.
[TNA: ADM.199/778; Jefferson pp69–70]

12 May MMS 89 motor minesweeper
Gosport 1941; 225 tons; 105ft × 23ft
Lieutenant Ronald Victor Porter Rogers RNVR
Stationed in the Mediterranean, she was 5 miles to the north-east of Cape Galite, acting as a follow-up ship to three other motor minesweepers, which were ahead of her, using magnetic and acoustic sweeps. At 05.45 a large explosion occurred aft, under the stern, believed to be a contact mine. This caused severe damage to the stern, the water rapidly entering the mess deck aft and filling the store room and battery room. The propeller shaft broke and was forced upwards, and she came to a stop, the stern awash. MMS 140 closed and came alongside to take men off and a tow was rigged. At 06.20 the after bulkhead of the engine room gave way and she rolled over and sank.
[TNA: ADM.267/115]

14 May HDML 1154 motor launch
Wroxham 1943; 46 tons; 70ft × 15ft; 1 × 2pdr
Sub-Lieutenant Leslie Robert Ward RNZVR†
Based in the Mediterranean, she was conducting a night-time patrol off Bizerte. At 22.48 a heavy explosion was heard and seen from the shore which appeared to be about 2 miles to the north of the detached mole of the harbour. Two other patrolling ships, the minesweepers Clacton and Stornaway, closed the area and when they sighted a darkened ship, it was engaged with 20mm fire,

but when a 'snowflake' illuminant was fired, the object was revealed to be the wreck of a motor launch. A search of the area was now initiated and the minesweeper Acute picked up one survivor from HDML 1154, and later three ratings made the shore from a Carley float. The wreck slowly drifted inshore and finally beached about 2 miles from the southern end of the detached mole. It was found that the stern had been blown off and the bridge wrecked. It was believed that she had struck a mine. Six men died.
[TNA: ADM.199/243]

20 May FANTOME minesweeper
Belfast 1942; 850 tons; 212.5ft × 35.5ft; 1 × 4in, 8 × 20mm
Captain John Wilfrid Boutwood
Sailed from Bizerte, Tunisia, in company with other minesweepers for Operation 'Antidote', the clearing of minefields along the North African coast. Whilst steaming at 10 knots with sweep gear out, there was an explosion under the stern, probably when the starboard propeller struck a mine. A large hole was blown in the hull, the rudder was blown away and the after compartments wrecked, with lower decks forced upwards to touch the upper deck. The after end of the ship flooded, and she started to settle, stern first, with the quarterdeck submerged and the shafts hanging down below the keel. All power was lost. However, bulkheads were shored up, and the ship remained stable, and a tow was rigged, and she was successfully towed into Bizerte. Temporary repairs were made, and she eventually returned to England, but by survey was written off as a constructive total loss. One man died of his wounds.
[TNA: ADM.267/116; CB.4273 p310]

26 May HONG LAM trawler
Singapore 1928 requisitioned 1941; 104 tons;
91.5ft × 17.4ft
Skipper George Knaggs RNR
A wooden-hulled vessel requisitioned for use as a loop layer/minesweeper, and based at Trincomalee, Ceylon. After completing a short refit at Colombo, she sailed 24 May to return to her base. The following morning the chief engineman reported that she was making water in the engine room. Initially it was not sufficient to be of concern, but by 10.00 the water was increasing and could not be kept under. A chain of buckets was organised to help clear the flood, but an inspection of the ship revealed that the forepeak was also flooding, and it became evident that the seams had opened, and the caulking was working out. At 12.00 the pump broke down and it was uncertain how much longer the engine would work, so she was turned inshore and made for a 4-fathom patch about 4 miles south-west of Dhanuskodi. At 16.30 the engines finally failed. With no working radio, she fired red flares at intervals

through the night, but this brought no response. At 07.00 the next day (26 May) the boat was manned and sent ashore to try and get assistance, meanwhile rafts and boats were prepared for lowering. To try and gain some control, a sail, made up from canvas awnings, was rigged and she moved slowly inshore, and was able to anchor off Dhanuskodi in 12ft of water at 10.00. At 10.25 she heeled over to port and sank. All the hands were able to take to the boats and rafts as she foundered.

[TNA: ADM.1/16867]

29 May **MGB 110** motor gun boat
Hythe 1942; 37 tons; 71.9ft × 20.6ft; 1 × 2pdr, 2 × 20mm
Lieutenant George Dick Kendall Richards DSC†

Ordered to screen a minelaying operation by motor launches, which was to be carried out off the coast of Belgium, a force of four gunboats were to loiter off the West Dyck Bank. At 02.30 tracer fire was seen to be lighting up the sky to the south, in the direction of Dunkirk. At the same time a signal was received from *MTB 221*, reporting that she was in action with four large armed trawlers. The gunboats left their station to head towards the gunfire. As they headed south, dark shapes loomed out of the dark, and they turned into attack. The enemy responded vigorously, with heavy fire. The gunboats returned the fire, and it seemed that two of the trawlers had been brought to a halt, although *110* was hit by a shell which exploded on the mast. As the British force disengaged, they encountered a force of enemy patrol boats, and another sharp engagement took place, during which *110* took further hits and burst into flames following a hit in the engine room. The burning gunboat was then abandoned, with five survivors being picked up by the enemy. Eleven men died.

[TNA: ADM.199/778; Scott pp141–4]

30 May **UNTAMED** submarine
Walker 1942; 545/735 tons; 180ft × 16ft; 1 × 3in,
4 × torpedo tubes
Lieutenant Gordon Maurice Noll†

Newly completed, the *Untamed* had arrived at Campbeltown on 29 May to conduct exercises and work up her newly joined crew to an operational state. The following day she sailed in company with the armed yacht *Shemara* to carry out diving exercises off Sanda Island. She dived at 13.50 and the *Shemara* fired dummy Hedgehog anti-submarine projectiles, using small buoys attached to the submarine's conning tower which were visible as markers as a target. At 14.36 it was noticed that the buoys had disappeared, so the yacht made the sound signal of dropping a small charge ordering the submarine to indicate her position, but there was no response, and a short time later a swirl of water was seen near her last known position. Several attempts were then made to order the submarine to surface, by dropping a series of small explosive charges, but without any result. By 16.00 staff on the yacht were concerned for the safety of the submarine and informed the shore authorities that all was not well. They gained an Asdic contact which they believed to be the *Untamed*, and the sound of engines being worked, and tanks being blown was heard, which seemed to indicate that she was in difficulty. All sounds from the submarine ceased at 17.45. The position, about 4.2 miles west of Ship Light House, was marked with dan buoys and the yacht anchored. At about midnight the diving tender *Tedworth* arrived on scene, and prepared to send down divers, but the tide and weather conditions were such that it was not until the following morning that they were able to descend. They found the submarine at 11.15, lying on an even keel and with no obvious damage. There was no response to tapping on the hull, and it was clear that all the crew were dead. It was decided to salvage the submarine and floating cranes and lifting craft were employed and on 15 June she was lifted from the seabed, but it was another week before she was at Campbeltown. She was pumped out, the bodies recovered, and an investigation commenced. It was believed that the most likely reason for her sinking was procedural error. The Ottway log, a device for measuring the speed through the water, had to be lowered through the hull into the sea. To raise the log, it would be wound back into a stowage tank, the valve beneath it shut, and it could then be lifted clear. It was found that an attempt had been made to close the valve, but the log was not completely retracted, meaning that the valve had not shut. The tank cover was open, which, as the bottom valve was still open, would have resulted in sea water pouring into the submarine at great pressure. It would seem that the bulkhead door to the machinery space, location of the flood, could not be properly closed as it was distorted. The bulk of the crew went to the control room and abandoned the fore ends to the sea, but two men had evidently stayed behind to try and secure the distorted door but failed. With the forward compartments flooding, the submarine would then have started to dive, but some tanks were evidently blown in an attempt to stabilise the dive or even bring her to the surface, but this failed, and she went to the bottom. It would then appear that a series of attempts were made to bring her to the surface, as evidenced by the sound of engines working and tanks blowing, heard by the *Shemara*. This was heard to cease at 17.45, and it is believed that at this time efforts to raise her were given up, and it was decided to escape from the submarine using the after escape hatch. This delay in attempting to escape immediately was considered to have been a major error, as the air would have been increasingly foul. The survivors evidently then faced another problem, as it was found that the flap valve to the escape hatch had failed to work correctly, apparently having assembled 90

degrees from the correct position. How this happened is unknown, as it had apparently been checked as correct earlier. It may have been removed for maintenance and cleaning and wrongly reassembled. What it meant was that the engine room could not be flooded rapidly to equalise the pressure and allow an escape. An alternative means of flooding was evidently found, but the underwater drain cock, which allowed water out of the compartment had not been closed, which meant that any water that did enter simply flowed out. The fact that this was not noticed, or any corrective action taken would seem to be evidence that the mental processes of the crew were being affected by CO_2. The causes of her loss may therefore be attributed to poor drill, a lack of appreciation of the situation, deficient training and, towards the end, CO_2 poisoning. Thirty-six men died.
[TNA: ADM.1/14943; Evans pp.359–69]

3 June LCT (2) 129 landing craft, tank
Deptford 1941; 296 tons; 143ft × 31ft; 2 × 2pdr
Listed in the *Statement of Losses* as being 'lost', cause and place unknown, in November 1944, *LCT 129* was actually paid off on this date at Malta, with extensive damage, and as repairs were not deemed practicable, she was ordered be employed locally as a dumb lighter.
[TNA: ADM.199/774]

6 June SARGASSO yacht
Govan 1926 (*Atlantis*) requisitioned 1939; 223 tons; 116.3ft × 20.6ft
Lieutenant Francis Cecil Corbet Knight RNVR
Employed as a dan layer, she was attached to the Ninth Minesweeping Flotilla based at Portsmouth. During the night of 5/6 June shore-based radar had detected hostile surface ship movements to the south and west of the Isle of Wight, and it was suspected that the enemy had been engaged in laying mines. This was confirmed when a mine was discovered the following morning. The flotilla proceeded to the area to commence sweeping operations, accompanied by the *Sargasso*. At 14.25 as the group approached the area declared as hazardous, she detonated a mine and sank in 2 minutes. Two men were lost. Her position was noted at the time as 50.31.32N 01.42.12W. A subsequent enquiry found that the extent of the designated danger area had been established by plotting radar tracks, and it was actually too small an area. The mines had been laid by a German torpedo boat flotilla.
[TNA: ADM.199/243]

11 June WALLAROO minesweeper
Sydney 1942; 650 tons; 162ft × 31ft; 1 × 4in, 1 × 20mm
Lieutenant Eric Sinclair Ross RANR
Royal Australian Navy. Ordered to escort two American Liberty ships clear of the coast of Western Australia, the ships took up a line ahead formation, with the *Wallaroo*

leading. The plan was for the ships to be escorted until midnight, when they would be dispersed to proceed independently. At 23.55, then being in position 31.25S 114.33E, the order to disperse was passed by flashing light to the ship immediately astern of the escort, the *John Whittier*, and at the same time the minesweeper commenced a turn to starboard. Soon after they had done so, a ship was sighted looming out of the darkness, and it was realised that this was the second ship in the convoy, the *Henry Gilbert Costin*. The helm was put over to port, but it was too late, and the *Costin* struck the *Wallaroo* on the starboard side under the bridge. The ship was damaged, but remained afloat but steadily settled, and finally sank at 07.10. Three men were lost. At the subsequent court martial, it was found that the cause of the collision was the dispersal order, which was also the order for the ships to steer new courses. The *Costin* had dutifully turned to her new course, and *Wallaroo*, instead of maintaining her course until the merchant ships were clear, by immediately putting her helm over had turned into the oncoming steamer. Lieutenant Ross was severely reprimanded.
[TNA: ADM.156/245]

12 June LCF 13 landing craft, flak
Meadowside 1942; 470 tons; 175ft × 31ft; 4 × 2pdr, 8 × 20mm
Lieutenant Bernard James Bryant Morris RANVR
Deployed to the Mediterranean, she supported the landings on the Italian island of Pantelleria. With the island secured, she remained in the harbour as a guardship with her sister *LCF 9*. The island then became the target for repeated German air raids. During the morning of 12 June there was a series of raids, mostly by Fw 190 aircraft and during one of these at 12.15 she was straddled by a number of bombs which peppered her with shrapnel. Later that afternoon she was again shaken by a number of near misses, with one bomb exploding close to the ship, adjacent to the bridge. This caused widespread damage, with a 2pdr gun mounting being blown overboard and several plates sprung by the shock. The engine room reported that water was entering, and all power was lost. She drifted across the harbour to lie alongside the seaboard side of the mole, where she again came under air attack and suffered more damage from near misses. The following day efforts were made to haul her off, but all failed and she was abandoned as a wreck.
[TNA: ADM.199/639; ADM.202/448]

14 June MGB 648 motor gun boat
Hamworthy 1943; 90 tons; 110ft × 21.3ft; 1 × 6pdr, 1 × 2pdr, 2 × 20mm
Lieutenant Kenneth Egremont Anson Bayley RNVR
The island of Pantellaria was taken by an Allied force on 11 June, and 2 days later *MGB 648* in company with

MTB 656 was deployed to the island from Malta. They arrived at first light and went alongside a moored water tanker, which had been abandoned. They had scarcely done so when the harbour came under air attack from a pair of Fw 190 aircraft, and during this a bomb exploded under the boat amidships. The boat was covered in water and smoke and was so badly shaken that water was reported entering. She was run into shallow water to prevent her sinking but was found to be so severely damaged that she was written off as a total loss.
[Reynolds, Dog Boats pp57–8]

18 June LCT (3) 358 landing craft, tank
Thornaby 1942; 350 tons; 175ft × 31ft; 2 × 2pdr
Having taken part in the landings on the island of Pantellaria on 11 June, she remained to support those ashore by ferrying supplies. During 11 June as she attempted to enter the harbour, she ran hard aground and started to fill with water. Efforts to free her failed and she was subsequently abandoned as a total loss.
[TNA: ADM.199/639]

18 June LCT (3) 395 landing craft, tank
Meadowside 1942; 350 tons; 175ft × 31ft; 2 × 2pdr
Having taken part in the landings on Pantellaria on 11 June, the landing craft sailed on 17 June with a detachment of the Royal Army Service Corps embarked. The following morning at 08.20, then being about 2 miles off Monastir, the ship detonated a mine, which exploded under the hull amidships. Several men were blown overboard, and the hold was wrecked, killing and trapping many of the troops. Another landing craft closed to take off the surviving soldiers. The landing craft was later towed inshore and run aground but written off as a total loss. Thirty-five soldiers were killed.
[TNA: ADM.199/639; WO.361/445]

26 June MGB 644 motor gun boat
Teddington 1942; 90 tons; 110ft × 21.3ft; 1 × 2pdr,
2 × 20mm
Lieutenant Ernest Michael Thorpe
A group of coastal forces craft, gunboats and a torpedo boat, were deployed from Bizerte to carry out an offensive patrol off Marsala, Sicily. Before they reached their target however, when between Marsala and Mazzara, *644* detonated a mine, suffering serious damage and starting a fire in the engine room. The other boats closed to take off the crew, and then fired several rounds into the wreck to ensure that she sank in position 37.30N 12.10E. One man lost his life.
[Reynolds, Dog Boats p60]

3 July LST 429 landing ship, tank
Baltimore 1942; 1,625 tons; 316ft × 50ft; 1 × 12pdr,
6 × 20mm
Lieutenant Commander Jack Jenkins RNR
Ordered to the Mediterranean she was employed supporting the Allied forces in North Africa. Having loaded 200 tons of ammunition and trucks and a small number of soldiers, she was also towing a pontoon causeway when she sailed from Sousse bound for Sfax. At 20.55 a fire was discovered under the engine of one of the trucks and the alarm was raised. Fighting the fire promptly got under way, but despite this the fire spread and as a precaution both of the boats were lowered, and preparations made for abandoning the ship. At 21.30 small-arms ammunition started to explode, and it was decided to leave her, the crew and the troops taking to the boats, assisted by the boats of *LST 303* that was in company. By 22.00 all were clear, by which time she was well alight. She continued to burn until a large explosion occurred, and she broke in half, her bows remaining afloat for some time before sinking. There were no casualties.
[MacDermott p30]

8 July LCT (4) 547 landing craft, tank
Middlesbrough 1942; 200 tons; 171ft × 38.8ft; 2 × 20mm
In Convoy SBS1 bound for the landing areas in Sicily loaded with six Sherman tanks, she pounded in heavy weather, with several leaks developing, until she finally foundered in position 34.48N 12.15E.
[TNA: ADM.199/640]

10 July Operation 'Husky' – invasion of Sicily
During the early hours of 10 July, amphibious landings were carried out on twenty-six beaches spread along 100 miles of the south–eastern coastline of Sicily. Surprise was achieved and there were few casualties during the landings. Air raids on the landing forces commenced during the morning, and during one air raid, by a mix of Ju 88 and Fw 190 aircraft during the early afternoon, two landing craft on 'Acid' beaches near Syracuse were reported to have been damaged by near misses. From secondary sources, both of these craft were subsequently written off. These would appear to be:

LCT (3) 300 landing craft, tank
Thornaby 1942; 350 tons; 175ft × 31ft; 2 × 2pdr
Three men killed.

LCT (3) 410 landing craft, tank
Meadowside 1942; 350 tons; 175ft × 31ft; 2 × 2pdr
Four men killed.
[TNA: ADM.358/4306; Winser p88; London Gazette 28 April 1950; www.robpedley.co.uk/world-war-2-navy-diary.html]

★ ★ ★

12 July SILVER CLOUD channel patrol boat
1933 requisitioned 1941; 53 tons; 65ft × 15.6ft
Lieutenant Richard Eric Breydon RANVR
Royal Australian Navy. Employed as a local patrol vessel at Sydney, she was so damaged by fire that she was subsequently written off as a total loss. There were no casualties.
[Cassells p67]

15 July MGB 641 motor gun boat
Bo'ness 1942; 90 tons; 110ft × 21.3ft; 1 × 2pdr, 2 × 20mm
Lieutenant Peter Hughes SANF
In company with *MGB 643* and *MGB 646*, she was on a night patrol to the south of Messina when they sighted a surfaced submarine. All of the boats altered course inshore to engage, but their target submerged before their fire could take effect. They now came under heavy fire from a shore battery, and with the third salvo it scored a direct hit amidships on *641*. The other boats laid smoke and initially cleared the area, but later returned to pick up the crew. Before they did so, the commanding officer and several of the crew managed to swim ashore where they were taken prisoner.
[Reynolds, Dog Boats p64; Pope p119]

17 July MTB 316 motor torpedo boat
Bayonne NJ 1942 (*PT 58*); 34 tons; 77ft × 20ft; 1 × 20mm, 2 × torpedo tubes
Lieutenant Richard Brittain Adams RNVR[†]
Based at Augusta, Sicily, she was one of a group of four torpedo boats conducting a night patrol along the eastern coast of the island, up to the approaches to the straits of Messina. As they neared the northern end of the patrol line a large warship was seen approaching through the channel. The boats split up and tried to work their way into attacking positions on either side of the target. *316* in company with *315* went to the east to attack the enemy on the port side, but the target turned towards them and opened fire with large and small-calibre weapons with increasing accuracy. *316* was hit, and very quickly caught fire and then blew up. Although the other boats launched torpedoes, no hits were obtained, and the enemy ship, which was the Italian cruiser *Scipio Africano*, was not damaged. There were no survivors, eleven men being lost.
[Pope pp121–2; Reynolds & Cooper, Mediterranean MTBs at War pp71–2]

22 July MTB 288 motor torpedo boat
Bristol 1942; 40 tons; 72.6ft × 19.3ft; 1 × 20mm, 2 × torpedo tubes
Lieutenant Peter Ronald Archie Taylor DSC RNR
Stationed in the Mediterranean she was alongside at Augusta, Sicily, when that port came under air attack.

At 03.45 a bomb exploded close to her stern and she subsequently foundered. There were no casualties.
[Pope p125; Reynolds & Cooper, Mediterranean MTBs at War p73]

27 July LCT (3) 353 landing craft, tank
Thornaby 1942; 350 tons; 175ft × 31ft; 2 × 2pdr
LCT 353 was secured alongside the merchant ship *Empire Austin* in the harbour at Syracuse, Sicily, when the harbour came under repeated air attacks. During a raid at 11.00 *LCT 353* received a direct hit and sank. One man was lost.
[TNA: ADM.199/640]

(early) August PARTHIAN submarine
Chatham 1929; 1,475/2,040 tons; 270ft × 29.11ft; 1 × 4in, 8 × torpedo tubes
Lieutenant Cyril Astell Pardoe RNR[†]
Sailed from Malta 21 July to carry out a patrol in the southern Adriatic but never heard or seen again. The submarine was due to arrive at Beirut on completion of the patrol on 11 August but failed to arrive and was posted missing on that day. She had failed to report by radio when ordered to do so on 6 August, and it was presumed that she was lost before that date, the most likely cause hitting a mine. However, there is an outside possibility that an air attack was responsible – an Italian aircraft reported sighting a submarine at 19.30 on 5 August, 16 miles south-east of Point Linguetta, and patches of oil were seen following a depth-charge attack. Four officers and sixty-one men were lost.
[Evans p370; TNA: DEFE3/868 p126; https://www.uboat.net/allies/warships/ship/3400.html]

5 August RED GAUNTLET trawler
Stockton 1930 requisitioned 1939; 338 tons; 133.7ft × 25ft; 1 × 12pdr
Lieutenant James Noel Childs RNVR[†]
Based at Ipswich, she was ordered to carry out a night patrol in company with another armed trawler, the *Hornbeam*, in the vicinity of number 52 buoy, off Felixstowe. At 02.08 the bridge staff on the *Hornbeam* heard a loud explosion, and then realised that the *Red Gauntlet* seemed to be sinking rapidly. A few minutes later firing was heard, and tracer seen to the north-east, and after some confusion a single star shell was fired in that direction, but nothing could be seen. The *Hornbeam* then carried out a perfunctory search of the area, but could find no sign of her consort, until at first light they found a patch of wreckage and four men were subsequently picked up, the only survivors. They reported that at about 02.00 hydrophone effect (HE) was reported, apparently from engine noises, on the port beam. This was, however, lost, but then a few minutes later HE was again reported, but this time on

the starboard beam. This bearing was ordered to be checked, but before this could be confirmed a torpedo track was seen on the starboard side, and she was hit on the starboard bow. The ship broke up and rapidly sank, disappearing in less than a minute. The pair had been the target for an attack by enemy torpedo boats, *S 86* having fired the torpedo that sank *Red Gauntlet*. The firing seen by *Hornbeam* to the north-east had been trawlers in the next patrol area engaging the enemy boats. The commanding officer of the *Hornbeam*, Lieutenant Walter Parker RNVR, was subsequently criticised for his actions. He had been slow to react to the events of the night, and seemed unsure of what to do, having to be prompted to carry out certain actions. He was informed that he had incurred their Lordships' displeasure and was relieved of his command.
[TNA: ADM.178/306]

8 August   MGB 64   motor gun boat
Hythe 1941; 28 tons; 70ft × 20ft; 1 × 20mm
Sub-Lieutenant Eoin Cameron Glennie RNVR
Based at Felixstowe she had undertaken a night patrol off the Essex/Suffolk coast in company with other boats, but poor weather forced the early abandonment of the work. In high seas all the boats pounded heavily, and *64* started to make water, and it was feared that she had suffered a broken back. When it was clear that she was sinking the crew were removed by *MGB 58* and she was abandoned. A later search of the area by aircraft failed to find any trace of her, indicating that she had indeed foundered.
[Reynolds, Home Waters MTBs p103; Hichens p337]

9 August   CORY BROS   tug
38 tons; requisitioned 1942
Employed locally at Algiers, at 15.40 an oil barge caught fire in the harbour, and this spread to threaten a nearby cargo ship, the *Empire Commerce*, and in attempting to assist, the tug also caught fire and was a total loss.
[TNA: ADM.199/640]

14 August   SARACEN   submarine
Birkenhead 1942; 715/990 tons; 201ft × 23.9ft; 1 × 3in, 6 × torpedo tubes
Lieutenant Michael Geoffrey Rawson Lumby DSO
The submarine sailed from Algiers 6 August for a patrol off the western coast of Italy and Corsica. On 13 August she was loitering off the port of Bastia in a flat calm sea and a clear blue sky. At 22.30 she came to the surface to recharge batteries, finding the sea as still as glass and a large full moon. At 23.45 ships were sighted closing from the north which appeared to be Italian patrol boats, and the boat was dived. The vessels were the corvettes *Euterpe* and *Minerva*, and they were conducting an anti-submarine sweep. At 00.14 the

Minerva gained a sonar contact at 700m and carefully manoeuvred to confirm and then attack the target. The attack commenced at 00.46 and over the next 3 minutes, thirty-six depth charges were dropped by the *Minerva* in a small area. This caused considerable damage to the submarine, which was 'whipped' badly, with glass breaking and fittings coming loose and the after ends were found to be filling with water and were sealed off. The submarine took a pronounced bows-up attitude and became difficult to control and she 'porpoised' up and down, coming to the surface and then plummeting to 400ft. Lieutenant Lumby decided that she could not be saved and ordered her to be taken to the surface and abandoned. At 00.59 she came to the surface and immediately came under fire from the corvettes. The crew hastily scrambled onto the casing and then into the sea, with Lumby the last to leave, first ensuring that the main vents had been opened, which ensured that she sank. The corvettes spent some time in the area picking up the survivors, but two men were found to be missing, believed drowned.
[Evans pp371–7]

14 August   NORDNES   drifter
1902 requisitioned 1941
A former Norwegian fishing vessel that successfully escaped from Norway in January 1941 and evidently subsequently employed as a harbour duty vessel, she is listed as being lost 'cause and place unknown' but it is believed to have been in Iceland.
Note: the name is wrongly spelled 'Nornes' in the official list.
[Statement of Losses p28]

15 August   MTB 665   motor torpedo boat
Appledore 1943; 95 tons; 110ft × 21.4ft; 1 × 2pdr, 2 × 20mm
Lieutenant Peter Andrew Ruttan Thompson RCNVR
Part of the 33rd MTB Flotilla based at Augusta, Sicily, she was ordered to conduct a night patrol along the Straits of Messina in company with two other MTBs. At 01.24 as they crept along the coast, they were illuminated by a searchlight from the shore. Other searchlights were soon focussed on the boats, which then became the target for fierce fire from shore batteries. The boats were turned through 180 degrees and making smoke, tried to clear the area. As they withdrew *665* received a direct hit in the engine room and came to a halt in a cloud of flames and smoke, the main fuel tank having been set on fire. She was ordered to be abandoned, Carley floats being put over the side. Unable to stop and give assistance in the hail of intense and accurate fire, the other boats were able to get clear. Thirty minutes after the incident they met with a flotilla of 'short' torpedo boats, which moved closer inshore and steered north

to try and render assistance. They sighted the burning wreck of *665*, drifting towards the Sicilian coast, but could not get close enough to help and had to clear the area as dawn broke. Two men were killed, but the survivors were picked up by the Germans, and taken prisoner.

[Pope p126; Reynolds, Dog Boats pp65–6]

15 August LST 414 landing ship, tank
Baltimore 1942; 1,625 tons; 316ft × 50ft; 1 × 12pdr, 6 × 20mm
Lieutenant Commander Harold Robert Austin King RNR
Part of a small convoy of landing ships bound for Bizerte from Malta, she was towing *LST 416*. They were about 4 miles from Cani Island light when at 01.30 they came under air attack. The attack achieved surprise, as the first they knew of the danger was when an aircraft was seen just as it dropped a torpedo and then passed ahead of the ship. Manoeuvring was almost impossible due to the tow, and moments later she was hit amidships by a torpedo. A fire was started, spreading thick fumes throughout the ship and the auxiliary engine space was flooded. The tow was slipped, and fire fighting started which was successful in getting the flames under control and *LST 425* closed to give assistance. By 03.00 she was in tow behind *425* and continued towards Bizerta. At 07.00 *LST 414* was run ashore to the north of Bizerte. On inspection it was found that the torpedo had blown a hole 50ft long and 15ft deep, there were extensive cracks in the hull and her back was broken. It was therefore decided to abandon her as a total loss, and she was later cannibalised for spares. One man was killed in the attack.

[MacDermott p35; www.bbc.co.uk/history/ww2peopleswar/ stories/86/a7971186.shtml]

22/23 August LEVANT SCHOONER NUMBER 4
Requisitioned 1942
Lieutenant Hubert Phillips RANVR†
Sailed 22 August from Haifa in company with *Levant Schooner Number 3*, both of them locally-acquired Greek caiques, bound for Paphos in Cyprus, they parted company during the afternoon, and she was last seen by her consort about 90 miles from the Syrian coast. *Number 3* arrived the following afternoon without incident, but nothing was seen of *Number 4*. Motor launches searched along the track but could find no trace of her. Five men were lost.

[TNA:ADM.199/774]

27 August EGRET sloop
Cowes 1938; 1,250 tons; 276ft × 37.6ft; 6 × 4in, 2 × 20mm
Commander John Valentine Waterhouse DSO
Part of the Fifth Escort Group, which were tasked to carry out an offensive anti-U-boat sweep in the Bay of Biscay, at 12.45 on 27 August they were in position 42.10N 09.18W, steering south at 15 knots in a line abreast formation, the *Egret* being in the centre. At 12.55 a large group of eighteen aircraft were seen approaching from astern. The ships took up a new, defensive formation, with *Grenville* and *Rother* forming one line, and *Jed* and *Athabaskan* another. The *Egret* took up a 'roving' position, to give support to whichever column was under attack. The aircraft broke up into groups, to attack from each side of the formation. At 13.05 the first attack took place on the port side. When at a range of about 3 miles they were seen to release what appeared to be a rocket-assisted bomb. Although most missed, one hit the *Athabaskan*, causing considerable damage. By now the other aircraft were attacking and also launched rocket-assisted bombs. Several appeared to be aimed at *Egret*, but the helm was put over to starboard and speed increased and two of the guided bombs sailed past to explode astern, whilst a third exploded about 30ft from the starboard side. She again altered course and was turning to starboard as a further two missiles were seen approaching. One fell harmlessly into the sea astern, but the second, which was apparently going to miss altered course –' … the bomb banked sweetly and turned smoothly to starboard like a well piloted fighter aircraft and so continued straight for the bridge' (from Commander Waterhouse's statement). The bomb struck the ship between the funnel and the after Oerlikon position with a violent explosion. The port side of the ship was blown open over a large area of the engine and boiler rooms and fires were started. The ship took a list to port and then she continued to roll slowly over. Commander Waterhouse immediately ordered the ship to be abandoned, and in less than a minute after being hit, she rolled over onto her beam ends and then floated bottom up. She remained in this position until 14.30 when she finally sank. One hundred and ninety-four men were killed. The group had been attacked by Dornier Do 217 aircraft from II/KG 100 using the Hs 293 missile.

[TNA:ADM.1/14507]

28 August LCT (3) 416 landing craft, tank
Meadowside 1942; 350 tons; 175ft × 31ft; 2 × 2pdr
Lieutenant James Matthew William Ruffell RNVR
Lying at Tripoli, the landing craft had embarked a large quantity of stores for the army, including ammunition and shells. At 09.00 as she was preparing to sail, smoke was seen rising from the cargo amidships, where smoke generators had been stowed. Within a short time, the smoke was very thick and spread, which hampered fire-fighting efforts, and within minutes a large fire had broken out. When the flames reached the ammunition, she was ordered to be abandoned, and at 09.12 there was a large explosion, scattering burning debris and

shells across the harbour. She continued to burn, with a series of explosions, until 14.00 when a fire float was brought alongside and extinguished the fire, but the craft was burnt out.

[TNA: ADM.1/15021; ADM.199/640]

28 August LCT (3) 301 landing craft, tank
Thornaby 1942; 350 tons; 175ft × 31ft; 2 × 2pdr
Lieutenant Stanley Albert Harrison RNVR

Moored alongside *LCT 416* at Tripoli when a fire broke out (see above). When *416* blew up, burning debris started fires in the cargo which soon spread, and she was also abandoned due to the threat of exploding ammunition. At 14.00 the *Ah Kwang* fire float came alongside and doused the flames, but it was found that the centre section of the landing craft was seriously damaged, with buckled and split plates, and she was written off as a total loss.

[TNA: ADM.1/15021; ADM.199/640]

2 September LCI (L) 107 landing craft, infantry, large
Orange 1942; 238 tons; 150ft × 23.8ft; 4 × 20mm

Driven ashore in poor weather at Reggio, Italy, and written off as a total loss.

[TNA: ADM.199/949]

5 September ML 108 motor launch
St Monance 1940; 57 tons; 110ft × 17.6ft; 1 × 3pdr,
6 × mines
Lieutenant Dennis Alfred Jefferis RNVR

In company with other motor launches, *108* was tasked to lay mines about 3 miles off the French coast in the vicinity of Le Touquet. At 00.05 she had just laid her sixth and last mine when there was a violent explosion about 20ft astern, which shook the ship considerably, shattering fittings, stopping the engines and putting the steering gear out of action. *ML 101* closed and a tow was quickly rigged, but almost immediately parted. *ML 104* had now joined, and another tow was rigged, this time successfully. Water was slowly entering aft, and the engine room reported that it was slowly filling and attempts to restart the engines failed. Hand pumps were used, and a chain of buckets formed to assist with clearing the water. The weather was poor, and as they slowly headed north the rising sea caused waves to break over the stern and quarterdeck, adding to the water entering the launch. By moving stores and ammunition the weight was shifted forward but by 05.30 she was well down by the stern and seas were now regularly breaking over her. At 06.15 she lurched and heeled to starboard, and it was decided to abandon her, the men being taken off by the other launches. She slowly rolled over and floated bottom up; *ML 104* then sank the wreck by gunfire. It was believed that she was sunk by her own mine. The last one launched

probably sank straight to the bottom instead of floating and detonated when it hit.

[TNA: ADM.1/15079]

6 September PUCKERIDGE escort destroyer
Cowes 1941; 1,050 tons; 264.2ft × 31.6ft; 6 × 4in, 4 × 2pdr,
2 × 20mm
Lieutenant John Cecil Cartwright DSC

Sailed from Gibraltar at 18.00 bound for Algiers, she was zigzagging at 22 knots when at 20.15 in position 36.06N 04.44E there was a violent explosion aft as she was hit by a torpedo, followed seconds later by a second detonation of greater magnitude as another torpedo hit. Engines stopped, all power was lost, and the engine room flooded rapidly. The ship began to go down by the stern, and she heeled over to port, both conditions worsening rapidly. The bows rose up and she had sunk within 10 minutes. The Spanish steam ship *Antiquera* stopped to pick up the survivors which she transferred to the armed trawler *Anglia* later. She had been attacked by *U 617* (Brandi). Sixty-one men died.

[TNA: ADM.267/94]

7 September STARFISH channel patrol boat
Sydney 1936 (*Corsair*) requisitioned 1942; 19 tons;
38ft × 11.5ft
Royal Australian Navy. Employed as a local patrol boat at Sydney, she ran aground 2 miles south of Wollongong Lighthouse, and was subsequently written off as a total loss.

[Cassells p69]

8 September MTB 77 motor torpedo boat
Portsmouth 1942; 38 tons; 71ft × 19.2ft; 2 × torpedo tubes
Lieutenant John Brian Sturgeon DSC RNVR

As part of the campaign in Italy, Allied naval forces gave support to the army in their advance northwards. Following successful landings near Reggio, a further amphibious landing was planned at Vibo Valentia, codenamed Operation 'Ferdy'. Resistance was stronger than had been anticipated, and the attacking forces came under fire from the shore and air attack. *MTB 77* was part of the force covering the landings, with Rear Admiral Rhoderick McGrigor (Flag Officer, Sicily) embarked. At 08.00 the MTB was closing a landing craft about 3 miles west of the harbour when an air attack developed, and a bomb dropped by an Fw 190 exploded under the starboard quarter. The boat was lifted violently stern first into the air, throwing the Admiral off the bridge and injuring several others. Badly shattered, with her bottom blown out from the stern up to the forward mess deck, the boat settled and started to sink immediately. *HDML 1128* came alongside and took off the crew before she sank.

[TNA: ADM.267/121; Pope pp128–9; Reynolds & Cooper, *Mediterranean MTBs at War* p77]

8 September LCT (4) 624 landing craft, tank
Middlesbrough 1942; 200 tons; 171ft × 38.8ft
[Sub-Lieutenant John Arthur Norton RNVR?]
Sailed from Bizerte with a large number of other landing craft on 4 September as Convoy FSS1 for Italy, and they arrived off Palermo on 6 September. They sailed the following day to make their way towards the landing beaches for the assault at Salerno. The ships came under regular air attack, and at 16.30 on 8 September, the convoy was again attacked, a group of Fw 190 aircraft concentrating on the rear ships of the group. At 16.50 a bomb landed close to *LCT 624*, apparently exploding under the hull, breaking her back and throwing much of the deck cargo overboard. The tug *Resolute* closed to take off the crew, as the craft was now settling and had caught fire. She sank about 30 minutes after the attack.
[TNA: ADM.199/641; http://www.ibiblio.org/hyperwar/USCG/ X-Sicily-Italy/USCG-X-M.html]

9 September Operation 'Avalanche' – Allied landings at Salerno, Italy
With the Allied forces in Sicily making good progress, followed by an unopposed landing at Calabria, a landing in force further north in Italy was planned. Salerno was chosen it was close to the port of Naples and within range of Allied aircraft. A number of troop carrying convoys sailed from North African ports, to arrive off the landing beaches in the early hours of 9 September. The landings went ahead under very heavy fire from German shore positions during which some landing craft were lost.

LCT (2) 154 landing craft, tank
Paisley 1941; 296 tons; 175ft × 30ft; 2 × 2pdr
As she closed the shoreline towards 'Roger' beach, she detonated a mine and sank, the survivors being picked by a motor launch.
Note: this loss is not included in the official *Statement of Losses*.
[TNA: ADM.199/949]

LCT (3) 391 landing craft, tank
Middlesbrough 1942; 350 tons; 175ft × 31ft; 2 × 2pdr
Loaded with tanks and men from the Royal Scots Greys, she was heading in the landing area, when the force came under heavy fire from the shore. At 04.40 she was hit by a heavy-calibre shell and set on fire. Unable to control the flames, and clearly sinking, she was ordered to be abandoned. She sank about 30 minutes after being hit. Three soldiers were killed.
Note: the *Statement of Losses* gives date of 1 October as the date of being paid off.
[TNA: WO.361/479]

LCT (4) 572 landing craft, tank
Thornaby 1943; 200 tons; 171ft × 38.8ft; 2 × 20mm
Lieutenant John Wade RNVR
Sailed from Tripoli loaded with two tanks and two field guns plus jeeps and the associated crews, she arrived off the beaches at Salerno to approach 'Roger Green' beach. She was about 4 miles offshore when at 04.30 there was a large explosion under the craft as she detonated a mine. The cargo was thrown around, wrecking the vehicles and causing several casualties amongst the soldiers. *ML 565* and *MTB 605* were called alongside to take off the troops as she settled and started to sink. The crew searched the wrecked hold to try and find any wounded survivors but could see only dead bodies. *ML 247* took off the crew just before she rolled over and sank. Fifteen soldiers were killed.
[TNA: WO.361/464]

LCT (4) 626 landing craft, tank
Middlesbrough 1943; 200 tons; 171ft × 38.8ft; 2 × 20mm
No details have been found for the loss, but the date would suggest lost during Salerno landings.
[Statement of Losses p54]

★ ★ ★

9 September NOSS HEAD drifter
Requisitioned 1940; 22 tons
Lieutenant Richard Archdall Vicars RNVR
Based at Freetown, Sierra Leone, she foundered after the securing strops holding a tank engine which was being lowered into the hold broke. The engine smashed through the wooden hull.
[http://www.naval-history.net/WW2BritishLossesbyName3.htm]

10 September ABDIEL minelayer
Cowes 1940; 2,650 tons; 400.6ft × 40ft; 6 × 4in, 4 × 2pdr 6 × 20mm, 156 mines
Captain David Orr-Ewing DSO
Laden with 400 troops of the First Airborne Division, along with 150 tons of stores, including seven field guns, eight jeeps and several motorbikes, she arrived at Taranto during the evening of 9 September, as part of Operation 'Slapstick', the occupation of that port. At 19.45 she anchored 3.6 cables (720 yards) from Castel St. Angelo in the harbour, in 12 fathoms, it being intended to land the troops and equipment the following day. At 00.15 there was a deep roar followed by a powerful whipping motion which shook the ship violently as there was an explosion directly under the ship. The force was such that the multiple 2pdr 'pom-pom' mounting was seen to leave its mounting and disappear in the direction of the quarterdeck. She heeled over to port, and the stern immediately started to settle. After about 30 seconds she righted herself for a short time, and then slowly heeled over to port again, breaking in half as she did

so. The two pieces remained afloat at a steep angle for several minutes before sinking. No more than 2 minutes had elapsed from the explosion to her demise. Seven officers and forty-two ratings of the *Abdiel* were killed, along with fifty-eight soldiers. Several TMC (or GN) influence mines were subsequently found nearby, some of which had been set to fire on a time-delay fuse; the torpedo boats *S 54* and *S 61* having laid them as they left the harbour immediately before the British arrival. [TNA: ADM.199/243]

10 September MTB 284/MTB 285
Annapolis 1943; 37 tons; 71ft × 19.3ft
Borne as deck cargo on the merchant vessel *Larchbank* from Baltimore, USA, bound for Colombo and Calcutta, both craft were lost when the *Larchbank* was torpedoed by the Japanese submarine *I-27* (Fukumura) in the Indian Ocean, in position 07.38N 74E and sank very quickly.
[Lloyd's War Losses p705; Rohwer, Axis Submarine Successes p270]

11 September ROSA drifter
Findochty 1908 (*Desire*) requisitioned 1940; 83 tons; 86.7ft × 18.3ft
Skipper Joseph Smith RNR
Listed as being 'lost, cause & place unknown'. She had been based in Scottish waters, at Granton, but is understood to have foundered in the Clyde. She was later salvaged and sold in April 1944.
[Statement of Losses p28; TNA: ADM.1/24129; http://canmore.org.uk/event/941019]

19 September BYMS 2019 minesweeper
Bellingham 1942; 207 tons; 130ft × 24.6ft;
1 × 3in, 2 × 20mm
Lieutenant Henry Francis Defrates RNR
Part of the minesweeping flotilla working in the Gulf of Taranto clearing mines, she was acting as the dan layer for the group as they working off the port of Crotone. At 15.30 there was a large explosion under the bows which carried away the forepart of the ship as far back as the bridge. Although damaged, she remained afloat, and the minesweeper *Poole* closed to lift off the survivors and then rigged a tow. The wreck was towed into the harbour at Crotone where she settled and finally sank at 04.00. Four ratings were killed. It was believed that she had struck a contact mine which had been rigged with a snag line.
[TNA: ADM.199/243; Minett p239]

20 September LAGAN frigate
Middlesbrough 1942; 1,370 tons; 283ft × 36.5ft; 2 × 4in,
10 × 20mm
Lieutenant Commander Albert Ayre RNR†
Part of Escort Group C2, that formed the escort to Convoy ON202, thirty-eight ships bound for North

America that sailed from Liverpool 15 September, *Lagan* initially escorted the Norwegian merchant ship *Elizabeth Bakke* from the Clyde to join the convoy during 17 September. Allied intelligence became aware of a large number of enemy submarines that were being formed in patrol lines in the mid-Atlantic, and it was decided to join ON202 with another convoy, ONS18. Just before the conjunction took place, the attacks commenced. At 02.23, the ships then being in position 57.09N 27.28W *Lagan* was ordered to detach and investigate a radio intercept (HF/DF) to the west and gained a radar contact at a range of 4,100 yards. A few moments later, the contact disappeared, evidently as the submarine had dived. As she continued to close the datum at 15 knots, at 03.05 there was an explosion under the stern of the ship. The screws, rudder and steering gear were blown off and about 30ft of her stern disappeared. Forward of this, minor damage occurred, mostly caused by the whipping effect of the blast. A fire was started by the ignition of calcium flares, but this was quickly brought under control. The ship remained stable, and was taken in tow by the tug *Destiny*, and arrived at Liverpool on 24 September. One officer and twenty-eight ratings were lost. Her attacker had been *U 270* (Otto), who had used the T5 acoustic homing torpedo, the first time the weapon had been employed in action. The ship was found to be so severely damaged that repairs were not worthwhile and was declared a constructive total loss.
[TNA: ADM.267/30; CB.4273 p277]

20 September ST CROIX destroyer
Hingham 1919 (*McCook*) transferred 1940; 1,190 tons; 311ft × 30.7ft; 3 × 4in, 1 × 12pdr, 2 × 20mm, 3 × torpedo tubes
Lieutenant Commander Andrew Hedley Dobson, RCNR†
Royal Canadian Navy. Acting as senior ship of Ocean Escort Group C9, *St Croix* was assigned to provide extra protection to the combined convoy ON202/ONS18. The attacks on the convoy started during the early hours of 20 September with the sinking of two merchant ships and the escort *Lagan* being damaged (see above). At 19.00 a patrolling RCAF Liberator aircraft attacked a U-boat sighted on the surface, astern of the convoy, and the *St Croix*, with *Itchen* and *Narcissus*, were detached to investigate. At 19.51 as they approached the datum point, stretching ahead of her consorts, there was a large explosion under the stern, when she was hit by a T5 homing torpedo fired by *U 305* (Bahr). This was followed by a several other explosions evidently as depth charges, dislodged by the blast, detonated. The ship came to a stop and assumed a list to port. She remained stable but was clearly sinking and abandon ship was ordered. This was underway when she was hit by a second torpedo at 20.44. This produced a large explosion, and

she broke up. The stern section immediately sank, the bows sinking minutes later. The *Itchen* picked up eighty-one survivors, but all of these were lost when the *Itchen* was sunk (see 23 September). The merchant ship *Wisla* picked up one man, who was to be the only survivor. One hundred and forty-seven men died.

[Morgan & Taylor pp338–40]

20 September POLYANTHUS corvette

Leith 1940; 940 tons; 190ft × 33ft; 1 × 4in, 2 × 20mm
Lieutenant John Gordon Aitken RNR[†]

Part of Ocean Escort Group C2 which joined the escort to westbound Atlantic Convoy ON202 which sailed from Liverpool on 15 September. When the Canadian destroyer *St Croix* was torpedoed (see above), the *Polyanthus* was ordered to search for survivors. She was reported to be on scene at 22.30 and almost immediately she sighted a submarine diving and then gained an Asdic contact at 2,500 yards. She was zigzagging down the line of contact when at 22.36 she was hit by a T5 acoustic homing torpedo fired by *U 952* (Curio) and sank immediately. One survivor was picked up by the *Itchen* but was lost when that ship was torpedoed (see 23 September). Seven officers and seventy-seven men were lost.

[TNA: ADM.267/118]

21 September DE ZEE MEEUW trawler

Ostend 1930 requisitioned 1940; 100 tons

Former Belgian fishing vessel, she formed part of the Thames Auxiliary Patrol, she sank following a collision with the American tanker *Pan-Maine* (7,237 tons) at 14.30 in Gravesend reach. There were no casualties.

[TNA: ADM.199/2278]

22 September BRAE FLETT drifter

1902 requisitioned 1942; 54 tons

Listed as being 'lost, cause and place unknown'; she appears to have been based at Greenock and used as a harbour tender, so presumably in the Clyde area.

[Statement of Losses p28; http://canmore.org.uk/event/581737]

22 September OCEAN RETRIEVER drifter

Lowestoft 1912 requisitioned 1940; 94 tons; 87.5ft × 19.6ft
Chief Skipper William Alfred Capps DSC RNR[†]

One of a number of drifters on patrol in the Edinburgh Channel off Sheerness, they had been lying to for some time, having taken the opportunity to put nets over the side for fish. At 19.00 the group started to haul in the nets and were getting under way when at 19.07 there was a vivid flash, and a cloud of black smoke engulfed the vessel as she detonated a mine. She broke up and sank immediately, with the other drifters closing to pick survivors out of the water. Her position was noted as

51.29.54N 01.04.00E. Ten men lost their lives. It was believed that whilst fishing she had drifted out of the swept channel into a danger area.

[TNA: ADM.199/243]

22 September Operation 'Source' – Attack on the Tirpitz in Altenfjord

During 1942–3 a plan to attack German heavy units which were based in Norway using small manned submersibles was formed. An attempt was made using Chariot 'manned torpedoes' in November 1942, but this failed when the Chariots were lost from the fishing vessel carrying them. In September 1943, an attack was planned by a force of midget submarines, which were to be towed across the North Sea from Loch Cairnbawn to the entrance of the Altenfjord. After slipping their tow, the boats would proceed independently whilst dived to take up positions in the shelter of the fjords, recharging batteries before commencing the attack. This would take place during the early hours of 22 September, with charges being set to explode at 08.30. During the afternoon of 11 September, the towing submarines *Truculent* (with X 6), *Syrtis* (with X 9), *Thrasher* (with X 5), *Seanymph* (with X 8), *Stubborn* (with X 7) and *Sceptre* (with X 10) sailed, with passage crews embarked, with high hopes that three large German ships, *Tirpitz*, *Scharnhorst* and *Lützow*, would be in the fjords. The passage was quiet until the weather deteriorated during 15 / 16 September. Over the next hours *Syrtis* lost X 9 and the *Seanymph* lost her tow with X 8. Despite these losses the remaining boats pressed ahead. Only three of these were able to carry out an attack, with X 10 having to abandon the attack, but was lost later (see 3 October). Details of the individual boats are as follows:

16 September X 9 midget submarine

Barrow 1943; 26/29 tons; 51.7ft × 5.9ft
Lieutenant Edward Kearon RNVR[†]

Under tow by the *Syrtis*, the passage was uneventful, and at 01.20 on 16 September, X 9 dived after her scheduled period on the surface for battery charging; the position noted a short while later was 70.49N 11.40E. At 09.07 charges were dropped by *Syrtis* as the signal for the midget to surface, but there was no response. The tow was recovered but found to have parted. The *Syrtis* reversed course and searched along the track but could not find her missing charge. An oil track, running east, towards the slipping position was seen at 15.45, which was thought may have been from a midget, but a further search failed to find any trace of X 9 and it was presumed that she had foundered with all four members of the passage crew.

18 September **X 8** midget submarine
Barrow 1943; 26/29 tons; 51.7ft × 5.9ft
Lieutenant Brian Mahoney McFarlane RAN

At 04.00 on 15 September, the towline parted between *X 8* and the towing submarine, whilst the former was submerged. The loss was not immediately realised by the *Seanymph*, but *X 8* was brought to the surface. Although the submarine reversed course and searched along the track when the loss was realised, it was the *Stubborn*, with *X 7* in tow that found *X 8* at 16.30. She stayed in company with her new supporter, to rendezvous with *Seanymph*, but at 23.59 contact was again lost. This was because a shouted course change had been misheard in the wind, and she steered 146° instead of 046°. *Seanymph* meanwhile had been searching the area, but it was not until 17.00 on 16 September that she finally found her missing charge, and the tow was re-connected. However, this was not the end of her troubles. At 07.25 the next morning *X 8* reported that she was experiencing difficulty in maintaining trim. This did not improve during the day, and it was realised that the buoyancy chambers of the explosive charge on the starboard side were leaking, making the craft unstable. It was decided to release the charge, and at 16.30 this was done, the charge being set to 'safe'. Despite this, the charge was heard and felt exploding sometime later, but no damage was caused. Difficulty was still being experienced with keeping trim, and it was suspected that the second, port charge, was also leaking. It was decided to release this charge also, but as the 'safe' setting was not trusted, a 2-hour fuse was set before releasing the charge at 16.55. At 18.40 there was a large explosion as the charge detonated. Although *X 8* was about 3.5 miles from the release point, she was 'whipped' by the force of the blast, and this caused considerable damage, breaking lights, distorting doors and fracturing pipes. At first light on 18 September an assessment was made of the situation, and as it was clear that she was of no further use, having lost her charges, and in poor material state, it was decided to scuttle her. By 03.45 all the crew had been removed and she sank in position 71.41N 18.11E.

The remaining boats slipped from their parent submarines between 18.45 and 20.00 on 20 September, to submerge and pass the minefields off Soroy Island and through the Stjernsund to take up positions off Brattholm Island. Here they surfaced, to recharge batteries and make final preparations for the attack.

22 September **X 6** midget submarine
Barrow 1943; 26/29 tons; 51.7ft × 5.9ft
Lieutenant Donald Cameron

Lieutenant Cameron left his position off Brattholm Island at 01.45 for his run into the anchorage, despite discovering that the periscope had become flooded, making observations blurred and distorted. As they approached the nets which formed a barrier, they took advantage of the passage of a small coaster to pass through the obstruction at 05.05. She then went deep, and tried to clear the periscope, to no avail, and then the periscope hoisting brake motor burnt out, adding to Cameron's problems. By 07.05 they were approaching the anchorage where the battleship *Tirpitz* lay, but then ran aground on the north shore near the battleship and broke surface. She managed to free herself and submerge, only to break surface again, now close to her target. She was seen from the *Tirpitz*, which launched a motor boat to investigate, and small-arms fire was opened. Cameron was in a precarious position, with no working periscope; the gyrocompass had just failed, and the boat had clearly been seen. Realising that the situation was hopeless it was decided that she should be abandoned after laying the charges, and at 07.30 after destroying some equipment, the side explosive charges were released, and she was brought to the surface close by the port bow of the battleship. The crew of four were taken off by the motor launch as the submarine slipped under the surface.

X 7 midget submarine
Barrow 1943; 26/29 tons; 51.7ft × 5.9ft
Lieutenant Basil Charles Godfrey Place DSC

She left the shelter of Brattholm at 00.45 to commence the penetration of the Kaafjord. By 03.40 she was approaching a screen of anti-submarine nets, and with a patrolling launch in the area she went deep but fouled the nets. An hour was spent working the boat backwards and forwards, in attempts to free herself from the barrier and find a way through. By violent action she finally broke through the barrier, possibly through an overlapping gap, and after another incident with a wire across her periscope standard, she was able to proceed and headed towards their target, the battleship *Tirpitz*. They trimmed for 40ft and Place took the boat close to their target, actually hitting the battleship approximately below 'B' turret. He then gently pushed the boat under the keel of his target and the starboard explosive charge was released. The boat had swung to port, so by going slowly astern, the *X 7* moved further along the battleship's keel before releasing the second charge under 'X' turret. This complete, she moved to get clear, only to foul an anti-submarine net. For the next 45 minutes she worked to free herself, but at 07.40 with the air running out she came to the surface and scraped over the top of the net. The crew of the *Tirpitz* and other ships in the anchorage were now on full alert following the adventures of *X 6*, and she was seen and attracted a hail of small-arms fire. Place took her down to 60ft, only to run into another net. There was no time to deal with this, as at 08.12 there were two huge explosions, close together, as the explosive charges dropped by *X 6* and *X 7* exploded. The shock wave threw the midget clear of the nets but caused considerable damage; all compasses and gauges were out of action, she had no periscope and no air, so at 08.30 she was brought to the surface, finding themselves close to a practice target moored in the centre of the fjord. Place climbed out onto the casing, despite coming under small-arms fire. The boat, still with way on, struck the target and the bows dipped, throwing water into the boat and she lost buoyancy and sank, the hatch slamming shut as it went under, sinking to the bottom of the fjord. Place, who had scrambled onto the target was immediately taken prisoner, but the other crew members had to wait for 2 hours before the pressure equalised in the submarine, with the air becoming increasingly foul. Two of the men passed out, leaving only Sub-Lieutenant Robert Aitken able to raise the hatch and come to the surface. She was subsequently salvaged by the Germans, minus her bows, on 1 October, finding one body, that of Lieutenant Whittam, who was buried with full military honours. The remains of ERA Whitley were never found. The charges laid by the X-craft failed to sink the battleship, as had been hoped, but did considerable harm, with split and distorted plates, several compartments flooded, two turrets were lifted off their roller paths, rangefinders and electrical equipment put out of action and there was widespread shock damage, all of which put her out of service for 6 months, not being able to move until April 1944.

X 5 midget submarine
Barrow 1942; 26/29 tons; 51.7ft × 5.9ft
Lieutenant Henty Henty-Creer RNVR[†]
After leaving her towing submarine, the *X 5* was last seen at 23.15 by the crew of *X 7* off Soroy Island, heading towards the layup position off Brattholm Island. Her movements after that are unknown, but at 08.43 the periscope of a midget submarine was clearly seen from the *Tirpitz*, about 500 yards from the anti-submarine nets, being observed both by the Germans, and Lieutenant Lorimer of *X 6* who was then being held on the upper deck of the battleship as a prisoner. A fierce fire was opened on the craft, and the destroyer *Z-27* dropped several depth charges onto the position and no further activity was seen. This can only have been *X 5*. Whether she had laid her charges and was making her escape or attempting to carry out an attack is unknown. No trace of the boat or her crew has ever been found.
[*Supplement to the London Gazette 11 February 1948*]

★ ★ ★

22 September HULDA tender
Sydney 1937; requisitioned 1942; c10 tons; 38ft × 9.6ft
Royal Australian Navy. A motor launch, employed as a tender in Papua New Guinea, she had been damaged by fire in September 1942, but was rebuilt. When off Buna, she was attacked and sunk by a Japanese aircraft. There were no casualties.
[*Cassells p33*]

23 September GOLDEN EFFORT drifter
Banff 1914 requisitioned 1939; 86 tons; 88.8ft × 19.1ft
Listed as having sunk off Greenock; cause unknown.
[*Statement of Losses p28; http://canmore.org.uk/event/864650*]

23 September ITCHEN frigate
Paisley 1942; 1,370 tons; 283ft × 36.6ft; 2 × 4in, 10 × 20mm
Commander Clement Edward Bridgeman DSO RNR[†]
Part of the Ninth Escort Group, which during the morning of 19 September, had joined the escort to the combined convoys ON202/ONS18. The convoy came under sustained attack from a wolf pack of U-boats from 20 September (see above). The *Itchen* had rescued eighty-one survivors from the Canadian *St Croix*, and one officer from the *Polyanthus*. During the night of 22/23 September the attacks continued, and the escorts were stretched, investigating Asdic and radar contacts. At 23.55 in approximate position 53.30N 39.45W, HMCS *Gatineau* reported a small contact ahead of the convoy, suspected to be a surfaced submarine. She investigated, and was joined by other escorts, including the *Itchen* which was stationed just ahead of number 3 column. At 00.02 the *Itchen* illuminated the contact with her searchlight, clearly picking out a submarine and fire was opened on the target. There was then a large explosion which scattered debris over a wide area and caused some confusion as it was not clear which ship had been hit, whether merchant ship, escort or submarine. Only when all escorts were called did it become clear that the *Itchen* had gone. She had been hit by a T5 acoustic homing torpedo fired by the submarine, *U 666* (Engel), which probably triggered a magazine explosion; the U-boat survived and later found debris from the frigate on her conning tower. Just two survivors were picked up by the Polish merchant ship *Wisla*, and 148 officers and men died.
[*TNA:ADM.267/118*]

24 September MMS 70 motor minesweeper
Lowestoft 1940; 225 tons; 105ft × 23ft; 1 × 20mm
Lieutenant Lionel Claude Evans RNVR
Based in the Mediterranean, she was at Taranto, when they were informed that there was an urgent need for minesweepers at Brindisi. She sailed at 19.00 in company with the minesweeper-whalers *Swona* and *Sahra*, forming

up astern of the landing craft *LCI (L) 313*, which was carrying an Italian pilot. None of the minesweepers had a copy of the route, and only a sketchy knowledge of the local minefields. All trusted that the landing craft would lead the way, believing that she must be the senior officer. In line ahead, the landing craft leading, they proceeded along the Italian coast, but Lieutenant Evans noted that they seemed to have altered course earlier than he had expected. He was correct; the landing craft had overestimated the speed and led the group into a minefield. At 02.15, off the port of Gallipoli, in approximate position 39.59.15N 17.47.15E there was a large explosion under *MMS 70* which blew her apart. All personnel below deck were killed, and the commanding officer and nine ratings that had been on the upper deck were thrown into the water. The other ships appeared to take no notice and steamed on, leaving the survivors struggling in the water. They were eventually picked up at 14.00 by a local fishing boat, having spent the day clinging to the wreckage. Ten men were killed. The subsequent inquiry found that the voyage had been poorly organised. No ship had been detailed as the senior officer, so everybody assumed someone else must be. No one had been properly briefed over the route to be taken or on the presence of unswept minefields. Far too much trust had been placed in the Italian pilot embarked in the landing craft. The inquiry found that he relied heavily on shore lights, but all of these were extinguished, apart from one, making him useless. When *70* was mined, confusion had followed; the *Sahra* had seen the explosion and stopped, but on asking the presumed leader in the landing craft for assistance was told they should investigate, whilst the landing craft steamed on. The *Sahra*, fearing that it had been a mine felt that they could not enter a danger area, and with the leader disappearing into the night, decided to abandon the search and follow. It was judged that all of the commanding officers had shown a lack of initiative with the commanding officer of the landing craft displaying a 'lamentable lack of judgement' in failing to report the explosion and subsequent disappearance of *MMS 70* and leaving the scene. Lieutenant Evans should also bear some responsibility. His navigation had been 'casual', simply following the ship ahead and although he realised that the group had altered course too early, failed to do anything about it. All the officers were informed that they had incurred the displeasure of the Commander-in-Chief.
[TNA: ADM.1/15086; ADM.358/1796]

25 September **FRANC TIREUR** trawler
Selby 1916 requisitioned 1940; 314 tons; 137ft × 24ft;
1 × 12pdr
Lieutenant Commander Leslie Rawson Greenwood RNVR
During the night of 24/25 September there were indications of enemy surface activity in the North Sea,

with intercepted radio transmissions being followed by reports of contacts from shore radar. Armed trawlers and coastal forces on the east coast were warned that enemy vessels were operating between 54B and B8 buoys (Harwich to Orfordness). This was actually a sortie by Dutch-based torpedo boats to lay mines. At about 01.00 the *Franc Tireur* found the enemy craft near number 52 buoy, off Lowestoft. She altered towards the threat, but the enemy had already responded by firing torpedoes. She was hit amidships by a torpedo, probably fired by *S 96* and she sank very quickly with the loss of fifteen men.
[TNA: ADM.267/132]

25 September **DONNA NOOK** trawler
Selby 1915 requisitioned 1939; 307 tons; 132ft × 24ft;
1 × 12pdr
Skipper Frank Emmitt RNR
As with the *Franc Tireur* (above), the *Donna Nook* was one of the armed trawlers patrolling off the Essex/ Suffolk coast when they encountered a group of minelaying patrol boats. After the loss of the *Franc Tireur*, there were a series of confused actions, involving the armed trawlers, motor gun boats and motor launches, with star shell and flares being fired. During this period, one of the enemy torpedo boats, *S 96*, that had torpedoed the *Franc Tireur* was rammed twice by motor launches, and subsequently abandoned in a sinking condition. At 02.27 during another engagement with the enemy boats as they attempted to clear the area, the *Donna Nook* was rammed by another trawler, the *Stella Rigel*, whilst the latter was turning to engage; she rolled onto her beam ends and subsequently sank. All the crew were rescued by *Stella Rigel*.
[TNA: ADM.267/132]

27 September **INTREPID** destroyer
Cowes 1936; 1,370 tons; 312ft × 33ft; 2 × 4.7in, 2 × 6pdr,
6 × 20mm
Commander Charles Arthur de Winton Kitcat
Following the surrender of Italy, in mid-September the Eighth Destroyer Flotilla, including *Intrepid*, deployed to the eastern Mediterranean, to give support to campaign to occupy the various islands in the Aegean that had been occupied by Italian forces. The *Intrepid*, in company with the Greek destroyer *Vasilissa Olga* was ordered to proceed to Leros, which they reached on 26 September. On arrival the ships secured to buoys at the head of the harbour, and Commander Kitcat went ashore to meet the senior officer. Soon after he had landed a large formation of Ju 88 aircraft was seen approaching which then commenced a dive bombing attack on both ships. The *Olga* was hit aft and her after magazine exploded blowing off her stern and she sank. The *Intrepid* was surrounded by bomb splashes, but only

received one hit, which struck the port side to puncture the bulkhead between number 3 boiler room and the engine room. Despite the suddenness of the attack the ships engaged the attackers, and one plane was shot down before they cleared the area. The ship was towed by motor launches into shallow water under a cliff to receive better protection whilst work went on to repair the damage. At 16.30 another air raid commenced, again by a large number of Ju 88 aircraft which concentrated on the *Intrepid*. One bomb hit her aft that blew her stern off up to 'X' gun, and she heeled over to port and started to settle by the stern. Motor launches were called alongside, and she was ordered to be abandoned. She continued to slowly sink until she was resting on the bottom of the harbour, her upper works and bows remaining visible for some time, until she finally rolled over and sank at 07.25 the following day (27th). Fifteen men were killed.
[TNA: ADM.267/109]

29 September LCT (4) 621 landing craft, tank

Middlesbrough 1942; 350 tons; 175ft × 31ft; 2 × 2pdr

Deployed to the Mediterranean, she had taken part in the landings at Salerno. At the end of September, the weather was poor, and this culminated in 2 days of gale force winds, gusting up to 80 mph. During this storm, a number of small craft were driven ashore; one of these was *LCT 621*, which received such damage as to be written off as a total loss.

Note; the *Statement of Losses* gives the date 7 October, which is likely to be the date of being written off charge.
[TNA: ADM.199/641]

30 September LST 79 landing ship, tank

Jeffersonville 1943; 1,625 tons; 316ft × 50ft; 1 × 12pdr, 6 × 20mm

Lieutenant Commander Ralph Palmer Robertson Taylor RNR

Based in the Mediterranean, she sailed from Algiers on 28 September fully loaded with vehicles and a number of Allied soldiers, bound for Ajaccio, Corsica. They arrived at that port during 30 September and having secured to a jetty bows first, disembarkation began. As they were unloading, the harbour came under surveillance by a Ju 88 aircraft. At around 17.00 another Ju 88 was seen overhead, and a few minutes later a force of Do 217 aircraft were seen approaching from the south. Although Spitfire aircraft were now on scene, the attackers launched several glider bombs. At least two of the bombs seemed to be aimed at the LST, with one being guided towards her until it struck the mole about 500ft to port. The second bomb struck *79* on the port side amidships, exploding in a fuel tank. A large fire was started, and the ship took a list of 5 degrees to port. Not only was there a major fuel fire burning, but the damage was extensive, with the decks

buckled and folded back. Finding that the engines were still working, Taylor got under way to take the burning ship clear of the jetty, until she was brought up by the stern anchor. At 18.15, when it was clear that nothing more could be done, she was ordered to be abandoned. She continued to burn until she finally sank at 23.00. Four men were killed in the attack.
[MacDermott p51]

30 September LCT (5) 2231 landing craft, tank

Memphis 1943 (*LCT 231*); 143 tons; 112.3ft × 32.9ft; 2 × 20mm

Apparently being carried as cargo in *LST 79* when she was sunk by a glide bomb (see above)
[MacDermott p51]

2 October LCT (4) 618 landing craft, tank

Middlesbrough 1942; 350 tons; 175ft × 31ft; 2 × 2pdr

Busily employed in the Mediterranean supporting the landings in Italy, she was used to ferry supplies to the 'Avalanche' beaches at Salerno, despite the poor weather. During 2 October, the strong winds drove her into shallow water and was written off as a total loss.
[TNA: ADM.199/641]

3 October X 10 midget submarine

Barrow 1943; 26/29 tons; 51.7ft × 5.9ft

Lieutenant Kenneth Robert Hudspeth RANVR

Part of the force of midget submarines that took part in Operation 'Source' in late September, they had been slipped from their towing submarine, the *Sceptre*, at 20.00 on 20 September. A number of defects became apparent as they made their way towards the Norwegian coast, which included the failure of the gyrocompass. It was therefore decided to head into Smajfjord, on the north coast of Stjernoy and remedy the defects before proceeding any further. After lying on the bottom all day, she was able to get under way at 17.50 with most of the defects cleared. She steered along the shoreline on the surface and was able to enter the Altenfjord, with the intention of reaching Kaafjord, and the *Tirpitz* by first light on 22 September. However, at 01.40 she was forced to dive by the approach of a surface vessel, and when she attempted to raise the periscope, the motor burnt out, filling the submarine with smoke. It was then found that both the gyro and magnetic compasses were not working. She was forced to surface to clear the boat of smoke. This done, they submerged again, and the boat was taken to lie on the bottom, at 195ft, off Tommerholm Island. An assessment of the situation made it clear that they were in no fit state to carry out an attack, but it was decided to work on the defects and hoped to continue with the operation if possible. They heard the big explosion as the charges laid under the *Tirpitz* went off, and the numerous explosions of depth charges being

dropped. By nightfall it was clear they would not be able to proceed, and any hopes of attacking were abandoned. They surfaced at 18.00 and made for the entrance to the fjord and for the next 2 days, vainly searched for an escort. After again taking shelter in an isolated fjord, they made one last effort to find one of the towing submarines and was sighted at 01.00 by the *Stubborn*, which took her in tow, a towing crew replacing the operational. At 12.30 on 3 October the towline parted, and it was with much difficulty that it was re-rigged, during which the submarine had struck the midget a glancing blow. The opportunity was taken at this time for the operational crew to take over the manning. At 17.00, just as the tow was getting underway again, a severe weather warning was received, and this was followed by an order to scuttle the craft as it was considered unlikely that it would survive a gale. The crew were therefore removed to the *Stubborn* and at 20.40 with the Kingston valves and hatches open she was abandoned, sinking 5 minutes later in position 66.13N 04.02E.
[Supplement to the London Gazette 11 February 1948]

3 October ARACARI trawler
Beverley 1908 requisitioned 1943; 245 tons; 120.5ft × 22ft
Skipper Reginald John William Brown RNR
Employed as a water boat, she dragged her anchors in a strong gale and was wrecked on Filicudi Island, Sicily.
[TNA: ADM.199/641]

3 October MEROR trawler
Selby 1905 (*Emperor*) requisitioned 1939; 250 tons; 127ft × 22.1ft; 1 × 12pdr
Skipper Harry James May RNR
Part of an escort to an east coast convoy, as they cleared the Humber estuary, at 08.25 there was a large explosion under the stern of the trawler. The nearest vessel, the tanker RFA *War Nizam*, which was immediately astern, stopped and as the trawler was slowly settling took the crew off and rigged a tow. It was hoped to reach Grimsby, but within minutes of commencing the tow she took an alarming list to starboard, forcing the small number of men who stayed onboard as a towing crew to jump overboard. She continued to heel over until she capsized and sank. They had been steering along a channel that had been swept the day before, and it was thought likely that she had fallen victim to an acoustic mine laid overnight.
[TNA: ADM.199/243]

3 October LCT (1) 3 landing craft, tank
Walker 1940; 226 tons; 135ft × 29ft; 2 × 2pdr
Sub-Lieutenant Robert Edward Fletcher RNVR
On 3 October, the island of Kos, recently occupied by the British, was attacked and rapidly overwhelmed by a German force. Landing craft that had gathered in the port of Kos were ordered to sail at nightfall and make for safety in Turkish waters. By 17.30 the enemy was reported to be only a mile away and the harbour was coming under mortar fire, so it was decided to sail immediately rather than wait for dusk. *LCT 3* had suffered a severe petrol leak and desperate efforts to repair this and get the engines started failed, and when a fire broke out in the engine room, it was decided to abandon her. Confidential books were destroyed, and guns thrown overboard before the crew moved to other landing craft. She was subsequently taken into German service as a prize and renamed *GD-06* and allocated to the *Küstenschutzflottille Dodekanes*. She was recovered in May 1945 and returned to RN service, to be converted to a maintenance vessel, *NSC(L) 94*.
[TNA: ADM.1/20020; ADM.199/1040]

9 October CARLISLE light cruiser
Govan 1918; 4,290 tons; 425ft × 43.5ft; 8 × 4in, 4 × 2pdr
Captain Harold Fielding Nalder
During September Allied forces commenced a campaign in the Aegean, with the intention of taking islands formerly held by Italian forces, and this led to a German counter-attack. A force of destroyers led by *Carlisle* carried out a sweep through the Scarpanto Strait (Karpathos). As they withdrew to the south, they became the target of Ju 87 dive bombers. From mid-day the force was without fighter cover for a short time, and it was during this period that they came under air attack. At 12.00 then being in position 35.34N 27.39E, a group of Ju 87 aircraft was seen to be closing from astern and commenced a dive-bombing attack. *Carlisle* suffered two direct hits – the first hit struck a 4in gun mounting, the second bomb hit the after funnel. Both caused extensive splinter damage and started a fire in ready-use ammunition. A series of near-misses caused further damage, with two bombs exploding under the hull and others abreast the after boiler room. Plating and framing on the starboard side abreast the after fuel tanks were blown in, the after magazines flooded, steering gear failed, and the starboard shaft and propeller was lost with the port shaft distorted. Power was lost and she came to a stop. Fortunately, air cover arrived to drive off the attackers. *Carlisle* was taken in tow by the *Rockwood* and arrived at Alexandria on 16 October, where a survey decided that she was a constructive total loss. The ship remained in the port, acting as a local base ship. Twenty-four men were killed or died of their wounds.
[TNA: ADM 267/14]

9 October PANTHER destroyer
Govan 1941; 1,640 tons; 328.9ft × 35ft; 4 × 4in, 4 × 2pdr, 6 × 20mm, 8 × torpedo tubes
Lieutenant Commander Robert William, the Viscount Jocelyn
Having been engaged in an offensive sweep in the Dodecanese, searching for enemy shipping, she was in

company with the light cruiser *Carlisle*, and destroyers *Petard*, *Rockwood* and *Miaoulis*, returning to Alexandria. At 07.50 the force sighted two low-flying Arado seaplanes which shadowed them for some time before being driven off by the arrival of friendly fighter aircraft. Just after noon the group was closed by a number of Ju 87 dive bombers. They initially concentrated on the *Carlisle*, inflicting considerable damage on her (see above), before a group of five aircraft turned on the *Panther*. The first bomb was a direct hit, just abaft the funnel, the others being near misses, exploding all around her. The ship's back was broken, and within minutes she had broken apart, the bow and stern both rising clear of the water to stand vertically for some moments before sinking. Three officers and thirty-three men were killed. American P-38 Lightning fighter aircraft arrived on scene soon afterwards and shot down several of the Ju 87s.

[TNA: ADM.267/110]

11 October HYTHE minesweeper
Troon 1941; 656 tons; 165.6ft × 28.6ft; 1 × 12pdr, 2 × 2pdr, 2 × 20mm
Lieutenant Commander Leslie Beara Miller
Part of the escort to Convoy MKS27 from Alexandria to Gibraltar, the ships were off the coast of Algeria, in position 37.02N 05.04E, when at 01.00 the *Hythe* gained an Asdic contact. Reported to be on the starboard bow at 2,000 yards, the alarms were sounded, and the ship altered course towards the threat. The range was down to 400 yards and she was preparing to carry out a depth-charge attack, when at 01.12 she was hit by a torpedo. The explosion was under the bridge, between the boiler room and the forward provision room on the port side. She broke in half, the mast came down, a fire broke out, and she sank very quickly on an even keel. Sixty-two men lost their lives. She had been hit by a T5 acoustic homing torpedo fired by *U 371* (Mehl).

[TNA: ADM.267/116]

11 October LCT (4) 553 landing craft, tank
Middlesbrough 1942; 350 tons; 175ft × 31ft; 2 × 2pdr
Sank in the Gulf of Salerno, Italy, in approximate position 39.57N 14.28E after a submerged attack by *U 616* (Koitschka), which fired T5 homing torpedoes at a column of landing craft at 05.44 and 05.47 with one explosion observed on the last vessel.

[Rohwer, *Axis Submarine Successes* p15]

October USURPER submarine
Walker 1942; 540/730 tons; 180ft × 16ft; 1 × 3in, 4 × torpedo tubes
Lieutenant David Roger Oakley Mott†
Sailed from Algiers for a patrol in the Gulf of Genoa on 24 September and failed to return as expected on 12

October. The place and time of her loss is not known. A submarine carried out a torpedo attack on a transport in the early hours of 1 October, which although marginally outside her patrol area, must have been *Usurper*. On 3 October she was ordered to shift patrol area, but nothing was heard from her. It is probable that she struck a mine whilst in transit. There is an outside possibility that an attack by the German patrol vessel *Uj 2208* was responsible. She reported gaining an Asdic contact in the Gulf of Genoa during the morning of 4 October, in the region of 44.15N, 09.06E, which was attacked, although no results were observed. This was outside her patrol areas.

[Evans p378; https://www.uboat.net/allies/warships/ship/3561.html]

12 October ML 835 motor launch
Cairo 1943; 85 tons; 112ft × 18.4ft; 1 × 3pdr
Lieutenant Brian Close RANR
Part of the Third ML Flotilla based in the Mediterranean, from September 1943 they had been deployed to the Aegean. At the beginning of October *ML 835* was ordered to conduct an extended patrol in the vicinity of the island of Leros, which she did with some success, attacking and setting on fire an Italian cargo ship, the *Volta*, and shooting down an inquisitive Ju 88 aircraft. On 12 October they steered for Levitha Island, where it was intended that they lay up during the day, to allow the crew some rest before resuming their night patrols. At 06.25 a number of Ju 88 aircraft were seen approaching, which promptly attacked the launch. Although by vigorous manoeuvring she avoided any direct hits, a near miss from a bomb shook the launch considerably, putting the port engine and the radio out of action. During the morning, the air attacks continued unabated, and the launch managed to run close inshore and was eventually hauled into a position under the foot of some cliffs. As the enemy aircraft were still clearly intent of attacking her, the crew were ordered off the launch to take shelter ashore. In the late afternoon they returned to the launch during a lull in the attacks, but as they prepared to move her to deeper water another air attack started, during which she was set on fire and in a few minutes, was ablaze. She eventually sank after an internal explosion. One man was wounded in the attacks.

[Pope pp180–1]

15 October HEDGEHOG 'schooner'
Requisitioned 1943; 60 tons
Sub-Lieutenant David Norman Harding RNVR
One of the numerous Levant Schooner Flotilla vessels, a motley collection of schooners, caiques and local fishing craft taken over to be used for clandestine missions in the eastern Mediterranean. She was sailed from Leros

to proceed to Stampalia (Astipalaia) to embark a patrol of the Long Range Desert Group and a small number of German soldiers that had been captured. On arrival they found that the numbers to be embarked were far greater than expected – forty-eight men in all. They sailed on 14 October for the return journey to Leros, but they suffered an engine breakdown and diverted to the island of Levitha. Nothing more was heard from her, and on 17 October, *ML 359*, searching for her, found her deserted and burning in the harbour. It later emerged that the crew had been overpowered by the German prisoners. The island of Levitha was occupied by German forces on 18 October.
[TNA: ADM.1/20020; ADM.199/1044]

15 October **MTB 636** motor torpedo boat
Rosneath 1943; 95 tons; 110ft × 21.3ft; 1 × 2pdr, 2 × 20mm, 2 × torpedo tubes
Lieutenant Frederick Archibald Warner RNVR

In company with *MTB 633* and *MGB 658*, she deployed from the base at Maddalena during the afternoon of 14 October to carry out an aggressive patrol in the Piombino Channel, between the island of Elba and the Italian mainland. During the long passage *MTB 633* developed engine trouble, but the remaining pair pushed on, with *636* embarking Lieutenant Commander Greene-Kelly as the senior officer. At 01.16, two ships were sighted, identified as armed flak lighters (*K-169* and *K-176*). The pair carried out an attack, with *636* firing both her torpedoes, but to no effect, and they disengaged. They decided to split up and approach from different directions to carry out a gun attack. *MGB 658* was the first to engage, confusing the enemy by repeating the challenge flashed by light as they approached. When close to the lighter they opened fire to great effect, setting their opponent ablaze. As *658* disengaged, a second vessel could be seen closing and was presumed to be the second flak lighter; they flashed the night challenge used earlier by the first target and received a stream of tracer fire in return. Still in the belief that they were tackling the second enemy vessel *MGB 658* opened fire on the stranger and scored hits which set her opponent on fire. The flames then revealed the silhouette of her consort, *MTB 636*. Gunfire was ceased immediately, and they closed to render assistance as men could be seen jumping into the sea. They were forced to break off as the other enemy vessel could then be seen looming out of the darkness. This was promptly tackled, and although *658* was hit and suffered casualties, she was able to silence her adversary, which was seen to be listing and burning. *658* then returned to pick up men from the sea around the burning *636* before clearing the area, now illuminated by searchlights from the shore. Seven men were lost.
[Reynolds, Dog Boats pp68–9]

16 October **MTB 356** motor torpedo boat
Belfast 1943; 37 tons; 72.6ft × 19.3ft; 1 × 20mm, 2 × torpedo tubes
Lieutenant Ian Clarence Trelawney RNVR

In company with four other torpedo boats ordered to carry out a night patrol between the Hook of Holland and Ijmuiden. At 23.38, a group of two armed trawlers with two armed coasters were sighted, and as they were expected to be heavily armed, the torpedo boats turned away to clear the area. However, they were sighted and after a challenge by light, were illuminated by a star shell. This was immediately followed by heavy fire from the enemy. The torpedo boats returned fire, increased speed and made smoke but *356* was hit in the engine room by a large-calibre shell. This destroyed one engine and burst a petrol tank. The boat lost way and started to settle by the stern. *MTB 349* ran alongside to lift off all the crew and she was abandoned; scuttling charges being set before they left to ensure that she sank.
[Reynolds: Home Waters MTBs p110; TNA: ADM.199/536]

(14–16) October **TROOPER** submarine
Greenock 1942; 1,090/1,575 tons; 245.6ft × 26.6ft; 1 × 4in, 11 × torpedo tubes
Lieutenant John Somerton Wraith DSO DSC†

Sailed from Beirut for a patrol in the Aegean on 26 September and posted as missing when she failed to return on 17 October. On 30 September she landed agents in Kalamos Bay, Euboa, and on 14 October one of the Levant Schooner Flotilla craft sighted her in Alinda Bay, Leros. She is presumed to have been lost soon after this, probably from hitting a mine to the east of Leros. Six officers and fifty-eight men lost.
[Evans p379]

17 October **GLADMOR** auxiliary patrol
Perth 1907 (*Minnehaha*) requisitioned 1942; 7 tons; 32ft × 7ft
Skipper William Horace Paddon RANVR

Royal Australian Navy. Based at Fremantle, Western Australia, where she acted as a local patrol craft, she caught fire and was burnt out. There were no casualties.
[Cassells p31]

21 October **CHEDABUCTO** minesweeper
Vancouver 1941; 673 tons; 171.5ft × 28.6ft; 1 × 12pdr, 1 × 2pdr
Lieutenant John Herbert Bowen Davies RCNR

Royal Canadian Navy. Attached to the Gaspé force in Quebec, she was ordered to escort the tug *Citadelle* to join the inward-bound Convoy QS68. At 05.45 staff on the bridge observed the green or starboard lights of a ship to port. The minesweeper altered 10 degrees to starboard, the radar operator reporting that the contact was about 2,200 yards distant. The officer of the watch,

Sub-Lieutenant John Ross Morrison RCNVR, went to the bridge wing, just in time to see the bows of a ship looming out of the dark. Engines were ordered full ahead and the wheel put over, but at 05.55 she was rammed amidships by the cable ship *Lord Kelvin*, which went astern, leaving a large gash in the ship's side. She took a 10-degree list to port and started filling with water. Most of the crew were transferred to the *Lord Kelvin*, while efforts went on to try and control the water. Help arrived in the shape of the US Coastguard Cutter *Buttonwood*, which managed to take her in tow. She was moved inshore until at 13.30 she ran aground about 1.5 miles above St Simeon, the list steadily increasing. The remainder of her crew were then removed and later that day she rolled over and settled into the mud. One man died in the collision. The subsequent inquiry found that Sub-Lieutenant Morrison was not a qualified bridge watchkeeper, and should take no blame, as he should not have been placed in such a difficult position. The commanding officer, Lieutenant Davies, was advised that he had incurred 'the severe displeasure' of the Board by not ensuring that a qualified and more experienced officer had a night watch in busy narrow waters.
[McKee & Darlington p196]

21 October HDML 1015 motor launch
Bideford 1941; 46 tons; 70ft × 15ft; 1 × 3pdr
Based at Alexandria, Egypt, she foundered in heavy seas whilst supporting operations on the island of Leros, in the Aegean.
[TNA: ADM.116/5817; ADM.1/20020]

22 October HURWORTH destroyer
Walker 1941; 1,050 tons; 264.2ft × 31.6ft; 6 × 4in, 4 × 2pdr, 2 × 20mm
Commander Royston Hollis Wright DSC
During October 1943, following the successful landings in Italy and consequent surrender of that country, the attention of the Allies in the Mediterranean shifted to the Aegean. Many of the islands in the Aegean were garrisoned by Italian troops, and the British decided to take control of those islands before the Germans could do so. The moves were vigorously opposed by the Germans, based in mainland Greece. On the night of 21 October, the *Hurworth*, accompanied by the Greek destroyer *Adrias* were in the vicinity of the island of Leros, to create a diversion for a force which was to land stores on the island. At 21.56 when they were to the east of Kalimnos, at approximately 36.59.03N 027.06.08E, the *Adrias* detonated a mine which blew her bows off, but she remained afloat. *Hurworth* closed to take off casualties, and manoeuvred to come alongside, but was about 200 yards on the starboard quarter of *Adrias* when there was a terrific explosion on the starboard side under the bridge. The explosion broke her back,

the fore part sinking rapidly, the after part remaining afloat for some 15 minutes before disappearing, which allowed the motor boat to be released. The *Adrias*, damaged herself, could not assist, but did release floats and lifebuoys before moving away to run into shallow water at Gumusluk Bay, Turkey. The motor boat made it to the Turkish coast with thirty-eight survivors and several others, clinging to rafts and floats made it to Kalimnos and Leros, but six officers and 127 men lost their lives. The minefield had been laid by the German *Drache*.
[TNA: ADM.199/243; Rogers pp93–6]

22 October ORFASY trawler
Aberdeen 1942; 545 tons; 150ft × 27.6ft; 1 × 12pdr, 3 × 20mm
Skipper-Lieutenant George Alfred Whichelo RNR†
Orfasy had departed Lagos on 16 October bound for Freetown escorting the Norwegian tanker *Litiopa*. The last time she was seen was at dusk on the 21st when she took up a night screening position astern of the tanker. At 23.00 several explosions were heard by the crew of the tanker, and another explosion at 00.30, which they believed to be depth charges, presumably dropped by *Orfasy* who was in contact with a submarine. At 01.30 a large explosion was both seen and felt by the *Litiopa*, and this was believed to have been the trawler exploding after being hit by a torpedo. At 03.00 the tanker was attacked and sunk by a surfaced U-boat. Their attacker had been the *U 68* (Lauzemis). All thirty men onboard were lost.
[TNA: ADM.199/635]

23 October CHARYBDIS cruiser
Birkenhead 1940; 5,600 tons; 485ft × 50.6ft; 8 × 4.5in, 8 × 2pdr, 8 × 20mm, 6 × torpedo tubes
Captain George Arthur Wallace Voelcker†
After intelligence suggested that an enemy convoy would attempt to pass between Brest and St Malo, the cruiser was tasked to take charge of a group of destroyers and carry out an offensive sweep along the Brittany coast. Such sweeps, known as Operation 'Tunnel', had been carried out before and due to the efficient radar systems established along the French coast the Germans were well aware that these sweeps usually followed a similar track. The enemy were also fully alert to the possibility of a British intervention. Therefore, when the German tanker *Münsterland*, bound for St Malo, with a close escort of patrol vessels and minesweepers sailed from Brest, a covering force of five large torpedo boats acted as distant escort, prepared to react to any British activity, being assisted by the shore radar stations. The British force was not helped by being a group of ships that had not worked together before and were plagued with communications difficulties and misunderstandings.

The British force steered for Les Heaux light on the coast of Brittany and then at 00.30 altered course to the west and reduced speed to 13 knots. The Germans detected the British force as it approached the coast of Brittany, and the torpedo boats (*T22, T25, T26, T27* and the leader *T23*) were manoeuvred to bring the British 'up-moon' before closing to carry out a torpedo attack, which took their opponents by surprise. The escort destroyers in the British force intercepted German communications, indicating at least five hostile warships in the area, but it was not until 01.30, when they were off Triagoz that *Charybdis* detected surface contacts on radar, ahead of them at a range of 7 miles. These were the force of torpedo boats, but they were mistakenly identified by *Charybdis*, which was leading the force in line, as being the enemy convoy, and continued to close until the contacts were 4.5 miles distant, at which she altered course by 13 degrees to starboard to parallel the apparent enemy course. This course alteration order was not received by most of the escorting destroyers, who were uncertain of what was happening. The situation became more confused at 01.41, when, just as *Charybdis* altered round, *Talybont* detected several more radar contacts which she presumed was the convoy escort. The alteration of course presented the enemy with a good target, and at 01.45 with the radar contacts at 2 miles, just as *Charybdis* fired star shell to illuminate the target, she was hit on the port side by a torpedo fired by *T23*, which exploded under the torpedo tubes. This put the dynamo room out of action, putting the lights out, and 'B' boiler room started to flood, the ship taking an immediate list of 20 degrees to port. About 5 minutes later she was hit again, by a torpedo fired by *T27*, again on the port side, but further aft, exploding at 135 station. This caused extensive damage, losing all power and the engine room reported being flooded. The list increased rapidly and very soon the upper deck was awash. Floats were ordered to be released and the ship ordered to be abandoned. The bows steadily rose as she went down by the stern until they were vertical as she sank. She remained in this position for about half an hour with a third of her length out of water, and then sank with the loss of 462 men. This was at approximately 02.30. The commanding officers of the destroyers testified that it had been a confusing and difficult night. The CO of one of the group, the *Talybont*, later stated that none of the force ever saw the enemy and the CO of the destroyer *Grenville* stated that it was clear that the Germans ' … knew we always run along the same patrol line'. All COs testified that communications were unreliable; manoeuvring signals were not passed in time, and changes of course and speed had to be judged by observation.

[TNA: ADM.1/12488; ADM.199/541; ADM.267/75]

23 October **LIMBOURNE** destroyer

Linthouse 1942; 1,050 tons; 264.2ft × 31.6ft; 4 × 4in, 4 × 2pdr; 3 × 20mm 2 × torpedo tubes
Commander Walter John Phipps

One of escort destroyers that sailed from Devonport to join the *Charybdis* to take part in the doomed Operation 'Tunnel' to intercept an enemy convoy off Brittany (see above), she was the fourth ship in line as they approached the French coast. On board the *Limbourne*, the first indication that they were in contact with the enemy came with a report from 'Headache' (radio intercept of enemy communications) at 01.18. That it was 'loud and clear' showed that naval units were close by. At 01.35 the *Charybdis* had signalled that she had a radar contact to the west, and just 3 minutes later 'Headache' was reporting constant radio traffic, which indicated at least three enemy units were close by. When the cruiser altered course, the manoeuvring signal was not heard and the leading destroyers, *Grenville* and *Rocket*, uncertain of where the enemy was or the intentions of the cruiser, held their course, with *Limbourne* following them. This meant the cruiser was actually out of the line and exposed. 'Headache' was now reporting hearing firing reports, and just as *Limbourne* fired rockets to illuminate a shadowy contact on her port bow the *Charybdis* was hit by a torpedo. The destroyers ahead of her could now be seen to be leading round to port, so the *Limbourne* duly followed them, but as she was swinging round a torpedo track was seen. The wheel was put hard over but there was a large explosion forward. The hit was in the low power room, and then the forward magazine blew up, which demolished the forward section of the ship. She immediately took a list to starboard, but the bulkheads held, and she still had power. Both the commanding and executive officers were concussed and put out of action. Sub-Lieutenant Cunliffe-Owen took charge and despite the damage, some order was brought back to the ship, but it was found to be impossible to steer her. Dark shapes then loomed up out of the dark, which proved to be the other ships of the force, and the *Limbourne* was prepared for towing. *Talybont* managed to rig a tow, but it parted soon after as the ship was yawing wildly. The position was now judged to be impossible, with the likelihood of a successful tow being negligible. It was therefore decided to abandon her, and the after magazines were flooded and at 06.40 *Talybont* and *Rocket* fired torpedoes into her and she was left, decks awash. The torpedo boat *T22* claimed the hit on *Limbourne*. Forty-two men were lost.

[TNA: ADM.1/12488; ADM.199/541; ADM.267/75]

23 October CROMARTY minesweeper
Blyth 1941; 673 tons; 171.6ft × 28.6ft; 1 × 12pdr, 1 × 2pdr,
2 × 20mm
Lieutenant Commander Charles George Palmer DSC
RNZVR

In company with other ships of the 14th Minesweeping
Flotilla, she had been tasked to sweep for moored
contact mines in the western approaches to the Strait
of Bonifacio, between Corsica and Sardinia. They sailed
from Maddalena at 06.30 and at 11.15 formed up to
commence the work, employing Oropesa sweeps to
starboard, the force being led by an Italian motor launch,
followed by the *Cromarty* with *Poole*, *Seaham* and *Boston*,
with the whaler *Kai* and two motor minesweepers
acting as dan layers. Almost immediately the *Cromarty*
observed two mines come to the surface, evidently
having been cut free by the leading motor launch. Both
mines floated away down the port side, being left to be
dealt with by the dan layers. Then a third mine surfaced,
immediately ahead of the *Cromarty*. The helm was put
over, but it was too late and there was a large explosion
as she ran over the mine. The whole ship was lifted up,
the engines stopped, and she heeled over to starboard in
a bows–down attitude. The boats were cleared away and
Carley floats released as the ship slowly righted herself.
She continued to roll over, taking a sharp list to port,
and then broke in two. The bow portion quickly sank,
and the remaining half floated for a moment or two
before capsizing and sinking. Five officers and fifteen
ratings were killed.
[TNA: ADM.199/243]

23 October LCI (L) 309 landing craft, infantry, large
New Jersey 1943; 234 tons; 150ft × 23.8ft; 4 × 20mm
Lieutenant Raymond Longbottom RNVR

One of a group of seven landing craft that was returning
to UK from the Mediterranean, the group were found
by a German reconnaissance aircraft during the
morning of 23 October, to the north-west of Cape
Finisterre. The shadowing aircraft stayed in contact until
early afternoon when a group of enemy aircraft closed
to commence an attack. *LCI 309* received a direct hit
and broke in half, the stern section staying afloat for
some time before sinking in position 47.10N 13.55W.
Five men were killed.
[TNA: ADM.199/2281; ADM.358/4281]

24 October ECLIPSE destroyer
Dumbarton 1934; 1,405 tons; 318.3ft × 33.3ft; 4 × 4.7in,
1 × 12pdr, 4 × 20mm, 4 × torpedo tubes
Commander Edward Mack DSO

In company with the destroyer *Petard* and the escort
destroyers *Exmoor* and *Rockwood*, she sailed from
Alexandria in the early hours of 23 October, to carry
troops and stores to the Aegean island of Leros. At 14.00

the escort destroyers were detached to return to Egypt,
but the *Eclipse* and *Petard* continued, to enter the Kos
straits, between the island and the mainland at 23.30. The
troops embarked, from the Royal East Kent Regiment,
were called up on deck soon after, and prepared to
disembark, it being intended to transfer them into
small boats when about 10 miles from Leros. At 00.50
when in position 37.01.27N 027.11E there was a large
explosion under the hull as she detonated a mine,
followed a few seconds later by a second detonation,
believed to be a second mine. The ship heeled over to
port and then slowly rolled over until she lay on her
beam ends. There was considerable confusion on the
upper deck as the troops were jammed against the guard
rails by falling stores, and others were thrown into the
sea. The *Petard* closed and lowered boats, but the *Eclipse*
sank quickly, leaving a large patch of debris and a thick
slick of oil. Before clearing the area, the *Petard* picked
up thirty-two survivors and the following morning *ML
337* and an air-sea rescue launch, found more, but five
officers and 123 ratings were lost, with 135 soldiers of
the East Kents.
[TNA: ADM.199/243; ADM.199/1040; Rogers pp97–100]

25 October WILLIAM STEPHENS trawler
Aberdeen 1917 requisitioned 1939; 235 tons;
119.8ft × 22.6ft; 1 × 12pdr
Skipper Samuel Salenius RNR†

During the night of 24/25 October German torpedo
boats staged a determined attack in strength on east
coast shipping. A total of thirty-two boats approached
the coast of Norfolk from the east to attack coastal
convoy FN1160 in the early hours of the morning. A
series of actions ensued which saw little success for the
attackers, being driven off by the escorting destroyers
and a force of torpedo and gun boats from Lowestoft,
and two German craft were sunk. The sole British
casualty was the *William Stephens*, which had straggled
astern of the convoy and was hit by a torpedo at 01.10
fired from *S 74* when in position 52.59.17N 01.46E.
Fifteen members of the crew were picked up by their
attackers to be taken prisoner, but sixteen men were
lost.
[TNA: ADM.267/118; Scott pp171–3; Foyle pp289–90]

26 October ML 579 motor launch
St Monance 1943; 73 tons; 112ft × 18.3ft; 1 × 3pdr
Lieutenant James Bain RNVR†

Supporting the Allied campaign in the Aegean, the
motor launch was berthed in a small cove on the island
of Arkoi, to the north of Lipsoi, fully camouflaged, but
leaving a gun cleared away. Several enemy aircraft were
seen to pass overhead during the morning, evidently
without seeing her, but then one Ju 88 spotted her, and
carried out a determined bombing run. Four bombs

were dropped, which exploded around her, with one direct hit. She listed heavily to port and sank quickly, three men being lost, the rest swimming to safety ashore although another died of his wounds later.
[TNA: ADM.1/20020]

26 October MTB 669 motor torpedo boat
Shoreham 1943; 95 tons; 110ft × 21.3ft; 1 × 2pdr, 2 × 20mm
Lieutenant James Galloway Fletcher RNVR
Based at Lerwick, where the torpedo boats regularly made the long voyage across the North Sea to carry out operations on the coast of Norway, *MTB 669* was in company with the Norwegian *MTB 688* when ordered to the area of Trondheim. At 07.25 the pair sighted two coasters, which they attacked with gunfire, and drove one of them, the *Kystraum*, ashore. As they were withdrawing, they were intercepted by a German patrol vessel, the *ND 16/Möwe*, and they made off at speed. The pair cleared the coast, but at 09.30 they were sighted by a flight of three fighter aircraft which carried out a series of attacks, during which both boats were hit and damaged. About 10 minutes later another three fighters appeared, to carry out more attacks. *MTB 669* was badly hit, with bullets piercing the sides, putting one engine out of action and starting a fire which spread to the forward petrol tank. She was clearly doomed, so *MTB 688* closed to lift off the crew and she was abandoned, last being seen listing to port covered with flames and smoke. One man died of his wounds. Despite the attentions of a float plane which carried out more attacks, *688* evaded any serious damage and reached Lerwick the following morning.
[Reynolds, *Dog Boats* p105]

26 October TIEN HSING tug
Shanghai 1935 requisitioned 1942; 268 tons; 118.2ft × 24.6ft
On passage from Suez to Massawa, she ran hard aground on the Abu Galawa Kebir reef off Hamata, Egypt. The Australian minesweeper *Gawler* was despatched to the scene, but confirmed that salvage was hopeless, and took off all the crew and she was abandoned as a wreck.
Note: wrongly listed as 'Tientsin' in *Statement of Losses*
[TNA: ADM.199/774]

28 October LCT (2) 115 landing craft, tank
Leith 1941; 296 tons; 143ft × 31ft; 2 × 20mm
Travelling from Haifa to Kaselorizo in company with *LCT 104*, she was carrying anti-aircraft guns and vehicles and their crews and was escorted by two armed trawlers. At 17.15 when about 35 miles from her destination aircraft were seen approaching and she came under attack from about twelve enemy aircraft, including Ju 87s. The troops were ordered below, but

the ship was almost immediately straddled by a stick of bombs. Two exploded close alongside, with another hitting amidships. The ship was shaken violently by the explosions, and started to heel over, eventually capsizing. The wreck floated upside down for about 10 minutes before sinking. The survivors were all picked up by *la Reine des Flots*, but twenty-two soldiers were killed.
[TNA: ADM.199/774; WO.361/470]

30 October CHANCELLOR drifter
1916 requisitioned 1941; 24 tons
Under tow from Inverness to Grimsby by the tug *Stoke*, she foundered at 08.00 in poor weather when about 6 miles north of Troup Head, Aberdeenshire. The towing crew of two had been taken off the previous evening.
[TNA: ADM.199/2281]

1 November HDML 1054 motor launch
Wroxham 1941; 46 tons; 70ft × 15ft; 2 × 20mm
Lieutenant Gerald Guy Pindar RNVR
Attempting to enter Hartlepool harbour, she ran aground at 19.20 on the Parton rocks, to the west of Heugh Lighthouse and was wrecked. The crew took to a small dinghy and were rescued by the Hartlepool lifeboat.
[TNA: ADM.199/770]

4 November MTB 606 motor torpedo boat
Wallasea 1942; 90 tons; 110ft × 21.3ft; 1 × 2pdr, 2 × 20mm
Lieutenant Donald George Dowling RNVR
During the night of 4/5 November a force gathered from two torpedo boat flotillas was ordered to carry out a commando operation on the Dutch coast, aiming to land a small party ashore from a dory, but with the proviso that if they encountered any enemy vessels, the landing was to be abandoned and an offensive sweep made instead. As they arrived off the coast at about 21.00 dark shapes were seen ahead which flashed a challenge, and on failing to respond correctly, fire was opened on them. These were actually two German torpedo boats, and a short but sharp exchange of fire took place, until the German craft disengaged and headed inshore under the cover of smoke. With surprise now gone, they decided to abandon the special operation and conduct a sweep to the north, towards the Hook of Holland. At 23.04 several shapes were seen ahead which they believed could be a convoy and minutes later they started to engage with gunfire. The strangers were actually a vessel laying buoys with three escorts. The torpedo boats scored hits on the enemy, but *606* was hit on the bridge, probably by an 88mm round fired by one of the armed trawlers. This killed one man and wounded all other personnel on the bridge and wrecked the controls. Another two hits struck the engine room, killing the motor mechanic and stoker,

and stopping two of the engines and further hits struck the petrol space and the tiller flat, the latter disabling the steering gear, the boat swinging round in a circle out of control. A fire had broken out in the engine room and as this spread, she came to a halt, covered in smoke. *MTB 630* found her, and an attempt was made to rig a tow, but this proved too difficult, and as they were again coming under fire, she was abandoned, scuttling charges having been set off before the last man left her. One officer and nine men were killed.
[TNA: ADM.199/537; Scott pp164–7; Reynolds, Dog Boats pp78–80]

4 November LCT (4) 583 landing craft, tank
Thornaby 1942; 200 tons; 171ft × 38.8ft
Deployed to the Mediterranean, on 28 October she was driven ashore by strong winds onto a beach near Naples. She was refloated and towed into Naples harbour, but on inspection found to be not worth repairing and was written off as a constructive total loss.
[TNA: ADM.199/641]

6 November AELDA yacht
1932 requisitioned 1939; 37 tons
Lieutenant John William Shannon RNVR
Based at Aultbea, on Loch Ewe, she was assisting in marshalling the ships of an outward-bound convoy. She was to the south of the Isle of Ewe, heading north at 4 knots when the lights of another Aultbea-based vessel, the 122 ton steam drifter *Neves* was seen approaching from the starboard bow. As no appreciable change in bearing was noted, Lieutenant Shannon ordered an alteration of course to starboard. However, the bearing remained steady, and as she was now uncomfortably close, Shannon ordered the wheel hard over to starboard and put his engines to full ahead. As they did so, the *Neves* was heard to blow two blasts on her siren and could be seen turning to port, into the oncoming steam yacht. She struck the *Aelda* on the port quarter, carrying away her boat, and punching a hole in the side. Mats and blankets were hung over the side in an effort to stem the flow of water but had little effect. Shannon therefore decided to head for shallow water, but the stern of the yacht settled quickly, forcing the engines to be stopped and the vessel to be hastily abandoned. Men were still jumping into the water as she disappeared. Four men were drowned. Skipper Findlay of the *Neves* was found to be at fault, having altered course in the wrong direction when he sighted the *Aelda*. He was informed that he had incurred their Lordships' displeasure.
[TNA: ADM.178/358]

10 November MTB 230 motor torpedo boat
Clynder 1942; 39 tons; 72.6ft × 19.3ft; 1 × 20mm, 2 × torpedo tubes
Lieutenant Michael Vernon Rout RNZVR
In company with *MTB 93*, *MTB 222* and *MTB 238*, engaged in a night patrol off the Dutch coast. Nothing was seen or heard until 04.30, when off Texel, when radar contact was made on three vessels in a wide 'V' formation. Course was altered to the south, and the torpedo boats formed up in line astern to manoeuvre into an attacking position using a blanket of fog to make their approach. By 05.17 this was complete, and the targets were on the starboard beam of the torpedo boats. They then turned towards the enemy and increased speed to commence an attack. However, it soon became clear that they had wrongly estimated their distance, and they found themselves far closer to the nearest enemy ship than they realised, and they were in danger of being run down. *MTB 222* was forced to take violent avoiding action, and in doing so rammed *230*, hitting her with some force at the after end of the engine room. The engine compartments and fuel tanks rapidly flooded, and she started to settle. As it was clear that she was sinking, a demolition charge was fired in the after mess deck which speeded her demise.
[TNA: ADM.199/541]

10 November MTB 222 motor torpedo boat
Renfrew 1942; 39 tons; 72.6ft × 19.3ft; 1 × 20mm, 2 × torpedo tubes
Lieutenant Eric Edwin James Whife RNVR
One of the group of torpedo boats that was patrolling the Dutch coast (see *MTB 230* above). In the confusion of attempting to avoid one of the enemy ships, *MTB 222* had suddenly altered course and rammed *230*. It was found that she could still go astern, but as they were so close to the enemy coast scuttling charges were fired to sink her, but they failed to go off. She was able to proceed to the west, initially under her own power, but when the engines failed, a tow was rigged by *MTB 238*. When in position 52.57N 03.15E it was decided to abandon her, due to the deteriorating weather. The engine room hatch had been carried away, and she was flooding due to seas constantly washing over her and by this time the boat was awash from aft as far forward as the bridge. The crew were taken off by the other boats and she was sunk by gunfire.
[TNA: ADM.199/541]

11 November HDML 1244 / HDML 1289 motor launch
Renfrew (*1244*), Hampton (*1289*) 1943; 70ft × 15ft
Being carried as deck cargo on the merchant ship *Indian Prince* (8,587 tons), bound for India, she was part of Convoy KMS31 which sailed from Gibraltar

10 November. The convoy was soon located by enemy aircraft, and when to the north-east of Oran, despite having a fighter escort came under sustained attack from German aircraft. After an initial attack at 18.10, there was a second determined attack at 18.40 by torpedo carrying He 111 aircraft. The *Indian Prince* was hit by a torpedo and damaged and was taken in tow by the corvette *Coltsfoot* but broke up and sank 4 hours later in position 36.10N 00.06W, taking the launches with her.
[TNA: ADM.237/5; Lloyd's War Losses p719]

12 November BYMS 2072 minesweeper
Whitestone 1942; 215 tons; 130ft × 24.6ft; 1 × 3in, 2 × 20mm
Lieutenant Edwin Harold Taylor RNR

Fully loaded with stores and personnel for the garrison on the island of Leros in the Aegean, she sailed on the evening of 8 November from Beirut in company with *BYMS 2073*, the pair taking advantage of sheltered bays in the Turkish coast to anchor during the day, wary of enemy aircraft. They arrived at Alinda Bay in the island in the early hours of 11 November where *2073* successfully offloaded her cargo, but *2072* had not fully discharged her load by daylight. They therefore returned to the shelter of the coast of Turkey, to spend the daylight hours at anchor in Guvenchlik Bay. At 18.00 *2072* again made her way to the island, this time on her own, to complete offloading. At 20.00 as the minesweeper approached Leros from the south-east, in a bright moonlit night, she came under attack from a number of aircraft including several Do 217s dropping Hs 293 guided bombs. At 20.30 there was a large explosion on the port side forward as a guided bomb detonated close alongside. The blast blew the port 20mm gun overboard and knocked down the mast which collapsed onto the starboard gun platform. The bridge and the forward compartments suffered badly from shock damage, the 3in gun was disabled and she suffered a steering gear breakdown, which meant that she performed a complete circle before regaining control. Although damaged, she remained stable and a radio call to the shore authorities at Alinda Bay brought *ML 299* and *MTB 315* to her assistance, and she was successfully brought into the anchorage. After discharging her cargo and clearing herself of debris and landing the dead and wounded, she was ordered to proceed to Portolago (Laki), an anchorage on the western side of the island to carry out repairs. Still using emergency steering, she sailed from Alinda Bay at 01.00 on 12 November. However, in the dark and without local charts, the minesweeper missed the entrance to the anchorage and continued steaming south where she blundered into a force of German vessels, loaded with troops, which were en-route from the island of Kalymnos to land on Leros. At about 02.00 *2072*

approached an oncoming German patrol boat, quite ignorant of her true identity, and believing that it was a British motor launch sent to guide her to a safe haven. The patrol boat was the *R 210*, and its commanding officer, Oberleutnant Weissenborn, realised that the strange ship was British and was clearly unaware of the danger so instead of opening fire he shouted a challenge in English. The unsuspecting Lieutenant Taylor replied that he was looking for a quiet place to anchor, at which Weissenborn took advantage of his opponents' ignorance and shouted an order, in English, for the minesweeper to follow him. Taylor duly obliged, whilst Weissenborn manoeuvred *R 210* to take station close on the port side. At 02.25 the Germans opened a fierce fire on the unprepared minesweeper, raking her fore and aft. Unable to respond and with several crew members killed or wounded, the hull riddled with holes and the engine stopped and a fire started, *2072* had little choice but to surrender, a white cloth being shown. This brought about a stop to the firing and a boat from the patrol vessel *Uj 2101* put a prize crew onboard. The minesweeper was settling at this time and it was thought that she would sink, and several members of the crew jumped overboard, but tow lines were rigged, and she was towed into shallow water. Four crewmen had been killed or died of injuries after the bomb hit and another two men had died when she was captured. The survivors were taken prisoner, but three ratings that had jumped overboard made it to the island of Kalymnos where they evaded capture to link up with the local resistance movement and eventually escaped to Egypt. *BYMS 2072* was subsequently taken to Portolago and renamed *GD-07* for local service, but she remained laid up. Her final fate is uncertain, but it would appear that she either sank or was scuttled off Portolago later in the war. More importantly for the Germans was the capture of classified material that could not be destroyed before being taken over; the full extent of the loss is uncertain, but it would appear to include signal codes. The Germans did not announce her capture, in order to exploit the secret material. Similarly, the Admiralty suppressed the details of her loss – she was not listed in the official *Statement of Losses*.
[Minett pp242–53]

12 November ML 358 motor launch
Cairo 1943; 73 tons; 112ft × 18.3ft; 1 × 3pdr
Lieutenant Edward Digby Lee Lander RNVR†

Ordered to proceed from Leros to an anchorage in Turkish water, *358* sailed in company with *ML 299* and *ML 461*, but lost contact with the others during the night. At 05.15 a brief radio message was received from *358* indicating that she was in contact with an enemy convoy, but nothing more was heard from her, and it was assumed that she had been sunk by either shore batteries or the enemy naval force. She is probably the motor launch that was sighted by German patrol boat *R 195* about 4 nautical miles off Alinda Bay, Leros at 05.00. The patrol vessel was part of an escort to a powerful German force that was en-route to a make a landing at Alinda. The launch evidently mistook *R 195* for a friendly unit and altered course towards and flashed the night recognition signal. The German vessel promptly repeated the challenge whilst closing to 100m when it opened fire on the unsuspecting launch. Hit repeatedly, the launch quickly altered course and disappeared into the night. At dawn, the German force successfully landed on the island where they discovered the battle damaged motor launch and sank it. Eleven men lost their lives.

[Rogers pp122–3; TNA: ADM.1/20020]

13 November DULVERTON escort destroyer

Linthouse 1941; 1,050 tons; 264.2ft × 31.6ft; 6 × 4in, 4 × 2pdr, 2 × 20mm

Commander Stuart Austen Buss

On 12 November, the Germans commenced landing on the island of Kos, and the *Dulverton* in company with the cruiser *Phoebe* and destroyers *Echo* and *Belvoir* were part of the naval forces in the Aegean tasked to find and destroy the transports. Despite hugging the Turkish coast, they were spotted at 23.00 by an enemy reconnaissance aircraft, which shadowed them at a distance, regularly dropping flares. At 01.40, then being about 6 miles east of Kos, the *Dulverton* was hit by an Hs 293 guided bomb, which had been dropped from a Do 217 aircraft. There was little warning, the missile only being seen a moment before it struck, detonating on the port side by the Oerlikon mounting. It penetrated through to the magazine which exploded, the fore part of the ship being blown away before the bridge. A fierce fire was started, and she steadily settled by the head. Her consorts closed to pick up the survivors, which were now leaving the stricken ship. At 03.20 when no more survivors could be found, the *Belvoir* torpedoed the burning wreck, and she sank, her position being noted as 30.50.3N 27.30. Seventy-eight officers and ratings were killed.

[TNA: ADM 267/110]

13 November LCT (3) 343 landing craft, tank

Thornaby 1942; 350 tons; 175ft × 31ft; 2 × 20mm

Lieutenant Arthur Charles Prince RNVR

On 5 November, a group of twenty-five landing craft sailed from Gibraltar, escorted by the corvette *Bluebell* and the armed trawler *Man of War*, bound for Falmouth. Designated 'Flight-P', they initially experienced good weather with calm seas and little wind, but during 12 November the wind steadily freshened and by the morning of 13 November there was a full gale from

the north-west. Several of the craft were in a poor material state, due to a chronic lack of spares, and engine breakdowns regularly occurred. At 00.30 a large sea was shipped by *343* which split the canvas cover over the hold. Although one pump failed, with the remaining pump and hand bailing, the water was kept under control and reduced until 02.30 when another heavy sea washed over her, which collapsed the hatch covers, fore and aft, whilst at the same time the starboard engine failed. The vessel became uncontrollable and swung broadside on to the sea, shipping several heavy seas. The *Bluebell* closed and released Carley floats, with lines attached down to *343*, which allowed all the crew to leave her, being hauled back to the corvette. During this operation, one of the floats capsized, throwing the occupants into the sea; all regained the float except for one rating, the only man lost. The *Bluebell* then closed the derelict craft to drop two depth charges alongside, set to explode at shallow depth. However, these seemed to have little effect, and so a depth charge was fired at her, but this dropped into the hold, and did not explode. A fourth charge was then fired, and this exploded close under the vessel and she settled and sank at 03.10 in position 49.40N 07.56W.

[TNA: ADM.1/15024]

14 November LCT (3) 385 landing craft, tank

Middlesbrough 1942; 350 tons; 175ft × 31ft; 2 × 20mm

Lieutenant Donald Kenneth Hogg RNVR

Part of the 'Flight-P' convoy returning to England from Gibraltar, she was battered by the storm during the early hours of the 13th, and at 04.30 the bilge pump failed, and this was followed soon after by the starboard engine stopping. Battered by heavy seas washing over her, she steered away from the group to the south-west, filling with water. The trawler *Man of War* closed to stand by her, until that evening when it was decided to abandon her. In a fine feat of seamanship, the trawler placed her bows alongside the starboard quarter of *385* and successfully lifted off all the crew. This was completed by 22.00. *Man of War* remained nearby the derelict, which was seen to roll over at 02.30 and float upside down for several minutes before she sank. The position was noted as 50.13N 10.13W.

[TNA: ADM.1/15024]

14 November LCT (3) 333 landing craft, tank

Thornaby 1942; 350 tons; 175ft × 31ft; 2 × 20mm

Lieutenant Kenneth Bertie Porteous RNVR

Another of the 'Flight-P' vessels, on board *333*, the port engine stopped at 10.00 on 13th, and this was followed 2 hours later by a very heavy sea which washed over her, smashing the stanchions supporting the canvas spread over the tank deck. A large amount of water was shipped through the split covers and she

took water in the hold. The rescue tug *Dexterous* was summoned and during the evening took the landing craft in tow. At 04.00 the towline parted, but *333* was able to proceed under limited power, but was unable to make any headway, and she steered away from the convoy to the south-east, before the wind. The water in the hold could not be cleared, and this worsened when the bilge pump failed. The *Dexterous*, still standing by her, skilfully ran her bows alongside the craft and took off the crew. She was abandoned, in a sinking condition, with her decks awash, in position 50.50N 09.45W.
[TNA: ADM.1/15024]

16 November LCT (3) 332 landing craft, tank
Thornaby 1942; 350 tons; 175ft × 31ft; 2 × 20mm
Lieutenant Derek Luke RNVR
Sailed from Gibraltar in the ill-fated 'Flight-P' convoy bound for England, but she suffered a cracked cylinder head in the starboard engine on 11 November. She struggled to keep up with the other ships, and when the weather worsened the next day, the crew were constantly pumping the hull space free of water. During 13 November she became detached from the convoy, falling astern of the group and the next day, with a number of oil pipes leaking and unable to make headway, it was decided to run for the shelter of the Spanish coast. During the morning of 16 November, she was heading for a beach near Gijon, intending to run her onto the shore, but as they approached, they struck an outcrop of rocks and was wrecked. There was no loss of life.
[NA ADM.199/176]

16 November LCT (3) 418 landing craft, tank
Meadowside 1943; 350 tons; 175ft × 31ft; 2 × 20mm
Skipper-Lieutenant Alexander Ord Tavendale RNR
Another of the 'Flight-P' craft, she was battered by the storm as the ships progressed northwards to England. During the evening of 12 November, the canvas cover over the tank hold spilt and the spreaders collapsed. This caused the hold to flood, but with hand bailing and pumping the water was kept under control. She struggled to make headway however, and by the morning of 16 November it was clear that the water was gaining, and by the afternoon the hold was full of water, and then the engines stopped. The escort destroyer *Talybont* was now standing by her, and at 19.15 she released a Carley float down to the landing craft with a line attached, and this was used to take off all the crew without loss. When this was complete, she was left in a sinking condition, her decks awash, in position 48.59N 06.30W.
[TNA: ADM.1/15024]

18 November CHANTICLEER sloop
Dumbarton 1942; 1,350 tons; 283ft × 38.5ft; 6 × 4in, 12 × 20mm
Lieutenant Commander Robert Henry Bristowe DSO
Part of the escort to the large homeward-bound Convoy SL139 that sailed from Freetown, Sierra Leone on 2 November and which then joined Convoy MKS30 on 16 November, to form a joint convoy of over sixty ships. They faced a series of attacks by enemy submarines, but were successful in countering the assault, the convoy being protected by the aggressive support groups and patrolling aircraft. During 18 November, Asdic contacts were gained, and during the afternoon *Chanticleer* was joined by the *Crane* to prosecute a promising contact the sloop held. As *Crane* was approaching the datum, at 15.24 in position 40.06N 19.48W there was a large explosion under the stern of *Chanticleer*, which demolished the after part of the ship, leaving the ship abaft the engine room open to the sea, with the rudder blown unto the upper deck. The ship took a list to port and fire broke out in 'X' magazine, and all power was lost. She remained stable, and whilst the *Crane* continued to carry out a series of attacks on Asdic contacts a tow was rigged. The ship was towed 250 miles to Ponta Delgado, in the Azores. She was declared a constructive loss, and later moved to Horta where she was hulked, to become a base ship. The attacker had been *U 515* (Henke) which had fired two T5 acoustic homing torpedoes at the escorts, one of which found *Chanticleer*. Twenty eight men were killed.
[TNA: ADM.1/15837; CB.4271 p344]

22 November BARFLAKE boom defence vessel
Dartmouth 1942; 730 tons; 150ft × 32.3ft; 1 × 12pdr
Skipper-Lieutenant Peter Henderson RNR
Based at Naples, Italy, she was ordered to sail to Pozzuoli. At 11.45, having steered along the coast, she altered course to go into the harbour, but 5 minutes later there was a large explosion aft, and the vessel started to sink by the stern, with a heavy list to starboard. Attempts were made to launch the boats on board, but there was no time as she sank rapidly. An Italian motor launch closed to pick up the twelve survivors, but three men were lost. It was found that she had detonated a mine, probably a contact mine. Skipper-Lieutenant Henderson was admonished to ensure that in future he should 'navigate with greater care and to ensure that adequate lookouts are available'.
[TNA: ADM.1/15867]

22 November HEBE minesweeper
Devonport 1936; 815 tons; 230ft × 33.6ft; 2 × 4in, 2 × 20mm
Lieutenant Arthur Lewis Gulvin
In company with the minesweeper *Sharpshooter*, sailed from Bari, Italy, to carry out a sweep between that port

and Brindisi for magnetic and acoustic mines. They were on their third 'lap' of the designated area when a mine exploded at 11.20 close to the ship. The explosion was abreast the bulkhead separating 'A' and 'B' boiler rooms on the port side and she at once took a list to port, the forward 4in gun breaking away from its mounting and sliding overboard as she did. A second explosion took place immediately after the first, probably her boilers exploding. She started to sink by the bows, the stern rising clear of the water very quickly. She continued to roll over whilst going down by the bows and had disappeared in 4 minutes. Her position was noted as 41.08.46N 15.60.45E. Thirty–eight men were killed.
[TNA: ADM.199/243; ADM.199/253]

22 November **MTB 686** motor torpedo boat
Littlehampton 1943; 95 tons; 110ft × 21.3ft; 1 × 2pdr, 2 × 20mm, 2 × torpedo tubes
Lieutenant Archibald McDougall RNVR
Based at Lerwick, in the Shetland Islands, she was part of the 30th MTB Flotilla, which was tasked to carry out offensive operations on the coast of Norway. To make the long journey across the North Sea and return, it was the normal practice to stow several 4–gallon petrol cans on the upper deck. During the afternoon of 22 November, *686* had embarked her deck cargo ready for a mission that evening, when an explosion occurred at one of the 20mm Oerlikon guns and a fire was started. This rapidly spread to the cargo of full petrol cans which exploded with some violence, and this triggered an explosion of ammunition, which destroyed the boat. The Norwegian boat *MTB 626* which was lying alongside her also caught fire and was burnt out. Seven men lost their lives.
[Reynolds, Dog Boats pp105–06]

22 November **EMPIRE ARTHUR** water carrier
Grangemouth 1942 Requisitioned 1942; 784 tons; 193ft × 30.7ft
Master Fraser Ernest Smith[†]
Capsized and sank at 20.00 alongside Kissy jetty at Freetown, West Africa when loading with fresh water, with the loss of two men. The wreck remained blocking the jetty until 1948 when she was salvaged and rebuilt.
[TNA: ADM.199/2284]

23 November **SANTA** whaler
Middlesbrough 1936 requisitioned 1941; 355 tons; 134.8ft × 26.3ft
Skipper-Lieutenant James Leslie Everett RNR[‡]
Attached to the mine clearance force at Maddalena, Sardinia, she was detailed to act as a dan layer to the 14th Minesweeping Flotilla which was working to clear the Straits of Bonifacio. The force sailed at 07.30 and proceeded to the position of the last lap of the previous day's sweeping, marked by a dan buoy. Work then

commenced, with *Poole* and *Boston* sweeping, and *Seaham* and *Santa* acting as dan layers and one mine was seen to be brought to the surface, which was duly marked with a buoy. At 10.29 with the weather deteriorating, sweeps were ordered to be hauled in, and the *Santa* detailed to dispose of the floating mine that had been exposed earlier. Ten minutes after this, the order to the *Santa* was countermanded, as it was clear that the mine was being carried inshore, so she headed back to the main group, to start recovering the marker buoys, with the exception of those that marked the last lap swept. At 11.13 as she was manoeuvring to pick up a buoy there was a large explosion close to her. As the smoke and spray subsided, to the others in the group she initially seemed to be all right, but a boat and a raft were seen to be put into the water, and she did not respond to a call by flashing light. At 11.18 there was a second explosion, right under the *Santa* and she disintegrated, the last of her, her bows, disappearing in seconds; the boat also disappeared. The raft with two men on board was seen to be carried clear by the wind and sea and they were later picked up by *MGB 658*. They were the only survivors, two officers and twenty men being killed. It was believed that she had just lifted a buoy clear of the water, and was recovering it on board, when she drifted with the high winds and sea into an unswept area.
[TNA: ADM.1/15870]

23 November **LCT (3) 329** landing craft, tank
Thornaby 1942; 350 tons; 175ft × 31ft; 2 × 20mm
Written off on this date as being 'damaged beyond economical repair' after grounding heavily at Messina in September, and then being driven onto rocks at Salerno during October; she was hauled off but found to be so damaged that she was considered a constructive total loss.
[Statement of Losses p54; http://www.robpedley.co.uk/world-war-2-navy-diary.html]

24 November **MTB 73** motor torpedo boat
Portsmouth 1941; 39 tons; 72.6ft × 19.3ft; 2 × torpedo tubes
Sub-Lieutenant Ronald Aitchison RNVR
Stationed in the Mediterranean, she was alongside at the port of Maddalena, Sardinia, recently occupied by the Allies, when that place came under air attack during which she was sunk. Two members of the crew were lost.
[Reynolds & Cooper, Mediterranean MTBs at War p82]

27 November **ML 126** motor launch
St Monance 1940; 73 tons; 112ft × 18.4ft; 1 × 3pdr
Lieutenant Charles Howard Pearse RNVR
Patrolling the entrance to Naples harbour, she was damaged at 14.46 when 1.5 miles to the south of the harbour by an explosion under the bows of the ship

which blew the forward part away. Although recovered, she was declared a constructive total loss and paid off 4 December. The area had been swept for mines, and it was believed likely that she had struck a floating torpedo, several of which had been dropped during an air raid earlier that day.
[TNA:ADM.199/642]

November SIMOOM submarine
Birkenhead 1942; 715/990 tons; 201ft × 23.9ft; 1 × 3in, 6 × torpedo tubes
Lieutenant Geoffrey Deryck Nicholson Milner DSC†
Ordered to conduct a patrol in the Aegean, she sailed from Port Said on 2 November and was never heard from again and when she failed to arrive at Beirut as expected on 19 November, she was presumed to have been lost with all hands – six officers and forty-two men. Claims have been made that she may have been responsible for attacking shipping on 7 and 10 November, but these are in error as the vessels identified as victims are now known to have been lost during a bombardment of Saseno by Allied destroyers. For some time, it was thought that she may have been sunk by the German submarine *U 565*, which reported attacking a surfaced submarine on the evening of 15 November off the island of Kos with two homing torpedoes and heard one explosion after the correct running time. However, modern research has ruled this as most unlikely, and the loss has been re-assessed as being caused by striking a mine. In October 2016 Turkish divers found the wreck of the *Simoom* off Tenedos Island (Bozcaada). There was extensive damage near the starboard hydroplane which would indicate that a mine was indeed responsible.
[Evans p380; Hezlet vol 1 p257; https://uboat.net/allies/warships/ship/3443.html]

1 December AVANTURINE trawler
Beverley 1930 requisitioned 1940; 296 tons; 128.9ft × 24ft; 1 × 12pdr
Skipper Edward Gillard RNR†
During the night of 30 November/1 December there were indications of enemy fast patrol boat activity in the eastern Channel, and several torpedo and gun boats were sailed from Dover to screen the passage of coastal Convoy CE226, due to pass through the straits that night. The attack on the convoy failed to develop, but a smaller eastbound group of vessels, about 5 miles astern of the convoy was attacked off Beachy Head. This included the *Avanturine*, which had been damaged when she ran ashore a few days earlier. Now under tow of the tug *Fairplay*, they were escorted by the trawlers *Peter Carey* and *Florio*. The *Avanturine* was hit by a torpedo at 22.30 fired by *S 142* and sank very quickly with the loss of all hands; twenty-four men died.
[TNA:ADM.199/630]

8 December RYSA trawler
Selby 1941; 545 tons; 150ft × 27.6ft; 1 × 12pdr
Lieutenant Commander John Handley Cooper RNVR†
Deployed to the Mediterranean, she was part of the mine clearance force assembled to clear the heavily mined waters around Sardinia and Corsica. She was busily employed sweeping a channel to the east of Corsica, using Oropesa sweeps to port and starboard, when at 09.15 the starboard sweep parted and very soon after there was a large explosion on the port side amidships. It cut the ship in half, breaking up in the region of the boiler room. The after part sank first, very quickly and the fore part, floating bows up, remained afloat for 20 minutes before it sank. Her position was approximately 41.21N 09.17E. The *Rysa* had put up a mine 2 days before this, close to this position, but sweeping subsequent to the loss found nothing, so it was thought that she had struck the only mine remaining within the channel. Nineteen men were killed.
[TNA:ADM.1/15870]

11 December CUCKMERE frigate
Montreal 1942; 1,370 tons; 283ft × 36.5ft; 2 × 4in, 10 × 20mm
Lieutenant Arthur Johnson RNVR
Part of the escort to Convoy KMS34 that sailed from Gibraltar on 9 December, bound for Port Said, at 13.04 in position 36.55N 03.01E, she was hit by a torpedo which exploded on the port side forward of the bridge. The explosion wrecked the forward compartments and the bows dropped about 8ft. The forward compartments of the ship, including oil tanks were flooded and lighting failed as the starboard generator was put out of action. Shock damage put the radio and radar out of operation. The ship was unable to steam ahead due to the damaged bow but could proceed astern under her own power at slow speed. She was taken in tow for Algiers, where she was declared a constructive total loss. Sixteen men were lost. The attacker had been *U 223* (Wächter) that had fired an acoustic homing torpedo.
[TNA:ADM. 267/117; CB.4273 p278]

12 December TYNEDALE escort destroyer
Linthouse 1940; 1,000 tons; 264.2ft × 29ft; 4 × 4in, 4 × 2pdr, 2 × 20mm
Lieutenant Commander James John Simon Yorke DSC
Part of the escort to Mediterranean Convoy KMS34 that had sailed from Gibraltar on 9 December for Port Said. She was steering east, zigzagging at 12.5 knots, when at 07.10 in position 37.10N 06.05E, with no warning, there was an explosion on the starboard side beneath the funnel as she was hit by a torpedo that had been fired by the *U 593* (Kelbling). The ship rapidly broke up, the bow portion rolling over to port and sinking, the bows pointing skyward before it disappeared. The

after part remained afloat slowly settling before it sank. The corvette *Hyderabad* and tug *Hengist* closed to pick up the survivors, but seven officers and sixty-six ratings were lost.

[TNA:ADM.267/95]

12 December **HOLCOMBE** escort destroyer
Linthouse 1942; 1,050 tons; 264.2ft × 31.6ft; 4 × 4in,
4 × 2pdr, 3 × 20mm, 2 × torpedo tubes
Lieutenant Frank Maclear Graves

Like the *Tynedale* (above), part of the escort to Convoy KMS34. After the attack on *Tyndedale*, the hunt started for her attacker, and at about 14.55 in position 37.20N 05.50E, the *Holcombe* gained an Asdic contact at 1,700 yards. She turned to port towards the contact to make an attack, but only 15 seconds later there was a large explosion under her stern, with a large sheet of flame going up from her after part, about 200ft into the air. The ship immediately heeled to port and she started to go down by the stern. After the flames died down, a huge mushroom cloud of light-coloured smoke remained hanging over the ship. The bows rose clear of the water until they were vertical, and she sank, about 4 minutes after the explosion. The USS *Niblack* (DD.424) picked up the survivors. Seventy-six men died. She had been hit by an acoustic homing torpedo fired by the *U 593* (Kelbling). The torpedo had evidently exploded by the after oil fuel tank, the flash penetrating the after magazine. It was believed that the large sheet of flame was probably caused by the contents of the magazine igniting. *U 593* was sunk later that day by USS *Wainwright* (DD.419) and the *Calpe*.

[TNA:ADM.267/97]

16 December **ROSE VALLEY** drifter
Findochty 1918 (*Silt*) requisitioned 1939; 100 tons;
87ft × 20ft

Acting as a local tender, she foundered in Gutter Sound after a collision in Scapa Flow. The wreck has been found at 58.49N 03.09W.

[Statement of Losses p28; http://www.scapaflowwrecks.com/wrecks/other/]

18 December **FELIXSTOWE** minesweeper
Renfrew 1941; 673 tons; 171.6ft × 28.6ft; 1 × 12pdr,
1 × 2pdr, 2 × 20mm
Lieutenant Charles Geoffrey Powney RNVR

Part of the force assembled at Maddalena, Sardinia, tasked to clear the extensive minefields in the area. On 18 December she was in company with the minesweepers *Rothesay*, *Stornaway* and *Polruan*, conducting an Oropesa sweep in the approaches to the harbour in a line abreast formation. At 09.04 when in position 41.08N 09.35E there was a large explosion under the stern which shook the ship violently and then she rolled over to take a heavy list to starboard. The after compartments were reported to be flooding fast, and a fracture opened up across the quarterdeck. The *Stornaway* closed to take off non-essential personnel and a tow was rigged. This had scarcely been completed when the ship took a further sudden lurch to starboard, at which the tow was abandoned, and the small number of men left on board went over the side. She continued to roll over until she was laying on her beam ends; she remained in this position for some time until at 09.47 she sank, stern first. It was believed that she must have run over a contact mine which had probably hit her propeller or rudder. There were no casualties.

[TNA:ADM.1/15870]

18 December **CECIL** water boat
No details found

Listed as being written off as a constructive total loss – no further detail known of the vessel or the loss.

[Statement of Losses p29; TNA:ADM.1/24129]

22 December **BV 42** barrage vessel
Millwall 1918; 270 tons; 96ft × 25ft; 1 × 12pdr
Chief Skipper Richard Cowling RNR

Originally built during the First World War for use as a barrage vessel, *BV 42* was 'dumb', without propelling machinery, her role being to tend to net barriers, and was fitted with four powerful searchlights to illuminate the barrier. The searchlights were powered by dynamos driven by 4-cylinder petrol engines, each of which had a petrol tank, situated amidships. At the end of 1942 *BV 42* was being used as a trials vessel, being fitted with a depth-charge launcher. During the morning of 22 December, she was in the West Old Dock at Leith preparing for sea and waiting for the arrival of a tug to tow her out to commence the trials. At 09.40 there was a violent explosion, a large sheet of flame being seen amidships. This started a fierce fire, and there was a second explosion about 30 minutes later. These explosions did considerable damage, splitting side plates and driving out rivets. This, plus the large amounts of water which was pumped onto her as part of the fire-fighting efforts, caused her to sink. It was found that the most likely cause of the explosion was an ignition of petrol vapour. She had filled her petrol tanks on 16 December, and it was believed that some petrol had spilled into the bilges. This had partly evaporated over the next few days and formed a concentration of fumes in the tank compartment and trunk leading to the tanks. It was found that the hatch on the upper deck, which led to the trunk, could not be fully closed. It was probably in this area that the spark which ignited the petrol vapour and triggered the explosion had occurred. Seven men were killed or died of their injuries. Chief Skipper Cowling was found to be at fault. He had

showed a lack of appreciation of the necessity to ventilate compartments containing petrol.
[TNA:ADM.178/327;ADM.199/259]

24 December HURRICANE destroyer

Barrow 1939; 1,350 tons; 312ft × 33ft; 3 × 4.7in, 1 × 12pdr, 4 × 20mm, 4 × torpedo tubes
Commander John Rowe Westmacott

As part of Escort Group B1, sailed in company with the destroyers *Watchman* and *Wanderer* and the frigate *Glenarm* on 17 December to support the passage of Atlantic Convoys OS62/MKS36. They joined the convoy during the night of 23 December. In the early hours of the next morning the American destroyer *Leary*, part of the supporting US escort carrier group, was sunk by submarine torpedo, and the *Hurricane* and *Glenarm* were ordered to the area to carry out a search. At 19.02 an HF/DF intercept was made on a U-boat radio transmission, and the ships altered course to steam down the bearing. This was rewarded at 19.45 when a small radar contact was detected at just over 9,000 yards ahead of them, which disappeared 10 minutes later, when less than a mile away, indicative of a submarine submerging. As they swept over the area conducting an Asdic search, at 20.02 there was a large explosion under the stern, when she was hit by a T5 acoustic homing torpedo, fired by the *U 415* (Neide). There were two further explosions as depth charges that had been thrown clear exploded. The ship developed a slight list and settled aft as her after magazines flooded, so that her quarterdeck was awash. Top weight was reduced by jettisoning torpedoes and depth charges, and with bulkheads shored and pumping underway, she remained stable, but lost power and had damaged or possibly lost her propellers, making it impossible to steam. The *Glenarm* remained standing by her as the *Watchman* steamed to join the pair. Fearing that the crippled destroyer would only attract more attacks, at 22.14 the CinC, Western Approaches, ordered that the ship's company be removed, and the ship sunk. During the night, the destroyer settled further by the stern and the list to port increased. At first light the *Watchman* and *Glenarm* started to take off the men, which was complete by 12.00, but as they prepared to sink her with a torpedo, she rolled over to port and slowly sank, stern first, in position 45.10N 22.05W. Five men were lost.
[TNA:ADM.237/877;ADM.267/95]

24 December HDML 1388 motor launch

Sittingbourne 1943; 46 tons; 70ft × 15ft; 2 × 20mm
Lieutenant Derric Armstrong Breen RNVR

On passage from the Humber to Hartlepool she ran hard aground at 19.22, north of Heugh light, as she attempted to enter the harbour. She was successfully refloated at 19.49 on 26 December, but then sank, 2 cables (400 yards) to the south-south-east of Hartlepool breakwater. It was later ordered that her wreck should be lifted to a sheltered position and then broken up, with the engines and fittings salvaged.
[TNA:ADM.199/253;ADM.199/770]

24 December MTB 357 motor torpedo boat

Belfast 1943; 37 tons; 72.6ft × 19.3ft; 1 × 20mm, 2 × torpedo tubes
Lieutenant Norman Steel Gardner RNVR

Whilst shifting berth in Dover harbour during the night of 24/25 December a leak became evident in the engine room, which soon flooded. She was taken in tow but sank near number 1 buoy. The cause of the flooding was uncertain but was probably due to damage when leaving her berth.
[TNA:ADM.199/259]

25 December KINGSTON BERYL trawler

Beverley 1928 requisitioned 1939; 352 tons; 140.3ft × 24ft; 1 × 12pdr
Skipper-Lieutenant Alan William John Baker RNR†

Part of an escort to a group of thirty ships that sailed from Loch Ewe on 24 December to rendezvous with Convoy ON217 that had sailed from Liverpool. She was last seen at 04.35 on the 25th, when she was about 15 miles west-south-west of Skerryvore. At 04.45 the Canadian destroyer *Calgary* saw a flash in her last known direction but could not ascertain the cause. *Calgary* had a radar contact which they believed to be the *Kingston Beryl*, so they assumed that she was safe. Only later when it was discovered that the radar contact had been misidentified did anyone realise that she had disappeared. Her estimated position when lost was 56.12N 07.30W, and as no U-boat subsequently claimed an attack, it was assumed that she was lost by striking a mine. There were no survivors. The officers of the *Calgary* were criticised by the enquiry team – they should have been more curious about the flash and had been too trusting in their assumption of the identity of the radar contact. Twenty-eight men died.
[TNA:ADM.199/243]

31 December CLACTON minesweeper

Troon 1941; 656 tons; 165.6ft × 28.6ft; 1 × 12pdr, 1 × 2pdr, 2 × 20mm
Lieutenant Commander Leonard Seymour Shaw DSC RNR

By late December 1943 it was hoped that the heavily-mined waters around Sardinia and Corsica had been sufficiently cleared to allow some traffic between Maddalena and Bastia. On 30 December, a small convoy of *LST 411* and the *Empire Lass*, escorted by the armed trawler *Hoy* sailed from Maddalena, accompanied by the fleet minesweepers *Polruan* and *Clacton* heading for Bastia, being ordered to keep to a narrow swept channel. As the force steamed along the eastern coast of Corsica the weather worsened, with a freshening wind gusting to Force 8 and regular squalls of rain. At 08.30 on 31 December, they estimated that they were at the rendezvous point, some 6 miles to the west of Bastia – subsequently it was found that they were actually 3 miles short and slightly to seaward of the point. *LST 411* signalled *Clacton* that they proposed heaving to in this position and the minesweeper concurred. A few minutes later there was a large explosion and the *Clacton* disappeared in a cloud of smoke and spray. The explosion had occurred on the starboard side, directly underneath her, and the bottom of the ship under the boiler and engine rooms was blown out. She heeled over onto her beam ends and then sank stern first. Thirty-three men were killed. It was believed that she had drifted slightly out of the swept channel and had 'sat' on top of a contact mine.

[TNA: ADM. 1/15870]

31 December LST 411 landing ship, tank
Baltimore 1942; 1,468 tons; 300ft × 50ft; 1 × 12pdr,
6 × 20mm
Lieutenant Commander John Douglas RNR
Loaded with US Army personnel and equipment, including vehicles, she had sailed in the small convoy from Maddalena to Bastia that the *Clacton* had escorted (see above). She saw the *Clacton* blown up, but could do little to assist, as she was rolling deeply, up to 30 degrees, in the heavy swell. Equipment was being tossed around and some vehicles had broken loose. At 10.02 there was a large explosion as she struck a mine, and the engine room reported that the compartment was flooding. All troops were ordered on deck and Carley floats were heaved overboard. The soldiers were put into the floats and the ships whaler was launched to gather the floats together. The arrival of a US Navy PT-boat and a motor launch (ML) was welcome as they worked to pick up the troops. She continued to settle until she heeled over onto her beam ends and then slowly sank, stern first. Three US soldiers and two members of the crew were lost.

[TNA: ADM. 1/15870; ADM. 199/259; MacDermott p53]

31 December HDML 1121 motor launch
Shoreham 1942; 46 tons; 70ft × 15ft; 1 × 2pdr, 2 × 20mm
Lieutenant Arthur Henry Lawlor RNVR
Based in the Mediterranean, she entered the harbour of Pantellaria Island during the morning and was secured alongside the northern mole. During the day, the wind steadily increased, and by early afternoon, there was a heavy swell being driven into the harbour by gale force winds. Lines were doubled up, but at 15.30, with the launch moving in the swell, two of the lines parted. These

were replaced, and by now she had six stern lines and four head-lines out. Despite this, she continued to 'surge' alongside the mole, being battered by the high winds and increasing swell. When another two lines parted, the cable was unshackled from the anchor, led aft, passed around the Oerlikon mounting and then passed out astern to the shore. She was still being thrown heavily against the wall, and soon after 16.15 all the shore lines parted, only the cable around the gun mounting holding. Efforts to re-secure her failed, and although her engines were now being worked to try and gain control, she was constantly being smashed against the wharf and eventually swung out to struck a rock some distance off the wall. By 17.00 she had been driven into shallow water, about 10ft from the mole, and swung her bows to the south-east, her stern slewing around to face the wall. The crew then left her, having to perform a perilous leap at the furthest point of the roll. She was slowly taken across the harbour, water constantly breaking over her. She finally filled and sank by the stern.

[TNA: ADM. 1/16891]

1944

6 January WALLASEA trawler
Leith 1943; 545 tons; 150ft × 27.6ft; 1 × 12pdr, 3 × 20mm
Lieutenant Edward James Hill RNVR[†]
At 03.01 British shore radar detected a group of small contacts to the south of Mounts Bay. These were assumed to be fishing vessels, known to be operating in that area. The group continued to be monitored until at 03.47 the vessels plotted increased speed and headed straight towards an oncoming westbound coastal convoy, WP457. Warning signals were hastily sent, and the escort destroyer *Talybont* was sailed from Plymouth. It was far too late, and at 03.50 one of the escorts to the convoy, the armed trawler *Asie*, reported she was engaging enemy torpedo boats. The action continued for the next 40 minutes, to the south of the Longships, and although the convoy was turned to the north, three merchant ships were hit and sunk during a well-conducted attack by seven torpedo boats of the Fifth S-boat Flotilla. Acting as part of the escort to the convoy, the *Wallasea* was hit by a torpedo fired by *S 138* at about 04.40 and rapidly sank. Thirty-five men were lost, with three survivors.

[TNA: ADM. 199/1393; Warship 1996 p48]

7 January TWEED frigate
Pointhouse 1942; 1,370 tons; 283ft × 36.8ft; 2 × 4in,
10 × 20mm
Lieutenant Commander Robert Stevenson Miller DSC RNR
Part of the Fifth Escort Group made up of British and Canadian frigates and corvettes, which had been

ordered to conduct a patrol in the Bay of Biscay, in company with a Liberator patrol aircraft, to search for possible blockade runners. The *Tweed*, in company with the *Nene* and *Wakeskiu*, was steaming south at 13 knots in line abreast when at 16.13 in position 44.18N 21.17W she was hit by a torpedo which exploded under her stern. Immediately before the explosion an echo of a contact on the Asdic was heard on the repeater on the bridge. On being questioned, the operator, influenced by numerous false echoes that had been experienced over the previous 24 hours, stated that it was a 'non-sub'. Sub-Lieutenant Oates, the junior officer of the watch, doubted this and investigated, shouting 'That's a good trace'. Seconds later the Asdic operator reported hydrophone effect (HE) on the same bearing, indicating a torpedo. The alarm was sounded, and course altered towards the bearing, but the order had scarcely been given when she was hit. The torpedo had hit near 'Y' magazine, but this did not explode. The engine room bulkhead, however, gave way and about 30 seconds after the torpedo hit at least one of a pattern of ten dislodged depth charges exploded underwater and probably caused further damage. The ship started to break up, with the quarterdeck appearing to float away. The ship was ordered to be abandoned as she took a heavy list to starboard, and the bows lifted clear of the water. She continued to sink by the stern until the bows were vertical. She hung in this position for some time, being submerged from the funnel aft, until a depth charge exploded, and she sank. Fifty-two survivors were picked up by the *Nene*, eighty-three men died. Her attacker had been the *U 305* (Bahr).
[TNA:ADM.1/15871]

11 January NOTMANN drifter
(Norway) acquired 1941; No details
A former fishing boat (SF255G) which escaped from Norway to Lerwick in August 1941 and subsequently employed as a tender in Iceland (Reykjavik/Hvalfjordur). Listed in the *Statement of Losses* as being lost, cause unknown and no further details have been found.
[Statement of Losses p33; TNA:ADM.208/23]

14 January ADHERENT tug
Selby 1941; 700 tons; 142.6ft × 33.4ft; 1 × 12pdr, 1 × 20mm
Lieutenant Stanley Wilfred Potter RNR†
Foundered at 10.45 in very heavy weather in position 43.25N 35.50W when proceeding to join convoy HX274. Nineteen men were rescued by the *Northern Pride*, but ten men, including the commanding officer, were lost.
[TNA:ADM. 199/260; ADM.199/1392]

16 January LCT (4) 1029 landing craft, tank
Thornaby 1943; 200 tons; 171ft × 38.9ft; 2 × 20mm
Lieutenant Henry Edward Clark RNVR
One of a small convoy of landing craft heading south in the North Sea, they encountered thick fog and decided to anchor for the night off Skegness. The fog eventually cleared to a bright moonlight night. The peace was disturbed at 05.00 when there was an explosion under the starboard side, the blast blowing one of the Oerlikon guns overboard. She heeled over to starboard and immediately started sinking rapidly by the stern, the bows rising until they were vertical. It was believed that a drifting mine was the most likely cause. Nine men lost their lives.
[TNA:ADM.199/259]

23 January JANUS destroyer
Wallsend 1938; 339.6ft × 35.8ft; 6 × 4.7in, 1 × 4in, 4 × 2pdr, 4 × 20mm, 5 × torpedo tubes
Lieutenant Commander William Brabazon Robert Morrison†
One of the large force of Allied ships gathered off the beaches at Anzio to support the landings, the *Janus* was in company with her sister *Jervis* off 'Peter' beach, conducting an anti-torpedo boat patrol. At sunset, then being about 2 miles off San Lorenzo tower, the sound of aircraft engines was heard and soon after, at 17.46, an aircraft, identified as an He 111, suddenly appeared from low cloud and headed straight towards the *Janus*. The aircraft was quickly engaged by gunfire, but it released a torpedo before passing close to *Jervis* and escaping. The destroyer was under helm to port, but was unable to avoid being hit, the torpedo exploding on the port side under the bridge. Moments later there was a large sheet of flame, probably as the forward magazines blew up, with debris being thrown over a large area, the *Jervis* being struck by some large chunks of metal. The ship was blown in half, the bow section being seen to break off and float down the starboard side before sinking. The ship was covered in smoke and steam as the wreckage of the stern section sank by the bow with a heavy list to port. She had disappeared by 17.53. One hundred and sixty men died, with eighty survivors.
[TNA:ADM.267/95]

26 January LST 422 landing ship, tank
Baltimore 1942; 1,468 tons; 300ft × 50ft; 1 × 12pdr, 6 × 20mm
Lieutenant Commander Colin Lowe Broadhurst RNR
Detailed to take supplies to Anzio on the west coast of Italy where Allied forces had landed on 22 January. Fully laden with trucks, petrol, ammunition and 517 US Army personnel, she sailed from Naples on 25 January and arrived at Anzio to anchor at 00.15, with the intention of unloading at first light. The weather

was poor with winds gusting to Force 8. At 05.20 there was an explosion as a mine detonated, apparently under the starboard side amidships, between the main and auxiliary engine rooms. Many of the vehicles had their fuel tanks split and a fire started which rapidly spread. Moments later the after hatch collapsed, which scattered ammunition into the blaze. The fire was spreading rapidly, and within minutes the bridge was on fire and thick smoke spread throughout the ship. Attempts to start the fire foam motor failed when it was found to have been damaged by shrapnel from the explosion. The ship was ordered to be abandoned, and Carley floats were released and any floatable material thrown overboard. The US Navy tug *ATR-1* came alongside to assist with fire-fighting, but it was clear that she could not be saved, at 07.40 the commanding officer and the last of the crew left her. She continued to burn until she sank at 14.30. Twenty-nine men of the crew and 454 US Army personnel died.
[TNA: ADM.199/259; ADM.358/2454; MacDermott p59]

29 January SPARTAN cruiser
Barrow 1942; 5,770 tons; 485ft × 50.6ft; 8 × 5.25in.
12 × 2pdr, 12 × 20mm, 6 × torpedo tubes
Captain Patrick Vivian McLaughlin
Having provided gunfire support to the Allied landings at Anzio, Italy on 22–23 January, she returned to the area on 27 January, anchoring off the town at sunset to give air protection during the twilight period. At 17.30 on 29 January, she again came inshore, anchoring in position 41.26.2N 12.41.2E. She had barely secured herself when at 17.50 'Air raid warning Red' was called, and a number of aircraft were observed closing from over the land. The Type 285 gunnery control radar acquired the targets as they closed, at between 6,000 and 8,000 yards (3 to 4 nautical miles), and fire was opened. At about the same time glider bombs were observed to be released from the aircraft, which were now on her starboard beam. At 17.56 a glider bomb was seen to be heading for the cruiser, and seemed to be likely to pass astern, but it altered course during its final stage and struck the ship just abaft the after funnel, starting a large fire in the vicinity. The bomb then passed through the ship to explode in the port side of 'B' boiler room, blowing a hole in the side. The boiler room and the adjacent spaces, which included the main switchboard, were flooded and the ship heeled 10 degrees to port. The main watertight bulkhead between stations 99 and 117 was damaged. All power was lost, and the portable diesel pump was destroyed. On the upper deck the mainmast collapsed over the side to port a few minutes after the blast and the fire caused the warheads of the port torpedoes to explode. The ready-use 2pdr and 20mm ammunition caught fire and exploded. The fire spread rapidly to the after galley and the pom-pom

magazine. The loss of power meant that the ship was plunged into darkness, and the fires spread thick smoke throughout the ship. By 18.10 a fire-fighting tug was alongside playing hoses onto the ship, but her own efforts to tackle the blaze were hampered by a lack of power and it was not until 18.20 that some power had been restored and the hoses rigged to tackle the fires could have some effect. However, the fires had a firm hold and the list was steadily increasing as the water continued to flood into the ship unchecked. By 19.00 the list had reached 30 degrees and the ship was ordered to be abandoned. About 5 minutes later the ship rolled over onto her beam ends, stayed there for about 10 minutes and then sank. The board of enquiry concluded that the ship had sunk owing to the inability of the crew to stop the flooding of the lower deck spaces or correct the steadily increasing list. The severe fire and exploding ammunition had dislocated communications between the after and forward parts of the ship; the death of key personnel, such as the executive officer, had delayed a response; the initial absence of steam and electrical power had prevented the correction of the list and the lack of portable generators had impeded the fire-fighting efforts. Seven officers and 112 men were killed in the loss. The Hs 293 guided bombs had been launched by Do 217K aircraft of Gruppe 111/KG 100.
[TNA: ADM.1/15928]

29 January ORACLE yacht
1929 (*Osprey*) purchased 1939; 745 tons; 184.5ft × 28ft;
1 × 12pdr
Lieutenant Commander Ian Kerr RNR
Accidentally caught fire during the night of 28/29 January, whilst in Wallasey Dock, Birkenhead, and was eventually scuttled to prevent damaging other ships. One officer lost his life. She settled into the mud listing at an angle of 40 degrees and remained there until raised in November 1947, after salvage teams had removed twenty-three depth charges and ammunition. The wreck was sold for scrap.
[TNA: ADM.199/2288; www.britishnewspaperarchive.co.uk: Liverpool Echo 9 June & 26 November 1947]

30 January HARDY destroyer
Clydebank 1943; 1,808 tons; 339.6ft × 35.8ft; 4 × 4.7in,
2 × 40mm, 8 × 20mm, 8 × torpedo tubes
Captain William George Arthur Robson DSO
Having provided support for the Russian convoy JW56A that had arrived in the Kola Inlet on 28 January, the escorting destroyer force, including *Hardy*, sailed at 21.00 to escort the next convoy, JW56B, into Russian waters. During 29 January, several HF/DF radio intercepts were made indicating a U-boat presence. At 03.47 a strong HF/DF intercept was made, and *Hardy* steamed down the bearing to investigate.

At 04.04 there was a heavy explosion aft when she was hit by a torpedo. The ship shuddered violently, trimmed by the stern and assumed a 10 degree list to starboard. The port engine stopped, and it was believed that the starboard shaft was broken, and the propeller had probably been lost. About 3 minutes after the first explosion there was a second, larger detonation, probably when the after magazines exploded. She started to flood rapidly, and the engine and boiler rooms were ordered to be evacuated. Although clearly settling by the stern, with the bows rising clear of the water, she remained upright, and all the crew were ordered to go forward. The *Virago* and *Venus* closed, to take off the wounded and non-essential personnel and then the *Venus* started to lift off the remainder of the survivors. When this had been complete, she fired a single torpedo into the wreck at 05.51 to ensure her sinking, the ship breaking in two as she disappeared. Her position was then approximately 73.37N 18.06E. Thirty-eight men were lost. It is not entirely certain who the successful attacker was – three U-boats carried out attacks in a similar time frame, *U 957* reported attacking a destroyer at 03.54 and 03.56 and *U 472* fired at a destroyer at 03.57. Both boats reported hearing subsequent detonations, but on the balance of probabilities it was *U 278* (Franze) that was most likely to have been responsible. It fired a T5 acoustic homing torpedo at 03.57 at a destroyer and witnessed a hit on her target beneath the after superstructure.
[TNA: ADM.199/957; ADM.267/95; Morgan & Taylor pp372–5]

31 January PINE trawler
Aberdeen 1940; 530 tons; 150ft × 27.6ft; 1 × 12pdr
Lieutenant John Hird RNVR
Part of the escort to coastal convoy CW243 through the English Channel, they were approaching Selsey Bill when at 01.23 they were warned by shore radar of three groups of vessels moving toward them at high speed from the south. The eastern group of hostiles were tackled by the escort destroyer *Quorn*, whilst the *Albrighton* intercepted the centre group. The third group passed to the west, crossing the head of the convoy before turning to close from the inshore side. These were torpedo boats of the Fifth S-boot Flotilla, and in the subsequent torpedo attack, two ships in the convoy, the *Emerald* and *Caleb Sprague*, were torpedoed and at 02.45 the *Pine* had her bows blown off by a torpedo launched by *S 142*. The trawler *Rehearo* closed and took her in tow, and later that morning was relieved by the tug *Resolve*, but at 13.25 she sank, then being 6 miles to the west of Selsey Bill. Ten men were killed.
[TNA: ADM.199/259]

February LCT (3) 375 landing craft, tank
Bo'ness 1942; 350 tons; 175ft × 31ft; 2 × 20mm
Listed in the *Statement of Losses* as being 'sunk in the Mediterranean' but with no details provided. She was part of the Seventh LCT Flotilla in the central Mediterranean and was deleted from the Landing Craft List during the first week of February, probably being written off through damage.
[TNA: ADM.210/6; Statement of Losses p58]

2 February LCI (S) 511 landing craft, infantry, small
Oulton Broad 1943; 63 tons; 100ft × 21.6ft; 2 × 20mm
Damaged when beached at Portslade, Sussex, a subsequent examination showed her to be unsalvageable and she was written off as a constructive total loss.
[TNA: ADM.199/2289]

7 February X 22 midget submarine
Chesterfield 1944; 30/32 tons; 51.4ft × 5.9ft
Lieutenant Brian Mahoney McFarlane RAN[†]
As a training exercise, the submarine *Syrtis* was ordered to take *X 22* in tow, from Kames Bay, Isle of Bute, to Scapa Flow, to allow the midget submarine to make an 'attack' on ships stationed there. The weather was poor and deteriorated during the passage until it was a Force 8 gale from the west. At 03.30 when in position 58.43N 03.18W, the *Syrtis* was 'pooped', with successive waves smashing over the boat, sweeping the officer of the watch, Lieutenant Charles Blythe, overboard and partly flooding the control room as water washed down the tower. An object, believed to be Blythe, was seen in the water and the submarine was turned to recover him, altering round to port whilst going slow ahead to close. When the object was directly ahead it was illuminated by Aldis lamp and found to be their tow, *X 22*, now apparently acting independently, with induction mast raised and hatches shut. This was a shock, as she was still thought to be on tow. The submarine went full astern, but at 03.50 the *Syrtis* hit *X 22* and rode over her. Several hard bumps were felt, and the midget submarine disappeared. It was thought likely that the tow had been lost either when 'pooped' or when the turn had commenced. Lieutenant Blythe was not found, and four men were lost in *X 22*.
[TNA: ADM.1/16893; Evans p381]

13 February CAP D'ANTIFER trawler
Wyandotte 1917 seized 1940; 294 tons; 251ft × 43.6ft; 1 × 12pdr
Lieutenant James Wright Neill RNVR[†]
During the night of 12/13 February there was a large deployment of enemy torpedo boats into the North Sea to lay mines off the Humber and Grimsby. The movement was detected although there was some confusion over their precise course and position. Radio

monitoring stations ashore heard the groups deploy and heard them carry out unsuccessful torpedo attacks on patrol vessels at 00.59 and 01.16. Further radio traffic intercepted at 01.21 reported a torpedo hit. Patrolling trawlers had been warned of the presence of the enemy craft, but most saw little. The *Chalcedony* and *Monimia* patrolling near 57B buoy saw a burst of star shell and tracer to the north-west at 01.23, but it was not until dawn that it became clear that the *Cap d'Antifer*, which had been patrolling near number 57D buoy was overdue and had been the target. A search of the area found some wreckage, a patch of oil and the ships nameboard. There were no survivors from a crew of twenty-four men. Her attackers were the *S 65* and *S 99*. The wreck has been found in position 53.17N 01.06E.
[*TNA:ADM.199/265;ADM.199/1436*]

14 February SALVIKING salvage vessel
Renfrew 1942; 1,440 tons; 200.3ft × 37.9ft; 4 × 20mm
[Civilian Master]
Admiralty owned, she was civilian manned, by Risdon Beazley, and was ordered to proceed to Addu Attoll in the Indian Ocean to assist the destroyer *Paladin* that had been beached with a damaged hull after she had rammed an enemy submarine. She sailed from Colombo during the evening of 12 February, escorted by the armed trawler *Fara*, but was attacked at 16.30 in position 03.30N 76.30E by the submarine *U 168* (Pich), which fired three torpedoes. The first hit her forward, blowing off the bows and a moment later a second hit her amidships, after which she 'disintegrated'. The third torpedo was seen to pass astern. The *Fara* picked up thirty-eight survivors, but seventeen men were killed.
[*TNA:ADM.199/259*]

16 February LST 418 landing ship, tank
Baltimore 1942; 1,468 tons; 316ft × 50ft; 1 × 12pdr; 6 × 20mm
Lieutenant Commander Cyril Charles Reynolds RNR
Deployed to the Mediterranean to support the Allied landings in Italy, she sailed from Anzio during the early afternoon, loaded with fifty-three vehicles and approximately seventy-five military personnel, bound for Naples. At 15.12 there was a large explosion under the stern as she was hit by a submarine-fired torpedo. The engines stopped, and they lost all power, the ship being plunged into darkness. The bridge structure was blown upwards, and a split could be seen across the upper deck near the main hatch; both ship's boats had been damaged, preventing them being lowered. Water started to flood into the after sections, rapidly filling the engine room. At 15.37 she was hit by a second torpedo, again exploding aft. The ship now took a pronounced list to starboard and started to settle by the stern and

she was ordered to be abandoned. The bows continued to rise until clear of the water before she sank. Twenty-one men were killed, the survivors being picked up by US Navy landing craft. Her attacker had been *U 230* (Siegmann).
[*MacDermott p6;TNA:ADM.358/2471*]

18 February PENELOPE cruiser
Belfast 1935; 5,220 tons; 480ft × 51ft; 6 × 6in, 8 × 4in, 8 × 2pdr, 6 × 20mm, 6 × torpedo tubes
Captain George Devereux Belben DSO DSC†
Having completed a fire support mission near Anzio, the cruiser was returning to Naples at 26 knots, when at 07.00 in position 40.55N 13.25E she was hit on the starboard side aft, at 134 station abreast 'Y' turret by an acoustic homing torpedo fired by the submarine *U 410* (Fenski). The explosion fractured oil tanks and caused immediate flooding of the aft engine room and adjacent compartments, all power failed, steering was lost, and she took a list to starboard. Damage control work started by preparing to counter-flood and landing ships nearby were signalled to close. Ten minutes after the first explosion she was hit by a second torpedo, which hit between the after-engine room and boiler room. This caused catastrophic flooding of both those spaces very rapidly and she capsized to starboard and sank in less than a minute, breaking in two as she sank. The escort destroyer *Wilton* and landing craft closed and rescued 206 survivors, but 419 men were lost.
[*TNA:ADM.199/1430; Morgan & Taylor pp377–9*]

18 February BREDA yacht
Clydebank 1912 (*Sapphire*) purchased 1939; 1,207 tons; 256.1ft × 35.1ft
Commander Gerald Gordon Slade
Attached to the Seventh Submarine Squadron in western Scotland, she was tasked to carry out a night exercise with the submarine *Proteus*. The purpose was to exercise officers on the Commanding Officers' Qualifying Course (COQC) in gaining contact on a surface vessel and then carrying out an attack. The exercise got under way in Kilbrennan Sound and continued uneventfully until another 'run' commenced at 01.20 with the vessels some miles apart and then closing each other. At 01.22 the Asdic operator on the yacht reported hydrophone effect (HE) ahead, and after 5 minutes the HE was still being held, now right ahead. Soon after this the starboard light of the surfaced submarine was seen. The yacht stood on, and 10 minutes later flashed the night challenge. At 01.38 as the submarine was still on a steady bearing, and realising that she was closing fast, Commander Slade ordered the navigation lights of the yacht to be switched on and then went full astern. Despite this, one minute later the *Proteus* struck the yacht on the port side forward. She immediately started

making water and assumed a bow-down angle. The bilge pumps were started, and a portable pump moved into the forward compartments, but she was still making water fast. The whaler *Boarhound* arrived about 30 minutes later and a tow was rigged, and they made their way towards Campbeltown. At 08.30 the tug *Saucy* took over the tow and passed suction hoses which helped to keep the water under control. By 10.30 she was in shallow water and anchored. Although work continued to try and clear her of water, it steadily gained and at 17.30 she started to heel over to starboard until she reached an angle of 45 degrees, at which she capsized over onto her side. The enquiry found that with HE being reported right ahead, Commander Slade should have appreciated earlier that the *Proteus* was on his track and could have altered course to ensure that she passed clear. Lieutenant Verschoyle of the *Proteus* was also at fault. He had believed that he would pass to starboard of the yacht, having relied too heavily on the reports from radar. The wreck lies in position 55.24.58N 05.34.59W.
[TNA: ADM.1/16873; Larn vol 4 sec 8]

20 February **WARWICK** destroyer
Hebburn 1917; 1,100 tons; 300ft × 29.6ft; 2 × 4in, 4 × 20mm
Commander Denys Arthur Rayner DSC RNVR
Converted to a long-range escort, she was ordered to carry out an anti-submarine patrol in company with the *Scimitar* off the coast of north Cornwall between Pendeen Head and Trevose Head. The patrol was hampered by a large convoy and the numerous fishing vessels in the area, which did not help the Asdic search, and the one firm contact that was attacked yielded only a quantity of fish. It was decided to re-tune the Asdic set, which meant that it was out of action. At 11.45, when about 15 miles off Trevose Head, an explosion occurred, generating a large upheaval of water and smoke, just abaft the captain's cabin. A few moments later there was a second smaller explosion, marked by a large flash as the warhead magazine blew up and she broke in half at bulkhead 136, abaft the captain's cabin. The after part floated away before the stern rose vertically into the air and sank. The fore part remained upright and stable, although several small fires broke out. These were tackled and brought under control, and there were hopes that this could be saved. However, the after-engine room bulkhead collapsed, and she rolled over to port and sank, her bows rising clear of the water. Her attacker had been *U 413* (Poel). Three officers and sixty-four ratings were killed. Wreck lies in position 50.29.20N 05.25.17W.
[TNA: ADM.199/957; Morgan & Taylor pp383–6; Larn vol 1 sec 1]

20 February **LST 305** landing ship, tank
Boston 1942; 1,468 tons; 300ft × 50ft; 1 × 12pdr, 6 × 20mm
Lieutenant Commander Ronald Maudsley Naylor RNR
With a radar-equipped van embarked on the tank deck, she was employed off the beaches at Anzio, Italy, as a control ship for fighter aircraft, several RAF personnel being on board to operate the equipment. Whilst stopped in approximate position 41.14N 12.31E, at 18.50 she was hit by a submarine-fired torpedo, which exploded starboard side aft, followed moments later by a second which blew a large hole in the starboard side. The upper deck and tank deck were both wrecked, with the deck plates being blown up into vertical positions, the radar van was demolished, and the ship took a heavy list to starboard as she rapidly flooded with water. The armed trawler *Sheppey* responded to her radio call for assistance and came alongside at 19.25. It was clear that the ship was sinking, and the crew were ordered to leave, embarking on the trawler. This was complete by 20.00. She settled and listed further, but remained afloat, and at 21.50 the tug *Prospect* arrived on scene, but in the darkness, it was decided to wait until daylight. The following morning it was clear that she was in her last minutes, her bows being almost underwater and almost on her beam ends, and at 07.15 she sank. Six RAF personnel were lost. The attacker had been *U 230* (Siegmann).
[MacDermott p63]

20 February **HDML 1083** motor launch
Bideford 1942; 46 tons; 70ft × 15ft; 1 × 2pdr, 1 × 20mm
Lieutenant John Frederick Ford RNVR
Engaged in Operation 'Fire Eater', a rolling programme of commando raids on German outposts in the Dodecanese Islands by Special Forces, she embarked a team of Special Boat Squadron personnel. Caught by bad weather she attempted to take shelter at Kefaluka on the Turkish coast, but ran aground and could not be freed, so was scuttled and abandoned.
[TNA: ADM.199/1428]

21 February **LE DUE PAOLE** drifter
No details
Listed as being lost, cause and place unknown; no further details of the vessel or incident have been found.
[Statement of Losses p33]

22 February **MFV 70** tender
Looe 1942; 50 tons; 61.6ft × 17.9ft
Petty Officer William Watt
Based in the eastern Mediterranean, Petty Officer Watt was ordered to take the tender from Cyprus to Castellorizo (Megisti). Sailing from Famagusta on 20 February she headed towards the Turkish coast, but the

following day suffered an engine breakdown, and was forced to rig sails. With little wind her progress was slow, but they passed Klides Island and expected to raise the mainland on the morning of 22 February. At 05.00 when they were about 10 or 12 miles from the shore, they struck an underwater object, which pierced the hull. Pumps were set to work, but the water steadily gained during the day and she was abandoned in a sinking condition in position 36.06N 33.47E.
[TNA: ADM.199/259]

25 February INGLEFIELD destroyer
Birkenhead 1936; 1,544 tons; 319ft × 34ft; 4 × 4.7in, 1 × 4in, 6 × 20mm, 8 × torpedo tubes
Commander Charles Fraser Harrington Churchill DSC
Deployed to support the Allied landings at Anzio, she had conducted several bombardments of shore positions, and was underway at slow speed off the port at dusk, in company with the US Navy ships *Charles Hughes* (DD 428) and *Herbert C Jones* (DE 137). At 17.55 she was warned of hostile air activity and at 18.10 the sound of aircraft could be heard. Speed was increased, the bows turned towards the direction of the sound and being aware of the danger of radio–controlled guided bombs (see *Spartan* above) radio jamming was ordered to be started. Before this could take effect, however, streaks of smoke were seen on the starboard bow, and it was realised that the bombs had already been released. The ship made smoke and the incoming missiles were engaged with 20mm gunfire, but the first bomb after appearing to likely to miss astern, banked steeply and altered course to come straight for the destroyer. At 18.12 it hit the ship, blowing a hole in the side from the after superstructure to the forward torpedo tubes. The searchlight platform and the after tubes were blown overboard. The second bomb struck the sea nearby. The ship took an immediate list to port and settled by the stern, the centre of the ship being enveloped in a cloud of steam and smoke. The bulkhead between the engine room and the forward cabin flat was destroyed by the blast and the next bulkhead, by the CO's cabin collapsed soon after, causing extensive flooding aft. She was clearly sinking, and she was ordered to be abandoned. She then evidently broke in half, the stern disappearing under the water, the bows rising clear. She had disappeared completely by 19.30. Thirty–five men were lost.
[TNA: ADM.199/169]

25 February MAHRATTA destroyer
Greenock 1942; 1,920 tons; 345.6ft × 36.9ft; 6 × 4.7in, 4 × 2pdr, 8 × 20mm, 4 × torpedo tubes
Lieutenant Commander Eric Arthur Forbes Drought DSC†
On 22 February she was part of the escort force that joined Convoy JW57 that had sailed from Loch Ewe earlier, bound for Russia. During the evening of 25

February, the *Mahratta* was stationed at the rear of the convoy, the weather was poor, with low cloud and regular snow showers. At 21.00 there was an explosion under her stern and the shock caused both engines to stop. About 7 minutes later there was a second explosion just aft of centre, either a boiler exploding or the after magazine detonating. The blast blew the stern off, all the lights went out and all the after compartments and the engine room flooded. She heeled over to port and started to sink by the stern. The destroyer *Impulsive* was sent back to her aid, but before she could render any assistance, *Mahratta* rolled over and sank in position 71.12N 13.30E. The conditions, with below freezing temperatures, a heavy swell and strong squalls of driving snow meant that much of the lifesaving equipment was frozen, and many of the men that escaped died of hypothermia. There were only sixteen survivors, with 220 men lost. Her attacker had been *U 990* (Nordheimer).
[TNA: ADM.267/95]

26 February LST 407 landing ship, tank
Baltimore 1942; 1,468 tons; 300ft × 50ft; 1 × 12pdr, 6 × 20mm
Lieutenant William Roy Gordon Carling RNVR
Arrived at Baia, Naples, on 25 February and anchored a short distance from the shore. During the night, the wind increased to gale force and drove several landing ships and craft into shallow water, with *LST 407* grounding on rocks at Nisida. Most of the craft were successfully salvaged, but *407* was found to have been damaged beyond repair and she was eventually written off as a constructive total loss on 24 April and stripped of all useful equipment.
[TNA: ADM.199/2290: MacDermott p114]

27 February WOODPECKER sloop
Dumbarton 1942; 1,475 tons; 283ft × 38.6ft; 6 × 4in, 10 × 20mm
Commander Henry Leslie Pryse RNR
Part of the Second Escort Group, commanded by Captain Walker, which had been deployed to the south of Iceland to carry out aggressive hunts for submarines in support of the passage of Atlantic convoys. The group had considerable success, sinking *U 762* on 8 February; *U 424* on 11 February and *U 264* on 19 February. On the evening of 19 February, the group was in position 44.49N 22.38W, in line abreast formation, sweeping down the line of an HF/DF bearing of an intercepted submarine radio transmission, which had been obtained at 21.55. At 22.16 an Asdic contact was obtained at 600 yards on the starboard quarter, but before any action could be taken there was a large explosion under the stern. The explosion blew her stern off, with the quarterdeck peeled back, but despite some flooding she

remained stable and upright. The other ships stood by her all night, and at first light an inspection revealed that deck plates had been split and the sides buckled badly but she seemed to be in no immediate danger of sinking. The *Starling* rigged a tow. The following day all non-essential personnel were taken off as the salvage tug *Storm King* arrived on scene to take over towing duties. The tow went on for the next few days, with slow but steady progress being made. The weather however was worsening all the time and by the morning of 26 February they were experiencing high winds and heavy seas, with a Force 9 gale forecast. The deep rolling of the sloop strained at the tow and that afternoon it was decided to take off the last of the men. This was completed by 18.30, in heavy, driving rain. The *Storm King* kept the tow through the night, but at first light the sloop could be seen to be low in the water and at 07.15 she cast off the tow. The sloop capsized at 07.21, but remained afloat, bottom up. The corvettes *Azalea* and *Chilliwack*, which had been acting as escorts fired several rounds into her to make her sink. Her last position was 49.54N 06.40W. Her attacker had been *U 256* (Brauel), which had fired a pair of T5 acoustic homing torpedoes, one of which had found the *Woodpecker*. There were no casualties.
[TNA:ADM.199/175]

I March **GOULD** frigate
Boston 1943; 1,140 tons; 283.6ft × 35.2ft; 3 × 3in, 2 × 40mm, 9 × 20mm
Lieutenant David William Ungoed

With other ships of the First Escort Group, the *Gould* was tasked to carry out an aggressive anti-submarine sweep to the south-west of Ireland to assist the passage of Atlantic convoys. During the morning of 29 February contact was made with a submarine and this contact was held throughout the day and the following night, with regular attacks made by depth charge. The prosecution continued through the next day and although at 16.00 *Gore* and *Garlies* had been detached to refuel, the *Gould* remained on scene in company with the *Affleck*. The weather was poor and was worsening with difficult Asdic conditions, but the pair hung on to their contact, working together to ensure contact was maintained. At 19.20 *Gould* lost the echo on her port quarter, but the *Affleck* immediately gained contact on her port beam. The contact was good and improved, and it was believed that the submarine may be coming to the surface. Then there was a large explosion as the *Gould* was hit by a torpedo on the port side, the after motor room taking the full impact of the blast. The ship broke in half, the stern section breaking away and sinking quickly. With a large cloud of smoke still hanging over the frigate, a submarine then broke surface about 1,500 yards on the port beam of *Affleck*. The frigate promptly altered course towards the threat and engaged with 20mm and 3in guns, scoring hits on the conning tower. As she turned, she fired two shallow-set depth charges which straddled the U-boat, one exploding on the port side amidships, the other by the port bow. *Affleck* was now close to her opponent, and her port quarter grazed the stern of the submarine which she raked with gunfire. A further two shallow-set depth charges were released which exploded 'with a most spectacular effect'. The submarine lifted out of the water and with a broken back did a vertical nose dive beneath the waves. The *Affleck* then turned back towards the fore end of *Gould* which was still afloat but low in the water and listing to starboard. With a heavy sea running it was difficult to render assistance, but she managed to pick men out of the water as they jumped overboard. At 19.45 the wreck rolled over and sank. Thirty-six of the ship's company were picked up, although one subsequently died of his wounds. One survivor from the submarine, which was the *U 358*, was also rescued. One hundred and twenty-three men died.
[TNA:ADM.267/117]

2 March **LST 362** landing ship, tank
Quincy 1942; 1,468 tons; 300ft × 50ft; 1 × 12pdr, 6 × 20mm
Lieutenant Commander Reginald Harry Clark RNR

Sailed from Gibraltar on 21 February in Convoy MKS40 bound for England, joining another homeward-bound convoy, SL149, the following day. At 21.00 on 1 March the landing ships in the group were ordered to detach and proceed to their destination ports, accompanied by the escort destroyer *Rockwood*. The latter was not in full operational condition, having been damaged in the Mediterranean, and was operating on only one shaft, and had no functioning radar. At 03.45 on 2 March, in approximate position 48N 17.23W, the radar-equipped *LST 324* reported a surface contact 1,600 yards on the starboard beam. *Rockwood* turned towards the contact and fired a star shell. This revealed the shape of a submarine on the surface, and the destroyer headed straight for the threat, intending to ram. Before she could reach her object, *LST 362* was hit by a torpedo on the starboard side amidships. The explosion had a devastating effect, the ship rapidly breaking in half. The bow section rose vertically and floated away into the darkness but the after section remained afloat, although listing to starboard. The submarine, however, had dived, the restricted speed of *Rockwood* not having allowed her to reach her in time, and the destroyer had to content herself with running over the scene and dropping a pattern of depth charges. The surviving section of *362* meanwhile remained afloat, and at first light *LST 324* came alongside, to take off seventy-three survivors, before the wreck rolled over and sank at about 07.20.

Fifteen men of her crew were lost, and another died later of his injuries, whilst seventy-four soldiers were killed. Her attacker had been *U 744* (Blischke).
[TNA: WO.361/493; MacDermott p65]

5 March **ML 387** motor launch
Cairo 1943; 75 tons; 112ft × 18.4ft; 1 × 3pdr, 2 × 20mm
Lieutenant Douglas Matthew Connor RNVR†
Based in the eastern Mediterranean, she was berthed alongside at Beirut when there was a fuel spillage in the engine room, which triggered a petrol vapour explosion and fire. Several local dockyard workers and French sailors went to fight the fire, but the flames spread rapidly and at 18.45 her depth charges exploded in the heat. This resulted in the death of Lieutenant Connor and six French sailors with over twenty other people injured. A small harbour tug that had gone to the scene was sunk and there was widespread damage to dockyard buildings and property. *HDML 1007* berthed nearby was peppered with shrapnel.
[TNA: ADM.199/253]

9 March **ASPHODEL** corvette
Greenock 1940; 940 tons; 190ft × 33ft; 1 × 4in, 2 × 20mm
Lieutenant Michael Albert Halliday RNZVR†
Part of the escort to Convoy SL150/MKS41 which sailed from Freetown, Sierra Leone on 2 March bound for Liverpool. At 00.56 the *Asphodel*, being stationed on the starboard bow of the convoy, which was then in position 45.24W 18.09W, gained a small radar contact at a range of 4,000 yards on her starboard beam. This was believed to be a submarine on the surface, probably attempting to close the convoy before diving to attack. The corvette manoeuvred to parallel the contacts course and at 01.20 fired a star shell to illuminate the area. At the same time, the Foxer (noisemaker) was streamed, to decoy any homing torpedoes. The submarine, now lit up, dived, whilst the corvette altered course to open the range to 6,000 yards before turning towards with the intention of attacking with Hedgehog anti-submarine projectiles. An Asdic contact was made at 01.28, but before she could carry out her attack, there was an explosion on the starboard side aft. The stern apparently broke away and sank immediately, whilst the forward portion settled and heeled rapidly to port. Seconds after the main explosion, a series of other separate explosions engulfed her stern, probably dislodged depth charges. Within a minute of being hit, *Asphodel* had disappeared. Fellow escort *Clover* was soon on scene, but only five survivors were picked up from the water, and two of these subsequently died of their injuries. Ninety-two men died. The first lieutenant was one of those who survived, and he believed that the corvettes' Foxer was not working correctly, leaving her open to attack. The

submarine was *U 575* (Boehmer), who had fired a T5 acoustic homing torpedo at her opponent.
[TNA: ADM.237/245; CB.4273 p356]

March **STONEHENGE** submarine
Birkenhead 1943; 715/990 tons; 201ft × 23.9ft; 1 × 3in, 7 × torpedo tubes
Lieutenant David Stuart McNeil Verschoyle-Campbell DSO DSC†
Based at Trincomalee in Ceylon (Sri Lanka), she sailed for a patrol on 25 February, but failed to return as expected on 22 March and was posted missing. Her patrol area was in the northern part of the Malacca Straits and she was presumed to have been lost by accident or by hitting a mine.
[Evans p382]

16 March **MTB 417** motor torpedo boat
Hythe 1942; 46 tons; 71.9ft × 20.7ft; 1 × 2pdr, 2 × 20mm, 2 × torpedo tubes
Sub-Lieutenant Thomas Graham Hughes RNVR†
Based at Dover, she sailed in company with MTBs *362*, *418* and *443*, with Lieutenant Ralph Bonfoy Rooper (Senior Officer, Motor Gun Boats, Dover) embarked, to carry out an offensive night sweep along the French coast between Calais and Boulogne, with a further group of gunboats were ordered to operate nearby. At 20.00 shore-based radar informed them that a group of ships had been detected leaving Calais and the torpedo boats prepared to intercept them. In the darkness, the group became separated, and it was only *MTB 417* with *MTB 418* that sighted the enemy at 20.41, about 5 miles off Cap Griz Nez, when star shells fired from the shore revealed a small convoy, which consisted of a single ship being escorted by six armed trawlers. As the torpedo boats approached the enemy, the noise of the engines was heard, which led to a night challenge being flashed, and then star shell being fired. As the British pair altered course to carry out an attack, they came under heavy shellfire from the escorts and *417* was hit by a large shell, probably an 88mm round fired by either *Vp 1810* or *Vp 1811*. This started a fire and she burnt fiercely, her companion reported seeing 'a great sheet of flame'. *418* attempted to close, but found only burning debris, and as she also came under heavy concentrated fire was forced to leave the area. All nineteen officers and men on board were lost.
[TNA: ADM.199/261; ADM.267/124; Reynolds, *Home Waters MTBs* p122]

17 March **LCI (L) 273** landing craft, infantry, large
New Jersey 1943; 234 tons; 150ft × 23.8ft; 4 × 20mm
Lieutenant Maurice Herbert Holifield RNVR
Acting as harbour guardship at Anzio, she also served as a local depot for the smaller landing craft, the crews

using her troop spaces as accommodation. That harbour came under regular and often intensive air attacks after the landings on 22 January. During one air raid at 03.50 a large bomb struck the jetty close to *273* and then glanced upwards to explode against her side, detonating just forward of the watertight bulkhead between the troop spaces. The force of the explosion blew the bows away and she took a list to starboard. More than twenty men were trapped in the troop space, all of whom were injured or killed by the blast, and were piled up amongst twisted wreckage, the deck having been blown up to within 2ft of the deckhead. Lieutenant Christopher Finlayson and Stoker Thomas Forrester entered the space, and despite the ship filling with water managed to haul three of the men to safety before the ship capsized. Finlayson was subsequently awarded the DSC, Forester the DSM. Twenty men were killed.
[TNA: ADM.199/1430; ADM.1/29571]

20 March GRAPH (P715) submarine
Hamburg 1941 (*U 570*), captured 1941; 769/883 tons; 165.8ft × 20.2ft; 1 × 88mm, 1 × 20mm, 5 × torpedo tubes
The submarine was captured in August 1941 after being disabled by depth charges from an RAF Hudson aircraft, and served in the Royal Navy from October 1941 as HMS *Graph*. A growing list of defects coupled with the lack of spares led to her being decommissioned in June 1943. In March 1944 she was listed for disposal and she was towed away from Chatham by the tug *Empire John*, bound for the Clyde, for use in a series of shock trials. By 18 March, the tug was finding towing conditions difficult, with a heavy swell and strong wind from the south-west, which made the tow sheer considerably from port to starboard. By 04.00 no headway was being made at all, and a short time later the tow parted, then being in position 56.09N 07.23W. At first light an attempt was made to get alongside and re-connect the tow, but all efforts failed. The Canadian corvette *Longbranch* came into sight during the morning and assisted the tug by releasing oil onto the water, and although a rope was thrown over the bits, it immediately parted. By nightfall, the weather was deteriorating further, with strong winds accompanied by squalls of snow and sleet. The next morning another tug, the *Allegiance* arrived, to be joined by the frigate *Bullen*. Again, oil was released to calm the waves, and again a line was secured, but immediately parted. During further efforts to get near the submarine both tugs suffered damage, forcing *Empire John* to leave the area and make for Campbeltown. The *Bullen* and *Allegiance* stood by the submarine during the night, but at 05.00 she was driven by the heavy swell and high seas onto Islay, south of Saligo Bay, and was wrecked in position 55.48N 06.27W.
[TNA: ADM.199/509]

(23–27) March SYRTIS submarine
Birkenhead 1943; 715/990 tons; 201ft × 23.9ft; 1 × 3in, 7 × torpedo tubes
Lieutenant Michael Hugh Jupp DSC†
Sailed from Lerwick on 16 March to conduct a patrol off the Norwegian coast but failed to return as expected. She attacked a steamer with gunfire on 22 March in position 66.45N 13.11E but failed to respond to radio calls on 28 March and was presumed lost between those dates, probably because of hitting a mine. Forty-eight men were lost.
[Evans pp381–2]

26 March MTB 352 motor torpedo boat
Wivenhoe 1943; 44 tons; 72.7ft × 19.2ft; 1 × 20mm, 2 × torpedo tubes
Lieutenant John Michael Moore RNVR
In company with five other torpedo boats sailed to carry out a night patrol in the southern North Sea heading east in a broad 'V' formation at 23 knots. At 21.55 *MTB 351* started making smoke when her smoke canisters on the stern suddenly and unexpectedly activated. A moment later the senior officer, in *MTB 355*, signalled the group to reduce speed, and then stop. This was done by flashing light, with each boat passing on the command. The smoke from *351* was thick and drifted across the group and mingling with the steam from the exhausts formed a dense cloud, making visual communications difficult. At 21.57, *352* had stopped abreast her leader when *MTB 454* emerged from the cloud of smoke. *454* was aware of the signal to slow, but had not received the message to stop and rammed *352*, crushing her stern. The engine room started to fill with smoke and started to flood. *454* managed to disengage herself, but as the crew of *352* worked to clear the debris they were hampered by a new cloud of thick smoke, as her own smoke making apparatus had been split by the collision. She started to sink quickly by the stern and all hands were moved forward. *454* came alongside and lifted off four men, and *355* ran alongside and passed a towing hawser, but it soon became clear that this was not a practicable proposition, so all remaining hands were taken off. As they did so her bows rose into the air. She remained afloat and an attempt was made to tow her in this condition, but it failed. She slowly settled and finally sank at 23.40 in position 52.05N 02.32E.
[TNA: ADM.1/16896]

27 March MAALØY whaler
Moss 1935 (*Globe VI*) requisitioned 1941; 249 tons; 115.9ft × 23.9ft
Lieutenant Frederick James Perkins RNVR†
Originally manned by the Royal Norwegian Navy, but transferred to the Royal Navy in June 1942, and was based in India. In early 1944 she was sent to the Maldive

Islands carrying an RAF officer who was tasked to investigate reports of food shortages. Having completed the investigation, she sailed to return to Trincomalee, Ceylon, with Hassan Fareed, the Prime Minister of the Maldives as a passenger, but disappeared whilst en-route. All seventeen members of the crew were lost, as were the two passengers. A search of the area found only wreckage and an empty life raft. It later emerged that she had been torpedoed and sunk by *U 510* (Eick) in position 05.25N 77.32E.
[TNA:ADM.199/265]

30 March **LAFOREY** destroyer
Scotstoun 1941; 1,935 tons; 345.6ft × 37ft; 6 × 4.7in, 4 × 2pdr, 8 × 20mm, 8 × torpedo tubes
Captain Harold Thomas Armstrong DSO DSC†
Conducting an aggressive anti-submarine sweep to the north of Sicily in company with the destroyers *Ulster* and *Tumult*, they successfully located *U 223* (Gerlach) during 29 March and commenced a long prosecution of the boat. The hunt went on for several hours with a series of depth-charge attacks until at 01.00 in position 38.45N 14E.18E the submarine was forced to the surface. She was sighted by *Laforey* on her port bow and was illuminated by searchlight, and the destroyer fired star shell and opened fire with 2pdr and 20mm guns. As she altered course to close the submarine there was a large explosion on the port side amidships, next to number 1 boiler room as she was hit by a T5 homing torpedo, fired by the submarine as she surfaced. This broke her back and she started to sink very quickly, breaking up as she did so, the bow and stern sections rising clear of the water. She sank in 2 minutes, taking 189 men with her. The other ships of the force, which had now been joined by the escort destroyers *Hambledon* and *Blencathra*, sank the submarine with gunfire.
[TNA:ADM.267/94]

31 March **MTB 241** motor torpedo boat
Teignmouth 1942; 47 tons; 72.6ft × 19.2ft; 1 × 20mm, 2 × torpedo tubes
Lieutenant James Rowntree Macdonald RNZVR
In company with three other torpedo boats, sailed from Harwich to carry out a night operation, sweeping along the Dutch coast in search of an enemy convoy reported leaving the Hook of Holland. By 23.37 the group were off Ijmuiden and located a group of ships ahead of them. Dividing into pairs, they attacked from different directions. *241* was in the group that crossed the bows of the convoy, but as they did so, came under heavy fire from the enemy. *241* was hit by a large-calibre shell in the engine room, but manage to extricate herself, despite the compartment starting to flood. When clear, she was taken in tow by *224* and *244*, but at 06.55 the tow parted. *241* now had a heavy list to starboard

and her stern was awash. The tow was reconnected, but again parted. Soon after this, at 08.00 she rolled over and sank, in position 52.22N 03.12E.
[TNA:ADM.199/259]

10 April **FORECAST** drifter
Lowestoft 1925 requisitioned 1939; 96 tons; 84.1ft × 19.2ft
Listed as being sunk at Greenock, no further details found, but the wreck was apparently broken up and cleared by July.
[Statement of Losses p33; https://canmore.org.uk/site/112158/forecast-greenock-upper-firth-of-clyde]

14 April **EL HIND** landing ship, infantry
Glasgow 1939 requisitioned 1943; 5,319 tons; 400ft × 52ft
Lieutenant Commander Frederick George Sharp
Royal Indian Navy. Laying at Bombay, she was destroyed as a result of the devastation caused when the merchant vessel *Fort Stikine* blew up. The *Stikine* had arrived in Karachi on 12 April and loaded a cargo of cotton on top of a mixed cargo, which included 1,400 tons of explosives. At about 13.30 smoke was seen rising from the ventilators of number 2 hold, and the crew, later assisted by dockyard fire-fighters, deployed hoses in an attempt to tackle the fire but were unable to reach the source of the smoke, which evidently lay in the stored bales of cotton. Hopes that the *Stikine* could be moved out of the harbour or scuttled were frustrated by defective engines and shallow water. By 15.45 flames were bursting out of the hold and the ship was ordered to be abandoned. At 16.03 there was a massive explosion, which blew the ship apart and scattered debris over a wide area. A second explosion occurred at 16.41, which was even greater than the first, scattering burning cotton bales. The combination of the explosions and fire set the dockyard and surrounding area on fire, and eleven ships in the harbour were damaged or sunk. One of them was the *El Hind* which was berthed nearby and caught fire when showered with burning debris and was subsequently flooded to sink by the stern.
[TNA:ADM.1/16317]

17 April **MTB 266** motor torpedo boat
Bayonne NJ 1940 (*PT 17*); 32 tons; 70ft × 20ft; 4 × torpedo tubes
Stationed in the eastern Mediterranean, she was one of a group that had been involved in a night patrol on the night of 9/10 March during which they intercepted a small enemy convoy. As the group closed, they were seen and came under heavy fire, and *266* received several hits, one exploding on the bridge killing her commanding officer, Lieutenant Broad RNZVR. After careering out of control, she was eventually brought under command and made the port at Casteloriso. Taken to Alexandria, she foundered in the harbour whilst awaiting repairs,

and although raised, was written off as a constructive total loss.

[Reynolds & Cooper, Mediterranean MTBs at War p113]

18 April **MTB 707** motor torpedo boat

Falmouth 1943; 95 tons; 110ft × 21.3ft; 1 × 2pdr,
2 × 20mm, 2 × torpedo tubes
Lieutenant Osmond Joseph Edward Fountaine

Sent to Larne, Northern Ireland, to carry out exercises in company with several surface ships, she was carrying out a mock attack on the French frigate *l'Escarmouche*, which involved passing ahead of the target to simulate dropping a depth charge in its path. The pass was evidently mistimed, and she was rammed and cut in half. The sections remained afloat and were eventually beached at Larne. Four men died.

[TNA: ADM.199/2293; ADM.358/4334]

20 April **LEVANT SCHOONER 24** caique

Requisitioned fishing vessel
Sub-Lieutenant Allan Lane Tuckey RNVR[†]

Part of the irregular forces that were employed in the Aegean, the caique sailed from Yedi Adalar with a patrol of commandos from the Special Boat Squadron (SBS), who were to be landed on the island of Alimnia, to carry out a reconnaissance. This was successfully completed but their presence had become known to the enemy, and as the caique waited to pick up the men, several German patrol boats appeared, and the vessel was captured and set on fire. Tuckey, along with his RN telegraphist, four commandos and three Greek crewmen were all taken prisoner, interrogated and then executed.

[TNA: ADM.199/267]

24 April **ROODE ZEE** tug

Kinderdijk 1938 requisitioned 1940; 468 tons;
148.5ft × 26.7ft
Master Jacob Klinge[†]
Sub-Lieutenant Harry Orme Dooyewaard RNVR[†] (senior RN officer)

During the night of 23/24 April, shore-based radar detected movement by German fast torpedo boats as they closed the English coast. The contacts were plotted closing Beachy Head, then splitting into three groups which proceeded on parallel courses to the north-east. Warnings of enemy presence were broadcast, and groups of MTBs and MLs were vectored to intercept them. At 02.55 the first contact was made by British patrol craft and for the next 2 hours there was a confused series of contacts between the groups of German torpedo boats and British warships. The *Roode Zee* was en-route to Portsmouth towing a section for a Mulberry harbour and was 2.2 miles to the south-east of Dungeness when she was found by the German *S 100* which hit her

with a single torpedo. The destroyer *Halstead*, busy engaging another group of enemy craft nearby, heard the dull thud of the explosion and closed the area, but could find no survivors, only the abandoned caisson. Seven members of the Royal Navy and fifteen civilians died. The wreck has been found and lies in position 51.53.12N 01.00.22E.

[TNA: ADM.199/2293; Larn vol 2. sec 4]

24 April **MTB 671** motor torpedo boat

Bangor 1943; 95 tons; 110ft × 21.3ft; 1 × 2pdr, 2 × 20mm,
2 × torpedo tubes
Lieutenant Lawrence Edson Toogood RNVR[†]

Based at Gosport with the 55th MTB Flotilla, she joined other boats of the flotilla, *617* and *632*, to conduct a night patrol in the English Channel to the east of Cherbourg. That night saw sorties by enemy torpedo boats, with one group attacking British shipping off Dungeness (see *Roode Zee*) and the second fought an action with British destroyers off Hastings. At 01.00 the large torpedo boats *Möwe*, *Kondor* and *Greif* deployed from Cherbourg to screen their return, and deal with any patrolling British coastal craft. Almost immediately they encountered and engaged a group of British MTBs, and in a sharp exchange of fire drove them off. This action had been seen by the boats of the 55th in the distance and they anticipated that the enemy units might move along the coast. At 03.46 this proved correct when they were detected by the torpedo boat's radar moving along the coast towards them. The British vessels deployed to seaward until they observed them at which they increased speed and closed. Apparently alerted by the noise of the engines, the German units altered course towards them and fired star shell, which illuminated the area, followed by a barrage of fire. Any hope of closing the targets had now gone, and the torpedo boats turned away, making smoke as they did, but *671* was hit twice, first in the wheelhouse and then in the engine room. The latter stopped the engine and stared a fire. One of the enemy torpedo boats closed and fired repeatedly into the burning wreck until her petrol tanks blew up and she disappeared. The survivors had to cling to pieces of floating wood and mattresses, but by the time a searching frigate found them the following morning, only two men were left alive. Twenty-five men died.

[Reynolds, Dog Boats pp99–100]

29 April **ATHABASKAN** destroyer

Walker 1941; 1,880 tons; 355.6ft × 36.5ft; 6 × 4.7in, 2 × 4in,
4 × 2pdr, 4 × torpedo tubes
Lieutenant Commander John Hamilton Stubbs DSO DSC RCN[†]

Royal Canadian Navy. On the night of 28/29 April the *Athabaskan* in company with sister ship *Haida*, were ordered to provide cover for a force of motor launches that were conducting a minelaying operation to the east of the Île de Batz, Brittany. By 03.00 the operation was complete, but at 03.13 the pair were advised by Plymouth shore radar that they had detected two surface contacts heading west along the coast. The Canadian pair shaped course to intercept and made radar contact at 14 miles. This enabled them to place themselves in an ideal position to intercept and at 04.00 *Athabaskan* fired star shell to illuminate the area, revealing the contacts as German *Elbing*-class ocean-going torpedo boats. The enemy reacted very quickly, turning away and firing torpedoes. The Canadians, realising the danger, altered towards the threat to 'comb the tracks', whilst continuing to fire star shell. At 04.15 there was a large explosion on the port side aft of *Athabaskan* as one of the torpedoes hit. She lost all power, and a fire broke out amidships. The fire was intense, evidently fuelled by a split oil tank, and the boats were ordered to be turned out. Just as a portable pump had been brought into use to fight the fire, there was a tremendous explosion as the after magazine blew up. She then rolled over to port and sank by the stern. Meanwhile, the *Haida* had put herself between the *Athabaskan* and the threat and laid smoke, then pursued the German ships, successfully hitting the *T27*, leaving it aground and burning, before turning back to pick up survivors. By now it was becoming light, and after loitering for 20 minutes, *Haida* left the scene, to ensure she was clear of the coast and the threat from air attack. Her motor boat had been lowered, and it remained on scene picking up more survivors, and then made the long journey back to Plymouth. German surface craft were on scene soon after and picked up more survivors, but 128 men died.

[*McKee & Darlington p142*]

1 May HDML 1380 motor launch
Clynder 1943; 46 tons; 70ft × 15ft; 1 × 40mm, 1 × 20mm
Lieutenant Donald Cameron MacDonald RNVR[†]
Based in the Aegean, *1380*, in company with *HDML 1398*, was ordered to proceed to the island of Ios where *1398* was to land a detachment from the Greek Sacred Heart Squadron. During the night of 30 April *1398* successfully closed the island to land the raiders, whilst *1380* patrolled offshore, and contact was lost between the pair. After landing her patrol, *1398* proceeded independently towards the rendezvous at Amorgos, but as the weather was poor, with strong winds and high seas, diverted to the island of Irakleia. At 05.40 in the morning, as they closed a sheltered bay, a vessel was seen ahead. Believing it could be the missing *1380* the single-letter night recognition code was flashed, but the stranger replied with single letters, which were not recognised. The silhouette of the vessel could be made out, and as it did not have the expected mast,

1398 feared that it was actually a German patrol boat, which seemed to be confirmed when the stranger got underway. *1398* therefore went to action stations and engaged the stranger, which replied soon after. It was quickly realised that the return fire being received was from a Bofors 40mm gun, and *1398* ceased fire and flashed 'What Ship' and received the reply '*1380*'. The pair then closed, and it was discovered that *1380* had lost her mast in the poor weather which explained the unusual outline and the boats had different sets of night recognition signals. *1380* had been hit several times and one rating was wounded. The holes were plugged, and she got under way on one engine, the other being out of action, intending to return to base. *HDML 1398* had to return to Ios to collect the men of the Sacred Heart, so *1380* was on her own. The weather remained poor, and at 23.00 it was found that the engine room was making water and soon after the remaining engine stopped. With the boat flooding, the dinghy was launched with as many men as possible embarked, but both officers and five ratings remained on board. She was last seen firing tracer bullets into the air and firing rockets. The dinghy reached Stampalia (Astypalaia), but *1380* was not seen again and was presumed to have foundered with the loss of all five men on board.
[*TNA: ADM.199/260; ADM.358/2227*].

4 May ELGIN minesweeper
Renfrew 1919; 710 tons; 231ft × 28.5ft; 1 × 4in, 2 × 12pdr
Lieutenant Nicholas Psaroudis RNR
Engaged in sweeping to the east of Portland, she was steaming at 12 knots with sweeps out, when in position 50.28N 02.11W an acoustic mine exploded 50 yards off the starboard quarter. Badly whipped by the detonation, although there was no major hull damage, the bottom plates split under the engine room, resulting in a slow flood of that compartment. The shock damage caused the engines to stop, and all power was lost. The ship was towed to the safety of Portland. After temporary repairs locally, the ship was then towed to Chatham for repairs. However, these were suspended in June, as it was considered that she was not worth the expense and the ship was written off a constructive loss. There were no fatalities.
[*TNA: ADM.267/117; CB.4273 p316; Warship Supplement 66*]

5 May MTB 708 motor torpedo boat
Glampton 1943; 95 tons; 110ft × 21.3ft; 1 × 2pdr,
2 × 20mm, 2 × torpedo tubes
Lieutenant Commander George Clifford Fanner RNVR
In company with *MTB 720*, the pair were returning to Portland in the early morning after an uneventful night patrol in the English Channel. The weather was good, with a clear blue sky and a calm sea. At 07.20 when they were about 26 miles south-east of Anvil Point a

flight of aircraft approached from ahead which were identified as RAF Beaufighters, evidently searching for enemy shipping. To the horror of crews of the torpedo boats, after passing them on the port side, the aircraft then turned and headed straight for them, evidently determined to attack. The Beaufighters made three runs, using cannon and rockets to great effect, setting *708* on fire and seriously wounding several of the crew. The torpedo boats fired flares as a recognition signal when the attack commenced, but this had no effect, and finally they replied, 'with all available guns'. The fire spread until it was out of control and thankfully the patrolling escort destroyer *Cottesmore* saw the smoke, closed, and took off the crew and then sank the burning hull of *708*. *MTB 720* was also hit and damaged but survived to make it back to Portland. One man later died of his wounds.
[TNA: ADM.199/259; Reynolds, Dog Boats pp100–01]

6 May 1944 VALLEYFIELD frigate
Quebec 1943; 1,445 tons; 283ft × 36.5ft; 2 × 4in, 8 × 20mm
Lieutenant Commander Dermot Thomas English RCNR
Royal Canadian Navy. Part of Ocean Escort Group C1, which had successfully escorted westbound Convoy ONM243 into North American waters. The group then headed north for St Johns, Newfoundland, steaming at 13 knots in line abreast, one mile apart. There was a lot of floating ice, much of it partly submerged, which led the group to stop zigzagging, At 23.40 Asdic on *Valleyfield* picked up HE (hydrophone effect) on the port beam, but before they could investigate the ship was hit on the port side by a torpedo, which exploded under the boiler room. The ship broke up, the bows immediately rolling over to starboard before rising vertically and sinking. The after section was afloat for a little longer, but within 2 minutes she had disappeared. So quick was her demise that the other ships of the group were uncertain what had happened, and it was only when the *Giffard* investigated after *Valleyfield* had failed to respond to radio calls and found wreckage and men in the water, did they realise that she had been sunk. Thirty men survived, but 125 were lost. The subsequent Inquiry was critical of the actions of the group: CAT noise makers were not streamed; no zigzag was ordered and there was a slow reaction to the torpedoing. Her attacker had been *U 548* (Zimmerman) that had fired a single acoustic homing torpedo.
[Morgan & Taylor pp398–401]

20 May WYOMING trawler
Selby 1915 (*Veresis*) requisitioned 1940; 302 tons; 135ft × 23.5ft; 1 × 12pdr
Skipper George Nelson Spencer RNR
Based at Harwich, she was conducting sweeping operations off that port in company with other trawler-minesweepers, employing Oropesa sweeps. At midday when in position 52.02.17N 01.48.54E 'in sweeps' was ordered, and the speed was reduced to 3–4 knots and the crew commenced heaving in. As they did so a mine was seen to break surface nearby clearly having snagged on the wire. Despite a prompt order to stop heaving in, there was a large explosion close to the starboard side and she sank, stern first, in a few minutes. Just before heaving in, she had fouled a dan buoy with her sweep, and this had been dragged to the end of the lap, and this was believed to have prevented the mine being cut free. Five men were killed.
[TNA: ADM.199/253]

28 May MTB 732 motor torpedo boat
Hamworthy 1944; 95 tons; 110ft × 21.3ft; 1 × 2pdr, 2 × 20mm, 10 × mines
Lieutenant Albert Henry Randall RNVR[†]
Modified for minelaying, with the torpedo tubes removed, *732* in company with *739* were patrolling off Beachy Head, when at 23.59, shore radar reported two groups of fast-moving enemy vessels closing from the south. The Free French destroyer *la Combattante* and frigate *Seymour*, patrolling off Selsey were directed to attack one group, whilst *732* and *739* were diverted to intercept the second group. At 01.00 the *Combattante* obtained a radar contact to the east of her at 4 miles and altered course to intercept and 5 minutes later she fired illuminant which revealed two small fast-moving torpedo boats. Believing these to be the enemy she had been seeking, she opened fire. The contact was actually *732* and *739*, and she very quickly found the range and *732* was hit twice by 4in shells. She immediately caught fire and soon after this blew up. One officer and twelve ratings were killed, and five of the ten survivors were wounded. It later emerged that none of the units had activated their IFF systems.
[TNA: ADM.199/259; Reynolds, Dog Boats p101]

30 May FIRMAMENT whaler
Middlesbrough 1930 (*Kos IX*) requisitioned 1940; 248 tons; 115.1ft × 24.1ft; 1 × 40mm, 2 × 20mm
Skipper John Muttitt RNR
Having completed a refit at Alexandria, the whaler sailed at 14.10 to conduct engine and gunnery trials. During the afternoon she experienced difficulty with the engines, an air pump having failed. This reduced her speed to 3 knots, and she headed back to harbour, and the assistance of a tug was requested. She proceeded slowly along the Great Pass Channel, and they were able to increase speed as the engine room reported that they had affected a repair to the pump. When they were abreast number 4 buoy the ship suddenly swung to starboard. The helm was put hard to port, but she failed to respond and at 16.50 with a sharp thud and

a screeching noise, they ran onto the Hydrographer's Shoal (31.09.45N 29.48.45E). She started to pound on the rocks and soon assumed a 40-degree list to port. The RAF launch *HSL 2731* closed the wreck at 18.00 and took the crew off. By then the engine room had flooded and the main decks were submerged. A later examination of the wreck found that although the wheel showed that the helm had been put to port, but the rudder was amidships, and it was probable that a fracture of the steering gear had occurred. Continuing to pound on the rocks, she was declared a constructive total loss.
[TNA: ADM.1/16907]

6 June Operation 'Neptune': amphibious landings in northern France as part of Operation 'Overlord'

In the early hours of 6 June the long-awaited landings in northern France got under way, with several hundred ships making their way across the English Channel, the way cleared by a force of minesweepers. The landings went remarkably well, with few losses in the escorting forces, although inevitably several of the amphibious craft were lost.

WRESTLER destroyer
Wallsend 1918; 1,100 tons; 300ft × 29.6ft; 4 × 4in, 4 × 20mm, 6 × torpedo tubes
Lieutenant Commander Reginald William Beecroft Lacon DSC
The destroyer sailed from the Solent during the afternoon of 5 June, being part of the escort to Convoy J7 which arrived off Juno Beach in the early hours of the following day. At 06.37 with the crew closed up at action stations, closing the beachhead, there was a large explosion under the forward part of the hull as she detonated a mine. The force of the explosion blew open hatches, and the flash travelled fore and aft, setting light to hammocks and killing two men and injuring several ratings. A fire broke out in the galley flat and number 1 oil tank was briefly ablaze. The ship was turned into wind to carry the smoke clear as fire–fighting efforts got under way. These were successful as the fires were quickly got under control and finally extinguished. Meanwhile flooding was being reported amidships, but bulkheads were quickly shored and pumping started. With the ship stabilised, she was taken in tow, being able to leave at 08.45 for Portsmouth. She anchored at 23.50 the same night. Subsequent examination found that the bottom was severely damaged, with a hole 12ft by 9ft exposing oil fuel tanks and various compartments to the sea, making it clear that it was good damage control work that had saved the ship from foundering. The damage was such, however, that repairs were considered uneconomical,

and she was declared a constructive total loss and sold for scrapping in July.
[TNA: ADM.267/96]

MTB 248 motor torpedo boat
Cowes 1943; 41 tons; 73ft × 18ft; 2 × torpedo tubes
Lieutenant Brian Marius MacGinty RNVR
During the night of 5/6 June a force of MTBs carried out Operation 'Monastic', laying mines off Cap d'Antifer. The mine laying was performed by 'D' class torpedo boats, screened by the boats of the 14th MTB Flotilla, which included *248*. The operation was carried out successfully, but whilst reforming to return to England *248* was involved in a collision and sank some hours later.
[TNA: ADM.179/509]

LCF 31 landing craft, flak
Thornaby 1943; 415 tons; 171ft × 38.8ft; 4 × 2pdr, 8 × 20mm
The Green List indicates that she was 'loaned to, manned by, the U.S. Navy for the Western Task Force'. She was sunk off Utah Beach at approximately 07.30, when she sank after a large explosion. The cause was uncertain, but probably after detonating a mine near the Cardonet shoal. She was not actually written off until 5 September.
[ADM 210/8]

LCT (3) 317 landing craft, tank
Middlesbrough 1942; 350 tons; 175ft × 31ft; 2 × 20mm
Sub-Lieutenant Arthur Vernon RNVR
Running towards 'Nan' sector, Juno Beach, she detonated a mine as she neared the beach, and was then hit repeatedly by shellfire and was abandoned. Two men were lost.
[TNA: ADM.199/1650]

LCT (3) 496 landing craft, tank
Old Kilpatrick 1943; 350 tons; 175ft × 31ft; 2 × 20mm
She made a successful landing on Gold Beach, discharging her cargo of tanks, and then made several subsequent trips ferrying troops from the *Empire Battleaxe* to the shore. The regular running onto the beach evidently placed a strain on the hull and by late afternoon she had developed several leaks. She eventually foundered 7 miles offshore.
[TNA: ADM.199/1650]

LCT (4) 524 landing craft, tank
Bo'ness 1942; 200 tons; 171ft × 38.8ft
Lieutenant Daniel Gilmour Scouller RNVR
Hit a mine as she approached Juno Beach and then raked by shellfire.
[TNA: ADM.199/1650]

LCT (4) 715 landing craft, tank
Middlesbrough 1943; 200 tons; 171ft × 38.8ft
Lieutenant James Kenneth Luykn Watts RNVR
During the night of 6 June, she was en-route to Juno Beach, but when 10 miles offshore there was a large explosion amidships, apparently when she was hit by a torpedo fired by an enemy torpedo boat. The ship caught fire and broke in half before she sank.
[TNA: ADM.199/1650]

LCT (4) 717 landing craft, tank
Middlesbrough 1943; 200 tons; 171ft × 38.8ft
Sub-Lieutenant James MacDonald RNVR
Loaded with artillery and tanks, she ran onto Juno Beach to unload her cargo. That complete, she was going astern to clear the beach when she ran over a mine which exploded under her stern and she sank.
Note: omitted from the *Statement of Losses.*
[TNA: ADM.199/186]

LCT (4) 750 landing craft, tank
Chepstow 1943; 200 tons; 171ft × 38.8ft
Sub-Lieutenant George Edward Cash RNVR
Damaged when she set off a mine on Sword Beach, she was then repeatedly hit by shellfire, and was abandoned.
[TNA: ADM.199/1650]

LCT (4) 809 landing craft, tank
Old Kilpatrick 1943; 200 tons; 171ft × 38.9ft
Detonated a mine as she approached Gold Beach which broke her back and she was then hit repeatedly by mortar and shellfire.
[TNA: ADM.199/1650; ADM.199/1651]

LCT (4) 886 landing craft, tank
Meadowside 1943; 200 tons; 171ft × 38.9ft
Approaching Gold Beach, she was hit by an 88mm shell which exploded in the engine room, disabling her; she drifted onto the beach, being hit repeatedly by large and small-calibre fire.
[TNA: ADM.199/1650]

LCT (5) 2039 landing craft, tank
Kansas 1943 (*LCT 39*); 143 tons; 105ft × 32.8ft; 2 × 20mm
Sub-Lieutenant Kenneth Croxton RNVR
Part of the assault force designated to land at 'King' sector, Gold Beach, she was still 20 miles from the shore when she was swamped by heavy seas and turned turtle and was abandoned as a wreck; two men were lost. The wreck continued to drift until 8 June when she became the target for shore batteries and was sunk.
Note: the *Statement of Losses* gives only June and 'cause and place unknown'
[TNA: ADM.199/1650; ADM.199/1652]

LCT (5) 2052 landing craft, tank
Kansas City 1943 (*LCT 52*); 143 tons; 112.4ft × 32.8ft; 2 × 20mm
Lieutenant Claude Elliott Woodham RNVR
Ran onto Sword Beach, close to *LCT 2191* (see below); she successfully offloaded her tanks but was hit by an 88mm shell. She was then 'peppered' with mortar and small-arms fire and set on fire.
[TNA: ADM.199/1650]

LCT (5) 2191 landing craft, tank
North Tonawanda 1943 (*LCT 191*); 143 tons; 112.4ft × 32.8ft; 2 × 20mm
Sub-Lieutenant Julian Roney RNVR†
Assigned to Sword Beach, she had discharged her cargo of tanks, when she was hit by an 88mm shell, which struck her bow doors killing two men and making her swing round broadside-on to the sea. This exposed her to more fire, and she was hit again, a large shell striking the bridge killing Sub-Lieutenant Roney. Hit several more times, the munitions stored on board ignited and she drifted off the beach burning fiercely.
[TNA: ADM.199/1650]

LCT (5) 2428 landing craft, tank
Camden 1943 (*LCT 428*); 143 tons; 112.4ft × 32.8ft; 2 × 20mm
Sub-Lieutenant – RNVR
Assigned to Juno Beach, she suffered an engine breakdown whilst still off the Isle of Wight, and she returned to anchor off the Nab Tower. The tug *Jaunty* closed to stand by her, but as she had developed several leaks, the landing craft steadily settled, and all the crew and army personnel were removed before she capsized. The hulk was sunk by gunfire from the *Jaunty*.
[TNA: ADM.199/1650]

LCT (5) 2439 landing craft, tank
Camden 1943 (*LCT 439*); 143 tons; 112.4ft × 32.8ft; 2 × 20mm
Sub-Lieutenant Ian Bruce Smith RNVR
Approaching Juno Beach, she detonated a mine which exploded under the engine room. Her back was broken, and she was run onto the beach and abandoned, being written off as a constructive total loss.
[TNA: ADM.199/1650]

LCT (5) 2498 landing craft, tank
Camden 1943 (*LCT 498*); 143 tons; 112.4ft × 32.8ft; 2 × 20mm
Sub-Lieutenant Dennis William Bowers RNVR
Suffered an engine breakdown she developed several leaks as she crossed the Channel, and eventually capsized and sank. US Navy destroyer *Barton* (DD-722) and *YMS-549* rendered assistance.
[TNA: ADM.199/1650]

LCT (5) 2049 – 2229 – 2273 – 2301 – 2307 – 2402 landing craft, tank
Kansas City (*2049*); Memphis (*2229*); Evansville (*2273*); Omaha (*2301, 2307*)
Camden (*2402*); 143 tons; 112.4ft × 32.8ft; 2 × 20mm
Several US–built landing craft that had been passed to the Royal Navy under the Lend-Lease scheme, were passed back to the control of the US Navy for the Normandy landings to become part of the Gunfire Support Group. They are included here for the sake of completeness:

2049 – Ensign Bassell USN. Assigned Omaha Beach, 'Easy Red' sector; sank in the Channel
2229 – Carpenter Hill USN. Lost on Omaha Beach, 'Dog Red' sector
2273 – Lieutenant (jg) Holtman USN. Assigned Omaha Beach, 'Dog Green' sector but broke up and sank in the Channel
2301 – – Kaman. assigned to Utah Beach, 'Uncle Red' sector; during the channel crossing she lost power. The crew was taken off by another vessel before she rolled over and sank.
2307 – Ensign Blein USN. Omaha Beach, 'Easy Green' sector; sank on the beach
2402 – – Gold. assigned to Utah Beach, Tare Green sector; during the passage across the Channel, she lost power due to salt water in the fuel. Although a minesweeper was sent to assist, an attempt to tow her was unsuccessful and she was abandoned, the crew and tank personnel being taken off by a US Coastguard cutter before she sank.
[TNA:ADM.199/2299:
http://www.combinedops.com/US%20LANDING%20CRAFT%20ROCKET.htm
http://ww2LCT org/history/stories/JSuozzo_report.htm]

LCI (L) 131 landing craft, infantry, large
Orange 1942; 234 tons; 150ft × 23.4ft; 4 × 20mm
Sub-Lieutenant Herbert William Smith RNVR
Approaching Sword Beach, she was hit by an 88mm shell on the bows. The craft came to a stop and was then hit several more times.
[TNA:ADM.199/1652]

LCI (S) 512 landing craft, infantry, small
Oulton Broad 1943; 63 tons; 100ft × 21.5ft; 2 × 20mm
Lieutenant John Waldron RNVR
Struck a submerged obstruction as she ran into Sword Beach which holed her; leaking, she was run onto the beach in a sinking condition.
[TNA:ADM/199/1650]

LCI (S) 517 landing craft, infantry, small
Cockenzie 1943; 63 tons; 100ft × 21.5ft; 2 × 20mm
Sub-Lieutenant John Gaunt RNZVR
Fouled an underwater obstruction as she closed Sword Beach, she subsequently detonated a mine and was hit several times by shore fire.
[TNA:ADM.199/1651]

LCI (S) 524 landing craft, infantry, small
Bo'ness 1943; 63 tons; 100ft × 21.5ft; 2 × 20mm
Lieutenant Alan Nigel Cromar RNVR
She landed her troops on Sword Beach, but was hit several times by shellfire, killing or wounding many of the crew. She cleared the beach but when about 2 miles off Ouistreham she received a heavy shell hit which caused an explosion and fire in the petrol tanks. She broke up and sank, with Cromar and three ratings picked up by a US Coastguard cutter. Nine men were killed.
[TNA:ADM 1/29713; Burns p219]

LCI (S) 531 landing craft, infantry, small
Grimsby 1943; 63 tons; 100ft × 21.5ft; 2 × 20mm
Lieutenant Stanley Ivan Tasker RNVR
Having struck an underwater object as she approached the beachhead, she was then hit repeatedly by shore fire, causing her to be abandoned in a sinking condition.
[TNA:ADM.199/1651]

LCI (S) 537 landing craft, infantry, small
Horning 1944; 63 tons; 100ft × 21.6ft
Sub-Lieutenant Roland Lister RNVR
Assigned to land at 'Nan' sector, Juno Beach, she closed the shore during the early afternoon, but when about one cable (200 yards) from the beach she detonated a mine and sank immediately. Several of the embarked troops were thrown into the water, most were saved, but nine lost their lives.
Note: the *Statement of Losses* only gives a vague date of June with 'damaged beyond economical repair'.
[Statement of Losses p56; TNA: WO.361/661]

LCI (S) 540 landing craft, infantry, small
Cockenzie 1943; 63 tons; 100ft × 21.5ft; 2 × 20mm
Lieutenant Douglas Coburn Wilson RNZVR
Running into the landing area, struck an underwater object and then became the target for mortar and small-arms fire which caused her to sink.
[TNA:ADM.199/1650]

★ ★ ★

7 June LCT (3) 427 landing craft, tank
Meadowside 1943; 350 tons; 175ft × 31ft; 2 × 2pdr
Sub-Lieutenant George Templeton Guthrie†
Took part in the landings at Normandy and having successfully landed her troops and equipment she set off to return to Spithead. There was a steady stream of vessels returning, and *427* was initially in company with *432, 433* and *454*, but they became separated during the night, and she finally lost contact at 01.30 as they approached the Nab tower. She then teamed up with another pair of returning landing craft, *643* and *884*,

and the group headed north-west, threading their way through the numerous ships anchored at Spithead, with *884* leading, *427* and *643* following. At 03.00 the bridge staff on *884* saw lights approaching, but the crowded anchorage and dark night made it difficult to ascertain the range. When they realised that it was a large warship that was approaching, *884* altered to port. The last ship in line, *643*, also claimed that it was difficult to work out the distance, and it was not until the unmistakable long fo'c'sle and tower superstructure could be seen was it realised that a battleship was bearing down on them, and hastily put the helm over. *427* presumably also had the same problems but failed to react. On board the battleship *Rodney*, steaming through a narrow channel between ships, making for the open sea, at 03.04 a column of landing craft was seen, which emerged from the anchorage and crossed her bows. The second craft in the line was close and could not be avoided and she was struck heavily. She reared up on the stem of the battleship, hung for a moment, and then rolled over and disappeared. *634* following saw her break into two and was forced to put the wheel over again to try and avoid the wreckage but struck a floating section of hull and was then struck a glancing blow by the *Rodney*. The battleship did not stop, but released some lifebelts, but a search by her companions found no survivors. Fourteen men died. [*TNA: ADM.1/16909*]

8 June **LAWFORD** frigate

Boston 1943; 1,140 tons; 283.6ft × 35.2ft; 3 × 3in, 2 × 40mm, 9 × 20mm
Lieutenant Commander Michael Charles Morris

Acting as Captain (Patrols), with Captain Pugsley embarked, the *Lawford* patrolled the seaward approaches to the landing beaches in Normandy and ensured that a defence line of escort ships and minesweepers was established at night. During the night of 7/8 June she anchored at the junction of Sword and Juno Beaches. At 02.00 reports were received of enemy torpedo boat activity and by 02.30 this had resolved into two hostile groups of craft about 8 miles to the north of the defence line. *Lawford* therefore weighed to commence patrolling. By 04.40 the surface threat had receded, and she headed back for her anchorage. At 04.55 the sound of an aircraft was heard approaching, evidently very low. This was initially presumed to be friendly, as they had been warned of Allied air movements at about this time. However, a minute later a stream of tracer fire hit the port side amidships as an aircraft passed low overhead. Shortly after this there was a violent explosion on the port side, abreast the funnel. The ship came to a stop and heeled over to starboard, covered in smoke, and she started to break up amidships. At 05.03 she broke in half; both ends sank until they touched the bottom with bow and stern showing above the water for some

time before sinking. The minesweeper *Pique* picked up the survivors, but twenty-four men died. The wreck has been found and lies in position 49.25.43N 00.23.47.W. It would appear likely that she had fallen victim to an attack by an aircraft employing an Hs 293 guided bomb. [*TNA: ADM.179/502*]

8 June **LCI (L) 105** landing craft, infantry, large

Orange 1942; 234 tons; 153ft × 23.8ft; 4 × 20mm
Lieutenant Arthur Joseph Cramp RNVR

Laden with troops and equipment, she sailed late on 7 June from the anchorage at Spithead, for the journey across the English Channel to the Normandy beaches, as part of Convoy Starlight S-23. At 04.00 the convoy was attacked by enemy fast torpedo boats, and a sharp action ensued between the escorting motor launch and the enemy, the landing craft engaging when they could. At 04.23 the track of a torpedo was seen on the port side, but despite putting the helm hard to port, she was hit aft. A second explosion occurred moments later when the magazine exploded. She subsequently sank, then being about 3.5 miles off Cap d'Antifer. Seven members of the ship's company and twenty soldiers were killed. [*TNA: ADM.179/502; ADM.199/1651*]

8 June **LCT (4) 875** landing craft, tank

Thornaby 1943; 200 tons; 171ft × 38.8ft
Sub Lieutenant Valentine Knight RNVR[†]

Fully loaded with stores for the Normandy beachhead, she was part of Convoy Starlight S-23, which came under attack by enemy fast torpedo boats. During the attack she suffered a direct hit from a torpedo and sank with the loss of twelve men, in approximate position 49.55N 00.45W. [*TNA: ADM.199/2295*]

8 June **LCT (3) 390** landing craft, tank

Middlesbrough 1943; 350 tons; 175ft × 31ft; 2 × 2pdr
Lieutenant Roy Harold Richard RNVR[†]

Fully loaded with trucks and troops, she headed for the beaches of northern France. However, she was apparently taken further to the east than she expected, and at 05.30 as she approached the coastline, she came under fire from a shore battery. She was hit twice, just forward of the bridge and with the engine room flooding she sank quickly. Six men were killed. *Note*: the *Statement of Losses* gives the wrong date (9 July) and 'cause & place unknown'. [*TNA: ADM.199/186*]

8 June **MINSTER** net layer

Partick 1924, requisitioned 1940; 682 tons; 220.4ft × 33.6ft
Lieutenant Commander Walter Jackson RNR

Deployed to Omaha Beach, Normandy, to lay mooring buoys, she arrived during the morning. At 12.00, guided

by a survey boat, she commenced laying her first line of moorings. By 13.05 this was complete, and she was returning to the designated anchorage when she detonated a mine on her port side, in position 49.26.5N 01.2W. She rolled over to port and quickly sank, the top of her deckhouse and funnel remaining visible for several days after. Fifty–eight men were lost.
[TNA: ADM.199/1652]

10 June MTB 681 motor torpedo boat
Lowestoft 1943; 102 tons; 110ft × 21.3ft; 1 × 2pdr; 2 × 20mm, 2 × torpedo tubes
Lieutenant Edward Stuart Forman RNVR

Conducting a patrol in the southern North Sea in company with five other boats, the weather was poor, with a swell and regular rain squalls. At 23.40 they detected a group of enemy ships off the Dutch coast and 'stalked' the enemy for some time, the poor visibility hampering their progress. Finally, at 01.15 they could make out four ships, escorted by seven armed trawlers. The torpedo boats divided into two groups of three and closed without being detected. The attack by the first group went very well, with two armed trawlers being hit by torpedoes and sunk. With the enemy now fully alerted, the attack by the second group, which included *681*, met very heavy fire. One enemy ship was hit and sunk, but *681* received a hit in the starboard wing fuel tank which started a fire. She managed to steer out of the action, but the flames rapidly spread until the fire was out of control. At 02.25 there was a large explosion, and now burning fiercely, with the superstructure wrecked and the upper deck ripped up, she was abandoned, *687* and *683* closing to pick up the survivors. She continued to burn fiercely until at 04.31 when she blew up and disappeared. Two men were killed.
[TNA: ADM.267/124; Reynolds, Dog Boats p169]

11 June MTB 448 motor torpedo boat
Hythe 1943; 41 tons; 71.9ft × 20.7ft; 1 × 6pdr, 2 × 20mm
Lieutenant Rodney Tatton Sykes RNVR

In the immediate aftermath of the landings in Normandy, coastal forces were active in protecting the forces assembled off the beaches from surface attack. On the night of 10/11 June *MTB 448* was patrolling in company with *MTB 453* off the Normandy coast when a group of enemy patrol boats were detected. Both of the torpedo boats had landed their torpedo tubes to be replaced by depth charges, and it was decided to attack the enemy at high speed, dropping charges as they passed through the line. *MTB 448* successfully closed to run close under the stern of the leading enemy vessel, releasing a depth charge as they did. However, as they cleared the area, they were hit by several 40mm shells in the hull, and she started to fill with water. *453* followed and after they had disengaged it became clear that *448*

was sinking, so her crew was taken off and *453* fired several rounds into the wreck to ensure that it sank. One man, a war correspondent, was killed in the fire.
[Reynolds, Home Waters MTBs p137]

11 June HALSTEAD frigate
Hingham 1943; 1,300 tons; 300ft × 36.9ft; 3 × 3in, 8 × 20mm
Commander John Rowe Westmacott

During the night of 10/11 June, there were a series of confused actions between enemy surface forces and the various ships screening the invasion area. *Halstead* with the *Stayner* intercepted a group of five fast torpedo boats following their encounter with British torpedo boats (see *MTB 448*). A salvo of torpedoes was fired at the British escorts, and one found *Halstead*. The torpedo struck the fore end abreast the forward 3in gun on the port side. The forward superstructure and the 3in gun platforms were wrecked and forced back against the bridge and about 80ft of the bow structure forward of the bridge disappeared. Several small fires were started, and smoke and toxic fumes spread through the ship, leading to the evacuation of machinery spaces. The fires were extinguished, and bulkheads shored. Steam was later raised in the after boiler room, and the ship was able to proceed very slowly, stern first. The escort destroyer *Fernie* closed, and a tow was rigged, to take her back to Portsmouth. Some temporary repairs were made, but the ship was declared a constructive total loss. Thirty-four men were lost.
[CB.4273 p280]

11 June MGB 17 motor gun boat
Hythe 1940; 31 tons; 70ft × 20ft; 1 × 2pdr
Lieutenant Royce Henry Payne RNVR

Caught fire following an explosion, and eventually blew up and sank at 11.30, whilst close to the western end of Gooseberry-II, off Gold Beach, Normandy. The exact cause was uncertain, although it was probably after striking a mine. Three men were lost.
[TNA: ADM.199/1397]

11 June SESAME tug
Selby 1943; 700 tons; 142.6ft × 33.3ft; 1 × 12pdr
Lieutenant John Cowley RNR

Towing a 'whale link' – a pier section for a Mulberry harbour – she was proceeding south across the English Channel towards the Normandy beaches. At 02.20 when about 20 miles from the French coast there was a large explosion on the starboard side amidships. The towing party on the 'whale' saw a flash and a cloud of smoke, and when it had cleared the tug had disappeared. The escort destroyer *Fernie* picked up several survivors, but eighteen men were lost. She had been torpedoed by a German torpedo boat.
[TNA: ADM.199/1650]

11 June DORRIMEE motor launch
Rosneath 1934 requisitioned 1941; 33 tons; 50.1ft × 12ft
Lieutenant John Campbell Cameron RNVR
Based at Alexandria, Egypt, following an accidental petrol vapour explosion a fierce fire broke out which engulfed the launch, seriously injuring several members of the crew. Despite fire-fighting efforts by the ship's company and the shore fire party, she was burned out. Three ratings later died of their injuries.
[TNA: ADM.199/1428]

(14–16) June SICKLE submarine
Birkenhead 1942; 715/990 tons; 201ft × 23.9ft; 1 × 3in, 7 × torpedo tubes
Lieutenant James Robert Drummond DSO DSC[†]
Ordered to conduct a patrol in the Aegean, she sailed from Malta on 31 May. On 4 June she surfaced to engage shipping off Mytilene but was forced to dive by two German patrol boats, which scored hits on the conning tower. One seaman was blown overboard in this action and was picked up – he was to be the only survivor. Over the next few days there were several more attacks on local shipping, and the last known radio contact was on 12 June. On 14 June, a caique was sunk by a submarine near Mytilene and that same afternoon a submarine shelled the Potamos shipyard at Mytilene; these actions must have been by *Sickle*. She failed to respond to a call ordering the termination of her patrol on 16 June, and it was presumed that she was lost, probably by hitting a mine at some time between 14 and 16 June.
[Evans pp382–3; http://uboat.net/allies/warships/ship/3442.html]

13 June BOADICEA destroyer
Hebburn 1930; 1,360 tons; 312ft × 32.3ft; 4 × 4.7in, 1 × 12pdr, 2 × 20mm, 4 × torpedo tubes
Lieutenant Commander Frederick William Hawkins[†]
Engaged in escorting supply ships from England to the Normandy beachheads, she had sailed from Milford Haven on 12 June, in company with a corvette and an armed trawler, with Convoy EBC8 consisting of six merchant ships. As dawn broke the convoy was in the English Channel heading eastwards toward the Isle of Wight and the rendezvous point to head south for France. Numerous aircraft were noted flying overhead, but all were Allied, until at 05.00 a twin-engined aircraft broke away from a stream of aircraft and headed straight for the convoy. It was identified as a Ju 88, but before any avoiding action could be taken, it dropped two torpedoes. One of them was seen to 'porpoise' across the surface out of control, but the second struck the destroyer forward, just under the bridge. There followed a tremendous explosion as the forward magazine exploded, and the forward part of the ship disappeared

in a huge cloud of smoke. The stern quickly rose out of the water and within minutes had slid beneath the surface, leaving a large patch of debris, covered in an expanding slick of sticky oil. One of the convoy, the merchant ship *Freeman Hatch*, lowered boats, which picked up twelve survivors. One hundred and seventy-six men lost their lives. The wreck lies in position 50.25.38N 02.45.50W.
[TNA: ADM.199/1651; Hawkins p290; Larn vol 1 sec 6]

13 June LCT (4) 967 landing craft, tank
Old Kilpatrick 1943; 200 tons; 171ft × 38.8ft
Sub-Lieutenant Ernest Rowland Barker RNVR[†]
Sailed 12 June from Portland loaded with army trucks and their drivers, bound for the Normandy beaches. She arrived off the British sector beachhead at 09.00 and prepared to run ashore. As she approached the beach there was a large explosion under the hull aft as she ran over a mine and she started to sink immediately by the stern. Within minutes she had sunk, breaking in half as she did. Eight men were lost.
[TNA: ADM.199/186]

13 June MMS 229 minesweeper
Grimsby 1942; 225 tons; 105ft × 23.5ft
Lieutenant Peter Marfell Smith RNVR
The centre vessel in a three-ship formation of sweepers that was working to clear mines from the eastern end of the Banc du Cardonnet off Utah Beach, Normandy, when at 18.30 a mine, probably an acoustic one, detonated close by. She broke up and sank in 7 minutes, and her consorts performed a smart piece of seamanship to rescue the survivors. Two men were killed.
[TNA: ADM.179/375; ADM.199/1397]

13 June BIRDLIP trawler
Beverley 1941; 750 tons; 166.4ft × 28.3ft; 1 × 12pdr, 3 × 20mm
Lieutenant Iorweth Brian Evan Humphrey RNVR[†]
Based in west Africa, she was ordered to escort the French ship *Saint Basile* from Takoradi to Freetown in company with the armed trawlers *Inkpen* and *Turcoman*. At 23.25 she obtained a radar contact ahead of her at 2,000 yards, and hydrophone effect from a ship's propellers could also be heard, so action stations was piped. A few moments later a dim object could be made out ahead and it was at first thought to be a motor launch, so the night challenge was made. No reply was received before she was hit by a torpedo fired by the U 547 (Niemayer) and she rapidly sank. The U-boat then went on to successfully attack the *Saint Basile*. Thirty-five men died, with sixteen men surviving, although Lieutenant Humphrey later died of his wounds.
[TNA: ADM.199/2530]

14 June LCG (L) 831 landing craft, gun, large
Old Kilpatrick 1943; 570 tons; 171ft × 38.8ft; 2 × 4.7in,
10 × 20mm
Having sailed from Southampton as part of the
Normandy invasion fleet, she was busily engaged from
6 June onwards, bombarding targets onshore, surviving
an attack by friendly aircraft on 7 June. On 14 June she
was ordered to the mouth of the river Seine to bombard
enemy positions. As she neared the shore, they detonated
a mine and began to sink. Another LCG was able to come
alongside and lift off the crew before she disappeared.
Note: the *Statement of Losses* gives the incorrect and
vague date of 'July–Aug' for her loss.
[TNA: ADM.199/176]

15 June GLEAM drifter
Oulton Broad 1922 requisitioned 1941; 57 tons;
69.9ft × 19.6ft
Skipper Andrew Stephen Buchan RNR
Listed as being sunk in collision, but no further details
of the incident found. The drifter was part of the
Greenock Pool, but listed as being based at Ayr, for
duties with *Varbel*, the midget submarine base.
[Statement of Losses p33: TNA ADM.208/25]

15 June BLACKWOOD frigate
Boston 1942; 1,140 tons; 283.6ft × 35.2ft; 3 × 3in,
2 × 40mm, 9 × 20mm
Lieutenant Commander Leslie Tillman Sly RNR[†]
Part of the Third Escort Group, she sailed in company
with the others of the group on 7 June to carry out
an offensive anti-submarine sweep in the western end
of the English Channel. Several contacts were gained
over the next few days, but all were found to be non-
submarine contacts. On 15 June, the group were to
the south of Portland and were refuelled at sea. This
operation was complete by 19.00 and the group were
reforming to resume the sweep when at 19.11 in
position 50.07N 02.15W, the *Blackwood* was rocked by
a large explosion as she was hit by a torpedo on the
starboard side, forward, fired by *U 764* (von Bremen).
She was covered in a thick cloud of brown and yellow
smoke and when this cleared the forward part of the
ship could be seen to have been blown away, evidently
as the forward magazine had exploded. The mast had
collapsed, and the bridge structure flattened, but the
ship remained upright and stable. The *Essington* stood
by her whilst the remainder of the group hunted the
submarine, and tugs were summoned from Portland.
The wreck steadily settled, and during the night the
survivors were removed by the tugs, which then left her.
The hunting group found her drifting and abandoned
hulk, but she sank at 04.15 in position 50.13N
02.15.30W. Fifty-eight men were killed.
[TNA: ADM.199/957]

15 June MOURNE frigate
Middlesbrough 1942; 1,370 tons; 283ft × 36.8ft; 2 × 4in,
10 × 20mm
Lieutenant Commander Raymond Spun Holland RNR
Part of the effort to counter any submarine threat to the
forces gathered off the northern French coast, *Mourne* was
attached to the Fifth Escort Group, tasked to carry out an
offensive anti-submarine sweep in the western approaches
to the English Channel. During the morning of 15 June,
the group were in position 49.40N 05.29W, about 50
miles to the north-west of Ushant, formed in line abreast,
the *Mourne* being stationed on the port wing. At 11.15 a
lookout reported sighting a puff of smoke on the horizon,
which was believed to be a submarine using a snort mast at
periscope depth. The ships turned together to investigate,
and at 11.30 a good Asdic contact was gained. The
Mourne prepared to carry out an attack using Hedgehog
projectiles, but at 11.39 there was a large explosion as a
torpedo struck the ship on the port side by the boiler
room, followed about 2 seconds later by a second, larger
explosion, marked by a huge flash of flame. The ship
heeled over to port, covered in smoke, but did not recover,
slowly rolling over until she capsized, and moments later
she sank, bows first. One hundred and ten men were lost.
Her attacker had been *U 767* (Dan[k]leff), which had fired
a T5 acoustic homing torpedo. The second explosion was
believed to be her magazines exploding.
[TNA: ADM.199/260; ADM.267/117]

16 June LCT (4) 589 landing craft, tank
Chepstow 1943; 200 tons; 171ft × 38.8ft
Lieutenant Herbert Aubrey Dale RNVR
Ordered to carry out an operation to land a small army
reconnaissance team, with twelve jeeps, behind enemy
lines on the eastern coast of Italy, the landing craft was
accompanied by a motor launch and an MFV tender.
The group arrived undetected late in the evening and
ran onto a beach, about 1,000 yards south of the mouth
of the Tenna River. However, it soon became clear that
the German army was present in strength nearby, so it
was decided to withdraw. On attempting to move off, it
was found that the landing craft was firmly aground, and
despite vigorous use of the engines, the craft broached to
and swung broadside on to the shore. At 02.00 attempts to
refloat her were abandoned and after demolition charges
were left on board, the crew and embarked troops were
taken off by the supporting craft. There were no casualties.
[Peniakoff pp367–75; TNA: ADM.199/1432]

16 June LCF 15 landing craft, flak
Meadowside 1942 (*LCT 406*); 470 tons; 175ft × 31ft;
4 × 2pdr, 8 × 20mm
Lieutenant Edward Sims RNVR[†]
Stationed in the Mediterranean, she was part of the
force assembled to carry out an assault on the island of

Elba. She took up station at the rear of a small convoy of landing ships, being about 1.5 cables (300 yards) astern of the centre column. She evidently lost touch with her group during the night, and fell astern, but proceeded independently. At 02.25 when about 10 miles to the east of Elba, there was a large explosion under the ship, below the engine room, as she detonated a mine. The engine room rapidly flooded, and she started to sink by the stern. With the ship's officers apparently dead or incapacitated, it was Lieutenant Philip Roome of the Royal Marines who took charge, and as it was clear that the ship was sinking, ordered boats and floats to be hoisted out or released, and then for her to be abandoned. As the survivors scrambled over the side she sank, the bows rising until they were vertical. Nineteen men lost their lives and fifty-one were rescued.
[TNA: ADM.199/260]

16 June SOUTHERN PRIDE whaler
Middlesbrough 1936 requisitioned 1940; 582 tons; 161.6ft × 31.1ft
Lieutenant Geoffrey Barratt Angus RNVR

Based at Freetown, Sierra Leone, she was conducting a patrol between the 10 and 20-fathom lines off the Marshall anchorage, about 30 miles from Monrovia, in company with an armed trawler, the *Pict*. During the afternoon of 15 June, the *Pict* anchored to carry out urgent repairs to her engine, the whaler continuing on her own. At 19.04 she was about 2 miles offshore, and at the southern end of her patrol line and commenced a turn to port to reverse course. About 3 minutes later, still under helm the ship shuddered as she touched the ground, and then with a more violent shudder came to stop as she ran aground. The engines were ordered to be stopped, watertight doors and hatches closed. She appeared to be stable, with no obvious breakers or rocks in sight, soundings ordered to be taken all around her which revealed 15ft forward, slightly deeper aft. The engines were put full astern and at 20.15 she came free of the obstruction. Having found deeper water, she anchored to take stock of her situation. Water was now reported entering the engine room, and this was soon gaining on the pumps. It was decided to run inshore and beach her in shallow water, so at 20.25 she weighed and steered inshore, but just 5 minutes later the engines were forced to stop as the water was reaching the furnaces. She drifted until she finally came to a halt in mud and sand just offshore. There was little to be done until first light, but during the night the swell increased until by 01.30 on 16 June the sea was breaking over her. The ship was also settling aft and was beginning to list to port. As her consort the *Pict*, having been alerted by radio, was now on scene, it was decided that she should be abandoned. The boats of the *Pict* were launched, and several men jumped into the sea to gain them, others

launching a Carley float which was taken inshore. One man was found to be very drunk as this was happening, and although he was helped to the upper deck, he was knocked over by a heavy sea that washed over the ship, and was drowned, the only casualty. The captain was the last to leave, jumping into the water to swim to a boat at just after 05.00. The Salvage Officer arrived some days later to examine her and found that she was lying in position 06.08.4N 10.27W and in a poor state, having started to break up in the surf. All valuable items were therefore removed, and she was declared a constructive total loss. Lieutenant Angus and his executive officer, Lieutenant William Gill RNVR, were court-martialled for the loss. Both were found guilty of negligence. It was found that the ship had run onto a bank known as Hooper's Patch, a well-known local hazard. The ship had been further inshore than they had estimated, with an insufficient number of fixes being taken, the one fix that had been taken during the afternoon being very inaccurate. Angus was dismissed his ship, severely reprimanded and suffered the loss of one years' seniority. Gill was severely reprimanded.
[TNA: ADM.178/361; ADM 156/253]

17 June LCI (L) 132 landing craft, infantry, large
Orange 1942; 234 tons; 150ft × 23.8ft; 4 × 20mm
Lieutenant Stanley Christopher Cole RNVR†

In the early hours of 17 June Operation 'Brassard' got underway, to capture the island of Elba, which was occupied by a sizeable German garrison. French colonial troops would be the main force, but Royal Navy Commandos were given the task of both capturing the flak ship *Köln*, berthed at Marina di Campo and securing the jetty area, using two LCI craft. As *LCI 132* closed the *Köln*, she came under very heavy fire, and was hit repeatedly, being set on fire, ran aground and eventually sank close inshore with the loss of thirteen men.
[http://www.combinedops.com/Elba%20-%20Op%20Brassard.htm]

18 June QUAIL destroyer
Hebburn 1942; 1,692 tons; 339.6ft × 35.8ft; 4 × 4.7in, 4 × 2pdr, 10 × 20mm, 8 × torpedo tubes

When returning to Bari, southern Italy on 15 November 1943 under the command of Lieutenant Commander Robert Jenks after a night patrol in company with the *Quilliam*, she was preparing to anchor, when at 11.05 a mine detonated under her stern. The explosion was violent, blowing the after gun turret overboard, and her after compartments flooded. She was eventually stabilised and taken into harbour, but the damage was severe, and she was decommissioned. In early 1944 it was decided to move her to the naval dockyard at Taranto, and under the tow of the tug *Capodistria*, she left Bari on 17 June with a small towing crew embarked. At 04.05 there was a dull explosion under the hull, apparently directly under the engine room, which filled with smoke and fumes and she started to fill with water. The explosion was muted, and the tug did not even realise that anything was amiss until the ship's bow rose out of the water, forcing the tug to go astern to release the strain. The bows continued to rise until they were vertical and then sank. She was then off Gallipoli, in position 40.07N 14.49E. It was found that she had been taken outside the designated swept channel and into a known minefield. One man was killed in the explosion. [TNA: ADM.199/243; ADM.199/253]

20 June LCT (4) 947 landing craft, tank
Middlesbrough 1943; 200 tons; 171ft × 38.9ft
Lieutenant Lionel Watson RNVR
In constant use on Juno Beach, Normandy, she was carrying a cargo of seven Churchill tanks for the beaches, but due to the poor weather she was ordered to stay in deep water. As she approached the designated anchorage, she detonated a mine off Courseuilles, which exploded under the engine room. This caused considerable damage, with everything moveable being blown overboard, and she settled and quickly sank. There were no casualties. [TNA: ADM.199/1651; Burns p219]

20 June LCT (5) 2040 landing craft, tank
Kansas City 1943 (LCT 40): 143 tons; 112.3ft × 32.9ft; 2 × 20mm
Suffered from several leaks caused by the constant use on the Normandy beaches, eventually her back broke, and she foundered in the English Channel. [TNA: ADM.199/1651]

(20?) June MATAFELE store carrier
Hong Kong 1938 requisitioned 1943; 186 tons; 115.5ft × 26.6ft; 1 × 12pdr
Lieutenant Commander Walter Charles Frederick Symonds[†] Royal Australian Navy. Sailed on 18 June from Townsville for Milne Bay, New Guinea, but failed to arrive as expected on 22 June and presumed lost by unknown cause on or around 20 June. Some wreckage, consisting of an oar and two boats, identified as being from Matafele was later washed ashore on the south coast of Papua. Four officers and thirty-three ratings, thirteen of them Pacific Island seamen, were lost. [Cassells p39; http://navynews.realviewdigital. com/?iid=121536#folio=18]

21 June FURY destroyer
Cowes 1934; 1,405 tons; 318.3ft × 33.3ft; 4 × 4.7in, 2 × 20mm, 4 × torpedo tubes
Lieutenant Commander Thomas Frederick Taylor DSC
Having been stationed off Sword Beach in the Normandy landing area, at 09.30 she weighed to shift to Juno area. At 10.39 when in position 49.26.2N 00.30.8W, she set

off a ground mine which detonated close to her stern, throwing up a large quantity of water, drenching the ship, and caused a considerable amount of shock damage to the ship. She heeled to port, lost steam and flooding was reported, with water entering the after shell room and the engine room. She promptly anchored and pumps were set to work to clear the water, and the destroyer Scorpion closed to render assistance. At 13.25 the tug Thames arrived to take her in tow, the anchor being slipped, the intention being to take her to Mulberry 'B'. The tow went on during the afternoon, with top weight being reduced by heaving overboard ammunition and depth charges. At 21.14, still under tow, they were approaching the Mulberry harbour, but in the rising winds she proved difficult to control and she collided with the anchored merchant ship Berryden, inflicting some minor damage to the port side of the hull – but worse was to follow. At 21.49 the tow parted, apparently when it snagged the bows of the Sea Salvor which was at anchor. The Fury, now out of control, drifted down onto the Salvor, further damaging her hull. When clear, the port anchor was let go to bring her up and another tug came alongside as did the salvage vessel Lincoln Salvor. Another tow was rigged, and she again got under way, hoping to make for the anchored cruiser Despatch, but in the increasing winds, the tow again parted. She was now carried by the strong wind and tide and despite more efforts by tugs to secure another line, all parted soon after being passed. She continued her passage, striking a floating crane, a ship loaded with petrol and another with ammunition before clearing the anchorage. A BYMS minesweeper then finally succeeded in passing a line which held, but she could not control the destroyer, which was now being carried down towards the shore, so she was cast off. At 01.30 she drove ashore onto a rocky beach with spray breaking over her. The ship's company stayed onboard the wreck until first light when, with some difficulty, made it over the side to safety. Efforts were made over the next several days to free her, several bulldozers being employed in clearing rocks to the seaward of her, helped by about 150 sailors and marines manually moving obstacles. The propellers were cut off and eventually, at 21.40 on 5 July she was hauled off the beach and refloated. Towed by the tug Zwarte Zee, she arrived at Portsmouth on 7 July, but examination of the hull revealed extensive damage, from both the mine and her time onshore. She was written off as a constructive total loss and sold for scrap in September. [TNA: ADM.267/96]

24 June SWIFT destroyer
Cowes 1943; 1,710 tons; 339.6ft × 35.8ft; 4 × 4.7in, 2 × 40mm, 8 × 20mm, 8 × torpedo tubes
Lieutenant Commander John Ronald Gower
Having conducted a night patrol off the Normandy beaches, she was heading into the Sword Beach area to

re-store and take on ammunition, when at 07.10 there was a large explosion, probably caused by an influence mine, under number 1 boiler room. She was then about 5 miles to the north of Ouistreham Lighthouse. This broke her back and blew several men who were on the upper deck into the water. She heeled over to port and her head swung round to port, almost colliding with a small landing craft that was steaming alongside her. The port anchor was promptly let go which brought her up. Her back was broken, and the bow and stern slowly rose into the air to an angle of about 30 degrees, with her amidships section being submerged. Life rafts were cleared away, but she was not immediately abandoned. The landing craft and *ML 197* closed her and several larger ships, including the cruiser *Belfast* and destroyer *Venus* sent boats to her assistance. She was then abandoned in good order. Captain Gower was the last to leave after checking that no one was left on board the ship. She steadily settled until she disappeared about an hour after the explosion, the top of the foremast still showing. Eighteen men lost their lives.
[TNA: ADM.267/95; ADM.199/1651]

24 June MMS 8 minesweeper
Lowestoft 1941; 225 tons; 105ft × 23.5ft
Lieutenant Jack Hardy Barrett RNVR†
Sank after she detonated a mine which exploded close to her, whilst sweeping to clear a minefield off Juno Beach, Normandy. The position was noted as 49.24.4N 00.20.5W. Fourteen men were killed.
[TNA: ADM.199/1397; ADM.199/1172]

24 June LORD AUSTIN trawler
Selby 1937 requisitioned 1940; 473 tons; 164.3ft × 26.6ft; 1 × 4in
Lieutenant Edward Stirling Terence Robinson RNVR
Having formed part of the force that had covered the landings at Normandy, the trawler was retained in the area, conducting patrols of the anchorage off the beaches. She had been at anchor overnight, and at 04.30 weighed to proceed to her patrol area. At 05.55 when in position 49.24.51N 00.18W, there was a large explosion under the hull, the engine room taking the full force of the blast. The engines shuddered to a halt, she heeled over to port and it was clear that she was sinking. Lieutenant Robinson ordered the boat hoisted out, but it was found that the davits and tackle had been distorted by the blast. Floats and rafts were heaved overboard, and the men ordered to abandon her. The trawler settled quickly, briefly righting herself before sinking stern first, her bows lifting clear of the water. There were a further two dull explosions as she disappeared, probably her boilers exploding. Seven men were lost, the survivors quickly being picked up by a US Coastguard Cutter. It

was believed that she had detonated a mine, probably laid overnight by a German aircraft.
[TNA: ADM.199/1651; Lund & Ludlum, Trawlers Go to War, pp235–8]

25 June GOODSON frigate
Boston (USA) 1943; 1,085 tons; 289.5ft × 35ft; 3 × 3in, 10 × 20mm
Lieutenant Commander Jack Winston Cooper RNR
Part of the Fifth Escort Group engaged in anti-submarine patrols in the western approaches to the English Channel. The group were approaching Cherbourg, when at 15.14 she was struck by a torpedo which exploded under her stern, About 35ft of the stern was blown away, and the hull and superstructure forward of this was distorted and buckled by the blast. She heeled over 20 degrees to starboard and the bows lifted as the ship started to flood from aft, and several minor fires were started. The flooding was contained, the fires extinguished, and the heel was reduced by counterflooding, but the ship was immobilised. Taken in tow by the *Bligh*, they successfully reached Portland. Survey revealed that the damage was too extensive for repair and the ship was written off as a constructive total loss. Her attacker had been the *U 984* (Sieder), who had fired a T5 acoustic homing torpedo at the escort group. There were no fatalities.
[TNA: ADM.267/134; CB.4273 p281]

25 June LCH 185 landing craft, headquarters
Newark 1943; 234 tons; 150ft × 23.8ft; 4 × 20mm
Lieutenant James Gordon Shepherd RNVR†
Approaching Sword Beach, Normandy, loaded with stores, at 13.00 she detonated a mine, probably acoustic, which exploded under her stern, and she sank very quickly. The US Army tug *ST-771* was nearby and went to her assistance and picked up a few survivors, one of her men jumping into the water to rescue some seen struggling in the water, but thirty-five men were killed.
[TNA: ADM.1/30319]

26 June MTB 734 motor torpedo boat
Bo'ness 1944; 95 tons; 110ft × 21.3ft; 1 × 2pdr, 2 × 20mm, 2 × torpedo tubes
Lieutenant Commander Harold William Paton DSC RNVR
Conducting a patrol in the southern North Sea in company with *612*, when the pair was attacked by a Swordfish aircraft that mistook them for enemy patrol boats. The rocket attack left *734* severely damaged, and the crew were taken off by her companion and she was sunk by gunfire.
[Reynolds, Dog Boats p169]

27 June PINK corvette
Leith 1942; 935 tons; 190ft × 33ft; 1 × 4in, 1 × 2pdr
Commander George Victor Legassick RNR
Conducting an anti-submarine patrol off the coast of Normandy, at 14.23 in position 29.48N 00.49W there was an explosion under her stern, which blew away most of the after part of the ship, and the rudder, propeller and shaft were lost. The upper deck remaining abaft the superstructure was blown upwards, and shock damage was widespread through the ship. All power was lost, but the ship was stabilised and was taken in tow for Portsmouth. The damage was such that the ship was written off as a constructive total loss. There were no fatalities. The cause of the explosion is uncertain; at the time it was believed to have been a contact mine, and this remains the most likely cause, although the possibility of a submarine torpedo remains, although no candidates for the attack have been confirmed, with modern research discounting an earlier theory that *U 988* may have been responsible.
[TNA: ADM.267/1117; CB.4273 p356; www.uboat.net/boats/u988.htm]

27 June MTB 640 motor torpedo boat
Wallasea 1942; 95 tons; 110ft × 21.3ft; 1 × 2pdr, 2 × 20mm, 2 × torpedo tubes
Lieutenant Campbell Martin MacLachlan RCNVR
Stationed in the Mediterranean and based at Bastia in Corsica, she was returning from a patrol off the Italian coast in company with other boats to try and intercept enemy minelayers reported to be active off San Vicenzo, when she detonated a mine. Her bows were blown off as far back as the bridge, but she remained afloat, although awash. *MTB 658* in company closed, took off the survivors, and then sank the wreck with gunfire. Five men were lost.
[Pope p237; Reynolds: Dog Boats p148]

28 June MGB 326 motor gun boat
Rosneath 1941; 110ft × 17.5ft; 2 × 2pdr, 6 × 20mm
Lieutenant William John Kempner RNVR
Part of the forces deployed to the Normandy beaches, at 21.30 she was proceeding to join *MTB 324* and *MTB 317*, secured astern of the frigate *Waveney* when there was a large explosion under the bridge, which blew a massive hole in the hull. She broke up and sank in less than 2 minutes. She was believed to have triggered an influence mine. There were no casualties.
[TNA: ADM.179.502; 199/1650]

28 June LCT (4) 529 landing craft, tank
Bo'ness 1943; 200 tons; 171ft × 38.9ft
Lieutenant Dennis Medwin Bolton RNVR
Having been worked hard on the Normandy beaches *529* was ordered to return to England. She was in a poor

state, and the leaks that were already evident worsened during the passage, and when she was approaching Spithead, it became clear that her port rudder had fallen off. She settled and finally sank about 1 mile to the north-north-west of the Nab tower.
[TNA: ADM.199/1651]

28 June LCT (5) 2238 landing craft, tank
Decatur 1943 (*LCT 238*); 143 tons; 112.3ft × 32.9ft; 2 × 20mm
Sub-Lieutenant Douglas Hubert Alexander RNVR
Strained by constant work on the Normandy beaches, she was further strained in poor weather, and developed several leaks. She was run onto the beach near le Hamel, Arromanches, where she pounded in the surf, and was abandoned and subsequently written off as a constructive total loss.
[TNA: ADM.199/1651]

1 July ML 287 motor launch
Barking 1941; 73 tons; 112ft × 18.4ft; 1 × 3pdr, 1 × 20mm
Lieutenant Ronald James Cotton RNVR
Lying at anchor in Kline Bay, Freetown, West Africa, with several other motor launches moored alongside, when there was a large explosion in the engine room, probably caused by ignition of petrol vapour. This started a large fire, which gutted the launch. Two men were killed.
[TNA: ADM.199/2530]

1 July ML 265 motor launch
Northam 1941; 73 tons; 112ft × 18.4ft; 1 × 3pdr, 1 × 20mm
Lieutenant Mervyn Gilbert Morris Smith RNVR
Lying alongside *ML 287* at Freetown, West Africa, when that launch was rocked by a petrol vapour explosion, the subsequent fire quickly spread to *265* and she was burnt out. *ML 296* was also set alight but managed to extinguish the flames. Two men died in the fire.
[TNA: ADM.199/2530]

2 July MMS 1019 minesweeper
Brixham 1943; 360 tons; 126ft × 26ft; 2 × 20mm
Lieutenant William Balfour RNVR†
Detonated a mine 1 mile to the north of the western entrance to Cherbourg, at about 10.30, whilst sweeping the approaches to the port and sank within minutes. *ML 137* quickly closed to pick up survivors, but six men were lost.
[TNA: ADM.199/1398]

2 July MTB 460 motor torpedo boat
Hythe 1944; 41 tons; 71.9ft × 20.7ft; 1 × 6pdr, 2 × 20mm, 2 × torpedo tubes
Lieutenant David Allison Killam DSC RCNVR†
Royal Canadian Navy. In company with *MTB 459* and *MTB 465*, carried out a night patrol off the coast of

Normandy, but *459* was forced to return after running over a submerged object. The remaining pair continued an uneventful patrol and turned for home, when *460* blew up and disappeared in a large explosion, evidently after hitting a mine. *465* immediately closed the scene and picked up six survivors and two bodies. Ten men died.

[McKee & Darlington p164]

3 July LCT (3) 313 landing craft, tank
Middlesbrough 1942; 350 tons; 175ft × 31ft; 2 × 20mm
Lieutenant Lionel White RNVR

In a poor state after the initial landings, the constant beaching that followed and the storms that swept the Normandy area in late June had caused numerous leaks to develop, and she was run onto Omaha Beach and written off as a constructive total loss.

[TNA: ADM.199/1651]

4 July MTB 666 motor torpedo boat
Hamworthy 1944; 95 tons; 110ft × 21.3ft; 1 × 2pdr, 2 × 20mm; 2 × torpedo tubes
Lieutenant Donald Napier Buller RNVR

One of a group of five torpedo boats conducting an offensive anti-shipping sweep along the Dutch coast, at 00.47 radar contact was made with enemy surface units. They closed until at 01.32, then being about a mile and a half from Ijmuiden. They stalked the contacts until at 02.12 a large-calibre shell was fired from the shore followed by star shells from seaward. This served to illuminate the targets, and they accelerated to attack, firing torpedoes before turning away to clear the area, the enemy ships opening a fierce fire as they did. At 02.25, *666* received a direct hit in the engine room, probably by a 37mm shell fired by *Vp 1415*, which started a fire. The engines came to a stop, and she drifted. The fire was tackled, and this was brought under control, but she was still without power. The other British torpedo boats had altered round to search for her, but two of the enemy vessels, *Vp 1401* and *Vp 1418*, had already closed and opened a fierce fire which prevented any assistance. As the German vessels approached Lieutenant Buller ordered the boat to be abandoned, and having set demolition charges, Carley floats were launched, and the crew jumped into the water, to be picked up after several hours in the water by the Germans to be made prisoners. The enemy escorts managed to get alongside the wreck, and as the demolition charges had failed to work, were able to rig a tow, and the following day the torpedo boat was taken into Ijmuiden as a prize. A few hours later, there was a large internal explosion, presumably as the demolition charges finally detonated, and she rolled over, and to settle, with her keel showing. The Germans attempted to salvage the wreck, and later that same day she was successfully raised by rigging slings

under her and taken into a floating dock. The next morning at 07.00 there was another explosion which wrecked what was left of her. An enquiry found that the most likely cause of the second explosion was the ignition of petrol fumes; fuel had leaked into the bilges, and when workmen boarded her to inspect the craft, they switched a light on which triggered an explosion.

[TNA: ADM.267/123; Reynolds, Dog Boats pp170–2]

5 July GANILLY trawler
Beverley 1943; 545 tons; 150ft × 27.8ft; 1 × 12pdr, 3 × 20mm
Lieutenant Maurice William Hampson RNVR

Whilst escorting the southbound cross-Channel convoy EBC30, she sank following a large explosion at 08.21 when to the north-east of Cap Barfleur, in position 50.28.06N 00.58.18W. The detonation was so large that all trace of the ship disappeared in less than a minute. The commanding officer and three ratings, the only survivors, were picked up by HMS *Watchman*. Three officers and thirty-six ratings were missing presumed killed. The cause of the explosion was uncertain; it was assumed at the time to be a mine, although it is likely that she was torpedoed by *U 390* (Geissler), which was operating in the area at the time, and was herself sunk later that day.

[TNA: ADM.199/1394; ADM.199/1398; ADM.358/3338]

6 July TROLLOPE frigate
Hingham 1943; 1,300 tons; 300ft × 36.9ft; 3 × 3in, 8 × 20mm
Lieutenant Commander Harry Westacott[†]

Following the successful landings at Normandy, German torpedo boats made several sorties against the Allied ships assembled off the beachheads. During the night of 5/6 June, two groups of torpedo boats from Le Havre were involved in engagements off the coast, and it was during one of these, at 01.30 the *Trollope* was hit by a torpedo which struck the ship in the vicinity of the forward magazine, which then exploded. About 130ft of the ship before the forward engine room, including the bridge and foremast, was blown away. The forward engine room flooded and the after boiler room leaked. The ship heeled over about 3 degrees to starboard. The wreck was towed by a US Navy tug inshore, where it was run into shallow water near Arromanches-les-Bains and subsequently written off as a constructive total loss. Sixty-four men lost their lives.

[TNA: ADM.267/118; CB.4273 p282]

6 July MAGIC minesweeper
Savannah 1943; 890 tons; 215ft × 32.2ft; 1 × 3in, 6 × 20mm
Lieutenant Commander John Percy Davies RNR

Laying at anchor off Sword Beach, Normandy, with several other minesweepers, the *Magic* was part of the

'Trout' defence line, set up to protect the anchorage from attack; the ship was closed up at action stations as it was suspected that torpedo–boat activity was likely. At 03.52 there was an explosion under the after engine room. The ship took a heavy list to starboard and rapidly settled by the stern and at 03.58 she sank, stern first, rolling over in the process and lay with her bows above water. The *Cato* was the nearest ship in the line and quickly weighed anchor to render assistance, picking up several survivors, being joined in the rescue efforts by the *Catherine* and *Grecian*. Twenty-five men were lost. She had been the victim of an attack by a *Neger* human torpedo.

[TNA: ADM.267/118]

6 July CATO minesweeper
Seattle 1942; 890 tons; 215ft × 32.2ft; 1 × 3in, 6 × 20mm
Lieutenant Robert William Edward Harris

Like her sister, *Magic*, the *Cato* was laying at anchor off Sword Beach, Normandy, as part of the defence line to protect the beach. When the *Magic* blew up, she immediately rendered assistance, picking up several men from the water. At 05.08 she became another victim of a *Neger* human torpedo, when there was a large explosion under the break of the forecastle. She quickly settled by the bows and heeled over to port, swathed in smoke. It was hoped that a tow might be rigged, but she was settling fast. The *Chamois* closed and took off all the survivors before standing clear. At 07.25 she returned to the wreck, to see if it could be towed, but at 07.45 as she was attempting to secure herself alongside the *Cato* lurched and in 2 minutes had lost her stability, slowly rolling over to port until she capsized to sink bows first, her stern rising clear of the water. Twenty-six men were lost.

[TNA: ADM.267/118]

7 July FDT 216 fighter direction tender
Seneca 1943 (*LST 216*); 1,468 tons; 316ft × 50ft; 1 × 12pdr, 12 × 20mm
Lieutenant Commander George Dudley Kelly RNR

A former landing ship fitted with RAF-manned radar and radio equipment to direct friendly fighter aircraft, she was deployed to the Normandy coast for the D-Day operations, being stationed off Omaha Beach. They continued these duties over the next few weeks, with *FDT 216* moving to take up station off Cap Barfleur, being accompanied by the corvette *Burdock*. In the early hours of 7 July, a radar contact was noted closing the pair, and at 00.53 the noise of an aircraft was heard but could not be seen due to low cloud and a misty drizzle. The aircraft appeared to fly around the pair, and then resolved itself as a Ju 88 aircraft as it emerged from the low cloud. Despite both ships opening fire, the aircraft flew towards *216* from the port side. When about half a

mile away the splash of a torpedo was seen after release from the aircraft, and moments later, at 00.59 there was a large explosion when *216* was hit on the port side forward. A large hole was blown in the side, a fire was started, and she took a list to port. The *Burdock* closed, and as it was clear that she was sinking at 01.07 the order was given to abandon her. *216* continued to heel further to port and settle by the head until at 01.45 the pig iron deck ballast carried on the upper deck started moving and she capsized onto her beam ends, hung for about 90 seconds and then rolled over completely to float, bottom up, for some minutes before sinking. Five men were lost.

[TNA: ADM.199/169]

8 July MTB 463 motor torpedo boat
Hythe 1944; 41 tons; 71.9ft × 20.7ft; 1 × 6pdr, 2 × 20mm, 2 × torpedo tubes
Lieutenant Douglas Glen Creba RCNVR

Royal Canadian Navy. Conducting a night patrol off the coast of Normandy in company with *MTB 466*, at 05.00 as they were off Sword Beach, there was a large explosion under the stern as she triggered a mine. *466*, immediately astern, found herself steering through the waterspout of the explosion, but despite being shaken, was able to be put alongside *463* to take off the injured men and rig a tow, but she was too badly shattered, and 2 hours after the explosion, she foundered.

[McKee & Darlington p164]

8 July PYLADES minesweeper
Savannah 1943; 890 tons; 215ft × 32.2ft; 1 × 3in, 6 × 20mm
Lieutenant Montague Harris

Deployed off the Normandy beachhead, she was engaged with two other minesweepers and an armed trawler in patrolling the approaches to the beaches. At 06.50, just after weighing anchor, there was a large explosion under the stern and the ship was lifted out of the water by the blast. She settled on an even keel, but it was clear that she had suffered considerable damage aft; fittings were torn out of the deck, the deck and hull was rippled and distorted, and water was reported entering the after engine room. A tow was ordered to be prepared, but this could not be carried out as there was a second explosion and she took a distinct dip by the stern and her bows rose clear of the water. The ship started to roll over to port, and did not recover, and slowly but continuously heeled over until she capsized to float bottom up before sinking stern first. The *Cockatrice* closed to pick up the survivors. Eleven men were killed. It was believed that she had been attacked by a *Neger* human torpedo.

[TNA: ADM.267/117; ADM.199/1651]

9 July LCT (4) 511 landing craft, tank
Old Kilpatrick 1943; 200 tons; 171ft × 38.8ft
Lieutenant Walter Ellis Eason RNVR
Badly strained by constant use on the Normandy
beaches and the poor weather, she was ordered back
to England under tow. Further leaks became evident
during the voyage and it became clear that her back was
broken. The tow was cast off as she started to sink, and
the wreck was despatched by gunfire from a destroyer.
[TNA:ADM.199/1651]

9 July MTB 434 motor torpedo boat
Hythe 1943; 37 tons; 71.9ft × 20.7ft; 1 × 6pdr, 2 × 20mm
Sub-Lieutenant Eric Archer RNVR
In company with *MTB 430*, she was lying about 3 miles off
the coast of France, to the north of Le Havre, with another
group of boats about 7 miles to the south, watching for any
movement of enemy surface forces towards the landing
beaches in Normandy. The pair detected a group of ships,
believed to be enemy patrol craft, moving along the coast
and headed towards them, working up to full speed.
As the pair ran in to attack, they were heavily engaged
by the enemy and *434* was hit in the 20mm magazine,
starting a serious fire which spread to a petrol tank. She
disengaged and cleared the area, but despite operating fire
extinguishers the blaze spread, forcing them to abandon
ship. Four men were picked up by *MTB 430* and others
by *MTB 459*. One man was killed.
[Reynolds, Home Waters MTBs pp143–4]

10 July LCT (4) 757 landing craft, tank
Chepstow 1943; 200 tons; 171ft × 38.8ft
Employed supporting the landings at Omaha Beach,
Normandy, she was badly strained by constant work and
bad weather. The leaks increased, and it became clear
that her back was broken, and she settled and finally
broke up and sank off the beach.
[TNA:ADM.199/1651]

10 July LCT (4) 1076 landing craft, tank
Middlesbrough 1943; 200 tons; 171ft × 38.8ft
After taking part in the Normandy landings, she
continued to supply Juno Beach. Whilst on passage back
to England at 20.30 the hull worked in the sea, and it was
thought that her back was broken. With leaks increasing
she was abandoned in position 50.22N 00.58W as she
started to break up. The wreck was evidently salvaged,
but she was written off 5 August as a total loss.
[TNA:ADM.199/2297; ADM.210/8]

10 July MMS 55 minesweeper
Peterhead 1941; 255 tons; 105ft × 23ft
Lieutenant Frederick William Holton RNVR
Employed with other minesweepers in clearing
minefields in the eastern area of the landing area in

Normandy, it proved a hazardous task, with the fields
reported as being 'very sensitive' with frequent multiple
explosions being triggered, and a total of twenty-five
mines were found and disposed of during the day. At
11.21 there was a large explosion close to *55* as she
triggered an influence mine, and the ship sank very
quickly, with sixteen men killed and four survivors.
[TNA:ADM.199/1398; ADM.358/2340]

12 July ML 443 motor launch
Oulton Broad 1941; 73 tons; 112ft × 18.4ft; 1 × 3pdr,
1 × 20mm
Lieutenant Adam Nicholson Robertson RNVR
Stationed in the Mediterranean, she was engaged in
sweeping for mines between Piombino and Livorno,
when she was damaged when she detonated a contact
mine in position 43.18.12N 10.14.12E, off the Vada
rocks. The explosion blew the bows off the launch,
but the stern section remained afloat and was towed to
Civitavecchia, but the damage was so great that she was
written off as a total loss. There were no casualties.
[TNA:ADM.199/1433]

15 July LCT (5) 2263 landing craft, tank
Evansville 1943 (*LCT 263*); 143 tons; 105ft × 32.8ft;
2 × 20mm
The landing craft had taken part in the Normandy
landings, on Juno Beach as part of the 105th LCT
Flotilla and the subsequent constant work strained
the hull, and the craft was beached and subsequently
written off as a constructive total loss.
[TNA:ADM.210/8]

16 July LCT (4) 1020 landing craft, tank
Thornaby 1943; 200 tons; 171ft × 38.3ft
Having taken part in the Normandy landings, she
was damaged by regular beaching in the re-supply
operations. She was beached and written off as a total
constructive loss.
[TNA:ADM.199/1398]

16 July LCT (3) 7057 landing craft, tank
Southwick 1943; 350 tons; 175ft × 31ft; 2 × 20mm
As part of the 16th LCT Flotilla, she took part in the
Normandy landings on Omaha Beach. During the
storm which struck the landing area 19–22 June she
was driven into one of the artificial 'Mulberry' harbours
and damaged so badly that she was subsequently written
off as a constructive total loss.
[TNA:ADM.210/8]

16 July LCT (3) 7064 landing craft, tank
Blyth 1944; 350 tons; 175ft × 31ft; 2 × 20mm
Lieutenant Arthur Leon Pullen RNVR
Damaged in the storm which hit the Normandy beaches
in late June, she was in poor condition and was towed

back to England full of water and was condemned as a constructive total loss.

[http://www.ddaymuseum.co.uk/normandy-veterans-photos.html]

17 July LCT (3) 387 landing craft, tank

Middlesbrough 1942; 350 tons; 175ft × 31ft; 2 × 2pdr
Lieutenant Frederick William Marshall Horsley RNVR

Loaded with American troops, she sailed from Civitavecchia bound for Naples, joining a small convoy of nine other LCTs, with three LCMs and two LCIs. As 387 had developed steering problems, she was lashed alongside LCT 587. However, 587 then experienced engine problems, and the pair fell astern of the group, and finally at 23.15 LCT 587 broke down completely. This left only 387 providing the power, and steering proved difficult, but they progressed slowly until at 04.10 there was a large explosion under the bow ramp of 387 as she detonated a mine. The explosion blew away the bow door, the watertight door and distorted bulkheads and deck plating. She immediately started to fill with water, but 587 assisted by passing across a portable pump, and a little later US Navy LCI 945 appeared and came alongside to assist with pumping. This kept the water at bay, and the group headed inshore towards Ischia. Despite the work, it became clear that she could not be kept afloat, and the soldiers were transferred to the other landing craft. At 08.00 she rolled over and sank bows first. Position noted as 41.04N 13.16E.

[TNA: ADM.199/260]

19 July TEXAS trawler

Ontario 1919 (TR 57) requisitioned 1940; 275 tons; 125.6ft × 23.6ft
Lieutenant Johan Ingvald Olsen RNR†

Foundered after a collision at 03.00 in the South Kingston Channel, Jamaica; two men lost their lives.

[TNA: ADM.199/2298].

20 July ISIS destroyer

Scotstoun 1937; 1,370 tons; 312ft × 33ft; 2 × 4.7in, 2 × 6pdr, 6 × 20mm, 5 × torpedo tubes
Lieutenant Henry Dumaresq Durell

Carrying out an anti-submarine patrol off Omaha Beach, Normandy, she was about 10 miles offshore when at 18.02 a bump was distinctly felt by those on board, as if she had struck something. A few seconds later there was a large explosion amidships, under number 1 boiler room, followed almost immediately by another two explosions either underneath her or close by her port side. The ship rolled over to starboard at once and the upper deck amidships was soon awash, and it was obvious that her back had been broken. Her bow and stern rose clear, the ship being swathed in smoke from a fire that had broken out in the galley. She was

ordered to be abandoned, men jumping into the sea and some Carley floats were released before she disappeared. The survivors spent several uncomfortable hours before being picked up in the early hours of the next morning, some by the minesweeper Hound and others by a US Coastguard cutter. One hundred and fifty-five officers and men died. The cause of the explosions was uncertain; a contact mine was believed to be the most likely cause, but an attack by a manned Neger craft is a possibility.

[TNA: ADM.267/95]

20 July LCT (4) 689 landing craft, tank

Bo'ness 1943; 200 tons; 171ft × 38.8ft
Sub-Lieutenant Brian Elmer Cotton RNVR

Part of the 54th LCT Squadron based at Portland, she was reported to have been 'destroyed by an explosion in the assault area', but no further details have been found. Nine men were lost.

[TNA: ADM.358/4380; Statement of Losses p58]

21 July CHAMOIS minesweeper

Seattle 1942; 890 tons; 215ft × 32ft; 1 × 3in, 6 × 20mm
Lieutenant Commander Denys Philip Richardson RNVR

With her sister minesweepers, Chamois had taken part in the Normandy landings, and was afterwards engaged in sweeping the numerous minefields off the beachheads. They had completed a sweep off Sword Beach and were heading towards the designated night anchorage, when there was a large explosion as they detonated a mine about 12ft from the port side, abreast the bridge. The engines stopped and all power was lost, the steering gear was broken, and the radio, radar and Asdic were wrecked by the shock. The ship remained stable, and she was taken in tow by the Grecian, and power was later restored to both engine rooms and she was able to maintain a reduced speed of 6 knots. She made her way back across the Channel to Plymouth where it was found that the hull on the port side was rippled and corrugated, and many of the internal fittings and fixtures were broken. The ship was declared a constructive total loss and paid off. There were no fatalities.

[TNA: ADM.267/116; CB.4273 p320]

21 July LCT (5) 2331 landing craft, tank

Decatur 1943 (LCT 331); 143 tons; 105ft × 32.8ft, 2 × 20mm
Sub-Lieutenant James Francis Oakley RNVR

Having taken part in the Normandy landings and the subsequent support landings, by July the landing craft was showing the strain, and following a survey in mid-June she was ordered to be towed back to England for repairs. However, half-way across the Channel cracks opened in the hull, and it was clear that her back was broken. The tow was slipped as she broke up and a destroyer was summoned to the scene and sank the sections by gunfire.

[Personal recollections of Signalman Mike Crumpton at: http:// www.combinedops.com/LCT%202331.htm]

23 July LCT (4) 1023 landing craft, tank
Thornaby 1943; 200 tons; 171ft × 38.8ft

In June *1023* had taken part in the Normandy operations, allocated to Sword Beach. Damaged by this and subsequent beaching to support the landings, she returned to Cardiff where she was written off as a constructive total loss and cannibalised.

[TNA: ADM.210/8]

24 July GOATHLAND escort destroyer
Govan 1942; 1,087 tons; 264.2ft × 31.5ft; 4 × 4in, 4 × 2pdr, 2 × torpedo tubes

Lieutenant Breon Buckie Bordes DSC

Fitted as a temporary HQ ship for the Normandy landings, she covered the landings at Sword Beach. She was then engaged in patrols off the beachhead, until she detonated a mine which exploded under the ship near the after magazine. The magazine and the aft fuel tank flooded, and the ship immediately heeled over to starboard. There was extensive shock damage to engines, boilers and generators, and radio and radar equipment was put out of action. She remained stable and was towed to Portsmouth. A subsequent survey found that the shafts were bent, and the hull was distorted. It was determined that repairs were uneconomical, and she was paid off as a constructive total loss. There were no fatalities.

[TNA: ADM.267/90; CB.4273 p260]

24 July LCT (4) 901 landing craft, tank
London 1943; 200 tons; 171ft × 38.8ft

As part of the 23rd LCT Flotilla she had landed at Gold Beach during the Normandy invasion. The damage suffered during this and the follow-up support operations led her back being broken on 21 July and subsequently she was written off.

[TNA: ADM.199/2298; ADM.210/8]

24 July MTB 372 motor torpedo boat
Annapolis 1943; 37 tons; 72.7ft × 19.2ft; 1 × 20mm, 2 × torpedo tubes

Lieutenant Kenneth Dunston Golding RNVR

Part of the 20th MTB Flotilla stationed in the Mediterranean, which was now based at Bari in southern Italy. On the night of 23/24 July *MTB 372* in company with *MTB 81* and *MTB 297* was conducting a patrol near the island of Korcula in the Adriatic. The pair encountered a small coastal convoy, with a strong escort of five torpedo boats and they attempted to manoeuvre closer to carry out an attack. However, the bright moonlight revealed their position, and as they closed, they came under heavy fire from the escorts. *372* was hit by a large shell in the engine room and she came to a halt and a fire broke out. The boat immediately astern of her, *MTB 81* could not avoid her and collided with her port quarter. With the fire spreading, *81* took the crew off and she was abandoned, although one man, finding himself in the water, swam to the shore where he contacted the partisans. One rating was killed in the engine room. The following morning a Spitfire was sent to search the area, and on finding the smoking wreck, dispatched it with gunfire.

[Reynolds & Cooper, Mediterranean MTBs pp125–6; Pope p222]

27 July MTB 430 motor torpedo boat
Hythe 1942; 37 tons; 71.9ft × 20.7ft; 1 × 6pdr, 2 × 20mm

Lieutenant Trevor John Mathias RNVR

MTB 430 was in company with two other boats, *MTB 412* and *MTB 431*, loitering on patrol off Cap d'Antifer, when a group of six enemy torpedo boats were encountered. Mathias, the senior officer, led the other boats in a high-speed attack, passing through the enemy line. As he did so, he collided with one of the enemy craft, *S 182*. Both craft were damaged, and spilled fuel on board *430* triggered an explosion and started a fierce fire. The wreck of *430* was then rammed by *412* (see below). The survivors abandoned her to be picked up by *431*; it was some consolation that *S 182* also sank. Eleven men were lost.

[Reynolds, Home Waters MTBs pp145–6]

27 July MTB 412 motor torpedo boat
Hythe 1942; 46 tons; 71.9ft × 20.7ft; 1 × 2pdr, 2 × 20mm, 2 × torpedo tubes

Lieutenant Walter Gordon Lindsay Salmon RNVR

On patrol in company with *MTB 430* and *MTB 431* off Cap d'Antifer when they were in contact with a group of six enemy torpedo boats (see *MTB 430* above). When *430* led the assault on the enemy line, *412* was immediately astern of her and could not avoid a collision when *430* exploded into flames. *412* managed to disengage and clear the area but was so damaged that she had to be sunk later. One man was killed.

[Reynolds, Home Waters MTBs pp145–6]

29 July PRINCE LEOPOLD landing ship, infantry
Hoboken 1930 requisitioned 1940; 2,950 tons; 347ft × 46.3ft; 2 × 12pdr, 2 × 2pdr, 6 × 20mm

Lieutenant Commander John Alverdus Lowe DSO DSC RNR

Having embarked 515 Royal Engineers, she sailed from St Helens at 04.00 to make her way across the Channel to northern France in company with three other troop transports, being escorted by two frigates. At 06.48 there

was an explosion under her stern, a Carley float being blown 100ft into the air. The ship came to a halt and it soon became clear that she had lost her propellers, and flooding was reported in the after compartments. Ten members of the crew and five soldiers were killed by the blast and shock. Bulkheads were shored, and work started to pump the water clear, and hopes were high that she could be saved. An attempt was made by the *Chelmer* to take her in tow, but in the increasingly choppy seas this proved difficult. However, at 08.30 the tug *Amsterdam* arrived on scene and an hour later she was under tow for Spithead at 6 knots. The wind continued to freshen, and the seas became choppier, and during the afternoon the pumps were losing the battle to keep the water in check. As a precaution the landing craft were lowered and manned, keeping in convoy with her. At 15.45 the ship took a lurch to port and it was clear that she was sinking. All hands were called to the upper deck and the embarked soldiers and crew started leaving her, taking to the landing craft and boats sent by the *Chelmer*. The tug slipped the tow and at 16.18 she finally sank, rolling over to port, then slowly coming back to the upright before she submerged, then being 5.8 miles to the south of the Nab Tower. In all, twenty-three men died. She had been torpedoed by *U 621* (Struckmann).
[TNA: ADM.267/123]

29 July LORD WAKEFIELD trawler
Selby 1933 requisitioned 1939; 418 tons; 152.6ft × 25.6ft;
1 × 12pdr
Skipper-Lieutenant Henry Edward Dodd RNR†
Whilst lying at anchor in the convoy assembly area off the 'Omaha' beachhead, Normandy, she suffered a direct hit at 10.20 from a bomb during an air attack and rapidly sank. Thirty-four men were lost. Eight survivors were picked up by the *Northern Sun*.
[TNA: ADM.199/1652; ADM.358/2363]

29 July LCG (L) 1062 landing craft, gun, large
Middlesbrough 1943; 570 tons; 171ft × 38.8ft; 2 × 4.7in,
10 × 20mm
Engaged in shelling enemy shore batteries near Le Havre, as she manoeuvred off shore she detonated a mine, which exploded amidships, and she rapidly broke in half. Both sections remained afloat for several hours before sinking. Six men were lost.
Note; the *Statement of Losses* gives the wrong date, of 1 July, for her loss.
[TNA: ADM.199/1652]

30 July LCT (3) 7036 landing craft, tank
Aberdeen 1944; 625 tons; 175ft × 31ft; 2 × 20mm
Lieutenant Henry George Richard Falconar RNVR
Bound for the beaches of northern France, she sailed from Southampton on 29 July loaded with motor

vehicles. Heading for a beach about 20 miles north from Cherbourg, they arrived that evening and anchored overnight. At 09.00 the next morning they weighed and headed in for the beach, but almost immediately there was a large explosion under the hull as she ran over a mine, and with extensive engine room damage, she began to sink. A US Navy boat came alongside to lift off most the crew before she was run into shallow water and beached. Two men were killed in the blast.
Note: this loss is not noted in the *Statement of Losses*.
[TNA: ADM.199/176; ADM.358/2411]

July LCT (3) 324 landing craft, tank
Middlesbrough 1942; 625 tons; 175ft × 31ft; 2 × 20mm
Sub-Lieutenant Kenneth Tarry RNVR
Engaged in the Normandy landings and subsequent support operations, she was damaged by constant beachings, and was eventually written off as a constructive total loss.
[Warships Supplement 182 p23]

3 August QUORN destroyer
Cowes 1940; 1,000 tons; 264.2ft × 31.6ft; 4 × 4in, 5 × 2pdr,
2 × 20mm
Lieutenant Ivan Hall
To defend the Normandy beachhead from attacks by German surface vessels, a patrol line was set up at the eastern flank, running approximately 6 miles north of the town of Ouistreham, and then 2 miles in a north–easterly direction. This was the 'Trout Line' and employed LCG and LCF ships at anchor 700 yards apart, and these were backed by patrolling vessels. There were several attempts on the patrol ships (see 7 July), but a determined attack was made by a large number of explosive motor boats and 'human torpedoes' on the night of 2/3 August. It was a bright moonlit night when the assault commenced at 02.00 when an attack was made on a scuttled blockship. Fifteen minutes later, as the *Quorn* came to the end of her southerly leg and was under helm to turn to the north–east, there was a tremendous explosion on the starboard side amidships. The ship rolled over to starboard and in less than a minute was on her beam ends. The ship then started to slowly right herself, but then broke apart, with both ends rising clear of the water to the vertical and sinking. Four officers and 126 ratings were lost. Her attacker was uncertain, as both *Linsen* explosive boats and *Neger* manned torpedoes were deployed that evening.
[TNA: ADM.267/95; ADM.199/957]

3 August GAIRSAY trawler
Ardrossan 1942; 545 tons; 150ft × 27.6ft; 1 × 12pdr,
3 × 20mm
Lieutenant Charles Henry Homer-Lindsay RNR
The attack on the *Quorn* (see above), started what became known as the 'Battle of the Trout Line'. For

the next 2 hours there were continuous attacks on the line by explosive motor boats and submersibles. At 03.25 the patrolling launch *HDML 1378* felt the shock of an explosion and saw a sheet of flame. She steered towards the disturbance and found a patch of floating debris and several men in the water, which marked the end of *Gairsay*. The commanding officer and nine men were picked up, but thirty-one men were lost. Survivors indicated that they had heard the sound of an engine before the explosion, but too late for any action to be taken. In all thirty-two explosive motorboats and twenty-one 'human torpedoes' were destroyed that night.
[TNA: ADM.199/396]

3 August LCG (L) 764 landing craft, gun, large
Middlesbrough 1943; 570 tons; 171ft × 38.8ft; 2 × 4.7in, 10 × 20mm
Lieutenant William Philip Webb RNVR
Lying at anchor about 5 miles to the north of Ouistreham, Normandy, as part of the defensive 'Trout Line', when the ships came under attack from 'human torpedoes' and radio-controlled explosive motor boats. At 04.40 a small motorboat was observed closing her at about 20 knots; it struck her but failed to explode and was sunk under the bows by small-arms fire. Soon after this, at 05.05, engine noises were heard and then a second boat was seen coming towards her. This hit her forward and exploded, wrecking everything forward of the bridge. She dipped by the bows and then sank quickly. Eight men were lost.
[TNA: ADM.199/1396; ADM.199/1652]

5 August LCT (4) 1039 landing craft, tank
Meadowside 1943; 200 tons; 171ft × 38.8ft
Having taken part in the Normandy landings as part of the 51st LCT Flotilla at Gold Beach, in July she was ordered to return to Plymouth, but she broke her back whilst under tow in English Channel and was subsequently written off as a constructive total loss.
[TNA: ADM.210/8]

8 August REGINA corvette
Sorel 1941; 940 tons; 190ft × 33ft; 1 × 4in
Lieutenant Jack Whiles Radford RCNR
Royal Canadian Navy. Escorting Convoy EBC66 to the Normandy beaches, they departed from Barry on 8 August, and that evening were off Trevose Head, Cornwall, when at 21.30 there was a large explosion in the starboard column of ships. On investigation, *Regina* found the damaged American cargo ship *Ezra Weston*, with the ship's back broken, and advised that they should steer inshore and try and beach the ship. *LCT 644* was also in the convoy and joined the *Regina*. It was believed that the most likely cause of the explosion was a mine, so both LCT and corvette stayed close by as the merchantman

moved slowly ahead. Eventually her engines stopped, and the LCT closed to rig a tow. At 22.48 with no warning the *Regina* exploded, and she broke up and sank in less than a minute. *LCT 248* and the armed trawler *Jacques Morgand* were quickly on scene and rescued seventy men, but thirty men died. It remained unclear at the time whether mine or torpedo was responsible, but *U 667* (Lange) reported attacking the convoy, dispatching the escort with an acoustic homing torpedo.
[McKee & Darlington p169]

10 August KUTUBTARI auxiliary patrol vessel
Calcutta 1915 (*Dharacottah*) requisitioned 1939; 237 tons; 115.4ft × 23.9ft; 1 × 12pdr
Lieutenant Ibrahim Daud Naqua RINVR
Royal Indian Navy. Grounded off Chittagong and subsequently written off as a constructive total loss.
[https://uboat.net/allies/warships/ship/22368.html]

10 August LCT (4) 1092 landing craft, tank
Alloa 1943; 200 tons; 171ft × 38.8ft
Lieutenant Thomas Esmond Wigley RNVR
On 17 June on her way back to Portsmouth from the beaches of Northern France, she broke her back at 14.30 in the heavy swell. By 15.00 the ship was working badly, and the bows were only held on by side railings. The tug *Empire Sara* arrived to assist her, and commenced a tow towards Arromanches, where she anchored. The craft eventually broke apart and sank.
[TNA: ADM.199/1651]

14 August LCI (L) 99 landing craft, infantry, large
Orange 1942; 380 tons; 150ft × 23.8ft; 4 × 20mm
Lieutenant Arthur John Reynolds RNVR†
Part of Convoy EBC72, which was bound for Falmouth from Milford Haven, and consisting of two columns of American and British amphibious craft escorted by the *Londonderry* and *Azalea*. At 16.54, then being in position 50.56N 04.47W, an American landing ship, *LST 921*, was hit by a torpedo, with a large amount of water and debris being thrown into the air and 2 minutes later, another torpedo hit *LCI 99* amidships. The craft immediately broke up and started to sink. The *Londonderry* went to the scene and lowered boats to pick up survivors before carrying out an Asdic search. A depth-charge and Hedgehog attack was carried out on a suspected contact, but without result. The attacker had been *U 667* (Lange). Nine men were lost.
[TNA: ADM.358/4381]

14 August ML 430 motor launch
Sydney 1943; 85 tons; 112ft × 18.3ft; 1 × 2pdr, 1 × 20mm
Lieutenant Arthur Alan Wordsworth RANVR
Royal Australian Navy. In company with several other motor launches, she was ordered to take part in Operation

'Hunter', designed to disrupt enemy communications around the island of Biak, New Guinea, as the battle to secure the island was nearing its end. It was suspected that an enemy submarine was active in the area, and when, at 22.00, look–outs onboard *ML 819* reported the noise of a diesel engine, it was suspected to be a submarine on the surface. A short time later the outline of a vessel was sighted about a mile distant. *ML 819* raised *ML 430* by radio, and ordered her to close, as she believed she was in contact with the enemy. At 23.10 *ML 819* increased speed and opened fire on the stranger, but moments later *ML 430* reported that she was being fired on, and it was realised that *819* had fired on her companion. She closed, and removed the crew, as the launch was burning fiercely. After this was complete, *819* fired several more rounds into the stricken vessel to ensure that it sank. Two men were wounded in the incident.

[http://www.navy.gov.au/ml-819]

15 August **LST 404** landing ship, tank
Meadowside 1943; 350 tons; 190.7ft × 31ft; 2 × 2pdr
Lieutenant Commander Henry Bruff Shaw RNR
Having taken part in the Normandy landings, *LST 404* embarked 138 casualties, many of them stretcher–bound, with several prisoners of war. In company with two merchant ships and escorted by a destroyer, they made up Convoy FTM69 which departed from the beaches to head for England. At 16.32 when in position 50.03.12N 00.37.36W, she was hit by a torpedo on the starboard side; all the lights went out and the engines stopped. The starboard side was blown in between frames 19 and 25, the upper deck was peeled back, side plates were cracked and buckled, and there was a dangerous split in the hull which seemed to extend from the upper deck to below the water line. All the stretcher cases were ordered to be brought to the upper deck, and the anchor was let go which brought her head to the sea and steadied the ship. *LST 413* was then seen approaching, and she was signalled to close, which she did and at 17.20 she came alongside to lift off the casualties. The US Navy tug *ATR-4* was now on scene and a tow was rigged aft, and at 17.48 she weighed anchor and was towed stern first towards the Isle of Wight. Later that evening she was run ashore in shallow water on Ryde Sands. Subsequent inspection condemned her as a constructive total loss. Seven men were killed. Her attacker had been *U 741* (Palmren), which was hunted and destroyed by the corvette *Orchis* later that same evening.

[TNA: ADM.199/957]

16 August   **MGB 313** motor gun boat
St. Monance 1941; 72 tons; 110ft × 17.5ft; 2 × 2pdr
Lieutenant Anthony Calvert Lewis RANVR
Carrying out a night patrol off the Normandy beaches, she was in company with *MGB 322* and *MGB 334*, lying with engines cut, maintaining a radar and hydrophone watch. At 05.20 HE (hydrophone effect) was reported astern, and a moment later there was a large explosion under the stern. This triggered a larger explosion as ammunition and petrol ignited and within seconds the ship was engulfed in flames. *MGB 322* closed to run close alongside the burning craft to take off the crew, before *313* rolled over to float keel up. The wreck slowly sank, stern first the bows remaining vertical out of the water, to be sunk by gunfire from the other gunboats. Seven men were killed. The cause of the blast was uncertain; the hydrophone effect strongly suggested it was a torpedo, and *Neger* human torpedoes were deployed that night, but the firer remained unidentified, and a drifting mine may have been responsible.

[TNA: ADM.199/1652]

16 August **BYMS 2022** minesweeper
Seattle 1942; 207 tons; 130ft × 24.6ft; 1 × 3in, 2 × 20mm
Skipper-Lieutenant George Garden RNR
In company with several other sweepers, she was ordered to cover the Allied landings in the south of France, being tasked to work in the area designated 'Camel' between Fréjus and St Raphael. Several mines had been brought to the surface by sweeping and *2022* in company with her sister *2026* were ordered to dispose of them. The pair moved inshore and closed *BYMS 2172* and the US Navy *YMS 24*, which had a group of five mines in sight. *2022* closed to 600 yards from the nearest and engaged with rifle fire. This continued with difficulty, as the other ships were also firing on the mines, and much of the shot was falling uncomfortably close to *2022*, and then a US Navy YMS steamed in between the firing ships and the mines. It was decided to clear the area, and reposition the ship, so at 19.30 she went astern. As she did so there was a large explosion aft, which demolished much of the stern. She heeled over to port and began to sink. *2026* closed to lift off the crew, the upper deck being awash, and she sank shortly after. Two men died in the explosion. The court of enquiry opined that the range at which the mines had been engaged was too distant and that a greater effort could have been made to save the vessel.

[TNA: ADM.199/227]

16 August **ML 563** motor launch
Sarisbury Green 1943; 73 tons; 112ft × 18.4ft; 1 × 3pdr, 1 × 20mm
Lieutenant Ronald Harry Boulter RNVR
With Lieutenant Commander Pierce RNVR, senior officer Third ML Flotilla, embarked, she was supporting the landings at Fréjus, in the south of France. The launch witnessed the explosion that sank *BYMS 2022* (see above) and shortly after this the American minesweeper *YMS 24* was also mined in the same area. She closed

and picked up several survivors from the YMS and attempted to rig a tow but as she was manoeuvring clear she detonated a mine herself, blowing the stern off and had to be abandoned; position noted as 43.20N 06.45E. [TNA: ADM.199/1433; Pope p240]

17 August LCF 1 landing craft, flak
Middlesbrough 1941; 539 tons; 143ft × 31ft; 4 × 4in, 3 × 20mm
Lieutenant Robert Blane Gray RNVR[†]
Whilst lying at anchor off Langrune, Normandy, with several other ships, they came under attack from *Marder* midget submarines. At 05.30 there was an explosion nearby when the wrecked merchant ship *Iddesleigh* was attacked, and at 06.18 it was approved for her to move out of the anchorage. As she was preparing to weigh anchor at 06.32 there was a large explosion under the stern, sending a sheet of flame 300ft into the air. The ship was covered in smoke and when it cleared only the bows were visible which rose out of the sea before sinking. Seventy men were lost.
[TNA: ADM.199/1652]

17 August LCT (4) 631 landing craft, tank
Thornaby 1943; 200 tons; 171ft × 38.8ft
Listed as being lost after she broke her back; she is shown as being part of the 33rd LCT Flotilla based at Portland and probably written off as a constructive total loss on this date, following numerous beachings at Normandy.
[Statement of Losses p58; TNA: ADM.210/9]

18 August FRATTON examination vessel
Glasgow 1925 requisitioned 1940; 757 tons; 220.3ft × 33.6ft; 1 × 12pdr
Commander Kenelm Jocelyn Townesend Hutchings RNR
Employed as a barrage balloon vessel off the Normandy assault beaches, she was laying at anchor 3.4 miles off the town of Arromanches when 05.40 there was a large explosion on the port side aft. She settled rapidly by the stern, the after part of the ship soon being underwater, and she heeled over to port. She was ordered to be abandoned, sinking stern first within 5 minutes. *HDML 1415* and *HDML 1421* were quickly on scene to pick up survivors, but thirty-one men were killed. The cause of the explosion was presumed to have been a torpedo, a mine being thought unlikely, as she had been at anchor for several days with engines stopped. It is likely that she was the victim of an attack by a *Marder* midget submarine.
[TNA: ADM.199/957; ADM.358/3329]

18 August MTB 93 motor torpedo boat
Lymington 1943; 47 tons; 72.7ft × 19.2ft; 1 × 20mm, 2 × torpedo tubes
Part of the 22nd MTB Flotilla, based at Lowestoft, she was returning from a night-time patrol in the North Sea

with when at approximately 05.00 she was in collision with *MTB 729*, and she subsequently sank. Two ratings lost their lives.
[TNA: ADM.199/1440]

21 August KITE sloop
Birkenhead 1942; 1,475 tons; 283ft × 38.6ft; 6 × 4in, 10 × 20mm
Lieutenant Commander Andrew Neil Gillespie Campbell[†]
As part of the escort to Russian Convoy JW59, a substantial escort was provided, with escort aircraft carriers and both close escorts and distant support being given. The *Kite*, in company with the destroyer leader *Keppel*, worked together initially to cover the right flank of the convoy out to 10 miles. In the early hours of 21 August, they were ordered to take station on the starboard quarter of the carrier *Vindex*. *Kite* was positioned some 5,000 yards on the starboard bow of the *Keppel*, and both units had Foxer noisemaking devices streamed astern, to decoy any homing torpedoes. At 05.00 the *Keppel* requested that *Kite* turn off her noisemaker, as it was interfering with her Asdic. This was done, and soon after 06.00 the sloop slowed to 6 knots to clear the Foxer wire which had become snagged. She was getting under way again, when moments later she was hit by two torpedoes on the starboard side. Her position then was 73.01N 03.57E. The first struck by the break of the boat deck, the second further aft. The ship rapidly broke up, and while the fore part listed heavily to starboard, the stern floated away in an upright position until it sank. The bow remained afloat for some time, assuming a steep angle before disappearing. Survivors reported that a submarine broached briefly after the explosion, but this was not seen by other vessels, and no Asdic contact was gained in a subsequent search. Although *Keppel*, aided by *Peacock* and *Mermaid*, closed the scene, they could find only nine survivors in the freezing, oil covered water; 217 men died. The attacker had been *U 344* (Pietsch).
[TNA: ADM.1/16879]

21 August ORCHIS corvette
Belfast 1940; 940 tons; 190ft × 33ft; 1 × 4in, 1 × 2pdr
Lieutenant Commander Bryan Webster Harris DSC RNVR
Stationed off Juno Beach, Normandy, she weighed anchor at 07.15 to escort a small convoy from Arromanches. At 08.15 there was a large explosion as she detonated a mine under the starboard bow, which blew away the forward part of the ship as far back as the 4in gun. The ship immediately came to a stop and heeled over to port which prompted several men on the upper deck to jump overboard, and several Carley floats were released. Commander Harris had been knocked unconscious by the blast, but on coming around

realised that the ship remained stable and ordered the abandonment to stop. The chief engineer reported that steam was still available, despite some flooding. The ship's head was turned inshore and about 10 minutes after the explosion she ran aground in shallow water off Corseuilles. Poor weather hampered salvage operations, but an inspection on 18 September found that the fore part of the ship had been destroyed; much of the side plating torn away or buckled and the deck plating was distorted with numerous breaks and fractures. It was decided that it was uneconomical to repair her, and she was written off as a constructive total loss and to be cannibalised. Twenty-eight men were killed.
[TNA: ADM.199/260; ADM.267/117]

21 August **ALBERNI** corvette
Esquimalt 1940; 940 tons; 190ft × 33ft; 1 × 4in, 2 × 20mm
Lieutenant Commander Ian Hunter Bell RCNVR
Royal Canadian Navy. Ordered to carry out an anti-submarine patrol to the east of the Normandy beaches, she proceeded along one of the swept channels at 14 knots, when at 11.43, with no warning, she was hit by a torpedo on the port side, aft of the engine room. Very quickly she started to sink by the stern, heeling over to port. With her internal bulkheads collapsing, in less than a minute she had sunk stern first. With no time to release floats, survivors had to cling to pieces of wreckage until *MTB 469* and *MTB 470* arrived on scene 45 minutes later, picking up thirty-one survivors, but fifty-nine men were lost. Her attacker had been *U 480* (Förster) who had fired a single acoustic homing torpedo.
[Morgan & Taylor p410]

21 August **HDML 1179** motor launch
Newport News 1943; 46 tons; 70ft × 15.10ft; 1 × 2pdr
Sub-Lieutenant John Basil Spaven RNVR
The Caribbean was affected by a hurricane, which struck Jamaica on 20/21 August, which destroyed several buildings and destroyed crops. *1179* was based in the West Indies, and was lost at Rio Bueno, Jamaica, being driven 20 yards above the high-water mark. There were no casualties.
[TNA: ADM.267/259]

22 August **NABOB** escort aircraft carrier
Tacoma 1943 (*Edisto*); 11,420 tons; 468.5ft × 69.5ft; 2 × 4in, 16 × 40mm, 24 aircraft
Captain Horatio Nelson Lay OBE RCN
Largely manned by Canadian personnel, *Nabob* took part in Operation 'Goodwood', a series of air attacks on the battleship *Tirpitz*, anchored in Kaafjord, Norway. The first raid took place on 22 August, with limited success, and after recovering her aircraft, *Nabob*, in company with another escort carrier, *Trumpeter*, and the

ships of the Fifth Escort Group, was detached from the main force to refuel the escorting destroyers. At 17.15 she was struck by a torpedo on the starboard side about 50ft abaft the engine room. A hole 32ft long was blown in the ship's side and there was considerable internal damage in the vicinity of the blast. Electrical power failed and main engines stopped, and the engine room had to be evacuated when it filled with steam. Some of the after fuel tanks and after magazines were flooded and the ship took a list to starboard and trimmed down by the stern. Some boats and floats were launched, and non-essential personnel were transferred to the other ships in company. The flooding was controlled, and by the evening power was restored, and she was able to get under way, at very reduced speed, and successfully arrived at Scapa Flow on 27 August. She was subsequently declared to be a constructive total loss and was cannibalised for spare parts. In spite of that, in 1947, after being sold for scrap, she was rebuilt as merchant vessel, and survived until 1977. Twenty-one men were killed. Her attacker had been *U 354* (Sthamer), which had fired a salvo of pattern-running FAT torpedoes at the group, one of which had hit *Nabob*, and then attempted another attack using an acoustic homing torpedo, but this found one of the escorts, *Bickerton* (qv).
[TNA: ADM. 267/77; CB.4273 p31]

22 August **BICKERTON** frigate
Lynn 1943; 1,400 tons; 300ft × 36.7ft; 3 × 3in, 2 × 40mm, 8 × 20mm
Commander Donald George Frederick Wyville MacIntyre DSO
Senior officer of the Fifth Escort Group that was detailed to provide cover for the escort carriers *Nabob* and *Trumpeter* that were supporting an attack by larger fleet carriers on the *Tirpitz* in northern Norway. During the afternoon of 22 August, the group prepared to refuel from the carriers as the withdrawal from the area began. At 17.15, the *Nabob* was hit by a torpedo on the starboard side aft. The *Bickerton*, with the *Bligh* and *Aylmer*, being on the starboard side of the group, responded by turning towards the threat direction, and forming up in line abreast, commenced a search. Just 5 minutes later the *Bickerton* was herself hit, the explosion being right aft, under her stern. The ship shuddered violently whilst an immense plume of smoke and water rose to a great height, and she came to a stop. The steam siren jammed 'on' and the loud piercing wail drowned out all attempts to communicate normally. Worse still, the smoke-generating apparatus had burst and the ship was covered with thick acrid smoke. For some time, the situation onboard was confused and chaotic, and there was some panic, with the whaler being hoisted out without orders, and some men jumped into the sea. Eventually order was restored; the siren shut

off bringing merciful silence, and the smoke cleared somewhat, but she was settling by the stern. Non-essential personnel were transferred to the *Kempthorne*, and this was completed by 19.15. The ship was still afloat, and it was hoped that she could be towed, but the force commander had a difficult decision to make; they were a long way from home, and the *Nabob* was also damaged and was the more important unit. It was therefore decided to concentrate on saving the carrier and sink the *Bickerton* rather than waste efforts in trying to save both. At 20.55 the destroyer *Vigilant* closed and fired a torpedo into her to ensure that she sank. Her position was approximately 71.49N 20.07E. The court of enquiry was not impressed with the performance of the engineer officer, Lieutenant James Edwin Lloyd RNR; it was found that he had failed to ascertain the state of the machinery compartments and had joined those attempting to abandon the ship. Her attacker had been *U 354* (Sthamer), who had already hit the *Nabob*, and was trying a second attack, using a T5 homing torpedo which diverted to hit the *Bickerton*. One officer and thirty-seven ratings were lost.
[*TNA:ADM.1/18925*]

22 August LOYALTY minesweeper
Belfast 1942 (*Rattler*); 850 tons; 212.6ft × 35.6ft; 1 × 4in, 4 × 20mm
Lieutenant Commander James Edward Maltby RNR†
In company with other ships of the 18th Minesweeping Flotilla, she departed from the beaches of Normandy to carry out an Oropesa sweep across the English Channel to Spithead, with another ship ahead of the group. During the afternoon, the *Loyalty*'s sweep wire became foul of the *Hydra*'s, when the latter was forced to alter course to avoid shipping and it subsequently parted. The *Loyalty* therefore hauled out formation to recover sweeps, and she fell behind her companions. By 16.00 this was complete, and she got under way to rejoin, but at 16.10 in position 50.15N 00.43W there was a large explosion under the stern of the ship on the starboard side. She immediately heeled over to starboard, and it could be seen that the stern was damaged, the quarterdeck having been lifted clear of the hull and folded back into a distorted position. Floats and rafts were ordered to be released and about 4 minutes after the explosion she rolled over to starboard and capsized the keel showing. She floated upside down for 15 minutes before sinking. The trawler *Doon* and two landing craft picked up the survivors, but nineteen men were lost. At the time it was uncertain whether she had struck a mine or had been torpedoed, but it was later confirmed that she had been the victim of a T5 acoustic homing torpedo from *U 480* (Förster).
[*TNA:ADM.1/19/957;ADM.267/117*]

25 August LCT (4) 1074 landing craft, tank
Middlesbrough 1943; 200 tons; 171ft × 38.8ft
Sub-Lieutenant Anthony Downham Belairs RNVR†
Part of a 'Starlight' convoy of landing craft re-supplying the Normandy beaches, she was in the swept channel approaching the beachhead when at 07.15 in position 49.50N 00.45W, she was shaken by a large explosion aft, which blew her stern off. The shattered bow section remained afloat and was towed inshore to Utah Beach by *LCT 800*, and initially placed alongside the American troopship *Thomas B Robertson*, which treated the wounded. The wreck was later run onto Utah Beach. It was presumed at the time that a mine was responsible, but it later emerged that she had fallen victim to *U 764* (von Bremen), which had fired two acoustic homing torpedoes at a convoy of landing craft. Ten members of the crew died, with one US Army passenger.
[*TNA:ADM.199/1652;ADM.358/4390*]

25 August CHOICE trawler
Beverley 1899 (*Jeria*) requisitioned 1944; 197 tons; 114ft × 21ft; 1 × 6pdr
Employed off the Normandy beaches as a fuel depot, she was in collision with the tug *Empire Samson*. She was holed so badly that the water could not be controlled by pumps and she rolled over and sank on her side. There were no casualties.
[*TNA:ADM.199/2300*]

26 August HDML 1381 motor launch
Clynder 1943; 46 tons; 70ft × 15ft; 1 × 2pdr
Lieutenant George Forbes Young RNVR
During the night of 25/26 August *1381* landed a commando patrol on Scarpanto (Karpathos) for a reconnaissance mission, but the patrol encountered a minefield and were forced to return, with one man missing and three wounded. *1381* withdrew with the wounded men and decided to lay up for the day in a sheltered cove in the island of Sirina (Nisida Syrna), but that evening as she was getting underway to leave, part of the camouflage netting that had been spread over the launch became entangled with the screw, leaving her powerless. When two German patrol vessels approached, she had little choice but to surrender, and she was boarded and captured. She was refitted by her captors for German service as the patrol boat *KJ 25*. Returned to British control in May 1945, she seems not to have been re-commissioned and was sold locally.
[*TNA:ADM.199/1433*]

27 August Attack on the First Minesweeping Flotilla by own forces
The attack on minesweepers off the northern coast of France was the worst case of 'friendly fire' that the Royal Navy suffered during the war. The First

Minesweeping Flotilla had been engaged since the invasion of Normandy in sweeping the approaches to Arromanches but on 22 August were moved to clear an area of the coast between Cap d'Antifer and Fécamp. This was to allow heavy units to close the coast to give gunfire support to the army. This continued until the evening of 25 August when they were ordered to return to the Arromanches area. However, as Commander Trevor Crick, senior officer of the flotilla, indicated that the work was not complete, the following day the orders were amended, allowing them to remain sweeping the Fécamp area. On 27 August the *Jason*, *Salamander*, *Hussar* and *Britomart* resumed their work after a 24-hour rest break. They were accompanied by 2 armed trawlers, the *Colsay* and *Lord Ashfield*, which would act as dan layers, marking the areas swept with buoys. The *Jason* took station in the centre of the line, with the *Salamander* to port and *Britomart* to starboard as the group commenced a sweep for influence mines. The *Hussar* was astern, and the trawlers were working on the port side of the group. At 12.20 a lone Spitfire passed low overhead, but otherwise the day was quiet. At 13.30 in dazzling sunshine and a calm sea, the ships were attacked by a group of aircraft which had approached out of the sun. The attackers achieved complete surprise and concentrated their attack on the *Britomart* and the *Hussar* using rockets and gunfire. As the aircraft pulled away, they were recognised as British Typhoon aircraft. The *Jason* immediately sent a signal that they were being attacked by friendly aircraft. When the attack started, *Salamander* had fired recognition flares, but these had no effect, and 5 minutes after the initial attack a second strike took place, the *Jason* firing recognition flares, but again to no effect. The *Jason* had by now ordered all ships to slip sweeps and manoeuvre independently. The second attack concentrated on the *Salamander* and *Colsay*. This attack was resisted, with ships firing anti-aircraft guns, but the aircraft pressed home their attack, hitting the *Salamander* aft, and the *Colsay* disappeared for some moments as she was covered in water spouts and smoke. The *Jason* and *Lord Ashfield* then came under attack, being raked by cannon fire. As this second attack ceased, the smoke cleared to reveal the *Britomart* stopped and burning, the *Hussar* under way but on fire; the *Colsay* dead in the water and not responding to visual signals. Five minutes later there was another pass by the aircraft, which was resisted by the *Jason* firing her 20mm guns, which seemed to act as a deterrent, but the *Hussar* was seen to be rocked by an explosion. The aircraft then circled and cleared away. The *Britomart and Hussar* were so damaged that they sank; the *Salamander* had her stern wrecked, but the *Jason* was able to take her in tow as she was drifting dangerously near to the coast, which attracted gunfire from shore batteries. The *Colsay* had survived her attack

and was able to get under way after a short while. Several ships had responded to the signals from *Jason* and within a short while the *Gozo*, *Catherine* and *Pytchley* were on scene, and rendered assistance. The *Jason* lost two killed and the *Salamander*, *Colsay* and *Lord Ashfield* all had wounded. In all seventy-eight officers and ratings were killed and 149 were injured, many seriously. The *Salamander* was successfully towed to Portsmouth but was paid off. On investigation it was found that the attackers had been twelve Typhoon aircraft from 263 and 266 Squadrons that had been tasked to attack shipping that had been detected by shore radar. Flag Officer, British Assault Area (FOBAA), the senior naval authority in the area, indicated that they had no knowledge of any friendly forces in the area. A Spitfire was sent to identify the contacts, which reported that they appeared to be friendly minesweepers. Attempts to contact Captain (Minesweeping) failed as the telephone lines were down. Believing them to be hostile, a strike was ordered, and at 13.05 the Typhoons took off to carry out an attack. When they were on scene, the leader, Wing Commander Baldwin, was not convinced that the ships were hostile and asked for confirmation that the ships were hostile, and this was given. After the first attack the recognition flares were seen, and they again queried whether the ships were German, and were again assured they were. Three officers were subsequently court-martialled; Lieutenant Commander Robert Franks DSO, Staff Officer, Operations, at FOBAA, Captain the Lord Teynham, Captain (Minesweepers) and Commander Dennis Venables DSC, deputy to Teynham. It was found that Teynham was absent from his base on the day, and it was Venables who was the senior officer responsible for the movement of minesweepers. Venables had authorised the continued deployment of the minesweepers to the Fecamp area, and had detailed a junior officer, Lieutenant Edward Shaw, to inform the relevant authorities by signal. Shaw did so but missed out one important address from the signal – FOBAA – and this had not been noticed by Venables. Teynham was acquitted of any blame, but Venables was found guilty of negligence, and severely reprimanded. Lieutenant Commander Franks was accused of not making sufficient effort to contact Captain (Minesweepers) to confirm whether the area was clear, but he was acquitted.
[TNA: ADM. 1/30555; ADM. 156/212; ADM. 156/213]

BRITOMART minesweeper

Devonport 1938; 815 tons; 230ft × 33.6ft; 2 × 4in, 2 × 20mm
Lieutenant Commander Arthur James Galvin DSC RNR†
Britomart was the first of the ships to be attacked, being hit by rockets and cannon fire in the first pass of the Typhoons; the bridge took the full force and everyone on

the bridge was killed or seriously wounded. The bridge was wrecked, the funnel was blown away and the upper deck and sides were ripped up by the missiles. The ship lurched over to starboard and then rolled back to the upright before taking a 10 degree list to port. She started to settle quickly by the stern and a fire broke out below, with ready-use ammunition exploding. The steering gear was jammed, and she started to circle around to port. The engineer officer, Warrant Officer Grigson, bravely used an axe to hack through the LL or electric cable sweep wire, although still electrically live. She continued to heel over and settle by the stern and the order was given to abandon her. At 14.00 she capsized over to port and floated keel up for some time before she disappeared. Twenty men were killed. Her wreck has been found and lies in position 49.40.29N 00.06.77W

[www.halcyon-class.co.uk/FriendlyFire/hms_britomart.htm]

HUSSAR minesweeper

Woolston 1934; 815 tons; 230ft × 33.6ft; 2 × 4in,
2 × 20mm
Lieutenant John Robert Nash RNR

The second ship to be attacked, she also suffered badly by being raked by rocket and cannon fire, which wrecked the upper deck and penetrated the sides to explode in the engine room. She rolled over to port with the force of the assault, and did not recover, continuing to heel over to an angle of 45 degrees. A fierce fire broke out below decks and she was ordered to be abandoned. She was hit again during the second pass of the Typhoons, and an explosion speeded her demise as she sank by the stern, covered in smoke, her bows remaining clear of the water for several minutes before disappearing. Fifty-seven men died. Her wreck lies in position 49.40.85N 00.05.96W.

[www.halcyon-class.co.uk/FriendlyFire/hms_hussar.htm]

SALAMANDER minesweeper

Cowes 1936; 815 tons; 230ft × 33.6ft; 2 × 4in, 2 × 20mm
Lieutenant Commander Harold Graham King RNVR

As the attacks continued, Salamander increased speed and commenced a zigzag, and avoided the first strikes, with rockets exploding in the water alongside. An aircraft then hit the minesweeper with a salvo of rockets striking the stern, setting the minesweeping store on fire, and wrecking the steering gear and rudder. The after magazines were flooded as damage control parties tackled the blaze, which was controlled and then extinguished. Taken in tow by Jason initially for Arromanches, the damaged ship was later towed back to England, but was written off as a constructive total loss. Eleven men were wounded in the attack.

[www.halcyon-class.co.uk/FriendlyFire/hms_salamander.htm]

* * *

1 September HURST CASTLE corvette
Dundee 1944; 1,010 tons; 225ft × 36.8ft; 1 × 4in,
10 × 20mm
Lieutenant Harold Greeves Chesterman DSC RNR

In company with her sister Oxford Castle, she sailed from Londonderry during the evening of 30 August, to join Force 33, a group of corvettes and the destroyer Ambuscade, providing support for the passage of Convoy CU36. Following a torpedo attack on the convoy the group commenced a search, concentrating on the area to the north of Tory Island. At 08.25 in position 55.35N 08.11W, without warning, she was hit by a torpedo on the port side aft, an oil fuel tank taking the full blast. The after compartments rapidly flooded and very soon after the after engine room bulkhead collapsed. The ship took a list to port and settled by the stern. It was obvious that she was sinking and was ordered to be abandoned. The Carley floats were launched, but an attempt to lower the dinghy failed when it was swamped in the rising sea. The ship sank stern first, the bows rising vertically out of the water and hung for some minutes before disappearing. Ambuscade picked up 102 survivors, but seventeen men lost their lives. Her attacker had been U 482 (von Matuschka) which had fired a single homing torpedo at the group.
[TNA:ADM.267/117]

1 September MMS 117 minesweeper
Grimsby 1941; 225 tons; 105ft × 23ft
Lieutenant Commander George Edwin Johnson RNVR†

The harbour of Civitavecchia, Italy, was captured by the Allies in July 1944 and was believed to be clear of mines as several ships had used the port since that time. However, on 31 August there was a large underwater explosion in the harbour near the mole. This was believed to have been caused by a delayed-action mine, probably using a 50 or 80-day fuse. MMS 117 was ordered to carry out a sweep for magnetic and acoustic mines at first light on 1 September. Work commenced at 06.30 and she worked across the harbour without incident until at 11.40 there was an explosion in the middle of the Bacino Michelangelo. The explosion was under the stern, as they were under helm to starboard preparatory to starting another lap, and they were recovering the LL magnetic sweep lines. She sank rapidly by the stern, and despite several boats closing the area, only two survivors were picked up alive, but one of those later died of his injuries; seventeen men were lost. It was believed that a magnetic mine was responsible, probably having been 'cocked' by the first pass of the sweeper and then triggered by the second.
[TNA:ADM.199/253]

2 September GLEN AVON auxiliary anti-aircraft ship
Troon 1912 requisitioned 1939; 509 tons; 220ft × 27.1ft;
1 × 12pdr, 2 × 2pdr, 4 × 20mm
Lieutenant Commander Edward Terrise Symonds RNVR
A small paddle steamer, normally employed in sheltered waters, she was ordered to proceed to Arromanches, Normandy, for examination duties as a relief for the *Fratton*, sunk on 18 August (qv). On 2 September she was at anchor off Ver-sur-Mer light in poor weather, with strong winds which by 21.00 were a Force 8 gale and increasing. The ship was pitching and rolling deeply in the heavy swell, and shipping water. She was given permission to shift to a more sheltered position, but it was found to be impossible to weigh the anchor, the ship being driven by the storm over her anchor chain, forcing her bows down. At 21.30 water was reported entering the forward magazine and it was found the water was entering through the hawse pipes to flood the capstan flat and surrounding compartments. Despite plugging with hammocks, the water still came in, and with the pumps unable to cope, a human chain with buckets was organised. Tugs were called for and eventually distress rockets were fired as the ship heeled over in the wind. When a particularly strong squall hit her, she heeled over further, and the port sponson door burst open which allowed water to flood onto the main deck. The tug *Stormking* was now on scene and ran alongside and *MMS 266* was standing by, as the men were taken off. She continued to heel over until she was at 45 degrees and started to sink. She disappeared at 23.51. One officer and twelve men were drowned.
[TNA: ADM.199/1652]

5 September FAIRHAVEN drifter
Lymington 1919 (*Maelstrom*) requisitioned 1940; 96 tons;
87ft × 19.7ft
Employed at Reykjavik as a tender, she was damaged when she grounded, and was ordered to return to the UK. During the passage from Iceland several leaks became evident, and she was eventually abandoned in a sinking condition near the Westman islands, the crew being taken off by an armed whaler.
[http://www.harry-tates.org.uk/veteranstales35.htm]

12 September MGB 657 motor gun boat
St Helens 1943; 90 tons; 110ft × 21.3ft; 1 × 6pdr,
2 × 20mm
Lieutenant John Douglas Maitland, RCNVR
Conducting a night patrol along the Italian coast between Ancona and Rimini, when at 02.45 she detonated a mine. Her stern was blown off, the deck being peeled upwards, the gun being thrown forward to land on the petrol compartment and the after mess deck demolished. Despite the damage, she remained afloat. Her consorts *MGB 633* and *MGB 658* closed

and managed to rig a tow and they were able to return to Rimini by the afternoon. The damage was such that she was written off as a total loss. Three men were killed.
[TNA: ADM.267/123]

13 September MFV 1032 tender
Grimsby 1944; 114 tons; 69.3ft × 19.9ft
Foundered while under tow; no further details found, but she had been assigned to the Mediterranean, to act as a tender at Oran, having previously been stationed at Greenock.
[Statement of Losses p32; TNA: ADM.208/25]

14 September MMS 278 minesweeper
Peterhead 1942; 165 tons; 105ft × 23ft
Lieutenant Edward Harwood Batt RNVR
Ran aground at 12.00 on rocks at the entrance to the river Rance, near St Malo. Initial efforts to free her failed and she subsequently sank 7 cables (1,400 yards) off Moulin de la Roche. There were no casualties.
[TNA: ADM.199/1172; ADM.199/2301]

17 September MIRABELLE trawler
Aberdeen 1918 (*Edward Barker*) requisitioned 1939;
203 tons; 115.4ft × 22.1ft; 1 × 12pdr
Rammed at 17.55 by the merchant ship *Sampa* (7,219 tons), whilst laying alongside Tilbury Dock, causing so much damage that she subsequently sank.
[TNA: ADM.199/1440]

27 September ROCKINGHAM destroyer
Squantum 1919 (USS *Swasey*), loaned 1940; 1,190 tons;
309ft × 30.10ft; 1 × 4in, 1 × 3in, 5 × 20mm, 3 × torpedo tubes
Lieutenant Commander John Cecil Cooper RNVR
Ex-US Navy destroyer acquired by the Royal Navy under the Lend-Lease scheme and converted to a long-range escort, from 1943 she had been employed as a training/target vessel for the Fleet Air Arm. She sailed from Rosyth at 15.30 on 25 September to carry out range safety duties off RNAS Crail, patrolling between 56.28N and 56.43N at longitude 00.7W. The weather was poor and worsened preventing any flying, and at 20.08 on 26 September she was ordered to return. They set course to the west, but their position was uncertain, as no sun sights had been taken, and they were relying on bearings taken from a shore-based radio beacon. At 04.00 there was a loud explosion on the port side aft as she detonated a mine. The tiller flat immediately flooded, and it became clear that the port propeller had been lost and water was flooding into the engine room. Damage control got under way, with pumps set to work and bulkheads shored. At 05.00 she let go her starboard anchor and called for assistance. At 08.50 she slipped her cable and drifted, but although she was down by the stern,

she remained stable. Later that morning the destroyer *Lancaster* arrived on scene and made several attempts to connect a tow, which finally succeeded at 14.17. By mid-afternoon, several ships were in company, but the weather continued to worsen and was now blowing Force 8, and she was pitching and rolling deeply, and it was difficult to control the entry of water. At 16.35 the tow line parted and it was with considerable difficulty that the trawler *Robert Stroud* succeeded in passing a new line at 19.15. In the meantime, all non-essential personnel were evacuated to the ships standing by. When the tow line again parted, the destroyer *Vanity* placed herself alongside to lift off the remaining crew. She continued to settle until at 20.38 her bows rose out of the water and she sank stern first. The position was noted as 56.26N 00.21W. One man was lost in the explosion. An enquiry found that she had strayed into the defensive British minefield QZX604 due to navigational difficulties. The commanding officer was judged to have exercised poor judgement in electing to return to harbour, which involved passing through a narrow channel in a minefield, in poor weather and relying on beacon fixes.
[TNA: ADM.1/16150]

28 September ML 216 motor launch
Isleworth 1941; 65 tons; 112ft × 18.4ft; 1 × 3pdr
Sub-Lieutenant George Arthur Bailey RNVR
Entering the port of Ostend on 19 September, at 10.35 she was abreast the seaward end of the eastern pier and approximately 15 yards from it, when she detonated a mine. The entire fo'c'sle forward of the wheelhouse disappeared and there was widespread flooding of all compartments. She remained afloat and was taken in tow and run ashore. Compartments were pumped dry, and the surviving forward bulkhead shored up and on 21 September she was towed off the beach and anchored, preparatory to making the voyage back to England. The weather deteriorated and as she was making water, she was taken alongside the minesweeper *Postillion*, but in the heavy seas she sustained further damage as she bumped alongside, staving in the transom and damaging the starboard quarter. She was again pumped clear of water and temporary repairs made, and on 27 September she was taken in tow of the *Postillion*. The tow was a difficult one, the line parting on several occasions, but each time was reconnected, until at 05.45 on 28 September she took a lurch, rolled over and sank.
[TNA: ADM.199/153]

1 October MTB 360 motor torpedo boat
Teignmouth 1943; 44 tons; 72.7ft × 19.2ft; 1 × 20mm, 2 × torpedo tubes
Lieutenant Douglas Arthur Hall RNVR
Part of the 11th MTB Flotilla based at Lowestoft, *360* was in company with four other boats from the flotilla to carry out an offensive patrol in the southern North Sea. They sighted the Dutch coast at 20.43 and then turned to the south, staying about 7 miles off shore. At just before midnight on 30 September, a convoy was sighted, which appeared to consist of two or three merchant ships with a heavy escort of flak-lighters and armed trawlers. The boats split into divisions and spent an hour slowly manoeuvring to carry out an attack. *360* followed the leader, *MTB 349*, and successfully passed unseen through the screen of escorts to carry out a torpedo attack. As they did so they were seen, and a heavy fire was opened on them as they attempted to disengage at high speed to starboard, making smoke. As they did so *360* was hit repeatedly by small and heavy calibre shells which jammed her steering and started a fire on the bridge. When she received a further hit in the engine room, she lost power and as the fire was spreading, and it was clear that she was sinking, the crew abandoned her. Nine men were lost.
[Reynolds, Home Waters MTBs pp153–4; TNA: ADM.199/265]

1 October MTB 347 motor torpedo boat
Portchester 1943; 44 tons; 72.7ft × 19.2ft; 1 × 20mm, 2 × torpedo tubes
Lieutenant Alexander Dunlop Foster RNVR
Another of the units from the 11th MTB Flotilla, which carried out an attack on a convoy off the Dutch coast (see *MTB 360* above), she was in company with *MTB 350* which had separated from the other boats to act as a second division. After firing flares to create a distraction they commenced their own attack but were seen and came under heavy fire. *347* was hit almost immediately, with her torpedo tubes and bridge being damaged. She disengaged, altering course at speed to take her clear, but was hit again, this time by two large-calibre shells which struck her amidships, putting two of the engines out of action and blowing a hole in the bottom of the boat. Under her one remaining engine she managed to pull herself clear of the action but as it was clear that she was sinking, she was abandoned, all the crew taking to the Carley float, to be picked up by the other boats of the flotilla.
[Reynolds, Home Waters MTBs pp153–4; TNA: ADM.199/265]

(2/3) October LCT (3) 377 landing craft, tank
Meadowside 1942; 350 tons; 175ft × 31ft; 2 × 2pdr
Skipper Cecil Leonard Barber RNR[†]
On passage from Marseilles in the south of France to Maddalena in Sardinia, when she failed to arrive on 4 October it was presumed that she had been lost with all hands. A search aircraft reported sighting two halves of a landing craft about 25 miles to the south of the southern tip of Sardinia, but subsequent searches

were unsuccessful. It was presumed that she had either broken up due to stress of weather or had strayed into a minefield. Thirteen men were lost.

[TNA: ADM.199/2303; ADM.199/2304]

2 October LCT (3) 7084 landing craft, tank

Barrow 1944; 350 tons; 175ft × 31ft; 2 × 2pdr

In gale-force winds, 7084 was driven onto the beach about a mile to the east of the entrance to Ostend harbour. She then detonated a beach mine which caused serious damage, and no tow was available owing to the wind and surf. She was written off as a constructive total loss, although much of her stores were later salvaged.

[TNA: ADM.267/123]

4 October CHEBOGUE frigate

Esquimalt 1943; 1,370 tons; 283ft × 36.5ft; 2 × 4in, 10 × 20mm

Lieutenant Commander Maurice Faulkman Oliver RCNR

Royal Canadian Navy. Atlantic Convoy ONS33 departed Liverpool on 29 September for North America, with Escort Group C1, which included Chebogue providing the escort. At 22.05, in position 49.20N 24.20W, there was an explosion under the stern, when she was hit by an acoustic homing torpedo fired by U 1227 (Altmeier), which blew away the rudder, propellers and shafts, with part of the rudder landing on the fo'c'sle and going through the upper deck. It penetrated an oil fuel tank and finally came to rest on the ship's bottom. The after superstructure was wrecked and blown upwards with part of the upper deck forced forward over a gun mounting. There was immediate flooding of the stern compartments, and widespread shock damage from the blast. Although the stern was open to the sea, the bulkheads held, and the ship remained stable. A tow was rigged, and a succession of escorts towed her nearly 900 miles, before finally handing over to the tug Earner. Her troubles were not over. On 11 October, the pair arrived off the Mumbles, south Wales, in poor weather, and the tow parted. Chebogue anchored, but the weather deteriorated, with a strong south-westerly gale with regular squalls of rain. At around 17.00 it was found that the anchor was dragging, and she was blown across Swansea Bay and ran aground in the shallow waters off Port Talbot. The Mumbles lifeboat was called out, and in darkness and extreme weather conditions, the lifeboat ran alongside repeatedly to take off all the crew. The lifeboat coxswain was awarded the RNLI Gold Medal for his actions. The ship was later hauled free but was deemed irreparable and written off as a constructive total loss. Seven men were killed when she was torpedoed.

[TNA: ADM.267/117; ADM.1/16823; CB.4273 p284]

5 October BYMS 2255 minesweeper

Orange 1943; 215 tons; 130ft × 24ft; 1 × 3in, 2 × 20mm

Skipper-Lieutenant Sidney Spore RNR

Having been busily employed in sweeping along the northern French coast, at the beginning of October she was at Boulogne in company with several other minesweepers. During the day, the group had swept the approaches to the harbour and had also noted several moored mines near the southern breakwater but had been instructed to only mark them for future attention. At 17.30 the group entered harbour and anchored uneventfully, 2255 being positioned about 500 yards from the fort on the breakwater. At 21.15 without any warning there was a large explosion under the vessel, the engine room taking the full force of the detonation. The force of the blast lifted the port engine upwards through the upper deck and blew a large hole in the starboard side. She immediately took a sharp list to starboard and started to sink by the stern. In less than a minute the upper deck was awash the length of the starboard side. The men were quickly mustered and at 21.35 she was ordered to be abandoned, men taking to a small boat and Carley floats, the stern dipping under the surface as they did so. BYMS 2050, anchored nearby, had got underway and closed along with ML 450 which came alongside to lift off more survivors. As the last men left her, a fire broke out in the generator room. The smoking wreck lay on her side for some time until she finally disappeared under the water at 00.30. There were no casualties. The subsequent enquiry found that she had probably detonated an unswept contact mine as she swung round her anchor, probably one of those seen earlier, but which had been left.

[TNA: ADM.199/1652; Minett pp196–8]

5 October HDML 1227 motor launch

Sittingbourne 1942; 46 tons; 70ft × 15ft; 2 × 20mm

Sub-Lieutenant Douglas Spencer Cole RNVR

Having landed a patrol on Makronisi Island in the Aegean, as she moved back towards the island in the early hours of the morning, she encountered two large enemy torpedo boats, TA 38 and TA 39, which promptly engaged her. Outgunned, she was hit several times and set on fire. All the crew were picked up by their attackers. British MGBs saw the engagement at some distance and closed but found only burning wreckage and debris.

[TNA: ADM.199/889; Rohwer, Chronology of the War at Sea p360]

7 October VIDONIA trawler

Selby 1907 requisitioned 1940; 276 tons; 128ft × 22ft; 1 × 6pdr

Skipper Henry Greenwood RNR

Converted for use as a fuel carrier, she was laying at anchor off Utah Beach, Normandy. The weather was

poor, with strong winds, so it was decided on 6 October to move into deeper water and re-anchor. This was achieved, but it proved to be no safer, as at 05.15 she was rammed by the US Liberty ship *Jose Artigas* (14,245 tons). She was badly holed, and eventually broke up and sank about 20 minutes later. Eight men were lost.
[TNA:ADM.199/260]

7 October   HDML 1119   motor launch
Calcutta 1944; 46 tons; 70ft × 15ft; 1 × 2pdr
Royal Indian Navy. Part of the force supporting operations in Burma, she was laying at anchor in company with *HDML 1118* in the Naaf River off Maungdaw, when at 06.30, two Spitfire aircraft were sighted approaching from the south. To the surprise of both vessels, the aircraft then commenced a series of attacks, using cannon and machine guns. Both launches were damaged, and *1119* foundered, with the loss of one officer and four ratings killed. It was believed that the Spitfires, from Cox's Bazar, had mistaken the Naaf River for the Mayu, which was then still in Japanese hands.
[TNA:ADM.199/1438; https://www.ibiblio.org/hyperwar/UN/India/RIN/RIN-13.html]

8 October   MULGRAVE   minesweeper
Port Arthur 1942; 672 tons; 171.5ft × 28.5ft; 1 × 3in, 1 × 2pdr
Lieutenant Ralph Morton Meredith RCNR
Royal Canadian Navy. Engaged in sweeping off the north coast of France when an explosion occurred close off her starboard quarter as she detonated a mine. The ship was badly whipped by the blast, which stopped the main engines and jammed the rudder. The side plating was rippled, and several rivets sheared off. The engine room was evacuated due to steam escaping from damaged pipes and both boilers were shut down within 10 minutes. The ship came to a stop and the after compartments started to flood and this could not be tackled due to the lack of power. The ship was abandoned, but a tow was rigged, and the ship taken inshore to be run into shallow water near le Havre, where she beached. By then the quarterdeck was awash and the engine room full of water. She underwent temporary repairs, and on 3 November was towed to Portsmouth, but written off as a constructive total loss.
[TNA:ADM.267/135; CB.4273 p322]

8 October   BYMS 2030   minesweeper
New Bern 1942; 207 tons; 130ft × 24.6ft; 1 × 3in, 2 × 20mm
Skipper-Lieutenant Sidney Henderson Duffield RNR
In company with other BYMS sweeping for magnetic and acoustic mines at the entrance to the river Seine. At 15.32 a mine exploded under the stern of *2030*,

then being about 5 miles off Le Havre, in position 49.28N 00.02.12W. She began to settle by the stern and the other sweepers closed to take men off her before she rolled over and sank about 35 minutes after the explosion. Four men were injured but there were no deaths.
[TNA:ADM.199/253]

10 October   MGB 663   motor gun boat
Littlehampton 1943; 90 tons; 110ft × 21.3ft; 1 × 2pdr, 2 × 20mm
Lieutenant William Roy Darracott DSC* RNVR
Based in the Adriatic, she was in company with *MGB 649* and was returning to base at Vis after a night patrol off Venice when she ran over a mine, which exploded amidships. The force of the explosion blew the men off the bridge, including Lieutenant Darracott, who found himself 'doubled over a guard rail' and she rapidly sank. Three men were killed.
[Pope p246; Reynolds, Dog Boats p219]

12 October   LOYAL   destroyer
Greenock 1941; 1,920 tons; 345.5ft × 36.7ft; 6 × 4.7in, 4 × 2pdr, 2 × 20mm, 8 × torpedo tubes
Commander Godfrey Ransome
In company with her sister *Lookout*, the pair conducted a bombardment of the harbour at Cesenatico on the north-east coast of Italy. As the pair cleared the area, they were steaming at 20 knots when there was an explosion about 10 yards off the starboard side amidships. The hull plating was spilt, rivets were sheared or driven through the hull, and the upper deck was lifted slightly by the blast, which resulted in flooding of the engine and gearing rooms. The starboard after fuel tanks were ruptured, which led to surrounding compartments being flooded with oil and seawater. All steam and electrical power failed, and the ship heeled over to port. The ship came to a stop but remained stable, and damage control parties managed to stop the flooding. Taken in tow by *Lookout*, she was towed to Ancona initially, and later transferred to Taranto. Here, a survey confirmed the extent of the damage to the bottom plating, and she was paid off as being beyond repair.
[TNA:ADM.267/96; CB.4273 p265]

12 October   MMS 170   minesweeper
Par 1942; 225 tons; 105ft × 23ft
Lieutenant Robert Henry Frank Savage RNVR†
Taking part in a joint RN/RAF exercise designated 'Sparkle' off the island of Gorgona, she had sailed from Livorno at 19.30. The aim was to exercise the intercept of a convoy, using aircraft and coastal forces, with the minesweeper acting the part of the convoy. At 20.35 as the sweeper passed to the north of the

island of Gorgona there was an explosion under the port bow, and she sank bows–first in less than a minute. The twelve survivors managed to gain a Carley float and spent an uncomfortable night before being rescued. Seven men were killed. It was found that she had taken a route through a known minefield under the mistaken impression that it had been swept. Position noted as 43.30N 10.20E.
[TNA: ADM.199/253]

13 October HDML 1057 motor launch
Littlehampton 1941; 46 tons; 70ft × 15ft; 1 × 3pdr
Sub-Lieutenant Nigel John Snelson Carr RNR
Based at Mombasa, Kenya, she was carrying out a practice firing off Kilindini, in position 04.36S 39.35E, when an explosion occurred in the tiller flat, starting a fierce fire. She settled by the stern and in 2 minutes the bows had pitched up into a vertical position before sinking. One rating was lost. It was believed that the explosion had almost certainly been due to a detonation of demolition charges which were stored in the tiller flat. There was no proper storage for the charges, and they had been stowed covered with a tarpaulin, but would still have been subject to high temperatures.
[TNA: ADM.1/18921]

13 October LCT (5) 2454 landing craft, tank
Camden, 1944 (LCT 454); 143 tons; 105ft × 32.8ft;
2 × 20mm
Sub-Lieutenant Leonard William Hood RNVR[†]
Proceeding from Dartmouth to Rosyth, she sailed on 12 October in poor weather, and by the time they reached Lyme Bay, with the wind gusting to Force 9, no headway was being made at all. At 14.00 it was decided to anchor off Portland, but 2 hours later the cable parted and in a heavy sea she was taken inshore and driven onto Chesil Beach. With waves breaking over her, the craft started to break up and some men were washed overboard from the upper deck. The local Coastguard attended the scene and attempted to fire a line on board with rockets, but these were constantly blown away in the high winds or became fouled. Attempts were made by the Coastguards to carry a line to the wreck, but they failed, with the men being swept away in the surf. Two of the crew managed to get ashore over the stern before Coastguard Cyril George Brown managed to clamber up the side with a line around his waist, despite being battered by fierce winds and with seas washing over him. The line was secured on board and by this, another two men were hauled ashore. With no more crew evident, Mr Brown then had to jump overboard to make his own escape. Nine crewmen lost their lives, in addition to two members of the Coastguard who were drowned. Mr Brown was subsequently awarded the Stanhope Gold Medal for saving life and another two

of the Coastguard team were awarded Bronze Medals by the Royal Humane Society.
[TNA: ADM.199/1652; www.wykecoastguard.co.uk/about.php]

14 October MAGOG frigate
Montreal 1943; 1,370 tons; 283ft × 36.5ft; 2 × 4in,
10 × 20mm
Lieutenant Lewis Dennis Quick RCNR
Royal Canadian Navy. On 14 October Atlantic Convoy ONS33 arrived off Halifax, Nova Scotia, and several ships formed up into a new convoy, GONS33, for the Gulf of Mexico, for which Magog would be one of the escorts. At 19.25, in the Gulf of St Lawrence in position 49.12N 68.19W, without warning, there was an explosion under her stern. The force of the blast demolished about 60ft of the stern, and the rudder and propellers were lost. The engine room after bulkheads held and, apart from shock damage, the ship remained stable. Immobilised, she was taken in tow and run into shallow water near Quebec City where she was condemned as a constructive total loss. Three men were killed. Her attacker had been the U 1223 (Kniep), who had fired a pair of T5 acoustic homing torpedoes, one of which found Magog.
[TNA: ADM.267/118; CB.4273 p284]

14 October MFV 117 tender
Fareham 1943; 50 tons; 61.6ft × 17.8ft
Whilst proceeding from Dorema to Khios in the Aegean, she sank following an explosion, very probably a mine, off Pasha Island; four men were lost.
[TNA: ADM.199/889; ADM.199/1434]

15 October ML 870 motor launch
Cairo 1944; 73 tons; 112ft × 18.4ft; 1 × 3pdr
Lieutenant Joseph William John Cahill RNVR[†]
On 15 October Operation 'Manna' got underway, the landing of British forces in the area around Athens. The main difficulty was the minefields laid in the approaches to Piraeus. The main force was preceded by numerous minesweepers and initially the work to clear the way went well, but off Cape Turlo they found a very thickly laid field, with the Greek minesweepers, GYMS 2191 and GYMS 2074 both being lost to mines and the British minesweeper Larne damaged. Several motor launches, including 870 moved to the area, to assist with the sweep, but she also detonated a mine and sank, with the loss of three men.
[TNA; ADM.199/1434; Minett pp279–80]

15 October PETRONELLA water carrier
Glasgow 1927 requisitioned 1943; 2,770 tons;
305.3ft × 50.2ft
Part of the force assembled for Operation 'Manna', the occupation of Athens. Tasked to carry a full load

of fresh water to the city, she had been routed clear of the menace of the minefield off Cape Turlo (see above). She was off Cape Kalauri, near Poros, about 27 miles south of Pireaus when at about 11.00 she detonated a mine which exploded under her stern. She immediately developed a heavy list to starboard, and slowly rolled over to float bottom up before sinking. The whole episode took less than 3 minutes. Four of the ship's civilian officers, along with eleven Chinese crew and three British naval ratings, were lost in addition to seven soldiers on board.
[TNA: WO.361/747]

18 October   GEELONG   minesweeper
Williamstown 1941; 650 tons; 162ft × 31ft; 1 × 4in, 1 × 20mm
Lieutenant Maxwell Ernest Mathers RANR

Royal Australian Navy. On passage from Milne Bay to Madang, Papua New Guinea, the ship was darkened, and although the weather was good, failed to see the dimmed lights of the American tanker *York* (10,488 tons) approaching. The American ship only saw the warship when it was very close, and although putting engines astern and the helm over, she struck the *Geelong* on the port quarter. The minesweeper heeled over and started to sink. The tanker lowered lifeboats to assist, and all the crew were successfully evacuated before *Geelong* sank at 21.51. The position was noted as 006.4S 147.45E, to the north of Langemak, New Guinea. There were no casualties.
[Cassells p30]

18/19 October   Loss of six landing craft through stress of weather
On 14 October the first ships for Convoy OS92/KMS66 sailed from the Clyde bound for Freetown, joining others in the Irish Sea off Liverpool the following day. Among them were five merchant ships which were towing landing craft. The weather was poor and worsened, with gale-force winds and a heavy swell. By the 17th the landing craft were being thrown about with some violence, and over the next few hours six of the nine landing craft were lost.
[TNA ADM.1/16922; ADM.217/48]

LCT (3) 480   landing craft, tank
Meadowside 1943; 350 tons; 175ft × 31ft; 2 × 2pdr
Sub-Lieutenant George Pennell Sample RNVR

In the tow of the 7,063-ton *City of Lyons* she had an uncomfortable time, and at 10.00 on the 18th she shipped a big sea which broke the securing strops for the barrels and stores on the tank deck. These tumbled out and rolled around, and it proved impossible to resecure all of them. It was also found that the welds around the bow doors were failing due to the constant

pounding, allowing water to enter. With the tank deck filling with water, repeated efforts were made to contact the *City of Lyons* to tell her to heave to, but she failed to respond. By 16.00 she had 7ft of water in the tank deck and the pumps could not cope. She then heeled over to port and remained in the position, but still under power. Soon after this the *Lyons* heaved to, and the landing craft managed to claw herself alongside her quarter. Heaving lines were repeatedly thrown, but could not be secured, and the *Lyons* eventually sheered off. It was then decided to abandon her, taking to the Carley floats and the men had to endure several uncomfortable hours until the *Allington Castle* picked them up at 22.00.

LCT (3) 488   landing craft, tank
Old Kilpatrick 1943; 350 tons; 175ft × 31ft; 2 × 2pdr
Sub-Lieutenant Arthur Paul Philip Thomas RNVR[†]

Towed by the 7,243-ton *Samfoyle* along with *LCT 489*, she suffered badly during the night of 17/18 October, with several barrels breaking free on the tank deck. The galley funnel was carried away and the mast was dislodged, and in the constant pounding she was shipping a lot of water. At 10.00 on the 18th her tow was slipped, and she got under way under own power, but had great difficulty in manoeuvring. It was found that not only were the seas breaking over her, but the welds around the hatch coamings were parting allowing even more water to enter. When the forward pump failed, it became doubtful that they could survive. The frigate *Knaresborough Castle* closed, and an attempt was made to abandon her. Carley floats were lowered but they drifted onto the weather side of the landing craft and several men were forced to scramble back onboard, but the frigate did manage to pick up others. She urged those onboard to jump across, but this was refused as being too dangerous. The remaining crew, three officers and seven men, spent an uncomfortable night onboard, using buckets and hand pumps to try and keep the water under control. Despite their efforts, by 04.15 the tank space was full of water and it was impossible to handle her. She fired red flares and the frigate closed. However, as they did so the landing craft was seen to take a big sea on the beam and she rolled over and sank, stern first, her bows pointing skywards. The *Knaresborough Castle* could find only one man alive in the water, nine men being drowned.

LCT (3) 491   landing craft, tank
Old Kilpatrick 1943; 350 tons; 175ft × 31ft; 2 × 2pdr
Lieutenant William Colin Gray RNVR

Under tow of the 7,134-ton *Fort Finlay*, she initially found the conditions uncomfortable but bearable. This changed during the afternoon of the 18th when the tow was slipped, without warning, along with another landing craft, *LCT 7015*. She struggled on under her own power for some time until at 15.00 she shipped a big sea over the bow door, and this fractured the welding around the doors. Several bigger seas followed, and the tank deck was flooded. She took a bows-down attitude and swung broadside-on to the sea as the port engine stopped. She lay in this position for some time with spray and seas breaking over her, with loose barrels and other objects being tossed about. At 01.00 the frigate *Allington Castle* came into sight and closed to stand by her, urging her crew to hang until daylight. However, at 03.30 she was clearly sinking so the frigate initially attempted to pass a Carley float with a line attached to the landing craft, but this was too difficult. It was decided that there was no alternative but to run alongside. Despite both ships being thrown about by the sea, this was done, all the crew jumping across to the heaving deck of the frigate. One stoker was found to be very drunk and had to be unceremoniously hauled across. This complete, the *Allington Castle* fired several rounds into the craft followed by a pattern of Squid mortars to ensure that she sank. Lieutenant Phillip Read, commanding officer of the frigate, was later praised for his skilful ship handling.

LCT (3) 494 landing craft, tank
Old Kilpatrick 1943; 350 tons; 175ft × 31ft; 2 × 2pdr
Lieutenant John Murts RNVR†
Being towed by the *Nairnbank* (5,156 tons), she parted her tow at 08.45 on the morning of 18 October but was evidently able to proceed under her own power, although clearly in distress. She was last seen during the afternoon and disappeared in the evening. All seventeen men on board were lost.

LCT (3) 7014 landing craft, tank
Meadowside 1943; 350 tons; 175ft × 31ft; 2 × 2pdr
Sub-Lieutenant James Farrell RNVR†
The second craft in tow of the *Nairnbank*, the tow parted during the morning of 18 October, but the main engines had been started successfully and she attempted to steer inshore. However, she pounded heavily in the high seas and by noon power had been lost and as she was wallowing, she was abandoned in a sinking condition. Some men were picked up by the rescue ship *Dundee*, but nine men lost their lives.

LCT (3) 7015 landing craft, tank
Meadowside 1943; 350 tons; 175ft × 31ft; 2 × 2pdr
Sub-Lieutenant Dennis Henry Condick RNVR†
In tow of the *Fort Finlay* (7,130 tons) she was labouring heavily when she was cast off at 15.00 on the afternoon of the 18th and disappeared; all eighteen men on board lost their lives.

★ ★ ★

24 October LCT (4) 943 landing craft, tank
Middlesbrough 1943; 200 tons; 171ft × 38.8ft
As she headed back for Portsmouth from the Normandy beaches, the craft encountered poor weather, and she laboured heavily. At 00.50 she reported that she was in danger of breaking up, then being about 19 miles east of St Catherine's Point. The merchant vessel *Arthur Sewell* stood by her and managed to lift off the crew, whilst the tug *St Mellons* arrived, intending to take the craft in tow. However, *943* broke in half, and the tug could only secure the stern section, which was towed into Spithead. The destroyer *Vanquisher* found the forward half and sank it with gunfire.
[TNA: ADM.199/1396]

24 October LCT (4) 1171 landing craft, tank
Old Kilpatrick 1944; 200 tons; 171ft × 38.8ft
Sub-Lieutenant Ronald Stewart Park RNVR
Sailed from Utah Beach during the afternoon of 23 October for Portland, with a load of marine engines, the weather steadily deteriorated during the passage until it was blowing a full gale. The ship strained in the heavy swell and splits started to appear in the hull. At 23.00 the ship broke in half, with about 100ft of the bow floating away. *LCT 929* managed to manoeuvre alongside and despite the treacherous conditions lifted off the crew and rigged a tow to the remaining stern half. The tow eventually parted and at 02.00 she was abandoned in a sinking condition, then being about 18 miles south-west of the Isle of Wight. The destroyer *Vesper* found the forward part and sank it with gunfire.
[TNA: ADM.199/1652; ADM.199/1396; info from survivor Austin Prosser on: http://www.combinedops.com/My_World_War.htm]

25 October SKEENA destroyer
Woolston 1930; 1,337 tons; 309ft × 32.3ft; 4 × 4.7in, 1 × 12pdr, 2 × 20mm, 4 × torpedo tubes
Lieutenant Commander Patrick Francis Xavier Russell RCN
Royal Canadian Navy. Part of the 11th Canadian Escort Group, in storm force conditions in the North Atlantic, the ships sought shelter at Reykjavik for the night. Ordered to anchor off Videy Island, this caused some concern onboard *Skeena*, as it was known that the ground was a poor holding ground, being loose volcanic ash. Nevertheless, they anchored, but paid out with extended cable to give extra weight on the bottom. Constant checks on bearings of points ashore were ordered. The weather during the night became worse, with high winds and regular flurries of snow and hail, obscuring visibility. In the early hours it was noted that the bearings were changing, indicating that they were dragging the anchor. Half ahead was ordered on both engines, but when this did not seem to have any

effect, full speed ahead was ordered. Soon after this the ship shuddered as she touched the ground, then swung round onto rocks, with a list to starboard. Assistance was requested from shore and the ship's company ordered onto the upper deck. There then followed some confusion, as Carley floats were ordered to be dropped as a precaution but were to remain secured to the ship. This was to be in preparation for the ship to be abandoned, but in the confusion, some men thought that the order to abandon had been given and jumped overboard. Three of the floats had their securing lines either cut or parted and were swept away into the night. At 03.00, two landing craft approached but could not get near the stranded vessel. Finally, a party was put onto the island, and a gunline was successfully fired from the ship to shore, to which a Carley float was attached, and the men ferried ashore. Inspection of the ship in calmer weather showed that her bottom was pierced in several places, and she was written off as a constructive total loss. Fifteen men died either from drowning or exposure.

[McKee & Darlington p189]

25 October LCT (4) 1045 landing craft, tank
Meadowside 1944; 200 tons; 171ft × 38.8ft
Sub-Lieutenant Alexander Charles Liddle RNVR
In a poor state after being in constant use on the Normandy beaches, by October it was decided to return to UK, and after being made ready for towing, on 23 October she left the Utah Beach anchorage in tow of LCT 1015. Almost immediately she started making water, and by 08.00 the next morning both the engine room and mess decks were flooding. The weather was poor and deteriorating and it was decided to turn back and headed to Utah anchorage. The tug Empire Winnie arrived at first light on the 25th and the US Army tug ST-740 joined to stand by them, taking off the crew. The landing craft continued to settle until the quarterdeck was awash, and at 19.15 when about 2 miles off the French coast she broke in half and sank.
[TNA: ADM.199/1652]

25 October BYMS 2077 minesweeper
Whitestone 1943; 207 tons; 130ft × 24.6ft; 1 × 3in, 2 × 20mm
Lieutenant Commander Frederick James Call RNR[†]
In company with BYMS 2020, part of a group of Aegean-based minesweepers that had been busily employed sweeping Greek coastal waters and was ordered to deploy from Patras into the Gulf of Corinth. When in position 38.20N 22E there was a large explosion under 2077 as she unexpectedly triggered a mine, and she broke up and sank very quickly. There were seven survivors and twenty dead.
[Minett p282]

30 October LCT (4) 936 landing craft, tank
Middlesbrough 1943; 200 tons; 171ft × 38.8ft
Whilst in convoy from Harwich to Lowestoft, she broke her back through stress of weather and was abandoned in a sinking condition. The tug Diversion was despatched but was unable to assist before the wreck went ashore at 17.30 about half a mile south of Pakefield Cliffs and broke up.
[TNA: ADM.199/1440; ADM.199/2304]

1 November Operation 'Infatuate' – landings at Walcheren
In order to clear the river Scheldt of the enemy and open the waterway to Antwerp, a landing on the island of Walcheren at the mouth of the West Scheldt was devised. As well as a direct assault from the mainland, amphibious landings were made on the western and southern ends of the island. The defences were strong, well manned and alerted, and the attackers met very stiff resistance.

LCF 37 landing craft, flak
Middlesbrough 1943; 415 tons; 171ft × 38.9ft; 4 × 2pdr, 8 × 20mm
Lieutenant Commander George Leslie Carlton RNVR
Leading ship of a group of three flak ships, she closed the beach until she was about 1 mile off the shore, and had commenced engaging shore positions, when at 09.00 she was hit by a heavy shell which brought her to a stop. She was subsequently hit another four times, killing thirty-five marines and seven of the RN crew. The last shell that hit her evidently detonated her magazine, as there was a large explosion, throwing debris far into the air. When the smoke cleared, the upper works had disappeared, and the wreck was filled with smoke and sinking, and she was abandoned by the survivors.
[TNA: ADM.199/186; ADM.199/1652]

LCF 38 landing craft, flak
Middlesbrough 1943; 415 tons; 171ft × 38.9ft; 4 × 2pdr, 8 × 20mm
Lieutenant Alfred George Whittington Wilkes RNVR
She took up position off Westkappelle and was busily employed off the beaches engaging shore positions, when at 09.45 she was struck by a large shell on the waterline. A few moments later a second shell hit the starboard gun position and she was then hit repeatedly as she lost power. With her wheelhouse smashed, steering jammed and a fire started, LCF 36 closed to tow her out of range, but she was still being hit and was filling with water. LCF 36 came alongside to take off the survivors before she blew up and sank. Five men were killed.
[TNA: ADM.199/176; ADM.199/1652]

LCG (L) 1   landing craft, gun, large
Meadowside 1942; 491 tons; 175ft × 31ft; 2 × 4.7in,
5 × 20mm
Lieutenant Arthur Hunter Ballard RNVR
Bombarding targets onshore, she was about 1,000 yards from the shoreline when hit on the water line by a heavy shell. Soon after this she was hit for a second time, on the port bow, and she started to sink. Hit by another two shells, one of which detonated a ready-use locker which started fires. She was now being hit repeatedly, the bridge being demolished, wounding the commanding officer. With all the guns out of action, all the officers wounded and the fuel pipes severed she drifted away from the assault area. An attempt was made by *LCG(L) 17* to take her in tow, but this failed, and she foundered. Two men were killed and twenty wounded.
[TNA: ADM.1991/86; Lund & Ludlam, War of the Landing Craft p206]

LCG (L) 2   landing craft, gun, large
Middlesbrough 1942; 491 tons; 175ft × 31ft; 2 × 4.7in,
5 × 20mm
Lieutenant Arthur Cheney RNVR
Closed to within 500 yards of the beach and despite being hit by three stray rockets fired from other landing craft was able to engage a large gun emplacement, coming under heavy fire as she did. She eventually received a hit in the engine room from a large shell, and with water entering, she turned out to seawards. The engines stopped when about 2,000 yards off shore, and she started to drift back towards the shore, but *LCT 789* approached and after securing herself alongside, started to haul her clear. All this time, she was still being constantly shelled and was returning the fire when she could. As they were clearing the danger zone, she detonated a mine which exploded amidships and brought her to a halt, and moments later she drifted down onto another mine, after which she went down very quickly. Six men were lost.
[TNA: ADM.199/1652; Lund & Ludlam, War of the Landing Craft pp206–07]

LCG (M) 101   landing craft, gun, medium
Middlesbrough 1944; 270 tons; × 154.6ft × 22.4ft;
2 × 17pdr, 2 × 20mm
Lieutenant George Alexander Flamank RNVR
Designed to be run into shallow water and fire from reported map references, two LCG(M)s were employed at Walcheren. *101* ran in towards her target, but when 2 miles offshore she came under heavy fire from the shore batteries. She continued to close until by 09.40 she was close inshore and engaged a fortified pillbox, but under constant fire and was hit repeatedly. At 09.50 with casualties mounting, and several guns out of action, it was decided to withdraw, and still being hit

she managed to haul herself clear with a kedge anchor, although one officer and one rating were killed doing so. She reached deep water, but steadily settled and finally sank.
[TNA: ADM.199/1652; Lund & Ludlam, War of the Landing Craft pp205–06]

LCG (M) 102   landing craft, gun, medium
Middlesbrough 1944; 270 tons; × 154.6ft × 22.4ft;
2 × 17pdr, 2 × 20mm
Lieutenant Donald Ralph Victor Flory RNVR†
Ran in close to the shore and engaged a large pillbox but was hit repeatedly by heavy shells and was seen to be on fire. The crew got the fire under control and continued to engage, but after being hit once more the fire broke out again and she drifted ashore where she burnt out. Thirty-two men were killed.
[TNA: ADM.358/3277; Lund & Ludlam, War of the Landing Craft p205]

LCT (4) 789   landing craft, tank
Meadowside 1943; 200 tons; 171ft × 38.8ft
Lieutenant John Phillipson RNVR
LCT 789 assisted *LCG (L) 2* after she had been damaged by shellfire (see above) and managed to secure herself alongside and then hauled her out of fire. However, as they reached the collecting area clear of the beaches, *LCG(L) 2* detonated another mine which caused considerable shock damage to *LCT 789* which drifted clear. She drifted out of control until she collided with *LCT 461* and then there was a further explosion under *789* as she touched another mine before sinking.
[TNA: WO.205/865A]

LCT (4) 839   landing craft, tank
Old Kilpatrick 1943; 200 tons; 171ft × 38.8ft
Sub-Lieutenant William Kennedy Stead RNVR
Fully loaded with troops and their equipment, she beached herself to discharge her cargo. At 10.20 as she went astern to clear the beach, she was hit by a heavy shell in the engine room and was then hit repeatedly as she steamed clear which started fires and she started to sink. By 11.45 the fires were spreading, and she was clearly sinking and was abandoned, then being about 2 miles offshore.
[TNA: ADM.199/186; ADM.199/1652]

LCT (4) 1133   landing craft, tank
Middlesbrough 1944; 200 tons; 171ft × 38.8ft
Sub-Lieutenant Denis Henry Till RNVR
She successfully made the beach, but as she did so was hit by a large-calibre shell, which caused several casualties. Despite this she landed her cargo and then cleared the beach, to make for *LCT 461* which was acting as a hospital ship. Having transferred her wounded, she was

drawing away when she detonated a mine and rolled over and sank. An LCI(L) picked up the survivors, but two men died.
[TNA: ADM.199/1652]

LCT (3) 7011 landing craft, tank
Meadowside 1944; 625 tons; 175ft × 31ft; 2 × 20mm
Sub-Lieutenant George Scales RNVR
At 10.05, as she approached the beach, she detonated a mine, rolled over and rapidly sank.
[TNA: ADM.199/1652; WO.361/750]

LCS (L) 252 landing craft, support (large)
Sarisbury Green 1944; 112 tons; 105ft × 21.6ft; 1 × 4in, 1 × 6pdr, 2 × 20mm
Lieutenant Sidney Nielsen Orum RNVR[†]
Successfully ran onto the beach despite being hit several times by heavy shells and was seen to be on fire at 10.00. She attempted to pull clear but sank at 10.25 after being hit repeatedly by shore batteries; thirty men were killed.
[TNA :ADM.358/2627]

LCS (L) 256 landing craft, support (large)
Maldon 1944; 112 tons; 105ft × 21.6ft; 1 × 4in, 1 × 6pdr, 2 × 20mm
Lieutenant Douglas Frederick Maurice Sexton RNVR[†]
As she ran into the beach, she was hit by shore fire, one of the first shells hitting the bridge, killing both the commanding and executive officers. By 09.45 all her guns were out of action and her steering gear out of order. She was abandoned at 10.15, then being about 200 yards off the beach. Eleven men were lost.
[TNA: ADM.199/1652]

LCS (L) 258 landing craft, support (large)
Sarisbury Green; 112 tons; 105ft × 21.6ft; 1 × 4in, 1 × 6pdr, 2 × 20mm
Sub-Lieutenant Hubert Wills Woodnoth RNVR[†]
Repeatedly hit by heavy shellfire as she approached the beach, she was set on fire and foundered just off the shoreline at 10.25. Twenty-four men killed.
[TNA: ADM.358/2627]

LCI (S) 532 landing craft, infantry, small
Lowestoft 1943; 63 tons; 100ft × 21.6ft; 2 × 20mm
Lieutenant Kenneth Burnard Wright RANVR
At 10.00 ran ashore at West Capelle and successfully discharged her troops. Whilst she was lying on the beach, she was struck by two shells. She was moved off the beach, but when about a mile offshore the starboard petrol tank, damaged by the earlier hit, exploded and she caught fire. She was abandoned and sank.
[TNA ADM.199/176]

1 November WHITAKER frigate
Hingham 1943; 1,300 tons; 300ft × 36.7ft; 3 × 3in, 8 × 20mm
Lieutenant Glynn Percy Watkin Edwards[†]
Part of the escort to Convoy SC159, which had sailed from Halifax on 18 October, bound for Liverpool, the ships were off Malin Head, approaching the Clyde when at 02.07 there was a large explosion in the fore end of the ship. This was followed a few seconds later by another explosion of considerably greater violence than the first. The forward part of the ship before the bridge disappeared, and the upper deck as far as the funnel was blown up and over the superstructure. The bridge, forward boiler room and surrounding compartments were wrecked, and there was widespread shock damage caused by the blast. A fire broke out near the funnel caused by burning fuel oil. The *Gore* closed to render assistance, as did the convoy rescue ship *Aboyne*. The fire was extinguished and bulkheads were shored, and the ship remained stable, which allowed a tow to be rigged, initially by *Gore*, later taken over by the tug *Earner*, and the ship was towed into Moville, County Donegal. Later moved to Belfast, the damage was so extensive that she was declared a constructive total loss. Eight officers and eighty-four members of the crew were killed. There was some uncertainty at the time for the cause of the explosion, and a floating mine was thought possible. It was later determined that the convoy had been attacked by *U 483* (von Morstein), which had fired two pattern-running FAT torpedoes, one of which had hit *Whitaker*. The second explosion was probably due to the detonation of the forward magazine, used to hold cordite and propellant for the Hedgehog anti-submarine mortars.
[TNA: ADM.267/135; CB.4273 p286]

2 November COLSAY trawler
Beverley 1943; 545 tons; 150ft × 27.6ft; 1 × 4in
Lieutenant John Henry Lloyd Sulman DSC RNVR[†]
Part of the First Minesweeping Flotilla, she had survived an attack by friendly aircraft on 27 August (q.v.) and after repairs had rejoined the flotilla to continue the work of sweeping the French and Belgian coasts of mines. On completion of a day's sweeping, the flotilla anchored at the western end of Ostend outer anchorage. At 00.48 without any warning there was a large explosion and the ship disintegrated. Her consorts lowered boats to go to the scene but found only one survivor in the debris and wreckage. Thirty-six men were lost. It was presumed that she had been torpedoed, possibly as a result of an attack or by a *Neger* or *Biber* midget submarine. The wreck lies in position 51.14.48N 02.47.51E.
[TNA: ADM.199/1652]

★ ★ ★

3 November LCT (4) 976 landing craft, tank
Bo'ness 1943; 200 tons; 171ft × 38.8ft
Lieutenant James Mark Boyle RNVR
Sailed from Ostend and joined a convoy for Southampton, the weather was poor and worsened as she progressed, labouring in the heavy seas. At 21.25 she broke her back. The engines were stopped as she settled and by 22.00 her bows were under water and the crew was taken off by *LCT 944*.
Note: the *Statement of Losses* gives the incorrect loss date as 7 November
[TNA: WO.205/865A]

4 November SUPPORTER drifter
Lowestoft 1914 requisitioned 1939; 88 tons; 84.6ft × 19.1ft
Chief Skipper William Smith RNR
The drifter ran aground off Newhaven and subsequently foundered, the crew all being taken off by the Newhaven lifeboat.
[TNA: ADM.199/2305]

5 November LCT (4) 1002 landing craft, tank
Chepstow 1944; 586 tons; 171ft × 38.7ft
Lieutenant Wilfred Joseph Kernutt RNVR
Having been worked hard on the beaches of northern France, *1002* was in a poor material state; both rudders had gone, her propellers were damaged, seams had opened, and she was constantly making water. She was prepared for towing and on 3 November *LCT 1077* started to tow her back across the Channel. Progress was slow, and the pumps were in constant use, but by the morning of 5 November she had 6ft of water in the engine room and had developed a list. The tug *Empire Harry* arrived to take over the tow, removing the crew for their own safety at the same time, as it was feared that she could founder at any moment. She was taken inshore and was run into shallow water at Cracknore Hard, Southampton where she was subsequently written off as a constructive total loss.
[TNA: ADM.199/1652]

5 November LCT (R) 457 landing craft, tank (rocket)
Meadowside 1943; 350 tons; 175ft × 31ft; 2 × 20mm, multiple rocket launchers
Lieutenant Maurice Tedcastle RNVR†
The craft sailed from Ostend at 16.00 on 4 November to make the return journey to England in company with several landing craft and supply ships. The weather was poor, and the amphibious craft were making heavy weather of it, and later that evening they were ordered to return to the anchorage off Ostend. The following morning, she got underway, the last ship in a group, but at 10.30, then being about 13 miles to the north-west of Ostend there was an explosion under the engine room as she detonated a mine. She rapidly broke up and had

disappeared in 15 minutes. Position noted as 51.24.8N 02.44E. Twenty-four men were killed.
[TNA: ADM.199/1652; ADM.267/124]

6 November LCT (4) 609 landing craft, tank
Meadowside 1943; 200 tons; 171ft × 38.8ft
Sub-Lieutenant James Rae Halliday RNVR
In the same convoy as *LCT 457* (see above), the landing craft laboured in the heavy seas, and when the starboard engine became defective *LCT 960* took her in tow. This parted twice but, on each occasion, it was re-secured in difficult conditions. Water was now entering at numerous points and the hold was flooding freely. When the tow parted for a third time at 14.30, she was abandoned in position 51.20N 02.52E in a sinking condition.
[TNA: WO.205/865A]

7 November LST 420 landing ship, tank
Baltimore 1942; 1,625 tons; 316ft × 50ft; 1 × 12pdr; 6 × 20mm
Lieutenant Commander Douglas Harold Everett RNR†
One of a convoy of five tank landing ships that sailed from Southend bound for Ostend, *420* was carrying an RAF base signals and radar unit. The weather was poor and steadily deteriorated, until it was blowing a Force 7 to 8 with heavy seas. Arriving off Ostend, they were advised that due to the poor weather conditions, they could not enter, and so headed for the Downs to take shelter. As they headed across the Channel they pitched and rolled heavily, and vehicle lashings had to be tightened to prevent them moving. At 15.20 when off the Middle Kerke bank, in position 51.17.44N 02.41.40E, as she was approaching OD2 buoy, there was a large explosion under *420* as she hit a mine. A second explosion occurred, probably as petrol fumes ignited. All power was lost, and she settled quickly and as the stern lifted clear of the water she broke in half, with fire breaking out in both halves before sinking. The other LSTs closed to give assistance and picked up several survivors struggling in the water with difficulty in the high seas, but fifty-five men were lost.
[TNA: ADM.199/253; WO.361/741; MacDermott p81]

8 November ML 916 motor launch
Cockenzie 1944; 85 tons; 112ft × 18.3ft; 1 × 3pdr
Lieutenant George Gordon MacPherson RNVR
Attached to the 19th Minesweeping Flotilla, the group were employed in clearing the river Scheldt and the approaches to Antwerp of mines. At 10.20 a group of five vessels, with *916* the second in line, were sweeping in line ahead, using single Oropesa sweeps alternately to port and starboard, when there was a large explosion under *916* and she quickly foundered. She was then off

Magere Merrieschor, near Walsoorden. Nineteen men were killed.
[TNA: ADM.199/253]

8 November LCT (3) 469 landing craft, tank
Meadowside 1943; 350 tons; 175ft × 31ft; 2 × 2pdr
Lieutenant David Neville Wilfred Witts RNVR
Attempting to return to England from Ostend in poor weather, she lost power, drifted and filled with water before being abandoned off West Kapelle, Walcheren Island.
[TNA: ADM.358/3277]

10 November HYDRA minesweeper
Renfrew 1942; 850 tons; 212.5ft × 35.6ft; 1 × 4in, 8 × 20mm
Lieutenant Commander Charles Thomas Jegon Wellard, RNR
In company with other ships of the 18th Minesweeping Flotilla, *Hydra* was tasked to clear the approaches to Ostend and was steaming at 8 knots when a mine detonated on the starboard side under the after boiler room. A 6ft hole was blown in the bottom, and the outer plating was forced inboard for 35ft. Both after and forward boiler rooms flooded, and the ship heeled over to port. All power was lost, and the ship was ordered to be abandoned as it was feared that she was about to sink, but when it became clear that she was stable, a party returned onboard and a tow rigged. Towed back to Sheerness, a survey confirmed that the damage was extensive, and she was declared a constructive total loss. Six men were killed.
[TNA: ADM.1/18913; CB.4273 p325]

12 November MARLEAN channel patrol boat
Sydney 1938 requisitioned 1942; 30 tons; 70ft × 15ft
Lieutenant Harry John Courtney RANVR
Royal Australian Navy. Employed as a local patrol vessel, she was a tender to the shore establishment at Garden Island, Sydney. She caught fire and was burnt out in Sydney Harbour. There were no casualties.
[Cassells p38]

14 November LCT (4) 1359 landing craft, tank
Alloa 1944; 200 tons; 171ft × 38.3ft
Driven ashore in Kirkcaldy Bay in very stormy weather, the entire crew of thirteen were rescued by breeches buoy from the shore.
[TNA: ADM.199/1391]

16 November LCT (3) 7094 landing craft, tank
Walker 1944; 350 tons; 175ft × 31ft
On 8 November, in poor weather she swung broadside on to the beach and broached at West Kapelle, Walcheren Island, and was subsequently written off as a total loss.
[TNA: ADM.358/3277; WSS Warship Supplement 185.41]

17 November LCT (4) 856 landing craft, tank
Alloa 1943; 200 tons; 171ft × 38.8ft
Lieutenant Shirley Carr Smith RNVR
Attempting to return to England from northern France, she encountered very heavy seas and strong winds. At 08.40, when the craft was 12 miles south of the Nab Tower off Portsmouth, she broke in half. The destroyer *Vidette* came to her aid and managed to tow the stern half into Spithead, but the forward part was driven ashore at Selsey Bill.
[TNA: ADM.199/1396]

17 November LCT (4) 1022 landing craft, tank
Thornaby 1944; 200 tons; 171ft × 38.8ft
Driven ashore in poor weather at Galloways Lookout, Lydd, the ship swinging broadside to at high water. The craft was surveyed and found to be in poor condition, with the port side buried into the shingle to a depth of 6ft. She was written off as a total loss, being stripped of useable fittings where she lay.
[TNA: ADM.199/2306]

18 November TRANSVAAL trawler
Selby 1917 requisitioned 1939; 125.3ft × 22.5ft
Skipper Thomas Threlfall RNVR†
Part of the escort to cross-Channel Convoy EBC38 the ships were affected by a storm as they left the English coast, and during the late afternoon turned back inshore to take shelter in Torbay. The *Transvaal* was last seen at 02.30 about 6 miles to the south-west of Portland, and when first light revealed that she was not with the other ships in Torbay, it was presumed that she had gone into Portland, but this was found not to be the case. At 07.30 the American Liberty ship *Charles Henderson* reported that she had earlier seen a ship in distress in position 49.48W 03.32W, but was unable to help, due to the high seas. The destroyer *Brissenden* and frigate *Annan* were sailed to carry out a search but found nothing. On the morning of 21 November, the frigate *Bayntun* recovered the bodies of four men, identified as ratings from the *Transvaal*. Nineteen men were lost.
[TNA: ADM.199/1394]

20 November ML 827 motor launch
Brisbane 1944; 85 tons; 112ft × 18.3ft; 1 × 2pdr
Lieutenant Ian Fairley Graham Downs RANVR
Royal Australian Navy. Based at Port Moresby, New Guinea, she was deployed to New Britain, to support the re-occupation of the island. On 17 November she ran aground in Jacquinot Bay and was damaged. Taken in tow by a salvage tug, she capsized and sank 3 days later off Cape Kawai.
[Cassells p41]

22 November STRATAGEM submarine
Birkenhead 1943; 715/990 tons; 201ft × 23.9ft; 1 × 3in,
7 × torpedo tubes
Lieutenant Clifford Raymond Pelly DSC[†]
Based at Trincomalee she sailed on 10 November for a patrol in the Malacca Straits. At 08.30 on 22 November, she was 3 miles south-west of Malacca when her periscope was sighted by a patrolling Japanese aircraft, and the submarine chaser *CH.35* began a search of the area. At 12.10 the chaser evidently gained sight of her periscope in the flat calm sea and running over her position carried out a depth-charge attack. One charge exploded under her stern and another close amidships, these shattered fittings and made splits in the hull, allowing water to flood in with some considerable force. She took a pronounced bow-down attitude and plummeted downwards until she struck the seabed with some force. Main ballast tanks were blown but had no effect. With the submarine rapidly flooding desperate efforts were made to don escape apparatus and clear access to the escape hatches, but the only group that seems to have escaped came from the forward compartment. As the clips were released the pressure inside the submarine blew the hatch open and it is believed that ten men made an ascent to the surface. *CH.35* was seen to circle the area for some considerable time before they lowered a boat to pick up survivors, only eight men then being alive. They were landed in Singapore and subsequently suffered badly at the hands of their captors, being severely maltreated, and when prisoners were liberated at the end of the war, only three men were still alive, the other five survivors having died in captivity. Forty-five men had been lost during the sinking.
[Evans pp384–9]

24 November SHAWINIGAN corvette
Lauzon 1941; 940 tons; 190ft × 33ft; 1 × 4in
Lieutenant William James Jones RCNR[†]
Royal Canadian Navy. Ordered to escort the passenger ferry *Burgeo*, which plied between Sydney, Nova Scotia, and Newfoundland, she saw the ferry safely into Port-aux-Basques during the afternoon of 24 November. She then intended to patrol the local area, to return to the harbour in the morning to cover the return journey but failed to arrive at the rendezvous. Not until the ferry arrived at Sydney alone did the authorities realise that she was missing. Subsequent searches found some wreckage and recovered six bodies. The cause of her loss was not discovered until after the war, when *U 1228* (Marienfeld) was identified as being the attacker. At 02.30 Central European Time – 21.30 local time – the submarine had fired a single acoustic homing torpedo at a warship and observed a large explosion and the disappearance of the target, followed by several

detonations as her depth charges exploded. There were no survivors; ninety-one men died.
[Morgan & Taylor p420]

24 November MTB 287 motor torpedo boat
Bristol (USA) 1943; 37 tons; 72.7ft × 19.2ft; 1 × 20mm,
2 × torpedo tubes
Sub-Lieutenant Jack Reed RNVR
Based in the Adriatic, a group of torpedo boats, *287*, *298* and *371*, were returning to Vis in thick fog after a night patrol, when two of the group, *287* and *371* ran hard aground off the island of Levrera, Croatia. The third boat left them to bring assistance, and later that morning other MTBs arrived on scene and attempted to tow them off. Despite all their efforts, this failed, and so it was decided to abandon the boat. Stores and equipment were removed, and they were set on fire by several rounds fired by the other boats.
[Pope pp261–2; Reynolds & Cooper, Mediterranean MTBs at War pp146–7]

24 November MTB 371 motor torpedo boat
Annapolis 1943; 37 tons; 72.7ft × 19.2ft; 1 × 20mm,
2 × torpedo tubes
Lieutenant Barry George Syrett RNVR
Companion to *287*, she also ran hard aground off Levrera and could not be moved, despite the attempts to tow her free by other MTBs. After removing stores, she was destroyed by gunfire from the other boats.
[Pope pp261–2; Reynolds & Cooper, Mediterranean MTBs at War pp146–7]

26 November LCT (4) 721 landing craft, tank
Middlesbrough 1943; 200 tons; 171ft × 38.8ft
Lieutenant Charles John Cooke RNVR
One of the large number of hard-worked landing craft employed in ferrying men and supplies between England and northern France, her badly strained hull finally gave out at 00.30 when she broke in half when 7 miles off the French coast. The stern half was taken in tow by *LCT 791* and taken into Le Havre, and the forward half was sunk by gunfire from the destroyer *Vanquisher* in position 49.44N 00.29E at 10.58.
[TNA: ADM.199/1396]

29 November MMS 101 minesweeper
Port Greville 1941; 225 tons; 105ft × 23ft
Lieutenant William Henry Sturtridge RNVR[†]
In company with two other motor minesweepers, she was employed clearing a minefield near Salonika, Greece. The group had performed several laps during the day, and as it was nearing sunset, decided to sweep towards the designated anchorage. At 17.10, when off Panomi lighthouse, the starboard ship of the team, *MMS 101* exploded, the ship completely disintegrating.

All the ships stopped and lowered boats, and three survivors were picked up from the floating wreckage. It was believed that a contact mine had been responsible. Fifteen men were lost.
[TNA:ADM.199/165]

29 November LCI (L) 102 landing craft, infantry, large
Orange 1943; 234 tons; 150ft × 23.8ft; 4 × 20mm
Lieutenant Henry Murray Sterling RNVR
Based in the Adriatic, she was anchored with other landing craft off the island of Vis, Croatia, when the weather deteriorated. The wind steadily increased, and *LCF 4* nearby lost her anchor and was blown broadside on the beach, fouling *LCI 102*, and as the pair bumped together *102* was holed. The collision also caused *102* to lose her kedge anchor and she drifted away, filling with water, and sank, with only her bridge visible.
Note: the *Statement of Losses* has the incorrect date of the loss as 11 November, a mistake copied by others
[TNA:ADM.199/176]

30 November DUFF frigate
Hingham 1943; 1,300 tons; 300ft × 36.9ft; 3 × 3in, 8 × 20mm
Lieutenant Roland Allan Harry RNVR
Returning to Harwich on completion of a patrol in the North Sea, when at 07.45 there was an explosion under the forward boiler room as she struck a contact mine. A large hole was torn in the bottom, measuring 11ft by 10ft, and the forward boiler room was wrecked. The boiler room and fuel tanks consequently flooded, and the shock caused widespread damage to radio and radar equipment. Damage control parties successfully controlled the flooding, and the ship was able to proceed under her own power to reach Harwich. The damage was such that it was deemed not worth repairing, and the ship was declared a constructive total loss. Three men lost their lives.
[TNA:ADM.267/124; CB.4273 p286]

30 November BEVER whaler
Oslo 1930 (*Hektor-10*) requisitioned 1941; 252 tons; 115.1ft × 23.9ft; 1 × 3in
Lieutenant William Edward Gleave SANF
South African Navy. Fitted as a minesweeper, *Bever* was deployed to the Aegean in 1944, and with her sister *Seksern* and two other ships was tasked to sweep areas in the Gulf of Nauplia (Nafplio). Several mines were located and destroyed during 29 November, and the work continued the following day. At 14.00 as the ships stopped to repair sweep gear damaged during the morning, the *Bever*, stationed astern of the main group was dealing with an unexploded mine seen nearby. As she manoeuvred, there was a large explosion as she

triggered an unseen mine, which detonated under her stern. The bows came clear of the water and she quickly sank, stern first in seconds. Seventeen men died.
[TNA:ADM.358/3066; https://samilhistory.com/tag/hmsas-bever/]

November LCT (5) 2461 landing craft, tank
Camden 1943 (*LCT 461*); 143 tons; 105ft × 32.8ft; 2 × 20mm
Reported to have capsized and the hulk sunk by gunfire, Bay of Bengal; no further details found.
[Statement of Losses p59]

2 December NORTHCOATES trawler
Falmouth 1918 (*George Corton*) requisitioned 1939; 277 tons; 125.4ft × 23.5ft; 1 × 12pdr
Lieutenant Arnold Geoffrey Hallows RNVR
Having suffered an engine breakdown, she was under tow of the tug *Resolve* across the Channel from Le Havre to Portland. The weather worsened, and she was abandoned before she sank at 12.06. The wreck has been found and lies in position 50.39.41N 00.35.19W.
[TNA:ADM.179/375; Larn vol 2 sec 3]

5 December LCT (3) 328 landing craft, tank
Thornaby 1942; 350 tons; 175ft × 31ft; 2 × 2pdr
Lieutenant Colin Ernest Polden RNVR
Stationed in the Aegean, she was initially ordered to take a load of sixteen vehicles, with twenty soldiers from the Indian Army, to Krioneri, but as this area was considered unsafe, this was altered to Missolonghi. They sailed from Patras at 07.50 and proceeded along the swept channel until they arrived at the approaches to Missolonghi. The entrance was taken carefully, as the wreck of the transport *Empire Dace*, sunk by mine on the 1st, could clearly be seen. As they passed the wreck there was a large explosion as they detonated a mine, which covered the landing craft in water and debris. As this cleared, it was seen that the bow ramp and doors had disappeared, along with two vehicles. The ship was going down, bows first, quite quickly, so all floats were ordered to be released and she was abandoned, the survivors being assisted by some local small boats. The ship steadily sank bows first, rolling over to starboard as she disappeared. Two members of the crew and thirteen Indian soldiers were lost.
[TNA:ADM.199/165]

5 December CYRUS mine destructor
Wallsend 1943; 3,980 tons; 359.2ft × 60ft
Designed to counteract pressure mines, she was operated under tow and with no crew. Taken across the English Channel, she was employed to clear the approaches to various northern French ports. When strong gales cancelled all operations, she was anchored

at the entrance to the river Seine, but broke adrift from her moorings and ran aground on the Banc D'Amfard where she broke up.
[TNA:ADM.179/375;ADM.199/1400]

6 December BULLEN frigate
Lynn 1943; 1,300 tons; 300ft × 36.6ft; 3 × 3in, 2 × 40mm, 8 × 20mm
Lieutenant Commander Anthony Heron Parish†
In company with other vessels of the 19th Escort Group, conducting an anti-submarine patrol to the north-west of Cape Wrath. The group were zigzagging, when at 10.00, in position 58.30N 05.03W, just as they had commenced a 30-degree turn to port in accordance with the zigzag pattern when there was an explosion on the starboard side amidships. The bulkhead between the engine room and number 2 boiler room took the full force of the detonation. This caused rapid flooding of both compartments and broke the ships back. There followed some confusion, and the damage control efforts were not well co-ordinated; it was later stated that not all watertight doors had remained closed, allowing water to pass between compartments. The hull broke amidships, and the bow and stern rose vertically out of the water. The forward part listed over to port slightly before sinking but the after part remained afloat on an even keel for some time. Seventy-two men died. Her attacker had been U 775 (Taschenmacher), which had fired a single homing torpedo at the group.
[TNA:ADM.1/18039]

6 December LCT (3) 7089 landing craft, tank
Barrow 1944; 350 tons; 175ft × 31ft; 2 × 20mm
Whilst attempting to enter Boulogne harbour in a heavy rain squall, at 19.15 she ran onto the submerged end of the northern breakwater. Holed in the engine room, she rapidly made water, and although she was freed, she went onto rocks at low water and became a total loss.
[TNA:ADM.199/1396]

11 December MMS 257 minesweeper
St. Andrews 1943; 225 tons; 105ft × 23ft
Skipper-Lieutenant Charles Walter Snape RNR
Engaged in working to clear the river Scheldt of mines, in company with three other motor minesweepers, the group were sweeping towards Flushing. The work went on all day until 22.17, when 257 exploded as she detonated a mine under the hull. She was covered with spray and smoke; the foremast was seen to fall across the side before she sank. It was believed that she was just outside the existing swept channel, in water which may not have been covered by the sweeps of the Oropesa sweepers that had swept the channel earlier that day. Two men were lost.
[TNA:ADM.199/253]

14 December ALDENHAM escort destroyer
Birkenhead 1941; 1,050 tons; 264.2ft × 31.6ft; 4 × 4in, 4 × 2pdr, 3 × 20mm, 2 × torpedo tubes
Commander James Gerald Farrant
Stationed in the Adriatic, she had been engaged in providing support for Yugoslav partisans, bombarding shore positions on the island of Pag in company with her sister Atherstone. During the afternoon of 14 December, the pair had completed their task and left the area, setting course to pass about 1 mile to the north of Skerda Island. At 15.45 course was altered to close Olib Island, and the ship was still under helm when there was an explosion amidships by the funnel as she detonated a mine. She broke in half, the after part of the ship sinking very quickly, the stern rising out of the water before it disappeared, the screws still turning. The fore part capsized and remained afloat for several minutes before sinking. The Atherstone anchored to leeward of her and lowered boats, and a motor launch also came to the scene, and between them sixty-seven men were rescued, but 126 were lost.
[TNA:ADM.199/260]

16 December WAR DIWAN oiler
Port Glasgow 1919; 5,551 tons; 400.2ft × 52.2ft
Master Stanley C Kernick
Having crossed the North Sea from Southend in Convoy TAM19, she spent the night at anchor off Flushing. During the morning she left her anchorage to proceed at low speed through a buoyed channel towards the river Scheldt. At 13.20 when steaming towards number 15 buoy there was a large explosion under the hull as she detonated an influence mine. A large column of water and smoke was thrown up and as it cleared it was seen that she had broken her back, the midships portion sagging with the bow and stern rising. Approximately 1 minute later there was a second explosion, probably another mine detonating, and this broke the ship in half. The separate portions drifted apart, the after section grounding whilst the forward part continued to drift. The escort destroyers Cowdray and Blencathra had closed, and they fired several shells into the drifting section to ensure that it sank. The fore part was noted as lying in position 51.25.45N 003.29.37E whilst the after section lay in position 51.25.31N 003.27.21E. Five men were killed.
[TNA:ADM.267/122]

17 December MANORA harbour defence craft
Built 1936 requisitioned 1940
A small craft employed locally at Portsmouth, she was wrecked in heavy weather when driven onto the eastern boom defences. There were no casualties.
[TNA:ADM.199/1396]

24 December CLAYOQUOT minesweeper
Prince Rupert 1940; 673 tons; 171.5ft × 28.5ft; 1 × 12pdr,
1 × 2pdr
Lieutenant Commander Alexander Craig Campbell
RCNVR

Royal Canadian Navy. In company with another minesweeper and a frigate, the group were conducting an anti-submarine sweep near Sambro Light Vessel off Halifax, the intention being to cover the passage of two convoys through the area. At 11.40, as they were screening the passage of Convoy XB139 through the area, *Clayoquot* was hit by a torpedo which exploded under her stern. The explosion set off a depth charge, scattering debris over a large area and twisting over 30ft of the stern into a vertical position, and the ship was covered in smoke and steam. She slowly rolled over to starboard and in 10 minutes had capsized and then sank, stern first, her depth charges detonating as she did so. Several ships were quickly on scene and rescued survivors, but eight men died. Her attacker had been *U 806* (Hornbostel) which had fired an acoustic homing torpedo.
[McKee & Darlington p187]

25 December DAKINS frigate
Hingham 1943; 1,300 tons; 300ft × 36.9ft; 3 × 3in,
8 × 20mm
Lieutenant Michael Geoffrey Henderson Arbuthnot RNVR

On patrol off the coast of Belgium, the ship was about 14 miles north-west of Ostend when at 21.10 an explosion occurred under the starboard side forward as she detonated a mine. The ship was whipped by the force of the explosion, and the hull plating was badly buckled, with splits opening, and the forward section of the ship started to flood. The boiler and engine rooms filled with steam from fractured pipes and power was lost. Damage control work stemmed the flood and power was restored, allowing the ship to get under way, stern first, and successfully made the safety of Harwich. After temporary repairs, she was taken to Hoboken, Belgium, for docking, but as deemed to be a constructive total loss. There were no fatalities.
[TNA: ADM.267/122; CB.4273 p287]

26 December CAPEL frigate
Boston 1943; 1,140 tons; 283.6ft × 35.2ft; 3 × 3in,
2 × 40mm, 9 × 20mm
Lieutenant Brian Bevil Heslop DSC†

In company with other ships of the First Escort Group arrived at Cherbourg on 23 December to carry out offensive anti-submarine sweeps of the western approaches to the English Channel. Over the following 2 days they hunted off the northern French coast, gaining several contacts, but none substantial enough to be prosecuted. At 12.35 the group was in line abreast in position 49.48N 01.43W, steaming at 8 knots, when without warning she was hit forward by a torpedo. Seconds later there was a second explosion as the forward Hedgehog projectiles exploded. As the huge cloud of grey smoke that had covered her cleared, it could be seen that the bows were wrecked with her bridge flattened, and she was settling by the head. The engines had stopped, and she had lost all power, the ship being plunged into darkness. The survivors collected on deck aft and launched floats and rafts and she was abandoned. The ship went down slowly by the head, and finally sank at 16.02, the stern rising out of the water and she sank bows first. Seventy-seven men were lost. About 8 minutes after the *Capel* had been hit, the *Affleck* was hit aft by a torpedo but was able to make port. Their attacker had been the *U 486* (Meyer), which had fired a salvo of three acoustic homing torpedoes at the group.
[TNA: ADM.199/957]

26 December AFFLECK frigate
Hingham 1943; 1,300 tons; 300ft × 36.9ft; 3 × 3in,
10 × 20mm
Commander Clive Gwinner

Acting as senior officer of the First Escort Group in their aggressive anti-submarine hunt in the English Channel, the ships were off Cherbourg when attacked by the *U 486* (Meyer) and the *Capel* was torpedoed (see above). The submarine had fired three acoustic homing torpedoes at the group, and 8 minutes after the first hit, there was an explosion under the stern of *Affleck*. About 50ft of the stern was wrecked, with the deck forced upward, and the after compartments flooded, the ship heeling over to starboard. The starboard propeller had evidently been lost, and the steering gear wrecked. Some smoke containers burst, filling the midships section with acrid smoke. The ship remained stable, and bulkheads held, and the shop was able to proceed to safety. The ship was not repaired but written off as a constructive total loss. Nine men were lost.
[CB.4273 p288]

29 December MTB 782 motor torpedo boat
Wallasea 1944; 95 tons; 110ft × 21.3ft; 1 × 2pdr 2 × 20mm,
2 × torpedo tubes
Lieutenant Paul William Rickards RNVR

Sank after she detonated a mine in position 51.24N 03.27E, about 2 miles to the west of Nieuwe Sluis, in the river Scheldt estuary. *MTB 753* was damaged in collision with the wreckage when she closed the site, but successfully picked up the survivors, but three men were lost, and a fourth man later died of his injuries.
[TNA: ADM.267/124; ADM.358/4399; Reynolds, Dog Boats p186]

1945: Losses 1 January to 15 August

2 January HAYBURN WYKE trawler

Selby 1917 (*Robert Barton*) requisitioned 1940; 324 tons; 138.5ft × 23.7ft; 1 × 12pdr

Skipper-Lieutenant Francis Wilson RNR[†]

During 1 and 2 January, German *Seehund* midget submarines were used for the first time, several units being deployed against Allied shipping gathered off the Dutch and Belgian coasts. They achieved little, their only success coming at 22.25 when the *Hayburn Wyke* suffered a large explosion when hit by a torpedo about 4 miles off Ostend and quickly sank. It is likely that her attacker had been the *Seehund U 5304* (Paulsen). The wreck lies in position 51.15.27N 02.48.44E. Twenty-two men lost their lives, with four survivors.

[*TNA: ADM.199/1441; Rohwer, Axis Submarine Successes p187*]

4 January HDML 1163 motor launch

Christchurch 1942; 45 tons; 70ft × 15ft; 1 × 2pdr, 1 × 20mm

Sub-Lieutenant Russell Kenyon Howden SANF[†]

Stationed in the Adriatic, she was ordered to carry out a night patrol in the Maknare Channel off the coast of Croatia, and intercept any craft attempting to pass through. At 21.30 a radio message was received from *1163* which indicated that four craft had been sighted, but nothing further was heard, and she failed to respond to repeated radio calls. A motor launch and two motor torpedo boats were despatched to the area, but could find no trace of her, until at daybreak wreckage was found in Brgulje Bay, Molat Island. The bows were the only recognisable section, and there was a considerable quantity of scattered debris. A party was sent to the location overland and found that an army patrol had already buried three bodies that had been found. On enquiring with locals, they reported hearing an explosion on that night, and torpedoes had been found on the beach. It was ascertained that she had encountered a number of enemy fast patrol boats and had been torpedoed by *S 33*, with no survivors. Eleven men died.

[*TNA: ADM.199/165*]

6 January WALPOLE destroyer

Sunderland 1918; 1,100 tons; 300ft × 29.5ft; 2 × 4in, 1 × 3in, 4 × 20mm

Lieutenant George Clement Crowley

Engaged in patrolling the southern North Sea, when in position 52.33N 03.06E there was an explosion on the port side, abreast the forward boiler room, when she hit a contact mine. A hole 30ft long was blown in the side, bulkheads were distorted by the blast and there was widespread shock damage. The forward boiler room flooded, and the ship heeled over to assume a 12-degree list to starboard. Power was lost, and the steering gear was blown away with the rudder jammed at 30 degrees. The frigate *Rutherford* closed to stand by her, and a tow was rigged. She was taken initially to Sheerness, and later moved to Chatham for survey, where she was written off as a constructive total loss. Two men were killed.

[*TNA: ADM.267/97; CB.4273 p270*]

(11/12) January PORPOISE submarine

Barrow 1932; 1,500/2,053 tons; 267ft × 29.10ft; 1 × 4in, 6 × torpedo tubes, 50 mines

Lieutenant Commander Hugh Bentley Turner DSC[†]

Tasked to lay a minefield in the vicinity of Penang, she sailed from Trincomalee 2 January. When she failed to return as expected on 19 January she was posted as missing. She reported that she had conducted her mine lay on 9 January, and some of her mines seem to have been the cause of sinking of three Japanese ships, so she must have been lost after this date. Japanese sources indicate that during the morning of 11 January in position 05.30N 098.39E a B6N 'Jill' aircraft discovered a submarine on the surface and dropped two small bombs, one scoring a direct hit. A second attack was carried out later that morning by a second B6N on a submerged submarine, and more attacks were made by aircraft on a submerged object leaking oil. This may well have been the *Porpoise*, and the initial attack may have damaged her, with the later attacks completing her demise.

[*TNA: HW.27/22; Evans p390; http://uboat.net/allies/ warships/ship/3412.html*]

12 January REGULUS minesweeper

Toronto 1943 (*Longbranch*); 1,010 tons; 212.6ft × 35.6ft; 1 × 4in, 8 × 20mm

Commander Roger William David Thomson

Leader of the Eighth Minesweeping Flotilla, she was stationed in the Aegean, engaged in clearing minefields in the sea around Corfu. At 08.00 she sailed from her anchorage, accompanied by a mixture of fleet and yard minesweepers, with two motor launches and two trawlers, to re-commence the work. During the morning, several mines were brought to the surface, twenty-one on the first lap alone. At 13.30 they started another lap, with *Regulus* steering along the line of danbuoys laid to mark the end of the previous sweep. Just as she was passing the fifth buoy there was a violent explosion under the stern. She lost all power but remained upright and stable. *BYMS 2026* closed and quickly had her in tow, as she was in danger of drifting further into the minefield. Flooding was reported from the after compartments and the engine

room, and she started to settle by the stern and a list to starboard developed. As the list increased the whaler was cleared away and floats prepared for launch. With the list increasing alarmingly, all hands were ordered up from below and she was abandoned, men jumping into the water as she rolled over to assume a 70-degree list. She hung in this position for some time before sinking by the stern, the bow rising up clear before sinking. One man lost his life. It was believed that she had struck a moored contact mine, which was close to the unswept side of the line.
[TNA: ADM.199/165]

12 January TREERN whaler

Oslo 1929 requisitioned 1941; 247 tons; 115.7ft × 23.9ft; 1 × 3in
Lieutenant Patrick Byrne SANF†
South African Navy. Fitted out as a minesweeper, she was part of the 166th Minesweeping Group supporting operations in the Aegean. Ordered to escort a caique laden with fuel to Oreoi, they sailed from Skiathos, but as they entered the Trikeri Channel, at about 08.30 there was a large explosion as she detonated a mine. She rolled over to starboard, and there was a second explosion as she detonated another mine and quickly sank. The caique, which was following, was hit by the shock wave of the explosion, which blew overboard one man, and after recovering him they searched the area, but found just one survivor. Later that day the destroyer *Musketeer*, searching for the missing minesweeper, found the caique and recovered the wounded survivor. The Board of Inquiry believed it probable that Lieutenant Byrne had assumed that a line marked on the chart supplied to him was a safe route, whereas it was actually the northern limit of a swept area. A small deviation from the line would take the ship into a known minefield. Twenty-three men died.
[TNA: ADM.1/18929]

15 January THANE escort aircraft carrier

Seattle 1943; 11,420 tons; 468.5ft × 69.5ft; 2 × 5in, 16 × 40mm
Captain Edmund Russell Goldney Baker
Employed on aircraft ferrying duties, she had loaded Corsair aircraft and Hoverfly helicopters in the United States and sailed from New York 3 January. She arrived at Belfast on 14 January to offload part of her cargo and sailed the following morning for the Clyde. At 13.28 as she was approaching the Clyde Light Vessel at 17 knots, she was hit by a torpedo on the starboard side abreast the after magazines below the waterline. The after 5in gun and sponson were blown away, and the starboard side plating for 48ft along the waterline was blown inboard several feet, and the internal structure was wrecked. The flight deck was fractured and the after

aircraft lift was distorted and fixed in the raised position. The after compartments flooded and steering gear was out of action. The ship remained stable, and work by damage control parties shored bulkheads and later that night she was towed into Greenock. She was declared a constructive total loss and was later towed to Faslane and laid up. The attacker had been *U 1172* (Kuhlmann).
[TNA: ADM.267/134; CB.4273 p31]

15 January GOLDEN WEST drifter

Sandhaven 1914 requisitioned 1940; 88 tons; 89.1ft × 19.4ft
Foundered in Aberdeen harbour; no further details found.
[Statement of Losses p36]

18 January MTB 690 motor torpedo boat

Falmouth 1943; 95 tons; 110ft × 21.3ft; 1 × 2pdr, 2 × 20mm, 2 × torpedo tubes
Sub-Lieutenant Frederick Norman Haslett RNVR
Whilst returning from patrol in the North Sea, at 05.18 she struck an underwater object when off Lowestoft, believed to be a submerged wreck. Efforts went on throughout the day to stabilise her, but she steadily settled and finally sank at 15.08.
[TNA: ADM.199/1441]

19 January NORTHERN ISLES trawler

Bremerhaven 1936 requisitioned 1939; 655 tons; 188ft × 28ft; 1 × 4in
Lieutenant David LeFleming Dobson RNVR
Based at Durban in South Africa, the crew decided to take the opportunity during a quiet patrol to supplement their rations with fresh fish. The trawler was taken close inshore for lines to be put out, but at 08.12 she ran aground in position 29.52.38S 31.03.44E. Tugs were sent to her aid, but they failed to move her, and as she had developed a heel, it was decided at 13.00 to leave her. Efforts to get a line to the trawler by rocket from shore had failed due to strong winds, but a line was successfully floated off the ship to the beach on the tide. This allowed a breeches buoy to be rigged, and all the crew were taken off. Over the next few days, she was re-boarded using the breeches buoy, and stores were removed, but on 26 January the Salvage Officer declared her to be a total loss.
[TNA: ADM.199/1442; Lund & Ludlam, Trawlers go to War pp248–50]

21 January COMPUTATOR trawler

Beverley 1919 (*Egilias Akerman*) requisitioned 1939; 286 tons; 125.5ft × 23.5ft
Skipper Alfred Frederick Meacock RNR
Foundered at 10.30 after a collision with the destroyer *Vanoc* in Seine Bay, the impact also severely damaged

the destroyer. The wreck lies in position 49.42.4N 00.37.1W.
[TNA: ADM.199/1172]

24 January **ML 891** motor launch
Cape Town 1944; 73 tons; 112ft × 18.4ft; 1 × 3pdr, 2 × 20mm
Lieutenant John George Weston RNVR
In January 1945 Operation 'Matador' was launched, to land troops in the area around Ramree Island, Burma, and *ML 891* was one of several launches deployed to support the landings. On 24 January troops were landed with little resistance and disembarkation proceeded smoothly until the destroyer *Rapid* reported sighting a line of moored mines. The area was ordered to be avoided, but at 11.01 *LCA 2086* was blown up when she hit a mine with the loss of two of her crew and twenty-four embarked troops, with many more being thrown into the water. *ML 891*, along with other launches. went to her aid and after picking up several survivors was clearing the area when she struck a mine, and sank rapidly, breaking up as she foundered. Three ratings were killed.
[TNA: ADM.358/2672; London Gazette 23 April 1948; Goulden p109]

26 January **MANNERS** frigate
Boston (USA) 1943; 1,085 tons; 289.5ft × 35ft; 3 × 3in, 10 × 20mm
Commander John Valentine Waterhouse DSO
In late January, a number of enemy submarines were ordered to operate in the Irish Sea, and anti-submarine escort groups were deployed to tackle the threat. Whilst prosecuting a promising Asdic target, at 09.45, when about 20 miles from the Isle of Man, an explosion occurred under the stern. Seconds later there was a second explosion, probably of a dislodged depth charge. The ship was whipped by the blast, with electrical equipment failing, and the stern plating was buckled. Way was lost as it became clear that the propellers had probably been lost in the blast. Thirteen minutes after the first explosion a third and much heavier explosion occurred about 30ft from the stern, and about 60ft of the ship's stern was blown away. The ship remained stable, and was taken in tow, to reach Barrow-in-Furness, but was deemed to be a constructive total loss. Four officers and thirty-nine ratings were killed. Her attacker had been *U 1051* (Holleben), which was located and prosecuted by the other ships in the group and sunk.
[TNA: ADM.1/19136; CB.4273 p289]

30 January **MMS 248** minesweeper
Shelburne 1943; 165 tons; 105ft × 23ft
Lieutenant Ian Merritt McLean RCNVR
In company with other motor minesweepers, the group was working to clear the extensive minefields laid in the river Scheldt. The weather was poor, with strong winds, a choppy sea and regular snow showers. At 09.35 as the ships were off Terneuzen, steering to the west in a line abreast ('Q') formation using LL and SA sweeps to tackle magnetic and acoustic mines, there was a large explosion under the stern of *248*. The sea boat was immediately ordered to be hoisted out, and floats were prepared for launching, but *MMS 228* came alongside and as it was clear that she was sinking lifted off all the men. Eleven minutes after the detonation, she had disappeared. It was thought that an acoustic mine was the most likely cause of the explosion.
[TNA: ADM 199/165]

3 February **ARLEY** trawler
Middlesbrough 1914 requisitioned 1939; 304 tons; 130.4ft × 24ft; 1 × 12pdr
Skipper William Limb RNR
In company with several other minesweeping trawlers, she had been tasked to sweep along the east coast, from the East Dudgeon light to Sheringham. By late afternoon they were approaching the South Sheringham bell buoy, and at 17.57 were ordered to haul in sweeps. The ships slowed to recover the wires, but as the float neared the stern it was seen that a mine was caught in the bight of the wire. The sweep winch was veered immediately, and all hands were ordered forward, but a moment later there was a large explosion as the mine detonated. The ship was covered in water, smoke and steam as the force of the explosion had forced the boiler off its mounts. She started settling by the stern and floats were prepared for launching and all hands were ordered on deck. The armed trawlers *Mount Keen* and *John Cattling* closed, and a tow was attempted by the former, but the towline parted almost immediately, as did a second attempt by *John Cattling*. The stern of the *Arley* was now awash and the *Cattling* came alongside to take off the crew. She sank a short time later at 18.45. One man was lost.
[TNA: ADM.199/165]

4 February **MMS 68** minesweeper
Lowestoft 1941; 165 tons; 105ft × 23ft
Lieutenant Frank Cecil Villiers Murray RNVR[†]
Based in the Aegean, she sailed from Patras to proceed to Taranto, joining two landing craft and a merchant ship under the escort of the destroyer *Easton* for the passage. The ships formed up in line ahead, with *MMS 68* being the fourth ship, behind the destroyer and landing craft. At 13.25 in position 38.02.3N 20.37.8E, as they passed Cape Skinari there was a large explosion which engulfed the minesweeper. She was broken in half by the detonation, breaking at the forward side of the wheelhouse. The *Easton* reversed course and steamed to the scene to find the fore part still afloat, and the sea littered with wreckage. Boats were lowered which

picked up seven men, the only survivors, eighteen men being lost. It was believed that she was the victim of a mine that had drifted out of a known minefield.
[TNA:ADM.199/165]

9 February **HESPERIA** tug
Leith 1942; 1,120 tons; 190ft × 38.6ft; 1 × 12pdr, 2 × 20mm
In late 1944 the 18,000-ton floating dock *AFD.24* was ordered to be transferred from Freetown, West Africa to Trincomalee, Ceylon. By January 1945 she had reached Gibraltar and the tugs *Hesperia* and *Empire Sandy* took over the tow through the Mediterranean. The group sailed from Oran 26 January. During 9 February, the dock broke the tow in poor weather and was taken inshore before grounding in shallow water 60 miles west of Derna. In the efforts to prevent her being wrecked the *Hesperia* ran aground herself at 15.00. Several ships closed the scene to render assistance, the Salvage Officer embarking in the *Empire Sandy*. They found the *Hesperia* had been holed and her stern was submerged. The *Prince Salvor* salvage vessel arrived on scene, but all efforts to free the tug and dock failed and both were written off as total losses and were later sold for scrap where they lay.
[TNA:ADM.199/2311]

11 February **PATHFINDER** destroyer
Hebburn 1941; 1,540 tons; 338.5ft × 35ft; 4 × 4.7in, 8 × 20mm, 8 × torpedo tubes
Lieutenant Commander Thomas Frederick Hallifax
Part of the substantial force employed in the re-occupation of Burma, *Pathfinder* covered the landing of troops and bombarded coastal positions. Whilst stationed in the mouth of the Pakseik Taungnaw river, to the south of Akyab, with her sister *Paladin*, the pair came under air attack. A bomb exploded in the water about 50ft from the starboard side abreast the after magazine, and probably detonated under the ship. The ship was covered in water and mud and the whipping effect of the blast split the hull plating and caused extensive distortion and buckling of the hull and superstructure. The after magazines flooded and after fuel tanks leaked into surrounding compartments. Temporary repairs were made and using the port engine only managed to steam to Colombo. Docking revealed the extent of the damage, and she was declared a constructive total loss. She was subsequently able, despite limited power, to return to England in June, to be later sold for breaking up.
[TNA:ADM.267/110; CB.4273 p271]

11 February **ML 183** motor launch
Bangor 1941; 73 tons; 112ft × 18.4ft; 1 × 3pdr, 2 × 20mm
Lieutenant Arthur John Wright RNVR
Whilst entering the harbour at Dieppe, she struck the East Pier heavily, her port side being crushed. She

rapidly filled with water and subsequently sank with the loss of three lives.
[TNA:ADM.199/1445]

13 February **DENBIGH CASTLE** corvette
Aberdeen 1944; 1,060 tons; 225ft × 36.8ft; 1 × 4in, 10 × 20mm
Lieutenant Commander Graham Butcher DSC RNVR
Part of the escort to Russian Convoy JW64 which had sailed from the Clyde on 3 February, and had successfully reached northern waters without loss, despite heavy air attacks. By 12 February, the convoy was approaching the Kola Inlet, *Denbigh Castle* being stationed on the port quarter of the convoy which was deployed in two long columns. The radar picture was complicated by returns from the land mass, but at 23.46, in position 69.20.30N 33.37.30E, a small echo was detected astern of the ships at about 2,500 yards, which then faded. It was regained a little after, only to again disappear. The identity of the contact was uncertain; suspicions were aroused that it may be a submarine but thought more likely to be a Russian patrol boat. At 00.08 there was a large explosion forward which wrecked the bows, threw the 4in gun off its mount and buckled the deck plates. She remained stable and upright, with watertight doors closed, and damage control parties started shoring up bulkheads. The corvette *Bluebell* came alongside to lift off casualties and preparations were made for towing. At 02.17 the corvette started to tow her, stern first, towards the land and they were joined an hour later by the Russian *Burevistnik*, which transferred a 100-ton pump before taking over the tow. The pump was set to work, and several flats were cleared of water, but despite this she was perceptibly settling by the head. All non-essential personnel were evacuated, with a towing party remaining onboard. At 07.30 she grounded in Bolshaya Volokovaya bay, in position 69.15.2N 33.34.9E; her bows now deep in the water, and her stern clear of the surface. At 09.00 she could be seen to be listing to port and 10 minutes later she capsized to float bottom up. Eleven men were killed. Her attacker had been *U 922* (Falke).
[TNA:ADM.199/175]

14 February **Fire at Ostend**
At the end of 1944 as the Allies continued to advance through the Low Countries, the liberated ports were occupied and used by Allied naval forces. Ostend became the base for coastal forces, but on 14 February it became the scene of the greatest single loss of torpedo boats in the war, following a disastrous fire. A number of torpedo boats were berthed at Ostend, with eleven 'short' boats and five of the larger 'D' boats being in the area known as the creek, with another thirteen of the 'D' boats in the main harbour. A number of the

boats were carrying out maintenance on their engines. During the afternoon, the Canadian-manned *MTB 464* entered harbour to join the others, and Petty Officer (Motor Mechanic) Arthur Frederick Walden took the opportunity to tackle the problem of water in the petrol tanks – a number of the boats had suffered contaminated fuel since being refuelled some days before. Requests for assistance from the Fleet Maintenance Unit ashore were refused, as they were overloaded with work, so Walden decided to take the defect in hand himself. He, along with other engineers of the affected boats, had already tried employing a hand pump and bucket to clear the problem, throwing the water overboard. Understanding that the boat must be ready for operations that night, he decided to employ the bilge pump and a length of hose, which discharged directly overboard. The pump ran from 15.15 to 15.35 which meant that about 50 gallons of fluid went overboard. However, there was apparently not as much water in the tank as Walden had feared, and much of what went into the basin was actually gasoline. From 15.30 several of the boats noticed a distinct smell of petrol, but all presumed it was internal to their boat. Exactly what caused the initial explosion was not discovered, but at 16.02 the petrol vapour ignited between *MTB 465* and *MTB 462*. The flames spread very quickly across the creek and in less than 3 minutes, seventeen boats, all moored close together, were on fire. At 16.05 there was a huge explosion, when *465* blew up, shattering windows in the town and throwing debris over a large area; this was followed a moment or so later by a second explosion as *462* blew up. Smaller explosions continued for some time, as ammunition exploded. Quick thinking by some of the crews saved their boats – on board *MTB 485* a stoker started the engines and powered the boat clear – and others were towed out of danger. In all twelve torpedo boats were lost and a total of sixty-four men were killed and sixty-five injured on board the boats. Nine civilians ashore were killed and dozens of people in the area were injured. The subsequent enquiry identified Petty Officer Walden as being responsible for the fire, and he was ordered to be 'severely admonished'. However, it was recognised that he had done the job in his zeal to get his craft ready; he had received no support from the shore maintenance facility, and ' … it was the general laxity and lack of interest shown by his superior officers that in a large measure contributed to the disaster' (*ADM.1/5493*). Lieutenant Lennox Bishop DSC RCNVR and Sub-Lieutenant George Hobart RCNVR, the officers of *MTB 464*, were both informed that they had incurred their Lordships' displeasure. Bishop had shown insufficient interest in the condition of his craft whilst Hobart had been aware of the unofficial tank cleaning but had allowed it to continue unsupervised. Several other officers, either of the MTB Flotilla or at the maintenance unit, were similarly reprimanded for either failing to ensure that proper procedures were followed or giving support. [TNA: ADM.1/5493; ADM116077; Reynolds, Dog Boats pp187–8]

The following motor torpedo boats were lost:

MTB 255
Cowes 1943; 41 tons; 73ft × 18ft; 2 × torpedo tubes
Lieutenant Peter Aspinall DSC RNVR

MTB 438
Hythe 1943; 37 tons; 71.9ft × 20.7ft; 1 × 2pdr, 2 × 20mm, 2 × torpedo tubes
Lieutenant Edward William Augustus Bostock RNVR

MTB 444
Hythe 1943; 37 tons; 71.9ft × 20.7ft; 1 × 2pdr, 2 × 20mm, 2 × torpedo tubes
Sub-Lieutenant Peter Richard Davis DSC RNVR

MTB 776
Shoreham 1944; 95 tons; 110ft × 21.3ft; 1 × 2pdr, 2 × 20mm, 2 × torpedo tubes
Lieutenant Ian Andrew Bryant Quarrie RNVR

MTB 789
Northam 1944; 95 tons; 110ft × 21.3ft; 1 × 2pdr, 2 × 20mm, 2 × torpedo tubes
Lieutenant Albert Arthur Friswell RNVR

MTB 791
Bo'ness 1944; 95 tons; 110ft × 21.3ft; 1 × 2pdr, 2 × 20mm, 2 × torpedo tubes
Lieutenant Peter Alvidge Robinson RNVR

MTB 798
Barking 1944; 95 tons; 110ft × 21.3ft; 1 × 2pdr, 2 × 20mm, 2 × torpedo tubes
Lieutenant James Galloway Fletcher RNVR

The following five Canadian torpedo boats of the Canadian 29th MGB Flotilla were lost, and the flotilla was disbanded.

MTB 459
Hythe 1944; 41 tons; 71.9ft × 20.7ft; 1 × 6pdr, 2 × 20mm, 2 × torpedo tubes
Lieutenant John Shand RCNVR

MTB 461
Hythe 1944; 41 tons; 71.9ft × 20.7ft; 1 × 6pdr, 2 × 20mm, 2 × torpedo tubes
Lieutenant Clement Vernon Barlow RCNVR

MTB 462

Hythe 1944; 41 tons; 71.9ft × 20.7ft; 1 × 6pdr, 2 × 20mm,
2 × torpedo tubes
Lieutenant Richard Paddon RCNVR

MTB 465

Hythe 1944; 41 tons; 71.9ft × 20.7ft; 1 × 6pdr, 2 × 20mm,
2 × torpedo tubes
Lieutenant Charles Donald Chaffey RCNVR

MTB 466

Hythe 1944; 41 tons; 71.9ft × 20.7ft; 1 × 6pdr, 2 × 20mm,
2 × torpedo tubes
Lieutenant Joseph Murray Adams RCNVR

★ ★ ★

15 February HDML 1417 motor launch

Clynder 1944; 46 tons; 70ft × 15ft; 1 × 2pdr
Sub-Lieutenant Malcolm Ernest Harold Pitstow RNVR
Ordered to proceed to Terneuzen, the launch had entered
the river Scheldt, and secured to a buoy to await the fog
that had affected the area to clear. Just after 14.00, as it
seemed to have cleared a little, she slipped and steered her
way past several temporary wreck marker buoys, but the
fog closed in again, and seemed to become worse, and
the launch was again stopped to await it clearing. A short
time later HDML 1392 emerged from the mist and 1417
got under way and took station astern of her. The fog
intervened and by 14.53 she lost sight of her leader. Speed
was reduced to 5 knots and soundings were ordered.
These showed that the water was shallowing rapidly, so
engines were put to full astern, but it was too late, and
she ran aground. Efforts to go astern failed to move her,
and water was reported to be entering the engine room.
Some wooden piles were dimly discernible ahead, so the
dinghy was launched which took a line to be secured to
one of the stakes which marked the edge of a low bank.
The confidential books and non-essential personnel were
then ferried ashore. At 15.30 HDML 1402 appeared out
of the murk in response to 1417's call for assistance, to be
joined a short while later by 1392. A tow was rigged by
1402 and at 16.30 her bows swung free to starboard as she
was hauled free of the ground, to be taken alongside 1392.
Water, however, was reported to still be entering, and by
17.00 she had a pronounced list to starboard. At 17.09 she
rolled over and sank, then being about half a mile to the
east-south-east of Flushing East dolphin.
[TNA: ADM.199/175]

17 February BLUEBELL corvette

Paisley 1940; 940 tons; 190ft × 33ft; 1 × 4in, 2 × 20mm
Lieutenant Geoffrey Herbert Walker DSC RNVR†
Part of the escort to Convoy RA64 that had sailed from
the Kola Inlet, Russia, on 17 February, she was stationed
on the port beam of the convoy. At 15.20 she was seen to

be altering course and increasing speed and was believed
to be in contact with a submarine. No signal had been
received from her, however, before she was blown apart
just 2 minutes later. An observer on the destroyer Opportune
reported seeing an explosion aft and then seconds later
a second explosion, probably caused by her own depth
charges and ammunition, which seem to spread forward
engulfing the whole ship. The destroyer Zest immediately
responded to close the scene but could find only a large
patch of debris and thick oil. Zest dropped several floats to
men that were seen in the water, and then carried out an
unsuccessful Asdic search of the area. On returning to the
wreck site only three men still alive could be found, and
two of these died after being recovered. Ninety men died.
Her attacker had been U 711 (Lange).
[TNA: ADM.199/175]

17 February MTB 605 motor torpedo boat

Littlehampton 1942; 95 tons; 110ft × 21.3ft; 1 × 2pdr,
2 × 20mm, 2 × torpedo tubes
Lieutenant John Allan May RNVR
Carrying twelve passengers, senior officers who had
visited Ostend to investigate the 14 February fire, she
sailed from that harbour at 13.00 to return to Dover. She
passed through the anchorage and then set course to the
north-west and increased to 20 knots. She passed OD3
buoy at 13.40, and moments later the ship shuddered as
she struck an underwater object. Engines were stopped,
and the engine room reported that a shaft seemed to
have come adrift, and the shaft had come up through
the after compartment as a result. She was making water
fast, and power failed after 2 minutes. All weights were
shifted forward, and pumping was started by hand. As a
precaution, the floats and dinghies were lowered over
the side, and the passengers put into them. To attract
attention, they fired red flares and bursts of machine-
gun fire. This brought MTB 511 and MTB 486 to their
aid. They removed the passengers and when the trawler
Herschell arrived, a tow was rigged. However, before this
could take effect, she rolled over and was eventually
sunk by gunfire from the other boats. An investigation
found that she had hit the wreck of LST 420, sunk on 7
November 1944. The officers of 605 were found to be
at fault; she was outside the swept channel; the wreck
was known but the position had been wrongly marked
on their chart; the wreck was marked by a buoy, but
they had failed to alter course in time after sighting it.
[TNA: ADM.1/5493; Reynolds: Dog Boats p188]

17 February LARK sloop

Greenock 1943; 1,475 tons; 283ft × 38.6ft; 6 × 4in,
10 × 20mm
Commander Hedworth Lambton
Part of the Seventh Escort Group that had covered
the passage of a convoy to Russia, on 16 February the

Group sailed to carry out an offensive anti-submarine sweep prior to the departure of Convoy RA64 from the Kola Inlet. The group had immediate success, with *Lark* and *Alnwick Castle* sinking *U 425*. During the 17th, the sweep continued, the ship in line abreast, a mile apart, the *Lark* being the outermost ship on the port side. At 12.25 in position 69.31.5N 34.31.5E, without warning she was hit by a torpedo which exploded under her stern. The starboard engine stopped, followed soon after by the port, and it became apparent that the propellers had gone. With the after part of the ship blown off, she settled by the stern, but with prompt work to shore up bulkheads and ready-use ammuntion stowed aft thrown overboard, there was little flooding and she remained stable. At 16.00 a Russian destroyer arrived, and a tow was secured, but this parted at 16.44, the ship constantly yawing. The *Alnwick Castle* and *Bamborough Castle* closed to take off non-essential personnel. At 18.34 a minesweeper was secured alongside, and progress was made towards the shore. In the early hours of 18 February, a tug was secured forward, and a further two arrived during the morning. The tow went on through the day until she was able to anchor in shallow water at 19.24 at Pyetenshikin Inlet. The assessment of the damage revealed that it was extensive. The stern abaft 105 station had been blown away; there was extensive buckling and splitting of the hull and side plates; bottom plates were buckled and bent and both shafts and propellers were missing. It was clear that very extensive repair work would be required, and it was decided that it was not worth repairing her. She was therefore stripped of all useful machinery and stores, being finally abandoned on 13 June. Her attacker had been *U 968* (Westphalen) which had fired a T5 acoustic homing torpedo. Three men were lost.
[TNA: ADM.1/18932]

20 February VERVAIN corvette
Belfast 1941; 940 tons; 1 × 4in, 2 × 20mm
Lieutenant Commander Robert Alwyn Howell RNVR†
Part of the escort to Convoy HX337 from New York to Liverpool, she was in position 51.56N 07.06W when at 12.50 she was hit by a torpedo, which exploded on the starboard side forward, between 24 and 30 stations. The bridge took the force of the blast, and all of the bridge staff were killed or seriously wounded. The forward end of the ship was destroyed, the mast came down, the Hedgehog projector collapsed, and the ship immediately took a steep list to port. Carley floats were launched as the ship broke in half under the 4in gun platform, the bows sinking quickly, and she had disappeared by 13.10. Sixty men were lost. Her attacker had been the *U 1276* (Wendt) which was immediately disposed of by another escort – after the attack, the frigate *Amethyst* searched the area, gained a good Asdic contact and conducted an

attack with Hedgehog projectiles, which resulted in an underwater explosion and oil bubbled up to the surface.
[TNA: ADM.199/186]

22 February TRENTONIAN corvette
Kingston 1943; 976 tons; 193ft × 33ft; 1 × 4in, 1 × 2pdr, 2 × 20mm
Lieutenant Colin Stinson Glassco RCNVR
Royal Canadian Navy. Part of Escort Group 41, she was tasked to escort Convoy BTC76 en-route to Antwerp from Milford Haven. At 13.20, when they were about 12 miles east of Falmouth, one of the ships in the port column of the convoy was hit by a torpedo and just as the corvette was altering course to investigate, they gained an Asdic contact ahead of the convoy. As she emerged from the columns of ships, she was hit on the starboard side aft by a torpedo. Flooding quickly spread through the after part of the ship and within 4 minutes had reached the engine room. She settled steadily by the stern, allowing the crew to leave in good order before she sank, about 14 minutes after being hit. Six men lost their lives. The attacker was *U 1004* (Hinz).
[McKee & Darlington p208]

22 February LST 364 landing ship, tank
Quincy 1942; 1,625 tons; 316ft × 50ft; 1 × 12pdr, 6 × 20mm
Lieutenant Commander Cecil Dick Bluett Coventry RNR
Loaded with over sixty motor vehicles and three tanks she sailed from Margate at 02.45 to join Convoy TAM87 bound for Antwerp, taking up station at the rear of the port column. At 05.45 she was rocked by an explosion on the starboard side, between frames 35 and 41. The damage was extensive; a large hole was blown in the side extending from the waterline to the upper deck; fresh water tanks burst, and the port shaft alley flooded causing the engine room to flood; all power failed, and the lights went out. The petrol tanks in some of the vehicles ruptured and the petrol vapour exploded, causing a large fire. The ship heeled over, and she settled rapidly by the stern, her bows rising out of the water. The armed trawler *Turquoise* came alongside and lifted off 220 men, the operation being complete at 07.00 just before she sank. There was no loss of life. Her attacker was uncertain but believed to be a midget *Seehund* submarine.
[TNA: ADM.199/175; MacDermott p83]

24 February LST 178 landing ship, tank
Evansville 1943; 1,625 tons; 316ft × 50ft; 1 × 12pdr, 6 × 20mm
Lieutenant Commander John Sutherland Watt DSC RNR
Based in the eastern Mediterranean, she was bound for Corfu, having sailed from Patras, loaded with army vehicles. At 09.30 there was a dull explosion on the

port side forward, and this was followed by a louder detonation on the port quarter as the ship detonated mines. The second explosion blew the port rudder off and distorted the port shaft. The hull was dented and creased, with several small cracks and splits developing, but she did not lose power, and with an MTB in company, she continued on her journey, although taking on water, and successfully made Patras harbour that afternoon. Subsequent examination found that she was too severely damaged to be worth repairing and was written off as a constructive total loss.
[MacDermott p88]

24 February ELLESMERE whaler
Middlesbrough 1939; 560 tons; 138.6ft × 26.6ft; 1 × 4in, 1 × 20mm
Lieutenant Thomas Henry Lloyd-Jones RNVR[†]
In company with the sloop *Bideford*, sailed from Plymouth to act as escort to 'Appian Flight-Q', the passage of a number of landing craft to Malta. At 23.40 when in position 49.04N 05.31W a large explosion was heard, and the *Ellesmere* was seen to be covered in smoke and spray. The sloop altered course to close the position, as did *LCI 299* but they could find only a large patch of oil, with splintered life rafts and an upside down boat. There were no survivors; thirty-seven men died. She had been attacked by *U 1209* (Seeger), that had fired a single acoustic homing torpedo at the group.
[TNA: ADM 199/175; ADM.358/3254]

March ALLIGATOR tug
Hessle 1940; 395 tons; 105ft × 26.6ft; 1 × 12pdr
Lieutenant Dudley William Bonney RNVR
In the official *Statement of Losses* listed as being reported lost, date and place unknown during this month. No further details have been found, although she was based at Trincomalee and acting as the station tug at Addu Attoll at this time.
[Statement of Losses p36; TNA ADM.208/33]

3 March SOUTHERN FLOWER whaler
Middlesbrough 1928 requisitioned 1940; 328 tons; 132ft × 26.2ft; 1 × 12pdr
Skipper William George Brown RNR
Torpedoed at 12.15 by *U 1022* (Ernst) whilst on patrol off the eastern coast of Iceland, 4 miles to the south-west of Skaggi Light, in position 64.05N 23.15W, she broke up and sank very quickly. Twenty-five men lost their lives with just one survivor, the skipper, who could say nothing apart from the ship blew up and sank very quickly.
[TNA: ADM.267/118; ADM.358/2747]

3 March STEADY HOUR air-sea rescue boat
Sydney 1940 requisitioned 1941; 35 tons; 58ft × 14.6ft
Skipper John Alison Sykes RANVR
Royal Australian Navy. Originally used as a patrol vessel, from 1944 she was employed at Darwin on air/sea rescue duties. She caught fire and was burnt out in Melville Bay; there were no casualties.
[Cassells p70]

6 March XE 11 midget submarine
Chesterfield 1944; 30 tons; 53.4ft × 5.9ft
Lieutenant Aubrey Staples SANF (V)[†]
Ordered to carry out instrument calibrations, she sailed from her base at *Varbel*, Loch Striven, with a crew of five. They submerged and went to 100ft, then slowly ascended, stopping every 10ft to re-trim the boat, calibrating instruments at each step. They had almost completed the exercise and had reached a depth of 10ft when there was loud crash as she struck something. She had been brought up directly underneath the boom defence vessel *Norina*, having strayed out of her exercise area. This first impact was followed by scraping noises as she slid along the keel of the *Norina*, which had just started her engines as the impact occurred, and the turning screws then pierced the hull of the submarine on the port side aft which started to flood. The boat sank quickly, hitting the bottom of the loch in about 180ft, at a steep angle, with water pouring in, which fused the electrics, putting out all the lights. Lieutenant Staples handed out escape apparatus breathing sets as they sank. Sub-Lieutenant Morrison had been in the heads (toilet) when the impact occurred, the compartment also doubling as the escape compartment. As the pressure equalised, he was able to open the hatch. Before he escaped, Morrison reached back into the control room, grabbing ERA Swatton, pulling him into the compartment. Both men became briefly jammed in the escape hatch, until Morrison dropped back into the boat, to be hauled out by Swatton. The pair then shot to the surface. No one else escaped. The boat was raised some days later and the bodies of the three dead crewmen recovered, but the vessel was not put back into service, being scrapped.
[Mitchell pp52–4]

6 March LCT (3) 492 landing craft, tank
Old Kilpatrick 1944; 350 tons; 175ft × 31ft; 2 × 2pdr
In tow of the Liberty ship *Samur*, which was also towing another landing craft, *LCG 5*, from Suez to Aden, *LCT 492* laboured in poor weather and started filling with water. During the evening of 5 March all nineteen men on board were taken off and the following morning she capsized, about 140 miles east-south-east of Massawa, in position 14.48N 42.02E. The hulk did not immediately sink and the cutter *Landguard* closed the scene, to speed

the end by gunfire, and was able to confirm that she finally sank at 13.54 in position 14.53N 42.06E.
[TNA: ADM.199/2313; ADM.199/772]

17 March GUYSBOROUGH minesweeper
Vancouver 1941; 673 tons; 171.5ft × 28.5ft; 1 × 12pdr, 1 × 2pdr
Lieutenant Benjamin Thomas Robert Russell RCNR
Royal Canadian Navy. Following a refit in Canada, she was heading for Plymouth, pausing in the Azores for fuel. Sailing alone she was steering north-east at 13 knots. The CAT noisemaker was streamed astern, but the ship was not zigzagging. At 18.50, in position 46.30N 09.30W, with no warning she was hit by a torpedo which detonated under the stern. She settled by the stern and assumed a list to port and the engines stopped but she remained stable. Damage control parties shored up damaged bulkheads and pumps were started, boats and floats lowered. At 19.35 she was again attacked, a torpedo hitting her amidships. She steadily settled and sank stern first about 30 minutes later. Although the boats had been destroyed most of the crew were able to gain the floats. They had to survive a cold and wet night and morning before searching ships arrived on scene, by which time many had died from hypothermia. Forty-one survivors were picked up, but fifty-one men died. Her attacker had been *U.868* (Turre).
[McKee & Darlington p214]

18 March DAFFODIL landing ship carrier
Newcastle 1917 (*Train Ferry 1*) requisitioned 1940; 2,683 tons; 350.6ft × 58.7ft; 4 × 2pdr, 5 × 20mm
Commander Spencer Francis Russell
Having offloaded a cargo of railway rolling stock, she sailed from Dieppe at 22.00 on 17 March, to proceed to Southampton. At 22.59 there was a violent explosion under the ship as she detonated a mine. The engines stopped and all electrical power failed. Both the engine and boiler rooms reported they were full of steam and they were evacuated. An examination of the ship found that she was watertight, with the exception of the engine and boiler rooms, which had clearly taken the full force of the blast. After a reasonable time had elapsed, entry was made into the boiler room and steam valves closed, which eased the situation, but it was clear that water was entering. At midnight, *MGB 333* came alongside and took off injured personnel and transferred them to the shore and at 01.45 the tug *Lynch* arrived to take her in tow, aiming to return to Dieppe. The flooding, however, was increasing, and could not be kept under by pumps, and it was being made worse by the forward movement of the tow. It was therefore decided to anchor, and this was done at 03.40. By 05.10 the ship had taken a pronounced list, and the rate of flooding was increasing. All spare hands were therefore

ordered into the tug, and all the boats were lowered. Ten minutes later she suddenly heeled over to starboard and sank. Five men were killed in the initial explosion, and a further twenty-seven died when she capsized.
[TNA: ADM.199/176]

20 March LAPWING sloop
Greenock 1943; 1,475 tons; 283ft × 38.6ft; 6 × 4in, 10 × 20mm
Commander Edward Campbell Hulton
Part of the escort to the Russian Convoy JW65, which was approaching the Kola Inlet, she was in company with five 'Castle' class corvettes which formed a screen ahead of the main body of the convoy. At 09.15 a ship in the convoy was torpedoed, and two of the corvettes were detached to assist in the hunt for the submarine. At 10.15 a further two ships of the screen were detached, to prosecute a contact that had been gained by the *Alnwick Castle*. The remaining pair, *Lapwing* and *Allington Castle*, continued, zigzagging at 12 knots. At 11.15 there was a severe explosion on the starboard side of the sloop, abreast the funnel. The motor boat and whaler were destroyed, along with the Carley floats on that side of the ship and major structural damage was caused. She immediately took a list to port; all power was lost and as she sagged in the middle, it was clear that her back was broken. The remaining Carley floats were slipped, and wooden shores and planking were thrown into the water, along with fenders and anything that would float, as the ship heeled further to port. At 11.25 the ship broke in two, both halves rolling over before sinking. The *Allington Castle* quickly closed the scene to pick up the survivors, but many died in the freezing water. Nine officers and 149 ratings died. Her attacker had been the *U 968* (Westphalen).
[TNA: ADM.199/176]

20 March LST 80 landing ship, tank
Jeffersonville 1943; 1,468 tons; 316ft × 50ft; 1 × 12pdr, 6 × 20mm
Lieutenant Commander Frederick Arthur Smyth RNR†
Sailed from Antwerp at 14.00 on 19 March in company with *LST 366* and joined Convoy ATM97 to return to England. At 18.38 as they passed NF12 buoy there was a large explosion under a merchant ship, the *Samselbu*, ahead of the landing ships. The immediate thought was that she had been torpedoed, and several of the ships in convoy started firing at suspicious objects seen in the water, and the destroyer *Versatile* commenced an anti-submarine search. *LST 80* and *LST 366* closed the *Samselbu*, which was sinking rapidly, to pick up survivors. By 19.00 this was complete, the survivors had been transferred to a motor launch, and the pair steamed to rejoin the convoy. At 20.12 as the ships passed NF9 buoy there was a large detonation under

the hull of *LST 80* as she detonated a mine. The ship started to flood, the engine room filling rapidly, and she settled by the stern. Despite a rough sea, *LST 366* came alongside and took off several men, and it was decided to try and tow the damaged ship to safety. In the poor weather conditions, this was difficult, but a tow was rigged by midnight. She proved difficult to tow, and at 02.00 the tow parted. Undeterred, *LST 366* again came alongside, took off all the crew except for fourteen men, and continued to stand by her until the tug *Antic* arrived on scene. At 08.30 with another tow line rigged, the *Antic* commenced the tow, but at 09.00 there was a large explosion on the starboard side forward of *LST 80*, which blew Lieutenant Smyth and a rating overboard. She immediately took a list to starboard and was clearly sinking. *Antic* rapidly slipped the tow and picked up men from the water as *LST 80* disappeared by the head. Four men were lost.
[TNA: ADM.199/175; MacDermott p83]

21 March MTB 655 motor torpedo boat
Littlehampton 1943; 95 tons; 110ft × 21.3ft; 1 × 2pdr, 2 × 20mm, 2 × torpedo tubes
Lieutenant Derrick Holden Brown RNVR
In company with *MGB 643* and *MGB 674* conducting a night patrol in the Adriatic, the trio steamed along the Istrian coast until 03.30 when they moved off towards Levrera Island where they were to land a detachment from the Special Boat Squadron. At 04.15, in position 44.50N 14.11.12E, there was a large detonation and *655* was enveloped in flames as she ran over a mine. This first explosion was followed by a second, as her ruptured fuel tanks exploded scattering burning wreckage and she broke in two. Her consorts closed to pick up survivors, picking their way through patches of burning fuel. Only one substantial piece of the boat was found, a section of the bows. One man was found, severely injured, still on board. Before moving off several rounds were fired into the wreck to leave it burning fiercely. Seven men were killed.
[TNA: ADM.199/175; Reynolds, Dog Boats p233]

23 March MTB 705 motor torpedo boat
Littlehampton 1942; 95 tons; 110ft × 21.3ft; 1 × 6pdr, 2 × 20mm, 2 × torpedo tubes
Lieutenant Peter Maxwell Davies RNVR
Based in the Adriatic, she was ordered to proceed from Ancona to Zara in company with *MTB 634*. The pair sailed at 10.30 and steered for the swept channel. At 14.30 on position 44.08.35N 14.43.05E, there was a large explosion under *705*, which blew her stern off, and with the engine room flooding fast, she started to settle, her bows rising clear of the water. *MTB 634* closed to lift off all the men and then stood off, as *705* slowly rolled over to port, the bows lifted until they were vertical and then she sank. Two men were lost. Both Lieutenant

Davies and Lieutenant W E A Blount of *MTB 634* were criticised over the loss. Davies was informed that he had incurred their Lordships' displeasure; he had been advised by the officer of the watch that they were steering the incorrect course but had failed to represent this fact to his senior officer. Blount, as senior officer, incurred severe displeasure. He had been guilty of careless navigation by steering a course that took the pair through known hazardous waters.
[TNA: ADM.199/175; Reynolds, Dog Boats p233]

25 March ML 466 motor launch
Itchenor 1942; 73 tons; 112ft × 18.4ft; 1 × 3pdr
Lieutenant Charles MacLennan Smith RNVR[†]
Patrolling off Walcheren, she was 4.6 miles to the west of Westkappele when she triggered a mine which exploded underneath her. A large column of water was seen by her consort, *ML 445*, which covered the launch and a cloud of thick black smoke rose from the centre. Less than a minute after the explosion the launch was seen to have been reduced to a mass of burning wreckage. *ML 445* closed, but only a small part of the bows was recognisable. There were no survivors. Two officers and eighteen ratings died.
[TNA: ADM.199/175; ADM.358/4437]

26 March PUFFIN sloop
Govan 1936; 510 tons; 234ft × 26.5ft; 1 × 4in
Lieutenant Alfred Stapledon Miller RNZNVR
During February and March 1945 there were repeated sorties by German midget submarines against shipping in the southern North Sea, but with little success. At 02.31, then being close to number 4 buoy, to the east of Lowestoft, *Puffin* gained an Asdic contact. As they closed the datum at 12 knots a midget *Seehund* submarine surfaced immediately ahead of her, which the sloop rammed. Almost immediately afterwards a heavy explosion occurred, thought to have been the detonation of the submarine's torpedo warheads. *Puffin* was lifted bodily, and the blast whipped the ship severely and she was showered with burning oil fuel. About 13ft of the fore end of the ship, from the keel to the lower deck, was blown away and the bow structure sagged and buckled, and much of the forepart of the ship was open to the sea. The ship remained upright and stable, and power was not lost, and she was able to return to Harwich, but was declared a constructive total loss.
[TNA ADM.267/134; CB.4273 p360]

26 March TERKA stores carrier
Newcastle NSW 1925 (*Sir Dudley de Chair*) requisitioned 1941; 420 tons; 147ft × 26.7ft; 1 × 12pdr
Lieutenant Frank Bruce Bragg RANVR
Royal Australian Navy. At Madang, Papua New Guinea, the ship had completed coaling, and was still secured

alongside the hulk *Rona*, when at 22.05 without warning she lurched to starboard and started settling. Water flooded the boiler and engine rooms and she righted herself as she slowly sank. No immediate cause was found for the loss.

[*Cassells p85*]

29 March **TEME** frigate

Teeside 1943; 1,370 tons; 283ft × 36.5ft; 2 × 4in, 10 × 20mm

Lieutenant Dennis Pearce Harvey RCNR

Royal Canadian Navy. Part of the escort to coastal Convoy BTC111, they were to the north of Land's End in position 50.07N 05.45W, when she investigated an Asdic contact, but failed to regain contact after it was lost. Steaming at 8 knots to rejoin, she was astern of the main body of the convoy when at 08.22 there was an explosion under her stern. About 30ft of the stern was blown away and a further 30ft, to the after end of the superstructure, was seriously damaged. Rudder, propellers and shafts were lost. The after end was exposed to the sea, but bulkheads held, and a tow was rigged. The weather deteriorated and 9 hours later, the 30ft of damaged stern broke away and sank but the ship reached safety at Falmouth. The ship was subsequently declared a constructive total loss. Four men lost their lives. The identity of the attacker was uncertain for some time, but modern research indicates that *U 315* (Zoller) would have been responsible, probably employing an acoustic homing torpedo.

[*TNA: ADM. 267/118; CB.4273 p291*]

30 March **HIGH TIDE** drifter

Lowestoft 1919 requisitioned 1940; 106 tons; 86.2ft × 18.5ft; 1 × 6pdr

Master Arthur Oswald Harris[†]

Based at Holyhead, Anglesey, for general duties, during the afternoon of 29 March she was ordered to proceed to Pwllheli in company with *MFV 720* to assist with the salvage work at a stranded vessel. Salvage gear was embarked with extra personnel, and she sailed at 00.30 on 30 March. The weather at this time was fair, with fresh breezes from the south-west and a moderate swell. The pair made 4 knots until they were about 1.5 miles west of South Stack when *720* reported that she was having difficulty in steering due to the increasing seas and high swell and turned back. About 5 minutes after *720* had altered course, it appeared that *High Tide* had altered also, or was having difficulty steering, as both steaming and bow lights became visible. They remained in sight for about 15 minutes and then only a white light could be seen, so *720* presumed that she must have resumed her course. This was the last seen of her. When she failed to arrive at Pwhelli, a search was initiated, and wreckage was reported coming ashore; later two bodies were washed

onto the beach at Rosscolin. It was thought likely that she had capsized, due to instability. When first requisitioned, some concern had been expressed over her stability, and an additional 3 tons of ballast were taken onboard, and a strict rule imposed that the maximum amount of coal embarked should not be more than 12 tons. It was found that Mr Harris had taken on board 13 tons, and as she already had remaining some 6–7 tons, she actually had some 19–20 tons of coal on board, well in excess of her limit. In addition, she had embarked two heavy pumps, several cans of petrol and two large towing hawsers, all of which were stowed on the upper deck. In the heavy swell, rolling in her condition would have caused her to react badly. It was found that Mr Harris was to blame for the loss. There were no survivors, four naval ratings and ten civilians being lost.

[*TNA: ADM.1/16927*]

7 April **MTB 5001** motor torpedo boat

St Helens 1944; 95 tons; 110ft × 21.3ft; 2 × 6pdr, 2 × 20mm, 2 × torpedo tubes

Lieutenant Alasdair Macdonald Watson RNVR

During the night of 6/7 April a force of six enemy torpedo boats made a sortie to the approaches to the river Humber, but they were detected at 22.50 by airborne reconnaissance. This allowed friendly forces to be deployed to intercept them, and at 00.40 as they closed the swept channel to the north-east of Great Yarmouth, they were intercepted by the frigate *Cubitt* and escort destroyer *Haydon* and turned away at high speed. They then encountered *MTB 781* and *MTB 5001* and a sharp gun engagement commenced at close range, with *5001* passing through the line of enemy craft. The running fight continued until *5001* received a hit in the engine room which started a fierce petrol fire, and the British pair were forced to break off. *781* ran her bows alongside *5001*'s fo'c's'le to allow her crew to escape before it sank. Three men were killed.

[*TNA: ADM.267/124; Reynolds, Home Waters MTBs p162; www.britishnewspaperarchive.co.uk: The Scotsman 17 May 2007 Watson obit.*]

7 April **MTB 494** motor torpedo boat

Hythe 1944; 41 tons; 71.9ft × 20.7ft; 1 × 6pdr, 2 × 20mm, 2 × torpedo tubes

Lieutenant Jack May RNVR[†]

Part of the 22nd MTB Flotilla based at Lowestoft, she was on patrol in the North Sea in company with *MTB 493* and *MTB 497* when they were advised by a Wellington aircraft of the encounter further to the north, which had seen the sinking of *MTB 5001* (see above). The aircraft tracked the enemy craft as they headed south and directed the torpedo boats to allow them to intercept. At 02.02 they sighted the six enemy craft to the west of them and prepared to engage with guns. The range was actually far shorter than they had realised and within minutes it became clear that the British column was actually about to pass through the German line. It was far too late to take avoiding action and *494* collided with one of the enemy craft, *S 176*. She quickly rolled over to float bottom up. As she lay wallowing in this position, she was struck again by *MTB 493*, which had also collided with one of the enemy, but had survived. The three surviving crew members abandoned her, either swimming to *493* or taking to Carley floats, but fourteen men died. The Germans lost two boats in the encounter – *S 176* which had been rammed, and *S 177*.

[TNA: ADM.267/124; Reynolds, Home Waters MTBs pp162–4]

10 April MTB 710 motor torpedo boat

Littlehampton 1943; 95 tons; 110ft × 21.3ft; 1 × 2pdr, 2 × 20mm, 2 × torpedo tubes

Lieutenant Anthony Watney Bone RNVR†

Whilst on patrol in the Adriatic, she detonated a mine off Sansego Island which exploded directly underneath her. The amidships section of the boat disintegrated, and she rapidly sank. Two officers and thirteen ratings were lost.

[TNA: ADM.267/124; Pope p271; Reynolds: Dog Boats p234]

16 April EKINS frigate

Hingham 1943; 1,300 tons; 300ft × 36.9ft; 3 × 3in, 8 × 20mm

Lieutenant Anthony John Taudevin RNVR

Patrolling off the Dutch coast, the ship was about 13 miles north-west of Ostend when at 21.25 there was an explosion under the engine room as she detonated a mine. All power was lost, and the ship drifted out of control for 15 minutes, when there was a second explosion, under the port bow. The ship heeled over to port and the after engine room, boiler room and fuel tanks were flooded. Shock damage caused the loss of most of the radar and radio aerials and the Asdic was wrecked. The flooding was controlled, and the ship remained stable. A tug arrived on scene in the morning to secure alongside, and she was safely taken to Chatham, pumping all the while. When docked, it was found that the hull aft was distorted for over 140ft with several splits, whilst forward, the side was corrugated and broken below the waterline. It was believed that two 'oyster' or pressure mines had been responsible, and the ship was declared a constructive total loss. There were no fatalities.

[TNA: ADM.267/134; CB.4273 p292]

16 April ESQUIMALT minesweeper

Sorel 1941; 592 tons; 162ft × 28ft; 1 × 4in, 1 × 2pdr

Lieutenant Robert Cunningham MacMillan DSC RCNVR

Royal Canadian Navy. Carrying out a patrol in the approaches to Halifax harbour, she was using Asdic

and had not streamed the CAT noisemaker because it caused too much interference. At 06.30, without making any Asdic contact, she was hit by a torpedo on the starboard side aft. She lost all power and rolled over to starboard and sank quickly, disappearing in 4 minutes. Her rapid demise meant that no signal could be sent, and it was not until later that day that it was realised that she was missing, and a search instigated by which time several men had died of hypothermia; forty-four men died in all. The attacker had been *U 190* (Reith), which had fired a single acoustic homing torpedo.

[McKee & Darlington p220]

17 April MTB 697 motor torpedo boat

St Helens 1943; 95 tons; 110ft × 21.3ft; 2 × 6pdr, 2 × 20mm, 2 × torpedo tubes

Lieutenant Dennis Hamilton Booth RNVR

Stationed in the Adriatic, in company with *MTB 670*, *MGB 633* and *MGB 658* sailed from Rab Island to carry out a patrol to the north-west of Krk, to prevent the enemy reinforcement of the area. As they negotiated a gap between the islands in line ahead, there was a flash and a large explosion as *697*, second in line, detonated a mine. She was split in two and the forward section caught fire, burning fiercely. Both of the other boats stopped to assist, having to avoid floating mines and burning debris to pick men from the sea. Ten ratings were lost. The position was noted as 44.59N 14.55E.

[Pope pp277–8]

27 April REDMILL frigate

Hingham 1943; 1,300 tons; 300ft × 36.7ft; 3 × 3in, 2 × 40mm, 8 × 20mm

Lieutenant John Richard Alured Denne

In company with *Fitzroy* and *Rupert*, the *Redmill* was conducting an anti-submarine sweep off the north-west of Ireland, actively investigating Asdic contacts. The group were about 25 miles west of the coast of Mayo, when there was an explosion under her stern. About 50ft of her stern was blown away. Forward of this a further 20ft, including a 3in gun and its support, was wrecked and blown upwards to an angle of about 45 degrees. The compartments immediately forward of the damage flooded and the ship was open to the sea. With the loss of propellers and shafts, the ship came to a stop, but bulkheads held. The *Rupert* towed the damaged ship, screened by *Fitzroy*, until relieved by the tug *Jaunty*, which towed *Redmill* to Londonderry, where she was later declared a constructive total loss. The attacker had been *U 1105* (Schwarz). Twenty-two men were killed.

[TNA: ADM.267/133; CB.4273 p293]

28 April BYMS 2053 minesweeper
Jacksonville 1942; 215 tons; 130ft × 24ft; 1 × 3in, 2 × 20mm
Lieutenant Peter Erington Davies RNVR
One of a large group of minesweepers employed in the Adriatic, sweeping along the northern Italian coast from Cesenatica to Porto Corsino, by 28 April they were working to clear the approaches to the latter port. The day was overcast, but with little wind and a calm sea. A group of five BYMS ships with two motor launches were sweeping, with another two BYMS and two landing craft acting as dan layers and for mine disposal. One mine had been put up and disposed of by rifle fire during their second lap, when at 13.23 in position 44.41N 12.37E, about 20 miles off the coast there was a large explosion near *2053* when a mine detonated. The ship was 'whipped' and badly shaken and water started to enter as she heeled over. *BYMS 2028* closed and managed to pass a tow, but it parted. Undeterred, the tow was re-rigged, but *2053* was settling all the time, making towing increasingly difficult. By 14.30 it was clear that she was sinking, and she was ordered to be abandoned. Ten minutes later she rolled over to starboard and sank. Two men died.
[*Minett pp285–6*]

29 April GOODALL frigate
Boston 1943 (USS *Reybold*); 1,140 tons; 283.6ft × 35.2ft; 3 × 3in, 2 × 40mm, 9 × 20mm
Lieutenant Commander James Vandalle Fulton RNVR
As part of the escort group which were providing screening duties ahead of Convoy RA66 she sailed from the Kola Inlet, Russia. The group of five ships were in line abreast, 4,000 yards apart, steaming at 12 knots with noisemakers streamed. During the early evening it became evident that they were passing through a line of U-boats. At 19.00 one of the group, the *Loch Insh* reported an Asdic contact and carried out an attack using the Squid anti-submarine mortar and soon after this the *Anguilla* also gained a contact, and she was detached to prosecute. The remaining three ships continued, until 19.35 when the *Goodall* gained an Asdic contact. She had barely reported this and was preparing to alter course to fire a pattern of Hedgehog projectiles when there was a large explosion under the bridge. The forward part of the ship disappeared, the bridge was folded over the funnel and the mast was blown overboard. A constant series of detonations followed, with tracer shells erupting out of her, and it was clear that her forward magazine had exploded following a torpedo hit. The survivors hastily scrambled into Carley floats as the *Loch Shin* turned to close, gaining an Asdic contact as she did, which resulted in another Squid attack before she closed to pick up survivors. The wreck was left burning. The following day, after the convoy had passed out of the area the group returned to the scene and the

Anguilla sank what remained of the wreck by gunfire. At that time the wreck was afloat but burning fiercely. When hit by the gunfire there was another tremendous explosion and only a small section of the stern then remained above water. The approximate position of the attack was 69.15N 33.38E. Sixty-one men lost their lives. After the war it was discovered that she had actually been attacked twice. The *U 968* (Westphalen) had missed with a T5 acoustic homing torpedo earlier, and just over an hour later she was hit by another T5 fired by the *U 286* (Dietrich).
[*TNA: ADM.199/176*]

April MGB 99 motor gun boat
Nantes 1940 (*VTB 12*); 28 tons; 65.7ft × 13ft; 2 × torpedo tubes
Listed as being written off during April as a constructive total loss, but with no further details.
[*Statement of Losses p35*]

3 May LCT (4) 1238 landing craft, tank
Bo'ness 1944; 200 tons; 171ft × 38.8ft
Lieutenant Commander Edward Walter Kennard[†]
Part of the force assembled on the coast of Burma to take part in Operation 'Dracula', the landing at Rangoon, she sailed with other amphibious force ships from Kyaukpyu on 28 April arriving in the approaches to Rangoon on 2 May. It soon emerged that the Japanese occupiers had already abandoned the area, and landings went on unopposed, there were, however, still hazards, as at 11.00 *LCT 1238* detonated a mine and sank when off Elephant Point at the entrance to Rangoon River. Eight men were killed.
[*London Gazette 6 April 1951; TNA: ADM.223/58*]

2 May EBOR WYKE trawler
Selby 1929 requisitioned 1940; 348 tons; 140.3ft × 24ft; 1 × 12pdr
Chief Skipper Hans Albert Jensen DSC RNR[†]
In company with the minesweeping trawler *Clevela*, carrying out a combined acoustic and magnetic mine (SA/LL) sweep off the east coast of Iceland. At 11.33 when they were 6.6 miles to the south of Skagi light, she was engulfed by a large explosion. She appeared to have been hit in the engine room, with debris scattered over a large area, and she was shrouded in a thick pall of black smoke. When the smoke cleared, she could be seen to be rapidly sinking by the stern and had disappeared in 10 seconds. The *Clevela* closed and lowered her sea boat, to pick up one survivor, twenty-three men being lost. She had been torpedoed by *U 979* (Meermeier).
[*TNA: ADM.199/175*]

5 May CORIOLANUS trawler
Selby 1940; 545 tons; 150ft × 27.8ft; 1 × 12pdr, 3 × 20mm
Lieutenant George Rundle RNVR
Deployed to the Adriatic coast of Italy to help clear the
coast of mines, she was based at Ancona. Ordered to
clear an area of shallow water, a force of five motor
launches were employed as minesweepers, with the
Coriolanus following the group acting a dan layer. At
about noon the group had completed a lap and were
re-positioning themselves to conduct another and the
Coriolanus had just laid a buoy to mark the edge of the
swept area. She started to manoeuvre around the dan
to take up her position astern of the sweepers, when
at 12.09 there was a large explosion. The blast was on
the starboard side, just under the bridge, and the force
of the explosion forced up the deck plates and blew a
hole in the side, demolishing a watertight bulkhead. She
rolled over to port and started filling with water. It was
clear that she was sinking rapidly and was ordered to be
abandoned; she sank at 12.14, her position then being
47.17.36N 13.22.40E. There were no casualties. It was
assessed that the most likely cause of the loss was that
during the manoeuvring to re-position herself, she must
have strayed outside the swept channel. An alternative
solution was that a mine may have been missed during
the last sweeping lap when one of the MLs had briefly
hauled out of position to deal with a mine snagged on
her sweep.
[TNA: ADM1/18938]

5 May ML 558 motor launch
Itchenor 1942; 73 tons; 112ft × 18.4ft; 1 × 3pdr
Lieutenant William Alfred Merrick RNVR
Stationed in the Adriatic, she was the lead ship of a
group of four motor launches ordered to assist with
sweeping mines between from Corsini to San Giovanni.
The launches would precede a group of three motor
minesweepers. During the afternoon several 'snag lines'
were encountered – wires designed to catch on a sweep
wire and then pull a contact mine towards the sweeper.
They were all avoided and cut until at 15.23 another
snag line was spotted close ahead. The wheel was put
over, but it was too late and moments later a mine
exploded under the stern on the starboard side. The
whole of the stern as far as the tank space bulkhead was
blown off, but remarkably, the engines kept running.
Other launches closed and took off the injured and
non-essential personnel, and a tow was rigged by *ML
459*. She was towed inshore and dragged into shallow
water in San Giovanni Bay where she was beached and
abandoned as a wreck. One man died of his wounds.
[TNA: ADM.199/175]

9 May PROMPT minesweeper
Toronto 1944; 950 tons; 212.5ft × 35.5ft; 1 × 4in,
8 × 20mm
Lieutenant Commander Robert Kenley Hart RANVR
Leading a force of eighteen minesweepers, with six
motor launches fitted for sweeping, *Prompt* was tasked
to clear the approaches to the port of Rotterdam of
mines. She was about 12 miles north-west of Ostend,
when at 17.05, underway at 11 knots with sweep gear
out, she detonated a mine abaft the engine room under
the bottom. The hull plating was split and distorted, and
flooding commenced in all the compartments abaft the
engine room, and the flooding slowly spread through
fractured bulkheads. All power was lost, and fractured
oil pipes caused a fire to break out in the forward
boiler room. After an hour of hard work, the fires were
extinguished and the flooding controlled, and some
power restored. She was towed to Sheerness, but on
survey was declared a constructive total loss, not being
worth repairing. There were no fatalities.
[TNA: ADM.267/118; CB.4273 p328]

9 May ML 591 motor launch
Looe 1944; 73 tons; 112ft × 18.4ft; 1 × 6pdr
Lieutenant Paul Prosser SANF
Following the successful occupation of Rangoon, the
army consolidated their positions and requested that
the Navy gave support by preventing fleeing Japanese
troops escaping across the Sittang River. To that end, a
force of motor launches entered the river in the early
hours of the morning, but *ML 591* along with *ML 905*,
ran aground in the darkness and were left high and dry
by the falling tide. When the tide turned, they were
both caught by the tidal bore and were capsized. All of
the crew managed to swim ashore.
[TNA: ADM.199/260; http://www.burmastar.org.uk/merrett.
htm]

9 May ML 905 motor launch
Cockenzie 1944; 73 tons; 112ft × 18.4ft; 1 × 2pdr
Lieutenant Harry Leslie DSC RNVR
In company with *ML 591* (above), she was supporting
army operations in the river Sittang, Burma, when she
was capsized by a powerful wave after running aground.
All managed to swim ashore.
[TNA: ADM.199/260]

12 May MGB 2002 motor gun boat
Northam 1943 (*MGB 502*); 95 tons; 117ft × 20.3ft;
1 × 2pdr, 2 × 20mm
Lieutenant Commander Robert Marshall RNVR†
Sailed from Aberdeen on 11 May to proceed to
Gothenburg in Sweden with four passengers, but not
heard from afterwards, and it was feared that she had
hit a mine. Wreckage from the boat was washed ashore

at Lista, and floating wreckage was seen by a searching aircraft in position 57.36N 07.00E. It was feared that all had been lost, but on 16 May two survivors, who had been in a raft for 4 days, were picked up by a Norwegian merchant ship in the Skaggerak. They were able to confirm that there was a large explosion under the vessel at 03.45 which demolished the forward part of the boat and she quickly sank. Twenty-four men died.
[TNA: ADM.199/260]

14 May WATCHER auxiliary
Brisbane 1939 (*Lookout*) requisitioned 1942; 72 tons; 93ft × 18ft
Commissioned Warrant Officer Francis Gerald Squire RANR
Royal Australian Navy. Fitted as a mobile port wireless telegraphy and signal station for service in New Guinea, she ran aground on Harvey Rocks, north-east of Thursday Island, off the coast of Queensland, whilst towing the ketch *Stingray*. She was subsequently written off as a total loss.
[Cassells p105]

16 May FAURO CHIEF auxiliary schooner
Botany Bay 1930 requisitioned 1942; 19 tons; 65ft × 16ft
Lieutenant Keith Dawson Kershaw RANR
Royal Australian Navy. Assigned to air-sea rescue duties a Port Moresby, New Guinea, she foundered when a jetty collapsed at Port Milne. There were no casualties.
[Cassells p29]

21/22 May Storm and Fire at Genoa
During 22 May a number of landing craft were lying off the Italian port of Genoa, when the weather worsened until by the afternoon it was blowing a full gale. Several landing craft found they were dragging their anchors, and there were numerous collisions, resulting in the loss of one of the landing craft. Others broached, swinging broadside-on to the beach where they suffered extensive damage. Worse was to follow, as one of the craft, laden with petrol, caught fire after a fuel spillage and then exploded, setting several other craft on fire. In all nine landing craft were lost.
[TNA: ADM.199/2318; ADM.199/1449]

LCT (4) 548 landing craft, tank
Middlesbrough 1942; 200 tons; 171ft × 38.8ft
Lieutenant Robert Vernon Donaldson RNVR
Suffered severe damage after being rammed 'with great force' by an Italian landing craft which had lost her anchor, she was written off as a total loss.

LCT (4) 552 landing craft, tank
Middlesbrough 1942; 200 tons; 171ft × 38.8ft
Caught fire after a fuel spillage during the storm and subsequently blew up and sank.

LCT (4) 554 landing craft, tank
Middlesbrough 1942; 200 tons; 171ft × 38.8ft
Laying alongside *552* and caught fire after the explosion and subsequently written off.

LCT (4) 615 landing craft, tank
Thornaby 1943; 200 tons; 171ft × 38.8ft
Also laying alongside *552* when it caught fire and blew up, she was written off after catching fire.

The following were written off either as a result of the fire or being driven ashore during the storm:

LCT (4) 550 landing craft, tank
Middlesbrough 1943; 200 tons; 171ft × 38.8ft

LCT (4) 559 landing craft, tank
Thornaby 1942; 200 tons; 171ft × 38.8ft

LCT (4) 561 landing craft, tank
Thornaby 1943; 200 tons; 171ft × 38.8ft

LCT (4) 578 landing craft, tank
Thornaby 1942; 200 tons; 171ft × 38.8ft

LCT (4) 586 landing craft, tank
Thornaby 1942; 200 tons; 171ft × 38.8ft

★ ★ ★

22 May MGB 2007 motor gun boat
Northam 1943 (*MGB 507, Gay Corsair*); 95 tons; 117ft × 20.3ft; 1 × 2pdr, 2 × 20mm
Originally completed as a merchant-manned blockade runner, it was intended to make clandestine trips to Sweden to collect ball bearings. This mission had mixed success, and in late 1944 she was converted to a motor gun boat. Late in the afternoon she was entering Aberdeen harbour, but encountered a confused sea and heavy swell as she entered Navigation Channel. Difficult to control, she swung to port and struck rocks about 150 yards to the east of the old South Breakwater. Efforts to free her failed, and with waves breaking over her in a rising sea, the local lifeboat was launched to stand by her, and the local rocket brigade turned out to fire a line, and this enabled an injured man to be lifted off by breeches buoy. By 21.30 heavy seas were now breaking over her and she was pounding badly. Despite the dangerous conditions, the lifeboat was taken in, and after three attempts, in which she suffered considerable damage, finally secured alongside to lift off all the crew. She was abandoned as a wreck two days later.
[TNA: ADM.199/2318; WSS Small Craft Group Journal 29 p14]

26 May LCT (3) 357 landing craft, tank
Thornaby 1942; 350 tons; 175ft × 31ft; 2 × 2pdr
Lieutenant Roger Meyrick Beauchamp RNVR
Sent to Suda Bay, Crete, as part of the force to take the surrender of German forces in the area, she was subsequently employed in embarking stocks of enemy ammunition for subsequent dumping at sea. A fire broke out when loading and the ammunition began to explode, and she eventually blew up. Sub-Lieutenant Ian Hay SANF was awarded an OBE for taking an open boat alongside the burning craft to rescue the crew.
[TNA: ADM.199/1449; London Gazette 16 November 1945]

6 June BROADLAND drifter
Lowestoft 1913 requisitioned 1939; 76 tons;
80.8ft × 17.9ft; 1 × 3pdr
Escort to Convoy RUN6 off the coast of Northern Ireland she became increasingly unstable, apparently having been overloaded with coal. The crew were taken off and she was sunk by gunfire from the armed whaler *Stora*.
[TNA: ADM.1/16928; ADM.199/2319]

13 June LOLITA air-sea rescue boat
Sydney 1937 requisitioned 1941; 18 tons; 54ft × 13.5ft
Lieutenant John Trim RANR
Royal Australian Navy. A motor launch, initially employed as a local patrol vessel, she was later employed as an air-sea rescue boat. She caught fire following an engine room explosion and foundered in Sydney Harbour. Two motor mechanics were killed.
[Cassells p37]

21 June HILDASAY trawler
Beverley 1941; 545 tons; 150ft × 27.6ft; 1 × 12pdr;
3 × 20mm
Lieutenant Wilfred Clennel Wilkinson (Kenyan) RNVR
Ran aground on a reef near Kilindini, East Africa, at 23.55 on 20 June whilst carrying out salvage operations on a wrecked lighter and all subsequent efforts to free her failed. She was ordered to be paid off and was written off as a constructive total loss.
[TNA: ADM.199/772]

25 June MMS 168 minesweeper
Par 1942; 165 tons; 105ft × 23ft
Skipper-Lieutenant Albert Henry Tucker DSC RNR[†]
When the Allies occupied the northern ports of Italy, they found that they had been heavily mined by the departing Germans. An intensive effort was made to clear the menace, involving several minesweeping flotillas. At Genoa, several motor minesweepers were used. *MMS 168* had already made several sweeps, and on 25 June was ordered to carry out a sweep for magnetic and acoustic mines in Genoa, between Ponte Eritrea and Avamporto. At 08.07 the ship had just completed a turn at the end of one leg and was steadying up on a new course when a mine detonated directly under the bows. The ship broke up and sank immediately with the loss of fifteen men.
[TNA: ADM.1/18770]

8 July LA NANTAISE trawler
Beverley 1933 (*St Arcadius*); 403 tons; 151.5ft × 25.6ft;
1 × 12pdr
Skipper Lieutenant Sidney John Cory RNR
Whilst on passage from Portsmouth to the Tyne, towing a small fishing vessel, the *Betty York*, they had followed several other ships that were part of a northbound convoy. At 00.20 she was in collision with the *Helencrest* (5,233 tons), about 5 cables (1,000 yards) to the north of the North Goodwin Buoy. The merchant ship had mistakenly presumed the trawler was part of the convoy and failed to realise that she was steering an independent course. The tug *Empire Henchman* was sent to the scene and picked up fifteen survivors who were transferred to *MTB 757* to be taken to Ramsgate. Walmer lifeboat was launched and the RAF launch *HSL2668* sailed from Ramsgate to carry out a search for any more survivors, but no one was found, nine ratings being lost.
[TNA: ADM.199/1441]

10 July KURD trawler
Selby 1930 requisitioned 1939; 352 tons; 140.3ft × 24.6ft;
1 × 12pdr
Lieutenant Commander Roy Barrett RNR[†]
One of a group of three minesweeping trawlers tasked to clear a defensive British minefield, QZX1600, in the vicinity of Lizard Point. At 12.46, as they were recovering sweeps, a mine was seen to have become snagged on the port Oropesa wire and was brought to the surface when only 6ft from the side, and despite the cable being instantly veered out, it exploded. She rolled over to starboard, slowly righted herself and then sank rapidly by the stern, disappearing in less than a minute. Her position was noted at 49.51.48N 05.01.55W. Sixteen men died, with eleven survivors.
[TNA: ADM.1/18940]

17 July ATHLETE tug
Orange 1943 (*ATR.92*); 783 tons; 135ft × 33.3ft; 1 × 3in,
2 × 20mm
Lieutenant Henry Cresswell RNR
Sank after she detonated a mine in the northern approaches to Livorno harbour at 07.15 in position 43.35.10N 10.15.12E. One man was killed with two missing.
[TNA: ADM.199/260; ADM.358/3030]

(?) July **MTB 242** motor torpedo boat

Portchester 1942; 47 tons; 72.6ft × 19.3ft; 1 × 20mm,
2 × torpedo tubes

Stationed in the Mediterranean, she had been based in the Adriatic with the 24th MTB Flotilla. She was under tow to Malta when she foundered.

[Statement of Losses p35]

24 July **SQUIRREL** minesweeper

Belfast 1943; 940 tons; 212.6ft × 35.6ft; 1 × 4in, 8 × 20mm
Lieutenant Commander Malcolm Buist

Part of a group of minesweepers that had arrived in the Indian Ocean in April 1945, they were tasked during mid-July to start the clearance of minefields around Phuket island, off the coast of Thailand, designated Operation 'Livery'. Distant cover for the operation was provided by the aircraft carriers *Ameer* and *Empress*, and more direct cover by the cruiser *Sussex*, destroyers from the 11th Destroyer Flotilla and units from the Royal Indian Navy. During 24 July, the minesweepers had completed three laps, bringing up several mines, and were about to commence a fourth. As they did so a mine exploded in the sweep of the *Plucky*, and as she hauled out of line to replace the sweep wire, the *Squirrel* took her place as the guide ship. The ships lined up to commence the next lap, approaching the line of buoys marking the edge of the last sweep, when there was a large explosion under the bows of the *Squirrel*. Her bows promptly dipped, and within a minute her fo'c'sle was awash as far aft as the breakwater and she assumed a list of 10 degrees to starboard. Boats and floats were put into the water as flooding was reported to be spreading aft. She lost electrical power, and with the boiler room reporting flooding, she was ordered to be abandoned; all the crew were taken off by the other ships. The ship continued to slowly settle and the list increased, but she remained stubbornly afloat. At 19.00 a destroyer closed and after several rounds were fired into the wreck, she sank. Seven men were lost.

[TNA:ADM.199/778]

26 July **VESTAL** minesweeper

Belfast 1943; 940 tons; 212.6ft × 35.6ft; 1 × 4in, 8 × 20mm
Lieutenant Commander Charles William Porter DSC

Part of the group of minesweepers taking part in Operation 'Livery', sweeping off the island of Phuket, (see *Squirrel* above), she was in company with her sisters *Pincher*, *Plucky* and *Rifleman*. Accompanied by two Indian Navy units, the *Deccan* and *Punjab* which acted as dan layers, the group had been sweeping all day under the protection of the cruiser *Sussex*. Late in the afternoon they came under air attack, when two aircraft, believed to be either Mitsubishi Ki51 'Sonia' or Aichi D3A 'Val', approached the group, heading for the cruiser. They were engaged by anti-aircraft fire from all the ships, and one of the aircraft was hit and crashed into the sea off the starboard side of *Sussex*. The second aircraft veered away and then altered course to head for the minesweepers, initially making for the *Plucky*. Still under fire from the minesweepers, the attacker was seen to be hit, but carried on, passing astern of the *Plucky* and then banked, to come round to head for the *Vestal*. The aircraft then dived straight into the ship, hitting her amidships on the port side, exploding as it hit. This wrecked the amidships section; strips of the deck were folded back and hung over the side; the funnel was still upright, but the deck around it had been blown away; the fo'c'sle deck was badly distorted; watertight doors were blown in and a fire started. The *Deccan* and *Punjab* closed and played fire hoses onto her for 30 minutes, but it was clear they were fighting a losing battle, as the centre section of the ship had disappeared. She was then abandoned. The destroyer *Racehorse* was summoned to the scene and after firing a number of rounds into the wreck dispatched her with a torpedo. Twenty men were lost.

[TNA:ADM.1/19611]

3 | Losses between 16 August 1945 and 24 April 1984

WITH THE END OF HOSTILITIES, the Royal Navy adjusted to peacetime restrictions. With a large fleet of wartime-built ships there was no need for new construction for several years, and the steady move away from Empire reduced the need to maintain fleets on foreign stations. The 1950s saw the confrontation with the Soviet Union develop into the Cold War, and the emphasis on deep-water anti-submarine work and mine warfare.

For completeness, I have included the losses suffered by the Royal Australian Navy in this section, but not the wider community of Commonwealth navies.

1945

17 August ML 230 motor launch
Oulton Broad 1941; 73 tons; 112ft × 18.4ft; 1 × 2pdr, 2 × 20mm
Lieutenant Jack Kenneth Cook RNVR
Part of a large naval force assembled at Trincomalee to take part in Operation 'Zipper', the landing in Malaya, which sailed on 15 August. The news of the surrender of Japan caused the cancellation of the operation, and the force was diverted to the Nicobar Islands to await developments. During this period *ML 230* was employed as a despatch vessel, moving between the ships of the force. When coming alongside the tanker *Cromwell* she was sucked against the hull and severely damaged. The crew was removed, and she was sunk by gunfire from destroyers.
[Winser, British Invasion Fleets p141; Goulden p218]

26 August MTB 261 motor torpedo boat
Bayonne NJ 1940 (*PT 12*); 32 tons; 70ft × 20ft; 4 × torpedo tubes
Out of commission, she foundered at her moorings in Alexandria harbour and was later 'destroyed' to clear the area.
[WSS Warship Supplement no 65 p10]

4 October HDML 1226 motor launch
Hamworthy 1942; 46 tons; 70ft × 15ft; 1 × 20mm
Lieutenant John Aubrey Clarendon Latham RNVR
In company with a group of trawlers and other motor launches, the ships were engaged in clearing minefields in the northern Aegean, around the island of Samothraki. During the afternoon, the launches moved to close the coast of the mainland, to work along the 15-fathom line, and immediately had some success, with a mine being found and disposed of. Soon after this *1226* snagged her sweep wire on an obstruction, which was found to be a float and chain mooring. She stopped to stream a new sweep and it was then decided to locate the disturbed float and recover it. As they were in the middle of signalling her intentions by light there was a large explosion under her stern which lifted her out of the water. She was clearly severely damaged, and water flooded into her, but she remained upright and stable. The other motor launches closed her to take off the crew, many of whom were injured, and a tow was rigged, but the engine room was filling fast and at 16.41 the bows rose up vertically and she sank, then being 2.8 miles to the south of Alexandropoulos light. Three men were killed.
[TNA: ADM.267/123]

5 October MFV 118 tender
Fareham 1943; 50 tons; 61.6ft × 17.9ft
Following an accidental fire whilst at Portsmouth, she was sufficiently damaged to be written off as a constructive total loss.
[WSS Warship Supplement 'The Naval MFVs of World War 2' p9]

12 October LOCH ERIBOL trawler
Beverley 1939 (*Beverlac*) purchased 1939; 352 tons; 140.3ft × 24ft
Sub-Lieutenant Leonard Francis Watts RNVR
Whilst anchored in thick fog off Start Point, Devon, she was rammed by the American Liberty ship *Sidney Sherman* (7,176 tons), which was on passage from Rotterdam to New York. The trawler subsequently sank about 18 miles east of Start Point, the crew being taken off by the trawler *Varanga*. There were no casualties.
[TNA: ADM.199/260]

16/17 October LCT (3) 7020 landing craft, tank
Meadowside 1944; 350 tons; 175ft × 31ft; 2 × 20mm
Sub-Lieutenant Dennis William Bowers RNVR[†]
Based in India, she sailed from Madras on 15 October bound for Vizagapatam, but failed to arrive as expected. The weather was bad, with cyclonic winds and high seas, and this initially prevented any air searches taking place. A subsequent air and surface search failed to find any trace of the craft which was presumed to have

foundered due to stress of weather, with the loss of all thirteen men on board.

[TNA: ADM.199/260; ADM.358/2857]

25 October LST 405 landing ship, tank

Baltimore 1942; 1,468 tons; 316ft × 50ft; 1 × 12pdr, 6 × 20mm

Lieutenant Commander James Clifford Anderson RNR

Collided with the American troopship *General M M Patrick (AP.150)* in the approaches to Colombo Harbour, she suffered some structural damage – the side plates and upper deck about 30ft from the bows were buckled and the degaussing cable was crushed. Despite the relatively slight damage it was decided that she would not be repaired and was written off as a constructive total loss. It would appear that she was towed out and scuttled at sea on 27 March 1946.

[TNA: ADM.199/2325; MacDermott p113]

5 November LST 199 landing ship, tank

Seneca 1943; 1,468 tons; 316ft × 50ft; 1 × 12pdr, 6 × 20mm

Commander Jack Trelawny Hamlyn RNR DSC

Proceeding to Batavia (Jakarta) with 400 soldiers of the 6/5 Maharati Regiment embarked, she was 5 miles to the north of Karang Jamuang light, Java, when at 18.00 she detonated a mine. The blast whipped and shook the ship violently, and she quickly anchored to check for damage. After a quick survey, she appeared stable, but there was extensive shock damage; the sides and decks were split, distorted and buckled, machinery and equipment had moved off their mountings and many internal fittings were broken. The former Japanese Navy supply ship *Arasaki* was brought alongside to take off the troops, and when that was completed the frigate *Loch Tarbert* rigged a tow and she was brought into Surabaya. On closer examination the hull was found to be seriously damaged, and she was condemned as a constructive total loss on 30 November and ordered to be disposed of locally.

[TNA: ADM.267/124]

12 November ERISKAY trawler

Paisley 1942; 545 tons; 150ft × 27.6ft; 1 × 12pdr, 3 × 20mm

Lieutenant Eric Henry Andrews RNVR

Based in the Azores, she was ordered to proceed from Angra on the island of Terceira to Horta on Faial. Departing at 22.00, the passage was uneventful until at 03.15 when she ran hard aground, the impact waking the commanding officer. A boat was lowered to sound around her, and this showed that she was in shallow water and a rocky shore was visible ahead. A check of the ship showed that the fore peak was flooded, and other forward compartments were making water. A kedge anchor was prepared and laid out astern but

attempts to haul her free failed. The engines were now put astern, but despite full power and hauling on the kedge wire, she would not move. Ammunition was now jettisoned, and other weighty objects heaved overboard, but all efforts to move her failed. By 07.00 the water was reported to be gaining on the pumps, and a boat successfully made it to the shore where a number of local people could be seen gathering and a wire was passed and secured. With the engine room reporting that it was flooding, it was decided to leave her, and a bosun's chair was rigged and by 09.30 all the crew had been landed. The subsequent enquiry found that she had run aground on the southern side of San Jorge island, in position 38.37.45N 28.06.30W due to a combination of errors. The officer of the middle watch, Sub-Lieutenant Alexander Oag RNVR, had altered course following a running fix on a light. Not only was the fix not reliable enough to have ordered a course change, but he had then applied the compass deviation the wrong way and ordered a course of N43W instead of N57W. This had taken her inshore instead of running along the coast. This mistake had been compounded by the failure of Oag to call the commanding officer when the visibility decreased and by the failure of the lookout to promptly report the sighting of a light at 02.30. Oag had sighted land ahead at 03.05 and ordered the engines full astern and put the helm over, but it was far too late. The wreck was later stripped of all useful gear before being sold for £800.

[TNA: ADM.1/19917; ADM.1/19327]

4 December MFV 1218 tender

Peterhead 1945; 114 tons; 69.9ft × 19.9ft

Foundered off the coast of Norfolk, following a collision with *MFV 1161* off North Scroby.

[WSS Warship Supplement, 'The Naval MFVs of World War 2' p 37]

19 December AIR MIST air-sea rescue launch

San Pedro (USA) 1944; 24 tons; 63ft × 15ft

Sub Lieutenant James Needle RANVR

Royal Australian Navy. On completion of air-sea rescue duties in Indonesia, she was under tow back to Sydney, with the minesweeper *Geraldton* taking over towing duties from 14 December at Brisbane, taking both *Air Mist* and her sister *Air Master* in tow. When to the north of Newcastle NSW, the tow parted, and the launch drifted away until the crew were able to anchor in shallow water. The launch subsequently dragged her anchor and went ashore on rocks near Morna Point, New South Wales, the crew having been taken off by *Air Master*.

[http://www.navy.gov.au/hmas-air-mist]

1946

1 January ALATNA tender
Sydney 1943; 28 tons; 62ft × 14.5ft
Royal Australian Navy. Originally built as a fast supply launch for the Australian Army, she was employed by the Navy as part of the Services Reconnaissance Department in Celebes (Sulawesi), supporting the work of the army. With the cessation of hostilities, she was paid off, and in December the destroyer *Quickmatch* was ordered to tow the launch to Labuan Island to be handed back to the control of the army. The pair were off the northern coast of Borneo, when at 10.00 they encountered an American merchant ship, the *Happy Runner*, which altered course towards them, apparently intending to pass astern, but struck the launch and cut it in two. One man was lost.
[https://www.navyhistory.org.au/ranships/hmas-alatna/]

4 January FT 4 tender
Warren (RI) 1943 (*APc54*); 165 tons; 99.3ft × 21.3ft
Written off and declared a constructive total loss on this date; apparently damaged by fire whilst lying at Colombo.
[WSS Warships Supplement no.75 p3]

8 January ADC 527 ammunition dumping craft
Glasgow 1942 (*LCT 527*); 200 tons; 171ft × 38.9ft
Master John Bertram Ross†
One of a number of naval landing craft that were placed under the control of the RASC water transport company, to be employed as an ammunition dumping craft (ADC). Manned by a civilian crew, she sailed in company with two other craft from Silloth, Cumberland on 6 January, bound for Cairnryan, loaded with explosives and ammunition for disposal. The weather was poor and *527* became separated and disappeared in heavy seas in the early hours of 8 January. Wreckage was later washed ashore at Garlieston and two bodies also came ashore in Wigtown Bay and another at Muncraig; twelve men died. The wreck has been found, lying to the south of Burrow Head.
[www.britishnewspaperarchive.co.uk/: Hull Daily Mail 12 January 1946; Angus Evening Telegraph 12 January 1946]

26–27 January Foundering of motor torpedo boats on passage
MTB 633 /MTB 634 / MTB 637 / MTB 638 / MTB 642 / MTB 643 / MTB 658 / MTB 659 / MTB 670 / MTB 674 / MTB 698 / MTB 700
Hamworthy 1942 (*633*), Littlehampton 1943 (*634*, *700*); Sandbank 1943 (*637*); Bangor (*638*); Appledore 1942 (*642*); St. Helens 1942 (*643*); Brixham 1943 (*658*); Falmouth 1943 (*659*); Wallasea 1943 (*670, 698*), Teddington (*674*); 95 tons; 110ft × 21.3ft

With the end of hostilities, the numerous small craft in the Mediterranean were disarmed and laid up in a variety of naval ports. A number of torpedo boats were at Malta, but in January 1946, twelve were ordered to be towed to Egypt – the reason is somewhat unclear, but probably for transfer to the local authorities for use as customs vessels. The destroyers *Jervis*, *Chequers*, *Chaplet* and *Chevron* were detailed to tow the craft, each ship towing three boats in line astern. They sailed during 25 January, despite threatening weather, and were soon in trouble, the boats corkscrewing in the high wind and waves. Some became swamped and others parted tows. To prevent them becoming a hazard to shipping, over the next 2 days, one by one they were despatched by gunfire from the destroyers. Only eleven numbers are listed in most sources, but it would seem likely that *MTB 674* was also involved as the twelfth boat.
[TNA: ADM.53/121581; Reynolds, Dog Boats pp239–40]

30 January MFV 1512 tender
Lowestoft 1945; 200 tons; 90ft × 22.3ft
At midday on 28 January a group of fourteen MFVs sailed from Cochin, southern India, bound for Penang and Singapore, under the escort of the frigate *Loch Tarbert*. During the early hours of the following morning, one of them, *MFV 1512*, reported that they were making water, apparently through the seams of the hull planking in the fore peak and hold. *Loch Tarbert* closed to stand by her, and at first light brought her alongside to pass a pump. This quickly cleared the water, and at 10.47 the frigate slipped the tender and the group continued. During the afternoon, *MFV 1512* reported that she was again making water, and although her bilge pump did not seem to be working, she was coping. By 18.00 the frigate was back alongside, and despite a swell, managed to transfer three men to help repairing the bilge pump, but it was decided to take the tender in tow, rather than let her fall behind. Despite the best efforts of the repair team, the pump remained obstinately defective, and although hand bailing was being used, the water steadily gained during the night. By 05.00 it was clear that *1512* was settling, being low in the water and down by the bow. The crew were removed, apart from an officer and two ratings, and the tow re-rigged to the stern. At 11.55 the tow had to be slipped as she was now very low, and she was ordered to be abandoned. This had scarcely been completed when at 12.06 she sank, her position being 07.08N 78.55E. The crew were landed at Colombo and the remaining tenders then resumed their journey.
[TNA: ADM.1/19600]

3 February CAPTIVE rescue tug
Hamburg 1923 (*Max Berendt*) prize 1943; 766 tons;
159.1ft × 32.2ft
Lieutenant John Watson RNR
On 23 January reports were received that the troopship
Gradisca, carrying over 1,200 troops with a small
number of women and children homeward-bound
from Egypt, had run aground on Gavdos Island, south
of Crete. The cruiser *Orion* and the minesweeper *Fancy*
went to the scene and began a rescue effort. The rescue
tugs *Brigand* and *Captive* were despatched to the scene
from Malta. On arrival they found that the *Gradisca* was
hard aground and beginning to break up, and could not
be salvaged, but were busily employed in transferring the
passengers, with their baggage and stores, to the *Orion*
and the escort carrier *Trumpeter* which had arrived. It
was in the course of these transfers that the *Captive* was
damaged. On 26 January, as she was going alongside the
cruiser, she misjudged the speed of the large ship and
struck the side, the blow being taken by the top strake of
the tug. No result of this was evident at the time, but it
was almost certainly the cause of her loss. On 28 January,
the tug was employed alongside the side of the *Gradisca*,
removing more baggage and stores, and completed
loading at 14.00. She then went alongside the *Orion*
to discharge her cargo, but the engine room reported
that it was filling with water. She was therefore turned
inshore into shallow water and work started to pump
her free, but this proved to be difficult, the pump suction
constantly being choked. The following day, 29 January,
she was run ashore in Potomas Bay. Over the next few
days efforts continued to clear the water, but it proved
impossible, and as the weather worsened, the ship started
pounding in the surf. By 31 January she was being swept
by gale force winds, the ' … seas smashed over her and
poured into the engine room'. On 2 February it was
decided to abandon her, and it was during the evacuation
that one man was lost, Sub-Lieutenant H A Colbourne
RNVR being drowned when he attempted to swim to
the shore through the surf. The following day she was
abandoned, the crew being taken off by the *Cardigan
Bay*. The tug had originally been a German vessel that
had been sunk at Tobruk and salvaged by the British and
an old 'war wound' had probably been re-opened by the
'swipe' from the *Orion*, resulting in a hole or split under
the coal bunker.
[TNA:ADM.1/19962]

4 March MFV 411 tender
Rockhampton 1945; 50 tons; 64.5ft × 17.9ft

MFV 812 tender
Leigh on Sea 1945; 28 tons; 45ft × 16.2ft
Three tenders, all MFVs were reported to have been
lost, apparently foundered, at Brisbane, Australia, in
storm force winds, widespread heavy rains and flooding
which affected Queensland. One of them, *MFV 424*,
was subsequently raised and returned to service, but the
other two were written off.
[WSS Warship Supplement, 'The Naval MFVs of World War
2' p19]

3 May CROCODILE tug
Hessle 1940; 395 tons; 105ft × 26.5ft
Having spent some time based at Trincomalee, she
was ordered to return to home waters for transfer to
Rosyth. However, whilst under tow of the civilian tug
Assistance, she broke her tow in poor weather soon after
leaving Ceylonese waters and was driven ashore on the
Sind coast, Pakistan, in position 23.54N 67.34E. Plans
were drawn up to salvage the vessel, but the wreck
attracted the attention of local opportunists who were
soon stripping it of anything valuable. By the end of
June, it was found that although the hull and machinery
were still intact, most of the fittings, including propeller
blades, had been looted. There was little choice but to
write her off as a constructive total loss, and the remains
were sold for scrap in April 1947.
[Maclean p161]

5 May ZZ 12 estuary minesweeper
Alexandria 1944; 97 tons; 52.6ft × 18.6ft
Capsized and sank in poor weather whilst transiting the
Firth of Forth under tow.
[SCG Journal 17 p33]

26 August BUCCANEER tug
Paisley 1937; 840 tons; 165ft × 32ft; 1 × 12pdr, 1 × 20mm
Lieutenant Commander Stephen Ernest Veal MBE
Based at Portland, she was ordered to tow a battle
practice target for a practice shoot by the destroyer *St
James*. At 11.50 the destroyer commenced the shoot at a
range of 6 miles and eight salvoes had been fired when a
shell struck the tug, hitting her under the rubbing strake
at the after end of the engine room. A second shell
landed close under her stern. She immediately signalled
that she had been hit, which brought the exercise to
a halt and the destroyer closed. The shell, which was a
practice round, did not explode but punched a hole in
her side through which a powerful jet of water entered.
The force was such that it was knocking down anyone
who tried to approach the damage. A collision mat was
placed over the side to try and stem the flow, but it
proved ineffective. The *St James* was soon alongside and
passed across a portable pump to assist with clearing
the water, and preparations were made for a tow. But
she was settling fast and at 12.20 all hands were ordered
to move onto the destroyer. She sank by the stern, her
bow standing vertically out of the water before heeling
over and sinking, striking the destroyer a glancing blow

as she disappeared. The fault was found to be a series of mistakes in the drill onboard the destroyer, which had allowed the director to yaw. In 'B' turret, which was firing, the rating acting as safety number blew a whistle to check fire as he saw his line of sight was coming onto the tug, but this was not heard before the final rounds were fired. The wreck lies in position 50.29.20N 02.41.41W

[TNA: ADM.1/19963; Larn vol 1 sec 6]

20 September TID 62 tug
Hessle 1944; 54 tons; 65ft × 17ft

Under tow from Portsmouth to Sheerness by the tug *Tenacity*, with a small towing crew onboard, in storm force winds she broke her tow when off Beachy Head. The Eastbourne and Hastings lifeboats were launched to stand by her, and the destroyer *Zephyr* closed which managed to secure a tow. Taken towards Folkstone, they heaved too in the high seas, but she capsized and sank, then being about 5 miles south-east of Folkstone pier. One man was lost.

[www.britishnewspaperarchive.co.uk/: Hampshire Telegraph 27 September 1946; Maclean p39]

September ZZ 16 estuary minesweeper
Alexandria 1944; 97 tons; 52.6ft × 18.6ft

Written off as a constructive total loss, after being damaged by fire at Port Said, Egypt.

[SCG Journal 17 p33]

22 October SAUMAREZ destroyer
Hebburn 1942; 1,730 tons; 339.5ft × 35.7ft; 4 × 4.7in, 2 × 40mm, 8 × 20mm
Captain William Halford Selby DSC

During May 1946, British cruisers had been fired on by Albanian shore batteries when en-route to the island of Corfu; no damage had been caused, but the subsequent claim by Albania that the ships had entered their territorial waters was disputed by the United Kingdom, which believed the channel was in international waters. The British government decided to back their view by sending a small naval force through the channel. This was to consist of the cruisers *Mauritius* and *Leander* with the destroyers *Saumarez* and *Volage*, whilst the aircraft carrier *Ocean* would be available to provide distant support. The ships sailed from Corfu harbour with *Mauritius* leading followed closely by the *Saumarez*, whilst the *Volage* took station astern of the *Leander*. The ships headed north, intending to pass through the narrow waters between Corfu and Albania, before turning west to skirt around the north of the island. The ships were closed up at action stations, it being thought possible that the Albanian shore batteries might again open fire. At 14.49 the *Mauritius* leading the line, altered course, followed moments later by the *Saumarez*. At 14.53, just as she was

steadying to follow in the wake of the cruiser, there was a large explosion on the starboard side, abreast the forward superstructure. She was then 3.9 miles from the nearest point on the Albanian coast. The ship was enveloped in smoke, lurched violently to starboard, took a sheer to port and then stopped, settling by the bows. A fire broke out forward, and a large quantity of fuel oil spilled out from ruptured tanks and this caught fire, surrounding the ship with flame and smoke. The *Mauritius* steamed on with the *Leander*, ordering the *Volage* to go to the assistance of *Saumarez*. The *Volage* initially passed under the stern of the stricken ship but attempts to pass a line were frustrated by the large fires still burning. On board the *Saumarez*, there had been considerable damage, with a 60ft hole blown in the starboard side and fuel tanks breached, which not only poured oil into the sea but flooded number 1 boiler room. After initially heeling to starboard, she came upright, and then assumed a pronounced list to port, at the same time settling by the bows. All power was lost, and amongst the casualties was the forward damage control party. Despite the difficulties, the fires were brought under control and shoring limited the spread of water and at 15.40 the *Saumarez* was clear of the burning fuel, and the *Volage* had rigged a tow. However, at 16.16 there was a second explosion, this time under the forefoot of the *Volage*. The destroyer took a bow-down attitude but did not lose power. The tow was slipped whilst the *Volage* dealt with her own problems, which were eased when about 40ft of her bow section broke off and sank. The ship stabilised herself and within a short time was able to re-connect the tow and get under way. At 19.45 the destroyer *Raider* came on scene and sent parties across to both ships to relieve the damage control and fire-fighting teams, and as they approached Corfu harbour the *Ocean* was able to assist by sending more men onboard, who quickly got the last of the fires out and were able to transfer many of the wounded to the carrier. The pair arrived in Corfu at 03.10. After temporary repairs both destroyers moved to Malta, and the *Volage* was later repaired to continue in service, but the *Saumarez* was found to be severely damaged and was written off as a constructive total loss. Thirty-six men were killed on board the *Saumarez*, and eight were lost on the *Volage*. Examination of fragments recovered from the destroyers showed that former German mines were likely to have been responsible, and this was confirmed by a subsequent investigation of the area, which found that a substantial minefield had been laid. This led to Operation 'Retail', to clear the channel, and this swept twenty-two German 'GY' type contact mines. Albania was blamed for laying the minefield in a shipping channel, without any warnings or announcements.

[TNA: ADM.116/5542; ADM.1/20901; ADM.267/97; ADM.1/22686]

27 October NSC (E) 101 servicing craft, engineering
Paisley 1944 (*LCT 311*); 625 tons; 190.8ft × 31ft
Lieutenant Commander Arthur Lennox Dodd RNVR

Ordered to sail from Malta to Suda Bay in Crete in company with two other support vessels, the boom defence vessel *Barcroft* and tender *MFV 85*, the trio set off during the afternoon of 25 October, being escorted by the minesweeper *Espiegle*. The following day the wind started to pick up and the swell increased, and seas occasionally broke over her. This resulted in some water being forced through the bow doors, and it proved difficult to manoeuvre pumps into place to clear the water. Despite this, as the wind and seas did not increase further, there was no immediate concern. At 01.20 on the 27th the wind veered to the east-south-east, and within the hour the swell had shifted to the starboard bow. This made steering difficult and she rolled incessantly, making it uncomfortable. It was also found that she was again making water and was developing a list to starboard. Portable pumps were now in use to try and clear the water, but there seemed to be no noticeable improvement in the list, and the flooding appeared to be worsening. At 07.00 the port engine stopped, owing to the failure of a circulating pump. She was now running before the wind as steering was impossible and the situation worsened at 08.45 when the starboard engine also stopped. She broached too, swinging round beam-on to the sea. The *Espiegle* had stayed with her and moved up-weather to lay oil on the water in an effort to try and reduce the rolling. The list steadily increased until by 09.40 it was at 20 degrees. The minesweeper closed and passed a line with the intention of rigging a tow, but this was frustrated by the line parting. Several more attempts were made by *Espiegle* to pass a line, but all failed with the line being broken by the movement of *101*. By mid-afternoon it was clear that she was sinking, and it was decided to abandon her before nightfall. The crew left in an orderly fashion by float and boat, and although some ended up in the sea, all were picked up by the escorting vessels. She was not seen to sink but disappeared from radar at 22.45 in approximate position 36N 18.08E. The cause of her loss was flooding which could not be stemmed, probably as a result of some of her bottom plates on the starboard side having opened up.
[TNA:ADM.1/20846]

21 December ENTICER tug
Selby 1944; 868 tons; 160ft × 36ft
Master Albert George Adcock†

On 15 December, the salvage vessel *King Salvor* was despatched from Hong Kong to proceed to the assistance of the merchant ship *Rosebank*, which was in distress, having been disabled in a tropical storm near Hainan. *King Salvor* was unable to make any headway due to the poor weather and 4 days later requested assistance, The sloop *Alacrity* and the *Enticer* were ordered to the scene. They arrived during 20 December but several attempts to pass a tow failed as the tug was rolling violently and she was shipping water. Now in difficulties herself, the locally employed Chinese crew of the tug were reluctant to make further efforts, and the sloop could do little in the Force 8 winds and high seas. By that evening *Enticer* reported that the pumps were unable to clear the water and she had developed a list to port. She foundered at about 02.49 in position 18.43 N 111.40 E. Three officers and eight ratings were saved, but two officers and seventeen ratings were lost.
[TNA:ADM.358/3262]

24 December AIRE frigate
Paisley 1943; 1,370 tons; 283ft × 36.8ft; 2 × 4in, 10 × 20mm
Lieutenant Commander John Plomer Somervaille

Aire had been laid up at Hong Kong in reserve, being used as an accommodation ship when she was ordered to be transferred to Singapore. A small 'steaming crew' was assembled under the command of Lieutenant Commander Somervaille, and after a very brief time for trials, sailed from Hong Kong on 18 December. The following day they passed the RFA *Fort Dunvegan*, and on request they provided a position, which disturbed Somervaille, as it was 14 miles from his own estimated position. The weather was poor and at noon an attempt to obtain a sun sight was frustrated by clouds, although a snap bearing was taken on the sun when it briefly appeared 40 minutes later, and this appeared to support his estimated position. However, a good stellar observation that night cast doubt on this, as it demonstrated that the 'snap' bearing was probably inaccurate. Now uncertain of his position, Somervaille decided to plot all the possible positions – those derived from the stellar sighting, the snap bearing and the *Fort Dunvegan* position and then use the one he considered the potentially least dangerous to set a safe course for the night. At 04.55 the following morning (20 December) bridge watchkeepers saw breakers ahead. Alarm bells were sounded, and the wheel was put hard over, but a minute later she struck the ground. With the ship surrounded by breaking surf, engines were stopped. All hands were called, and boats were hoisted out as a precaution whilst all compartments were ordered to be checked. The ship was found to be dry, and engines and propellers appeared unharmed, but all power had been lost. At first light she attempted to go astern but would not move. During the morning more attempts were made to drive her off the reef, but although she seemed to move, her head swinging round, it was realised that she was swinging around a pinnacle of rock. At 15.15 during an attempt to light number 1 boiler, an oil fire broke out in the boiler room. With a limited number of

hands available this was difficult to tackle, and despite being put out twice, the fire flared up again and took hold. All hands were now directed to tackling the fire, and this proved a long and difficult task, with flames seen to be leaping out of the funnel at one stage. The fire was successfully contained to the boiler room and burnt for 24 hours until at 18.00 on 21 December the fire was finally declared to be out. The following day was spent clearing up the mess generated by fire. Relief finally arrived during that afternoon in the shape of the depot ship *Bonaventure*. After an assessment of the situation, it was decided to abandon her, and during 24 December boats were organised to take all the crew off. Somervaille was court-martialled for the loss and was found guilty of hazarding and stranding his ship by negligence on the Bombay Reef, Paracel Islands in position 16.03N 112.34E. Although the plotting of the three potential positions to judge the planned course was a correct course of action, he had failed to make any allowance for the prevailing set of the sea or the strong local currents and had also allowed a speed higher than was being achieved. He was severely reprimanded.
[TNA: ADM.156/259]

1947

6 June LCT (4) 1068 landing craft, tank
Middlesbrough 1943; 200 tons; 171ft × 38.8ft; 2 × 20mm
Damaged by gunfire during firing trials on 4 June, she was under tow for Portsmouth for repairs when she sank in Stokes Bay. Her wreck lies in position 50.46.43N 01.10.31W.
[Larn vol 2 sec 1]

1948

19 January ORIANA tug
Glasgow 1945 (*Empire Frieda*); 295 tons; 116ft × 28ft
Master Albert Boland†
Towing a minesweeper from Chatham to Harwich in company with the tug *Vagrant*, she was 1.5 cables (300 yards) to the north-east of number 2 Wallet Buoy, near the Knoll buoy, off Brightlingsea when at 14.00 there was a large explosion, and she rapidly sank. All fifteen crew members were killed; it was believed that she had detonated a magnetic mine.
[The Times 20 and 21 January 1948]

1950

12 January TRUCULENT submarine
Barrow 1942; 1,090/1,567 tons; 265ft × 26.7ft; 1 × 4in, 11 × torpedo tubes
Lieutenant Charles Philip Bowers
Having completed a refit at Chatham, the submarine proceeded to sea for trials, carrying eighteen dockyard employees in addition to her usual crew. With the day's trials over, she headed back along the Thames Estuary, steering for Sheerness and an overnight anchorage. At 19.00 the lights of a vessel came into sight, but these confused the bridge staff, as they could see not only both red (port) and green (starboard) lights, but a third red light over them. It was presumed to be a stationary ship, and with shallow water to starboard, course was altered to port. As the submarine started to swing round the bridge staff suddenly realised that the strange ship was not only underway, but it was closer than they had estimated. Lieutenant Bowers ordered stop, then full astern and the wheel hard to starboard, but it was too late and at 19.04 the 643-ton Swedish tanker *Dvina* struck the submarine on the starboard side just forward of the conning tower. The force of the impact threw five men, including Bowers, off the bridge into the sea. The submarine rapidly flooded through the hole caused by the collision and she sank. The *Dvina* had seen the lights of an oncoming vessel just before the collision on her port bow and when it was realised that the stranger was altering to cross her bows, course had been altered to starboard, but she was still under helm at the time of the collision. Uncertain of what she had struck, she immediately stopped and after throwing lifebelts into the sea lowered a lifeboat, but they could find nothing in the cold pitch-black night. As she was not equipped with a radio, no shore authorities could be alerted. An inward-bound Dutch steamer, the *Almdyk*, arrived on scene about 30 minutes later and stopped to assist, lowering a boat, which successfully found the five men who had been thrown clear of the bridge. Only then was it realised that a submarine had been sunk, and a distress message sent asking for urgent assistance. At about 21.00 the crew of *Dvina* heard shouts from the darkness, and her searching boat discovered four men in the water who were rescued; a subsequent search found another survivor and two dead bodies, all of them clearly having successfully escaped from the sunken submarine. The bodies of several more were recovered from the water over the next few days. The survivors testified that when the collision happened, the forward compartments of the submarine had rapidly flooded, drowning the occupants, but survivors from the control room and after compartments had gathered in the engine room which remained watertight. The first

lieutenant, Lieutenant Frederick Hindes, with Chief ERA Francis Hine, took command of the situation and quickly organised an escape, using well-practised drills. Influenced by the loss of life in the *Untamed* in 1943 and *Thetis* in 1939 (q.v.), when delays had cost lives, they decided to exit quickly, the noise of ships propellers heard above convincing them that ships were gathering overhead. At 20.20 with the compartment flooded they started to leave the submarine by the escape hatches, all the men successfully escaping, CERA Hine being the last to leave. However, the men came to the surface to discover that apart from the *Dvina* and *Almdyk*, there was no rescue force, and with no searchlights to illuminate the area, and with only a ship's boat to search they were not seen. Apart from the ten men picked up by *Almdyk* and *Dvina*'s boats, all the rest died of exposure in the freezing water; sixty-four men lost their lives. Lieutenant Bowers was court-martialled for the loss. He was cleared of losing his ship by negligence or default, by failing to recognise the lights of the *Dvina* for what they were, that of a vessel carrying a dangerous cargo, and then turning across the channel instead of maintaining his course, he was found guilty of hazarding his ship. He was severely reprimanded. Lieutenant Hindes and CERA Hine were later posthumously awarded the Albert Medal for their conduct after the sinking. The *Truculent* was raised by lifting craft on 14 March and initially towed into shallow water for the recovery of ten bodies that were still inside her forward compartments, and on 23 March she was refloated and taken to Chatham dockyard. She was not repaired and sold for scrap on 8 May.

[TNA: ADM.116/6156; 116/6157; 1/22713; Evans pp393–401]

1951

16/17 April **AFFRAY** submarine

Birkenhead 1945; 1,120/1,620 tons; 1 × 4in, 10 × torpedo tubes

Lieutenant John Blackburn DSC[†]

The submarine sailed from Portsmouth at 16.15 on 16 April to take part in Exercise 'Training Spring'. This would involve her moving to the western approaches to the English Channel and at some stage closing the coast to land and later recover a party of Royal Marines at a suitable beach in Cornwall. That complete, she was to call at Falmouth during the night of 19 April to land her Marines and then conduct a simulated war patrol until the 23rd. In addition to the Marines, she was also carrying twenty officers under training who were to gain experience of a submarine in 'war' conditions. The last contact with her was at 21.15 that night when she signalled that she was diving, in position 50.10N

01.45W, about 30 miles to the south of the Isle of Wight. The first indication that something was wrong was the next morning at 09.00 when she failed to make her scheduled position report. When nothing had been heard from her, an hour later the submarine rescue organisation was alerted. This involved a large number of vessels and aircraft searching, and radio stations listening and calling regularly. With a huge area of sea to search, and no specific location it proved to be a frustrating and fruitless task. On 18 April, the submarine *Ambush* picked up sonar signals, which indicated a signal code for a submarine being trapped on the bottom, but no location could be ascertained. The hunt continued until 14 June when the diving vessel *Reclaim*, searching an area to the north-west of Alderney, investigated a contact discovered by the frigate *Loch Insh* in position 50.02N 02.34.5W. She used an underwater television camera to descend the 260ft to the bottom and it revealed the sunken *Affray*, which was sitting on an even keel on the seabed, at the edge of a depression known as Hurd's Deep. The wreck was then examined by divers, who could find no evidence of collision damage; her radar and periscope masts were raised, which indicated that she had been at periscope depth when she had foundered. However, her hydroplanes were set to 'rise' showing that an attempt had been made to stop a dive. The escape hatches were shut indicating that no attempt had been made to leave her. They also discovered that the snort mast, which allowed the submarine to draw air from the surface whilst submerged, had been broken off about 3ft above the deck and an examination of the site discovered the broken portion lying alongside the submarine. After much hard work the mast was recovered and sent for analysis. This revealed that there was poor welding in the joints connecting the mast, and evidence of a brittle fracture in one of the components. Subsequent examination of other 'A' class submarines found that welding on another two boats' snort masts was below standard. This would seem to offer the explanation that she had been running at periscope depth, snorting, when a catastrophic failure of the mast had occurred which had caused it to break, flooding the boat. However, there are considerable doubts over this. Other tests on those submarines with defective masts found that despite the faults, they remained strong enough to withstand the shocks liable to be expected at sea. Further, an induction valve was fitted, designed to close should the mast go beneath the water. For the submarine to flood it would require the failure of not just the mast but also the induction valve. Attempts were made by divers to discover whether the induction valve was open or closed, but all failed in difficult conditions. The fact that her broken mast was lying next to the wreck probably indicates that it had actually fractured when the boat hit the bottom. One possibility is a battery gas explosion, whilst snorting. This would have led to a partial loss of power and, if not immediately tackled, start an uncontrolled sequence of events which would cause her loss when the power in the diminished batteries was exhausted. Seventy-five men were lost. [TNA: ADM.1/22735; ADM.1/31032; ADM.116/5821; ADM.116/5826; ADM.116/5899; Evans pp401–05]

27 April BEDENHAM ammunition carrier
Troon 1938; 1,192 tons; 215ft × 37.5ft
Master Cyril Leslie Doughty
The naval armament vessel *Bedenham* arrived at Gibraltar on 24 April from Plymouth and secured at the Ordnance Wharf. She started to unload her cargo of ammunition the following day. On the 27th, *Lighter Number 10* was warped alongside her to take onboard a number of depth charges. The lighter was already partly loaded with some depth charges and also had onboard 1,450 cartridges of 4.5in, 20 of 5.25in and 820 of 4in ammunition. The transfer of *Bedenham's* cargo was well underway when at 09.54 an explosion occurred in the lighter amongst the depth charges; the explosion did not seem to be large, being described as a 'thud', accompanied by a flash of flame several feet high. There was then a burst of flames as the lighter caught fire with a larger explosion and within seconds it was ablaze from stem to stern. Hoses, already rigged as a precaution on board the *Bedenham*, were brought to play on the lighter and the dockyard fire service were very quickly on scene with a pump. Master Doughty realised the danger and ordered the crew to evacuate, and this proved to be a wise move as at 10.00 the lighter blew up with devastating force, throwing large pieces of debris over a wide area. The *Bedenham* was blown apart, the smaller portion, from the stem to number 1 hold was thrown bodily onto the quay, the ammunition, and the contents of the hold was strewn around the dockyard. The after part rolled over onto its port side and sank, spilling the cargo of ammunition into the sea around the wreck. Two cranes were knocked over, several vehicles wrecked, and there was widespread damage to surrounding buildings. Thirteen men were killed – nine dockyard employees and four civilians, including two street traders. A George Cross was later posthumously awarded to Sub-Officer George Henderson of the Gibraltar Fire Brigade, who had led the initial team of fire-fighters and remained in a position of extreme danger doing what he could to prevent the fire spreading but had been killed in the explosion. The cause of the blast was uncertain, all possibilities were examined, but it was believed that the most likely cause was the explosion of a depth charge. Why this should have happened could not be ascertained but was likely to be either a fault in manufacture or a defective filling or a combination of these faults. [TNA: ADM.116/5815; ADM.116/6414; COAG.10/120]

19 August LCT (3) 7009 landing craft, tank
Glasgow 1944; 350 tons; 175ft × 31ft; 2 × 20mm
Being transferred from the Clyde to Sheerness under tow of the tug *Jaunty*, when off the coast of Cornwall, the landing craft developed several leaks and filled with water. At seven o'clock it was clear that she was sinking, and the tow was slipped, the landing craft capsizing and sinking in position 51.17N 05.38W. [www.britishnewspaperarchive.co.uk/: Portsmouth Evening News 20 August 1951]

1952

31 January MTB 1602 patrol boat
Anglesey 1950 (*MTB 539*); 43 tons; 72ft × 19.9ft; 1 × 2pdr, 4 × torpedo tubes
In September 1951, the boat was damaged by an explosion in an exhaust pipe, which had caused her engine room to flood whilst lying at Portsmouth and after temporary repairs she was taken in tow by the tug *Enforcer* to be returned to her builders in Anglesey for a refit. The weather deteriorated and it was noticed that she was low in the water when off the north Wales coast. One of the tow ropes parted but the tow continued with a single rope, but in strong, gale force winds, this also parted, and the boat became swamped, and she foundered about 12 miles off the Anglesey shore. [Maclean p39]

28 March MTB 1030 patrol boat
Portchester 1946 (*MTB 530*); 48 tons; 72.6ft × 19.6ft; 1 × 6pdr, 2 × 20mm, 2 × torpedo tubes
Lieutenant James Samuel Dale Williams
Taking part in NATO Exercise 'Bandeau-III' in the southern North Sea, she was one of a group of seven torpedo boats that were to carry out a night attack during the night of 27 March on a group of ships off the coast of Holland that would simulate a coastal convoy. It was a dark night, with a sea from the stern, which made the boats yaw, and at 21.40 *1030* was in collision with her sister *MTB 1032*. The group came to a stop, and it was decided that whilst other boats would continue on with the exercise, *1032* should return to harbour, escorted by *MTB 5003*, whilst *MTB 5517* took the damaged *1030* in tow, escorted by *MTB 5035*. Despite bailing and pumping she slowly filled with water and by 23.55 water was washing over the upper deck. *5035* closed to lift off the crew. The minesweeper *Pincher* was now on scene, but little could be done. The boat continued to settle until at 02.03 she capsized, to float bottom up for some time, until she sank at 03.58 in position 52.03N 03.15E. [TNA: ADM.1/23759]

2 June MMS 1534 minesweeper
Fraserburgh 1941 (*MMS 35*); 225 tons; 105ft × 23ft;
1 × 20mm
Lieutenant Mark Henry MacAndrew

Part of the 108th Minesweeping Squadron based at Malta, which sailed on 26 May to take part in NATO Exercise 'Dragex-II', which involved sweeping the area between Kuriat Island and the coast of Tunisia. At 10.11 on 2 June, a fire broke out in the battery room of *1534*, which forced her to abandon the exercise sweep then under way and call for assistance. The *Fierce* and *Sursay* went to her aid, going alongside to pass pumps and fire-fighting equipment. The efforts went on throughout the day, and they were joined during the afternoon by the USS *Hambleton* (DMS 20) and USS *Gherardi* (DMS 30), both of which sent across powerful pumps as well as fire-fighting teams. By nightfall, the situation was under control and at 19.00 *1534* was declared to be out of danger, although work went on through the night to pump her clear of water. The following morning the *Sursay* rigged a tow and took her into the shelter of Kuriat Island where she anchored. The salvage vessel *Sea Salvor* arrived on scene on 4 June with the Admiralty Salvage Officer embarked and under his direction *1534* was prepared for sea and was towed back to Malta. However, she was so severely damaged, that she was written off as a constructive total loss.
[TNA: ADM.1/23800]

5 June ML 2582 patrol boat
Looe 1943 (*ML 582*); 73 tons; 112ft × 18.4ft; 1 × 3pdr,
2 × 20mm
Lieutenant John Ingles Shepherd†

Taking part in Exercise 'Bluebird' with other NATO forces in the North Sea, she came under a mock attack at 06.00 by Dutch Air Force F-84 Thunderjet aircraft about 2 miles off the Dutch coast near Mars Diep. The aircraft carried out attacks from about 1,500ft, but one of the aircraft failed to pull out of a dive and after striking her mast, crashed into the launch. There was a large explosion, with smoke and flames covering the ship. Local fishermen who had witnessed the crash closed the site, but found only a burning wreck, with the fore part already under water. They picked up one man, the only survivor, but fifteen men were killed. The cause of the aircraft crash was uncertain, a mechanical defect was possible, but an error of judgement by the pilot was not ruled out.
[TNA: ADM.1/23940]

21 October MMS 1788 minesweeper
Gosport 1943 (*MMS 288*); 225 tons;
105ft × 23ft × 1 × 20mm
Lieutenant Alistair Neil Campbell-Harris

Whilst on passage from Harwich to Rosyth, water flooded the engine room, apparently through leaking seams in the wooden hull. The crew were removed by the armed trawler *Gorregan* and she settled and sank off Winterton Ness, Norfolk.
[Maclean p235]

1953

1 February BERKELEY CASTLE frigate
Glasgow 1943; 1,060 tons; 252ft × 36.8ft; 1 × 4in,
10 × 20mm

During the night of 31 January/1 February a high spring tide coupled with a strong north-east gale combined to create a tidal surge which caused extensive flooding along the eastern coast of England, from the Humber to the Thames. The flood waters swept into the dockyard at Sheerness, submerging roads, flooding buildings to the depth of 3ft and filling dry docks. The sea was reported to have swept across the basin like a tidal wave. One of the dry docks was occupied by the submarine *Sirdar*, under refit; the dock was filled, and she flooded. Also, under refit was the frigate *Berkeley Castle*. As the tide swept into the dockyard, the water rose over the caisson into the dry dock. The ship began to fill through the numerous inlets in her hull and as the water filled the dock, she was swept off her blocks and fell over against the side of the dock and capsized onto her beam ends. She was finally cleared of water and righted on 16 February. The *Sirdar* was salvaged, but a survey of the *Berkeley Castle* found her to be too heavily damaged, and she was written off as a constructive total loss, being listed for disposal in September 1953.
[www.britishnewspaperarchive.co.uk/: Hampshire Telegraph 6 February 1953; Maclean p42]

17 May MTB 1023 torpedo boat
Portchester 1945 (*MTB 523*); 48 tons; 72.5ft × 19.5ft;
1 × 6pdr, 2 × 20mm, 2 × torpedo tubes
Lieutenant James Samuel Dale Williams

In company with five other torpedo boats *1023* sailed from Gosport on 7 May to take part in the NATO Exercise 'Cocktail', in the western Baltic. When lying alongside at Aarhus, in Denmark, a petrol vapour explosion took place in the engine room during the early hours of the morning which started a large fire, damaged the torpedo boat *Gay Archer* lying alongside, as well as blowing out windows in the surrounding area. Two men on the upper deck were blown into the water, and when it was clear that she could not be saved the others jumped into the water to be picked up. One leading stoker was treated for burns.
[www.britishnewspaperarchive.co.uk :Daily Herald 18 May 1953; TNA: ADM.116/5936]

22 October MFV 26 tender

Oulton Broad 1943; 50 tons; 61.6ft × 17.9ft

Based at Malta, she was acting as the base ship for Fort Ricasoli, Malta, when she foundered off that island.

[WSS Warship Supplement, 'The Naval MFVs of WW2' p7]

1954

17 April MMS 1558 minesweeper

Poole 1941 (MMS 58); 225 tons; 105ft × 23ft

Lieutenant Commander Peter William Thorn Warren DSC RNVR

Allocated to London Division Royal Naval Reserve for the use of a weekend training cruise, she sailed from the Thames during the evening of 16 April for 3 days exercising in the North Sea. Very soon after sailing the weather deteriorated and the ship rolled heavily during the night, during which lockers and cupboards broke loose and she was found to be making water. Early the next morning flames were seen to shoot out of the funnel and at the same time a fire was reported to have broken out in the engine room. The ship was then about 30 miles off Ostend. Fire-fighting was started, but the blaze was soon out of control, and a distress message was sent, which brought the French steamer *Tunisia* and the Dutch *Phoenix* to her aid. The French ship was first on scene and she launched a boat which came alongside and several of the crew were taken off, leaving an officer and thirteen men onboard to continue fighting the fire. They were defeated however, and as the ship was ablaze from stem to stern, the last men were taken off. She steadily settled and finally sank at 07.40. A subsequent enquiry found that the minesweeper was in poor material condition, and the fire had probably been started by electrical arcing caused by seawater.

[www.britishnewspaperarchive.co.uk/: Portsmouth Evening News 17 April 1954; Taylor pp112–13]

2 May LCT (4) 565 landing craft, tank

Thornaby 1943; 200 tons; 171ft × 38.8ft

While being towed by the tug *Thunderer*, the vessels were in the Bristol Channel when the tow parted in strong winds and high seas. With no crew onboard, she was driven onto Lundy Island, about a quarter of a mile north of Lundy Lighthouse and was wrecked.

[www.britishnewspaperarchive.co.uk/ : Western Mail 3 May 1954]

21 November MFV 1163 tender

Anstruther 1945; 114 tons; 69.3ft × 19.9ft

Attached as a tender to HMS *Pomona*, the boom defence depot at Crockness, Scapa Flow, she had recovered a practice torpedo and was returning to Scapa when she ran aground at Carness Point near Kirkwall. Low tide

left her high and dry and heeling over to starboard. Subsequent efforts to free her by the tug *Salveda* failed and she was subsequently written off as a total loss, the wreck being sold in January 1955.

[www.britishnewspaperarchive.co.uk/ : Dundee Courier 22 and 24 November 1954]

1955

16 June SIDON submarine

Birkenhead 1944; 715/990 tons; 201ft × 23.9ft; 1 × 4in, 6 × torpedo tubes

Lieutenant Commander Hugh Turrel Verry

One of several submarines berthed alongside the depot ship *Maidstone* in Portland harbour, the *Sidon* was preparing to sail to carry out torpedo firing trials in the local area. At 08.25 as *Sidon* prepared to cast off, there was a violent explosion in the torpedo tubes. A sheet of flame shot through the boat and vented up through the conning tower. The force of the blast wrecked the forward compartments and jammed debris against the control room bulkhead. The boat started to settle by the bows and filled with thick choking smoke and toxic gasses. The boat was rapidly cleared of men, but several were trapped in the forward compartments or had been stunned by the explosion and the thick smoke made it difficult to see, preventing them escaping. The officers who had been on the bridge went below to help men clear but had to don breathing apparatus in the noxious atmosphere. They were joined by Surgeon Lieutenant Charles Rhodes from the *Maidstone* who repeatedly went into the smoke to haul men out before he was also overcome and collapsed. The mooring vessel *Moordale* was nearby and after the explosion quickly went alongside to secure a wire around the stern of the submarine as it rose out of the water, but at 08.45 the submarine sank, bows first. Salvage work began that same day, with large buoyancy chambers being positioned overhead the wreck. Wires were positioned by divers under her hull to be secured to the buoys and in the early hours of 23 June she was raised. The following day she was towed into an area of shallow water and the work of recovering the dead began. She was written off as a constructive total loss and in June 1957 was scuttled off Portland for use as a target for training sonar operators. The subsequent enquiry found that the disaster had been caused by the explosion of a Mark 12 'Fancy' torpedo which had been embarked for trial firings. The 'Fancy' was powered by high-test peroxide (HTP) which although normally stable, in certain circumstances is potentially dangerous. When preparing the torpedo for the trial firing, the internal motor had been started which had over-pressurised the internal pipework causing a split in the HTP lines. This would have allowed the propellant to spray around inside the torpedo casing, coming into contact with copper fittings and would have decomposed into a lethal mixture of oxygen and steam and expanded rapidly in volume. This caused the explosion which had split the torpedo into bits, the rear end being catapulted back through the internal doors whilst the front half was blown through the bow doors of the tubes allowing water to enter and flood the boat. Three officers and ten ratings died, including Surgeon Rhodes, who was posthumously awarded the Albert Medal for his gallantry.

[TNA: ADM.1/25919; ADM.1/26286; ADM.1/26287; London Gazette 1 November 1955; Evans pp405–09]

1956

28 September Fire at Gosport

BISHAM minesweeper
Poole 1954; 120 tons; 100ft × 21ft; 1 × 40mm

BROADLEY minesweeper
Bideford 1953; 123 tons; 100ft × 21.9ft; 1 × 40mm

EDLINGHAM minesweeper
Cockenzie 1955; 120 tons; 100ft × 21ft; 1 × 40mm
A number of newly completed inshore minesweepers were laid up in reserve in Haslar Creek, Portsmouth, with protective wooden housings built over the superstructure. At 15.00 observers from the shore saw smoke rising from one of them, the *Broadley*. Fire-fighting teams from the shore bases at *Hornet* and *Dolphin* in addition to the Royal Dockyard attended, but fire had a firm hold and spread to the ships moored alongside her. The other minor war craft that were nearby were towed to safety by dockyard tugs as the fire-fighting went on. The fires were eventually brought under control and extinguished after 3 hours, but the *Broadley* was burnt out and two other minesweepers, the *Bisham* and *Edlingham* were so severely damaged that they were written off as total losses, and subsequently sold for scrap. It was believed that a discarded cigarette was the most likely cause of the fire.

[www.britishnewspaperarchive.co.uk/ :Hampshire Telegraph 5 October 1956]

1958

13 January **BARCOMBE** boom defence vessel
Goole 1938; 730 tons; 150ft × 32.3ft
Lieutenant Commander Derek Charles Godfrey
En route from the Clyde to Rosyth for a refit, in poor weather she ran aground at Loch Buie, a sea loch in the

south of the Isle of Mull. Initial positions given by the wrecked ship indicated that she was ashore on Oronsay, which led searching vessels to look in the wrong area, and it was not until the fishing vessel *Rosebud* saw the wrecked ship the following day that rescuers were directed to the scene. After she had grounded, she filled with water, and when the order to abandon ship was given the crew scrambled ashore onto the rocks but found themselves at the foot of a 300ft cliff face and they spent an uncomfortable night, cold and wet, until found the next day. The Islay lifeboat assisted by the salvage vessel *Kingfisher* took off all the crew. At subsequent courts martial, Lieutenant Roland Harvey, the first lieutenant, was reprimanded after being found guilty of negligence, by failing ensure that a complete account of movements was maintained in the ships log and Lieutenant Commander Derek Godfrey, the commanding officer, was found guilty of negligence and dismissed his ship.

[www.britishnewspaperarchive.co.uk/ : Aberdeen Evening Express 14 January; 16 January; 19 February & 20 February 1958]

1959

25 August **HOGUE** destroyer
Birkenhead 1944; 2,315 tons; 355ft × 40.2ft; 4 × 4.5in, 1 × 4in, 8 × 40mm
Commander James Ralph Pardoe
Part of the Far East Fleet, the *Hogue* was taking part in Exercise 'JET59' in the Indian Ocean. At dusk, the *Hogue* was stationed 2 miles on the port bow of the Indian cruiser *Mysore*. In order to conform with a manoeuvring signal, the ship was required to reposition herself on the starboard side of the cruiser, and the commanding officer, directing events from the operations room, ordered a turn to starboard. However, the azimuth stabilisation of the Type 974 radar was malfunctioning, and this presented a false picture, leading Commander Pardoe to believe that he was 20 degrees broader on the beam of the *Mysore* that was the case – if it had been correct the new course would have taken him safely under the stern of the cruiser. At this moment, a serious misunderstanding developed which caused some distraction. The bridge staff of the *Mysore*, concerned with the destroyer's movements, switched on the navigation lights. This confused the bridge staff onboard the *Hogue* and led to a distracting conversation between the officer of the watch and the commanding officer, during which the turn was allowed to continue. Before any corrective action could be taken the *Hogue* was across the stem of the cruiser, which despite ordering a turn to starboard, struck the bows of the destroyer. Severe damage was caused, crushing and folding the

bows of the *Hogue* backwards. One rating was killed and another two seriously injured. The damage was shored up and she was towed to Trincomalee. The following month, with a temporary bow, she made her way to Singapore where a survey condemned her as a constructive total loss, and she was sold for scrapping. [*TNA: ADM.1/28035*]

1960

11 October WOOMERA armament store carrier
Fremantle 1945 (*Ashburton*); 603 tons; 125ft × 24ft
Lieutenant Commander Douglas Marshall RAN
Royal Australian Navy. Having embarked several tons of obsolete reconnaissance flares and shells, the *Woomera* sailed at 05.00 from Sydney to a position approximately 20 miles off the coast to dispose of the outdated ordnance. Dumping of the ammunition overboard commenced, and went on uneventfully until at 09.40, when there was a small explosion in the hold as ratings were handling the flares, and a large quantity of smoke covered the ship. A fierce fire broke out in the hold and this rapidly spread, despite fire-fighting efforts. The destroyers *Quickmatch* and *Cavendish* were soon on scene as the crew abandoned ship, but two men lost their lives. The cause was not discovered but believed to have been due to the premature deployment of the parachute from an unstable flare which triggered the explosion.
[*http://www.navy.gov.au/hmas-woomera*]

1962

2 August BATTLEAXE destroyer
Scotstoun 1945; 2,043 tons; 341.6ft × 38ft; 4 × 4in,
6 × 40mm
Commander Oliver Peter Sullivan
In company with the frigate *Ursa*, the *Battleaxe* was engaged in an anti-submarine exercise in the approaches to the river Clyde. At midnight on 1 August, both ships were darkened, steaming at 15 knots towards the exercise area, the destroyer being on the starboard bow of the frigate. The weather was poor, and visibility was limited. At 00.26 the pair collided after the *Battleaxe* had performed a turn to port, the ships striking each other bow to bow. The bow of the destroyer was split open on the port side from the upper deck to below the waterline, whilst the stem of the *Ursa* was stove in. The impact of the collision threw men from their hammocks and bunks, causing injuries to seven men in the destroyer. The exercise was abandoned, both ships heading for Greenock. The *Ursa* was subsequently repaired, but the damage to the destroyer was such that

it was written off as a constructive total loss and sold for scrap in 1964. A series of courts martial followed, with five officers and one rating being charged with a range of offences based on negligence, and it became clear that the collision had happened because neither ship was clear of the position of the other. For the *Ursa*, Commander Samuel Brooks was found guilty of failing to remain on the bridge or operations room when he was aware of the inexperience of some of his officers. Petty Officer (Radar) William Overton was found guilty of one count of negligence and reprimanded; in charge of the local operations plot, he had failed to ensure that the position of the *Battleaxe* was kept up to date and failed to report when the radar contact had been lost in ground returns. Also reprimanded was Lieutenant Philip Stephens; as the operations room officer of *Ursa*, he had failed to ensure that the position of *Battleaxe* was tracked and reported and had failed to update the bridge with information. Three officers from *Battleaxe* were court-martialled; Commander Sullivan was reprimanded for failing to adequately supervise his staff. Lieutenant Anthony Patterson, the navigating officer, was reprimanded; he had failed to appreciate a 1-mile error in the ship's plotted position and had failed to realise that an alteration of course would take the ship dangerously close to *Ursa*. Lieutenant Edwin Brooks, officer of the watch, had failed to inform the operations room of the poor visibility and had failed to ascertain the position of the *Ursa* before executing a turn. He was reprimanded.
[*TNA: ADM.1/28035; The Times, 3 August; 20 October; 23 October; 26 October, 27 October, 31 October, 24 November 1962; Maclean p214*]

17 November GREEN RANGER oiler
Dundee 1941; 4,750 tons; 339.7ft × 48.3ft
Under tow from Plymouth to Cardiff by the tug *Caswel* with a small towing crew embarked, the weather had been poor from the outset, and the pair had anchored off Clovelly during the evening of 16 November. On getting underway the next morning the weather worsened, with the winds gusting to Force 10 and the tow was slipped as it was feared that both vessels would be driven ashore. The tanker was carried onto the shore at Mansley Cliff, Hartland Point. Local lifeboats were launched, the Appledore boat standing by her through the storm, until a breeches buoy was rigged to the shore to take off the crew. The ship subsequently broke up and was declared a total loss. The wreck was sold in September 1963 for scrap.
[*Larn vol 1 sec 1; The Times 19 November 1962*]

29 December TID 97 tug

Thorne 1944; 54 tons; 65ft × 17ft

Master Leslie Savage[†]

Employed at Chatham Dockyard, with other tugs she was assisting the RFA stores vessel *Hebe* to berth. The tug was secured alongside the starboard quarter of the store ship, but with a strong north–east wind it proved difficult to manoeuvre the ship alongside. To assist the tugs, the engines of the *Hebe* were put ahead at slow speed, but the forward movement caused the hawser securing *TID 97* to be hauled taut and pulled forward. Before it could be released the tug was pulled over and at 15.33, she capsized over to port. Two men on the upper deck jumped clear, but the master and two engine room men were trapped below and drowned. The tug was raised the following week by the salvage vessel *Swin*, but not put back into service, being written off and sold for scrap.

[*The Times 31 December 1962; Maclean p283*]

1964

10 February VOYAGER destroyer

Sydney 1952; 2,610 tons; 390ft × 43ft; 6 × 4.5in, 6 × 40mm

Captain Duncan Herbert Stevens RAN[†]

Royal Australian Navy. Conducting exercises in company with the aircraft carrier *Melbourne* some 20 miles off the New South Wales coast, during the early evening both ships were darkened as the carrier prepared for night flying exercises. For this, the *Voyager* would act as plane guard, prepared to deal with any ditched aircraft, which meant being stationed on the port quarter of the *Melbourne*. From 19.29 the pair manoeuvred to gain sufficient wind over the deck, until at 20.54 the carrier signalled the intended course and speed for air operations. The course changes had left the *Voyager* some 1,200 yards off the starboard bow of the carrier, and she was now required to take up her station on the port side of *Melbourne*. She was seen to start a turn to starboard, and bridge staff on *Melbourne* assumed that she would continue her turn to cross under the stern of the carrier and then take up her station. However, the turn was halted, and *Voyager* commenced a turn to port, across the course of the *Melbourne*. There was little time to react, and although the carrier bridge staff ordered engines astern it was too late, and the carrier struck the destroyer on the port side amidships, crushing the bridge superstructure and cutting the ship in half. The forward section passed down the port side of *Melbourne* before sinking, disappearing in 10 minutes. The after section went down the starboard side and remained afloat for about 3 hours. Eighty-two men lost their lives. The loss resulted in two Royal Commissions of Enquiry and spawned numerous articles and books. Why the *Voyager*

halted her turn to starboard and turned across the bows of *Melbourne* is unknown, as all the key bridge personnel were killed.

[*Maclean pp197–201; https://navalinstitute.com.au/melbourne-voyager-causes-and-inquiries/*]

1968

11 November EMPIRE ACE tug

Selby 1942; 274 tons; 105ft × 27ft

Employed in the Clyde area, in strong winds she was driven onto Davaar Island, 4 miles south of Campbeltown, all the crew were taken off by the salvage vessel *Mandarin* which was standing by the tug. She remained aground until March the following year, when she was finally refloated, but written off as a constructive total loss in June and sold for scrap.

[*Maclean p38; www.historicalrfa.org/rfa-empire-ace-ship-information*]

1970

1 June ENNERDALE oiler

Kiel 1963 (*Naess Scotsman*) chartered 1967; 30,112 tons; 710ft × 98.5ft

Master George Bray MBE

Having been at anchor off Port Victoria, Seychelles, she weighed at 07.00 to proceed to sea. Steaming at 12.5 knots, fixes were taken at 07.15 and 07.24 which showed that she was 2 or 3 cables (400 to 600 yards) off the planned track. It was realised that this would put her close to the shallowest depth shown on the charts, at 9 fathoms (54ft), but this was not thought to be significant, as the tanker was drawing 39ft and the echo sounder showed no indication of danger. At 07.34 a terrific rumbling sound was heard forward, which continued for about 45 seconds. Empty tanks began to vent with a roar, and an order for the engines to be put astern was stopped when the engine room reported they were flooding. After 15 minutes the ship began to heel over to starboard and it was decided to abandon her, the ship sinking very soon afterwards in position 04.29.36S 55.31.22E. Divers later investigated the site and discovered two pinnacles of rock, the tops of which showed signs of damage, having been broken off, and there was metallic debris remaining. When the wreck was investigated, it was found that the bottom of the ship had been ripped open over a great part of her length. The 'feet and fathoms' chart supplied to the tanker was based on a lead line survey conducted in 1870, which not only failed to show the pinnacles but failed to accurately reflect the series of reefs that existed across the planned track of the tanker. However, it was also noted that the chart carried a warning that it was imperfect and should be used with caution; the 9-fathom patch should have been regarded as a potential danger and it had been imprudent to plan a passage through the marked shoals. As a result of the sinking, 13.8 million gallons (46,940 tonnes) of fuel was spilled and the wreck was eventually blown up by an RN demolitions team.

[Information supplied by MoD; FCO.76/50]

1971

1 July ARTEMIS submarine
Greenock 1946; 1,120/1,620 tons; 221ft × 22.3ft;
6 × torpedo tubes
Lieutenant Commander Roger Godfrey

The submarine was in a maintenance and leave period at Portsmouth, which included a docking period in the floating dock *AFD 26*, prior to a deployment to the West Indies. During the morning of 1 July, she was undocked under the supervision of the 'Third Hand', the sonar officer, Lieutenant John Crawford, as the commanding officer was absent on duty at RAF Boscombe Down, and the First Lieutenant on leave. He was relatively inexperienced and relied on the knowledge of other officers and senior rates for this important manoeuvre. As the submarine was floated out of the dock, the dock master commented that the boat seemed rather light and the engineer officer advised that although number 4 main ballast tank was partly full, they partly fill number 5 main ballast tank, which was duly flooded to the waterline. This was accepted without question. She was then taken by a tug to HMS *Dolphin*, to be secured at a trot and another patrol submarine, the *Ocelot*, later secured alongside, outboard of her. During the day, some maintenance work was carried out for which the after loading hatch was opened, but it was never closed. Further, the after escape hatch, which had been opened, was closed, but not clipped and secured. Other openings – the torpedo loading hatch, gun tower hatch and conning tower lid were also left open or not properly secured. Finally, in an effort to get onboard a shore power cable, the engine room hatch had been used, preventing it from being closed. Thus, by late afternoon six hatches were open or insecure, when standing orders were clear, that no more than two hatches should be open at any one time. Late in the afternoon the engineers commenced 'first filling' the external fuel tanks with seawater, a move preparatory to fuelling, apparently unaware that one of the after main tanks was nearly full. Permission was not sought for this from Lieutenant Crawford, and neither was he informed. Crawford himself went

ashore late afternoon, to remain in *Dolphin*. No one seemed to be aware of the dangerous situation the boat was in; by filling the external fuel tanks when number 5 ballast tank was already full would actually remove all reserve of buoyancy abaft the fin of the submarine. As the filling continued, she steadily settled aft until the stern of the submarine went underwater, and water started to trickle into the open after escape hatch. This continued for at least 10 minutes with no one noticing. The trim of the submarine was now such that the waterline aft was up to the larger after loading hatch. The result was uncontrolled and rapid flooding. As this was happening, at 18.55 a small party of three young Sea Cadets had arrived, to request a visit. Chief Petty Officer Guest, acting as the duty petty officer, told the trot sentry to show them around, whilst he stayed on the casing with the leading hand carrying out the first fill. At 19.05 it was realised that something was wrong. The trot sentry on the *Ocelot*, alongside, noticed that the *Artemis* was down by the stern, and at the same time, CPO Guest and the leading hand grasped the seriousness of the situation. Guest quickly went below to order the Sea Cadets to get out, which they did, remarkably quietly, and then went aft shouting out a warning, which allowed several men to escape. The submarine was now sinking quickly, but CPO Guest with two ratings desperately tried to shut after hatches, but could not do so. With the boat now in near darkness, they made their way forward to take refuge in the torpedo compartment, which they sealed, the trot sentry above standing on the loading hatch as they clipped it shut. The boat sank, with the three ratings still inside. They remained inside for the next 10 hours until they made a successful escape. The submarine remained on the bottom until raised a week later, but was not repaired, and was sold for scrap the following year. The subsequent court of inquiry found that she had foundered due to a number of factors. There had been poor coordination between departments and failure to pass on vital information which had led to filling external tanks when ballast tanks were full; the commanding officer had failed to exercise proper supervision of an inexperienced team; there had been poor supervision of the boat during the day which had left several hatches open and overall, there was a lack of awareness of the dangers of submarine life. Lieutenant Commander Godfrey was cleared at a court martial of negligence, but Lieutenant Crawford was severely reprimanded, and Sub-Lieutenant Ian Mortimer, the engineer officer, was reprimanded for negligence. CPO Guest was awarded the George Medal for his actions.

[Various secondary; various editions of The Times; FOSM 'Lessons learned'; Evans p409]

1974

25 December ARROW patrol boat

Maryborough 1968; 146 tons; 107.6ft × 20ft; 1 × 40mm
Lieutenant Robert Dagworthy RAN

Royal Australian Navy. At the end of December, a strong tropical cyclone, which was given the name 'Tracy', was detected forming in the Timor Sea and the forecast track took it over the city of Darwin, which was the base for a patrol boat squadron, including *Arrow*. The crews were recalled from Christmas leave and the boats prepared for the storm, being secured to buoys in the outer harbour. The cyclone stuck the harbour during the early hours of the morning, with windspeeds reaching over 130mph, and although *Arrow* initially rode well, at 02.45 the securing shackle to the buoy parted. Main engines were started, and the head put into the wind, but the strain on the engines as she fought to maintain her position, soon began to tell, and they were overheating. Lieutenant Dagworthy decided that for the safety of the crew the patrol boat should be run into shallow water, and tried to make Frances Bay, but the strength of the wind took the boat onto a wharf and was then driven under the wharf with some force and the upperworks were crushed. The crew scrambled onto the wharf, although some men were washed into the sea, and two men were drowned. Several suffered injuries from flying debris. Cyclone 'Tracy' destroyed 70 per cent of the buildings in Darwin, and seventy-one people lost their lives.

[http://www.navy.gov.au/hmas-arrow]

1976

10 August REWARD patrol boat

Leith 1944; 1,120 tons; 190ft × 38.6ft; 1 × 40mm
Lieutenant Commander Ronald James Sandford

A former tug, she was employed as an offshore patrol vessel, and stationed at Rosyth. During the late afternoon of 10 August, she was returning to harbour having completed engine trials, the visibility was poor, with thick fog. Outward bound at the same time was the German-registered cargo ship *Plainsman*. At 19.00, between the rail and road bridges that span the Forth, a lookout on the *Reward* saw the cargo ship loom out of the mist about 200 yards away, and although the helm was ordered to be put over and the engines full ahead, before these took effect she was struck amidships. Water flooded into the engine room, but the *Plainsman* managed to keep some headway, partly plugging the hole, which slowed the flow somewhat. She steadily filled and as she started to heel over the crew rapidly transferred across to the cargo ship as she sank, stern first.

The subsequent investigation found that the *Plainsman* had failed to sound fog signals and was not burning navigation lights. Lieutenant Commander Sandford testified that they had detected the closing ship on radar and had broadcast a warning on radio that she was inbound at 6 knots, but the patrol boat's speed and manoeuvrability were restricted by unreliable engines. Further, the oncoming merchant ship was travelling at twice the recommended speed in the channel. Sandford was cleared of the charge of causing the loss by negligence but was found guilty of approving an unsafe entry plan into Rosyth and was reprimanded. The *Reward* was successfully raised 2 weeks later, but not repaired, and was sold for scrap.

[TNA: DEFE.69/204; The Times 11 August; 22 & 23 October 1976; Maclean p186]

20 September FITTLETON minesweeper

Southampton 1954; 360 tons; 140ft × 28.9ft; 1 × 40mm
Lieutenant Peter Valentine Paget RNR

Manned largely by reservists drawn from London Division RNR, the *Fittleton* had been participating in 'Teamwork-76', a NATO exercise in the North Sea, in company with six other reserve-manned minesweepers. On completion of the exercise the minesweepers steamed to rendezvous with the frigate *Mermaid*, which carried the flag of Admiral Commanding Reserves (ACR) prior to a port visit to Hamburg. At 14.45 the ships sighted each other and ACR ordered the minesweepers to form up in a column, the *Fittleton* leading, with the frigate being stationed on her beam. When this was complete, at 15.20 *Mermaid* informed the sweepers that they should close for a transfer of mail by heaving line 'when directed'. This involved the sweepers closing the frigate to steam a parallel course whilst a line was thrown to the fo'c'sle of the frigate; it was a well-established and practised manoeuvre. The order was taken by *Fittleton* as a warning, and they would be further advised when the transfer was to take place. However, only a few minutes later, at 15.24 ACR ordered her to comply with her earlier order. At this time, the sweepers did not have the men closed up or were prepared for a transfer, so were slow to react, prompting ACR to signal 'What are you waiting for?' The *Fittleton* increased speed to 12 knots and hauled out of line to approach the port quarter of the *Mermaid*, then started to move forward to position herself for the transfer from the fo'c'sle of the frigate. Lieutenant Paget found that he had difficulty in maintaining the required position. The *Mermaid* had an unusually short fo'c'sle which meant that the smaller ship had to sit in the disturbed water thrown up by the bows, which was very uncomfortable, and the smaller ship yawed about 5 degrees either side of the course steered. Heaving lines were thrown but bounced off the guardrails. To facilitate the fo'c'sle parties' task, Paget put the wheel to starboard for a moment then back to port, to bring his ship slightly closer to the frigate, but as she did so she found herself drawn closer into the frigate, due to the interaction between the ships. Despite the rudder being put over to port, she continued to close and struck the frigate under her bridge, the ships bumping side to side. Realising what was happening, the commanding officer of the sweeper ordered the helm hard over to port and increased speed, hoping to drive his ship out of danger, and she initially did pull away from the larger ship and moved ahead. However, as her bows entered the pressure wave from the bow of the frigate it pushed her stern out and her head to starboard. Now heeling over to port, she was dragged under the bows of the *Mermaid*. The commanding officer of the frigate had also realised the danger and ordered full astern and put the wheel hard to starboard, but despite their efforts the *Fittleton* remained trapped under her bows, slewing round to starboard. The *Mermaid* came into contact with *Fittleton*'s starboard side just below her amidships derrick, and then bounced along her side pushing her further over. When her bows were level with the minesweepers winch, she dug into her side. The sweeper heeled about 70 degrees to port, hung in that position for a few seconds until her port gunwale went underwater, and then rolled over onto her beam ends and capsized. Life rafts were released from the frigate and the other sweepers closed to lower boats to pick up the men seen swimming in the water. The *Crofton*, in a fine feat of seamanship, placed her stern next to the wreck to pick up a number of men. She remained afloat, upside down, and attempts were made to secure the wreck, but this proved difficult. Later that evening three German destroyers arrived on scene, but a plan to pass wires under the upturned hull was abandoned as the ship was settling further, and she finally sank at about 19.36. The position was marked by a dan buoy, the *Mermaid* remaining on scene until relieved by the frigate *Achilles*, which led a small force of ships that gathered at the scene. On 22 September, the salvage vessels *Magnus-1* and *Sea Leeuw* arrived on scene and they successfully raised the wreck, which was taken to Den Helder, arriving on 4 October. After being made seaworthy, she was towed to Chatham on 11 October, but was not repaired, being sold for scrap the following year. Twelve men died in the loss. Lieutenant Commander Paget was later court-martialled, being charged with negligence. Cleared of three charges, he was found guilty of the charge of hazarding his ship by failing to reduce speed and alter away earlier and was reprimanded. This was later quashed as an unsafe verdict.

[TNA: ADM.330/132; DEFE.13/1331; DEFE.24/963; DEFE.69/547]

1977

3 December EMPIRE ROSA tug
Blyth 1948; 292 tons; 116ft × 27.6ft

Employed as a stationary boundary marker on a bombing range in Luce Bay, Scotland, she was torn from her mooring during a gale, capsized and was driven ashore at Drummore. She was subsequently salvaged by *RMAS Mandarin* but was declared a constructive total loss and sold for scrap.

[Various secondary]

1982

The Falklands Conflict

On 2 April 1982 Argentina mounted an amphibious operation to occupy the Falkland Islands in the South Atlantic. This led to the rapid assembly and despatch of a task group to re-take the islands, which was successfully achieved in mid-June. The expected surface threat to the force evaporated following the sinking of the enemy cruiser *Belgrano* by the submarine *Conqueror* and a helicopter attack on an Argentine patrol boat, but a sub-surface threat remained. However, the ships found themselves very exposed to air attack, particularly when operating in close proximity to the land, and six ships were lost, in addition to one merchant vessel, all to aircraft bombs or missiles.

4 May SHEFFIELD guided missile destroyer
Barrow 1971; 3,850 tons; 392ft × 46ft; 1 × 4.5in, 1 × Sea Dart
Captain James Frederick Thomas George Salt

On 1 May the Task Group commenced operations inside the area designated the Total Exclusion Zone (TEZ). During the morning of 4 May the group was about 70 miles to the south-east of Port Stanley, with the aircraft carriers screened by several frigates and destroyers. with the *Sheffield* being the southernmost, and about 18 miles from the main body. During the morning, several Argentine aircraft had been detected closing from the mainland, but these had all proved to be Mirage aircraft on defensive Combat Air Patrol (CAP) duties over the islands and posed no threat to the force. This matched the scenario of the previous days, during which the ships had been dogged by false alarms, triggered by the detection of airborne radar transmissions, assessed as possibly emanating from a missile-carrying Super-Etendard attack aircraft. These alerts had led to ships taking the appropriate countermeasures, only to have them cancelled moments later when it was re-assessed as a CAP aircraft. At 13.56 the Type 42 destroyer *Glasgow* detected a brief radar transmission to the south-west, which was positively identified as being from a Super-Etendard; this was correlated to the brief appearance on radar of a contact at 40 miles from the main body, the *Invincible* also detecting the brief radar contacts. The *Glasgow* reported the raid by radio and passed the information by data link. A 'Zippo' call was broadcast, which initiated countermeasures, and several ships responded, which included firing chaff-dispensing rockets. At this point the Anti-Air Warfare Controller, borne in the *Hermes*, cancelled the actions, believing that this was yet another false alarm. *Sheffield* meanwhile had not detected the radar transmissions, as she had commenced transmitting on satellite communications, which interfered with her electronic warfare equipment; further she had failed to react to the alert from *Glasgow*. The incoming raid flying at very low level consisted of two Super-Etendard aircraft, which at 14.03 again 'popped-up' when they were about 30 miles from the main body of the Task Group, but only 15 miles from the nearest ship, which was the *Sheffield*. Both aircraft again briefly transmitted on radar, for just enough time to acquire a target, release their AM 39 Exocet missiles, and then split in opposite directions to clear the area. When the missiles were released, they were probably not more than 12 miles from the *Sheffield*. One missile failed to find a target, possibly deceived by one of the clouds of chaff that had been deployed from the earlier alert, the other locked on to the *Sheffield*. Less than a minute after release, it struck her amidships, exploding on 2 deck, between the galley and the forward auxiliary machinery room (FAMR). The impact smashed a hole 15ft wide by 4ft high, and the explosion blew open watertight doors and caused shock damage, the unspent fuel from the missile ignited, starting a large fire, with thick black smoke which rapidly spread throughout the ship, forcing many compartments to be evacuated. The firemain had been breached on impact which limited the initial fire-fighting efforts. Despite determined efforts to fight the fire, the blaze spread rapidly, both forward and aft the men being driven back by heat and smoke. The frigates *Arrow* and *Yarmouth* closed, stationing themselves on either side of the *Sheffield* to assist in fire-fighting efforts. By 17.50 there was still no firemain, the fires were spreading, and were now threatening the magazines, and Captain Salt took the decision to abandon her. Most clambered over onto the *Arrow*, but others were taken off by *Yarmouth*, with several being lifted off by helicopter from the *Hermes*. The ship remained upright and stable, and she was taken in tow by *Yarmouth*, hoping to reach South Georgia. However, the wind and sea increased, and she was evidently shipping water through the large hole in her side. On 10 May at 07.00 she was seen to take a distinct

list to starboard, and the tow was quickly slipped; shortly after this she rolled over and sank in position 52.11S 53.50W. Twenty men died in the loss.
[Sheffield Board of Inquiry; various secondary]

21 May **ARDENT** frigate
Scotstoun 1975; 3,100 tons; 360ft × 41.9ft; 1 × 4.5in, 4 × Exocet, 1 × Sea Cat, 2 × 20mm
Commander Alan William John West

On 21 May British forces commenced landing in San Carlos Sound on East Falkland, achieving complete surprise, the forces encountering no opposition. After the landing, several flights of aircraft were launched from mainland Argentina to attack the ships assembled at San Carlos. The *Ardent* had been conducting a gunfire support mission further to the south, on the area of Darwin/Goose Green, and was on her own in Grantham Sound when at 16.00 she came under attack by a single A-4B Skyhawk aircraft, which dropped a bomb, which missed. Some damage was caused to the Type 992Q radar which was struck a glancing blow by the aircraft as it passed low overhead. At 17.40 the next attack materialised in the shape of three Dagger aircraft, which approached the area keeping low over the land of West Falkland, and as they crossed over the coast saw the solitary *Ardent* ahead of them. They approached from astern, and pressed home an attack, each aircraft releasing two bombs. Still trying to manoeuvre to allow the 4.5in gun to engage, and the Sea Cat missile being unable to fire owing to the low angle of approach, the frigate could only engage with 20mm gunfire. Of the six bombs dropped, she was hit by two, one of which detonated on impact with the hangar, demolishing the Lynx helicopter and blowing the Sea Cat launcher off the ship. The second lodged, unexploded, in the after auxiliary machinery space. A fire was started, but the ship was able to move into clear water, and head towards the north, to join the other ships in San Carlos Sound, with damage control parties working hard to contain and control the fire, but 15 minutes later a third attack commenced, this time by three A-4Q Skyhawk aircraft. They closed from the starboard side in line astern, each aircraft dropping a pair of 500lb bombs. She was hit by three of them, all of which exploded. This started a large fire in the canteen area, the tiller flat was destroyed which meant that she had lost steering and there was flooding aft which could not be controlled. The other bombs exploded in the water close by her, causing the ship to 'whip'. The ship had lost steering, but the engines were still working, and she headed inshore, out of control until the engines were tripped and she came to a stop less than a mile offshore, and an anchor was let go to hold her steady. She continued to flood, and a dangerous list to starboard developed. When the ship gave a lurch, it became clear that she could not survive, and Commander West ordered the ship to be abandoned. The frigate *Yarmouth* closed to put her stern against the burning frigate's bow and took her men off, Commander West, being the last man to leave at 18.55. Twenty-two men were lost. None of the three Skyhawk aircraft survived the attack. Two were immediately shot down by Sea Harrier aircraft, and the third had been damaged by fire from the *Ardent* and then further damaged by gunfire from a Harrier, forcing the pilot to eject.

[Ardent Board of Inquiry; various secondary]

23 May ANTELOPE frigate

Southampton 1972; 3,100 tons; 360ft × 41.9ft; 1 × 4.5in, 4 × Exocet, 1 × Sea Cat, 2 × 20mm
Commander Nicholas John Tobin

Located off Fanning Head in San Carlos water, protecting the ships still offloading stores to support the landing, she became the target for an air attack during the afternoon by four A-4B Skyhawk aircraft, which appeared from over the surrounding hills of the land. At 12.40 the first pair closed, and each dropped a 1,000lb bomb, one of which struck the frigate forward on 2 deck, killing one man, but failing to explode. The pair of aircraft were damaged by small-arms fire and despite a missile exploding nearby, they escaped. The remaining two aircraft flew down the hills of Fanning Head, one passing astern, the other carried out an attack at low level from starboard. This was engaged by gunfire and crashed into the sea, but the bomb it released struck amidships on 2 deck. The last attack from astern was also engaged, but the bomb dropped wide. Neither of the bombs that had struck her exploded. One of the unexploded bombs lodged in the air conditioning compartment aft, the second in the petty officers' mess. The ship was moved into Ajax Bay and bomb disposal specialists from the Royal Engineers came onboard to defuse the weapons. They decided to tackle the bomb lodged in the air-conditioning compartment first and attempted to defuse it by withdrawing the firing pistol. Three attempts were made to so, but all failed to remove the mechanism. At 21.15 they decided to try and detach the pistol by using a small charge to cut the pistol free. The charge was successfully fired, but as the pair went to inspect the bomb it exploded, killing one of the officers, and severely wounding the second. The blast blew a hole 35ft wide in the side and severed the firemain, which meant that there was little pressure on hoses. A fierce fire was started which spread rapidly. Despite strenuous efforts to fight the blaze, including assistance by two small landing craft which came alongside, it was clear that they were fighting a losing battle. At 22.20 the order to abandon ship was given, and the men quickly and quietly left her by the landing craft. About 10 minutes after the last man had been taken off, the Sea

Cat magazines exploded, starting more fires, and there were continued explosions through the night. At dawn there was a second major explosion forward and in a cloud of smoke she broke in two and sank, her bows and stern showing above the water for some time. In addition to the bomb disposal officer, one member of the ship's company died.

[Antelope Board of Inquiry; various secondary]

25 May COVENTRY guided missile destroyer

Birkenhead 1974; 3,850 tons; 392ft × 46ft; 1 × 4.5in, 1 × Sea Dart
Captain David Hart-Dyke

On 22 May, in company with the Type 22 frigate, *Broadsword*, *Coventry* was ordered set up a joint patrol to the north of Pebble Island, West Falkland. The intention was to give assistance to the ships unloading in San Carlos Water which were coming under intense air raids, by intercepting targets as they closed the islands. This would be provided by the Sea Dart missile system carried by the Type 42 destroyer, and *Broadsword*, armed with the close-range, quick-reaction Sea Wolf system, would complement this. The pair established a patrol line 10 miles offshore on 23 May, but although several raids were detected over the next 2 days and CAP aircraft directed to intercept, none of the raids came into the engagement envelope. The proximity to land caused concern, as it was felt that it was certain that they had been observed and would be made a target for attack. Further, the radar was suffering from 'clutter' caused by ground returns, which would give minimal warning of a low-flying attacker approaching from the land. However, it was felt that the risk must be taken, both to provide protection to the ships in San Carlos Water, and to stay within radio range. At 12.30 GMT, another incoming air raid was detected closing from the west, and this was successfully tracked until it was engaged by *Coventry* with Sea Dart, resulting in the destruction of an A-4 Skyhawk. Another air raid was similarly tracked 3 hours later and engaged, with the successful downing of another A-4. At 17.15 GMT a further air raid was detected approaching the island, and was tracked closing West Falkland, when it dropped down to hug the ground, to be lost in the 'clutter' of returns from the hills. It was presumed that this was another raid for San Carlos Water, but the hostiles were then detected by *Broadsword* on her 967 Doppler radar, heading north, straight for the *Coventry* and *Broadsword*. The frigate continued to track them as they closed, but the destroyer did not detect the raid until they left the shadow of the land at a range of 10 miles. The raid was seen when about 8 miles distant and identified as two pairs of A-4 Skyhawk aircraft, flying low. The Sea Dart missile control radar had insufficient time to acquire the targets as they emerged from the clutter and the Sea Wolf control radar on *Broadsword*, having tracked the targets, malfunctioned and failed to engage. The first pair was engaged with gunfire, but flew through this to attack the *Broadsword*, which they strafed with gunfire and then dropped two bombs each. Three of the four bombs missed, but the fourth struck the frigate, passing through the side and up through the flight deck, damaging the helicopter as it continued on its way into the sea without exploding. The second pair now approached and these concentrated on the destroyer. As they closed the *Coventry* manoeuvred vigorously, to open gun arcs to allow the 4.5in gun to engage, and fired a Sea Dart missile, although a proper acquisition was impossible. As *Coventry* swung round the *Broadsword* followed, but the move had placed the destroyer between the frigate and the oncoming raid and although the frigate had now acquired the raid and was about to engage, she could not do so as the destroyer fouled the range. Each of the attacking aircraft strafed the destroyer with cannon fire, although the first aircraft suffered a hang-up with its bomb load, the second placed all three of its 1,000lb bombs accurately in the *Coventry*. The first bomb struck 3 deck to explode after a short delay in the conversion machinery room, destroying the adjacent computer room and blowing a hole in the ship's side. This effectively put out of action all the ships sensors. The second bomb penetrated 2 deck, but did not explode, probably lodging unexploded in the provisions room on 4 deck. The third bomb entered the ship by the engine intakes to explode in the forward engine room. Both of the bombs that exploded started fires and there was extensive flooding which affected several sections, causing the ship to heel to port, and she developed an increasing list. After some 15 minutes it became clear that she could not be saved, and an evacuation was ordered as she started to slowly roll over. Men left her quickly and calmly, the last to leave walking down the ship's hull into the water. The *Broadsword* was quickly on scene and she was joined by helicopters launched from the RFA *Fort Austin*. Nineteen men were lost.

[*Coventry Board of Inquiry; various secondary*]

8 June SIR GALAHAD landing ship, logistic

Govan 1966; 3,270 tons; 380ft × 59.8ft; 1 × 40mm
Captain Philip Jeremy George Roberts RFA

The successful landings at San Carlos Water led to an advance to the east across the island of East Falkland towards Port Stanley. On 2 June, an advance party had taken the settlements of Fitzroy and Bluff Cove, only 15 miles from Stanley, and these had to be reinforced rapidly. The troops found the going hard, marching with full equipment across boggy ground and rough terrain. Helicopters were used whenever possible, but there were never enough. Attempts were made to carry troops and equipment by sea, but this put the larger assault

ships at considerable risk, and it was decided to utilise the smaller LSLs. On 7 June, the *Sir Tristram* arrived in Fitzroy Cove, fully laden with ammunition and stores and the work of unloading her proceeded, although very slowly. The following morning, at 06.50 local time, the *Sir Galahad* arrived, carrying troops from the Welsh Guards and a Field Ambulance Unit. Unloading was painfully slow, as there was only one small utility landing craft and one motorised lighter available for both ships. A small number of Sea King helicopters was made available to assist, but they had limited lift capability. Work was concentrated on unloading the *Sir Tristram* and when that was complete, at noon, the landing craft was able to move to the *Sir Galahad*. It was decided to offload the Field Ambulance Unit first, but during this, the ramp of the landing craft was damaged, meaning that the disembarkation, already slow, was further delayed, as equipment had to be lifted off by crane. The *Sir Tristram* had been observed from Argentine observation positions on the shore the previous day, and the arrival of a second unit prompted an inevitable response. A determined effort was mounted by the Argentine Air Force with Dagger and A-4 Skyhawk aircraft, but only five of the latter managed to locate the landing ships. At 1.10pm they ran into the cove, splitting into groups of two and three aircraft to carry out the attack. *Sir Galahad* was hit by three bombs on the starboard side and was also raked by cannon fire. One bomb struck the after superstructure, under the funnel, another punctured the upper deck to enter the tank deck and the third hit the engine room and galley. They did not explode, rather they 'deflagrated', the casings bursting open on impact and the explosives burning rather than exploding. A 500-gallon diesel tank was ruptured, spilling its contents and fuelling a fierce fire in the funnel and engine room. The bomb that hit the tank deck triggered explosions in the ammunition stored there, and another fire broke out. All power was lost, and Captain Roberts ordered the ship to be abandoned. The landing craft, lighter and helicopters all closed the scene to assist with the evacuation, and life rafts and lifeboats were lowered. All the survivors were off in 30 minutes, but many were severely injured and burned. Forty-eight men died in the ship, thirty-two of them Welsh Guardsmen. The fires continued to burn for some time. Subsequent inspection confirmed that the damage was such that she was a constructive total loss and on 25 June she was towed out to sea and the following day sunk by torpedo from the submarine *Onyx*. *Sir Tristram* was hit by two bombs which failed to explode, and was temporarily abandoned, but later re-boarded and later repaired.

[*Sir Galahad Board of Inquiry and various secondary*]

8 June LCM 703 landing craft, medium
Lowestoft 1963, 175 tons; 84ft × 21ft
Colour Sergeant Brian Johnston[†]

Carrying the local identity of 'F.4', the craft had been disembarked from *Fearless* and was employed ferrying equipment along the southern coast of East Falkland. Whilst carrying a load of vehicles and their drivers from Goose Green to Fitzroy it was seen by a group of four enemy A–4 aircraft that were searching for the reported landing ships (see *Sir Galahad* above). The aircraft turned in to attack the craft, using cannon and one aircraft released bombs, one of which hit. The bomb did not explode, but the impact killed five men, including Colour Sergeant Johnston, and caused her to start settling. The local coaster *Monsunnen*, taken over by the Navy, was directed to her assistance, and a Sea King helicopter arrived to lift off the eleven survivors. *Monsunnen* took her in tow, but the landing craft steadily settled and at 23.00 sank.
[*Various secondary*]

1984

24 April LCVP 120 landing craft, vehicles and personnel
Poole 1959; 8.5 tons; 41.5ft × 10ft

Whilst under tow off Portland, she foundered when her bow ramp accidentally dropped open, causing her to flood and rapidly sink. The wreck lies in position 50.39.36N 01.50.42W.
[*Larn vol 1 sec 6*]

4 Losses of Minor Landing Craft 1939–1945

LANDING CRAFT WERE ORIGINALLY intended to be carried by larger ships to the area of operation, and as such were regarded as 'minor' vessels and were not detailed or listed in the contemporary Navy Lists. This makes any attempt to trace the history of an individual craft difficult. Further, the details of any loss were often poorly recorded. Although regular listings of minor craft were maintained (TNA ADM.210), craft were often simply deleted from the list with no explanation. The official *Statement of Losses during the Second World War* often has only the vaguest of detail, such as 'Lost in Middle East' with no date or 'cause and place unknown'.

The larger amphibious ships (LSI, LST, LCF, LCH, LCG, LCI (L), LCI(S), LCS (L), LCT and FDT) have been listed in the main section, but I have decided to follow the convention established in the *Statement of Losses* and list these minor craft separately, with what detail I have been able to ascertain.

Brief details of the types listed below:

LCA	Landing Craft Assault	11–13 tons, 38.9ft x 10ft
LCA (HR)	Landing Craft, Assault (Hedgerow)	12 tons, 38.9ft x 10ft
LCA (OC)	Landing Craft, Assault (Obstruction Clearance)	12 tons, 38.9ft x 10ft
LCE	Landing Craft, Emergency Repair	11 tons, 36.4ft x 10.6ft
LCM (1)	Landing Craft, Medium (Mark 1)	36 tons, 44.9ft x 14ft
LCM (3)	Landing Craft, Medium (Mark 3)	52 tons, 50ft x 14ft
LCP (S)	Landing Craft Personnel (Small)	5.5 tons, 28ft x 8.9ft
LCP (M)	Landing Craft Personnel (Medium)	7.5 tons, 39ft x 10ft
LCP (L)	Landing Craft Personnel (Large)	10.7 tons, 36.9ft x 10.9ft
LCP (R)	Landing Craft Personnel (Ramped)	10.7 tons, 36.9ft x 10.9ft
LCP (survey)	Landing Craft Personnel (Survey)	10.7 tons, 36.9ft x 10.9ft
LCS (M)(1)	Landing Craft Support (Medium Mark 1)	9–10 tons, 38.9ft x 10ft
LCS (M)(2)	Landing Craft Support (Medium Mark 2)	10–12 tons, 38.9ft x 10ft
LCS (M)(3)	Landing Craft Support (Medium Mark 3)	11–13 tons, 38.9ft x 10ft
LCV	Landing Craft Vehicle	11 tons, 36.4ft x 10.9ft
LCVP	Landing Craft, Vehicle & Personnel	11.5 tons, 36ft x 10.6ft

Barges – a large number of commercial barges were taken up from trade and converted for a variety of uses, Although numbered in a sequence and with prefix, they were not of a uniform size, but were grouped according to their role. Where known, the former commercial name is shown. The term dumb indicates that they were not powered.

LB	Landing Barge	c150–200-ton dumb
LBE	Landing Barge, Emergency Repair	c150–200 tons powered
LBF	Landing Barge, Flak	c150 tons powered
LBG	Landing Barge, Gun	c150 tons powered
LBK	Landing Barge, Kitchen	c150 tons powered
LBO	Landing Barge, Oil	c150–200 tons powered
LBR	Landing Barge, Ramped	c100–150-ton dumb with stern ramp
LBV (1)	Landing Barge, Vehicle, Mark 1	c100–150 tons, 70–78ft x 18–20ft dumb
LBV (2)	Landing Barge, Vehicle, Mark 2	c200 tons, c82ft x 23ft dumb
LBW	Landing Barge, Water	c150–200 tons powered

Information mainly from *Statement of Losses*, supplemented by War Diaries; details of barges from TNA: ADM.1/16255 and www.naval-history.net/WW2MiscRNLandingBarges2.htm

1940

Date	Name	Circumstances & Location
29 May	LCA 4	Carried onboard *Clan MacAlister* to Dunkirk; fell from ship when being unloaded.
	LCA 16	Sub-Lieutenant Robert Owen Wilcoxon RNVR†. Sunk by aircraft attack at Dunkirk.
	LCA 18	Crushed by LCA 4 when being unloaded from *Clan MacAlister* off Dunkirk and lost.
31 May	LCA 8	Lost off Dunkirk after tow parted.
	LCA 15	Sub-Lieutenant George Banfield Eyre RNVR. Abandoned at Dunkirk after striking submerged object
2 June	LCM (1) 12	Petty Officer Brinton. Abandoned at Dunkirk following engine failure
	LCM (1) 22	CPO Mitten. Abandoned off Dunkirk after tow parted.
3 June	LCM (1) 17	L/Seaman Coleman. Abandoned off Dunkirk after tow parted & engines failed.
May/June		Lost in operations around Narvik, Norway; one apparently capsized when embarking a tank and another was lost during an air raid. The remainder were sunk by own forces' gunfire during the final withdrawal:
	LCM (1) 10	
	LCM (1) 11	
	LCM (1) 14	
	LCM (1) 15	
	LCM (1) 18	
	LCM (1) 19	
	LCM (1) 20	
9 June	LCA 14	Lost in home waters.
11 June	LCA 11	Sunk off St Valery during evacuation.
14 June	LCA 1	Lost in home waters.
	LCA 2	Lost in home waters.
July	LCA 6	Lost, cause and place uncertain.
21 December	LCP (L) 30	Destroyed during air attack on Liverpool.

1941

Date	Name	Circumstances & Location
29 May	LCA 28	Abandoned in Crete following German invasion.
	LCM (1) 106	Abandoned in Crete following German invasion.
May	LCP (L) 107	Reported lost in home waters.
	LCP (L) 108	Reported lost in home waters.
	LCP (L) 109	Reported lost in home waters.
July	LCA 119	Sunk; home waters.
19 August	LCM (1) 82	Skipper Patrick Donald Jackson RNVR† Driven ashore and wrecked during air attack on Tobruk.
	LCM (1) 96	Skipper John James Fortune RNVR Driven ashore and wrecked during air attack on Tobruk.
31 August		A large number of amphibious craft were written off as being 'lost in the Middle East' – some of these would have been in Crete:
	LCA 31	
	LCA 32	
	LCA 38	
	LCA 39	
	LCA 45	
	LCA 48	
	LCA 49	
	LCA 51	

Date	Name	Circumstances & Location
	LCA 60	
	LCA 63	
	LCA 64	
	LCA 75	
	LCA 79	
	LCA 80	
	LCA 81	
	LCA 87	
	LCA 105	
	LCA 113	
	LCM (1) 32	
	LCM (1) 55	
	LCM (1) 67	
	LCM (1) 95	
	LCM (1) 97	
	LCM (1) 103	
	LCM (1) 107	
	LCM (1) 108	
	LCP (L) 63	
2 September	LCP (L) 59	Driven ashore at Sidi Barrani during a gale and lost.
	LCP (L) 71	Driven ashore at Sidi Barrani during a gale and lost.
24 December	LCA 121	Lost, location unknown.
31 December	LCP (L) 193	Lost overboard from parent ship in home waters.
	LCP (L) 194	Lost overboard from parent ship in home waters.

The following craft were written off, date and location unknown, in home waters:

LCP (L) 24
LCP (L) 25
LCP (L) 26
LCP (L) 27
LCP (L) 38
LCP (L) 82

Lost in the Middle East, date and location unrecorded:

LCA 70

The following were written off, time and place of loss unknown:

LCS (M) 1
LCM (1) 1

1942

Date	Name	Circumstances & Location
1 January		Attacked and destroyed by enemy aircraft near Port Swettenham, Malaya:
	LCP (L) 180	
	LCP (L) 181	
	LCP (L) 182	
	LCP (L) 183	
	LCP (L) 184	
	LCP (L) 185	
30 March	LCM (1) 51	Lost in the Middle East.
	LCM (1) 53	Lost in the Middle East.
	LCP (L) 57	Lost in a bombing raid at Tobruk.
	LCP (L) 117	Lost in home waters

Date	Name	Circumstances & Location
1 April	LCM (1) 38	Lost in the Mediterranean.
19 April	LCA 166	Lost in home waters.
	LCA 211	Lost in home waters.
5 May	LCM (1) 46	Capsized, in the East Indies.
20 June	Lost at the capture of Tobruk:	
	LCA 193	
	LCM (1) 110	Sunk by *S 56* and *S 58*
	LCM (1) 113	Sunk by *S 56* and *S 58*
	LCM (1) 145	Captured by *S 55*
	LCM (1) 146	Captured by *S 55*
	LCM (1) 148	Sunk by *S 56* and *S 58*
	LCP (L) 64	
	LCS (M)(1) 4	
	LCS (M)(1) 6	
	LCS (M)(1) 15	
	LCS (M)(1) 18	
	LCS (M)(1) 19	
	LCS (M)(1) 22	
June	LCA 138	Lost in home waters.
June	A number of craft in the Middle East were written off:	
	LCM (1) 84	
	LCM (1) 90	
	LCM (1) 93	
	LCM (1) 119	
	LCM (1) 122	
	LCM (1) 135	
	LCM (1) 137	
	LCM (1) 140	
30 June	LCP (L) 65	Foundered in bad weather at Alexandria
10 July	LCP (L) 93	Burnt out at Shoreham.
July	LCA 196	Lost, 'by enemy action', place unrecorded, but probably the LCA destroyed 7 July by air attack on LSI(S) *Princess Astrid* off Isle of Wight
19 August	Lost in the landings at Dieppe:	
	LCA 37	
	LCA 52	
	LCA 92	
	LCA 94	
	LCA 97	
	LCA 102	
	LCA 192	
	LCA 209	
	LCA 214	
	LCA 215	
	LCA 237	
	LCA 247	
	LCA 251	
	LCA 262	
	LCA 284	
	LCA 314	
	LCA 317	
	LCM (1) 56	
	LCP (L) 42	
	LCP (L) 45	
	LCP (L) 81	

Date	Name	Circumstances & Location
	LCP (L) 157	
	LCP (L) 164	
	LCP (L) 174	
	LCP (L) 210	
	LCP (L) 212	
	LCS (M)(1) 9	
31 August	LB 329	
August	(ex-*Destroyer*) Sunk during air raid, Stoke Gabriel.	
	Written off in the Middle East (some of these will have been at Tobruk):	
	LCM (1) 23	
	LCM (1) 24	
	LCM (1) 25	
	LCM (1) 34	
	LCM (1) 45	
	LCM (3) 501	
	LCM (3) 510	
	LCM (3) 516	
August	LCP (R) 1008	Foundered in heavy weather in home waters.
August	LCP (R) 1012	Sank after collision in home waters.
2 September	LCP (L) 83	Burnt out at Newhaven.
12 September	LCV 597	Lost in home waters.
15 September	LCP (L) 29	Burnt out, Middle East.
	LCP (L) 617	Lost in home waters.
19 September	Sunk at Salcombe during enemy air raid:	
	LB 232 (ex-*Peace*)	
	LB 332 (ex-*Bear*)	
	LB 362 (ex-*Buffalo*)	
24 September	LCP (R) 622	Lost in home waters.
	LCV 798	Wrecked after engine failure, Corsewall Point.
September	LB 382	Lost in home waters, cause and place unknown.
13 October	Lost when *Southern Empress*, the ship they were being carried on, was torpedoed by *U 221* in the North Atlantic:	
	LCM (3) 508	
	LCM (3) 509	
	LCM (3) 519	
	LCM (3) 522	
	LCM (3) 523	
	LCM (3) 532	
	LCM (3) 537	
	LCM (3) 547	
	LCM (3) 620	
14 October	Lost in the *Empire Tarpon*, which foundered 57.24N 07.45W following engine failure:	
	LCM (3) 611	
	LCM (3) 613	
	LCM (3) 632	
	LCM (3) 633	
	LCM (3) 634	
	LCM (3) 636	
19 October	Sunk by air raid at Stoke Gabriel, Dartmouth:	
	(*Note*: not listed as being lost in the official Statement of losses, so possibly salvaged)	
	LB 65 (ex-*Quits*)	
	LB 295 (ex-*Trust*)	
	LB 347 (ex-*Bodley*)	
	LB 485 (ex-*Watton*)	

Date	Name	Circumstances & Location
22 October	LCM (1) 89	Lost in tow in the Indian Ocean.
October	LCM (1) 31	Lost in home waters, date uncertain.
6 November	LCP (L) 209	Wrecked in Seaford Bay.
8–12 November		Lost during Operation 'Torch' landings, North Africa. Most of the LCAs were probably lost when their carriers *Viceroy of India*, *Ettrick* and *Karanja* were sunk:
	LCA 35	
	LCA 128	Wrecked on the beach.
	LCA 135	Wrecked on the beach.
	LCA 153	
	LCA 218	
	LCA 219	
	LCA 221	
	LCA 227	
	LCA 239	
	LCA 244	
	LCA 245	
	LCA 259	
	LCA 260	
	LCA 261	
	LCA 269	
	LCA 271	
	LCA 286	
	LCA 287	Wrecked on the beach.
	LCA 301	
	LCA 309	
	LCA 310	
	LCA 321	
	LCA 423	
	LCA 436	
	LCA 447	
	LCA 451	
	LCM (1) 63	
	LCM (1) 64	
	LCM (1) 65	
	LCM (1) 69	
	LCM (1) 72	
	LCM (1) 73	
	LCM (1) 120	
	LCM (1) 147	
	LCM (1) 153	
	LCM (1) 161	
	LCM (1) 169	
	LCM (1) 186	
	LCM (3) 518	
	LCM (3) 520	
	LCM (3) 528	
	LCM (3) 539	
	LCM (3) 543	
	LCM (3) 551	
	LCM (3) 555	
	LCM (3) 556	
	LCM (3) 558	
	LCM (3) 564	
	LCM (3) 567	

Date	Name	Circumstances & Location
	LCM (3) 569	
	LCM (3) 571	
	LCM (3) 572	
	LCM (3) 574	
	LCM (3) 581	
	LCM (3) 584	
	LCM (3) 590	
	LCM (3) 592	
	LCM (3) 593	
	LCM (3) 595	
	LCM (3) 596	
	LCM (3) 606	
	LCM (3) 609	
	LCM (3) 624	
	LCM (3) 635	
	LCP (L) 138	
	LCP (L) 507	
	LCP (L) 543	
	LCP (L) 550	
	LCP (L) 560	
	LCP (L) 562	
	LCP (L) 565	
	LCP (L) 566	
	LCP (L) 568	
	LCP (L) 573	
	LCP (L) 575	
	LCP (L) 576	
	LCP (R) 603	
	LCP (R) 620	
	LCP (R) 629	
	LCP (R) 721	
	LCP (L) 759	
	LCP (R) 783	
	LCP (R) 794	
	LCP (R) 837	
	LCP (R) 850	
	LCP (R) 901	
	LCP (R) 909	
	LCP (R) 1009	
	LCP (R) 1029	
	LCP (R) 1036	
	LCS (M)(1) 11	
	LCS (M)(1) 28	
12 November		Lost when the *Karanja* was sunk by air attack off Bougie:
	LCA 235	
	LCP (L) 544	
	LCP (R) 858	
14 November		Lost when the *Warwick Castle* was torpedoed and sunk by *U 413* off coast of Portugal:
	LCA 55	
	LCA 167	
	LCA 169	
	LCA 176	
	LCA 187	
	LCA 188	

Date	Name	Circumstances & Location
	LCA 189	
	LCA 266	
	LCA 307	
	LCA 375	
20 November	LCM (1) 139	Foundered in heavy weather at Ras Kanayis.
22 November	LCS (M)(1) 14	Sunk in air attack at Bougie.
November	LCA 226	Written of charge, Mediterranean.
6 December	LCM (1) 98	Lost at Benghazi.
13 December	LCP (R) 578	Lost at Inveraray.
	LCV 579	Lost at Inveraray.
24 December	LCP (L) 36	Burnt out at Chittagong.
30 December	Lost when the *Fidelity* was sunk by *U 435* in the North Atlantic:	
	LCV 752	
	LCV 754	

1943

Date	Name	Circumstances & Location
2 January	LCM (1) 26	Ran aground at Taifa, Libya.
3 January	LCP (L) 17	Lost by fire at Chittagong.
5 January	LCP (M) 17	Foundered in the Solent.
15 January	LCP (L) 80	Foundered in bad weather in home waters.
25 January	LCM (1) 58	Lost off Libya.
	LCP (L) 87	Lost in home waters.
January	Lost at Surabaya, Java (?): This is according to the *Statement of Losses* p 53 but makes little sense, as Java had been occupied by the Japanese since March 1942. Perhaps 1941 was meant.	
	LCP (L) 203	
	LCP (L) 204	
	LCP (L) 205	
	LCP (L) 206	
6 February	LCM (1) 80	Wrecked at Benghazi.
8 February	LCM (1) 61	Foundered in bad weather at Benghazi.
4 March	Lost when the *Marietta-E* was torpedoed by *U 160* in the Indian Ocean:	
	LCP (R) 673	
	LCP (R) 680	
	LCP (R) 684	
	LCP (R) 685	
	LCP (R) 689	
	LCP (R) 692	
	LCP (R) 693	
	LCP (R) 727	
4 March	LCP (L) 106	Wrecked at Tobruk.
15 March	LCV 584	Foundered off Inellan, Scotland.
March	LCP (L) 276	Lost in transit.
	LCP (L) 277	Lost in transit.
30 March	LCS (M)(1) 23	Sunk in the River Mayu, Burma.
17 April	Lost when the *Sembilan* was torpedoed by *Da Vinci* in the Indian Ocean:	
	LCP (R) 780	
	LCP (R) 782	
25 April	LCS (M)(1) 17	Sunk in the River Mayu, Burma.
April	LCA 272	Lost in the Mediterranean.
21 May	LCV 825	Sank after explosion during night exercise off west Scotland.
June	LCA 78	Lost in tow off the North African coast.
	LCA 222	Written off in the Mediterranean.

Date	Name	Circumstances & Location
	LCA 312	Written off in the Mediterranean.
	LCP (R) 769	Lost in the Mediterranean
29 August	LCA 446	Foundered in bad weather in the Mediterranean.
	LCS (M)(1) 16	Lost in India.
August	LCP (L) 126	Burnt out – location not recorded.
4 September	LCP (L) 325	Sunk at Bombay.
12 September	LCP (R) 879	Wrecked at Bombay.
	LCP (L) 316	Sunk at Bombay.
15 September	LCM (3) 1165	Caught fire whilst dumping ammunition off Syracuse.
24 September	LCA 675	Foundered in bad weather at Salerno.
28 September	LCP (R) 1019	Foundered in bad weather at Salerno.
September	LCS (L) 201	Foundered after collision in the English Channel.
5 October	LBV 229	
	(ex-*Benefactor*)	Written off, London.
October	LCE 1	Lost, Mediterranean.
October	LCE 9	Lost, Mediterranean.
October		All listed vaguely as being lost in the Mediterranean, they were probably those actually lost in July when the merchant ships *Devis*, *City of Venice* and *St Essylt* carrying LCMs as deck cargo were sunk:
	LCM (1) 232	
	LCM (3) 545	
	LCM (3) 938	
	LCM (3) 1044	
October	LCM (3) 1182	Lost in home waters.
1 November	LCVP 1040	Capsized after flooding, Newhaven.
11 November	LCM (3) 923	Captured when Leros occupied.
29 November	LCA 813	Foundered during exercises, Home waters.
November		The following reported to have been written off/lost, in the Mediterranean:
	LCA 212	
	LCA 316	
	LCA 505	
	LCA 545	
November	LCM (1) 181	Lost, Azores.
	LCM (3) 583	Lost, Mediterranean.
	LCP (M) 14	Lost; date, location and cause not recorded.
2 December	LCA 553	Foundered after collision in the Solent.
8 December	LCP (L) 136	Caught fire and blew up, Southampton.
19 December		Written off after damage during beaching exercises, home waters:
	LCP (R) 753	
	LCP (R) 771	
	LCP (R) 795	
20 December	LCM (1) 33	Damaged beyond repair, home waters.
21 December	LCA 645	Foundered in bad weather, English Channel.
	LCA 646	Foundered in bad weather, English Channel.
22 December		Lost overboard from the *Hilary*:
	LCP (R) 613	
	LCP (R) 661	
	LCP (R) 1035	
22 December	LCP (S) 116	Lost in exercises, home waters.
December	LCA 723	Wrecked after breaking adrift, Port Edgar.

1944

Date	Name	Circumstances & Location
17 January	LBV (1) 367	Wrecked between Dartmouth and Portland.
19 January	Reported lost off East Scotland:	
	LCA 783	
	LCA 790	
	LCA 865	
22 January	Lost during the landings at Anzio (Operation 'Shingle'):	
	LCA 323	
	LCA 364	
	LCA 382	
	LCA 394	
	LCA 398	
	LCA 417	
	LCA 428	
	LCA 433	
	LCA 440	
	LCA 487	
	LCA 697	
	LCM (3) 623	
	LCM (3) 910	
	LCM (3) 930	
	LCM (3) 1022	
	LCM (3) 1064	
	LCM (3) 1173	
	LCM (3) 1204	
	LCP (L) 66	
	LCP (L) 356	
	LCP (L) 373	
	LCS (M)(3) 46	
22 January	LCP (R) 616	Broke adrift and damaged beyond repair, home waters.
25 January	LCP (S) 60	Wrecked in the Azores.
29 January	LCA 845	Foundered during exercises off Leith.
9 February	LCA 552	Wrecked during exercises off east Scotland.
14 February	LCP (R) 781	Foundered after collision, home waters.
24 February	LCP (L) 152	Wrecked during exercises, home waters.
28 February	LCP (L) 541	Foundered off the Isle of Wight.
February	Written off, cause and place unrecorded:	
	LBV (1) 136	
	LBV (1) 149	
	LBV (1) 497	
February	Lost in home waters, date uncertain:	
	LCM (1) 192	
	LCM (1) 234	
	LCM (1) 254	
	LCM (1) 279	
	LCM (1) 282	
	LCM (1) 327	
	LCM (1) 329	
	LCM (1) 367	
February	LCV 894	Lost, training at Rothesay.
February	LCVP 1066	Wrecked during exercises, Richborough.

Date	Name	Circumstances & Location
1 March	LCA 726	Lost in home waters.
	LCA 908	Lost in home waters.
3 March	LCS (M)(3) 69	Foundered during exercises, Scotland.
13 March	LCA (HR) 689	Foundered, home waters.
	LCP (S) 76	Lost on passage.
23 March	LCP (R) 1026	Sunk in the Mediterranean.
March	LBV (1) 266	Lost, cause and place unknown.
	LCM (1) 76	Lost in the East Indies.
2 April	LCA (HR) 672	Foundered during exercises, Scotland.
	LCA (HR) 811	Foundered during exercises, Scotland.
6 April	LCP (S) 9	Wrecked at Weymouth.
14 April		Lost by fire & explosion at Bombay:
	LCP (L) 323	
	LCP (R) 866	
April	LCP (L) 360	Lost during exercises at Mandapam, Ceylon.
	LCP (L) 367	Lost during exercises at Mandapam, Ceylon.
April		Lost on passage from USA to India, presumably as deck cargo:
	LCM (3) 1313	
	LCM (3) 1314	
	LCM (3) 1373	
	LCM (3) 1378	
23 May	LBR 83	Foundered off Sheerness.
May	LCP (S) 74	Lost overboard from parent ship, Messina.
	LCA 130	Destroyed by fire at Marve beach, Bombay.
	LCP (R) 584	Lost in home waters.
May		Reported lost in the Mediterranean:
	LCM (3) 1380	
	LCM (3) 1381	
	LCP (R) 643	
May		Reported lost in the East Indies:
	LCM (1) 131	
	LCM (1) 182	
	LCM (1) 183	
	LCM (1) 207	
	LCM (1) 209	
May		Written off as being lost, cause and place unknown:
	LCA 459	
	LCA 492	
	LCA 526	
	LCA 573	
	LCA 761	
	LCE 14	
	LCE 21	
	LCE 5	
	LCM (1) 212	
	LCM (1) 215	
	LCM (1) 218	
	LCM (1) 219	
	LCM (1) 243	
	LCM (1) 272	
	LCM (1) 277	
	LCM (1) 285	
	LCM (1) 288	
	LCM (1) 324	

Date	Name	Circumstances & Location
	LCM (3) 527	
	LCM (3) 534	
	LCM (3) 540	
	LCM (3) 588	
	LCM (3) 1029	
	LCM (3) 1045	
	LCM (3) 1071	
	LCM (3) 1083	
	LCM (3) 1123	
	LCM (3) 1171	
	LCM (3) 1205	
	LCP (L) 8	
	LCP (S) 25	
	LCP (S) 50	
	LCP (S) 61	
	LCP (S) 73	
	LCP (S) 101	
	LCP (S) 135	
	LCP (S) 137	
	LCP (L) 263	
	LCP (L) 287	
	LCP (L) 577	
	LCP (R) 614	
	LCP (R) 634	
	LCP (R) 663	
	LCP (R) 824	
	LCP (R) 844	
	LCP (R) 912	
	LCP (R) 913	
	LCP (R) 995	
	LCS (M)(3) 59	
6 June	Lost in the Normandy landings:	
	LCA 171	Hit by mortar bomb approaching Gold Beach.
	LCA 208	Blown up by mine Juno Beach.
	LCA 303	Mined approaching Juno Beach.
	LCA 401	Blown up by mine, Omaha Beach.
	LCA 409	Broached on Gold Beach and abandoned.
	LCA 458	Stranded on Omaha Beach; broached at high tide.
	LCA 462	Struck underwater object Juno Beach and sank.
	LCA 530	Struck rocks and sank Juno Beach.
	LCA 579	Bottom ripped open by underwater obstruction, Gold Beach
	LCA 584	Fouled underwater obstruction and sank off Gold Beach.
	LCA 586	Hit mine 50 yards off Gold Beach.
	LCA 590	Damaged during landing Juno Beach and sank attempting to return to host ship.
	LCA 642	Hit by shellfire Juno Beach.
	LCA 683	Blown up by mine Juno Beach.
	LCA 704	Hit by shellfire Sword Beach.
	LCA 705	Struck metal stake and foundered Juno Beach
	LCA 721	Struck underwater object off Juno Beach
	LCA 729	Struck underwater object and then hit by shellfire Juno Beach.
	LCA 780	Struck underwater object 3 miles off Sword Beach
	LCA 791	Foundered after being launched off Sword Beach.
	LCA 792	Fouled underwater obstruction Sword Beach.
	LCA 796	Destroyed by mine when landing at Sword Beach.

Date	**Name**	**Circumstances & Location**
	LCA 869	Hit by a mortar bomb and sank Juno Beach.
	LCA 886	Holed by underwater object, Juno Beach.
	LCA 978	Destroyed by mine off Juno Beach.
	LCA 1000	Mined Juno Beach.
	LCA 1016	Mined Juno Beach.
	LCA 1017	Mined Juno Beach.
	LCA 1037	Mine and gunfire, Juno Beach.
	LCA 1063	Sunk by mortar and shellfire, Omaha Beach.
	LCA 1068	Sunk by mortar and shellfire, Omaha Beach.
	LCA 1093	Detonated mine and then hit by shore fire Juno Beach.
	LCA 1096	Mined Juno Beach.
	LCA 1108	Swamped and foundered under tow.
	LCA 1114	Swamped and foundered under tow.
	LCA 1131	Foundered when returning to parent ship off Juno Beach.
	LCA 1143	Struck underwater object Gold Beach.
	LCA 1146	Mined Juno Beach.
	LCA 1251	Struck underwater object Sword Beach.
	LCA 1252	Detonated mine off Juno Beach.
	LCA 1340	Destroyed by mine off Juno Beach.
	LCA 1341	Struck underwater obstruction Sword Beach.
	LCA 1379	Foundered off Sword Beach after landing troops.
	LCA 1382	Foundered off Juno Beach after landing troops.
	LCA 1383	Foundered off Gold Beach after collision with another LCA.
	LCA (HR) 671	Sub-Lt R D Bradshaw; damaged when lowered from *Empire Cutlass* and sank alongside.
	LCA (HR) 690	Sub-Lt A B Duffin; swamped whilst being towed across Channel.
	LCA (HR) 961	Swamped whilst being towed inshore Gold Beach.
	LCA (HR) 962	Swamped whilst being towed inshore Gold Beach.
	LCA (HR) 963	Swamped whilst being towed inshore Gold Beach.
	LCA (HR) 968	Sub-Lt Jessop; swamped and sank off Gold Beach.
	LCA (HR) 969	Sub-Lt Roberts; foundered off Gold Beach.
	LCA (HR) 972	Swamped whilst being towed inshore Gold Beach.
	LCA (HR) 977	Swamped whilst being towed inshore Sword Beach.
	LCA (HR) 1106	Sub-Lt B V Ashton RANVR; rammed and sunk by *LST 899* off Gold Beach.
	LCM (1) 128	
	LCM (1) 165	
	LCM (1) 191	
	LCM (1) 203	
	LCM (1) 216	
	LCM (1) 226	
	LCM (1) 229	Sub-Lt Pye RNVR; swamped and foundered mid-Channel.
	LCM (1) 231	
	LCM (1) 241	
	LCM (1) 251	
	LCM (1) 281	
	LCM (1) 316	
	LCM (1) 330	
	LCM (1) 335	
	LCM (1) 338	
	LCM (1) 346	Foundered after collision with LCM 303.
	LCM (1) 348	
	LCM (1) 355	
	LCM (1) 357	

Date	Name	Circumstances & Location
	LCM (1) 377	
	LCM (1) 382	
	LCM (1) 383	
	LCM (1) 408	
	LCM (1) 409	
	LCM (1) 419	
	LCM (1) 421	
	LCM (1) 425	Struck underwater obstruction and detonated mine.
	LCM (1) 443	Mined and shelled on Juno Beach.
	LCM (1) 444	Fouled underwater obstruction and sank.
	LCM (1) 466	
	LCM (3) 531	
	LCM (3) 535	
	LCM (3) 568	
	LCM (3) 577	
	LCM (3) 587	
	LCM (3) 627	
	LCM (3) 628	
	LCM (3) 631	
	LCM (3) 641	
	LCM (3) 908	
	LCM (3) 929	
	LCM (3) 1059	
	LCM (3) 1062	
	LCM (3) 1088	Sub-Lt M A Smith RNR; hit by heavy shell and sank, Sword Beach.
	LCM (3) 1098	
	LCM (3) 1108	
	LCM (3) 1120	
	LCM (3) 1127	
	LCM (3) 1139	
	LCM (3) 1145	
	LCM (3) 1189	
	LCM (3) 1200	Detonated mine and shelled.
	LCM (3) 1207	
	LCM (3) 1208	Swamped and foundered returning to UK after landings.
	LCM (3) 1212	
	LCM (3) 1220	
	LCM (3) 1221	
	LCM (3) 1233	
	LCM (3) 1240	
	LCM (3) 1282	Mined and then hit by several shells.
	LCM (3) 1293	Sword Beach: hit by 88mm shell and subsequently foundered.
	LCM (3) 1297	Sub-Lieut. Jackson RNVR; swamped and sunk en-route,
	LCM (3) 1397	
	LCP (L) 13	Being towed across Channel by *LCT 740*; tow parted taking cleat and part of the deck with it; props fouled by rope and abandoned in sinking condition.
	LCP (L) 14	
	LCP (L) 21	
	LCP (L) 22	
	LCP (L) 23	
	LCP (L) 40	
	LCP (L) 51	
	LCP (L) 84	
	LCP (L) 85	

Date	Name	Circumstances & Location
	LCP (L) 88	
	LCP (L) 97	
	LCP (L) 98	
	LCP (L) 110	
	LCP (L) 132	
	LCP (L) 137	
	LCP (L) 139	
	LCP (L) 145	
	LCP (L) 146	
	LCP (L) 149	
	LCP (L) 162	
	LCP (L) 163	
	LCP (L) 170	
	LCP (L) 175	
	LCP (L) 187	
	LCP (L) 189	
	LCP (L) 197	
	LCP (L) 198	
	LCP (L) 199	
	LCP (L) 200	
	LCP (L) 208	Sub-Lt S Gosling RNVR; struck underwater object approaching Sword Beach and sank.
	LCP (L) 230	
	LCP (L) 231	
	LCP (L) 232	
	LCP (L) 233	
	LCP (L) 235	
	LCP (L) 238	
	LCP (L) 239	
	LCP (L) 241	
	LCP (L) 242	
	LCP (L) 246	
	LCP (L) 247	
	LCP (L) 269	
	LCP (L) 272	
	LCP (L) 280	
	LCP (L) 282	
	LCP (L) 285	
	LCP (L) 286	
	LCP (L) 289	
	LCP (L) 293	
	LCP (L) 294	
	LCP (L) 309	
	LCP (L) 312	
	LCP (L) 528	
	LCP (L) 556	
	LCP (R) 892	
	LCP (R) 896	
	LCP(S) 136	
	LCS (M)(3) 47	Sub-Lt Pierre RANVR; mined and shelled Juno Beach.
	LCS (M)(3) 75	Sunk after gunfire damage when landing Gold Beach.
	LCS (M)(3) 83	Sub-Lt BWJS Brisby RNVR; foundered under tow by LCT.
	LCS (M)(3) 91	
	LCS (M)(3) 99	Foundered under tow after being mined.

Date	Name	Circumstances & Location
	LCS (M)(3) 101	Sub-Lt E T Fletcher RNVR; struck underwater object off Gold Beach, filled and sank.
	LCVP 1016	Hit a mine off Gold Beach.
	LCVP 1029	
	LCVP 1031	
	LCVP 1033	
	LCVP 1044	
	LCVP 1045	
	LCVP 1046	
	LCVP 1049	
	LCVP 1054	
	LCVP 1056	
	LCVP 1062	
	LCVP 1065	
	LCVP 1084	
	LCVP 1088	Swamped in mid-Channel.
	LCVP 1093	Swamped in mid-Channel.
	LCVP 1098	
	LCVP 1101	
	LCVP 1102	
	LCVP 1104	
	LCVP 1106	
	LCVP 1111	
	LCVP 1114	Swamped 12 miles off French coast.
	LCVP 1120	Broke down and foundered off Juno Beach.
	LCVP 1121	
	LCVP 1124	
	LCVP 1129	
	LCVP 1132	
	LCVP 1133	
	LCVP 1139	
	LCVP 1146	
	LCVP 1153	
	LCVP 1155	
	LCVP 1157	
	LCVP 1159	
	LCVP 1165	
	LCVP 1170	
	LCVP 1171	
	LCVP 1172	
	LCVP 1184	
	LCVP 1188	
	LCVP 1201	
	LCVP 1204	
	LCVP 1211	
	LCVP 1216	
	LCVP 1242	
	LCVP 1245	
	LCVP 1246	
	LCVP 1248	
	LCVP 1249	
	LCVP 1251	
	LCVP 1255	
	LCVP 1260	

Date	Name	Circumstances & Location
	LCVP 1262	
	LCVP 1264	
7 June	Lost during the day after the initial landings:	
	LCM (1) 381	Written off because of leaks; Gold Beach.
	LCM (3) 1128	Broke adrift and foundered on way back to England.
	LCM (3) 1244	Sub-Lt J V Brown RNVR; detonated a mine off Sword Beach.
	LCP (L) 299	Engine failure and run onto beach at Sword and abandoned.
	LCP (L) 303	Sank approaching Sword Beach.
	LCP (L) 304	Foundered en-route to Gold Beach
	LBO 53	
	(ex-*Celtic*)	Wrecked near Fecamp, Normandy
	LBV (1) 52	Sub-Lt W Thompson RNVR; swamped and foundered when 2 miles off the French coast.
	LBW 6	Sub-Lt J Alexander RNVR; swamped and foundered when 16 miles north of Cherbourg.
	LCVP 1108	Sunk in air raid off Gold Beach.
	LCVP 1230	Sunk on Sword Beach when she beached over a bomb crater, and flooded when ramp lowered
8 June	LCA 1058	Sunk by air attack off Normandy beaches.
	LCP (L) 176	Hit by shellfire and foundered 2 miles off Corseuilles.
	LCS (M)(3) 78	Beached and abandoned in a sinking condition.
9 June	LCM (3) 1195	Engine breakdown; drifted and finally sank off Normandy.
10 June	LCA 352	Scuttled off Gold Beach as unserviceable
12 June	LBV (1) 16	
	(ex-*Merthyr*)	Foundered in bad weather, Normandy.
	LBV (1) 51	
	(ex-*Thomas*)	Foundered in bad weather, Normandy.
	LBV (1) 49	Foundered in bad weather, Normandy.
13 June	LCP (L) 298	Beached and abandoned on Gold Beach after propeller broke.
	LCA 651	Foundered, poor material condition.
14 June	LCVP 1218	Struck underwater object off Gold Beach and foundered.
	LBO 73	
	(ex-*January*)	Wrecked near Le Havre (not written off until October)
15 June	LCA 59	Lost, Bombay area.
	LCA 69	Lost, Bombay area.
19 June	LCP (L) 53	Foundered in bad weather, Arromanches.
17 June	Either lost or written off as part of Operation 'Brassard', the assault on Elba:	
	LCA 112	
	LCA 183	
	LCA 248	
	LCA 258	
	LCA 400	
	LCA 625	
	LCA 802	
	LCS (M)(3) 42	
	LCS (M)(3) 44	
19 June	LCP (R) 905	Foundered in bad weather, home waters.
	LBV (1) 116	
	(ex-*Romany*)	Wrecked Juno Beach, Normandy.
20 June	Driven ashore and wrecked in bad weather, Normandy:	
	LBE 8	
	(ex-*East*)	Omaha Beach.
	LBE 26	
	(ex-*Excelsior*)	Omaha Beach.

Date	Name	Circumstances & Location
	LBE 27	
	(ex-*Dagonet*)	Sub-Lt Leonard Dyer RNVR; Omaha Beach.
	LBE 60	
	(ex-*Albemarle*)	Foundered in bad weather, Omaha Beach.
	LCA 1338	Foundered in bad weather off Gold Beach.
20–22 June	In poor material state from overwork and bad weather and run ashore at Arromanches and abandoned as wrecks:	
	LCS (M)(3) 75	Lt F R Sillitoe RM.
	LCS (M)(3) 76	Lt. J Finan RM.
	LCS (M)(3) 80	Lt. E A Jennings RM.
	LCS (M)(3) 81	Lt. W D Wilson RM.
	LCS (M)(3) 103	Lt. B Jones RM.
	LCS (M)(3) 108	
	LCS (M)(3) 114	Lt A E Garnett RM.
21 June	Foundered in bad weather, Normandy:	
	LBE 17 (ex-*Leo*)	Omaha Beach.
	LBE 19	
	(ex-*Hermitage*)	Foundered off Juno Beach.
	LBE 33	
	(ex-*Transport*)	Omaha Beach.
	LBE 34	
	(ex-*Pom*)	Omaha Beach.
	LCS (M)(3) 110	Lt Saunderson RM; at anchor, Arromanches.
22 June	Foundered in bad weather, Normandy:	
	LBE 57	
	(ex-*Kensing*)	Omaha Beach.
	LBO 13	Dragged her anchor and was washed ashore on Utah Beach.
	LBO 82	Utah Beach.
	LBV (2) 214	
	(ex-*E-4*)	Omaha Beach.
	LCVP 1122	Sword Beach.
25 June	Written off charge as a result of bad weather damage, Normandy:	
	LBE 25 (ex-*Garrick*)	
	LBO 10 (ex-*Canova*)	Omaha Beach.
	LBO 46 (ex-*Flagship*)	Omaha Beach.
	LBO 84 (ex-*Monitor*)	Omaha Beach.
	LBV (2) 3 (ex-*No.34*)	Omaha Beach.
	LBV (2) 27 (ex-*Devon*)	
	LBV (2) 49 (ex-*Falcon*)	
	LBV (2) 61 (ex-*Buccaneer*)	
	LBV (2) 67 (ex-*Colombo*)	
	LBV (2) 84 (ex-*Dreadnought*)	
	LBV (2) 89 (ex-*Cassia*)	
	LBV (2) 94 (ex-*Beech*)	
	LBV (2) 95 (ex-*Minorca*)	
	LBV (2) 103 (ex-*Fairway*)	
	LBV (2) 172 (ex-*Edgar*)	
	LBV (2) 176 (ex-*Steeleye*)	
	LBV (2) 206 (ex-*Admiral*)	
	LBV (2) 209 (ex-*David*)	
	LBV (2) 232 (ex-*Wear*)	
	LBW 7 (ex-*Elaine*)	
	LBW 15 (ex-*Baroda*)	

Date	Name	Circumstances & Location
26 June	LCVP 1117	Damaged by shellfire and abandoned, Normandy.
28 June	Lost when *Maid of Orleans* torpedoed and sunk:	
	LCA 812	
	LCA 931	
29 June	LBV (1) 56	
	(ex-*Fid*)	Wrecked, US beach, Normandy.
June	LBO 50	Lost, cause and place unknown.
	LBV (2) 20	
	(ex-*H-8*)	Foundered in the Channel.
	LBV (2) 51	Lost, cause and place unknown.
June	LCA 33	Lost in the East Indies.
	LCA 56	Lost in the East Indies.
	LCA 146	Lost in the East Indies.
	LCA 182	Lost, cause and place unknown.
	LCM (1) 91	Lost in the East Indies.
	LCM (1) 295	Lost 'overseas'.
	LCM (3) 1115	Lost in the Mediterranean.
	LCM (3) 1130	Lost in the Mediterranean.
	LCP (R) 723	Lost in the Mediterranean.
	LCP (R) 854	Lost, cause and place unknown.
	LCP (R) 867	Wrecked at Mandapam, Ceylon.
	LCP (R) 966	Damaged en-route to Anzio and foundered.
	LCP (R) 970	Lost in home waters.
	LCP (S) 154	Lost, cause and place unknown.
	LCV 719	Lost, cause and place unknown.
June–July:	Written off as lost, either through enemy action or through stress of weather supporting the Normandy landings:	
	LCA 279	Gold Beach.
	LCA 289	Juno Beach.
	LCA 320	Gold Beach.
	LCA 337	Sword Beach.
	LCA 339	Gold Beach.
	LCA 341	Sword Beach.
	LCA 349	Gold Beach.
	LCA 350	Gold Beach.
	LCA 360	Juno Beach.
	LCA 367	Gold Beach.
	LCA 383	Gold Beach.
	LCA 387	Sword Beach.
	LCA 418	Omaha Beach.
	LCA 424	Sword Beach.
	LCA 431	Gold Beach.
	LCA 434	Gold Beach.
	LCA 442	Gold Beach.
	LCA 463	Juno Beach.
	LCA 476	Juno Beach.
	LCA 485	Sword Beach.
	LCA 494	Juno Beach.
	LCA 496	Sword Beach.
	LCA 503	Gold Beach.
	LCA 509	Gold Beach.
	LCA 518	Juno Beach.
	LCA 519	Juno Beach.
	LCA 520	Juno Beach.

Date	Name	Circumstances & Location
	LCA 522	Juno Beach.
	LCA 525	Juno Beach.
	LCA 535	Juno Beach.
	LCA 540	Juno Beach.
	LCA 566	Juno Beach.
	LCA 581	Juno Beach.
	LCA 588	Gold Beach.
	LCA 589	Sword Beach.
	LCA 592	Gold Beach.
	LCA 593	Gold Beach.
	LCA 594	Gold Beach.
	LCA 611	Sword Beach.
	LCA 613	Gold Beach.
	LCA 623	Omaha Beach.
	LCA 637	Sword Beach.
	LCA 649	Omaha Beach.
	LCA 650	Juno Beach.
	LCA 652	Sword Beach.
	LCA 655	Omaha Beach.
	LCA 661	Juno Beach.
	LCA 664	Sword Beach.
	LCA 691	Juno Beach.
	LCA 692	Juno Beach.
	LCA 710	Juno Beach.
	LCA 717	Juno Beach.
	LCA 722	Omaha Beach.
	LCA 738	Juno Beach.
	LCA 748	Juno Beach.
	LCA 750	Omaha Beach.
	LCA 768	Juno Beach.
	LCA 775	Juno Beach.
	LCA 779	Sword Beach.
	LCA 788	Omaha Beach.
	LCA 795	Sword Beach.
	LCA 797	Gold Beach.
	LCA 803	Juno Beach.
	LCA 808	Juno Beach.
	LCA 809	Juno Beach.
	LCA 810	Juno Beach.
	LCA 814	Juno Beach.
	LCA 815	Juno Beach.
	LCA 821	Juno Beach.
	LCA 825	Juno Beach.
	LCA 827	Juno Beach.
	LCA 835	Juno Beach.
	LCA 849	Omaha Beach.
	LCA 853	Omaha Beach.
	LCA 857	Omaha Beach.
	LCA 859	Gold Beach.
	LCA 860	Omaha Beach.
	LCA 867	Sword Beach.
	LCA 870	Sword Beach.
	LCA 871	Gold Beach.
	LCA 879	Omaha Beach.

Date	Name	Circumstances & Location
	LCA 881	Juno Beach.
	LCA 900	Sword Beach.
	LCA 903	Sword Beach.
	LCA 911	Lt Anthony Drew; Omaha Beach.
	LCA 913	Omaha Beach.
	LCA 914	Omaha Beach.
	LCA 918	Juno Beach.
	LCA 919	Juno Beach.
	LCA 920	Gold Beach.
	LCA 929	Gold Beach.
	LCA 933	
	LCA 946	Juno Beach.
	LCA 949	Gold Beach.
	LCA 958	Juno Beach.
	LCA 984	Gold Beach.
	LCA 998	Utah Beach.
	LCA 999	Gold Beach.
	LCA 1005	Gold Beach.
	LCA 1008	Gold Beach.
	LCA 1013	Gold Beach.
	LCA 1021	Juno Beach.
	LCA 1024	Gold Beach.
	LCA 1026	Gold Beach.
	LCA 1027	Gold Beach.
	LCA 1028	Omaha Beach.
	LCA 1034	Juno Beach.
	LCA 1050	Gold Beach.
	LCA 1057	Juno Beach.
	LCA 1059	Juno Beach.
	LCA 1069	Omaha Beach.
	LCA 1074	Omaha Beach.
	LCA 1082	Omaha Beach.
	LCA 1086	Gold Beach.
	LCA 1088	
	LCA 1091	Juno Beach.
	LCA 1129	Juno Beach.
	LCA 1132	Gold Beach.
	LCA 1137	Juno Beach.
	LCA 1138	Juno Beach.
	LCA 1144	Omaha Beach.
	LCA 1149	Gold Beach.
	LCA 1150	Juno Beach.
	LCA 1151	Juno Beach.
	LCA 1155	Gold Beach.
	LCA 1156	Gold Beach.
	LCA 1213	Gold Beach.
	LCA 1215	Sword Beach.
	LCA 1216	Sword Beach.
	LCA 1253	Juno Beach.
	LCA 1256	Sword Beach.
	LCA 1339	Juno Beach.
	LCA 1343	
	LCA 1372	Juno Beach.
	LCA 1381	Sword Beach.

Date	Name	Circumstances & Location
	LCA (HR) 965	Juno Beach.
	LCA (HR) 1072	Juno Beach.
1 July	LBR 43	Lost; cause and place unknown.
	LBR 65	Lost, cause and place unknown.
	LCS (M)(3) 54	Lost, cause and place unknown.
2 July	LCP (R) 895	Whilst being hoisted back onboard LST 425, falls parted and craft fell bows first into sea and foundered.

2 July   Lost onboard the *Empire Broadsword*, when mined off Normandy:

	LCA 665	
	LCA 673	
3 July	LCA 1393	Lost in Normandy.
7 July	LCM (1) 138	Foundered off Gilkicker, Spithead, in poor weather.
8 July	LCP (L) 267	Sunk at 06.30 by mine, Petite Rade, Cherbourg.
9 July	LBV (1) 121 (ex-*Yankee*)	Written off, Omaha Beach.
	LBV (1) 175 (ex-*Condor*)	Written off, Utah Beach.
10 July	LBO 90 (ex-*Crawley*)	Foundered in storm off St Catherine's Point.
11 July	LBV (2) 140 (ex-*D-10*)	Beached 22 June during storm; salvaged but subsequently broke moorings and sank off Omaha Beach.
11 July	LBO 87 (ex-*Lupin*)	Foundered, Normandy.
13 July	LCE 15	Lost, cause and place unknown.
	LCVP 1288	Lost in home waters.
14 July	LCA 1304	Foundered in bad weather, home waters.

23 July   Foundered in bad weather in the English Channel, whilst returning to England from Normandy in Convoy Bluesky-25:

	LCM (1) 168	
	LCM (1) 180	
	LCM (1) 337	
	LCM (1) 345	
	LCM (3) 1227	
	LCM (3) 1232	
	LCM (3) 1053	
	LCM (3) 1146	
	LCM (3) 1161	Wreck sunk by gunfire from *Hound*.
	LCM (3) 1175	
	LCM (3) 1197	
	LCM (3) 1278	
25 July	LBV (2) 122 (ex-*Warsaw*)	Foundered off Normandy coast.
27 July	LBV (2) 76 (ex-*Endenen*)	Written off, US beach, Normandy.
28 July	LCM (1) 127	Swamped in bad weather, 8 miles off Normandy coast.
	LCP (R) 971	Lost in collision, home waters.
29 July	LBV (2) 19 (ex-*Glennifer*)	Written off, Juno Beach.
	LBV (2) 28	Written off, Juno Beach.
July	LCA 54	Written off in the East Indies.

July   Written off, lost in home waters, cause unknown:

	LCP (L) 229	
	LCP (L) 300	
	LCP (L) 305	

Date	Name	Circumstances & Location
	LCP (L) 308	
	LCP (L) 310	
July	LCP (S) 183	Reported wrecked, Mediterranean.
July	LCP (L) 683	Sunk in action off northern France.
8 August	LBV (1) 29	
	(ex-*Orwell*)	Foundered, Normandy.
9 August	LCM (3) 618	Lost, Mediterranean.
	LCM (3) 640	Lost, Mediterranean.
13 August	LBO 68	
	(ex-*Witham*)	Mined in the Grande Rade, Cherbourg.
14 August	LBV (1) 154	Foundered at her moorings, Portsmouth.
17 August	LBO 4	Lost, cause and place unknown.
19 August	LBV (1) 83	
	(ex-*Damara*)	Sank in tow off Normandy.
29 August	LBW 14	
	(ex-*Croydon*)	Foundered in the Channel.
	LCV 816	Foundered in heavy seas off Gilkicker Point.
31 August	LBO 30	Lost, cause and place unknown.
11 September	LCM (1) 263	Wrecked, Normandy.
13 September	LBW 11	
	(ex-*Bill*)	Foundered whilst in tow off Nab Tower.
	LBV (2) 42	
	(ex-*Paris*)	Written off charge as non-effective; US beach, Normandy.
15 September	LCP (L) 348	Destroyed by fire, India.
17 September	Written off, Normandy:	
	LBO 63 (ex-*E-27*)	
	LBO 69 (*Waveney*)	
	LBO 79 (ex-*Madge*)	
	LBO 88 (ex-*Gladys*)	
	LBV (2) 11	
	(ex-*No.33*)	Omaha Beach.
	LBV (2) 15	
	(ex-*Suffolk*)	Utah Beach.
	LBV (2) 33 (ex-*Sid*)	
	LBV (2) 72 (ex-*Marconi*)	
	LBV (2) 78 (ex-*Nen*)	
	LBV (2) 137 (ex-*Logic*)	
	LBV (2) 157 (ex-*Severn*)	
	LBV (2) 211 (ex-*D-15*)	
26 September	LCA 848	Foundered in heavy weather, home waters.
	LCA 1378	Foundered in heavy weather, home waters.
	LCP (R) 999	Foundered in heavy weather, home waters.
September	LCA 577	Written off, believed lost Mediterranean.
6 October	LCP (L) 7	Lost in home waters.
	LCP (L) 18	Lost in home waters.
11 October	LCP (R) 52	Destroyed by fire, Portsmouth.
18 October	LCV 801	Broke adrift and sank, Portsmouth.
21 October	LCP (R) 1011	Lost in collision, home waters.
2 November	Lost in Operation 'Infatuate', landings at Walcheren:	
	LCA 713	
	LCA 725	
	LCA 817	
	LCA 831	
	LCA 843	

Date	Name	Circumstances & Location
	LCA 1018	
	LCA 1079	
	LCA 1125	
	LCA 1260	
	LCP (L) 127	
	LCP (L) 134	
2 November	Written off, US beaches, Normandy:	
	LBO 56 (ex-*Dingwall*)	
	LBV (2) 9 (ex-*Obi*)	
	LBV (2) 16 (ex-*Lion*)	
5 November	LCP (L) 133	Lost in the river Scheldt, between Westkapelle and Breskens.
	LCP (L) 302	Wrecked, east of Ostend.
7 November	LCA 551	Foundered in bad weather, river Blackwater.
10 November	LCP (S) 129	Destroyed by fire at Hythe.
15 November	LCM (3) 1101	Wrecked near Aden.
	LCA 1030	Hit by shellfire and sunk at Breskens, Belgium.
16 November	LCA 149	Lost in India.
19 November	LCM (1) 340	Lost overboard from the *John L Manson* in Mounts Bay.
	LCM (1) 424	Lost overboard from the *John L Manson* in Mounts Bay.
20 November	LCVP 1103	Wrecked at Chichester.
21 November	LBV 123	Damaged in poor weather and went onshore Juno Beach.
25 November	LCVP 1199	Foundered near Portsmouth.
27 November	LCVP 1228	Lost in 'home waters'.
29 November	LCA 614	Foundered in bad weather, English Channel.
November	LCP (R) 805	Lost, cause and place unknown.
	LCP (R) 806	Lost, cause and place unknown.
December	LCA 1188	Lost in the Solomon Islands.
December	LCA 326	Lost, Mediterranean.
December	Written off as presumed lost, cause and place unknown:	
	LCA 254	
	LCA 347	
	LCA 696	
	LCA 753	
	LCM (3) 525	
	LCM (3) 559	
	LCM (3) 591	
	LCM (3) 650	
	LCM (3) 907	
	LCP (L) 540	
	LCP (L) 760	
	LCP (R) 640	
	LCP (R) 652	
	LCP (R) 669	
	LCP (R) 735	
	LCP (R) 978	
	LCP (R) 982	
	LCP (R) 987	
	LCP (R) 989	
	LCP (R) 991	
	LCP (R) 993	
	LCP (R) 1023	
	LCP (S) 1	
	LCS (M)(3) 49	

1945

Date	Name	Circumstances & Location
18 January	LCP (L) 11	Foundered on passage between Brest and Cherbourg.
20 January	LBO 17	Foundered during a gale in Arromanches harbour.
23 January	LCM (3) 1131	Foundered, Arromanches.
24 January	LCA 2086	Mined off Ramree Island, Burma.
26 January	LCP (R) 1018	Lost in the river Scheldt.
30 January	LCV 814	Lost, 'home waters'.
	LCVP 1191	Written off; cause and place of loss unknown.
22 February	LCP (R) 707	Lost 'by enemy action'; home waters.
26 February	LCA 1161	Foundered in poor weather, Leyte.
28 February	LCA (HR) 829	Written off.
February	LCM (1) 136	Lost, cause and place unknown.
February	Lost overboard from *Asa Lothrop*:	
	LCM (1) 270	
	LCM (1) 339	
	LCM (1) 359	
	LCM (1) 422	
5 March	LCP (R) 979	Lost in the Far East.
18 March	LCP (L) 764	Lost in home waters.
27 March	LCA 1433	Sunk in heavy weather at Leyte.
28 March	LCP (R) 840	Lost 'by enemy action', home waters.
March	LCM (3) 1011	Lost, Mediterranean.
March	Written off as presumed lost, place and cause unknown:	
	LCA 1112	
	LCA 1153	
9 April	LCP (R) 738	Foundered in poor weather, Mediterranean.
22 April	LCA 841	Foundered, coast of Holland.
April	LCVP 1358	Wrecked eastern Mediterranean.
April	Lost on the Arakan coast, Burma:	
	LCM 1319	
	LCM 1327	
April	Written off as presumed lost, in the Mediterranean:	
	LCA 1346	
	LCA 1396	
29 May	LCP (L) 344	Sunk at Akyab, Burma.
	LCP (L) 378	Sunk at Akyab, Burma.
May	LCP (2) 1110	Lost in the Aegean.
	LCP (2) 1121	Lost in the Aegean.
May	Written off, presumed lost, date, cause and place unknown:	
	LBV (2) 152	
	LCA (OC)1211	
5 June	LCM (3) 1092	Broke adrift from parent craft and wrecked.
June	Lost in operations on the Arakan coast, Burma:	
	LCM (1) 354	
	LCM (1) 493	
	LCS (M)(2) 30	
	LCS (M)(3) 148	
June	LCP (2) 1113	Written off following weather damage at Maddalena.
	LCM (R) 832	Lost in tow, Mediterranean.
June	Written off, presumed lost, date, cause and place unknown:	
	LBE 12	
	LBE 20	

Date	Name	Circumstances & Location
	LBE 32	
	LBO 11	
	LBO 21	
	LBO 24	
	LBO 26	
	LBO 37	
	LBO 77	
	LBO 92	
	LBO 95	
	LBO 96	
	LBR 114	
	LBV (2) 1	
	LBV (2) 5	
	LBV (2) 31	
	LBV (2) 35	
	LBV (2) 73	
	LBV (2) 75	
	LBV (2) 118	
	LBV (2) 170	
	LBV (2) 212	
	LBW 1	
13 July	LBV (2) 99	Foundered off Arromanches in tow of *Empire Race*.
14 July	LBO 5	In sinking condition off Arromanches, sunk by a destroyer.
15 July	LCVP 1167	Lost, Channel Islands.
29 July	LBV (2) 132	Written off.
31 July	LBK 8	Foundered in tow, English Channel, returning from Juno Beach.
July	LCP (R) 965	Foundered in tow, Mediterranean.
July	LCM (3) 1185	Written off, presumed lost, cause and place unknown.
2 August	LCV 802	Foundered in tow, home waters.

Bibliography

Primary Sources

Unpublished Papers: The National Archives (TNA), Kew

ADM 1/8597-9749	Admiralty correspondence 1921–1938
ADM 1/9750-10235	Admiralty correspondence 1939
ADM 1/10236-10975	Admiralty correspondence 1940
ADM 1/10985-11669	Admiralty correspondence 1941
ADM 1/11670-12641	Admiralty correspondence 1942
ADM 1/12642-15624	Admiralty correspondence 1943
ADM 1/15625-17224	Admiralty correspondence 1944
ADM 1/17225-19191	Admiralty correspondence 1945
ADM 53/ –series	Admiralty; ship's logs
ADM 116/ –series	Admiralty; Cases – miscellaneous papers
ADM 156/ –series	Admiralty: Courts-martial cases and files
ADM 178/ –series	Admiralty: Courts-martial and Boards of Inquiry
ADM 199/360-429	War Diaries, various theatres
ADM 199/627-659	War Diaries, various theatres
ADM 199/766-774	War Diaries, various theatres
ADM 199/1050-1051	War Diaries, various theatres
ADM 199/1388-1400	War Diaries, various theatres
ADM 199/1426-1453	War Diaries, various theatres
ADM 199/2195-2383	War Diaries; daily summaries
ADM 210/–series	Admiralty: Lists of Landing Ships, Crafts and Barges (Green List)
ADM 267/1-140 A	Admiralty: damage reports and files 1939–1945
ADM 358/1-4530	Admiralty: Casualty Branch: Enquiries into Missing Personnel, 1939–1945
CAB 66/1-67	War Cabinet minutes and papers 1939–1945
WO.205/ –series	War Office: Military HQ papers
WO.361/ –series	War Office: Enquiries into Missing Personnel 1939–1945

Published Papers

CB 4273 *H M Ships Damaged or Sunk by Enemy Action 3 Sept. 1939 to 2 Sept. 1945* [*Accessed at: http://www.navy.gov. au*]

Ships of the Royal Navy: Statement of losses during the Second World War (HMSO, London, 1947).

Statement of losses: Amendment no.1 (HMSO, London, 1949).

The London Gazette, various dates [*accessed at: https://www.thegazette.co.uk/*].

Lloyd's War Losses: The Second World War vol 1 (London, 1989 [reprint].

Naval Staff Histories

Gardner, W J R (ed), *The Evacuation from Dunkirk Operation Dynamo, 26 May – 4 June 1940.*

Brown, D (ed), *Naval Operations of the Campaign in Norway, April – June 1940.*

Navy Records Society

Simpson, Michael (ed), *The Somerville Papers* (Aldershot, 1996).

Secondary Sources

Books

Brown, David, *Warship Losses of World War Two* (London, 1990).

Burn, Lambert, *Down Ramps* (London, 1947).

Cassells, Vic, *For those in peril …* (Kenthurst NSW, 1995).

Dawson, Lionel, *Mediterranean Medley* (London, 1933).

Dickens, Peter, *Night Action, MTB Flotilla at War* (Barnsley, 2008).

Dittmar, F J, & Colledge, J J, *British Warships 1914–1919* (London, 1972).

Dorrian, James G, *Storming St Nazaire* (London, 1998).

Evans, A S, *Beneath the Waves* (London, 1986).

Foynes, J P, *Battle of the East Coast* (Privately published, 1994).

Gardiner, Robert (ed), *Conway's All the World's Fighting Ships 1922–1946* (London, 1980).

——, *Conway's All the World's Fighting Ships 1947–1982* (London, 1983).

Goulden, O A, *From Trombay to Changi's a Helluva Way* (Privately published, 1987).

Haar, Geirr, *The German Invasion of Norway* (2 vols) (Barnsley 2010–11).

Hardy, Hilbert, *The Minesweepers' Victory* (Weybridge, 1976).

Hewitt, Nick, *Coastal Convoys 1939–1945* (Barnsley, 2008).

Hezlet, Sir Arthur, *British and Allied Submarine Operations in World War II* (Royal Navy Submarine Museum, 2001).

Hichens, Antony, *Gunboat Command* (Barnsley, 2007).

Jefferson, David, *Coastal Forces at War* (London, 1996).

Kemp, Paul, *The Admiralty Regrets: British Warship Losses of the 20th Century* (London, 1999).

Larn, Richard & Bridget, *Shipwreck Index of the British Isles* (6 vols) (London, 1995).

Lenton, H T, *British and Empire Warships of the Second World War* (London, 1998).

Lund, Paul, & Ludlam, Harry, *The War of the Landing Craft* (London, 1976).

——, *Trawlers go to War* (London, 1972).

Maclean, Malcolm, *Naval Accidents since 1945* (Liskeard, 2008).

Mcdermott, Brian, *Ships Without Names* (London, 1992).

McKee, Fraser, & Darlington, Robert, *The Canadian Naval Chronicle 1939-45* (Ontario, 1966).

Minett, Eric, *The Coast is Clear: The Story of the BYMS* (Great Yarmouth, 1995).

Mitchell, Pamela, *The Tip of the Spear* (Huddersfield, 1995).

Morgan, Daniel, & Taylor, Bruce, *U boat Attack Logs* (Barnsley, 2011).

Peniakoff, Vladimir, *Popski's Private Army* (Oxford University Press, 1991).

Pope, Dudley, *Flag 4* (London, 1998).

Reynolds, Leonard, *Dog Boats at War* (Stroud, 1998).

——, *Home Waters MTBs and MGBs at War 1939–1945* (Stroud, 2000).

——, & Cooper, H F, *Mediterranean MTBs at War 1939–45* (Stroud, 1999).

Rohwer, Jurgen, *Chronology of the War at Sea 1939–1945* (3rd edition, London, 2005).

——, *Axis Submarine Successes of World War Two* (London, 1999).

Roskill, Stephen W, *The War at Sea 1939 – 1945* (reprint: Uckfield, 2004).

Scott, Peter, *The Battle of the Narrow Seas* (White Lion edition, London, 1974).

Shores, Christopher, *Fledgling Eagles; Complete Account of Air Operations During the "Phoney War" and the Norwegian Campaign* (London, 1992).

——, & Cull, Brian, *Bloody Shambles: The Drift to War to the Fall of Singapore* (London, 1992).

Sigwart, E, *Royal Fleet Auxiliary* (London, 1969).

Smith, Peter C, *Naval Warfare in the English Channel 1939 – 1945* (Barnsley, 2007).

Williams, Jack, *Fleet Sweepers at War* (Blackpool, 1997).

Winser, John de S, *BEF Ships before, at and after Dunkirk* (Gravesend, 1999).

——, *British Invasion Fleets: The Mediterranean and Beyond* (Gravesend, 2002).

Woodman, Richard, *Arctic Convoys 1941–1945* (London, 1994).

Young, John M, *Britain's Sea War: A Diary of Ship Losses 1939–1945* (Wellingborough, 1989).

Periodicals

WSS Warship Supplement: quarterly by the World Ship Society.

SCG Journal: occasionally by the Small Craft Group of the World Ship Society

Websites

ASW Trawlers   http://www.royal-naval-reserve.co.uk

Australian National Archives   http://www.naa.gov.au/collection/fact-sheets

Australian Naval Institute   https://navalinstitute.com.au

Australian War Memorial — https://www.awm.gov.au/
Defence Department, Australia — http://www.defence.gov.au
BBC WW2 People's War — http://www.bbc.co.uk/ww2peopleswar
Clyde built ships — http://www.clydesite.co.uk
Combined operations in WW2 — http://www.combinedops.com/
Far East prisoners of war — https://www.cofepow.org.uk
Historic Environment Scotland — https://canmore.org.uk/
Japanese Navy WW2 — http://www.combinedfleet.com
Maidstone sub-aqua club — www.msac.org.uk/wrecks
National Monuments Record of Wales — https://www.coflein.gov.uk/
National Record of the Historic
    Environment — http://www.pastscape.org.uk/
National Trust for Scotland (Canna) — www.nts.org.uk/stories/john-lorne-campbells-canna-diaries
Naval History Net — http://www.naval-history.net/index.htm
Naval Historical Society of Australia: — https://www.navyhistory.org.au/ranships-index/
New Zealand Electronic Text Collection — http://www.nzetc.org/tm/scholarly/tei-WH2Navy
Navy Records Society — https://www.navyrecords.org.uk
Royal Australian Navy — http://www.navy.gov.au
Royal Canadian Navy history — www.forposterityssake.ca/RCN.htm
Royal Fleet Auxiliary — www.historicalrfa.org
Royal Indian Navy in WW2 — http://www.ibiblio.org/hyperwar/UN/India/RIN/
Scapa Flow wrecks — http://www.scapaflowwrecks.com
South African Navy in WW2 — https://samilhistory.com/category/war-at-sea-ww2/
U-boat net — https://www.uboat.net/
Warsailors — http://www.warsailors.com
World online wreck database — http://www.wrecksite.eu

Contemporary Newspapers

The British Newspaper Archive is a partnership between the British Library and findmypast.com to make available the British Library's newspaper collection, and is available at: http://www.britishnewspaperarchive.co.uk/ Among the titles used were:

Aberdeen Evening Express
Aberdeen Journal
Angus Evening Telegraph
Daily Herald
Dundee Courier
Dundee Evening Telegraph
Exeter & Plymouth Gazette
Fleetwood Chronicle
The Globe
Hampshire Telegraph
Hull Daily Mail
Liverpool Echo
Portsmouth Evening News
The Scotsman
Western Mail
Western Morning News
Yorkshire Post

The Times Digital Archive – available at https://www.gale.com/intl/c/the-times-digital-archive

Alphabetical Index of Ships Lost

Name	Type	Date of loss
Abdiel	minelayer	10 September 1943
Abel Tasman	coaster	13 June 1940
Abingdon	minesweeper	5 April 1942
Acasta	destroyer	8 June 1940
Achates	destroyer	31 December 1942
Acheron	destroyer	17 December 1940
ADC 527	landing craft	8 January 1946
Adele	examination vessel	7 May 1943
Adept	tug	17 March 1942
Adherent	tug	14 January 1944
Adonis	trawler	15 April 1943
Adversus	patrol vessel	20 December 1941
Aelda	yacht	6 November 1943
Affleck	frigate	26 December 1944
Affray	submarine	16 April 1951
Afridi	destroyer	3 May 1940
Agate	trawler	6 August 1941
Air Mist	air–sea rescue	19 December 1945
Aire	frigate	24 December 1946
Airedale	escort destroyer	15 June 1942
Aisha	yacht	11 October 1940
Akranes	trawler	4 July 1941
Alaisia	tug	20 June 1942
Alarm	minesweeper	2 January 1943
Alatna	launch	1 January 1946
Alberic	trawler	3 May 1941
Alberni	corvette	21 August 1944
Aldenham	destroyer	14 December 1944
Alder	trawler	22 October 1941
Aldersdale	oiler	7 July 1942
Aldgate	boom defence vessel	19 December 1941
Algerine	minesweeper	15 November 1942
Alice	coaster	28 May 1940
Alliance	tug	19 December 1941
Alligator	tug	30 February 1945
Almond	trawler	2 February 1941
Alouette	trawler	19 September 1942
Amethyst	trawler	24 November 1940
Amulree	yacht	1 June 1940
AN 2	whaler	8 November 1940
Andania	armed merchant cruiser	16 June 1940
Andromeda	tug	18 April 1942
Anking	base ship	4 March 1942
Antelope	frigate	23 May 1982
Antoine Willy	boom defence vessel	15 December 1940
Appletree	drifter	15 October 1940
Aracari	trawler	3 October 1943
Aragonite	trawler	22 November 1939
Arbutus	corvette	5 February 1942
Arctic Pioneer	trawler	27 May 1942
Arctic Trapper	trawler	3 February 1941
Ardent	destroyer	8 June 1940
Ardent	frigate	21 May 1982
Argyllshire	trawler	1 June 1940
Ark Royal	aircraft carrier	14 November 1941

Name	Type	Date of loss
Arley	trawler	3 February 1945
Armidale	minesweeper	1 December 1942
Arrow	patrol vessel	25 December 1974
Arsenal	trawler	16 November 1940
Artemis	submarine	1 July 1971
Asama	trawler	21 March 1941
Ash	trawler	5 June 1941
Asphodel	corvette	2 March 1944
Assurance	tug	18 October 1941
Aston Villa	trawler	1 May 1940
Astronomer	boom carrier	2 June 1940
Athabaskan	destroyer	29 April 1944
Athlete	tug	17 July 1945
Attendant	yacht	30 October 1940
Auckland	sloop	24 June 1941
Audacity	auxiliary aircraft carrier	21 December 1941
Auricula	corvette	6 April 1942
Aurora II	drifter	24 May 1941
Avenger	escort carrier	15 November 1942
Aventurine	trawler	1 December 1943
Bahram	drifter	3 April 1941
Baia	tug	3 November 1942
Bandolero	trawler	30 December 1940
Banka	minesweeper	10 December 1941
Barbara Robertson	trawler	28 December 1939
Barcombe	boom defence	13 January 1958
Barflake	boom defence	22 November 1943
Barham	battleship	25 November 1941
Barlight	boom defence	19 December 1941
Basilisk	destroyer	1 June 1940
Battleaxe	destroyer	2 August 1962
Bayonet	boom defence	21 December 1939
Bedenham	store ship	27 April 1951
Bedfordshire	trawler	11 May 1942
Bedouin	destroyer	15 June 1942
Beech	trawler	22 June 1941
Belmont	destroyer	30 January 1942
Ben Ardna	trawler	13 May 1942
Ben Gairn	trawler	4 May 1941
Bengali	trawler	5 December 1942
Benvolio	trawler	23 February 1940
Berkeley	escort destroyer	19 August 1942
Berkeley Castle	frigate	1 February 1953
Bever	whaler	30 November 1944
Beverley	destroyer	11 April 1943
Bickerton	frigate	22 August 1944
Birchol	oiler	29 November 1939
Birdlip	trawler	13 June 1944
Bisham	minesweeper	28 September 1956
Bittern	sloop	30 April 1940
Blackburn Rovers	trawler	2 June 1940
Blackwood	frigate	15 June 1944

Name	Type	Date of loss
Blanche	destroyer	13 November 1939
Blean	escort destroyer	11 December 1942
Bloodhound	trials	31 January 1943
Blue Sky	drifter	13 June 1922
Bluebell	corvette	17 February 1945
Boadicea	destroyer	13 June 1944
Boardale	oiler	30 April 1940
Bonaventure	cruiser	31 March 1941
Boomerang VI	yacht	8 June 1940
Borealis	barrage balloon vessel	8 August 1940
Botanic	trawler	18 February 1942
Boy Alan	drifter	10 February 1941
Boy Andrew	drifter	9 November 1941
Boy Peter	auxiliary	5 February 1942
Boy Roy	drifter	27 May 1940
Boy Roy	drifter	11 February 1942
Bradman	trawler	25 April 1940
Brae Flett	drifter	22 September 1943
Bramble	minesweeper	31 December 1942
Branlebas	torpedo boat	14 December 1940
Bras d'Or	trawler	19 October 1940
Brazen	destroyer	20 July 1940
Breconshire	stores	26 March 1942
Breda	yacht	18 February 1944
Bredon	trawler	8 February 1943
Brighton Belle	minesweeper	28 May 1940
Brighton Queen	minesweeper	1 June 1940
Britomart	minesweeper	27 August 1944
Broadland	drifter	6 June 1945
Broadley	minesweeper	28 September 1956
Broadwater	destroyer	18 October 1941
Brodrene	tender	26 December 1942
Broke	destroyer	8 November 1942
Brora	trawler	6 September 1941
Buccaneer	tug	26 August 1946
Buffalo	mooring vessel	4 April 1941
Bullen	frigate	6 December 1944
BV 42	barrage vessel	22 December 1943
BYMS 2019	minesweeper	19 September 1943
BYMS 2022	minesweeper	16 August 1944
BYMS 2030	minesweeper	8 October 1944
BYMS 2053	minesweeper	28 April 1945
BYMS 2072	minesweeper	12 November 1943
BYMS 2077	minesweeper	25 October 1944
BYMS 2255	minesweeper	5 October 1944
C 64/Rosa	lighter	28 April 1930
C 308	tug	11 May 1942
Cachalot	submarine	30 July 1941
Cairndale	oiler	30 May 1941
Cairo	cruiser	12 August 1942
Calanthe	yacht	25 April 1941
Calcutta	cruiser	1 June 1941
Calverton	trawler	29 November 1940
Calvi	trawler	29 May 1940
Calypso	cruiser	12 June 1940
Cambrian	boom defence	30 May 1940
Cameron	destroyer	5 December 1940
Camito	ocean boarding vessel	6 May 1941

Name	Type	Date of loss
Campbeltown	destroyer	28 March 1942
Campeador	yacht	22 June 1940
Campina	trawler	22 July 1940
Campobello	trawler	16 March 1943
Canberra	cruiser	9 August 1942
Canna	trawler	5 December 1942
Cap d'Antifer	trawler	13 February 1944
Cape Chelyuskin	trawler	29 April 1940
Cape Finisterre	trawler	2 August 1940
Cape Howe	special service	21 June 1940
Cape Passaro	trawler	21 May 1940
Cape Siretoko	trawler	28 April 1940
Cape Spartel	trawler	2 February 1942
Capel	frigate	26 December 1944
Capricornus	trawler	7 December 1940
Captive	tug	3 February 1946
Carinthia	armed merchant cruiser	7 June 1940
Carlisle	cruiser	9 October 1943
Caroline Moller	tug	7 October 1942
Carry On	drifter	17 December 1940
Catherine	drifter	8 June 1942
Cato	minesweeper	6 July 1944
Caulonia	trawler	31 March 1943
Cayton Wyke	trawler	8 July 1940
Cecil	water boat	18 December 1943
CH 06	submarine chaser	12 October 1940
CH 07	submarine chaser	12 October 1940
Chabool	tug	16 March 1941
Chakdina	armed boarding vessel	5 December 1941
Chakla	convoy service ship	29 April 1941
Chamois	minesweeper	21 July 1944
Chancellor	drifter	30 October 1943
Changteh	minesweeper	13 February 1942
Chantala	armed boarding vessel	7 December 1941
Chanticleer	minesweeper	18 November 1943
Charde	drifter	21 June 1940
Charles Boyes	trawler	25 May 1940
Charlottetown	corvette	11 September 1942
Charybdis	cruiser	23 October 1943
Chebogue	frigate	4 October 1944
Chedabucto	minesweeper	21 October 1943
Chestnut	trawler	30 November 1940
Choice	trawler	25 August 1944
Chorley	boom defence	25 April 1942
Christine Rose	drifter	10 September 1941
Cicala	river gunboat	21 December 1941
City of Rochester	minesweeper	19 May 1941
Clacton	minesweeper	31 December 1943
Clayoquot	minesweeper	24 December 1944
Cloughton Wyke	trawler	2 February 1942
CMB 99	coastal motor boat	9 September 1920
Cobbers	trawler	3 March 1941
Cocker	whaler	3 June 1942
Codrington	destroyer	27 July 1940

Name	Type	Date of loss
Colsay	trawler	2 November 1944
Comet	trawler	30 September 1940
Comfort	drifter	29 May 1940
Comorin	armed merchant cruiser	6 April 1941
Computator	trawler	21 January 1945
Conquistador	trawler	25 November 1940
Cor Jesu	drifter	8 June 1941
Coral	trawler	30 April 1942
Corburn	mine destructor	21 May 1940
Corfield	mine destructor	8 September 1941
Coringa	tug	23 June 1940
Coriolanus	trawler	5 May 1945
Corncrake	minelayer	25 January 1943
Cornflower	sloop	19 December 1941
Cornwall	cruiser	5 April 1942
Cortina	trawler	7 December 1940
Cory Bros	tug	9 August 1943
Cossack	destroyer	27 October 1941
Courageous	aircraft carrier	17 September 1939
Coventry (i)	cruiser	14 September 1942
Coventry (ii)	GMD	25 May 1982
Cramond Island	trawler	2 April 1941
Crested Eagle	anti-aircraft ship	29 May 1940
Crestflower	trawler	19 July 1940
Cricket	river gunboat	30 June 1941
Crispin	ocean boarding vessel	3 February 1941
Crocodile	tug	3 May 1946
Cromarty	minesweeper	23 October 1943
Cromer	minesweeper	9 November 1942
Culver	cutter	30 January 1942
Curacoa	cruiser	2 October 1942
Curlew	cruiser	26 May 1940
Cyrus	mine destructor	5 December 1944
Daffodil	landing ship	18 March 1945
Dainty	destroyer	24 February 1941
Daisy	tug	2 January 1942
Daisy	degaussing	25 April 1942
Dakins	frigate	25 December 1944
Daneman	trawler	8 May 1943
Danube III	tug	13 October 1940
D'Arcy Cooper	drifter	9 April 1941
Daring	destroyer	18 February 1940
Darkdale	oiler	22 October 1941
Darogah	trawler	27 January 1941
Dasher	escort carrier	27 March 1943
De Zee Meeuw	trawler	21 September 1943
Defender	destroyer	11 July 1941
Delight	destroyer	29 July 1940
Denbigh Castle	corvette	13 February 1945
Dervish	trawler	9 September 1940
Desiree	trawler	16 January 1941
Devon County	drifter	1 July 1941
Devonia	minesweeper	31 May 1940
Dewy Eve	drifter	9 June 1940
Diamond	destroyer	27 April 1941

Name	Type	Date of loss
Dinsdale	oiler	31 May 1942
Donna Nook	trawler	25 September 1943
Dorrimee	launch	11 June 1944
Dorsetshire	cruiser	5 April 1942
Dowgate	boom defence	15 February 1942
Dox	trawler	20 March 1941
Dragonfly	river gunboat	14 February 1942
Dromio	trawler	22 December 1939
Drummer	trawler	4 August 1940
Duchess	destroyer	12 December 1939
Dulverton	destroyer	13 November 1943
Dundalk	minesweeper	17 October 1940
Dundee	sloop	15 September 1940
Dunedin	cruiser	24 November 1941
Dungeness	trawler	15 November 1940
Dunoon	minesweeper	30 April 1940
Dunvegan Castle	armed merchant cruiser	28 August 1940
Dusky Queen	drifter	9 January 1941
Duthies	drifter	25 October 1940
Eagle	aircraft carrier	11 August 1942
Ebonol	oiler	19 December 1941
Ebor Wyke	trawler	2 May 1945
Eclipse	destroyer	24 October 1943
Eddy	drifter	26 May 1942
Edinburgh	cruiser	2 May 1942
Edlingham	minesweeper	28 September 1956
Effingham	cruiser	18 May 1940
Egeland	whaler	29 November 1941
Egret	sloop	27 August 1943
Eileen Duncan	trawler	30 September 1941
Ekins	frigate	16 April 1945
El Hind	landing ship	14 April 1944
Electra	destroyer	27 February 1942
Elgin	minesweeper	4 May 1944
Elizabeth Angela	trawler	13 August 1940
Elk	trawler	27 November 1940
Ellesmere	trawler	24 February 1945
Elphinstone	sloop	29 January 1925
Embrace	drifter	2 August 1940
Emelle	yacht	31 August 1940
Emilion	trawler	24 October 1941
Emily	tug	7 April 1942
Empire Ace	tug	11 November 1968
Empire Arthur	water carrier	22 November 1943
Empire Rosa	tug	3 December 1977
Encounter	destroyer	1 March 1942
Englishman	rescue tug	21 January 1941
Ennerdale	oiler	1 June 1970
Enticer	tug	21 December 1946
Erica	corvette	9 February 1943
Eridge	escort destroyer	29 August 1942
Erin	trawler	18 January 1942
Eriskay	trawler	12 November 1945
Escaut	store ship	4 August 1941
Escort	destroyer	11 July 1940
Esk	destroyer	1 September 1940
Eskimo Nell	schooner	20 June 1942

Name	Type	Date of loss	Name	Type	Date of loss
Esquimalt	minesweeper	16 April 1945	*Gatling*	tug	16 December 1941
Ethel Taylor	trawler	22 November 1940	*Gaul*	trawler	1 May 1940
Evelina	trawler	16 December 1939	*Geelong*	minesweeper	18 October 1944
Evesham	trawler	27 May 1941	*Gemas*	whaler	3 March 1942
Exeter	cruiser	1 March 1942	*Giang Bee*	patrol vessel	14 February 1942
Exmoor	destroyer	25 February 1941	*Gipsy*	destroyer	21 November 1939
Exmouth	destroyer	21 January 1940	*Girl Helen*	drifter	6 November 1940
Fabious	boom defence	16 January 1943	*Girl Pamela*	drifter	28 May 1940
Fair Breeze	drifter	1 June 1940	*Gladiolus*	corvette	16 October 1941
Fairhaven	drifter	5 September 1944	*Gladmor*	patrol vessel	17 October 1943
Fairplay Two	tug	2 March 1940	*Gleam*	drifter	15 June 1944
Fanling	motor launch	15 February 1942	*Glen*	armament lighter	22 November 1940
Fantome	minesweeper	20 May 1943	*Glen Avon*	A/A ship	2 September 1944
Farouk	schooner	13 June 1942	*Glenalbyn*	armed drifter	23 December 1939
Fastnet	boom defence	20 April 1942	*Gloaming*	drifter	3 March 1921
Fauro Chief	schooner	16 May 1945	*Gloaming*	drifter	20 March 1941
FDT 216	fighter direction	7 July 1944	*Glorious*	aircraft carrier	8 June 1940
Fearless	destroyer	23 July 1941	*Gloucester*	cruiser	22 May 1941
Felixstowe	minesweeper	18 December 1943	*Glowworm*	destroyer	8 April 1940
Fermoy	minesweeper	3 May 1941	*Gnat*	river gunboat	21 October 1941
Fertile Vale	drifter	17 July 1941	*Go Ahead*	drifter	18 November 1940
Fidelia	trawler	5 May 1941	*Goathland*	escort destroyer	24 July 1944
Fidelity	special service	30 December 1942	*Godetia*	corvette	6 September 1940
Fifeshire	trawler	20 February 1940	*Golden Dawn*	drifter	4 April 1940
Fiji	cruiser	22 May 1941	*Golden Effort*	drifter	23 September 1943
Fiona	convoy service ship	18 April 1941	*Golden Gift*	drifter	6 April 1943
Firedrake	destroyer	16 December 1942	*Golden Sunbeam*	drifter	19 August 1942
Firmament	whaler	20 May 1944	*Golden West*	drifter	15 January 1945
Fisher Girl	drifter	25 November 1941	*Goodall*	frigate	29 April 1945
Fittleton	minesweeper	20 September 1976	*Goodson*	frigate	25 June 1944
Fitzroy	minesweeper	27 May 1942	*Goodwill*	drifter	2 November 1940
Fleming	trawler	24 July 1940	*Goorangai*	trawler	20 November 1940
Fleur de Lys	corvette	14 October 1941	*Gossamer*	minesweeper	24 June 1942
Flotta	trawler	6 November 1941	*Gould*	frigate	25 February 1944
Fontenoy	trawler	19 November 1940	*Gowan Hill*	drifter	7 May 1941
Force	trawler	27 June 1941	*Gracie Fields*	minesweeper	30 May 1940
Forecast	drifter	30 March 1944	*Grafton*	destroyer	29 May 1940
Forerunner	drifter	14 October 1941	*Grampus*	submarine	16 June 1940
Foresight	destroyer	13 August 1942	*Graph*	submarine	20 March 1944
Forfar	armed merchant cruiser	2 December 1940	*Grasshopper*	river gunboat	14 February 1942
Fort Royal	trawler	9 February 1940	*Gray Ranger*	oiler	22 September 1942
Fortuna	trawler	2 April 1941	*Green Ranger*	oiler	17 November 1962
Foxglove	sloop	9 July 1940	*Grenade*	destroyer	29 May 1940
Foylebank	anti-aircraft ship	4 July 1940	*Grenville*	destroyer	19 January 1940
Franc Tireur	trawler	25 September 1943	*Greyhound*	destroyer	22 May 1941
Francol	oiler	4 March 1942	*Grimsby*	sloop	25 May 1941
Francolin	trawler	12 November 1941	*Grinder*	tug	26 December 1941
Fraser	destroyer	25 June 1940	*Grive*	yacht	1 June 1940
Fratton	examination	18 August 1944	*Grove*	escort destroyer	12 June 1942
FT 4	tender	4 January 1946	*Guardsman*	tug	15 November 1940
Fuh Wo	minesweeper	14 February 1942	*Gullfoss*	trawler	9 March 1941
Fumarole	drifter	11 November 1927	*Gulzar*	yacht	29 July 1940
Fury	destroyer	21 June 1944	*Gurkha*	destroyer	9 April 1940
Gael	yacht	24 November 1940	*Gurkha*	destroyer	17 January 1942
Gairsay	trawler	3 August 1944	*Guysborough*	minesweeper	17 March 1945
Galatea	cruiser	14 December 1941	*Gypsy*	accommodation	11 May 1941
Gallant	destroyer	10 January 1941	*H 29*	submarine	9 August 1926
Ganilly	trawler	5 July 1944	*H 31*	submarine	21 December 1941
Gardenia	corvette	9 November 1942			

Name	Type	Date of loss
H 42	submarine	23 March 1922
H 47	submarine	9 July 1929
H 49	submarine	18 October 1940
Haideri	patrol vessel	2 April 1943
Halstead	frigate	11 June 1944
Hammond	trawler	25 April 1940
Han Wo	auxiliary patrol	19 December 1941
Hanyards	yacht	21 May 1941
Hardy (i)	destroyer	10 April 1940
Hardy (ii)	destroyer	30 January 1944
Harlequin	accommodation	30 September 1942
Harmony	drifter	15 November 1941
Hartland	cutter	8 November 1942
Harvest		
Gleaner	drifter	28 October 1940
Harvester	destroyer	11 March 1943
Hasty	destroyer	15 June 1942
Havant	destroyer	1 June 1940
Havock	destroyer	6 April 1942
Hayburn		
Wyke	trawler	2 January 1945
HDML 1003	motor launch	20 April 1941
HDML 1011	motor launch	24 May 1941
HDML 1015	motor launch	21 October 1943
HDML 1030	motor launch	28 May 1941
HDML 1037	motor launch	20 April 1941
HDML 1039	motor launch	20 June 1942
HDML 1054	motor launch	1 November 1943
HDML 1057	motor launch	13 October 1944
HDML 1062	motor launch	16 February 1942
HDML 1063	motor launch	1 March 1942
HDML 1069	motor launch	20 June 1942
HDML 1083	motor launch	20 February 1944
HDML 1090	motor launch	11 July 1942
HDML 1092	motor launch	4 May 1941
HDML 1093	motor launch	4 May 1941
HDML 1094	motor launch	4 May 1941
HDML 1095	motor launch	4 May 1941
HDML 1096	motor launch	13 February 1942
HDML 1097	motor launch	14 February 1942
HDML 1119	motor launch	7 October 1944
HDML 1121	motor launch	31 December 1943
HDML 1153	motor launch	30 September 1942
HDML 1154	motor launch	14 May 1943
HDML 1157	motor launch	22 March 1943
HDML 1163	motor launch	4 January 1945
HDML 1167	motor launch	14 February 1942
HDML 1168	motor launch	14 February 1942
HDML 1169	motor launch	14 February 1942
HDML 1170	motor launch	14 February 1942
HDML 1179	motor launch	21 August 1944
HDML 1212	motor launch	22 March 1943
HDML 1213	motor launch	14 February 1942
HDML 1214	motor launch	14 February 1942
HDML 1215	motor launch	14 February 1942
HDML 1216	motor launch	14 February 1942
HDML 1217	motor launch	14 February 1942
HDML 1218	motor launch	14 February 1942
HDML 1219	motor launch	14 February 1942

Name	Type	Date of loss
HDML 1220	motor launch	14 February 1942
HDML 1226	motor launch	4 October 1945
HDML 1227	motor launch	5 October 1944
HDML 1244	motor launch	11 November 1943
HDML 1289	motor launch	11 November 1943
HDML 1380	motor launch	18 April 1944
HDML 1381	motor launch	26 August 1944
HDML 1388	motor launch	24 December 1943
HDML 1417	motor launch	15 February 1945
HDML 2582	motor launch	5 June 1952
Hebe	minesweeper	22 November 1943
Hebe-II	coaster	12 June 1940
Hecla	depot ship	12 November 1942
Hector	armed merchant cruiser	5 April 1942
Hedgehog	schooner	15 October 1943
Helen Barbara	tug	21 October 1941
Hellespont	tug	7 April 1942
Helvellyn	A/A ship	20 March 1941
Henriette	trawler	30 December 1941
Herald	survey ship	9 February 1942
Hereward	destroyer	29 May 1941
Hermes	aircraft carrier	9 April 1942
Hermione	cruiser	16 June 1942
Herring	trawler	22 April 1943
Hesperia	tug	9 February 1945
Heythrop	escort destroyer	20 March 1942
Hickory	trawler	22 October 1940
High Tide	drifter	30 March 1945
Highland		
Queen	drifter	20 June 1942
Hildasay	trawler	21 June 1945
Hogue	destroyer	25 August 1959
Holcombe	destroyer	12 December 1943
Hollyhock	corvette	9 April 1942
Hong Lam	trawler	26 May 1943
Honjo	trawler	18 January 1942
Hood	battlecruiser	24 May 1941
Hopper 39	minesweeper	6 February 1941
Horatio	trawler	7 January 1943
Horsa	tug	16 March 1943
Horst	coaster	31 May 1940
Hostile	destroyer	23 August 1940
Hua Tong	minesweeper	13 February 1942
Hulda	tender	22 September 1943
Hungjao	auxiliary patrol	14 February 1942
Hunter	destroyer	10 April 1940
Huntley	minesweeper	31 January 1941
Hurricane	destroyer	24 December 1943
Hurst Castle	corvette	1 September 1944
Hurworth	destroyer	22 October 1943
Hussar	minesweeper	27 August 1944
Hydra	minesweeper	10 November 1944
Hyperion	destroyer	22 December 1940
Hythe	minesweeper	11 October 1943
Ibis	sloop	10 November 1942
Imbat	drifter	4 February 1941
Imogen	destroyer	16 July 1940
Imperial	destroyer	29 May 1941
Indira	auxiliary patrol vessel	15 December 1941

Name	Type	Date of loss
Indus	minesweeper	6 April 1942
Inglefield	destroyer	25 February 1944
Insolent	tender	1 July 1922
Intrepid	destroyer	27 September 1943
Intrepide	drifter	13 August 1942
Inverclyde	trawler	16 October 1942
Irini Vernicos	tug	2 June 1941
Irvana	trawler	16 January 1942
Isis	destroyer	20 July 1944
Isleford	armament carrier	25 January 1942
Itchen	frigate	23 September 1943
Ivanhoe	destroyer	1 September 1940
Jackal	destroyer	11 May 1942
Jade	trawler	21 April 1942
Jaguar	destroyer	26 March 1942
James Fennel	trawler	16 January 1920
James Ludford	trawler	14 December 1939
Janus	destroyer	23 January 1944
Jarak	minesweeper	16 February 1942
Jardine	trawler	30 April 1940
Jasper	trawler	1 December 1942
Jeram	whaler	2 March 1942
Jerantut	whaler	15 February 1942
Jersey	destroyer	2 May 1941
Jervis Bay	armed merchant cruiser	5 November 1940
Jewel	drifter	18 May 1941
Joseph Button	trawler	21 October 1940
Juniper	trawler	8 June 1940
Juno	destroyer	21 May 1941
Jupiter	destroyer	27 February 1942
Jura	trawler	7 January 1943
Justified	drifter	16 June 1942
K 5	submarine	20 January 1921
Kalgah	water carrier	24 September 1942
Kampar	auxiliary A/S vessel	13 December 1941
Kandahar	destroyer	20 December 1941
Kantara	schooner	26 September 1941
Karalee	lighter	5 March 1942
Karanja	landing ship	12 November 1942
Kashmir	destroyer	22 May 1941
Keith	destroyer	1 June 1940
Kelana	motor launch	16 January 1942
Kelat	coal hulk	19 February 1942
Kelly	destroyer	23 May 1941
Kennymore	trawler	25 November 1940
Kephallinia	schooner	13 August 1941
Keryado	trawler	6 March 1941
Khartoum	destroyer	13 June 1940
Kheir-el-Dine	schooner	20 June 1942
King Henry	gate vessel	13 June 1941
King Orry	armed boarding steamer	30 May 1940
Kingston	destroyer	11 April 1942
Kingston Alalite	trawler	10 November 1940
Kingston Beryl	trawler	25 December 1943
Kingston Cairngorm	trawler	18 October 1940

Name	Type	Date of loss
Kingston Ceylonite	trawler	13 June 1942
Kingston Cornelian	trawler	5 January 1940
Kingston Galena	trawler	24 July 1940
Kingston Jacinth	trawler	12 January 1943
Kingston Sapphire	trawler	5 October 1940
Kipling	destroyer	11 May 1942
Kite	sloop	21 August 1944
Klias	minesweeper	15 February 1942
Knight of Malta	transport	2 March 1941
Kopanes	trawler	19 April 1941
Kos XVI	whaler	24 August 1941
Kos XXII	whaler	27 May 1941
Kos XXIII	whaler	20 May 1941
Kuala	auxiliary A/S	13 February 1942
Kudat	auxiliary patrol vessel	26 December 1941
Kung Wo	minelayer	14 February 1942
Kurd	trawler	10 July 1945
Kuttabul	accommodation ship	1 June 1942
Kutubtari	patrol vessel	10 August 1944
Kylemore	net layer	21 August 1940
L 9	submarine	18 August 1923
L 24	submarine	10 January 1924
La Nantaise	trawler	8 July 1945
Lady Craddock	drifter	16 October 1942
Lady Lilian	trawler	16 March 1941
Lady Shirley	trawler	11 December 1941
Lady Slater	examination vessel	30 July 1940
Lady Somers	ocean boarding vessel	15 July 1941
Ladybird	river gunboat	12 May 1941
Laertes	trawler	25 July 1942
Laforey	destroyer	27 March 1944
Lagan	frigate	20 September 1943
Lance	destroyer	9 April 1942
Lantaka	tug	15 February 1942
Lantau	minesweeper	19 December 1941
Lapwing	sloop	20 March 1945
Lark	sloop	17 February 1945
Lars Riisdahl	schooner	20 June 1942
Larut	armed trader	22 January 1942
Larwood	trawler	26 April 1940
Latona	minelayer	25 October 1941
Laurentic	armed merchant cruiser	3 November 1940
Lawford	frigate	8 June 1944
LCF 1	landing craft	17 August 1944
LCF 2	landing craft	19 August 1942
LCF 13	landing craft	12 June 1943
LCF 15	landing craft	16 June 1944
LCF 31	landing craft	1 September 1944
LCF 37	landing craft	1 November 1944
LCF 38	landing craft	1 November 1944
LCG(L) 1	landing craft	1 November 1944
LCG(L) 2	landing craft	1 November 1944

Name	Type	Date of loss	Name	Type	Date of loss
LCG(L) 15	landing craft	25 April 1943	LCT 126	landing craft	19 August 1942
LCG(L) 16	landing craft	25 April 1943	LCT 129	landing craft	3 June 1943
LCG(L) 101	landing craft	1 November 1944	LCT 137	landing craft	4 November 1941
LCG(L) 102	landing craft	1 November 1944	LCT 143	landing craft	30 November 1941
LCG(L) 764	landing craft	3 August 1944	LCT 145	landing craft	19 August 1942
LCG(L) 831	landing craft	14 June 1944	LCT 150	landing craft	21 June 1942
LCG(L) 1062	landing craft	29 July 1944	LCT 154	landing craft	9 September 1943
LCG(M) 101	landing craft	1 November 1944	LCT 155	landing craft	2 March 1942
LCG(M) 102	landing craft	1 November 1944	LCT 159	landing craft	19 August 1942
LCH 185	landing craft	25 June 1944	LCT 300	landing craft	10 July 1943
LCI(L) 7	landing craft	21 April 1943	LCT 301	landing craft	28 August 1943
LCI(L) 99	landing craft	14 August 1944	LCT 313	landing craft	3 July 1944
LCI(L) 102	landing craft	29 November 1944	LCT 317	landing craft	6 June 1944
LCI(L) 105	landing craft	8 June 1944	LCT 324	landing craft	30 July 1944
LCI(L) 107	landing craft	2 September 1943	LCT 326	landing craft	2 February 1943
LCI(L) 131	landing craft	6 June 1944	LCT 328	landing craft	5 December 1944
LCI(L) 132	landing craft	17 June 1944	LCT 329	landing craft	23 November 1943
LCI(L) 162	landing craft	7 February 1943	LCT 332	landing craft	16 November 1943
LCI(L) 273	landing craft	16 March 1944	LCT 333	landing craft	14 November 1943
LCI(L) 309	landing craft	23 October 1943	LCT 343	landing craft	13 November 1943
LCI(S) 511	landing craft	2 February 1944	LCT 353	landing craft	27 July 1943
LCI(S) 512	landing craft	6 June 1944	LCT 357	landing craft	26 May 1945
LCI(S) 517	landing craft	6 June 1944	LCT 358	landing craft	18 June 1943
LCI(S) 524	landing craft	6 June 1944	LCT 375	landing craft	1 February 1944
LCI(S) 531	landing craft	6 June 1944	LCT 377	landing craft	2 October 1944
LCI(S) 532	landing craft	2 November 1944	LCT 381	landing craft	27 February 1943
LCI(S) 537	landing craft	6 June 1944	LCT 385	landing craft	14 November 1943
LCI(S) 540	landing craft	6 June 1944	LCT 387	landing craft	17 July 1944
LCM 703	landing craft	8 June 1982	LCT 390	landing craft	8 June 1944
LCS(L) 252	landing craft	2 November 1944	LCT 391	landing craft	25 September 1943
LCS(L) 256	landing craft	2 November 1944	LCT 395	landing craft	18 June 1943
LCS(L) 258	landing craft	2 November 1944	LCT 403	landing craft	24 February 1943
LCT 1	landing craft	24 April 1941	LCT 410	landing craft	10 July 1943
LCT 2	landing craft	12 October 1941	LCT 416	landing craft	28 August 1943
LCT 3	landing craft	3 October 1943	LCT 418	landing craft	16 November 1943
LCT 5	landing craft	28 April 1941	LCT 427	landing craft	7 June 1944
LCT 6	landing craft	28 May 1941	LCT 457	landing craft	5 November 1944
LCT 7	landing craft	12 October 1941	LCT 469	landing craft	8 November 1944
LCT 8	landing craft	29 July 1941	LCT 480	landing craft	19 October 1944
LCT 10	landing craft	17 July 1941	LCT 488	landing craft	19 October 1944
LCT 11	landing craft	16 December 1941	LCT 491	landing craft	19 October 1944
LCT 12	landing craft	12 June 1941	LCT 492	landing craft	6 March 1945
LCT 14	landing craft	12 August 1941	LCT 494	landing craft	19 October 1944
LCT 15	landing craft	28 April 1941	LCT 496	landing craft	6 June 1944
LCT 16	landing craft	27 May 1941	LCT 511	landing craft	9 July 1944
LCT 19	landing craft	26 April 1941	LCT 524	landing craft	6 June 1944
LCT 20	landing craft	28 May 1941	LCT 529	landing craft	28 June 1944
LCT 102	landing craft	10 October 1941	LCT 547	landing craft	8 July 1943
LCT 103	landing craft	10 October 1941	LCT 548	landing craft	22 May 1945
LCT 105	landing craft	4 November 1941	LCT 550	landing craft	22 May 1945
LCT 106	landing craft	6 January 1943	LCT 552	landing craft	22 May 1945
LCT 107	landing craft	6 January 1943	LCT 553	landing craft	11 October 1943
LCT 109	landing craft	4 November 1941	LCT 554	landing craft	22 May 1945
LCT 115	landing craft	28 October 1943	LCT 559	landing craft	22 May 1945
LCT 117	landing craft	20 June 1942	LCT 561	landing craft	22 May 1945
LCT 119	landing craft	20 June 1942	LCT 565	landing craft	2 May 1954
LCT 120	landing craft	20 November 1942	LCT 572	landing craft	9 September 1943
LCT 121	landing craft	19 August 1942	LCT 578	landing craft	22 May 1945
LCT 124	landing craft	19 August 1942	LCT 583	landing craft	4 November 1943

Name	Type	Date of loss
LCT 586	landing craft	22 May 1945
LCT 589	landing craft	16 June 1944
LCT 609	landing craft	6 November 1944
LCT 613	landing craft	3 May 1943
LCT 615	landing craft	22 May 1945
LCT 618	landing craft	2 October 1943
LCT 621	landing craft	29 September 1943
LCT 624	landing craft	8 September 1943
LCT 626	landing craft	9 September 1943
LCT 631	landing craft	17 August 1944
LCT 689	landing craft	20 July 1944
LCT 715	landing craft	6 June 1944
LCT 717	landing craft	6 June 1944
LCT 721	landing craft	26 November 1944
LCT 750	landing craft	6 June 1944
LCT 757	landing craft	10 July 1944
LCT 789	landing craft	2 November 1944
LCT 809	landing craft	6 June 1944
LCT 839	landing craft	2 November 1944
LCT 856	landing craft	17 November 1944
LCT 875	landing craft	8 June 1944
LCT 886	landing craft	6 June 1944
LCT 901	landing craft	24 July 1944
LCT 936	landing craft	30 October 1944
LCT 943	landing craft	24 October 1944
LCT 947	landing craft	20 June 1944
LCT 967	landing craft	13 June 1944
LCT 976	landing craft	3 November 1944
LCT 1002	landing craft	5 November 1944
LCT 1020	landing craft	16 July 1944
LCT 1022	landing craft	17 November 1944
LCT 1023	landing craft	23 July 1944
LCT 1029	landing craft	16 January 1944
LCT 1039	landing craft	5 August 1944
LCT 1045	landing craft	25 October 1944
LCT 1068	landing craft	6 June 1947
LCT 1074	landing craft	25 August 1944
LCT 1076	landing craft	10 July 1944
LCT 1092	landing craft	10 August 1944
LCT 1133	landing craft	2 November 1944
LCT 1171	landing craft	24 October 1944
LCT 1238	landing craft	3 May 1945
LCT 1359	landing craft	14 November 1944
LCT 2006	landing craft	14 October 1942
LCT 2039	landing craft	6 June 1944
LCT 2040	landing craft	20 June 1944
LCT 2049	landing craft	6 June 1944
LCT 2052	landing craft	6 June 1944
LCT 2054	landing craft	30 December 1942
LCT 2187	landing craft	30 November 1942
LCT 2190	landing craft	29 October 1942
LCT 2191	landing craft	6 June 1944
LCT 2192	landing craft	20 October 1942
LCT 2229	landing craft	6 June 1944
LCT 2231	landing craft	21 July 1943
LCT 2238	landing craft	28 June 1944
LCT 2239	landing craft	17 January 1943
LCT 2263	landing craft	15 July 1944
LCT 2267	landing craft	17 January 1943

Name	Type	Date of loss
LCT 2273	landing craft	6 June 1944
LCT 2281	landing craft	27 October 1942
LCT 2284	landing craft	29 October 1942
LCT 2301	landing craft	6 June 1944
LCT 2307	landing craft	6 June 1944
LCT 2312	landing craft	20 November 1942
LCT 2331	landing craft	20 July 1944
LCT 2335	landing craft	8 February 1943
LCT 2341	landing craft	10 March 1943
LCT 2344	landing craft	17 January 1943
LCT 2398	landing craft	11 March 1943
LCT 2402	landing craft	6 June 1944
LCT 2428	landing craft	6 June 1944
LCT 2439	landing craft	6 June 1944
LCT 2454	landing craft	13 October 1944
LCT 2461	landing craft	30 November 1944
LCT 2480	landing craft	8 March 1943
LCT 2498	landing craft	6 June 1944
LCT 7009	landing craft	19 August 1951
LCT 7011	landing craft	2 November 1944
LCT 7014	landing craft	19 October 1944
LCT 7015	landing craft	19 October 1944
LCT 7020	landing craft	16 October 1945
LCT 7036	landing craft	30 July 1944
LCT 7057	landing craft	16 July 1944
LCT 7064	landing craft	16 July 1944
LCT 7084	landing craft	2 October 1944
LCT 7089	landing craft	6 December 1944
LCT 7094	landing craft	16 November 1944
LCVP 120	landing craft	24 April 1984
Le Due Paole	drifter	21 February 1944
Leda	minesweeper	20 September 1942
Legion	destroyer	26 March 1942
Lena	coaster	4 June 1940
Lettie	tug	9 November 1941
Levant Schooner 4	schooner	22 August 1943
Levant Schooner 24	schooner	20 April 1944
Levanter	drifter	13 October 1926
Levis	corvette	19 September 1941
Leyland	trawler	25 November 1942
Li Wo	minesweeper	14 February 1942
Lightning	destroyer	12 March 1943
Limbourne	destroyer	23 October 1943
Lincoln City	trawler	20 February 1941
Lipis	armed trader	11 February 1942
Listrac	trawler	12 October 1940
Lively	destroyer	11 May 1942
Loch Alsh	trawler	30 January 1942
Loch Assater	trawler	22 March 1940
Loch Doon	trawler	25 December 1939
Loch Eribol	trawler	12 October 1945
Loch Inver	trawler	23 September 1940
Loch Naver	trawler	6 May 1940
Loch Shin	boom defence vessel	26 May 1940
Lolita	air sea rescue	13 June 1945
Lord Austin	trawler	24 June 1944
Lord Cavan	drifter	1 June 1940

Name	Type	Date of loss
Lord Hailsham	trawler	27 February 1943
Lord Howard	drifter	24 December 1940
Lord Inchcape	trawler	25 October 1940
Lord Selborne	trawler	31 March 1941
Lord Snowden	trawler	13 April 1942
Lord St Vincent	drifter	7 July 1941
Lord Stamp	trawler	14 October 1940
Lord Stonehaven	trawler	2 October 1942
Lord Wakefield	trawler	29 July 1944
Lorinda	trawler	20 August 1941
Lormont	guardship	7 December 1940
Louisburg	corvette	6 February 1943
Loyal	destroyer	12 October 1944
Loyalty	minesweeper	22 August 1944
LST 79	landing ship	30 September 1943
LST 80	landing ship	20 March 1945
LST 178	landing ship	24 February 1945
LST 199	landing ship	5 November 1945
LST 305	landing ship	20 February 1944
LST 362	landing ship	27 February 1944
LST 364	landing ship	22 February 1945
LST 404	landing ship	15 August 1944
LST 405	landing ship	25 October 1945
LST 407	landing ship	26 February 1944
LST 411	landing ship	31 December 1943
LST 414	landing ship	15 August 1943
LST 418	landing ship	16 February 1944
LST 420	landing ship	7 November 1944
LST 422	landing ship	26 January 1944
LST 429	landing ship	3 July 1943
Lucienne Jeanne	trawler	24 October 1941
Luda Lady	trawler	22 January 1941
Ludgate	boom defence vessel	15 February 1942
Lyemun	minesweeper	19 December 1941
M 1	submarine	12 November 1925
M 2	submarine	26 January 1932
MAC 5	motor attendant craft	26 December 1940
MA/SB 3	motor A/S boat	28 February 1941
MA/SB 30	motor A/S boat	14 December 1941
M A West	drifter	14 May 1941
Maaloy	whaler	20 March 1944
Magic	minesweeper	6 July 1944
Magog	frigate	14 October 1944
Mahratta	destroyer	25 February 1944
Maida	drifter	16 March 1940
Malacca	minesweeper	17 February 1942
Malvernian	ocean boarding vessel	19 July 1941
Mamari	fleet tender	4 June 1941
Man Yeung	auxiliary minelayer	14 December 1941
Manchester	cruiser	13 August 1942
Manistee	ocean boarding vessel	24 February 1941
Manners	frigate	26 January 1945
Manor	trawler	9 July 1942
Manora	harbour defence	17 December 1944
Manx Lad	drifter	16 August 1940

Name	Type	Date of loss
Manx Prince	trawler	28 November 1940
Maori	destroyer	11 February 1942
Marcelle	boom defence vessel	10 November 1940
Marconi	trawler	20 September 1941
Margaree	destroyer	22 October 1940
Maria de Giovanni	schooner	22 November 1941
Marigold	corvette	9 December 1942
Marjoram	sloop	17 January 1921
Marlean	patrol vessel	12 November 1944
Marmion	minesweeper	9 April 1941
Maroubra	store ship	10 May 1943
Marsona	trawler	4 August 1940
Martin	destroyer	10 November 1942
Mashobra	base ship	25 May 1940
Mashona	destroyer	28 May 1941
Mastiff	trawler	20 November 1939
Mata Hari	auxiliary A/S	15 February 1942
Matabele	destroyer	17 January 1942
Matafele	store ship	20 June 1944
Matchlock	tug	19 December 1941
Mavie	patrol vessel	19 February 1942
Medway	depot ship	30 June 1942
Melbourne	trawler	22 May 1940
Mercury	paddle minesweeper	25 December 1940
Meror	trawler	3 October 1943
MFV 26	tender	22 October 1953
MFV 70	tender	22 February 1944
MFV 117	tender	14 October 1944
MFV 118	tender	5 October 1945
MFV 411	tender	4 March 1946
MFV 812	tender	4 March 1946
MFV 1032	tender	13 September 1944
MFV 1163	tender	21 November 1954
MFV 1218	tender	4 December 1945
MFV 1512	tender	30 January 1946
MGB 12	motor gun boat	3 February 1941
MGB 17	motor gun boat	11 June 1944
MGB 18	motor gun boat	30 September 1942
MGB 19	motor gun boat	6 November 1942
MGB 62	motor gun boat	9 August 1941
MGB 64	motor gun boat	8 August 1943
MGB 76	motor gun boat	6 October 1942
MGB 78	motor gun boat	3 October 1942
MGB 79	motor gun boat	28 February 1943
MGB 90	motor gun boat	16 July 1941
MGB 92	motor gun boat	16 July 1941
MGB 98	motor gun boat	10 March 1941
MGB 99	motor gun boat	30 April 1945
MGB 109	motor gun boat	7 February 1943
MGB 110	motor gun boat	29 May 1943
MGB 313	motor gun boat	16 August 1944
MGB 314	motor gun boat	28 March 1942
MGB 326	motor gun boat	28 June 1944
MGB 328	motor gun boat	21 July 1942
MGB 335	motor gun boat	11 September 1942
MGB 501	motor gun boat	27 July 1942
MGB 601	motor gun boat	24 July 1942
MGB 641	motor gun boat	15 July 1943

Name	Type	Date of loss	Name	Type	Date of loss
MGB 644	motor gun boat	26 June 1943	*ML 432*	motor launch	17 February 1942
MGB 648	motor gun boat	14 June 1943	*ML 433*	motor launch	15 February 1942
MGB 657	motor gunboat	12 September 1944	*ML 434*	motor launch	26 December 1941
MGB 663	motor gun boat	10 October 1944	*ML 435*	motor launch	26 December 1941
MGB 2002	motor gun boat	12 May 1945	*ML 443*	motor launch	12 July 1944
MGB 2007	motor gun boat	22 May 1945	*ML 446*	motor launch	28 March 1942
Michael			*ML 447*	motor launch	28 March 1942
Maloney	trawler	19 February 1920	*ML 457*	motor launch	28 March 1942
Midas	drifter	3 February 1941	*ML 466*	motor launch	25 March 1945
Milford Earl	trawler	8 December 1941	*ML 558*	motor launch	5 May 1945
Minicoy	launch	14 May 1941	*ML 563*	motor launch	16 August 1944
Minnie	auxiliary patrol	19 December 1941	*ML 579*	motor launch	26 October 1943
Minnie Moller	tug	26 December 1941	*ML 591*	motor launch	9 May 1945
Minster	net layer	8 June 1944	*ML 827*	motor launch	20 November 1944
Mirabelle	trawler	17 September 1944	*ML 835*	motor launch	12 October 1943
Mistletoe	drifter	15 October 1940	*ML 870*	motor launch	15 October 1944
ML 103	motor launch	24 August 1942	*ML 891*	motor launch	24 January 1945
ML 108	motor launch	5 September 1943	*ML 905*	motor launch	9 May 1945
ML 109	motor launch	30 October 1940	*ML 916*	motor launch	8 November 1944
ML 111	motor launch	25 November 1940	*ML 1100*	motor launch	30 April 1942
ML 126	motor launch	27 November 1943	*ML 1101*	motor launch	30 April 1942
ML 127	motor launch	22 November 1940	*MMS 8*	minesweeper	24 June 1944
ML 129	motor launch	22 March 1942	*MMS 39*	minesweeper	7 August 1941
ML 130	motor launch	7 May 1942	*MMS 51*	minesweeper	4 March 1942
ML 132	motor launch	22 March 1942	*MMS 55*	minesweeper	10 July 1944
ML 133	motor launch	11 May 1943	*MMS 68*	minesweeper	4 February 1945
ML 144	motor launch	22 September 1941	*MMS 70*	minesweeper	24 September 1943
ML 156	motor launch	28 March 1942	*MMS 89*	minesweeper	12 May 1943
ML 160	motor launch	6 May 1942	*MMS 93*	minesweeper	14 February 1942
ML 169	motor launch	15 February 1942	*MMS 94*	minesweeper	14 February 1942
ML 177	motor launch	28 March 1942	*MMS 95*	minesweeper	26 December 1941
ML 183	motor launch	11 February 1945	*MMS 96*	minesweeper	26 December 1941
ML 192	motor launch	28 March 1942	*MMS 101*	minesweeper	29 November 1944
ML 196	motor launch	29 August 1922	*MMS 117*	minesweeper	1 September 1944
ML 216	motor launch	28 September 1944	*MMS 123*	minesweeper	26 December 1941
ML 219	motor launch	21 November 1941	*MMS 124*	minesweeper	26 December 1941
ML 230	motor launch	17 August 1945	*MMS 125*	minesweeper	14 February 1942
ML 242	motor launch	29 November 1942	*MMS 126*	minesweeper	14 February 1942
ML 251	motor launch	6 March 1943	*MMS 127*	minesweeper	14 February 1942
ML 262	motor launch	28 March 1942	*MMS 128*	minesweeper	14 February 1942
ML 265	motor launch	1 July 1944	*MMS 147*	minesweeper	March 1942
ML 267	motor launch	28 March 1942	*MMS 153*	minesweeper	March 1942
ML 268	motor launch	28 March 1942	*MMS 156*	minesweeper	March 1942
ML 270	motor launch	28 March 1942	*MMS 161*	minesweeper	March 1942
ML 287 (i)	motor launch	28 February 1926	*MMS 162*	minesweeper	March 1942
ML 287 (ii)	motor launch	1 July 1944	*MMS 163*	minesweeper	March 1942
ML 288	motor launch	11 October 1941	*MMS 164*	minesweeper	March 1942
ML 298	motor launch	28 March 1942	*MMS 168*	minesweeper	25 June 1945
ML 301	motor launch	9 August 1942	*MMS 170*	minesweeper	12 October 1944
ML 306	motor launch	28 March 1942	*MMS 180*	minesweeper	13 February 1942
ML 307	motor launch	23 January 1925	*MMS 229*	minesweeper	13 June 1944
ML 310	motor launch	14 February 1942	*MMS 248*	minesweeper	30 January 1945
ML 311	motor launch	15 February 1942	*MMS 257*	minesweeper	11 December 1944
ML 339	motor launch	7 October 1942	*MMS 278*	minesweeper	14 September 1944
ML 352	motor launch	14 September 1942	*MMS 1019*	minesweeper	2 July 1944
ML 353	motor launch	14 September 1942	*MMS 1534*	minesweeper	2 June 1952
ML 358	motor launch	12 November 1943	*MMS 1558*	minesweeper	17 April 1954
ML 387	motor launch	1 March 1944	*MMS 1788*	minesweeper	21 October 1952
ML 430	motor launch	14 August 1944			

Name	Type	Date of loss	Name	Type	Date of loss
Moa	minesweeper	7 April 1943	MTB 248	motor torpedo boat	28 May 1944
Mohawk	destroyer	16 April 1941	MTB 255	motor torpedo boat	14 February 1945
Mollusc	yacht	17 March 1941	MTB 259	motor torpedo boat	14 June 1942
Monarda	drifter	8 November 1941	MTB 261	motor torpedo boat	26 August 1945
Montenol	oiler	21 May 1942	MTB 262	motor torpedo boat	24 February 1943
Moor	mooring vessel	8 April 1941	MTB 264	motor torpedo boat	10 May 1943
Moorberry	mooring vessel	26 December 1941	MTB 266	motor torpedo boat	31 March 1944
Moorview	mooring vessel	24 March 1920	MTB 267	motor torpedo boat	2 April 1943
Moorwind	mooring vessel	15 February 1942	MTB 284	motor torpedo boat	10 September 1943
Moravia	trawler	14 March 1943	MTB 285	motor torpedo boat	10 September 1943
Moray	trawler	13 March 1943	MTB 287	motor torpedo boat	24 November 1944
Mosquito	river gunboat	1 June 1940	MTB 288	motor torpedo boat	22 July 1943
Moth	river gunboat	12 December 1941	MTB 308	motor torpedo boat	14 September 1942
Mourne	frigate	15 June 1944	MTB 310	motor torpedo boat	14 September 1942
MTB 6	motor torpedo boat	16 November 1939	MTB 311	motor torpedo boat	2 May 1943
MTB 7	motor torpedo boat	26 December 1941	MTB 312	motor torpedo boat	14 September 1942
MTB 8	motor torpedo boat	16 December 1941	MTB 314	motor torpedo boat	14 September 1942
MTB 9	motor torpedo boat	26 December 1941	MTB 316	motor torpedo boat	17 July 1943
MTB 10	motor torpedo boat	26 December 1941	MTB 338	motor torpedo boat	16 May 1942
MTB 11	motor torpedo boat	26 December 1941	MTB 347	motor torpedo boat	1 October 1944
MTB 12	motor torpedo boat	19 December 1941	MTB 352	motor torpedo boat	16 March 1944
MTB 15	motor torpedo boat	24 September 1940	MTB 356	motor torpedo boat	16 October 1943
MTB 16	motor torpedo boat	31 October 1940	MTB 357	motor torpedo boat	24 December 1943
MTB 17	motor torpedo boat	21 October 1940	MTB 360	motor torpedo boat	1 October 1944
MTB 26	motor torpedo boat	19 December 1941	MTB 371	motor torpedo boat	24 November 1944
MTB 27	motor torpedo boat	26 December 1941	MTB 372	motor torpedo boat	24 July 1944
MTB 28	motor torpedo boat	7 March 1941	MTB 412	motor torpedo boat	27 July 1944
MTB 29	motor torpedo boat	6 October 1942	MTB 417	motor torpedo boat	9 March 1944
MTB 30	motor torpedo boat	18 December 1942	MTB 430	motor torpedo boat	27 July 1944
MTB 41	motor torpedo boat	14 February 1941	MTB 434	motor torpedo boat	9 July 1944
MTB 43	motor torpedo boat	18 August 1942	MTB 438	motor torpedo boat	14 February 1945
MTB 44	motor torpedo boat	7 August 1942	MTB 444	motor torpedo boat	14 February 1945
MTB 47	motor torpedo boat	17 January 1942	MTB 448	motor torpedo boat	11 June 1944
MTB 61	motor torpedo boat	9 May 1943	MTB 459	motor torpedo boat	14 February 1945
MTB 63	motor torpedo boat	2 April 1943	MTB 460	motor torpedo boat	2 July 1944
MTB 64	motor torpedo boat	2 April 1943	MTB 461	motor torpedo boat	14 February 1945
MTB 67	motor torpedo boat	23 May 1941	MTB 462	motor torpedo boat	14 February 1945
MTB 68	motor torpedo boat	14 December 1941	MTB 463	motor torpedo boat	8 July 1844
MTB 73	motor torpedo boat	24 November 1943	MTB 465	motor torpedo boat	14 February 1945
MTB 74	motor torpedo boat	28 March 1942	MTB 466	motor torpedo boat	14 February 1945
MTB 77	motor torpedo boat	8 September 1943	MTB 494	motor torpedo boat	7 April 1945
MTB 87	motor torpedo boat	31 October 1942	MTB 605	motor torpedo boat	17 February 1945
MTB 93	motor torpedo boat	18 August 1944	MTB 606	motor torpedo boat	4 November 1943
MTB 105	motor torpedo boat	1 January 1943	MTB 622	motor torpedo boat	10 March 1943
MTB 106	motor torpedo boat	16 October 1940	MTB 633	motor torpedo boat	26 January 1946
MTB 108	motor torpedo boat	10 January 1941	MTB 634	motor torpedo boat	26 January 1946
MTB 201	motor torpedo boat	15 June 1942	MTB 636	motor torpedo boat	15 October 1943
MTB 213	motor torpedo boat	23 May 1941	MTB 637	motor torpedo boat	26 January 1946
MTB 214	motor torpedo boat	23 May 1941	MTB 638	motor torpedo boat	26 January 1946
MTB 215	motor torpedo boat	29 March 1942	MTB 639	motor torpedo boat	28 April 1943
MTB 216	motor torpedo boat	23 May 1941	MTB 640	motor torpedo boat	27 June 1944
MTB 217	motor torpedo boat	23 May 1941	MTB 642	motor torpedo boat	26 January 1946
MTB 218	motor torpedo boat	18 August 1942	MTB 643	motor torpedo boat	26 January 1946
MTB 220	motor torpedo boat	13 May 1942	MTB 655	motor torpedo boat	21 March 1945
MTB 222	motor torpedo boat	10 November 1943	MTB 658	motor torpedo boat	26 January 1946
MTB 230	motor torpedo boat	10 November 1943	MTB 659	motor torpedo boat	26 January 1946
MTB 237	motor torpedo boat	7 August 1942	MTB 665	motor torpedo boat	15 August 1943
MTB 241	motor torpedo boat	28 March 1944	MTB 666	motor torpedo boat	4 July 1944
MTB 242	motor torpedo boat	30 July 1945	MTB 669	motor torpedo boat	26 October 1943

Name	Type	Date of loss	Name	Type	Date of loss
MTB 670	motor torpedo boat	26 January 1946	*Odin*	submarine	14 June 1940
MTB 671	motor torpedo boat	24 April 1944	*Oleander*	oiler	8 June 1940
MTB 674	motor torpedo boat	26 January 1946	*Olna*	oiler	18 May 1941
MTB 681	motor torpedo boat	10 June 1944	*Olympus*	submarine	8 May 1942
MTB 686	motor torpedo boat	22 November 1943	*Oracle*	yacht	29 January 1944
MTB 690	motor torpedo boat	18 January 1945	*Orchis*	corvette	21 August 1944
MTB 697	motor torpedo boat	17 April 1945	*Orfasy*	trawler	22 October 1943
MTB 698	motor torpedo boat	26 January 1946	*Oriana*	tug	19 January 1948
MTB 700	motor torpedo boat	26 January 1946	*Ormonde*	trawler	16 February 1941
MTB 705	motor torpedo boat	23 March 1945	*Orpheus*	submarine	19 June 1940
MTB 707	motor torpedo boat	10 April 1944	*Oswald*	submarine	1 August 1940
MTB 708	motor torpedo boat	24 April 1944	*Oswaldian*	trawler	4 August 1940
MTB 710	motor torpedo boat	10 April 1945	*Othello*	boom defence vessel	11 April 1941
MTB 732	motor torpedo boat	5 May 1944	*Ottawa*	destroyer	13 September 1942
MTB 734	motor torpedo boat	26 June 1944	*Otter*	yacht	26 March 1941
MTB 776	motor torpedo boat	14 February 1945	*Ouse*	trawler	20 February 1941
MTB 782	motor torpedo boat	29 December 1944	*Ouzel*	yacht	3 November 1941
MTB 789	motor torpedo boat	14 February 1945	*Oxley*	submarine	10 September 1939
MTB 791	motor torpedo boat	14 February 1945	*P 32*	submarine	18 August 1941
MTB 798	motor torpedo boat	14 February 1945	*P 33*	submarine	18 August 1941
MTB 1023	motor torpedo boat	17 May 1953	*P 36*	submarine	1 April 1942
MTB 1030	motor torpedo boat	28 March 1952	*P 38*	submarine	23 February 1942
MTB 1602	motor torpedo boat	31 January 1952	*P 39*	submarine	26 March 1942
MTB 5001	motor torpedo boat	7 April 1945	*P 48*	submarine	25 December 1942
Mulgrave	minesweeper	8 October 1944	*P 222*	submarine	12 December 1942
Mundon	boom defence	27 April 1941	*P 311*	submarine	1 January 1943
Muria	tug	8 November 1940	*P 514*	submarine	21 June 1942
Murmansk	trawler	17 June 1940	*P 615*	submarine	18 April 1943
Myrtle	trawler	14 June 1940	*Pahlawan*	motor launch	15 February 1942
Nabob	escort aircraft carrier	22 August 1944	*Pakenham*	destroyer	16 April 1943
Naiad	cruiser	11 March 1942	*Pandora*	submarine	1 April 1942
Napia	tug	20 December 1939	*Panglima*	motor launch	13 February 1942
Narwhal	submarine	23 July 1940	*Panorama*	boom defence vessel	30 October 1942
Nautilus	drifter	29 May 1940	*Panther*	destroyer	9 October 1943
Neptune	cruiser	19 December 1941	*Parktown*	whaler	21 June 1942
Nereus	patrol vessel	2 July 1942	*Parramatta*	sloop	27 November 1941
Nestor	destroyer	16 June 1942	*Parthian*	submarine	1 August 1943
New Spray	drifter	3 January 1941	*Partridge*	destroyer	18 December 1942
Niger	minesweeper	5 July 1942	*Parvati*	patrol	30 April 1941
Nogi	trawler	23 June 1941	*Pathan*	sloop	23 June 1940
Nordnes	drifter	14 August 1943	*Pathfinder*	destroyer	11 February 1945
Northcoates	trawler	2 December 1944	*Patia*	fighter catapult ship	27 April 1941
Northern Isles	trawler	19 January 1945	*Patricia Cam*	store ship	22 January 1943
Northern Princess	trawler	8 March 1942	*Patroclus*	armed merchant cruiser	4 November 1940
Northern Rover	trawler	30 October 1939	*Paxton*	drifter	27 May 1940
Noss Head	drifter	9 September 1943	*Pellag II*	yacht	1 June 1940
Notmann	tender	11 January 1944	*Pelton*	trawler	24 December 1940
Notts County	trawler	8 March 1942	*Penelope*	cruiser	18 February 1944
NSC 101	service craft	27 October 1946	*Pengail*	motor launch	18 February 1942
Nyken	harbour tender	10 December 1941	*Pengawal*	tug	14 February 1942
Nyula	yacht	2 May 1941	*Penghambat*	motor launch	11 February 1942
Ocean Lassie	drifter	4 June 1940	*Peningat*	motor launch	14 February 1942
Ocean Retriever	drifter	22 September 1943	*Pentland Firth*	trawler	19 September 1942
Ocean Reward	drifter	28 May 1940	*Penylan*	escort destroyer	3 December 1942
Ocean Sunlight	drifter	13 June 1940	*Penzance*	sloop	24 August 1940
			Peridot	trawler	15 March 1940
			Perseus	submarine	6 December 1941
			Persevere	drifter	27 October 1940
			Perth	cruiser	1 March 1942

Name	Type	Date of loss
Peterel	river gunboat	8 December 1941
Petersfield	sloop	11 November 1931
Petronella	water boat	15 October 1944
Peuplier	tug	30 April 1941
Phineas Beard	trawler	8 December 1941
Phoenix	submarine	16 July 1940
Picotee	corvette	12 August 1941
Pierre		
Descalliers	trawler	13 August 1942
Pilot Vessel 4	examination vessel	29 November 1940
Pilot Vessel 10	examination vessel	7 June 1941
Pine	trawler	31 January 1944
Pink	corvette	27 June 1944
Pintail	corvette	10 June 1941
Placidas		
Faroult	gate vessel	1 November 1940
Plumleaf	oiler	4 April 1942
Poet Chaucer	tug	19 December 1941
Polly Johnson	trawler	29 May 1940
Polyanthus	corvette	20 September 1943
Porcupine	destroyer	9 December 1942
Porpoise	submarine	11 January 1945
Port Napier	minelayer	27 November 1940
Poseidon	submarine	9 June 1931
Pozarica	auxiliary A/A ship	13 February 1943
Prabhavati	patrol vessel	8 December 1941
Premier	drifter	3 February 1943
Prince Leopold	landing ship	29 July 1944
Prince of Wales	battleship	10 December 1941
Prince		
Philippe	raiding craft carrier	15 July 1941
Princess	yacht	11 January 1940
Princess		
Victoria	minelayer	18 May 1940
Proficient	drifter	19 December 1940
Promotive	armed drifter	23 December 1939
Prompt	minesweeper	9 May 1945
Puckeridge	destroyer	6 September 1943
Punjabi	destroyer	1 May 1942
Puriri	minesweeper	14 May 1941
Pylades	minesweeper	8 July 1944
Pyrope	trawler	12 August 1940
Quail	destroyer	18 June 1944
Queenworth	mine destructor vessel	9 May 1941
Quentin	destroyer	2 December 1942
Quorn	destroyer	3 August 1944
Raccoon	yacht	7 September 1942
Rahman	whaler	1 March 1942
Rainbow	submarine	4 October 1940
Rajputana	armed merchant cruiser	13 April 1941
Raleigh	cruiser	8 August 1922
Raub	trader	22 January 1942
Rawalpindi	armed merchant cruiser	23 November 1939
Ray of Hope	armed drifter	10 December 1939
Receptive	drifter	3 July 1941
Recoil	trawler	28 September 1940
Red Gauntlet	trawler	5 August 1943
Redmill	frigate	27 April 1945
Redstart	minelayer	19 December 1941

Name	Type	Date of loss
Reed	drifter	7 November 1940
Refundo	trawler	18 December 1940
Regent	submarine	18 April 1943
Regina	corvette	8 August 1944
Regulus (i)	submarine	6 December 1940
Regulus (ii)	minesweeper	12 January 1945
Relonzo	trawler	20 January 1941
Remillo	trawler	27 February 1941
Repulse	battlecruiser	10 December 1941
Resmilo	trawler	20 June 1941
Resolvo	trawler	12 October 1940
Resparko	trawler	20 August 1940
Reward	patrol vessel	10 August 1976
Rhodora	yacht	7 September 1940
Rhu	minelayer	14 February 1942
Riant	drifter	27 January 1940
Rifsnes	trawler	20 May 1940
Rinovia	trawler	2 November 1940
Ristango	boom defence vessel	14 November 1940
River Clyde	trawler	5 August 1940
Robert Bowen	trawler	9 February 1940
Robin	river gunboat	24 December 1941
Roche Bonne	trawler	7 April 1941
Rockingham	destroyer	27 September 1944
Rodino	trawler	24 July 1940
Roode Zee	tug	24 April 1944
Rosa	drifter	11 September 1943
Rosabelle	yacht	11 December 1941
Rosaura	armed boarding vessel	18 March 1941
Rose Valley	drifter	16 December 1943
Rosemonde	trawler	19 January 1942
Rowan Tree	drifter	21 November 1941
Royal Oak	battleship	14 October 1939
Royalo	trawler	1 September 1940
Rubens	trawler	13 February 1941
Ruby	harbour tender	9 October 1942
Rutlandshire	trawler	20 April 1940
Rysa	trawler	8 December 1943
Saguenay	destroyer	15 November 1942
Sahib	submarine	24 April 1943
St Abbs	tug	1 June 1940
St Achilleus	trawler	31 May 1940
St Angelo	tug	30 May 1942
St Apollo	trawler	22 November 1941
St Boswells	tug	10 June 1920
St Breock	tug	14 February 1942
St Briac	training/target	12 March 1942
St Cathan	trawler	11 April 1942
St Colomb	tug	16 January 1920
St Croix	destroyer	20 September 1943
St Cyrus	tug	22 January 1941
St Donats	trawler	1 March 1941
St Fagan	tug	1 June 1940
St Genny	tug	12 January 1930
St Goran	trawler	1 May 1940
St Issey	tug	28 December 1942
St Just	tug	15 February 1942
St Olaves	tug	21 September 1942
St Sampson	tug	7 March 1942

Name	Type	Date of loss
Salmon	submarine	9 July 1940
Salopian	armed merchant cruiser	13 May 1941
Salvage King	tug	12 September 1940
Salvia	corvette	23 December 1941
Salviking	salvage vessel	14 February 1944
Sambhur	whaler	5 May 1942
Samphire	corvette	30 January 1943
Santa	whaler	23 November 1943
Sappho	yacht	29 September 1940
Saracen	submarine	14 August 1943
Sargasso	yacht	6 June 1943
Sarna	whaler	25 February 1941
Saturnus	barrage balloon vessel	23 April 1941
Saucy	tug	4 September 1940
Saumarez	destroyer	22 September 1946
Scorpion	river gunboat	13 February 1942
Scotch Thistle	drifter	6 October 1940
Scotstoun	armed merchant cruiser	13 June 1940
Scott Harley	minesweeper	4 March 1942
Sea Angler	yacht	19 May 1941
Sea King	trawler	9 October 1940
Seagem	tug	30 October 1940
Seahorse	submarine	7 January 1940
Seal	submarine	5 May 1940
Sedgefly	trawler	16 December 1939
Senateur Duhamel	trawler	6 May 1942
Sesame	tug	13 June 1944
Sevra	whaler	6 November 1940
SGB 7	steam gun boat	19 June 1942
Shark	submarine	6 July 1940
Shashi III	yacht	7 September 1940
Shawinigan	corvette	24 November 1944
Sheffield	GMD	4 May 1982
Shera	whaler	9 March 1942
Shipmates	drifter	14 November 1940
Shu Kwang	auxiliary A/S	14 February 1942
Shun On	auxiliary patrol	26 January 1942
Shun Wo	auxiliary patrol	19 December 1941
Siang Wo	auxiliary A/S	13 February 1942
Sickle	submarine	14 June 1944
Sidon	submarine	18 June 1955
Siesta	patrol vessel	23 September 1942
Sikh	destroyer	14 September 1942
Silicia	trawler	8 May 1941
Silver Cloud	patrol vessel	12 July 1943
Silvia	yacht	15 February 1942
Simoom	submarine	30 November 1943
Sin Aik Lee	minesweeper	2 March 1942
Sindonis	trawler	29 May 1941
Sir Galahad	landing ship	8 June 1982
Sirocco	patrol vessel	26 January 1942
Sisapon	trawler	12 June 1940
Skeena	destroyer	25 October 1944
Skilful	tug	26 December 1941
Skipjack	minesweeper	1 June 1940
Skudd 3	whaler	27 August 1941
Slavol	oiler	26 March 1942
Snaefell	minesweeper	5 July 1941

Name	Type	Date of loss
Snapdragon	corvette	19 December 1942
Snapper	submarine	11 February 1941
Soizic	drifter	20 March 1941
Solomon	trawler	1 April 1942
Somali	destroyer	24 September 1942
Sona	yacht	4 June 1942
Sophie Marie	patrol vessel	1 March 1942
Sotra	whaler	29 January 1942
South Sea	trawler	19 December 1942
Southampton	cruiser	11 January 1941
Southern Floe	whaler	11 February 1941
Southern Flower	whaler	3 March 1945
Southern Pride	whaler	16 June 1944
Southsea	minesweeper	16 February 1941
Southwold	escort destroyer	24 March 1942
Spaniard	trawler	5 December 1942
Sparsholt	mooring lighter	13 March 1942
Spartan	cruiser	29 January 1944
Spearfish	submarine	1 August 1940
Speedy	destroyer	24 September 1922
Sphinx	minesweeper	3 February 1940
Spikenard	corvette	10 February 1942
Splendid	submarine	21 April 1943
Springbank	fighter catapult ship	27 September 1941
Squirrel	minesweeper	24 July 1945
Staghound	distilling	27 March 1942
Stanley	destroyer	19 December 1941
Star of Deveron	trawler	30 September 1941
Starfish (i)	submarine	9 January 1940
Starfish (ii)	patrol vessel	7 September 1943
Staunton	trawler	27 July 1940
Steady	mooring vessel	17 July 1940
Steady Hour	air-sea rescue	3 March 1945
Stella Capella	trawler	11 March 1942
Stella Dorado	trawler	1 June 1940
Stella Orion	trawler	11 November 1940
Stella Sirius	trawler	25 September 1940
Sterlet	submarine	18 April 1940
Stoke	minesweeper	7 May 1941
Stonehenge (i)	destroyer	1 November 1920
Stonehenge (ii)	submarine	5 March 1944
Stora	whaler	1 June 1941
Stratagem	submarine	22 November 1944
Strathborve	trawler	6 September 1941
Stronghold	destroyer	2 March 1942
Stronsay	trawler	5 February 1943
Sturdy	destroyer	30 October 1940
Sui Wo	accommodation ship	14 February 1942
Sulla	whaler	24 March 1942
Summer Rose	drifter	13 October 1940
Sun VII	tug	6 March 1941
Sun IX	tug	21 December 1940
Sundown	drifter	30 August 1939
Sunset	drifter	1 April 1942
Supporter	drifter	4 November 1944
Surf	yacht	6 April 1941

Name	Type	Date of loss
Surprise	yacht	28 February 1942
Sursum Corda	coaster	31 May 1940
Susarion	trawler	7 May 1941
Svana	whaler	8 April 1942
Swift	destroyer	24 June 1944
Sword Dance	trawler	5 July 1942
Swordfish	submarine	7 November 1940
Sydney	cruiser	19 November 1941
Syrtis	submarine	26 March 1944
Syvern	whaler	27 May 1941
Taikoo	tug	12 September 1941
Taitam	minesweeper	19 December 1941
Talisman	submarine	16 September 1942
Tamar	base ship	12 December 1941
Tamarisk	trawler	12 August 1940
Tanjong Penang	auxiliary	17 February 1942
Tanjore	trawler	June 1942
Tapah	minesweeper	17 February 1942
Tarpon	submarine	10 April 1940
Teme	frigate	29 March 1945
Tempest	submarine	14 February 1942
Tenedos	destroyer	5 April 1942
Terka	store ship	26 March 1945
Tern	river gunboat	19 December 1941
Terror	monitor	23 February 1941
Tervani	trawler	7 February 1943
Tetrach	submarine	27 October 1941
Texas	trawler	19 July 1944
Thalia	yacht	11 October 1942
Thames	submarine	3 August 1940
Thane	escort aircraft carrier	15 January 1945
Thanet	destroyer	27 January 1942
The Boys	drifter	14 November 1940
Thetis	submarine	1 June 1939
Thistle (i)	submarine	10 April 1940
Thistle (ii)	drifter	8 May 1941
Thomas Bartlett	trawler	28 May 1940
Thomas Connolly	trawler	17 December 1940
Thora	drifter	26 April 1943
Thorbryn	whaler	19 August 1941
Thorgrim	whaler	8 April 1942
Thorn	submarine	7 August 1942
Thracian	destroyer	16 December 1941
Thunderbolt	submarine	14 March 1943
Thuringia	trawler	28 May 1940
Tiberio	schooner	23 December 1941
TID 62	tug	20 September 1946
TID 97	tug	29 December 1962
Tien Hsing	tug	26 October 1943
Tien Kwang	auxiliary A/S	15 February 1942
Tigris	submarine	27 February 1943
Tilbury Ness	trawler	1 November 1940
Tobago	destroyer	12 November 1920
Token	drifter	21 December 1941
Tonbridge	net layer	22 August 1941
Topazes'	trawler	20 April 1941

Name	Type	Date of loss
Torbay II	drifter	1 November 1940
Torrent	yacht	6 April 1941
Tourmaline	trawler	5 February 1941
Trang	whaler	15 February 1942
Tranio	trawler	27 June 1941
Tranquil	trawler	16 June 1942
Transvaal	trawler	18 November 1944
Transylvania	armed merchant cruiser	10 August 1940
Traveller	submarine	1 December 1942
Treern	whaler	12 January 1945
Trentonian	corvette	22 February 1945
Triad	submarine	15 October 1940
Trinidad	cruiser	15 May 1942
Triton	submarine	6 December 1940
Triumph	submarine	2 January 1942
Trollope	frigate	6 July 1944
Trooper	submarine	16 October 1943
Truculent	submarine	12 January 1950
True Accord	drifter	26 December 1940
Trusty Star	drifter	10 June 1942
Tuna	store ship	13 July 1941
Tung Wo	examination vessel	13 December 1941
Tunisian	trawler	9 July 1942
Turbulent	submarine	22 March 1943
Tweed	frigate	7 January 1944
Twente	coaster	12 June 1940
Tynedale	destroyer	12 December 1943
Tynwald	anti-aircraft ship	12 November 1942
Uberous	drifter	11 January 1941
Uberty	drifter	8 May 1941
Ullswater	whaler	19 November 1942
Ulster Prince	store ship	25 April 1941
Umpire	submarine	19 July 1941
Unbeaten	submarine	11 November 1942
Undaunted	submarine	12 May 1941
Undine	submarine	7 January 1940
Unicity	drifter	31 January 1942
Union	submarine	20 July 1941
Unique	submarine	13 October 1942
Unity	submarine	29 April 1940
Untamed	submarine	30 May 1943
Upholder	submarine	14 April 1942
Urge	submarine	28 April 1942
Usk	submarine	26 April 1941
Usurper	submarine	30 October 1943
Ut Prosim	drifter	2 March 1943
Utmost	submarine	24 November 1942
Vaillant	tug	2 February 1942
Valdora	trawler	12 January 1940
Valentine	destroyer	15 May 1940
Valerian	sloop	22 October 1926
Valleyfield	frigate	6 May 1944
Vampire	destroyer	9 April 1942
Van Dyck	armed boarding steamer	10 June 1940
Van Meerlant	convoy escort	4 June 1941
Van Orley	trawler	4 May 1941
Vandal	submarine	24 February 1943
Vassiliki	tender	24 July 1942
Velia	trawler	19 October 1940

Name	Type	Date of loss
Venetia	destroyer	19 October 1940
Vervain	corvette	20 February 1945
Vestal	minesweeper	26 July 1945
Veteran	destroyer	26 September 1942
Victoria I	drifter	25 March 1942
Vidonia	trawler	7 October 1944
Viking	salvage vessel	6 April 1941
Vimiera	destroyer	9 January 1942
Vision	tug	18 June 1942
Viva II	yacht	8 May 1941
Vixen	tug	17 June 1942
Voltaire	armed merchant cruiser	4 April 1941
Vortigern	destroyer	15 March 1942
Voyager (i)	destroyer	25 September 1942
Voyager (ii)	destroyer	10 February 1964
Vyner Brook	armed trader	14 February 1942
Waglan	minesweeper	19 December 1941
Wakeful	destroyer	29 May 1940
Wallaroo	minesweeper	11 June 1943
Wallasea	trawler	6 January 1944
Walney	cutter	8 November 1942
Walpole	destroyer	6 January 1945
Walrus	destroyer	12 February 1938
War Diwan	oiler	16 December 1944
War Mehta	oiler	20 November 1941
War Sepoy	oiler	19 July 1940
War Sirdar	oiler	1 March 1942
Warland	trawler	18 February 1942
Warrior II	yacht	11 July 1940
Warwick	destroyer	20 February 1944
Warwick		
Deeping	trawler	12 October 1940
Warwickshire	trawler	30 April 1940
Washington	trawler	6 December 1939
Watcher	auxiliary	14 May 1945
Waterfly	trawler	17 September 1942
Watergate	boom defence vessel	19 December 1941
Waterhen	destroyer	30 June 1941
Wave	tug	26 December 1941
Waveflower	trawler	21 October 1940
Waverley	minesweeper	29 May 1940
Wayward	despatch vessel	11 November 1922
Welshman	minelayer	1 February 1943
Wessex	destroyer	24 May 1940
West Cocker	tug	9 April 1942
Westella	trawler	2 June 1940
Weyburn	corvette	22 February 1943
Whippet	whaler	4 October 1941
Whirlwind	destroyer	5 July 1940

Name	Type	Date of loss
Whitaker	frigate	1 November 1944
White Daisy	drifter	25 September 1940
White Fox II	yacht	27 August 1940
Whitley	destroyer	19 May 1940
Widnes	minesweeper	20 May 1941
Wild Swan	destroyer	17 June 1942
Willamette		
Valley	special service	29 June 1940
William		
Hallett	trawler	13 December 1939
William		
Stephens	trawler	25 October 1943
William		
Wesney	trawler	7 November 1940
William		
Willmot	trawler	9 September 1920
Wilna	yacht	24 March 1941
Windflower	corvette	7 December 1941
Winsome	drifter	18 November 1942
Wo Kwang	tug	5 March 1942
Woodpecker	sloop	27 February 1944
Woomera	armament carrier	11 October 1960
Wren	destroyer	27 July 1940
Wrestler	destroyer	7 June 1944
Wryneck	destroyer	27 April 1941
Wyoming	trawler	1 May 1944
X 5	midget submarine	22 September 1943
X 6	midget submarine	22 September 1943
X 7	midget submarine	22 September 1943
X 8	midget submarine	18 September 1943
X 9	midget submarine	16 September 1943
X 10	midget submarine	3 October 1943
X 22	midget submarine	7 February 1944
XE 11	midget submarine	6 March 1945
Xmas Rose	drifter	21 November 1940
Yampi Lass	lighter	11 April 1943
Yarra	sloop	4 March 1942
Yin Ping	tug	15 February 1942
York	cruiser	26 March 1941
Yorkshire Belle	yacht	11 April 1941
Young Ernie	drifter	18 April 1941
Young		
Fisherman	drifter	29 November 1940
Young Sid	drifter	10 August 1940
Ypres	trawler	12 May 1940
Zinnia	corvette	23 August 1941
Zulu	destroyer	14 September 1942
ZZ 12	minesweeper	5 May 1946
ZZ 16	minesweeper	September 1946

Index of Minor Amphibious Vessels Lost

Landing Barges

Type & Number	Date	Type & Number	Date
Landing barge		LBO 92	June 1945
LB 329	31 August 1942	LBO 95	June 1945
LB 382	30 September 1942	LBO 96	June 1945
LB 485	19 October 1942		
		Landing barge, ramped	
Landing barge, emergency repair		LBR 43	1 July 1944
LBE 8	20 June 1944	LBR 65	1 July 1944
LBE 12	June 1944	LBR 83	23 May 1944
LBE 17	21 June 1944	LBR 114	June 1945
LBE 20	June 1944		
LBE 25	25 June 1944	Landing barge, vehicle	
LBE 26	20 June 1944	LBV 1	May 1945
LBE 27	20 June 1944	LBV (1) 3	25 June 1944
LBE 32	June 1944	LBV (2) 3	17 September 1944
LBE 33	21 June 1944	LBV 5	May 1945
LBE 34	21 June 1944	LBV 9	2 November 1944
LBE 57	22 June 1944	LBV 11	17 September 1944
LBE 60	20 June 1944	LBV 15	17 September 1944
		LBV (1) 16	12 June 1944
Landing barge, kitchen		LBV (2) 16	2 November 1944
LBK 8	31 July 1945	LBV 19	29 July 1944
		LBV 20	June 1944
Landing barge, oiler		LBV 27	25 June 1944
LBO 4	17 August 1944	LBV 28	29 July 1944
LBO 5	14 July 1945	LBV 29	8 August 1944
LBO 10	25 June 1944	LBV 31	May 1945
LBO 11	June 1945	LBV 33	17 September 1944
LBO 13	June 1945	LBV 35	May 1945
LBO 17	20 January 1945	LBV 42	13 September 1944
LBO 21	June 1945	LBV (1) 49	12 June 1944
LBO 24	June 1945	LBV (2) 49	25 June 1944
LBO 26	June 1945	LBV 51	12 June 1944
LBO 30	31 August 1944	LBV 52	7 June 1944
LBO 37	June 1945	LBV 56	29 June 1944
LBO 46	25 June 1944	LBV 61	25 June 1944
LBO 50	June 1944	LBV 65	19 October 1942
LBO 53	7 June 1945	LBV 67	25 June 1944
LBO 56	2 November 1944	LBV 72	17 September 1944
LBO 63	17 September 1944	LBV 73	May 1945
LBO 68	13 August 1944	LBV 75	May 1945
LBO 69	17 September 1944	LBV 76	27 July 1944
LBO 73	14 June 1944	LBV 78	17 September 1944
LBO 77	June 1945	LBV 83	19 August 1944
LBO 79	17 September 1944	LBV 84	25 June 1944
LBO 82	June 1945	LBV 89	25 June 1944
LBO 84	25 June 1944	LBV 94	25 June 1944
LBO 87	11 July 1944	LBV 95	25 June 1944
LBO 88	17 September 1944	LBV 99	13 July 1945
LBO 90	10 July 1944	LBV 103	25 June 1944

Type & Number	Date	Type & Number	Date
LBV 116	19 June 1944	LBV 214	22 June 1944
LBV 118	May 1945	LBV 229	5 October 1943
LBV 121	9 July 1944	LBV (1) 232	19 September 1942
LBV 122	25 July 1944	LBV (2) 232	25 June 1944
LBV 123	21 November 1944	LBV 266	March 1944
LBV 132	29 July 1945	LBV 295	19 October 1942
LBV 136	February 1944	LBV 329	31 August 1942
LBV 137	17 September 1944	LBV 332	19 September 1942
LBV 140	11 July 1944	LBV 347	19 October 1942
LBV 149	February 1944	LBV 362	19 September 1942
LBV 152	May 1945	LBV 367	17 January 1944
LBV 154	14 August 1944	LBV 497	February 1944
LBV 157	17 September 1944		
LBV 170	May 1945	**Landing barge, water**	
LBV 172	25 June 1944	LBW 1	June 1944
LBV 175	9 July 1944	LBW 6	7 June 1944
LBV 176	25 June 1944	LBW 7	25 June 1944
LBV 206	25 June 1944	LBW 11	13 September 1944
LBV 209	25 June 1944	LBW 14	29 August 1944
LBV 211	17 September 1944	LBW 15	25 June 1944
LBV 212	May 1945		

Landing Craft, Assault

Type & Number	Date	Type & Number	Date
LCA 1	14 June 1940	LCA 78	June 1943
LCA 2	14 June 1940	LCA 79	31 August 1941
LCA 4	29 May 1940	LCA 80	31 August 1941
LCA 6	July 1940	LCA 81	31 August 1941
LCA 8	31 May 1940	LCA 87	31 August 1941
LCA 11	11 June 1940	LCA 92	19 August 1942
LCA 14	9 June 1940	LCA 94	19 August 1942
LCA 15	31 May 1940	LCA 97	19 August 1942
LCA 16	29 May 1940	LCA 102	19 August 1942
LCA 18	29 May 1940	LCA 105	31 August 1941
LCA 28	29 May 1941	LCA 112	17 June 1944
LCA 31	31 August 1941	LCA 113	31 August 1941
LCA 32	31 August 1941	LCA 119	July 1941
LCA 33	June 1944	LCA 121	24 December 1941
LCA 35	November 1942	LCA 128	November 1942
LCA 37	19 August 1942	LCA 130	May 1944
LCA 38	31 August 1941	LCA 135	November 1942
LCA 39	31 August 1941	LCA 138	June 1942
LCA 45	31 August 1941	LCA 146	June 1944
LCA 48	31 August 1941	LCA 149	16 November 1944
LCA 49	31 August 1941	LCA 153	November 1942
LCA 51	31 August 1941	LCA 166	19 April 1942
LCA 52	19 August 1942	LCA 167	14 November 1942
LCA 54	July 1944	LCA 169	14 November 1942
LCA 55	14 November 1942	LCA 171	6 June 1944
LCA 56	June 1944	LCA 176	14 November 1942
LCA 59	15 June 1944	LCA 182	June 1944
LCA 60	31 August 1941	LCA 183	17 June 1944
LCA 63	31 August 1941	LCA 187	14 November 1942
LCA 64	31 August 1941	LCA 188	14 November 1942
LCA 69	15 June 1944	LCA 189	14 November 1942
LCA 70	1941	LCA 192	19 August 1942
LCA 75	31 August 1941	LCA 193	20 June 1942

Type & Number	Date	Type & Number	Date
LCA 196	July 1942	LCA 375	14 November 1942
LCA 208	6 June 1944	LCA 382	22 January 1944
LCA 209	19 August 1942	LCA 383	June 1944
LCA 211	19 April 1942	LCA 387	June 1944
LCA 212	November 1943	LCA 394	22 January 1944
LCA 214	19 August 1942	LCA 398	22 January 1944
LCA 215	19 August 1942	LCA 400	17 June 1944
LCA 218	November 1942	LCA 401	6 June 1944
LCA 219	November 1942	LCA 409	6 June 1944
LCA 221	November 1942	LCA 417	22 January 1944
LCA 222	June 1943	LCA 418	June 1944
LCA 226	November 1942	LCA 423	November 1942
LCA 227	November 1942	LCA 424	June 1944
LCA 235	12 November 1942	LCA 428	22 January 1944
LCA 237	19 August 1942	LCA 431	June 1944
LCA 239	November 1942	LCA 433	22 January 1944
LCA 244	November 1942	LCA 434	June 1944
LCA 245	November 1942	LCA 436	November 1942
LCA 247	19 August 1942	LCA 440	22 January 1944
LCA 248	17 June 1944	LCA 442	June 1944
LCA 251	19 August 1942	LCA 446	29 August 1943
LCA 254	December 1944	LCA 447	November 1942
LCA 258	17 June 1944	LCA 451	November 1942
LCA 259	November 1942	LCA 458	6 June 1944
LCA 260	November 1942	LCA 459	May 1944
LCA 261	November 1942	LCA 462	6 June 1944
LCA 262	19 August 1942	LCA 463	June 1944
LCA 266	14 November 1942	LCA 476	June 1944
LCA 269	November 1942	LCA 485	June 1944
LCA 271	November 1942	LCA 487	22 January 1944
LCA 272	April 1943	LCA 492	May 1944
LCA 279	June 1944	LCA 494	June 1944
LCA 284	19 August 1942	LCA 496	June 1944
LCA 286	November 1942	LCA 503	June 1944
LCA 287	November 1942	LCA 505	November 1943
LCA 289	June 1944	LCA 509	June 1944
LCA 301	November 1942	LCA 518	June 1944
LCA 303	6 June 1944	LCA 519	June 1944
LCA 307	14 November 1942	LCA 520	June 1944
LCA 309	November 1942	LCA 522	June 1944
LCA 310	November 1942	LCA 525	June 1944
LCA 312	June 1943	LCA 526	May 1944
LCA 314	19 August 1942	LCA 530	6 June 1944
LCA 316	November 1943	LCA 535	June 1944
LCA 317	19 August 1942	LCA 540	June 1944
LCA 320	June 1944	LCA 545	November 1944
LCA 321	November 1942	LCA 551	7 November 1944
LCA 323	22 January 1944	LCA 552	9 February 1944
LCA 326	December 1944	LCA 553	2 December 1943
LCA 337	June 1944	LCA 566	June 1944
LCA 339	June 1944	LCA 573	May 1944
LCA 341	June 1944	LCA 577	September 1944
LCA 347	December 1944	LCA 579	6 June 1944
LCA 349	June 1944	LCA 581	June 1944
LCA 350	June 1944	LCA 584	6 June 1944
LCA 352	10 June 1944	LCA 586	6 June 1944
LCA 360	June 1944	LCA 588	June 1944
LCA 364	22 January 1944	LCA 589	June 1944
LCA 367	June 1944	LCA 590	6 June 1944

Type & Number	Date	Type & Number	Date
LCA 592	June 1944	LCA 803	June 1944
LCA 593	June 1944	LCA 808	June 1944
LCA 594	June 1944	LCA 809	June 1944
LCA 611	June 1944	LCA 810	June 1944
LCA 613	June 1944	LCA (HR) 811	2 April 1944
LCA 614	29 November 1944	LCA 812	28 June 1944
LCA 623	June 1944	LCA 813	29 November 1943
LCA 625	17 June 1944	LCA 814	June 1944
LCA 637	June 1944	LCA 815	June 1944
LCA 642	6 June 1942	LCA 817	2 November 1944
LCA 645	21 December 1943	LCA 821	June 1944
LCA 646	21 December 1943	LCA 825	June 1944
LCA 649	June 1944	LCA 827	June 1944
LCA 650	June 1944	LCA (HR) 829	28 February 1945
LCA 652	June 1944	LCA 831	2 November 1944
LCA 655	June 1944	LCA 835	June 1944
LCA 661	June 1944	LCA 841	22 April 1945
LCA 664	June 1944	LCA 843	2 November 1944
LCA 665	2 July 1944	LCA 845	29 January 1944
LCA (HR) 671	6 June 1944	LCA 848	28 September 1944
LCA (HR) 672	2 April 1944	LCA 849	June 1944
LCA 673	2 July 1944	LCA 853	June 1944
LCA 675	24 September 1943	LCA 857	June 1944
LCA 683	6 June 1944	LCA 859	June 1944
LCA (HR) 689	13 March 1944	LCA 860	June 1944
LCA (HR) 690	6 June 1944	LCA 865	19 January 1944
LCA 691	June 1944	LCA 867	June 1944
LCA 696	December 1944	LCA 869	6 June 1944
LCA 692	6 June 1944	LCA 870	June 1944
LCA 697	22 January 1944	LCA 871	June 1944
LCA 704	6 June 1944	LCA 879	June 1944
LCA 705	6 June 1944	LCA 881	June 1944
LCA 710	June 1944	LCA 886	6 June 1944
LCA 713	2 November 1944	LCA 900	June 1944
LCA 717	June 1944	LCA 903	June 1944
LCA 721	6 June 1944	LCA 908	1 March 1944
LCA 722	June 1944	LCA 911	June 1944
LCA 723	December 1943	LCA 913	June 1944
LCA 725	2 November 1944	LCA 914	June 1944
LCA 726	1 March 1944	LCA 918	June 1944
LCA 729	6 June 1944	LCA 919	June 1944
LCA 738	June 1944	LCA 920	June 1944
LCA 748	June 1944	LCA 929	June 1944
LCA 750	June 1944	LCA 931	28 June 1944
LCA 753	December 1944	LCA 933	June 1944
LCA 761	May 1944	LCA 946	June 1944
LCA 768	June 1944	LCA 949	June 1944
LCA 775	June 1944	LCA 958	June 1944
LCA 779	June 1944	LCA (HR) 961	6 June 1944
LCA 780	6 June 1944	LCA (HR) 962	6 June 1944
LCA 783	19 January 1944	LCA (HR) 963	6 June 1944
LCA 788	June 1944	LCA (HR) 965	June 1944
LCA 790	19 January 1944	LCA (HR) 968	6 June 1944
LCA 791	6 June 1944	LCA (HR) 969	6 June 1944
LCA 792	6 June 1944	LCA (HR) 972	6 June 1944
LCA 795	June 1944	LCA (HR) 977	6 June 1944
LCA 796	6 June 1944	LCA 978	6 June 1944
LCA 797	June 1944	LCA 984	June 1944
LCA 802	17 June 1944	LCA 998	June 1944

Type & Number	Date	Type & Number	Date
LCA 999	June 1944	LCA 1137	June 1944
LCA 1000	6 June 1944	LCA 1138	June 1944
LCA 1005	June 1944	LCA 1143	6 June 1944
LCA 1008	June 1944	LCA 1144	June 1944
LCA 1013	June 1944	LCA 1146	6 June 1944
LCA 1016	6 June 1944	LCA 1149	June 1944
LCA 1017	6 June 1944	LCA 1150	June 1944
LCA 1018	2 November 1944	LCA 1151	June 1944
LCA 1021	June 1944	LCA 1153	March 1945
LCA 1024	June 1944	LCA 1155	June 1944
LCA 1026	June 1944	LCA 1156	6 June 1944
LCA 1027	6 June 1944	LCA 1161	26 February 1945
LCA 1028	June 1944	LCA 1188	December 1944
LCA 1030	15 November 1944	LCA (OC) 1211	May 1945
LCA 1034	June 1944	LCA 1213	June 1944
LCA 1037	6 June 1944	LCA 1215	June 1944
LCA 1050	June 1944	LCA 1216	June 1944
LCA 1057	June 1944	LCA 1251	6 June 1944
LCA 1058	8 June 1944	LCA 1252	6 June 1944
LCA 1059	June 1944	LCA 1253	June 1944
LCA 1063	6 June 1944	LCA 1256	6 June 1944
LCA 1068	6 June 1944	LCA 1260	2 November 1944
LCA 1069	June 1944	LCA 1304	14 July 1944
LCA (HR)1072	June 1944	LCA 1338	20 June 1944
LCA 1074	June 1944	LCA 1339	June 1944
LCA 1079	2 November 1944	LCA 1340	6 June 1944
LCA 1082	June 1944	LCA 1341	6 June 1944
LCA 1086	June 1944	LCA 1343	June 1944
LCA 1088	June 1944	LCA 1346	April 1945
LCA 1091	June 1944	LCA 1372	June 1944
LCA 1093	6 June 1944	LCA 1378	26 September 1944
LCA 1096	6 June 1944	LCA 1379	6 June 1944
LCA (HR) 1106	6 June 1944	LCA 1381	June 1944
LCA 1108	6 June 1944	LCA 1382	6 June 1944
LCA 1112	March 1945	LCA 1383	6 June 1944
LCA 1114	6 June 1944	LCA 1393	3 July 1944
LCA 1125	2 November 1944	LCA 1396	April 1945
LCA 1129	June 1944	LCA 1433	27 March 1945
LCA 1131	6 June 1944	LCA 2086	24 January 1945
LCA 1132	June 1944		

Landing Craft Emergency Repair

Type & Number	Date	Type & Number	Date
LCE 1	October 1943	LCE 14	May 1944
LCE 5	May 1944	LCE 15	13 July 1944
LCE 9	October 1943	LCE 21	May 1944

Landing Craft Mechanised

Type & Number	Date	Type & Number	Date
LCM (1) 1	1941	LCM (1) 18	June 1940
LCM (1) 10	June 1940	LCM (1) 19	June 1940
LCM (1) 11	June 1940	LCM (1) 20	June 1940
LCM (1) 12	2 June 1940	LCM (1) 22	2 June 1940
LCM (1) 14	June 1940	LCM (1) 23	August 1942
LCM (1) 15	June 1940	LCM (1) 24	August 1942
LCM (1) 17	3 June 1940	LCM (1) 25	August 1942

Type & Number	Date	Type & Number	Date
LCM (1) 26	2 January 1943	LCM (1) 169	November 1942
LCM (1) 31	October 1942	LCM (1) 180	23 July 1944
LCM (1) 32	31 August 1941	LCM (1) 181	November 1943
LCM (1) 33	20 December 1943	LCM (1) 182	May 1944
LCM (1) 34	August 1942	LCM (1) 183	May 1944
LCM (1) 38	1 April 1942	LCM (1) 186	November 1942
LCM (1) 45	August 1942	LCM (1) 191	6 June 1944
LCM (1) 46	5 May 1942	LCM (1) 192	February 1944
LCM (1) 51	30 March 1942	LCM (1) 203	6 June 1944
LCM (1) 53	30 March 1942	LCM (1) 207	May 1944
LCM (1) 55	31 August 1941	LCM (1) 209	May 1944
LCM (1) 56	19 August 1942	LCM (1) 212	May 1944
LCM (1) 58	25 January 1943	LCM (1) 215	May 1944
LCM (1) 61	8 February 1943	LCM (1) 216	6 June 1944
LCM (1) 63	November 1942	LCM (1) 218	May 1944
LCM (1) 64	November 1942	LCM (1) 219	May 1944
LCM (1) 65	November 1942	LCM (1) 226	6 June 1944
LCM (1) 67	31 August 1941	LCM (1) 229	6 June 1944
LCM (1) 69	November 1942	LCM (1) 231	6 June 1944
LCM (1) 72	November 1942	LCM (1) 232	October 1943
LCM (1) 73	November 1942	LCM (1) 234	February 1944
LCM (1) 76	March 1944	LCM (1) 241	6 June 1944
LCM (1) 80	6 February 1943	LCM (1) 243	May 1944
LCM (1) 82	19 August 1941	LCM (1) 251	6 June 1944
LCM (1) 84	June 1942	LCM (1) 254	February 1944
LCM (1) 89	22 October 1942	LCM (1) 263	11 September 1944
LCM (1) 90	June 1942	LCM (1) 270	February 1945
LCM (1) 91	June 1944	LCM (1) 272	May 1944
LCM (1) 93	June 1942	LCM (1) 277	May 1944
LCM (1) 95	31 August 1941	LCM (1) 279	February 1944
LCM (1) 96	19 August 1941	LCM (1) 281	6 June 1944
LCM (1) 97	31 August 1941	LCM (1) 282	February 1944
LCM (1) 98	6 December 1942	LCM (1) 285	May 1944
LCM (1) 103	31 August 1941	LCM (1) 288	May 1944
LCM (1) 106	29 May 1941	LCM (1) 295	June 1944
LCM (1) 107	31 August 1941	LCM (1) 316	6 June 1944
LCM (1) 108	31 August 1941	LCM (1) 324	May 1944
LCM (1) 110	20 June 1942	LCM (1) 327	February 1944
LCM (1) 113	20 June 1942	LCM (1) 329	February 1944
LCM (1) 119	June 1942	LCM (1) 330	6 June 1944
LCM (1) 120	November 1942	LCM (1) 335	6 June 1944
LCM (1) 122	June 1942	LCM (1) 337	23 July 1944
LCM (1) 127	28 July 1944	LCM (1) 338	6 June 1944
LCM (1) 128	6 June 1944	LCM (1) 339	February 1945
LCM (1) 131	May 1944	LCM (1) 340	19 November 1944
LCM (1) 135	June 1942	LCM (1) 345	23 July 1944
LCM (1) 136	February 1945	LCM (1) 346	6 June 1944
LCM (1) 137	June 1942	LCM (1) 348	6 June 1944
LCM (1) 138	7 July 1944	LCM (1) 354	June 1945
LCM (1) 139	20 November 1942	LCM (1) 355	6 June 1944
LCM (1) 140	June 1942	LCM (1) 357	6 June 1944
LCM (1) 145	20 June 1942	LCM (1) 359	February 1945
LCM (1) 146	20 June 1942	LCM (1) 367	February 1944
LCM (1) 147	November 1942	LCM (1) 377	6 June 1944
LCM (1) 148	20 June 1942	LCM (1) 381	7 June 1944
LCM (1) 153	November 1942	LCM (1) 382	6 June 1944
LCM (1) 161	November 1942	LCM (1) 383	6 June 1944
LCM (1) 165	6 June 1944	LCM (1) 408	6 June 1944
LCM (1) 168	23 July 1944	LCM (1) 409	6 June 1944

Type & Number	Date	Type & Number	Date
LCM (1) 419	6 June 1944	LCM (3) 613	14 October 1942
LCM (1) 421	6 June 1944	LCM (3) 618	9 August 1944
LCM (1) 422	February 1945	LCM (3) 620	13 October 1942
LCM (1) 424	19 November 1944	LCM (3) 623	22 January 1944
LCM (1) 425	6 June 1944	LCM (3) 624	November 1942
LCM (1) 443	6 June 1944	LCM (3) 627	6 June 1944
LCM (1) 444	6 June 1944	LCM (3) 628	6 June 1944
LCM (1) 466	6 June 1944	LCM (3) 631	6 June 1944
LCM (1) 493	June 1945	LCM (3) 632	14 October 1942
LCM (3) 501	August 1942	LCM (3) 633	14 October 1942
LCM (3) 508	13 October 1942	LCM (3) 634	14 October 1942
LCM (3) 509	13 October 1942	LCM (3) 635	November 1942
LCM (3) 510	August 1942	LCM (3) 636	14 October 1942
LCM (3) 516	August 1942	LCM (3) 640	9 August 1940
LCM (3) 518	November 1942	LCM (3) 641	6 June 1944
LCM (3) 519	13 October 1942	LCM (3) 650	December 1944
LCM (3) 520	November 1942	LCM (3) 907	December 1944
LCM (3) 522	13 October 1942	LCM (3) 908	6 June 1944
LCM (3) 523	13 October 1942	LCM (3) 910	22 January 1944
LCM (3) 525	December 1944	LCM (3) 923	11 November 1943
LCM (3) 527	May 1944	LCM (3) 929	6 June 1944
LCM (3) 528	November 1942	LCM (3) 930	22 January 1944
LCM (3) 531	6 June 1944	LCM (3) 938	October 1943
LCM (3) 532	13 October 1942	LCM (3) 1011	March 1944
LCM (3) 534	May 1944	LCM (3) 1022	22 January 1944
LCM (3) 535	6 June 1944	LCM (3) 1029	May 1944
LCM (3) 537	13 October 1942	LCM (3) 1044	October 1943
LCM (3) 539	November 1942	LCM (3) 1045	May 1944
LCM (3) 540	May 1944	LCM (3) 1053	23 July 1944
LCM (3) 543	November 1942	LCM (3) 1059	6 June 1944
LCM (3) 545	October 1945	LCM (3) 1062	6 June 1944
LCM (3) 547	13 October 1942	LCM (3) 1064	22 January 1944
LCM (3) 551	November 1942	LCM (3) 1071	May 1944
LCM (3) 555	November 1942	LCM (3) 1083	May 1944
LCM (3) 556	November 1942	LCM (3) 1088	6 June 1944
LCM (3) 558	November 1942	LCM (3) 1092	5 June 1945
LCM (3) 559	December 1944	LCM (3) 1098	6 June 1944
LCM (3) 564	November 1942	LCM (3) 1101	15 November 1944
LCM (3) 567	November 1942	LCM (3) 1108	6 June 1944
LCM (3) 568	6 June 1944	LCM (3) 1115	June 1944
LCM (3) 569	November 1942	LCM (3) 1120	6 June 1944
LCM (3) 571	November 1942	LCM (3) 1123	May 1944
LCM (3) 572	November 1942	LCM (3) 1127	6 June 1944
LCM (3) 574	6 June 1944	LCM (3) 1128	7 June 1944
LCM (3) 577	6 June 1944	LCM (3) 1130	June 1944
LCM (3) 581	November 1942	LCM (3) 1131	23 January 1944
LCM (3) 583	November 1943	LCM (3) 1139	6 June 1944
LCM (3) 584	November 1942	LCM (3) 1145	6 June 1944
LCM (3) 587	6 June 1944	LCM (3) 1146	23 July 1944
LCM (3) 588	May 1944	LCM (3) 1161	23 July 1944
LCM (3) 590	November 1942	LCM (3) 1165	15 September 1943
LCM (3) 591	December 1944	LCM (3) 1171	May 1944
LCM (3) 592	November 1942	LCM (3) 1173	22 January 1944
LCM (3) 593	November 1942	LCM (3) 1175	23 July 1944
LCM (3) 595	November 1942	LCM (3) 1182	October 1943
LCM (3) 596	November 1942	LCM (3) 1185	July 1945
LCM (3) 606	November 1942	LCM (3) 1189	6 June 1944
LCM (3) 609	November 1942	LCM (3) 1195	9 June 1944
LCM (3) 611	14 October 1942	LCM (3) 1197	23 July 1944

Type & Number	Date	Type & Number	Date
LCM (3) 1200	6 June 1944	LCM (3) 1278	23 July 1944
LCM (3) 1204	22 January 1944	LCM (3) 1282	6 June 1944
LCM (3) 1205	May 1944	LCM (3) 1293	6 June 1944
LCM (3) 1207	6 June 1944	LCM (3) 1297	6 June 1944
LCM (3) 1208	6 June 1944	LCM (3) 1313	April 1944
LCM (3) 1212	6 June 1944	LCM (3) 1314	April 1944
LCM (3) 1220	6 June 1944	LCM (3) 1319	April 1945
LCM (3) 1221	6 June 1944	LCM (3) 1327	April 1945
LCM (3) 1227	23 July 1944	LCM (3) 1373	April 1944
LCM (3) 1232	23 July 1944	LCM (3) 1378	April 1944
LCM (3) 1233	6 June 1944	LCM (3) 1380	May 1944
LCM (3) 1240	6 June 1944	LCM (3) 1381	May 1944
LCM (3) 1244	7 June 1944	LCM (3) 1397	6 June 1944

Landing Craft, Personnel, Large

Type & Number	Date	Type & Number	Date
LCP (L) 7	6 October 1944	LCP (L) 98	6 June 1944
LCP (L) 8	May 1944	LCP (L) 106	4 March 1943
LCP (L) 11	18 January 1944	LCP (L) 107	May 1941
LCP (L) 13	6 June 1944	LCP (L) 108	May 1941
LCP (L) 14	6 June 1944	LCP (L) 109	May 1941
LCP (L) 17	3 January 1943	LCP (L) 110	6 June 1944
LCP (L) 18	6 October 1944	LCP (L) 117	30 March 1942
LCP (L) 21	6 June 1944	LCP (L) 126	August 1943
LCP (L) 22	6 June 1944	LCP (L) 127	2 November 1944
LCP (L) 23	6 June 1944	LCP (L) 132	6 June 1944
LCP (L) 24	1941	LCP (L) 133	5 November 1944
LCP (L) 25	1941	LCP (L) 134	2 November 1944
LCP (L) 26	1941	LCP (L) 136	8 December 1943
LCP (L) 27	1941	LCP (L) 137	6 June 1944
LCP (L) 29	15 September 1942	LCP (L) 138	November 1942
LCP (L) 30	21 December 1940	LCP (L) 139	6 June 1944
LCP (L) 36	24 December 1942	LCP (L) 145	6 June 1944
LCP (L) 38	1941	LCP (L) 146	6 June 1944
LCP (L) 40	6 June 1944	LCP (L) 149	6 June 1944
LCP (L) 42	19 August 1942	LCP (L) 152	24 February 1944
LCP (L) 45	19 August 1942	LCP (L) 157	19 August 1942
LCP (L) 51	6 June 1944	LCP (L) 162	6 June 1944
LCP (L) 52	11 October 1944	LCP (L) 163	6 June 1944
LCP (L) 53	19 June 1944	LCP (L) 164	19 August 1942
LCP (L) 57	30 March 1942	LCP (L) 170	6 June 1944
LCP (L) 59	2 September 1941	LCP (L) 174	19 August 1942
LCP (L) 63	31 August 1941	LCP (L) 175	6 June 1944
LCP (L) 64	20 June 1942	LCP (L) 176	8 June 1944
LCP (L) 65	30 June 1942	LCP (L) 180	1 January 1942
LCP (L) 66	22 January 1944	LCP (L) 181	1 January 1942
LCP (L) 71	2 September 1941	LCP (L) 182	1 January 1942
LCP (L) 80	15 January 1943	LCP (L) 183	1 January 1942
LCP (L) 81	19 August 1942	LCP (L) 184	1 January 1942
LCP (L) 82	1941	LCP (L) 185	1 January 1942
LCP (L) 83	2 September 1942	LCP (L) 187	6 June 1944
LCP (L) 84	6 June 1944	LCP (L) 189	6 June 1944
LCP (L) 85	6 June 1944	LCP (L) 193	31 December 1941
LCP (L) 87	25 January 1943	LCP (L) 194	31 December 1941
LCP (L) 88	6 June 1944	LCP (L) 197	6 June 1944
LCP (L) 93	10 July 1942	LCP (L) 198	6 June 1944
LCP (L) 97	6 June 1944	LCP (L) 199	6 June 1944

Type & Number	Date	Type & Number	Date
LCP (L) 200	6 June 1944	LCP (L) 303	7 June 1944
LCP (L) 203	January 1943 (?)	LCP (L) 304	7 June 1944
LCP (L) 204	January 1943 (?)	LCP (L) 305	July 1944
LCP (L) 205	January 1943 (?)	LCP (L) 308	July 1944
LCP (L) 206	January 1943 (?)	LCP (L) 309	6 June 1944
LCP (L) 208	6 June 1944	LCP (L) 310	July 1944
LCP (L) 209	6 November 1942	LCP (L) 312	6 June 1944
LCP (L) 210	19 August 1942	LCP (L) 316	12 September 1943
LCP (L) 212	19 August 1942	LCP (L) 323	14 April 1944
LCP (L) 229	July 1944	LCP (L) 325	4 September 1943
LCP (L) 230	6 June 1944	LCP (L) 344	29 May 1945
LCP (L) 231	6 June 1944	LCP (L) 348	15 September 1944
LCP (L) 232	6 June 1944	LCP (L) 356	22 January 1944
LCP (L) 233	6 June 1944	LCP (L) 360	April 1944
LCP (L) 235	6 June 1944	LCP (L) 367	April 1944
LCP (L) 238	6 June 1944	LCP (L) 373	22 January 1944
LCP (L) 239	6 June 1944	LCP (L) 378	29 May 1945
LCP (L) 241	6 June 1944	LCP (L) 507	November 1942
LCP (L) 242	6 June 1944	LCP (L) 528	6 June 1944
LCP (L) 246	6 June 1944	LCP (L) 540	December 1944
LCP (L) 247	6 June 1944	LCP (L) 541	28 February 1944
LCP (L) 263	May 1944	LCP (L) 543	November 1942
LCP (L) 267	8 July 1944	LCP (L) 544	12 November 1942
LCP (L) 269	6 June 1944	LCP (L) 550	November 1942
LCP (L) 272	6 June 1944	LCP (L) 556	6 June 1944
LCP (L) 276	March 1943	LCP (L) 560	November 1942
LCP (L) 277	March 1943	LCP (L) 562	November 1942
LCP (L) 280	6 June 1944	LCP (L) 565	November 1942
LCP (L) 282	6 June 1944	LCP (L) 566	November 1942
LCP (L) 285	6 June 1944	LCP (L) 568	November 1942
LCP (L) 286	6 June 1944	LCP (L) 573	November 1942
LCP (L) 287	May 1944	LCP (L) 575	November 1942
LCP (L) 289	6 June 1944	LCP (L) 576	November 1942
LCP (L) 293	6 June 1944	LCP (L) 577	May 1944
LCP (L) 294	6 June 1944	LCP (L) 578	13 December 1942
LCP (L) 298	13 June 1944	LCP (L) 617	15 September 1942
LCP (L) 299	7 June 1944	LCP (L) 683	July 1944
LCP (L) 300	July 1944	LCP (L) 760	December 1944
LCP (L) 302	5 November 1944	LCP (L) 764	18 March 1945

Landing Craft Personnel Medium

Type & Number	Date
LCP (M) 14	November 1943
LCP (M) 17	5 January 1943

Landing Craft Personnel Ramped

Type & Number	Date	Type & Number	Date
LCP (R) 584	May 1944	LCP (R) 640	December 1944
LCP (R) 603	November 1942	LCP (R) 643	May 1944
LCP (R) 613	22 December 1943	LCP (R) 652	December 1944
LCP (R) 614	May 1944	LCP (R) 661	22 December 1943
LCP (R) 616	22 January 1944	LCP (R) 663	May 1944
LCP (R) 620	November 1942	LCP (R) 673	4 March 1943
LCP (R) 622	24 September 1942	LCP (R) 680	4 March 1943
LCP (R) 629	November 1942	LCP (R) 684	4 March 1943
LCP (R) 634	May 1944	LCP (R) 685	4 March 1943

Type & Number	Date	Type & Number	Date
LCP (R) 689	4 March 1943	LCP (R) 892	6 June 1944
LCP (R) 692	4 March 1943	LCP (R) 895	2 July 1944
LCP (R) 693	4 March 1943	LCP (R) 896	6 June 1944
LCP (R) 707	22 February 1945	LCP (R) 901	November 1942
LCP (R) 721	November 1942	LCP (R) 905	19 June 1944
LCP (R) 723	June 1944	LCP (R) 909	November 1942
LCP (R) 727	4 March 1943	LCP (R) 912	May 1944
LCP (R) 735	December 1944	LCP (R) 913	May 1944
LCP (R) 738	9 April 1944	LCP (R) 965	July 1945
LCP (R) 753	19 December 1943	LCP (R) 966	June 1944
LCP (R) 759	November 1942	LCP (R) 970	June 1944
LCP (R) 769	June 1943	LCP (R) 971	28 July 1944
LCP (R) 771	19 December 1943	LCP (R) 978	December 1944
LCP (R) 780	17 April 1943	LCP (R) 979	5 March 1945
LCP (R) 781	14 February 1944	LCP (R) 982	December 1944
LCP (R) 782	17 April 1943	LCP (R) 987	December 1944
LCP (R) 783	November 1942	LCP (R) 989	December 1944
LCP (R) 794	November 1942	LCP (R) 991	December 1944
LCP (R) 795	19 December 1943	LCP (R) 993	December 1944
LCP (R) 805	November 1944	LCP (R) 995	May 1944
LCP (R) 806	November 1944	LCP (R) 999	26 September 1944
LCP (R) 824	May 1944	LCP (R) 1008	August 1942
LCP (R) 832	June 1945	LCP (R) 1009	November 1942
LCP (R) 837	November 1942	LCP (R) 1011	21 October 1944
LCP (R) 840	28 March 1945	LCP (R) 1012	August 1942
LCP (R) 844	May 1944	LCP (R) 1018	26 January 1944
LCP (R) 850	November 1942	LCP (R) 1019	28 September 1943
LCP (R) 854	June 1944	LCP (R) 1023	December 1944
LCP (R) 858	12 November 1942	LCP (R) 1026	23 March 1944
LCP (R) 866	14 April 1944	LCP (R) 1029	November 1942
LCP (R) 867	June 1944	LCP (R) 1035	22 December 1943
LCP (R) 879	12 September 1943	LCP (R) 1036	November 1942

Landing Craft Personnel Small

Type & Number	Date	Type & Number	Date
LCP (S) 1	December 1944	LCP (S) 101	May 1944
LCP (S) 9	6 April 1944	LCP (S) 116	22 December 1943
LCP (S) 25	May 1944	LCP (S) 129	10 November 1944
LCP (S) 50	May 1944	LCP (S) 135	May 1944
LCP (S) 60	25 January 1944	LCP (S) 136	6 June 1944
LCP (S) 61	May 1944	LCP (S) 137	May 1944
LCP (S) 73	May 1944	LCP (S) 154	June 1944
LCP (S) 74	May 1944	LCP (S) 183	July 1944
LCP (S) 76	13 March 1944		

Landing Craft Personnel Mark 2

Type & Number	Date
LCP (2) 1110	May 1945
LCP (2) 1113	June 1945
LCP (2) 1121	May 1945

Landing Craft Support Medium

Type & Number	Date	Type & Number	Date
LCS (M) 1	1941	LCS (M) 49	December 1944
LCS (M) 4	20 June 1942	LCS (M) 54	1 July 1944
LCS (M) 6	20 June 1942	LCS (M) 59	May 1944
LCS (M) 9	19 August 1942	LCS (M) 69	3 March 1944
LCS (M) 11	November 1942	LCS (M) 75	6 June 1944
LCS (M) 14	22 November 1942	LCS (M) 76	20 June 1944
LCS (M) 15	20 June 1942	LCS (M) 78	8 June 1944
LCS (M) 16	29 August 1943	LCS (M) 80	20 June 1944
LCS (M) 17	25 April 1943	LCS (M) 81	20 June 1944
LCS (M) 18	20 June 1942	LCS (M) 83	6 June 1944
LCS (M) 19	20 June 1942	LCS (M) 91	6 June 1944
LCS (M) 22	20 June 1942	LCS (M) 99	6 June 1944
LCS (M) 23	30 March 1943	LCS (M) 101	6 June 1944
LCS (M) 28	November 1942	LCS (M) 103	20 June 1944
LCS (M) 30	June 1945	LCS (M) 108	20 June 1944
LCS (M) 42	17 June 1944	LCS (M) 110	22 June 1944
LCS (M) 44	17 June 1944	LCS (M) 114	20 June 1944
LCS (M) 46	22 January 1944	LCS (M) 148	June 1945
LCS (M) 47	6 June 1944		

Landing Craft Vehicle

Type & Number	Date	Type & Number	Date
LCV 579	13 December 1942	LCV 801	18 October 1944
LCV 584	15 March 1943	LCV 802	2 August 1945
LCV 597	12 September 1942	LCV 814	30 January 1945
LCV 719	June 1944	LCV 816	29 August 1944
LCV 752	30 December 1942	LCV 825	21 May 1943
LCV 754	30 December 1942	LCV 894	February 1944
LCV 798	24 September 1942		

Landing Craft Vehicle & Personnel

Type & Number	Date	Type & Number	Date
LCVP 1016	6 June 1944	LCVP 1104	6 June 1944
LCVP 1029	6 June 1944	LCVP 1106	6 June 1944
LCVP 1031	6 June 1944	LCVP 1108	7 June 1944
LCVP 1033	6 June 1944	LCVP 1111	6 June 1944
LCVP 1040	1 November 1943	LCVP 1114	6 June 1944
LCVP 1044	6 June 1944	LCVP 1117	26 June 1944
LCVP 1045	6 June 1944	LCVP 1120	6 June 1944
LCVP 1046	6 June 1944	LCVP 1121	6 June 1944
LCVP 1049	6 June 1944	LCVP 1122	22 June 1944
LCVP 1054	6 June 1944	LCVP 1124	6 June 1944
LCVP 1056	6 June 1944	LCVP 1129	6 June 1944
LCVP 1062	6 June 1944	LCVP 1132	6 June 1944
LCVP 1065	6 June 1944	LCVP 1133	6 June 1944
LCVP 1066	February 1944	LCVP 1139	6 June 1944
LCVP 1084	6 June 1944	LCVP 1146	6 June 1944
LCVP 1088	6 June 1944	LCVP 1153	6 June 1944
LCVP 1093	6 June 1944	LCVP 1155	6 June 1944
LCVP 1098	6 June 1944	LCVP 1157	6 June 1944
LCVP 1101	6 June 1944	LCVP 1159	6 June 1944
LCVP 1102	6 June 1944	LCVP 1165	6 June 1944
LCVP 1103	20 November 1944	LCVP 1167	15 July 1945

Type & Number	Date	Type & Number	Date
LCVP 1170	6 June 1944	LCVP 1230	7 June 1944
LCVP 1171	6 June 1944	LCVP 1242	6 June 1944
LCVP 1172	6 June 1944	LCVP 1245	6 June 1944
LCVP 1184	6 June 1944	LCVP 1246	6 June 1944
LCVP 1188	6 June 1944	LCVP 1248	6 June 1944
LCVP 1191	30 January 1945	LCVP 1249	6 June 1944
LCVP 1199	25 November 1944	LCVP 1251	6 June 1944
LCVP 1201	6 June 1944	LCVP 1255	6 June 1944
LCVP 1204	6 June 1944	LCVP 1260	6 June 1944
LCVP 1211	6 June 1944	LCVP 1262	6 June 1944
LCVP 1216	6 June 1944	LCVP 1264	6 June 1944
LCVP 1218	14 June 1944	LCVP 1288	13 July 1944
LCVP 1228	27 November 1944	LCVP 1358	April 1945